Richard Wright

Richard Wright

*An Annotated Bibliography of
Criticism and Commentary,
1983–2003*

KENETH KINNAMON

McFarland & Company, Inc., Publishers
Jefferson, North Carolina, and London

LIBRARY OF CONGRESS CATALOGUING-IN-PUBLICATION DATA

Kinnamon, Keneth.
Richard Wright : an annotated bibliography of criticism and
commentary, 1983–2003 / Keneth Kinnamon.
p.   cm.
Includes index.

ISBN 0-7864-2135-5 (softcover : 50# alkaline paper) ∞

1. Wright, Richard, 1908–1960 — Bibliography.   2. African Americans
in literature — Bibliography.   3. Wright, Richard, 1908–1960 — Criticism
and interpretation — Bibliography.   I. Title.
Z8986.323.K56   2006   [PS3545.R815]   016.813'54 — dc22   2005001717

British Library cataloguing data are available

Cover photograph ©2006 PhotoSpin

Manufactured in the United States of America

*McFarland & Company, Inc., Publishers
Box 611, Jefferson, North Carolina 28640
www.mcfarlandpub.com*

I dedicate this book to my compañera
de la vida y de la barrera sombra.

¡Va por ti, Paquita!

TABLE OF CONTENTS

PREFACE

This book, a bibliography of nearly 10,000 annotated items concerning Richard Wright, is a sequel to my *A Richard Wright Bibliography: Fifty Years of Criticism and Commentary* (New York, 1988). As such, it covers the period from 1983 to 2003, but also includes addenda of scores of earlier items that surfaced after 1988. Taken together, this volume and its predecessor constitute the most comprehensive secondary bibliography ever compiled for any American writer, reflecting my expansive view of literary reputation as all published mentions of a writer and his works.

Each entry consists of bibliographical information followed by my annotation. In the case of Japanese items, however, the veteran Wright scholars Yoshinobu Hakutani and Toru Kiuchi supplied the annotations.

A bibliography of this scope requires the help of expert librarians, an excellent interlibrary loan service, and tireless typists. Such help has been generously provided by Ann Marie Candido, Steve Chism, Robin Ruggio, Sheila Nance, and Mark Harris.

THE BIBLIOGRAPHY

1983

1. Adolph, Robert. "Marginality and After: The Making of Modern American Literature." *The Canadian Review of American Studies*, 14 (Winter), 481–487. Mentions W briefly (p. 483).

2. Aithal, S.K. "Blacks." *Abstracts of English Studies*, 26 (December), 385. Abstracts an article by John M. Reilly mentioning W.

3. _____. "Richard Wright." *Abstracts of English Studies*, 26 (June), 211. Abstracts an article by Michel Fabre.

4. _____. "Richard Wright." *Abstracts of English Studies*, 26 (December), 409. Abstracts articles by Charles De Arman, Diane Long Hoeveler, and Melvin G. Williams.

5. Alexander, Margaret Walker, and John Griffin Jones. "Margaret Walker Alexander," in *Mississippi Writers Talking*. Vol. 2. Ed. by John Griffin Jones. Jackson: University Press of Mississippi, pp. 120–146. Interview dated 13 March 1982 including discussion of Alexander's relation to Wright and his characteristics as a writer.

6. Allen, Mary, *Animals in American Literature*. Urbana: University of Illinois Press, pp. 135–150. In a chapter entitled "Tortured Animals: Richard Wright," Allen treats *BB*, *LD*, "The Man Who Was Almost a Man," "Big Boy Leaves Home," "The Man Who Killed a Shadow," "The Man Who Lived Underground," *NS*, "How Bigger Was Born," "The Man Who Went to Chicago," and *PS*, showing that W is empathetic to the suffering of animals, which is analogous to the suffering of blacks.

7. Angelou, Maya, and Claudia Tate. "Maya Angelou," in Tate's *Black Women Writers at Work*. New York: Continuum, pp. 1–11. In this interview Angelou mentions W briefly (pp. 2, 5). Reprinted: 1989.

8. Anon. "American Literature — 1914 to the Present: A Proposed Course," in *Reconstructing American Literature: Courses, Syllabi Issues*. Ed. Paul Lauter. Old Westbury, NY: The Feminist Press, pp. 123–125. Course plan including "Long Black Song," "Bright and Morning Star," and "Almos'a Man."

9. Anon. *Bibliographic Guide to Black Studies: 1982*. Boston: G.K. Hall, p. 131. Lists one primary and two secondary items concerning W in the New York Public Library, supplementing the *Dictionary Catalog of the Schomburg Collection of Negro Literature and History*.

10. Anon. "Ebony Book Shelf." *Ebony*, 38 (August), 31. Lists Allison Davis's *Leadership, Love and Aggression*, mentioning W briefly.

11. Anon. "The Black Scholar Publishers Listing of Black Interest Books." *The Black Scholar*, 14 (Summer), 24–40. Lists *Critical Essays on Richard Wright* edited by Yoshinobu Hakutani (p. 29) and *Richard Wright: A Primary Bibliography* (p. 29).

12. Anon. "A Check List of Explication (1981)." *The Explicator*, 41 (Winter), 3–60. Lists three items s.v. W.

13. Anon. "Checklist: Contributions to Literary History and Biography, 1982," in *Dictionary of Literary Biography: 1982*. Ed. Richard Ziegfeld. Detroit: Gale, pp. 404–409. Lists Margaret Walker's *The Daemonic Genius of Richard Wright*.

14. Anon. "Chicago." *Journal of Black Studies*, 14 (December) [263]. Includes a publisher's review of Houston Baker's *The Journey Back* mentioning W briefly.

15. Anon. "Kilson, Martin. *Politics and Identity Among Black Intellectuals*." *American History and Life*, 20A, 152. Abstract of the article.

16. Anon. "New Scholarly Books." *The Chronicle of Higher Education* (6 July), p. 19. Includes a notice of Allison Davis's *Leadership, Love, and Aggression*, which contains a "psychobiography" of Wright.

17. Anon. "St. James Theatre," in *The Critical Temper of Alain Locke: A Selection of His Essays on Art and Culture*. Ed. Jeffrey C. Stewart. New York: Garland, p. 92. Reprint of 1941.

18. Anon. "Wright, Richard," in *The Concise Columbia Encyclopedia*. Eds. Judith S. Levey and Agnes Greenhall. New York: Columbia University Press, p. 932. Very brief biographical entry. Reprinted: 1989, 1994.

19. Anon. "Wright, Richard," in *The Cambridge Guide to English Literature*. Ed. Michael Stapleton. Cambridge: Cambridge University Press, 1983, pp. 979–980. Biographical sketch with photograph. Mentions W's works through *EM*.

20. Andrews, William. "American Autobiography," in *Reconstructing American Literature: Courses, Syllabi, Issues*. Ed. Paul Lauter. New York: The Feminist Press, pp. 133–135. Course plan including *AH* and *BB*.

21. Baker, Houston A., Jr. "To Move Without Moving: An Analysis of Creativity and Commerce in

Ralph Ellison's Trueblood Episode." *PMLA*, 98 (October), 828–845. Begins with a quotation from "Richard Wright's Blues." Reprinted.

22. Bambara, Toni Cade, and Claudia Tate. "Toni Cade Bambara," in Tate's *Black Women Writers at Work*. New York: Continuum, pp. 12–38. In this interview Bambara mentions W briefly (p. 20).

23. Bandler, Michael J. "The Good Old Boy's Taste in Books." *Chicago Tribune Book World* (20 November, 1983), pp. 35–36. In an interview Willie Morris states that he read W while at the University of Texas, met him and corresponded with him thereafter. Reprinted: 2000.

24. Baraka, Imamu Amiri. "A Reply to Saunders Redding's 'The Black Revolution in American Studies'," in *Sources for American Studies*. Eds. Jefferson B. Kellogg and Robert H. Walker. Westport, CT: Greenwood, pp. 15–24. Reprint of 1979. 34.

25. Barnett, Ursula A. *A Vision of Order: A Study of Black South African Literature in English (1914–1980)*. London: Sinclair Brown, pp. 119, 143. Notes the influence of W on Peter Abrahams and the role of *UTC* in Ezekiel Mphahlele's novel *The Wanderers*.

26. Barrax, Gerald W. "The Head and Heart of Melvin Dixon." *Callaloo*, 6 (Spring-Summer), 135–144. Review of Melvin Dixon's *Change of Territory* commenting on his poems on W.

27. Berry, Faith. *Langston Hughes: Before and Beyond Harlem*. Westport, CT: Lawrence Hill, pp. 229, 245, 246, 252–253, 285, 292, 300, 302–303, 322, 352, 356. Recounts meeting of W and Ellison through Hughes, the composition of "Red Clay Blues," W's favorable response to *The Big Sea*, the publication of "Not My People's War," and the W-Baldwin quarrel.

28. Bertens, Hans, and Theo D'haen. *Geschiedenis van de Amerikaanse literatur*. Amsterdam: Uitgeverij De Arbeiderspers, pp. 328, 330–332, 341. Contains two paragraphs discussing *NS* (pp. 330–332) and mentions also *O*, *BB*, and *WML*.

29. _____. Amsterdam: Uitgeverij Ve Arbeiderspers, pp. 328, 330–332, 341. In a chapter entitled "Richard Wright ende naturalisten (pp. 330–332) the authors treat *NS*,

stating that it brought an end to the Harlem Renaissance. They also find Wrightian naturalism in Attaway, Himes, and Petry. They also mention briefly *BB*.

30. Berthoff, Warner. "The American Story-Chronicle," in *Reconstructing American Literature: Courses, Syllabi, Issues*. Ed. Paul Lauter. Old Westbury, NY: The Feminist Press, pp. 141–145. Course plan including *UTC*, *AH*, and *NS*.

31. Blount, Marcellus. "A Woman Speaks." *Callaloo*, 6 (Spring-Summer), 118–122. Mentions *NS* briefly.

32. Bosmajian, Haig. "Introduction," in his *Censorship, Libraries, and the Law*. New York: Neal-Schuman, pp. xi–xxiv. Mentions *BB* in connection with the Island Trees case.

33. Bradbury, Malcolm. *The Modern American Novel*. Oxford: Oxford University Press, pp. 98, 103–105, 132, 133. Sketches W's early career, mentioning *UTC* and *LT* and comments on *NS* and *O*, emphasizing their existential themes.

34. Brennan, William. "Justice Brennan's Opinion Notes," in *Censorship, Libraries, and the Law*. Ed. Haig Bosmajian. New York: Neal-Schuman, pp. 113–115. Mentions *BB* in the Island Trees case.

35. Brewton, Butler E. "The Functions of the Feminine in Richard Wright's 'Big Boy Leaves Home,' a Novella in *Uncle Tom's Children*." *African American Journal of Philosophy Quarterly Review*, 1 (Winter 1982-1983), 95–104. Analyzes the characterization of Bigger's mother, the white woman at the swimming hole, and the women in the lynch mob in terms of racism and sexual fantasy.

36. Brignano, Russell C. "*Critical Essays on Richard Wright*. Ed. with Intro., Yoshinobu Hakutani." *MELUS*, 10 (Winter), 83–86. Favorable review commenting on the individual essays.

37. Brooks, A. Russell. "The *CLA Journal* as a Mirror of Changing Ethnic and Academic Perspectives." *CLA Journal*, 26 (March), 265–276. Mentions W briefly.

38. Brown, Carolyn T. "The Myth of the Fall and the Dawning of Consciousness in George Lamming's *In the Castle of My Skin*." *World Literature Today*, 57 (Winter), 38–43. Comments briefly on W's introduction to Lamming's novel (p. 41).

39. Bryant, Earle V. "Sexual Initiation and Survival in Richard Wright's *The Long Dream*." *The Southern Quarterly*, 21 (Spring), 57–66. Analyzes the relation between sex and race in *LD*. The taboo on sexual contact between black men and white women stimulates Fishbelly's attraction to whiteness and jeopardizes his survival. Reprinted: 1993.

40. Butler, Robert J. "The Quest for Pure Motion in Richard Wright's *Black Boy*." *MELUS*, 10 (Fall), 5–17. Places Wright in the open road tradition of both American literature and the blues. In *Black Boy* the quest for nonteleological movement is developed by repeated contrasts between images of shifting stasis and images of a motion that promises possibility. Wright's commitment to energizing movement "helps to account for his triumph as a man and an artist" (p. 8).

41. Callahan, John, "American Literature: 1900–1940 and 1940–1980," in *Reconstructing American Literature: Courses, Syllabi, Issues*. Ed Paul Lauter. Old Westbury, NY: The Feminist Press, pp. 113–117. Course plan including "The Man Who Was Almost a Man" and selections from *BB*.

42. Carr, Virginia Spencer, and Joseph R. Millichap. "Carson McCullers," in *American Women Writers: Bibliographical Essays*. Eds. Maurice Duke, Jackson R. Bryer, and M. Thomas Inge. Westport, CT: Greenwood Press, pp. 297–319. Quotes from W's review of *The Heart Is a Lonely Hunter* (p. 307).

43. Carter, Purvis M. "The Negro in Periodical Literature, 1973–1974 — Part II." *The Journal of Negro History*, 68 (Summer), 318–353. Contains an annotated entry for an article on *UTC* by James R. Giles.

44. Charters, Ann. "Richard Wright," in her *The Story and Its Writer: An Introduction to Short Fiction*. New York: St. Martin's Press, pp. 826–827. Biographical-critical headnote to "The Man Who Was Almost a Man." Reprinted: 1987, 1990, 1995 (2).

45. Chew, Martha, Beverly Vlark, Brian Gallagher, Joan Hedrick, and Eleanor Tignor. "Survivals — A Thematic Course," in *Reconstructing American Literature: Courses, Syllabi, Issues*. Ed. Paul Lauter. Old Westbury, NY: The Feminist Press, pp.

219–222. Course plan includes selections from *EM*.

46. Childrey, Frank W. "Mississippi Writers Anthology." *The Southern Register*, 2 (Summer), 4. Mentions W briefly.

47. Coleman, James W., and Joanne Veal Gabbin. "The Legacy of George E. Kent." *Black American Literature Forum*, 17 (Winter), 143–147. Includes consideration of Kent's W criticism.

48. Coles, Robert A. "Richard Wright's *The Outsider*: A Novel in Transition." *Modern Language Studies*, 13 (Summer), 53–61. Disputes critical disparagement of *O* and Wright's exile. Granville Hicks's review of the novel is sound, but Coles gives even greater emphasis to the theme of alienation. Wright's use of "nonfiction technique," i.e., philosophical monologues of Cross Damon and Ely Houston, looks forward to his nonfiction books on the Third World.

49. Conn, Peter. *The Divided Mind: Ideology and Imagination in America, 1898–1917*. Cambridge University Press, pp. 143, 146. Mentions W briefly.

50. Conner, Tim. "Wright, Richard (Nathaniel) 1908–1960," in *Contemporary Authors: A Bio-Bibliographical Guide*. Vol. 108. Ed. by Hal May, Diane L. Dupuis, Debra G. Jones, Lillian S. Sims, and Susan M. Trosky. Detroit: Gale, pp. 530–535. Contains information under the following rubrics: Personal, Career, Writings, Sidelights, Bibliographical Sources. The following critics are quoted: James A. Page; Malcolm Cowley, Houston A. Baker, Margaret Marshall, Edward Margolies, Sheldon Brivic, James Baldwin, Darryl Pinckney, Ralph Ellison, Morris Dickstein, David Littlejohn, Howard Mumford Jones, Warren French, Granville Hicks, Phoebe Adams, Stanley Edgar Hyman, Nathan A. Scott, Jr., Tillman Durdin, and Charles Shapiro. Reprinted in revised form: 1989.

51. Cox, Virginia. "Modern American Literature," in *Reconstructing American Literature: Course, Syllabi, Issues*. Ed Paul Lauter. Old Westbury, NY: The Feminist Press, pp. 117–121. Course plan including "Almos' a Man" and the film version.

52. Crunden, Robert M. "Ralph Ellison's New World Symphony." *Indian Journal of American Studies*,

13 (January), 45–54. Quotes from "Richard Wright's Blues" and distinguishes Ellison's artistic goals from W's (pp. 50–51).

53. Dance, Daryl C. "Zora Neale Hurston," in *American Women Writers: Bibliographical Essays*. Eds. Maurice Duke, Jackson R. Bryer, and M. Thomas Inge. Westport, CT: Greenwood Press, pp. 321–351. Mentions Hurston's review of *UTC* and W's review of *Their Eyes Were Watching God*, as well as June Jordan's article on the two authors (pp. 329, 339, 345, 348, 349).

54. Davis, Allison. "Mightier Than the Sword: Richard Wright, Creator of *Native Son*," in his *Leadership, Love, and Aggression*. New York: Harcourt Brace Jovanovich, pp. 153–180, 248–249. Psychological interpretation of Wright's personality and its reflection in his work. The basic formative influence was "his sadistic maternal family" (p. 156). Beaten by his mother and rejected by his father, W developed a self-hatred which he projected on blacks generally. His anger and distrust — and consequent guilt feelings — generate his fictional protagonists.

55. Dennis, Frank Allen. "A Bibliography of Theses and Dissertations Relating to Mississippi, 1983." *The Journal of Mississippi History*, 45 (February), 73–77. Lists a dissertation by Anthony S. Magistrale treating W and others (see 1982.95).

56. Dewsnap, Terence. "Watergate Endings and Initiations." *Biography: An Interdisciplinary Quarterly*, 6 (Fall), 342–352. Compares the ending of *BB* favorably to endings of autobiographies written by Watergate conspirators.

57. Dixon, Melvin. *Change of Territory*. Lexington, Kentucky: Callaloo Poetry Series, pp. [1, 3]. Dedication is to "Richard" and others. Epigraph is from *BB*.

58. _____. "Climbing Montmartre," in his *Change of Territory*. Lexington: Callaloo Poetry Series, University of Kentucky, pp. 24–25. Poem mentioning W briefly. Reprinted: 1992.

59. _____. "Kin of Crossroads," in his *Change of Territory*. Lexington, KY: Callaloo Poetry Series, p. 17. Reprint of 1976.57.

60. _____. "Richard, Richard: American Fuel," in his *Change of Territory*. Lexington: Callaloo Po-

etry Series, University of Kentucky, p. 19. Poem on W's last days, death, and cremation. Reprinted: 1992.

61. _____. "Richard, Richard: An American Hunger," in his *Change of Territory*. Lexington: Callaloo Poetry Series, University of Kentucky, pp. 20–21. Poem about examining W's papers in Paris in 1975 with Michel Fabre and Ellen Wright. Reprinted: 1992.

62. Donlan, Dan. "Getting Dialogue for Stories from Real Life, Not Schlock." *English Journal*, 72 (December), 16–18. Quotes a passage from "The Man Who Saw the Flood."

63. Eastman, John. *Who Lived Where: A Biographical Guide to Homes and Museums*. New York: Bonanza Books, pp. 77, 125, 355, 506. Lists and comments on residences of W in Brooklyn, Manhattan, Mississippi, and Memphis.

64. Ellis, Grace W. "UnSouthern Times." *Southern Exposure*, 11 (January/February), 65–67. Notes that a microfiche program for high schools by a subsidiary of *The New York Times* does not include W among "50 Great American Writers."

65. Ellison, Mary. "Black Perceptions and Real Images: Indian and Black Literary Links." *Phylon*, 44 (First Quarter), 44–55. Comments briefly on Bigger Thomas as a trickster figure.

66. Eno-Belinga, Martin. "Alioune Diop: L'homme de la rencontre." *Présence Africaine*, No. 125 (First Quarter), 302–306. Mentions W briefly.

67. Ensslen, Klaus. "Das Getto in der afroamerikanischen literatur nach 1945," in *Amerikanische Gettoliteratur zur Literatur ethnischer, marginaler und unterdrukter gruppen in Amerika*. Darmstadt: Wissenschaftliche Buchgesellschaft, pp. 234–292. Contains a discussion of *NS* noting its influence on Petry (pp. 239–241). Mentions briefly W (pp. 246, 248, 252) as well as *BB* and *AH* (pp. 282, 283).

68. _____. "Diedrich, Maria, *Kommunismus im afro-amerikanischen roman: Der Verhältnis afroamerikanischer Schriftsteller zur Kommunistischen Partei der USA zwischen Weltkriegen*; Eckhard Breitinger, Hg., *Black Literature: Zur afrikanischen und afro-amerikanischen literatur*." *Amerikastudien*, 28, no. 2, 253–255. Review commenting on Diedrich's treatment of W and Kurt Otten's essay on W in the Breitinger collection.

69. Evans, Veichal J. "Chester Himes on Miscegenation." *Western Journal of Black Studies*, 7 (Summer), 74–77. Mentions briefly Bigger Thomas and Mary Dalton (p. 76).

70. Fabre, Michel. "Craig H. WERNER.—*Paradoxical Resolutions: American Fiction Since James Joyce.*" *Revue françaises d'études américaines*, 16 (February), 177. Review mentioning W.

71. Faulkner, Howard. "Richard Wright," in *Critical Survey of Long Fiction.* Vol. 7. Ed. Frank N. Magill. Englewood Cliffs, NJ: Salem Press, pp. 2974–2984. After commenting on the short fiction and autobiographical writing, Faulkner assesses W's achievement, sketches his life, and analyzes his novels. A brief bibliography concludes the essay. "In his best work, Wright gives American literature its strongest statement of the existential theme of alienated man defining himself" (p. 2975).

72. Fenster, Valmai Kirkham. *Guide to American Literature.* Littleton, CO: Libraries Unlimited, Inc., pp. 224–225. Selective bibliographical guide to primary and secondary sources.

73. Fontenot, Chester J. "American Novel Since the Modern Age," in *Reconstructing American Literature: Courses, Syllabi, Issues.* Ed. Paul Lauter. Old Westbury, NY: The Feminist Press, p. 149. Course plan including *NS*.

74. Forrest, Leon. "Forged in Injustice." *Chicago*, 32 (November), 146, 148, 150, 152. Review of Allison Davis's *Leadership, Love and Aggression* praising highly its treatment of W (p. 152). Reprinted: 1994.

75. Foster, E.C. "Books Received." *The Journal of Negro History*, 68 (Fall), 390–399. Mentions treatment of W by Charles T. Davis in *Black Is the Color of the Cosmos* (p. 391).

76. Frank, Joseph. "Ralph Ellison and a Literary 'Ancestor': Dostoevski." *The New Criterion*, 2 (September), 11–21. Comments briefly on Ellison's relation to W (p. 11). Reprinted.

77. French, Warren. "Introduction," in *American Writers Since 1900*, Ed. James Vinson. Chicago:

St. James Press, pp. 1–20. Reprint of 1980.102.

78. Gates, Henry Louis, Jr. "The 'Blackness of Blackness': A Critique of the Sign and the Signifying Monkey." *Critical Inquiry*, 9 (June), 685–723. Discusses Ellison's relation to W: "Ellison in his fiction signifies upon Wright by parodying Wright's literary structures through repetition and difference" (p. 696), especially in *NS*, *BB*, and "The Man Who Lived Underground." Reprinted: 1984 1987.

79. Gentsch, Günter. *Faulkner zwischen Schwarz und Weiss.* Berlin: Akademie-Verlag, pp. 28, 89. Mentions *BB* and comments briefly on *UTC*.

80. Gilmore, Al-Tony. "The Myth, Legend, and Folklore of Joe Louis: The Impression of Sport on Society." *The South Atlantic Quarterly*, 82 (Summer), 256–268. Quotes and comments on W's "King Joe" (p. 264).

81. Giovanni, Nikki, and Claudia Tate. "Nikki Giovanni," in Tate's *Black Women Writers at Work.* New York: Continuum, pp. 60–78. In this interview Giovanni comments briefly on W's expatriation (pp. 74–75).

82. Girlin, Rhoda. "Richard Wright: 'The Man Who Was Almost a Man'," in the Instructor's Manual for *The Borzoi Book of Short Fiction.* New York: Alfred A. Knopf, pp. 180–182. Provides a plot summary and emphasizes "Dove's empty dreams." Includes seven study questions.

83. Göbel, Walter. "Identität und Mythos in Toni Morrison's *Song of Solomon.*" *English Amerikanische Studien*, 5 (September), 424–430. Mentions briefly *BB* (p. 424).

84. Gray, Rockwell. "Albert E. Stone. *Autobiographical Occasions and Original Acts: Versions of Identity from Henry Adams to Nate Shaw.*" *Biography*, 6 (Fall), 358–367. Review mentioning W briefly (p. 364).

85. Hamamoto, Takeo. "Ellison and Baldwin," in *America Bungako no shin Tenkai Go no Shosetsu* [The New Development of American Literature: Post-World War II Fiction]. Kyoto: Yamaguchi Shoten, pp. 192–202. Ellison and Baldwin were both influenced by their mentor W but later outgrew his influence. Surveys Baldwin's career, beginning with his meeting with W and ending with

the publication of *Just Above My Head.* Considers *Go Tell It On the Mountain* representative of Baldwin's work [Y.H. and Toru Kiuchi].

86. _____. "Wright, Ellison, and Baldwin," in *The New Development in American Literature: Novels After World War II.* Kyoto: Yamaguchi Shoten, pp. 185–202. Places W, Ellison, and Baldwin, noting the indebtedness of the younger two. W strove for black liberation and employed realism [T.K., R.B. and Y.H.].

87. Hanawalt, Jean Allen. "Black and Ethnic Literature," in *Reconstructing American Literature: Courses, Syllabi, Issues.* Ed. Paul Lauter. Old Westbury, New York: The Feminist Press, pp. 176–178. Course plan including *BB*.

88. Harper, Michael S. "Don't They Speak Jazz." *MELUS*, 10 (Spring), 3–6. Mentions reading W as a youth in Brooklyn.

89. Hart, James D. *The Oxford Companion to American Literature.* Fifth edition. New York: Oxford University Press, p. 850. Revised reprint of 1941.760.

90. Hedrick, John P. "Introduction to American Literature: Civil War to the Present," in *Reconstructing American Literature: Courses, Syllabi, Issues.* Ed. Paul Lauter. Old Westbury, NY: The Feminist Press, pp. 48–49. Course plan including *NS*.

91. Hellenbrand, Harold. "Bigger Thomas Reconsidered: 'Native Son,' Film and 'King Kong.'" *Journal of American Culture*, 6, 84–95. Treats the general influence of film and photography on Wright and the specific influences of *King Kong* on *NS*. Although Hellenbrand does not know that W actually saw the film, it summarized many racial issues also reflected in the novel. "Mythically and sociologically, the movie and the novel tell the same story. The movie, though, tells it largely from the white point of view; and the novel largely from the black" (p. 92).

92. Hobson, Fred. *Tell About the South: The Southern Rage to Explain.* Baton Rouge: Louisiana State University Press, p. 12. Mentions W briefly.

93. Holman, C. Hugh. "No More Monoliths, Please: Continuities in the Multi-Souths," in *Southern Literature in Transition: Heritage and*

Promise. Memphis: Memphis State University Press, pp. xiii–xxiv. Mentions W briefly (p. xxiii).

94. Hopkins, Ellen. "Where They Lived." *New York*, 16 (7 March), p. 42. Explains the difficulties W had in 1945 while living at 82 Washington Place, including racial indignities.

95. Hovet, Grace Ann, and Barbara Lounsberry. "Flying as Symbol and Legend in Toni Morrison's *The Bluest Eye, Sula,* and *Song of Solomon.*" *CLA Journal,* 27 (December), 119–140. Mentions briefly Bigger's desire to fly in *NS* (p. 120).

96. Hughes, Langston, Milton Meltzer, and C. Eric Lincoln. *A Pictorial History of Blackamericans.* Fifth edition. New York: Crown, pp. 281, 286, 352. Reprint of 1958.161 plus an additional brief mention of W.

97. Hunter, Kristin, and Claudia Tate. "Kristin Hunter," in Tate's *Black Women Writers at Work.* New York: Continuum, pp. 79–88. In this interview Hunter mentions W briefly (p. 87).

98. Hull, Gloria T. "What Is It I Think She's Doing, Anyhow": A Reading of Toni Cade Bambara's *The Salt Eaters,* in *Home Girls: A Black Feminist Anthology.* Ed. Barbara Smith. New York: Kitchen Table Women of Color Press, 1983, pp. 124–142. Mentions briefly *NS.* Reprint in revised form: 1985.

99. Hyatt, Marshall. *The Afro-American Cinematic Experience: An Annotated Bibliography and Filmography.* Wilmington, Delaware: Scholarly Resources, pp. 37, 117. Lists Thomas Cripp's article on the film *NS* and two reviews.

100. Johnson, Diane. *Dashiel Hammett: A Life.* New York: Random House, p. 202. Quotes Hammett calling W "a blackface Cliff Odets who never had any rolling skates either."

101. Jones, John Griffin. "Margaret Walker Alexander," in *Mississippi Writers Talking.* Vol. II Jackson: University Press of Mississippi, pp. 120–146. Interview dated 13 March 1982, including discussion of Walker's relation to W and his characteristics as a writer.

102. _____. "Walker Percy," in *Mississippi Writers Talking.* Vol. II. Jackson: University Press of Mississippi, pp. 3–45. Percy mentions briefly *NS* as a novel that survives

"despite the passionate ideology" (p. 39).

103. Joyce, Joyce A. "Nella Larsen's *Passing.*" *Western Journal of Black Studies,* 7 (Summer), pp. 68–73. Contrasts briefly *NS* and Bigger with Larsen's Novel (p. 72). Reprinted: 1994.

104. Joyce, Joyce Ann. "Introduction to American Literature After 1865," in *Reconstructing American Literature: Courses, Syllabi, Issues.* Ed. Paul Lauter. Old Westbury, NY: The Feminist Press, pp. 53–55. Course plan including *NS.*

105. Kaiser, Ernest. "Recent Books." *Freedomways,* 23 (Fourth Quarter), 297–303. Notes that W is treated in *Black Novelists and the Southern Literary Traditions* (p. 298).

106. Kaplan, Amy. "The City in American Literature," in *Reconstructing American Literature: Courses, Syllabi, Issues.* Ed. Paul Lauter. Old Westbury, NY: The Feminist Press, pp. 202–203. Course plan including *NS* and "The Man Who Lived Underground."

107. Karcher, Carolyn L. "Male and Female Tradition in American Fiction," in *Reconstructing American Literature: Courses, Syllabi, Issues.* Ed. Paul Lauter. Old Westbury, NY: The Feminist Press, pp. 154–156. Course plan including *NS* in opposition to *Their Eyes Were Watching God.*

108. Karl, Frederick R. *American Fictions, 1940–1980.* New York: Harper & Row, pp. xiii, 47, 75–77, 79, 80, 82–84, 129, 131, 145–146, 160, 161, 196–197, 247–249, 274, 291–295, 317, 340, 343, 567. Values W's achievement in *NS,* though it "is clearly a product of the 1930s" (p. 83). But W "moves beyond the matrix of determinism to establish individual identity." Discusses W's relation to Baldwin (pp. 145–146), Ellison, and other black writers. Mentions W elsewhere and comments on *BB* (p. 160).

109. Kaye, Fran, "Introduction to Later American Literature," in *Reconstructing American Literature: Courses, Syllabi, Issues.* Ed. Paul Lauter. Old Westbury, NY: The Feminist Press, pp. 55–58. Course plans including *NS.*

110. Kellogg, Jefferson B. "Redding and Baraka: Two Contrasting Views on Afro-American Studies," in *Sources for American Studies.* Eds.

Jefferson B. Kellogg and Robert H. Walker. Westport, CT: Greenwood, pp. 3–7. Mentions briefly Fabre's work on W.

111. _____. and Robert H. Walker. "General Bibliography and Author Index," in their *Sources for American Studies.* Westport, CT: Greenwood, pp. 561–766. Lists *AH, BB, UTC,* and "Blueprint for Negro Literature" (p. 764).

112. Kinnamon, Keneth. "Ellison, Ralph (Waldo)," in *American Writers Since 1900.* Ed. James Vinson. Chicago: St James Press, pp. 192–194. Reprint of 1980.138.

113. Kiernan, Robert F. *American Writing Since 1945: A Critical Survey.* New York: Frederick Ungar, p. 46. Mentions briefly *BB.*

114. Kimura, Shoji. "A Study of Black Boy," in *Oksaka Gakuin University Essays on Foreign Languages.* Osaka: pp. 50–71. Considers American social structure in W's formative years to 1940 through *BB* [T.K., R.B. and Y.H.].

115. Kishino, Junko. "Black Women Now Write: *The Bluest Eye* and *Meridian.*" *Literary Space* (9 June) [T.K., R.B., and Y.H.]. While *NS* is a critical appeal to the dominant society, *The Bluest Eye* is directed to a black female audience [T.K., R.B., and Y.H.].

116. Krupat, Arnold, "The Complex Fate," in *Reconstructing American Literature: Courses, Syllabi, Issues.* Ed. Paul Lauter. Old Westbury, NY: The Feminist Press, pp. 10–15. Plan for a course in American Literature given in 1982–1983. *NS* is on the syllabus.

117. Kubitschek, Missy Dehn, "Masterpieces of American Literature," in *Reconstructing American Literature: Courses, Syllabi, Issues.* Ed. Paul Lauter. Old Westbury, NY: The Feminist Press, pp. 18–22. Course plan including *UTC.*

118. _____. "'Tuh de Horizon and Bak': The Female Quest in *Their Eyes Were Watching God.*" *Black American Literature Forum,* 17 (Fall), 109–115. Mentions W briefly (p. 113). Reprinted: 1987.

119. Kumai, Hironao, Tokuji Otani, and Keiko Fujita, eds. *Encyclopedia of Black American Miscellany.* Tokyo: Jazu Hihyosha, Special Issue of *Jazzy Criticism.* Refers to *NS* and includes hiroshi Kanzaki's "The History of Black Literature," treating W [T.K., R.B., and Y.H.].

120. Lamming, George. "Introduction to the Schocken Edition," in his *In the Castle of My Skin*. New York: Schocken Books, pp. ix–xx. Quotes from W's introduction to the first American edition of this novel.

121. Lamont, Bridget L., ed. *Illinois Authors: A Publication of Read Illinois*. Springfield: Illinois State Library, pp. 223–224. Contains a list of W's works.

122. Laryea, Doris L. "A Black Poet's Vision: An Interview with Lance Jeffers." *CLA Journal*, 26 (June), 422–433. Jeffers acknowledges W as one of his favorites: "I profoundly respect him for the depth and power of his rage" (p. 424).

123. Lauter, Paul. "Race and Gender in the Shaping of the American Literary Canon." *Feminist Studies*, 9 (Fall), 435–463. Mentions W briefly (pp. 437, 459, 462). Reprinted: 1991.

124. _____. "Race and Gender in the Shaping of the American Literary Canon: A Case Study from the Twenties." *Feminist Studies*, 9 (Fall), 435–463. Mentions W briefly (p. 462). Reprinted: 1996.

125. Lawhn, Juanita, and Sandra Mondin. "American Literature: Whitman to the Present," in *Reconstructing American Literature: Courses, Syllabi, Issues*. Ed. Paul Lauter. Old Westbury, NY: The Feminist Press, pp. 58–63. Course plan including "Big Boy Leaves Home."

126. Lee, A. Robert. *Black American Fiction Since Richard Wright*. London: BAAS Pamphlets in American Studies, pp. 5, 10–16, 17, 19, 23, 24, 29, 38, 42, 43, 46. The second chapter, "Richard Wright and the Wright Tradition," treats *UTC, NS, O, SH, LD, LT, EM*, and "The Man Who Lived Underground," followed by briefer consideration of Himes, Petry, Motley, Willard Savoy, Julian Mayfield, and William Gardner Smith. W's presence pervades the entire pamphlet.

127. _____. "Richard Wright's Inside Narratives," in *American Fictions: New Readings*. Edited by Richard Gray. London: Vision, pp. 200–221. After reviewing various oversimplified versions of W and his work, Lee examines most of the fiction to show that a mythic, hallucinatory dimension co-exists with naturalistic protest. "Big Boy Leaves

Home," "The Man Who Lived Underground," *NS*, and *The Long Dream* are most successful in combining this "inside narrative" with a realistic story. Reprinted: 1987.

128. Lee, Brian. "Marcus Klein, *Foreigners: The Making of American Literature 1900–1940*." *Journal of American Studies*, 17 (April), 138–139. Review mentioning W briefly.

129. _____. "Marcus Klein, Foreigners: *The Making of American Literature 1900–1940. Journal of American Studies*, 17 (April 1983), 138–139. Review mentioning briefly.

130. Lenz, Gunter. "Gettofahrung, Gettokultur, Gettoliteratur: Zur Afroamerikanischen Literatur zwischen den Weltkrieg (1914–1945),in *Amerikanische Gettoliteratur zur Literatur ethnischer, marginaler und unterdrükter gruppen in Amerika*. Darmstadt: Wissenschaftliche Buchgesellschaft, pp. 149–233. Contains a substantial treatment of "Richard Wright's Quest for Community" after he moved to Chicago, with special attention to "How Bigger Was Born," *LT*, and *TMBV* (pp. 217–229). Also mentions W briefly (pp. 150, 174, 181, 183, 186, 191, 205, 214).

131. Levine, Alan H. "Petitioners' Brief for a Writ of Certiorari in *Presidents Council, Dist. 25* v. *Community School Bd. No. 25*," in *Censorship, Libraries, and the Law*. Ed. Haig Bosmajian. New York: Neal-Schuman, pp. 21–24. Mentions W briefly (p. 24).

132. Lewis, David Levering. "*Black Messiahs and Uncle Toms: Social and Literary Manipulations of a Religious Myth*. By Wilson Jeremiah Moses." *The Journal of American History*, 69 (March), 955–956. Review mentioning W briefly.

133. Link, Franz. *Geschichte der amerikanischen Erzählkunst 1900–1950*. Stuttgart: Verlag W. Kohlhammer, pp. 12, 114, 120–127, 246. Includes a biographical sketch with emphasis on the influence of Mencken and Farrell. Discusses *LT, NS*, "The Man Who Lived Underground," and *BB*. Also mentions *O* and *LD*.

134. Liston, Carolyn Olivia. "Black Positivism Through Character Growth and Development in the Short Stories of Richard Wright." *Dissertation Abstracts International*, 43 (January), 2349A. Abstracts a 1982 University of Colorado disser-

tation. W "produces characters and a fictional short story world that are aesthetically complimentary to black life."

135. Litzinger, Boyd. "Richard Wright," in his *The Heath Reader*. Lexington, MA: Heath, pp. 302–309. Very brief headnote to an excerpt from *BB*.

136. _____. "Vocabulary, Questions, Topics for Writing," in his *The Heath Reader*. Lexington, MA: Heath, pp. 308–309. Study aids for an excerpt from *BB*.

137. Locke, Alain. "Broadway and the Negro Drama," in *The Critical Temper of Alain Locke: A Selection of His Essays on Art and Culture*. Ed. Jeffrey C. Stewart. New York: Garland, pp. 93–98. Reprint of 1941. 796.

138. _____. "A Critical Retrospect of the Literature of the Negro for 1947," in *The Critical Temper of Alain Locke: A Selection of His Essays on Art and Culture*. Ed. Jeffrey C. Stewart. New York: Garland, pp. 329–336. Reprint of 1948.190.

139. _____. "Deep River: Deeper Sea: Retrospective Review of the Literature of the Negro for 1935," in *The Critical Temper of Alain Locke: A Selection of His Essays on Art and Culture*. Ed. Jeffrey C. Stewart. New York: Garland, pp. 237–244. Reprint of 1936.

140. _____. "Dry Fields and Green Pastures: Part I," in *The Critical Temper of Alain Locke: A Selection of His Essays on Art and Culture*. Ed. Jeffrey C. Stewart. New York: Garland, pp. 285–297.

141. _____. "From *Native Son* to *Invisible Man*: A Review of the Literature of the Negro for 1952," in *The Critical Temper of Alain Locke: A Selection of His Essays on Art and Culture*. Ed. Jeffrey C. Stewart. New York: Garland, pp. 385–393. Reprint of 1953.174.

142. _____. "God Save Reality! Retrospective Review of the Literature of the Negro: 1936," in *The Critical Temper of Alain Locke: A Selection of His Essays on Art and Culture*. Ed. Jeffrey C. Stewart. New York: Garland, pp. 245–255. Reprint of 1937.29.

143. _____. "Jingo, Counter-Jingo and Us: Retrospective Review of the Literature of the Negro: 1937, Part I," in *The Critical Temper of Alain Locke: A Selection of His Essays on Art and Culture*. Ed. Jeffrey C.

Stewart. New York: Garland, pp. 257–266. Reprint of 1938.232.

144. _____. "The Negro: 'New' or Newer: A Retrospective Review of the Literature of the Negro for 1938," in *The Critical Temper of Alain Locke: A Selection of His Essays on Art and Culture.* Ed. Jeffrey C. Stewart. New York: Garland, pp. 271–283. Reprint of 1939.92.

145. _____. "Of Native Sons: Real and Otherwise: Part I," in *The Critical Temper of Alain Locke: A Selection of His Essays on Art and Culture.* Ed. Jeffrey C. Stewart. New York: Garland, pp. 299–308. Reprint of 1941.790.

146. _____. "Propaganda — Or Poetry?" in *The Critical Temper of Alain Locke: A Selection of His Essays on Art and Culture.* Ed. Jeffrey C. Stewart. New York: Garland, pp. 55–61. Reprint of 1936.

147. _____. "Who and What Is 'Negro'?" in *The Critical Temper of Alain Locke: A Selection of His Essays on Art and Culture.* Ed. Jeffrey C. Stewart. New York: Garland, pp. 309–318. Reprint of 1942.

148. Lowe, John. "American Literature of Social Justice," in *Reconstructing American Literature: Courses, Syllabi, Issues.* Ed. Paul Lauter. Old Westbury, NY: The Feminist Press, pp. 179–182. Course plan including *NS*.

149. Mahle, Benjamin. "Why I Teach *Black Boy*." *English Journal*, 72 (December), 19–21. A Minnesota ninth-grade teacher emphasizes the work's universal themes and its revelation of support by blacks of social oppression while minimizing its attack on racism.

150. Manganyi, Noel Chabani. "Psychobiography and the Truth of the Subject." *Biography: An Interdisciplinary Quarterly*, 6 (Winter), 34–52. Quotes from and comments on the first page of *BB* (pp. 39–40).

151. Mangione, Jerre. *An Ethnic at Large: A Memoir of America in the Thirties and Forties.* Philadelphia: University of Pennsylvania Press, pp. 124, 263–264. Reprint of 1978.156.

152. Mansfield, Walter. "Appendix," in *Censorship, Libraries, and the Law.* Ed. Haig Bosmajian. New York: Neal-Schuman, pp. 106–108. Includes two excerpts from *BB* considered objectionable by the school board in the Island Trees case.

153. Martin, Tony. *Literary Garveyism: Garvey, Black Arts and the Harlem Renaissance.* Dover, MA: The Majority Press, p. 77. Mentions briefly W's renunciation of Communist support.

154. McCluskey, John, Jr. "Two Steppin': Richard Wright's Encounter with Blue-Jazz." *American Literature*, 55 (October), 332–344. Examines W's "commentary on and use of blues forms and allusions in selected poems, essays, and fiction" (p. 333). Although W recognizes the expressive power of such folk forms as blues and jazz, his fiction does not adequately utilize this tradition. His isolated, alienated protagonists are a powerful indictment of racism, but he does not achieve "the grand fusion — synthesizing verbal attack with a nourishing cultural tradition" (p. 344).

155. McDowell, Deborah." Major American Authors, II," in *Reconstructing American Literature: Courses, Syllabi, Issues.* Ed. Paul Lauter. Old Westbury, NY: The Feminist Press, pp. 61–61. Course plan including "Long Black Song."

156. McGrath, Daniel F., ed. *Bookman's Price Index.* Vol. 23. Detroit: Gale, p. 784. Lists *NS* at $45.

157. _____. *Bookman's Price Index.* Vol. 24. Detroit: Gale, p. 782. Lists *NS* at $27.50, *NS* at $25, *TMBV* at $25, and *UTC* at $37.50.

158. _____. *Bookman's Price Index.* Vol. 25. Detroit: Gale, pp. 766–767. Lists *BB* at $15, *How "Bigger" Was Born* at $65, *NS* at $25, *NS* at $75 (twice), and *TMBV* at $40.

159. McWilliams, John P., Jr. "Innocent Criminal or Criminal Innocence: The Trial in American Fiction," in *Law and American Literature: A Collection of Essays.* By Carl S. Smith, John P. McWilliams, Jr., and Maxwell Bloomfield. New York: Knopf, pp. 45–124.

160. Mebane, Mary E. *Mary, Wayfarer.* New York: The Viking Press, pp. 16, 68, 92–93. Mentions reading *NS* and writing a paper on existential themes in *Invisible Man* and *O*. Relates the death threats directed at W in Chapel Hill in 1940, including Paul Green's effort to protect him. Reprinted: 1999.

161. Méral, Jean. *Paris dans la littérature américaine.* Paris: Editions du CNRS, pp. 273, 274, 285, 290–291. Comments on "Island of Hallucination" and *LD*. Translated: 1989.

162. Miller, Charles H. *Auden: An American Friendship.* New York: Charles Scribner's Sons, p. 127. Mentions W briefly.

163. Miller, Eugene E. "Folkloric Aspects of Wright's 'The Man Who Killed a Shadow.'" *CLA Journal*, 27 (December), 210–223. Claims that Wright "inadvertently and yet consciously" gave "folkloric characteristics" to the story. The librarian's screams are analogous to the screeches of an owl, in black folklore an old maid metamorphosed. Saul Saunders is himself a folk character. The story's structure follows closely the pattern described by Axel Olrik in his 1909 essay "Epic Traces of Folk Narrative." The story's haunting quality derives from its folkloric aspects.

164. Miller, M. Sammye. "The National Endowment for the Humanities: A Selected Bibliography for Two Years of Funded Projects on the Black Experience, 1977–1978." *The Journal of Negro History*, 68 (Winter), 59–79. Lists grants to Susan L. Blake and Thadious Davis for projects on W.

165. Miller, Wayne Charles. "Editor's Column." *MELUS*, 10 (Fall), 1–3. Praises Robert J. Butler's "The Quest for Pure Motion in Richard Wright's *Black Boy*," included in this issue of the journal.

166. Milligan, Ian. *The Novel in English: An Introduction.* New York: St. Martin's Press, p. 11. Mentions W briefly.

167. Milloy, Sandra D. "Dilsey: Faulkner's Black Mammy in *The Sound and The Fury*." *Negro History Bulletin*, 46 (July-August-September), 70–71. Contains a paragraph comparing the treatment of the young W by his mother and grandmother in *BB* to Dilsey's treatment of Luster in the Faulkner novel.

168. Mootry, Maria K. "J. Saunders Redding: A Case Study of the Black Intellectual." *The Western Journal of Black Studies*, 7 (Summer), 62–67. Mentions W several times.

169. Murata, Kaoru. "Chapter 26 in *Invisible Man*." *Bulletin of Waseda Daigaku Daigakuin*, 9 (1 April), 121–132 [T.K., R.B., and Y.H.]. Praises Ellison's disagreement with Irving Howe concerning W [T.K., R.B., and Y.H.].

170. Mveng, Engelbert. "Chemins vers la solidarité." *Présence Africaine*,

No. 125 (First Quarter), 307–309. Mentions W briefly.

171. Naison, Mark. *Communists in Harlem During the Depression.* Urbana: University of Illinois Press, pp. xv, xvi, xx, 203–204, 206, 208, 210–211, 218, 224, 258, 294, 300, 312, 316. Discusses W's relation to the Communist Party, quoting from his *Daily Worker* journalism and "Blueprint for Negro Writing" and mentioning *UTC*. Notes W's refusal to idealize Communists and comments on the Party's response to *NS*.

172. Namekata, Hitoshi. "An Essay on *The Outsider:* In Search of Freedom." *Bulletin of Musashino College for Music,* 14 (1 April), 121–132. Treats Cross Damon as an existentialist searching for absolute freedom. Notes his struggle with the communists and mentions Ely Houston [T.K., R.B., and Y.H.].

173. Nash, Charles C. "*Literature at the Barricades: The American Writer in the 1930s.* Ralph F. Bogardus and Fred Hobson, eds." *The Georgia Review,* 37 (Spring), 224–226. Review mentioning W briefly.

174. Nicosia, Gerald. *Memory Babe: A Critical Biography of Jack Kerouac.* New York: Grove Press, p. 467. Mentions W briefly.

175. Oates, Joyce Carol. "'At Least I Have Made a Woman of Her': Images of Women in Twentieth-Century Literature." *The Georgia Review,* 37 (Spring), 7–30. Comments briefly on Bigger's murder of Mary Dalton in *NS* (p. 26).

176. Okolie, M.A.E. "Nostalgia and Creative Secret: The Case of Camara Laye." *Okike: An African Journal of New Writing,* No. 23 (February), 8–15. Mentions briefly W's *Black Child* [sic].

177. Olney, James. "*Aké:* Wole Soyinka as Autobiographer." *The Yale Review,* 73 (Autumn), 72–93. Mentions briefly *AH* and *BB* (pp. 76–77).

178. O'Meally, Robert G. "'The Countless Possibilities of Music as a Way of Life.'" *Callaloo,* 6 (February), 153–155. Review of Al Young's *Snakes* mentioning briefly *BB*.

179. Ostendorf, Berndt. "Einleitung," in his *Amerikanische Gettoliteratur zur Literatur ethnischer, marginaler und unterdrükter gruppen in Amerika.* Darmstadt: Wissenschaftliche Buchgesellschaft, pp. 1–26. Mentions W's phrase "banker's daughters" (p. 9).

180. Ozick, Cynthia. "Literary Blacks and Jews," in her *Art & Ardor: Essays.* New York: Knopf, pp. 90–112. Reprint of 1972.157.

181. Pannill, Linda. "'I Consulted Myself.'" *Callaloo,* 6 (Spring–Summer), 130–131. Mentions W briefly.

182. Percy, Walker, and John Griffin Jones. "Walker Percy," in *Mississippi Writers Talking.* Vol. II. Ed. John Griffin Jones. Jackson: University Press of Mississippi, pp. 3–45. Mentions briefly *NS* (p. 39).

183. Peters, Erskine. *William Faulkner: The Yoknapatawpha World and Black Being.* Darby, Pennsylvania: Norwood Editions, p. 208. Comments on Faulkner's response to *NS* and *BB*.

184. _____. *William Faulkner: The Yoknapatawpha World and Black Being.* Darby, PA: Norwood Editions, p. 208. Comments on Faulkner's correspondence with W and his opinions on *NS* and *BB*.

185. Phillips, Robert L., Jr. "*MLA.*" *S.S.S.L.: The News-Letter of the Society for the Study of Southern Literature,* 16 (November), 4–5. List a paper by Trudier Harris on "Ritual Violence and the Formation of an Aesthetic: Richard Wright's 'Between the World and Me.'"

186. _____. "Reprints." *S.S.S.L.: The News-Letter of the Society for the Study of Southern Literature,* 16 (April), 14–15. Lists the paperback reprint of *AH.*

187. Phillips, William. *A Partisan View: Five Decades of the Literary Life.* New York: Stein and Day, p. 187. Mentions knowing W in America and seeing him in Paris in the winter of 1949-1950. "Unlike his books, Wright was sweet and gentle. But he lived in his own limbo, for he was in his anti–American phase and therefore not part of the American contingent, nor could he become French."

188. Piccinato, Stefania. "Ralph Waldo Ellison," in *I Contemporanei: Novecento Americano.* Ed. Elémire Zolla. Vol. 2. Rome: Lucarini Editore, pp. 617–634. Mentions W briefly (p. 620).

189. Podhoretz, Norman. "Why *The God That Failed* Failed." *Encounter,* 60 (January), pp. 28–34. Mentions W briefly (p. 29). Reprinted: 1986.

190. Pollard, Leslie T. "*The Grapes of Wrath* and *Native Son*: Literary Criticism as Social Definition." *Dis-*

sertation Abstracts International, 44 (October), 1136A. Abstracts a 1983 University of Kansas dissertation. Analyzing the milieu and issues of the two novels, as well as the critical response to them from 1939 to 1941.

191. Portelli, Alessandro. "Richard Wright," in *I Contemporanei: Novecento Americano.* Ed. Elémire Zolla. Vol. 2. Rome: Lucarini Editore, pp. 395–402. Biographical sketch, critical survey, and a primary and secondary bibliography with a list of Italian translations.

192. Pratt, George C. "*Pico v. Board of Ed., Island Trees Union Free School,* 474 F. Supp. 387 (1979)," in *Censorship, Libraries, and the Law.* Ed. Haig Bosmajian. New York: Neal-Schuman, pp. 61–67. Refers several times to *BB,* one of the books at issue.

193. Pudaloff, Ross. "Celebrity as Identity: Richard Wright, *Native Son* and Mass Culture." *Studies in American Fiction,* 11 (Spring), 3–18. Examines the influence of popular media on "Long Black Song," *LT,* and *NS.* Such fiction "describes worlds in which mass culture serves as the locus of personal identity" (p. 5). Image becomes more important than character, especially in the case of Bigger Thomas.

194. Rahming, Melvin B. "Complacency and Community: Psychocultural Patterns in the West Indian Novel." *CLA Journal,* 26 (March), 288–302. Quotes briefly from W's introduction to George Lamming's *In the Castle of My Skin* (p. 293).

195. Rampersad, Arnold. "Biography, Autobiography, and Afro-American Culture." *The Yale Review,* 73 (October), 1–16. Mentions briefly Addison Gayle's biography of W (p. 2) and *BB* (p. 12).

196. Reagan, Bette A. "The Outsider: An Underground Man's Burden of Complete Freedom." *Journal of the American Studies Association of Texas,* 14. pp. 39–45. Presents a detailed plot summary of *O* to demonstrate that Cross Damon corresponds to Dostoevsky's Underground Man.

197. Richter, David H. "Richard Wright," in his *The Borzoi Book of Short Fiction.* New York: Knopf, p. 1419. Biographical headnote to "The Man Who Was Almost a Man."

198. Ro, Sigmund. "'Desecrators' and 'Necromancers': Black American Writers and Critics in the Nineteen Sixties and the Third World Perspective." *American Studies in Scandinavia*, 15, 15–33. Mentions briefly W and *NS*.

199. Robinson, Cedric. *Black Marxism: The Making of the Black Radical Tradition*. London: Zed Press, pp. 258, 260, 264, 416–440. The chapter "Richard Wright and the Critique of Class Theory" is subdivided as follows: Marxist Theory and the Black Radical Intellectual, The Novel as Politics, Wright's Social Theory, Blacks as the Negation of Capitalism, and *The Outsider* as a Critique of Christianity and Marxism. Robinson concludes that although W had reservations about Marxism as a theory of society and as an ideology, "as a method of social analysis he found it compelling" (p. 434).

200. Ross, Jean W. "The Island Trees Case: A Symposium on School Library Censorship," in *Dictionary of Literary Biography: Yearbook: 1982*. Ed. Richard Ziegfeld. Detroit: Gale, pp. 17–18. Considers a 1975 case in which *BB* was one of eleven books proposed by a Long Island school board for removal. Nine were removed, but *BB* remained.

201. Rubin, Louis D., Jr. "Scholarship in Southern Literature: Its History and Recent Developments." *American Studies International*, 21 (April), 3–34. Mentions briefly W (p. 25) and *NS* (p. 27).

202. Salaam, Yusef. "The Schomburg Library Then and Now." *Freedomways*, 23 (First Quarter), 29–36. Notes that the Schomburg has signed copies of books by W.

203. Sallis, James. "In America's Black Heartland: The Achievement of Chester Himes." *Western Humanities Review*, 37 (Autumn), 191–206. Mentions W briefly (p. 192). Reprinted: 1999.

204. Samuels, Wilfred D. "Going Home: A Conversation with John Edgar Wideman." *Callaloo*, 6 (February), 40–59. Wideman mentions reading W.

205. Sanders, Leslie. "Text and Contexts in Afro-American Criticism." *Canadian Review of American Studies*, 14 (Fall), 344–352. Contains a review of Addison Gayle's *Richard Wright: Ordeal of a Native Son*. Valuable for its account of governmental harassment of W, Gayle's biography is too reluctant to engage ideological issues.

206. Seed, David. "Craig Hansen Werner, *Paradoxical Resolutions: American Fiction Since James Joyce*; Charles Clerc (ed.), *Approaches to 'Gravity's Rainbow.'*" *Journal of American Studies*, 17 (December), 475–477. Review mentioning briefly *LT*.

207. _____. "Craig Hansen Werner, *Paradoxical Resolutions: American Fiction Since James Joyce*. *Journal of American Studies*, 17 (December 1983), 475–476. Review noting that *LT* imitates Joyce.

208. Seidel, Kathryn L. "Southern Literature," in *Reconstructing American Literature: Courses, Syllabi, Issues*. Ed. Paul Lauter. Old Westbury, NY: The Feminist Press, pp. 204–205. Course plan including W.

209. Sekora, John, and Houston A. Baker, Jr. "Written-Off: Narratives, Master Texts, and Afro-American Writing from 1760 to 1945." *Komparatische Hefte* 7, 39–52. The first section shows how early African American autobiography was forced to conform to dominant white values. The second section is a post-structuralist treatment of *BB* showing how it broke from these restraints to achieve a liberated narrative. Sekora and Baker's trope for this process is the black hole. Reprinted: 1984

210. Shange, Ntozake. "Take the A Train," in her *A Daughter's Geography*. New York: St. Martin's Press, p. 18. Poem containing the following line: "Bigger is not a black boy yearning for an airplane."

211. Sheidley, William E., and Ann Charters. *Instructor's Manual to Accompany the Story and Its Writer: An Introduction to Short Fiction*. New York: St. Martin's Press, pp. 129–130. Two paragraphs of interpretive comment on "The Man Who Was Almost a Man" are followed by a dozen study questions, four topics for writing, and suggested readings (1980.94 and 1969.167).

212. Shiroma, Mikio. "Richard Wright: Hunger for 'Knowledge' and 'Violence.'" *Bulletin of Ryuku University School of Education*, 26 (6 January), 237–245. Considers W's remarkable emergence from deprivation to become a writer [T.K., R.B., and Y.H.].

213. _____. "Violence in Wrights's *Uncle Tom's Children*," *Bulletin of Ryukyu University School of Educa-* *tion*, 26 (6 January), 227–36. Studies violence in *UTC* [T.K., R.B., and Y.H.].

214. Shourie, Usha. "The Image of the Black Woman as Reflected in Black American Fiction." *Indian Journal of American Studies*, 13 (January), 184–188. Includes consideration of Gladys in *LD*.

215. Sifton, Charles P., Walter R. Mansfield, and Jon O. Newman. "*Pico* v. *Board of Ed., Island Trees Union Free School*, 628 F.2d404 (1980)," in *Censorship, Libraries, and the Law*. Ed. Haig Bosmajian. New York: Neal-Schuman, pp. 68–93. A circuit court decision on a censorship case involving *BB* and works by other authors.

216. Singh, Amritjit. "Richard Wright's *The Outsider*: Existentialist Exemplar or Critique?" in *Existentialism in American Literature*. Ed. by Ruby Chatterji. Atlantic Highlands, NJ: Humanities, pp. 134–146. Places *O* in the context of W's intellectual development. Its origin is in his "attempt to resolve the dilemma of the individual *versus* society, the mind *versus* materialism" (p. 134). The influence of Sartre and the urgency of Third World politics are reflected in the novel. *O* does not fulfill W's humanistic search because he cannot reconcile his allegiances to Western thought with his Third World sympathies. Reprinted: 1984.

217. Sirlin, Rhoda. "Richard Wright: 'The Man Who Was Almost A Man,'" in Instructor's Manual for *The Borzoi Book of Short Fiction*. New York: Alfred A. Knopf, pp. 180–182. Provides a plot summary emphasizing "Dave's Empty Dreams." Includes seven study questions.

218. Smith, Valerie Ann. "'The Singer in One's Soul': Storytelling in the Fiction of James Weldon Johnson, Richard Wright, Ralph Ellison, and Toni Morrison." *Dissertation Abstracts International*, 43 (January), 2350A. Abstracts a 1982 University of Virginia dissertation. Argues that "learning to tell his story convinces Bigger Thomas both of the coherence of his individual life and his connection to other people."

219. Stone, Albert E. "Autobiography in American Culture: Looking Back at the Seventies," in *Sources for American Studies*. Eds. Jefferson B. Kellogg and Robert H. Walker.

Westport, CT: Greenwood, pp. 389–400. Mentions W briefly, p. 392.

220. Story, Ralph. "Paul Lawrence Dunbar: Master Player in a Fixed Game." *CLA Journal*, 27 (September), 30–55. Mentions briefly W and *EM* (p. 43).

221. Stout, Janis P. *The Journey Narrative in American Literature: Patterns and Departures.* Westport, CT: Greenwood Press, pp. 33, 95. Mentions briefly "The Man Who Lived Underground."

222. Suda, Minoru. "Could White Writers Portray Black People? An Attempt at Solution." *Ritsumeikan University Foreign Literature Studies*, 58 (31 May), 1–47. Compares the images of black people in *The Street, A Raisin in the Sun*, and "Bright and Morning Star" with ghose in fiction by Faulkner, McCullers and Styron [T.K., R.B., and Y.H.].

223. Sundquist, Eric. *Faulkner: The House Divided.* Baltimore: Johns Hopkins University Press, pp. 64, 86–87, 89, 92, 94. Compares *NS* to *Light in August*, with additional comparisons to Styron's *The Confessions of Nat Turner* and to *Uncle Tom's Cabin*.

224. Tate, Claudia. "Introduction," in her *Black Women Writers at Work.* New York: Continuum, pp. xv–xx. Mentions briefly Cross Damon's journey in *O.*

225. _____. "Margaret Walker," in her *Black Women Writers at Work.* New York: Continuum, pp. 188–204. Includes an interview with Walker discussing her friendship with W (p. 193) and her biography of him (pp. 193–201).

226. _____. "Maya Angelou," in her *Black Women Writers at Work.* New York: Continuum, pp. 1–11. Angelou mentions W briefly. Reprinted in *Conversations with Maya Angelace.* Jackson: University Press of Mississippi, pp. 147, 150.

227. Taylor, Gordon O. *Chapters of Experience: Studies in 20th Century American Autobiography.* New York: St. Martin's Press, pp. 41–43, 47, 48–52, 53–58, 60, 63, 64, 71, 142, 154, 155. In a chapter on twentieth-century black autobiography, Taylor discusses *BB* and *AH*, noting W's "increasing emphasis on his effort to become a writer, and on the act of writing as the way to become oneself" (p. 48). He also comments on *NS* and relates W to DuBois, Baldwin, and Malcolm X.

228. Taylor, Walter. *Faulkner's Search for a South.* Urbana: University of Illinois Press, pp. 65–67, 70–71, 79–85, 213. Extensive comparison of *NS* and *Light in August.* Includes discussion of Baldwin's view of *NS.*

229. Tignor, Elanor Q. "American Literature: From the Late Nineteenth Century to the 1970's," in *Reconstructing American Literature: Courses, Syllabi, Issues,* Ed. Paul Lauter. Old Westbury, NY: The Feminist Press, pp. 103–107. Course plan including *NS.*

230. Traore, Bakary. "Témoignage." *Présence Africaine,* No. 125 (First Quarter), 356–359. Mentions W briefly.

231. Traylor, Eleanor W. "The Fabulous World of Toni Morrison: *Tar Baby,*" in *Confirmation: An Anthology of African American Women.* Eds. Amiri Baraka and Amina Baraka. New York: William Morrow, pp. 333–352. Mentions briefly *NS* (p. 341). Reprinted: 1988.

232. Wald, Alan M. *The Revolutionary Imagination: The Poetry and Politics of John Wheelwright and Sherry Morgan.* Chapel Hill: The University of North Carolina Press, pp. 4, 14–15. Mentions W briefly and comments on elements of "radical modernism" in *NS* comparable to Brecht's epic theater."

233. Walker, Alice. "Beyond the Peacock: The Reconstruction of Flannery O'Connor," in her *In Search of Our Mothers' Gardens.* San Diego: Harcourt Brace Jovanovich, pp. 42–59. Reprint of 1975.197a.

234. _____. "The Black Writer and the Southern Experience," in her *In Search of Our Mothers' Gardens.* San Diego: Harcourt Brace Jovanovich, 1983, pp. 15–21. Reprint of 1970.

235. _____. "Breaking Chains and Encouraging Life," in her *In Search of Our Mothers' Gardens: Womanist Prose.* San Diego: Harcourt Brace Jovanovich, pp. 278–289. Reprint of 1980.

236. _____. "Choosing to Stay at Home: Ten Years After the March on Washington," in *In Search of Our Mothers' Gardens.* San Diego: Harcourt Brace Jovanovich, pp. 158–170. Deplores W's lack of a choice to stay in or depart from Mississippi (p. 164).

237. _____. "From an Interview," in her *In Search of Our Mothers' Gar-*

dens: *Womanist Prose.* San Diego: Harcourt Brace Jovanovich, pp. 244–272. Partial reprint of 1973. 289.

238. _____. "If the Present Looks Like the Past, What Does the Future Look Like?" in her *In Search of Our Mothers' Gardens: Womanist Prose.* San Diego: Harcourt Brace Jovanovich, pp. 290–312. Reprint of 1982. 138.

239. _____. "In Search of Our Mothers' Gardens," in her *In Search of Our Mothers' Gardens: Womanist Prose.* San Diego: Harcourt Brace Jovanovich, pp. 231–243. Mentions W briefly (p. 239). Reprint of 1974.

240. _____. "The Unglamorous but Worthwhile Duties of the Black Revolutionary Artist, or the Black Writer Who Simply Works and Writes," in her *In Search of Our Mothers' Gardens.* San Diego: Harcourt Brace Jovanovich, pp. 130–138. Mentions favorably *BB*, "The Ethics of Living Jim Crow," and Bigger Thomas (pp. 131, 137).

241. _____. "A Talk: Conversation 1972," in her *In Search of Our Mothers' Gardens.* San Diego: Harcourt Brace Jovanovich, pp. 33–41. Reprint of 1972.203a.

242. Walker, Margaret, and Claudia Tate. "Margaret Walker," in Tate's *Black Women Writers at Work.* New York: Continuum, pp. 188–204. Interview containing much material on W (pp. 193–200), most of it in her biography of W. She emphasizes her qualifications and disparages Constance Webb and Michel Fabre.

243. Walker, Marshall. *History of American Literature.* Chicago: St. James Press, pp. 150–151, 164, 220. Mentions briefly *NS, BB, WML,* and *EM.*

244. _____. *History of American Literature.* Chicago: St. James Press, pp. 150–151, 164. Comments briefly on *NS* and *BB.*

245. Walkiewicz, E.P. "1957–1968: Toward Diversity of Form," in *The American Short Story: 1945–1980.* Boston: Twayne, pp. 35–75. Mentions *EM* and asserts that "Wright's fiction is marked by the use of broad symbolism and characterized by what is sometimes a heavy didacticism" (p. 56).

246. Warner, Anne Bradford. "The Southern Renaissance," in *Reconstructing American Literature: Courses, Syllabi, Issues.* Ed. Paul

Lauter. Old Westbury, New York: The Feminist Press, pp. 206–208. Course plan including "Long Black Song" and "The Man Who Was Almost a Man."

247. Weaver, Gordon. "Chronology," in his *The American Short Story: 1945–1980*. Boston: Twayne, pp. vii–ix. Lists W's death and the publication of *UTC*.

248. Webb, Constance. "Wright, Richard Nathaniel," in *Collier's Encyclopedia*. Ed. William D. Halsey. New York: Macmillan Educational Company, vol. 23, p. 638. Biographical sketch noting "his profound influence on contemporary black writers."

249. Weidman, Bette S. "Regionalism, Realism, and Naturalism in American Fiction," in *Reconstructing American Literature." Courses, Syllabi, Issues*." Ed. Paul Lauter. Old Westbury, NY: The Feminist Press, pp. 108–111. Course plan including *NS*.

250. Williams, Sherley Anne, and Claudia Tate. "Sherley Anne Williams," in Tate's *Black Women Writers at Work*. New York: Continuum, pp. 205–213. In this interview Williams mentions W briefly (p. 206).

251. Yarborough, Richard. "The American Political Novel," in *Reconstructing American Literature: Courses, Syllabi, Issues*. Ed. Paul

Lauter. Old Westbury, New York: The Feminist Press, pp. 160–162. Course plan including *O*.

252. Yellin, Jean Fagan, "Criticisms of American Culture," in *Reconstructing American Literature: Courses, Syllabi, Issues*. Ed. Paul Lauter. Old Westbury, NY: The Feminist Press, pp. 223–230. Course plan including *NS* and *AH*.

253. _____. "Model Chronology," in *Reconstructing American Literature: Courses, Syllabi, Issues:* Ed. Paul Lauter. Old Westbury, NY: The Feminist Press, pp. 231–246. Lists *UTC, NS* and *BB*.

1984

254. Abcarian, Richard, and Marvin Klotz. *Instructor's Manual to Accompany Literature: The Human Experience*. New York: St. Martin's Press, pp. 18–19. Reprint of 1973.5.

255. Alexander, Margaret Walker. "Richard Wright," in *Richard Wright: A Collection of Critical Essays*. Eds. Richard Macksey and Frank E. Moorer. Englewood Cliffs, NJ: Prentice-Hall, pp. 21–36. Reprint of 1971.4.

256. Allen, William Rodney. *Instructor's Guide to Accompany The Heath Introduction to Literature, Second Edition*. Lexington, MA: D.C. Heath, pp. 28–29. Includes two discussion questions for "The Man Who Was Almost a Man."

257. Alvarez-Pereyre, Jacques. *The Poetry of Commitment in South Africa*. Trans. Clive Wake. London: Heinemann, p. 49. Quotes Sipho Sepamla's desire to read W and other black protest writers, unavailable in South Africa.

258. Anon. *Arts and Humanities Citation Index 1984*. Vol. 2. Philadelphia: Institute for Scientific Information, pp. 10165–10166. Lists seventy-four items s.v. WRIGHT R, not all on W.

259. Anon. *Bibliographic Guide to Black Studies: 1983*. Boston: G.K. Hall, p. 116. Lists one secondary

item concerning W in the New York Public Library, supplementing the *Dictionary Catalog of the Schomburg Collection of Negro Literature and History*.

260. Anon. "Bibliographie." *Notre Librairie*, 77 (November-December), 112–115. Lists works in French translation of fifty-three African American writers as well as a dozen critical works. Thirteen works by W are included.

261. Anon. "British Association for American Studies: Pamphlets in American Studies." *Journal of American Studies*, 18 (December 1984) p. iv. Lists A. Robert Lee's "Black Fiction Since Richard Wright."

262. Anon. "*The Black Scholar* Publishers Listing of Black Interest Books." *The Black Scholar*, 15 (September-October), 34–49. Contains a Howard University Press notice of Margaret Walker's *The Daemonic Genius of Richard Wright* (p. 37).

263. Anon. *Comprehensive Dissertation Index Ten-Year Cumulation 1973–1982*. Vol. 30. Ann Arbor: University Microfilms International, pp. 879–880. Lists dissertations treating W by Charles J. Evans, Anthony Magistrale, William Joseph Barnette, John Oliver Hodges, Kandi Baba Kumasi, Elizabeth Ciner, Catherine Daniels Hurst,

Joyce Ann Joyce, Earle Vincent Bryant, Annette O. Shands, Paul Victor Olsen, Robert A. Coles, Butler Emmanuel Brewton, Annette Lois Conn, Jerry W. Ward, Maryemma Graham, Claudia Tate, Eleanor E. Traylor, Chukwedi Maduka, Theresa Haynon, Darrell Rhea Shreve, Evelyn Gross Avery, Jean Lovell Bauerly, James A. Miller, Walter Anthony Eden, Rebecca McBride, Alvin J. Starr, Arlene Joan Crewdson, Esther A. Terry, Anne Hudson Jones, Moylan C. Mills, Katherine Sprandell, Mary E. Mebane, Brian J. Benson, and Hugh Gloster. Reprinted: 1999.

264. Anon. "Hellenbrand, Harold. *Bigger Thomas Reconsidered: Native Son, Film and King Kong*." *American History and Life*, 21A, 285. Abstract of the article.

265. Anon. *Index Translationum 32*. Paris: Unesco, pp. 311, 563, 569, 616, 899, 1254. Lists translations of *NS* into Danish and Russian; *SH* into French; *AH* into French; and *BB* into Hungarian and Korean.

266. Anon. "Lenz, Günter H. *Southern Exposures: The Urban Experience and the Re-Construction of Black Folk Culture and Community in the Works of Richard Wright and Zora Neale Hurston*." *American History and Life* 21A, 85. Abstract of the article.

267. Anon. "Repères bibliographiques: Traductions françaises de romans et nouvelles écrits par des auteurs noirs américains (1930–1984)." *Focus*, pp. [20–21]. Lists ten works by W.

268. Anon. "Wright (Richard)," in *Grand Dictionnaire Encyclopedique Larousse*. Paris: Librarie Larousse, 1985, vol. 10, p. 10940. Brief biographical note.

269. Baker, Houston A., Jr. "Introduction," in his *Blues, Ideology, and Afro-American Literature: A Vernacular Theory*. Chicago: The University of Chicago Press, pp. 1–14. Mentions briefly *BB*.

270. _____. "Reassessing (W)right: A Meditation on the Black (W)hole," in his *Blues, Ideology, and Afro-American Literature: A Vernacular Theory*. Chicago: The University of Chicago Press, pp. 139–172. Disputing disparagement of W's achievement by Baldwin and Ellison, Baker offers "a tropological perspective on Wright" (p. 144) in terms of the black hole of physics: "a massive concentration of energy that draws all objects to its center" (p. 145). After analyzing *BB*, "Big Boy Leaves Home," and — at length — "The Man Who Lived Underground," Baker concludes that W's use of the ludic trickster makes him "the Black Symbolist par excellence" and places him at "the very center of that dark (and powerfully invisible) area of Afro-American life that constitutes its underground expressive (w)holiness" (p. 172). Reprinted: 1987.

271. _____. "A Yea and an Announcement: Notice of a New Black Playwright and His Work." *Black American Literature Forum*, 18 (Fall), 113–116. Mentions briefly Baldwin's criticism of W.

272. Baldwin, James, Jordan Elgrably, and George Plimpton. "The Art of Fiction LXXVIII." *The Paris Review*, No. 91 (Spring), pp. 49–82. Baldwin discusses his relationship to W (pp. 71, 81).

273. Baraka, Amiri. "Afro-American Literature and Class Struggle," in his *Daggers and Javelins: Essays, 1974–1979*. New York: William Morrow, pp. 310–334. Reprint of 1980.39.

274. _____. "*Black Boy* as Slave Narrative, *Black Boy* as Anti-Imperialist Narrative," in his *Daggers and Javelins: Essays, 1974–1979*. New York: William Morrow, pp. 172–181.

Marxist-Leninist interpretation of W's autobiography. Though similar in many ways to the slave narrative, *BB* is really a story of "national oppression" during "the development of the Post-Reconstruction, twentieth-century, modern Afro-American sensibility in the face of … imperialism" (p. 176). But W's individualism was excessive.

275. _____. "Howdy Doody and the Mind Bandits," in his *Daggers and Javelins: Essays, 1974–1979*. New York: William Morrow, pp. 297–309. Mentions W briefly (p. 308).

276. _____. "Introduction," in his *Daggers and Javelins: Essays, 1974–1979*. New York: William Morrow, pp. 9–15. Notes that the essay on W included in the collection derives from lectures at Yale and George Washington University.

277. _____. "Langston Hughes and the Harlem Renaissance," in his *Daggers and Javelins: Essays, 1974–1979*. New York: William Morrow, pp. 149–165. Mentions W's exile (p. 164) and ranks him with Hughes and Du Bois as "perhaps the most eminent of the Afro-American authors" (p. 165).

278. _____. "Not Just Survival: Revolution (Some Historical Notes on Afro-American Drama)," in his *Daggers and Javelins: Essays, 1974–1979*. New York: William Morrow, pp. 30–52. Mentions W briefly (p. 43).

279. _____. "A Reply to Saunders Redding's 'The Black Revolution in American Studies,'" in his *Daggers and Javelins: Essays, 1974–1979*. New York: William Morrow, pp. 279–287.

280. _____. "The Revolutionary Tradition in Afro-American Literature," in his *Daggers and Javelins: Essays, 1974–1979*. New York: William Morrow, pp. 137–148. Reprint of 1979.35.

281. Bawer, Bruce. "The Novel in the Academy: A Paean to Perplexity." *The New Criterion*, 2 (May), 20–30. Review of *American Fictions 1940–1980: A Comprehensive History and Critical Evaluation* quoting a long sentence on *NS*.

282. Benoist, Mary Anne. "Black Studies." *S.S.S.L.: The News-Letter of The Society for the Study of Southern Literature*, 17 (November), 13–14. Lists Margaret Walker's *The Daemonic Genius of Richard Wright*.

283. Benston, Kimberly W. "Con-

trolling the Dialectical Deacon: The Critique of Historicism in *Invisible Man*." *Delta*, 18 (April), 89–103. Mentions briefly W (p. 91) and *NS* (p. 93).

284. _____. "I Am What I Am: The Topos of Un(naming) in Afro-American literature," in *Black Literature and Literary Theory*. Ed. Henry Louis Gates, Jr. New York: Methuen, 1984, pp. 151–172. Includes discussion of naming in *BB*, especially in the case of W's grandfather.

285. Bergreen, Laurence. *James Agee: A Life*. New York: E.P. Dutton, p. 289. Notes the powerful impact of *BB* on Agee.

286. Bischof, Phyllis. *Afro-Americana: A Research Guide to Collections at the University of California at Berkeley*. Berkeley: University of California at Berkeley, pp. 8, 48. Mentions W briefly.

287. Blair, Dorothy S. *Senegalese Literature: A Critical History*. Boston: Twayne, p. 116. Mentions the "indirect influence" of *UTC* on Cheik Ndao's play *La Décision*.

288. Blount, Marcellus. "Studies in Afro-American Literature: An Annual Annotated Bibliography, 1983." *Callaloo*, 7 (Fall), 104–139. Includes eleven items on W with cross-references to seven others. Also mentions W briefly in the introduction.

289. Blumberg, Rhoda Lois. *Civil Rights: The 1960s Freedom Struggle*. Boston: Twayne, p. 31. Mentions briefly *NS*.

290. Boorstein, Karen. "Beyond *Black Macho*: An Interview with Michele Wallace." *Black American Literature Forum*, 18 (Winter), 163–167. Wallace mentions briefly W's "experience of true marginality."

291. Bordarier, Françoise. "Michel Fabre. *La Rive Noire*." *Notre Librairie*, 77 (November–December), 120–121. Mentions W briefly.

292. Bordman, Gerald. "Welles, Orson," in his *The Oxford Companion to American Theatre*. New York: Oxford University Press, p. 707. Biographical sketch mentioning briefly the play *NS*.

293. Brazinsky, Judith Giblin. "The Demands of Conscience and the Imperatives of Form: The Dramatization of *Native Son*." *Black American Literature Forum*, 18 (Fall), 106–109. Investigates the differences between the novel and Paul Green's play. They are attributable not only to Green's rejection of determinism, but even more to the exigencies of dramatic form. In the novel W could elicit understanding and sympathy for Bigger, but Bigger had to be simplified for the theater. Brazinsky analyzes the first scene and the characterization of Mary and Bessie to make her case.

294. Breen, Jon L. *Novel Verdicts: A Guide to Courtroom Fiction*. Metuchen, NJ: The Scarecrow Press, p. 233. Lists *NS*.

295. Brignano, Russell C. *Black Americans in Autobiography*. Revised and expanded edition. Durham, NC: Duke University Press, pp. 130–131. Revised reprint of 1974.33.

296. Bröck, Sabine. "'Talk as a Form of Action': An Interview with Paule Marshall," in *History and Tradition in Afro-American Culture*. Ed. Günter H. Lenz. Frankfurt: Campus Verlag, pp. 194–206. Marshall mentions reading W (p. 194) and Bröck asks a question mentioning an essay by Robert Stepto on W.

297. Brown, Beth. "Five from Lotus." *CLA Journal*, 28 (September), 102–109. Mentions briefly *O* (p. 104).

298. Brown, Jeanine Barrett. "Richard Wright." *Abstracts of English Studies*, 27 (June), 198. Abstracts an article by Oliver Conant.

299. Brown, Susan Love. "*The Sage in Harlem; H.L. Mencken and the Black Writers of the 1920s* by Charles Scruggs." *Lincoln Review*, 5 (Summer), 63–65. Review quoting Scruggs mentioning W.

300. Burgum, Edwin Berry. "The Art of Richard Wright's Short Stories," in *Richard Wright: A Collection of Critical Essays*. Eds. Richard Macksey and Frank E. Moorer. Englewood Cliffs, NJ: Prentice-Hall, pp. 194–206. Reprint of 1944.64.

301. Bus, Heiner. "Jean Toomer and the Black Heritage," in *History and Tradition in Afro-American Culture*. Ed. Günter H. Lenz. Frankfurt: Campus Verlag, pp. 56–83. Quotes Robert Bone on *NS*.

302. Butler, Robert James. "Wright's *Native Son* and Two Novels by Zola: A Comparative Study." *Black American Literature Forum*, 18 (Fall), 100–105. Without definitely asserting that W used *Thérèse Racquin*, and *La Bête Humaine* as sources for *NS*, Butler finds many similarities. An atmosphere of fear pervades *NS* and *Thérèse Racquin*, and the characterization of the protagonists is similar. Motifs and image patterns correspond in striking ways. *NS* and *La Bête Humaine* depict the ambivalence of love and hate in human character and focus on the psychology of violence. Despite their common grimness, W's vision of life is finally less despairing than Zola's.

303. Campbell, Diane H. "Richard Wright." *Abstracts of English Studies*, 27 (September), 321. Abstracts an article by M.E. Grenander.

304. Cheney, Anne. *Lorraine Hansberry*. Boston: Twain, p. 19. Mentions W briefly.

305. [Childrey, Frank W.]. "Profile: Ronald Bailey, Director, Afro-American Studies." *The Southern Register*, 2 (Winter), 11. Notes that a course on W is taught at the University of Mississippi.

306. Coale, Samuel. *William Styron Revisited*. Boston: Twayne, p. 29. Mentions W briefly.

307. Coe, Richard N. *When the Grass Was Taller: Autobiography and the Experience of Childhood*. New Haven, CT: Yale University Press, pp. 234, 287. Mentions and quotes from *BB*.

308. Cohen, Milton A. "Black Brutes and Mulatto Saints: The Racial Hierarchy of Stein's 'Melanctha.'" *Black American Literature Forum*, 18 (Fall), 119–121. Mentions W's admiration of Stein.

309. Cooke, Michael G. *Afro-American Literature in the Twentieth Century: The Achievement of Intimacy*. New Haven, CT: Yale University Press, pp. xii, 22, 38, 39, 40, 70, 83, 85, 86–97, 98, 107, 109, 121, 125, 142, 173, 211, 220. Cooke traces a literary evolution out of signifying and the blues through the stages of self-veiling, solitude, kinship, and intimacy. Along with Hurston and Ellison, W represents the stage of solitude. Chapter 3 analyzes *BP* and *NS* from this perspective.

310. Cracroft, Richard H. "Research in Western American Literature: 1982." *Western American Literature*, 18 (Winter), 335–342. Lists a dissertation treating W by Mary Cathleen Gallagher (p. 337).

311. Cruse, Harold. *The Crisis of the Negro Intellectual*. New York: Quill, pp. 3, 51, 69, 115, 181, 183–184, 187, 237, 267, 269, 271, 273, 275–277, 500, 510. Reprint of 1967.25.

312. Cudjoe, Selwyn R. "Maya Angelou and the Autobiographical Statement," in *Black Women Writers (1950–1980): A Critical Evaluation*. Ed. Mari Evans. New York: Doubleday, pp. 6–24. Mentions briefly *NS* (p. 10).

313. _____. "Maya Angelou and the Autobiographical Statement," in *Black Women Writers (1950–1980)*. Ed. Mari Evans. New York: Doubleday, pp. 6–24. Mentions briefly *NS* (p. 10).

314. Cutrer, Thomas W. *Parnassus on the Mississippi: The Southern Review and the Baton Rouge Literary Community 1935–1942*. Baton Rouge: Louisiana State University Press, p. 155. Mentions briefly W and *UTC*.

315. Davis, George. *Coming Home*. Washington: Howard University Press, p. [vii].

316. Davis, Jane Maria. "This Peculiar Kind of Hell: The Role of Power in the Novels of Richard Wright." *Dissertation Abstracts International*, 45 (September), 844A. Abstracts a 1984 Stanford dissertation arguing that W portrays "power as an almost exclusively destructive force."

317. Davis, Lenwood G. *Black-Jewish Relations in the United States, 1752–1984: A Selected Bibliography*. Westport, CT: Greenwood Press, p. 20. Contains an annotated entry for *BB*.

318. Daziron, Héliane. "Richard Wright. *Une faim d'egalité*." *Notre Librairie*, No. 77 (November-December), 122–123. Review of *AH* explaining its relation to *BB* and stressing the theme of disillusion, both with the North as a racial haven and with the Communist Party.

319. De Beauvoir, Simone. *Adieux: A Farewell to Sartre*. London: André Deutsch and Weidenfeld and Nicholson, p. 239.

320. DeMott, Robert J. *Steinbeck's Reading: A Catalogue of Books Owned and Borrowed*. New York: Garland, pp. 124, 181. Lists *NS* and *UTC* in Steinbeck's personal library and comments on the W-Steinbeck relationship in Mexico in 1940.

321. _____. *Steinbeck's Reading: A Catalog of Books Owned and Borrowed*. New York: Garland Publishing, p. 124. Lists *NS* and *UTC*.

322. Dent, Tom. "Marcus B. Christian: A Reminiscence and an

Appreciation." *Black American Literature Forum*, 18 (Spring), 22–26. Includes an entry from Christian's diary dated 1 May 1957 commenting on "Bright and Morning Star" and its political implications.

323. Dietze, Rudolf F. "Ralph Ellison and the Literary Tradition," in *History and Tradition in Afro-American Culture*. Ed. Günter H. Lenz. Frankfurt: Campus Verlag, pp. 118–129. Comments on W's response to Ellison's first short story (p. 124) and mentions W several times elsewhere.

324. Dorsinville, Roger. "Mémoire des dispersés." *Notre Librairie*, 77 (November-December), 3–5. Mentions W briefly.

325. Downs, Robert B., and Ralph E. McCoy. "School Censorship Cases," in their *The First Freedom Today: Critical Issues Relating to Censorship and to Intellectual Freedom*. Chicago: American Library Association, pp. 70–74. Mentions briefly *BB* as a book censored in Island Trees, New York (p. 72).

326. Doyle, Mary Ellen, S.C.N. "A *MELUS* Interview: Ernest J. Gaines – 'Other Things to Write About.'" *MELUS* 11 (Summer), 59–81. Mentions W briefly (p. 60). Reprinted: 1995.

327. Dust, Alvin I. "Richard Wright." *Abstracts of English Studies*, 27 (December), 399. Abstracts an article by Al Starr.

328. Elgrably, Jordan. "The Art of Fiction LXXVIII: James Baldwin." *The Paris Review*, 26 (Spring) 48–82. Baldwin comments (pp. 71, 81) on his early relation to W ("I adored him"), *NS* ("too simple-minded"), and *LT* ("his greatest novel"). Reprinted: 1989.

329. Ellison, Ralph. "Remembering Richard Wright." *Delta*, No. 18 (April), 1–13. Delivered at the W Conference at the University of Iowa in 1971, this lecture relates Ellison's early friendship with W. Topics include friction with the Communist Party and the *Daily Worker* occasioned by W's independence, the *New Challenge* episode, W's Mississippi and Chicago background, and the composition of *NS*. "He had as much curiosity about how writing is written as I had about how music is composed and our curiosity concerning artistic creation became the basis of our friendship" (p. 11).

330. Fabre, Michel. "Entretien avec Frank Yerby." *Notre Librairie*, 77 (November-December), 101–103. Yerby mentions W briefly.

331. _____. "'Looking at the Naked Blonde – Closely' (or Scrutinizing Ellison's Writing)." *Delta*, 18 (April), 119–131. Compares briefly the belly dancer scene early in *Invisible Man* to episodes in W's work (p. 119).

332. _____. "Quelques tendances du roman noir contemporain." *Notre Librairie*, 77 (November-December), 84–89. Mentions briefly "The Man Who Lived Underground" (p. 86).

333. _____. "Regards sur les contemporains." *Focus*, pp. 12–16. Comments on W and the tradition he established (p. 12).

334. _____. "Richard Wright et l'Afrique." *Notre Librairie*, No. 77 (November-December), 41–46. After noting references to Africa in *LT*, *NS*, and *LD*, Fabre discusses *BP*, emphasizing W's ambivalence toward the ancestral homeland. The trip to the Gold Coast was a search for identity, but W views Africa from a Western rationalist perspective. The article ends with an excerpt from a letter to Fabre by Leopold Sedar Senghor expressing admiration for W because he was "*l'incarnation même de la <<passion>> noire.*"

335. _____. "Richard Wright: The Man Who Lived Underground," in *Richard Wright: A Collection of Critical Essays*. Eds. Richard Macksey and Frank E. Moorer. Englewood Cliffs, NJ: Prentice-Hall, pp. 207–220. Reprint of 1971.110.

336. Farnsworth, Robert M. *Melvin B. Tolson, 1898–1966: Plain Talk and Poetic Prophecy*. Columbia: University of Missouri Press, pp. 39–40, 95, 137, 214, 220, 227–228, 250, 253. Discusses Tolson's praise of W for *UTC* and *NS*, quotes W's praise of Tolson's *Rendezvous with America*, mentions W and Tolson discussing Sartre's *No Exit*, and notes appearance of W in Tolson's *Harlem Gallery*.

337. Faulkner, Howard. "Homespun Justice: The Lynching in American Fiction." *South Dakota Review*, 22 (Winter), 104–119. Contains a paragraph (pp. 116–117) on "Big Boy Leaves Home" and mentions the story elsewhere.

338. Fetrow, Fred M. *Robert Hayden*. Boston: Twayne, pp. 6, 55, 148–149. Mentions briefly "The Ethics of Living Jim Crow," "I Have Seen Black Hands," *BB*, and *NS*.

339. Fontenot, Chester J. "Visionaries, Mystics, and Revolutionaries: Narrative Postures in Black Fiction." *Studies in Black American Literature*. Vol. 1: *Black American Prose Theory*. Eds. Joe Weixlmann and Chester J. Fontenot. Greenwood, Florida: Penkevill, pp. 63–87. Includes comments on *NS* in relation to Fanon's theories of language (pp. 74–75).

340. Ford, Nick Aaron. "The Ordeal of Richard Wright," in *Richard Wright: A Collection of Critical Essays*. Eds. Richard Macksey and Frank E. Moorer. Englewood Cliffs, NJ: Prentice-Hall, pp. 139–148. Reprint of 1953.126.

341. Frye, Charles A., Charlyn Harper, Linda James Myers, Eleanor W. Traylor. "How to Think Black: A Symposium on Toni Cade Bambara's *The Salt Eaters*." *Contributions in Black Studies*, 6, 33–48. Traylor mentions W briefly (p. 44).

342. Gallagher, Kathleen. "Bigger's Great Leap to the Figurative." *CLA Journal*, 27 (March), 293–314. *NS* is a novel about the way Bigger, a criminal because he is black in a racist society, reacts to images. In Book One they dominate him. In Book Two he "learns to manipulate the images" (p. 300). In Book Three W presents two stories without linking them adequately: the public story of the trial and the private story of Bigger's effort to discover the meaning of his life. "At the end, he breaks through to a comprehension of the metaphor of his life" (p. 313), but it is too late for him to act on his understanding.

343. Garrett, George. *James Jones*. San Diego: Harcourt Brace Jovanovich, p. 4. Quotes Budd Schulberg mentioning W and *NS*.

344. Gates, Henry Louis, Jr. "'The Blackness of Blackness': A Critique of the Sign and the Signifying Monkey." *Studies in Black American Literature*. Vol. 1 *Black American Prose Theory*. Eds. Joe Weixlmann and Chester J. Fontenot. Greenwood, FL: Penkevill, pp. 129–181.

345. _____. "The blackness of blackness: a critique of the sign and the signifying Monkey," in his *Black Literature and Literary Theory*. New York: Methuen, pp. 285–321.

346. _____. "Criticism in the Jungle," in his *Black Literature and Literary Theory*. New York: Methuen, pp. 1–24. Quotes Sartre on W (pp. 8–9).

347. Gayle, Addison, Jr. "Gwendolyn Brooks: Poet of the Whirlwind," in *Black Women Writers (1950–1980): A Critical Evaluation*. Ed. Mari Evans. New York: Doubleday, pp. 79–87. Quotes W briefly (p. 83).

348. _____. "Gwendolyn Brooks: Poet of the Whirlwind," in *Black Women Writers (1950–1980)*. Ed. Mari Evans. New York: Doubleday, pp. 79–87. Quotes W that "the man on the corner with the machine gun" is symbolic of the twentieth century.

349. Gibson, Donald B. "Wright's Invisible Native Son," in *Richard Wright: A Collection of Critical Essays*. Eds. Richard Macksey and Frank E. Moorer. Englewood Cliffs, NJ: Prentice-Hall, pp. 95–105.

350. Giddings, Paula. *When and Where I Enter: The Impact of Black Women on Race and Sex in America*. New York: William Morrow, pp. 239, 322. Mention *NS* and quotes from *O*.

351. Gounard, Jean-François. *Le Probleme noir dans les oeuvres de Richard Wright et de James Baldwin*. Sherbrooke, Québec, 333 pp. Contains five chapters on W: The Life of Richard Nathaniel Wright (1908–1960), Conditions in the South, Conditions in the North, Flight and Conclusion. Throughout the effort is to relate W's life and work to social and racial conditions, relying mainly on summary and paraphrase rather than analysis. The bibliography contains nothing on W after 1977. Translation 1992.

352. Graham, Maryemma. "Barak Tells, but Not All." *Freedomways*, 24 (Second Quarter), 144–148. Mentions briefly W and *AH* (p. 144).

353. Gunner, Elizabeth. *A Handbook for Teaching African Literature*. London: Heinemann, p. 9. Lists *BB* with very brief annotation. Reprinted: 1987.

354. Hairston, Loyle. *A Gathering of Old Men. By Ernest J. Gaines.*" *Freedomways*, 24 (First Quarter), 57–60. Includes favorable comment on W, who dared to dig deeper by proposing that racism is a systemic function of the capitalist social order" (p. 59).

355. _____. "Alice in the Mainstream: An Essay Review." *Freedomways*, 24 (Third Quarter), 182–190. Includes three brief mentions of W (pp. 182, 183).

356. _____. "New South Tragi-Comedy." *Freedomways*, 24 (First Quarter) 57–60. Review of Ernest Gaines's *A Gathering of Old Men* praising W highly.

357. Hajek, Friederike. "From Slave Narrative to Contemporary Afro-American Autobiography: Some Remarks on the Contribution of Black People to the Origins and Originality of American Culture," in *The Origins and Originality of American Culture*. Ed. Tibor Frank. Budapest: Akadémiai Kiadó, pp. 621–630. Mentions W briefly (p. 626).

358. Hansen, Chadwick. "*Rediscoveries: Literature and Place in Illinois*. By Robert C. Bray." *American Studies*, 25 (Fall), 84. Review mentioning W briefly.

359. Harris, Trudier. "Ritual Violence and the Formation of an Aesthetic," in her *Exorcising Blackness: Historical and Literary Lynching and Burning Rituals*. Bloomington: Indiana University Press, pp. 95–128. Argues that the ritual of lynching shapes W's artistic vision, creating a pervasive atmosphere of apprehension. "The ritual also determines communal and individual character and provides the symbolic unifying structure for 'Between the World and Me' (1935), 'Big Boy Leaves Home' (1938), *Native Son* (1940), and *The Long Dream* (1958)." Harris analyzes the role of lynching in these works.

360. Hatcher, John. *From the Auroral Darkness: The Life and Poetry of Robert Hayden*. Oxford: George Ronald, pp. 13, 15, 61, 66, 67, 81. Notes the influence of W's poetry on Hayden's early verse. Mentions *UTC* and W's radicalism.

361. Henderson, Mae G. "In Another Country: Afro-American Expatriate Novelists in France, 1946–1974." *Dissertation Abstracts International*, 45 (September), 845A. Abstracts a 1983 Yale dissertation. W "provides a personal and artistic model for his exiled compatriots." Includes a chapter on *O*, which "extends the concept of expatriation from a social and geographical to a spiritual and psychological plane."

362. Hernton, Calvin. "Postscript," in *A Case of Rape* by Chester Himes. Washington: Howard University Press, pp. 107–140. Mentions briefly *NS*, *O*, and *LD* (p. 118).

363. _____. "The Sexual Mountain and Black Women Writers." *Black American Literature Forum*, 18 (Winter), 139–145. Comments briefly on W's depiction of black women in *NS*.

364. Hill, George H. *Black Media in America: A Resource Guide*. Boston: G.K. Hall, pp. 21, 49, 184, 273. Lists items on W by George A. Sewell, Gwendolyn Louise King, Michel Fabre, and Greg Morris.

365. Holton, Sylvia Wallace. "Black English in Fiction, 1900–1945: Dialect and Social Change," in her *Down Home and Uptown: The Representation of Black Speech in American Fiction*. Rutherford, Madison, Teaneck, NJ: Fairleigh Dickinson University Press, pp. 95–142. Comparing passages from "Big Boy Leaves Home" and *NS*, Holton shows that Wright's representation of dialect changes from phonological to grammatical. The same change typifies African American literature as a whole.

366. Holtzclaw, Robert Fulton. "Richard Nathaniel Wright," in his *A Brief History of the Afro-Mississippian, 1865–1980*. Shaker Heights, OH: The Keeble Press, pp. 181–184. Biographical sketch emphasizing the Mississippi connection and comparing W favorably to Faulkner. Mentions briefly most of W's books.

367. Horvath, Brooke K. "Richard Wright." *Abstracts of English Studies*, 27 (June), 198. Abstracts an article by Jerry H. Bryant.

368. Howard, William. "Richard Wright's Flood Stories and the Great Mississippi River Flood of 1927: Social and Historical Backgrounds." *Southern Literary Journal*, 16 (Spring), 44–62. Analyzes "Silt" ("The Man Who Saw the Flood") and "Down by the Riverside" in the context of the 1927 flood. Although W's specific knowledge of the social history of this catastrophe derived mainly from biased white Memphis newspapers, his account of its racial consequences is strikingly similar to that of black journalists because of inferred and intuitive judgments based on his own racial experience.

369. [Hurt, James]. "James Baldwin (1924–)," in his and Brian Wilkie's *Literature of the Western*

World. Vol. II: Neoclassicism Through the Modern Period. New York: Macmillan, pp. 2202–2204. Comments on W's early help to Baldwin.

370. _____. "Ralph Ellison (1914–)," in his and Brian Wilkie's *Literature of the Western World*. Vol. II: Neoclassicism Through the Modern Period. New York: Macmillan, pp. 2171–2173. Comments on W's early encouragement of Ellison's literary efforts.

371. Jackson, Blyden. "Richard Wright in a Moment of Truth," in *Richard Wright: A Collection of Critical Essays*. Eds. Richard Macksey and Frank E. Moorer. Englewood Cliffs, NJ: Prentice-Hall, pp. 182–193.

372. Jackson, Esther Merle. "The American Negro and the Image of the Absurd," in *Richard Wright: A Collection of Critical Essays*. Eds. Richard Macksey and Frank E. Moorer. Englewood Cliffs, NJ: Prentice-Hall, pp. 129–138.

373. Jackson, Jacquelyn L. "The Black Novelist and the Expatriate Experience: Richard Wright, James Baldwin, Chester Himes." *Dissertation Abstracts International*, 45 (July), 183A. Abstracts a 1983 University of Kentucky dissertation. Contrary to American critical opinion, expatriation "had positive effects on their lives and art."

374. James, C.L.R. "Black Studies and the Contemporary Student," in his *At the Rendezvous of Victory: Selected Writings*. London: Allison & Burley, pp. 186–201. Relates an anecdote about a visit to W at his farm in Normandy. Showing James numerous books by Kierkegaard on his shelf, W commented: "Everything that he writes in those books, I knew before I had them" (p. 196). Reprinted: 1992.

375. JanMohamed, Abdul. "Humanism and Minority Literature: Toward a Definition of Counterhegemonic Discourse." *Boundary 2*, 12/13 (Spring/Fall), 281–299. Mentions W briefly (p. 286).

376. Jařab, Joseph. "Black Aesthetic: A Cultural or Political Concept?" in *The Origins and Originality of American Culture*. Ed. Tibor Frank. Budapest: Akadémiai Kiadó, pp. 631–640. Mentions W briefly (pp. 632, 633).

377. Johnson, Barbara. "Metaphor, Metonomy and Voice in *Their Eyes Were Watching God*," in *Black Literature and Literary Theory*. Ed. Henry Louis Gates, Jr. New York: Methuen, pp. 205–219. Quotes from W's review of the Hurston novel.

378. Johnson, Charles. "Whole Sight: Notes on New Black Fiction." *Callaloo*, 7 (Fall), 1–6. Mentions W briefly (p. 1).

379. Jones, Rhett S. "Social Scientific Perspectives on the Afro-American Arts." *Black American Literature Forum*, 18 (Fall), 128–130. Mentions W briefly.

380. Jones, Steven Swann. *Folklore and Literature in the United States: An Annotated Bibliography of Studies of Folklore in American Literature*. New York: Garland, p. 259. Mentions W briefly.

381. Julien, Claude. "*Regards sur la littérature noire americaine—French Approaches to Black American Literature*. Essais réunis par Michel Fabre." *Notre Librairie*, 77 (November-December), 118–119. Mentions Fabre's essay on "The Man Who Killed a Shadow."

382. Kaiser, Ernest. "Recent books." *Freedomways*, 24 (First Quarter), 72–78. Mentions briefly David Ray and Robert M. Farnsworth's *Richard Wright: Impressions and Perspectives*.

383. Kavanagh, James H., and Fredric Jameson. "The Weakest Link," in *The Left Academy: Marxist Scholarship on American Campuses*. Vol. 2. Eds. Bertell Oldman and Edward Vernoff. New York: Praeger, pp. 1–23. Mentions briefly Paul Siegel's work on W (p. 8).

384. _____. "Recent Books." *Freedomways*, 24 (Second Quarter), 156–160. Mentions an essay on W in *Afro-American Journal of Philosopy*.

385. Kellner, Bruce. "Green, Paul," in his *The Harlem Renaissance: A Historical Dictionary for the Era*. Westport, CT: Greenwood Press, p. 143. Mentions W briefly.

386. Kent, George E. "Richard Wright and the Adventure of Western Culture," in *Richard Wright: A Collection of Critical Essays*. Eds. Richard Macksey and Frank E. Moorer. Englewood Cliffs, NJ: Prentice-Hall, pp. 37–54. Reprint of 1969.141.

387. Kinnamon, Keneth. "*Native Son*: The Personal, Social, and Political Background," in *Richard Wright: A Collection of Critical Essays*. Eds. Richard Macksey and Frank E. Moorer. Englewood Cliffs, NJ: Prentice-Hall, pp. 87–94.

388. Kiuchi, Toru. "Richard Wright's 'Between the World and Me': An Annotated Japanese Translation." *Bulletin of Aichi Shukutoku Junior College*, 23 (25 March), 59–63. Provides notes on the background of the poem and demonstrates its relationship to the poem's structure [T.K., R.B. and Y.K.].

389. _____. "The Critical Reception of Richard Wright in Japan: A Checklist, 1940–1983." *Waseda Review*, 23 (10 December), 94–114. List of essays, reviews, translations, oral reports, and college textbooks concerning W published in Japan between 1940 and 1983 [T.K., R.B. and Y.H.].

390. Klehr, Harvey. *The Heyday of American Communism: The Depression Decade*. New York: Basic Books, pp. 351, 472, 473. Mentions W in the American Writers' Congress, identifies Harry Haywood as the "Buddy Nealson" of "I Tried to Be a Communist," and quotes briefly from *AH*.

391. Kodama, Sanehide. *American Poetry and Japanese Culture*. Hamden, CT: Archon Books, pp. 155, 156–162. Quotes twenty of W's haiku poems with very favorable commentary. "Each poem is endorsed with subtlety, freshness, suggestiveness, delicacy, and a sense of commitment, quite close to Japanese sensiblity" (p. 158).

392. _____. "Richard Wright and His Haiku," in his *American Poetry and Japanese Culture*. Hamden, CT: Archon Press, pp. 156–162. Comparative Study of the influence of Japanese haiku on W's.

393. Landy, Alice S. *Instructor's Guide to Accompany the Heath Introduction to literature*. Second Edition. Lexington, Mass: D.C. Heath, pp. 28–29. Comment and discussion questions on "The Man Who Was Almost a Man."

394. Langer, Elinor. *Josephine Herbst*. Boston: Little, Brown, p. 185. Mentions W briefly.

395. Lattin, Patricia H., and Vernon E. Lattin. "Dual Vision in Gwendolyn Brooks's *Maud Martha*." *Critique*, 25 (Summer), 180–188. Mentions briefly Bigger Thomas and *NS*.

396. Lauter, Paul. "Reconstructing

American Literature: A Synopsis of an Educational Project of The Feminist Press." *MELUS*, 11 (Spring), 33–43. Mentions W briefly (p. 39).

397. _____. "Society and the Profession, 1958–83." *PMLA*, 99 (May), 414–425. Relates experience in teaching *NS* to a group of black students in a freedom school in Mississippi in 1964 (p. 424).

398. Lawson. Lewis A. "Cross Damon: Kierkegaardian Man of Dread," in his *Another Generation: Southern Fiction Since World War II*. Jackson: University Press of Mississippi, pp. 38–57.

399. Lee, Sonia. *Camara Laye*. Boston: Twayne, pp. 5, 16. Mentions briefly W's sponsorship of *Présence Africaine* and Mongo Beti's unfavorable comparison of *L'Enfant noir* to *BB*.

400. Lehan, Richard. "Dreiser and the Hostile Critics." *The Old Northwest*, 10 (Fall), 307–317. Contains three paragraphs on *NS*, which Lehan compares unfavorably to *An American Tragedy* (pp. 314–315).

401. Lenz, Günter H. "Black Poetry and Black Music; History and Tradition: Michael Harper and John Coltrane," in his *History and Tradition in Afro-American Culture*. Frankfurt: Campus Verlag, pp. 277–326. Mentions W briefly (p. 281) and discusses Harper's treatment of W in *Debridement* (pp. 306–307).

402. _____. "Southern Exposures: The Urban Experience and the Re-Construction of Black Folk and Cultural Community in the Works of Richard Wright and Zora Neale Hurston," in his *History and Tradition in Afro-American Culture*. Frankfurt, New York: Campus Verlag, pp. 84–117.

403. Lester, Julius. "James Baldwin — Reflections of a Maverick." *The New York Times Book Review* (27 May), pp. 1, 22–24. Baldwin discusses his early relationship with W and his belief that W "was much, much better than ... the French existentialists" (p. 22). Mentions *UTC*, *NS*, and "Bright and Morning Star."

404. Lewis, Vashti Crutcher. "The Declining Significance of the Mulatto Female as Major Character in the Novels of Zora Neale Hurston." *CLA Journal*, 28 (December), 127–149. Mentions W briefly (p. 146).

405. Libby, Anthony. "Conceptual Space, The Politics of Mod-

ernism." *Chicago Review*, 34 (Spring), 11–26. Contains a brief comparison of W and *Light in August*.

406. Linkfield, T.P. "McCluskey, John, Jr. *Two Steppin': Richard Wright's Encounter with Blue-Jazz*." *American History and Life*, 21A, 485. Abstract of the article.

407. Longest, George C. et al. "A Checklist of Scholarship on Southern Literature for 1983." *The Mississippi Quarterly*, 37 (Spring), 210–322. Lists nine items on W and cross-references to eighteen other items dealing partially with W.

408. Macksey, Richard, and Frank E. Moorer. "Introduction," in their *Richard Wright: A Collection of Critical Essays*. Englewood Cliffs, NJ: Prentice-Hall, pp. 1–20. Biographical-critical essay turning on W's need and quest for "space," both geographical and psychological. Includes commentary on most of the essays included in the volume and urges treatment of W from the perspective of the ideas of René Girard.

409. _____. eds. *Richard Wright: A Collection of Critical Essays*. Englewood Cliffs, NJ: Prentice-Hall, 240 pp. Contains an introduction, original essays by Horace A. Porter and Maria K. Mootry, reprinted essays by Margaret Walker Alexander, George E. Kent, Harold T. McCarthy, Keneth Kinnamon, Donald B. Gibson, Paul N. Siegel, Esther Merle Jackson, Nick Aaron Ford, Nathan A. Scott, Jr., Darwin T. Turner, Kingsley Widmer, Blyden Jackson, Edwin Berry Burgum, and Michel Fabre, and a chronology, notes on contributors, and a bibliography.

410. Maduka, Chidi. "Irony and Vision in Richard Wright's *The Outsider*." *Western Humanities Review*, 38 (Summer), 161–169. *O* reveals W as "an artist who subtly manipulates the ironic mode in his quest for meaningful values that could fertilize the cultural landscape of America. The quest is revealed through a network of ironic situations which revolve around three foci: the communists and their attitude to the existing social institutions; Houston's role as a District Attorney; and Damon's fight for self-autonomy." W's irony is finally moral, not nihilistic.

411. Marable, Manning. *Race, Reform, and Rebellion: The Second Reconstruction in Black America:*

1945–1982. Jackson: University Press of Mississippi, pp. 48–49, 51, 53, 104. Discusses W's career and influence, mentioning *NS*, *BB*, *O*, and *BP*, and quotes from "Blueprint for Negro Writing" and *O*. Notes Lorraine Hansberry's rejection of W's existentialism.

412. McCarthy, Harold T. "Richard Wright: The Expatriate as Native Son," in *Richard Wright: A Collection of Critical Essays*. Eds. Richard Macksey and Frank E. Moorer. Englewood Cliffs, NJ: Prentice-Hall, pp. 68–85.

413. McElvaine, Robert S. *The Great Depression: America, 1929–1941*. New York: *Times* Books, p. 270. Comments briefly on W and the Writer's Project.

414. McGrath, Daniel F., ed. *Bookman's Price Index*. Vol. 27. Detroit: Gale, pp. 909–910. Lists *BB* at $60, *BB* at $60, and the French translation at $60.

415. _____. *Bookman's Price Index*. Vol. 28. Detroit: Gale, p. 866. Lists *BB* at $75 and *TMBV* at $60.

416. Meltzer, Milton. *The Black Americans: A History in Their Own Words, 1619–1983*, New York: Thomas Y. Crowell, pp. 171–185. "My First Lesson," an introductory note on W, precedes excerpts from *UTC* and *TMBV*.

417. Miller, R. Baxter. "An Authentic Contribution." *Callaloo*, 7 (Winter), 159–161. Review of Trudier Harris's *From Mammies to Militants* mentioning briefly "Man of All Work."

418. _____. "Charles T. Davis. *Black Is the Color of the Cosmos: Essays on Afro-American Literature and Culture, 1942–1981*. Ed. Henry Louis Gates, Jr." *Black American Literature Forum*, 18 (Winter), 178–181. Mentions Davis's work on W.

419. _____. "Double Mirror: George E. Kent and the Scholarly Imagination." *The Journal of the Midwest Modern Language Association*, 17 (Fall), 13–23. Includes references to the bullfighter as "the highly neglected touchstone of Richard Wright's prose" (p. 14) and quotes from "Blueprint for Negro Writing" (p. 17). Comments on Kent's views on W and quotes Kenny J. Williams on *NS*.

420. _____. "The Wasteland and the Flower: Through Blyden Jackson — A Revised Theory for Black

Southern Literature." *The Southern Literary Journal*, 17 (Fall), 3–11. Compares Jackson as literary scholar and W as creative writer.

421. _____. "Who Knows But, That on the Equal Frequencies, We Speak for Ourselves?: A Response to a Statement by Katharine D. Newman, *MELUS* Editor Emeritus." *MELUS*, 11 (Spring), 75–79. Quotes from *NS*.

422. Mitchell, Carolyn. "'A Laying on of Hands': Transcending the City in Ntozake Shange's *for colored girls who have considered suicide/ when the rainbow is enuf*," in *Women Writers and the City*. Ed. Susan Merrill Squier. Knoxville: The University of Tennessee Press, pp. 230–248. Comments on Fred Daniels in "The Man Who Lived Underground" (pp. 236, 237).

423. Mnthali, Felix. "Common Grounds in Literatures of Black America and Southern Africa," in *American Studies in Africa*. Eds. Andrew Horn and George E. Carter. Roma: University Press of Lesotho, pp. 37–54. Includes a comparison of *NS* and Alex La Guma's *A Walk in the Night* (pp. 41–47). Mnthali finds many similarities.

424. Mootry, Maria K. "Bitches, Whores, and Woman Haters: Archetypes and Typologies in the Art of Richard Wright," in *Richard Wright: A Collection of Critical Essays*. Eds. Richard Macksey and Frank E. Moorer. Englewood Cliffs, NJ: Prentice-Hall, pp. 117–127. Describes W's heroes: "Narcissistic, they value the company of men above all; they are childless; and they define themselves in opposition to women, either by using them, by perceiving themselves to be used by them, or in extreme situations, by transmuting the impulse to love to the impulse to violence and even death" (p. 118). Analyzes *LT* and *NS* in these terms.

425. Morrison, Toni. "Rootedness: The Ancestor as Foundation," in *Black Women Writers (1950–1980): A Critical Evaluation*. Ed. Mari Evans. New York: Doubleday, pp. 339–345. Mentions W briefly (p. 343).

426. Mphahlele, Es'kia. *Afrika My Music: An Autobiography, 1957–1983*. Johannesburg: Ravan Press, p. 18. Relates his discovery of *UTC*. W's depiction of blacks in the South was strikingly similar to the situation of blacks in South Africa.

427. _____. "My Experience as a Writer," in *Momentum: On Recent South African Writing*. Eds. M.J. Daymond, J.V. Jacobs, and Margaret Leota. Poetermaritzburg: University of Natal Press, pp. 75–82. Mentions reading *UTC* and acknowledges W's influence (p. 78).

428. Muller, Gilbert H., and *John A. Williams*. Boston: Twayne, pp. 19, 23, 25, 28–30, 33, 36, 66, 77, 141, 160. Discusses *The Most Native of Sons* (pp. 28–30) and emphasizes throughout Williams's high regard for W.

429. Munoz-Moreau, Emmanuel. "Richard Wright. *Black Boy*." *Notre Librairie*, No. 77 (November-December), 121–122. Review noting that *BB* is W's most popular book for French readers. Munoz-Moreau praises the work's representative quality: as a geographical and spiritual itinerary for African Americans and a voice for all oppressed and marginalized people. The reviewer is also impressed by W's account of the liberating effect of reading.

430. Nama, Charles Atangana. "Aesthetics and Ideology in African and Afro-American Fiction: Ngugi Wa Thiong'o, Ayi Kwei Armah, Toni Morrison, and Richard Wright." *Dissertation Abstracts International*, 45 (October), 1110A. Abstracts a 1984 State University of New York at Binghamton dissertation. The fifth chapter illustrates "Wright's indebtedness to the Afro-American oral tradition in some of his works." His neglected novels, *Lawd Today* and *The Long Dream*, are also analyzed in detail."

431. Neuman, Shirley. "Autobiography and American Characters." *The Canadian Review of American Studies*, 15 (Winter), 421–431. Mentions W briefly (p. 430).

432. Newby, James E. "Language, Literature, and Communication: An Annotated Bibliography of Books by Black Authors." *Journal of Black Studies*, 15 (December), 155–176. Mentions W briefly in entries on Arthur Davis's *From the Dark Tower* and James O. Young's *Black Writers of the Thirties*.

433. Newman, Richard. *Black Access: A Bibliography of Afro-American Bibliographies*. Westport, CT: Greenwood, pp. 30, 32, 33, 42, 46, 67, 68, 75, 108, 112, 114, 120, 159, 160, 161, 181, 182, 199. Lists 1971.54, 1969.46, 1960.126, 1977.89, 1971.147, 1982.40, 1965.59, 1968.211, 1969.76, 1971.112, 1973.137, 1973.133, 1969.107, 1968.145, 1971.251A, 1977.221, 1978.208, 1971.260, 1970.33, 1970.328, 1953.231.

434. Ngandu Nkashama, Pius. "La présence noire américaine dans la littérature africaine." *Notre Librairie*, 77 (November-December), 105–111. Mentions briefly *UTC* (p. 108) and *BP* (p. 111).

435. Okada, Seiichi. "Wright's Encounter with G. Stein: A Note." Saita University Heron (15 March), 13–19. Notes that W's style and his decision to go to Paris were influenced by Stein, drawing on an unpublished letter from W to Stein [T.K., R.B., and Y.H.].

436. Olney, James. "'I Was Born': Slave Narratives, Their Status as Autobiography and as Literature." *Callaloo*, 7 (Winter), 46–73. Relates *BB* to slave narratives, which it resembles in theme and form but surpasses in literary quality (pp. 65–67).

437. O'Meally, Robert G. "Le Roman invisible de Ralph Ellison." *Focus*, pp. 9–11. Mentions W briefly (p. 11).

438. Oren, Michel. "A '60s Saga: The Life and Death of Umbra." *Freedomways*, 24 (Third Quarter), 167–181. Mentions W briefly, p. 169.

439. _____. "A '60s Saga: The Life and Death of Umbro, Part 1" in *Freedomways*, 24 (Third Quarter), 167–181. Mentions W briefly (p. 169).

440. Perry, Thomas Amherst. *A Bibliography of American Literature Translated Into Romanian with Romanian Commentary* New York: Philosophical Library, p. 312. Lists "I Have Been Black Hands" and selected haiku.

441. Piccinato, Stefania. "Da Langston Hughes a Richard Wright: Percorso di una ideologica e di una poetica." *Letterature d'America*, 24/25 (Autumn), 153–165. Analyzes similarities during the thirties between Hughes and W in their reconciliation of nationalist and radical literary perspectives. Discusses "Blueprint for Negro Writing" in this context.

442. Pingree, Elizabeth E., ed. *Humanities Index: April 1983 to March 1984*. New York: H.W. Wilson, p. Lists six items s.v. W.

443. Pinsker, Sanford. "A Conversation with Etheridge Knight."

Black American Literature Forum, 18 (Spring), 11–14. Includes comments by Knight on W's rootlessness and expatriation.

444. Pointer, Fritz A. "Laye, Lamming, and Wright: Mother and Son." *African Literature Today*, 14, 19–33. Analyzes the mother-son relationship in the three writers, noting the similarity of W and Lamming and their difference from Laye. W and Lamming "reveal the rootlessness, ambiguity of identity, and individualism ... of the deculturized" (p. 27). W's existentialism has biographical origins.

445. Porter, Horace A. "The Horror and the Glory: Richard Wright's Portrait of the Artist in *Black Boy* and *American Hunger*," in *Richard Wright: A Collection of Critical Essays*. Eds. Richard Macksey and Frank E. Moorer. Englewood Cliffs, NJ: Prentice-Hall, pp. 55–67. Places W's autobiography in the tradition of the *Künstlerroman*, emphasizing the relation of language to development. "Wright's incredible struggle to master words is inextricably bound to his defiant quest for individual existence and expression" (p. 56). Words became for W both a weapon against oppression, familial and social, and a source of redemption.

446. Puckett, John Rogers. *Five Photo-Textual Documentaries from the Great Depression*. Ann Arbor, MI: UMI Research Press, pp. 3, 14, 61–81, 122. Chapter 5 analyzes both the photographs and text of *TMBV*. Puckett criticizes W for oversimplification and abstraction, comparing the work unfavorably to *BB* and "The Ethics of Living Jim Crow." Mentions briefly *NS, WML*, and the introduction to *Black Metropolis*.

447. Ramos, Marcos A. "Wright, Richard," in *12,000 Minibiographies*. Ed. Maria Eloisa Álvarez del Real. Panama City, Panama: Editorial América, p. 658. Brief entry mentioning *O, WML, LD, BB,* and *NS.*

448. Rampersad, Arnold. "*Adventures of Huckleberry Finn* and Afro-American Literature." *Mark Twain Journal*, 22 (Fall), 47–52. Mentions W's use of dialect in *UTC*, his comments on folk expression in "Blueprint for Negro Writing," his use of a child's consciousness in "Big Boy Leaves Home" and "Almos' a Man," "Voodoo of Hell's Half-Acre," *BB, LT, NS* and Bigger Thomas, *O* and

Cross Damon, and "How 'Bigger' Was Born," relating them all to Twain's novel.

449. Rich, R. Bruce. "School Censorship Cases: Kanawha County and Island Trees," in *The First Freedom Today*. Eds. Robert B. Downs and Ralph E. McCoy. Chicago: American Library Association, 1984, pp. 71–74. Notes that in Island Trees, New York, textbook vigilantes objected to *BB*.

450. Ro, Sigmund. *Rage and Celebration: Essays on Contemporary Afro-American Writing*. Atlantic Highlands, NJ: Humanities Press, pp. 11, 16–18, 25, 42, 57, 69, 96, 116. Discusses W's universalism in relation to Baldwin's (pp. 16–18) and mentions briefly W's poetry, *BB, NS* and Bigger Thomas, *O* and Cross Damon, *WML*, "The Man Who Lived Underground" and Fred Daniels, and "How 'Bigger' Was Born."

451. Romanet, Jérôme de. "Pour qui chante Ralph Ellison?" *Notre Librairie*, 77 (November-December), 47–52. Mentions W briefly (p. 50).

452. Roper, John Herbert. *U.B. Phillips: A Southern Mind*. Macon, GA: Mercer University Press, pp. 130–131. Comments briefly on "Down by the Riverside."

453. Saporta, Marc. "L'histoire de la littérature romanesque afro-américaine." *Focus*, pp. 1–8. Contains seven paragraphs on W, adopting Nathan A. Scott's reservations about protest fiction (see 1979.231) and commenting on *NS, UTC,* and *O* (pp. 4–5). Mentions W elsewhere.

454. Schultz, Elizabeth. "*Ralph Ellison: The Genesis of an Artist*. By Rudolph Dietze." *American Studies*, 25 (Fall), 85. Review mentioning W briefly.

455. Scott, Nathan A., Jr. "The Dark and Haunted Tower of Richard Wright," in *Richard Wright: A Collection of Critical Essays*. Eds. Richard Macksey and Frank E. Moorer. Englewood Cliffs, NJ: Prentice-Hall, 149–162. Reprint of 1964.113.

456. Scruggs, Charles. *The Sage in Harlem: H.L. Mencken and the Black Writers of the 1920s*. Baltimore: The Johns Hopkins University Press, pp. 16, 24, 25, 137, 147, 157, 166–169, 172, 205. Discusses W's response to Mencken as recorded in *BB* (p. 25) and his development beyond the realism Mencken prescribes (pp. 166–169). Also mentions *NS* and Bigger Thomas.

457. Sekora, John, and Houston A. Baker, Jr. "Written-Off: Narratives, Master Texts, and Afro-American Writing from 1760 to 1945." *Studies in Black American Literature*. Vol. 1: *Black American Prose Theory*. Ed. by Joe Weixlmann and Chester J. Fontenot. Greenwood, FL: Penkevill, pp. 43–62. Reprint of 1983.72.

458. Sewell, George A., and Margaret L. Dwight. "Margaret Walker Alexander, Educator and Author," in their *Mississippi Black History Makers*. Revised and enlarged edition. Jackson: University Press of Mississippi, pp. 267–269.

459. _____. "Richard Nathaniel Wright, Novelist," in their *Mississippi Black History Makers*. Revised and enlarged edition. Jackson: University Press of Mississippi, pp. 252–267. A photograph of W appears preceding p. 309.

460. Shucard, Alan R. *Countee Cullen*. Boston: Twayne, pp. 8, 79, 83. Brief mentions of W and *NS.*

461. Siegel, Paul N. "The Conclusion of Richard Wright's *Native Son*," in *Richard Wright: A Collection of Critical Essays*. Eds. Richard Macksey and Frank E. Moorer. Englewood Cliffs, NJ: Prentice-Hall, pp. 106–116. Reprint of 1974.158.

462. Silver, James W. *Running Scared: Silver in Mississippi*. Jackson: University Press of Mississippi, pp. 136, 226, 227, 229. Mentions W, advocates reading "Down by the Riverside" as an antidote to William Alexander Percy's *Lanterns on the Levee*, relates an anecdote about W's being told by a Memphian that "you act mighty bright to be from there" (Jackson, MS), and quotes from *BB.*

463. Singh, Amritjit. "Richard Wright's *The Outsider*: Existentialist Exemplar or Critique?" *CLA Journal*, 27 (June), 357–370. Reprint of 1983.75.

464. Smith, Carl S. *Chicago and the American Literary Imagination, 1880–1920*. Chicago: University of Chicago Press, pp. 175, 181. Mentions briefly W and Bigger Thomas.

465. Snead, James. "Thadious M. Davis. *Faulkner's 'Negro': Art and the Southern Context*." *Black American Literature Forum*, 18 (Fall), 131–132. Quotes W's statement that "the Negro is America's metaphor."

466. [Snell, Susan]. "Books." *S.S.S.L.: The News-Letter of the*

Society for the Study of Southern Literature, 17 (November), 9–20. Lists Margaret Walker's *The Daemonic Genius of Richard Wright* (p. 14).

467. Stepto, Robert B. "L'épanouissement d'une littérature." *Focus*, pp. 17–20. Mentions *NS* and *BB*. Comments on Toni Morrison's characterization of black women as corrective of W's portrayal of them (p. 17). Reprinted: 1992.

468. Stevick, Philip. "Articles and Books by and Devoted to Specific Authors," in his *The American Short Story: 1900–1945*. Boston: Twayne, pp. 193–201. Lists *UTC*, *EM*, and six secondary sources.

469. _____. "Chronology," in his *The American Short Story: 1900–1945*. Boston: Twayne, pp. vii–xi. Lists *UTC*.

470. _____. "Introduction," in his *The American Short Story: 1900–1945*. Boston: Twayne, pp. 1–31. Mentions briefly W and "The Man Who Lived Underground" (pp. 6, 7, 20).

471. Suda, Minoru. "Mothers in Black American Autobiographies" *Bulletin of Ritsume University of Humanity Studies*, 37 (20 March), 61–122. Outlines treatment of mothers and grandmothers in *BB* and other autobiographies [T.K. R.B., and Y.H.].

472. Suzuki, Atsumi. "On Richard Wright's *Native Son*." *Treatises of Central Japan Junior College for Automobiles*, 14 (1 March), 167–170. Maintains that protest in *NS* is, if anything, conservative [T.K., R.B., and Y.H.].

473. Tamada, Yoshiyuki. "Onomatopoeia in Richard Wright's "The Man Who Lived Underground." *Hyogo College for Education Studies of Language and Expression*, 2 (27 February), 1–14. The success of W's novella derives from his art of expression-sound effects; as well as from his theme and vision.

474. _____. "Onomatopaeia in Richard Wright's 'The Man Who Lived Underground.'" *Bulletin of Osaka Institute of Technology*, 29 (April) p. 4 [T.K., R.B.] Translation to English of 1984.

475. _____. "Richard Wright and *Lawd Today*. "*Black Studies*, 54 (15 December), 33–38. W's apprentice novel protests against the corruption of materialism among black workers [T.K., R.B., and Y.H.].

476. _____. "Richard Wright and

Savage Holiday." *Black Studies*, 53 (28 June), 1–4. Sees the novel as a prelude to *The Long Dream* and maintains that the problem it deals with is similar to that of *O*. W's intention is to show that only when one becomes an outsider can one cope with the problem of daily living [T.K., R.B. and Y.H.].

477. Tindall, George Brown. *America: A Narrative History*. New York: Norton, pp. 1013, 1015–1016. Contains two paragraphs on W, mentioning *UTC*, *BB*, and "The Ethics of Living Jim Crow." Also mentions his affiliation with the American Writers' Congress.

478. Tingley, Donald F. "*The WPA Guide to Illinois: The Federal Writers' Project Guide to 1930s Illinois*. Edited with a new Introduction by Neil Harris and Michael Conzen." *Journal of the Illinois State Historical Society*, 77 (Summer), 147–148. Mentions W briefly.

479. Turner, Darwin T. "*The Outsider*: Revision of an Idea," in *Richard Wright: A Collection of Critical Essays*. Eds. Richard Macksey and Frank E. Moorer. Englewood Cliffs, NJ: Prentice-Hall, pp. 163–172. Reprint of 1969.239.

480. Vauthier, Simone. "'Not quite on the beat': An Academic Interpretation of the Narrative Stances in Ralph Ellison's *Invisible Man*." *Delta*, 18 (April), 69–85. Mentions W briefly (p. 76).

481. Verner-Carlsson, Jan, ed. *USA Poesi: 700 Dikter från 1010–1983*. Göteborg: Café Existens, pp. 278, 304, 843. Contains a photograph of W, a Swedish translation of "Between the World and Me" by Heli Parland, and a biographical sketch.

482. Vickery, John B. "American Literature: The Twentieth Century," in *The Year's Work in English Studies*, 62, pp. 423–448. Contains a notice of Marcus Klein's *Foreigners* mentioning W briefly (p. 426).

483. _____. "American Literature to 1900," in *The Year's Work in English Studies*, 62, pp. 406–422. Contains a notice of Ladell Payne's *Black Novelists and the Southern Literary Tradition* mentioning W briefly (pp. 416–417).

484. Walker, Warren S. "Bibliography." *Studies in Short Fiction*, 21 (Summer), 289–326. Lists three items on W (p. 322).

485. _____. *Twentieth-Century*

Short Story Explication. Supplement II to Third Edition. Hamden, CT: The Shoe String Press, p. 303. Lists 21 items on W.

486. Wallace, Eunice Ewer. "Richard Wright." *Abstracts of English Studies*, 27 (December), 399. Abstracts an article by Ross Pudaloff.

487. Ward, Jerry W., Jr. "Lance Jeffers on the Art and Act of Fiction." *Black American Literature Forum*, 18 (Winter), 169–173. Includes favorable comments by Jeffers on *UTC*.

488. Washington, Mary Helen. "The House Slavery Built." *The Nation*, 238 (14 January), 22–24. Review of Ernest Gaines's *A Gathering of Old Men* mentioning W and "The Ethics of Living Jim Crow."

489. _____. "Taming all that anger down': rage and silence in Gwendolyn Brooks's *Maud Martha*," in *Black Literature and Literary Theory*. Ed. Henry Louis Gates, Jr. New York: Methuen, pp. 249–262. Mentions briefly Brooks's criticism of W for his "clumsy prose" (p. 254).

490. Watson, James G. "The American Short Story: 1930–1945," in *The American Short Story: 1900–1945*. Ed. Philip Stevick. Boston: Twayne, pp. 103–146. Includes treatment of "Big Boy Leaves Home" and "Down by the Riverside" (pp. 112–115). W uses "Adamic forms" and Biblical images to serve his purpose of racial protest.

491. Wedertz-Furtado, Utelinde. "Historical Dimensions in Toni Morrison's *Song of Solomon*," in *History and Tradition in Afro-American Culture*. Ed. Günter H. Lenz. Frankfurt: Campus Verlag, pp. 222–241. Quotes from *BB* the disparaging passage about black life, noting that Morrison's character Pilate refutes it.

492. Weixlmann, Joe. "*The Oxford Companion to American Literature*. James D. Hart. 5th ed." *MELUS*, 11 (Spring), 103–105. Review mentioning *NS* and *BB*.

493. White, Ray Lewis. *Gertrude Stein and Alice B. Toklas: A Reference Guide*. Boston: G.K. Hall, pp 115, 123, 156, 199. Annotated entries for W's writings on Stein.

494. Whitfield, Stephen J. *Voices of Jacob, Hands of Esau: Jews in American Life and Thought*. Hamden, CT: Archon, pp. 253–254, 308. Quotes from *BB* on black anti-Semitism.

495. Widmer, Kingsley. "Black Existentialism," in *Richard Wright: A Collection of Critical Essays*. Eds. Richard Macksey and Frank E. Moorer. Englewood Cliffs, NJ: Prentice-Hall, pp. 173–181. Reprint of 1971.315.

496. Wilkie, Brian, and James Hurt. "Chronology," in their *Literature of the Western World*. Vol. II: Neoclassicism Through the Modern Period. New York: Macmillan, pp. [2277–2291]. Lists W (pp. [2285, 2289]).

497. Wintz, Cary D. *Black Culture and the Harlem Renaissance*. Houston: Rice University Press, pp. 2, 217. Mentions W briefly.

498. Wittenberg, R. Charles. "A Bibliography of Theses and Dissertations Relating to Mississippi — 1984." *The Journal of Mississippi History*, 46 (February), 57–60. Lists dissertations treating W by Charles J. Evans, Carolyn Olivia Liston, and Valerie Ann Smith.

499. Yarborough, Richard. "'In the Realm of the Imagination': Afro-American Literature and the American Canon." *ADE Bulletin*, No. 78 (Summer), pp. 35–39. Mentions W briefly.

500. Young, Thomas Daniel. "Foreword," in *Another Generation: Southern Fiction Since World War II* by Lewis A. Lawson. Jackson: University Press of Mississippi, ix–xiv. Includes comment on Lawson's essay on *O*.

1985

501. Abbott, Dorothy. "Mississippi Writers," in her *Mississippi Writers: Reflections of Childhood and Youth*. Vol. I. Jackson: University Press of Mississippi, pp. 725–785. Contains a biographical sketch of W (pp. 783–784). This collection includes "Almos' a Man" and the last three sections of "Big Boy Leaves Home."

502. Adachi, Mariko, et al. "Richard Wright's Native Son: A List of Word Frequency." *Aichi Shukutoku Junior College Athena*." 19 (March), 81–132. Concordance to *NS*.

503. Adams, Timothy Dow. "I Do Believe Him Though I Know He Lies: Lying as Genre and Metaphor in Richard Wright's *Black Boy*." *Prose Studies*, 8 (September), 172–187. Argues that although W often departs from autobiographical fact, *BB* is convincing in its narrative truth. It is a collective autobiography of black boys, in which "Wright creates a version of himself whose metaphor for survival and for sustenance is falsehood" (pp. 185–186).

504. Adler, Jacob H. "Modern Southern Drama," in *The History of Southern Literature*. Eds. Louis D. Rubin, Jr., Blyden Jackson, Rayburn S. Moore, Lewis Simpson, and Thomas Daniel Young. Baton Rouge: Louisiana State University Press, pp. 436–442. Mentions briefly the play *NS* (p. 437).

505. Amuta, Chidi. *Towards a So-ciology of African Literature*. Oguta, Nigeria: Zim Pan African Publishers, p. 98. Mentions Bigger Thomas as an "outlaw hero."

506. Anon. "'Afro Scholar' to Be Hosted by U. of Miss." *Afro-American Studies: Newsletter of the Afro-American Studies Program, The University of Mississippi*, No. 4 (Fall), p. [2]. Mentions the cover photograph of W.

507. Anon. *Arts & Humanities Citation Index 1984*. Vol. 2. Philadelphia: Institute for Scientific Information, pp. 9417–9418. Lists fifty-one items s.v. WRIGHT R, not all on W.

508. Anon. *Bibliographic Guide to Black Studies: 1984*. Boston: G.K. Hall, p. 227. Lists three primary and one secondary item concerning W in the New York Public Library, supplementing the *Dictionary Catalog of the Schomburg Collection of Negro Literature and History*.

509. Anon. "Conferences." *Afro Scholar*, 4 (Fall), 2–3. Lists the international symposium on W at the University of Mississippi. A photograph of W appears on the cover of this issue.

510. Anon. "Governor Declares Sept. [sic] 21–28 'Richard Wright Week.'" *Afro-American Studies: Newsletter of the Afro-American Studies Program, The University of Mississippi*, No. 4 (Fall), p. [1]. Announces both the proclamation and the international symposium on W.

511. Anon. "Historical News & Notices." *The Journal of Mississippi History*, 47 (November), 334–341. Mentions the international W symposium at the University of Mississippi.

512. Anon. *Index to Periodical Articles by and About Blacks: 1982*. Boston: G.K. Hall, p. 229. Lists seven items about W.

513. Anon. *Index Translationum 33*. Paris: Unesco, pp. 129, 500, 604, 702. Lists translations of *AH* into German, *BB* into French and Italian, *LT* into French, *O* into French, and *NS* into Polish.

514. Anon. "Mississippi's Native Son: An International Symposium on Richard Wright." *Black American Literature Forum*, 19 (Summer), 89.

515. Anon. "Mississippi's Native Son: An International Symposium on Richard Wright." *Callaloo*, 8 (Spring-Summer), 506. Announcement of the University of Mississippi conference, 21–23 November 1985.

516. Anon. "Mississippi's Native Son: An International Symposium on Richard Wright." *Indian Journal of American Studies*, 15 (Winter), 134. Announcement of the University of Mississippi conference.

517. Anon. "*Mississippi Writers: Reflections of Childhood and Youth. Vol. I: Fiction*, edited by Dorothy Abbott." *The Virginia Quarterly Review*, 61 (Autumn), 120. Notice mentioning W briefly.

518. Anon. "Photographic Essay." *Sage: A Scholarly Journal on Black Women*, 2 (Spring), 4–8. Contains a photograph of Margaret Walker with a caption mentioning her forthcoming biography of W.

519. Anon. "Publications Relating to Mississippi." *The Journal of Mississippi History*, 47 (August), 221–230. Lists *Richard Wright: A Collection of Critical Essays* edited by Richard Macksey and Frank E. Moorer.

520. Anon. "Richard Wright Week Proclaimed." *The Oxford* (Miss.) *Eagle* (20 November), p. 10. Quotes from Governor Bill Allain's proclamation.

521. Anon. "*The World of Richard Wright* By Michel Fabre," in *Books for Fall and Winter 1985-1986*. Jackson: University Press of Mississippi, p. 7. Full-page publisher's notice. Includes a photograph of W.

522. Asante, Moleti Kete. "Rhetorical Alliances in the Civil Rights Era." *Negro Educational Review*, 36 (January), 6–12. Compares NS and "The Man Who Lived Underground" to *Invisible Man* (p. 7).

523. Ashanti, Asa Paschal. "Dust to Dust." *Black American Literature Forum*, 19 (Fall), 102. Poem mentioning W briefly.

524. Atkins, Joe. "Mississippians Are Proving That You Can Go Home Again." *The Clarion Ledger/Jackson* (Miss.) *Daily News* (1 December), p. 31. Comments on W's departure from Mississippi and quotes from *BB*.

525. Awazu, Masahiro. "Up from Uncle Tom." Okayama University Persica, 12 (March), 23–28. Discussion in English of *UTC* as protest literature [T.K., R.B., and Y.H.].

526. Axelrod, Rise B., and Charles R. Cooper. "Narrating," in their *The St. Martin's Guide to Writing*. New York: St. Martin's Press, pp. 386–403. In a section on dialogue the authors quote and comment on a passage from *BB* (p. 396).

527. ____. *The St. Martin's Guide to Writing*. New York: St. Martin's Press, p. 396. Quotes and comments on a passage from *BB* in a discussion of dialogue.

528. Baker, Houston A., Jr. "Autobiographical Acts and the Voice of the Southern Slave," in *The Slave's Narrative*. Eds. Charles T. Davis and Henry Louis Gates, Jr. New York: Oxford University Press, pp. 242–261.

529. ____. "The Black Man of Culture: W.E.B. Du Bois and *The Souls of Black Folk*," in *Critical Essays on W.E.B. Du Bois*. Ed. William L. Andrews. Boston: G.K. Hall, pp. 129–139.

530. ____. "Critical Change and Blues Continuity: An Essay on the Criticism of Larry Neal." *Callaloo*, 8 (Winter), 70–84. Mentions Neal's essay on W and W's "Blueprint for Negro Writing" (p. 74).

531. Baldwin, James. *The Price of the Ticket: Collected Nonfiction, 1948–1985*. New York: St. Martin's/Marek, pp. 1–11, 27–33, 41–64, 65–78, 237–244, 269–288, 449–552, 557. Reprints of 1948.125; 1949.79; 1951.129; 1957.136; 1961.107, 108, 109, 110; 1972.30; 1976.29.

532. Bamikunle, Aderemi. "The Harlem Renaissance and White Critical Tradition." *CLA Journal*, 29 (September), 33–51. Mentions briefly Ellison's "Richard Wright's Blues" (p. 40).

533. Banes, Ruth A. "Southerners Up North: Autobiographical Indications of Southern Ethnicity." *Perspectives on the American South: An Annual Review of Society, Politics, and Culture*, 3, 1–16. Discusses W on the South quoting from *BB* and "Early Days in Chicago" (pp. 11–13) and notes his acquaintance with Willie Morris (p. 9).

534. Baraka, Amiri. "What About Literature? W-15." *The Southern Review*, 21 (July), 801–804. Poem mentioning W briefly.

535. Basie, Count. *Good Morning Blues: The Autobiography of Count Basie as Told to Albert Murray*. New York: Random House, pp. 250–251. Explains the origin of "King Joe," which was an idea of John Hammond, a friend of Paul Roberson, Joe Louis, and W.

536. [Baym, Nina]. "American Literature Between the Wars, 1914–1945," in *The Norton Anthology of American Literature*. Second edition. Ed. Nina Baym et al. Vol 2. New York: Norton, pp. 861–875. Mentions briefly W and NS (pp. 866, 871).

537. ____. "Preface to the Second Edition," in her *The Norton Anthology of American Literature*. Second edition. New York: W.W. Norton, pp. xxvii–xxxi. Mentions W briefly (p. xxix).

538. Baym, Nina. "Richard Wright, 1908–1960," in *The Norton Anthology of American Literature*." Eds. Baym, Ronald Gottesman, Laurence B. Holland, Francis Murphy, Hershel Parker, William H. Pritchard, and David Kalstone. Second edition. Vol. 2. New York: W.W. Norton, pp. 1747–1748. Biographical-critical headnote to "The Man Who Was Almost a Man."

539. ____, and Laurence B. Holland. "American Literature Between the Wars, 1914–1945," in *The Norton Anthology of American Literature*. Eds. Nina Baym, Ronald Gottesman, Laurence B. Holland, Francis Murphy, Hershel Parker, William H. Pritchard, and David Kalstone. Second edition. Vol. 2. New York: W.W. Norton, pp. 861–875. Mentions briefly W and NS (pp. 866, 871).

540. ____. "Richard Wright," in *The Norton Anthology of American Literature*. Eds. Nina Baym, Ronald Gottesman, Laurence B. Holland, Francis Murphy, Hershel Parker, William H. Pritchard, and David Kalstone. Second edition. Vol. 2. New York: W.W. Norton, pp. 2632–2633. Brief bibliographical note.

541. Bell, Bernard W. "Ann Petry's Demythologizing of American Culture and Afro-American Character," in *Conjuring: Black Women, Fiction, and Literary Tradition*. Eds. Marjorie Pryse and Hortense J. Spillers. Bloomington: Indiana University Press, pp. 105–115. Compares Petry and W on several points, concluding that she "moves beyond [his] naturalistic vision" (p. 115).

542. ____. "Ann Petry's Demythologizing of American Culture and Afro American Character," in *Conjuring: Black Women, Fiction, and Literary Tradition*. Eds. Marjorie Pryse and Hortense J. Spillers. Bloomington: Indiana University Press, pp. 105–115. Argues that Petry moves beyond W's naturalism. Partially.

543. Benoist, Mary Anne. "Major Southern Authors." *S.S.S.L.: The News-Letter of the Society for The Study of Southern Literature*, 18 (November), 11–12. Lists Michel Fabre's *The World of Richard Wright*.

544. ____. "1985 Meetings and Conferences." *S.S.S.L.: The News-Letter of The Society for the Study of Southern Literature*, 18 (November), 6–7. Announces "Mississippi's *Native Son*" at the University of Mississippi, 21–23 November 1985.

545. Bigsby, C.W.E. *A Critical*

Introduction to Twentieth-Century American Drama. Vol. 3: *Beyond Broadway.* Cambridge: Cambridge University Press, pp. 357, 381. Quotes from "Blueprint for Negro Literature" and mentions briefly *NS.*

546. Bloom, Lynn Z. *Fact and Artifact: Writing Nonfiction.* San Diego: Harcourt Brace Jovanovich, 1985, pp. 71–86. Analyzes and comments on changes made by W in successive drafts of his commentary on *BB.* Draws on work by Linda Peterson.

547. Bowles, Paul. *Without Stopping: An Autobiography.* New York: The Ecco Press, p. 233. Reprint of 1972.

548. Bradley, David. "Looking Behind *Cane.*" *The Southern Review,* 21 (July), 682–694. Mentions W briefly (p. 683).

549. Breit, Anitra D. "Cumulative Index, Volume 1–20, 1963–83, *Studies in Short Fiction.*" *Studies in Short Fiction,* 22 (Winter), 1–187. Lists four articles on W (p. 104).

550. Brittin, Ruth L. "Samuel W. Allen," in *Afro-American Poets Since 1955.* Eds. Trudier Harris and Thadious M. Davis. Detroit: Gale, pp. 8–17. Comments on W's help in getting Allen published and introducing him to the negritude poets (p. 10).

551. Brooks, A. Russell. "*The Sage in Harlem: H.L. Mencken and the Black Writers of the 1920's.* By Charles Scruggs." *CLA Journal,* 29 (September), 100–106. Mentions W briefly.

552. Brown, Lloyd W. "The Black Literary Experience in Games and Sports," in *American Sport Culture: The Humanistic Dimensions.* Ed. Wiley Lee Umphlett. Lewisburg, PA: Bucknell University Press, pp. 246–254. Contains two paragraphs on the game of "playing white" in *NS* (pp. 247–248).

553. Brown, Soi-Daniel W. "'Black Opheus': Langston Hughes Reception in German Translation (An Overview)." *The Langston Hughes Review,* 4 (Fall), 30–38. Mentions W briefly (p. 31).

554. Bruccoli, Matthew J. *Nelson Algren: A Descriptive Bibliography.* Pittsburgh: University of Pittsburgh Press, pp. 9, 10, 11, 13, 116, 153, 155, 207. Mentions W's introduction to Algren's *Never Come Morning* and lists Algren's essays and reviews concerning W.

555. Bruning, Eberhard. "New York und Paris," *Weimarer Beiträge,* 31 (June), 917, 922. Mentions briefly *NS.*

556. Bryant, Jerry H. "Wright, Ellison, Baldwin — Exorcising the Demon," in *The American Classics Revisited: Recent Studies of American Literature.* Eds. P. C. Kar and D. Ramakrishna. Hyderabad: American Studies Research Center, pp. 681–695. Reprint of 1976.43.

557. Burger, Nash K. "Eudora Welty's Jackson," in *Mississippi Writers: Reflections of Childhood and Youth.* Vol. 2. Ed. Dorothy Abbott. Jackson: University Press of Mississippi, pp. 16–23.

558. Burns, Dan E. "*Mississippi Writers: Reflections of Childhood and Youth.* Volume I: Fiction. Ed. Dorothy Abbott." *South Central Review,* 2 (Winter), 101–103. Mentions "the pace and drama of Richard Wright."

559. Burns, Landon C., Janet P. Alwang, and Elizabeth Buckmaster. "The Eleventh (1984) Supplement to a Cross-Referenced Index of Short Fiction Anthologies and Author-Title Listings." *Studies in Short Fiction,* 22 (Spring), 259–293. Lists "The Man Who Was Almost a Man" in two anthologies.

560. Butler, Robert James. "Open Movement and Selfhood in Toni Morrison's *Song of Solomon.*" *The Centennial Review,* 29 (Fall), 58–75. Contains a paragraph on the entrapment and journey motifs in W (pp. 61–62).

561. Byerman, Keith E. *Fingering the Jagged Grain: Tradition and Form in Recent Black Fiction.* Athens: The University of Georgia Press, pp. 11, 41, 157, 276, 278. Mentions briefly W, his naturalism, his use by Alice Walker, and his relation to "a modernist sensibility."

562. _____. "Zora Neale Hurston. *Dust Tracks on a Road.* Eds. Robert Hemenway and Mari Evans. *Black Women Writers (1950–1980): A Critical Evaluation*; Sylvia Wallace Holton. *Down Home and Uptown: The Representation of Black Speech in American Fiction*; Trudier Harris. *Exorcising Blackness: Historical and Literary Lynching and Burning Rituals*; Houston A. Baker, Jr. *Blues, Ideology, and Afro-American Literature.*" *Modern Fiction Studies,* 31 (Winter), 730–735. Review commenting on Trudier Harris's treatment of "Big Boy Leaves Home." Mentions also *NS.*

563. Caldeira, Maria Isabel. "Jean Toomer's *Cane*: The Anxiety of the Modern Artist." *Callaloo,* 8 (Fall), 544–550. Mentions W briefly (p. 549).

564. Calloway, Earl. "Writers Seminar Highlights Four Black Authors." *Chicago Defender* (5 October), p. 25. Announces a discussion of W by Danielle Taylor-Guthrie at the DuSable Museum of African American History. Includes a biographical sketch of W.

565. _____. "Writers Seminar Highlights Four Black Authors." *Chicago Defender* (5 October), p. 25. Includes a sketch of W's life and works. This seminar features Danielle Taylor-Guthrie on W.

566. Cappetti, Carla. "Sociology of an Existence: Richard Wright and the Chicago School." *MELUS,* 12 (Summer), 25–43. Analyzes *BB* and *AH* in relation to concepts of the Chicago sociologists, especially W. I. Thomas and F. Znaniecki in *The Polish Peasant in Europe and America.* The theme of W's autobiography is the conflict between "environment" (family, church, school, white racism, the Communist Party) and "personality." In developing this theme, W found useful the sociological "conceptualization of two important points of view: the informant and the participant-observer" (p. 36). Thus W was able to understand and render the sociology of his own existence.

567. Carpenter, Charles A. "Modern Drama Studies: An Annual Bibliography." *Modern Drama,* 28 (June), 223–327. Lists the 1984 article by Judith G. Brazinsky (p. 238).

568. Carter, Steven R. "Lorraine Hansberry," in *Afro-American Writers After 1955: Dramatists and Prose Writers.* Eds. Thadious M. Davis and Trudier Harris. Detroit: Gale, pp. 120–134. Mentions W briefly (p. 132).

569. Chénetier, Marc. "Charting Contemporary American Fiction: A View from Abroad." *New Literary History,* 16 (Spring), 653–669. Mentions W briefly (p. 655).

570. [Childrey, Frank W., Jr.]. "Bibliographic Projects at the Center." *The Southern Register: The Newsletter of the Center for the Study of Southern Culture,* 3 (Spring/Summer), 9. Mentions briefly Michel Fabre's *The World of Richard Wright.*

571. _____. "Mississippi Heritage Institute." *The Southern Register: The Newsletter of the Center for the Study of Southern Culture*, 3 (Spring/Summer), 2–3. Mentions briefly *BB* and the film version of "Almos' a Man."

572. _____. "Mississippi Writers Day." *The Southern Register: The Newsletter of the Center for the Study of Southern Culture*, 3 (Spring/Summer), 1–2. Mentions W as one of the five writers "who established the state's literary reputation."

573. _____. "Richard Wright Symposium Attracts International Audience." *The Southern Register*, 4 (Fall), 1–2. Reports on the conference held at the University of Mississippi, 21–23 November. Mentions the speakers and their topics.

574. Christian, Barbara. "An Angle of Seeing: Motherhood in Buchi Emecheta's *The Joys of Motherhood* and Alice Walker's *Meridian*," in her *Black Feminist Criticism: Perspectives on Black Women Writers*. New York: Pergamon Press, pp. 211–252. Mentions Mrs. Thomas in *NS* (p. 225).

575. _____. "The Contrary Women of Alice Walker: A Study of Female Protagonists in *In Love and Trouble*," in her *Black Feminist Criticism: Perspectives on Black Women Writers*. New York: Pergamon Press, pp. 31–46. Reprint of 1981.

576. _____. "Images of Black Women in Afro-American Literature: From Stereotype to Character," in her *Black Feminist Criticism: Perspectives on Black Women Writers*. New York: Pergamon Press, pp. 1–30. Compares briefly *NS* and Ann Petry's *The Street* (p. 11) and mentions *NS* and *O* elsewhere (p. 15).

577. _____. "Nuance and the Novella: A Study of Gwendolyn Brooks's *Maud Martha*," in her *Black Feminist Criticism: Perspectives on Black Women Writers*. New York: Pergamon Press, pp. 127–141. Mentions briefly *O* and *NS* (pp. 130, 133).

578. Clark, Norris B. "Michael S. Harper," in *Afro-American Poets Since 1955*. Eds. Trudier Harris and Thadious M. Davis. Detroit: Gale, pp. 152–166. Discusses Harper's treatment of W in *Debridement* and *Images of Kin* (pp. 162, 164).

579. Cohen-Solal, Annie. *Sartre*. Paris: Gallimard, pp. 319, 320, 383, 398–399, 402, 433. Comments on Sartre's friendship with W, who enhanced his understanding of racial

issues in the U.S.; mentions *BB*; notes that W has included in *Les Temps Modernes* and quotes from W's speech for the R.D.R. on 13 December 1948. Translated into English.

580. Coleman, Edwin L., II. "Conrad Kent Rivers," in *Afro-American Poets Since 1955*. Eds. Trudier Harris and Thadious M. Davis. Detroit: Gale, pp. 282–296. Mentions briefly *The Wright Poems* (p. 286).

581. Cramer, William S. "The Federal Writers' Project: Work Relief That Preserved a National Resource." *Publishing History*, 18, 49–68. Mentions briefly the attack of Rep. Joseph Starnes of the Dies Committee on W (p. 61).

582. Cunningham, James. "Sterling D. Plumpp," in *Afro-American Poets Since 1955*. Eds. Trudier Harris and Thadious M. Davis. Detroit: Gale, pp. 257–265. Mentions briefly W as an influence on Plumpp (p. 258).

583. Dandjinou, Pierre. "*Les Ecrivains noirs américaines et l'Afrique*. Numéro 77 (novembre 1985) de *Notre Libraire*." *Revue française d'études américaines*, 26 (November), 464. Review mentioning W briefly.

584. Daniels, Douglas Henry. "The Significance of Blues for American History." *The Journal of Negro History*, 70 (Winter, Spring), 14–23. Quotes from and comments on W's introduction to *Blues Fell This Morning* (pp. 21–22).

585. Davis, Angela. "For a People's Culture," *Political Affairs*, 64 (March), 17–24.

586. Davis, Charles T., and Henry Louis Gates, Jr. "Introduction: The Language of Slavery," in their *The Slave's Narrative*. New York: Oxford University Press, pp. xi–xxxiv. Mentions briefly *BB* (p. xxxiii).

587. Davis, Thadious M., and Trudier Harris. "Foreword," to their *Afro-American Writers After 1955: Dramatists and Prose Writers*. Detroit: Gale, pp. xi–xiii. Mentions W briefly.

588. DeCosta-Willis, Miriam. "*No Crystal Stair: Visions of Race and Sex in Black Women's Fiction*. By Gloria Wade-Gayles." *CLA Journal*, 28 (June), 464–467. Mentions W briefly.

589. Drabble, Margaret. "Wright, Richard," in her *The Oxford Companion to English Literature*. Fifth

edition. Oxford: Oxford University Press, p. 1087. Biographical entry mentioning *NS* and *O*.

590. Eakin, Paul John. *Fictions in Autobiography: Studies in the Art of Self-Invention*. Princeton, NJ: Princeton University Press, p. 172. Mentions briefly W as autobiographer.

591. Edwards, Paul. "Black Writers of the Eighteenth and Nineteenth Centuries," in *The Black Presence in English Literature*. Ed. David Dabydeen. Manchester: Manchester University Press, p. 59. Mentions W briefly.

592. Erickson, Peter B. "June Jordan," in *Afro-American Writers After 1955: Dramatists and Prose Writers*. Eds. Thadious M. Davis and Trudier Harris. Detroit: Gale, pp. 146–162. Mentions briefly Jordan's essay on W and Hurston [1981.70] (p. 161).

593. Fabre, Michel. "Richard Wright: De l'existentialisme au tiers-mondisme," in his *La Rive noire: de Harlem à la Seine*. Paris: Editions Lieu Commun, pp. 173–196. Discusses W's favorable opinion of Paris, his interest in existentialism and his relation to Sartre and de Beauvoir, and his connections with African intellectuals in Paris.

594. _____. "Richard Wright, poète." *Présence Africaine*, 135, 39–55. Traces W's poetic impulse throughout his career: the agit-prop verse of the thirties (mentioned briefly), the prose-poetry of *TMBV* and *BB*, the "Celebrations" project, and the haiku at the end of his life. Emphasizes W's nature mysticism, spiritual quality, and symbolic imagination, noting parallels with blues, spirituals, Baudelaire, Whitman, and the Bible.

595. _____. *The World of Richard Wright*. Jackson: University Press of Mississippi, 268 pp. Contains reprints of 1970.54, 124, 282; 1971.103, 110, 111; 1973.132; 1975.71; 1977.122; 1978.95; 1980.84, 87; two previously unpublished essays, "Wright's South," and "Wright, Negritude, and African Writing"; W's early story "Superstition"; and W's published poetry. The "Introduction" (pp. 3–11) reviews the essays included within the framework of W's life and career.

596. _____. "Wright, Negritude, and African Writing," in his *The World of Richard Wright*. Jackson: University Press of Mississippi, pp. 192–213. Discusses W's role in

Présence Africaine and his friendships with Alioune Diop, Peter Abrahams, and George Padmore. Recounts W's disagreements with Senghor and with the American Society for African Culture. In general, W's approach to Africa was political rather that cultural or literary. Reprinted: 1986.

597. ____. "Wright, Richard (1908–1960)," in *Modern American Literature.* Eds. Paul Schlueter and June Schlueter. *A Library of Literary Criticism*, Vol. V: Second Supplement to the Fourth Edition. New York: Frederick Ungar, pp. 579–580.

598. ____. "Wright's South," in his *The World of Richard Wright.* Jackson: University Press of Mississippi, pp. 77–92. Examines W's generally negative attitude toward his native region. Formed by the South, his feelings were at times ambivalent, but the pain of racism overcame rural pleasures. Fabre treats *BB, TMBV, LD*, and shorter works, as well as W's opinion of Faulkner.

599. Felgar, Robert. "Wright, Richard (1908–1960)," in *Modern American Literature.* Eds. Paul Schlueter and June Schlueter. *A Library of Literary Criticism*, Vol. V: Second Supplement to the Fourth Edition. New York: Frederick Ungar, pp. 580–581. Partial reprint of 1980.94.

600. Ferris, William. "Director's Column." *The Southern Register*, 4 (Fall), 2. Mentions the W symposium at the University of Mississippi and Michel Fabre's *The World of Richard Wright.*

601. Fishburn, Katherine. "Wright, Richard (1908–1960)," in *Modern American Literature.* Eds. Paul Schlueter and June Schlueter. *A Library of Literary Criticism*, Vol. V: Second Supplement to the Fourth Edition. New York: Frederick Ungar, pp. 578–579. Partial reprint of 1977.131.

602. Fleming, Robert E. "O'Neill's *The Hairy Ape* as a Source for *Native Son.*" *CLA Journal*, 28 (June), 434–443. Argues that "Wright was influenced by O'Neill in his creation of Bigger Thomas and Mary Dalton, in his attacks on religion and leftist political movements, and perhaps even in certain surrealistic elements in the setting of *Native Son.*" Fleming adduces many details to support the connection while ad-

mitting that Wright also used other sources, literary and social.

603. Fleming, Thomas J. "An Unbroken Circle." *Modern Age*, 29 (Summer), 265–268. Review mentioning Lewis A. Lawson's treatment of *O.*

604. Forman, James. *The Making of Black Revolutionaries.* Washington, DC: Open Hand, pp. 4, 35, 75.

605. F[owler], C[arolyn]. "Black Writers of Recent Decades." *Phylon*, 46 (December), 374–375. Review of *Afro-American Fiction Writers After 1955* noting the absence of W from this volume.

606. Frye, Northrop, Sheridan Baker, and George Perkins. *The Harper Handbook to Literature.* New York: Harper & Row, pp. 8, 27, 552, 553. Calls *NS* "the single most influential work of Afro-American Literature" (p. 8), mentions W in the section on "American Literature" (p. 27), and lists *NS* and *BB* in a "Chronology of Literature and World Events" (pp. 552, 553).

607. Gabbin, Joanne V. *Sterling A. Brown: Building the Black Aesthetic Tradition.* Westport, CT: Greenwood Press, pp. 13, 71, 103, 108, 109. Comments on W's work on the Writers' Project (p. 71) and on Brown's review of *NS* (p. 109). Mentions W elsewhere. Reprinted: 1994.

608. Gaffney, Floyd. "Amiri Baraka (LeRoi Jones)," in *Afro-American Writers After 1955: Dramatists and Prose Writers.* Ed. Thadious M. Davis and Trudier Harris. Detroit: Gale, pp. 22–42. Mentions W briefly (p. 24).

609. Gayle, Addison. "Introduction: *The Way of the New World,* in *Afro-American Writing: An Anthology of Prose and Poetry.* Eds. Richard Long and Eugenia W. Collier. University Park: The Pennsylvania State University Press, pp. 650–659. Partial reprint of 1975.85.

610. ____. "Wright, Richard," in *Academic American Encyclopedia.* Danbury, CT: Grolier, 1995, vol. 20, pp. 290–291. Biographical sketch with a photograph of W. Emphasizes W's racial protest and his influence on subsequent black writers.

611. Gilbert, Sandra M., and Susan Gubar. "Zora Neale Hurston (c. 1901–1960)," in their *The Norton Anthology of Literature by Women: The Tradition in English.* New York:

W.W. Norton, pp. 1637–1639. Notes W's criticism of *Their Eyes Were Watching God* (p. 1639).

612. Gilyard, Keith. "The Sociolinguistics of Underground Blues." *Black American Literature Forum*, 19 (Winter), 158–159. Analyzes the sociolinguistics of "The Man Who Lived Underground," with comparisons to *NS* and *O.* While underground, Fred Daniels is "empowered ... through metalinguistic struggle," but he "dies because he does not possess a voice with which to secure his existence in the face of aboveground oppression."

613. Goodin, George. *The Poetics of Protest: Literary Form and Political Implication in the Victim-of-Society Novel.* Carbondale and Edwardsville: Southern Illinois University Press, pp. 105–111. Analyzes Bigger's conflicting selves to demonstrate that "a major achievement of *NS* consists of showing the confusion which oppression can foster in its victims, a confusion in which the various alternatives for remedy tend to cancel each other out" (p. 107).

614. Graham, Maryemma. "Introduction: Mississippi's Living Presence," in *Mississippi Writers: Reflections of Childhood and Youth.* Vol. 2. Ed. Dorothy Abbott. Jackson: University Press of Mississippi, xvii–xxx. Contains a paragraph on W (p. xviii) and mentions him elsewhere.

615. Greene, Lee. "Black Novelists and Novels, 1930–1950," in *The History of Southern Literature.* Eds. Louis D. Rubin, Jr., Blyden Jackson, Rayburn S. Moore, Lewis P. Simpson, and Thomas Daniel Young. Baton Rouge: Louisiana State University Press, pp. 383–398. Contains numerous comments on W and *NS* in relation to such novelists as George Wylie Henderson, George Washington Lee, Waters Turpin, William Attaway, and Saunders Redding.

616. Greenspon, Joanna, ed. *Humanities Index: April 1984 to March 1985.* New York: H. W. Wilson, p. 992. Lists six items s.v. W.

617. Gresset, Michel. *A Faulkner Chronology.* Trans. Arthur B. Scharff. Jackson: University Press of Mississippi, p. 68. Dates Faulkner's letter to W as 11 September 1945.

618. Grossman, Anita Susan. "Art Versus Truth in Autobiography: The Case of Lillian Hellman." *Clio*, 14 (Spring), 289–308. Includes discussion of fictionalization of autobiography in *BB* (pp. 300–301).

619. Hakutani, Yoshinobu. "Creation of the Self in Richard Wright's *Black Boy*." *Black American Literature Forum*, 19 (Summer), 70–75. Argues that *BB* is a sociological autobiography, not an autobiographical novel. W is spokesman and representative in the work of "the voiceless Negro boys," oppressed by white racism. In opposition to such a society, W turned inward to create a self, and "in so doing he discovered the new world" (p. 75).

620. Hall, Donald, and D.K. Emblen. "Considerations," in their *A Writer's Reader*. Fourth edition. Boston: Little, Brown, p. 475. Reprint of 1976.

621. _____. "Richard Wright *The Library Card*," in their *A Writer's Reader*. Fourth edition. Boston: Little, Brown, p. 466.

622. Hanna, Archibald. *A Mirror for the Nation: An Annotated Bibliography of American Social Fiction, 1901–1950*. New York: Garland, p. 387. Lists *NS* and *UTC*.

623. Hannush, Mufid J. "The Methodology of Phenomenological Psychobiography: The Case of Richard Wright's *Black Boy* Revisited." *Journal of Phenomenological Psychology*, 16 (Spring), 39–68. Critiquing Ralph R. White's 1951 value analysis of *BB*, Hannush develops and applies a nine-step methodology. After much paraphrase and summary, Hannush concludes: "These interrelated value structures (apartness-fear and anger-ambivalence and independence-safety capture Richard Wright's affective and motivational modes of being present to his world as they are disclosed in his autobiographical work *Black Boy*" (p. 63).

624. Harris, Norman. "Larry Neal," in *Afro-American Writers After 1955: Dramatists and Prose Writers*. Eds. Thadious M. Davis and Trudier Harris. Detroit: Gale, pp. 225–230. Quotes Addison Gayle mentioning W briefly (p. 228).

625. Harris, Trudier. *Black Women in the Fiction of James Baldwin*. Knoxville: The University of Tennessee Press, p. 206. Contrasts W and Ellison unfavorably to Baldwin in their literary depiction of black women.

626. _____. "Black Writers in a Changed Landscape, Since 1950," in *The History of Southern Literature*.

Eds. Louis D. Rubin, Jr., Blyden Jackson, Rayburn S. Moore, Lewis P. Simpson, and Thomas Daniel Young. Baton Rouge: Louisiana State University Press, pp. 566–577. Mentions briefly W and *UTC* (pp. 566, 569).

627. Harris, William J. *The Poetry and Poetics of Amiri Baraka: The Jazz Aesthetic*. Columbia: University of Missouri Press, pp. 16, 63, 126, 149. Mentions briefly W, *BB*, and *NS*.

628. Harrison, Paul Carter. "Larry Neal/*the genesis of vision*." *Callaloo*, 8 (Winter), 170–194. Mentions W briefly (p. 173).

629. Haslam, Gerald. "A Regional-Ripple Approach to American Literature." *English Journal*, 74 (April), 55–57. Mentions W briefly.

630. Hays, William S. "*Mississippi Writers: Reflections of Childhood and Youth, Volume I: Fiction*. Dorothy Abbott, editor." *The Journal of Mississippi History*, 47 (August), 215–216. Mentions Faulkner, Welty, and W as the "old icons" of Mississippi fiction.

631. Hendricks, Fredric Jefferson. "*Accent*, 1940–1960: The History of a Little Magazine." *Dissertation Abstracts International*, 45 (May), 3350A. Abstracts a 1984 University of Illinois dissertation. Mentions W briefly.

632. Henry, Joseph K. "The Public, Spiritual, and Humanistic Odyssey of Malcolm X: A Critical Bibliographical Debate." *The Western Journal of Black Studies*, 9 (Summer), 115–125. Mentions W briefly (p. 116).

633. Hernton, Calvin. "The Sexual Mountain and Black Women Writers." *The Black Scholar*, 16 (July/August), 2–11. Reprint of 1984.70.

634. Higginson, William J. *The Haiku Handbook*. New York: McGraw-Hill, pp. 65, 88–89. Notes that W studied R.H. Blyth and wrote many haiku at the end of his life. Quotes and briefly analyzes "In the falling snow." Mentions briefly *BB* and *NS*.

635. Higham, Charles. *Orson Welles: The Rise and Fall of an American Genius*. New York: St. Martin's Press, pp. 165–167, 168, 172, 174. Comments on the novel *NS*, relates the adaptation by W and Paul Green, explains the argument between Green and Welles on changes during production of the play, and evaluates favorably Welles's staging, casting, and direction.

636. Hobson, Fred. "The Savage South: An Inquiry Into the Origins, Endurance, and Presumed Demise of an Image." *The Virginia Quarterly Review*, 61 (Summer), 377–395. Mentions briefly W, *UTC*, and *BB* (pp. 389, 393).

637. Hodges, John O. "An Apprenticeship to Life and Art: Narrative Technique in Wright's *Black Boy*." *CLA Journal*, 28 (June), 415–433. Analyzes *BB* as a *bildungsroman*. In addition to the genre's usual theme of the development of self-consciousness, W's book has the task of exposing Southern racism in all its brutality.

638. Hodges, LeRoi S., Jr. *Portrait of an Expatriate: William Gardner Smith, Writer*. Westport, CT: Greenwood Press, pp. 6, 20, 33–35, 39–40, 50, 53, 55–56, 58, 61, 91, 97, 101. Treats W's expatriation, quoting from his articles "American Negroes in France" and "Les noirs americaines et la France." Comments on W's friendships with Ollie Harrington and Chester Himes. Also treats the Gibson affair.

639. Hogue, W. Lawrence. "History, the Feminist Discourse, and Alice Walker's *The Third Life of George Copeland*." *MELUS*, 12 (Summer), 45–62. Compares briefly the notion of psychological liberation through violence in Walker's novel and *NS* (pp. 52–53).

640. Holcomb, Phillip A. "Black Studies." *Abstracts of English Studies*, 28 (September), 293. Abstracts an article by Barbara Foley mentioning W.

641. [Holland, Laurence B. and Nina Baym]. "Richard Wright 1908–1960," in *The Norton Anthology of American Literature*. Second edition. Ed. Nina Baym et al. Vol. 2. New York: Norton, pp. 1747–1748, 2632–2633. Biographical-critical headnote to "The Man Who Was Almost a Man," with a bibliographical note on pp. 2632–2633.

642. Horne, Gerald C. "The Hansberry Example." *Freedomways*, 25 (Summer), 120–122. Comments on Hansberry's criticism of W's anti-communism.

643. Howard, Lillie P. "Sherley Anne Williams," in *Afro-American Poets Since 1955*. Eds. Trudier Harris and Thadious M. Davis. Detroit: Gale, pp. 343–350. Comments on Ellison's "Richard Wright's Blues" (p. 348).

644. Hubbard, Dolan. "An Interview with Richard K. Barksdale." *Black American Literature Forum*, 19 (Winter), 139–145. Comments on W's attitude toward women (p. 141) and relates W's emergence to the Harlem Renaissance (p. 143).

645. Hudson, Theodore R. "Ralph Ellison," in *The History of Southern Literature*. Eds. Louis D. Rubin, Jr., Blyden Jackson, Rayburn S. Moore, Lewis P. Simpson, and Thomas Daniel Young. Baton Rouge: Louisiana State University Press, pp. 510–512. Mentions W briefly (p. 511).

646. Hughes, Langston. "The Writer's Position in America." *The Langston Hughes Review*, 4 (Spring), 18–19. Reprint of 1957.

647. ____, "The Twenties: Harlem and Its Negritude." *The Langston Hughes Review*, 4 (Spring), 29–36. Reprint of 1966.80.

648. Hull, Gloria T. "What It Is I think She's Doing Anyhow": A Reading of Toni Cade Bambara's *The Salt Eaters*, in *Conjuring: Black Women, Fiction and Literary Tradition*. Bloomington: Indiana University Press, pp. 216–232.

649. Hurd, Myles Raymond. "Rhetoric Versus Eloquence in the Afro-American Double Narrative: Perspectives on Audience, Ambivalence, and Ambiguity." *Dissertation Abstracts International*, 46 (August), 421A. Abstracts a 1985 City University of New York dissertation. "Long Black Song" is one of the works treated.

650. Inman, Arthur Crew. *The Inman Diary: A Public and Private Confession*. Ed. Daniel Aaron. Vol. II. Cambridge, MA: Harvard University Press, p. 1284. The entry for 2 July 1945 discusses *BB* and Southern race relations generally.

651. Jackson, Blyden. "Richard Wright," in *The History of Southern Literature*. Eds. Louis D. Rubin, Jr., Blyden Jackson, Rayburn S. Moore, Lewis P. Simpson, and Thomas Daniel Young. Baton Rouge: Louisiana State University Press, pp. 443–449. After sketching W's biography, Jackson emphasizes his Southernness, defends his style from detractors, praises his creation of the epic figure of Bigger Thomas, and points out his influence on other black writers.

652. Jařab, Josef. "Black Aesthetic: A Cultural or Political Concept?" *Callaloo*, 8 (Fall), 587–593. Mentions W briefly (p. 588).

653. Jenkinson, Edward B. "Protecting Holden Caulfield and His Friends from the Censors." *English Journal*, 74 (January), 26–33. Mentions *BB* briefly.

654. Jeyifo, Biodun. "Tragedy, History, and Ideology," in *Marxism and African Literature*. Ed. Georg M. Gugelberger. London: James Currey, pp. 94–109. Quotes from *BP* and compares the passage to Wole Soyinka's *Death and the King's Horseman* (p. 99).

655. Johnson, Carolyn M. "Twentieth Century U.S. General." *Abstracts of English Studies*, 28 (December), 405. Abstracts an article by Leslie Sanders mentioning W.

656. Jones, Jacqueline. *Labor of Love, Labor of Sorrow: Black Women, Work, and the Family from Slavery to the Present*. New York: Basic Books, pp. 198, 222. Quotes from *TMBV*.

657. Jones, Lola E. "Sex and Sexuality in Richard Wright's 'Big Boy Leaves Home,'" in *Amid Visions and Revisions: Poetry and Criticism on Literature and the Arts*. Ed. Burney J. Hollis. Baltimore: Morgan State University Press, pp. 102–108. Uses the "sexual game-song" at the beginning of the story as the key to its theme of psychosexual racism.

658. Jordan, June. "Richard Wright Was Wrong," in her *Living Room*. New York: Thunder's Mouth, pp. 64–65. Poem arguing the real Bigger Thomas is a racist "whiteman."

659. Joyce, Joyce Ann. "Style and Meaning in Richard Wright's *Native Son*," in *The American Classics Revisited: Recent Studies of American Literature*. Eds. P.C. Kar and D. Ramakrishna. Hyderabad: American Studies Research Centre, pp. 696–703.

660. Kaiser, Ernest. "Recent Books." *Freedomways*, 25 (Fall), 240. Comments on Margaret Walker's *The Daemonic Genius of Richard* and mentions also Michel Fabre's *The World of Richard Wright*.

661. Kiernan, Maureen Brigid. "Novelists/Scenarists: Four Case Studies of Writers Adapting Their Own Fiction to Film." *Dissertation Abstracts International*, 45 (May), 3350A. Abstracts a 1984 University of Illinois dissertation. *NS* is one of the four.

662. Kiuchi, Toru. "Richard Wright's Early Poems: From Revolution to Art." Waseda University English Literature, 61 (15 February), 231–244. Traces W's spiritual development from Communism to literary art as depicted in his poems [T.K., R.B., and Y.H.].

663. ____. "A Trend of African American Studies in the United States, and Bibliographies: In Reference to Richard Wright." *Bibliography and Index Perspective*, 9 (1 February), 34–35. Examines a trend in African American literature focusing on its uniquely autobiographical emphasis [T.K., R.B., and Y.H.].

664. ____. "Translation of Richard Wright's Early Poems, II." *Aichi Shukutoku Junior College Athena*, 19 (March), 21–33. Translation into Japanese of "Old Habit and New Love" and other poems.

665. ____. "An introduction to Richard Wright's Article in Ebony." *Waseda Review*, 24 (December), 93–103. Japanese translation of "The Shame of Chicago," *Ebony*, 7 December 1952.

666. Klotman, Phyllis R. "'Tearing a Hole in History': Lynching as Theme and Motif." *Black American Literature Forum*, 19 (Summer), 55–63. Contains three paragraphs recounting "Big Boy Leaves Home."

667. Kodama, Sanehide. "Japanese Influence on Richard Wright in His Last Years: English Haiku as a New Genre." *Tamking Review*, 15 (Autumn 1984-Summer), 63–73. Quotes and comments on nineteen of W's haiku, explains their relation to his illness, notes his reading of R.H. Blyth's *Haiku*, and discusses briefly other American writers of haiku.

668. Kostelanetz, Richard. "Fictions for a Negro Politics: The Neglected Novels of W.E.B. Du Bois," in *Critical Essays on W.E.B. Du Bois*. Ed. William L. Andrews. Boston: G.K. Hall, pp. 173–194. Reprint of 1968.145a.

669. Krause, David. "Faulkner's Blues." *Studies in the Novel*, 17 (Spring), 80–94. Review article on books on Faulkner mentioning W several times and quoting Faulkner on W (p. 90).

670. Lauter, Paul. "Race and Gender in the Shaping of the American Literary Canon: A Case Study from the Twenties," in *Feminist Criticism and Social Change: Sex, Class, and Race in Literature and Culture*. New York: Methuen, pp. 19–44. Mentions W briefly (p. 21).

671. Leaming, Barbara. *Orson Welles: A Biography.* New York: Viking, pp. 212, 213, 214. Comments on the play *NS*, quoting from reviews. After the play Welles became a target of red-baiters.

672. [Levine, Stuart]. "Obnafrucepbopitroas." *American Studies*, 26 (Spring), 47–49. Mentions briefly A. Robert Lee's pamphlet *Black American Fiction Since Richard Wright.*

673. Lewis, David Levering. "*Leadership, Love, and Aggression.* By Allison Davis." *The Journal of Southern History*, 51 (February), 131–132. Review commenting on the work's treatment of W.

674. Lewis, Pamela Masingale. "Victor Hernández Cruz," in *Afro-American Poets Since 1955.* Eds. Trudier Harris and Thadious M. Davis. Detroit: Gale, pp. 74–84. Mentions W as an influence on Cruz (p. 76).

675. Liebowitz, Herbert. "Richard Wright's *Black Boy*: Styles of Deprivation." *Southwest Review*, 70 (Winter), 71–94. Places *BB* in the context of black autobiography. Its "central motif ... is hunger" (p. 72), for words as well as food. Liebowitz analyzes W's style in numerous passages, finding it "intuitive, lyrical, morose, tender, haughty, tormented, didactic," but always artful. Also considers W's treatment of family and society in *BB*.

676. Lindsey, Victor. "Richard Wright." *Abstracts of English Studies*, 28 (June), 216. Abstracts an article by Robert F. Moss.

677. Litzinger, Boyd, and Joyce Carol Oates. "Questions," in their *Story: Fictions Past and Present.* Lexington, MA: D.C. Heath, pp. 612–613. Study questions to accompany "The Man Who Killed a Shadow."

678. Lockwood, Alan L., and David E. Harris. "Stealing North," in their *Reasoning with Democratic Values: Ethical Problems in United States History.* Vol. 2. New York: Teachers College Press, pp. 92–104. After background information on race relations in the nineteenth and twentieth centuries, the authors quote extensively from *BB* and provide numerous study exercises.

679. Logan, Maureen F. "Star-Crossed Platonic Lovers, or Bowdler Redux." *English Journal*, 74 (January), 53–55. Mentions *BB* briefly.

680. Long, Richard, and Eugenia W. Collier. "The Forties to 1970," in their *Afro-American Writing: An Anthology of Prose and Poetry.* University Park: The Pennsylvania State University Press, pp. 440–449. Includes a brief discussion of W mentioning *NS, BB, O, EM,* and *LT.*

681. _____. "James Baldwin (b. 1924)," in their *Afro-American Writing: An Anthology of Prose and Poetry.* University Park: The Pennsylvania State University Press, pp. 526–527. Mentions briefly the "Wright-Ellison Generation" (p. 526).

682. Longest, George C., et al. "Checklist of Scholarship on Southern Literature for 1984." *The Mississippi Quarterly*, 38 (Spring), 154–273. Lists nine items on W and cross-references to eighteen other items dealing partially with W.

683. Lynch, John. "Richard Wright 'The Man Who Was Almost a Man,'" in his *Instructor's Manual to Accompany Muller/Williams The McGraw-Hill Introduction to Literature.* New York: McGraw-Hill, p. 35. Paragraph on the story with suggested questions and a reference to Brignano (1970.68).

684. MacShane, Frank. *Into Eternity: The Life of James Jones, American Writer.* Boston: Houghton Mifflin, p. 234. Mentions W briefly.

685. McDowell, Edwin, "Mississippi Honors a 'Native Son' Who Fled." *The New York Times* (23 November), pp. 1, 11. Reports the W conference at the University of Mississippi, emphasizing its social and racial significance.

686. Maduka, Chidi T. "The Revolutionary Hero and Strategies for Survival in Richard Wright's *The Outsider.*" *Présence Africaine*, 135, 56–70. Comparing Cross Damon to Frederick Douglass, Dr. Miller in *The Marrow of Tradition*, and the protagonist of *Invisible Man*, Maduka studies "his confrontation with the power structure ... in three parts: first, an examination of his socio-political consciousness; second, a study of the various strategies deployed by him in confronting the system; third, the significance of his political activism" (p. 61).

687. Marable, Manning. *Black American Politics from the Washington Marches to Jesse Jackson.* London: Verso, pp. 184, 214. Quotes from *BB* and *AH.*

688. Martin, Charles H. "The International Labor Defense and Black America." *Labor History*, 26 (Spring), 165–194. Mentions briefly *AH* (p. 167).

689. Mason, Julian. "Wright Companions." *The Mississippi Quarterly*, 38 (Winter 1984-85), 87–90. Favorable review of Yoshinobu Hakutani's *Critical Essays on Richard Wright* and Charles T. Davis and Michel Fabre's *Richard Wright: A Primary Bibliography.*

690. McDowell, Edwin. "Mississippi Honors a 'Native Son' Who Fled." *The New York Times* (23 November), pp. 1, 14. Reports on the international symposium on W at the University of Mississippi, emphasizing the state's background of racism and recent changes. Includes statements on W by Ralph Ellison, Irving Howe, and others.

691. McGrath, Daniel F., ed. *Bookman's Price Index.* Vol. 29. Detroit: Gale, p. 983. Lists *NS* at $125 and *TMBV* at $25.

692. _____. *Bookman's Price Index.* Vol. 30. Detroit: Gale, p. 929. Lists *How "Bigger" Was Born* at $65, *NS* at $100, and *NS* at $40.

693. _____. *Bookman's Price Index.* Vol. 31. Detroit: Gale, p. 1003. Lists *BB* at $50, *NS* at $425, *NS* at $100, *NS* at $75, *NS* at $60, and *NS* at $55.

694. McMichael, George. "James Baldwin 1924–," in his *Anthology of American Literature.* Third edition. Vol. II. New York: Macmillan, pp. 1771–1772. Revised reprint of 1974. 125.

695. _____. "Ralph Ellison 1914–," in his *Anthology of American Literature.* Third edition. Vol. II. New York: Macmillan, p. 1552. Revised reprint of 1974.126.

696. _____. "Richard Wright 1908–1960," in his *Anthology of American Literature.* Third edition. Vol. II. New York: Macmillan, pp. 1513–1514. Revised reprint of 1974. 128.

697. Melhem, D. H. "Black Nationalism and the Poet Activist: An Interview with Haki R. Madhubuti." *The Western Journal of Black Studies*, 9 (Summer), 106–114. Madhubuti acknowledges W's great effect on him, mentioning *BB, NS, O,* and *BP* (p. 111).

698. Miller, Wayne C., ed. *Minorities in America: The Annual Bibliography, 1976.* University Park: The Pennsylvania State University

Press, 1985, pp. 149–150. Contains annotated entries for works on W by W.J. Feuser, Trudier Harris, Blyden Jackson, Chukwodi Thomas Maduka, and Joan Lovell Bayerly Maxwell.

699. [Miller, Wayne Charles]. "Editor's Column." *MELUS*, 12 (Summer), 1–5. Mentions W briefly (p. 1).

700. Millican, Arthenia J. Bates. "Kalamu ya Salaam (Valery Ferdinand III)," in *Afro-American Writers After 1955: Dramatists and Prose Writers*. Eds. Thadious M. Davis and Trudier Harris. Detroit: Gale, pp. 231–239. Notes that Salaam won the 1971 Richard Wright Award for literary criticism given by *Black World* (p. 239).

701. Mitchell, Mozella G. "Nikki Giovanni," in *Afro-American Poets Since 1955*. Eds. Trudier Harris and Thadious M. Davis. Detroit: Gale, pp. 135–151. Mentions Giovanni's reading of *BB* when she was a seventh grader (p. 136).

702. Montgomery, Glenn. "Center Asking for Some Friends." *The Southern Register: The Newsletter of the Center for the Study of Southern Culture*, 3 (Winter), 1–2. Mentions Michel Fabre's collection of essays on W.

703. Muller, Gilbert H., ed. *The McGraw Hill Reader*, second editon. New York: McGraw-Hill, pp. 245–249. Reprints W's "The Psychological Reactions of Oppressed People," followed by ten study questions.

704. Muller, Gilbert H., and John A. Williams. "Questions," in his *The McGraw-Hill Reader*. Second edition. New York: McGraw-Hill, p. 249.

705. _____. "Richard Wright 'The Man Who Was Almost a Man,'" in their *The McGraw-Hill Introduction to Literature*. New York: McGraw-Hill, p. 288. Biographical headnote.

706. _____. "Topics for Writing," in their *The McGraw-Hill Introduction to Literature*. New York: McGraw-Hill, p. 297. Four topics concerning "The Man Who Was Almost a Man."

707. Muller, Gilbert, and Richard McAdams. "Richard Wright, The Psychological Reactions of Oppressed People," in his *The McGraw-Hill Reader*. Second edition. New York: McGraw-Hill, p. 245.

708. Muller, Gilbert H., and John A. Williams. "Questions," in their

The McGraw-Hill Introduction to Literature. New York: McGraw-Hill, p. 297. Seven study questions on "The Man Who Was Almost a Man."

709. Muller, Gilbert H., and Richard McAdams. "Richard Wright, The Psychological Reactions of Oppressed People," in Muller's *Instructor's Manual to Accompany the McGraw-Hill Reader*. New York: McGraw-Hill, pp. 106–107.

710. Namekata, Hitoshi. "Community and Individual: Duality in Richard Wright." *Bulletin of Musashino College for Music*, 16 (31 March), 81–94. Observes that W grounds *NS* on black folklore to appeal to the Black masses. Argues that Bigger dies as an accomplice in the crime that the whole world commits [T.K., R.B., and Y.H.].

711. Nash, Charles C. "'The Man Who Lived Underground': Richard Wright's Parable of the Cave." *Interpretations*, 16 (Fall), 62–74. Relates W's story to Plato's parable in *The Republic*. Nash emphasizes W's anti–Communism and individualism. Provides a full plot summary.

712. Neal, Larry. "The Glorious Monster in the Bell of the Horn." *Callaloo*, 8 (Winter), 87–169. Mentions W briefly (pp. 128).

713. Nichols, Charles H. "The Slave Narrators and the Picaresque Mode: Archetypes for Modern Black Personae," in *The Slave's Narrative*. Eds. Charles T. Davis and Henry Louis Gates, Jr. New York: Oxford University Press, pp. 283–298. Includes discussion of W relating *BB*, *NS*, "The Man Who Lived Underground," and *O* to the traditions of the picaresque tale and the slave narrative. Nichols makes large claims for *O*.

714. O'Brien, Robert, with Harold H. Martin. *The Encyclopedia of the South*. New York: Facts on File, pp. 172, 458. Contains a brief entry on W mentioning *UTC* and *BB*. Also mentions W s.v. Green, Paul Eliot.

715. Oehlschlaeger, Fritz. "Robert Hayden's Meditation on Art: The Final Sequence of "*Words in the Mourning Time*." *Black American Literature Forum*, 19 (Fall), 115–119. Mentions W briefly (p. 115).

716. Ohmann, Richard. "*English in America*, Ten Years Later (with an aside on dechairing the department)." *ADE Bulletin*, No. 82

(Winter), pp. 11–17. Mentions W briefly (p. 16).

717. Okada, Seiichi. "Richard Wright's Unpublished Work, 'Tarbaby's Dawn.'" *Saitama University Heron*, 19 (27 February), 11–16. W's story "Almos' a Man" is part of this unpublished autobiographical novel, in which the portrayal of the south is peaceful [T.K., R.B., and Y.H.].

718. Olney, James. "'I Was Born': Slave Narratives, Their Status as Autobiography and as Literature," in *The Slave's Narrative*. Eds. Charles T. Davis and Henry Louis Gates, Jr. New York: Oxford University Press, pp. 148–175. Reprint of 1984.119.

719. O'Meally, Robert G. "The Ruler of Magic: Hemingway as Ellison's 'Ancestor.'" *The Southern Review*, 21 (July), 751–769. Uses W's influence on Ellison as a point of departure for a study of Hemingway's deeper influence, concluding that Invisible Man is "much more like Hemingway's Jake and Nick than like Bigger Thomas."

720. Onoge, Omafume F. "The Crisis of Consciousness in Modern African Literature: A Survey (1974)," in *Marxism and African Literature*. Ed. Georg M. Gugelberger. London: James Currey, pp. 21–49. Comments on "Blueprint for Negro Literature" (pp. 43, 48).

721. Page, James A., and Jae Min Roh. *Selected Black American, African, and Caribbean Authors: A Bio-Bibliography*. Littleton, CO: Libraries Unlimited, pp. 308–309. Contains an entry on W.

722. Perkins, Barbara M. "Chronology of Literature and World Events," in *The Harper Handbook to Literature*. New York: HarperCollins, pp. 493–563. Lists *NS* and *BB* (pp. 552, 553).

723. [Perkins, George.] "After the Second World War," in *The American Tradition in Literature*. Eds. George Perkins, Sculley Bradley, Richmond Croom Beatty, and E. Hudson Long. Sixth edition. Vol. 2. New York: Random House, pp. 1389–1395.

724. _____. "Richard Wright (1908–1960)," in *The American Tradition in Literature*. Eds. George Perkins, Sculley Bradley, Richmond Croom Beatty, and E. Hudson Long. Sixth edition. Vol. 2. New York: Random House, p. 1378. Reprint of 1974.142.

725. _____. "Richard Wright

(1908–1960)," in *The American Tradition in Literature*. Sixth edition (shorter edition). Eds. Sculley Bradley, Richmond Croom Beatty, E. Hudson Long, and George Perkins. New York: Random House, p. 1373. Revised reprint of 1974.142.

726. _____, Sculley Bradley, Richmond Croom Beatty, and E. Hudson Long. "After the Second World War," in their *The American Tradition in Literature*. Sixth edition (shorter edition). New York: Random House, pp. 1383–1389.

727. Peterson, Linda. "Repetition and Metaphor in the Early Stages of Composing." *College Composition and Communication*, 36 (December), 429–443. Analyzes drafts of an interview statement by W about *BB* to show the generative function of repetition and metaphor. In the statement, reproduced as an appendix, W acknowledges the importance of his reading of *The House of the Dead*, *Confessions of a Young Man*, *The Portrait of the Artist as a Young Man*, and *Sons and Lovers* in helping him to understand his Southern experience. Reprinted: 1991.

728. Pinsker, Sanford. *Conversations with Contemporary American Writers*. Amsterdam: Rodopi, pp. 106–116.

729. Podhoretz, Norman. "The Dialectic of Blame: Some Reflections on Anti-Americanism." *Encounter*, 65 (July/August), pp. 6–68. Mentions W briefly.

730. Pritchard, William H. "James Baldwin, 1924–," in *The Norton Anthology of American Literature*. Eds. Nina Baym, Ronald Gottesman, Laurence B. Holland, Francis Murphy, Hershel Parker, David Kalstone, and Pritchard. Second edition. Vol. 2. New York: W.W. Norton, pp. 2111–2113.

731. _____. "Ralph Ellison, 1914–," in *The Norton Anthology of American Literature*. Eds. Nina Baym, Ronald Gottesman, Laurence B. Holland, Francis Murphy, Hershel Parker, David Kalstone, and Pritchard. Second edition. Vol. 2. New York: W.W. Norton, pp. 1879–1880.

732. Ramanan, M.G., Andrew Horn, George E. Carter (eds.) *American Studies in Africa*. Tibor Frank (ed.), *The Origins and Originality of American Culture*, 15 (Summer), 142–145. Mentions briefly a paper by Felix Mnthali mentioning *NS*.

733. Rampersad, Arnold. "The Complexity of Southern Literary History." *Southern Literary Journal*, 18 (Fall), 110–115. Briefly contrasts *BB* and Hurston's *Dust Tracks on a Road* (p. 111).

734. _____. "The Literary Blues Tradition." *Callaloo*, 8 (Spring-Summer), 498–500. Review of Houston A. Baker's *Blues, Ideology, and Afro-American Literature* praising its treatment of "The Man Who Lived Underground."

735. _____. "W.E.B. Du Bois as a Man of Literature," in *Critical Essays on W.E.B. Du Bois*. Ed. William L. Andrews. Boston: G.K. Hall, pp. 57–72. Reprint of 1979.210.

736. Ramsey, Priscilla R. "Alexis Deveaux," in *Afro-American Writers After 1955: Dramatists and Prose Writers*. Eds. Thadious M. Davis and Trudier Harris. Detroit: Gale, pp. 92–97. Calls W Deveaux's "aesthetic grandfather" (p. 92).

737. _____. "E. Ethelbert Miller," in *Afro-American Poets Since 1955*. Eds. Trudier Harris and Thadious M. Davis. Detroit: Gale, pp. 233–240. Includes comparison of Miller's views to those W expresses in *How "Bigger" Was Born*, p. 235.

738. Redding, Saunders. "The Negro Writer and His Relationship to His Roots," in *Afro-American Writing: An Anthology of Prose and Poetry*. Eds. Richard Long and Eugenia W. Collier. University Park: The Pennsylvania State University Press, pp. 462–468. Reprint of 1960.222.

739. Richards, Rhonda. "Chicago an 'Important Chapter of Wright's Life.'" *The Daily Mississippian* (21 November), pp. 1, 5. Reports on W's life in Chicago, especially as recalled by Margaret Walker. Also mentions *UTC*, *NS*, W's relation to communism, and his expatriation.

740. Ro, Sigmund. "'Desecrators' and 'Necromancers': Black American Writers and Critics in the Nineteen-Sixties and the Third World Perspective." *Callaloo*, 8 (Fall), 563–576. Comments briefly on *NS*.

741. _____. "Henry Louis Gates, Jr., ed., *Black Literature and Literary Theory*." *American Studies in Scandinavia*, 17, 81–84. Mentions W briefly.

742. Rorabacher, Louise E., and Georgia Dunbar. "A Loaf of Bread and the Stars *Richard Wright*," in their *Assignments in Exposition*. Eighth edition. New York: Harper & Row, pp. 45–47. Reprints an excerpt from *BB* with a brief headnote and four study questions.

743. Rowell, Charles H. "An Interview with Larry Neal." *Callaloo*, 8 (Winter), 11–35. Neal mentions W briefly (pp. 17, 22).

744. _____, and William Lyne. "Studies in Afro-American Literature: An Annual Annotated Bibliography, 1984." *Callaloo*, 8 (Fall), 630–660. Lists twelve items on W with cross-references to seven others.

745. Ruas, Charles. *Conversations with American Writers*. New York: Knopf, pp. 215–243. Expresses admiration for W's books, but they did not seem addressed to *her*.

746. Sadler, Lynn Veach. "Richard Wright's *Savage Holiday*: The Criminal Minds [sic] Its Own Best Detective." *Journal of Popular Literature*, 1 (Fall-Winter), 61–72. Analyzes the novel as a combination of crime fiction and Freudian existentialism. Sandler points out W's use of Dostoevsky, Victor Hugo, Nietzsche and Theodor Reik as well as Freud.

747. Sagarin, Edward, and Robert J. Kelly. "Responsibility and Crime in Literature." *The Annals of the American Academy of Political and Social Science*, 477 (January), 12–24. Includes a discussion of Bigger Thomas. He is not responsible for the social conditions driving him to crime, but he is responsible for his criminal acts (pp. 20–22).

748. Salzberg, Joel. *Bernard Malamud: A Reference Guide*. Boston: G.K. Hall, p. 80. Lists Robert Stanton's article (1969.226).

749. Schlueter, Paul, and June Schlueter. "Bibliographies," in their *Modern American Literature* in *A Library of Literary Criticism*. Vol. V: Second Supplement to the Fourth Edition. New York: Frederick Ungar, pp. 587–603. Includes a list of W's books from 1954.

750. Schultz, Elizabeth. "Albert L. Murray," in *Afro-American Writers After 1955: Dramatists and Prose Writers*. Eds. Thadious M. Davis and Trudier Harris. Detroit: Gale, pp. 214–224. Mentions briefly W and Bigger Thomas (pp. 216, 220).

751. Scruggs, Charles W. "Finding Out About This Mencken: The Impact of *A Book of Prefaces* on

Richard Wright." *Menckeniana*, 95 (Fall), 1–11. Comprehensive treatment of the W-Mencken relationship, showing that the affinity was even stronger than that of the Harlem Renaissance writers. W responded to Mencken's love of books, his satire on an anti-intellectual culture, his sense of wonder at the adventure of life, and his tragic view. Scruggs analyzes *NS* from a Menckenian perspective.

752. Scully, James. "Scratching Surfaces." *The Minnesota Review*, 24 (Spring), 9–36. Quotes from *BB* in an endnote (p. 34).

753. Shourie, Usha. *The Black American Literature.* New Delhi: Cosmo Publications, pp. 4, 10–20, 24, 27–29, 76, 95–121, 152, 153, 167, 172, 176, 178, 205. The chapter on W shows Marxist ideas in its analysis of *UTC*, *NS*, and *LT*, but *O* reflects his withdrawal from the Communist Party. Shourie notes W's use of irony and symbols. The introduction reviews W scholarship, and W is mentioned frequently throughout the book.

754. _____. *The Black American Literature.* New Delhi: Cosmo Publications, pp. 4, 10–20, 24, 27–29, 76, 95–121, 152, 153, 167, 176. Chapter 4 surveys W's work, emphasizing the Marxist element. Mentions W frequently elsewhere.

755. Shrodes, Caroline, Harry Finestone, and Michael Shugrue. "Richard Wright *The Ethics of Living Jim Crow*," in their *The Conscious Reader.* Third edition. New York: Macmillan, p. 500. Brief headnote.

756. _____. "Suggestions for Discussion, Suggestions for Writing," in their *The Conscious Reader.* Third edition. New York: Macmillan, pp. 508–509.

757. Silberman, Charles E. *A Certain People: American Jews and Their Lives Today.* New York: Summit Books, pp. 340, 341, 437. Quotes from *BB* to illustrate black anti–Semitism.

758. Sisney, Mary F. "The Power and Horror of Whiteness: Wright and Ellison Respond to Poe." *CLA Journal*, 29 (September), 82–90. Discusses W's use of Poe's "The Black Cat" as a source for *NS*. Considers also W's use of the color white.

759. Skei, Hans H. "The Reception and Reputation of 'Minor' Mis-

sissippi Writers in Norway." *Notes on Mississippi Writers*, 17, No. 1, 19–33. Includes publication data on the two works translated into Norwegian (*NS* and *BB*), a survey of reviews, and a summary of four University of Oslo theses.

760. Smith, Robert P., Jr. "Publications by CLA Members: 1984." *CLA Journal*, 29 (December), 243–247. Mentions W briefly.

761. [Snell, Susan]. "Books." *S.S.S.L.: The News-Letter of The Society for the Study of Southern Literature* (18 April), 13–22. Notes that *The American Short Story 1900–1945: A Critical History* treats W (p. 13).

762. _____. "Books." *S.S.S.L.: The News-Letter of The Society for the Study of Southern Literature*, 18 (November), 11–21. Lists Michel Fabre's *The World of Richard Wright* (p. 12).

763. Solomon, Charlotte, D. "Native Son," in *Academic American Encyclopedia*. Danbury, CT: Grolier, 1985, vol. 14, p. 47. Synopsis of the novel, which "is considered a landmark in 20th century black American literature."

764. Sorkin, Adam J. "Politics, Privatism and the Fifties: Ring Lardner, Jr.'s 'The Ecstasy of Owen Muir.'" *Journal of American Culture*, 8 (Fall), 59–73. Quotes briefly from *AH* (p. 61).

765. Spack, Ruth. "Literature, Reading, Writing, and ESL: Bridging the Gaps." *TESOL Quarterly*, 19 (December), 703–725. Mentions briefly "The Man Who Was Almost a Man" (p. 721).

766. Spillers, Hortense. "Afterword," in *Conjuring: Black Women, Fiction, and Literary Tradition.* Eds. Marjorie Pryse and Hortense Spillers. Bloomington: Indiana University Press, pp. 249–261. Mentions Bigger Thomas and *NS*.

767. _____. "Afterword: Cross-Currents, Discontinuities: Black Women's Fiction," in her and Marjorie Pryse's *Conjuring: Black Women, Fiction, and Literary Tradition.* Bloomington: Indiana University Press, pp. 249–261. Mentions briefly *NS* (p. 253).

768. Spradling, Mary Mace, ed. *In Black and White Supplement: A Guide to Magazine Articles, Newspaper Articles, and Books Concerning More Than 6,700 Black Individuals and Groups.* Third edition. Detroit: Gale, p. 426. Biographical data and listing of eleven research sources.

769. Steeves, Edna L. "Richard Wright." *Abstracts of English Studies*, 28 (March), 94. Abstracts an article by Robert A. Coles.

770. Stepto, Robert B. "I Rose and Found My Voice: Narration, Authentication, and Authorial Control in Four Slave Narratives," in *The Slave's Narrative.* Eds. Charles T. Davis and Henry Louis Gates, Jr. New York: Oxford University Press, pp. 225–241. Partial reprint of 1979. 243.

771. Stuckey, W.J. "Rose Ann C. Fraistat. *Caroline Gordon as Novelist and Woman of Letters*; Lewis A. Lawson. *Another Generation: Southern Fiction Since World War II*; Peggy Whitman Prenshaw, ed. *Conversations with Eudora Welty*." *Modern Fiction Studies*, 31 (Summer), 400–402. Review noting Lawson's reprinted essay on *O*.

772. Tallack, Douglas. "American Short Fiction: A Bibliographical Essay." *American Studies International*, 23 (October), 3–59. Comments on Burgum and Margolies on W's short stories (p. 35) and lists a few others in a bibliography (p. 53).

773. Tamada, Yoshiyuki. "Richard Wright and *Black Power*." *Black Studies*, 55 (30 September), 26–32. Revaluates W's non-fiction, which is not well known in Japan. Explains *BP* with reference to Kwame Nkrumah [T.K., R.B., and Y.H.].

774. _____. "Richard Wright and Kwame Nkrumah: On *Black Power*." *Newsletter of the Black Studies Association in Japan*, 22 (15 December), 6. Brief comment on W's nonfiction, a compelling message to the third world [T.K., R.B., and Y.H.].

775. Taylor, Clyde. "Black Writing as Immanent Humanism." *The Southern Review*, 21 (July), 790–800. Applies the ideas of "Blueprint for Negro Writing" to black writing after W, finding the essay prophetic and perspicacious (except for overlooking womanist literature). Also praises *NS*.

776. Thaddeus, Janice. "The Metamorphosis of Richard Wright's *Black Boy*." *American Literature*, 57 (May), 199–214. The concluding pages of *BB* seem to define the experiences narrated to that point, changing the work from an "open" autobiography, in which the writer attempts to speak the painful truth, to a "defined" autobiography, in which the writer resolves tensions and provides a teleological structure. *AH*, however, continues in an "open" mode. The explanation, as revealed in unpublished papers, is that the hopeful conclusion of *BB* was added so that the work would be selected by the Book-of-the-Month Club. Thaddeus also analyzes the relation of the epigraphs of W's autobiography (*BB* and *AH*) to its imagery.

777. Tidwell, John Edgar. "An Interview with Frank Marshal Davis." *Black American Literature Forum*, 19 (Fall), 105–108. Davis discusses his friendship with W, their association in the League of American Writers, his introduction of photography to W, and his reading galley proof of *NS*, "part of which was left out by the publisher as too pornographic for that era" (p. 107).

778. Tracy, Steven C. "*Blues, Ideology, and Afro-American Literature.* Houston A. Baker." *MELUS*, 12 (Summer), 97–102. Comments favorably on Baker's treatment of *W* (p. 101).

779. _____. "A MELUS Interview: Etheridge Knight." *MELUS*, 12 (Summer), 7–23. Knight comments on the lack of a sense of place in W, referring to his life and to *O* (p. 15).

780. Traylor, Eleanor W. "'And the Resurrection, Let It Be Complete': The Achievement of Larry Neal (A Biobibliography of a Critical Imagination)." *Callaloo*, 8 (Winter), 36–69. Mentions W briefly (pp. 38, 53, 56, 58, 59).

781. _____. "An Annotated Bibliography of the Works of Larry (Lawrence Paul) Neal." *Callaloo*, 8 (Winter), 265–273. Lists Neal's essay on W.

782. Trimmer, Joseph F., and C. Wade Jennings. "Richard Wright *The Man Who Was Almost a Man*," in their *Fictions*. San Diego: Harcourt Brace, Jovanovich, pp. 1242–1251. Reprints the story with a headnote and five "Questions for Discussion and Writing."

783. Van Deburg, William L., *Slavery and Race in American Popular Culture." Journal of American Studies*, 19 (April 1985), pp. 138–139. Review mentioning W briefly.

784. Vickery, John B. "American Literature: The Twentieth Century," in *The Year's Work in English Studies*, 63, pp. 438–461. Contains notices of *Literature at the Barricades*

and an article by Raymond Hedin, both mentioning W briefly (pp. 438–439, 451).

785. _____. American Literature to 1900," in *The Year's Work in English Studies*, 63, pp. 417–437. Contains a notice of *American Novelists Revisited* mentioning W briefly (p. 420).

786. Vinson, Audrey. "The Other World of Toni Morrison" in her and Bessie W. Jones's *The Worlds of Toni Morrison: Explorations in Literary Criticism*. Dubuque, IA: Kendall/Hunt, pp. 7–21. Mentions briefly W and the tradition of the grotesque (p. 7).

787. Wald, Alan. "The Politics of Culture: The New York Intellectuals in Fiction." *The Centennial Review*, 29 (Summer), 353–369. Argues that Lionel Trilling's story "The Other Margaret" may be a response to *NS* (p. 367).

788. Walker, Alice. "Beyond the Peacock: The Reconstruction of Flannery O'Connor," in *Critical Essays on Flannery O'Connor*. Eds. Melvin J. Friedman and Beverly Lyon Clark. Boston: G.K. Hall, pp. 71–81.

789. Walker, Warren S. "Bibliography." *Studies in Short Fiction*, 22 (Summer), 371–419. Lists an item on "Big Boy Leaves Home" and an item on "The Man Who Lived Underground."

790. Walls, Doyle W. "The Clue Undetected in Richard Wright's *Native Son*." *American Literature*, 57 (March), 125–128. In the particular sense, whites in the novel fail to detect the Black English verb form in Bigger's ransom note ("*Do what this letter say*."). In a general sense, they fail to recognize his humanity.

791. Walton, Hanes, Jr. *Invisible Politics: Black Political Behavior*. Albany: State University of New York Press, pp. 279, 355. Notes W's attendance at the Bandung Conference. The endnote incorrectly cites *BP*.

792. Ward, Jerry W., Jr. "Lenard D. Moore. *The Open Eye*." *Black American Literature Forum*, 19 (Fall), 133–134. Review mentioning briefly W's haiku.

793. _____. "Selected Bibliography for the Study of Southern Black Literature in the Twentieth Century." *The Southern Quarterly*, 23 (Winter), 94–115. Lists fifteen items s.v. W.

794. Watson, Carole McAlpine. *Prologue: The Novels of Black American Women, 1891–1965*. Westport, CT: Greenwood Press, pp. 56, 106, 158. Quotes from "Blue Print for Negro Writing," comments briefly on *NS*, and lists "I Bite the Hand That Feeds Me."

795. Watson, Douglas. "James Andrew Emanuel," in *Afro-American Poets Since 1955*. Eds. Trudier Harris and Thadious M. Davis. Detroit: Gale, pp. 103–117. Lists an article on W by Emanuel (p. 103).

796. Weaver, Gordon. "A Sense of Place and Time: Common Experience, Common Values," in *Mississippi Writers: Reflections of Childhood and Youth*. Ed. Dorothy Abbott. Vol. I. Jackson: University Press of Mississippi, pp. xix–xxxvii. Rates W with Faulkner, Welty, and Walker Percy (p. xix) and contains a paragraph on "Almos' a Man" (p. xxx).

797. [Weixlmann, Joe]. "Volume II of *Studies in Black American Literature* Published." *Black American Literature Forum*, 19 (winter), 146. Lists Keneth Kinnamon's article on W and Maya Angelou.

798. Werner, Craig. "Nellie Y. McKay. *Jean Toomer, Artist: A Study of His Literary Life and Work, 1894–1936*; Gloria Wade-Gayles. *No Crystal Stair: Visions of Race and Sex in Black Women's Fiction*; Sigmund Ro. *Rage and Celebration: Essays on Contemporary Afro-American Writing*; William Luis, ed. *Voices from Under: Black Narrative in Latin America and the Caribbean*; Joe Weixlmann and Chester J. Fontenot, eds. *Studies in Black American Literature*. Volume I: *Black American Prose Theory*." *Modern Fiction Studies*, 31 (Summer), 420–424. Review mentioning Fabre's biography of W and Sekora and Baker's article on Douglass and W.

799. _____. "The Old South, 1815–1840," in *The History of Southern Literature*. Eds. Louis D. Rubin, Jr., Blyden Jackson, Rayburn S. Moore, Lewis P. Simpson, and Thomas Daniel Young. Baton Rouge: Louisiana State University Press, pp. 81–91. Mentions W briefly (p. 91).

800. West, Cornel. "Communism in Harlem." *Monthly Review*, 37 (December), 48–51. Review of Mark Naison's *Communists in Harlem During the Depression* mentioning W briefly.

801. Westling, Louise. *Sacred*

Groves and Ravaged Gardens: The Fiction of Eudora Welty, Carson McCullers, and Flannery O'Connor. Athens: The University of Georgia Press, pp. 38–39. Mentions briefly *BB.*

802. White, Barbara A. *Growing Up Female: Adolescent Girlhood in American Fiction.* Westport, CT: Greenwood Press, p. 96. Compares Bigger to Frankie in Carson McCullers's *The Member of the Wedding.*

803. White, John. *Black Leadership in America, 1895–1968.* London: Longman, p. 83. Quotes from *AH* on Marcus Garvey.

804. _____. "William L. Van Deburg, *Slavery and Race in American Popular Culture.*" *Journal of American Studies,* 19 (April), 138–139. Review mentioning W briefly.

805. Williams, John. "*Afro-American Literature in the 20th Century: The Achievement of Intimacy.* Michael G. Cooke." *The Black Scholar,* 16 (July/August), 66–67. Review mentioning W briefly.

806. _____. "*Afro-American Literature in the 20th Century: The Achievement of Intimacy.*" *The Black Scholar,* 16 (July/August), 66–67. Mentions W briefly.

807. Williams, Sherley Anne. "Roots of Privilege: *New Black Fiction.*" *Ms.,* 13 (June), 69–72. Mentions briefly *BB* (p. 71). Reprinted: 1993.

808. _____. "Roots of Privilege: *New Black Fiction.*" *MS* (June), pp. 69–72. Includes comment on *BB.*

809. _____. "Langston Hughes and the Negro Renaissance." *The Langston Hughes Review,* 4 (Spring), 37–39. Mentions W briefly W and *NS.*

810. Willis, Susan. "Alice Walker's Women." *New Orleans Review,* 12 (Spring), 33–41. Mentions W briefly (p. 35).

811. Winchel, Mark Royden. *Leslie Fiedler.* Boston: Twayne, p. 68. Comments briefly on *NS.*

812. Winterowd, W. Ross, and Patricia Y. Murray. "Model: Personal Essay-Commentary," in their *English: Writing and Skills.* Teacher's edition. San Diego: Coronado, p. 28. Quotes a paragraph from the hospital episode of *AH* with a prefatory note and two study questions.

1986

813. Adams, Timothy Dow. "I Do Believe Him Though I Know He Lies: Lying as Genre and Metaphor in Richard Wright's *Black Boy,*" in *Modern Selves: Essays on Modern British and American Autobiography.* Ed. Philip Dodd. London: Frank Cass, pp. Revised reprint of 1985.3.

814. Aithal, S.K. "Richard Wright." *Abstracts of English Studies,* 29 (September), 325–326. Abstracts articles by Judith Giblin Brazinsky and Robert James Butler.

815. Andrews, William L. *To Tell a Free Story: The First Century of Afro-American Autobiography, 1760–1865.* Urbana: University of Illinois Press, p. 291. Mentions briefly *BB.*

816. Anon. "About the Author," in *Going to the Territory.* By Ralph Ellison. New York: Random House, p. 339. Biographical sketch of Ellison mentioning W briefly.

817. Anon. *Arts & Humanities Citation Index, 1985.* Vol. 2. Philadelphia: Institute for Scientific Information, pp. 11418–11419. Lists sixty-four items s.v. WRIGHT R, not all on W.

818. Anon. "*Black Boy,*" in *The Encyclopedia Americana.* Ed. Bernard S. Cayne. Danbury, CT: Grolier, vol. 4, p. 29. Describes *BB* as a social document.

819. Anon. "*Callaloo*: 'Ole Miss' salutes a native son! Richard Wright." *Obsidian II,* 1 (Winter), 195. Advertisement for the special W issue of *Callaloo.* Includes a photograph of W.

820. Anon. *Index to Periodical Articles by and About Blacks: 1983.* Boston: G.K. Hall, p. 170. Lists one item about W.

821. Anon. *Index Translationum 34.* Paris: UNESCO, pp. 89, 366, 807. Lists translations of *BB* into German and Finnish and *AH* into Russian.

822. Anon. "*Kaffir Boy* by Mark Mathabane." *The Nation,* 242 (3 May), 623. Advertisement claiming that "if Richard Wright had grown up in South Africa, this is the book he would have written."

823. Anon. "Mississippi Writers Share Childhood Memories." *The Southern Register,* 4 (Winter/Spring), 3–4. Notes W's inclusion in *Mississippi Writers: Reflections of Childhood and Youth.*

824. Anon. "Publications Relating to Mississippi." *The Journal of Mississippi History,* 48 (May), 165–169. Lists an article on *BB* by Yoshinobu Hakutani and a book on W by Margaret Walker.

825. Anon. "Publications Relating to Mississippi." *The Journal of Mississippi History,* 48 (November), 315–318. Lists articles on W by Lynn Veach Sadler and Louis Tremaine.

826. Anon. "This Week's N.Y. Showcase." *Variety* (31 December), p. 10. Reports gross receipts of $110,000 for the new *NS* film during the first week.

827. Anon. "Your invitation to see *Native Son.*" New York: Harper & Row. Flyer providing free admission to the New York screening of the film *NS.*

828. Appiah, Anthony. "Are We Ethnic? The Theory and Practice of American Pluralism." *Black American Literature Forum,* 20 (Spring-Summer), 209–224. Review of *Beyond Ethnicity: Consent and Descent in American Culture* mentioning W briefly (p. 216).

829. Awazu, Masahiro. "An Impossible Dream." *Okayama University Persica,* 13 (31 March), 33–39. Discussion of racial prejudice in *LD* [T.K., R.B., and Y.H.].

830. Axelrod, Rise B., and Charles R. Cooper. "Narrative," in their *The St. Martin's Guide to Writing*. Short edition. New York: St. Martin's Press, pp. 386–403. Reprint of 1985.15.

831. Baker, Miriam, Donald McQuade, and Nancy Sommers. "Richard Wright, 'Discovering Books,'" in their *Instructor's Manual to Accompany Student Writers at Work and Student Writers at Work and in the Company of Other Writers*. New York: St. Martin's Press, pp. 137–138. Pedagogical notes on an excerpt from *BB*.

832. Baraka, Amiri. "*Raisin in the Sun's* Enduring Passion." *Washington Post* (16 November), pp. F 1, 3. Favorable review emphasizing Hansberry's politics and mentioning W. Reprinted: 1996

833. Barksdale, Richard K. "Margaret Walker: Folk Orature and Historical Prophecy," in *Black American Poets Between Worlds, 1940–1960*. Ed. R. Baxter Miller. Knoxville: The University of Tennessee Press, pp. 104–117. Mentions W briefly (p. 106). Reprinted: 1992.

834. [Baym, Nina]. "American Literature Between the Wars, 1914–1945," in *The Norton Anthology of American Literature*. Second edition, shorter. Ed. Nina Baym et al. New York: Norton, pp. 1637–1671. Reprint of 1985.22.

835. Bellman, Samuel Irving. "*The American Short Story 1900–1945: A Critical History*, edited by Philip Stevick." *Studies in Short Fiction*, 23 (Winter), 124–125. Review mentioning W briefly.

836. Benoist, Mary Anne. "News, Projects, and Research." *S.S.S.L.: The News-Letter of The Society for the Study of Southern Literature*, 19 (April), 7–9. Mentions a project by Lola E. Jones involving W.

837. Benson, Peter. *Black Orpheus, Transition, and Modern Cultural Awakening in Africa*. Berkeley and Los Angeles: University of California Press, pp. 25, 26. Notes coverage in *Black Orpheus* of the W-Césaire debate and comments on Ulli Beier's discussion in the same magazine of *BB* and *BP*.

838. Bernstein, Margaret. "Breaking Hollywood's Race Barrier." *USA Today* (30 December), pp. 1D–2D. Notes that the 1986 film version of *NS* has been criticized for its "negative images of blacks."

839. Berry, Faith. "A Question of Publishers and a Question of Audience." *The Black Scholar*, 17 (March–April), 41–49. Mentions Margaret Walker's biography of W and notes prurient interests of some early white readers of *NS*.

840. _____. "Saunders Redding as Literary critic of Langston Hughes." *The Langston Hughes Review*, 5 (Fall), 24–28. Mentions W briefly (p. 28).

841. Blake, Susan L. "Old John in Harlem: The Urban Folktales of Langston Hughes," in *Critical Essays on Langston Hughes*. Ed. Edward J. Mullen. Boston: G.K. Hall, pp. 167–176.

842. Blau, Robert. "Starring Role a Labor of Love." *Chicago Tribune* (10 April), Sec. 5, pp. 1, 3. Article on Victor Love, who plays Bigger in the film *NS*. Contrasts the actor with his privileged middle-class background to Bigger.

843. Bloom, Alexander. *Prodigal Sons: The New York Intellectuals and Their World*. New York: Oxford University Press, pp. 59, 65. Mentions W early in his career.

844. Bloom, Harold. "Bibliography," in his *American Fiction 1914 to 1945*. New York: Chelsea House, pp. 437–446. Contains nine items s.v. Richard Wright (p. 446).

845. _____. "Biographical Notes," in his *American Fiction 1914 to 1945*. New York: Chelsea House, pp. 425–432. Includes a biographical note on W (p. 432).

846. _____. "Richard Wright," in his *American Fiction 1914 to 1945*. New York: Chelsea House, 1986, p. 432. Biographical note.

847. Bohner, Charles H. "Richard Wright, 'The Man Who Was Almost a Man,'" in his *Instructor's Manual Classic Short Fiction*. Englewood Cliffs, NJ: Prentice-Hall, pp. 125–126. Emphasizes W's technique of the limited omniscient point of view and the symbolism of the gun.

848. Bone, Robert. "Richard Wright and the Chicago Renaissance." *Callaloo*, 9 (Summer), 446–468. Argues for a Chicago Renaissance (1935–1950) following the Harlem Renaissance (1920–1935) as an integral part of African American literary history. W was its central figure and guiding spirit, but Bone deals also with its other creative writers, its social milieu of migrants, its sociological connections (Park, Wirth, Cayton, Drake), its patrons (Embree, Rosenwald, Stark),

and its journals (*Abbott's Monthly*, *Left Front*, *New Challenge*, and *Negro Story*). Whereas the Harlem Renaissance looked back to folklore and the Southern past, the Chicago group, under W, looked toward the urban future and existential freedom.

849. Bonetti, Kay. "An Interview with John Edgar Wideman." *The Missouri Review*, 9, No. 2, 77–103. Mentions W briefly (pp. 80, 98). Reprinted: 1998.

850. Booth, James. "African, Caribbean, Canadian, Indian, and Australian Literature in English: Africa," in *The Year's Work in English Studies*. Vol. 64. London: John Murray, pp. 531–550. Comments favorably on a book by Kinfe Abraham comparing W and Peter Abrahams.

851. Bracy, William. "Wright, Richard Nathaniel," in *The Encyclopedia Americana*. Ed. Bernard S. Cayne. Danbury, CT: Grolier, Vol. 29, pp. 555–556. Biographical sketch mentioning all of W's books except *WML*.

852. _____. "Wright Richard Nathaniel," in *The Encyclopedia Americana*. Ed. Bernard S. Cayne. Danbury, CT: Grolier, Vol. 29, pp. 555–556. Reprint of 1969.

853. Bradley, David. "On Rereading 'Native Son.'" *The New York Times Magazine*, 7 December, pp. 68, 70, 71, 74, 78–79. Relates his four readings of the novel over a period of fifteen years. He originally hated it: "The plot was improbable, the narrative voice intrusive, the language often stilted and the characters ... were stereotypical beyond belief" (p. 70). Even worse, Bigger's brutality was repulsive. The realization that whites thought Bigger plausible was frightening. Bradley finally regarded *NS* as a book of its time, a sad reminder of the racism of the past and the blurred vision it created. Also comments on *BB* and *NS*.

854. Brotman, Barbara. "New 'Native Son' Sad Old Truth to Guests." *Chicago Tribune* (11 December), Sec. 2, pp. 1, 4. Interviews with members of the audience at the premier of the film *NS*, a benefit for the United Negro College Fund. Most confirmed the work's portrayal of racism in Chicago.

855. Brown, Beth. "*A Daughter's Geography*. By Ntozake Shange; *Black Women Writers at Work*. By Claudia

Tate; *Our Nig; Or, Sketches from the Life of a Free Black.* Ed. Henry Louis Gates." *CLA Journal*, 29 (March), 378–386. Mentions briefly W in Ntozake Shange's poem "Take the A Train."

856. Burns, Edward, ed. *The Letters of Gertrude Stein and Carl Van Vechten, 1913–1946.* Vol. 2. New York: Columbia University Press, pp. 768, 769, 771, 772, 775–776, 778, 780, 781, 784, 786, 788–789, 790, 796, 798, 806, 808, 811, 816, 819–823, 825, 826, 827, 829. Van Vechten and Stein comment extensively on W from March 1945 to Stein's death sixteen months later. Both express admiration for W and his work, Stein saying of *UTC* that "I'm mad about it, there is a tremendous mastery in the thing" (p. 789). By late June of 1946, however, Stein is expressing reservations because W "does not seem to me very Negro" (p. 827).

857. Burns, Landon C., Janet P. Alwang, and Elizabeth Buckmaster. "The Twelfth (1985) Supplement to a Cross-Referenced Index of Short Fiction Anthologies and Author-Title Listings." *Studies in Short Fiction*, 23 (Spring), 225–363. Lists two items on W (p. 263).

858. Burnshaw, Stanley. *Robert Frost Himself.* New York: Braziller, p. 51. Burnshaw mentions W's poetry and states that he urged W to move from Chicago to New York.

859. Burr, Nelson R. "New Eden and New Babylon: Religious Thoughts of American Authors: A Bibliography VII." *Historical Magazine of the Protestant Episcopal Church*, 55 (September), 213–247. Notes dissertations treating W by Richard Lehan (p. 217), Cynthia Janis Smith (p. 244), Esther Alexander Terry (p. 245), Ramona Kumar Singh (p. 245), and Evelyn Gross Avery (p. 245).

860. Burrison, William. "Another Look at *Lawd Today*: Richard Wright's Tricky Apprenticeship." *CLA Journal*, 29 (June), 424–441. After reviewing criticism of the novel, Burrison analyzes its comic pattern of fool/trickster. W uses colors (especially green), numbers (especially three), and objects as devices to enhance this pattern. The novel is structurally sound, balancing comic and tragic elements.

861. Butler, Robert James. "The Function of Violence in Richard Wright's *Native Son.*" *Black American Literature Forum*, 20 (Spring-Summer), 9–25. Far from being gratuitous, violence in W's novel is carefully controlled to express Bigger's personality split between romantic aspiration and naturalistic entrapment. His relation to Mary reveals the first, his relation to Bessie the second. In killing them, he is also destroying two aspects of himself. In Book Three he strives to transcend both "shallow romanticism" and "confining naturalism" so as to achieve wholeness, but the final scene shows that he falls short.

862. Byrd, Rudolph. "Continued Relevance." *Callaloo*, 9 (Fall), 751–752. Favorable review of Michel Fabre's *The World of Richard Wright*.

863. Canby, Vincent. "Screen: 'Native Son,' Based on Wright's Novel." *The New York Times* (24 December), p. C14. Mixed review criticizing the film's softening of the novel, but praising most of the performances. The residual power testifies "to the headlong simplicity and mysterious durability of Wright's classic" as well as to the screenplay.

864. Chametzky, Jules. *Our Decentralized Literature: Cultural Meditations in Selected Jewish and Southern Writers.* Amherst: The University of Massachusetts Press, p. 9. Mentions W briefly.

865. Clark, Georgene. "*The World of Richard Wright.* By Michel Fabre." *The Journal of Mississippi History*, 48 (May), 156–157. Favorable review praising Fabre's treatment of the whole range of W's writings.

866. Coles, Nicholas. "Democratizing Literature: Issues in Teaching Working-Class Literature." *College English*, 48 (November), 664–680. Mentions briefly W and *NS* (p. 675).

867. Colter, Cyrus. "Wright Revisited." *Chicago Tribune* (21 December), Sec. 14, pp. 1, 4, 10. Sketches W's life, focusing on *NS*. Colter recalls seeing W in Chicago in 1936, then meeting him in 1941 and attending with him and others a Marian Anderson concert. Describes W's dress, demeanor, and appearance, thinking, "can this urbane, agreeable personage ... be the man who created that native son and archetype Bigger Thomas?"

868. Corbin, Raymond M. *1999 Facts About Blacks: A Sourcebook for African-American Accomplishment.*

Providence: Beckham House, p. 68. Mentions briefly *BB*.

869. Core, George. "The Southern Country of the American Imagination." *The Virginia Quarterly Review*, 62 (Summer), 519–523. Review of *The History of Southern Literature* praising Blyden Jackson's essay on W (p. 521).

870. Cornell, Charles R., ed. *Biography Index: A Cumulative Index to Biographical Material in Books and Magazines, September 1984–August 1986.* New York: H.W. Wilson, p. 767. Lists three items on W.

871. Couturier, Maurice. "'Le continent postmoderne': Le Nouveau Roman américain." *Les Langues Modernes*, 80, no. 3, 27–36. Mentions W briefly (p. 29).

872. Cunliffe, Marcus. *The Literature of the United States.* Fourth edition. Harmondsworth, Middlesex: Penguin Books, pp. 366–367, 386–388. Contrasts W and Thomas Wolfe. Sketches W's career, mentioning *BB* and most of the fiction.

873. Dacy, Elo. "Rapport général du colloque," in his *L'Actualité de Frantz Fanon.* Paris: Editions Karthala, pp. 313–315. Mentions W briefly.

874. Davis, David Brion. "Violence in American Literature," in his *From Homicide to Slavery: Studies in American Culture.* New York: Oxford University Press, pp. 41–51. Reprint of 1966.42.

875. Davis, Jane. "More Force Than Human: Richard Wright's Female Characters." *Obsidian II*, 1 (Winter), 68–83. Argues that power is the main issue between men and women in W's fiction. "Women's power can result from either their independence or dependence" (p. 82), and both threaten male independence. So threatened, W's male characters lash back, often violently.

876. Davis, Thadious M. "Separating Fact from Self-Created Fiction," in *The Challenges of Writing Black Biography.* Eds. Leo Hamalian and James V. Hatch. New York: Hatch-Billops Collection, pp. 5–9. Mentions W "rewriting his family history in order to emphasize the singularity of his individual achievement."

877. _____. "Wright, Faulkner, and Mississippi as Racial Memory." *Callaloo*, 9 (Summer), 469–478. Relates W and Faulkner to the social and historical context of their native state, which they must reconstitute imaginatively and then transcend. Faulkner must come to terms with the past and a closed society, even while criticizing them. W could achieve his human potential only by rejecting the state's past with its racism and oppression. But both were indelibly marked by Mississippi.

878. Davis, Ursula Broschke. *Paris Without Regret: James Baldwin, Kenny Clarke, Chester Himes, and Donald Byrd.* Iowa City: University of Iowa Press, pp. 10–11, 12–15, 43, 84, 85–86, 91–92, 96. Discusses the relation of Baldwin and Himes to W. Notes that Himes considered *SH* W's best novel "because its characters seemed real and they were absurd" (p. 92).

879. Dearborn, Mary V. *Pocahontas's Daughters: Gender and Ethnicity in American Culture.* New York: Oxford University Press, p. 63. Comments on W's criticism of *Their Eyes Were Watching God.*

880. DeCosta-Willis, Miriam. "Avenging Angels and Mute Mothers: Black Southern Women in Wright's Fictional World." *Callaloo,* 9 (Summer), 540–549. Examines W's black women characters not as realistic representations, but as "the dark side of a Southern womanhood that has been violated and distorted in the crucible of racism and sexism" (p. 548). So considered, they fall into the categories of the Mother Avenger (Aunt Sue), the Mother Sufferer (W's own mother and Lulu), and the Earth Mother (Sarah).

881. DelFattore, Joan. "Contemporary Censorship Pressures and Their Effect on Literature Textbooks." *ADE Bulletin,* No. 83 (Spring), pp. 35–40. Notes that Ginn removed "the first and fifth stanzas from Richard Wright's "Hokku poems" (p. 38).

882. Demougin, Jacques. *Dictionnaire historique, thématique et technique des littératures.* Vol. 2. Paris: Librairie Larousse, p. 1791. Entry for W lists seven of his works.

883. Dessner, Lawrence J. "Richard Wright." *Abstracts of English Studies,* 29 (December), 414. Abstracts an article by Clyde Taylor.

884. Dickstein, Morris. "The Critics Who Made Us: Lionel Trilling and *The Liberal Imagination.*" *Sewanee Review,* 94 (Spring), 323–334. Mentions W briefly (p. 327).

885. Dinnerstein, Leonard. "The Origins of Black Anti-Semitism in America." *American Jewish Archives,* 38 (November), 113–122. Quotes from *BB* (pp. 113–114).

886. Dissanayake, Wimal. "Richard Wright: A View from the Third World." *Callaloo,* 9 (Summer), 481–489. Points out that W's appeal to Third World intellectuals resides in "his concept of power and its implications for those who are marginal members of society" (p. 481). Like Foucault, W understood the "need for subverting the dominant cultural discourse so as to create a more satisfying human one" (p. 483). In this context Dissanayake comments on *NS* and *BB* as well as *BP, CC,* and *WML.*

887. Dodson, Howard, Jr. *The Schomburg Center for Research in Black Culture.* New York: The New York Public Library, pp. 19, 31. Mentions W materials at the Schomburg, including the manuscript and reviews of *NS.*

888. Duff, Gerald. "Reed, Ishmael (1938–)," in *Postmodern Fiction: A Bio-Bibliographical Guide.* Ed. Larry McCaffery. Westport, CT: Greenwood, pp. 493–496. Mentions W briefly.

889. Early, Gerald. "Book Review." *Obsidian II,* 1 (Winter), 162–170. Mentions W briefly (p. 168).

890. _____. "Guest Editor's Note: First Catch." *Cottonwood,* 38/39 (Summer/Fall), 7–9. Mentions W briefly.

891. _____. "Working Girl Blues: Mothers, Daughters, and the Image of Billie Holiday in Kristin Hunter's *God Bless the Child.*" *Black American Literature Forum,* 20 (Winter), 423–442. Quotes briefly from *BB* (p. 429).

892. Ebert, Roger. "Movies." *New York Post* (24 December), p. 17. Favorable review of the 1986 film version of *NS* Summarizes the plot and praises the performance of Victor Love as Bigger.

893. Ellison, Ralph. "On Initiation Rites and Power: Ralph Ellison Speaks at West Point," in his *Going to the Territory.* New York: Random House, pp. 39–63.

894. _____. "Remembering Richard Wright," in his *Going to the Territory.* New York: Random House, pp. 198–216. Reprint of 1984.47.

895. _____, James Thompson, Lennox Raphael, and Steve Cannon.

"'A Very Stern Discipline,'" in Ellison's *Going to the Territory.* New York: Random House, pp. 275–307. Reprint of 1967.29.

896. Engel, Leonard W. "Alienation and Identity: Richard Wright's Outsider in 'The Man Who Lived Underground.'" *Philological Papers,* 32, 72–78. Emphasizes W's use of the device of enclosure in developing his existential theme. He is indebted to Poe in this respect.

897. Ensslen, Klaus. "Michael G. Cooke, *Afro-American Literature in the Twentieth Century: The Achievement of Intimacy*; Mary Frances Berry and John W. Blassingame, *Long Memory: The Black Experience in America.*" *Amerikastudien,* 31, no. 4, 477–480. Review noting Cooke's treatment of W.

898. Estes, David C. "An Interview with James Baldwin." *New Orleans Review,* 13 (Fall), 59–64. Estes mentions W briefly in an introductory note.

899. Estes-Hicks, Onita. "Jean Toomer and the Politics and Poetics of National Identity." *Contributions in Black Studies,* 7 (1985–1986), 22–44. Mentions W briefly (p. 24). Reprinted: 1996.

900. Fabre, Michel. "Frantz Fanon et Richard Wright," in *L'Actualité de Frantz Fanon.* Ed. Elo Dacy. Paris: Editions Karthala, pp. 169–177. Discusses Fanon's reading of W and cites his letter to him of 6 January 1956. Among their common interests were the psychological stress inflicted on blacks by colonialism and racism, especially as formulated by Octavio Mannoni, and Sartrean existentialism. Fabre also notes W's influence on Fanon's writings.

901. _____. "Richard Wright, Negritude and African Writing," in *European-Language Writing in Sub-Saharan Africa.* Ed. Albert S. Gérard. Vol. 2. Budapest: Akadémiai Kiadó, pp. 1155–1168. Reprint of 1985.60.

902. Feuser, Willfried F. "French-English-Portuguese: The Trilingual Approach: 1. The Rise of an Urban Civilization in African Fiction," in *European-Language Writing in Sub-Saharan Africa.* Ed. Albert S. Gérard. Budapest: Akadémiai Kiadó, pp. 1088–1105. Briefly compares Alex La Guma's *A Walk in the Night* (p. 1101) and Ezekiel Mphahlele's *Down Second Avenue* to *BB* (pp. 1104–1105).

903. _____. "Richard Wright's *Native Son* and Ousmane Sembène's [sic] *Le Docker Noir*." *Komparatische Hefte*, 14, 103–116. Although *Le Docker Noir* has been compared to Claude McKay's *Banjo*, it is much more similar to *NS*. Feuser discusses similarities in theme (alienation, exploitation), structure (point of view, time, space, action), style, characterization, and world-view. *NS* had a profound effect on Sembène Ousmane's novel.

904. Fleming, Robert E. "*Kingsblood Royal* and the Black 'Passing' Novel," in *Critical Essays on Sinclair Lewis*. Ed. Martin Bucco. Boston: G.K. Hall, pp. 213–221. Mentions briefly *NS* and *BB* (p. 213).

905. Foley, Barbara. *Telling the Truth: The Theory and Practice of Documentary Fiction*. Ithaca, NY: Cornell University Press, pp. 46, 108, 255, 256–257. Comments on *NS*, *UTC*, and W as Harry Ames in *The Man Who Cried I Am*.

906. Forkner, Ben, and Patrick Samway, S.J. "Biographical Notes," in their *A Modern Southern Reader*, Atlanta: Peachtree, pp, 721–731. Includes a note on W (p. 731) and reprints "The Man Who Was Almost a Man" (pp. 226–235).

907. Franklin, V.P. "*Black Marxism: The Making of a Black Radical Tradition* by Cedric Robinson." *Phylon*, 47 (Fall), 250–251. Review mentioning W briefly.

908. Gallantz, Michael. *Richard Wright's Native Son & Black Boy*. Woodbury, NY: Barron's Educational Series, x + 134 pp. Study guide to the two works including plot summaries, character analysis, discussion of themes and style, biographical background, sample test and answers, topics for writing, a brief bibliography, and four quotations from critics.

909. Garrow, David J. *Bearing the Cross: Martin Luther King, Jr. and the Southern Christian Leadership Conference*. New York: William Morrow, p. 113. Mentions King's meeting with W.

910. Gates, Henry Louis, Jr. "Talkin' That Talk." *Critical Inquiry*, 13 (Autumn), 203–210. Mentions W briefly (p. 207).

911. Gayle, Addison, Jr. "The Outsider," in *Zora Neale Hurston*. Ed. Harold Bloom. New York: Chelsea House, pp. 35–46. Partial reprint of 1975.85.

912. Gelmis, Joseph. "'Native Son' As Unconsoling as It Is Disturbing." Long Island *Newsday* (24 December), Part II, p. 9. Unfavorable review of the film *NS* criticizing the contrived melodrama, superficial characterization, and unimaginative screenplay and direction.

913. Gérard, Albert S. "Birth and Early Growth of a New Branch of Learning," in his *European-Language Writing in Sub-Saharan Africa*. Vol.2. Budapest: Akadémiai Kiadó, pp. 1239–1257.

914. _____. "Black Consciousness," in his *European-Language Writing in Sub-Saharan Africa*. Vol. 1. Budapest: Akadémiai Kiadó, pp. 333–339. Mentions W briefly (p. 336).

915. _____. "Comparative Vistas: Introduction," in his *European-Language Writing in Sub-Saharan Africa*. Vol.2. Budapest: Akadémiai Kiadó, pp. 1013–1020. Mentions briefly W's correspondence (p. 1018).

916. Gibson, Donald B. "Richard Wright's *Black Boy* and the Trauma of Autobiographical Rebirth." *Callaloo*, 9 (Summer), 492–498. Analyzes the first chapter of *BB* to show how it is arranged to emphasize parental rejection and failure. The result is the early development of self-reliance in W. His individualism allowed him to resist authority — parental, social, racial, or other.

917. Gibson, Morgan. "*American Poetry and Japanese Culture*. By Sanehide Kodama." *Comparative Literature Studies*, 23 (Spring), 85–90. Notes Kodama's treatment of W (p. 89).

918. Gill, Walivy. "The Western Film: Hollywood Myths and One Black Reality." *The Western Journal of Black Studies*, 10 (Spring), 1–4. Mentions briefly the film *NS*.

919. Graham, Maryemma. "Introduction." *Callaloo*, 9 (Summer), 439–445. Introducing a special W issue deriving from the November 1985 symposium at the University of Mississippi, Graham emphasizes the need for new critical approaches that examine "aesthetic concerns within the context of the social and political realities that shaped Wright's world and being" (p. 439).

920. _____. "Mississippi's Native Son: An International Symposium on Richard Wright (1908–1960)." *Sage: A Scholarly Journal on Black Women*, 3 (Spring), 66. Description of the conference highlighting the talks by Margaret Walker Alexander, Maria Mootry, and Gerald McWorter.

921. Green, Leonard. "Joanne V. Gabbin. *Sterling A. Brown: Building the Black Aesthetic Tradition*." *Black American Literature Forum*, 20 (Fall), 327–334. Mentions W briefly (p. 332).

922. Greenspon, Joanna, ed. *Humanities Index: April 1985 to March 1986*. New York: H.W. Wilson, p. 1160. Lists eleven items s.v. W.

923. Griffith, Kelley, Jr. *Writing Essays About Literature: A Guide and Style Sheet*. Second edition. San Diego: Harcourt Brace Jovanovich, p. 40. Reprint of 1982.

924. Gubert, Betty, ed. *Index to the Schomburg Clipping File*. Alexandria, VA: Chadwick-Healey, p. 154. Lists W.

925. Guerin, Wilfred L., Michael L. Hall, Earle Labor, Lee Morgan, Barry Nass, and John R. Willingham. "Discussion Topics," in their *LIT: Literature and Interpretive Techniques*. New York: Harper & Row, p. 277. Three topics following "The Man Who Was Almost a Man."

926. _____. "Richard Wright," in their *LIT: Literature and Interpretive Techniques*. New York: Harper & Row, p. 268. Brief biographical headnote to "The Man Who Was Almost a Man."

927. Hakutani, Yoshinobu. "Richard Wright's Experiment in Naturalism and Satire: *Lawd Today*." *Studies in American Fiction*, 14 (Autumn), 165–178. Maintains that *LT* fails as a naturalistic novel because it does not develop the tensions between social determinism and individual will. It is more successful as a satire on the average man, black or white. Irony is the predominant mode of Wright's satire. The effort to combine naturalism and satire fails, however.

928. _____, and Toru Kiuchi. "The Critical Reception of Richard Wright in Japan: An Annotated Bibliography." *Black American Literature Forum*, 20 (Spring-Summer), 27–61. Consists of 134 items, "all of the critical books and articles of substance on Richard Wright published in Japan through 1984." The introductory paragraphs (pp. 27–29) trace W's reputation in Japan.

929. Harmetz, Aljean. "Problems of Filming 'Native Son.'" *The New York Times* (23 December), Sec. C, p. 14. Discusses producer Diane Silver's omission of Bessie's murder in the film *NS* over the objection of director Jerrold Freedman. Quotes comments by Richard Yarborough and Arnold Rampersad on the importance of the novel and by Valerie Smith on W's unfavorable portrayal of black women, as well as comments by Silver, Freedman, and Lindsay Law on the film.

930. Harris, Norman. "The Black University in Contemporary Afro-American Fiction." *CLA Journal*, 30 (September), 1–13. Mentions briefly *NS*.

931. Hazard, Geoffrey C., Jr. "Rising Above Principle." *University of Pennsylvania Law Review*, 135 (December), 153–191. Mentions briefly W, *BB*, and *NS* (pp. 158–159).

932. Hedgepeth, Chester, Jr. *Theories of Social Action in Black Literature*. New York: Peter Lang, pp. 3, 11, 15–21, 30, 32, 34, 38–43, 144–145, 154. Explains *NS* as exemplifying both the "Samson Syndrome" of self-destruction and a "Sartrian nihilism."

933. Hellenbrand, Harold. "Speech, After Silence: Alice Walker's *The Third Life of Grange Copeland.*" *Black American Literature Forum*, 20 (Spring-Summer), 113–128. Includes discussion of the reworking of racial confrontation in *NS* and "Big Boy Leaves Home" by Walker in her novel.

934. Hemenway, Robert E. "Crayon Enlargements of Life," in *Zora Neale Hurston*. Ed. Harold Bloom. New York: pp. 71–81. Partial reprint of 1977.172.

935. _____. "That Which the Soul Lives By," in *Zora Neale Hurston*. Ed. Harold Bloom. New York: Chelsea House, pp. 83–95. Partial reprint of 1977.172.

936. High, Peter B. *An Outline of American Literature*. London: Longman, pp. 214–215. Comments on *UTC*, *BB*, *NS*, and "The Man Who Lived Underground."

937. Hoberman, J. "Bigger Than Life." *The Village Voice* (30 December), pp. 64, 77. Review of both film versions of *NS*. The first "is a documentary of a novelist trapped in his own myth." The second is poorly directed and badly acted. Hober-

man also comments on the novel *NS*: "A product of '30s political culture that looks forward to the turmoil of the '60s, a philosophical tract with lurid tabloid immediacy, and a Dreiserian exposé that anticipates French existentialism, *Native Son* takes the 'proletarian realism' of its era into a hallucinatory realm."

938. Hodges, John O. "'Wondering About the Art of a Wanderer': Langston Hughes and His Critics." *The Langston Hughes Review*, 5 (Fall), 19–23. Mentions briefly W, *NS*, and *BB* (p. 19).

939. Hogue, W. Lawrence. *Discourse and the Other: The Production of the Afro-American Text*. Durham, NC: Duke University Press, pp. 8–9, 13, 14, 26, 29–31. Discusses W as an integrationist writer, quoting from "The Literature of the Negro in the United States," noting his treatment in Arthur P. Davis's *From the Dark Tower* and Robert Stepto's *From Behind the Veil*, and contrasting the favorable reception of *NS* to the unfavorable reception of *Their Eyes Were Watching God*.

940. [Holland, Laurence B., and Nina Baym]. "Richard Wright 1908–1960," in *The Norton Anthology of American Literature*. Second edition, shorter. Ed. Nina Baym et al. New York: Norton, pp. 2183–2184, 2636. Reprint of 1985.91.

941. Homberger, Eric. *American Writers and Radical Politics, 1900–39*. New York: St. Martin's Press, pp. 129, 138, 228. Mentions W and the John Reed Club.

942. Horne, Gerald. *Black and Red: W.E.B. Du Bois and the Afro-American Response to the Cold War, 1944–1963*. Albany: State University of New York Press, pp. 260, 273, 341. Quotes Du Bois to George Padmore sharply criticizing *BP*.

943. Houseman, John. *Unfinished Business: A Memoir*. London: Chatto & Windus, pp. 227, 229–232, 233–234, 269. Recalls reading *NS* and discusses meeting W in Chapel Hill, comments on the disparate views of W and Paul Green on dramatizing *NS*, accuses Green of distorting W's meaning, and mentions picketing of the play by the Urban League and elements of the Communist Party angry at W for refusing to make changes in *NS* that they had proposed.

944. Houston, Helen R. "Weixlmann, Joe, and Chester J. Fontenot,

eds. *Belief vs. Theory in Black American Literary Criticism.*" *Obsidian II*, 1 (Winter), 174–178. Includes a paragraph on Keneth Kinnamon's "Call and Response: Intertextuality in Two Autobiographical Works by Richard Wright and Maya Angelou."

945. Howland, Jacob. "*Black Boy*: A Story of Soul-Making and a Quest for the Real." *Phylon*, 47 (June), 117–127. "In the first part ... I try to set forth the general character and significance of the quest which gives *Black Boy* its special form, and which I describe as a quest for the real. In the second part, I attempt to state how *Black Boy* displays the development of Wright's soul and the nature of his own specifically artistic quest" (p. 117). Howland analyzes at length the opening scene, stressing the metaphor of fire.

946. Howorth, Lisa N. "A Bibliography of Dissertations Relating to Mississippi—1986" *Journal of Mississippi History*, 48 (February), 67–70. Lists Jacquelyn Logan Jackson's 1983 dissertation on "The Black Novelist and the Expatriate Experience: Richard Wright, James Baldwin, Chester Himes" and Charles Atangana Noma's 1984 dissertation on "Aesthetics and Ideology in African and Afro-American Fiction: Ngugi Wa Thiong'O, Ayi Kwei Armah, Toni Morrison, and Richard Wright."

947. Hudson-Withers, Clenora. "Toni Morrison's World of Topsy-Turvydom: A Methodological Explication of New Black Literary Criticism." *The Western Journal of Black Studies*, 10 (Fall), 132–136. Concludes with a quotation from an article on W by Hudson-Withers.

948. Irele, Abiola. "The Negritude Debate," in *European-Language Writing in Sub-Saharan Africa*. Ed. Albert Gérard. Vol. 1. Budapest: Akadémiai Kiadó, p. 387. Comments on W's attitude toward Senghor and negritude.

949. Jackson, Richard L. "The Human Legacy of Black Latin-American Literature." *CLA Journal*, 30 (December), 154–170. One of four epigraphs is a quotation from the end of *AH*. In the essay Jackson cites Julius Lester on *NS*.

950. Jemie, Onwuchekwa. "Hughes's Black Esthetic," in *Critical Essays on Langston Hughes*. Ed.

Edward J. Mullen. Boston: G.K. Hall, pp. 95–120. Partial reprint of 1976.108.

951. Jeyifo, Biodun. "Tragedy, History, and Ideology," in *Marxism and African Literature*. Ed. Georg M. Gugelberger. Trenton, NJ: Africa World Press, pp. 94–109. Quotes a passage from p. 153 of *BP* and compares it to Wole Soyinka's play *Death and the King's Horseman*, written twenty years later (pp. 99, 108).

952. Johnson, Barbara, "Metaphor, Metonymy, and Voice in Zora Neale Hurston's *Their Eyes Were Watching God,"* in *American Fiction 1914 to 1945.* Ed. Harold Bloom. New York: Chelsea House, pp. 361–374.

953. _____. "Metaphor, Metonymy, and Voice in Zora Neale Hurston's *Their Eyes Were Watching God,* in *American Fiction 1914 to 1945.* Ed. Harold Bloom. New York: Chelsea House, 1986, pp. 361–374.

954. Johnson, Carolyn M. "Prose." *Abstracts of English Studies*, 29 (December), 397. Abstracts an article by Shirley Newman mentioning W.

955. Johnson, Joe. "Books." *The Crisis*, 93 (February), 12–13, 64. Review of James Baldwin's *The Price of the Ticket* mentioning briefly W, *NS*, and Bigger Thomas.

956. _____. "Books." *The Crisis*, 93 (March), 14–15, 48. Includes a review of James Baldwin's *The Evidence of Things Not Seen* comparing Wayne Williams, convicted of killing children in Atlanta, to Bigger Thomas.

957. _____. "A Crisis Report on Literature." *The Crisis*, 93 (January), 11–15, 44. Discusses and quotes from "Blueprint for Negro Writing" before commenting on dissent from W's position by Ellison and Baldwin. Mentions *NS* and *BB.*

958. _____. "*Going to the Territory* By Ralph Ellison." *The Crisis*, 93 (December), 10–11. Review discussing the Ellison-W relationship and commenting on "Blueprint for Negro Writing."

959. Jordan, Jennifer. "Cultural Nationalism in the 1960s: Politics and Poetry," in *Race, Politics, and Culture: Critical Essays on the Radicalism of the 1960s.* Ed. Adolph Reed, Jr. Westport, CT: Greenwood Press, pp. 29–60. Quotes from *BB* (pp. 33–34).

960. Joyce, Donald Franklin. *Blacks in the Humanities, 1750–1984: A Selected Annotated Bibliography.* Westport, CT: Greenwood, pp. 7, 108, 148, 149, 150, 151–152, 156–157, 158, 159–160. Lists a bibliographical guide to W and dissertations by Allan Gordon, as well as works treating W by Jane M. Davis, Mae G. Henderson, and Valerie Smith; and books by Charles T. Davis, Carl M. Hughes, A. Robert Lee, Ladell Payne, and Michel Fabre. Also lists the Chicago Public Library as a repository of some W manuscripts.

961. Joyce, Joyce Ann. *Richard Wright's Art of Tragedy.* Iowa City: University of Iowa Press, 129 + xvii pp. Taking issue with biographical, social, naturalistic, and existential interpretations of W, Joyce stresses his artistry in developing *NS* as a tragedy. Her concluding paragraph summarizes her argument: "The structure of the novel (the arrangement of parts that result in the ironic reversal of roles between Bigger and Max), Bigger's ambiguous personality, and the paradoxical nature of the image patterns all function integrally as a well-orchestrated discord that becomes harmonized in Bigger's suffering as his consciousness grows. The complexity of Wright's symphonic characterization of Bigger reaches a crescendo in the rhythmical repetition and interlocking relationship between the sentence patterns, the colors black, white, and yellow, the image of the wall, and the metaphors of the snow, the sun, and blindness. The polarity expressed in these weblike linguistic chords synthesized in Max's speech captures the tension in Bigger's psyche, a tension that evokes the awe and power responsible for the success and lastingness of *Native Son*" (pp. 119–120).

962. Julien, Claude. "*Michel FABRE.— La Rive Noire de Harlem à la Seine.*" *Revue française d'études américaines*, 27/28 (February), 171–172. Review mentioning W briefly.

963. Kart, Larry. "To Play Bigger, Love Belies His Name." *Chicago Tribune* (22 December), Sec. 5, p. 3. Article on the actor in the film *NS*. Love interprets Bigger's personality and background, contrasting them to his own. Notes a conflict between the producer and director: "Silver wanting to portray Bigger Thomas in relatively sympathetic terms, while [Jerrold] Freedman hoped to retain the brutality of Wright's original vision." Love notes that the murder of Bessie was filmed but subsequently cut.

964. Katrak, Ketu H. "Trudier Harris. *Black Women in the Fiction of James Baldwin.*" *Black American Literature Forum*, 20 (Winter), 449–458. Mentions W briefly.

965. Katz, Alan. "Transition Is Tugging at a Local Avant-Garde Author." *The Denver Post* (15 June), p. 18 Clarence Major comments on W's emphasis on race.

966. Kehr, Dave. "'Native Son' Absurd Rendering of Famous Book." *Chicago Tribune* (26 December), Sec. 7, pp. A, H, L. Extremely unfavorable review of the film *NS*. Praises Victor Love's acting as Bigger, but pans all other aspects of the production. The film dilutes W's rage, resulting in "a dim weepie" (p. L).

967. Keller, Ulrich. *The Highway as Habitat: A Roy Stryker Documentation, 1943–1955.* Santa Barbara: University Art Museum, p. 30. Quotes Edwin Rosskam mentioning W and *Two* [sic] *Million Black Voices.*

968. Kinnamon, Keneth. "Call and Response: Intertextuality in Two Autobiographical Works by Richard Wright and Maya Angelou," in *Belief vs. Theory in Black American Literary Criticism.* Eds. Joe Weixlmann and Chester J. Fontenot. *Studies in Black American Literature,* vol. 2. Greenwood, FL: Penkeville, pp. 121–134. Compares *BB* and *I Know Why the Caged Bird Sings* "to ascertain how gender may affect genre in these two autobiographical quests for freedom and literacy and, in Angelou's case, community as well" (p. 123). Numerous similarities, both general and specific, are revealed. The difference is in the treatment of childhood episodes: W emphasizes white racism and the hostility of his own family; Angelou shows the same racism at work, but treats respectfully black cultural patterns designed to survive it. Reprinted: 1995

969. Kiuchi, Toru. "The Japanese Translation of English Haiku: The Case of Richard Wright." *Sable: A Haiku Magazine,* 23 (20 June), 24–25. Translates six of W's published Haiku into Japanese with an analysis.

970. _____. "The International Richard Wright Symposium." *Black Studies*, 56 (28 June), 68–70. Reports on the symposium at the University of Mississippi in 1985, summarizing each presentation [T.K., R.B., Y.H.].

971. _____. "The International Richard Wright Symposium." *Newsletter of the Black Studies Association in Japan*, 23 (24 May), 3. Reports on the symposium in November 1985 at the University of Mississippi.

972. _____. "On the Dramatization of *Native Son*." *Bulletin of Aichi Shukutoku Junior College*, 25 (25 March), 73–84. Compares W's dramatization of *NS* with that of Ellen Wright and Paul Green, noting a slight difference in theme [T.K., R.B., and Y.H.].

973. Klamkin, Lynn, and Margot Livesey. "Biographical Notes," in their *Writing About Literature: An Anthology for Reading and Writing*. New York: Holt, Rinehart and Winston, pp. 977–991. Includes a brief note on W.

974. _____. "Suggestions for Writing and Discussion," in their *Writing About Literature: An Anthology for Reading and Writing*. New York: Holt, Rinehart and Winston, p. 440. Seven suggestions to accompany an excerpt from "The Man Who Saw the Flood."

975. Klehr, Harvey. "Haywood, Harry (1898–1985)," in *Biographical Dictionary of the American Left*. Westport, CT: Greenwood Press, pp. 189–190. States that as chairman of the Communist Party in Cook County, Haywood's "rigid policies helped drive Richard Wright out of the Party."

976. Koguchi, Hiroyuki. "*Native Son*: Bigger Thomas as a New Hero." *Studies in American Literature*, 23 (February) 87–100. Writing in English, Koguchi reinterprets Bigger as a symbol of black experience and the liberation movement [T.K., R.B., and Y.H.].

977. Köster, Patricia. "Richard Wright." *Abstracts of English Studies*, 29 (June), 211. Abstracts an article by John Vassilowitch, Jr.

978. Kraft, Eugene. "An Interview with Gwendolyn Brooks." *Cottonwood*, 38/39 (Summer/Fall), 52–69. Mentions briefly *NS* (p. 55).

979. Kroeber, Karl. "Novel: 7, United States," in *The Encyclopedia*

Americana. Ed. Bernard S. Cayne. Danbury, CT: 1986, vol. 20, p. 511b. Notes the influence of W on Ellison and Baldwin.

980. Krupnick, Mark. *Lionel Trilling and the Fate of Cultural Criticism in America*. Evanston, IL: Northwestern University Press, pp. 87–88. Comments on and quotes from Trilling's review of *BB*.

981. Laguardia, Gari, and Bell Gale Chevigny. "Introduction," in their *Reinventing the Americas: Comparative Studies of Literature of the United States and Spanish America*. Cambridge: Cambridge University Press, pp. 3–59. Mentions briefly W and *NS* (p. 25).

982. Lara, Oruno D. "*La rive noire: de Harlem a la Seine*, par Michel Fabre." *Présence Africaine*, Nos. 137–138 (First and Second Quarter), 262–263. Review mentioning W briefly.

983. Lauter, Paul. "Looking a Gift Horse in the Mouth." *San Jose Studies*, 12 (Winter), 6–19. Mentions briefly "Bright and Morning Star" (p. 7).

984. Lee, A. Robert. "Introduction," in his *The Nineteenth-Century American Short Story*. London: Vision Press, pp. 7–11. Mentions briefly *UTC* and *EM* (p. 9).

985. Lemann, Nicholas. "The Origins of the Underclass." *The Atlantic*, 257 (June), 31–43, 47–55. Mentions W briefly (p. 49).

986. Lester, Julius. "Some Tickets Are Better: The Mixed Achievement of James Baldwin." *Dissent*, 33 (Spring), 189–192, 214. Quotes from a taped conversation with Baldwin commenting on W's relation to young Third World writers in Paris (p. 191).

987. _____. "Some Tickets Are Better Than Others." *Dissent*, 33 (Spring), 189–192, 214. Reports that in a taped conversation in 1984 Baldwin discusses W as a black witness in Paris around whom younger blacks collected as they did for Baldwin himself later. Reprinted: 1988.

988. Levine, Lawrence W. "Comment," in *The State of Afro-American History: Past, Present, and Future*. Ed. Darlene Clark Hine. Baton Rouge: Louisiana State University Press, pp. 123–129. Relates an anecdote about W talking to a white Frenchman and an African at a Paris café (pp. 128–129).

989. [Levitt, Morton P.]. "1985-

1986 Annual Review." *Journal of Modern Literature*, 13 (November), 347–584. Lists nineteen items on W in whole or in part.

990. Lindfors, Bernth. "*Black Orpheus*," in *European-Language Writing in Sub-Saharan Africa*. Ed. Albert S. Gérard. Vol. 2. Budapest: Akadémiai Kiadó, pp. 669–679.

991. Loftis, John E. "Domestic Prey: Richard Wright's Parody of the Hunt Tradition in 'The Man Who Was Almost a Man.'" *Studies in Short Fiction*, 23 (Fall), 437–442. Contrasts W's story to Faulkner's hunting story "The Old People" with respect to naming and identity, the relationship of the protagonists to guns, and the presence or absence of a male model. Faulkner's initiation story is typical of the subgenre, but W parodies the hunt as rite of passage in his story.

992. Longest, George C., et al. "A Checklist of Scholarship on Southern Literature for 1985." *The Mississippi Quarterly*, 39 (Spring), 137–298. Lists eleven items on W and cross-references to nineteen other items partially on W.

993. Ludwig, Richard M., and Clifford A. Nault, Jr. *Annals of American Literature, 1602–1983*. New York: Oxford University Press, pp. 173, 176, 178, 183, 194, 195, 198, 200, 201, 206, 210. Lists all of W's books through *LT* except *SH*.

994. Lynch, Michael Francis. "Richard Wright, Ralph Ellison, and Dostoevsky: The Choice of Individual Freedom and Dignity." *Dissertation Abstracts International*, 47 (July), 179A. Abstracts a 1985 Kent State University dissertation. Compares the move from collectivism to individualism in the three writers.

995. Macksey, Eileen M., ed. *1985 MLA International Bibliography of Books and Articles on the Modern Languages and Literatures. Volume I: British Isles, British Commonwealth, English-Caribbean, New Zealand, and American Literatures*. New York: The Modern Language Association of America, pp. 253, A451. Lists seventeen items on W.

996. Maddock, Lawrence. "Richard Wright." *Abstracts of English Studies*, 29 (March), 86. Abstracts an article by Earl V. Bryant.

997. Magistrale, Tony. "From St. Petersburg to Chicago: Wright's *Crime and Punishment*." *Comparative*

Literature Studies, 23 (Spring), 59–70. Having read *Crime and Punishment* a decade before he wrote *NS*, W used it imaginatively for his own fictional purposes. The theme of crime leading to spiritual growth and plot similarities are obvious, but Magistrale notes also that "Wright's use of parallel characters, atmospheric effects, and a similar belief in the power of the human spirit to transform itself bear a marked resemblance to *Crime and Punishment*" (p. 68).

998. Major, Clarence. *My Amputations*. Boulder, CO: Fiction Collective, pp. 6, 8, 91, 181, 187, 189. Novel mentioning briefly W, *BP* (p. 181), and Cross Damon (p. 187).

999. Marable, Manning. "Black Studies: Marxism and the Black Intellectual Tradition," in *The Left Academy: Marxist Scholarship on American Campuses*. Vol. 3. Eds. Bertell Ollman and Edward Vernoff. New York: Praeger, pp. 35–66. Mentions W briefly (pp. 41, 48).

1000. Martinez, Nancy C., et al. "A Check List of Explication (1984)." *The Explicator*, 44 (Summer), 3–52. Lists one item concerning W.

1001. Mathabane, Mark. *Kaffir Boy*. New York: Macmillan, p. 234. Includes W in a list of names of blacks of achievement in America.

1002. McGrath, Daniel F., ed. *Bookman's Price Index*. Vol. 32. Detroit: Gale, p. 1035. Lists *Bright and Morning Star* at $75, *How "Bigger" Was Born* at $45, *TMBV* at $40, and *TMBV* at $85.

1003. _____. *Bookman's Price Index*. Vol. 33. Detroit: Gale, p. 1171. Lists *NS* at $85.

1004. Meese, Elizabeth A. *Crossing the Double-Cross: The Practice of Feminist Criticism*. Chapel Hill: The University of North Carolina Press, pp. 41, 42. Mentions W briefly in a chapter on Zora Neale Hurston.

1005. Menand, Louis. "Literature and Liberation." *The New Republic*, 195 (4 August), 37–40. Review of Ralph Ellison's *Going to the Territory* containing a paragraph on W (p. 37) and mentioning W and *NS* elsewhere.

1006. Michaelson, Judith. "Wright's Daughter Approves." *Los Angeles Times* (24 December), pp. 1, 3. Interview with Julia Wright on both versions of the film *NS*. The original version was a failure, but the Diane Silver production is "honest"

and Victor Love's portrayal of Bigger is excellent. Julia Wright also speaks of "a Columbia Pictures project several years ago [that] ... fell through."

1007. Miller, James A. "Bigger Thomas's Quest for Voice and Audience in Richard Wright's *Native Son*." *Callaloo*, 9 (Summer), 501–506. Taking issue with critics who believe that Max is an authorial spokesman and that Bigger is inarticulate, Miller uses Bakhtinian concepts to argue that Bigger, quite articulate in his own black street environment, must cope with the "authoritative discourse" of the white world to achieve voice and audience. In doing so he repudiates Max as well as white racists, ending in isolation, "a soloist listening to the sound of his own song."

1008. _____. "'I Investigate the Sun': Amiri Baraka in the 1980s." *Callaloo*, 9 (Winter), 184–192. Mentions W briefly (p. 188).

1009. Miller, R. Baxter. "'Define ... the Whirlwind': Gwendolyn Brooks' Epic Sign for a Generation," in his *Black American Poets Between Worlds, 1940–1960*. Knoxville: The University of Tennessee Press, pp. 160–173. Mentions briefly W's naturalism (p. 163).

1010. _____. "The 'Intricate Design' of Margaret Walker: Literary and Biblical Re-Creation in Southern History," in his *Black American Poets Between Worlds, 1940–1960*. Knoxville: The University of Tennessee Press, pp. 118–135. Reprint of 1982.

1011. _____. "'One Prime Obligation': The Example of Therman B. O'Daniel." *The Langston Hughes Review*, 5 (Fall), 5–10. Mentions briefly W, *NS*, and *BB* (pp. 5, 9).

1012. Miller, Wayne C. *Minorities in America: The Annual Bibliography, 1977*. University Park: The Pennsylvania State University Press, pp. 130, 145. Contains annotated entries for works on W. by James R. King, Alfred R. Ferguson, Robert Fleissner, Gordon Querry Freeman, Maryemma Graham, Barry Gross, Rebecca and David McBride, Robin McNallie, Vimala Rao, John M. Reilly, Alvin Starr, Robert B. Stepto, Melvin G. Williams, and an entry on *AH*.

1013. _____, ed. *Minorities in America: The Annual Bibliography, 1978*. University Park: The Pennsyl-

vania State University Press, pp. 45, 142–143. Annotated entries for works on W by Butler Emmanuel Brewton, Owen Brady, Nina Kressner Cobb, Annette Lois Conn, Charles De Arman, Michel Fabre, J.F. Gounard, Australia Tarver Henderson, Dianne Long Hoeveler, Steven J. Rubin, James Edward Walton, and Ellen Wright. Also lists a reprint of *WML*.

1014. Morris, Daphne. "Roger Mais (1905–1955)," in *Fifty Caribbean Writers: A Bio-Bibliographical Critical Sourcebook*. Ed. Daryl Cumber Dance. Westport, CT: Greenwood Press, pp. 303–317. Mentions W's help to Mais in setting up an exhibition of his paintings in Paris in 1954.

1015. Morton, Brian. "Paul Oliver, *Songsters and Saints: Vocal Traditions on Race Records*." *Journal of American Studies*, 20 (April), 113–115. Review beginning with a quotation from W's foreword to Oliver's *Blues Fell This Morning*.

1016. Moylan, Tom. *Demand the Impossible: Science Fiction and the Utopian Imagination*. New York: Methuen, p. 219. Mentions W briefly.

1017. _____. "Paul Oliver: *Songsters and Saints: Vocal Traditions on Race Records*." *Journal of American Studies*, 20(April 1986), 113–115. Quotes from W's foreword to Oliver's *Blues Fell This Morning*.

1018. Mullen, Edward J. "Introduction," in his *Critical Essays on Langston Hughes*. Boston: G.K. Hall, pp. 1–35. Mentions W briefly (pp. 1–2, 21) and quotes "Forerunner and Ambassador," W's review of *The Big Sea* (p. 18) and reprints it in full (pp. 67–68).

1019. Munro, Ian H. "George Lamming (1927–)," in *Fifty Caribbean Writers: A Bio-Bibliographical Critical Sourcebook*. Ed. Daryl Cumber Dance. Westport, CT: Greenwood Press, pp. 264–275. Mentions W's view of *In the Castle of My Skin* (p. 270).

1020. Mur[phy], A.D. "Native Son (Color)." *Variety* (17 December), p. 20. Unfavorable review of "a corny adaptation" of the novel. Includes credits and cast for the play *NS* and the first film version as well as this one.

1021. Namekata, Hitoshi. "Fred's Travels: 'The Man Who Lived Underground.'" *Bulletin of Musashino College for Music*, 18 (31 March),

143–156. Argues that Fred Daniel is a prototype of Cross Damon. The novella shows W trying to transcend racial problems [T.K., R.B., and Y.H.].

1022. Nisula, Dasha Culic. "Dostoevsky and Richard Wright: From St. Petersburg to Chicago," in *Dostoevsky and the Human Condition After a Century*. Eds. Alexej Ugrinsky, Valija K. Ozolius, and Pete Hamill. New York: Greenwood, pp. 163–170. Compares "The Man Who Lived Underground" to *Notes from Underground* and *O* to *Crime and Punishment*. Nisula finds structural, thematic, and philosophical similarities. Like Dostoevsky, W came to believe that the regeneration of the individual must precede social reform.

1023. Onoge, Omafume F. "The Crisis of Consciousness in Modern African Literature: A Survey (1974)," in *Marxism and African Literature*. Ed. Georg M. Gugelberger. Trenton, NJ: Africa World Press, pp. 21–49. Claims that "we can speculate with some confidence that had the later Richard Wright lived long enough to write a blueprint for African literature in our contemporary epoch, the uneasy tension between race and class which runs as an undercurrent in his 1937 *Blueprint for Negro Literature* would have been overcome" (p. 43). In an endnote Onoge elaborates the point (p. 48).

1024. Paravisini, Lizabeth. "*Mumbo Jumbo* and the Uses of Parody." *Obsidian II: Black Literature in Review*, 1 (Spring Summer), 113–125. Mentions *O* as "an early parodic adaptation of the hard-boiled detective story" (p. 124).

1025. Parrill, William. "An Interview with Ernest Gaines." *Louisiana Literature* (Fall), 17–44. Mentions briefly *NS* (p. 20). Reprinted: 1995.

1026. Payne, Ethel. "Wright Book Delayed by Legal Questions." *The Baltimore Afro-American* (5 April), p. 5. Reviews Margaret Walker's relation to W and recounts her difficulties with Howard University Press in publishing *The Daemonic Genius of Richard Wright*.

1027. Pearson, Norman Holmes. "American Literature," in *The Encyclopedia Americana*. Ed. Bernard S. Cayne. Danbury, CT: Grolier, vol. 1, pp. 691–706. Notes that *NS*, a naturalistic novel, contrasts with the

symbolism of *Invisible Man*, but is of equal importance.

1028. _____. "American Literature: The Twentieth Century," in *The Encyclopedia Americana*. Ed. Bernard S. Cayne. Vol. 1, pp. 703–710.

1029. Perry, Evelyn. "Dorothy ABBOTT, ed.—*Mississippi Writers: Reflections of Childhood and Youth, Volume I: Fiction.*" *Revue française d'études américaines*, 30 (November), 512. Review mentioning W briefly.

1030. Peterson, Larry. "The Intellectual World of the IWW: An American Worker's Library in the First Half of the 20th Century." *History Workshop: A Journal of Socialist and Feminist Historians*, 2 (Autumn), 153–172. Notes that *BB* was included.

1031. Pfeil, Fred. "Policiers Noirs." *The Nation*, 243 (15 November), 523–525. Article on Chester Himes mentioning W briefly (p. 523).

1032. _____. "Policiers Noirs." *The Nation*, 243 (15 November), 523–525. Article on Chester Himes mentioning W briefly. Reprinted: 1999.

1033. Pickering, James H., and Jeffrey D. Hoeper. "The Elements of Fiction," in their *Literature*. Second edition. New York: Macmillan, pp. 19–74. Mentions briefly "The Man Who Was Almost a Man" as an initiation story with "archetypal overtones" (p. 59).

1034. Podhoretz, Norman, "Why *The God That Failed* Failed, in his *The Bloody Crossroad: Where Literature and Politics Meet*. New York: Simon and Schuster, pp. 17–32.

1035. Pondrom, Cyrena N. "The Role of Myth in Hurston's *Their Eyes Were Watching God.*" *American Literature*, 58 (May), 181–202. Contains a footnote reference to W's review of Hurston's novel (p. 181).

1036. Rahming, Melvin B. *The Evolution of the West Indian's Image in the Afro-American Novel*. Millwood, NY: Associated Faculty Press, pp. 49, 73, 154. Compares briefly Bigger Thomas to Leo Proudhammer in James Baldwin's *Tell Me How Long the Train's Been Gone* (p. 49) and mentions W elsewhere.

1037. Rampersad, Arnold. "Foreword," in *Lawd Today* by Richard Wright. Boston: Northeastern University Press, pp. 1–6. Appreciation of *LT* rating it next to *NS* among

W's novels. Comments on its relation to naturalism and on its modernist technique. While noting its pessimism, Rampersad praises its honesty and its comic sense.

1038. _____. "Langston Hughes and His Critics on the Left." *The Langston Hughes Review*, 5 (Fall), 34–40. Quotes briefly from W's *New Republic* review of Hughes (p. 40).

1039. _____. "Langston Hughes's *Fine Clothes to the Jew.*" *Callaloo*, 26 (Winter), 144–157. Mentions W briefly as poet (p. 157).

1040. _____. *The Life of Langston Hughes*. Vol. 1: 1902–1941. *I, Too Sing America*. New York: Oxford University Press, pp. 281, 304, 321, 324, 338, 339, 340, 360, 382–384, 387, 388, 389, 392. Discusses Hughes's friendship with W and their good professional literary relationship, even though Hughes disliked *NS* and was jealous of W's success (pp. 382–384). W is briefly mentioned elsewhere in political, literary, and social contexts.

1041. _____. "Psychoanalysis and Black Biography," in *The Challenges of Writing Black Biography*. Eds. Leo Hamalian and James V. Hatch. New York: Hatch-Billops Collection, pp. 34–42. Includes criticism of Allison Davis's application of psychoanalysis to W. Also mentions Frederic Wertham and *SH*.

1042. Reardon, Patrick. "'Native Son': New Film's Racial Message as Valid Today as in 1949 [sic]." *Chicago Tribune* (10 April), Sec. 5, pp. 1, 3. Emphasizes continuing relevance of the work. Includes plot summary, quotations from the novel, and comments of the film writer, Richard Wesley, and producer, Diane Silver.

1043. Reed, Adolph L., Jr. *The Jesse Jackson Phenomenon: The Crisis of Purpose in Afro-American Politics*. New Haven: Yale University Press, p. 118. Mentions W briefly.

1044. Reed, Ishmael. "Hyped or Hip?" *California Magazine* (March), pp. 36, 39–40. Article on the detective fiction of Chester Himes mentioning W briefly.

1045. Reilly, John M. "Richard Wright and the Art of Non-Fiction: Stepping Out on the Stage of the World." *Callaloo*, 9 (Summer), 507–520. Interprets *CC* as an autobiographical reading of history. From the disillusion and despair expressed in *O*, W turned to emerging African and Asian nations as the "compelling subject" needed "to restore optimism of will" (p. 510), allowing him to speak as an intellectual voice and agent of contemporary history. Interpreting the Bandung Conference, he developed a paradigm of history as consciousness, his own consciousness and experience providing the key to understanding his alter egos, the Westernized leaders of the Third World.

1046. Reising, Russell J. *The Unusable Past: Theory and the Study of American Literature*. New York and London: Methuen, pp. 30–31. Comments briefly on *UTC*.

1047. Rollins, Judith. "Part of a Whole: The Interdependence of the Civil Rights Movement and Other Social Movements." *Phylon*, 47 (Spring), 61–70. Comments on W's response to the Bandung Conference and quotes from *CC* (pp. 63–64).

1048. Rosenblatt, Roger. "*Their Eyes Were Watching God*," in *Zora Neale Hurston*. Ed. Harold Bloom. New York: Chelsea House, pp. 29–33. Partial reprint of 1974.153.

1049. Rowe, Anne E. *The Idea of Florida in the American Literary Imagination*. Baton Rouge: Louisiana State University Press, p. 21. Quotes from *WML*.

1050. Rowell, Charles H., and Kimberly Chambers. "Studies in Afro-American Literature: An Annual Annotated Bibliography." *Callaloo*, 9 (Fall), 583–622. Contains ten items on W with cross-references to six others.

1051. Salzman, Jack, ed. *American Studies: An Annotated Bibliography*. Volume 1. Cambridge: Cambridge University Press, pp. 761, 766, 772, 775, 788, 793, 807, 813, 815, 817, 829, 831, 835, 838, 847, 852, 857. Mentions W in annotations on books by Daniel Aaron, Nelson Manfred Blake, Ralph F. Bogardus and Fred Hobson, Malcolm Cowley, Warren French, Marcus Klein, Edward Margolies, Craig Werner, Houston Baker, C.W.E. Bigsby, Robert Bone, Addison Gayle, Donald B. Gibson, Trudier Harris, Carl Milton Hughes, A. Robert Lee, Ladell Payne, Roger Rosenblatt, and Robert Stepto.

1052. _____, et al., eds. *The Cambridge Handbook of American Literature*. Cambridge: Cambridge University Press, pp. 75, 175–176, 261, 268. Contains entries on W and *NS*. Mentions W in entries on Ralph Ellison and John A. Williams.

1053. Sandarg, Robert. "Jean Genet and the Black Panther Party." *Journal of Black Studies*, 16 (March), 269–282. Quotes Genet mentioning W (p. 279).

1054. Sandomir, Richard. "If a Film Flies, the Book Sells." Long Island *Newsday* (24 December), Part II, p. 9. Reports that Harper & Row has printed 150,000 copies of the paperback *NS* to accompany the release of the film. "Since buying the rights to 'Native Son' 20 years ago, Harper & Row's Perennial Library imprint has sold 1.6 million copies."

1055. Saunders, James Robert. "Greater 'Truth' in Fiction: A Study of Four Black Writers." *Dissertation Abstracts International*, 47 (December), 2161A. Abstracts a 1986 University of Michigan dissertation. W is one of the four.

1056. Sazawa, Masahiro. "On an Essay About *Native Son*: 'The Meaning of Believing' in Black Community." *Quarterly of New English and American Studies*, 17 (February), 48–49. Rebuts an essay on *NS*, whose conclusion is "not acceptable" [T.K., R.B., and Y.H.].

1057. Scarpa, Harriet Jackson. "Margaret Walker Alexander." *American Visions*, 1 (March/April), 48–52. Reviews Walker's relation to W and comments extensively on her forthcoming biography. Based on interview with Walker, who is quoted extensively.

1058. Shaw, Harry B. "Perceptions of Men in the Early Works of Gwendolyn Brooks," in *Black American Poets Between Worlds, 1940–1960*. Ed. R. Baxter Miller. Knoxville: The University of Tennessee Press, pp. 136–159. Quotes Eugene Redmond mentioning W briefly (p. 143) and mentions Bigger and his family in *NS* (p. 144).

1059. _____. "Perceptions of Men in the Early Works of Gwendolyn Brooks," in *Black American Poets Between Worlds, 1940–1960*. Ed. R. Baxter Miller. Knoxville: The University of Tennessee Press, p. 143. Mentions W. briefly.

1060. Smith, Frank E. "Dale Mullen and Modern Mississippi Literature." *Journal of Mississippi History*, 48 (November), 257–270. Contains a letter dated 19 June 1937 from W to Mullen, editor of a new magazine, *River*, published in Oxford, Mississippi. W discusses his own short stories, *Challenge*, and the possibility of publishing black writers in white literary magazines in the South. W mentions that he is reading *Absalom, Absalom!*

1061. Smith, Robert P., Jr. "Rereading *Banjo*: Claude McKay and the French Connection." *CLA Journal*, 30 (September), 46–58. Mentions W briefly (p. 57).

1062. Sollors, Werner. *Beyond Ethnicity: Consent and Descent in American Culture*. New York: Oxford University Press, pp. 9, 53, 102, 263. Mentions Wright's relation to sociology and his Christian symbolism. Quotes from "Transcontinental" on Amerindians.

1063. _____. "A Critique of Pure Pluralism," in *Reconstructing American Literary History*. Ed. Sacvan Bercovitch. Harvard English Studies 13. Cambridge, MA: Harvard University Press, pp. 250–279. Mentions W briefly (p. 257).

1064. _____. "'Never Was Born': The Mulatto, an American Tragedy?" *The Massachusetts Review*, 28 (Summer), 293–316. Mentions briefly *NS* (p. 306).

1065. Sommers, Nancy. "Questions for Reading and Revising, Questions on Connections, Suggestions for Writing," in their *Student Writers at Work and in the Company of Other Writers*. Second series. New York: St. Martin's Press, pp. 610–612. Nine questions and three suggestions to accompany an excerpt from *BB*.

1066. _____, and Donald McQuade. "Richard Wright," in their *Student Writers at Work and in the Company of Other Writers*. Second series. New York: St. Martin's Press, p. 602. Biographical headnote to an excerpt from *BB*.

1067. Spivey, Ted R. *Revival: Southern Writers in the Modern City*. Gainesville: University Presses of Florida, pp. 141, 143, 144. Notes W's relation to Ellison, but denies his influence on the younger writer.

1068. St. Andrews, B.A. "*Exorcising Blackness: Historical and Literary Lynching and Burning Rituals*. By Trudier Harris." *The Georgia Review*, 40 (Winter), 1040–1042. Review mentioning W briefly (p. 1040).

1069. Stepto, Robert B. "Distrust

of the Reader in Afro-American Narratives," in *Reconstructing American Literary History*. Ed. Sacvan Bercovitch. Harvard English Studies 13. Cambridge, MA: Harvard University Press, pp. 300–322. Includes a comparison of W and Douglass with respect to their distrust of their white audience (pp. 301–304).

1070. _____. "Sharing the Thunder: The Literary Exchanges of Harriet Beecher Stowe, Henry Bibb, and Frederick Douglass," in *New Essays on Uncle Tom's Children*. Ed. Eric J. Sundquist. Cambridge: Cambridge University Press, pp. 135–153. Mentions briefly Baldwin on Stowe and W (p. 151).

1071. _____. "I Thought I Knew These People: Richard Wright and the Afro-American Literary Tradition," in *American Fiction 1914 to 1945*. Ed. Harold Bloom. New York: Chelsea House, pp. 389–403. Reprint of 1979.244

1072. Sterritt, David. "Wright's Novel 'Native Son' Brought to the Screen." *The Christian Science Monitor* (26 December), pp. 21–22. Generally favorable review of the film. It is uneven, but it is serious and the issues it raises are still relevant. Victor Love's portrayal of Bigger is good, though the film softens the novel's characterization.

1073. Summer, Bob. "The Irony of Illiteracy." *Southern Magazine*, 1 (December), 25–26. Mentions W briefly.

1074. Sundquist, Eric J. "Introduction," in his *New Essays on Uncle Tom's Cabin*. Cambridge: Cambridge University Press, pp. 1–44. Mentions briefly *UTC* (p. 5).

1075. Swindell, Warren C. "The Role of Criticism in Black Popular Culture." *The Western Journal of Black Studies*, 10 (Winter), 185–192. Mentions the F.B.I. report that W "was obsessed with solving the problems of Black people," adding that "this is the type of Black writer needed by Blacks" (p. 191).

1076. Tamada, Yoshiyuki. "From Natchez, Mississippi." *English and American Literature Notebook*, 24 (13 November), 72–73. Notes on impressions on a visit to W's birthplace [T.K., R.B., and Y.H.].

1077. _____. "Richard Wright and *12 Million Black Voices*." *Black Studies*, 56 (28 June), 50–54. Argues that W's relationship to the North and the South is a key to understanding his writing.

1078. _____. "Richard Wright and *Black Power*." *Bulletin of Osaka Institute of Technology*, 31 (April), 37–48. English translation of 1985 [T.K., R.B., and Y.H.].

1079. _____. "Richard Wright and *The Color Curtain*." *Newsletter of the Black Studies Association in Japan*, 24 (30 November), 9. Brief note on the Bandung Conference [T.K., R.B., and Y.H.].

1080. _____. "Symbolical and Metaphorical Expressions in the Opening Scene in *Native Son*." *Osaka Institute of Technology Central Laboratory Report*, 19 (February), 29–45. English translation of 1986 [T.K., R.B., and Y.H.].

1081. _____. "Symbolical and Metaphorical Expressions in the Opening Scene in *Native Son*." *Hyogo College for Education Studies of Language and Expression*, 4 (22 February), 29–45. Considers the opening scene of *NS* symbolic of the South side world of the Thomas family.

1082. Taneja, G.R. "Richard Wright." *Abstracts of English Studies*. 29 (March), 86. Abstracts an article by Charles W. Scruggs.

1083. Taylor, Clyde. "Brer Baker's Post-Opec Blues." *American Quarterly*, 38 (Spring), 114–119. Review of Houston A. Baker's *Blues, Ideology, and Afro-American Literature: A Vernacular Theory* praising its "stunning" reading of "The Man Who Lived Underground."

1084. Thomas, Kevin. "Movie Review: A Prodigal 'Native Son' Returns." *Los Angeles Times* (24 December), Part VI, pp. 1, 3. Unfavorable review complaining that the film makes "a molehill out of a mountain," lacking as it does "the raw tragic power of the novel." It starts well but becomes plodding and predictable. The acting is good, however, especially Victor Love's as Bigger. Reprinted: 1987.

1085. Tidwell, John Edgar. "Charles Scruggs. *The Sage in Harlem: H.L. Mencken and the Black Writers of the 1920s*." *Black American Literature Forum*, 20 (Fall), 341–344. Mentions W briefly (p. 344).

1086. Tremaine, Louis. "The Dissociated Sensibility of Bigger Thomas in Wright's *Native Son*." *Studies in American Fiction*, 14 (Spring), 63–76. Argues that Bigger's basic problem is a "conflict between experience and expression" (p. 64) that prevents

understanding of his emotions by himself or others. He wants to know the meaning of his life, but is afraid of that knowledge. He wants to communicate his real self to others, but fear causes him to dissemble instead. Tremaine analyzes character, plot, and narrative voice to show how they work expressionistically, not naturalistically, to express Bigger's sensibility.

1087. Vanderbilt, Kermit. *American Literature and the Academy: The Roots, Growth, and Maturity of a Profession*. Philadelphia: University of Pennsylvania Press, p. 518. Mentions W briefly.

1088. Vaughn, Christopher. "*Native Son*: A Film Version of the Classic." *Essence*, 17 (December), 30. Favorable review praising the performances of Victor Love as Bigger and Oprah Winfrey as his mother.

1089. Vickery, John B. "American Literature: The Twentieth Century," in *The Year's Work in English Studies*. Vol. 64. London: John Murray, pp. 502–530. Comments on articles on W by Ross Pudaloff and John McClusky, Jr.

1090. _____. "American Literature to 1900," in *The Year's Work in English Studies*. Vol. 64. London: John Murray, pp. 478–502. Mentions favorably an essay on W by A. Robert Lee (p. 479).

1091. Walker, Alice. "A Cautionary Tale and a Partisan View," in *Zora Neale Hurston*. Ed. Harold Bloom. New York: Chelsea House, pp. 63–69. Reprint of 1977.332.

1092. Wallace, Michelle. "Female Troubles: Ishmael Reed's Tunnel Vision." *The Village Voice Literary Supplement*, No. 51 (December), pp. 9, 11. Mentions W briefly.

1093. Ward, Jerry W., Jr. "The Wright Critical Paradigm: Facing a Future." *Callaloo*, 9 (Summer), 521–528. Discusses the past and future of W criticism and scholarship. Using reviews of *UTC* by Granville Hicks, Sterling Brown, and John Lovell as examples, Ward shows how current critical patterns continue earlier trends. Also notes recent books by Houston Baker and Henry Louis Gates as evidence that poststructuralist criticism is compatible with black cultural imperatives.

1094. Washington, James Melvin. "Editor's Introduction," in his *A Testament of Hope: The Essential Writings of Martin Luther King, Jr.*

San Francisco: Harper and Row, pp. xi–xxvi. Mentions W briefly as one of the "black cultural heroes" (p. xv).

1095. Washington, Johnny. *Alain Locke and Philosophy: A Quest for Cultural Pluralism.* Westport, CT: Greenwood Press, p. 176. Mentions W briefly.

1096. Washington, Mary Helen. "A Woman Half in Shadow," in *Zora Neale Hurston.* Ed. Harold Bloom. New York: Chelsea House, pp. 123–138. Reprint of 1979.275.

1097. Watkins, Mel. "Essay, Novel and Biography: Tools for Exploring Black Identity." *American Visions,* 1 (September/October), 53–56. Includes a review of Ralph Ellison's *Going to the Territory* mentioning his essay "Remembering Richard Wright" (p. 54).

1098. _____. *"The Price of the Ticket: Collected Nonfiction 1948–1985.* By James Baldwin; *The Evidence of Things Not Seen.* By James Baldwin." *American Visions,* 1 (March/April), 60–64. Review discussing Baldwin's treatment of W in "Many Thousands Gone" and mentions W elsewhere.

1099. _____. "Sexism, Racism and Black Women Writers." *The New York Times Book Review* (15 June), pp. 1, 35–36. Mentions briefly Bigger Thomas.

1100. Werner, Craig. "'The In-surrection of Subjugated Knowledge': Poe and Ishmael Reed," in *Poe and Our Times: Influences and Affinities.* Ed. Benjamin Franklin Fisher IV. Baltimore: The Edgar Allan Poe Society, pp. 144–156. Discusses Reed's use in *The Last Days of Louisiana Red* of W's use of Poe in *NS,* quoting from "How 'Bigger' Was Born."

1101. _____. "LeRoy S. Hodges, Jr. *Portrait of an Expatriate: William Gardner Smith, Writer;* Preston M. Yancy. *The Afro-American Short Story: A Comprehensive, Annotated Index with Selected Commentaries.* Marjorie Pryse and Hortense Spillers, eds. *Conjuring: Black Women, Fiction, and Literary Tradition.*" *Modern Fiction Studies,* 32 (Winter), 638–641. Review mentioning W as expatriate and "Big Black Good Man."

1102. Westling, Louise. "The Loving Observer of *One Time, One Place.*" *The Mississippi Quarterly,* 39 (Fall), 587–604. Includes comparison of Welty's book of photographs with *TMBV* and James Agee's *Let Us Now Praise Famous Men.*

1103. Williams, John A. "Black Biography Compared to White," in *The Challenges of Writing Black Biography.* Eds. Leo Hamalian and James V. Hatch. New York: Hatch-Billops Collection, pp. 43–47. In-cludes discussion of Margaret Walker's projected biography of W and Williams's own *The Most Native of Sons* (pp. 43, 44–45).

1104. _____. "The Use of Communications Media in Four Novels by Richard Wright." *Callaloo,* 9 (Summer), 529–539. Catalogs W's use of media, especially newspapers, in *LT, NS, O,* and *LD.*

1105. Williams, Sherley Anne. "Janie's Burden," in *Zora Neale Hurston.* Ed. Harold Bloom. New York: Chelsea House, pp. 97–102.

1106. _____. "Some Implications of Womanist Theory." *Callaloo,* 9 (Spring), 303–308. Comments on *NS* (p. 306).

1107. Wright, William. *Lillian Hellman: The Image, the Woman.* New York: Simon and Schuster, pp. 129, 139, 167. Mentions W briefly in relation to radical politics and to *PM.*

1108. Yarborough, Richard. "Strategies of Black Characterization in *Uncle Tom's Cabin* and the Early Afro-American Novel," in *New Essays on Uncle Tom's Cabin.* Ed. Eric J. Sundquist. Cambridge: Cambridge University Press, pp. 45–84. Comments on W's repudiation of Stowe's novel in *UTC* and *NS* (p. 67).

1987

1109. Aaron, Daniel. "The Unholy City: A Sketch," in *American Letters and the Historical Consciousness: Essays in Honor of Lewis P. Simpson.* Baton Rouge: Louisiana State University Press, p. 187. Mentions W briefly.

1110. Abbott, Philip. *States of Perfect Freedom: Autobiography and American Political Thought.* Amherst: University of Massachusetts Press, pp. 19, 21–22, 146–155, 188, 189, 190, 194, 205–206. Discusses W's autobiographical writings. His brutal childhood led to "defensive living" in order to survive, but he also developed a "Lockean individualism." Includes comment on *NS,* "The Man Who Lived Underground," *WML, BP,* and *PS* as well as *BB* and *AH.*

1111. Achebe, Chinua. "James Baldwin, 1924–1987." *The Massachusetts Review,* 28 (Winter), 552–554. Mentions persuading the United States Information Services Library in Lagos to acquire Baldwin and W.

1112. Adler, Thomas P. *Mirror on the Stage: The Pulitzer Plays as an Approach to American Drama.* West Lafayette: Purdue University Press, p. 73. Mentions briefly the W-Green collaboration on the play *NS.*

1113. _____. Untitled speech. *The Massachusetts Review,* 28 (Winter), 554–556. Mentions W briefly in a tribute to James Baldwin.

1114. Anon. "Adams, Timothy Dow. *I Do Believe Him Though I Know He Lies: Lying as Genre and Metaphor in Richard Wright's Black Boy.*" *American History and Life,* 24A, 356. Abstract of the article.

1115. Anon. *Arts & Humanities Citation Index 1986,* Vol. 2. Philadelphia: Institute for Scientific Information, p. 11913. Lists forty-nine items s.v. WRIGHT R, not all on W.

1116. Anon. *Bibliographic Guide*

to Black Studies: 1987 Boston: G.K. Hall, p. 215. Lists three secondary items concerning W in the New York Public Library, supplementing the *Dictionary Catalog of the Schomburg Collection of Negro Literature and History.*

1117. Anon. "Black Boy." *The Encyclopedia Americana.* Ed. Bernard S. Cayne. Vol. 4. Danbury, CT: Grolier, p. 29. Entry on *BB* calling it "an important document in the struggle for equal rights."

1118. Anon. "The Black Scholar Black Books Roundup #14." *The Black Scholar,* 18 (July/August-September/October), 30–49. Includes notices of *EM* (p. 42), Joyce A. Joyce's *Richard Wright's Art of Tragedy* (p. 45), and Michel Fabre's *The World of Richard Wright* (p. 48).

1119. Anon. "Center Book Chosen." *The Southern Register,* 5 (Summer), 9. Notes that Michel Fabre's *The World of Richard Wright,* sponsored by the Center for the Study of Southern Culture, won designation by *Choice* magazine as one of the Outstanding Scholarly Books of 1987.

1120. Anon. "Contributors." *Cultural Critique,* 6 (Spring), [225]. Mentions briefly Abdul JanMohamed's work-in-progress on W.

1121. Anon. "Contributors." *Cultural Critique,* 7 (Fall), [273]. Mentions briefly Abdul JanMohamed's work-in-progress on W.

1122. Anon. "Contributors." *The Langston Hughes Review,* 6 (Spring), v–vii. Entry on Michel Fabre mentions two of his books on W.

1123. Anon. "Cover." *Ebony,* 42 (March), 4. Mentions the second film version of *NS.*

1124. Anon. "Ebony Book Shelf." *Ebony,* 43 (November), 25. Highly favorable notice of Margaret Walker's *Richard Wright: Daemonic Genius.* Emphasizing Walker's "rich backdrop of personal experience," the reviewer calls it "a major work of biography *and* art" that will "Stimulate debate and discussion."

1125. Anon. "Family Studies: Past and Present." *American Visions,* 2 (August), 54–55. Lists *BB.*

1126. Anon. "50 Top-Grossing Films." *Variety* (7 January), p. 9. Places the new film *NS* in seventeenth place for its first week of December 1986 with $201,000.

1127. Anon. "50 Top-Grossing Films." *Variety* (14 January), p. 15.

Places the new film *NS* in seventeenth and twenty-first place for its first and second weeks with $201,000 and $90,500.

1128. Anon. "50 Top-Grossing Films." *Variety* (21 January), p. 11. Places the new film *NS* in twenty-first and twentieth place for its second and third weeks with $90,500 and $111,000.

1129. Anon. "50 Top Grossing Films." *Variety* (28 January), p. 9. Places the new film *NS* in twentieth and twenty-first place for its third and fourth weeks with $111,000 and $117,400.

1130. Anon. "50 Top-Grossing Films." *Variety* (4 February), p. 13. Places the new film *NS* in twenty-first and twenty-fourth place in its fourth and fifth weeks with $17,400 and $67,000.

1131. Anon. "50 Top Grossing Films." *Variety* (11 February), p. 9. Places the new film *NS* in twenty-fourth and twenty-ninth place in its fifth and sixth weeks with $67,000 and $49,700.

1132. Anon. "The Gathering of a Great Tradition." New York: Harper & Row, 4 pp. Publisher's brochure containing a pictorial sketch of W and mention of the publication of *NS.*

1133. Anon. "Hakutani, Yoshinobu. 'The Creation of the Self in Richard Wright's *Black Boy.*'" *Prospects,* 11— Bibliography, 61. Annotated notice.

1134. Anon. "Historical News and Notices." *The Journal of Mississippi History,* 49 (May), 173–178. Includes an announcement of the special *Callaloo* issue on W.

1135. Anon. "*Native Son.*" *Ebony,* 42 (March), 27. Brief notice of a paperback reprint edition.

1136. Anon. "1940's Novel, 'Native Son,' Brought to the Screen." Little Rock *Arkansas Gazette* (11 January), p. 9G. Comments on the 1941 play and the previous film version. Includes quotations by the producer of the new version, Diane Silver, and the actor who plays Bigger, Victor Love, and a still photograph of Bigger and Max.

1137. Anon. "Publications Relating to Mississippi." *The Journal of Mississippi History,* 49 (February), 73–76. Lists a bibliography of W's Japanese reception compiled by Yoshinobu Hakutani and Toru Kiuchi and an article by Robert J. Butler.

1138. Anon. "Publications Relating to Mississippi," *The Journal of Mississippi History,* 49 (May), 169–172. Lists articles on W by Yoshinobu Hakutani and Louis Tremaine.

1139. Anon. "*Richard Wright and Racial Discourse.*" Hakutani, Yoshinobu *Reference and Research Book News,* 11, p. 73. Describes coverage of the book.

1140. Anon. "Thaddeus, Janice. 'The Metamorphosis of Richard Wright's *Black Boy.*'" *Prospects,* 11— Bibliography, 63. Annotated notice.

1141. Anon. "This Week's N.Y. Showcase." *Variety* (7 January), p. 8. Reports gross receipts of $75,000 for the new *NS* film during the second week.

1142. Anon. "This Week's N.Y. Showcases." *Variety* (14 January), p. 14. Reports gross receipts of $116,507 for the first week of January and $105,000 for the second week for the new *NS* film.

1143. Anon. "This Week's N.Y. Showcases." *Variety* (21 January), p. 10. Reports gross receipts of $59,932 for the second week of January and $35,000 for the third week for the new *NS* film.

1144. Anon. "This Week's N.Y. Showcases." *Variety* (28 January), p. 8. Reports gross receipts of $25,824 for the third week of January and $11,000 for the fourth week for the new *NS* film.

1145. Anon. "This Week's N.Y. Showcases." *Variety* (4 February), p. 12. Reports gross receipts of $11,651 in the fifth week and $15,000 in the sixth week for the new *NS* film.

1146. Anon. "A Wrap-Up of BOMC Classics for Your Last-Minute Gift Giving." *Book-of-the-Month Club News* (December), p. 5. Includes *NS* with a blurb.

1147. Anon. "Wright R," in *Social Sciences Citation Index: 1986 Annual,* Part 3. Philadelphia: Institute for Scientific Information, p. 16829. Lists twenty-three items, most of them not on W.

1148. Appiah, Kwame Anthony. "A Long Way from Home: Wright in the Gold Coast," in *Richard Wright.* Ed. Harold Bloom. New York: Chelsea House, pp. 173–190. Analyzes *BP* in the context of prior Afro-Americans who returned to Africa. Unlike Crummell and Blyden, however, W rejects mere racial identification with the ancestral homeland. He also rejects, in his "paranoid hermeneutic," African traditional religion and the African physical self. His political advice to Nkrumah is also wrong. W persistently distances himself from Africa, almost willing not to understand it.

1149. Aptheker, Herbert. "Racism and Historiography," in his *Racism, Imperialism, & Peace.* Eds. Marvin J. Berlowitz and Carol E. Morgan. Minneapolis: Marxist Educational Press, pp. 69–72.

1150. Armstrong. Roberta R. Houston A. Baker, Jr. "*Blues, Ideology, and Afro-American Literature: A Vernacular Theory.*" *The Western Journal of Black Studies,* 11 (Fall), 149. Favorable review with special praise for Baker's treatment of *BB.*

1151. Asante, Molefi Kete. *The Afrocentric Idea.* Philadelphia: Temple University Press, p. 120. Quotes Houston Baker on W.

1152. Athas, Daphne. "The Wrong Side of the Tracks: Carrboro, 1940: Notes of a Native Daughter." Raleigh *Spectator* (30 April), pp. 5–6. Includes an account of W's visit to Chapel Hill, N.C., in 1940. A party for W was cancelled when a death threat was received.

1153. Atkinson, Michael. "Richard Wright's 'Big Boy Leaves Home' and a Tale from Ovid: A Metamorphosis Transformed." *Studies in Short Fiction,* 24 (Summer), 251–261. Compares W's story to the myth of Actaeon and Diana. "Ontology and difference, seeing and being seen, idyll and isolation, speech and silence, transformation and wounding — these are the structures of understanding that emerge to guide us when we bring Richard Wright's story into alignment with its mythic source" (p. 261).

1154. Avery, Laurence G. "Paul Green (1894–1981)," in *Fifty Southern Writers After 1900.* Eds. Joseph M. Flora and Robert Bain. Westport, CT: Greenwood Press, pp. 235–246. Contains two paragraphs on the play *NS* (pp. 241–242).

1155. Awazu, Masaharu. "Wright's View of Christianity." *Okayama University Persica,* 14 (31 March), 117–124. Discusses the influence of Christianity on *UTC, NS* and *O* [T.K., R.B., and Y.H.].

1156. Baber, Willie L. "Psychocultural Perspectives on Afro-American Leadership Style," in *Expressively Black: The Cultural Basis of*

Ethnic Identity. Eds. Geneva Gay and Willie E. Baber. New York: Praeger, pp. 266–292. Mentions briefly W and *NS* (pp. 268, 270).

1157. Baker, Houston A., Jr. "In Dubious Battle." *New Literary History,* 18 (Winter), 362–369. Quotes from W's "The History of the Negro in the United States" (pp. 364–365).

1158. _____. *Modernism and the Harlem Renaissance.* Chicago: The University of Chicago Press, pp. 81, 95, 100, 103, 106, 115. Mentions briefly W and *BB.*

1159. _____. "Reassessing (W)right: A Meditation on the Black (W)hole," in *Richard Wright.* Ed. Harold Bloom. New York: Chelsea House, pp. 127–161. Reprint of 1984.10.

1160. _____. "To Move Without Moving: An Analysis of Creativity and Commerce in Ralph Ellison's Trueblood Episode," in *Speaking for You: The Vision of Ralph Ellison.* Ed. Kimberly W. Benston. Washington, DC: Howard University Press, pp. 322–348. Reprint of 1983.6.

1161. Baldwin, James. "Introduction," in *Duties, Pleasures, Conflicts.* By Michael Thelwell. Amherst: The University of Massachusetts Press, xvii–xxii. Notes that two of Thelwell's pieces borrow W's title "Bright and Morning Star."

1162. Banta, Martha, and Robert Atwan. "The Literature of an Expanding Nation: 1865–1912," in *The Harper American Literature.* Vol. 2. Eds. Donald McQuade, Robert Atwan, Martha Banta, Justin Kaplan, David Minter, Cecilia Tichi, and Helen Vendler. New York: Harper & Row, pp. 1–28. Mentions W briefly (p. 8).

1163. Baraka, Amiri. "In the Tradition," in his and Amini Baraka's *The Music: Reflections on Jazz and Blues.* New York: William Morrow.

1164. Bardrick, Cameron, et al. "Literature." *Prospects: An Annual of American Cultural Studies,* 10 — Bibliography, 220–244. Mentions W in annotations on works by Michael G. Cooke, Theodore L. Gross, Trudier Harris, Sanehide Kodama, Lewis A. Lawson, and R. Baxter Miller.

1165. _____. "Literature." *Prospects: An Annual of American Cultural Studies,* 11 — Bibliography, 201–229. Mentions W in annotations on works by Mary F. Sisney and Clyde Taylor.

1166. Bartlett, Lee. "Poetry: The 1940s to the Present," in *American Literary Scholarship: An Annual/ 1985.* Ed. J. Albert Robbins. Durham, NC: Duke University Press, pp. 323–345. Includes mention of Sanehide Kodama's treatment of W in *American Poetry and Japanese Culture* (p. 328).

1167. Baskett, Sam S. "Beyond Native Grounds: American Literary Expatriation." *Centennial Review,* 31 (Spring), 192–211. Contains a paragraph on W concluding that expatriation caused him to lose "the passion of *Native Son* and *Black Boy*" (p. 207). Also quotes Baldwin on W (p. 208).

1168. Bell, Bernard W. *The Afro-American Novel and Its Tradition.* Amherst: The University of Massachusetts Press, pp. xiv, xv, xviii, 23, 25, 57, 102, 150–151, 153–168, 171, 177, 179, 183, 185–186, 189, 191, 194, 215–216, 218–219, 233, 236, 247–248, 250, 257–258, 279, 284–286, 301, 307, 315, 321, 329, 339. In the chapter on "Richard Wright and the Triumph of Naturalism," Bell argues that W rejected "both the concept of black nationalism and the values of Afro-American culture" (p. 155). After a full commentary on *NS,* Bell concludes that "Wright's most significant contributions to the tradition of the Afro-American novel are threefold: his complex and controversial naturalistic vision of urban black characters and culture, his creation of the best-known character in black fiction by a synthesis of white and black myths of the Bad Nigger, and his projection of the Afro-American as the metaphor for America and modern man" (pp. 166–167).

1169. Bennett, Lerone, Jr. *Before the Mayflower: A History of Black America.* Sixth ed. Chicago: Johnson, pp. 533, 536, 560. Chronology listing *NS,* W's Spingarn Medal, and W's death.

1170. Benoist, Mary Anne. "Black Studies." *The Society for The Study of Southern Literature News-Letter,* 20 (November), 12–14. Lists Maryemma Graham's *The Afro-American Novel: A Study Guide,* Wendy Lesser's *The Life Below Ground: A Study of the Subterranean in Literature and History,* and Margaret Walker's *Richard Wright: Daemonic Genius.*

1171. _____. "Executive Council Nominees." *The Society for the Study* *of Southern Literature News-Letter*, 20 (November), 1–2. Notes work on W by Thadious M. Davis.

1172. Benston, Kimberly W., ed. *Speaking for You: The Vision of Ralph Ellison*. Washington, DC: Howard University Press, x + 438 pp. Includes essays by Michel Fabre and Joseph T. Skerrett, Jr., on the W-Ellison relationship as well as numerous other essays mentioning W.

1173. Bigsby, C.W.E. "Improvising America: Ralph Ellison and the Paradox of Form," in *Speaking for You: The Vision of Ralph Ellison*. Ed. Kimberly W. Benston. Washington, DC: Howard University Press, pp. 173–183. Mentions and quotes from W (pp. 173, 176, 183).

1174. Bloom, Harold. "Bibliography," in his *American Fiction 1914 to 1945*. New York: Chelsea House, pp. 437–447. Includes eight books and one article on W.

1175. _____. "Biographical Notes," in his *American Fiction 1914 to 1945*. New York: Chelsea House, pp. 425–432. Includes an entry for W.

1176. _____. "Editor's Note," in his *American Fiction 1914 to 1945*. New York: Chelsea House, pp. ix–xi. Comments favorably on Robert B. Stepto's "I Thought I Knew These People: Richard Wright and the Afro-American Literary Tradition."

1177. _____. "Editor's Note," in his *Richard Wright*. New York: Chelsea House, p. vii. Provides one-sentence summaries of the eleven essays collected in the volume, which Bloom considers "the best criticism available" on W.

1178. _____. "Introduction," in his *Richard Wright*. New York: Chelsea House, pp. 1–6. Argues that the aesthetic shortcomings of *NS* derive from W's "bad authorial ear," but admits the social importance of the work. *BB* also has social importance, but is perhaps more interesting for its Oedipal theme. Emphasizes Dreiser's influence on W.

1179. _____, ed. *Richard Wright*. New York: Chelsea House, vii + 246 pp. Contains an introduction by Bloom, original essays by Kwame Anthony Appiah and Abdul JanMohamed, reprinted material by Edward Margolies, George E. Kent, Michel Fabre, Robert B. Stepto, A. Robert Lee, Houston A. Baker, Jr., and Michael G. Cooke, and a chronology, notes on contributors, and a bibliography.

1180. Bloom, Lynn Z. "Review: *Life Studies: Interpreting Autobiography*." *College English*, 49 (March), 345–352. Mentions W briefly (p. 346).

1181. _____. "Richard Wright Interview Comments on *Black Boy*," in her *The Lexington Reader*. Lexington, MA: D.C. Heath. Headnote to an early and late draft of "*Black Boy* and Reading," an unpublished interview statement.

1182. Boyd, Herb. "Bigger Is Back: An Assessment of *Native Son* as Book and Movie." *EM: Ebony Man*, 2 (June), 42–43. Discuss the success and importance of the novel and reviews unfavorably both film versions. The new film is "minimalist" and emphasizes the personal element at the expense of the social. Deplores the deletion of Bigger's murder of Bessie.

1183. Bracy, William. "Wright, Richard Nathaniel," *The Encyclopedia Americana*. Ed. Bernard S. Cayne. Vol. 29. Danbury, CT: Grolier, pp. 555–556.

1184. Bradley, David. "Foreword," in *Eight Men*. New York: Thunder's Mouth Press, pp. ix–xxv. Traces the evolution of *EM* from W's projected *Seven Men* in 1944 to the posthumously published work. Although Bradley discusses or comments on each of the stories, his emphasis is on their place in W's career, a career impeded and altered by agents, editors, and publishers. Comments on *UTC, NS, BB, O, BP, CC, PS,* and *WML* as well as *EM*.

1185. Brewer, Betty. "Are We Ready for the Truth About Southern Racism from the Eyes of Richard Wright's *Black Boy*?" *Mount Olive Review*, 1 (Spring), 61–69. Examines *BB* with emphasis on its continuing relevance and its unpalatable truth. Notes the Howe-Ellison debate on the validity of W's depiction of black life.

1186. B[rosnahan], J[ohn]. "Walker, Margaret. Richard Wright, daemonic genius: a portrait of the man, a critical look at his work." *Booklist*, 84 (15 November), 533–534. Mixed notice complaining of Walker's "uncharitable and doctrinaire" dismissal of her predecessors in W criticism and her "strident" psychologizing, but praising her "highly informed and reliable" personal perspective on W and his times.

1187. Brown-Guillory, Elizabeth.

"Black Women Playwrights: Exorcising Myths." *Phylon*, 48 (Fall), 229–239. Mentions briefly Bessie in *NS* (p. 233).

1188. Brumm, Ursula. "William Faulkner and the Southern Renaissance," in *American Literature Since 1900*. Ed. Marcus Cunliffe. New York: Peter Bedrick Books, pp. 173–203. Mentions W briefly (p. 181).

1189. Bryan, Violet Harrington. "An Interview with Brenda Marie Osbey." *The Mississippi Quarterly*, 40 (Winter), 33–45. Osbey mentions W briefly (p. 36).

1190. Buckmaster, Elizabeth, Landon C. Burns, and Janet P. Alwang. "The Thirteenth (1986) Supplement to a Cross-Referenced Index of Short Fiction Anthologies and Author-Title Listings." *Studies in Short Fiction*, 24 (Spring), 185–241. Lists three items on "The Man Who Was Almost a Man" (p. 241).

1191. Buncombe, Marie H. "Legacy from the Past, Agenda for the Future: The College Language Association, 1937–1987." *CLA Journal*, 31 (September), 1–11. Mentions W briefly (p. 9).

1192. Byrd, Rudolph. "Book Review: Michel Fabre, *The World of Richard Wright*." *CAAS Newsletter*, 10 (May), 14. Favorable review except for unfavorable response to "Fantasies and Style in Wright's Fiction."

1193. Callahan, John F. "Chaos, Complexity, and Possibility: The Historical Frequencies of Ralph Waldo Ellison," in *Speaking for You: The Vision of Ralph Ellison*. Ed. Kimberly W. Benston. Washington, DC: Howard University Press, pp. 125–143. Reprint of 1979.56a.

1194. _____. "'Riffing' and Paradigm-Building: The Anomaly of Tradition and Innovation in *Invisible Man* and *The Structure of Scientific Revolutions*." *Callaloo*, 10 (Winter), 91–102. Mentions W briefly (p. 98).

1195. Campbell, Diane H. "Richard Wright." *Abstracts of English Studies*, 30 (March), 98. Abstract of an article by John McClusky, Jr.

1196. Carby, Hazel V. *Reconstructing Womanhood: The Emergence of the Afro-American Woman Novelist*. New York: Oxford University Press, p. 175. Mentions W briefly. Reprinted: 1990.

1197. Carr, Virginia Spencer. "Carson McCullers," in *Fifty Southern*

Writers After 1900: A Bio-Bibliographical Sourcebook. Eds. Joseph M. Flora and Robert Bain. Westport, CT: Greenwood Press, 301–312. Mentions W briefly (p. 303).

1198. Chambers, Kimberly R. "Right on Time: History and Religion in Alice Walker's *The Color Purple*." *CLA Journal*, 31 (September), 44–62. Mentions briefly *NS* (p. 47).

1199. Charters, Ann. "Richard Wright," in her *The Story and Its Writer: An Introduction to Short Fiction*. Second edition. New York: St. Martin's Press, pp. 758–759. Biographical headnote to "The Man Who Was Almost a Man."

1200. _____, William E. Sheidley, and Martha Ramsey. "Richard Wright 'The Man Who Was Almost a Man,'" in their *Instructor's Manual to Accompany the Story and Its Writer: An Introduction to Short Fiction*. Second edition. New York: St. Martin's Press, pp. 129–130. Contains two analytical paragraphs on the story, a dozen questions for discussion, three topics for writing, and two secondary sources.

1201. Chase-Riboud, Barbara. "Why Paris?" *Essence*, 18 (October), 65–66. Mentions W briefly.

1202. Chénetier, Marc. "Foreign Scholarship: French Contributions," in *American Literary Scholarship: An Annual/1985*. Ed. J. Albert Robbins. Durham, NC: Duke University Press, pp. 454–464. Mentions briefly Michel Fabre's *The World of Richard Wright* (p. 463).

1203. Christian, Barbara. "Nuance and the Novella: A Study of Gwendolyn Brooks's *Maud Martha*," in *A Life Distilled: Gwendolyn Brooks, Her Poetry and Fiction*. Eds. Maria K. Mootry and Gary Smith. Urbana: University of Illinois Press, pp. 239–253.

1204. _____. "The Race for Theory." *Cultural Critique*, 6 (Spring), 54, 55. Mentions briefly W and "Blueprint for Negro Writing."

1205. Cohen-Solal, Annie. *Sartre: A Life*. Trans. Norman MacAfee. New York: Pantheon Books, pp. 242, 305, 307.

1206. Collier, Eugenia. "The Black Person in Art: How Should S/he Be Portrayed? (Part II)." *Black American Literature Forum*, 21 (Fall), 318–321. Mentions briefly *NS*.

1207. _____. "Some Thoughts on the Black Aesthetic," in *Nommo: A Literary Legacy of Black Chicago (1967–1987)*. Ed. Carole A. Parks. Chicago: OBAhouse, pp. 320–325. Mentions briefly Bigger Thomas.

1208. Comprone, Joseph J. "*The Library Card* Richard Wright," in his *Perspectives: Turning Reading Into Writing*. Boston: Houghton Mifflin, pp. 627–628. Headnote to an excerpt from *BB*.

1209. _____. "Questions and Activities," in his *Perspectives: Turning Reading Into Writing*. Boston: Houghton Mifflin, pp. 636–637. Nine study questions and two writing suggestions on an excerpt from *BB*.

1210. Cooke, Michael G. "The Beginnings of Self-Realization," in *Richard Wright*. Ed. Harold Bloom. New York: Chelsea House, pp. 163–171.

1211. Cooper, Wayne F. *Claude McKay: Rebel Sojourner in the Harlem Renaissance: A Biography*. Baton Rouge: Louisiana State University Press, pp. 82, 259, 320, 338, 361. Quotes briefly from *BB* (p. 82), mentions W briefly (p. 259, 320, 338), quotes Melvin B. Tolson comparing W favorably to McKay (p. 320), and mentioning briefly *NS* (p. 361). Reprinted: 1996.

1212. Costanzo, Angelo. *Surprising Narrative: Olaudah Equinano and the Beginnings of Black Autobiography*. Westport, CT: Greenwood Press, p. 3. Mentions W briefly.

1213. Dance, Daryl. *Long Gone: The Mecklenburg Six and the Theme of Escape in Black Folklore*. Knoxville: The University of Tennessee Press, pp. 3, 4. Mentions W briefly.

1214. Davis, Charles T. "The Mixed Heritage of the Modern Black Novel: Ralph Ellison and Friends," in *Speaking for You: The Vision of Ralph Ellison*. Ed. Kimberly W. Benston. Washington, DC: Howard University Press, pp. 272–282. Reprint of 1982.37.

1215. Davis, Thadious M. "From Jazz Syncopation to Blues Elegy: Faulkner's Development of Black Characterization," in *Faulkner and Race: Faulkner and Yoknapatawpha, 1986*. Eds. Doreen Fowler and Ann J. Abadie. Jackson: University Press of Mississippi, pp. 70–92. Quotes W calling the blues "fantastically paradoxical" (p. 90).

1216. _____. "Richard Wright (1908–1960)," in *Fifty Southern Writers After 1900: A Bio-Bibliographical Sourcebook*. Eds. Joseph M. Flora and Robert Bain. Westport, CT: Greenwood Press, pp. 535–559. Contains sections on biography, major themes, survey of criticism, and bibliography (primary and secondary). Davis identifies W's major themes as "alienation, flight, becoming, rebellion, oppression, freedom, and self-actualization, all within the emotional nexus of fear, dread, pain, anger or rage, and in a few instances ... despair" (p. 552). W's place in American literature is secure.

1217. Dinnerstein, Leonard. *Uneasy at Home: Antisemitism and the American Jewish Experience*. New York: Columbia University Press, pp. 219, 249. Quotes from *BB* in a chapter entitled "Black Antisemitism."

1218. Dixon, Melvin. *Ride Out the Wilderness: Geography and Identity in Afro-American Literature*. Urbana: University of Illinois Press, pp. 4, 57–69, 82, 83, 85, 98, 100, 123–124, 134, 157, 161, 164, 166. Discusses actual and imaginary space in W, especially in "Between the World and Me," *BB*, and "The Man Who Lived Underground." Comments also on W in relation to Frederick Douglass, Zora Neale Hurston, James Baldwin, and Alice Walker.

1219. Donald, David Herbert. *Look Homeward: A Life of Thomas Wolfe*. Boston: Little Brown, p. 179. Mentions W briefly.

1220. Douglas, Robert L. "Religious Orthodoxy and Skepticism in Richard Wright's *Uncle Tom's Children* and *Native Son*." *Griot*, 6 (Fall), 44–51. Compares *UTC* and *NS* with respect to "the treatment of the minister, the concept of religion or religious worldview, and the use of religious music" (p. 44). Ambivalent in his attitude toward black Christianity, W fluctuates between orthodoxy and skepticism.

1221. Drake, Sandra E. "The Black Person in Art: How Should S/he Be Portrayed (Part II)." *Black American Literature Forum*, 21 (Fall), 324–329. Compares briefly W and Alice Walker (p. 324).

1222. Drake, William. *The First Wave: Women Poets in America, 1915–1945*. New York: Macmillan, p. 251. States that Margaret Conklin befriended W "when he arrived unknown in New York."

1223. Drimmer, Melvin. *Issues in Black History: Reflections and Commentaries on the Black Historical Experience*. Dubuque, IA: Kendall/Hunt, pp. 179, 189. Notes W's role in making Chicago the center of African American culture, mentioning *UTC*, *NS*, and *BB*. Notes also W's relation with the Communist Party.

1224. Eagles, Brenda M. "A Bibliography of Dissertations Relating to Mississippi—1987." *Journal of Mississippi History*, 49 (February), 65–67. Lists a dissertation by Michael Francis Lynch on W, Ellison, and Dostoevsky.

1225. Early, Gerald. "*Fingering the Jagged Grain: Tradition and Form in Recent Black Fiction*. By Keith E. Byerman." *American Studies* 28 (Spring), 104. Review mentioning W briefly.

1226. _____. "*Richard Wright's Art of Tragedy*. By Joyce Ann Joyce." *American Studies*, 28 (Fall), 65–66. Unfavorable review calling her reading of W "too simplistic."

1227. Egan, Susanna. "Changing Faces of Heroism: Some Questions Raised by Contemporary Autobiography." *Biography*, 10 (Winter), 20–38. Mentions briefly *BB* (pp. 22, 24).

1228. Egerton, John. "Keepers." *Southern Magazine*, 1 (May), 26, 28–29. Article on book collecting mentioning W briefly.

1229. Elbow, Peter. "Closing My Eyes as I Speak: An Argument for Ignoring Audience." *College English*, 49 (January), 50–69. Includes a parenthetical reference to an incident in *BB*.

1230. Ellison, Ralph. "Remembering Richard Wright," in *Speaking for You: The Vision of Ralph Ellison*. Ed. Kimberly W. Benston. Washington, DC: Howard University Press, pp. 187–198. Reprint of 1984.47.

1231. Ensslen, Klaus. "Der afro-amerikanische Roman nach 1945," in *Der amerikanische Roman nach 1945*. Ed. Arno Heller. Darmstadt: Wissenschaftliche Buchgesellschaft, pp. 223–255. Discusses *NS*, *LT*, *O*, *SH*, *UTC*, and *LD* (pp. 224–226, 236–237) and mentions W elsewhere (pp. 229, 231, 233, 246, 247, 249, 250).

1232. Evans, James H., Jr. *Spiritual Empowerment in Afro-American Literature*. Lewiston, NY: The Ed-

win Mellen Press, pp. 19, 95–130, 165, 166–167. In a chapter entitled "The Veil of Faith: Richard Wright's *Native Son*," Evans "offers a critical analysis ... in which the use of religious language is seen as the key to the development of ... Bigger Thomas" (p. 19). Bigger's self-realization is finally achieved through openness to faith when in Jan's example "the word had become flesh." Bigger's faith is "restless" and "questioning," however, not firm or traditionally Christian.

1233. Fabre, Michel. "Beyond Naturalism?" in *Richard Wright*. Ed. Harold Bloom. New York: Chelsea House, pp. 37–56. Reprint of 1975.71.

1234. _____. "From *Native Son* to *Invisible Man*: Some Notes on Ralph Ellison's Evolution in the 1950's," in *Speaking for You: The Vision of Ralph Ellison*. Ed. Kimberly W. Benston. Washington, DC: Howard University Press, pp. 199–216. Traces the early development of Ellison's political, racial, and literary ideology during his friendship with W, quoting liberally from letters to W, especially concerning *TMBV* and *BB*. Fabre concludes that Ellison was much closer to W's Marxism than his later writings would indicate.

1235. _____. "Hughes's Literary Reputation in France." *The Langston Hughes Review*, 6 (Spring), 20–27. Mentions W's recommendation of Hughes to *Présence Africaine* and Hughes's visit to W in 1960 (pp. 21, 25).

1236. Farley, Reynold, and Walter R. Allen. *The Color Line and the Quality of Life in America*. New York: Russell Sage Foundation, pp. 189, 467. Quotes from *TMBV* in a chapter on "The Schooling of America: Black-White Differences in Education."

1237. Fleming, Robert E. *James Weldon Johnson*. Boston: Twayne, pp. 91, 108. Mentions briefly *BB* and "The Man Who Lived Underground."

1238. Flora, Joseph M., and Robert Bain. "Introduction," in their *Fifty Southern Writers After 1900: A Bio-Bibliographical Sourcebook*. Westport, CT: Greenwood Press, pp. 1–8. Contains a paragraph on W, "the major black writer of the South and the nation" (p. 7).

1239. Flynn, Joyce. "Introduction," in *Frye Street & Environs: The*

Collected Works of Marita Bonner. Boston: Beacon Press, pp. xi–xxvii. Mentions briefly *NS* (p. xxii).

1240. _____. "Marita Bonner Occomy," in *Afro-American Writers from the Harlem Renaissance to 1940*. Ed. Trudier Harris. Detroit: Gale, pp. 222–228. Claims that Occomy's story "Tin Can" influenced W.

1241. Foley, Barbara. "The Politics of Poetics: Ideology and Narrative Form in *An American Tragedy* and *Native Son*," in *Narrative Poetics*. Ed. James Phelan. *Papers in Comparative Studies*, 5 (1986–1987), 55–67. Compares Dreiser's novel of "the tragic consequences of false consciousness" to W's "grotesque rather than tragic ... bitter social commentary" to support the view that proletarian fiction should be judged by a proletarian, not bourgeois, aesthetic.

1242. Foster, Frances Smith. "Donnarae MacCann and Gloria Woodard. *The Black American in Books for Children: Readings in Racism*." *Black American Literature Forum*, 21 (Spring-Summer), 199–204. Mentions W briefly (p. 201).

1243. Fox, Robert Elliott. *Conscientious Sorcerers: The Black Postmodernist Fiction of LeRoi Jones/Amiri Baraka, Ishmael Reed, and Samuel R. Delany*. Westport, CT: Greenwood Press, pp. 32, 35. Mentions *AH*, *NS*, and "The Man Who Lived Underground."

1244. Fraden, Rena. "Feels Good, Can't Hurt: Black Representation on the Federal Arts Project." *Journal of Popular Culture*, 10 (Winter), 21–29. Comments on *NS* and Bigger Thomas (p. 21).

1245. Frank, Joseph. "Ralph Ellison and a Literary 'Ancestor': Dostoevski," in *Speaking for You: The Vision of Ralph Ellison*. Ed. Kimberly W. Benston. Washington, DC: Howard University Press, pp. 231–244. Reprint of 1983.34.

1246. Freibert, Lucy M. "Southern Song: An Interview with Margaret Walker." *Frontiers*, 9, no. 3, 50–56. Includes comments on Walker's relation to W and her use of the word *daemonic* in describing him (pp. 50, 51).

1247. _____. "Southern Song: An Interview with Margaret Walker." *Frontiers*, 9 (March), pp. 50–56. Includes discussion of Walker's relation to W and her biography.

1248. French, Warren. "American

Literature Since 1900," in *Reference Guide to American Literature*. Second edition. Ed. D. L. Kirkpatrick. Chicago: St. James Press, pp. 14–29. Reprint of 1980.102.

1249. Fuller, Hoyt. "Racism in Literary Anthologies." *The Black Scholar*, 18 (January/February), 35–39. Quotes Martha Foley mentioning W (see 1971).

1250. Gates, Henry Louis, Jr. *Figures in Black: Words, Signs, and the "Racial" Self*. New York: Oxford University Press, pp. xxvi, xxviii, 29, 30, 55–56, 233, 242, 245–246, 248. Contains a reprint of 1983.35 and comments on and quotes from W in the "Introduction" and the first chapter on "Literary Theory and the Black Tradition."

1251. _____, ed. "The Black Person in Art: How Should S/he Be Portrayed? (Part I)." *Black American Literature Forum*, 21 (Spring-Summer), 3–24. Includes responses mentioning W by Blyden Jackson, Ishmael Reed, and, in the fall issue, by Eugenia Collier, Sandra E. Drake, and Jerry Ward, Jr.

1252. Gayle, Addison. "Hoyt Fuller and the Black Aesthetic," in *Nommo: A Literary Legacy of Black Chicago (1967–1987)*. Ed. Carole A. Parks. Chicago: OBA house, pp. 310–313. Mentions W's views on "the art of dissimulation" in a racist society.

1253. Gilbert, Susan. "Maya Angelou's *I Know Why the Caged Bird Sings*: Paths to Escape." *Mount Olive Review*, 1 (Spring), 39–50. Mentions briefly *NS* (pp. 44–45), comments on and quotes from *BB* (pp. 45–46), and notes that Angelou rejects W's bleak view of black life in the South (p. 47).

1254. Gilroy, Paul. "*There Ain't No Black in the Union Jack: The Cultural Politics of Race and Nation*. Chicago: The University of Chicago Press, front matter and p. 25. One of three epigraphs is a quotation from *O*. Also quotes briefly George Padmore quoting W.

1255. Glazier, Lyle. *Great Day Coming*. New Delhi: Raajprakashan, pp. 4, 115, 149–171, 172, 173, 179–180, 184, 240. The section on W (pp. 150–171) sketches his life and career and discusses *UTC* (especially its skillful use of language), *NS*, and *LD*. "No writer of fiction has caught better than Richard Wright the poetry and tragedy, the violence and

aspirations of the American Negro's experience" (p. 154).

1256. Goldman, Arnold. "A Remnant to Escape: The American Writer and the Minority Group," in *The New History of Literature: American Literature Since 1900*. Ed. Marcus Cunliffe. New York: Peter Bedrick Books, pp. 283–311. Discusses W's early writing including *UTC*, *NS*, and *BB* (pp. 299–302), and mentions W elsewhere.

1257. Gordon, Lois, and Alan Gordon. *American Chronicle: Six Decades in American Life 1920–1980*. New York: Atheneum, pp. 178, 200, 206, 209, 245, 321, 339, 391. Lists *UTC*, *NS*, the play *NS*, *TMBV*, *BB*, *O*, *BP*, and W's death (s.v. 1961 by mistake).

1258. Greene, J. Lee. "Ralph Ellison," in *Fifty Southern Writers After 1900: A Bio-Bibliographical Sourcebook*. Eds. Joseph M. Flora and Robert Bain. Westport, CT: Greenwood Press, pp. 147–157. Notes Ellison's friendship with W and mentions W elsewhere (pp. 149–150, 152, 155).

1259. Greenspon, Joanna, ed. *Humanities Index: April 1986 to March 1987*. New York: H.W. Wilson, p. 995. Lists five items s.v. W.

1260. Grimwood, Michael. *Heart in Conflict: Faulkner's Struggles with Vocation*. Athens: The University of Georgia Press, p. 323. Comments on W's flood stories, referring to William Howard's essay.

1261. Gunner, Elizabeth. *A Handbook for Teaching African Literature*. Second edition. Oxford: Heinemann, p. 9.

1262. Hakutani, Yoshinobu. "The Artistry of Richard Wright's *Black Boy*." *Chiba Review*, 9 (November), 19–28. Observes that *BB* is not only a unique autobiography, but also the most influential racial discourse in America because of its style and artistry. W's prose is enriched by poetry, irony, and rhetoric [T.K., R.B., and Y.H.].

1263. Harap, Louis. *Creative Awakening: The Jewish Presence in Twentieth-Century American Literature, 1900–1940s*. Westport, CT: Greenwood Press, pp. 92, 107. Mentions briefly *NS*.

1264. _____. *Dramatic Encounters: The Jewish Presence in Twentieth-Century American Drama, Poetry, and Humor and the Black-Jewish Literary Relationship*. Westport, CT:

Greenwood Press, pp. 5–6, 7, 13, 18, 25. Discusses the role of Boris Max and anti-Semitism in *NS*.

1265. Harding, Vincent. "Power from Our People: The Sources of the Modern Revival of Black History." *The Black Scholar*, 18 (January/February), 40–51. Comments on and quotes from "The Literature of the Negro in the United States" (p. 41) and mentions W elsewhere.

1266. Harrington, Richard. "Diluted 'Native Son.'" *The Washington Post* (16 January), p. B8. Unfavorable review of the film comparing it to the novel. Without the rage and complexity of the novel, the film turns it into "a pious liberal document." Victor Love's acting is good, however.

1267. Hatch, James V. "Owen Dodson: Excerpts from a Biography in Progress." *The Massachusetts Review*, 28 (Winter), 627–641. Mentions W briefly (p. 638).

1268. Hayman, Ronald. *Sartre: A Life*. New York: Simon and Schuster, pp. 220, 264, 269. Mentions W in connection with the racial issue and with the R.D.R.

1269. Heller, Arno. "Einführung in den amerikanischen Roman nach 1945 und dessen kritische Rezeption," in his *Der amerikanische Roman nach 1945*. Darmstadt: Wissenschaftliche Buchgesellschaft, pp. 1–39. Comments on W and *NS* and their influence on subsequent African American fiction (pp. 4, 25, 26, 27).

1270. Helmbold, Lois Rita. "Beyond the Family Economy: Black and White Working-Class Women During the Great Depression." *Feminist Studies*, 13 (Fall), 629–655. Mentions W and relatives living together in Chicago, citing *AH* (p. 645).

1271. Hernton, Calvin C. *The Sexual Mountain and Black Women Writers*. New York: Anchor Press/Doubleday, pp. 10, 39, 50, 61–65. Mentions "The Ethics of Living Jim Crow," comments on the depiction of women in *NS*, notes W's incorporation of "Marxism in a formulated black male aesthetic statement," and discusses *NS* in relation to Ann Petry's *The Street*.

1272. Hersey, John. "'A Completion of Personality': A Talk with Ralph Ellison," in *Speaking for You: The Vision of Ralph Ellison*. Ed. Kimberly W. Benston. Washington,

DC: Howard University Press, pp. 285–307. Includes discussion by Ellison of his friendship and literary relation with W (pp. 301–305).

1273. Hitt, Greg. "Maya Angelou: Vibrant Professor-Writer Shares Her Talent, Her Search, Her Self." *Winston-Salem Journal* (6 December), pp. A13, A16. Notes that Angelou included W at a reading at Mount Zion Baptist Church.

1274. Holloway, Clayton G. "When a Pariah Becomes a Celebrity: An Interview with James Baldwin." *Xavier Review*, 7 (Fall), 1–10. Baldwin mentions briefly the play *NS* (p. 8).

1275. Holloway, Karla F.C. *New Dimensions of Spirituality: A Biracial and Bicultural Reading of the Novels of Toni Morrison.* Westport, CT: Greenwood Press, p. 122. Comments on *EM*.

1276. Hönnighausen, Lothar. "Black as White Metaphor: A European View of Faulkner's Fiction," in *Faulkner and Race: Faulkner and Yoknapatawpha, 1986.* Jackson: University Press of Mississippi, pp. 192–208. Quotes W's statement that "the Negro is America's metaphor" (p. 193).

1277. Hungerford, Lynda. "Dialect Representation in *Native Son.*" *Language and Style*, 20 (Winter), 3–15. Demonstrates that W "represented black speech in two contrasting ways to delineate two groups of black characters and underline the thematic content of the novel" (p. 3). For the first group (Bigger and his family and friends) W presents Black English Vernacular through grammatical patterns, especially negative concord, the absence of *are*, and the absence of *have, do*, and *did*. For the second group, Reverend Hammond and the two black workers in Book II, Jack and Jim, W represents dialect orthographically. The result is realistic portrayal of the first group, deliberately stereotypical portrayal of the Tomish second group.

1278. Hunter, Jefferson. *Image and Word: The Interaction of Twentieth-Century Photographs and Texts.* Cambridge, MA: Harvard University Press, pp. 14–16, 86. Discusses *TMBV* unfavorably, complaining of the "florid prose text, half sermon, half populist history," which is ill-suited to the understated photographs.

1279. Hyman, Lawrence W. "Is Cary Nelson Really 'Against English'?" *ADE Bulletin*, No. 88 (Winter), pp. 80–81. Letter to the editor mentioning W briefly.

1280. Inove, Kenji. "Lament for Baldwin's Death." *Library Newspaper* (19 December). Notes that like Baldwin, W has been less praised than women writers recently.

1281. Jackson, Blyden. "Blyden Jackson responds," in "The Black Person in Art: How Should S/he Be Portrayed?" Ed. Henry Louis Gates, Jr. *Black American Literature Forum*, 21 (Spring-Summer), 3–24. Mentions briefly *NS* and Bigger Thomas (p. 18).

1282. Jackson-Opoku, Sandra. "Preface," in *Nommo: A Literary Legacy of Black Chicago (1967–1987).* Ed. Carole A. Parks. Chicago: OBAhouse, pp. xiii–xiv. Mentions W briefly.

1283. JanMohamed, Abdul R. "Negating the Negation as a Form of Affirmation in Minority Discourse: The Construction of Richard Wright as Subject." *Cultural Critique*, 7 (Fall), 245–266. Examines *BB* as "a testament to the struggle over the formation of black subjectivity in a racist society" (p. 246). By negating the South's effort to dehumanize him as a "black boy," W achieves his own subjectivity, thus escaping the "social death" of accommodation while risking the physical death threatening black rebels. Literature provides a way out, and "the literary success of *Black Boy* becomes an affirmation, a vindication of his strategy of negating the racist negation" (p. 264).

1284. _____. "Rehistoricizing Wright: The Psychopolitical Function of Death in *Uncle Tom's Children*," in *Richard Wright*. Ed. Harold Bloom. New York: Chelsea House, pp. 191–228. Analyzes the five stories of the expanded version in the light of Orlando Patterson's study of slavery as a kind of "social death" which could be escaped only by rebellion and, usually, actual death, often violent. JanMohamed also places his treatment of the stories in the context of W's own life and the general social conditions of the South in the early twentieth century.

1285. Johnson, Barbara. "Metaphor, Metonymy, and Voice in Zora Neale Hurston's *Their Eyes Were Watching God*," in *American Fiction 1914 to 1945*. Ed. Harold Bloom. New York: Chelsea House, pp. 361–374.

1286. _____. "Metaphor, Metonymy, and Voice in *Their Eyes Were Watching God*," in her *A World of Difference*. Baltimore: The Johns Hopkins University Press, pp. 155–171.

1287. _____. "Metaphor, Metonymy, and Voice in *Their Eyes Were Watching God*," in Harold Bloom, ed. *Zora Neale Hurston's Their Eyes Were Watching God.* New York: Chelsea House, pp. 41–57. Reprint of 1984.

1288. Johnson, Charles, *Being and Race: Black Writing Since 1970.* Bloomington: Indiana University Press, pp. 5, 8, 12–15, 21, 24, 28, 31, 78, 86, 93, 96, 118. Discusses *NS* as a fully achieved "drama of consciousness" in which "everything *means* something; every physical, historical object is a metaphor for feeling" (p. 14). Johnson also mentions *AH, O*, and W's influence on Ellison and John A. Williams.

1289. Johnson, Joe. "*Mating Birds* by Lewis Nkosi." *The Crisis*, 94 (June/July), 18, 62–63. Review mentioning briefly *NS*.

1290. Jones, Kenneth M. "The Lion Never Sleeps: Black Male Writers in America." *EM: Ebony Man*, 2 (July), 64–69. Mentions Gayle's biography of W, quotes a New York literary agent on W as an archetypal black writer, includes a sketch of W and three other male writers, and presents a photograph of several books by black men, one of which is *O*.

1291. Joyce, Joyce A. "The Black Canon: Reconstructing Black Literary Criticism." *New Literary History*, 18 (Winter), 335–344. Mentions W and *NS*. Quotes from *WML* (p. 338).

1292. _____. "Structural and Thematic Unity in Toni Morrison's *Song of Solomon*." *The CEA Critic*, 49 (Winter 1986-Summer 1987), 185–198. Mentions *NS* briefly (p. 185).

1293. _____. "'Who the Cap Fit': Unconsciousness and Unconscionableness in the Criticism of Houston A. Baker, Jr., and Henry Louis Gates, Jr." *New Literary History*, 18 (Winter), 371–384. Mentions W briefly (p. 378).

1294. Kempley, Rita. "Love's Labor

Lost in 'Son.'" *The Washington Post* (16 January), Weekend sec., p. 17. Unfavorable review of the film *NS*. "It's a magnanimous, modestly budgeted, morally medicinal adaptation of Richard Wright's classic novel of race and rage." The acting is generally good, but the film is too stagey and didactic.

1295. Kennedy, Adrienne. *People Who Led to My Plays*. New York: Knopf, pp. 70, 89, 104. Recalls reading *NS* in college, and trying later to imagine W's expatriation. "As an exiled writer who lived in France, Wright provided for me an immeasurable personal symbol, a powerful Negro artist" (p. 104). Contains a photograph of W.

1296. Kent, George E. "Blackness and the Adventure of Western Culture," in *Richard Wright*. Ed. Harold Bloom. New York: Chelsea House, pp. 19–36. Reprint of 1969.141.

1297. Kimizuka, Tunichi. "Innocence, Protest, and Myths: A Comparison of Michael Gold and Richard Wright." *Black Studies*, 57 (26 September) 12–17. Compares *BB* and *NS* with *Jews Without Money* in terms of American Society as Seen through children's eyes [T.K., R.B., and Y.H.].

1298. King, Anne Mills, and Sandra Kurtinitis. "Richard Wright," in their *Being and Becoming: An Introduction to Literature*. New York: Random House, p. 1109. Biographical note to accompany "The Man Who Was Almost a Man" (reprinted on pp. 14–22).

1299. Kitamura, Takao. "Langston Hughes and Japan." *The Langston Hughes Review*, 6 (Spring), 8–12. Mentions briefly *BB* and *NS* (p.12).

1300. _____. "Langston Hughes and Japan." *The Langston Hughes Review*, 6 (Spring), 8–12 Mentions briefly W, *NS* and *BB* (p. 12).

1301. Kiuchi, Toru. "Richard Wright's *Uncle Tom's Children*: A Revaluation." *Bulletin of Aichi Shukutoku Junior College*, 26 (10 March), 29–40. Considers *UTC* as a novel rather than a collection of short stories [T.K., R.B., and Y.H.].

1302. Klawans, Stuart. "All of Me." *The Nation*, 244 (24 January), 90–92. Mentions briefly *NS* and W.

1303. Kreyling, Michael. *Figures of the Hero in Southern Narrative*. Baton Rouge: Louisiana State University Press, pp. 185–186. Discusses briefly "Big Boy Leaves Home" in relation to "the narrative tradition of southern heroic."

1304. _____. "A Southern Dissensus?" *The Southern Literary Journal*, 19 (Spring), 102–107. Mentions briefly *BB* (p. 103).

1305. Kroeber, Karl. "Novel." *The Encyclopedia American*. Ed. Bernard S. Cayne. Vol. 20. Danbury, CT: Grolier, pp. 505–511b. Mentions briefly *NS* and *BB* (p. 511b.

1306. Kubitschek, Missy Dehn. "'Tuh de Horizon and Back': The Female Quest in *Their Eyes Were Watching God*," in *Zora Neale Hurston's Their Eyes Were Watching God*. Ed. Harold Bloom. New York: Chelsea House, pp. 19–33.

1307. Kutzinski, Vera M. *Against the American Grain: Myth and History in William Carlos Williams, Joy Wright, and Nicolas Guillen*. Baltimore: The Johns Hopkins University Press, pp. 161, 244, 271. Mentions W in comparison to Nicolás Guillén, quotes from *AH*, and comments on the Howe-Ellison controversy.

1308. _____. "Re-Reading Nicolás Guillén: An Introduction." *Callaloo*, 10 (Spring), 161–167. Mentions W briefly (p. 163).

1309. Lee, A. Robert. "Inside Narratives," in *Richard Wright*. Ed. Harold Bloom. New York: Chelsea House, pp. 109–126.

1310. Lee, Brian. *American Fiction 1865–1940*. London: Longman, pp. 114, 128–131, 262, 292. Sketches W's relation to the Communist Party and discusses *LT* and *NS*. Includes a brief bio-bibliographical note.

1311. Leibowitz, Herbert. "Arise Ye Pris'ners of Starvation: On Richard Wright's *American Hunger*." *Pequod*, 23/24, 250–265. Summarizes *AH*, especially as it treats W's relations with the Communist party. Compares W's prose style quite unfavorably with that of *BB*.

1312. Lenz, Günter H. "History, Folk Tradition, and Fictional Voice: Die schwarze Südstaatenliteratur seit dem Civil Rights Movement." *Gulliver: Deutsche-Englische Jahrbücher*, 21, 93–113. Mentions briefly W (pp. 93, 94, 95) and *NS* (p. 102).

1313. Lesser, Wendy. *The Life Below the Ground*. Boston: Faber and Faber, pp. 102–125, 207. Analyzes "The Man Who Lived Underground" and Ellison's *Invisible Man* in relation to Dostoevsky's *Notes from Underground* and Douglass's *My Bondage and My Freedom* in a chapter entitled "Darkness and Invisibility."

1314. Levine, Paul. "The Intemperate Zone: The Climate of Contemporary American Fiction," in *Der amerikanische Roman nach 1945*. Ed. Arno Heller. Darmstadt: Wissenschaftliche Buchgesellschaft, pp. 73–92.

1315. [Levitt, Morton P.]. "Comparative Studies — Two or More Authors." *Journal of Modern Literature*, 14 (Fall/Winter), 227–236. Lists a dissertation (p. 232) and an article treating W.

1316. _____. "Criticism of Fiction." *Journal of Modern Literature*, 14 (Fall/Winter), 261–269. Lists one dissertation treating W (p. 268).

1317. _____. "Regional, National, and Ethnic Literatures." *Journal of Modern Literature*, 14 (Fall/Winter), 203–227. Lists three dissertations treating W and other writers (pp. 221, 223).

1318. _____. "Richard Wright." *Journal of Modern Literature*, 14 (Fall/Winter), 405. Lists five articles on W in the annual bibliography.

1319. Lewis, R.W.B. "Ellison's Essays," in *Speaking for You: The Vision of Ralph Ellison*. Ed. Kimberly W. Benston. Washington, DC: Howard University Press, pp. 45–48. Reprint of 1964.

1320. Lewis, Vashti Crutcher. "African Tradition in Toni Morrison's *Sula*." *Phylon*, 48 (March), 91–97. Quotes briefly from "Blueprint for Negro Writing" (p. 97).

1321. Lipking, Lawrence. "Arnold Rampersad. *The Life of Langston Hughes. Volume I: 1902–1941; I, Too, Sing America*." *Black American Literature Forum*, 21 (Winter), 467–474. Mentions briefly *NS*.

1322. Litwack, Leon F. "Trouble in Mind: The Bicentennial and the Afro-American Experience." *The Journal of American History*, 74 (September), 315–337. Quotes from *BB* (p. 320) and "How 'Bigger' Was Born" (p. 330).

1323. Longest, George C., et al. "A Checklist of Scholarship on Southern Literature for 1986." *The Mississippi Quarterly*, 40 (Spring), 124–265. Lists twenty-one items on W and cross-references to nineteen other items dealing partially with W.

1324. Lubin, Maurice A. "Langston Hughes and Haiti." *The Langston*

Hughes Review, 6 (Spring), 4–7. Mentions W briefly (p. 6).

1325. _____. "Langston Hughes and Haiti." *The Langston Hughes Review*, 6 (Spring), 4–7. Mentions W briefly (p. 6).

1326. Lyons, Brenda. "Interview with Ntozake Shange." *The Massachusetts Review*, 28 (Winter), 687–696. Shange mentions W briefly (p. 690).

1327. Machor, James L. *Pastoral Cities: Urban Ideals and the Symbolic Landscape of America.* Madison: The University of Wisconsin Press, p. 215. Mentions briefly *NS*.

1328. MacKethan, Lucinda H. "Names to Bear Witness: The Theme and Tradition of Naming in Toni Morrison's *Song of Solomon.*" *The CEA Critic*, 49 (Winter 1986-Summer 1987), 199–207. Comments briefly on naming in *BB* (pp. 200, 201).

1329. Macksey, Eileen M. *1986 MLA International Bibliography of Books and Articles on the Modern Languages and Literatures. Volume I. British Isles, British Commonwealth, English-Caribbean, and American Literatures.* New York: The Modern Language Association of America, pp. 243–244, A 439. Lists twenty-seven items on W.

1330. Madhubuti, Haki R. "negro: an updated definition part 368," in his *Killing Memory, Seeking Ancestors.* Detroit: Lotus Press, pp. 50–51. Poem mentioning briefly the film *NS*.

1331. _____. "Poet: What Ever Happened to Luther?" in *Nommo: A Literary Legacy of Black Chicago (1967–1987).* Ed. Carole A. Parks. Chicago: OBAhouse, p. 236. Reprint of 1987.

1332. _____."Were Corners Made for Black Man to Stand On?" *The Black Scholar*, 18 (May/June), 25–32. Mentions W briefly (p. 32).

1333. Margolies, Edward. "Foreshadowings: *Lawd Today*," in *Richard Wright.* Ed. Harold Bloom. New York: Chelsea House, pp. 7–17. Partial reprint of 1969.167.

1334. Marius, Richard. "Ruling Passions, Falls from Grace." *Harvard Magazine*, 89 (March-April), 55–58. Mentions W briefly as an example of black self-hatred.

1335. Mathis, Steve. "The Black Dream." *The Black Collegian*, 18 (September/October), 26. Discusses *LD* in relation to available opportu-

nities in 1987, hoping that now black dreams can come true.

1336. McDowell, Deborah E. "'The Changing Same': Generational Connections and Black Women Novelists." *New Literary History*, 18 (Winter), 281–302. Mentions W briefly (p. 295).

1337. _____. "Conversations with Dorothy West," in *The Harlem Renaissance Re-examined.* Ed. Victor A. Kramer. New York: AMS Press, pp. 265–282. Includes discussion of W and *New Challenge.*

1338. _____. "Conversations with Dorothy West," in *The Harlem Renaissance Re-examined.* Ed. Victor A. Kramer. New York: AMS Press, pp. 265–282. Includes West's recollections of W, and *Challenge*, and *New Challenge* (pp. 271–272)

1339. McDowell, Margaret B. "The Black Woman as Artist and Critic: Four Versions." *The Kentucky Review*, 7 (Spring), 19–41. Mentions W as a friend of Margaret Walker and the subject of her *The Demonic* [sic] *Genius of Richard Wright* (pp. 21, 36). Also mentions briefly *BB* (p. 30).

1340. McHenry, Susan. "Producer Diane Silver and the Making of 'Native Son.'" *Ms.*, 15 (March), 15–17. Discusses Silver's background, her production of the film, and her dispute with the director, Jerrold Freedman.

1341. McMillen, Neil R. "Black Journalism in Mississippi: The Jim Crow Years." *The Journal of Mississippi History*, 49 (May), 129–138. Mentions that the Jackson *Southern Register* published W's first story (p. 137).

1342. McPherson, James Alan. "Indivisible Man," in *Speaking for You: The Vision of Ralph Ellison.* Ed. Kimberly W. Benston. Washington, DC: Howard University Press, pp. 15–29. Reprint of 1970.119.

1343. Melhem, D.H. *Gwendolyn Brooks: Poetry and the Heroic Voice.* Lexington: The University Press of Kentucky, pp. 16, 18, 20, 54, 245. Comments on W's favorable response to *A Street in Bronzeville* (except for the poem "The Mother") and notes Brook's admiration of *BB*.

1344. Meltzer, Milton. "Walker, Margaret. *Richard Wright: daemonic genius.*" *Library Journal*, 112 (November), 113. Review acknowledging its "fresh information and helpful insights" but criticizing its

pedantry, awkwardness, and repetitiveness.

1345. Merrill, Robert. *Joseph Heller.* Boston: Twayne, pp. 29, 32, 54. Mentions W briefly as a social critic.

1346. Meserve, Walter J. "Drama," in *American Literary Scholarship: An Annual/1985.* Ed. J. Albert Robbins. Durham, NC: Duke University Press, pp. 347–365. Includes comment on Robert E. Fleming's "O'Neill's *The Hairy Ape* as a Source for *Native Son*" (p. 358).

1347. Meyer, Michael, Ellen Darion, and Louise Kawada. "Symbolism," in their *Resources for Teaching the Bedford Introduction to Literature.* New York: St. Martin's Press, pp. 18–21. Contains an analysis of "The Man Who Was Almost a Man" (pp. 19–20).

1348. Middleton, David L. *Toni Morrison: An Annotated Bibliography.* New York: Garland, p. 22. Mentions W briefly.

1349. Miller, J.A. "Joyce, Joyce Ann. Richard Wright's art of tragedy." *Choice*, 24 (April), 1219. Favorable notice of "a new and refreshing interpretation [of *NS*], a welcome revisionist departure from standard readings of Wright's complex work."

1350. Miller, R. Baxter. "Baptized Infidel: Play and Critical Legacy." *Black American Literature Forum*, 21 (Winter), 393–414. Comments on "The Man Who Lived Underground" (p. 411).

1351. Minow, Martha. "Foreword: Justice Engendered." *Harvard Law Review*, 101 (November), 10–95. Mentions briefly *NS* (p. 69).

1352. Minter, David. "The Literature of Modernism: Prose 1912–1940," in *The Harper American Literature.* Eds. Donald McQuade, Robert Atwan, Martha Banta, Justin Kaplan, David Minter, Cecelia Tichi, and Helen Vendler. Vol. 2. New York: Harper & Row, pp. 1087–1110. Mentions W briefly (pp. 1090, 1101, 1105, 1108).

1353. _____. "Richard Wright 1908–1960," in *The Harper American Literature.* Ed. Donald McQuade et al. Vol. 2. New York: Harper & Row, pp. 1461–1464. Biographical-critical headnote to "Long Black Song" and an excerpt from *BB*. Emphasizes W's Mississippi background.

1354. Moore, Jack B. "The Art of *Black Power*: Novelistic or Documentary." *Revue Française d'Etudes Américaines*, 12 (February), 79–91. Argues that *BP* is "better read as a novel than as a realistic travel document or personal memoir" (p. 79). So read, W becomes a literary character searching for identity, a character presented as "alien to the scene he desperately desires to feel allegiance to" (p. 90). W the author "richly dramatizes the disordered world" (p. 90) within himself and in the Gold Coast.

1355. _____. "*Native Son*," in *Reference Guide to American Literature*. Second edition. Ed. D.L. Kirkpatrick. Chicago: St. James Press, p. 668. Critical treatment commenting on social significance, reception, character development, structure, and imagery.

1356. Muckley, Peter. "Joyce, Joyce Ann. *Richard Wright's Art of Tragedy*." *Journal of Modern Literature*, 14 (Fall/Winter), 405. Favorable notice of Joyce's New Critical approach that "reveals the intricate artistry of a work too often dismissed as social realist polemic."

1357. Murphy, John J. "Fiction: 1900 to the 1930s," in *American Literary Scholarship: An Annual/1985*. Ed. J. Albert Robbins. Durham, NC: Duke University Press, pp. 229–251. Includes comment on Charles W. Scruggs's "Finding Out About This Mencken: The Impact of *A Book of Prefaces* on Richard Wright" (p. 248).

1358. Namekata, Hitoshi. "On Richard Wright's 'The Man Who Lived Underground.'" *Poiesis*, 8 (25 July), 3–15. Considers the novella as W's effort to transcend racial issues and to reach a universal vision of life [T.K., and R.B., and Y.H.].

1359. Neal, Larry. "Ellison's Zoot Suit," in *Speaking for You: The Vision of Ralph Ellison*. Ed. Kimberly W. Benston. Washington, DC: Howard University Press, pp. 105–124.

1360. _____. "The Social Background of the Black Arts Movement." *The Black Scholar*, 18 (January/February), 11–22. Mentions W briefly (p. 12).

1361. Newman, Katharine. "An Evening with Hal Bennett: An Interview." *Black American Literature Forum*, 21 (Winter), 357–378. Bennett mentions briefly *NS* and *BB* (p. 359).

1362. Newman, Richard. "'The Only Great Revolutionary Poetry':

African Cultural Nationalism and Negritude," in his *Black Power and Black Religion: Essays and Reviews*. West Cornwall, CT: Locust Hill Press, p. 51. Mentions briefly W's connection to *Présence Africaine*.

1363. Norman, Dorothy. *Encounters: A Memoir*. San Diego: Harcourt Brace Jovanovich, pp. 189–201, 213. Norman gives her impressions of W; comments on his relation to Sartre, de Beauvoir, and Camus; and explains his connection with *Twice a Year*. Most importantly, she quotes extensively from letters to her from W dated 10 June, 1 July, 26 August, 30 September 1946, and 10 September 1947. Includes a reprint of "Operation: Richard Wright" (see 1946.248).

1364. Oates, Stephen B. *William Faulkner: The Man and the Artist*. New York: Harper & Row, p. 285. Notes Faulkner's favorable opinion of *NS*.

1365. Ochillo, Yvonne. "*Black Boy*: Structure as Meaning." *Griot*, 6 (Spring), 49–54. Structuring his work in two parts, before and after his departure to Memphis, W is more concerned in *BB* with the formation of his identity and his artistic imagination than with a complete and chronological factual account. Ochillo stresses W's encounter with racism, a representative experience.

1366. Oitate, Masatsugu. "Richard Wright's Use of Marxist Theory in *Native Son*." *Southern Review*, 2 (December), 69–84. Essay in English on W's application of Marxism to his novel [T.K., R.B., and Y.H.].

1367. Okada, Seiichi. "On Richard Wright: His Hate and Protest." *Saitama University Heron*, 21 (20 March), 23–28. Contends that W's hate and fear toward white people stem from his childhood [T.K., R.B., and Y.H.].

1368. O'Meally, Robert G. "The Rules of Magic: Hemingway as Ellison's 'Ancestor,'" in *Speaking for You: The Vision of Ralph Ellison*. Ed. Kimberly W. Benston. Washington, DC: Howard University Press, pp. 245–271. Contains several brief references to W.

1369. _____. "The Writings of Ralph Ellison," in *Speaking for You: The Vision of Ralph Ellison*. Ed. Kimberly W. Benston. Washington, DC: Howard University Press, pp.

411–419. Bibliography including works on W.

1370. [O'Neal, Jim]. "Wright Acceptance Letter Donated to Williams Library." *The Southern Register*, 5 (Spring), 8. Reports that Julia Wright donated to Williams Library of the University of Mississippi her father's letter of acceptance of the Spingarn Medal. Quotes from W's statement.

1371. Orr, John. *The Making of the Twentieth-Century Novel: Lawrence, Joyce, Faulkner, and Beyond*. New York: St. Martin's Press, pp. 15, 129, 164, 167, 169–173, 188. Applies a "psychocritical" approach to *NS*, emphasizing "Southern identity ... ostensibly suppressed, only to dominate the narrative through its haunting absences" (p. 170). Makes numerous comparisons to Faulkner, especially to themes of incest and miscegenation. Notes also W's influence on Ellison.

1372. Ozer, Jerome S. "*Native Son*," in his *Film Review Annual 1987*. Englewood, NJ: Jerome Ozer, pp. 921–927. Lists production details and cast members of *NS*; reprints reviews by David Sterritt, Kevin Thomas, Roger Ebert, Joseph Gelmis, and J. Hoberman; and lists four other reviews.

1373. Pace, Charles. "Theatre in Black," in *Expressively Black: The Cultural Basis of Ethnic Identity*. Eds. Geneva Gay and Willie E. Baber. New York: Praeger, pp. 164–194. Mentions W briefly (p. 177).

1374. _____. "Theatre in Black," in *Expressively Black: The Cultural Basis of Ethnic Identity*. Eds. Geneva Gay and Willie L. Baber. New York: Praeger, p. 177. Mentions W briefly.

1375. Painter, Nell Irvin. "Black Americans," in *The Encyclopedia Americana*. Ed. Bernard S. Cayne. Vol. 4. Danbury, CT: Grolier, pp. 28A–28p. Reprint of the.

1376. Peeler, David P. *Hope Among Us Yet: Social Criticism and Social Solace in Depression America*. Athens: The University of Georgia Press, pp. 150–157, 169–171, 172, 174, 180–182, 185–190, 269, 279. Discusses, in the context of social fiction in the Depression, "Long Black Song," *NS*, W's relation to Communism, and his belief in community.

1377. Perlin, Albert J., and Peggy Whitman Prenshaw. "A Conversation with Eudora Welty," in *Welty*:

A Life in Literature. Ed. Albert J. Devilin. Jackson: University Press of Mississippi, pp. 3–26.

1378. Perry, Evelyn. "Dorothy ABBOTT, ed.—*Mississippi Writers: Reflections of Childhood and Youth, Volume II: Nonfiction.*" *Revue française d'études américaines*, 32 (April), 331–332. Review mentioning W briefly.

1379. Pettingell, Phoebe. "Writers and Writing: Enigmatic Lives." *The New Leader*, 70 (12–26 January), 15–16. Contains a review of Volume I of Arnold Rampersad's *The Life of Langston Hughes* mentioning W.

1380. Pettis, Joyce. "Modernism in Black Writers." *The Southern Literary Journal*, 20 (Fall), 132–138. Mentions briefly Ellison's "Richard Wright's Blues" (p. 132).

1381. Phillips, Caryl. *The European Tribe.* London: Faber and Faber, pp. 7–8, 28, 41–42. Phillips attributes his determination to become a writer to his first reading of *NS*: "I felt as if an explosion had taken place inside my head" (p. 7). He begins a chapter on "A Pagan Spain" with an epigraph from *PS.* Also mentions W in Paris.

1382. Pinsker, Sanford. "Bashing the Liberals: How Neoconservative Essayists Make Their Point." *The Virginia Quarterly Review*, 63 (Summer), 377–392. Mentions briefly W and *The God That Failed* (p. 390).

1383. _____. "The Great American Book Review." *The Georgia Review*, 41 (Fall), 602–611. Quotes Monroe K. Spears mentioning W briefly in *American Ambitions.*

1384. Prescott, Peter S. "The Dilemma of a Native Son." *Newsweek*, 110 (14 December), 86. Obituary of James Baldwin mentioning briefly the quarrel with W.

1385. Rabinowitz, Peter J. *Before Reading: Narrative Conventions and the Politics of Interpretation.* Ithaca: Cornell University Press, pp. 80–82, 89, 122, 124, 128. Quotes and comments on a passage from "Down by the Riverside" illustrating shifts in narrative voice, style, and tense (pp. 80–82). Mentions *UTC* elsewhere (pp. 89, 122). Also comments on *NS* (pp. 124, 128).

1386. Rampersad, Arnold. "Future Scholarly Projects on Langston Hughes." *Black American Literature Forum*, 21 (Fall), 305–316. Mentions favorably the scholarship on W (p. 306).

1387. _____. "*Richard Wright's Art of Tragedy.* By Joyce Ann Joyce." *American Literature*, 59 (December), 671–672. Favorable review of "a challenging and assertive piece of criticism." Joyce perceives *NS* as a tragedy and Bigger as a tragic hero. Praises Joyce especially on W's language.

1388. Ravitch, Diane, and Chester E. Finn, Jr. *What Do Our 17-Year-Olds Know? A Report on the First National Assessment of History and Literature.* New York: Harper, pp. 104, 108, 116–119. Reports that to the question, "Who wrote *Native Son*, a novel of black life in Chicago, and *Black Boy*, which is highly autobiographical?" 32.3% answered correctly, but 34.2% of the girls and 50.2% of the blacks did so.

1389. Reed, Ishmael. "'Stephen Spielberg Plays Howard Beach' by Ishmael Reed," in "The Black Person in Art: How Should S/he Be Portrayed?" Ed. Henry Louis Gates, Jr. *Black American Literature Forum*, 21 (Spring-Summer), 3–24. Mentions briefly the film *NS* (p. 10).

1390. Reilly, John M. "Black Literature," in *American Literary Scholarship: An Annual/1985.* Ed. J. Albert Robbins. Durham, NC: Duke University Press, pp. 367–414. Includes comment on work on W by Houston Baker, Lee Greene, Clyde Taylor, Michel Fabre, Blyden Jackson, George Goodin, Robert E. Fleming, Lynn Beach Sadler, Keith Gilyard, Yoshinobu Hakutani, John O. Hodges, Timothy Dow Adams, Janice Thaddeus, and Linda Peterson. "The outstanding publishing event in Wright studies for this year is the appearance of Michel Fabre's *The World of Richard Wright.*"

1391. _____. "Jean Toomer," in *Fifty Southern Writers After 1900: A Bio-Bibliographical Sourcebook.* Eds. Joseph M. Flora and Robert Bain. Westport, CT: Greenwood Press, pp. 479–490. Mentions W briefly (p. 487).

1392. _____. "The Testament of Ralph Ellison," in *Speaking for You: The Vision of Ralph Ellison.* Ed. Kimberly W. Benston. Washington, DC: Howard University Press, pp. 49–62. Mentions W briefly (pp. 50, 58).

1393. _____. "Thinking History in *The Man Who Cried I Am.*" *Black American Literature Forum*, 21 (Spring-Summer), 25–42. Summa-rizes the scholarship on W's response to naturalism in *NS* (pp. 27–29) and analyzes the character Harry Ames, based on W, in the Williams novel.

1394. _____. "Wright, Richard (Nathaniel)," in *Reference Guide to American Literature.* Second edition. Ed. D.L. Kirkpatrick. Chicago: St. James Press, pp. 598–599. Reprint of 1979.213.

1395. Robins, Natalie. "Hoover and American Lit: The Defiling of Writers." *The Nation*, 245 (10 October), 367–370, 372. Lists W as one of 136 writers whose F.B.I. files were released to Robins.

1396. Rodgers, Carolyn M. "Black Poetry—Where It's At," in *Nommo: A Literary Legacy of Black Chicago (1967–1987).* Ed. Carole A. Parks. Chicago: OBAhouse, pp. 28–37. Reprint of 1969.211.

1397. Roemer, Marjorie Godlin. "Which Reader's Response?" *College English*, 49 (December), 911–921. Arguing for an expanded notion of reader response to reflect actual student diversity, Roemer comments at length on a classroom discussion and student paper on *BB.*

1398. Rogal, Samuel J. *A Chronological Outline of American Literature.* Westport, CT: Greenwood Press, pp. 179, 263, 270, 274, 286, 299, 307, 309, 314, 316, 319, 323, 329, 335, 377. Lists W's birth and death as well as *UTC, NS, TMBV, BB, The God That Failed, O, BP, CC, PS, LD, EM, LT,* and *AH.*

1399. Roper, John Herbert. *C. Vann Woodward, Southerner.* Athens: The University of Georgia Press, p. 93. Mentions briefly W's visit to Chapel Hill, North Carolina.

1400. Rosenberg, Ruth. "Seeds in Hard Ground: Black Girlhood in *The Bluest Eye.*" *Black American Literature Forum*, 21 (Winter), 435–445. Contrasts treatment of mother-child relationships in *The Bluest Eye* and *BB* (pp. 438–439).

1401. Rowell, Charles H., Elizabeth Alexander, Ursula Appelt, Herman Beavers, Kimberly Chambers, Barbara Green, Helen Lock, Melissa Pope, Doris Smith, and Cheryl Wall. "Studies in Afro-American Literature: An Annual Annotated Bibliography, 1986." *Callaloo*, 10 (Fall), 605–655. Lists twenty-three items on W with cross-references to twelve others.

1402. Rubeo, Ugo. "Langston Hughes's Critical Recognition in Italy." *The Langston Hughes Review*, 6 (Spring), 13–19. Discusses W's favorable reception in Italy during the postwar years (pp. 13–14). Mentions *BB, NS,* and *UTC*.

1403. _____. "Langston Hughes's Critical Recognition in Italy." *The Langston Hughes Review*, 6 (Spring), 13–19. Mentions briefly W, *NS,* and *BB* (p. 12).

1404. _____. *Mal d'America: da mito a realtà*. Rome: Editori Riuniti, p. 111. In an interview, Fernanda Pivano mentions W briefly.

1405. Ruderman, Judith. "Afterward: William Styron in the Kingdom of the Jews," in her *William Styron*. New York: Ungar, pp. 129–139. Mentions W as an exception to the usual anti–Semitism of the modern American novel (p. 131).

1406. Ruoff, James. "Katherine Anne Porter Comes to Kansas," in *Katherine Anne Porter: Conversations*. Ed. Joan Givner. Jackson: University Press of Mississippi, pp. 61–68.

1407. _____. "Katherine Ann Porter Comes to Kansas." in *Katherine Anne Porter: Conversations*. Jackson: University Press of Mississippi, pp. 61–68.

1408. Ryan, F.L. "*American Fiction, 1914–1945*, ed. and introd. by Harold Bloom." *Choice*, 25 (October), 304. Mentions W briefly.

1409. Salaam, Kalamu ya. "Making the Most of the Middle Passage," in *Nommo: A Literary Legacy of Black Chicago (1967–1987*. Ed. Carole A. Parks. Chicago: OBAhouse, pp. 306–307. Mentions briefly the W-Baldwin quarrel.

1410. Salzman, Jack, ed. *Prospects: An Annual of American Cultural Studies*. Volume 10 Bibliography. New York: Cambridge University Press, pp. 224, 228, 231, 235. Contains entries mentioning W for books by Michael Cooke, Theodore L. Gross, Trudier Harris, and Lewis A. Lawson, and for an article by R. Baxter Miller.

1411. Sato, Kazuo. "Richard Wright's Haiku," in his *From Japanese Haiku to English Haiku: The Reception of Haiku in America and Britain*. Tokyo: Nanundo, pp. 156–159. Introduction to the influence of Japanese culture on W's haiku [T.K., R.B., and Y.H.].

1412. Saunders, James Robert.

"The Social Significance of Wright's Bigger Thomas." *College Literature*, 14 (Winter), 32–37. Emphasizes the social import of *NS* and adduces classroom experience to demonstrate its universal appeal.

1413. Schechner, Mark, *After the Revolution: Studies in the Contemporary Jewish American Imagination*. Bloomington: Indiana University Press, pp. 28, 40. Mentions briefly W, *NS, BB,* and *O*.

1414. Scruggs, Charles. "H.L. Mencken and James Weldon Johnson: Two Men Who Helped Shape a Renaissance," in *Critical Essays on H.L. Mencken*. Ed. Douglas C. Stenerson. Boston: G.K. Hall, pp. 186–203. First paragraph treats W's discovery of Mencken.

1415. Shulman, Robert. *Social Criticism and Nineteenth-Century American Fictions*. Columbia: University of Missouri Press, p. 53. Includes a quotation on lynching from *BB*.

1416. Silk, John. "Racist and Anti-Racist Ideology in the Films of the American South," in *Race and Racism: Essays in Social Geography*. Ed. Peter Jackson. London: Allen & Unwin, pp. 326–344. Mentions briefly W's racism.

1417. Singh, Amritjit. "Beyond the Mountain: Langston Hughes on Race/Class and Art." *The Langston Hughes Review*, 6 (Spring), 37–43. Mentions briefly (p. 40).

1418. Skerrett, Joseph T., Jr. "The Wright Interpretation: Ralph Ellison and the Anxiety of Influence," in *Speaking for You: The Vision of Ralph Ellison*. Ed. Kimberly W. Benston. Washington, DC: Howard University Press, pp. 217–230.

1419. Smith, Curtis C. "Werner Sollors' *Beyond Ethnicity* and Afro-American Literature." *MELUS*, 14 (Summer), 65–71. Comments on the book's treatment of W and *NS* (pp. 65–66, 69).

1420. Smith, Valerie. *Self-Discovery and Authority in Afro-American Narrative*. Cambridge, MA: Harvard University Press, pp. 2, 65–87, 89, 161–162. W's alienated autobiographical persona is projected in most of the fictional protagonists. Like their creator, they learn to overcome their isolation and gain control of their lives by telling their stories. Smith comments on *LT, O,* and *LD* and analyzes *BB* and, at greater length, *NS*. Partially reprinted: 1993.

1421. [Snell, Susan]. "Books." *The Society for the Study of Southern Literature News-Letter*, 20 (April), 12–24. Lists Joyce Ann Joyce's *Richard Wright's Art of Tragedy* (p. 17).

1422. _____. "Executive Council Nominees." *The Society for the Study of Southern Literature News-Letter*, 20 (November), 1–2. Notes Thadious Davis's work on W.

1423. _____. "Black Studies." *The Society for the Study of Southern Literature News-Letter*, 20 (November), 12–14. Mentions coverage of W in Maryemma Graham's *The Afro-American Novel*.

1424. _____. "Recent Conferences." *The Society for the Study of Southern Literature News-Letter*, 20 (April), 7–9. Notes that George Lamming gave a lecture on "Reshaping the Imagination: Wright, Africa, and the African Diaspora" on a visit to the University of Mississippi, 26–27 April.

1425. _____. "Books." *S.S.S.L.: The News-Letter of the Society for the Study of Southern Literature*, 19 (April 1986), 11–20. Notes that *Modern Southern Reader*, edited by Ben Forkner and Patrick Samway, includes W (p. 11).

1426. Solomon, Barbara Probst. "The Spanish Scene." *The Review of Contemporary Fiction*, 7 (Spring), 150–153. Mentions W, alluding briefly to *PS*.

1427. Southern, David W. *Gunnar Myrdal and Black-White Relations: The Use and Abuse of an American Dilemma, 1944–1969*. Baton Rouge: Louisiana State University Press, pp. 94, 107, 227. Mentions W briefly.

1428. Spears, Monroe K. *American Ambitions: Selected Essays on Literary and Cultural Themes*. Baltimore: The Johns Hopkins University Press, p. 249. Mentions W briefly in an essay on Black English.

1429. _____. "The History of Southern Literature. Ed. Louis D. Rubin Jr., and Others." *The Journal of Southern History*, 53 (February), pp. 91–93. Mentions W briefly (p. 93).

1430. Spillers, Hortense. "Ellison's 'Usable Past': Toward a Theory of Myth," in *Speaking for You: The Vision of Ralph Ellison*. Ed. Kimberly W. Benston. Washington, DC: Howard University Press, pp. 144–158.

1431. Stein, Judith. "*Claude McKay: Rebel Sojourner in the Harlem*

Renaissance: A Biography. By Wayne F. Cooper." *The Journal of American History,* 74 (December), 1083–1084. Mentions W briefly.

1432. Stepto, Robert B. "After the 1960's: The Boom in Afro-American Fiction," in *Contemporary American Fiction.* Eds. Malcolm Bradbury and Sigmund Ro. London: Edward Arnold, pp. 89–104. Contrasts Toni Morrison's treatment of black women characters to W's in *NS* and *BB* (p. 91). Also contrasts Ernest Gaines to W.

1433. _____. "I Thought I Knew These People: Richard Wright and the Afro-American Literary Tradition," in *American Fiction 1914 to 1945.* Ed. Harold Bloom. New York: Chelsea House, pp. 389–403.

1434. _____. "I Thought I Knew These People: Wright and the Afro-American Literary Tradition," in *Richard Wright.* Ed. Harold Bloom. New York: Chelsea House, pp. 57–74. Reprint of 1977.294.

1435. _____. "Literacy and Ascent: *Black Boy,*" in *Richard Wright.* Ed. Harold Bloom. New York: Chelsea House, pp. 75–107. Partial reprint of 1979.243.

1436. _____. "Literacy and Hibernation: Ralph Ellison's *Invisible Man,*" in *Speaking for You: The Vision of Ralph Ellison.* Ed. Kimberly W. Benston. Washington, DC: Howard University Press, pp. 360–385.

1437. Sundquist, Eric J. "Faulkner, Race, and the Forms of American Fiction," in *Faulkner and Race: Faulkner and Yoknapatawpha, 1986.* Eds. Doreen Fowler and Ann J. Abadie. Jackson: University Press of Mississippi, pp. 1–34. Includes a discussion of *NS* (pp. 21–25) in relation to *Light in August* and other treatments of the black murderer. Mentions also *UTC, LD,* and *WML.*

1438. Tamada, Yoshiyuki. "Richard Wright and Africa," in *Noah's Ark: Toward the 21st Century.* Ed. Black Studies Association in Japan. Yokahama: Mondosha, pp. 147–170. Interprets W's reaction to the British government and to Kwame Nkrumah through *WML* and *BP.* Notes that W's African writings were not well received in Africa [T.K., R.B., and Y.H.].

1439. _____. "A Crinum Bloomed Behind a Hydrangea." *English and American Literature Notebook,* 25 (23 November), 123–124. Brief essay on a conversation with Margaret

Walker at the W symposium at the University of Mississippi in 1985 [T.K., R.B., and Y.H.].

1440. Tanner, Laura E. "Uncovering the Magical Disguise of Language: The Narrative Presence in Richard Wright's *Native Son.*" *Texas Studies in Literature and Language,* 29 (Winter), 412–431. Argues for a sharp distinction between Bigger and the narrative voice in the novel, which constantly moves from "the material substance of [Bigger's] actions into a symbolic universe in which they are reinscribed within the narrator's own language game" (p. 414). In Book 3 Max's voice becomes identical to the narrative voice. The narrative voice is unreliable, "white," at times almost racist.

1441. Taylor, Walter. "Faulkner's *Reivers*: How to Change the Joke Without Slipping the Yoke," in *Faulkner and Race: Faulkner and Yoknapatawpha, 1986.* Eds. Doreen Fowler and Ann J. Abadie. Jackson: University Press of Mississippi, pp. 111–129. Quotes Faulkner on W (p. 129, note 7).

1442. Thompson, James J., Jr. "Genuine Gifts." *The World & I,* 2 (April), 431–434. Review of Arnold Rampersad's biography of Langston Hughes mentioning W.

1443. Thelwell, Michael. *Duties, Pleasures, Conflicts: Essays in Struggle.* Amherst: The University of Massachusetts Press, pp. xxiii, xiv. Mentions briefly W and "Bright and Morning Star" and mentions W as a product of "the social ferment of the thirties."

1444. Toll, William. "Pluralism and Moral Force in the Black-Jewish Dialogue." *American Jewish History,* 77 (September), 87–105. Quotes from *WML* on cultural disadvantages of "traditional 'colored' cultures" (p. 94).

1445. Traylor, Eleanor W. "'Bolder Measures Crashing Through': Margaret Walker's Poem of the Century." *Callaloo,* 10 (Fall), 570–595. Mentions W briefly (pp. 571, 572, 592).

1446. Turner, Darwin T. "Introduction." *The Black Scholar,* 18 (January/February), front matter. Mentions briefly the 1971 conference on W at the University of Iowa.

1447. _____. "Retrospective of a Renaissance." *The Black Scholar,* 18 (January/February), 2–10. Mentions briefly *BP* (p. 7).

1448. _____. "Introduction." *The Black Scholar,* 18 (January/February), 1. Mentions briefly the University of Iowa conference on W.

1449. Twombly, Robert C. "Harlem Renaissance," in *Collier's Encyclopedia.* Ed. William D. Halsey. New York: Macmillan, vol. 11, pp. 654–655. Notes that W rejected the optimism of the Harlem Renaissance.

1450. Uruburu, Paula M. *The Gruesome Doorway: An Analysis of the American Grotesque.* New York: Peter Lang, 1987, p. 77. Mentions W briefly.

1451. Van Vechten, Carl. *Letters of Carl Van Vechten.* Ed. Bruce Kellner. New Haven: Yale University Press, pp. 196, 213, 220. Writing to Blanche Knopf, Van Vechten says that W "could write a humdinger" on the Negro question (c. 16 August 1943). Mentions *BB* early in 1945 and W on nuclear disaster late in the same year.

1452. Vernoff, Edward, and Rima Shore. "Wright, Richard," in their *The International Dictionary of 20th Century Biography.* New York: New American Library, p. 766. Biographical sketch mentioning *UTC, NS, BB, TMBV,* and *AH* as well as secondary works by Michel Fabre, Constance Webb, and Robert Felgar.

1453. Wald, Alan M. *The New York Intellectuals.* Chapel Hill: The University of North Carolina Press, p. 236. Contains a paragraph on *NS,* to which Lionel Trilling's story "The Other Margaret" "may be partially intended as a response."

1454. _____. "Theorizing Cultural Difference: A Critique of the 'Ethnicity School.'" *MELUS,* 14 (Summer), 21–33. Mentions W briefly (p. 21).

1455. _____. "Theorizing Cultural Difference: A Critique of the 'Ethnicity School.'" *MELUS,* 14 (Summer), 21–33. Mentions W briefly (p. 21).

1456. Walker, Marshall. "Chronology," in *Reference Guide to American Literature.* Second edition. Ed. D.L. Kirkpatrick. Chicago: St. James Press, pp. 707–722. Lists *NS* and *BB.*

1457. Walker, Warren S. "Bibliography." *Studies in Short Fiction,* 24 (Summer), 369. Lists two items on W.

1458. Ward, Jerry W., Jr. "The

Black Person in Art: How Should S/he Be Portrayed? (Part II)." *Black American Literature Forum*, 21 (Fall), 322–324. Mentions briefly W and *NS*.

1459. Washington, Mary Helen. "Anna Julia Cooper: The Black Feminist Voice." *Legacy*, 4 (Fall), 3–15. Refers to Cooper's criticism of the black critics afraid to criticize *NS* because of white support of the novel.

1460. _____, ed. *Invented Lives: Narratives of Black Women 1860–1960*. New York: Doubleday, pp. xvi, xix, xx, xxi, 80, 297, 298–299. Comments on W's review of *Their Eyes Were Watching God* and his relation to Ann Petry, and mentions W elsewhere.

1461. _____. "'The Darkened Eye Restored': Notes Toward a Literary History of Black Women," in her *Invented Lives: Narratives of Black Women 1860–1960*. Garden City, NY: Anchor/Doubleday, pp. xv–xxxi. Mentions W briefly (pp. xvi, xxix).

1462. Waters, Enoch P. *American Diary: A Personal History of the Black Press*. Chicago: Path Press, pp. 299–300. Relates a discussion Waters had with W concerning his expatriation.

1463. Waxman, Barbara Frey. "Canonicity and Black American Literature: A Feminist View." *MELUS*, 14 (Summer), 87–93. Mentions W's "forthright protesting and witnessing," especially in *BB* (p. 89).

1464. Webb, Suzanne. "Groping Toward That Invisible Light. Richard Wright," in her *The Resourceful Writer*. San Diego: Harcourt Brace Jovanovich, p. 225. Biographical headnote to an excerpt from *Black Boy*. Reprinted: 1990.

1465. _____. "Responding to the Whole Essay, Analyzing the Elements, Suggestions for Writing," in her *The Resourceful Writer*. San Diego: Harcourt Brace Jovanovich, pp. 235–237. Study aids to an excerpt from *Black Boy*.

1466. Werner, Craig. "*Blues, Ideology, and Afro-American Literature: A Vernacular Theory*, by Houston Baker." *The Mississippi Quarterly*, 40 (Winter), 46–48. Mentions briefly "The Man Who Lived Underground" and "Blueprint for Negro Writing."

1467. _____. "Minstrel Nightmares: Black Dreams of Faulkner's Dreams of Blacks," in *Faulkner and Race: Faulkner and Yoknapatawpha, 1986*. Eds. Doreen Fowler and Ann J. Abadie. Jackson: University Press of Mississippi, pp. 35–56. Compares Charlie Biggs of Ernest Gaines's *A Gathering of Old Men* to Big Boy and Bigger Thomas (p. 44) and elsewhere mentions W (pp. 41–42) and "Fire and Cloud" (p. 52).

1468. West, Hollie. "Through a Writer's Eyes," in *Speaking for You: The Vision of Ralph Ellison*. Ed. Kimberly W. Benston. Washington, DC: Howard University Press, pp. 91–94. Reprint of 1973.303.

1469. Westling, Louise. "The Loving Observer of *One Time, One Place*," in *Welty: A Life in Literature*. Ed. Albert J. Devlin. Jackson: University Press of Mississippi, pp. 168–187.

1470. Whitaker, Charles. "Oprah Winfrey: The Most Talked-About TV Show Host." *Ebony*, 42 (March), 38–40, 42, 44. Contains a photograph with Winfrey as Mrs. Thomas in the second film version of *NS*.

1471. Whitaker, Thomas R. "Speaking for Invisibility," in *Speaking for You: The Vision of Ralph Ellison*. Ed. Kimberly W. Benston. Washington, DC: Howard University Press, pp. 386–403. Quotes from *TMBV* (p. 390) and mentions briefly "The Man Who Lived Underground" (p. 398).

1472. White, John. "Richard A. Long & Eugenia W. Collier (eds.), *Afro-American Writing: An Anthology of Prose and Poetry*; Nellie Y. McKay, *Jean Toomer, Artist: A Study of His Literary Life and Work, 1894–1936*." *Journal of American Studies*, 21 (April), 153–154. Review noting that W is absent from the Long-Collier anthology because of the "executors' wishes."

1473. _____. "Richard A. Long & Eugenia W. Collier (eds.) *Afro-American Writing: An Anthology of Prose and Poetry* (second and enlarged edition). *Journal of American Studies*, 21 (April 1987), 153–154. Mentions W briefly.

1474. Whitfield, Stephen J. "A Critique of Leonard Dinnerstein's 'The Origins of Black Anti-Semitism in America.'" *American Jewish Archives*, 39 (November), 193–198. Mentions W briefly (p. 193).

1475. Wiehe, R.E. "The South." *Abstracts of English Studies*, 30 (June), 304. Abstract of an article by Fred Hobson treating W and others.

1476. Wiener, Harvey S., and Nora Eisenberg. "Meaning and Idea; Language, Form, Structure; Ideas for Writing," in their *Great Writing: A Reader for Writers*. New York: McGraw-Hill, pp. 75–76. Study questions for the first chapter of *NS*.

1477. _____. "Richard Wright, *Native Son*, Chapter 1," in their *Great Writing: A Reader for Writers*. New York: McGraw-Hill, p. 68. Biographical-critical headnote.

1478. Williams, Pontheolla T. *Robert Hayden: A Critical Analysis of His Poetry*. Urbana: University of Illinois Press, pp. 17–18, 118, 219. Notes that Hayden "was influenced by [W's] politics and literary style," especially in *UTC* (pp. 17–18). Mentions briefly *BB*, *NS*, and "The Man Who Lived Underground."

1479. Wolf, Howard. "Of Manhattan the Son: Autobiography as a Creative Form of American Writing." *Indian Journal of American Studies*, 17 (Winter/Summer), 45–51. Mentions briefly *BB* (pp. 50, 51).

1480. Wolfe, Charles. "Direct Address and the Social Documentary Photograph: 'Annie Mae Gudger' as Negative Subject." *Wide Angle*, 9 (Winter), 59–70. Mentions briefly *TMBV* (p. 64).

1481. Woll, Allen L., and Randall M. Miller. *Ethnic and Racial Images in American Film and Television: Historical Essays and Bibliography*. New York: Garland, pp. 135, 146. Lists two items on W.

1482. Wright, John. "Shadowing Ellison," in *Speaking for You: The Vision of Ralph Ellison*. Ed. Kimberly W. Benston. Washington, DC: Howard University Press, pp. 63–88. Reprint of 1980.269.

1483. Yamauchi, Tadashi. "Richard Wright's Alienated Negro Heroes." *Bulletin of Chubu Junior College for Women*, 17 (22 December), 19–31. Surveys the relationship between Bigger, Gus, and others by way of examining why he murders Bessie.

1484. Yarborough, Richard. "Afterword," in *Blood on the Forge*. By William Attaway. New York: Monthly Review Press, pp. 295–312. Notes Attaway's acquaintance with W, comments on and quotes from *TMBV*, and mentions *UTC* and *NS*.

1485. _____. "Selected Bibliography," in *Blood on the Forge*. By William Attaway. New York: Monthly Review Press, pp. 313–315. Lists *TMBV*.

1988

1486. Aaron, Daniel. "Literary Scenes and Literary Movements," in *Columbia Literary History of the United States*. Ed. Emory Elliott. New York: Columbia University Press, pp. 733–757. Notes that W was on the Federal Writers' Project (p. 752).

1487. Abbott, Dorothy, "Richard Wright," in her *Mississippi Writers: Reflections of Childhood and Youth*. Jackson: University Press of Mississippi, Vol. 3: Poetry, p. 42. Biographical sketch.

1488. Abcarian, Richard, and Marvin Klotz. *Instructor's Manual to Accompany Literature: The Human Experience*. New York: St. Martin's Press, pp. 63–64. Contains two analytical paragraphs on "Between the World and Me."

1489. Adams, Anne. "Straining to Make Out the Words to the 'Lied': The German Reception of Toni Morrison," in *Critical Essays on Toni Morrison*. Ed. Nellie Y. McKay. Boston: G.K. Hall, pp. 190–214 Mentions W briefly (p. 202).

1490. Adams, Katherine H., and John L. Adams. "Questions," in their *The Accomplished Writer: Observing, Judging, Reflecting*. Englewood Cliffs, NJ: Prentice-Hall, p. 220. Seven study questions to accompany "The Ethics of Living Jim Crow."

1491. Alexander, Sandra Carlton. "Ann Petry," in *Afro-American Writers, 1940–1955*. Eds. Trudier Harris and Thadious M. Davis. Detroit: Gale, pp. 140–147. Mentions W briefly (p. 143).

1492. Allen, Samuel. "[Review of *Song of Solomon*]," in *Critical Essays on Toni Morrison*. Ed. Nellie Y. McKay. Boston: G.K. Hall, pp. 30–32. Mentions W briefly.

1493. Allen, William Rodney. "Richard Wright, 'The Man Who Was Almost a Man,'" in his *Instructor's Guide to Accompany the Heath Introduction to Literature, Third Edition*. Lexington, MA: D.C. Heath, p. 27. Two discussion questions and answers.

1494. Als, Hilton. "Fathers and Sons." *The Village Voice* (12 January 1988), pp. 35, 39. Quotes from "Alas, Poor Richard" and applies James Baldwin's remarks on W to Baldwin himself.

1495. Anderson, James D. *The Education of Blacks in the South, 1860–1935*. Chapel Hill: University of North Carolina Press, pp. 149, 283, 285. Quotes from *TMBV*.

1496. Andrews, William L. "In Search of a Common Identity: The Self and the South in Four Mississippi Autobiographies." *The Southern Review*, 24 (Winter), 47–64. Compares *BB*, William Alexander Percy's *Lanterns on the Levee*, Willie Morris's *North Toward Home*, and Anne Moody's *Coming of Age in Mississippi*. All four autobiographers depict an effort to achieve personal coherence, but caste impedes them.

1497. Angelou, Maya, and Rosa Guy. "Maya Angelou Talking with Rosa Guy," in *Writing Lives: Conversations Between Women Writers*. Ed. Mary Chamberlain. London: Virago Press, pp. 1–23. Guy expresses admiration for W (p. 8).

1498. _____. "Maya Angelou Talking with Rosa Guy," in *Writing Lives: Conversations Between Women Writers*. Ed. Mary Chamberlain. London: Virago Press, pp. 1–23. Guy acknowledges the influence and importance of W (pp. 8–9).

1499. Anon. *Arts & Humanities Citation Index 1987*. Vol. 2. Philadelphia: Institute for Scientific Information, pp. 11026–11027. Lists forty-six items s.v. WRIGHT R, not all on W.

1500. Anon. *Bibliographic Guide to Black Studies: 1988*. Boston: G.K. Hall, pp. 385–386. Lists three primary and three secondary items concerning W in the New York Public Library, supplementing the *Dictionary Catalog of the Schomburg Collection of Negro Literature and History*.

1501. Anon. "The Black Scholar Publishers Listing of Black Interest Books." *The Black Scholar*, 19 (November/December), 45–57. Contains notices of paperback editions of the *TMBV* and *EM* (p. 52)

1502. Anon. "Contributors." *Modern Fiction Studies*, 34 (Spring), 2. The note on Craig Werner mentions W briefly.

1503. Anon. *Howard University Press Books 1988*. Washington: Howard University Press, pp. 2, 20, 21. Mentions W briefly.

1504. Anon. *Index to Black Periodicals: 1986*. Boston: G.K. Hall, pp. 208–209. Lists twelve items on W.

1505. Anon. *Index to Black Periodicals: 1985*. Boston: G.K. Hall, p. 209. Lists five items on W.

1506. Anon. *Index to Black Periodicals: 1984*. Boston: G.K. Hall, p. 180. Lists four items on W.

1507. Anon. *Index to Black Periodicals: 1987*. Boston: G.K. Hall, pp. 152–153. Lists two items on W.

1508. Anon. "Iowa." *The Black Scholar*, 19 (January/February), 8. Contains a publisher's notice of Joyce Ann Joyce's *Richard Wright's Art of Tragedy*.

1509. Anon. *Index to Black Periodicals: 1985*. Boston: G.K. Hall, p. 209. Lists five items on W.

1510. Anon. "Spring Titles from Thunder's Mouth Press." *The Black Scholar*, 19 (Fall), 113. Contain's a brief notice of *TMBV*.

1511. Anon. "*The Long Dream*. Richard Wright." *Literature and Language*. New York: Harper & Row, p. 3. Publisher's announcement of a paperback edition.

1512. Anon. "Other Books by Richard Wright." in *Literature and Language*. New York: Harper & Row, p. 6. Publisher's listing of paperback editions of *AH*, *BB*, *O*, and *UTC*.

1513. Anon. "*Richard Wright: Daemonic Genius*, Margaret Walker." *Publishers Weekly*, 234 (14 October), 54. Favorable notice claiming that "this excellent, flesh-and-blood portrait gets closer to the inner man than any previous volume."

1514. Anon. "Spingarn Medal," in *Notable Americans: What They Did, from 1620 to the Present*, ed. Linda S. Hubbard. Detroit: Gale Research, 1988, p. 561. Lists W as the 1941 recipient.

1515. Anon. "Spingarn Medal," in *Notable Americans: What They Did, from 1620 to the Present*, ed Linda S. Hubbard. Detroit: Gale Research, p. 561. Lists W as the 1941 recipient.

1516. Anon. "Spring Titles from Thunder's Mouth Press." *Black American Literature Forum*, 22 (Summer), 226. Contains an announcement of the paperback edition of *TMBV*.

1517. Anon. "Spring Titles from Thunder's Mouth Press." *The Black Scholar*, 19 (July–October), 113. Contains a publisher's notice of the paperback edition of *TMBV*.

1518. Anon. "Spring Titles from Thunder's Mouth Press." *The Nation*, 246 (28 May), 749. Contains a publisher's notice of the paperback edition of *TMBV*.

1519. Anon. "Valerie Smith on Richard Wright," in *Eminent Scholars/Teachers Video Lecture Series*. Detroit: Omnigraphics, p. 11. Publisher's notice.

1520. Anon. "Wright R," in *Social Sciences Citation Index: 1987 Annual*. Part 2. Philadelphia: Institute for Scientific Information, p. 15967. Lists fifty items, most of them not on W.

1521. Aswell, Edward C. *In the Shadow of the Giant, Thomas Wolfe: Correspondence of Edward C. Aswell and Elizabeth Nowell, 1949–1958*. Eds. Mary Aswell Doll and Clara Stites. Athens: Ohio University Press, p. xviii. Mentions W briefly.

1522. Atkinson, Michael. "Richard Wright's 'Big Boy Leaves Home' and a Tale from Ovid: A Metamorphosis Transformed," in *Richard Wright: Myths and Realities*. Ed. C. James Trotman. New York: Garland, pp. 43–57. Reprint of 1987.34.

1523. Awazu, Mashahiro. "A Symbol of Color in Wright's Novels." Okayamo *University Persica*, 15 (31 March), 75–83. Considers W's color symbolism of white symbolizing silent protest against white society [T.K., R.B., and Y.H.].

1524. Awkward, Michael. "Race, Gender, and the Politics of Reading." *Black American Literature Forum*, 22 (Spring), 5–27. Mentions W briefly (p. 8).

1525. _____. "Roadblocks and Relatives: Critical Revision in Toni Morrison's *The Bluest Eye*," in *Critical Essays on Toni Morrison*. Ed. Nellie Y. McKay. Boston: G.K. Hall,

pp. 57–68. Discusses Morrison's "refigurations of Baldwin's discussion of Wright in 'Many Thousands Gone'..." (p. 58).

1526. Baker, Houston A., Jr. *Afro-American Poetics: Revisions of Harlem and the Black Aesthetic*. Madison: The University of Wisconsin Press, pp. 52, 116, 149, 178. Quotes from *BB* in the concluding chapter.

1527. _____. "The Embattled Craftsman: An Essay on James Baldwin," in *Critical Essays on James Baldwin*. Eds. Fred L. Standley and Nancy V. Burt. Boston: G.K. Hall, pp. 62–77. Reprint of 1977.

1528. Baldwin, James. "From 'Many Thousands Gone,'" in *Twentieth-Century American Literature*. Ed. Harold Bloom. Vol. 7. New York: Chelsea House, pp. 4498–4501. Partial reprint of 1951.129.

1529. Barrax, Gerald. "Uniforms." *Callaloo*, 11 (Summer), 451–452. Poem with epigraph from *TMBV*.

1530. Battle, Thomas C. "The Moorland-Spingarn Research Center," in *Afro-American Writers, 1940–1955*. Eds. Trudier Harris and Thadious M. Davis. Detroit: Gale, pp. 237–242. Mentions W briefly (p. 242).

1531. Baughman, Ronald. "Finales: How American Writers Died; Where They're Buried; Epitaphs and Last Words," in *American Literary Almanac from 1608 to the Present*. Ed. Karen L. Rood. New York: Facts on File, pp. 335–375. Sketches circumstances of W's death (p. 350).

1532. Bellei, Sérgio Luiz Prado. "American Culture in Brazil: The Search for Strategies for Reading." *American Studies International*, 26 (October), 3–9 Comments on W's discussion of the "frog perspective" and quotes from *WML* (p. 7).

1533. Bennett, Joy, and Gabriella Hochmann, *Simone de Beauvoir: An Annotated Bibliography*. New York: Garland, p. 43. Contains an entry on 1982.51.

1534. Benoist, Mary Anne. "Black Studies." *The Society for the Study of Southern Literature Newsletter*, 20 (April), 24–25. Lists the reissue of *TMBV*.

1535. Bigsby, C.W.E. "The Divided Mind of James Baldwin," in *Critical Essays on James Baldwin*. Eds. Fred L. Standley and Nancy V. Burt. Boston: G.K. Hall, pp. 94–111.

1536. Bishop, Jack. *Ralph Ellison*. New York: Chelsea House, 110 pp. Juvenile biography of Ellison including discussion of W's influence and friendship.

1537. Bishop, Rand. *African Literature, African Critics: The Forming of Critical Standards, 1947–1966*. Westport, CT: Greenwood Press, pp. 48, 126, 132. Mentions W's assistance to *Présence Africaine* and Alexandre Biyidi's unfavorable comparison of Camara Laye's *L'Enfant noir* to *BB* (see 1954.79), and quotes M.S. Eno Belinga's comparison of Peter Abrahams to W.

1538. Bloom, Harold. "Editor's Note," in his *Richard Wright's Native Son*. New York: Chelsea House, pp. vii–viii. Provides brief summary statements about the eleven essays collected in the volume.

1539. _____. "Introduction," in his *Richard Wright's Native Son*. New York: Chelsea House, pp. 1–4. Reprint of the first two of three sections of 1987.54.

1540. _____. "Richard Wright," in his *Twentieth-Century American Literature*, Vol. 7. New York: Chelsea House, p. 4493. Biographical headnote.

1541. _____, ed. *Richard Wright's Native Son*. New York: Chelsea House, viii + 174 pp. Includes an introduction, chronology, and brief bibliography by the editor as well as essays or book excerpts by Dan McCall, Roger Rosenblatt, Joel Roache, Michael G. Cooke, Joyce Ann Joyce, Louis Tremaine, Valerie Smith, Barbara Johnson, Joseph T. Skerrett, Jr., and David Bradley.

1542. _____, ed. *Twentieth Century American Literature*. Vol. 8: Bibliographical Supplement and Index. New York: Chelsea House, pp. 4658, 4717. Lists W's books and four secondary sources.

1543. Bloom, Lynn Z. "Richard Wright," in her *The Essay Connection: Readings for Writers*. Second edition. Lexington, MA: D.C. Heath, pp. 325–337. Reprints an excerpt from *BB* with headnote, study questions, and suggestions for writing.

1544. _____. "Richard Wright, *The Power of Books*," in her *Instructor's Manual The Essay Connection: Readings for Writers*. Second edition. Lexington, MA: D.C. Heath, pp. 81–84. Pedagogical notes on an excerpt from *BB* s.v. "Content," "Strategies/Structures," and "Language."

1545. Bodziock, Joseph. "Richard Wright and Afro-American Gothic," in *Richard Wright: Myths and Realities.* Ed. C. James Trotman. New York: Garland, pp. 27–42. Analyzes W's use of the gothic mode in *NS*. With the American gothic of Poe and Hawthorne, W evokes psychosexual fears and phobias to achieve the special horror needed to shock readers into confronting the racist reality of American society.

1546. Bogle, Donald. "Native Son (1951)," in his *Blacks in American Film and Television: An Encyclopedia.* New York: Garland, pp. 152–153. Highly unfavorable evaluation of the Chenal film and brief dismissal of the 1986 version.

1547. Bone, Robert. *Down Home: Origins of the Afro-American Short Story.* New York: Columbia University Press. Reprint of 1975.27 with a new preface mentioning briefly Ellison's "Richard Wright's Blues" (p. x).

1548. _____. *Down Home: Origins of the Afro-American Short Story.* New York: Columbia University Press. Reprint of 1975.27 with a new preface mentioning Ellison's review of *BB*.

1549. Booth, Wayne C., and Marshall W. Gregory. "Questions for Discussion," in their *The Harper & Row Reader.* Second edition. New York: Harper & Row, p. 232. Five questions to accompany an excerpt from *BB*.

1550. _____. "Richard Wright," in their *The Harper & Row Reader.* Second edition. New York: Harper & Row, pp. 224–225. Headnote to "The Library Card," an excerpt from *BB*.

1551. _____. "Suggested Essay Topics," in their *The Harper & Row Reader.* Second edition. New York: Harper & Row, pp. 232–233. Two topics to accompany an excerpt from *BB*.

1552. Boozer, William. "Faulkner in Venezuela." *Faulkner Newsletter,* 8 (October–December), 1, 2, 3–4. On a visit to Venezuela in April 1961 Faulkner was asked a question about W: "His tragedy was his color ... something his soul couldn't stand. As we all do, in *Black Boy* he wrote of the human being in the human dilemma. But he gradually lost the concept of the tragedy of the human being (by putting emphasis on) the human being in a social condition;

in my opinion, that's when his work began to go down."

1553. Bradbury, Malcolm. "Neo-realist Fiction," in *Columbia Literary History of the United States.* Ed. Emory Elliott. New York: Columbia University Press, pp. 1126–1141. Mentions *O* briefly (p. 1139).

1554. Bradley, David. "David Bradley on *Native Son* by Richard Wright, 1940," in *Introducing the Great American Novel.* Ed. Anne Skillion. New York: Morrow, pp. 195–207. Reprint of 1986.20.

1555. _____. "On Reading *Native Son,*" in *Richard Wright's Native Son.* Ed. Harold Bloom. New York: Chelsea House, pp. 143–153. Revised reprint of 1986.20.

1556. _____. "Preface," in *12 Million Black Voices.* By Richard Wright. New York: Thunder's Mouth Press, pp. v–xvii. Reviews the history of the Great Migration and sketches W's early career. Among W's works, *TMBV* "stands out as a work of poetry, of passion, of lyricism and of love" (p. xvii).

1557. _____. "Richard (Nathaniel) Wright," in *Contemporary Literary Criticism.* Eds. Daniel G. Marowski and Roger Matuz. Detroit: Gale, pp. 428–430.

1558. Branch, Taylor. *Parting the Waters: America in the King Years, 1954–63.* New York: Simon and Schuster, p. 250. Mentions Martin Luther King's visit with W in Paris in 1959.

1559. Bröck, Sabine. *Der entkolonisierte Körper: Die Protagonistin in der Afroamerikanischen weiblichen Erzältradition der 30er bis 80er Jahre.* Frankfurt/Main: Campus Verlag, pp. 81–82. Quotes from an article on W and Hurston by Günter Lenz.

1560. Brown-Guillory, Elizabeth. *Their Place on the Stage: Black Women Playwrights in America.* Westport, CT: Greenwood Press, pp. 3, 113. Mentions briefly *NS*.

1561. Bryant, Jerry H. "From 'The Violence of *Native Son,*'" in *Twentieth-Century American Literature.* Ed. Harold Bloom, Vol. 7. New York: Chelsea House, pp. 4506–4510. Partial reprint of 1981.29.

1562. [Budd, Louis J.]. "Brief Mention." *American Literature,* 60 (October), 514–527. Includes a notice of *A Richard Wright Bibliography* (p. 524).

1563. Buhle, Paul. *C.L.R. James:*

The Artist as Revolutionary. London: Verso, pp. 68, 106, 117. Mentions W briefly.

1564. Bullock-Kimball, Susanne. "The Modern Minotaur: A Study of Richard Wright's *Native Son.*" *Notes on Mississippi Writers,* 20, No. 2, 41–48. Offers an interpretation of *NS* "from the mytho-metaphoric perception." Bigger is the Minotaur, Mr. Dalton "a modern Minos," Mary a sacrifice to the beast, Bessie "the Ariadne-figure," and the police "the collective Theseus." *NS* persuades its readers "that Bigger is part of us."

1565. Bulsterbaum, Allison. *H.L. Mencken: A Research Guide.* New York: Garland, pp. 151, 213, 226, 228, 232. Lists sources on the W-Mencken connection by Gayle, Scruggs, Fabre, Hakutani, and Donald Hall.

1566. Burnette, R.V. "Rescuing the Past: Black Theory and Black Research." *The CEA Critic,* 50 (Winter-Summer), 105–114. Disputes Houston Baker's claim that "Wright is a product of black culture" (p. 109).

1567. Burns, Landon C., Elizabeth Buckmaster, and Janet P. Alwang. "The Fourteenth Supplement (1987) to a Cross-Referenced Index of Short Fiction Anthologies and Author-Title Listings." *Studies in Short Fiction,* 25 (Spring), 175–246. Lists one item on "Big Black Good Man" and three items on "The Man Who Was Almost a Man" (p. 246).

1568. Butler, Johnnella E. "African American Studies and the 'warring ideals': The Color Line Meets the Borderlands." *Race and Reason,* 4, pp. 30–35. Mentions briefly W's identification with the West (p. 31).

1569. Butler, Robert. "Down from Slavery: *Invisible Man's* Descent Into the City and the Discovery of Self." *American Studies,* 29 (Fall), 57–67. Comments on W's attitude toward the city (p. 58).

1570. _____. "Making a Way Out of No Way: The Open Journey in Alice Walker's *The Third Life of Grange Copeland.*" *Black American Literature Forum,* 22 (Spring), 65–79. Comments on the journey motif in *LD*, mentioning also Bigger Thomas, Fred Daniels, and Cross Damon (p. 67).

1571. Butler-Evans, Elliott. "Constructing and Narrativizing the Black Zone: Semiotic Strategies of

Black Aesthetic Discourse." *The American Journal of Semiotics*, 6 (Winter), 19–35. Discusses "Blueprint for Negro Literature" as semiotic background of the Black Aesthetic. Motivated by W's radical politics, the essay emphasized an oppositional cultural stance.

1572. Byrd, Rudolph P. *"Living by the Word.* Alice Walker." *MELUS*, 15 (Spring), 109–115. Comments briefly on "Blueprint for Negro Writing" (p. 113).

1573. Cain, William E. *F.O. Matthiessen and the Politics of Criticism.* Madison: The University of Wisconsin Press, pp. 6, 195, 200–201, 207. Mentions W briefly and quotes from "How Bigger Was Born," showing how Mathiessen, despite his politics, ignored W and other black writers.

1574. _____. "Review: Literature, History, and Afro-American Studies." *College English*, 50 (February), 190–205. Mentions W briefly (pp. 191, 203).

1575. Callahan, John F. *In the African-American Grain: The Pursuit of Voice in Twentieth-Century Black Fiction.* Urbana: University of Illinois Press, pp. 113, 165, 187, 256–257, 264. Mentions W briefly and comments on a passage in *NS* (pp. 256–257).

1576. Carby, Hazel V. "Ideologies of Black Folk: The Historical Novel of Slavery," in *Slavery and the Literary Imagination.* Eds. Deborah McDowell and Arnold Rampersad. Baltimore: Johns Hopkins University Press, pp. 125–143. Comments briefly *BB* (p. 124) and W (pp. 138, 140). Quotes from W's review of *Black Thunder* (p. 138).

1577. Carr, Virginia Spencer. "Fiction: The 1930s to the 1960s," in *American Literary Scholarship: An Annual/1986.* Ed. David Nordloh. Durham, NC: Duke University Press, pp. 259–282. Comments on Joyce Ann Joyce's *Richard Wright's Art of Tragedy* and six articles on W.

1578. Caute, David. *The Fellow-Travellers: Intellectual Friends of Communism.* Revised edition. New Haven: Yale University Press, p. 81. Revision of 1973.

1579. Chamberlain, Mary. "A Conversation Between Rosa Guy and Maya Angelou," in her *Writing Lives.* London: Virago, pp. 218–240. Guy attributes her understanding of

Harlem and America to her reading of W.

1580. Chénetier, Marc. "Foreign Scholarship: French Contributions," in *American Literary Scholarship: An Annual/1986.* Ed. David J. Nordloh. Durham, NC: Duke University Press, pp. 414–427. Mentions Michel Fabre's essay "Frantz Fanon and Richard Wright" (p. 426).

1581. Ciner, Elizabeth J. "Richard Wright's Struggles with Fathers," in *Richard Wright: Myths and Realities.* Ed. C. James Trotman. New York: Garland, pp. 125–136. Asserts that "the struggle of the individual for self-possession, which is a struggle to be fully human and free, is the strongest unifying element in Wright's work" (p. 125). The struggle in *BB* is with the family, especially the paternal principle in all its manifestations.

1582. Claridge, Henry. "Chicago: 'The Classical Center of American Materialism'," in *The American City: Literary and Cultural Perspectives.* Ed. Graham Clarke. London: Vision, pp. 86–104. Comments on W's "nightmarish," deterministic depiction of Chicago. Mentions *LT* and *NS* (p. 101).

1583. Clark, Edward D. "Richard Wright," in *Afro-American Writers, 1940–1955.* Ed. Trudier Harris. *Dictionary of Literary Biography*, Vol. 76. Detroit: Gale, pp. 199–221. Biographical-critical essay with discussions of all of W's books, illustrations, and primary and secondary bibliographies. Concludes that "Richard Wright is undeniably one of the most important American writers of the twentieth century."

1584. Clary, Françoise. *L'espoir de vivre: violence et sexualité dans le roman afro-américain de Chester Himes à Hal Bennett.* Berne: Peter Lang, pp. 42, 72, 207, 342, 364. Mentions briefly W, *TMBV*, and *NS*, and lists nine of W's books in the bibliography.

1585. Clayton, John J. "Richard Wright (1906 [sic]–1960)," in his *The Heath Introduction to Fiction.* Third edition. Lexington, MA: D.C. Heath, p. 530. Headnote to "Bright and Morning Star."

1586. Cleveland, Jim. "World Interest in Southern Culture." *The Southern Register*, 6 (Summer). In an photograph accompanying this article, *NS* and *BB* are among books being sent to Bulgarian universities.

1587. Clift-Pellow, Arlene. "Literary Criticism and Black Imagery," in *Images of Blacks in American Culture: A Reference Guide to Information Sources.* Ed. Jessie Carney Smith. Westport, CT: Greenwood Press, pp. 139–189. Bibliographical essay mentioning W frequently.

1588. Colaiaco, James A. *Martin Luther King, Jr.: Apostle of Militant Nonviolence.* New York: St Martin's Press, p. 162. Notes W's use of the term "Black Power." Reprinted: 1993.

1589. Coles, Robert A. "Richard Wright's Synthesis." *CLA Journal*, 31 (June), 375–393. Examines W's early work (especially *NS* and the poetry) and career as an effort to synthesize literary forms, to unite art and social science, and to merge the black and white dispossessed in order to effect social change.

1590. Cooke, Michael G. "The Beginnings of Self-Realization," in *Richard Wright's Native Son.* Ed. Harold Bloom. New York: Chelsea House, pp. 57–65. Reprint of 1984. 35.

1591. Cornell, Charles, ed. *Biography Index: A Cumulative Index to Biographical Material in Books and Magazines, September 1986–August 1988.* New York: H.W. Wilson, p. 825. Lists two items on W.

1592. Crouch, Stanley. "The Rage of Race." *The Village Voice* (12 January), pp. 35, 38–39. Comments on James Baldwin's appraisal of W in "Princes and Powers."

1593. D., T. B. "Book Marks." *Essence*, 18 (March), 24. Contains a descriptive review of Margaret Walker's *Richard Wright: Daemonic Genius*, which "is sure to arouse controversy."

1594. Dance, Daryl Cumber. "'Learn It to the Younguns': Passing on Folk Wisdom," in *From Folklore to Fiction: A Study of Folk Heroes and Rituals in the Black American Novel.* Westport, CT: Greenwood Press, pp. ix–xii. Quotes briefly from "Blueprint for Negro Writing."

1595. _____. "You Can't Go Home Again: James Baldwin and the South," in *Critical Essays on James Baldwin.* Boston: G.K. Hall, pp. 54–62. Reprint of 1974.54.

1596. Davis, Jane. "Self-Hatred in the Novels of Richard Wright." *The Literary Griot*, 1 (Fall), 75–97. Examines "self-hatred and rejection of one's identity as a consequence of being successfully inferiorized" (p.

77) in *LT*, *NS*, and *LD*. W exemplifies Du Boisian double consciousness.

1597. Deutsch, Leonard J. "Ralph Ellison," in *Afro-American Writers, 1940–1955*. Eds. Trudier Harris and Thadious M. Davis. Detroit: Gale, pp. 37–56. Comments on Ellison's early friendship with W (p. 40); discusses W's life, autobiography, *NS*, and "The Man Who Lived Underground" as sources for *Invisible Man* (pp. 47–48); and mentions W elsewhere.

1598. Dick, Bruce Allen. "Struggle toward global humanism: The later works of Richard Wright." *Dissertation Abstracts International* 49 (December), 1455A. Abstracts a 1988 Florida State University dissertation defending the expatriate works, especially the nonfiction and *LD*.

1599. Diedrich, Maria. "George S. Schuyler's *Black No More*— The Black Conservative's Socialist Past." *The Western Journal of Black Studies*, 12 (Spring), 55–60. Mentions W briefly (p. 56).

1600. Dietzel, Susanne, and Maryemma Graham. "*Self-Discovery and Authority in Afro-American Narrative*. By Valerie Smith." *Legacy*, 5 (Spring), 59–60. Review with critical comments on Smith's treatment of W. Mentions briefly *NS* and *BB*.

1601. Diggins, John Patrick. *The Proud Decades: America in War and Peace, 1941–1960*. New York: Norton, pp. 171, 275, 276. Comments on W's rejection of communism.

1602. Dodson, Howard. "The Schomburg Center for Research in Black Culture," in *Afro-American Writers, 1940–1955*. Eds. Trudier Harris and Thadious M. Davis. Detroit: Gale, pp. 242–255. Notes that W used the Schomburg Collection in the forties (p. 244) and that it now contains manuscripts by W (p. 247).

1603. Donald, David Herbert. *Look Homeward: A Life of Thomas Wolfe*. New York: Ballantine Books, p. 179. Reprint of 1987.85.

1604. Donaldson, Scott. *John Cheever: A Biography*. New York: Random House, p. 75. Mentions W as a member of the New York Writers' Project.

1605. Douglas, Robert L. "Religious Orthodoxy and Skepticism in Richard Wright's *Uncle Tom's Children* and *Native Son*," in *Richard Wright: Myths and Realities*. Ed. C.

James Trotman. New York: Garland, pp. 79–88. Reprint of 1987.87.

1606. Doyle, Mary Ellen, SCN. "Ernest Gaines' Materials: Place, People, Author." *MELUS*, 15 (Fall), 75–93. Mentions W briefly (pp. 87, 90).

1607. Duberman, Martin Bauml. *Paul Robeson*. New York: Knopf, pp. 197, 225, 243, 626, 633, 642–643, 692. Records the opinion of C.L.R. James that W was more political and radical than Robeson, quotes from Robeson's foreword to the English edition of *UTC*, notes that Robeson served with W on the board of the Negro Playwrights Company, mentions "King Joe," quotes a letter from Waldo Frank praising W, states that Robeson and Van Vechten liked *UTC* but that Robeson liked and Van Vechten disliked *NS*, and mentions W's political disapproval of Robeson in 1949.

1608. Dunbar, Sybil J. "William Faulkner and Richard Wright: Two perspectives of the South, the female as focal point." *Dissertation Abstracts International*, 49 (August), 253A. Abstracts a 1987 University of Kentucky dissertation finding many similarities between Faulkner and W, especially in their treatment of women.

1609. Duval, Elaine I. "Reasserting and Raising Our History, An Interview with Amiri Baraka." *Obsidian II*, 3 (Spring), 1–19. The interviewer mentions W briefly (p.3).

1610. Eagles, Brenda M. "Recent Manuscript Accessions at Mississippi College and University Libraries." *Journal of Mississippi History*, 50 (February), 29–35. Notes the gift by Ellen and Julia Wright to the University of Mississippi of W's letter accepting the Spingarn Medal.

1611. Early, Gerald. "The Black Intellectual and the Sport of Prizefighting." *The Kenyon Review*, 10 (Summer), 102–117. Discusses W's three articles on Joe Louis, as well as W's interest in popular culture as shown in *NS*, *BB*, *BP*, *CC*, *LT*, and *AH* (pp. 109, 111–113).

1612. Ellison, Ralph. "Richard Wright's Blues," in *Twentieth-Century American Literature*. Ed. Harold Bloom. Vol. 7. New York: Chelsea House, pp. 4493–4498. Reprint of 1945.890.

1613. Ensslen, Klaus. "Fictionalizing History: David Bradley's *The Chaneysville Incident*." *Callaloo*, 11

(Spring), 280–296. Mentions briefly *BB* and *UTC*.

1614. Fabre, Michel. "Françoise Grellet. *An Introduction to American Literature*." *Afram Newsletter*, No. 26 (January), 61. Review noting that W is included in this anthology-history.

1615. ____. "From 'Introduction,'" in *Twentieth-Century American Literature*. Ed. Harold Bloom. Vol. 7. New York: Chelsea House, pp. 4501–4506. Partial reprint of 1978.93.

1616. ____. "Melvin Dixon. *Ride Out the Wilderness: Geography and Identity in Afro-American Literature*." *Afram Newsletter*, No. 26 (January), 58–59. Favorable review mentioning the treatment of W.

1617. ____. "Michael Thelwell. *Duties, Pleasures, and Conflicts: Essays in Struggle*." *Afram Newsletter*, No. 26 (January), 52. Review mentioning briefly W and "Bright and Morning Star."

1618. ____. Pontheolla T. Williams. "*Robert Hayden, A Critical Analysis of His Poetry*." *Afram Newsletter*, No. 26 (January), 55. Review noting W's influence on *Heart-Shape in the Dust*.

1619. ____. "Preface," in *L'Espoir de vivre: Violence et sexualité dans le roman afro-américain de Chester Himes à Hal Bennett* by Françoise Clary. Berne: Peter Lang, pp. 5–7. Mentions W briefly.

1620. Farnsworth, Robert M. "Melvin B Tolson," in *Afro-American Writers, 1940–1955*. Eds. Trudier Harris and Thadious M. Davis. Detroit: Gale, pp. 164–172. Notes that Tolson visited W in Paris in 1956 (p. 170). Quotes Tolson that "even in the violence of Richard Wright there is something that lifts you. There is no despair" (p. 171).

1621. Ferguson, SallyAnn H. "Dorothy West," in *Afro-American Writers, 1940–1955*. Eds. Trudier Harris and Thadious M. Davis. Detroit: Gale, pp. 187–195. Notes W's connection with West's magazine, where "Blueprint for Negro Writing" was published (p. 193).

1622. Ferris, William. "Director's Column." *The Southern Register*, 6 (Spring), 2. Notes that Michel Fabre taught a graduate seminar on W at the University of Mississippi in the fall semester, 1987.

1623. Feuser, Willfried F. "Wole Soyinka: The Problem of Authenticity." *Black American Literature Forum*, 22 (Fall), 555–575. Quotes W on his estrangement from Senghor (p. 560).

1624. Fiehrer, Thomas, "Narratives, Slave," in *Dictionary of Afro-American Slavery*. Eds. Randall M. Miller and John David Smith. Westport, CT: Greenwood Press, pp. 515–519. Mentions W briefly (p. 518).

1625. Fleischauer, Carl, and Beverly W. Brannan. "Introduction," in their *Documenting America, 1935–1943*. Berkeley: University of California Press, p. 8. Mentions briefly *TMBV*.

1626. Fleming, Robert E. "Willard Motley," in *Afro-American Writers, 1940–1955*. Eds. Trudier Harris and Thadious M. Davis. Detroit: Gale, pp. 113–121. Mentions W on the Writers' Project (p. 115) and notes comparisons of Motley's *Knock on Any Door* to *NS* (p. 117).

1627. Forrest, Leon. "In the Light of the Likeness — Transformed," in *Contemporary Authors Autobiography Series*. Ed. Mark Zadrozney. Vol. 7. Detroit: Gale, pp. 21–35. Mentions briefly W (p. 32) and "The Man Who Lived Underground" (p. 33).

1628. Foster, M. Marie Booth. *Southern Black Creative Writers, 1829–1953: Biobibliographies*. Westport, CT: pp. 70–71, 101. Lists fifteen items by W and provides minimal bibliographical information.

1629. Fraden, Rena. "The Cloudy History of *Big White Fog*: The Federal Theatre Project, 1938." *American Studies*, 29 (Spring), 5–27. Includes comments on W and the Southside Writer's Club (pp. 11, 26) and mentions W and *NS* elsewhere.

1630. France, Alan W. "Misogyny and Appropriation in Wright's *Native Son*." *Modern Fiction Studies*, 34 (Autumn), 413–423. In this feminist and poststructuralist reading of the novel about the repressed absence, sexism, is a theme as important as the authorial theme of racism. Bigger engages in "the struggle to appropriate (and thus dehumanize) women by reducing them … to property, valuable only to the extent they serve as objects of phallocentric status conflicts" (p. 414). To support this thesis, France examines the killing of the rat, the "symbolic rape-slaying of Gus, the partially effected rape and the murder of Mary Dalton, and the overt rape-killing of Bessie Mears" (p. 416).

1631. Franklin, John Hope, and Alfred A. Moss, Jr. *From Slavery to Freedom: A History of Negro Americans*. Sixth edition. New York: Knopf, pp. 374–375, 483. Reprint of 1956.158.

1632. Fromm, Harold. "Real Life, Literary Criticism, and the Perils of Bourgeoisification." *New Literary History*, 20 (Autumn), 49–64. Quotes Joyce A. Joyce mentioning W (p. 57).

1633. Gállego, Cándido Perez. *Historia de la literatura norteamericana*. Madrid: Taurus, pp. 235, 321, 323. Comments favorably on W and mentions most of his works. *PS* is "una valiente disección de la vida española en la época franquista" (p. 321).

1634. Gallup, Donald. *Pigeons on the Granite: Memories of a Yale Librarian*. New Haven, CT: The Beinecke Rare Book & Manuscript Library, Yale University, p. 79. Quotes from a letter dated 11 May 1946 from Gertrude Stein mentioning that W arrived in Paris "yesterday."

1635. Garren, Samuel B. "William Attaway," in *Afro-American Writers, 1940–1955*. Eds. Trudier Harris and Thadious M. Davis. Detroit: Gale, pp. 3–7. Mentions Attaway's friendship with W (p. 4) and compares Big Mat in *Blood on the Forge* to Bigger Thomas (p. 6).

1636. Garrow, David J. *Bearing the Cross: Martin Luther King, Jr., and the Southern Christian Leadership Conference*. New York: Vintage, p. 113.

1637. Gates, Henry Louis, Jr. *The Signifying Monkey: A Theory of Afro-American Literary Criticism*. New York: Oxford University Press, pp. ix, xxvii, 96–100, 105–107, 111–112, 115, 118–121, 122, 181–184, 192. Comments on signifying in W and quotes examples from *LT* and "Big Boy Leaves Home," discusses Ellison's parodying of *NS* and "The Man Who Lived Underground" in *Invisible Man*, criticizes W's attitude toward his "black textual antecedents," and contrasts narrative voice in W and Hurston.

1638. Gaudet, Marcia, and Carl Wooton. "Talking with Ernest J. Gaines." *Callaloo*, 11 (Spring), 229–243. Gaines discusses the influence of W and other black writers on his literary development.

1639. Govan, Sandra Y. "Black Women as Cultural Conservators:

Biographers and Builders of Our Cultural Heritage." *The Langston Hughes Review*, 7 (Fall), 1–14. Mentions briefly *BB* (p. 2) and comments on W's work on *New Challenge* (p. 11).

1640. Graham, Maryemma. "Introduction," in her *Complete Poems of Frances E.W. Harper*. New York: Oxford University Press, pp. xxxiii–lvii. Mentions briefly *BB* (p. lvi).

1641. Grant, Robert. "Absence Into Presence: The Thematics of Memory and 'Missing' Subjects in Toni Morrison's *Sula*," in *Critical Essays on Toni Morrison*. Ed. Nellie Y. McKay. Boston: G.K. Hall, pp. 90–103. Mentions briefly *UTC* (p. 90) and *NS* (p. 91).

1642. Greenspon, Joanna, ed. *Humanities Index April 1987 to March 1988*. New York: Wilson, p. 929. Lists two items on W.

1643. Guereschi, E. "Wright, Richard. Eight men: stories." *Choice*, 26 (July-August), 1696–1697. Mixed notice of the new edition of *EM* with a foreword by David Bradley.

1644. Hakutani, Yoshinobu. "*No Name in the Street*: James Baldwin's Image of the American Sixties," in *Critical Essays on James Baldwin*. Eds. Fred L. Standley and Nancy V. Burt. Boston: G.K. Hall, pp. 277–289. Mentions briefly *BB* (p. 277).

1645. _____. "Richard Wright and American Naturalism." *Zeitschrift für Anglistik und Amerikanistik*, 36, 217–226. After an exposition of conflicting views of literary naturalism, Hakutani posits the tensions between individual will and social determinism as characteristic of the best American versions. *NS* is analyzed as a success in this regard, *LT* as a failure.

1646. Hall, Donald, and D.L. Emblen. "Considerations," in their *A Writer's Reader*. Fifth edition. Glenview, IL: Scott, Foresman, pp. 489–490. Reprint of 1979.120.

1647. _____. "Richard Wright, 'The Library Card,'" in their *A Writer's Reader*. Fifth edition. Glenview, IL: Scott, Foresman, p. 481. Reprint of 1979.121.

1648. Halsey, William. "Signify(cant) Correspondences." *Black American Literature Forum*, 22 (Summer), 257–261. Notes some correspondences between works by Henry Dumas and "Between the World and Me" and *NS* (p. 259).

1649. Hamalian, Linda. "Other

Voices, Other Looms: Richard Wright's Use of Epigraphs in Two Novels." *Obsidian II*, 3 (Winter), 72–88. On the premise that epigraphs are an author's interpretive clues to the reader, Hamalian relates the epigraphs of *LT* (Van Wyck Brooks, Waldo Frank, and T.S. Eliot) and their contexts in the original source to the novels, after which she does the same with the epigraphs in *SH* (Oscar Wilde, Job, Exodus, Sandor Ferenczi, Freud, Nietzsche, Theodore Reik, Goethe, Euripides, Corinthians, and Christopher Marlowe).

1650. Hamill, Pete. "Breaking the Silence: A Letter to a Black Friend." *Esquire*, 109 (March), 91–94, 96, 98, 100, 102. Mentions W briefly (p. 98).

1651. Harding, Vincent. "Toward a Darkly Radiant Vision of America's Truth: A Letter of Concern, an Invitation to Re-Creation," in *Community in America: The Challenge of Habits of the Heart*. Eds. Charles H. Reynolds and Ralph V. Norman. Berkeley and Los Angeles: University of California Press, pp. 71–72. Quotes and comments on a passage from *TMBV*.

1652. Harris, Norman. "*The Afro-American Novel and Its Tradition*. By Bernard W. Bell." *The Georgia Review*, 42 (Winter), 870–871. Review mentioning briefly *NS*.

1653. _____. "Preface." *Modern Fiction Studies*, 34 (Spring), 3–4. The editor of a special issue on modern black fiction comments on Tracy Webb's essay on W.

1654. Harris, Trudier. "Foreword," in her and Thadious M. Davis's *Afro-American Writers, 1940–1955*. Detroit: Gale, pp. xi–xiii. Contains a paragraph on W, "the dominant voice in Afro-American fiction in the 1940s."

1655. Hatch, James V. "Owen Dodson," in *Afro-American Writers, 1940–1955*. Eds. Trudier Harris and Thadious M. Davis. Detroit: Gale, pp. 30–36. Notes that W was among Dodson's friends (p. 31). Mentions W briefly elsewhere (p. 35).

1656. Hawthorne, Evelyn. "On Gaining the Double-Vision: *Tar Baby* as Diasporean Novel." *Black American Literature Forum*, 22 (Spring), 97–107. Mentions W briefly (p. 99).

1657. Hemenway, Robert E. "Most

Public of Poets, Most Private of Men." *Callaloo*, 11 (Summer), 636–642. Review of the first volume of Arnold Rampersad's *The Life of Langston Hughes* mentioning briefly *NS* (p. 638).

1658. Henriksen, Louise Levitas. "*Anzia Yezierska: A Writer's Life*." New Brunswick: Rutgers University Press, pp. 261, 263. Comments on W and the Writers Project.

1659. Hirsch, E.D., Jr. *The Dictionary of Cultural Literacy*. Boston: Houghton Mifflin, p. 139. Contains an entry on W.

1660. Hodges, J.O. "Smith, Valerie. *Self-discovery and authority in Afro-American narrative*." *Choice*, 26 (September), 125. Mentions briefly *NS*.

1661. Holmes, John Clellon. "Arm: A Memoir," in his *Representative Men: The Biographical Essays*. Fayetteville: The University of Arkansas Press, pp. 243–262. Reports that Nelson Algren stated that "*Native Son*'s the only sure-as-hell existentialist novel we ever wrote over here. Don't anyone read Dick Wright anymore?" (p. 246).

1662. Holte, James Craig. *The Ethnic I: A Sourcebook for Ethnic-American Autobiography*. Westport, CT: Greenwood Press, pp. 196–201. Contains a biographical sketch of W, a summary of *BB*, quotations from three critics (Butterfield, Kinnamon, Margolies), and a primary and secondary bibliography of twelve primary and twenty-five secondary sources.

1663. Horne, Gerald. *Communist Front?: The Civil Rights Congress, 1946–1956*. Rutherford, Madison, Teaneck, NJ: Fairleigh Dickinson University Press, pp. 88, 173. Quotes Cedric Belfrage on W's protest against the execution of Willie McGee. Quotes from an unpublished letter from William Patterson to W expressing appreciation for "the many fine things you said about [*The Man Who Cried*] Genocide," and hope that W will say them publicly.

1664. Hubbard, Linda S., ed. *Notable Americans: What They Did, from 1620 to the Present*. Fourth edition. Detroit: Gale, p. 56. Lists W as a winner of the Spingarn Medal.

1665. Hug, W.J. "*Richard Wright's Art of Tragedy*. By Joyce Ann Joyce." *Southern Humanities Review*, 22 (Summer), 301–303. Favorable re-

view of Joyce's New Critical approach to *NS* with summaries of her prologue and four chapters. "She offers a convincing case for Richard Wright as a careful craftsman of modern tragedy."

1666. Huggins, Nathan Irvin. "'Here to Stay.'" *The Nation*, 247 (10 October), 316–320. Review of the first volume of Arnold Rampersad's biography of Langston Hughes, mentioning Hughes's envy of W's success and his distaste for *NS*.

1667. _____. "Modernism and the Harlem Renaissance." *Americana: Tijdschrift voor de Studie van Noord-Amerika*, 2, No. 1, 62–70. Mentions W and "Blueprint for Negro Writing." Reprinted: 1995.

1668. Hughes, Langston. "From Harlem to Paris," in *Critical Essays on James Baldwin*. Eds. Fred L. Standley and Nancy V. Burt. Boston: G.K. Hall, pp. 225–226.

1669. Hunt, Douglas. "Richard Wright (1908–1960) The Library Card," in his *The Riverside Anthology of Literature*. Boston: Houghton Mifflin, pp. 374–382. Reprints an excerpt from *BB* and appends an excerpt by Ellison from 1961.143.

1670. Ito, Yuko, *et al.* "Richard Wright's Five Episodes.'" *Aichi Shukutodu Junior College Athena*, 22 (March), 71–119. Analysis and translation of "Five Episodes," an excerpt from W's unpublished novel "Island of Hallucinations."

1671. Jackson, Jacquelyn. "William Gardner Smith," in *Afro-American Writers, 1940–1955*. Eds. Trudier Harris and Thadious M. Davis. Detroit: Gale, pp. 158–163. Mentions W briefly (p. 158) and notes that Smith met W in Europe.

1672. Jackson, Jocelyn Whitehead. "The Problem of Identity in Selected Early Essays of James Baldwin," in *Critical Essays on James Baldwin*. Eds. Fred V. Standley and Nancy V. Burt. Boston: G.K. Hall, pp. 250–267.

1673. J[ackson], P[aul] R. "Joyce, Joyce Ann. *Richard Wright's Art of Tragedy*." *Journal of Modern Literature*, 15 (Fall/Winter), 425–426. Favorable notice with some reservations: "an arguable reading of a central text."

1674. Jacoby, Jay. "Book Review." *Obsidian II*, 3 (Winter), 141–149 Comments briefly on Boris Max in *NS* (p. 142).

1675. _____. "Harap, Lewis.

Dramatic Encounters in Twentieth-Century American Drama, Poetry, and Humor and the Black-Jewish Literary Relationship." *Obsidian II*, 3 (Winter), 141–149. Comments on Harap's treatment of *NS* and *BB* (p. 142).

1676. Jay, Paul, ed. *The Selected Correspondence of Kenneth Burke and Malcolm Cowley, 1915–1981.* New York: Viking, pp. 262–263. In a letter dated 9 March 1944 Cowley discusses sin and retribution, rather than crime and punishment, in Dostoevsky, *NS*, and Arthur Koestler's *Darkness at Noon.*

1677. _____. *The Selected Correspondence of Kenneth Burke and Malcolm Cowley, 1915–1981.* New York: Viking, p. 262. Includes a letter from Cowley to Burke dated 9 March 1944 commenting on *NS* as it concerns "sin and retribution, crime and punishment."

1678. Johnson, Barbara. "The Re(a)d and the Black," in *Richard Wright's Native Son.* Ed. Harold Bloom. New York: Chelsea House, pp. 115–123. Analyzes Bigger's ransom note in relation to W's effort to combine Marxist vision with black experience as prescribed in "Blueprint for Negro Writing" (the red and the black). Comparing the scene of the ransom note in *NS*, in which Bessie infers that Mary has been killed, to the scene in *BB* in which W reads his story of the death of an Indian maiden to a black woman, Johnson argues that "the figure of the black woman as *reader* in his work is fundamental" (p. 123).

1679. Johnson, Charles. "Where Philosophy and Fiction Meet." *American Visions*, 3 (June), 36, 47–48. Comments on W's. philosophical interests and their expression in *NS* and "The Man Who Lived Underground.

1680. Johnson, Eloise McKinney. "Remembering Langston Hughes: Memories of a Langston Hughes Class." *The Langston Hughes Review*, 7 (Spring), 35–37. Mentions W briefly as a "social poet" (p. 36).

1681. Jones, Carolyn M., and Julia M. Hardy. "From Colonialism to Community: Religion and Culture in Charles H. Long's *Significations.*" *Callaloo*, 11 (Summer), 582–596. Long comments briefly on W.

1682. Jones, Norma R. "Robert Hayden," in *Afro-American Writers, 1940–1955.* Eds. Trudier Harris and Thadious M. Davis. Detroit: Gale, pp. 75–88. Mentions briefly W and Bigger Thomas (p. 85).

1683. Joyce, Joyce A. "The Aesthetic of E. Ethelbert Miller." *Occasional Paper #01.* Washington, DC: The Institute for the Preservation of African American Writing. Mentions briefly W and his misunderstanding of Hurston.

1684. _____. "The Tragic Hero," in *Richard Wright's Native Son.* Ed. Harold Bloom. New York: Chelsea House, pp. 67–87. Partial reprint of 1986.98.

1685. Juneja, Om P. "Afro-American Critical Theory: A Bricolage." *Indian Journal of American Studies*, 18 (Winter), 41–47. Mentions W briefly (p. 41).

1686. Kaname, Hiroshi. "Wright's *The Long Dream*: A Dream and a Failure," in *The Dream and the Failure in American Literature.* Ed. Hirotsugu Inove. Skaka: Sogensha, pp. 142–160. Kaname observes that the South never changes, even in the 1950's. The novel is a Bildungsroman depicting a young Southern black boy's deferred dream of male dignity [T.K., R.B., and Y. H.].

1687. Kaufman, Jonathan. *Broken Alliance: The Turbulent Times Between Blacks and Jews in America.* New York: Touchstone, pp. 36–37. Quotes the passage from *BB* about black anti-Semitism.

1688. Kazin, Alfred. *A Writer's America: Landscape in Literature.* New York: Alfred A. Knopf, pp. 8, 181, 183, 185–186. Mentions W briefly and relates him to the Chicago literary scene.

1689. Kent, George E. "Gwendolyn Brooks," in *Afro-American Writers, 1940–1955.* Eds. Trudier Harris and Thadious M. Davis. Detroit: Gale, pp. 11–24. Notes W's favorable prepublication response to *A Street in Bronzeville.*

1690. King, Richard. "Politics and Literature: The Southern Case." *The Virginia Quarterly Review*, 64 (Spring), 189–201. Comments briefly on W (pp. 193–194, 197).

1691. Kinnamon, Keneth, with the help of Joseph Benson, Michel Fabre, and Craig Werner. *A Richard Wright Bibliography: Fifty Years of Criticism and Commentary, 1933–1982.* Westport, CT: Greenwood Press, xiv + 983 pp. "This book is a bibliography of 13,117 annotated items published from 1933 to 1982

pertaining to Richard Wright." Items are included from more than fifty countries and in many languages. "The arrangement of entries is chronological by year. Within each year items are numbered and alphabetized by author." The format is double column with small but readable type. The uncommonly full index (209 pp.) uses asterisks to indicate items of special importance.

1692. _____. "*A Richard Wright Bibliography: Fifty Years of Criticism and Commentary, 1933–1982,*" in *Black Studies.* Westport, CT: Greenwood Press, p. 6. Publisher's announcement.

1693. Kiuchi, Toru. "Richard Wright and Asia." *Chiba Review*, 10, 35–42. Traces W's expanding knowledge of Asia from *LT* and *Daily Worker* journalism through *O* and *CC* to the haiku he wrote at the end of his life.

1694. _____. "Richard Wright and Asia." *Chiba Review*, 10 (6 November), 35–42. Article in English focusing on W's view of Asia, mainly as presented in *CC* [T.K., R.B., and Y.H.].

1695. Kreyling, Michael. "Southern Literature: Consensus and Dissensus." *American Literature*, 60 (March), 83–95. Mentions W briefly.

1696. Larson, Thomas. "A Political Vision of Afro-American Culture: Richard Wright's 'Bright and Morning Star,'" in *Richard Wright: Myths and Realities.* Ed. C. James Trotman. New York: Garland, pp. 147–159. Analyzes the relation between race and radicalism in W's story. He wishes to show the Party how it must recognize, respect, and use black cultural patterns. The story's success "directs us within Afro-American life to the place where the different paths of its religious-centered culture, its conditioned deference to whites, and its need for a working-class political vision can meet" (p. 158).

1697. Lee, A. Robert. "Harlem on My Mind: Fictions of a Black Metropolis," in *The American City: Literary and Cultural Perspectives.* Ed. Graham Clarke. London: Vision, pp. 62–85. Mentions W, *NS*, and protest fiction (p. 72).

1698. _____. "Introduction," in his *First Person Singular: Studies in American Autobiography.* London: Vision Press, pp. 7–15. Mentions briefly *BB* (p. 13).

1699. _____. "'The Stance of Self-Representation': Moderns and Contemporaries in Afro-American Autobiography," in his *First Person Singular: Studies in American Autobiography*. London: Vision Press, pp. 151–176. Includes discussion of *BB* and *AH* as records of events and, more importantly, self-representation through writing (pp. 160–163). Mentions W elsewhere.

1700. Leitch, Vincent B. *American Literary Criticism from the Thirties to the Eighties*. New York: Columbia University Press, pp. 3, 340, 344, 349, 363. Mentions W briefly, mainly in a chapter entitled "Black Aesthetics."

1701. Lemelle, Anthony J., Jr. "Killing the Author of Life, or Decimating 'Bad Niggers.'" *Journal of Black Studies*, 19 (December), 216–231. Article on juvenile delinquency with an epigraph from *NS* and comments on Bigger, "a key to understanding black American juvenile delinquency."

1702. Lenz, Günter H. "Symbolic Space, Communal Rituals, and the Surreality of the Urban Ghetto: Harlem in Black Literature from the 1920s to the 1960s." *Callaloo*, 11 (Spring), 309–345. Mentions briefly W and *NS* (pp. 332, 333).

1703. Lester, Julius. "Some Tickets Are Better: The Mixed Achievement of James Baldwin," in *Critical Essays on James Baldwin*. Eds. Fred L. Standley and Nancy V. Burt. Boston: G.K. Hall, pp. 244–250. Reprint of 1986.109.

1704. [Levitt, Morton P.]. "Regional, National, and Ethnic Literatures." *Journal of Modern Literature*, 15 (Fall/Winter), 192–211. Lists two articles treating W (pp. 207, 208).

1705. _____. "Richard Wright." *Journal of Modern Literature*, 15 (Fall/Winter), 425–426. Lists seven items on W.

1706. Lewis, Felice F. "Literary Censorship in America," in *American Literary Almanac from 1608 to the Present*. Ed. Karen L. Rood. New York: Facts on File, pp. 221–230. Mentions briefly *BB* (p. 230).

1707. Littlefield, Daniel, Houston A. Baker, Jr., Henry Louis Gates, Jr., and Gloria Naylor. "The Afro-American Writer and the South," in *The "Southern Review" and Modern Literature: 1935–1985*. Eds. Lewis P. Simpson, James Olney, and Jo

Gulledge. Baton Rouge: Louisiana State University Press, pp. 131–151. The point of departure of this wide-ranging discussion is the last paragraph of "How 'Bigger' Was Born." The consensus is that the South means more than "horror" to black writers.

1708. Ljungquist, Kent P. "Poe," in *American Literary Scholarship: An Annual/1986*. Ed. David J. Nordloh. Durham, NC: Duke University Press, pp. 41–52. Mentions W briefly (p. 45).

1709. Longest, George C., et al. "A Checklist of Scholarship on Southern Literature for 1987." *The Mississippi Quarterly*, 41 (Spring), 199–371. Lists nine items on W and cross-references to twenty-two other items dealing partially with W.

1710. Lowe, John. "Wright Writing Reading: Narrative Strategies in *Uncle Tom's Children*." *Journal of the Short Story in English*, 10 (Autumn), 49–71. Finds three interrelated strategies in the 1940 *UTC*: "the re-historicizing, through fiction, of the black experience ... the use of biblical narrative patterns in the service of Communism ... a narrative structure that dramatizes and inter-relates theses [sic] two systems, Wright's compelling appropriation of the structures of torture." Thus W uses folk material to enhance his art and advocate his political ideology.

1711. Lynch, Michael. "The Journey Toward Self and Community in Gloria Naylor's *The Women of Brewster Place* and *Linden Hills*." *The Literary Griot*, 1 (Fall), 98–113. Mentions briefly *NS* (p. 98).

1712. Lyra, F. "Foreign Scholarship: East European Contributions," in *American Literary Scholarship: An Annual/1986*. Ed. David J. Nordloh. Durham, NC: Duke University Press, pp. 403–414. Mentions Tamara Denisova's treatment of W in her book on existentialism in American literature.

1713. MacKethan, Lucinda H. "*Black Boy* and *Ex-Coloured Man*: Version and Inversion of the Slave Narrator's Quest for Voice." *CLA Journal*, 32 (December), 123–147. Argues that "Wright used the model of the slave narratives [especially *Narrative of the Life of Frederick Douglass*] in shaping his version of quest for a voice with which to announce and confirm his struggle for freedom" (p. 124).

1714. Mackey, Douglas A. *Philip K. Dick*. Boston: Twayne, p. 1. Mentions W as one of Dick's favorite writers.

1715. Maini, Darghan Singh. *The Spirit of American Literature*. New Delhi: Sterling, p. 16. Mentions W briefly.

1716. Mairowitz, David Zane, and Alain Korkos. *Introducing Camus*. New York: Totem Books, p. 129. Mentions W. briefly as a contributor to *The God That Failed*.

1717. Marovitz, Sanford E. "Images of American-Jewish Fiction," in *Handbook of American-Jewish Literature*. Ed. Lewis Fried. Westport, CT: Greenwood Press, pp. 315–356. Mentions W briefly (p. 325).

1718. _____. "Images of America in American-Jewish Fiction," in *Handbook of American-Jewish Literature: An Analytical Guide to Topics, Themes And Sources*. Westport, CT: Greenwood Press, pp. 315–356 Mentions W briefly (p. 324)

1719. Marowski, Daniel G., and Roger Matuz, eds. "Richard (Nathaniel) Wright," in their *Contemporary Literary Criticism*. Detroit: Gale Research Company, pp. 415–430. Introduction to W followed by critical excerpts from W, Baldwin, Kathleen Gallagher, Louis Tremaine, James A. Miller, and David Bradley.

1720. Marr, David. *American Worlds Since Emerson*. Amherst: The University of Massachusetts Press, p. 192. Mentions W briefly in a chapter on Ellison.

1721. Martin, Reginald. "New Ideas for Old: New Black Aesthetic." *The CEA Critic*, 50 (Winter-Summer), 90–104. Comments on W's high reputation among the black aesthetic critics (pp. 100–101).

1722. Martin-Ogunsola, Dellita L. "Ambivalence as Allegory in Langston Hughes's 'Simple' Stories." *The Langston Hughes Review*, 7 (Spring), 1–8. Mentions briefly Bigger Thomas (p. 1).

1723. Masilela, Ntongela. "Sterling A. Brown: The Last of the Harlem Renaissance Greats." *Présence Africaine*, No. 148 (Fourth Quarter), 170–175. Mentions W briefly (p. 171).

1724. Mason, Theodore O., Jr. "Between the Populist and the Scientist: Ideology and Power in Recent Afro-American Literary Criticism or, 'The Dozens as Scholarship.'" *Callaloo*, 11 (Summer), 606–615. Mentions briefly W's underground man (p. 613).

1725. _____. "Performance, History, and Myth: The Problem of Ishmael Reed's *Mumbo-Jumbo*." *Modern Fiction Studies*, 34 (Spring), 97–109. Criticizes Henry Louis Gates's elevation of Hurston and Ellison at the expense of W (pp. 105–106).

1726. Masuda, Mitsuko. "A Study of Richard Wright's Existentialism." *Nihon Women's University Veritas*, 10 (20 December), 49–62. Comparative Study of *O* and Sartre's *Les Chemins de la liberté*, concluding that W was not much influenced by existentialism [T.K., R.B., and Y.H.].

1727. Matsumoto, Noboru. "Baldwin's Flight." *Kokushikan Daigaku Kyoyo Ronshu [Journal of Kokushikan University School of General Education]*, 26 (January), 33–40. Examines Baldwin's relationships to his father David, W, and black Americans in light of his ten-year exile in Europe and return [Y.H. and T.K.].

1728. Mayfield, Julian. "A Love Affair with the United States," in *Critical Essays on James Baldwin*. Eds. Fred L. Standley and Nancy V. Burt. Boston: G.K. Hall, pp. 226–228. Reprint of 1961.

1729. McCall, Dan. "The Bad Nigger," in *Richard Wright's Native Son*. Ed. Harold Bloom. New York: Chelsea House, pp. 5–22.

1730. McGrath, Daniel F., ed. *Bookman's Price Index*. Vol. 34. Detroit: Gale, p. 852. Lists *BB* at $100, *NS* at $450, *NS* at $150, *TMBV* at $100, and *UTC* at $600.

1731. _____, ed. *Bookman's Price Index*. vol. 35. Detroit: Gale, p. 776. Lists *NS* at $175 and *UTC* at $250.

1732. _____, ed. *Bookman's Price Index*. Vol. 36. Detroit: Gale, p. 940. Lists *Bright and Morning Star* at $100 and *UTC* at $150.

1733. _____, ed. *Bookman's Price Index*. Vol 37. Detroit: Gale, p. 961. Lists *TMBV* at $100 and *NS* at $145.

1734. McKay, Nellie Y. "Introduction," in her *Critical Essays on Toni Morrison*. Boston: G.K. Hall, pp. 1–15. Mentions briefly *NS* (p. 4) and W (p. 8).

1735. _____. "Introduction," in *The Narrows* by Ann Petry. Boston: Beacon Press, pp. vii–xx. Includes comparison of *The Street* and *NS*, contrasting Lutie Johnson to Bigger.

1736. McQuade, Donald. "Intellectual Life and Public Discourse," in *Columbia Literary History of the United States*. Ed. Emory Elliott. New York: Columbia University Press, pp. 715–732. Mentions briefly W, *NS*, and *BB* (pp. 726–729).

1737. McSweeney, Kerry, *Invisible Man: Race and Identity*. Boston: Twayne, pp. xii, 5–6, 16, 19. Comments on the question of W's influence on Ellison, mentioning *NS*, *BB*, and "The Man Who Lived Underground."

1738. Merriam, Allen H. "Literature as Window: Developing Interracial Understanding Through Fiction." *Journal of Black Studies*, 19 (September), 61–69. Mentions W briefly (pp. 62, 69).

1739. Meserole, Harrison T. "A Selected, Annotated List of Current Articles on American Literature." *American Literature*, 60 (October), 528–536. Mentions W briefly (p. 528).

1740. Mitgang, Herbert. *Dangerous Dossiers: Exposing the Secret War Against America's Greatest Authors*. New York: Donald I. Fine, pp. 100, 155, 157. Mentions briefly *UTC* and *NS* but does not report on the FBI's dossier on W.

1741. Moffett, James. *Storm in the Mountains: A Case Study of Censorship, Conflict, and Consciousness*. Carbondale and Edwardsville: Southern Illinois University Press, p. 29. Mentions W briefly (p. 29).

1742. Monroe, Sylvester, and Peter Goldman. *Brothers*. New York: William Morrow, p. 11. Mentions W briefly.

1743. Moore, Jack B. "Black Power Revisited: In Search of Richard Wright." *The Mississippi Quarterly*, 41 (Spring), 161–186. Reports on 1971 interviews in Ghana with James Moxon, a white former Englishman who was Ghana's Director of Information Services and made most of W's arrangements for travel in the country; Hannah Kudjoe, Propaganda Secretary for the Convention People's Party, whom W interviewed; and Kofi Boako, Nkrumah's political secretary, whom W also interviewed. Their recollections vary in several ways from W's version of events in *BP*.

1744. _____. "*Richard Wright's Art of Tragedy*, by Joyce Ann Joyce." *The Mississippi Quarterly*, 41 (Winter), 94–99. Favorable review em-

phasizing Joyce's interpretation of Bigger Thomas as a tragic hero of dignity and stature. Disagrees with Joyce's belittling view of Boris Max, but generally praises her ability to display W's genius "in a new and bright light" (p. 99).

1745. _____. "*Richard Wright's Art of Tragedy*, Joyce Ann Joyce." *Afram Newsletter*, No. 26 (January), 41–46. Reprint of 1988.212.

1746. Mullen, Edward J. "The Dilemma in Selecting Representative Scholarship on Langston Hughes." *The Langston Hughes Review*, 7 (Fall), 43–48. Quotes from an essay on W by Jerry Ward, Jr. (p. 43) and mentions elsewhere *NS* (p. 46).

1747. Muller, Gilbert H. "Questions," in his *The McGraw-Hill Reader*. Third edition. New York: McGraw-Hill, p. 240. Reprint of 1982.

1748. _____. "Richard Wright, The Psychological Reactions of Oppressed People," in his *The McGraw-Hill Reader*. Third edition. New York: McGraw-Hill, p. 236.

1749. Nadel, Alan. *Invisible Criticism: Ralph Ellison and the American Canon*. Iowa City: University of Iowa Press, p. 154. Mentions W briefly.

1750. Nakajima, Yoshinobu. "In Memory of James Baldwin." *Kikan Shin Eibei Bungaku Kenkyo [Quarterly of New English and American Literary Studies]*, 19 (May), 46–47, 50. Nakajima summarizes Baldwin's literary career and considers his relationship with W [Y.H. and T.K.].

1751. _____. "In Memory of James Baldwin." *Quarterly of New English and American Literary Studies*, 19 (7 May), 46–47, 50. Summarizes Baldwin's literary career and considers his relationship with W.

1752. Namekata, Hitoshi. "In Search of the Past: On *The Chaneysville Incident*." *Black Studies*, 58 (29 October), 1–6. Contrasts David Bradley's protagonist, who searches for his heritage, to Cross Damon in *O*, who rejects his past [T.K., R.B., and Y.H.].

1753. Naylor, Gloria. "Love and Sex in the Afro-American Novel." *The Yale Review*, 78 (Autumn), 19–31. Mentions *NS* as a "classic" (pp. 26, 30).

1754. _____. "The Myth of the Matriarch." *Life*, 11 (Spring), 65. Comments on and quotes from "Man of All Work."

1755. Nazareth, Peter. "Arnold Rampersad. *The Life of Langston Hughes. 1: 1902–1941: I, Too, Sing America.*" *World Literature Today,* 62 (Summer), 132–133. Review mentioning W briefly.

1756. _____. "Valerie Smith. *Self-Discovery and Authority in Afro-American Narrative.*" *World Literature Today,* 62 (Autumn), 662. Review mentioning W and *BB.*

1757. Nelson, Cary. "The Diversity of American Poetry," in *Columbia Literary History of the United States.* Ed. Emory Elliott. New York: Columbia University Press, pp. 913–936. Mentions W's "Whitmanesque catalogues and broadsides of protest," such as "I Have Seen Black Hands," "We of the Street [sic]," "I am a Red Slogan," and "Child of the Dead and Forgotten Gods."

1758. Newlin, Paul. "Why 'Bigger' Lives On: Student Reaction to *Native Son,*" in *Richard Wright: Myths and Realities.* Ed. C. James Trotman. New York: Garland, pp. 137–146. Reports that *NS* over many years has elicited a stronger response from his university students than any other book he teaches. The reason is the confrontation of the students' sense of fairness and civic responsibility with "the horror of Negro life in the United States."

1759. Nielsen, Aldon Lynn. *Reading Race: White American Poets and the Racial Discourse in the Twentieth Century.* Athens: University of Georgia Press, pp. 21, 57, 132. Mentions briefly "The Man Who Lived Underground," *BB,* and W's relation to Gertrude Stein.

1760. Norris, Jerrie. *Presenting Rosa Guy.* Boston: Twayne, pp. 32, 33. Notes W's influence on Guy, who considers him and Dreiser "two of America's great writers."

1761. O'Meally, Robert G. "Johnson, Charles. *Being and race: black writing since 1970.*" *Choice,* 26 (November), 489. Mentions W briefly.

1762. _____. "Introduction," in his *New Essays on Invisible Man.* Cambridge: Cambridge University Press, pp. 1–23. Mentions W briefly (pp. 6, 11).

1763. O'Neale, Sondra A. "Fathers, Gods, and Religion: Perceptions of Christianity and Ethnic Faith in James Baldwin," in *Critical Essays on James Baldwin.* Eds. Fred L. Standley and Nancy V. Burt. Boston: G.K. Hall, pp. 125–143. States

that in an interview David Baldwin recalled the "benignly discourteous" treatment given by W to James Baldwin (p. 139). O'Neale also notes W's unhappy experience with religion (p. 143).

1764. Ostendorf, Berndt. "Ralph Waldo Ellison: Anthropology, Modernism, and Jazz," in *New Essays on Invisible Man.* Ed. Robert O'Meally. New York: Cambridge University Press, pp. 95–121. Mentions briefly Ellison's "Remembering Richard Wright" (pp. 99, 119).

1765. Pearson, Lynn. "Fabre Ford Foundation Professor." *The Southern Register,* 6 (Winter), 5. Comments on Fabre's extensive work on W.

1766. Peterson, Bernard L., Jr. *Contemporary Black American Playwrights and Their Plays: A Biographical Directory and Dramatic Index.* Westport, CT: Greenwood Press, pp. 304, 376. Lists Leslie Lee's adaptation of "Almos' a Man" and Rob Penny's adaptation of "Bright and Morning Star."

1767. Pettis, Joyce. "Margaret Walker," in *Afro-American Writers, 1940–1955.* Ed. Trudier Harris. *Dictionary of Literary Biography,* Vol. 76. Detroit: Gale, pp. 173–181. Discusses Walker's literary friendship with W (pp. 174–176).

1768. Pfaff, Françoise. *Twenty-five Black African Filmmakers.* Westport, CT: Greenwood Press, p. 238. Mentions briefly Ousmane Sembene's interest in W.

1769. Phillips, Caryl. "A Good Man and an Honest Writer.'" *Race Today,* 18 (January), 18. Mentions W briefly. Reprinted: 1988.234.

1770. Pinckney, Darryl. "Blues for Mr. Baldwin," in *Critical Essays on James Baldwin.* Eds. Fred L. Standley and Nancy V. Burt. Boston: G.K. Hall, pp. 161–166.

1771. Plumpp, Sterling D. "Toi Toi." *The Black Scholar,* 19 (July-October), 99. Poem mentioning W briefly.

1772. Pomerance, Alan. *Repeal of the Blues.* New York: Citadel Press, p. 198. Comments briefly on the film *NS.*

1773. Powers, Bernard E., Jr. "*Richard Wright's Art of Tragedy.* By Joyce Ann Joyce." *Illinois Historical Journal,* 81 (Spring), 67–68. Favorable review noting Joyce's attention to setting, irony, and paradox in establishing the tragic artistry of *NS.*

1774. Pratt, Louis H. "The Political Significance of James Baldwin's Early Criticism," in *Critical Essays on James Baldwin.* Eds. Fred L. Standley and Nancy V. Burt. Boston: G.K. Hall, pp. 267–277.

1775. Pratt, Louis H., and Darnell D. *Alice Malsenior Walker: An Annotated Bibliography: 1968–1986.* Westport, CT: Meckler, pp. 38, 39, 42, 56, 89, 134. Lists items commenting on W by Gayle R. Pemberton, Arnold Rampersad, Clyde Taylor, Robert Towers, and Susan Willis.

1776. Proffitt, Edward. "Questions, Writing Suggestions," in his *Reading and Writing About Short Fiction.* San Diego: Harcourt Brace Jovanovich, pp. 445–446. Five questions and two writing suggestions about "The Man Who Was Almost a Man."

1777. Rampersad, Arnold. "Henry Dumas's World of Fiction." *Black American Literature Forum,* 22 (Summer), 329–332. Mentions briefly W and "Down by the Riverside."

1778. _____. "Psychology and Afro-American Biography." *The Yale Review,* 78 (Autumn), 1–18. Mentions the biographies of W by Webb, Fabre, and Gayle; comments on W's interest in psychiatry, especially in *SH*; and discusses Allison Davis's psychological study of W in *Leadership, Love, and Aggression.*

1779. _____. *The Life of Langston Hughes.* Vol. 2: *1941–1967. I Dream a World.* New York: Oxford University Press, pp. 5, 13–14, 18, 23, 30, 44, 48, 80, 95–96, 99, 116, 117, 118–119, 128, 133, 143, 173, 179, 205, 206, 207, 224, 237, 296, 297, 307–308, 326, 360. Exhaustive record of Hughes's contacts with and opinion of W, of whose growing reputation he was jealous. Reprinted: 2002.

1780. Reckley, Ralph. "Chester Himes," in *Afro-American Writers, 1940–1955.* Eds. Trudier Harris and Thadious M. Davis. Detroit: Gale, pp. 89–103. Mentions briefly W and *NS* (pp. 95, 98).

1781. Reed, Ishmael. "Hyped or Hip?" in his *Writin' Is Fightin': Thirty-Seven Years of Boxing on Paper.* New York: Atheneum, pp. 123–131. Reprint of 1986.147.

1782. _____. "Killer Illiteracy," in his *Writin' Is Fightin': Thirty-Seven Years of Boxing on Paper.* New York: Atheneum, pp. 183–194.

1783. _____. "Soyinka Among

the Monoculturalists." *Black American Literature Forum*, 22 (Winter), 705–709. Mentions briefly *NS* (p. 708).

1784. _____. "300 Years of 1984," in his *Writin' Is Fightin': Thirty-Seven Years of Boxing on Paper*. New York: Atheneum, pp. 57–75. Mentions briefly *SH* (p. 60) and calls *NS* a "great work of art" (p. 74).

1785. Renek, Morris. "'Sex Was Their Way of Life': A Frank interview with Erskine Caldwell," in Edwin J. Arnold, ed. *Conversations with Erskine Caldwell*. Jackson: University Press of Mississippi, pp. 66–80.

1786. Rieke, Alison. "Articulation and Collaboration in Richard Wright's Major Fiction," in *Richard Wright: Myths and Realities*. Ed. C. James Trotman. New York: Garland, pp. 111–123. Examines the role of polemics in the narrative structure of *NS*, *O*, and "The Man Who Lived Underground." In these stories fear leads the protagonist to violence followed by concealment, then articulation, which involves white male collaborators. The final step, possible but never realized, is reintegration into society.

1787. Riis, Thomas. "Blacks on the Musical Stage," in *Images of Blacks in American Culture: A Reference Guide to Information Sources*. Ed. Jessie Carney Smith. Westport, CT: Greenwood Press, pp. 29–50. Comments on the play *NS* (p. 41).

1788. Roache, Joel. "'What Had Made Him and What He Meant': the Politics of Wholeness in 'How "Bigger" Was Born," in *Richard Wright's Native Son*. Ed. Harold Bloom. New York: Chelsea House, pp. 39–55.

1789. Rollyson, Carl. *Lillian Hellman: Her Legend and Her Legacy*. New York: St. Martin's Press, p. 159. Quotes from a letter of Hellman to W about *PM*.

1790. Rood, Karen L. "Schooldays," in her *American Literary Almanac from 1608 to the Present*. New York: Facts on File, pp. 45–152. Notes that Theodore Morrison invited W to lecture at the Bread Loaf Writers' Conference (p. 86). Also sketches W's education and early literary career (p. 152).

1791. Rosenblatt, Roger. "Bigger's Infernal Assumption," in *Richard Wright's Native Son*. Ed. Harold Bloom. New York: Chelsea House, pp. 23–37.

1792. Rowell, Charles H. "'Inscription at the City of Brass': An Interview with Romare Bearden." *Callaloo*, 11 (Summer), 428–446. Includes brief discussion of W and *NS* (p. 437).

1793. Sanders, Leslie Catherine. *The Development of Black Theater in America: From Shadows to Selves*. Baton Rouge: Louisiana State University Press, pp. 5, 16, 164, 186. Brief mentions of *NS*.

1794. Sasse, Mary Hawley. "Literature in a Multiethnic Culture," in *Literature in the Classroom: Readers, Texts, and Contexts*. Ed. Ben F. Nelms. Urbana, IL: National Council of Teachers of English, pp. 167–178. Mentions briefly "Bright and Morning Star" (p. 175).

1795. Sato, Hiroko. "Foreign Scholarship: Japanese Contributions," in *American Literary Scholarship: An Annual/1986*. Ed. David J. Nordloh. Durham, NC: Duke University Press, pp. 472–479. Mentions an article on *NS* by Hiroyuki Koguchi (p. 478).

1796. Schaub, Thomas. "Ellison's Masks and the Novel of Reality," in *New Essays on Invisible Man*. Ed. Robert O'Meally. New York: Cambridge University Press, pp. 123–156. Notes W's early stimulus to Ellison's literary career, and discusses how Ellison's differed from W's kind of fiction (pp. 123, 134–135).

1797. Schultz, Elizabeth A. "The Illumination of Darkness: Affinities Between *Moby-Dick* and *Invisible Man*." *CLA Journal*, 32 (December), 170–200. Mentions W briefly (p. 171).

1798. Schwartz, Lawrence H. *Creating Faulkner's Reputation: The Politics of Modern Literary Criticism*. Knoxville: University of Tennessee Press, pp. 3, 101, 109–110. Mentions W briefly.

1799. Seamon, Roger. "Naturalist Narratives and Their Ideational Context: A Theory of Naturalist Fiction." *The Canadian Review of American Studies*, 19 (Spring), 47–64. Quotes James Baldwin and Michel Fabre on W (pp. 50, 57).

1800. Seed, David. "American Literature: The Twentieth Century: Prose Fiction," in *The Year's Work in English Studies*, Vol. 66. London: John Murray, pp. 595–634. Contains a favorable review of Michel Fabre's *The World of Richard Wright* (pp. 622–633) and mentions W elsewhere (p. 633).

1801. Seelye, John. "If at First You Don't Secede, Try, Try Again: Southern Literature from Fenimore Cooper to Faulkner." *Proceedings of the American Antiquarian Society*, 98, Part 1, 51–68. Notes W's use of Poe in *NS*.

1802. Shapiro, Herbert. *White Violence and Black Response: From Reconstruction to Montgomery*. Amherst: The University of Massachusetts Press, pp. 255, 257, 291–297, 331, 336. Discusses the theme of violence in *BB*, *UTC*, and *NS*. Quotes W on the National Negro Congress and Harlem riot of 1943. Quotes Allison Davis on W.

1803. Shaw, Brenda R. "An Interview with Richard K. Barksdale." *CLA Journal*, 31 (June) 400–411. Barksdale mentions W briefly (p. 405).

1804. Showalter, Elaine. "Women Writers Between the Wars," in *Columbia Literary History of the United States*. Ed. Emory Elliott. New York: Columbia University Press, pp. 822–841. Mentions W in relation to communism and to Zora Neale Hurston.

1805. Shrodes, Caroline, Harry Finestone, and Michael Shugrue. "Richard Wright," in their *The Conscious Reader*. Fourth edition. New York: Macmillan, p. 707.

1806. _____. "Richard Wright *The Ethics of Living Jim Crow*," in their *The Conscious Reader*. Fourth edition. New York: Macmillan, p. 707.

1807. _____. "Suggestions for Discussion, Suggestions for Writing," in their *The Conscious Reader*. Fourth edition. New York: Macmillan, p. 716. Reprint of 1974.157.

1808. Sims-Wood, Janet. "The Black Female: Mammy, Jemima, Sapphire, and Other Images," in *Images of Blacks in Musical Culture: A Reference Guide to Information Sources*. Ed. Jessie Carney Smith. Westport, CT: Greenwood Press, pp. 235–256. Mentions Gloria Wade-Gayles's treatment of Mrs. Thomas in *NS* in a 1980 article.

1809. _____, et al. "Studies in Afro-American Literature: An Annual Annotated Bibliography, 1987." *Callaloo*, 11 (Fall), 720–771. Lists seven items on W and crosslists twelve additional items touching on W.

1810. Skerrett, Joseph T., Jr. "Composing Bigger: Wright and the

Making of *Native Son*," in *Richard Wright's Native Son*. Ed. Harold Bloom. New York: Chelsea House, pp. 125–142. Psychological approach arguing that the novel "objectified, in symbolic terms," W's own "conflicts and passions" (p. 126). These center around his rebellious nature, his rejection of family, women, religion, society, and finally the Communist Party. Like W, Bigger Thomas must create his own values.

1811. Smelstor, Marjorie. "Richard Wright's Beckoning Descent and Ascent," in *Richard Wright: Myths and Realities*. Ed. C. James Trotman. New York: Garland, pp. 89–109. Considers *BB* and *AH*, the first poetic and the second polemic. A complex autobiography, the total work "is blues and testimonial; it is Aristotelian and Longinian; it is product and process" (pp. 92–93). Smelstor considers such matters as structure, imagery, and narrative voice, as well as themes of education, self-creation, the journey, and purification through destruction.

1812. Smith, Valerie. "Alienation and Creativity in *Native Son*," in *Richard Wright's Native Son*. Ed. Harold Bloom. New York: Chelsea House, pp. 105–114.

1813. _____. "The Meaning of Narration in *Invisible Man*," in *New Essays on Invisible Man*. Ed. Robert O'Meally. Cambridge: Cambridge University Press, pp. 25, 70. Mentions briefly the Howe-Ellison exchange and Ellison's essay. "Remembering Richard Wright."

1814. Smith, Virginia Whatley. "Richard Wright's *Tarbaby Series*." *Dissertation Abstracts International*, 48 (February), 2063A. Abstracts a 1988 Boston University dissertation of mostly unpublished material that reflects the four periods of Tarbaby's life. "The history and composition of the *Tarbaby Series* is discussed in detail," and reading texts with apparatus are provided for "Tarbaby's Dawn" and "Tarbaby's Sunrise."

1815. S.[mith], W.R.[aymond]. "Richard Wright *The Library Card*," in *Instructor's Guide to the Riverside Anthology of Literature* by Melody Richardson Daily, Douglas Hunt, and W. Raymond Smith. Boston: Houghton Mifflin, pp. 93–95. Questions and answers concerning autobiographical verisimilitude, relation of autobiography and fiction, and polemicism in an excerpt from *BB*.

1816. [Snell, Susan]. "Black Studies." *The Society for the Study of Southern Literature News-Letter*, 21 (April), 24–26. Notes the reissue of *TMBV*.

1817. _____. "Books." *The Society for the Study of Southern Literature News-Letter*, 21 (November), 18–30. Lists Margaret Walker's biography of W and the reissue of *EM*.

1818. _____. "Fall 1988 Conferences." *The Society for the Study of Southern Literature News-Letter*, 21 (November), 7–8. Reports a symposium on W at Jackson State University "led by scholars Jerry Ward, Eugene Redman [sic] and Gloria Gayles."

1819. _____. "People, Projects, Etc." *The Society for the Study of Southern Literature News-Letter*, 21 (November), 10–11. Notes that Virginia Whatley Smith is working on W.

1820. Soitos, Stephen. "Black Orpheus Refused: A Study of Richard Wright's *The Man Who Lived Underground*," in *Richard Wright: Myths and Realities*. Ed. C. James Trotman. New York: Garland, pp. 15–25. Interprets W's novella "as a synthesis of Eurocentric myth and Afro-American sensibilities" (p. 15). W weaves into the myth of Orpheus racial themes constituting an indictment of white American society.

1821. Spofford, Tim. *Lynch Street: The May 1970 Slayings at Jackson State College*. Kent, OH: The Kent State University Press, pp. 9, 33, 104, 187. Notes that W lived on Lynch Street in Jackson, uses a quotation from *BB* as an epigraph to the third chapter, and states that W was discussed in black schools in Jackson in the 1960s.

1822. _____. *Lynch Street: The May 1970 Slayings at Jackson State College*. Kent, OH: Kent State University Press, pp. 9, 104, 187. Notes that W had once lived on Lynch Street in Jackson and that teachers at the black Line Street School often discussed W.

1823. Standley, Fred L. "James Baldwin as Dramatist," in *Critical Essays on James Baldwin*. Eds. Fred L. Standley and Nancy V. Burt. Boston: G.K. Hall, pp. 298–302.

1824. _____. "James Baldwin: The Artist as Incorrigible Disturber of the Peace," in *Critical Essays on James Baldwin*. Eds. Fred L. Stand-

ley and Nancy V. Burt. Boston: G.K. Hall, pp. 43–54. Reprint of 1970.329.

1825. _____, and Nancy V. Burt. "Introduction," in their *Critical Essays on James Baldwin*. Boston: G.K. Hall, pp. 1–33. Discusses Cleaver's essay on Baldwin and W (pp. 9, 10) and mentions W elsewhere (pp. 3, 14, 17).

1826. Steiner, Wendy. "The Diversity of American Fiction," in *Columbia Literary History of the United States*. Ed. Emory Elliott. New York: Columbia University Press, pp. 845–872. Mentions W's residence in Paris, his editorship of *New Challenge*, *NS*, and *BB*.

1827. Stepto, Robert B. "Afro-American Literature," in *Columbia Literary History of the United States*. Ed. Emory Elliott. New York: Columbia University Press, pp. 785–799. Mentions W frequently, mainly in relation to canonical issues. Mentions also *NS*, *UTC*, and *BB*.

1828. Stewart, Leisha. "Painful Truths of a SAMLA Convention." *Sage: A Scholarly Journal on Black Women*, 5 (Summer), 71–72. Reports on a paper by Virginia Whatley Smith comparing *BB* and Mark Mathabane's *Kaffir Boy*.

1829. Subryan, Carmen. "Circles: Mother and Daughter Relationships in Toni Morrison's *Song of Solomon*." *Sage: A Scholarly Journal on Black Women*, 5 (Summer), 34–36. Mentions briefly *NS* and *BB*.

1830. Sullivan, Sally. *Vision and Revision: The Process of Reading and Writing*. New York: Macmillan, pp. 29–30. Mentions briefly W and *BB* to illustrate that writers are avid readers.

1831. Sundquist, Eric J. "Realism and Regionalism," in *Columbia Literary History of the United States*. Ed. Emory Elliott. New York: Columbia University Press, pp. 501–524. Notes that Dunbar's *The Sport of the Gods* "presages Richard Wright" (p. 513).

1832. Taylor, Clyde. "Henry Dumas: Legacy of a Long-Breath Singer." *Black American Literature Forum*, 22 (Summer), 353–364. Notes that Taylor won *Black World's* Richard Wright Award for Literary Criticism (p. 353). Comments on "Hearst Headline Blues" and "Between the World and Me" (p. 355).

1833. Taylor, Willene P. "The Blindness Motif in *Native Son*." *The Literary Griot*, 1 (Fall), 59–74.

Examines blindness as a metaphor of racial relations in America. Also discusses "the motif of the forbidden fruit that brings a tragic vision of reality to the protagonist" (p. 59).

1834. Tener, Robert L. "Union with Nature: Rchard [sic] Wright and the Art of Haiku." *Chiba Review*, 10, 19–34. Discusses the circumstances of W's interest in the form during his last year, sketches the history and nature of haiku, and analyzes several of W's poems in the form. W's individualism and racial themes did not usually allow him "to attain the necessary austerity and selfless love of the ordinary" that characterizes the best haiku, but his 4000 haiku poems do illustrate his lifelong interest in the relation between human beings and nature.

1835. Thomas, H. Nigel. *From Folklore to Fiction: A Study of Folk Heroes and Rituals in the Black American Novel*. Westport, CT: Greenwood Press, pp. 9, 38, 39, 71–75, 92, 99–100, 123, 124–137, 165, 193–194. Analyzes Bigger Thomas as a Bad Nigger, making specific comparisons to the toast hero (pp. 71–75), discusses the use of folk rituals in *LT* (pp. 124–131), and shows "the bankruptcy of folklore" in *LD* (pp. 131–137). Thomas considers more briefly "Blueprint for Negro Writing," *BP, O, WML, UTC, BB, AH,* and *TMBV*.

1836. Thompson, Thelma Barnaby. "J. Saunders Redding," in *Afro-American Writers, 1940–1955*. Eds. Trudier Harris and Thadious M. Davis. Detroit: Gale, pp. 148–157. Uses W's introduction to Redding's *No Day of Triumph* as the point of departure. Lists Redding's essays on W.

1837. Tindall, George Brown. *America: A Narrative History*. Second edition. New York: Norton, pp. 1059, 1061–1062. Reprint of 1984 with a photograph of W added.

1838. _____. *America: A Narrative History*. Second Edition. New York: W.W. Norton, pp. 1059, 1061–1062. Mentions W's affiliation with the League of American Writers and provides a biographical sketch including a photograph of W. Mentions *NS* and "The Ethics of Living Jim Crosw".

1839. Trachtenberg, Alan. "From Image to Story: Reading the File," in *Documenting America, 1935–1943*. Berkeley: University of Cali-

fornia Press, p. 66. Comments on the relation of image and text in *TMBV*.

1840. Tracy, Steven C. *Langston Hughes and the Blues*. Urbana: University of Illinois Press, pp. 2, 98, 132, 212–215. Comments on and quotes from W's introduction to *Blues Fell This Morning* and discusses his alleged ignorance of the blues tradition. Also analyzes "Red Clay Blues."

1841. Traoré, Ousseynou B. "Like a Mask, Dancing." *The Literary Griot*, 1 (Fall), v–x. Comments on the essays by Willene P. Taylor and Jane Davis in this issue.

1842. Traylor, Eleanor W. "The Fabulous World of Toni Morrison: *Tar Baby*," in *Critical Essays on Toni Morrison*. Ed. Nellie Y. McKay. Boston: G.K. Hall, pp. 135–150.

1843. _____. "Henry Dumas and the Discourse of Memory." *Black American Literature Forum*, 22 (Summer), 365–378. Mentions "the native son" as a trope (p. 369). Mentions W as a "literary father" of Dumas.

1844. _____. "I Hear Music in the Air: James Baldwin's *Just Above My Head*," in *Critical Essays on James Baldwin*. Eds. Fred L. Standley and Nancy V. Burt. Boston: G.K. Hall, pp. 217–223.

1845. Tremaine, Louis. "The Dissociated Sensibility of Bigger Thomas," in *Richard Wright's Native Son*. Ed. Harold Bloom. New York: Chelsea House, pp. 89–104.

1846. Trimmer, Joseph F., and James M. McCrimmon. "Exercise," in their *Writing with a Purpose*. Ninth edition. Boston: Houghton Mifflin, pp. 237–238. Asks the reader to compare tone in passages from Walker Percy, Jan Morris, and *BB*.

1847. Trotman, C. James. "Our Myths and Wright's Realities," in his *Richard Wright: Myths and Realities*. New York: Garland, pp. xi–xvi. Introduction to a collection of papers from the Richard Wright Literary Symposium held in October 1985 at West Chester University. Trotman stresses W's contribution to expanded social awareness, even though his treatment of women characters is less than satisfactory.

1848. _____, ed. *Richard Wright: Myths and Realities*. New York: Garland, xvi + 163 pp. Contains an introduction by the editor ("Our Myths and Wright's Realities") and

essays by Michael Atkinson, Joseph Bodziock, Elizabeth J. Ciner, Robert L. Douglas, Thomas Larson, Paul Newlin, Alison Rieke, Marjorie Smelstor, Stephen Soitos, Robbie Jean Walker, and Nagueyalti Warren.

1849. Troupe, Quincy. "An Interview with James Baldwin." *The Village Voice* (12 January), p. 36. Baldwin mentions W briefly as the first writer he ever met.

1850. _____. "James Baldwin, 1924–1987: A Tribute–The Last Interview" *Essence*, 18 (March), 53, 114, 117, 119. Troupe mentions W briefly (p. 53).

1851. _____. "Last Testament: An Interview with James Baldwin." *The Village Voice* (12 January), p. 36. Baldwin mentions W briefly.

1852. _____. "The Last Interview." *Essence*, 18 (March), 53, 114, 117, 119. Interview with James Baldwin mentioning W briefly.

1853. Turner, Darwin T. "Civil Rights in the Second Renaissance — 1954–1970: Introduction." *The Black Scholar*, 19 (January-February), 2–3. Mentions briefly the 1971 Wright Conference at the University of Iowa.

1854. Turner, Joyce Moore. "Richard B. Moore and His Works," in *Richard B. Moore, Caribbean Militant in Harlem*. Eds. W. Burghardt Turner and Joyce Moore Turner. Bloomington: Indiana University Press, pp. 69, 71. Quotes from W's "Foreword" to George Padmore's *Pan-Africanism or Communism* and mentions sale of W's novels at Richard Moore's Book Center in Harlem.

1855. Wade-Lewis, Margaret. "Censorship of Black Books," in *The Bicentennial of the U.S. Constitution: Reflections on the Black Experience*. New York: New York University Institute of Afro-American Affairs, pp. 1–7. Notes that *BB* and *NS* have been targets of censors.

1856. Walden, Daniel. "From Image to Presence: Literary Merit and Social Value in Twentieth-Century American Jewish Literature." *American Jewish Archives*, 40 (April), 159–164. Mentions briefly *NS* (p. 164).

1857. Walker, Margaret. *Richard Wright: Daemonic Genius*. New York: Warner Books, 448 pp. Described as "A Portrait of the Man, A Critical Look at His Work," this book combines memoir and biography, criticism and intellectual history. The biographical approach is heavily psychological, emphasizing the wounds inflicted by racism and severe sexual strains in W's personality. W's literary relations are with naturalism, realism, black humanism, and Southern gothicism; his intellectual development assimilated Marx, Freud, Kierkegaard, Einstein, and Du Bois, the key thinkers of the twentieth century. The book concludes with a bibliographical essay and a conference speech delivered at the University of Mississippi.

1858. Walker, Marshall. *The Literature of the United States of America.* Second edition. London: Macmillan Education, pp. 157–225. Revised reprint of 1983.89.

1859. Walker, Robbie Jean. "Artistic Integration of Ideology and Symbolism in Richard Wright's 'Fire and Cloud,'" in *Richard Wright: Myths and Realities.* Ed. C. James Trotman. New York: Garland, pp. 3–14. Disputing the notion that art and propaganda are irreconcilable, Walker analyzes Biblical imagery in the story using the model Barthes proposes in "An Introduction to the Structural Analysis of Narrative." Imagery of dust, fire, and cloud is used effectively to develop theme in "Fire and Cloud."

1860. Walker, Warren S. "Bibliography." *Studies in Short Fiction,* 25 (Summer), 337–385. Lists three items on W.

1861. Wall, Cheryl A. "*Modernism and the Harlem Renaissance.* By Houston A. Baker, Jr.; *Ride Out the Wilderness: Geography and Identity in Afro-American Literature.* By Melvin Dixon." *American Literature,* 60 (December), 680–682. Mentions briefly W and "The Man Who Lived Underground."

1862. Wallace, Michelle. "Who Dat Say Who Dat When I Say Who Dat? Zora Neale Hurston Then and Now." *The Village Voice Literary Supplement,* 64 (April), pp. 18–21. Mentions W briefly.

1863. Ward, Jerry W., Jr. "Verbal Text Beyond a Pretext." *Callaloo,* 11 (Spring), 392–394. Mentions briefly *O.*

1864. Ward, Jerry W., Jr. "A Writer for Her People: An Interview with Dr. Margaret Walker Alexander." *The Mississippi Quarterly,* 41 (Fall), 515–527. Walker notes that

W had "that Gothic imagination" (p. 517), claims that W took the idea for *NS* from her *Goose Island* (p. 522), and states that W was a Trotskyist (p. 526).

1865. Ward, William S. *A Literary History of Kentucky.* Knoxville: The University of Tennessee Press, p. 425. Mentions briefly W and *NS.*

1866. Warren, Kenneth W. "Possessing the Common Ground: William Dean Howells' *An Imperative Duty.*" *American Literary Realism,* 20 (Spring), 23–37. Contains an epigraph from *BB* and begins and ends with references to W.

1867. Warren, Nagueyalti. "Black Girls and Native Sons: Female Images in Selected Works by Richard Wright," in *Richard Wright: Myths and Realities.* Ed. C. James Trotman. New York: Garland, pp. 59–77. Examines black women in W's work, finding that they are either nonfeminine stereotypes or whorish sex objects. Warren treats *NS, BB, O, LD,* and "Long Black Song," but not "Bright and Morning Star." She quotes from various critics and provides a lengthy bibliography.

1868. Wartts, Charles, Jr. "Henry Dumas: A Coat Spun of Race, Rivers, and Rainbows." *Black American Literature Forum,* 22 (Summer), 388–393. Mentions W briefly (p. 390).

1869. Washington, J. Charles. "Positive Black Males in Alice Walker's Fiction." *Obsidian II,* 3 (Spring), 23–48. Mentions W briefly (p. 24).

1870. Watkins, Mel. "The Fire Next Time This Time," in *Critical Essays on James Baldwin.* Eds. Fred L. Standley and Nancy V. Burt. Boston: G.K. Hall, pp. 232–238.

1871. Webb, Tracy. "The Role of Water Imagery in *Uncle Tom's Children.*" *Modern Fiction Studies,* 34 (Spring), 5–16. Examines W's extensive water and thirst imagery in each of the five stories of the expanded version. For Big Boy and Mann water has negative connotations. Thirst is important in "Long Black Song." Water has more favorable connotations in the last two stories. For Sue in "Bright and Morning Star," crossing a swollen creek is tantamount to gaining control of her life.

1872. Weissinger, Thomas. "Current Bibliography." *Black American Literature Forum,* 22 (Summer),

412–416. Lists Keneth Kinnamon's *A Richard Wright Bibliography* and the reprint edition of *TMBV.*

1873. Weixlmann, Joe. "Dealing with the Demands of an Expanding Literary Canon." *College English,* 50 (March), 273–283. Notes that Harold Kolb includes W among the eleven writers to be represented in all American literature surveys.

1874. Werner, Craig. *Adrienne Rich: The Poet and Her Critics.* Chicago: American Library Association, pp. 28, 166. Mentions briefly W and *NS.*

1875. _____. *Dubliners: A Pluralistic World.* Boston: Twayne, p. 8. Notes that Joyce anticipates later collections of short stories, such as *UTC,* "with the structural and thematic coherence usually associated with novels."

1876. _____. "Recent Books on Modern Black Fiction: An Essay-Review." *Modern Fiction Studies,* 34 (Spring), 125–135. Includes reviews of Joyce A. Joyce's *Richard Wright's Art of Tragedy* and Michel Fabre's *The World of Richard Wright.* Mentions W elsewhere.

1877. West, Cornel. "On Mark Naison's *Communists in Harlem During the Depression,*" in his *Prophetic Fragments: Illuminations of the Crisis in American Religion and Culture.* Grand Rapids, MI: Eerdman's, and Trenton, NJ: Africa World Press, pp. 90–93.

1878. West, Sandra. "Literary Civil War: Black American Poetry of the 1960s," in *The Bicentennial of the U.S. Constitution.* Ed. Earl S. Davis. New York: New York University Institute of Afro-American Affairs, pp. 15–40. Comments on and quotes from "Blueprint for Negro Writing" (p. 17).

1879. Whitfield, Stephen J. *American Space, Jewish Time.* Hamden, CT: Archon, pp. 48, 158, 213. Quotes W on "Melanctha" and notes that Hollywood wanted to make Bigger Thomas white.

1880. _____. "The Braided Identity of Southern Jewry." *American Jewish History,* 77 (March), 363–387. Comments on and quotes from the library episode in *BB* (p. 369).

1881. _____. *A Death in the Delta: The Story of Emmett Till.* Baltimore: The Johns Hopkins University Press, pp. 8, 79, 128. Comments on W's attitudes toward lynching and mentions his coverage of the Bandung Conference.

1882. Whitlow, Roger. "Baldwin's *Going to Meet the Man*: Racial Brutality and Sexual Gratification," in *Critical Essays on James Baldwin*. Eds. Fred L. Standley and Nancy V. Burt. Boston: G.K. Hall, pp. 194–198.

1883. Williams, John A. "Prior Restraints." *The Nation*, 246 (23 April), 574–577. Mentions W briefly (p. 576).

1884. Williams, Kenny J. *A Storyteller and a City: Sherwood Anderson's Chicago*. DeKalb: Northern Illinois University Press, pp. 27, 28, 40, 44, 96, 129, 154, 161, 164, 180. Mentions briefly W, *NS*, and Bigger Thomas.

1885. Williams, Ora. "Lorenz Graham," in *Afro-American Writers, 1940–1955*. Eds. Trudier Harris and Thadious M. Davis. Detroit: Gale, pp. 57–66. Mentions W briefly (p. 58).

1886. Wilson, M.L. *Chester Himes*. New York: Chelsea House, pp. 49, 50, 57, 61, 63, 66, 75, 86. Mentions W's friendship with and influence on Himes. Includes two photographs of W, one with Ellen and Lionel Stander (p. 57) and the other alone (p. 61).

1887. Wilson, Mark K. "A *MELUS* Interview: Ann Petry — The New England Connection." *MELUS*, 15 (Summer), 71–84. Petry states that she "had no contact with Richard Wright," but read and admired his fiction (pp. 79–80).

1888. Winegarten, Renee. *Simone de Beauvoir: A Critical View*. Oxford: Berg, p. 66. Mentions briefly W and *BB*.

1889. Wintz, Cary D. *Black Culture and the Harlem Rennaissance*. Houston: Rice University Press, pp. 2, 217. Mentions W briefly.

1890. Wright, John S. "The Conscious Hero and the Rites of Man: Ellison's War," in *New Essays on Ralph Ellison*. Ed. Robert O'Meally. Cambridge: Cambridge University Press, pp. 183, 185. Mentions briefly *BB* and *NS*.

1891. Wyatt-Brown, Bertram. "The Mask of Obedience: Male Slave Psychology in the Old South." *The American Historical Review*, 93 (December), 1228–1252. Recounts the episode of Shorty the elevator operator in *BB* (pp. 1245–1246).

1892. Yamagata, Toshio. "Passing as a White." *Journal of Komazawa University Faculty of Foreign Languages*, 28 (1 September), 173–183. Traces the history of Afro-American Literature from slave narratives to W and Baldwin.

1893. Yetman, Norman R. "Autobiographies," in *Dictionary of Afro-American Slavery*. Eds. Randall M. Miller and John David Smith. Westport, CT: Greenwood Press, pp. 70–71. Mentions W briefly.

1989

1894. Achebe, Chinua. "'Spelling Our Proper Name,'" in *Black Writers Redefine the Struggle*. Ed. Jules Chametsky. Amherst: The University of Massachusetts Press, pp. 5–12. Mentions W briefly (p. 8).

1895. _____. "Panel Discussion," in *Black Writers Redefine the Struggle: A Tribute to James Baldwin*. Jules Chametsky, ed. Amherst, MA: Institute for Advanced Study in the Humanities, pp. 72–74. Mentions W briefly.

1896. Abel, Richard M. "From the Director," in *Books for Fall and Winter 1989–1990*. Jackson: University Press of Mississippi, inside front cover. Mentions W briefly.

1897. Ailey, Alvin, James Baldwin, Romare Bearden, and Albert Murray. "To Hear Another Language." *Callaloo*, 12 (Summer), 431–452. Bearden mentions W briefly (p. 435).

1898. Altman, Susan. "James Baldwin, Playwright, 1924–1987," in her *Extraordinary Black Americans from Colonial to Contemporary Times*. Chi-

cago: Childrens Press, pp. 178–180. Mentions the W-Baldwin friendship.

1899. _____. "Richard Wright, Novelist, 1908–1960," in her *Extraordinary Black Americans from Colonial to Contemporary Times*. Chicago: Children's Press, pp. 150–152. Biographical sketch focusing on the American years.

1900. Andrews, William L. "Toward a Poetic of Afro-American Autobiography," in *Afro-American Literary Study in the 1990's*. Eds. Houston A. Baker, Jr., and Patricia Redmond. Chicago: The University of Chicago Press, pp. 78–104. Mentions briefly *BB*. (p. 81).

1901. Andreas, James R. "*Invisible Man* and the Comic Tradition," in *Approaches to Teaching Ellison's Invisible Man*. Eds. Susan Resneck Parr and Pancho Savery. New York: The Modern Language Association of America, pp. 102–106. Mentions briefly "The Man Who Lived Underground" (p. 105).

1902. Angelou, Maya, and Clau-

dia Tate. "Maya Angelou," in *Conversations with Maya Angelou*. Ed. Jeffrey M. Elliot, Jackson: University Press of Mississippi, pp. 146–156.

1903. Angelou, Maya, and Greg Hitt. "Maya Angelou," in *Conversations with Maya Angelou*. Ed. Jeffrey M. Elliot. Jackson: University Press of Mississippi, pp. 205–213. Winston-Salem Journal (6 Dec. 1987), Sec. A, 13, 16.

1904. Angelou, Maya, and Rosa Guy. "A Conversation Between Rosa Guy and Maya Angelou," in *Conversations with Maya Angelou*. Ed. Jeffrey M. Elliot. Jackson: University Press of Mississippi, pp. 218–240. Writing Lives, ed. Mary Chamberlain.

1905. Annable, H.D. *Annable's Treasury of Literary Teasers*. Cincinnati: Writer's Digest Books, pp. 189, 190. Asks which book W called his "literary Bible" and answers H.L. Mencken's *Book of Prefaces*.

1906. Anon. "A Book Lover's Trivial Pursuit." Envelope flap accompanying *Book-of-the-Month Club News* (December). Notice of H.D. Annable's *Annable's Treasury of Literary Teasers* mentioning as afterword its question "What was Richard Wright's literary bible?"

1907. Anon. "American Short Story: Almos' a Man," in *University of Illinois Video Sales Catalog*. Champaign: University of Illinois Film Center, p. 53. Notice and summary of the dramatic version of the short story.

1908. Anon. *Arts & Humanities Citation Index 1988*. Vol. 2 Philadelphia: Institute for Scientific Information, pp. 11408–11409. Lists sixty-six items s.v.: Wright R, not all on W.

1909. Anon. "Baker, Houston A., Jr., in *Black Writers: A Selection of Sketches from Contemporary Authors*. Ed. Linda Metzger. Detroit: Gale Research, pp. 23–24. Lists Baker's collection of interpretations of *NS*.

1910. Anon. Baldwin, James (Arthur), in *Black Writers: A Selection of Sketches from Contemporary Authors*. Ed. Linda Metzger. Detroit: Gale Research, pp. 24–30. Notes W's help to Baldwin at the beginning of his career.

1911. Anon. "Baraka, Amire (Leroi Jones), in *Black Writers: A Selection of Sketches from Contemporary Authors*. Ed. Linda Metzger. Detroit: Gale Research, pp. 33–42. Cites Arnold Rampersad citing W as one of the eight figures who have significantly affected the course of African-American literary culture." (p. 36).

1912. Anon. "Black Participation in American Society," in *A Common Destiny: Blacks and American Society*. Eds. Gerald David Jaynes and Robin M. Williams, Jr. Washington: National Academy Press, pp. 101, 167. Comments on W, mentioning *NS*, *UTC*, *BB* and *O*.

1913. Anon. "Brooks, Gwendolyn," in *Black Writers: A Selection of Sketches from Contemporary Authors*. Ed. Linda Megzger. Detroit: Gale Research, pp. 64–69. Cites a reviewer's opinion that the impact of *In the Mecca* is comparable to that of W's fiction (p. 66).

1914. Anon. "Chronology: A Historical Review," in *The Negro Almanac: A Reference Work on the African American*. Eds. Harry A. Ploski and James Williams. Detroit: Gale, p. 35. Notes that W became

editor of *Challenge* advocated social realism (p. 25).

1915. Anon. Davis, Charles T., in *Black Writers: A Selection of Sketches from Contemporary Authors*. Eds. Linda Metzger. Detroit: Gale Research, pp. 139–140. Mentions W briefly.

1916. Anon. Dust Jacket of *Conversations with James Baldwin*. Eds. Fred L. Standley and Louis H. Pratt. Jackson: University Press of Mississippi. Mentions W briefly.

1917. Anon. *"Eight Men,"* in *Thunder's Mouth Press: Fall 89*. New York: Thunder's Mouth Press, p. 18. Publisher's notice of a reprint edition.

1918. Anon. "Ellison, Ralph Waldo," in *Black Writers: A Selection of Sketches from Contemporary Authors*. Ed. Linda Metzger. Detroit: Gale Research, pp. 176–183. Substantial biographical-critical sketch mentioning W's tutelage. Also mentions *NS*.

1919. Anon. "Gayle, Addison, Jr.," in *Black Writers: A Selection of Sketches from Contemporary Authors*. Ed. Linda Metzger. Detroit: Gale Research, pp. 216–217. Lists Gayle's *Richard Wright: Ordeal of a Native Son*.

1920. Anon. Gibson, Donald B., in *Black Writers: A Selection of Sketches from Contemporary Authors*. Ed. Linda Metzger. Detroit: Gale Research, p. 217. Lists Gibson's *Five Black Writers: Essays on Wright, Ellison, Baldwin, Hughes, and LeRoi Jones*.

1921. Anon. "Guess Which One Has Been Censored." *Civil Liberties*, No. 367 (Summer), p. 5. Mentions the removal of *BB* from Island Trees, Long Island, schools in 1976.

1922. Anon. "Here's a Sampling of Poll Questions." *Tulsa World* (9 October), p. A-4. Includes a question from a Gallop survey of college seniors on the authorship of *BB* and *NS*.

1923. Anon. "Highlights of NAACP History 1909–1988." *The Crisis*, 96 (January), 78–79, 81–82, 84–90, 92–100, 102–107, 109–111, 113. Mentions the award of the Spingarn Medal to W (p. 90).

1924. Anon. "Himes, Chester (Bomar)," in *Black Writers: A Selection of Sketches from Contemporary Authors*. Ed. Linda Metzger. Detroit: Gale Research, pp. 273–276. Mentions W briefly (p. 274), calling him "Himes's literary model."

1925. Anon. "Hurston, Zora Neale," in *Black Writers: A Selection of Sketches from Contemporary Authors*. Ed. Linda Metzger. Detroit: Gale Research, pp. 287–288. Notes W's unfavorable review of *Their Eyes Were Watching God*.

1926. Anon. Johnson, Anne Janette. "Baldwin, James (Arthur)," in *Black Writers: A Selection of Sketches from Contemporary Authors*. Ed. Linda Metzger. Detroit: Gale Research, pp. 24–30. Notes W's help to Baldwin at the beginning of his career.

1927. Anon. "Madhubuti, Haki R. (Don L. Lee)," in *Black Writers: A Selection of Sketches from Contemporary Authors*. Ed. Linda Metzger. Detroit: Gale Research, pp. 370–372. Mentions W briefly (p. 371).

1928. Anon. "Morrison, Toni," in *Black Writers: A Selection of Sketches from contemporary Authors*. Ed. Linda Metzger. Detroit: Gale Research, pp. 411–417. Mentions briefly W and *NS* (p. 414).

1929. Anon. "Petry, Ann," in *Black Writers: A Selection of Sketches from Contemporary Authors*. Ed. Linda Metzger. Detroit: Gale Research, pp. 454–456. Quotes Arthur P. Davis placing Petry in "the tradition of hard-hitting social commentary which characterized the Richard Wright school of naturalistic protest writing."

1930. Anon. "Poignant portraits of the black experience." *Journal of Black Studies*, 19 (March), 382. Publisher's notice of Mark Mathabane's *Kaffir Boy* mentions briefly *BB*.

1931. Anon. "Publications Relating to Mississippi." *The Journal of Mississippi History*, 51 (February), 69–71. Lists *A Richard Wright Bibliography*.

1932. Anon. "Publications Relating to Mississippi." *The Journal of Mississippi History*, 51 (May), 157–159. Lists articles on W by Hal Blythe and Charlie Sweet and by Susanne Bullock-Kimball.

1933. Anon. "Publications Relating to Mississippi." *The Journal of Mississippi History*, 51 (November), 399–401. Lists an article on W by Lynda Hungerford.

1934. Anon. "Ralph Ellison, Novelist, Essayist, 1914," in *The Negro Almanac: A Reference Work on the African American*. Eds. Harry A. Ploski and James Williams. Detroit: Gale, 1989, pp. 1989–990. Biographical sketch mentioning Ellison's friendship with W.

1935. Anon. *"Richard Wright: Books and Writers.* By Michel Fabre," in *Books for Fall and Winter 1989–1990.* Jackson: University Press of Mississippi, p. 9. Publisher's full notice.

1936. Anon. *"Richard Wright: Books and Writers* by Michel Fabre," in *Mississippi Books in Print 1989–1990.* Jackson: University Press of Mississippi, p. 10. Publisher's brief notice.

1937. Anon. *"Richard Wright: Daemonic Genius.* Margaret Walker." *Publishers Weekly,* 234 (6 January), 50. Favorable retrospective notice of a "passionately committed portrait."

1938. Anon. "Richard Wright 1908–1960," in *Adventures in American Literature.* Orlando: Harcourt Brace Jovanovich, pp. 917–921. Headnote and study aids to a selection from *AH.*

1939. Anon. "Richard Wright, Novelist, 1908–1960," in *The Negro Almanac: A Reference Work on the African American.* Eds. Harry A. Ploski and James Williams. Detroit: Gale, pp. 1021–1022. Biographical sketch mentioning most of W's books. His "work is still used as the yardstick by which black novelist in America are measured."

1940. Anon. "Richard Wright Symposium Held in Moscow." *The Southern Register,* 7 (Summer), 11. Describes the symposium at the Gorky Institute of World Literature in Moscow in July 1989, mentioning the following speakers and their topics: Michel Fabre, Mae Henderson, Keneth Kinamon, Maryemma Graham, and William Ferris.

1941. Anon. "Rivers, Conrad Kent," in *Black Writers: A Selection of Sketches From Contemporary Authors.*" Ed. Linda Metzger. Detroit: Gale Research, p. 488. Lists *The Wright Poems* by Rivers.

1942. Anon. *"12 Million Black Voices,"* in *Thunder's Mouth Press: Fall 89.* New York: Thunder's Mouth Press, p. 14. Publisher's notice.

1943. Anon. "The University Press of Mississippi." *American Literature,* 61 (October), [iii]. Contains publisher's notices of Michel Fabre's *Richard Wright: Books and Writers* and Eugene E. Miller's *Voice of a Native Son: The Poetics of Richard Wright.*

1944. Anon. "The University Press of Mississippi." *The Virginia Quarterly Review,* 65 (Autumn), 119. Publisher's advertisement containing notices of Michel Fabre's *Richard Wright: Books and Writers* and Eugene A. Miller's *Voice of a Native Son: The Poetics of Richard Wright.*

1945. Anon. Untitled photograph with caption. *The Southern Register,* 7 (Winter), 6. The photograph shows Margaret Walker at an autograph party for her book on W. On 15 November 1989 a Richard Wright Day was proclaimed in Jackson, Mississippi, with a symposium on W at Jackson State University.

1946. Anon. *"Voice of a Native Son: The Poetics of Richard Wright.* By Eugene E. Miller in *Books for Fall and Winter 1989–1990.* Jackson: University Press of Mississippi, p. 8. Publisher's full notice.

1947. Anon. *"Voice of a Native Son: The Poetics of Richard Wright* By Eugene E. Miller," in *Mississippi Books in Print 1989–1990.* Jackson: University Press of Mississippi, p. 11. Publisher's brief notice.

1948. Anon. "Walker, Margaret Abigail," in *Black Writers: A Selection of Sketches from Contemporary Authors.* Ed. Linda Metzger. Detroit: Gale Research, pp. 575–578. Mentions briefly Walker's biography of W (p. 575).

1949. Anon. "Ward, Theodore," in *Black Writers: A Selection of Sketches from Contemporary Authors.* Ed. Linda Metzger. Detroit: Gale Research, pp. 581–582. Mentions W briefly (p. 582).

1950. Anon. *"The World of Richard Wright* by Michel Fabre," in *Mississippi Books in Print 1989–1990.* Jackson: University Press of Mississippi, p. 11. Publisher's brief notice.

1951. Anon. "Wright, Richard (Nathanial) 1908–1960," in *Black Writers: A Selection of Sketches from Contemporary Authors.* Ed. Linda Metzger. Detroit: Gale Research, 1989, pp. 607–612. Biographical, critical, and bibliographical sketch. Includes extracts from numerous critics.

1952. Anon. "Wright, Richard (Nathaniel)," in *Black Writers: A Collection of Critical Sketches from Contemporary Authors.* Ed. Linda Metzger. Detroit: Gale Research, 1989, pp. 607–612. Biographical critical essay listing W's works and including commentary by such critics as Sheldon Brivic, Darryl Pinck-

ney, Ralph Ellison, David Littlejohn, Howard Mumford Jones, Stanley Edgar Hyman, Nathan Scott, Edward Margolies, Tilman Durden, Charles Shapiro, Granville Hicks, and others.

1953. Anon. "Wright, Richard," in *The Concise Columbia Encyclopedia.* Eds. Judith S. Levey and Agnes Greenhall. Second edition. New York: Columbia University Press, p. 908.

1954. Anon. "Yale University Visiting Fellowships." *Black American Literature Forum,* 23 (Fall), 558. Mentions briefly the Beinecke Library's collection of W's papers.

1955. Appiah, Kwame Anthony. "The Conservation of 'Race.'" *Black American Literature Forum,* 23 (Spring), 37–60. Mentions W briefly (p. 53).

1956. Aubert, Alvin. "Kenneth A. McClane. *Take Five: Collected Poems, 1971–1986.*" *Black American Literature Forum,* 23 (Fall), 608–614. Mentions W briefly (p. 613).

1957. Awkward, Michael. *Inspiriting Influences: Tradition, Revision, and Afro-American Women's Novels.* New York: Columbia University Press, pp. 6, 58–60, 63, 70–71, 88, 98, 102, 141. Comments on intertextual relations of W to Baldwin, Ellison and Morrison.

1958. Bacigalupo, Massimo. "Foreign Scholarship: Italian Contributions," in *American Literary Scholarship: An Annual/1987.* Ed. James Woodress. Durham, NC: Duke University Press, pp. 467–475. Comments on an article on W and Langston Hughes by Stefania Piccinato (p. 472).

1959. Baker, Houston A. "Generational Shifts and the Recent Criticism of Afro-American Literature," in *The Critical Tradition: Classic Texts and Contemporary Trends.* Ed. David H. Richter. New York: St. Martin's Press, pp. 1344–1373. Reprint of 1981.11.

1960. Baraka, Amiri. "Jimmy!" in *James Baldwin: The Legacy.* Ed. Quincy Troupe. New York: Simon & Schuster, pp. 127–134. Mentions W briefly (p. 131).

1961. Basel, Marilyn K. "Williams, Sherley Anne," in *Black Writers: A Collection of Critical Sketches from Contemporary Authors.* Ed. Linda Metzger. Detroit: Gale Research, pp. 602–604. Notes that reading *BB* stimulated Williams's desire to be a writer.

1962. [Baym, Nina]. "American Literature Between the Wars, 1914–1945," in *The Norton Anthology of American Literature*. Third edition. Ed. Nina Baym et al. Vol. 2. New York: Norton, pp. 927–938.

1963. _____. "American Literature Between the Wars," in *The Norton Anthology of American Literature*. Third Edition, shorter. Ed. Nina Baym et al. New York: Norton, 1669–1681.

1964. _____. "Richard Wright," in *The Norton Anthology of American Literature*. Eds. Baym, Ronald Gottesman, Laurence B. Holland, Francis Murphy, Hershel Parker, William H. Pritchard, and David Kalstone. Third edition shorter. New York: W.W. Norton, p. 2680. Bibliographical note.

1965. _____. "Richard Wright 1908–1960," in *The Norton Anthology of American Literature*. Third edition. Ed. Nina Baym et al. Vol. 2. New York: Norton, pp. 1761–1762, 2824.

1966. _____. "Richard Wright 1908–1960," in *The Norton Anthology of American Literature*. Third edition, shorter. Ed. Nina Baym et al. New York: Norton, pp. 2116–2118, 2680.

1967. _____, and Laurence B. Holland. "American Literature Between the Wars, 1914–1945," in *The Norton Anthology of American Literature*. Eds. Nina Baym, Ronald Gottesman, Laurence B. Holland, Francis Murphy, Hershel Parker, William H. Pritchard, and David Kalstone. Third edition. Vol. 2. New York: W.W. Norton, pp. 927–938.

1968. Binder, Wolfgang. "James Baldwin, an Interview," in *Conversations with James Baldwin*. Eds. Fred L. Standley and Louis H. Pratt. Jackson: University Press of Mississippi, pp. 190–209.

1969. Bloom, Harold, "Introduction," in his *Langston Hughes*. New York: Chelsea House, pp. 1–3. Mentions W briefly (p. 1).

1970. Blount, Marcellus. "'A Certain Eloquence': Ralph Ellison and the Afro-American Artist." *American Literary History*, 1 (Fall), 675–688. Comments on essays dealing with the Wright-Ellison relation in Kimberly Benston's *Speaking for You: The Vision of Ralph Ellison* (p. 682).

1971. Blythe, Hal and Charlie

Sweet. "'Yo Mama Don Wear No Drawers': Suspended Sexuality in 'Big Boy Leaves Home.'" *Notes on Mississippi Writers*, 21 No. 1, 31–36. Freudian reading of the story noting sticks, "tangled vines and bushes," "piece of meat" and jelly-roll, rifle, train, kiln, snake, etc. Wright's purpose is to indict white racism for retarding black sexual maturation as well as for inflicting violence.

1972. Boesenberg, Eva. "Harold Bloom, ed. and intro *Modern Critical Views: Zora Neale Hurston*; _____, ed. and intro. *Modern Critical Interpretations: Zora Neale Hurston's Their Eyes Were Watching God*." *Black American Literature Forum*, 23 (Winter), 799–807. Review criticizing Bloom for not giving attention to the W-Hurston controversy.

1973. Bradley, David. "Foreword," in *A Different Drummer* by William Melvin Kelley (New York: Doubleday), pp. xi–xxxii. Quotes Dorothy Canfield on *NS* (p. xvi) and mentions W elsewhere.

1974. Braxton, Joanne M. *Black Women Writing Autobiography: A Tradition Within a Tradition*. Philadelphia: Temple University Press, pp. 139, 140, 150, 162, 165, 172, 180, 183, 192. Mentions *TMBV*, *BB*, and W's criticism of Zora Neale Hurston.

1975. Brockman, William S. "Richard Wright," in *American Reference Books Annual 1989*. Vol. 20. Ed. Bohdan S. Wynar. Englewood, Colorado: Libraries Unlimited, p. 438. Favorable review of *A Richard Wright Bibliography*.

1976. [Budd, Louis J.]. "Brief Mention." *American Literature*, 61 (October), 511–535. Includes notices of *Richard Wright: Myths and Realities*, edited by C. James Trotman (p. 524), and *Short Story Criticism* (p. 529) edited by Sheila Fitzgerald, mentioning Wright.

1977. Buell, Lawrence. "American Pastoral Ideology Reappraised." *American Literary History*, 1 (Spring), 1–29. Comments on "Big Boy Leaves Home," in which "white injustice is dramatized by the scene of exclusion from pastoral fulfillment" (p. 13).

1978. Butler-Evans, Elliott. "Constructing and Narrativizing the Black Zone: Semiotic Strategies of Black Aesthetic Discourse." *The American Journal of Semiotics*, 6, No.

1 (1988–1989), 19–35. Includes discussion of "Blueprint for Negro Literature," emphasizing its black nationalist emphasis and its interpretation of black culture as "a signifier of repressed political consciousness" (p. 24).

1979. _____. *Race, Gender, and Desire: Narrative Strategies in the Fiction of Toni Cade Bambara, Toni Morrison, and Alice Walker*. Philadelphia: Temple University Press, pp. 24–26, 29, 42, 44, 57, 91, 194, 202.

1980. Cain, William. "An Interview with Irving Howe." *American Literary History*, 1 (Fall), 554–564. Includes comments on Wright, whom Howe considers "An important if limited writer" (p. 559).

1981. Cain, William E. "Traditions, History, and the Afro-American Novel." *American Quarterly*, 41 (March), 178–183. In a generally very favorable review of Bernard Bell's *The Afro-American Novel and Its Tradition*, Cain takes issue with his criticism of W for not celebrating black culture. Cain comments on *O* and argues that *NS* should be placed in white as well as black literary traditions.

1982. Calloway, Earl. "Author Margaret Walker Talks About Poet Richard Wright." *Chicago Defender* (13 May), p. 32. In this interview Walker states that she was asked to write a W biography by Vincent Harding because Horace Cayton would not be able to finish his. She states that W "was a very angry man … a very insecure person."

1983. Cappetti, Carla. "Deviant Girls and Dissatisfied Women: A Sociologist's Tale," in *The Invention of Ethnicity*. Ed. Werner Sollors. New York: Oxford University Press, pp. 124–157. Mentions W briefly (pp. 156, 273).

1984. Carby, Hazel V. "The Canon: Civil War and Reconstruction." *Michigan Quarterly Review*, 28 (Winter), 35–43. Mentions briefly *BB* (p. 41).

1985. _____. "Ideologies of Black Folk: The Historical Novel of Slavery," in *Slavery and the Literary Imagination*. Edited by Deborah E. McDowell and Arnold Rampersad. Baltimore; The Johns Hopkins University Press, pp. 125–143. Mentions *BB* and W's review of *Black Thunder* (pp. 125, 138, 140, 143).

1986. Carr, Virginia Spencer.

"Fiction: The 1930s to the 1960s," in *American Literary Scholarship: An Annual/1987*. Ed. James Woodress. Durham, NC: Duke University Press, pp. 253–281. Comments on an article on W by Michael Atkinson (p. 254) and mentions W elsewhere.

1987. _____. "Fiction: The 1930s to the 1960s," in *American Literary Scholarship: An Annual/1987*. Ed. James Woodress. Durham, NC: Duke University Press, pp. 253–281. Includes discussion of articles on W by Michael Atkinson (p. 254).

1988. Cashman, Sean Dennis. *America in the Twenties and Thirties.* New York: New York University Press, pp. 257, 300. Quotes W's maxim: "The Negro is America's metaphor" and includes a brief summary of W's career through *NS* with a commentary on that novel.

1989. Chénetier, Marc. *Au-Dela du soupçon: la nouvelle fiction américaine de 1960 a nos jours.* Paris: Éditions de Seuil, pp. 29, 31. Mentions W briefly.

1990. Clark, Edward D. "Richard Wright," in *Concise Dictionary of Literary Biography: The Age of Maturity: 1929–1941.* Detroit: Gale Research, pp. 392–419.

1991. Cobb, James C. "The South's South: The Enigma of Creativity in the Mississippi Delta." *The Southern Review*, 25 (January), 72–85. Mentions Wright and quotes from *BB* (pp. 75, 76).

1992. Coleman, James W. *Blackness and Modernism: The Literary Career of John Edgar Wideman.* Jackson: University Press of Mississippi, pp. 8, 19, 67, 81, 140. Brief mention of W, *BB*, *NS*, and *UTC*.

1993. Coleman, Peter. *The Liberal Conspiracy: The Congress for Cultural Freedom and Struggle for the Mind of Postwar Europe.* New York: The Free Press, p. 7 Notes that W boycotted an anti-communist conference in 1949.

1994. Coles, Robert A., and Diane Isascs. "Primitivesm as a Therapeutic Pursuit: Notes toward a Reassessment of Harlem Renaissance Literature," in *The Harlem Renaissance: Revaluations.* Eds. Amritjit Singh, William S. Shiver, and Stanley Bradwin, New York: Garland Publishing, pp. 3–12. Mentions briefly W's criticism of Hurston (p. 10).

1995. Cripps, Thomas. "*Native Son*, Film and Book: A Few Thoughts on a 'Classic.'" *Mississippi Quarterly*, 42 (Fall), 425–427. Comments briefly on W's film version and more extensively on the Silver-Freedman 1986 version. It would be pointless to attempt to convey the novel's Marxist politics in a film, but Silver and Freedman would have improved their "honorable failure" by expressing Bigger's "prepolitical rage" in ways similar to such films as *Sweet Sweetback's Baad Assss Song, Up Tight*, and *Blast*.

1996. Davis, Angela Y. "Art on the Frontline: *Mandate for a People's Culture*, in her *Women, Culture, and Politics.* New York: Random House, pp. 199–218.

1997. Davis, Mary Kemp. "Arna Bontemps' *Black Thunder*: The Creation of an Authoritative Text of 'Gabriel's Defeat.'" *Black American Literature Forum*, 23 (Spring), 17–36. Quotes W's review of the Bontemps novel (p. 19).

1998. Davis, Robert Gorham. "Acts of Creation." *The New Leader*, 72 (11–25 December), 23–24. Review of Herbert Leibowitz's *Fabricating Lives* commenting on W.

1999. Deutsch, Leonard. "*Invisible Man* and the European Tradition," in *Approaches to Teaching Ellison's Invisible Man.* Eds. Susan Resneck Parr and Pancho Savery. New York: The Modern Language Association of America, pp. 96–101. Mentions W briefly (p. 97).

2000. Dick, Bruce. "Richard Wright and the Blues Connection." *The Mississippi Quarterly*, 42 (Fall), 393–408. Examines W's lifelong interest in the blues, his writing about the blues and blues singers, and his own blues compositions treating the full range of traditional themes. Dick draws on much unpublished material.

2001. Dolle, Raymond. "Freeing the First Person." *Black American Literature Forum*, 23 (Winter), 785–791. Review of Angelo Costanzo's *Surprising Narrative: Olaudah Equiano and the Beginnings of Black Autobiography* with a brief mention of *BB*.

2002. Dorsey, D.F. "Porter, Horace A. *Stealing the fire: the art of protest of James Baldwin*." *Choice*, 27 (September), 128. Mentions briefly Wright and *NS*.

2003. Drew, Bettina. *Nelson Algren: A Life on the Wild Side.* New York: G.P. Putnam's, pp. 50–53, 61, 76, 77, 80, 81, 90, 94, 100–104, 108, 118, 120–121, 125–126, 129–135, 140–142, 144, 152, 160, 179, 205–206, 209, 226, 227, 232, 253, 287, 301, 310. Discusses Algren's relation to the John Reed Club, including Abe Aaron's eviction from his apartment and job because W attended his literary sessions with Algren and others (pp. 50–53, 76–77, 80, 94); relates Algren's continuing friendship with W on the Illinois Writers' Project and in the League of American Writers (pp. 100–104); emphasizes Algren's strongly favorable response to *NS*, including excerpts from letters (pp. 120–121, 125–126); explains Wright's encouragement, criticism, and intercession with Edward Aswell during the writing of *Never Come Morning*, which W thought proved Algren to be the "Proust of the Proletariat" (pp. 129–135, 140–142); notes the final meeting of W and Algren, who disapproved of his expatriation (pp. 205–206, 227); and mentions W elsewhere.

2004. DePlessis, Rachel Blau. "Gates, Jr. Henry Louis. *The Signifying Monkey: A Theory of Afro-American Literary Criticism*." *Journal of Modern Literature*, 16 (Fall/Winter 1988-1989), 233–234. Review mentioning W briefly.

2005. Eagles, Brenda M., comp. "A Bibliography of Dissertations Relating to Mississippi—1989." *Journal of Mississippi History*, 51 (February), 51–53. Lists dissertations on W by Sybil J. Dunbar and Virginia Whatley Smith.

2006. Edwards, Walter. "Sylvia Wallace Holton. *Down Home and Uptown: The Representation of Black Speech in American Fiction*." *Black American Literature Forum*, 23 (Fall), 615–620. Comments briefly on *Native Son* (p. 618).

2007. Elgrably, Jordan, and George Plimpton. "The Art of Fiction LXXVIII: James Baldwin," in *Conversations with James Baldwin.* Eds. Fred L. Standley and Louis H. Pratt. Jackson: University Press of Mississippi, pp. 232–254.

2008. Elias, Khaliquzzaman. "The Legacies of Prospero: A Critique of the Colonial and the Neo-Colonial Experiences in Selected Writings of Richard Wright, Chinua Achebe, and George Lamming." *Dissertation Abstracts International*, 50 (December),

1651-A. Abstracts a 1989 Howard University dissertation arguing that all three writers effectively attack racism and colonialism, but they do not conceive an ideal society based on self-determination.

2009. Ellison, Mary. "Houston A. Baker, Jr., *Modernism and the Harlem Renaissance*; Wayne F. Cooper, *Claude McKay, Rebel Sojourner in the Harlem Renaissance: A Biography*; Henry Louis Gates, Jr. *Figures in Black: Words, Signs, and the Racial Self*; Claude McKay, *Home to Harlem.*" *Journal of American Studies*, 23 (December) 473–476. Review mentioning W briefly.

2010. Fabre, Michel. "Jean Méral. *Paris in American Literature.*" *Afram Newsletter* 30 (November), 31–32. Review mentioning W briefly.

2011. _____. "Response," in *Afro-American Literary Study* in the 1990's. Eds. Houston A. Baker, Jr., and Patricia Redmond. Chicago: The University of Chicago Press, pp. 208–214. Discusses the psychological approach to biography, especially as pertaining to W.

2012. _____. "Kinnamon, Kenneth. *A Richard Wright Bibliography: Fifty Years of Criticism and Commentary, 1933–1982.*" *Afram Newsletter*, No. 29 (June), pp. 28–29. Favorable review emphasizing the new way the work permits evaluation of literary reputation and praising it as "an indispensable tool ... heavy with entries but also with implications."

2013. _____. "A Man of the South." *Mississippi Quarterly*, 42 (Fall), 355. Headnote to W's tribute to Faulkner, first published in French translation in 1950.

2014. _____. "Margaret Walker's Richard Wright: A Wrong Righted or Wright Wronged?" *Mississippi Quarterly*, 42 (Fall), 429–450. Unfavorable essay-review of *Richard Wright: Daemonic Genius* pointing out dozens of factual errors, much awkward or unclear writing, some dubious psychoanalysis, and defective literary criticism. Self-serving and vindictive, the work presents an unattractive and distorted picture of W as man and writer.

2015. [_____]. "Nouvelles." *Afram Newsletter*, No. 30 (November), 1–4. Comments on the Wright Symposium at the Gorky Institute in Moscow.

2016. _____. "To French Readers." *Mississippi Quarterly*, 42 (Fall),

359. Headnote to W's introduction to the French edition of *WML*.

2017. Fetrow, Fred M. "Minority Reporting and Psychic Distancing in the Poetry of Robert Hayden." *CLA Journal*, 33 (December), 117–129. Notes Hayden's comparison of Malcolm X to Bigger Thomas.

2018. Fichtelberg, Joseph. *The Complex Image: Faith and Method in American Autobiography.* Philadelphia: University of Pennsylvania Press, pp. 1–2. Comments on James Olney's review of *Black Boy.*

2019. Fishman, Ethan. "James Baldwin's Blues," in his *Likely Stories: Essays on Political Philosophy and Contemporary American Literature.* Gainesville: University of Florida Press, pp. 79–92. Includes discussion of Baldwin's and Ellison's critique of *NS* (pp. 90–91).

2020. Fitzgerald, Sheila ed. "Richard (Nathaniel) Wright, 1908–1960," in her *Short Story Criticism.* Vol. 2. Detroit: Gale, pp. 358–394. Contains a biographical-critical introduction (pp. 358–359), an annotated bibliography of fifty items, and excerpts from works on Wright's short fiction by Farrell (1938.198), Hicks (1938.222), Brown (1938.164), Burgum (1944.64), Webb (1949.156), Howe (1963.113), Redding (1963.160), Littlejohn (1966.97), Kent (1969.141), Margolies (1969.167), McCall (1969.172), Wyman (1970.187), Stephens (1971.290), Timmerman (1971.296), Fabre (1971.110), Giles (1973.157), Rubin (1978.214), Agosta (1981.2), Bryant (1982.22), Lee (1983), Jan Mohamed (1987).

2021. Fleming, Robert E. "Introduction," in *Knock on Any Door.* By Willard Motley. DeKalb: Northern Illinois University Press, pp. ix–xix. Includes analysis of Motley's relation to W (p. xiv).

2022. Franklin, H. Bruce. *Prison Literature in America: The Victim as Criminal and Artist.* Expanded edition. New York: Oxford University Press, p. xxix. Reprint of 1978.102.

2023. Gallop, Jane. "Heroic Images: Feminist Criticism, 1972." *American Literary History*, 1 (Fall), 612–636. Includes comment on Florence Howe's experience of teaching *NS* in Mississippi. See 1972.101.

2024. Gates, Henry Louis, Jr. "Introduction: Darkly, As Through a Veil," in *The Souls of Black Folk* by W.E.B. Du Bois. New York: Ban-

tam Books, pp. vii–xxxix. Mentions briefly *BB* (p. xvii).

2025. Gayle, Addison. "Wright, Richard," in *Academic American Encyclopedia.* Ed. Bernard S. Cayne. Danbury, CT: Grolier, pp. 290–291. Biographical sketch emphasizing W's influence on subsequent black writers.

2026. _____. "Wright, Richard," in *Academic American Encyclopedia.* Danbury, CT: Grolier, 1989, Vol. 20, pp. 290–291. Reprint of 1985.

2027. Giddings, Paula. "Word Star." *Essence*, 19 (January), 30. Favorable review of Margaret Walker's *Richard Wright: Daemonic Genius.*

2028. Giles, James R. *Confronting the Horror: The Novels of Nelson Algren.* Kent, OH: The Kent State University Press, pp. 1, 5, 17, 22, 32, 38–39, 42, 44, 46, 54, 71, 72, 86, 92, 93, 97. Compares the movement from naturalism to existentialism in Algren and W (pp. 32, 72), notes similarities between *Somebody in Boots* and *NS* (pp. 38–39, 42, 44, 46) and *Never Come Morning* and *NS* (p. 54), points out W's influence on Willard Motley (p. 71), and mentions W elsewhere.

2029. Glikin, Ronda. *Black American Women in Literature: A Bibliography, 1976–1987.* Jefferson, NC: McFarland, p. 41. Lists Thadious Davis's article on W and Faulkner.

2030. Gregg, Joan Young and Beth M. Pacheco. "Essay for Analysis," in their *The Human Condition: A Rhetoric with Thematic Readings.* Belmont, CA: Wadsworth, pp. 10–16. Reprints an excerpt from *BB* with headnotes and marginalia, followed by two pages of analysis.

2031. _____. "Essay for Analysis: Richard Wright *Black Boy*," in *The Human Condition: A Rhetoric with Thematic Readings* (Belmont, CA: Wadsworth), pp. 10–16. An excerpt with headnote and analysis under the rubrics "Invention," "Focus," and "Formulating a Thesis."

2032. Gregg, Sandra R. "Weaving a New Spell in Mississippi." *American Visions*, 4 (August), 30–37. Mentions W briefly (p. 30).

2033. Gresham, Jewell Handy. "James Baldwin Comes Home," in *Conversations with James Baldwin.* Eds. Fred L. Standley and Louis H. Pratt. Jackson: University Press of Mississippi, pp. 159–167. Reprint of 1976.89A.

2034. Grimshaw, James A., Jr.

"Thomas Daniel Young, ed., *Modern American Fiction: Form and Function*." *South Central Review,* 6 (Winter), 104–105. Mentions Blyden Jackson's essay on "Big Boy Leaves Home."

2035. Grossman, James R. *Land of Hope: Chicago, Black Southerners, and the Great Migration.* Chicago: The University of Chicago Press, pp. 2–3, 18, 38, 116, 117, 155, 166. Grossman begins his book with a comparison of similar responses to Chicago by Richard Robert Wright and W twenty-eight years later. He cites W's Chicago experience several times thereafter, quoting from *BB* and *AH* and mentioning *NS*.

2036. Grosvenor, Verta Mae. "'Vous êtes Swing,'" in *James Baldwin: The Legacy.* Ed. Quincy Troupe. New York: Simon & Schuster, pp. 51–58. Mentions briefly seeing W at the Café Tournon (p. 54).

2037. Hakutani, Yoshinobu. "Richard Wright's *The Outsider* and Albert Camus's *The Stranger*." *The Mississippi Quarterly,* 42 (Fall), 365–378. Whereas most critics note affinities between the two novels, Hakutani stresses the differences. Naturalistic shame and determinism govern the action of *The Stranger,* but in contrast to the passive Meursault, the active Cross Damon kills with premeditated volition. Meursault accedes to the absurdity of society and existence; Damon rebels against society because it oppresses him and he seeks philosophical essence. Meursault welcomes death; Damon hungers for life, denies the past and hopes for the future. Damon, finally, is more an expression of Afro-American tradition than Camus's brand of French existentialism.

2038. Harris, Leonard. "Chronology: Alain Leroy Locke, 1885–1954," in his *The Philosophy of Alain Locke: Harlem Renaissance and Beyond.* Philadelphia: Temple University Press, pp. 293–300. Notes Locke's defense of *NS* (p. 298).

2039. _____. "Rendering the Subtext: Subterranean Deconstructive Project," in his *The Philosophy of Alain Locke: Harlem Renaissance and Beyond.* Philadelphia: Temple University Press, pp. 279–289. Notes Locke's support of proletarian literature and *NS*.

2040. _____. "Rendering the Text," in his *The Philosophy of Alain Locke: Harlem Renaissance and Beyond.* Philadelphia: Temple University Press, pp. 3–27. Mentions briefly W and *NS* (pp. 7, 21).

2041. Hashimoto, Fukuo. *Collected Essays by Fukuo Hashimo: On Black Literature.* Tokyo: Hayakawashobo, 313 pp. Reprint of his *The World of Black Literature* (Tokyo: Miraisha, 1967), with additional essays "On Richard Wright," "On *Native Son,* I and II, and "On *The Outsider*."

2042. Helmling, Steven. "T.S. Eliot and Ralph Ellison: Insiders, Outsiders, and Cultural Authority." *The Southern Review,* 25 (July), 841–858. Mentions briefly W as a passe' writer by 1952,

2043. Ichiki, Jun. "Bigger Thomas's Violence: A Study of *Native Son.* *Seinan Gakuin University Quest,* 8 (31 December), 27–41. Discusses the cause of Bigger's murder of Mary and his change after the incident [T.K., R.B., Y.H.].

2044. Hitt, Greg. "Maya Angelou," in *Conversations with Maya Angelou.* Ed. Jeffrey M. Elliot. Jackson: University Press of Mississippi, pp. 205–213.

2045. _____. "Maya Angelou," in *Conversations with Maya Angelou.* Ed. Jeffrey M. Elliott. Jackson: University Press of Mississippi.

2046. Hodges, Graham. 'Foreword," in *Lonely Crusade* by Chester Himes. New York: Thunder's Mouth Press, pp. vii–x. Mentions W briefly.

2047. Holder, Laurence. "Zora," in *New Plays for the Black Theatre.* Ed. Woodie King, Jr. Chicago: Third World Press, pp. 137–152. One-act play consisting entirely of a monologue by Zora [Hurston], in which there is sharp criticism of W (pp. 147, 149).

2048. Houseman, John. *Unfinished Business.* New York: Applause Theatre Book Publishers, pp. 227, 229–232, 233–234, 269. Discusses his friendship with W and his collaboration on the stage version of *NS,* especially in rejecting the tepid influence of Paul Green.

2049. Hubbard, Dolan, et al. "Studies in Afro-*American Literature,* 12 (Fall), 680–740. Contains thirteen annotated items on W with cross-references to ten others.

2050. Hudson, Robert J., and Robert P. Smith, Jr. "Publications by CLA Members 1988–89." *CLA Journal,* 33 (December), 215–225. Lists

items on Wright s.v. Kinnamon, Mackethan, and Warren.

2051. Jackson, Blyden, "Richard Wright in a Moment of Truth," in *Modern American Fiction: Form and Function.* Ed. Thomas Daniel Young. Baton Rouge: Louisiana State University Press, pp. 170–183. Reprint of 1971.178.

2052. Jacobs, J.U. "The Blues: An Afro-American Matrix for Black South African Writing." *English in Africa,* 16 (October), 3–17. Mentions briefly the influence of W on Es'kia Mphahlele and Don Mattera.

2053. Jaynes, Gerald David and Robin M. Williams, Jr., eds. *A Common Destiny: Blacks and American Society.* Washington, DC: National Academy Press, pp. 101, 167. Mentions briefly *NS* (novel and play), *BB,* and *O.* Quotes W on "the dulling impact of racism on blacks."

2054. _____. *A Common Destiny: Blacks and American Society.* Washington DC: National Academy Press, pp. 101, 167 Mentions and comments on *UTC, NS, BB,* and *O.*

2055. Jean-Pierre, Wendell A. "Léopold Sédar Senghor's Freedom I–Negritude and Humanism," in *The Harlem Renaissance: Revaluations.* Eds. Amritjit Singh, William S. Shiver, and Stanley Brodwin. New York: Garland. pp. 281–295. Notes that Senghor asserts that W's Poetry has African roots (p. 291).

2056. Jehlen, Myra. "How the Curriculum Is the Least of Our Problems." *ADE Bulletin,* No. 93 (Fall), pp. 5–7. Mentions teaching *NS.*

2057. Johnson, Charles. "Novelist of Memory." *Dialogue* (Washington, USIA). Includes comment on W, *NS,* and "Wright's tradition of protest fiction."

2058. Johnson, Charles R. "Richard Wright Loved, Lost, Hated, Missed." *Los Angeles Times Book Review* (19 February), p. 9. Mixed review of Margaret Walker's *Richard Wright: Daemonic Genius,* "a curious mixture of delightful remembrance and disappointing critical analysis."

2059. Jones, James *To Reach Eternity: The Letters of James Jones.* Ed. George Hendrick. New York: Random House, p. 285. In a letter to Norman Mailer dated 18 November 1959 Jones mentions seeing W at a cocktail Party given by Phil Brooks.

2060. _____. *To Reach Eternity: The Letters of James Jones.* New York:

Random House, p. 285. In a letter to Norman Mailer dated 18 November 1959, Jones mentions seeing W at a cocktail party in Paris.

2061. Joyce, Joyce Ann. "Richard Wright's 'Long Black Song': A Moral Dilemma." *Mississippi Quarterly*, 42 (Fall), 379–385. Analyzes Sarah as the protagonist and center of consciousness of the story. Through his sympathetic portrayal of her, Wright "illuminates the insanity of a racist society which confines all forms of human behavior within narrow, emotionally stultifying limits" (p. 380).

2062. Karl, Frederick R. *William Faulkner: Americas Writer*. New York: Weidenfeld & Nicolson, pp. 510, 647, 654, 728, 888, 919, 932. Comments on Faulkner's opinion of W (pp. 728, 919, 932) and mentions W, *NS*, Bigger Thomas, and *BB*.

2063. Kent, George E. "Richard (Nathaniel) Wright," in *Short Story Criticism*. Ed. Sheila Fitzgerald. Detroit: Gale Research, pp. 366–368.

2064. Kiernan, Robert F. "American Literature Since World War II," in *Encyclopedia of World Literature in the 20th Century*. Ed. Leonard S. Klein. Vol. 1. New York: Continuum, pp. 67–76.

2065. Kinnamon, Keneth. "A Selective Bibliography of Wright Scholarship and Criticism, 1983–1988." *Mississippi Quarterly* 42 (Fall), 451–471. Lists and annotates 144 items constituting "a highly selective updating of *A Richard Wright Bibliography*, similarly organized but sharply reduced in scope. Only new (not reprinted) items of substantial importance are included" (p. 451).

2066. Klevar, Harvey L. "Caldwell's Women." *The Southern Quarterly*, 27 (Spring), 15–35. Mentions briefly W's favorable review of *Trouble in July* (p. 24).

2067. Kostelanetz, Richard. "An Interview with Ralph Ellison." *The Iowa Review*, 19 (Fall), 1–10. Ellison comments briefly on meeting Wright and first writing fiction under his impetus. This interview was conducted in 1965.

2068. Kuehl, John. *Alternate Worlds: A Study of Postmodern Antirealistic American Fiction*. New York: New York University Press, pp. 144, 309. Brief mentions of W.

2069. Leo, John. *Guide to American Poetry Application. Volume 2: Modern and Contemporary*. Boston:

G.K. Hall, p. 491. Lists articles on W's poetry by Keneth Kinnamon and John McCluskey, Jr.

2070. Lester, Julius. "James Baldwin — Reflections of a Maverick," in *Conversations with James Baldwin*. Eds. Fred L. Standley and Louis H. Pratt. Jackson: University Press of Mississippi, pp. 222–231.

2071. Liebowitz, Herbert. *Fabricating Lives: Explorations in American Autobiography*. New York: Knopf, pp. xviii, xxiv, 30, 99, 269–306. In a chapter entitled "'Arise, Ye Pris'ners of Starvation': Richard Wright's *Black Boy* and *American Hunger*," Liebowitz reprints in revised form 1985 and treats also *AH*, which he considers stylistically inferior. Mentions W briefly elsewhere.

2072. Lindsey, Lydia. "*The European Tribe*. By Caryl Phillips." *Journal of Black Studies*, 20 (September), 113–115. Review mentioning W briefly.

2073. Lionnet, Françoise. *Autobiographical Voices: Race, Gender, Self-Portraiture*. Ithaca, NY: Cornell University Press, pp. 144, 155. Mentions *BB* in a chapter on Maya Angelou.

2074. Locke, Alain. "Who and What Is 'Negro'?" in *The Philosophy of Alain Locke: Harlem Renaissance and Beyond*. Ed. Leonard Harris. Philadelphia: Temple University Press, pp. 207–228. Reprint of 1942.270 and 1942.271.

2075. Lubiano, Wahneema. "Constructing and Reconstructing Afro-American Texts: The Critic as Ambassador and Referee." *American Literary History*, 1 (Summer), 432–447. Review of Hazel Carby's *Reconstructing Womanhood: The Emergence of the Afro-American Woman Novelist* and Valerie Smith's *Self-Discovery and Authority in Afro-American Narrative* commenting on W's "marginalization" of Zora Neale Hurston (pp. 434, 444) and mentions W elsewhere (p. 441).

2076. Lunsford, Andrea, and Robert Connors. *The St. Martin's Handbook*. New York: St. Martin's Press, pp. 439–440. Reprints a passage from *BB* to illustrate the effective use of commas.

2077. Major, Clarence. "Necessary Distance: Afterthoughts on Becoming a Writer." *Black American Literature Forum*, 23 (Summer), 197–212. Recalls that reading W "was an overwhelming experience"

that led him on to Dos Passos, Farrell, Toomer, Himes, William Gardner Smith, Petry, Larsen, and others (pp. 200, 201).

2078. Mann, Susan Garland. *The Short Story Cycle: A Genre Companion and Reference Guide*. New York: Greenwood Press, pp. 13, 208. Mentions *UTC* and notes the theme of union with poor whites to achieve change. Believes that "The Ethics of Living Jim Crow" weakens the unity of the cycle.

2079. Margolies, Edward. "Richard Wright's Opposing Freedoms." *The Mississippi Quarterly*, 42 (Fall), 409–414. Relates W's ambivalent feelings toward the Third World to his youthful ambivalence toward Black American culture. Rejecting white power, be also rejected black, Asian, or African acquiescence to racist control. Freedom brings power which destroys the freedom of others.

2080. Marovitz, Sanford E. "Images of America in American-Jewish Fiction," in *Handbook of American-Jewish Literature*. Ed. Lewis Fried. Westport, CT: Greenwood Press, pp. 315–356. Mentions W briefly (p. 325).

2081. Martin, Reginald. "Building the Afro-American Canon." *Callaloo*, 12 (Spring), 425–427. Review of Valerie Smith's *Self-Discovery and Authority in Afro-American Narrative* mentioning Wright briefly (p. 427).

2082. Marx, Steven. "Beyond Hibernation: Ralph Ellison's 1982 Version of *Invisible Man*." *Black American Literature Forum*, 23 (Winter), 701–721. Mentions W's "social pessimism" (p. 714) and compares Ellison's introduction to the thirtieth anniversary edition to "How 'Bigger' Was Born" (p. 719).

2083. Mason, Ernest D. "Attraction and Repulsion: Huck Finn, 'Nigger' Jim, and Black Americans Revisited." *CLA Journal*, 33 (September), 36–48. Mentions briefly Bigger Thomas (p. 44).

2084. Mason, Theodore O., Jr. "Alice Walker's *The Third Life of Grange Copeland*: The Dynamics of Enclosure." *Callaloo*, 12 (Spring), 297–309. Notes Walker's indebtedness in her novel to *Native Son* and *The Outsider* (p. 309).

2085. Masuda, Mitsuko. "Richard Wright and Dostoevsky." *Nikon Women's University Veritas*, 11 (25

December) 89–101. Comparative study of *O* and *Notes from Underground* and *Crime and Punishment*, contending that Dostoyevsky had a serious influence on W [T.K., R.B., and Y.H.].

2086. McDowell, Deborah E. "Boundaries: Or Distant Relations and Close Kin," in *Afro-American Literary Study in the 1990's*. Eds. Houston A. Baker, Jr., and Patricia Redmond. Chicago: The University of Chicago press, pp. 51–70. Mentions W briefly (p. 52).

2087. _____. "New Directions for Black Feminist Criticism," in *The Critical Tradition: Classic Texts and Contemporary Trends*. Ed. David H. Richter. New York: St. Martin's Press, pp. 1138–1146. Reprint of 1980.160.

2088. _____. "Reading Family Matters," in *Changing Our Own Words: Essays on Criticism, Theory, and Writing by Black Women*. New Brunswick, NJ: Rutgers University Press, pp. 75–97, 224–230. Criticizes a 1986 essay by Mel Watkins for praising W while disparaging black women writers (pp. 80, 227).

2089. McMillen, Neil R. *Dark Journey: Black Mississippians in the Age of Jim Crow*. Urbana: University of Illinois Press, pp. 25–26, 177, 227–228, 255, 283–284. Quotes from and refers to *BB* to illustrate proscribed topics of conversation, accommodation for survival, fear of lynching, and black resentment of whites. Mentions also W's story in the *Southern Register*.

2090. Méral, Jean *Paris in American Literature*. Trans. Laurette Long. Chapel Hill: The University of North Carolina Press, pp. 211, 212, 223, 229–230.

2091. Miller, R. Baxter. "A Deeper Literacy: Teaching *Invisible Man* from Aboriginal Ground," in *Approaches to Teaching Ellison, Invisible Man*. Eds. Susan Resneck Parr and Pancho Savery. New York: The Modern Language Association of America, pp. 51–57. Mentions W briefly (p. 56).

2092. _____. "No Crystal Stair: Unity Archetype, and Symbol in Hughes's Poems on Women" in *Langston Hughes*. Ed. Harold Bloom. New York: Chelsea House, pp. 93–102. Reprint of 1975.

2093. _____. *The Art and Imagination of Langston Hughes*. Lexington: The University Press of Ken-

tucky, p. 12. Quotes briefly from W's review of Hughes's *The Big Sea*.

2094. _____. "'No Crystal Stair': Unity, Archetype, and Symbol in Hughes's Poems on Women," in *Modern Critical Views: Langston Hughes*. Ed. Harold Bloom. New York: Chelsea House, pp. 93–102.

2095. Moore, Jack B. "The Voice in *12 Million Black Voices*." *Mississippi Quarterly*, 42 (Fall), 415–424. Complements John Reilly's treatment of *TMBV* as folk sermon (1982.117) with an analysis of the work's similarity to the documentary film. Considers such matters as the authoritative narrative voice, integration of text and pictures, use of montage, and musical effects.

2096. Moore, Jack B., and Michel Fabre. "Editors' Introduction." *The Mississippi Quarterly*, 42 (Fall), 353. Brief introduction to a special W issue with contributions by W himself, Yoshinobu Hakutani, Joyce Ann Joyce, Kathleen Ochshorn, Bruce Dick, Edward Margolies, the editors, Thomas Cripps, and Keneth Kinnamon. "Our standard was good, new work on Richard Wright."

2097. Moses, Wilson J. "*Invisible Man* and the American Way of Intellectual History," in *Approaches to Teaching Ellison's Invisible Man*. Eds. Susan Resneck Parr and Pancho Savery. New York: The Modern Language Association of America, pp. 58–64. Mentions W briefly (p. 58).

2098. Mossman, James. "Race, Hate, Sex, and Colour: A Conversation with James Baldwin and Colin MacInnes," in *Conversations with James Baldwin*. ed. Fred L. Standley and Louis H. Pratt. Jackson: University Press of Mississippi, pp. 46–58.

2099. Mueller-Hartmann, Andreas. "Houston A. Baker, Jr., The Development of a Black Literary Critic." *The Literary Griot*, 1 (Spring), 100–111. Comments on *BB* (p. 102) and mentions W elsewhere (pp. 106, 107).

2100. Muller, Gilbert H. *Chester Himes*. Boston: G.K. Hall, pp. 8, 9, 12, 17, 27, 28, 30, 40, 78, 86, 118–119. Comments on Himes's relation to W, emphasizing the friction between the two. Quotes from an unpublished 1952 letter from Himes to W.

2101. Naremore, James. *The Magic World of Orson Welles*. Revised edi-

tion. Dallas: Southern Methodist University Press, p. 116.

2102. Nazareth, Peter. "Ishmael Reed. 'Writin' is Fightin.'" *World Literature Today*, 63 (Summer), 483–484. Quotes Reed calling *NS* a great work of art.

2103. Nelson, Cary. *Repression and Recovery: Modern American Poetry and the Politics of Cultural Memory, 1910–1945*. Madison: The University of Wisconsin Press, pp. 108–109, 153, 285. Mentions several proletarian poems by W, commenting briefly on "Hearst Headline Blues," "Obsession," and "I Have Seen Black Hands."

2104. Newman, Robert P. *The Cold War Romance of Lillian Hellman and John Melby*. Chapel Hill & London: The University of North Carolina Press, p. 197. Mentions W briefly.

2105. Ochshorn, Kathleen. "The Community of *Native Son*." *The Mississippi Quarterly*, 42 (Fall), 387–392. Defends the women characters in the novel, asserting that "the black women in particular do represent a community" (p. 392) which Bigger, not W, underestimates.

2106. Olney, James, "The Founding Fathers — Frederick Douglass and Booker T. Washington," in *Slavery and the Literary Imagination*. Edited by Deborah E. McDowell and Arnold Rampersad. Baltimore: The Johns Hopkins University Press, pp. 1–24. Mentions briefly W (pp. 3, 21) and compares *BB* to *Their Eyes Were Watching God* (pp. 22–23).

2107. Olster, Stacey, *Reminiscence and Re-Creation in Contemporary American Fiction*. Cambridge: Cambridge University Press, pp. 5, 18, 20–21, 22, 27, 28, 30, 32, 33, 156. Treats *O*, *NS*, *AH*, and *The God That Failed* in relation to W's politics, which moved from Marxism to existentialism.

2108. O'Meally, R[obert] G. "The Rules of Magic: Hemingway as Ellison's 'Ancestor,'" in *Afro-American Writing Today*. Ed. James Olney. Baton Rouge: Louisiana State University Press, pp 164–182.

2109. _____. "*12 million black voices*, text by Richard Wright, photo direction by Edwin Rosskam." *Choice*, 26 (April), 1325. Favorable review of a reprint edition of "a powerful narrative portrait nearly a prose poem...." Praises also David Bradley's introduction.

2110. Ostendorf, Berndt. "Anette Houber, Ekkehard Jost, Klaus Wolbert, eds. *That's Jazz. Der Sound des 20. Jahrhunderts.*" *Afram Newsletter*, No. 30 (November) 14–19. Mentions W briefly (p. 18).

2111. Parker, David B. "*Southern Black Creative Writers, 1829–1953.* Compiled by M. Marie Booth Foster." *The Journal of Mississippi History*, 51 (May), 141–142. Unfavorable review including an analysis of the entry on W.

2112. Parr, Susan Resneck, "Introduction," in *Approaches to Teaching Ellison's Invisible Man.* Eds. Susan Resneck Parr and Pancho Savery. New York: The Modern Language Association of America, pp. 19–25. Mentions briefly "The Man Who Lived Underground" and *NS* (p. 21).

2113. Petesch, Donald. *A Spy in the Enemy's Country: The Emergence of Modern Black Literature.* Iowa City: University of Iowa Press, pp. 38, 39, 42, 49–50, 64, 68, 70–71, 116–117, 160–161, 162, 216, 231, 240, 243, 249–250. Mentions, quotes from, and makes comparisons to *LD, BB, LT,* and *NS.*

2114. Phillips, Caryl. "Dinner at Jimmy's," in *James Baldwin: The Legacy.* Ed. Quincy Troupe. New York: Simon & Schuster, pp. 59–64. Mentions W briefly (p. 62).

2115. Pinckney, Darryl. "Trickster Tales." *The New York Review of Books* (12 October), pp. 20, 22–24. Article on Ismael Reed mentioning briefly *BB* (p. 20) and *NS* (p. 23).

2116. Pollard, Phyllis. "African, Caribbean, Indian, Australian, and Canadian Literatures in English: Africa," in *The Year's Work in English Studies.* Vol. 67. London: John Murray, pp. 702–722. Comments favorably on Michel Fabre's "Richard Wright, Negritude, and African Writing (p. 703).

2117. Pritchard, William H. "James Baldwin, 1924–1987," in *The Norton Anthology of American Literature.* Eds. Nina Baym, Ronald Gottesman, Laurence B. Holland, David Kalstone, Francis Murphy, Hershel Parker, Patricia B. Wallace, and Pritchard. Third edition. Vol. 2. New York: W.W. Norton, pp. 2108–2109.

2118. _____. "James Baldwin, 1924–1987," in *The Norton Anthology of American Literature.* Eds. Nina Baym, Ronald Gottesman, Laurence B. Holland, David Kalstone,

Francis Murphy, Hershel Parker, Patricia B. Wallace, and Pritchard. Third edition shorter. New York: W.W. Norton, pp. 2267–2268.

2119. _____. "Ralph Ellison, 1914–," in *The Norton Anthology of American Literature.* Eds. Nina Baym, Ronald Gottesman, Laurence B. Holland, David Kalstone, Francis Murphy, Hershel Parker, Patricia B. Wallace, and Pritchard. Third edition. Vol. 2. New York: W.W. Norton, pp. 1910–1912.

2120. _____. "Ralph Ellison, 1914–," in *The Norton Anthology of American Literature.* Eds. Nina Baym, Ronald Gottesman, Laurence B. Holland, David Kalstone, Francis Murphy, Hershel Parker, Patricia B. Wallace, and Pritchard. Third edition shorter. New York: W.W. Norton, pp. 2221–2222.

2121. Pryse, Marjorie. *A Course Guide to Accompany The Norton Anthology of American Literature, Third Edition.* New York: Norton, pp. 21, 29, 31, 35, 60, 170, 176. Lists W and *UTC* in various curricular configurations and provides study questions for "The Man Who Was Almost a Man" (p. 170).

2122. Ramm, Hans-Christoph. *Modell für eine literarische Amerikakunde: Zügange zum modernen schwarzamerikanischen Roman am Beispiel von Ann Petrys The Street, James Baldwins Go Tell It on the Mountain and Ralph Ellisons Invisible Man.* Frankfurt am Main: Peter Lang, pp. 37–38, 45, 364, 371. Briefly compares *NS* and *The Street* and mentions W elsewhere.

2123. Rampersad, Arnold. "Langston Hughes and Approaches to Modernism in the Harlem Renaissance," in *The Harlem Renaissance: Revaluations.* Eds. Amritjit Singh, William S. Shiver and Stanley Brodwin: New York: Garland, pp. 49–71. Mentions W briefly and quotes from "Blueprint for Negro Writing" (pp. 49–50), and mentions W elsewhere (pp. 57, 68).

2124. Rampersad, Arnold. "Biography and Afro-American Culture," in *Afro-American Literary Study in the 1990's.* Eds. Houston A. Baker, Jr., and Patricia Redmond, Chicago: The University of Chicago Press, pp. 194–208. Mentions W briefly (p. 194).

2125. Reid, Robert L., and Larry A. Viskochil, eds. *Chicago and Downstate: Illinois as Seen by the Farm Se-*

curity Administration Photographers, 1936–1943. Urbana: University of Illinois Press, pp. 95–96. Discusses W's role in *TMBV*, especially his role in expanding the photographs to cover the urban scene of Chicago's Black Belt.

2126. Robbins, J. Albert. "General Performance Works," in *American Literary Scholarship: An Annual/1987.* Ed. James Woodress. Durham, NC: Duke University Press, pp. 497–501. Mentions W as one of the "literary stars' included in *Fifty Southern Writers After 1900: A Bio-Bibliographical Sourcebook* (p. 497).

2127. Rose, Phyllis. *Jazz Cleopatra: Josephine Baker in Her Time.* New York: Doubleday, p. 74. Notes briefly W's favorable opinion of life in France.

2128. Roses, Lorraine Elena, and Ruth Elizabeth Randolph. "West, Dorothy (1907–)," in their *The Harlem Renaissance and Beyond: Literary Biographies of 100 Black Women Writers, 1900–1945.* Boston: G.K. Hall, pp. 343–346. Biographical sketch mentioning W's work on *Challenge* and *New Challenge.*

2129. _____. "Walker, Margaret Abigail Alexander (1915–)," in their *The Harlem Renaissance and Beyond: Literary Biographies of 100 Black Women Writers, 1900–1945.* Boston: G.K. Hall, pp. 332–336. Biographical sketch with a bibliography listing two items on W.

2130. _____. "Petry, Ann Lane (1908–)," in their *The Harlem Renaissance and Beyond: Literary Biographies of 100 Black Women Writers, 1900–1945.* Boston: G.K. Hall, pp. 258–264. Biographical sketch mentioning W briefly (p. 258, 261).

2131. _____. "Tarry, Ellen (1906–)," in their *The Harlem Renaissance and Beyond: Literary Biographies of 100 Black Women Writers, 1900–1945.* Boston: G.K. Hall, pp. 304–309. Biographical sketch mentioning and quoting from her essay "Native Daughter," responding to *NS.*

2132. _____. "Hurston, Zora Neale (1891–1960)," in their *The Harlem Renaissance and Beyond: Literary Biographies of 100 Black Women Writers, 1900–1945.* Boston: G.K. Hall, pp. 181–192. Biographical sketch mentioning briefly W (p. 183) and Bigger Thomas (p. 188).

2133. Savery, Pancho. "Materials,"

in *Approaches to Teaching Ellison's Invisible Man*. Eds. Susan Resneck Parr and Pancho Savery. New York: The Modern Language Association of America, pp. 1–15. Mentions W briefly (pp. 5, 7, 11, 13).

2134. _____. "'Not like an arrow, but a boomerang': Ellison's Existential Blues," in *Approaches to Teaching Ellison's Invisible Man*. Eds. Susan Resneck Parr and Pancho Savery. New York: The Modern Language Association of America, pp. 65–74. Mentions briefly W and *NS* (p. 65).

2135. Schipper, Mineke. *Beyond the Boundaries: Text and Context in African Literature*. Chicago: Ivan R. Dee, p. 41. Notes that S.S.K. Adotevi quotes a statement from *BP*: "I was black and they were black but it did not help me at all."

2136. Schreiber, Norman. "'Tell about the South. What it's like there. What they do....'" *Smithsonian* 20 (September), 163–164, 166–168, 170, 172, 174, 176, 178, 180. Review of *Encyclopedia of Southern Culture*, edited by William Ferris and Charles Wilson, mentioning W briefly (p. 172).

2137. Seed, David. "American Literature: The Twentieth Century: Fiction," in *The Year's Work in English Studies*. Vol. 67. London: John Murray, pp. 656–691. Comments on articles on W by Louis Tremaine, Tony Magistrale, Robert Butler, Yoshinobu Hakutani and Toru Kiuchi, and John E. Loftis (p. 688), and mentions W elsewhere (p. 688, 689).

2138. _____. "American Literature: The Twentieth Century: General," in *The Year's Work in English Studies*, Vol. 67. London: John Murray, pp. 608–621. Mentions briefly Margaret Walker's acknowledgment of W's influence.

2139. Shepherd, Kenneth R. "Williams, John A. 1925," in *Black Writers: A Selection of Sketches from Contemporary Authors*. Eds. Linda Metzger, Hal May, Deborah A. Straub and Susan M. Trosky. Detroit: Gale, pp. 598–601. Lists Williams's biography of W.

2140. _____. "Williams, John Alfred," in *Black Writers: A Selection of Sketches from Contemporary Authors*. Ed. Linda Metzger. Detroit: Gale Research, 1989, pp. 598–601. Lists William's *The Most Native of Sons: A Biography of Richard Wright*.

2141. Silberman, Arlene. *Growing Up Writing: Teaching Children to Write, Think, and Learn*. New York: Random House, pp. 18–19. Mentions briefly *NS*.

2142. Skinner, Robert. "The Black Man in the Literature of Labor: The Early Novels of Chester Himes." *Labor's Heritage*, 1 (July), 51–65. Includes a comparison of *If He Hollers Let Him Go* and *NS* (p. 59).

2143. Smith, Judy R., "Ellison, Ralph (Waldo) 1914–," in *Black Writers: A Selection of Sketches from Contemporary Authors*. Eds. Linda Metzger, Hal May, Deborah A. Straub, and Susan M. Trosky. Detroit: Gale, pp. 176–183. Comments on Ellison's relation to W (p. 179).

2144. Smith, Valerie. "Black Feminist Theory and the Representation of the 'Other,'" in *Changing Our Own Words: Essays on Criticism, Theory, and Writing by Black Women*. New Brunswick, NJ: Rutgers University Press, pp. 38–57. Notes that Sherley Anne Williams compares Andrea Lee's Sarah Phillips to *BB* (p. 51).

2145. _____. "Black Feminist Theory and the Representation of the 'Other,'" in *Changing Our Own Words: Essays on Criticism, Theory, and Writing by Black Women*. Ed. Cheryl A. Wall. New Brunswick: Rutgers University Press, 1989, pp. 38–57. Mentions *BB* (p. 51). W and Bigger (p. 80)

2146. Snell, Susan. "African-American Studies." *The Society for the Study of Southern Literature Newsletter*, 22 (April), 32–35. Lists Keneth Kinnamon's *A Richard Wright Bibliography*.

2147. _____. "Literary Criticism." *The Society for the Study of Southern Literature Newsletter*, 22 (April), 27–31. Lists C. James Trotman's *Richard Wright: Myths and Realities* (p. 31).

2148. _____. "Literary Scholarship on the South and Its Major Authors." *The Society for the Study of Southern Literature Newsletter*, 22 (November), 20–22. Lists Eugene E. Miller's *Voice of a Native Son* and Michel Fabre's *Richard Wright: Books and Writers*.

2149. _____. "Southern Authors (Past and Present) on Audiocassettes." *The Society for the Study of Southern Literature Newsletter*, 22 (April), 31–32. Lists *BB* read by Brock Peters.

2150. Solomon, Charlotte, D.

"*Native Son*," in *Academic American Encyclopedia*. Ed. Bernard A. Danbury, CT: Grolier, vol. 14, p. 47. Brief plot summary of "a landmark in black American literature."

2151. _____. "*Native Son*," in *Academic American Encyclopedia*. Danbury, CT: Grolier, 1989, vol. 14, p. 47.

2152. Soyinka, Wole. "Foreword at the Welcome Table," in *James Baldwin: The Legacy*. Ed. Quincy Troupe. New York: Simon & Schuster, pp. 9–18. Mentions W briefly (p. 17).

2153. Spickard, Paul R. *Mixed Blood: Intermarriage and Ethnic Identity in Twentieth-Century America*. Madison: The University of Wisconsin Press, pp. 277, 369. Mentions W's intermarriage.

2154. Stam, Robert. 'Orson Welles, Brazil, and the Power of Blackness." *Persistence of Vision: The Journal of the Film Faculty of the City University of New York*, 7, pp. 93–112. Contains a paragraph on the play *NS* and *BB* in relation to Welles's racial attitudes (p. 107).

2155. Standley, Fred L., and Louis H. Pratt. "Chronology," in their *Conversations with James Baldwin*. Jackson: University Press of Mississippi, p. xi. Mentions W briefly.

2156. _____. "Introduction," in their *Conversations with James Baldwin*. Jackson: University Press of Mississippi, p. ix. Mentions W briefly.

2157. _____, eds. *Conversations with James Baldwin*. Jackson: University Press of Mississippi, 297 pp. Contains an introduction and chronology mentioning W. Reprints from the following items: 1961, 1965, 1969, 1976.89A, 1980, 1984 [2], 1986, 1988 [2].

2158. Steeves, Edna L. "Hazel V. Carby. *Reconstructing Womanhood: The Emergence of the Afro-American Woman Novelist*; Joe Weixlmann and Houston A. Baker, Jr., eds. *Studies in Black American Literature, Volume III: Black Feminist Criticisms and Critical Theory*; Richard L. Jackson, *Black Literature and Humanism in Latin America*; Bernard W. Bell. *The Afro-American Novel and Its Tradition.*" *Modern Fiction Studies*, 35 (Summer), 310–313. Mentions W briefly (p. 313).

2159. Sten, Christopher. "Losing It 'even as he finds it': The Invisible Man's Search for Identity," in

Approaches to Teaching Ellison's Invisible Man. Eds. Susan Resneck Parr and Pancho Savery. New York: The Modern Language Association of America, pp. 86–95. Mentions W briefly (p. 92).

2160. Stephens, Martha. "Richard (Nathaniel) Wright," in *Short Story Criticism.* Ed. Sheila Fitzgerald. Detroit: Gale Research, pp. 374–376.

2161. Stepto, Robert B. "Response," in *Afro-American Literary Study in the 1990's.* Ed Houston A. Baker, Jr., and Patricia Redmond, Chicago: The University of Chicago Press, pp. 121–128. Mentions W briefly (p. 122).

2162. Story, Ralph. "An Excursion Into the Black World: The 'Seven Days' in Toni Morrison's *Song of Solomon.*" *Black American Literature Forum,* 23 (Spring), 149–158. Comments briefly on "Down by the Riverside" and *NS* (p. 152).

2163. _____. "Gender and Ambition: Zora Neale Hurston in the Harlem Renaissance." *The Black Scholar,* 20 (Summer-Fall), 25–31. Discusses W's criticism of *Their Eyes Were Watching God* (pp. 28–29).

2164. _____. "Geader and Ambition: Zora Neale Hurston in the Harlem Renaissance." *The Black Scholar,* 20 (Summer/Fall), 25–31. Mentions briefly W's differences with Hurston (pp. 25, 28).

2165. Strout, Cushing. "'An American Negro Idiom': *Invisible Man* and the Politics of Culture," in *Approaches to Teaching Ellison's Invisible Man.* Eds. Susan Resneck Parr and Pancho Savery. New York: The Modern Language Association of America, pp. 79–85. Mentions briefly W and *NS* (pp. 79, 81).

2166. _____. "Going to Ellison Territory." *Black American Literature Forum,* 23 (Winter), 808–814. Review of *Going to the Territory* commenting on Ellison's relation to W. Claims that Bigger's rejection of Max is related to W's place in the American, rather than radical, literary and political tradition.

2167. Sylvander, Carolyn Wedin. "Baldwin, James," in *Encyclopedia of World Literature in the 20th Century* Ed. Leonard S. Klein. Vol. 1 New York: Continuum, p. 182.

2168. Tate, Claudia. "Allegories of Black Female Desire; or, Rereading Nineteenth-Century Sentimental Narratives of Black Female Au-

thority," in *Changing Our Own Words: Essays on Criticism, Theory and Writing by Black Women.* New Brunswick, NJ: Rutgers University Press, pp. 98–126, 230–234. Comments on W's stay in the Moss household in Memphis in *BB,* comparing it to Bigger and Bessie in *NS,* by way of illustrating the black male's fear of female entrapment and his desire for freedom (pp. 98–99, 231).

2169. _____. "Allegories of Black Female Desire; or Rereading Nineteenth-Century Sentimental Narratives of Black Female Authority," in *Changing Our Words: Essays on Criticism, Theory and Writing by Black Women.* Ed. Cheryl A. Wall. New Brunswick: Rutgers University Press, pp. 98–126. Comments on the passage in *BB* relating W's stay with the Moss family in Memphis (p. 98).

2170. _____. "Maya Angelou," in *Conversations with Maya Angelou.* Ed. Jeffrey M. Elliot. Jackson: University Press of Mississippi, pp. 146–155.

2171. Taylor, Gordon O. "Learning to Listen to Lower Frequencies," in *Approaches to Teaching Ellison's Invisible Man.* Ed Susan Resneck Parr and Pancho Savery. The Modern Language Association of America, pp. 43–50. Mentions briefly W and *AH* (pp. 47, 50).

2172. Terkel, Studs. "An Interview with James Baldwin," in *Conversations with James Baldwin.* Eds. Fred L. Standley and Louis H. Pratt. Jackson: University Press of Mississippi, pp. 3–23. Includes comment on "Man of All Work" (p. 10).

2173. Tidwell, John Edgar. "Sterling A. Brown Remembered." *Black American Literature Forum,* 23 (Spring), 109–111. Mentions briefly *NS.*

2174. Tindall, George B. "Separate Pasts: Growing Up White in the Segregated South. By Melton A. McLaurin." *Journal of American Ethnic History,* 9 (Fall), 155–157. Review mentioning briefly W and "The Ethics of Living Jim Crow."

2175. Traylor, Elizabeth. "Response," in *Afro-American Literary Study in the 1990's.* Eds. Houston A. Baker, Jr., and Patricia Redmond. Chicago: The University of Chicago Press, pp. 128–134. Mentions W briefly and quotesfrom "Blueprint for Negro Writing" (p. 128).

2176. Trimmer, Joseph F., and C.

Wade Jennings. "Richard Wright *The Man Who Was Almost a Man,*" in their *Fictions.* Second edition. San Diego: Harcourt Brace Jovanovich, pp. 1204–1213. Reprints the story with a headnote and five "Questions for Discussion and Writing."

2177. Troupe, Quincy. "Last Testament: An Interview with James Baldwin," in *Conversations with James Baldwin.* Eds. Fred L. Standley and Louis H. Pratt. Jackson: University Press of Mississippi, pp. 3–23.

2178. Urban, Joan. *Richard Wright,* New York: Chelsea House, 111 pp. Biography for juvenile readers in the "Black Americans of Achievement Series." Treats briefly all of W's books, emphasizing the theme of racial protest. Includes numerous photographs of people and places.

2179. Vowell, Faye Nell. "Minorities," in *Handbook of American Popular Culture.* Second edition. Ed. M. Thomas Inge. Vol. 2. Westport, CT: Greenwood, pp. 746–770.

2180. Wagner-Martin, Linda. *The Modern American Novel, 1914–1945.: A Critical History.* Boston: Twayne, pp. xvii, xviii, 91, 101, 117–121, 132–134. Discusses *NS* with emphasis on its literary connections, its ambivalence, its disbelief in American justice, and its hostility to women. Mentions briefly *UTC* and *BB.*

2181. Wainwright, Mary Katherine. "The Aesthetics of Community: The Insular Black Community as Theme and Focus in Hurston's. *Their Eyes Were Watching God,*" Eds. Amritjit Singh, William S. Shiver, and Stanley Brodwin. New York: Garland, pp. 233–243. Mentions briefly W and *NS* (p. 240).

2182. Walker, Margaret. "Preface," in her *This Is My Century: New and Collected Poems.* Athens: The University of Georgia Press, pp. xi-xiv. Comments on her association with W in Chicago.

2183. Wallace, Eunice E. "Richard Wright." *Abstracts of English Studies,* 30 (September), 421. Abstracts an article by Fritz H. Pointer.

2184. Walter, John C. *The Harlem Fox: J. Raymond Jones and Tammany, 1920–1970.* Albany: State University of New York Press, p. 244. Mentions W briefly.

2185. Walton, James E. "The Student and Teacher as Readers of *Invisible Man,*" in *Approaches to*

Teaching Ellison's Invisible Man. Eds. Susan Resneck Parr and Pancho Savery. New York: The Modern Language Association of America, pp. 26–30. Mentions briefly W, *NS*, and *BB*.

2186. Ward, Jerry W., Jr. "Alvin Aubert: The Levee the Blues, the Mighty Mississippi." *Black American Literature Forum*, 23 (Fall), 415–440. Aubert mentions Wright briefly (p. 436).

2187. _____. "A Writer for Her People: An Interview with Dr. Margaret Walker Alexander." *Mississippi Quarterly*, 41(Fall), 515–527. Walker states that W had a Gothic imagination and that he got the idea of *NS* from a collection of her stories. Reprinted: 2002.

2188. _____. "Signifying Possibility." *Callaloo*, 12 (Summer), 600–604. Book review mentioning W briefly.

2189. Watkins, Mel. "An Appreciation," in *James Baldwin: The Legacy*. New York: Simon & Schuster, pp. 107–123. Mentions W briefly (pp. 109–111) and comments on Baldwin's critique of W (pp. 118–119).

2190. Watkins, Patricia D. "The Paradoxical Structure of Richard Wright's 'The Man Who Lived Underground.'" *Black American Literature Forum*, 23 (Winter), 767–783. Emphasizes the often overlooked naturalistic element of the story. "At every level, from the dictional to the philosophical, Wright pairs contradictory and seemingly irreconcilable parts" (p. 767) — the naturalistic and the existential, the deterministic and the anti-deterministic. Fred Daniels is both animal and god. The result is a paradoxical meaning and structure throughout.

2191. Weatherby, W.J. *James Baldwin: Artist on Fire.* New York: Dell, pp. 9, 50, 53–57, 64–65, 71, 72, 75, 78–79, 82–91, 99, 103, 116–117, 119, 127–130, 140, 142, 143, 148, 150–151, 170, 182–184, 186, 189, 200, 217, 218, 251, 268, 302, 322, 332, 412, 426. Relates from Baldwin's perspective his relation to W in New York and Paris. Weatherby bases his information on Baldwin's writings and conversations, drawing from

such sources as Himes's autobiography and Fabre's biography of W.

2192. Weissinger, Thomas. "Current Bibliography." *Black American Literature Forum*, 23 (Winter), 815–823. Lists C. James Trotman's *Richard Wright: Myths and Realities.*

2193. _____. "Reference Books Relating to Afro-American Literature: A Selected Bibliography." *Black American Literature Forum*, 23 (Spring), 187–192. Lists *A Richard Wright Bibliography.*

2194. Weixlmann, Joe. "Doing Battle with the Wolf: A Critical Introduction to Wanda Coleman's Poetry." *Black American Literature Forum*, 23 (Fall), 539. Mentions W briefly.

2195. Werner, Craig. *Black American Women Novelists: An Annotated Bibliography.* Pasadena, CA: Salem Press, pp. 2, 3, 4, 6, 17, 29, 33, 41, 45, 56, 62, 63, 64, 68, 69, 70, 124, 132, 135, 136, 142, 219, 220, 221, 224, 225, 226, 242, 266. Comments on W in the "Introduction," includes entries on "Blueprint for Negro Writing" (p. 70) and "Between Laughter and Tears" (p. 142), and mentions W briefly elsewhere.

2196. _____. "James Baldwin, Politics, and the Gospel Impulse." *New Politics*, 2 (Winter), 106–124. Includes a substantial discussion of the W-Baldwin quarrel and its repercussions in the debate over "art" and "protest." Also discusses the reception of *NS.*

2197. Wilson, Charles Reagan. "Expatriates and Exiles," in *Encyclopedia of Southern Culture.* Eds. Charles Reagan Wilson and William Ferris. Chapel Hill: The University of North Carolina Press, pp. 542–545. Mentions W briefly (p. 544).

2198. _____. "Garden Patch," in *Encyclopedia of Southern Culture.* Eds. Charles Reagan Wilson and William Ferris, Chapel Hill: The University of North Carolina Press, pp. 21–22. Quotes briefly from *BB.*

2199. _____. "Manners," in *Encyclopedia of Southern Culture.* Eds. Charles Reagan Wilson and William Ferris. Chapel Hill: The University of North Carolina Press, pp. 634–637. Recounts the episode from *BB*

about the visiting preacher with a large appetite for fried chicken.

2200. Woll, Allen. *Black Musical Theatre: From "Coontown" to "Dream Girls."* Baton Rouge: Louisiana State University Press, pp. 206–207. Notes that Kurt Weill and Maxwell Anderson considered doing a musical version of the play *NS.*

2201. Woodward, C. Vann. *The Future of the Past.* New York: Oxford University Press, p. 209.

2202. Wright, John S. "To the Battle Royal: Ralph Ellison and the Quest for Black Leadership in Postwar America," in *Recasting America: Culture and Politics in the Age of the Cold War.* Ed. Larry May. Chicago: The University of Chicago Press, pp. 246–266. Mentions briefly W, Bigger and *BB.*

2203. Wyrick, Jean, and Beverly J. Slaughter, eds. *The Rinehart Reader.* New York: Holt, Rinehart and Winston, pp. 13, 43. Brief mention of W and a headnote to an excerpt from *BB.* Includes a photograph.

2204. Yamanami, Akira. "Richard Wright and *Native Son. Avant Garde [Zenei]*, 573 (March), 209. Notes that *NS* reveals how oppressed black people have been [T.K., R.B., Y.H.].

2205. Yarborough, Richard. "'In the Realm of the Imagination': Afro-American Literature and the American Canon," in *The Informed Reader: Contemporary Issues in the Disciplines.* Ed. Charles Bayerman. Boston: Houghton Mifflin, pp. 65–77.

2206. _____. "The First Person in Afro-American Fiction," in *Afro-American Literary Study in the 1990's* Eds. Houston A. Baker, Jr., and Patricia Redmond, Chicago: The University of Chicago Press, pp. 105–134. Mentions W briefly (pp. 106, 110). Also mentions *LT.*

2207. Yates, James. *Mississippi to Madrid: Memoir of a Black American in the Abraham Lincoln Brigade.* Seattle: Open Hand, pp. 72, 85, 133. Reports meeting W in Chicago in the early thirties, claiming that he participated in a protest march to Springfield. Also mentions W's support of the International Brigades in the Spanish Civil War.

1990

2208. Abarry, Abu. "The African-American Legacy in American Literature." *Journal of Black Studies*, 20 (June), 379–398. Mentions W briefly (p. 379).

2209. Adams, Timothy Dow. "Richard Wright: 'Wearing the Mask,'" in his *Telling Lies in Modern American Autobiography*. Chapel Hill: University of North Carolina Press, pp. 69–83.

2210. Adell, Sandra. "Reading the Aesthetics and Philosophies of Black Writing." *Dissertation Abstracts International*, 50 (April), 3219A–3220A. Abstracts a 1989 University of Wisconsin dissertation containing a reading of *O*.

2211. Alkalimat, Abdul. "Black Marxism in the White Academy: The Contours and Contradictions of an Emerging School of Black Thought," in his *Paradigms in Black Studies: Intellectual History, Cultural Meaning and Political Ideology*. Chicago: Twenty-First Century Books and Publishers, pp. 205–222. Mentions briefly W (pp. 209, 211) and *BB* (p. 214).

2212. ———. "Introduction," in his *Paradigms in Black Studies: Intellectual History, Cultural Meaning, and Political Ideology*. Chicago: Twenty-First Century Books and Publications, pp. 1–28. Mentions W briefly (p. 21).

2213. Andrews, William L. "Introduction." *Black American Literature Forum*, 24 (Summer), pp. 197–201. Mentions W briefly.

2214. ———. "Mark Twain, William Wells Brown, and the Problem of Authority in New South Writing," in *Southern Literature and Literary Theory*. Ed. Jefferson Humphries. Athens: The University of Georgia Press, pp. 1–21. Contrasts response to W and Faulkner by white Southern critics and black critics (p. 1).

2215. Annas, Pamela J., and Robert C. Rosen. "Richard Wright (1908–1960)," in their *Literature and Society: An Introduction to Fiction, Poetry, Drama, Nonfiction*. Englewood Cliffs, NJ: Prentice Hall, pp. 894–895. Biographical headnote to "The Man Who Went to Chicago."

2216. ———. "Study and Discussion Questions, Writing Exercises," in their *Literature and Society: An Introduction to Fiction, Poetry, Drama, Nonfiction*. Englewood Cliffs, NJ: Prentice Hall, p. 920. To accompany "The Man Who Went to Chicago."

2217. Anon. "Almos' a Man," in *Filmic Archives*. Botsford, CT: The Cinema Center, p. 3. Videocassette catalog entry for the television adaptation of the story.

2218. Anon. "American Writing: Into the 20th Century," in *The Random House Encyclopedia*. Ed. James Mitchell. New York: Random House, pp. 1374–1375.

2219. Anon. "Approaches Series Invites Contributors." *MLA Newsletter*, 22 (Winter), 12. Mentions a volume on teaching *NS* to be edited by James A. Miller.

2220. Anon. *Bibliographic Guide to Black Studies: 1989*. Boston: G.K. Hall, p. 387. Lists four primary and five secondary items concerning W in the New York Public Library, supplementing the *Dictionary Catalog of the Schomburg Collection of Negro Literature and History*.

2221. Anon. *Index to Black Periodicals: 1988*. Boston: G.K. Hall, p. 413. Lists three items on W.

2222. Anon. "James Baldwin," in *The Annual Obituary 1987*. Ed. Patricia Burgess. Chicago: St. James Press, pp. 625–629. Notes that W befriended Baldwin early in the latter's career.

2223. Anon. "*Located Lives: Place and Idea in Southern Autobiography*. Ed. J. Bill Berry," in *Books for Spring 1990*. Athens: The University of Georgia Press, p. 21. Comments briefly on James Olney's essay on W and Eudora Welty.

2224. Anon. "Memorable Photos: From the Ebony Files." *Ebony*, 45 (June), 154. Photograph of W in Paris in 1952 with a biographical caption.

2225. Anon. "The Natchez Trace: Its Literary Legacy." Natchez: Copiah-Lincoln Community College.

Poster announcing a literary celebration in Natchez, 7–9 June, including a paper by Margaret Walker Alexander on "Natchez in Southern American Literature with Emphasis on Richard Wright" and the dedication of an historic marker honoring W.

2226. Anon. "No. 40 Profiles in History: Richard Wright 1822–1901 [sic] Novelist." *Norfolk Journal and Guide* (5 September), p. 16. Biographical sketch.

2227. Anon. "Proletarian Novelist from Moberly Dies." *Macon* (Missouri) *Chronicle-Herald* (1 March), pp. 1–2. Obituary of Jack Conroy mentioning W briefly.

2228. Anon. "Publications Relating to Mississippi." *Journal of Mississippi History*, 52 (May), 147–150. Lists books on W by Michel Fabre and Eugene E. Miller.

2229. Anon. "Publications Relating to Mississippi." *Journal of Mississippi History*, 52 (November), 345–346. Lists items on W by Tommie L. Jackson and Jack B. Moore.

2230. Anon. "*Telling Lies in Modern American Autobiography* By Timothy Dow Adams," in *The University of North Carolina Press: Spring 1990*. Chapel Hill: The University of North Carolina Press, p. 13. Publisher's notice mentioning briefly *BB*.

2231. Anon. "*Telling Lies in Modern American Autobiography* by Timothy Dow Adams." *South Atlantic Review*, 55 (May), [218]. Publisher's notice mentioning W.

2232. Anon. "*Telling Lies in Modern American Autobiography* by Timothy Dow Adams." *The Virginia Quarterly Review*, 66 (Autumn), 118, 120. Notice mentioning briefly W and *BB*.

2233. Anon. *Thunder's Mouth Press: Spring '90*. New York: Thunder's Mouth Press, pp. 15, 19. Publisher's notice of reprint editions of *TMBV* and *EM*.

2234. Anon. "Winter and Wacaster Address Teacher Recruits." *The Southern Register* (Fall), p. 8. In an address to the Mississippi Teachers Corps, C. Thompson Wacaster mentions briefly W, Faulkner, and Welty.

2235. Anon. "Wright, Richard," in *The Cambridge Encyclopedia*. Ed. David Crystal. Cambridge: Cambridge University Press, p. 1315. Brief entry mentioning *NS, BB*, and *O*.

2236. Anon. "Wright, Richard," in *The Random House Encyclopedia*. Ed. James Mitchell. New York: Random House, p. 2749.

2237. Anon. "Wright, Richard," in *Cambridge Biographical Dictionary*. Ed. Magnus Magmusson. Cambridge: Cambridge University Press, p. 1585. Brief biographical sketch mentioning *BB*, "The Man Who Lived Underground," and *NS*.

2238. Anon. "Wright, Richard," in *The New Encyclopedia Britannica*. Chicago: Encyclopedia Britannica, Inc., vol. 12, pp. 733–744. Biographical sketch emphasizing the theme of protest. Mentions with brief comment *UTC, NS,* (novel and play), "The Man Who Lived Underground," *EM, BB, O, WML,* and *AH*.

2239. Anon. "Wright, Richard (Nathaniel)," in *Oxford Illustrated Encyclopedia of the Arts*. Oxford: Oxford University Press, vol. 5. p. 495. Brief critical sketch mentioning *UTC, NS* (novel and play), and *AH*.

2240. Anon. "Wright, Richard Nathaniel," in *Concise Dictionary of American Biography*. New York: Charles Scribner's, 1990, p. 1348. Biographical sketch.

2241. Anon. "Wright, Richard," in *The Random House Encyclopedia*. New York: Random House, 1990, p. 2749. Brief biographical sketch.

2242. Anon. "Wright Richard," in *Webster's Illustrated Encyclopedia Dictionary*. Montreal: Termont, p. 1896. Brief biographical note.

2243. Anon. "Zora!" Eatonville, FL: The Association to Preserve the Eatonville Community, Inc. Conference brochure of the second annual Zora Neale Hurston Festival of the Arts and Humanities, 24–27 January 1991, listing a paper by Bruce Dick entitled "Neglected Parallels: A Reexamination of Zora Neale Hurston and Richard Wright."

2244. Appiah, Anthony. "Alexander Crummell and the Invention of Africa." *The Massachusetts Review*, 31 (Autumn), 385–406. Mentions his own article on W in the Gold Coast (p. 406).

2245. Asante, Molefi Kete. *Kemet, Afrocentricity and Knowledge*. Trenton, NJ: Africa World Press, pp. 165–166. Notes Ellison's indebtedness to W.

2246. Awkward, Michael. "Introduction," in his *New Essays on Their Eyes Were Watching God*. Cambridge: Cambridge University Press, pp. 1–27. Comments on and quotes from W's review of *Their Eyes Were Watching God* (pp. 3, 11–12).

2247. _____. "Negotiations of Power: White Critics, Black Texts, and the Self-Referential Impulse." *American Literary History*, 2 (Winter), 581–606. Includes a quotation from a Werner Sollors essay (1986). mentioning W briefly.

2248. Bair, Deirdre. *Simone de Beauvoir: A Biography*. New York: Simon & Schuster, pp. 370, 371, 374, 388–389, 412, 413, 647. Quotes W on Arthur Koestler, notes that he encouraged de Beauvoir to visit Merida, mentions *BB*, quotes de Beauvoir on W's declining interest in race and his responsibility for wrecking his marriage, notes W's admiration for Sarte, and mentions W's connection with *Twice a Year*.

2249. Baker, Houston A., Jr. "Generational Shifts and the Recent Criticism of Afro-American Literature," in *Paradigms in Black Studies: Intellectual History, Cultural Meaning, and Political Ideology*. Ed. Abdul Alkalimat. Chicago: Twenty-First Century Books and Publications, pp. 71–117.

2250. _____. "Our Lady: Sonia Sanchez and the Writing of a Black Renaissance," in *Reading Black, Reading Feminist: A Critical Anthology*. Ed. Henry Louis Gates, Jr. New York: Meridian, pp. 318–347. Notes briefly Baldwin's view of Bigger Thomas.

2251. _____. "Required Questions and Cheney's Book of Hours: A Note on 'What Should Be Required?'" *College Literature*, 17, Nos. 2/3, 129–133. Mentions W briefly (p. 130).

2252. _____. "Richard Wright and the Dynamics of Place in Afro-American Literature," in *New Essays on Native Son*. Ed. Keneth Kinnamon. Cambridge: Cambridge University Press, pp. 85–116. Focuses on the concept of place in a new historicist treatment of black male and female roles in *NS* against the background of W's own interpretation

of African American history in *TMBV*. The resulting indictment of Bigger and endorsement of Bessie challenges much received opinion about W's protagonist.

2253. Banes, Ruth A. "Relentlessly Writing the Weary Song: Blues Legacies in Literature." *The Canadian Review of American Studies*, 21 (Summer), 57–71. Mentions W briefly (p. 59).

2254. Baraka, Amiri. "Afro-American Literature and Class Struggle," in *Paradigms in Black Studies: Intellectual History, Cultural Meaning and Political Ideology*. Ed. Abdul Alkalimat. Chicago: Twenty-First Century Books and Publications, pp. 119–142.

2255. Barnwell, Tom, and Leah McCraney. "Richard Wright, 'The Man Who Was Almost a Man,'" in their *Teaching Critical Reading: A Manual to Accompany Introduction to Critical Reading*. Fort Worth: Holt, Rinehart and Winston, pp. 36–37. Brief discussion of the story followed by three teaching suggestions.

2256. Barry, Michael Gordon. "Recovering Meaning from the Irony of History: American Political Fiction in Transition." *Dissertation Abstracts International*, 50 (June), 3949-A. Abstracts a 1989 State University of New York at Buffalo dissertation treating *NS* and *EM* as well as works by Steinbeck, Warren, and Trilling.

2257. Bartholomaus, Craig. "White Fog." *American Book Review*, 12, pp. 16, 18. Joint review of Bob Blauner's *Black Lives, White Lives* and the reissued *TMBV*, preferring the former. W's book is too gloomy, ignoring "the strength, dignity, and consummate humanity" of black people.

2258. Beauvais, Paul Jude. "*Native Son* in Prison: Rhetorical Performance in Restored Behavior." *Text and Performance Quarterly*, 10 (October), 306–315. Reports an experiment requiring student-prisoners to enact the role of prosecuting or defense attorney in Bigger's trial. The analysis centers on student behavior, not on the novel itself.

2259. Beauvoir, Simone de. *Lettres à Sartre*. Ed. Sylvie Le Bon de Beauvoir. Vol. 2. Paris: Gallimard, pp. 286, 289, 294, 296, 299–300, 303–304, 313, 314, 343–344, 345, 346, 349, 351, 354, 356, 357.

Writing about her American trip in 1947, de Beauvoir mentions W frequently, expressing much affection for him, Ellen, and Julia.

2260. Bell, Bernard W. "The African-American Literary Tradition," in *Encyclopedia of Literature and Criticism.* Eds. Martin Coyle, Peter Garside, Malcolm Kelsall, and John Peck. London: Routledge, pp. 1136–1147. Quotes from "Blueprint for Negro Writing" (p. 1137) and mentions *NS* (p. 1142).

2261. Benston, Kimberly W. "Facing Tradition: Revisionary Scenes in African American Literature." *PMLA*, 105 (January), 98–109. Examines the "figure by which the [African American] tradition constitutes itself at this conjunction of exegesis and inscription: the *face* catching its reflection in some version of the other" (p.99). Benston develops this "specular dynamic" in passages from *TMBV* (p. 146) and *BB* (pp. 30–31).

2262. Berry, J. Bill. "Introduction," in his *Located Lives: Place and Idea in Southern Autobiography.* Athens: The University of Georgia Press, pp. ix–xvii. Mentions briefly *BB*.

2263. Betts, Doris. "Introduction," in *Southern Women Writers: The New Generation.* Ed. Tonette Bond Inge. Tuscaloosa: The University of Alabama Press, pp. 1–8. Mentions W briefly (p. 5).

2264. Blair, Walter, and James R. Giles. "American Literature," in *The New Encyclopedia Britannica*, Chicago: Encyclopedia Britannica, vol. 13, pp. 414–422. Mentions W's protest in *UTC* and *NS* (p. 420).

2265. Bleikasten, André. *The Ink of Melancholy: Faulkner's Novels from The Sound and the Fury to Light in August.* Bloomington: Indiana University Press, p. 336. Briefly compares Bigger Thomas and Joe Christmas.

2266. Blockson, Charles L., ed. *Catalogue of the Charles L. Blockson Afro-American Collection.* Philadelphia: Temple University Press, pp. 60, 100, 104, 227, 239, 245, 258, 262, 274, 292, 298, 299, 308, 323. Contains entries for *BP, CC, PS, TMBV, AH, BB, Bright and Morning Star, Cross Section, EM, How "Bigger" Was Born, NS, O, SH, UTC.* Also lists numerous secondary works.

2267. Bloom, Harold, ed. *Bigger Thomas.* New York: Chelsea House, 189 pp. Contains "The Analysis of Character," "Editor's Note," and

"Introduction" by the editor; critical extracts by James Baldwin, Irving Howe, Ralph Ellison, Houston A. Baker, Jr., Sherley Anne Williams, Charles T. Davis, Nina Kressner Cobb, Henry Louis Gates, Jr., and Charles Johnson; critical essays by W, Edward Margolies, Edward A. Watson, Keneth Kinnamon, Dorothy S. Redden, Charles De Arman, Ross Pudaloff, Robert James Butler, Tony Magistrale, Laura E. Tanner, and Alan W. France; notes on contributors; and a bibliography.

2268. _____. "Editor's Note," in his *Bigger Thomas.* New York: Chelsea House, pp. xv–xvi. Comments briefly on each of the dozen essays in the collection.

2269. _____. "Introduction," in his *Bigger Thomas.* New York: Chelsea House, pp. 1–3. Argues that guilt feelings and ideology determine our response to Bigger, not the aesthetic quality of his characterization.

2270. Biola, Heather. "The Black Washerwoman in Southern Tradition," in *Black Women's History: Theory and Practice.* Vol. 1. Ed. Darlene Clark Hine. Brooklyn: Carlson Publishing, pp. 63–75.

2271. Bogumil, Mary L., and Michael R. Molino. "Pretext, Context, Subtext: Textual Power in the Writing of Langston Hughes, Richard Wright, and Martin Luther King, Jr." *College English*, 52 (November), 800–811. Analyzes a Simple sketch ("That Word *Black*"), the Mencken episode in *BB*, and "Letter from Birmingham Jail" according to theories expressed by Robert Scholes in *Textual Power.*

2272. Booth, Wayne C., and Marshall W. Gregory. "Questions for Discussion," in their *The Harper & Row Reader.* Brief edition. New York: Harper & Row, p. 135.

2273. _____. "Richard Wright," in their *The Harper & Row Reader.* Brief edition. New York: Harper & Row, pp. 128–129.

2274. _____. "Suggested Essay Topics," in their *The Harper & Row Reader.* Brief edition. New York: Harper & Row, pp. 135–136.

2275. Bradbury, Malcolm. "American Literature and the Coming of World War II," in *Looking Inward, Looking Outward: From the 1930s Through the 1940's.* Ed. Steve Ickringill. Amsterdam: VU University Press, pp. 8–21. Mentions briefly *O*, comparing it to Kafka.

2276. Brantlinger, Patrick. *Crusoe's Footprints: Cultural Studies in Britain and America.* New York: Routledge, pp. 153, 156, 166. Mentions briefly W and *NS.*

2277. Braxton, Joanne M. "Afra-American Culture and the Contemporary Literary Renaissance," in *Wild Women in the Whirlwind: Afra-American Culture and the Contemporary Literary Renaissance.* Eds. Joanne M. Braxton and Andrée Nicola McLaughlin. New Brunswick, NJ: Rutgers University Press, pp. xxi–xxx. Mentions W briefly (p. xxiii).

2278. Bredella, Lothar. "Das verstehen literarischer Texte im Fremdsprachenunterricht." *Die Neueren Sprachen*, 89 (December), 562–583. Analyzes the understanding process of "Almos' a Man" in terms of "schema-theory."

2279. Brett, Anitra D. "Cumulative Index: Volumes 21–25 (1984–1988)." *Studies in Short Fiction*, 27 (Winter), 127–176. Lists two items on W.

2280. Brooks, Roy L. *Rethinking the American Race Problem.* Berkeley: University of California Press, p. 146. Mentions W briefly.

2281. Brown, Dorothy H. "Conversations with James Baldwin. Eds. Fred L. Standley and Louis H. Pratt." *Christianity and Literature*, 39 (Winter), 208–210. Review mentioning W briefly.

2282. Brown-Guillory, Elizabeth. "Marita Bonner (1899–1971)," in her *Wines in the Wilderness: Plays by African American Women from the Harlem Renaissance to the Present.* New York: Praeger, pp. 1–3. Notes briefly that Bonner "may have had an influence on Richard Wright."

2283. Bryant, Earle V. "The Transfiguration of Personality in Richard Wright's 'The Man Who Lived Underground.'" *CLA Journal*, 33 (June), 378–393. Analyzes W's novella in terms of four stages of the descent into hell: separation, affliction, transition, and reintegration. The protagonist undergoes death and rebirth as the story proceeds. Bryant draws on Eliade, Jung, Freud, and Erich Neumann as well as W criticism in advancing his interpretation.

2284. Bucknell, Brad. "Henry Louis Gates, Jr. and the Theory of Signifyin(g)." *Ariel*, 21 (January), 65–84. Comments on Gates's treatment of Ellison and Ishmael Reed signifying on W (pp. 75, 76, 78–79). Mentions briefly *NS, BB,* and "The Man Who Lived Underground." Also quotes Charles T. Davis on W (pp. 80–81).

2285. Buhle, Paul. "Daily Worker (and Successors)," in *Encyclopedia of the American Left.* Eds. Mari Jo Buhle, Paul Buhle, and Dan Georgakas. New York: Garland, pp. 178–182. Praises W's work on the newspaper (p. 181).

2286. Burns, Landon C., Elizabeth Buckmaster, and Janet P. Alwang. "The Sixteenth (1989) Supplement to a Cross-Referenced Index of Short Fiction Anthologies and Author-Title Listings." *Studies in Short Fiction,* 27 (Spring), 279–319. Lists one item on "Silt" (p. 319).

2287. Busby, Mark. "Kimberly W. Benston, ed., *Speaking for You: The Vision of Ralph Ellison*; Robert O'Meally, ed. *New Essays on Invisible Man*; Alan Nadel, *Invisible Criticism: Ralph Ellison and the American Canon.*" *South Central Review,* 7 (Summer), 95–98. Review mentioning W's influence on Ellison.

2288. Byrd, Rudolph P. *Jean Toomer's Years with Gurdjieff: Portrait of an Artist, 1923–1936.* Athens: The University of Georgia Press, pp. 15, 45, 129. Mentions briefly *NS* and compares Toomer's "Harvest Song" to *AH.*

2289. Cain, William E. "Criticism and the People." *Monthly Review,* 41 (February), 59–63. Mentions W briefly (p. 61).

2290. _____. "New Directions in Afro-American Literary Criticism." *American Quarterly,* 42 (December), 657–663. Review of Henry Louis Gates's *The Signifying Monkey* noting his treatment of intertextuality involving *NS* and *BB.* Cain criticizes Gates's dismissive treatment of W in this book and in a *Dissent* article.

2291. _____. "W.E.B. Du Bois's *Autobiography* and the Politics of Literature." *Black American Literature Forum,* 24 (Summer), 299–313. Mentions W briefly (p. 303) and comments on W's relation to Communism as described in *AH* and *The God That Failed* (pp. 306–307).

2292. Campbell, James. "Black Boys and the FBI." *The* (London) *Times Literary Supplement,* no. 4574 (30 November to 6 December), pp. 1290, 1298. Relates FBI and other surveillance of W and James Baldwin, emphasizing W's resulting fear

and tension which caused him to act as an informer and contributed to his fatal heart attack.

2293. Cappetti, Carla Sofia. "Urbanism as a Way of Writing: Chicago Urban Sociology and Chicago Urban Literature, 1915–1945." *Dissertation Abstracts International,* 50 (April), 3271-A. Abstracts a 1989 Columbia University dissertation showing that the fiction of W, Farrell, and Algren and the urban sociology of Robert Park, Louis Wirth, and others are interrelated and complementary.

2294. Carr, Virginia Spencer. *Understanding Carson McCullers.* Columbia: University of South Carolina Press, pp. 10, 33. Mentions briefly W's residence in Brooklyn and quotes from his review of *The Heart Is a Lonely Hunter.*

2295. Carby, Hazel V. "The Blackness of Theory." London *Times Literary Supplement* (29 December–4 January), p. 1446. Takes issue with Gates's exclusion of W from the African American literary tradition.

2296. _____. "The Politics of Fiction: Anthropology and the Folk: Zora Neale Hurston," in *New Essays on Their Eyes Were Watching God.* Ed. Michael Awkward. Cambridge: Cambridge University Press, pp. 71–93. Comments on W and his review of *Their Eyes Were Watching God* (pp. 77, 79).

2297. _____. "The Quicksands of Representation: Rethinking Black Cultural Politics," in *Reading Black, Reading Feminist: A Critical Anthology.* Ed. Henry Louis Gates, Jr. New York: Meridian, pp. 76–90.

2298. Cartosio, Bruno. "*Chicago: City on the Make* di Nelson Algra: esperienza e memoria della città." *Contesti,* 2/3, 203–234. Review mentioning W briefly.

2299. Cassill, R.V. "Richard Wright," in his *The Norton Anthology of Short Fiction.* Fourth Edition. New York: Norton, p. 1694.

2300. Charters, Ann. "Richard Wright," in her *The Story and Its Writer: An Introduction to Short Fiction.* Shorter second edition. New York: St. Martin's Press, pp. 439–440. Headnote to "The Man Who Was Almost a Man."

2301. Christian, Barbara. "The Highs and Lows of Black Feminist Criticism," in *Reading Black, Reading Feminist: A Critical Anthology.* Ed. Henry Louis Gates, Jr. New

York: Meridian, pp. 44–51. Mentions W briefly (p.46).

2302. _____. "The Race for Theory," in *The Nature and Context of Minority Discourse.* Eds. Abdul R. Jan Mohamed and David Lloyd. Oxford: Oxford University Press, pp. 37–49. Mentions briefly W and "Blueprint for Negro Writing." (pp. 40, 41).

2303. Chupa, Anna Maria. *Anne, the White Woman in Contemporary African-American Fiction: Archetypes, Stereotypes, and Characterizations.* Westport, CT: Greenwood Press, pp. 25, 38, 44–47, 51, 52, 73–74, 82, 86–88, 113, 122. Considers only *NS,* noting Mary's racial guilt, politics, and witchlike qualities. Mrs. Dalton is treated as a white witch. Chupa's point of view is Jungian.

2304. Clark, Keith. "Man on the Margin: Lucas Beauchamp and the Limitations of Space." *The Faulkner Journal,* 6 (Fall), 67–79. Comments on Houston Baker on "Big Boy Leaves Home."

2305. Clary, Françoise. "Jeffrey M. Elliot ed. *Conversations with Maya Angelou.*" *Afram Newsletter,* No. 31 (June), 35–36. Review mentioning W briefly.

2306. Coe, Richard M. *Process, Form, and Substance: A Rhetoric for Advanced Writers.* Second Edition. Englewood Cliffs, NJ: Prentice-Hall, pp. 125–128. Quotes *BB* (pp. 63–64) and analyzes it to illustrate rhetorical relations between the general and the particular.

2307. Cohen, Philip G., David Krause, and Karl F. Zender. "William Faulkner," in *Sixteen Modern American Authors: Vol. 2: A Survey of Research and Criticism Since 1972.* Ed. Jackson R. Bryer. Durham: Duke University Press, pp. 210–300. Comment on essays and books on race in Faulkner and W by Blyden Jackson (p. 256), Erskine Peters (p. 259), and Craig Werner (p. 260).

2308. Compliment, Anne. "Matthew J. Bruccoli, Richard Layman, and C.E. Frazer Clark, Jr., eds., *The Age of Maturity, 1929–1941* (*Concise Dictionary of American Literary Biography Series*)." *American Studies International,* 28 (October), 115–116. Notes that W and Langston Hughes are included, but not Zora Neale Hurston.

2309. Cornish, Samuel. *1935.* Boston: Ploughshare Books, pp. 8, 26,

28, 30–31, 35, 55, 63, 66, 85, 86, 89, 96, 132, 144, 145, 175. Mentions W frequently; also mentions *UTC*, *NS*, and "The Man Who Lived Underground." Discusses W's circumstances and state of mind during his early days in Chicago (pp. 30–31).

2310. Cornwell-Giles, JoAnne. "Afro-American Criticism and Western Consciousness: The Politics of Knowing." *Black American Literature Forum*, 24 (Spring), 85–98. Mentions W briefly (p. 90).

2311. Cowart, David. "Faulkner and Joyce in Morrison's *Song of Solomon*." *American Literature*, 62 (March), 87–100. Mentions W briefly (p. 89).

2312. Crouch, Stanley. "The Rage of Race," in his *Notes of a Hanging Judge: Essays and Reviews, 1979–1989*. New York: Oxford University Press, pp. 231–236.

2313. Cudjoe, Selwyn R. "Maya Angelou: The Autobiographical Statement Updated," in *Reading Black, Reading Feminist: A Critical Anthology*. Ed. Henry Louis Gates, Jr. New York: Meridian, pp. 272–306. Mentions briefly *BB* and a conversation between W and Baldwin as recalled by Chester Himes (pp. 277, 283–284).

2314. Current-Garcia, Eugene, and Bert Hitchcock. "Richard Wright, 1908–1960," in their *American Short Stories*. Fifth edition. New York: HarperCollins, pp. 455–456. Headnote to "Big Black Good Man."

2315. _____. "Tradition and Experimentation, 1935–1975," in their *American Short Stories*. Fifth edition. New York: HarperCollins, pp. 441–454. Mentions W (p. 444) and comments on *UTC* and *EM*.

2316. Davenport, Doris. "Pedagogy &/of Ethnic Literature: The Agony & the Ecstasy." *MELUS*, 16 (Summer), 51–62. Mentions briefly Bigger Thomas and *NS* (pp. 52, 56).

2317. Davies, Carole Boyce. "*The Afro-American Novel and Its Tradition*. By Bernard W. Bell." *American Literature*, 62 (September), 499–501. Mentions briefly "the Richard Wright School."

2318. Deck, Alice A. "Autoethnography: Zora Neale Hurston, Noni Jabava, and Cross-Disciplinary Discourse." *Black American Literature Forum*, 24 (Summer), 237–256. Mentions briefly W and *BB* (pp. 238, 240, 256).

2319. De Jongh, James. *Vicious Modernism: Black Harlem and the Literary Imagination*. Cambridge: Cambridge University Press, pp. 79, 82, 83, 85. Mentions briefly W as editor of *New Challenge* and as author of *NS*.

2320. Dick, Bruce. "*Richard Wright: Books and Writers* by Michel Fabre." *Afram Newsletter*, No. 32 (December), 39–40. Favorable review emphasizing the importance of Fabre's annotations and the stimulus this book will give to W studies.

2321. _____. "*Voice of a Native Son* by Eugene E. Miller." *Afram Newsletter*, No. 31 (June), 26–27. Favorable review emphasizing the originality of Miller's treatment of Wright's aesthetics. "The 'visionary and semi-mystical' Wright he presents serves to complement the numerous sociological and political studies done on Wright in the past."

2322. Doughty, Peter. "A Fiction for the Tribe: Toni Morrison's *The Bluest Eye*," in *The New American Writing: Essays on American Literature since 1970*. London: Vision Press, pp. 29–50. Mentions briefly *BB* (p. 33).

2323. Doyle, Mary Ellen. "Ernest J. Gaines: An Annotated Bibliography, 1956–1988." *Black American Literature Forum*, 24 (Spring), 125–150. Lists Charles Atangana's 1984 dissertation on W and three other writers.

2324. Durham, Joyce R. "The City in Recent American Fiction: Listening to Black Urban Voices." *College English*, 52 (November), 764–775. Comments on *NS*, citing Charles Johnson's favorable opinion of it, then describes Baldwin's urban fiction, showing how it differs from W's.

2325. Eagles, Brenda M. "A Bibliography of Dissertations Relating to Mississippi—1989." *Journal of Mississippi History*, 52 (February), 49–51. Lists Bruce Dick's dissertation on W.

2326. Early, Gerald. "The Unquiet Kingdom of Providence: The Patterson-Liston Fight." *The Antioch Review*, 48 (Winter), 44–65. Mentions briefly W and *BB* (p. 53) and compares briefly Liston to Bigger Thomas (p. 54).

2327. Edwards, Thomas R. "Underground Man." *The New York Review of Books* (28 June), pp. 22–24. Article on Nelson Algren including

a comment W made after reading a draft of *Never Come Morning*: "I think some plot would not hurt at all, Nelson" (p. 22).

2328. Escott, Paul D., and David R. Goldfield. "Documents," in their *Major Problems in the History of the American South*. Vol. II. Lexington, MA: D.C. Heath, p. 323. Comments briefly on an excerpt from *BB* included on pp. 341–344.

2329. Estes-Hicks, Onita. "The Quest for a Place in Two Mississippi Autobiographies: *Black Boy* and *Coming of Age in Mississippi*." *CLA Journal*, 34 (September), 59–67. Compares the quest for a home in the two works. W's grandmother's home in Jackson and Moody's first room of her own at the age of seventeen provide some satisfaction, but both authors are leaving Mississippi at the end of their books.

2330. [Fabre, Michel]. "Activités du CETANLA." *Afram Newsletter*, No. 31 (June), 1–3. Mentions briefly Virginia Whatley Smith's research on W.

2331. [_____]. "Charles Reagan Wilson et William Ferris, co-editors, Ann Abadie et Mary L. Hart, associate editors. *Encyclopedia of Southern Culture*." *Afram Newsletter*, No. 31 (June), 29–30. Review mentioning W briefly.

2332. _____. *Richard Wright: Books and Writers*. Jackson: University Press of Mississippi, 312 pp. After an introduction emphasizing the importance of intertextuality in the study of W, explaining W's reading and book-buying habits, and setting forth his own method in compiling this volume, Fabre provides an annotated list of books that W owned or was otherwise familiar with. Four appendices reprint W's book reviews and a bibliography on the Negro in Chicago he compiled in 1936 as well as providing book lists and notes by W.

2333. _____. "Eugene E. Miller.— *Voice of a Native Son. The Poetics of Richard Wright*." *Revue française d'etudes americaines*. No. 46 (November), 309–310. Highly favorable review praising Miller's use of unpublished sources, especially "Memories of My Grandmother" and "Personalism."

2334. _____. "Françoise Clary.— *L'Espoir de vivre: Violence et sexualité dans le roman afro-americain, de Chester Himes à Hal Bennett*." *Études*

Anglaises, 43 (July–September), 367–368. Mentions briefly W and *NS*.

2335. [_____]. "Wright, Richard Nathaniel," in *Concise Dictionary of American Biography*. Fourth edition. Ed. Ann B. Toback. New York: Scribner's, p. 1348.

2336. Fanning, Charles. *The Irish Voice in America: Irish-American Fiction from the 1760's to the 1980's*. Lexington: The University Press of Kentucky, p. 292. Notes briefly W's indebtedness to James T. Farrell.

2337. Ferguson, SallyAnn. "Book Review." *Obsidian II*, 5 (Winter), 123–126. Unfavorable review of Joyce Ann Joyce's *Richard Wright's Art of Tragedy*. Her argument that *NS* "is a tragedy remains unconvincing because it inadvertently reinforces the old established views" (p. 123) emphasizing naturalism or existentialism.

2338. Fitch, Noël Riley. *Met Hemingway in Paris: Vandelingen voor de literaire reiziger*. Trans. Lon Falger. Den Haag: Strengholt, p. 79.

2339. _____. *Walks in Hemingway's Paris: A Guide to Paris for the Literary Traveler*. New York: St. Martin's Press, p. 82. Mentions briefly W, *BB*, and *NS*.

2340. Fitzgerald, Margaret E., and Joseph A. King. *The Uncounted Irish in Canada and the United States*. Toronto: P.W. Meany, p. 322. Mentions briefly *NS*.

2341. Fodde, Luisanna, and Paola Boi. "Zora Neale Hurston, The Black Woman Writer in the Thirties and Forties (Part 1); Moses, Man of Power, Man of Knowledge (Part 2)," in *Looking Inward, Looking Outward: From the 1930s Through the 1940s*. Ed. Steve Ickringill. Amsterdam: VU University Press, pp. 127–150. Includes brief mention of W (pp. 127, 131, 134).

2342. Foley, Barbara. "Race and Class in Radical African-American Fiction of the Depression Years." *Nature, Society, and Thought*, 3 (July), 305–324. Discusses Marxist discourse in the Depression years on race and class, then analyzes *NS*, arguing that it shows how close W was to the Communist Party's position. Both "Blueprint for Negro Writing" and *TMBV* reflect the same view. Foley also defends Max's speech in Book Three of the novel.

2343. _____. "Subversion and Oppositionality in the Academy."

College Literature, 17 (June/October), 64–79. Contrasts briefly *UTC* and *Absalom, Absalom!* (p. 73).

2344. Fonteneau, Yvonne. "Ralph Ellison's *Invisible Man*: A Critical Reevaluation." *World Literature Today*, 64 (Summer), 408–412. Comments on Ellison's debt to W (p. 408), citing Richard Barksdale and Keneth Kinnamon on the subject.

2345. Foster, Frances Smith. "African American Progress-Report Autobiographies," in *Redefining American Literary History*. Eds. A. LaVonne Brown Ruoff and Jerry W. Ward, Jr. New York: The Modern Language Association of America, pp. 270–283. Mentions briefly *BB* (p. 283).

2346. _____. "Calvin C. Hernton. *The Sexual Mountain and Black Women Writers: Adventures in Sex, Literature, and Real Life*; Anne Allen Shockley. *Afro-American Women Writers, 1746–1933: An Anthology and Critical Guide*." *Black American Literature Forum*, 24 (Spring), 151–160. Mentions W briefly (pp. 156, 157).

2347. Fox-Genovese, Elizabeth. "Between Individualism and Fragmentation: American Culture and the New Literary Studies of Race and Gender." *American Quarterly*, 42 (March), 7–34. Comments on W in Alice Walker's "A Sudden Trip Home in Spring" (pp. 13–14).

2348. Frank, Joseph. *Through the Russian Prism*. Princeton: Princeton University Press, pp. 34, 46–47. Discusses Ellison's criticism of W.

2349. Franklin, Benjamin V. *Dictionary of American Literary Characters*. New York: Facts on File, 542 pp. Jeffrey D. Parker identifies sixty-three characters from all of Wright's published works.

2350. Fried, Lewis. *Makers of the City*. Amherst: The University of Massachusetts Press, pp. 119–158. Mentions W briefly (p. 120).

2351. Fried, Richard M. *Nightmare in Red: The McCarthy Era in Perspective*. New York: Oxford University Press, p. 11. Quotes W on the Communist Party.

2352. Friedman, Susan Stanford. *Penelope's Web: Gender, Modernity, H.D.'s Fiction*. Cambridge: Cambridge University Press, p. 368. Mentions W briefly.

2353. Fryar, Imani L.B. "Literary Aesthetics and the Black Woman Writer." *Journal of Black Studies*, 20

(June), 443–466. Mentions briefly James Baldwin and Eldridge Cleaver on W (p. 451).

2354. Fuchs, Lawrence H. *The American Kaleidoscope: Race, Ethnicity, and the Civic Culture*. Hanover, NH: Wesleyan University Press and the University Press of New England, pp. 176, 180. Quotes from *TMBV* and *BB*.

2355. Fuchs, Miriam. "*Fabricating Lives: Explorations in American Autobiography*. By Herbert Leibowitz." *American Literature*, 62 (September), 512–514. Review mentioning a chapter on W.

2356. Fullbrook, Kate. *Free Women: Ethics and Aesthetics in Twentieth-Century Women's Fiction*. Philadelphia: Temple University Press, p. 69. Mentions briefly W's favorable opinion of "Melanctha."

2357. Gabbin, Joanne V. "A Laying On of Hands: Black Women Writers Exploring the Roots of Their Folk and Cultural Tradition," in *Wild Women in the Whirlwind: Afra-American Culture and the Contemporary Literary Renaissance*. Eds. Joanne M. Braxton and Andrée Nicola McLaughlin. New Brunswick, NJ: Rutgers University Press, pp. 246–263. Mentions W briefly (p. 255).

2358. _____. "The Southern Imagination of Sonia Sanchez," in *Southern Women Writers: The New Generation*. Ed. Tonette Bond Inge. Tuscaloosa: The University of Alabama Press, pp. 185, 190. Mentions briefly W and *BB*.

2359. Gates, Henry Louis, Jr. "Introduction," in his *Reading Black, Reading Feminist: A Critical Anthology*. New York: Meridian, pp. 1–17. Mentions W briefly (pp. 2,9) and comments on Barbara Johnson's essay on W (p. 11).

2360. _____. "Introduction: 'Tell Me, Sir, … What *Is* 'Black' Literature?'" *PMLA*, 105 (January), 11–22. Notes W's place in the public school curriculum and the banning of *BB* (p. 13), takes exception to W's view that white racism elicited black literature (p. 20), and mentions W elsewhere.

2361. _____. "Zora Neale Hurston: 'A Negro Way of Saying,'" in *Their Eyes Were Watching God*. By Zora Neale Hurston. New York: Harper & Row, pp. 185–195. Includes comparison of W to Hurston with advantage to the latter.

Contrasts passages about a mother's death in *BB* and Hurston's *Dust Tracks on a Road*.

2362. _____. "Zora Neale Hurston and the Speakerly Text," in *Southern Literature and Literary Theory*. Ed. Jefferson Humphries. Athens: The University of Georgia Press, pp. 142–169.

2363. Gaudet, Marcia, and Carl Wooton. *Porch Talk with Ernest Gaines: Conversations on the Writer's Craft*. Baton Rouge: Louisiana State University Press, pp. 23, 33, 34, 35, 36. Gaines disavows W's influence, stating that he did not read him in college. Gaines describes himself as rural, not urban, a writer who finds room for humor, not an unremitting naturalist. Mentions *NS* and Bigger, *BB*, and *UTC*.

2364. Georgakas, Dan. "Proletarian and Radical Writers—1930s and 1940s," in *Encyclopedia of the American Left*. Eds. Mari Jo Buhle, Paul Buhle, and Dan Georgakas. New York: Garland, pp. 601–606. Mentions *UTC* and *NS* and notes W's later third world perspective (pp. 604, 605).

2365. Gill, Glenda E. "*White Dresses, Sweet Chariots, In Abraham's Bosom, The No 'Count Boy'* and *A Hymn*: Paul Green's Vehicles for the Black Actor." The *Southern Literary Journal*, 22 (Spring), 90–97. Notes W's high opinion of *Hymn to the Rising Sun*, quotes from a letter by W to Green dated 22 May 1940, and comments on their collaboration on the play *NS* and its reception. States that Green thought that Bigger Thomas was not a metaphor for hate but a metaphor of forgiveness (p. 96).

2366. Gilroy, Paul. "One Nation Under a Groove: The Cultural Politics of 'Race' and Racism in Britain," in *Anatomy of Racism*. Ed. David Theo Goldberg. Minneapolis: University of Minnesota Press, pp. 263–282. Mentions W briefly (p. 280).

2367. Goldfield, David R. *Black, White, and Southern: Race Relations and Southern Culture*. Baton Rouge: Louisiana State University Press, pp. 3, 5, 6, 7–8, 25, 280. Quotes from *BB* to illustrate racial etiquette and stereotypes. Mentions W elsewhere.

2368. _____. *Black, White, and Southern: Race Relations and Southern Culture*. Baton Rouge: Louisiana State University Press, pp. 3, 5, 6, 7,

7–8, 25. Quotes from *BB* on Southern racism.

2369. Gordon, Larry. "Anthology Rattles Tradition." *Los Angeles Times* (27 August), Sec. A, pp. 1, 24. Mentions W briefly.

2370. Gotera, Vicente F. "'Lines of Tempered Steel': An Interview with Yusef Komunyakaa." *Callaloo*, 13 (Spring), 215–229. Komunyakaa mentions W briefly (p. 216).

2371. Graham, Maryemma. "Bearing Witness to Black Chicago: A View of Selected Fiction by Richard Wright, Frank London Brown, and Ronald Fair." *CLA Journal*, 33 (March), 280–297. Examines and compares the three writers as social realists in the social context of black Chicago. They successfully combined social criticism and a race-specific aesthetic. Discusses W's Southern background, radical politics, and leadership in the Southside Writer's Group, as well as *NS*.

2372. _____. "Introduction," in her *How I Wrote Jubilee and Other Essays on Life and Literature* by Margaret Walker. New York: The Feminist Press, pp. xiii–xxi. Comments on Walker's relation to W.

2373. [_____]. "Northeastern University Celebrates Richard Wright." Boston: Northeastern University. Flyer for a conference held 4–5 May. Includes four photographs of W.

2374. [_____]. "Northeastern University Celebrates Richard Wright: 'Doing the (W)right thing.'" Boston: Northeastern University. Flyer for a conference held 4–5 May. Includes a photograph of W.

2375. _____. "Reginald Martin, *Ishmael Reed and the New Black Aesthetic Critics*." *Black American Literature Forum*, 24 (Fall), 590–593. Mentions W briefly (p. 593).

2376. Graham, Maryemma, with S.B. Dietzel and R.W. Bailey. "Review: Historicizing the Black Experience or Telling One's Own Story." *College English*, 52 (February), 194–202. Includes consideration of Melvin Dixon's *Ride Out the Wilderness*. His treatment of W ("The Man Who Lived Underground") is not as good as his treatments of Baldwin and Morrison.

2377. Gray, Richard. *American Poetry of the Twentieth Century*. London: Longman, p. 160. Mentions W briefly.

2378. Green, Jonathon. "Board of Education v. Pico (1982)," in his

The Encyclopedia of Censorship. New York: Facts on File, pp. 24–25. Records that *BB* was among the works cited as objectionable by a school board in New York State.

2379. _____. "*Native Son*," in his *The Encyclopedia of Censorship*. New York: Facts on File, p. 206. Notes that the film *NS* was banned by the Ohio State censorship board "on the grounds that 'it contributed to immorality and crime.'" The Supreme court overturned this censorship.

2380. Greenlee, Marcia. "Black Women and Oral History: Margaret Walker," excerpt from *Black Women: Oral History Project* at the Schlesinger Library, Radcliffe College. Ed. Ruth Edmonds Hill. New Providence, NJ: K.G. Saur, pp. 32–58. Walker comments on W, her interest in him, and his rejection of her.

2381. Greenspon, Joanna, ed. *Humanities Index: April 1989 to March 1990*. New York: H.W. Wilson, p. 1076. Lists two items s. v. W.

2382. Griffith, Kelley, Jr. *Writing Essays About Literature: A Guide and Style Sheet*. Third Edition. San Diego: Harcourt Brace Jovanovich, p. 42.

2383. Grigsby, John L. "On the Validity and Importance of the AAUP Censure List." *The CEA Forum*, 20 (Spring), 21–22. Reports pressure not to teach "Long Black Song" at an institution in the South Dakota system.

2384. Gross, Barry. "Using the *Heath Anthology*, Part I: Report from Chile." *The Heath Anthology of American Literature Newsletter* (Fall), pp. 8–9. Gross reports using W in his syllabus.

2385. Gruesser, John C. "Afro-American Travel Literature and Africanist Discourse." *Black American Literature Forum*, 24 (Spring), 5–20. In a theoretical framework derived from Foucault, Said, and Christopher Miller (*Blank Darkness: Africanist Discourse in French*), Gruesser analyzes *BP* (pp. 9–13) and works by other writers. Although W questions assumptions of the West about Africa, his treatment of the Gold Coast does not overcome them. "Binary oppositions ... and evolutionary language pervade *Black Power*" (p. 9).

2386. Guerrero, Edward. "Tracking 'The Look' in the Novels of Toni Morrison." *Black American Literature Forum*, 24 (Winter), 761–773. Mentions briefly "Big Boy Leaves Home" (p. 772).

2387. Guidry, Marc. "Richard Wright's Wrighting: The Autobiographical Comedy of *Black Boy*." *Publications of the Mississippi Philological Association*, pp. 104–108. Argues that although the social situation as depicted in *BB* is tragic, the autobiographical protagonist is comic because he escapes the general fate of black people. *NS*, on the other hand, is tragic because Bigger succumbs to his fate.

2388. Hajek, Friederike. "Alice Walker's 'Die Farbe Lila.'" *Weimarer Beiträge*, 36, No. 7, pp. 1116–1127. Mentions briefly W and *NS* (p. 1116).

2389. Hall, Robert L. "African Religious Retentions in Florida," in *Africanisms in American Culture*. Ed. Joseph E. Holloway. Bloomington: Indiana University Press, pp. 98–118. Quotes "Blueprint for Negro Literature" on the access the black church provided to "the shrine of Western culture" (p. 113).

2390. Hamalian, Leo. "D.H. Lawrence and Black Writers." *Journal of Modern Literature*, 16 (Spring), 579–596. Includes a section making strong claims for Lawrence's influence on W. "In many unexpected ways his strange and tormented genius is akin to Lawrence's…" (p. 593).

2391. Hampton, Henry, and Steve Fayer, with Sarah Flynn. *Voices of Freedom: An Oral History of the Civil Rights Movement*. New York: Bantam Books, p. 292. Quotes Floyd McKissick mentioning W briefly.

2392. Harper, Donna Akiba Sullivan. "Book Review." *Obsidian II*, 5 (Summer), 148–152. Review of Arnold Rampersad's biography of Hughes noting that he used Fabre's biography of W as one of his models.

2393. Harris, Laurie Lanzen. *Characters in 20th Century Literature*. Detroit: Gale, pp. 454–455. Comments on important characters in "Big Boy Leaves Home" and *NS*. Contains a short bibliography.

2394. Harris, Trudier. "Native Sons and Foreign Daughters," in *New Essays on Native Son*. Ed. Keneth Kinnamon. Cambridge: Cambridge University Press, pp. 63–84. Explores some of the social ironies involved in the unfavorable presentation of female characters in *Native Son*. As Bigger, responding to the American cultural values of individualism and freedom, aspires to soar, his mother, sister, and lover attempt to hold him down in the subservient place designated by society as appropriate for black people.

2395. Hazlett, John Downton. "The Situation of American Autobiography: Generic Blurring in 'Contemporary' Historiography." *Prose Studies*, 13 (September), 261–277. Mentions W briefly (p. 272).

2396. Heller, Arno. "Fictions of Violence in American Literature: A Probing Into Psycho-Historical Criticism," in *Reconstructing American Literary and Historical Studies*. Eds. Günter H. Lenz, Hartmut Keil, and Sabine Bröck-Sallah. Frankfurt am Main: Campus Verlag/New York: St. Martin's Press, pp. 268–284. Comments on W's linking of violence and identity in *NS*, contrary to the usual realistic and naturalistic view of violence as socially conditioned (p. 273).

2397. Helmbold, Lois Rita. "Beyond the Family Economy: Black and White Working-Class Women During the Great Depression," in *Black Women in American History: The Twentieth Century*. Vol. 2. Ed. Darlene Clark Hine. Brooklyn: Carlson, pp. 567–593.

2398. Hernton, Calvin. "Foreword," in *The Collected Stories of Chester Himes*. New York: Thunder's Mouth Press, pp. ix–xii. Mentions W briefly.

2399. _____. "The Sexual Mountain and Black Women Writers," in *Wild Women in the Whirlwind: Afra-American Culture and the Contemporary Literary Renaissance*. Eds. Joanne M. Braxton and Andrée Nicola McLaughlin. New Brunswick, NJ: Rutgers University Press, pp. 195–212.

2400. Herron, Carolivia. "Philology as Subversion: The Case of Afro-America." *Comparative Literature Studies*, 27 (Spring), 62–65. Mentions W briefly (p. 62).

2401. H[obson], F[red]. "Editorial Note." *The Southern Literary Journal*, 23 (Fall), 3–4. Includes W in a list of authors on whom submissions would be welcome.

2402. Homberger, Eric. "John Reed Clubs," in *Encyclopedia of the American Left*. Eds. Mari Jo Buhle, Paul Buhle, and Dan Georgakas. New York: Garland, pp. 649–650. Notes W's affiliation with the Chicago John Reed Club.

2403. Hornung, Alfred. "American Autobiographies and Autobiography Criticism: Review Essay." *Amerikastudien*, 35 (Fall), 371–407. Mentions briefly W and *BB*. Calls *NS* "autobiographical fiction."

2404. Howarth, William. "Writing Upside Down," in *Located Lives: Place and Idea in Southern Autobiography*. Ed. J. Bill Berry. Athens: The University of Georgia Press, pp. 3–19.

2405. _____. "Writing Upside Down: Voice and Place in Southern Autobiography." *Southwest Review*, 75 (Winter), 126–140. The epigraph is from *BB*, to which a paragraph is devoted (pp. 135–136). In it W creates "a powerful illusion of verity," though "many of the book's details are imaginary."

2406. Howe, Irving. "Black Boys and Native Sons," in his *Selected Writings 1950–1990*. San Diego: Harcourt Brace Jovanovich, pp. 119–139. Reprint of 1963.113.

2407. Hubbard, Dolan, et al. "Studies in African-American Literature: An Annual Annotated Bibliography, 1989." *Callaloo*, 13 (Fall), 910–954. Contains thirteen items on W with cross-references to seven others.

2408. Huke, Thomas. *Jazz and Blues im Afroamerikanischen Roman von der Jahrhundertwende bis zur Gegenwart*. Würzburg: Königshausen & Newmann, p. 132. Mentions W briefly.

2409. Hyles, Vernon. "*Modern American Fiction: Form and Function*. Edited by Thomas Daniel Young." *South Atlantic Review*, 55 (May), 163–165. Notes that the collection contains an article by Blyden Jackson on W and Mississippi.

2410. Ichiki, Jun. "Richard Wright's View of the Whites in *Black Boy*: A Possibility of Black Nationalism." *Seinan Gakuin University Literary Studies*, 10 (January), 43–61. Argues that W's view of white people will lead to black nationalism [T.K., R.B., and Y.H.].

2411. Ickstadt, Heinz. "Introduction: Looking Inward and Outward in the Thirties — The Construction of a National Identity," in his *Looking Inward — Looking Outward: From the 1930s Through the 1940s*. Amsterdam: VU University Press, pp. 1–7. Mentions W briefly (p. 5).

2412. Inge, Tonett Bond. "Preface," in her *Southern Women Writers: The New Generation.* Tuscaloosa: The University of Alabama Press, p. 5. Mentions W briefly.

2413. Jackson, Blyden. "A Postlude to a Renaissance." *The Southern Review,* 26 (October), 746–765. Mentions W's acquaintance with Arna Bontemps in Chicago (p. 759).

2414. Jackson, Walter A. *Gunnar Myrdal and America's Conscience: Social Engineering and Racial Liberalism, 1938–1987.* Chapel Hill: The University of North Carolina Press, pp. 246, 247, 259, 330. Notes and quotes W's praise of *An American Dilemma,* calls *BB* W's effort to do for black personality what Myrdal's book did for the social and political relations, discusses W's role in the Aptheker-Cayton controversy about Myrdal, and comments on W's acquaintance with Myrdal's Communist son Jan in Paris, quoting W's advice to "never turn your back on Jan no matter what hostile governments say. Blood is thicker than ideology and life is stronger than passing governmental policies."

2415. JanMohamed, Abdul R. "Negating the Negation as a Form of Affirmation in Minority Discourse: The Construction of Richard Wright as Subject," in his and David Lloyd's *The Nature and Context of Minority Discourse.* New York: Oxford University Press, pp. 102–123.

2416. Jennings, La Vinia. "Sexual Violence in the Works of Richard Wright, James Baldwin, and Toni Morrison." *Dissertation Abstracts International,* 50 (February), 2487-A. Abstracts a 1989 University of North Carolina dissertation. W emphasized the "sexualization of racism."

2417. Jennings, Regina B. "*Workings of the Spirit: The Poetics of Afro-American Women's Writing* by Houston A. Baker, Jr." *Sage: A Scholarly Journal on Black Women,* 7 (Fall), 75–76. Review mentioning W briefly.

2418. Johnson, Barbara. "Philology: What Is at Stake?" *Comparative Literature Studies,* 27 (Spring), 26–29. Comments on Bigger's ransom note in *NS* to illustrate the importance of close reading (p. 29).

2419. _____. "Euphemism, Understatement, and the Passive Voice: A Genealogy of Afro-American Poetry," in *Reading Black, Reading Feminist: A Critical Anthology.* Ed. Henry Louis Gates, Jr. New York:

Meridian, pp. 204–211. The point of departure is a passage from "Blueprint for Negro Writing" in which W criticizes prior black writing.

2420. _____. "The Re(a)d and the Black," in *Reading Black, Reading Feminist: A Critical Anthology.* Ed. Henry Louis Gates, Jr. New York: Meridian, pp. 145–154.

2421. Jones, Quincy. "Playboy Interview." *Playboy,* 37 (July), 57–60, 62–66, 164–166. Mentions meeting W in Paris through Nadia Boulanger (p. 60).

2422. Kennedy, Richard S. "Thomas Wolfe," in *Sixteen Modern American Authors: Vol. 2: A Survey of Research and Criticism Since 1972.* Ed. Jackson R. Bryer. Durham: Duke University Press, pp. 716–755. Comments on an article by Ladell Payne on W and Thomas Wolfe (p. 750).

2423. Kent, George E. *A Life of Gwendolyn Brooks.* Lexington: The University Press of Kentucky, pp. 4, 49, 54, 55, 56, 62–63, 64, 65, 75, 79, 99, 152, 156, 172, 179, 197. Quotes from *AH* on the social context of Chicago, discusses W and the South Side Writers Group to establish the literary context of Brooks's intellectual coming of age, paraphrases and quotes from W's letter on the manuscript of *A Street in Bronzeville,* reports Brooks's response to W's encouragement and to *NS* and *BB,* quotes from Brooks's review of *LT,* and mentions W elsewhere.

2424. King, Sigrid. "Naming and Power in Zora Neale Hurston's *Their Eyes Were Watching God.*" *Black American Literature Forum,* 24 (Winter), 683–696. Mentions briefly *BB* (p. 684).

2425. Kinnamon, Keneth. "How *Native Son* Was Born," in *Writing the American Classics.* Eds. James Barbour and Tom Quirk. Chapel Hill: University of North Carolina Press, pp. 209–234. Analyzes manuscripts, proofs, and unpublished letters to show that *NS* was shaped by external pressures as well as by the author's creative imagination, especially in the areas of sex and politics. Also discusses *How "Bigger" Was Born* and reviews the reception of *NS* through 1941.

2426. _____. "Introduction," in his *New Essays on Native Son.* Cambridge: Cambridge University Press, pp. 1–33. Revised version of 1990

adding a section on the influence of *NS* on subsequent black writers and on scholarship on the novel.

2427. _____, ed. *New Essays on Native Son.* Cambridge: Cambridge University Press, viii + 156 pp. Consists of an introduction by the editor; essays by John M. Reilly, Trudier Harris, Houston A. Baker, Jr., and Craig Werner; notes on contributors; and a selected bibliography.

2428. Kirkpatrick, Ken. "Recent African-American Scholarship." *College English,* 52 (November), 812–822. Mentions W briefly (p. 820).

2429. Kiuchi, Toru. "Richard Wright's *Native Son*: The Film and the Novel," in *Film and Society: Proceedings of the Eighth Annual Kent State University International Film Conference, April 17–18.* Ed. Douglas Radcliff-Umstead. Kent, OH: Romance Languages Department, Kent State University, pp. 62–68. Analyzes changes made from the novel in the 1986 Diane Silver production and notes its generally unfavorable reception. The most serious change was the elimination of the murder of Bessie in order not to forfeit audience empathy for Bigger.

2430. Klevar, Harvey L. "Caldwell's Women," in *Erskine Caldwell Reconsidered.* Ed. Edwin T. Arnold. Jackson: University Press of Mississippi, pp. 15–35. Mentions briefly W's review of *Trouble in July.*

2431. Kolb, Harold H., Jr. "Defining the Canon," in *Redefining American Literary History.* Eds. A. LaVonne Brown Ruoff and Jerry W. Ward, Jr. New York: The Modern Language Association of America, pp. 35–51. Proposes a first-level canon of American literature consisting of Hawthorne, Emerson, Thoreau, Melville, Whitman, Dickinson, Twain, James, Eliot, W, and Faulkner (p. 41).

2432. Kramer, Hilton. "Irving Howe at Seventy." *The New Criterion,* 9 (October), 6–9. Mentions W briefly (p. 9).

2433. Kutulas, Judy. "The League of American Writers, the Communist Party, and the Literary People's Front. *Journal of American Culture,* 13, no. 1, pp. 71–80. Mentions W briefly (p. 74).

2434. _____. "Becoming 'More Liberal': The League of American Writers, The Communist Party, and The literary People's Front." *Journal* *of American Culture*, 13, 71–80. Mentions W briefly. (p. 74).

2435. Kutzinski, Vera M. "Günter H. Lenz, ed. *History and Tradition in Afro-American Culture.*" *Amerikastudien*, 35 (Summer), 230–233. Discusses Lenz's essay on W and Zora Neale Hurston.

2436. LaSalle, Peter. "Artful Dodgers." *Commonweal*, 117 (9 February), 93–94. Review of Herbert Leibowitz's *Explorations in American Autobiography* mentioning W briefly.

2437. Lee, A. Robert. "'Ask Your Mama': Langston Hughes, the Blues and Recent Afro-American Literary Studies." *Journal of American Studies*, 24 (August), 199–209. Mentions W briefly (p. 203).

2438. _____. "Introduction," in his *William Faulkner: The Yoknapatawpha Fiction*. London: Vision Press, pp. 7–18. Mentions W briefly (p. 17).

2439. _____. "State of the Art: 'Ask Your Mama': Langston Hughes, the Blues and Recent Afro-American Studies." *Journal of American Studies*, 24 (August 1990), 199–209. Review of five books in the field. Mentions W briefly (p. 203).

2440. Lee, Don L. "The Achievement of Gwendolyn Brooks," in *Black Women in American History: The Twentieth Century*. Vol. 3. Ed. Darlene Clark Hine. Brooklyn: Carlson, pp. 826–835.

2441. Lentz, Richard. *Symbols, The News Magazines, and Martin Luther King*. Baton Rouge: Louisiana State University Press, p. 209. Mentions briefly W's use of the phrase "Black Power."

2442. Lenz, Günter H. "The Radical Imagination: Revisionary Modes of Radical Cultural Criticism in Thirties America in *"Looking Inward Looking Outward: From the 1930s Through the 1940s*. Ed. Steve Ickringill. Amsterdam: VU University Press, pp 94–126. Includes a substantial discussion of W's effort to treat "the ambiguous legacy of black folk life in the racist rural South and the paradoxical effects of living in the black ghetto" (p. 106). Considers W's relation to the Chicago School of Sociology and comments on *LT*, *NS* and *TMBV*. Also contrasts W and Hurston.

2443. _____. "Reconstructing American Literary Studies: History, Difference, and Synthesis," in *Reconstructing American Literary and*

Historical Studies. Eds. Günter H. Lenz, Hartmut Keil, and Sabine Bröck-Sallah. Frankfurt am Main: Campus Verlag/New York: St. Martin's Press, pp. 21–50. Mentions briefly *BB* (p. 39).

2444. Levitt, Morton P. "1989 Annual Review." *Journal of Modern Literature*, 17 (Fall/Winter), 189–442. Lists W issue of *The Mississippi Quarterly* and an article by Hal Blythe and Charlie Sweet (p. 425) and mentions W in notices of works on broader topics (pp. 191, 195, 253, 280, 310, 328).

2445. Lewis, Earl. "Acting in Their Own Interest: African-Americans and the Great Migration." *The Crisis*, 98 (February), 18–22, 44–45. Notes W's departure from the South, quoting from *BB* (p. 21).

2446. Lewis, Vashti Crutcher. "African Tradition in Toni Morrison's *Sula*," in *Wild Women in the Whirlwind: Afra-American Culture and the Contemporary Literary Renaissance*. Eds. Joanne M. Braxton and Andrée Nicola McLaughlin. New Brunswick, NJ: Rutgers University Press, pp. 316–325. Quotes briefly from "Blueprint for Negro Writing" (p. 323).

2447. Lhamon, W.T., Jr. *Deliberate Speed: The Origins of a Cultural Style in the American 1950's*. Cambridge: Harvard University Press, pp. 32, 64, 69, 140, 223. Notes W's attendance at the Banding Conference, comments on the W-Ellison relationship, and notes that "the last word in Wright's titles always reinforced stunted immaturity" (*UTC*, *NS*, *BB*).

2448. Lingeman, Richard. *Theodore Dreiser: An American Journey, 1908–1945*. New York: Putnam's, pp. 427, 451. Notes the influence of *An American Tragedy* on *NS*. Quotes W on Dreiser on the occasion of his farewell party in New York in 1944.

2449. Longest, George, ed. "A Checklist of Scholarship on Southern Literature for 1989." *The Mississippi Quarterly*, 43 (Supplement 2), 1–173. Lists six items on W and cross-references to twenty-four other items dealing partially with W.

2450. Loury, Glenn C. "Black Dignity and the Common Good." *First Things: A Monthly Journal of Religion and Public Life* (June/July), 12–19. Quoted Baldwin on Bigger in "Everybody's Protest Novel" (p. 17).

2451. Lupton, Mary Jane. "Dolly A. McPherson. *Order Out of Chaos: The Autobiographical Works of Maya Angelou.*" *Black American Literature Forum*, 24 (Winter), 809–814. Mentions briefly *BB* (p. 812).

2452. Lynch, Michael F. *Creative Revolt: A Study of Wright, Ellison, and Dostoevsky*. New York: Peter Lang, 194 pp. After discussing W's affiliation with the Communist party and his knowledge of Dostoevsky, relying mainly on secondary sources, Lynch analyzes the influence of *Crime and Punishment* on *NS* and *O*. In *NS*, W is moving away from deterministic naturalism and communism. Communism is attacked and individual freedom affirmed, thus achieving "greater power, complexity, and consistency" (p. 108) than in *NS*. Lynch also treats "The Man Who Lived Underground," finding in it parallels to *Crime and Punishment* and *The Brothers Karamazov*.

2453. _____. "Dostoevsky and Richard Wright: Choices of Individual Freedom and Dignity." *Chiba Review*, 12 (November), 25–40. Analyzes similarities and differences in *Crime and Punishment, The Brothers Karamozov, NS, O*, and "The Man Who Lived Underground."

2454. Lyons, Mary E. *Sorrow's Kitchen: The Life and Folklore of Zora Neale Hurston*. New York: Scribner's, pp. 97, 99–100. Treats the W-Hurston relationship, quoting her praise of *NS*.

2455. Macieski, Robert. "American Writers Congress," in *Encyclopedia of the American Left*. Eds. Mari Jo Buhle, Paul Buhle, and Dan Georgakas. New York: Garland, pp. 33–34. Notes that W was among the signers of the call for the Congress.

2456. Madden, David. "Questions and Commentaries for Discussion and Writing," in his *The World of Fiction*. Fort Worth: Holt, Rinehart, and Winston, pp. 1071–1191. Includes (pp. 1189–1191) three questions, a four-paragraph commentary, and a brief bibliography to accompany "The Man Who Was Almost a Man" (reprinted on pp. 1061–1070).

2457. Magistrale, Tony, and Patricia Ferreira. "Sweet Mama Wanda Tells Fortunes: An Interview with Wanda Coleman." *Black American Literature Forum*, 24 (Fall), 491–

507. The interviewers mention W briefly (pp. 492–498).

2458. Maland, Charles. "*Hope Among Us Yet: Social Criticism and Social Solace in Depression America.* David Peeler." *American Studies,* 31 (Spring), 129–130. Review mentioning W briefly.

2459. Marable, Manning. "Race, Class, and Conflict: Intellectual Debates on Race Relations Research in the United States Since 1960, a Social Science Bibliographical Essay," in *Black Studies: Intellectual History, Cultural Meaning, and Political Ideology.* Ed. Abdul Alkalimat. Chicago: Twenty-First Century Books, pp. 163–204.

2460. Marcuse, Michael J. *A Reference Guide for English Studies.* Berkeley: University of California Press, pp. 21, 400. Lists the W collection at Yale and John M. Reilly's bibliographical essay.

2461. Margolies, Edward. "Keneth Kinnamon, ed. *New Essays on Native Son.*" *Black American Literature Forum,* 24 (Winter), 821–828. Favorable essay-review treating the five essays individually. Takes exception to some of the points made by Trudier Harris, Houston Baker, and Craig Werner, but as a whole this "fine collection ... addresses ... issues with intelligence and real engagement" (pp. 821–822).

2462. _____. "Kinnamon, Keneth, ed. *New Essays on Native Son.*" *Afram Newsletter,* No. 32 (December), 41–42. Favorable review with comments on the editor's introduction and each of the four essays. "Thi [sic] fine collection is a fitting tribute to the enduring relevance of Wright's novel."

2463. Márquez, Roberto. "One Boricua's Baldwin: A Personal Remembrance." *American Quarterly,* 42 (September), 456–477. Comments on Baldwin's criticism of W, mentioning *NS* and *BB* (pp. 464–465.)

2464. Martin, Reginald. "An Interview with Michael Harper." *Black American Literature Forum,* 24 (Fall), 441–451. Harper comments briefly on W, praising "his commitment and his rigor" (p. 445).

2465. Martinez, Nancy, et al. "A Checklist of Explication (1988)." *The Explicator,* 49 (Fall), 3–66. Lists one item on W.

2466. _____. "A Checklist of Explication (1986–87)." *The Explica-*

tor, 48 (Winter), 66–170. Lists four items on W (p. 165).

2467. Mason, Theodore O., Jr. "Dreaming a World." *Callaloo,* 13 (Spring), 372–376. Review of the second volume of Arnold Rampersad's *The Life of Langston Hughes* commenting on Hughes's attitude toward W (p. 373).

2468. Masuda, Mitsuko. "Ralph Ellison and Richard Wright: A Comparison." *Nikon Women's University Veritas,* 12 (25 December) 81–87. Applies Freudian Psychology to a comparative study of Bigger and the protagonist of *Invisible Man.* Bigger is humorless, dogmatic, and pessimistic while "I' is clown-like and superegotistic [T.K., R.B., and Y.H.].

2469. May, Lee. "Turning a New Page in History." *Los Angeles Times* (14 May), pp. 1, 14–15. Mentions briefly W, *UTC,* and *NS.*

2470. McDowell, Deborah E. "'The Changing Same': Generational Connections and Black Women Novelists," in *Reading Black, Reading Feminist: A Critical Anthology.* Ed. Henry Louis Gates, Jr. New York: Meridian, pp. 91–115.

2471. McDowell, Margaret B. "The Black Woman as Artist and Critic: Four Versions," in *Black Women in American History: The Twentieth Century.* Vol. 3. Ed. Darlene Clark Hine. Brooklyn: Carlson, pp. 897–919.

2472. McGrath, Daniel F., ed. *Bookman's Price Index.* Vol. 40. Detroit: Gale, p. 859. Lists *NS* at $100 and *TMBV* at $300.

2473. McGrory, Mary. "Mississippi Starts Over with Kids." Little Rock *Arkansas Gazette* (28 January), p. 3C. Mentions W briefly.

2474. McKay, Nellie Y. "The Autobiographies of Zora Neale Hurston and Gwendolyn Brooks: Alternate Versions of the Black Female Self," in *Wild Women in the Whirlwind: Afra-American Culture and the Contemporary Literary Renaissance.* Eds. Joanne M. Braxton and Andrée Nicola McLaughlin. New Brunswick, NJ: Rutgers University Press, pp. 264–281. Mentions W and *BB* (pp. 265, 269, 272, 277).

2475. McLaughlin, Andrée Nicola. "A Renaissance of the Spirit: Black Women Remaking the Universe," in *Wild Women in the Whirlwind: Afra-American Culture and the Contemporary Literary Renaissance.*

Eds. Joanne M. Braxton and Andrée Nicola McLaughlin. New Brunswick, NJ: Rutgers University Press, pp. xxxi–xlix. Mentions briefly Margaret Walker Alexander's biography of W (p. xxxiv).

2476. McMillan, Terry. "Introduction," in her *Breaking Ice: An Anthology of Contemporary African-American Fiction.* New York: Penguin Books, pp. xv–xxiv. Mentions W briefly (p. xvi).

2477. McPartland, Scott. *Instructor's Manual to Accompany Wiener Reading for the Disciplines: An Anthology for College Writers.* New York: McGraw-Hill, pp. 7–8. Answers and comments for study questions and notes.

2478. McPherson, Dolly A. *Order Out of Chaos: The Autobiographical Works of Maya Angelou.* New York: Peter Lang, pp. 3, 11–12, 18–19, 45, 62, 125–126. Compares and contrasts Angelou's autobiographical writings to *BB.*

2479. McWilliams, John. "The Rationale for 'The American Romance.'" *Boundary 2,* 17 (Spring), 71–82. Mentions W briefly (p. 74).

2480. Melhem, D.H. "Amiri Baraka: Revolutionary Traditions," in his *Heroism in the New Black Poetry.* Lexington: The University Press of Kentucky, pp. 215–263. Mentions W briefly (p. 215) Baraka rates him with Du Bois and Hughes as the most eminent writers of the Harlem Renaissance (pp. 219–220).

2481. _____. "Foreword" to *A Life of Gwendolyn Brooks* by George E. Kent. Lexington: The University Press of Kentucky, pp. vii–viii. Mentions briefly Kent's work on W.

2482. _____. "Haki R. Madhubuti: Prescriptive Revolution," in his *Heroism in the New Black Poetry.* Lexington: The University Press of Kentucky, pp. 84–130). Madhubuti recalls his mother's love of literature, especially *BB* (p. 85) and acknowledges W as a major influence on him. Mentions *NS, O* and *BP.*

2483. _____. "Introduction," in his *Heroism in the New Black Poetry.* Lexington: The University Press of Kentucky, pp. 1–8. Mentions W briefly in a footnote (p. 7).

2484. Messent, Peter. *New Readings of the American Novel: Narrative Theory and Its Application.* New York: St. Martin's Press, p. 268. Quotes from W's review of *Their Eyes Were Watching God.*

2485. Mikolyzk, Thomas A. *Langston Hughes: A Bio-Bibliography.* New York: Greenwood Press, pp. 12, 19, 27, 77, 90, 92, 94, 95, 129, 185, 187, 188, 217. Mentions W briefly three times in the biographical section and ten times in the annotated bibliographical section.

2486. Miller, Eugene E. *Voice of a Native Son: The Poetics of Richard Wright.* Jackson: University Press of Mississippi, xxv + 264 pp. Studies the "intuitive, emotional, even visionary and semi-mystical Wright" (pp. xiv–xv), drawing on unpublished material and treating "The Man Who Killed a Shadow," *NS*, and the haiku poems. Miller argues for Mark Twain and Gertrude Stein as W's chief literary ancestors and Kenneth Burke as his primary intellectual mentor.

2487. Miller, R. Baxter. "Black Literature," in *American Literary Scholarship: An Annual/1989.* Ed. J. Albert Robbins. Durham, NC: Duke University Press, pp. 397–428. Reviews work published in 1988 on W, including Keneth Kinnamon's *A Richard Wright Bibliography* and essays by Alan W. Frances and Jack Moore (pp. 416–417). Mentions W elsewhere.

2488. Morales, Donald M. "Black Arts and Radical South African Theater: A Comparative View." *The Literary Griot*, 2 (Spring), 103–116. Mentions briefly *NS* (pp. 103–104).

2489. Moreland, Kim. "James Barlowe and Tom Quirk, eds. *Writing the American Classics.*" *American Studies International*, 28 (October), 114–115. Mentions briefly *NS*.

2490. Moses, Wilson Jeremiah. *The Wings of Ethiopia: Studies in African-American Life and Letters.* Ames: Iowa State University Press, pp. 103, 274, 279. Mentions briefly W and *TMBV*.

2491. Mulvey, Christopher. "Harlem: Entrance and Initiation." *European Contributions to American Studies*, 17 (*The Future of American Modernism: Ethnic Writing Between the Wars*), pp. 94–104. Quotes extensively from "How 'Bigger' Was Born" and comments on *NS* (pp. 216–217).

2492. Myers, D.G. "Sound and Fury." *The New Criterion*, 8 (February), 61–64. Review of Henry Louis Gates, Jr.'s *The Signifying Monkey* mentioning briefly *LT*.

2493. Namekata, Hitoshi. "Fred's Journey: Richard Wright's 'The Man Who Lived Underground,'" in *British and American Literature and Language: In Search of a New Horizon.* Ed. The Byblos Society. Tokyo: Homeros Sha, 366–382. Concludes that W tried to get over racial issues and reach universal problems [T.K., R.B, and Y.H.].

2494. Nelson, David. "M.A. Students in Southern Studies." *The Southern Register* (Fall), pp. 3–5. Notes that the first recipient of the Master of Arts in Southern Studies of the University of Mississippi was Guilan Wang of China, the translator of *BB* into Chinese.

2495. Nelson, Emmanuel S. "Black America and the Black South African Literary Consciousness," in *Perspectives of Black Popular Culture.* Ed. Harry B. Shaw. Bowling Green, OH: Bowling Green State University Popular Press, pp. 155–165. Mentions briefly W, *UTC*, and W's influence on Ezekiel Mphahlele (p. 160).

2496. Newman, Blaze. "*The Afro-Americans.* Howard Snead. *The Scotch-Irish Americans.* Robin Brownstein and Peter Guttmacher." *MELUS*, 16 (Summer), 111–115. Mentions W briefly (p. 111).

2497. Nixon, Will. "Black Male Writers: Endangered Species?" *American Visions*, 5 (February), 25–28. Quotes Florence Howe mentioning W briefly (p. 25).

2498. Njeri, Itabari. *Every Good-Bye Ain't Gone.* New York: Times Books, p. 67. The author notes that her father, Mark Marion Moreland, was an acquaintance of W in Harlem.

2499. _____. "Life with Father." *Harper's Magazine*, 280 (January), 34, 36, 38. Mentions W briefly.

2500. Nkrumah, Kwame. *Kwame Nkrumah: The Conakry Years.* Ed. June Milne. London and Atlantic Highlands, NJ: Panaf/Zed Press, pp. 17, 37, 134, 183, 185, 190, 202. Nkrumah comments on W and *BP*, especially in connection with the use of W's letter to Nkrumah in the latter's *Dark Days in Ghana.*

2501. Norman, Dorothy. *The Hero: Myth/Image/Symbol.* New York: Doubleday, pp. 172–174.

2502. Ochillo, Yvonne. "The Universal Black Experience: An Interview with C. Eric Lincoln." *The Journal of Negro History*, 75 (Summer, Fall), 112–119. Ochillo notes echoes of *NS* in Lincoln's novel *Clayton City* (p. 113).

2503. Olaniyan, Tejumola. "God's Weeping Eyes: Hurston and the Anti-Patriarchal Form." *Obsidian II*, 5 (Summer), 30–45. Comments on W's unfavorable review of *Their Eyes Were Watching God* (p. 30) and Hurston's review of *UTC* (p. 43).

2504. Olney, James. "Autobiographical Traditions Black and White," in *Located Lives: Place and Idea in Southern Autobiography.* Ed. J. Bill Berry. Athens: The University of Georgia Press, pp. 66–77. Argues that a Black Southern autobiographical tradition exists based on "the thematic triad of literacy, identity, and freedom," but that there is no white Southern autobiographical tradition. Analyses of *BB* and Eudora Welty's *One Writer's Beginnings* support the case. Olney states that it seems "altogether reasonable to argue that no American book of this century is more important than Wright's autobiography"(p. 68).

2505. _____. "The Founding Fathers—Frederick Douglass and Booker T. Washington." *Amerikastudien*, 35 (Fall), 281–296. Comments briefly on W and *BB* (pp. 295, 296).

2506. Ostenby, Peter M. "Paul Buhle, *C.L.R. James: The Artist as Revolutionary.*" *The Journal of Negro History*, 75 (Winter, Spring), 47–48. Review mentioning W briefly.

2507. Paquet, Sandra Pouchet. "The Ancestor as Foundation in *Their Eyes Were Watching God* and *Tar Baby.*" *Callaloo*, 13 (Summer), 499–515. Mentions W briefly (p. 500).

2508. Parks, Gordon. *Voices in the Mirror: An Autobiography* (New York: Doubleday), pp. 85, 87, 145–148, 171. Parks acknowledges the profound influence of *TMBV* on his life and work; reports an evening in Paris with W in 1959, including comments by W on *UTC* and *NS*; and mentions W elsewhere.

2509. Pauly, Thomas H. "Black Images and White Culture During the Decade Before the Civil Rights Movement." *American Studies*, 31 (Fall), 101–119. Comments on James Baldwin's early attitude toward W and *NS* (pp. 115–116).

2510. Peck, David. "New Masses," in *Encyclopedia of the American Left.* Eds. Mari Jo Buhle, Paul Buhle, and Dan Georgakas. New York: Garland, pp. 526–527. Notes that W published in the journal.

2511. Pemberton, Gayle. "The Hottest Water in Chicago." *The Yale Review*, 79 (Summer), 509–517. Mentions Bigger Thomas (p. 510).

2512. _____. "The Koan of Nana." *The Yale Review*, 79 (Summer), 534–552. Expresses distaste for W's view that literature is a weapon and rejects *NS* for its dehumanized characterization of Bigger. Calls *Invisible Man* "a comic *Native Son*" (p. 547).

2513. _____. "None of the Above." *The Yale Review*, 79 (Summer), 509–552. Mentions briefly Bigger Thomas (p. 510) and W (p. 544).

2514. Perkins, George, Sculley Bradley, Richmond Croom Beatty, and E. Hudson Long. "After the Second World War," in their *The American Tradition in Literature*. Seventh edition. Vol. 2. New York: McGraw-Hill, pp. 1369–1375.

2515. _____. "After the Second World War," in their *The American Tradition in Literature*. Seventh edition (shorter edition). New York: McGraw-Hill, pp. 1605–1611.

2516. [Perkins, George]. "Richard Wright (1908–1960)," in *The American Tradition in Literature*. Eds. Sculley Bradley, Richmond Croom Beatty, E. Hudson Long, and George Perkins. Seventh edition. Vol. 2. New York: McGraw-Hill, pp. 1358–1359. Revised reprint of 1974.142

2517. [_____]. "Richard Wright (1908–1960)," in *The American Tradition in Literature*. Seventh edition (shorter edition). Eds. Sculley Bradley, Richmond Croom Beatty, E. Hudson Long, and George Perkins. New York: McGraw-Hill, pp. 1594–1595.

2518. Perreault, Donna. "What Makes Autobiography Interrogative?" *Biography*, 13 (Spring), 130–142. Analyzes *BB* "as a questioning response to self hood" (p. 131). Constantly questioning himself and his social environment, the child Richard and the narrator are linked. Both are personae of the actual W. The questions are unanswerable, but the questioning defines the personality of character, narrator, and author.

2519. Peterson, Bernard L., Jr. *Early Black American Playwrights and Dramatic Writers: A Biographical Directory and Catalog of Plays, Films, and Broadcasting Scripts*. Westport, CT: Greenwood, pp. xiv, 19, 20, 185, 201–204. Includes a biographical sketch of W with notes on *NS* as drama and film, "Fire and Cloud," the play *LD*, *Daddy Goodness*, and unpublished dramatic writings. Mentions W elsewhere and notes Melvin B. Tolson's dramatic adaptation of *BB*.

2520. Petrie, Dennis W. "Timothy Dow Adams. *Telling Lies in Modern American Autobiography*." *Modern Fiction Studies*, 36 (Winter), 588–589. Review commenting on Adams's treatment of *BB*.

2521. Pettis, Joyce. "Margaret Walker: Black Woman Writer of the South," in *Southern Women Writers: The New Generation*. Ed. Tonette Bond Inge. Tuscaloosa: The University of Alabama press, p. 10. Mentions W briefly.

2522. Platt, Anthony M. "Racism in Academia: Lessons from the Life of E. Franklin Frazier." *Monthly Review*, 42 (September), 29–45. Mentions W briefly (pp. 30, 41).

2523. Powell, Timothy B. "Toni Morrison: The Struggle to Depict the Black Figure on the White Page." *Black American Literature Forum*, 24 (Winter), 747–760. Comments briefly on "The Man Who Lived Underground" and *NS* (pp. 748, 754–755).

2524. Prestianni, Vincent. "Bibliographical Scholarship on Three Black Writers." *Obsidian II*, 5 (Spring), 75–85. Mentions W briefly (p. 75).

2525. Prevost, Verbie Lovorn. "Theses and Dissertations for 1989." *South Atlantic Review*, 55 (November), 161–184. Lists a dissertation by La Vinia Delois Jennings, "Sexual Violence in the Works of Richard Wright, James Baldwin, and Toni Morrison" (p. 173).

2526. Proefriedt, William A. "The Immigrant or 'Outsider' Experience as Metaphor for Becoming an Educated Person in the Modern World: Mary Antin, Richard Wright and Eva Hoffman." *MELUS*, 16 (Summer), 77–90. Discusses W's ambivalent attitude toward his childhood as expressed in *BB*, comparing it to analogous experiences of two Jewish immigrants. Moving between cultures, Proefriedt believes, is probably educational.

2527. Rackham, Jeff, and Beverly J. Slaughter. "Fiction," in their *The Rinehart Reader*. New York: Holt, Rinehart and Winston, pp. 564–569. Includes comments on "The Man Who Was Almost a Man."

2528. _____. "*The Man Who Was Almost a Man* Richard Wright (1908–1960)," in their *The Rinehart Reader*. New York: Holt, Rinehart and Winston, pp. 678–679. Biographical headnote with a full-page photograph.

2529. _____. "Writing Assignments for Chapter Thirteen," in their *The Rinehart Reader*. New York: Holt, Rinehart and Winston, pp. 689–691. Includes one assignment on "The Man Who Was Almost a Man."

2530. _____. *The Rinehart Reader*. Fort Worth: Holt, Rinehart and Winston, pp. 565, 567, 569, 678–689, 691. Reprints "The Man Who Was Almost a Man" and comments on its technique, symbolism, and style. Includes a photograph of W, headnote, and topics for writing.

2531. Rampersad, Arnold. "V.S. Naipaul: Turning in the South." *Raritan: A Quarterly Review*, 10 (Summer), 24–47. Concludes the essay by comparing Naipaul and W in their alienation from their origins. Mentions *BB*, *O*, *SH*, *BP*, *PS*, and *CC*.

2532. Raper, Julius Rowan. "Inventing Modern Southern Fiction: A Postmodern View." *The Southern Literary Journal*, 22 (Spring), 3–18. Mentions briefly W (p. 6) and Bigger Thomas (p. 8).

2533. Rehin, George. "Jean Toomer, *Cane*; Robert K. Jones and Margery Toomer Latimer (eds.), *The Collected Poems of Jean Toomer*; Cynthia Earl Kerman and Richard Eldridge. *The Lives of Jean Toomer: A Hunger for Wholeness*." *Journal of American Studies*, 24 (April), 138–139. Review mentioning W briefly.

2534. _____. "Jean Toomer, *Cane*" (ed. Darwin T. Turner). Robert B. Jones and Margery Toomer (eds.), *The Collected Poems of Jean Toomer*, Cynthia Earl Kerman and Richard Eldridge, *The Lives of Jean Toomer: A Hunger for Wholeness*. *Journal of American Studies*, 24 (April 1990). Review mentioning W briefly.

2535. Reid, Calvin. "Ruling Allows Use of Unpublished Material to Establish Fact: Fair Use Case Won by R. Wright Biographer M. Walker." *Publishers Weekly*, 237 (12 October), 8. Explains the favorable ruling granted to Margaret Walker in a suit brought by Ellen Wright.

2536. Reilly, John M. "Giving Bigger a Voice," in *New Essays on Native Son*. Ed. Keneth Kinnamon. Cambridge: Cambridge University Press, pp. 35–62. Demonstrates how narrative techniques are carefully used to subvert conventional American racial discourses and to establish the authority and authenticity of the protagonist's voice. "Bigger's achievement of voice stands as a symbol of the purpose of Afro-American literature" (p. 62).

2537. _____. "Richard Wright 1908–1960," in *The Heath Anthology of American Literature*. Vol. 2. Ed. Paul Lauter et al. Lexington, MA: D.C. Heath, pp. 1786–1787. Headnote to "The Man Who Was Almost a Man" commenting on *UTC, NS, BB*, and *AH*. Rooted in Afro-American culture, W presents in "The Man Who Was Almost a Man" a "story for everyone."

2538. Rose, Mike. *Lives on the Boundary: A Moving Account of the Struggles and Achievements of America's Educational Underclass*. New York: Penguin, p. 36.

2539. Rowell, Charles H. "'Down Don't Worry Me': An Interview with Michael S. Harper." *Callaloo*, 13 (Fall), 780–800. Contains many comments by Harper on reading W and using him as a poetic subject.

2540. _____. "An Interview with John Edgar Wideman." *Callaloo*, 13 (Winter), 47–61. Both Rowell and Wideman mention W briefly (pp. 53, 55).

2541. Rubin, Louis D., Jr. "The High Sheriff of Yoknapatawpha County: A Study in the Genius of Place," in *Faulkner and Popular Culture*. Eds. Doreen Fowler and Ann J. Abadie. Jackson: University Press of Mississippi, pp. 242–264. Mentions W briefly (p. 247).

2542. Ruoff, A. LaVonne Brown, Jerry W. Ward, Jr., Richard Yarborough, Frances Smith Foster, Paul Lauter, and John W. Roberts. "African American Literature," in *Redefining American Literary History*. Eds. A. LaVonne Ruoff and Jerry W. Ward, Jr. New York: The Modern Language Association of America, pp. 287–326. Lists primary works (books) by W (p. 312), secondary works on W (pp. 325–326), and mentions W elsewhere.

2543. Ruppersburg, Hugh. *Rob-*

ert Penn Warren and the American Imagination. Athens: The University of Georgia Press, p. 187. Notes Warren's authorship of the W headnote in *American Literature: The Makers and the Making*.

2544. Salzman, Jack, ed. *American Studies: An Annotated Bibliography, 1984–1988*. Cambridge: Cambridge University Press, pp. 665, 674, 690, 692, 699, 701, 724. Mentions W in annotations on books by Bernard W. Bell, Michael G. Cooke, Theodore L. Gross, Trudier Harris, Sanehide Kodama, Lewis A. Larson, and Valerie Smith.

2545. Sanders, Leslie. "The Politics of Representation: Some Recent African-American Literary Criticism." *The Canadian Review of American Studies*, 21 (Fall), 247–260. Comments on Valerie Smith's treatment of *NS* (p. 255).

2546. Saunders, James Robert. "The Ornamentation of Old Ideas: Gloria Naylor's First Three Novels." *The Hollins Critic*, 27 (April), 1–11. Mentions briefly *NS* (p. 2).

2547. Savery, Pancho. "'Git a Stool. Let Me Tell You Something': Call and Response in *No Day of Triumph*." *Black American Literature Forum*, 24 (Summer), 277–298. Mentions briefly W, *NS*, and W's introduction to *No Day of Triumph*.

2548. _____. "The Third Plane at the Change of the Century: The Shape of African American Literature to Come," in *Left Politics and the Literary Profession*. Eds. Lennard J. Davis and M. Bella Mirabella. New York: Columbia University Press, pp. 236–253. Mentions briefly Fabre's work on W (p. 243).

2549. Sayre, Robert F. "*Fabricating Lives: Explorations in American Autobiography*. By Herbert Leibowitz." *The Journal of American History*, 77 (December), 983–984. Review mentioning W briefly.

2550. Seed, David. "American Literature: Twentieth Century: Prose Fiction," in *The Year's Work in English Studies*. Vol. 63. London: John Murray, pp. 632–675. Comments on work on W by David Bradley, Joyce Ann Joyce, Lynda Hungerford, Laura E. Tanner, Michael Atkinson, Jane Campbell, John M. Reilly, and Charles J. Wright (pp. 632, 636, 654–655, 656).

2551. Sharpe, Patricia, F.E. Mascia-Lees, and C.B. Cohen. "White Women and Black Men: Differential

Responses to Reading Black Women's Texts." *College English*, 52 (February), 142–153. Mentions briefly W's review of *Their Eyes Were Watching God* (p. 145).

2552. Shaw, Harry B. "Introduction," in his *Perspectives of Black Popular Culture*. Bowling Green, OH: Bowling Green State University Popular Press, pp. 1–6. Mentions briefly W and *NS* (p. 5).

2553. Sheppard, R.Z. "Foul Weather for Fair Use." *Time*, 135 (30 April), 86–87. Mentions Ellen Wright's suit against Margaret Walker. Mentions briefly *NS*.

2554. Shockley, Ann Allen. "The Negro Woman in Retrospect: Blueprint for the Future," in *Black Women's History: Theory and Practice*. Vol. 2. Ed. Darlene Clark Hine. Brooklyn: Carlson, pp. 575–579.

2555. Shorris, Earl. "Somebody in Books." *The Nation*, 250 (5 February), 174–175. Review of Bettina Drew's biography of Nelson Algren mentioning his friendship with W.

2556. Silk, Catherine, and John Silk. *Racism and Anti-racism in American Popular Culture: Portrayals of African-Americans in Fiction and Film*. Manchester: Manchester University Press, pp. 32, 74, 86, 87. Mentions briefly W and *NS* and refers to *BB*.

2557. Simpson, Paul. "English Language: Stylistics," in *The Year's Work in English Studies*. Vol. 68. London: John Murray, pp. 108–115. Comments on Lynda Hungerford's "Dialect Representation in *Native Son*" (p. 113).

2558. Smith, Carter, ed. *American Historical Facts on File: The Black Experience*. New York: Facts on File, pp. 4.61, 5.57. Large photograph of W with biographical note. *NS* is mentioned in a similar entry for Toni Morrison.

2559. Smith, Tracy E. "A Stronger Soul Within a Finer Frame': Portraying African-Americans in the Black Renaissance: An Introduction to the Exhibition," in her and John S. Wright's *A Stronger Soul Within a Finer Frame: Portraying African Americans in the Black Renaissance*. Minneapolis: University of Minnesota, pp. 46–64. Mentions briefly W and *NS* (p. 62).

2560. Snell, Susan. "African-American Studies." *The Society for the Study of Southern Literature Newsletter*, 33 (November), 26–27.

Lists Harold Bloom's *Bigger Thomas* and Eugene E. Miller's *Voice of a Native Son.*

2561. _____. "Audiocassettes." *The Society for the Study of Southern Literature Newsletter*, 23 (April), 39. Lists *NS* read by James Earl Jones.

2562. _____. "Reissues and Paperbacks for Classes in Southern and African-American Literature." *The Society for the Study of Southern Literature Newsletter*, 23 (November), 22–23. Lists *AD, BB, LD, NS, O,* and *UTC.*

2563. Sollors, Werner. "Anthropological and Sociological Tendencies in American Literature of the 1930's and 1940's: Richard Wright, Zora Neale Hurston, and American Culture," in *Looking Inward Looking Outward: From the 1930's Through the 1940's.* Ed. Steve Ickringgill. Amsterdam: VU University Press, pp. 22–93. Extensive comparison/contrast of "Long Black Song" and "The Gilded Six-Bits." Also deals with W's relation to Horace Cayton and the Chicago School of Sociology. Mentions other W works, cites numerous critics, and provides a joint chronology of W and Hurston."

2564. _____. "Culture, Southern?" *Appalachian Journal*, 17 (Summer), 408–418. Essay-review of *Encyclopedia of Southern Culture* mentioning W, *BB, UTC,* and "The Ethics of Living Jim Crow."

2565. _____. "Modernization as Adultery: Richard Wright, Zora Neale Hurston and American Culture of the 1930s and 1940s." *Hebrew University Studies in Literature and the Arts*, 18, pp. 109–155. Focusing on *NS*, "Long Black Song," and "The Gilded Six-Bits," this essay contrasts W and Hurston, the former sociological and urban, the latter anthropological and rural. W was a pessimistic modernist, Hurston a folkloric traditionalist. Sollors emphasizes differing approaches to time in the two authors and their personal relationships with social scientists. He draws on manuscript versions of the two short stories as well as the published texts.

2566. _____. "Of Mules and Mares in a Land of Differences; or, Quadrupeds All?" *American Quarterly*, 42 (June), 167–190. Notes W's criticism of Zora Neale Hurston as commented on by Elaine Showalter and Gilbert and Gubar (p. 170). Also

quotes an interesting unpublished publicity statement by W about *BB* (p. 189).

2567. Spencer, Norman. "Juju Jazz and Mojo Blues." *American Book Review*, 11 (January-February), 16, 25, 28. Mentions W briefly (p. 25).

2568. Strout, Cushing. *Making American Tradition: Visions and Revisions from Ben Franklin to Alice Walker.* New Brunswick, NJ: Rutgers University Press, pp. 164–176. In a chapter entitled "Invisible Men and Native Sons in Wright and Ellison," Strout examines their personal relationships and compares *Invisible Man* and *NS.* Ellison improves on W by his use of folklore and his rejection of political radicalism.

2569. Taylor, Walter, "The Priest Line," in *Critical Essays on William Faulkner: The McCaslin Family.* Ed. Arthur F. Kinney. Boston: G.K. Hall, pp. 245–258.

2570. Taylor, Willene P. "The Blindness Motif in Richard Wright's *Native Son.*" *CLA Journal*, 34 (September), 44–58. Examines literal and, especially, metaphorical blindness in the novel. Emphasizes imagery of darkness and light and the contrast between illusion and reality. Only Bigger and, to a lesser degree, Buddy and Max manage to gain some vision.

2571. Thornton, Jerome E. "The Paradoxical Journey of the African American in African American Fiction." *New Literary History*, 21 (Spring), 733–745. Mentions W briefly (pp. 734–735).

2572. Traoré, Ousseynou B. "Introduction." *The Literary Griot*, 2 (Spring), iv–viii. Comments on the essay by Nagueyalti Warren in this issue.

2573. Tuttleton, James W. "Fictions and Fabrications in Autobiography Today." *The New Criterion*, 8 (March), 32–40. Mentions briefly W and Communism (p. 39).

2574. Uba, George. "Only a Man: The Folkloric Subtext of Richard Wright's 'Down by the Riverside.'" *Essays in Literature*, 17 (Fall), 261–269. Since the story "compresses an entire history of oppression into … a single day," realistic plausibility is not an issue. As in black folklore, Mann makes morally right choices with calamitous results. Neither a trickster nor a Bad Nigger, he can-

not survive either physically or psychically.

2575. Unseld, Teresa S. "African Americans in Europe Conference." *Sage: A Scholarly Journal on Black Women*, 7 (Fall), 64. Notes events concerning W.

2576. Vaillant, Janet G. *Black, French, and African: A Life of Leopold Sedar Senghor.* Cambridge, MA: Harvard University Press, pp. 196, 213, 285, 286–287. Mentions W's belief that blacks could become French, notes his relation to *Présence Africaine*, and discusses his role, especially in relation to Senghor, at the First Congress of Black Writers and Artists in Paris (quoting from W's "Intervention" and "Tradition and Industrialization").

2577. Wald, Priscilla. "Becoming 'Colored': The Self-Authorized Language of Difference in Zora Neale Hurston." *American Literary History*, 2 (Spring), 79–100. Quotes from W's review of *Their Eyes Were Watching God* (p. 96).

2578. Walker, Alice. "The Black Writer and the Southern Experience," in *Emerging Voices: A Cross-Cultural Reader.* Eds. Janet Madden-Simpson and Sara M. Blake. Fort Worth: Holt Rinehart and Winston, pp. 346–349.

2579. Walker, Margaret. "A Brief Introduction to Southern Literature," in her *How I Wrote Jubilee and Other Essays on Life and Literature.* Ed. Maryemma Graham. New York: The Feminist Press, pp. 134–142. Compares W to Faulkner and Welty, emphasizing his "power and passion" (p. 140).

2580. _____. "The Humanistic Tradition of Afro-American Literature," in her *How I Wrote Jubilee and Other Essays on Life and Literature.* Ed. Maryemma Graham. New York: The Feminist Press, pp. 121–133.

2581. _____. "A Literary Legacy from Dunbar to Baraka," in her *How I Wrote Jubilee and Other Essays on Life and Literature.* Ed. Maryemma Graham. New York: The Feminist Press, pp. 69–83. States that Langston Hughes introduced her to W, who believed that Theodore Ward was a better playwright than Hughes. Also mentions W's death and comments on his relation to James Baldwin.

2582. _____. "Rediscovering Black Women Writers in the Mecca of the New Negro." in her *How I*

Wrote Jubilee and Other Essays on Life and Literature. Ed. Maryemma Graham. New York: The Feminist Press, pp. 91–101. Mentions briefly W, *New Challenge,* and "Blueprint for Negro Writing."

2583. _____. "Richard Wright," in her *How I Wrote Jubilee and Other Essays on Life and Literature.* Ed. Maryemma Graham. New York: The Feminist Press, pp. 33–49.

2584. _____. "Willing to Pay the Price," in her *How I Wrote Jubilee and Other Essays on Life and Literature.* Ed. Maryemma Graham. New York: The Feminist Press, pp. 15–25.

2585. Walker, Warren S. "Annual Bibliography of Short Fiction Interpretation." *Studies in Short Fiction,* 27 (Summer), 435–486. Lists one item on W.

2586. Wallace, Michelle. "Ishmael Reed's Female Troubles," in her *Invisibility Blues: From Pop to Theory.* London: Verso, pp. 146–154.

2587. _____. "Variations of Negation and the Heresy of Black Feminist Creativity," in her *Invisibility Blues: From Pop to Theory.* London: Verso, pp. 213–240.

2588. _____. "Variations on Negation and the Heresy of Black Feminist Creativity," in *Reading Black, Reading Feminist: A Critical Anthology.* Ed. Henry Louis Gates, Jr. New York: Meridian, pp. 52–67. Reprint of 1989.

2589. _____. "Who Owns Zora Neale Hurston?: Critics Carve Up the Legend," in her *Invisibility Blues: From Pop to Theory.* London: Verso, pp. 172–186.

2590. Walton, Anthony. "The Brief." *Callaloo,* 13 (Fall), 807–809. Mentions W briefly.

2591. Ward, Jerry W., Jr. "An Open Letter to Michel Fabre." *The Mississippi Quarterly,* 43 (Spring), 235–236. Takes issue with Fabre's unfavorable review of Margaret Walker's biography of W on poststructuralist grounds that "writing about another person's life is always already a social construction of reality."

2592. Warren, Nagueyalti. "Black Girls and Native Sons: Female Images in Selected Works by Richard Wright." *The Literary Griot,* 2 (Spring), 52–67. Feminist analysis of women characters in *NS, BB, O,* and *LD,* finding them "cast as nonfeminine asexual beings and as sex objects of little value" (p. 64). Warren attributes the attitudes of such characters as Bigger, Cross, Fishbelly, and Tyree to W himself: "the male-dominant aesthetic of Wright's novels not only stems from but reflects the ambivalence of his psychosexual self" (p. 65).

2593. Washington, Mary Helen. "'The Darkened Eye Restored': Notes Toward a Literary History of Black Women," in *Reading Black, Reading Feminist: A Critical Anthology.* Ed. Henry Louis Gates, Jr. New York: Meridian, pp. 30–43.

2594. Watkins, T.H. *Righteous Pilgrim: The Life and Times of Harold L. Ickes, 1874–1952.* New York: Holt, p. 644. Mentions W briefly.

2595. Webb, Constance. "Wright, Richard (1908–60)," in *Encyclopedia of the American Left.* Eds. Mari Jo Buhle, Paul Buhle, and Dan Georgakas. New York: Garland, pp. 860–861. Biographical sketch emphasizing W's radicalism. Mentions *UTC, NS, BB, TMBV,* and *WML,* but calls *CC* the *Bandung Conference.*

2596. Webb, Suzanne. "Groping Toward That Invisible Light, Richard Wright," in her *The Resourceful Writer.* Second edition. San Diego: Harcourt Brace Jovanovich, p. 196. Reprint of 1987

2597. _____. "Responding to the Whole Essay, Analyzing the Elements, Suggestions for Writing," in her *The Resourceful Writer.* Second edition. San Diego: Harcourt Brace Jovanovich, pp. 203–205.

2598. Weisbrot, Robert. *Freedom Bound: A History of American's Civil Rights Movement.* New York: Norton, pp. 8, 230. Mentions W briefly.

2599. Weissinger, Thomas. "Current Bibliography." *Black American Literature Forum,* 24 (Spring), 185–191. Lists C. James Trotman's *Richard Wright: Myths and Realities.*

2600. _____. "Current Bibliography." *Black American Literature Forum,* 24 (Fall), 605–612. Lists Harold Bloom, ed., *Bigger Thomas,* and Keneth Kinnamon, ed. *New Essays on Native Son.*

2601. Warren, Kenneth. "*The Signifying Monkey: A Theory of Afro-American Literary Criticism.* Henry Louis Gates, Jr." *Modern Philology,* 88 (November), 224–226. Review mentioning W briefly.

2602. Weixlmann, Joe. "African American Autobiography in The Twentieth Century: A Bibliographical Essay." *Black American Literature Forum,* 24 (Summer), 375–415. Includes discussion of books and essays treating *BB* and *AH.*

2603. Werner, Craig. "Bigger's Blues: *Native Son* and the Articulation of Afro-American Modernism," in *New Essays on Native Son.* Ed. Keneth Kinnamon. Cambridge: Cambridge University Press, pp. 117–152. Relates *NS* to modernism as a literary movement. Alienated and inarticulate, Bigger repeatedly struggles to tell as well as understand his story, becoming in the process a bluesy modernist black hero in a racist wasteland.

2604. _____. "The Framing of Charles W. Chesnutt: Practical Deconstruction in the Afro-American Tradition," in *Southern Literature and Literary Theory.* Ed. Jefferson Humphries. Athens: The University of Georgia Press, pp. 339–365. Mentions W briefly (pp. 341, 362).

2605. _____. "*From Folklore to Fiction: A Study of Folk Heroes and Rituals in the Black American Novel.* H. Nigel Thomas." *MELUS,* 16 (Spring), 113–115. Review mentioning Thomas's treatment of *LT* and *LD.*

2606. _____. "On the Ends of Afro-American 'Modernist' Autobiography." *Black American Literature Forum,* 24 (Summer), 203–220. Mentions briefly *BB* (p. 208).

2607. West, James L.W., III. "Theodore Dreiser," in *Sixteen Modern American Authors: Vol. 2: A Survey of Research and Criticism Since 1972.* Ed. Jackson R. Bryer. Durham: Duke University Press, pp. 120–153. Comments on an essay by Yoshinobu Hakutani on Dreiser and W (p. 148).

2608. White, John. *Black Leadership in America: From Booker T. Washington to Jesse Jackson.* London: Longman, pp. 21, 93.

2609. Whitehead, Fred. "Conroy, Jack (b. 1899)," in *Encyclopedia of the American Left.* Eds. Mari Jo Buhle, Paul Buhle, and Dan Georgakas. New York: Garland, pp. 163–164. Mentions W briefly.

2610. Wiener, Harvey S. "'How 'Bigger' Was Born' Richard Wright," in his *Reading for the Disciplines: An Anthology for College Writers.* New York: McGraw Hill, pp. 29, 32–34. Introduction, study questions and notes for a reprinted excerpt from W's essay.

2611. Williams, Juan. "The Fire This Time." *The New Republic*, 203 (1 October), 33–36. Review of Shelby Steele's *The Content of Our Character* mentioning W and *NS* (p. 33).

2612. Williams, Kenny J. "*The Life of Langston Hughes, Volume II, 1941–1967: I Dream a World.* By Arnold Rampersad." *American Literature*, 62 (September), 522–524. Review mentioning W briefly.

2613. Williams, Marjorie. "The Author's Solo Passage: Charles Johnson on Race and Writing." *The Washington Post* (4 December), pp. D1, D8. Comments briefly on W as racial spokesman.

2614. Williams, Sherley Anne. "Some Implications of Womanist Theory," in *Reading Black, Reading Feminist: A Critical Anthology.* Ed.

Henry Louis Gates, Jr. New York: Meridian, pp. 68–75. Comments briefly on *NS* (p. 73) and mentions W elsewhere (pp. 74, 75).

2615. Wills, Gary. *Under God: Religion and American Politics.* New York: Simon and Schuster, p. 248. Notes that Andrew Young "forced himself to read Richard Wright's *Native Son.*"

2616. Winchell, Mark Royden. "Inner Dark: or, The Place of Cormac McCarthy," *The Southern Review*, 26 (Spring), 293–309. Mentions W briefly (p. 302).

2617. Wolitzer, Meg. "The Invisible Family," *The New York Times Book Review* (4 February), p. 9. Review of Itabari Njeri's *Every Good-Bye Ain't Gone* with a quotation mentioning W briefly.

2618. Wright, John S. "A Scintil-

lating Send-Off For Falling Stars: The Black Renaissance Reconsidered," in his and Tracy E. Smith's *A Stronger Soul Within a Finer Frame: Portraying African Americans in the Black Rennaissance.* Minneapolis: University of Minnesota, pp. 13–45. Mentions briefly W and Blueprint for Negro Writing (pp. 40, 42).

2619. Yates, Gayle Graham. *Mississippi Mind.* Knoxville: The University of Tennessee Press, pp. 228–232, 233. Discusses W's life and *BB*, especially the contrast between a "black boy" and a "good old boy." Compares W to Faulkner and Willie Morris and comments on the 1985 W conference at the University of Mississippi and Julia Wright's visit to her father's home state.

1991

2620. Aaron, Daniel. "The Hoodlum's Friend." *The London Times Literary Supplement*, No. 4586 (22 February), p. 10. Review of Bettina Drew's biography of Nelson Algren mentioning briefly W and *NS*.

2621. Abbandonato, Linda. "'A View from Elsewhere': Subversive Sexuality and the Rewriting of the Heroine's Story in *The Color Purple.*" *PMLA*, 106 (October), 1106–1115. Comments on and questions W's realism (pp. 1109, 1114). Reprinted: 1996

2622. Abbott, Dorothy. "Map of Literary Mississippi," in her *Mississippi Writers: An Anthology.* Jackson: University Press of Mississippi, p. x. Map of the state with sketches of W and fifteen other writers.

2623. _____. "Mississippi Writers," in her *Mississippi Writers: An Anthology.* Jackson: University Press of Mississippi, pp. 497–515. Includes a biographical sketch of W, who is represented in the anthology by "Almos' a Man" and an excerpt from *BB*.

2624. _____. "Twentieth-Century Mississippi Writers," in her *Mississippi Writers: An Anthology.*

Jackson: University Press of Mississippi, pp. xi–xiii. List of towns and writers associated with them, including W under Natchez.

2625. Abbott, Dorothy, and Susan Koppleman. "Richard Wright," in their *The Signet Classic Book of Southern Short Stories.* New York: Penguin Books. Biographical headnote to "Big Boy Leaves Home" (p. 231).

2626. Abraham, Kinte. *Politics of Black Nationalism from Harlem to Soweto.* Trenton, NJ: Africa World Press, p. 164. Compares briefly W and Peter Abrahams.

2627. Abramson, Doris. "Foreword." *The Massachusetts Review*, 32 (Summer), 225–229. Mentions W briefly (p. 225).

2628. Adell, Sandra. "Richard Wright's *The Outsider* and the Kierkegaardian Concept of Dread." *Comparative Literature Studies*, 28, No. 4, 378–394. Argues that the origins of Cross Damon's characterization lie in the Kierkegaardian ideas first articulated in "How 'Bigger' Was Born." Bigger's fear and dread have white racism as a reference, but Cross's are ontological and

primal. Achieving a nihilistic freedom, Cross "dies unredemptive and pleading his innocence in face of the horror of the nothingness he encountered as an absolutely free man" (p. 392). In addition to Kierkegaard, W was influenced by Heidegger, Nietzsche, Jaspers, Husserl, and literary modernism in developing such a vision of the human condition.

2629. Aithal, S.K. "Richard Wright." *Abstracts of English Studies*, 34 (December), 314. Abstracts articles by Carolyn Camp and Lynda Hungerford.

2630. Alexander, Margaret Walker. "Natchez and Richard Wright in Southern American Literature." *The Southern Quarterly*, 29 (Summer), 171–175. Comments on history and myth in Southern culture. Born in Natchez, Wright was influenced by the racism of the South and by such Southern writers as Twain, Poe, Mencken, and Faulkner. Mentions briefly *UTC, NS, BB, TMBV,* and *LD*.

2631. Ammons, Elizabeth. *Conflicting Stories: American Women Writers at the Turn Into the Twentieth Century.* New York: Oxford

University Press, p. 67. Quotes Anzia Yezierska on W (see 1950).

2632. Andrews, William L. "African-American Autobiography Criticism: Retrospect and Prospect," in *American Autobiography: Retrospect and Prospect.* Ed. Paul John Eakins. Madison: University of Wisconsin Press, pp. 195–215. Reviews scholarship on *BB* (p. 202) and mentions W elsewhere (pp. 196, 209).

2633. Anon. "Advance Praise for *Richard Wright: Works.*" New York: The Library of America, 1 p. Promotional flyer with quotations by Henry Louis Gates, Jr., Roger Rosenblatt, and Charles Johnson.

2634. Anon. "1988 articles." *Afro Scholar Newsletter* (Fall), pp. 23–. Lists Robert A. Coles's "Richard Wright's Synthesis," Linda Hanrabon's "Other Voices, Other Looms: Richard Wright's Use of Epitaphs in Two Novels," "Lucinda H. MacKethan's "*Black Boy* and Ex-Colored Man: Version and Inversion of the Slave Narrators Quest for Voice."

2635. Anon. "1988 Books." *Afro-Scholar Newsletter* pp. 1–11. Lists Keneth Kinnamon's *A Richard Wright Bibliography* and C. James Trotman's *Richard Wright: Myths and Realities* (pp. 5, 10).

2636. Anon. "1989 Books." *Afro Scholar Newsletter* (Fall), pp. 12–22. Lists Joan Urban's *Richard Wright* (p. 21).

2637. Anon. "American Visions." *American Quarterly*, 43 (June), following p. 373. Publisher's advertisement of several books, including *The Signet Classic Book of Southern Short Stories*, to which W is listed as a contributor.

2638. Anon. "Angry Genius of Richard Wright." *Washington Afro-American* (19 January), p. B2. Reprint of 1991.

2639. Anon. "At last. Unexpurgated. Authoritative. Wright." *The New Republic*, 205 (14 October), 37. Publisher's advertisement for the Library of America edition. Includes a photograph of W and a blurb by Henry Louis Gates, Jr.

2640. Anon. *Bibliographic Guide to Black Studies: 1990.* Boston: G.K. Hall, p. 270. Lists four secondary items concerning W in the New York Public Library, supplementing the *Dictionary Catalog of the Schomberg Collection of Negro Literature and History.*

2641. Anon. "Booksearch: Out-of-Print Books That Should Still Be in Print." *English Journal*, 80 (December), 88–92. Contains an entry on *Black and White: Stories of American Life* mentioning W briefly (p. 91).

2642. Anon. "Cambridge University Press." *American Quarterly*, 43 (March), following p. 171. Publisher's advertisement including notices of Paul Oliver's *Blues Fell This Morning* (foreword by W) and *New Essays* on *Native Son*, edited by Keneth Kinnamon.

2643. Anon. "Cambridge." *Journal of American Studies.* 25 (April 1991), 65–67. Contains an advertisement for a new edition of Paul Oliver's *Blues Fell This Morning* mentioning W's foreword.

2644. Anon. *Comprehensive Dissertation Index 1990.* Ann Arbor: University Microfilms, p. 497. Lists dissertations treating W by Sandra A. Adell, Michael Gordon Berry, and La Vinia Delois Jennings.

2645. Anon. "Constitution." *The Richard Wright Newsletter*, 1 (Spring), 4. Consists of seven articles governing the Richard Wright Circle. "The object of this society shall be to stimulate and promote interest in the work and ideas of Richard Wright and to facilitate scholarship and criticism on Wright's works."

2646. Anon. "Contributors." *Callaloo*, 14 (Spring), 553–555. Mentions that Henry Louis Gates, Jr., "recently delivered the First Annual Richard Wright Lectures" at the University of Pennsylvania.

2647. Anon. "Contributors." *New Literary History*, 22 (Summer), [17]. Lists Joyce Ann Joyce and her *Richard Wright's Art of Tragedy.*

2648. Anon. "Court Dismisses Suit Over Richard Wright Biography." *Jet*, 81 (16 December), 14. Announces the result of Ellen Wright's suit against Margaret Walker for use of unpublished material in her biography of W.

2649. Anon. "'Doing the (W)right Thing!' 50th Anniversary of Richard Wright's Classic Novel *Native Son* Celebrated at Symposium at Northeastern University." *The Richard Wright Newsletter*, 1 (Spring), 1. Speakers included Joyce Scott, James Nagel, Hope Davis, Joyce Ann Joyce, Mae G. Henderson, Bernard Bell, Clyde Taylor, Samuel Allen, and George Lamming.

2650. Anon. *English 1992 Catalog.* New York: Merit Audio Visual, pp. 5, 11. Lists a videocassette of "Almos' a Man" and a film strip on W.

2651. Anon. "From Provincial Outpost to National Treasure: Natchez Celebrates Its 275th Anniversary." Natchez, Mississippi: The Natchez Literary Celebration. Brochure announcing a lecture by Michel Fabre on "Richard Wright and Natchez: An Enduring Connection," 1 June.

2652. Anon. *Fulbright Scholar Program 1992–93 Update of Available Awards.* Washington: Council for International Exchange of Scholars, p. 5. Contains a photograph of W.

2653. Anon. "General Announcements, Inquiries, Etc." *The Richard Wright Newsletter*, 1 (Spring), 2–3. Announces that James A. Miller is seeking contributors to his proposed volume on teaching *NS.*

2654. Anon. "History of American Literature: 1940–1960," in *Benet's Reader's Encyclopedia of American Literature.* Eds. George Perkins, Barbara Perkins, and Phillip Leininger. New York: HarperCollins, pp. 473–475. Mentions briefly W, *NS*, and *BB.*

2655. Anon. *Humanities Fall 1991.* Westport, CT: Greenwood, p. 7. Includes a publisher's announcement of *The Racial Problem in the Works of Richard Wright and James Baldwin* by Jean-François Gounard and Joseph J. Rodgers, Jr.

2656. Anon. *Index to Black Periodicals: 1989.* Boston: G.K. Hall, p. 336. Lists two items on W.

2657. Anon. *Index to Black Periodicals: 1990.* Boston: G.K. Hall, p. 291. Lists six items on W.

2658. Anon. *Language & Literature.* New York: HarperCollins, p. 11. Publisher's brochure listing paperback editions of *NS, BB, O, UTC, AH,* and *LD* "in a bright new format."

2659. Anon. "Library of America Edition." *The Richard Wright Newsletter*, 1 (Fall), 2. Announcement.

2660. Anon. "Library of America to Publish Edition of Wright's Works." *The Richard Wright Newsletter*, 1 (Spring), 1–2. Announces Volume One, containing *UTC, LT, NS,* and two essays; and Volume Two, containing *BB, AH,* and *O.* Notes restoration of material cut by publishers.

2661. Anon. *Literature 1990/1991.*

Westport, CT: Greenwood, pp. 14, 20. Publisher's catalog containing notices of Jean-François Gounard's *The Racial Problem in the Works of Richard Wright and James Baldwin* and Keneth Kinnamon's *A Richard Wright Bibliography*.

2662. Anon. "Literature Unit Plans." *English Journal*, 80 (September), 12. Lists *BB* and *NS* among high school lesson plans offered by Teacher's Pet Publications, Inc. Reprinted 1992, 1993

2663. Anon. "Literature Unit Plans." *English Journal*, 80 (November), 112. Lists *BB* among high school lesson plans offered by Teacher's Pet Publications, Inc. Reprinted: 1991, 1992.

2664. Anon. "Literature Unit Plans." *English Journal*, 80 (December), 121. Reprint of 1991.

2665. Anon. "Michel Fabre." *Richard Wright: Books and Writers. The Southern Register* (Winter), p. 13. Favorable review. "It serves as the key to understanding the development, the philosophies, and the aesthetics" of W, "and it provides accurate information for the study of intertextuality in his works."

2666. Anon. "*Native Son: The Emergence of a New Black Hero.* Robert Butler," in *G.K. Hall & Co./Twayne Publishers New Titles July–September 1991.* Boston: G.K. Hall, p. 5. Publisher's notice.

2667. Anon. "A New Tool for Teaching *Native Son.*" *The Richard Wright Newsletter*, 1 (Fall), 2. Favorable notice of Robert Butler's *Native Son: The Emergence of a New Black Hero.*

2668. Anon. "1988 Articles." *Afro Scholar Newsletter*, Fall, pp. 23–43. Lists articles on W by Robert A. Coles, Linda Hamalian, and Linda MacKethan.

2669. Anon. "1989 Articles." *Afro Scholar Newsletter*, Fall, pp. 44–59. Lists articles on W by Margaret Walker and Patricia Watkins.

2670. Anon. "1988 Books." *Afro Scholar Newsletter*, Fall, pp. 1–11. Lists books on W by Harold Bloom, James H. Evans, Keneth Kinnamon, and C. James Trotman.

2671. Anon. "1989 Books." *Afro Scholar Newsletter*, Fall, pp. 12–22. Lists a book on W by Joan Urban.

2672. Anon. "Perennial Library," in *Language & Literature.* New York: HarperCollins, p. 11. Publisher's catalog listing paperback editions of *NS, BB, O, UTC, AH,* and *LD.*

2673. Anon. "Principales publications depuis 1987 des membres de l'equipe ayant répondee à notre questionnaire à cette date." *Afram Newsletter*, Nos. 33–34 (October), pp. 58–69. Lists items on W by Michel Fabre.

2674. Anon. "Proletarian Literature," in *Benet's Reader's Encyclopedia of American Literature.* Eds. George Perkins, Barbara Perkins, and Phillip Leininger. New York: HarperCollins, pp. 883–884. Mentions W briefly.

2675. Anon. "Publications Relating to Mississippi." *The Journal of Mississippi History*, 53 (November), 363–366. Lists an article on W by Margaret Walker.

2676. Anon. "Recent Publications." *The Richard Wright Newsletter*, 1 (Spring), 3. Lists five books and twenty-three articles "published in the last three years."

2677. Anon. "Recent Publications." *The Richard Wright Newsletter*, 1 (Fall), 3. Lists ten books and fifteen articles on or by W.

2678. Anon. "Richard Wright Circle Membership." *The Richard Wright Newsletter*, 1 (Spring), 4. Includes an application form.

2679. Anon. "Richard Wright Is Selected for 'Gallery of Greats' Work." *The New York Amsterdam News* (5 January), p. 20. Biographical sketch occasioned by his inclusion in "a collection of portraits commissioned by the Miller Brewing Company." Reprinted: 1991.

2680. Anon. "Richard Wright Is Selected for 'Gallery of Greats' Work." *The New York Amsterdam News* (5 January), p. 20. Biographical sketch emphasizing racism in W's childhood and youth and his literary achievement. The occasion for the article is W's selection for a collection of portraits of twelve black authors commissioned by the Miller Brewing Company.

2681. Anon. "Richard Wright is selected for 'Gallery of Greats' Work." *The New York Amsterdam News* (5 January), p. 20. Treats W's life and work, except his final years and death. The "Gallery of Greats" (black authors), sponsored by the Miller Brewing Company is on a national tour of museums, art galleries and universities.

2682. Anon. "Richard Wright

Works," in *The Library of America Fall 1991.* New York: The Library of America, pp. [1–2]. Publisher's review explaining restoration of expurgated passages and dropped portions. Included are *LT, UTC, NS, BB, AH,* and *O.* Quotes Hemingway (mistakenly) on W and Henry Louis Gates, Jr., Roger Rosenblatt, and Julian Bond on this edition. Includes two photographs of W.

2683. Anon. "Richard Wright's Works Restored." *The Jackson Mississippi Advocate* (17–23 October), p. 1B. Favorable review of the Library of America edition of W together with a biographical sketch. Claims that W "singlehandedly transformed our nation's understanding of racism and its tragic consequences."

2684. Anon. "Sample Passages Restored in the Library of America Edition of Richard Wright's Works." New York: The Library of America, 11 pp. Prefatory note and restored passages in *NS* and *O.*

2685. Anon. "Special Book Offer for Course Adoption ... *The LeRoi Jones/Amiri Baraka Reader.*" New York: Thunder's Mouth Press. Publisher's flyer quoting Arnold Rampersad that Baraka "stands with Wheatley, Douglass, Dunbar, Hughes, Hurston, Wright and Ellison as one of the eight figures ... who have significantly affected the course of African-American literary culture."

2686. Anon. "Studying the African-American Experience at NU: A Retrospective." *Afro Chronicles*, 1 (Spring), pp. 4–8. Reports a visit by Margaret Walker Alexander to Northeastern University, 27 October–5 November 1989, including a presentation on "Richard Wright: Daemonic Genius."

2687. Anon. "Twayne's Masterwork Studies," in *New Titles in Literature.* Boston: G.K. Hall, pp. 9–11. Includes a notice of Robert Butler's *Native Son: The Emergence of a New Black Hero* (p. 10).

2688. Anon. "*12 Million Black Voices; Eight Men,*" in *Thunder's Mouth Press: Spring 1991.* New York: Thunder's Mouth Press, p. 19. Publisher's selected backlist advertisements for reprinted editions of the two books.

2689. Anon. "Unexpurgated, Authoritative New Texts." *American Literature*, 63 (December), page following 800. Advertisement for the Library of America edition of W with a blurb by Henry Louis Gates, Jr.

2690. Anon. "Unexpurgated, Authoritative New Texts." *The Nation*, 253 (9 December), 753. Advertisement for the Library of America edition.

2691. Anon. "Unexpurgated, Authoritative New Texts." *Transition*, No. 54, p. [188]. Full-page publisher's notice of the Library of America edition of W.

2692. Anon. Untitled. *Oxherding Tale* by Charles Johnson. New York: Grove Wiedenfeld, back cover. Places the Johnson novel "in the best tradition of Richard Wright and Ralph Ellison."

2693. Anon. "Upcoming Conferences." *The Richard Wright Newsletter*, 1 (Spring), 2. Announces conference on "African Americans and Europe" to be held in Paris on 5–9 February 1992. Notes special interest of this conference for W scholars.

2694. Appleby, Bruce C., Greg Johnson, and Robert M. Taylor. "Yet Another Old Standard: HBJ's *Adventures* Series." *English Journal*, 80 (November), 93–96. Mentions W briefly (p. 94).

2695. Asante, Molefi K., and Mark T. Mattson. *The Historical and Cultural Atlas of African Americans*. New York: Macmillan, pp. 107, 114, 146. Mentions briefly W, *NS*, and *BB*. Includes two photographs. Reprinted: 1992.

2696. Avery, Evelyn. "Remembrances of Malamud," in *Conversations with Bernard Malamud*. Ed. Lawrence Lasher. Jackson: University Press of Mississippi, pp. 145–151. Mentions W briefly (p. 145).

2697. Axelrod, Rise B., and Charles R. Cooper. "*Narrating*," in their *The St. Martin's Guide to Writing*. Third edition. New York: St. Martin's Press, pp. 417–428. Reprint of 1986.

2698. Babb, Valerie Melissa. *Ernest Gaines*. Boston: Twayne, pp. 112–113, 148–149, 157. Introducing her chapter on *A Gathering of Old Men*, Babb quotes from "How 'Bigger' Was Born" and comments on the theme of self-realization through violence in *NS*. The bibliography includes *NS*, comparing Bigger to Gaines's black male characters.

2699. Bailey, Frankie Y. *Out of the Woodpile: Black Characters in Crime and Detective Fiction*. Westport, CT: Greenwood Press, pp. 59–62, 68, 108, 149, 181. Discusses *NS* considering Bigger a "caricature ... black monster" (p. 61). Compares W to Twain, quotes Faulkner on W, and mentions *EM*.

2700. Bair, Barbara. "Wall, Cheryl A., ed. *Changing Our Words: Essays on Criticism, Theory, and Writing by Black Women.*" *Studies in the Novel*, 23 (Winter), 514–518. Mentions briefly Bigger's murder of Bessie in *NS* (p. 517).

2701. Baker, Houston A., Jr. *Workings of the Spirit: The Poetics of Afro-American Women's Writing*. Chicago: The University of Chicago Press, pp. 26, 41, 102, 105–130, 137, 142, 144, 208. Pages 105–130 are a revised version of 1990. Elsewhere W is mentioned briefly.

2702. Baldwin, Lewis V. *There Is a Balm in Gilead: The Cultural Roots of Martin Luther King, Jr.* Minneapolis: Fortress Press, pp. 45, 61. Mentions W briefly.

2703. Baraka, Amiri. "Jimmy!" in *The LeRoi Jones/Amiri Baraka Reader*. Ed. William J. Harris. New York: Thunder's Mouth Press, pp. 450–456. Eulogy of James Baldwin mentioning W briefly (p. 453).

2704. Barnet, Sylvan. "Richard Wright," in his *The Harper Anthology of Fiction*. New York: HarperCollins, pp. 789–790. Biographical headnote to "The Man Who Was Almost a Man."

2705. Barrett, Lindon. "Speaking of Failure: Undergraduate Education and Intersection of African-American Literature and Critical Theory." *Callaloo*, 14 (Summer), 619–630. Quotes the passage from *BB* in which W insults his grandmother (p. 624).

2706. Barton, Paul. "Censoring at 'All-Time' High." Little Rock *Arkansas Gazette* (29 August), p. 3A. Mentions *NS* as one of the books in American schools challenged by would-be censors.

2707. Bawer, Bruce. "Race and Art: The Career of James Baldwin." *The New Criterion*, 10 (November), pp. 16–26. Comments on Baldwin's criticism of W. Reprinted: 1993.

2708. Baxter, Karen. "An On-Going Dialogue with George Bass." *The Langston Hughes Review*, 9/10, 69–81. Bass mentions briefly "The Man Who Lived Underground" (p. 75).

2709. Beach, Richard, and James Marshall. *Teaching Literature in the Secondary School*. San Diego: Harcourt Brace Jovanovich, pp. 201, 444, 448, 449, 450, 452. Mentions briefly W and "The Man Who Was Almost a Man," *NS*, *O*, *BB*, and *AH*.

2710. Beauvoir, Simone de. *Letters to Sartre*. Ed. and trans. Quintin Hoare. New York: Arcade, pp. 417, 419, 420–421, 423, 425, 426, 430, 433, 455, 456. Partial translation of 1990.

2711. Bell, Bernard W. "The African-American Literary Tradition," in *Encyclopedia of Literature and Criticism*. Eds. Martin Coyle, Peter Garside, Malcolm Kelsall, and John Peck. Detroit: Gale, pp. 1136–1147. Reprint of 1990.

2712. _____. "Ellison, Ralph," in *The Reader's Companion to American History*. Eds. Eric Foner and John A. Garraty. Boston: Houghton Mifflin, pp. 349–350. Mentions W briefly.

2713. Bell, C. Rosalind. "Worlds Within: An Interview with Caryl Phillips." *Callaloo*, 14 (Summer), 578–606. Phillips recalls reading W at Oxford (p. 581) and acknowledges W's influence: "he was a man who really made me feel like I wanted to write after reading *Native Son*" (p. 591). *BB* is "a work of great, consummate genius" (p. 591).

2714. Beppu, Keiko, "Cultural Colonization?: American Studies in Jampan," in *As Others Read Us: International Perspectives on American Literature*. Ed. Huck Gutman. Amherst: The University of Massachusetts Press, pp. 161–175. Mentions W briefly (p. 173).

2715. Bergman, David. *Gaiety Transfigured: Gay Self-Representation in American Literature*. Madison: The University of Wisconsin Press, pp. 164, 184. Mentions briefly W and *BB*.

2716. Berry, J. Bill. "Introduction," in his *Home Ground: Southern Autobiography*. Columbia: University of Missouri Press, pp. 1–10. Mentions briefly *BB* (p. 8).

2717. Betts, Doris. "Many Souths and Broadening Scale: A Changing Southern Literature," in *The Future South: A Historical Perspective for the Twenty-First Century*. Eds. Joe P. Dunn and Howard L. Preston. Urbana: University of Illinois Press, pp. 158–187. Mentions briefly W, Mencken, and *NS* (pp. 158, 185).

2718. Blades, John. "The Uncut Vision of Richard Wright." *Chicago Tribune* (7 October), Tempo sec., pp. 1, 7. Favorable review of the Library of America edition of W. Discusses at length the deletions in *NS*, wondering why W did not protest them. At conclusion quotes Nelson Algren on W's enduring quality. Partially reprinted: 1991.

2719. Blair, Linda. "Developing Student Voices with Multicultural Literature." *English Journal*, 80 (December), 24–28. Mentions and comments on *BB* (pp. 24, 26).

2720. Blake, Caesar R. "On Richard Wright's *Native Son*," in *Rough Justice: Essays on Crime in Literature*. Ed. M. L. Friedland. Toronto: University of Toronto Press, pp. 187–199. Reviews criticism of *NS* by Irving Howe, Alfred Kazin, Baldwin, Ellison, David Bradley, Tony Magistrale, and Robert Butler. Also comments on naturalism and the social and racial context of the novel.

2721. Blau, Eleanor. "After 51 Years, You Can Finally Read Uncut 'Native Son.'" *The Bremerton Sun* (21 September), p. 4. Partial reprint of 1991.

2722. _____. "The Works of Richard Wright, as Written." *The New York Times* (28 August), p. C11. Favorable prepublication review of the Library of America edition of W, with explanation of restored cuts in *NS*, *BB*, *LT*, and *O*. Includes comments by Arnold Rampersad and Hanna M. Bercovitch. Reprinted: 1991.

2723. Bloom, Lynn Z. "Coming of Age in the Segregated South: Autobiographies of Twentieth-Century Childhoods, Black and White," in *Home Ground: Southern Autobiography*. Ed. J. Bill Berry. Columbia: University of Missouri Press, pp. 110–122. Mentions briefly *BB* (pp. 112) and compares it to Anne Moody's *Coming of Age in Mississippi* (p. 119).

2724. _____. "Content, Strategies/ Structures, Language," in her *The Essay Connection: Readings for Writers*. Third edition. Lexington, MA: D.C. Heath, pp. 170–171. Study notes to a reprint of 1985. 139.

2725. _____. "Content, Strategies/ Structures, Language, for Writing," in her *The Essay Connection: Readings for Writers*. Third edition. Lexington, MA: D.C. Heath, pp. 459–460. Reprint of 1988.

2726. _____. "Linda Peterson," in her *The Essay Connection: Readings for Writers*. Third edition. Lexington, MA: D. C. Heath, pp. 151–152. Headnote to a reprint of 1985. 139.

2727. _____. "Richard Wright," in her *The Essay Connection: Readings for Writers*. Third edition. Lexington, MA: D.C. Heath, p. 449. Reprint of 1988.

2728. Boelhower, William. "The Making of Ethnic Autobiography in the United States," in *American Autobiography: Retrospect and Prospect*. Ed. Paul John Eakin. Madison: The University of Wisconsin Press, pp. 123–141. States that Carlos Bulosan modeled his *America Is in the Heart* after "Wright's fictionally explored protest vision" (p. 130).

2729. Bok, Sissela. *Alva Myrdal: A Daughter's Memoir*. Reading, MA: Addison-Wesley, p. 135. States that W was a frequent visitor to the Myrdal household in New York as work was beginning on *An American Dilemma*.

2730. Boldridge, Effie J. "Harold Bloom, ed. *Bigger Thomas*." *CLA Journal*, 35 (December), 252–257. Favorable review summarizing the argument of each of the twenty-one essays and extracts in the collection.

2731. Boyer, Allen D. "James R. Giles. *Confronting the Horror: The Novels of Nelson Algren*; George Hendrick, ed. *To Reach Eternity: The Letters of James Jones*." *Modern Fiction Studies*, 37 (Summer), 266–267. Review mentioning W briefly.

2732. Breitwieser, Mitchell. "Early American Antigone," in *Theorizing American Literature: Hegel, The Sign, and History*. Eds. Bainard Cowan and Joseph G. Kronick. Baton Rouge: Louisiana State University Press, pp. 125–161. Mentions briefly Bigger and *NS* (p. 148n).

2733. _____. "The Great Gatsby: Grief, Jazz and the Eye-Witness." *Arizona Quarterly*, 47 (Autumn), 17–70. Contains a paragraph commenting on *NS* as a "counterpoint text" to Fitzgerald's novel (p. 53).

2734. Brinkley, Alan, Richard N. Current, Frank Freidel, and T. Harry Williams. *American History: A Survey*. Eighth edition. New York: McGraw-Hill, p. 737. Mentions briefly W and *NS*.

2735. [Budd, Louis]. "Brief Mention." *American Literature*, 63 (March), 172–185. Includes a favorable notice of Michel Fabre's *Richard Wright: Books & Writers* (p. 183).

2736. Burkett, Randall K., Nancy Hall Burkett, and Henry Louis Gates, Jr. *Black Biography, 1790–1950: A Cumulative Index*. Vol. 2. Alexandria, VA: Chadwyck-Healey, p. 671. The entry for W cites eight sources.

2737. Burns, Landon C., and Elizabeth Buckmaster. "The Seventeenth (1990) Supplement to a Cross-Referenced Index of Short Fiction Anthologies and Author-Title Listings." *Studies in Short Fiction*, 28 (Spring), 239–291. Lists one item on "Big Black Good Man" and four items on "The Man Who Was Almost a Man."

2738. Busby, Mark. *Ralph Ellison*. Boston: Twayne, pp. xiii, 8, 10, 12, 17, 18, 19, 22, 24, 65, 69, 78, 87–92, 95, 124, 128, 129, 133, 134, 140, 143. Discusses the W-Ellison relationship, both personal and literary, quoting from some of Ellison's early letters. *Invisible Man* is deeply indebted to "The Man Who Lived Underground," but Ellison has a "distinctly different vision" (p. 92). Also discusses Ellison's treatment of W in his essays.

2739. Bush, Clive. *Halfway to Revolution: Investigation and Crisis in the Work of Henry Adams, William James, and Gertrude Stein*. New Haven: Yale University Press, pp. 266, 353, 403–408, 425, 480. Examines the W-Stein relationship, analyzing W's review of *Wars I Have Seen* and paraphrasing extensively from W's letters to her. Bush concludes that the relation was "a fruitful one and helped make a bridge between two people of very different ideological convictions, but with a clear common cause of describing the new world of twentieth-century society" (p. 408).

2740. Butler, Robert. *Native Son: The Emergence of a New Black Hero*. Boston: Twayne, xiv + 133 pp. After a chronology of W's life and chapters on the cultural background, importance, and critical reception of *NS*, Butler provides an intensive, original reading of the novel (pp. 27–118) with chapters on setting, structure, characterization, point of view, tone, and theme. A selected, annotated bibliography is also included. Butler's reading argues that Bigger moves from victimization by a hostile racist environment through a psychological process of increasing self-understanding to the status of a black existential hero, master of his consciousness if not his circumstances. In *NS* W "achieved the originality, depth, and resonance of a genuine masterwork" (p. 118).

2741. Byerman, Keith. "Remembering History in Contemporary Black Literature and Criticism." *American Literary History*, 3 (Winter), 809–816. Mentions W briefly (p. 810).

2742. Cain, William E. "The Ethics of Criticism: Does Literature Do Any Good?" *College English*, 53 (April), 467–476. Includes a comparison of John Stuart Mill and W on the impact of their reading (p. 469).

2743. Campbell, James. *Talking at the Gates: A Life of James Baldwin*. New York: Viking, pp. 20, 21, 22–23, 29–32, 37, 40, 44–45, 52–53, 62–71, 73, 87, 93–94, 105, 107–108, 111, 112, 125, 129–130, 131, 139, 141, 144–145, 154, 201, 204–205, 265, 281. Narrates Baldwin's early admiration of W, the first meeting in Brooklyn and the early friendship, the renewal of the friendship when Baldwin moved to Paris, the quarrel over the *Zero* essay and the encounter in the Deux Magots in 1953 (with an extended quotation from W's unpublished account of the episode). Campbell mentions elsewhere *NS* (novel and play), *TMBV*, and W.

2744. _____. "The Wright Version," London *Times Literary Supplement* (13 December), p. 14. Unfavorable review of the Library of America edition of W. Lacking evidence that W was dissatisfied with changes made between proofs and first editions of *NS* and *BB*, Campbell objects to restoring passages in these new texts.

2745. Campbell, Jane. "Margaret Walker," in *African American Writers*. Ed. Valerie Smith. New York: Scribner's, pp. 459–471. Discusses Walker's friendship with W and her biography of him, pointing out some of its defects (pp. 461, 467–468).

2746. Carby, Hazel V. "Foreword," in *Seraph on the Suwanee*. New York: Harper-Collins, pp. vii-xviii. Mentions briefly *SH* (p. xii). Reprinted: 1999.

2747. _____. "The Politics of Fiction, Anthropology, and the Folk: Zora Neale Hurston," in *New Essays on Their Eyes Were Watching God*.

Ed. Michael Awkward. Cambridge: Cambridge University Press, pp. 71–93. Mentions W briefly (pp. 77, 90). Reprinted: 1999.

2748. Carlton-Alexander, Sandra. "Arna Bontemps: The Novelist Revisted." *CLA Journal*, 34 (March), 317–330. Quotes approvingly from W's review of *Black Thunder* (p. 328).

2749. Carter, Stephen L. *Reflections of an Affirmative Action Baby*. New York: Basic Books, p. 241. Mentions W briefly.

2750. Cashman, Sean Dennis. *African-Americans and the Quest for Civil Rights, 1900–1990*. New York: New York University Press, pp. 66–68, 96. Mentions briefly *UTC, TMBV*, and *BP*. Devotes four paragraphs to *NS*, a novel "about the social, psychological, and physical incarceration of the marginal man, Bigger Thomas" (p. 67).

2751. Chakovsky, Sergei. "The Work of Richard Wright in Soviet Literary Criticism." *Notes on Mississippi Writers*, 23 (June), 85–100. Treats the W criticism of Isidor Schneider, S. Vostokova, V. Nevelsky, V. Barsov, I. Beilin, E. Romanova, A. Startzev, T. Rokotov, M. Mendelson, Louisa Bashmakova, Chakovsky himself, Aleskei M. Zvergev, Tamara Denisova, and Boris Gilenson, while listing that of fourteen others. Soviet criticism of W became less political over the years.

2752. Charry, Ellen T. "Literature as Scripture: Privileged Reading in Current Religious Reflection." *Soundings*, 74 (Spring/Summer), 65–99. Discusses James Evans's discussion of *NS* (pp. 87, 89–90).

2753. Christian, Barbara. "Paule Marshall," in *African American Writers*. Ed. Valerie Smith. New York: Scribner's, pp. 289–304. Mentions briefly *BB* (p. 292).

2754. Christol, Hélène and Sylvie Mathé. *An Introduction to American Fiction*. Paris: Longman France, pp. 108, 113–116, 134, 135, 147, 183. Contains a biographical sketch relating W to racial history and commenting on *BB, AH, UTC, NS*, and *O*, followed by a passage from the opening scene of *NS* (pp. 113–116). Elsewhere the authors comment on *O* and "The Man Who Lived Underground" and mention W in various contexts.

2755. Clark, Vèvè A. "Develop-

ing Diaspora Literary and *Marasa* Consciousness," in *Comparative American Identities: Race, Sex, and Nationality in the Modern Text*. New York: Routledge, pp. 40–61. Mentions briefly Bigger Thomas (p. 42).

2756. Clark, William Bedford. *The American Vision of Robert Penn Warren*. Lexington: The University Press of Kentucky, p. 63. Mentions *NS* briefly.

2757. Coale, Samuel. *William Styron Boisited*. Boston: Twayne, p. 29. Mentions W briefly.

2758. Cobb, James C. "Does Mind No Longer Matter?: *The Mind of the South*, 1941–1991." *The Journal of Southern History*, 57 (November), 681–718. Quotes briefly from *BB* (p. 697).

2759. Colter, Cyrus. "Cyrus Colter Speaking with Charles Johnson and Reginald Gibbons on January 19, 1991." *Callaloo*, 14 (Fall), 887–897. Recalls meeting W in Chicago in 1940 through Horace Cayton. W was unmoved by Marian Anderson's rendition of "A City Called Heaven" (pp. 887–893).

2760. _____. "Cyrus Colter Speaking with Fred Shafer in February 1991." *Callaloo*, 14 (Fall), 864–886. Colter expresses admiration for W (p. 874).

2761. Compliment, Anne. "Baldwin, James (Arthur)," in *St. James Guide to Biography*. Ed. Paul E. Schellinger. Chicago and London: St. James Press, pp. 42–43. Comments on the treatment of the W-Baldwin relationship in biographies of the latter by Fern Maria Eckman and W.J. Weatherby.

2762. Cook, Sylvia Jenkins. *Erskine Caldwell and the Fiction of Poverty: The Flesh and the Spirit*. Baton Rouge: Louisiana State University Press, pp. 84, 143, 266, 271. Mentions *UTC* and cites W's review of *Trouble in July*.

2763. Cooper, Wayne F. "Claude McKay," in *African American Writers*. Ed. Valerie Smith. New York: Scribner's, pp. 305–319. Mentions W briefly (p. 305)

2764. Cox, James M. "Beneath My Father's Name." *The Sewanee Review*, 99 (Summer), 412–433. Discusses Faulkner, mainly *Light in August*, and W, mainly *NS*, as Southern writers. Notes W's relation to Dreiser, Poe, and Dostoevsky as well as Faulkner. In the reiterated phrase "I'm all right" in the final scene of *NS*, Cox believes, W is implying that he is Bigger's father and that Bigger is all Wright (p. 424). Reprinted: 1991.

2765. _____. "Beneath My Father's Name," in *Home Ground: Southern Autobiography*. Ed. J. Bill Berry. Columbia: University of Missouri Press, pp. 13–30. Reprint of 1991.

2766. Crews, Frederick. "The Strange Fate of William Faulkner." *The New York Review of Books*, 38 (7 March), 47–52. Mentions W briefly (p. 48). Reprinted: 1992.

2767. Cross, Gilton Gregory. "Fought for It and Paid Taxes Too." *Callaloo*, 14 (Fall), 855–861. Interview with Cyrus Colter in 1974. Colter expresses admiration for W (pp. 857, 859).

2768. Cross, William E., Jr. *Shades of Black: Diversity in African-American Identity*. Philadelphia: Temple University Press, p. 37. Mentions briefly Bigger Thomas.

2769. Crowley, John W. "Unmastering All We Survey." *ADE Bulletin*, No. 100 (Winter), pp. 31–34. Mentions teaching *NS* in relation to *Light in August* and *The Street*.

2770. Davis, Arthur P. "Survival Techniques as Expressed in Afro-American Literature," in *The New Cavalcade: African American Writing from 1760 to the Present*. Eds. Arthur P. Davis, J. Saunders Redding, and Joyce Ann Joyce. Vol. 1. Washington, DC: Howard University Press, pp. 673–688. Contains a paragraph on *O*.

2771. Davis, Arthur P., and J. Saunders Redding. "The New Negro Renaissance and Beyond: 1910–1954," in *The New Cavalcade: African American Writing from 1760 to the Present*. Eds. Arthur P. Davis, J. Saunders Redding, and Joyce Ann Joyce. Vol. 1. Washington, DC: Howard University Press, pp. 321–329. Reprint of 1971.82.

2772. Davis, Arthur P., J. Saunders Redding, and Joyce Ann Joyce. "Chester B. Himes," in their *The New Cavalcade: African American Writing from 1760 to the Present*. Vol. 1. Washington, DC: Howard University Press, pp. 759–760. Mentions W briefly.

2773. _____. "Dorothy West (1912–)," in their *The New Cavalcade: African American Writing from 1760 to the Present*. Vol. 1. Washington, DC: Howard University Press, p. 786. Mentions W briefly.

2774. _____. "Margaret Walker (1915–)," in their *The New Cavalcade: African American Writing from 1760 to the Present*. Vol. 1. Washington, DC: Howard University Press, pp. 827–828. Lists *The Daemonic Genius of Richard Wright*.

2775. _____. "Ralph Ellison," in their *The New Cavalcade: African American Writing from 1760 to the Present*. Vol. 1. Washington, DC: Howard University Press, pp. 888–889. Bio-bibliographical headnote to an excerpt from *Invisible Man* and "Hidden Name and Complex Fate" mentioning W briefly.

2776. _____. "Samuel W. Allen (Paul Vesey)," in their *The New Cavalcade: African American Writing from 1760 to the Present*. Vol. 1. Washington, DC: Howard University Press, pp. 866–867. Mentions W briefly.

2777. _____. "Selected Bibliography," in their *The New Cavalcade: African American Writing from 1760 to the Present*. Vol. 1. Washington, DC: Howard University Press, pp. 925–962. Includes items by and about W.

2778. Davis, Thadious M. "Race and Region," in *The Columbia History of the American Novel*. Ed. Emory Elliott. New York: Columbia University Press, pp. 407–436. Mentions briefly W and "The Man Who Killed a Shadow" (pp. 430–431) before discussing W's career, emphasizing *BB*, *NS*, *LT*, and *LD* and mentioning *UTC*, *EM*, and *SH*. Davis focuses on W's attack on white racism and his fictional black mothers and fathers (pp. 432–436).

2779. Dawley, Alan. *Struggles for Justice: Social Responsibility and the Liberal State*. Cambridge, MA: The Belknap Press of Harvard University Press, pp. 330, 346. Comments briefly on "Down by the Riverside" and mentions *BB*.

2780. Decker, Jeffrey Louis. "Preface," in his *The Black Aesthetic Movement*. Vol. 8 of *Dictionary of Literary Biography Documentary Series: An Illustrated Chronicle*. Detroit: Gale, pp. ix–xii. Mentions W briefly (p. x).

2781. Dent, Tom. "The Free Southern Theater: An Evaluation," in *Dictionary of Literary Biography: Documentary Series: An Illustrated Chronicle*. Vol. 8: *The Black Aesthetic Movement*. Ed. Jeffrey Louis Decker.

Detroit: Gale, pp. 46–50. Reprint of 1966.

2782. DeParie, Jason. "Poor Need a Dickens to Tell Their Story." Little Rock *Arkansas Gazette* (15 September), p. 1C. Mentions W briefly.

2783. De Weever, Jacqueline. *Mythmaking and Metaphor in Black Women's Fiction*. New York: St. Martin's Press, pp. 5, 96, 154. Mentions briefly "The Man Who Lived Underground" and comments on *NS*.

2784. Diawara, Manthia, and Phyllis R. Klotman. "*Ganja and Hess*: Vampires, Sex, and Addictions." *Black American Literature Forum*, 25 (Summer), 299–314. Quotes James Monaco comparing the film *Sweet Sweetback's Baadasssss Song* to *NS*.

2785. Dickstein, Morris, William Phillips, Jean Bethke Elshtain and Joe Flynn, "The Crisis in Our Culture." *Partisan Review*, 58 (Spring), 192–226. Dickstein and Flynn mention W briefly (pp. 218, 225).

2786. Diedrich, Maria. "James A. Baldwin — Obituaries for a Black Ishmael," in *James Baldwin: His Place in American Literary History and His Reception in Europe*. Ed. Jakob Köllhofer. Frankfurt am Main: Peter Lang, pp. 129–140. Discusses the W-Baldwin relationship in the context of intraracial intellectual politics.

2787. Dowie, William. *Peter Matthiessen*. Boston Twayne, p. Mentions W briefly as a literary expatriate in Paris.

2788. Dudley, David L. *My Father's Shadow: Intergenerational Conflict in African American Men's Autobiography*. Philadelphia: University of Pennsylvania Press, pp. 1–3, 31, 35, 94, 101–135, 137–149, 151, 153, 157, 163–165, 178, 187, 190, 192, 202–206. Chapter 4, "Runaway Son: Richard Wright," is a substantial treatment of *BB* and *AH*, emphasizing the themes of fear and alienation. Here and elsewhere Dudley makes numerous comparisons of W to Douglass, Washington, Du Bois, Baldwin, Cleaver, and Malcolm X. The general thesis of intergenerational conflict draws on Freud and Harold Bloom.

2789. Durczak, Jerzy. "Timothy Dow Adams. — *Telling Lies in Modern American Autobiography*." *Revue Française d'etudes américaines*," No. 47 (February), pp. 98–99. Review mentioning W briefly.

2790. Eagles, Brenda M. "A Bibliography of Dissertations Related to Mississippi —1990." *The Journal of Mississippi History*, 53 (February), 51–56. Lists a dissertation on W, Chinua Achebe, and George Lamming by Khaliquzzaman M. Elias.

2791. Early, Gerald. "Introduction," in his *My Soul's High Song: The Collected Writings of Countee Cullen, Voice of the Harlem Renaissance.* New York: Doubleday, pp. 1–73. Mentions W briefly (p. 53).

2792. Elliott, Emory. "Introduction," in his *The Columbia History of the American Novel.* New York: Columbia University Press, pp. ix–xviii. Mentions W briefly (p. xvii).

2793. Elliott, Joan C. "Race and Ethnicity in the Curriculum." *New Directions*, 18 (Spring), 16–17. Mentions W briefly.

2794. Erickson, Stephanie, and Deborah Hatheway. "Biographies of American Authors," in *The Columbia History of the American Novel.* New York: Columbia University Press, pp. 753–820. The W entry mentions briefly *NS, BB, UTC, O, SH, LD,* and *EM* (p. 820).

2795. Fabre, Michel. "Blyden Jackson. *A History of Afro-American Literature. Volume I: The Long Beginning, 1746–1895.*" *Afram Newsletter*, Nos. 33–34 (October), p. 27. Favorable review mentioning the parallel Jackson draws between W and the attorney Charles Houston.

2796. ____. *From Harlem to Paris: Black American Writers in France, 1840–1980.* Urbana: University of Illinois Press, pp. 5, 6, 7, 53, 166, 167–169, 175–193, 195, 198, 202, 204, 206, 207, 208, 215, 218, 219, 223, 224, 228, 239, 240, 242, 243, 249, 250, 251, 252, 271, 273, 279, 280, 283, 296, 298, 299, 301, 303, 305, 306, 343. Chapter 12, "Richard Wright, An Intellectual in Exile," treats his first trip to France and his subsequent residence there. Among matters treated are his initial response, his relations with French intellectuals and with the negritude group, his involvement with RDR and anticolonial politics, and his continuing interest in American racial affairs. Numerous brief references to W relate to a variety of contexts.

2797. ____. "Houston A. Baker. *Workings of the Spirit. The Poetics of Afro-American Women's Writing.*" *Afram Newsletter*, Nos. 33–34 (Oc-

tober), pp. 31–32. Review mentioning the work's treatment of *TMBW.*

2798. ____. "James Baldwin in Paris: Hardship and Romance," in *James Baldwin: His Place in American Literary History and His Reception in Europe.* Ed. Jakob Köllhofer. Frankfurt am Main: Peter Lang, pp. 45–56. Mentions W briefly (pp. 45, 56).

2799. ____. "James Campbell. *Talking at the Gates. A Life of James Baldwin.*" *Afram Newsletter*, Nos. 33–34 (October), pp. 30–31. Review mentioning briefly W's response to "Everybody's Protest Novel."

2800. ____. "*New Essays on Native Son.* Ed. Keneth Kinnamon." *The Southern Quarterly*, 29 (Winter), 154–156. Favorable review praising each of the five essays.

2801. ____. "*The Literary Griot.*" *Afram Newsletter*, Nos. 33–34 (October), p. 38. Mentions W briefly.

2802. Feaster, John. "James Baldwin and the Village of Modernism." *The Cresset*, 54 (January), 4–8. Includes comment on the W-Ellison relation and discussion of that between W ("the documentary social realist") and Baldwin ("the modern subjective formalist").

2803. Filene, Benjamin. "'Our Singing Country': John and Alan Lomax, Leadbelly, and the Construction of an American Past." *American Quarterly*, 43 (December), 602–624. Quotes W on Leadbelly (pp. 611, 622).

2804. Filreis, Alan. *Wallace Stevens and the Actual World.* Princeton: Princeton University Press, p. 273. Mentions W briefly.

2805. Fitz, Earl E. *Rediscovering the New World: Inter-American Literature in a Comparative Context.* Iowa City: University of Iowa Press, p. 166. Mentions briefly *NS.*

2806. Foeller-Pituch, El_bieta. "Catching Up: The Polish Critical Response to American Literature," in *As Others Read Us: International Perspectives on American Literature.* Ed. Huck Gutman. Amherst: The University of Massachusetts Press, pp. 205–218. Mentions W briefly (p. 206).

2807. Folks, Jeffrey J. "Ernest Gaines and the New South." *The Southern Literary Journal*, 24 (Fall), 32–46. Notes W's "bitterly ironic response to the 'New South'" (p. 33). Reprinted: 1993.

2808. Foster, Edward. "Poems, Made or Found?" *American Book Review*, 13 (April–May), pp. 8–9. Mentions briefly W as poet in a review of Cary Nelson's *Repression and Recovery: Modern American Poetry and the Politics of Cultural Memory, 1910–1945.*

2809. Foster, Frances Smith. "Parents and Children in Autobiography by Southern Afro-American Writers," in *Home Ground: Southern Autobiography.* Ed. J. Bill Berry. Columbia: University of Missouri Press, pp. 98–109. Mentions briefly *BB* (p. 108).

2810. Freccero, Carla. "June Jordan," *African American Writers.* Ed. Valerie Smith. New York: Scribner's, pp. 245–261. Mentions briefly Jordan's essay on W and Hurston (p. 252).

2811. Freese, Peter. "Some Remarks on the Reception of James Baldwin's Work in the Federal Republic of Germany," in *James Baldwin: His Place in American Literary History and His Reception in Europe.* Ed. Jakob Köllhofer. Frankfurt am Main: Peter Lang, pp. 11–32. Mentions W briefly (p. 11).

2812. [Frick, Judie]. "A Soviet View of William Faulkner and Richard Wright." Fayetteville: University of Arkansas. Flyer announcing a lecture by Sergei Chakovsky of the Gorky Institute of World Literature delivered on 19 April.

2813. Gates, Henry Louis, Jr. "Introduction: On Bearing Witness," in his *Bearing Witness: Selections from African-American Autobiography in the Twentieth Century.* New York: Pantheon, pp. 3–9. Mentions briefly *BB* (p. 4).

2814. ____. "Ishmael Reed," in *African American Writers.* Ed. Valerie Smith. New York: Scribner's, pp. 361–377. Comments on Reed's signifying on W's naturalism (pp. 363, 364, 371), mentioning *BB* and *NS.*

2815. ____. "Richard Wright," in his *Bearing Witness: Selections from African-American Autobiography in the Twentieth Century.* New York: Pantheon, p. 38. Biographical caption to a photograph of W preceding "The Ethics of Living Jim Crow."

2816. Gayle, Addison, Jr. "The Black Aesthetic: Defender," in *Dictionary of Literary Biography: Documentary Series: An Illustrated*

Chronicle. Vol. 8: *The Black Aesthetic.* Ed. Jeffrey Louis Decker. Detroit: Gale, pp. 70–77. Reprint of 1974.

2817. _____. "Cultural Strangulation: Black Literature and the White Aesthetic," in *Dictionary of Literary Biography: Documentary Series: An Illustrated Chronicle.* Vol. 8: *The Black Aesthetic Movement.* Ed. Jeffrey Louis Decker. Detroit: Gale, pp. 27–31. Reprint of 1969.101.

2818. Gibson, Richard. "Richard Wright." *The London Times Literary Supplement,* No. 4588 (8 March), p. 13. Responds to Julia Wright's letter to the editor by attributing the belief that he was involved in W's death to "various Communist sympathizers." Emphasizes W's rejection of Communism and his adherence to Pan-Africanism.

2819. Gilroy, Paul. *There Ain't No Black in the Union Jack.* Chicago: The University of Chicago Press, pp. [v] and p. 25. The epigraph is a quotation from *O.* Quotes George Padmore quoting W.

2820. Gilyard, Keith. *Voices of the Self: A Study of Language Competence.* Detroit: Wayne State University Press, p. 113. Notes the opposition of Marva Collins to *BB.*

2821. Glazer, Nathan. "In Defense of Multiculturalism." *The New Republic,* 205 (2 September), 18–20, 22. Mentions W briefly (p. 19).

2822. Glover, David. "John Clellon Holmes, *Displaced Person: The Travel Essays*; *Representative Men: The Biographical Essays*; and *Passionate Opinions: The Cultural Essays.*" *Journal of American Studies,* 25 (August), 272–273. Review mentioning briefly *NS.*

2823. _____. "John Clellon Holmes, *Displaced Person: The Travel Essays*: John Clellon Holmes, *Representative Men: The Biographical Essays.* John Clellon, Holmes, *Passionate Opinions: The Cultural Essays.'* *Journal of American Studies,* 25 (August 1991), pp. 272–273. Quotes Holmes's opinion that *NS* is "the most purely existentialist novel ever written by an American."

2824. Goncalves, Joe. "When State Magicians Fail: An Interview with Ishmael Reed," in *Dictionary of Literary Biography: Documentary Series: An Illustrated Chronicle.* Vol. 8. *The Black Aesthetic Movement.* Ed. Jeffrey Louis Decker. Detroit: Gale, pp. 265–270. Reprint of 1969.

2825. Goode, Stephen. "Title Search." *Northeastern University Magazine* 16 (May), 20–23. Reprint of 1990.

2826. Gordon, Mary. "Good Boys and Dead Girls," in her *Good Boys and Dead Girls and Other Essays.* New York: Viking, pp. 3–23. Mentions Bigger's murders of two women in *NS* (p. 17).

2827. Graham, Maryemma. "Butler-Evans, Elliott. *Race, Gender, and Desire: Narrative Strategies in the Fiction of Toni Cade Bambara, Toni Morrison, and Alice Walker.*" *Studies in American Fiction,* 19 (Spring), 120–122. Mentions W briefly.

2828. Graham, Maryemma, and Jerry Ward. "The Constitution of the Richard Wright Circle." *Richard Wright Newsletter,* 1 (Spring), 3 pp. Sets forth the purpose of the organization, names the charter members, stipulates annual dues of $10.00, and announces that a newsletter will be published twice a year and an annual meeting held.

2829. Graham, Maryemma, and Jerry W. Ward, Jr. "Letter from the Editors." *The Richard Wright Newsletter,* 1 (Fall), 1. Reviews activities pertaining to W during the past year and announces forthcoming activities.

2830. Graham, Maryemma and Jerry Ward. "Recent Publications." *Richard Wright Newsletter,* 1 (Spring), [3]. Lists five books and twenty-three articles.

2831. Graham, Maryemma and Jerry Ward. "Richard Wright Circle Membership." *Richard Wright Newsletter.* (Spring) [3]. States the purpose of the organization and includes an application form.

2832. Grant, Nathan. "Delta Scalene: A Passage through *Mississippi Triangle.*" *Black American Literature Forum,* 25 (Summer), 409–416. Mentions W briefly (p. 410).

2833. Greenberg, Cheryl Lynn. *"Or Does It Explode?": Black Harlem in the Great Depression.* New York: Oxford University Press, pp. 74, 100, 105, 196. Quotes from *LT,* mentions W's membership in the Communist Party, and quotes from *TMBV.*

2834. Greenberg, Douglas. "Worlds Not Our Own: Centrifugal and Centripetal Forces in the Humanities." *The Massachusetts Review,* 32 (Summer), 297–313. Mentions W briefly (p. 301).

2835. Greenlee, Marcia. "Interview with Margaret Walker Alexander, January 22, 1977," in *The Black Women Oral History Project,* Vol. 2 Ed. Ruth Edmonds Hill. Westport: Meckler, pp. 6–64. Includes discussion of her attraction to W and her traumatic response when he ended their friendship. Claims that W told her that he was going to marry white (pp. 28, 29, 34, 39). Reprinted: 2002.

2836. Greenspon, Joanna, ed. *Humanities Index April 1990 to March 1991.* New York: Wilson, pp. 1131–1132. Lists two primary and fifteen secondary items on W.

2837. Gretlund, Jan Nordby. "The Danes and American Literature," in *As Others Read Us: International Perspectives on American Literature.* Ed. Huck Gutman. Amherst: The University of Massachusetts Press, 65–78. Mentions W briefly (p. 76).

2838. Griffin, Noah W. "The Uncut Richard Wright: Repaying the Posthumous Debt." *San Francisco Review of Books,* 16 (April), pp. 11–12. Favorable review of the Library of America edition of W. Emphasizes race and sex in *NS* and the two parts of *AH.* Also mentions *O* and "The Ethics of Living Jim Crow."

2839. _____. "The Uncut Richard Wright: Repaying the Posthumous Debt." *San Francisco Review of Books,* Favorable review of the Library of America edition of W Focusing on sex and violence in *NS.* Treats more briefly *LT, BB,* and *O.*

2840. Hajek, Friederike. "Historical Aspects of the Reception of James Baldwin in the German Democratic Republic," in *James Baldwin: His Place in American Literary History and His Reception in Europe.* Ed. Jakob Köllhofer. Frankfurt am Main: Peter Lang, pp. 33–43. Mentions briefly W (pp. 33, 34) and *NS* (pp. 35, 36).

2841. Hakutani, Yoshinobu. "Richard Wright (4 September 1908–28 November 1960)," in *American Short-Story Writers, 1910–1945, Second Series.* Ed. Bobby Ellen Kimbel. Vol. 102 of *Dictionary of Literary Biography.* Detroit: Gale, pp. 378–386. Consists of a biographical sketch with a list of W's works, summaries of all the stories in *UTC* and *EM,* comments on the critical reception of W's short stories, and a brief bibliography of secondary sources.

2842. ____. "Two on Wright." *The Mississippi Quarterly*, 44 (Fall), 491–497. Review of Eugene E. Miller's *Voice of a Native Son: The Poetics of Richard Wright* and Keneth Kinnamon's *New Essays on Native Son*.

2843. Hakutani, Yoshinobu, and Toru Kiuchi. "The Critical Reception of James Baldwin in Japan: An Annotated Bibliography." *Black American Literature Forum*, 25 (Winter), 753–779. Contains 195 items, including 19 mentioning W.

2844. Hall, Donald, and D.L. Emblen. "Considerations," in their *A Writer's Reader*. Sixth edition. New York: HarperCollins, pp. 537–538. Reprint of 1979.120.

2845. ____. "Richard Wright The Library Card," in their *A Writer's Reader*. Sixth edition. New York: HarperCollins, p. 529. Reprint of 1979.121.

2846. ____. "Richard Wright The Library Card," in their *Instructor's Manual to Accompany A Writer's Reader* (bound with *A Writer's Reader*). New York: HarperCollins, pp. I-158-I-159. Answers to "Considerations," the study questions.

2847. Hamalian, Leo. "God's Angry Man." *Black American Literature Forum*, 25 (Summer), 417–420. Review of the documentary film *James Baldwin: The Price of the Ticket* mentioning W.

2848. Hamalian, Linda. *A Life of Kenneth Rexroth*. New York: W.W. Norton, pp 79, 308. Mentions W briefly and states that Rexroth's "Who Am I? Where Am I Going???" (1961.244)." was written in part as a eulogy for Richard Wright."

2849. Hamamoto, Takeo. "Richard Wright's Haikiu." *Public Opinion: A Monthly*, 24 (1 September), 83–86. After a summary of W's literary career, Hamamoto provides a detailed account of W's composition of haiku, in which he explores Japanese culture in a genuine manner [T.K., R.B., and Y.H.].

2850. Harding, Vincent. "Back to the Movement (1979–mid-1980's)," in *The Eyes on the Prize: Civil Rights Reader*. Eds. Clayborne Carson, David J. Garrow, Gerald Gill, Vincent Harding, and Darlene Clark Hine. New York: Penguin, pp. 656–662. Mentions W briefly (p. 658).

2851. ____. "We the People: The Long Journey Toward a More Perfect Union," in *The Eyes on the Prize: Civil Rights Reader*. Eds. Clay-borne Carson, David J. Garrow, Gerald Gill, Vincent Harding, and Darlene Clark Hine. New York: Penguin, pp. 1–34. Mentions W briefly (pp. 23–24).

2852. Harrington, Oliver W. *Why I Left America*. Detroit: Walter O. Evans, pp. 12–14, 16–17. Discusses the W-Harrington friendship in Paris, with brief comment on his mysterious death. Also includes brief comments by Julia Wright. Reprinted: 1993.

2853. Harrison, Alferdteen. "Introduction." in his *Black Exodus: The Great Migration from the American South*. Jackson: University Press of Mississippi, p. xv. Mentions briefly W and *NS*.

2854. Harrison, Elizabeth Jane, Knoxville: The University of Tennessee Press, p. 8. Mentions briefly W and *BB*.

2855. Hartman, S.V. and Farah Jasmine Griffin. "Are You as Colored as that Negro?: The Politics of Being Seen in Julie Dash's *Illusions*." *Black American Literature Forum*, 25 (Summer), 361–373. Includes an epigraph from *NS* and a brief mention of Bigger (p. 362).

2856. Hatch, James V. "Anthologies of African-American Plays." *Black American Literature Forum*, 25 (Spring), 185–192. Lists *NS* among the plays included in James V. Hatch and Ted Shine's *Black Theater USA: Forty-Five Plays, 1847–1974*.

2857. ____. "Introduction: Two Hundred Years of Black and White Drama," in his and Leo Hamalian's *The Roots of African American Drama: An Anthology of Early Plays, 1856–1939*. Detroit: Wayne State University Press, pp. 15–37. Comments briefly on the play *NS* and on "Big Black Good Man."

2858. Heath, Gordon. "Deep Are the Roots: Memoirs of a Black Expatriate." *The Massachusetts Review*, 32 (Summer), 230–279. Mentions briefly the play *NS* (p. 256).

2859. Hedgepeth, Chester M., Jr. "Baldwin, James A. (1924–1987)," in his *Twentieth-Century African American Writers and Artists*. Chicago: American Library Association, pp. 14–15. Mentions W briefly.

2860. ____. "(Baldwin, James A. (1924–1987)," in his *Twentieth-Century African-American Writers and Artists*. Chicago: American Library Association, pp. 14–15. Notes W's help to Baldwin.

2861. ____. "Hines, Chester Bomar (1909–1984)," in his *Twentieth-Century African American Writers and Artists*. Chicago: American Library Association, pp. 140–142. Notes W's influence on Hines.

2862. ____. "Hines, Chester Bomar," in his *Twentieth-Century African-American Writers and Artists*. Chicago: American Library Association, pp. 140–141. Places Kines in "the Richard Wright School of Urban Realists."

2863. ____. "Motley, Willard," in his *Twentieth-Century African American Writers and Artists*. Chicago: American Library Association, pp. 226–227. Briefly compares Motley and W.

2864. ____. "Motley Willard," in his *Twentieth-Century African-American Writers and Artists*. Chicago: American Library Association, pp. 226–227. Notes Motley's affinity to W.

2865. ____. "Murray, Albert (1916–)," in his *Twentieth-Century African American Writers and Artists*. Chicago: American Library Association, pp. 227–228. Notes that Murray criticizes Baldwin for criticizing W.

2866. ____. "Petry, Ann (1912–)," in his *African-American Writers and Artists*. Chicago: American Library Association, pp. 239–240. Mentions W briefly.

2867. ____. "Petry, Ann," in his *Twentieth-Century African-American Writers and Artists*. Chicago: American Library Association, pp. 239–240. Notes Petry's affinity to W.

2868. ____. "Pharr, Robert Deane (1916–), in his *African American Writers and Artists*. Chicago: American Library Association, pp. 240–241. Mentions W briefly.

2869. ____. "Redding, Jay Saunders," in his *African American Writers and Artists*. Chicago: American Library Association, pp. 250–252. Mentions briefly *The Alien Land of Richard Wright*.

2870. ____. "Redding, Jay Saunders," in his *Twentieth-Century African-American Writers and Artists*. pp. 250–251. Comments on Redding's "The Alien Land of Richard Wright."

2871. ____. "Walker, Margaret Abigail (Alexander, 1915–), in his *African American Writers and Artists*. Chicago: American Library Association, pp. 293–295. Mentions briefly Walkers's book on W.

2872. _____. "Walker, Margaret," in his *Twentieth-Century African-American Writers and Artists.* Chicago: American Library Association, pp. 293–295. Mentions briefly Walker's *Richard Wright: Daemonic Genius.*

2873. _____. "Williams, John Alfred (1925–)" in his *African American Writers and Artists.* Chicago: American Library Association, pp. 302–304. Lists Williams's *The Most Native of Sons, A Biography of Richard Wright.*

2874. _____. "Wright, Richard Nathaniel (1908–1960)," in his *African American Writers and Artists.* Chicago: American Library Association, pp. 314–315. Biographical sketch with a list of W's work and a short secondary bibliography.

2875. Hedrick, Joan D. *Making American Tradition: Visions and Revisions from Ben Franklin to Alice Walker.* By Cushing Strout." *The Journal of American History,* 77 (March), 1321–1322. Review praising the treatment of W.

2876. Hernton, Calvin. "Foreword," in *The Collected Stories of Chester Himes.* New York: Thunder's Mouth Press, pp. ix–xii. Mentions W briefly (pp. x, xii).

2877. Herron, Carolivia. "Introduction," in her *Selected Works of Angelina Weld Grimke.* New York: Oxford University Press, pp. 3–22. Notes briefly that Grimke anticipates W in her depiction of violence (p. 21).

2878. Hinojosa, Rolando. "Foreword: Redefining American Literature," in *Criticism in the Borderlands: Studies in Chicano Literature, Culture, and Ideology.* Eds. Hector Calderon and José David Saldívar. Durham, NC: Duke University Press, pp. xi–xv. Mentions W briefly (p. xiv).

2879. _____. "Foreword: Redefining American Literature," in *Criticism in the Borderlands: Studies in Chicano Literature, Culture, and Ideology.* Eds. Hector Calderon and José David Saldívar. Durham, NC: Duke University Press, pp. xi–xv. Mentions W briefly (p. xv).

2880. Hobson, Fred. *The Southern Writer in the Postmodern World.* Athens: The University of Georgia Press, pp. 6, 94. Mentions briefly W and *BB.*

2881. _____. "Surveyors and Boundaries: Southern Literature and Southern Literary Scholarship After Mid-Century." *The Southern Review,* 27 (October), 739–755. Mentions W briefly (pp. 745, 748, 755).

2882. Hooks, Bell, and Cornel West. *Breaking Bread: Insurgent Black Intellectual Life.* Boston: South End Press, pp. 55, 173–174. Mentions W briefly and lists *AH, BB, BP, LD,* and *NS.*

2883. Hord, Fred Lee. *Reconstructing Memory: Black Literary Criticism.* Chicago: Third World Press, p. 23. Contains a paragraph on "Blueprint for Negro Writing" emphasizing "collectivity" regarding social consciousness and responsibility, perspective, and theme."

2884. Hornsby, Alton, Jr. *Chronology of African-American History: Significant Events and People from 1619 to the Present.* Detroit: Gale, p. 85. Reprint of 1977.

2885. Horton, James Oliver. "In Search of Identity: James Baldwin and the Black American Intellectual Tradition," in *James Baldwin: His Place in American Literary History and His Reception in Europe.* Ed. Jakob Köllhofer. Frankfurt am Main: Peter Lang, pp. 95–108. Mentions W briefly (p. 97).

2886. Howe, Irving. "New Black Writers," in *Dictionary of Literary Biography: Documentary Series: An Illustrated Chronicle.* Vol. 8. *The Black Aesthetic Movement.* Ed. Jeffrey Louis Decker. Detroit: Gale, pp. 282–283. Partial reprint of 1969.

2887. _____. "The Value of the Canon." *The New Republic,* 204 (18 February), 40–44, 46–47. Mentions briefly W's reading Dreiser (p. 47).

2888. Hubbard, Dolan. "Society and Self in Alice Walker's *In Love and Trouble.*" *Obsidian II,* 6 (Summer), 50–75. Quotes from W's "The Literature of the Negro in the United States" (p. 69) and mentions Kinnamon's article on W and Angelou (p. 72).

2889. Hunt, Douglas. "Growing Up in America: 10 Lives," in his *The Riverside Guide to Writing.* Boston: Houghton Mifflin, p. 96. Includes comment on *BB,* "a milestone in both social history and literature."

2890. Hurd, Myles Raymond. "Between Blackness and Bitonality: Wright's 'Long Black Song.'" *CLA Journal,* 35 (September), 42–56.

Analysis of the "complex double story" focusing on both Silas and Sarah. The former is both cuckold and chauvinist; the latter is both victim and villainess. It "exhibits problematic disharmonies between technique and theme."

2891. Ichiki, Jun. "A Study of Richard Wright: His View of White People in *Black Boy: A Possibility of Black Nationalism.*" Seinan Gakuin University Literary Studies, *10 (January),* 43–61. Traces W's growth from boyhood to youth in *BB* in terms of his view of Southern whites, which develops into black nationalsim [T.K., R.B., and Y.H.].

2892. Inge, Tonette Bond. "Preface," in her *Southern Women Writers: The New Generation.* Tuscaloosa: The University of Alabama Press, pp. xvii–xviii. Mentions W briefly.

2893. Jackson, Blyden. "Introduction: A Street of Dreams," in *Black Exodus: The Great Migration from the American South.* Ed. Alferdteen Harrison. Jackson: University Press of Mississippi, pp. xi–xviii. Mentions briefly *NS* (p. xv).

2894. Jackson, Walter A. "Between Socialism and Nationalism: The Young E. Franklin Frazier." *Reconstruction,* 1, No. 3, 124–134. Mentions W briefly (p. 133).

2895. Johnson, Charles. "Black Fiction's Father Figure." *Chicago Tribune* (17 November), Sec. 14, pp. 1, 4. Favorable review of the Library of America edition of W with an assessment of W's place in African American literature. Analyzes the restored passages in *NS.*

2896. Jones, Gayl. *Liberating Voices: Oral Tradition in African American Literature.* Cambridge, MA: Harvard University Press, pp. 30–31, 58, 90–91, 105–106, 113, 118–119, 134, 146, 152–154, 156, 158–160, 188–189, 201. Quotes from "I Tried to Be a Communist," *BB,* "Blueprint for Negro Writing," and *NS;* notes W's unfavorable response to Zora Neale Hurston; contrasts briefly the old man in Ellison's "Flying Home" to Bigger Thomas; makes a brief connection between W and Joyce; and discusses the intertextuality of Alice Walker's *The Third Life of Grange Copeland* and *NS.*

2897. Jones, LeRoi. "Black Writing," in *Dictionary of Literary Biography: Documentary Series: An Illustrated Chronicle.* Vol. 8. *The Black*

Aesthetic. Ed. Jeffrey Louis Decker. Detroit: Gale, pp. 86–88. Reprint of 1964.

2898. _____. "The Myth of 'Negro Literature,'" in *Dictionary of Literary Biography: Documentary Series: An Illustrated Chronicle.* Vol. 8. *The Black Aesthetic.* Ed. Jeffrey Louis Decker. Detroit: Gale, pp. 81–86. Reprint of 1963.121.

2899. Jones, Suzanne, W. "Introduction, in her *Growing Up in the South.* New York: Penguin, pp. xiii–xx. Comments on "The Man Who Was Almost a Man," included in this autholgy.

2900. Jordan, June. "On Richard Wright and Zora Neale Hurston: Notes Toward a Balancing of Love and Hatred," in *Dictionary of Literary Biography: An Illustrated Chronicle.* Vol. 8. *The Black Aesthetic Movement.* Ed. Jeffrey Louis Decker. Detroit: Gale, pp. 335–338. Reprint of 1974.102.

2901. Joyce, Joyce A. "Black Woman Scholar, Critic, and Teacher: The Inextricable Relationship Among Race, Sex, and Class," in *(En)Gendering Knowledge: Feminists in Academe.* Eds. Joan E. Hartman and Ellen Messer-Davidow. Knoxville: The University of Tennessee Press, pp. 159–178. Revised reprint of 1991.

2902. _____. "Black Woman Scholar, Critic, and Teacher: The Inextricable Relationship Between Race, Sex, and Class." *New Literary History,* 22 (Summer), 543–565. Mentions W briefly (p. 553) and comments on her *Richard Wright's Art of Tragedy,* adding that "the sublimity of *NS* lies in the inextricable relationship between Wright's perceptions of racial realities and his adroit skill at shaping his creative vision" (p. 559). Reprinted in revised form: 1991.

2903. _____. "Richard Wright," in *African American Writers.* Ed. Valerie Smith. New York: Scribner's, pp. 505–523. Reviews W's life and career, discussing or commenting on all the books. Emphasizes W's effort to give voice to "the inexpressibly human." His iconoclasm is the source of much of his literary power. Joyce also praises his creative diversity and his "ability to synthesize politics and art."

2904. [_____]. "Richard Wright (1908–1960)," in *The New Cavalcade: African American Writing from 1760 to the Present.* Eds. Arthur P.

Davis, J. Saunders Redding, and Joyce Ann Joyce. Vol. 1. Washington, DC: Howard University Press, pp. 706–707. Bio-bibliographical headnote to an except from *BB* and "Bright and Morning Star."

2905. Julien, Claude. "Keneth Kinnamon — *New Essays on Native Son.*" *Revue française d'études américaines,* No. 46 (February), pp. 100–101. Favorable brief review emphasizing the collection's emphasis on social discourse.

2906. Kammen, Michael. *Mystic Chords of Memory: The Transformation of Tradition in American Culture.* New York: Alfred A. Knopf, p. 461. Mentions favorably "The Ethics of Living Jim Crow" as a product of the Federal Writers' Project.

2907. Karrer, Wolfgang. "Discursive Strategies in James Baldwin's Essays," in *James Baldwin: His Place in American Literary History and His Reception in Europe.* Ed. Jakob Köllhofer. Frankfurt am Main: Peter Lang, pp. 113–128. Mentions W and quotes Baldwin on W (pp. 114, 116, 119, 124, 126).

2908. Kazin, Alfred. "Too Honest for His Own Time." *The New York Times Book Review* (29 December), pp. 3, 18–19. Favorable review of the Library of American edition of W. "Richard Wright was a most extraordinary writer, with two masterpieces to his credit, the novel 'Native Son' (1940) and 'Black Boy' (1945), that are more overwhelming today now that they are judged by their literary power, than they were in a period when it was easy to accept them as 'news,' shocking and even thrilling." Compares W to Dostoevsky, comments on W and Baldwin, and discusses *NS.*

2909. _____. "William Faulkner and Religion: Determinism, Compassion, and the God of Defeat," in *Faulkner and Religion.* Eds. Doreen Fowler and Ann J. Abadie. Jackson: University Press of Mississippi, pp. 3–20. Comments on Faulkner's attitude toward W and quotes from "The Man Who Went to Chicago."

2910. Kelly, Lionel. "American Literature: The Twentieth Century," in *The Year's Work in English Studies.* Vol. 69. Oxford: Basil Blackwell, pp. 583–624. Mentions W briefly (p. 606).

2911. Kennedy, Randall. "'Keep the Nigger Down!': The Age of Segregation in Mississippi." *Reconstruc-*

tion, 1, No. 3, 115–136. Review of Neil McMillen's *Dark Journey* citing an incident in *BB* (p. 117).

2912. Khimes, Chester B. "From *The Quality of Hurt,*" in *The New Cavalcade: African American Writing from 1760 to the Present.* Eds. Arthur P. Davis, J. Saunders Redding, and Joyce Ann Joyce. Vol. 1. Washington, DC: Howard University Press, pp. 768–785. Partial reprint of 1972.97.

2913. Kinnamon, Keneth. "Hemingway, Wright, and the Forge of Injustice." *The Richard Wright Newsletter,* 1 (Fall), 3. Corrects an error on the dust jacket of the Library of America edition of W by showing that Hemingway did not have W in mind when he wrote that "writers are forged in injustice as a sword is forged."

2914. _____. "Three Black Writers and the Anthologized Canon." *American Literary Realism,* 23 (Spring), 42–51. Mentions briefly W (pp. 47, 48, 49) and "Between the World and Me" (p. 48).

2915. _____. "*Voice of a Native Son: The Poetics of Richard Wright.* By Eugene E. Miller." *American Literature,* 63 (December), 762–764. Unfavorable review taking issue with Miller's emphasis on the visionary W and complaining of lack of evidence, awkward writing, factual mistakes, and typographical errors.

2916. Kirszner, Laurie G., and Stephen R. Mandell. "Reading and Reacting," in their *Literature: Reading, Reacting, Writing.* Fort Worth: Harcourt Brace, Jovanovich, p. 752. Reprinted: 1994.

2917. Kitt, Eartha. *Confession of a Sex Kitten.* Fort Lee, NJ: Barricade Books, p. 63. Mentions briefly conversations with W in Paris.

2918. Kiuchi, Toru. "Richard Wright's *Native Son*: The Film and the Novel," in *Film & Society: Proceedings of the Eighth Annual Kent State University International Film Conference, April, 7–18, 1990.* Ed. Douglas Radcliff-Ulmstead. Kent, OH: Department of Romance Languages, Kent State University, pp. 62–68. Compares the 1951 and 1986 film versions of *NS,* reviews the critical response to the latter, and analyzes differences between it and the novel emphasizing producer Diane Silver's effort to reach whites and blacks who had not read the book and did not know each other.

2919. Klissourska, Nataliz. "One More Window to the World: American Literature in Bulgaria," in *As Others Read Us: International Perspectives on American Literature.* Ed. Huck Gutman. Amherst: The University of Massachusetts Press, p. 40. Mentions W briefly.

2920. Kostelanetz, Richard. *Politics in the African-American Novel: James Weldon Johnson, W.E.B. Du Bois, Richard Wright, and Ralph Ellison.* Westport, CT: Greenwood Press, pp. 3, 5, 66, 69–108, 113, 140, 153, 154, 155. Reprints 1969.150 (pp. 69–105), comments on W and Ellison (pp. 107–108), and mentions elsewhere *NS, BB, O, EM,* and "The Man Who Lived Underground."

2921. Kramer, Hilton. "Thinking About 'The Forties.'" *The New Criterion,* 9 (May), 4–8. Mentions W briefly (p. 8).

2922. Kramer, Victor A. *Agee and Actuality: Artistic Vision in His Work.* Troy, NY: Whitston, p. 164. Mentions W briefly.

2923. Kriegel, Leonard. "Summer Dreams." *The Sewanee Review,* 99 (Spring), 202–211. Mentions W briefly (p. 205).

2924. Kubitschek, Missy Dehn. *Claiming the Heritage: African-American Women Novelists and History.* Jackson: University Press of Mississippi, pp. xxi, 53, 91. Mentions "Big Boy Leaves Home," notes W's criticism of Zora Neale Hurston, and quotes Shirley Anne Williams on *BB.*

2925. Kutzinski, Vera M. "*The Life of Langston Hughes.* By Arnold Rampersad." *The Journal of American History,* 78 (September), 701–702. Review mentioning W briefly.

2926. Lamar, Jake. *Bourgeois Blues: An American Memoir.* New York: Summit Books, p. 65. Mentions W briefly.

2927. Lauter, Paul. "American Proletarianism," in *The Columbia History of the American Novel.* Ed. Emory Elliott. New York: Columbia University Press, pp. 331–356. Mentions W briefly (p. 344), comments on "Bright and Morning Star" (p. 348), and mentions *UTC* and *NS* (p. 348).

2928. _____. *Canons and Contexts.* New York: Oxford University Press, pp. 8, 18, 24, 42, 45, 70, 99, 244, 245, 268. Contains reprints of 1983 (3), 1984, and 1986. Also mentions W in the penultimate chapter: "Whose Culture?, Whose Literacy?"

2929. Lee, Don L. "Black Poetry: Which Direction?" in *Dictionary of Literary Biography: Documentary Series: An Illustrated Chronicle.* Vol. 8. *The Black Aesthetic Movement.* Ed. Jeffrey Louis Decker. Detroit: Gale, pp. 185–189. Reprint of 1968.148.

2930. _____. "Black Writing: this is u, thisisu," in *Dictionary of Literary Biography: Documentary Series: An Illustrated Chronicle.* Vol. 8. The Black Aesthetic *Movement.* Ed. Jeffrey Louis Decker. Detroit: Gale, pp. 189–192. Reprint of 1969.

2931. Leeming, David. "Baldwin, James," in *Benet's Reader's Encyclopedia of American Literature.* Eds. George Perkins, Barbara Perkins, and Phillip Leininger. New York: HarperCollins, pp. 62–63. Biographical sketch mentioning Baldwin's essays on W.

2932. Lemann, Nicholas. *The Promised Land.* New York: Knopf, pp. 46, 51–52, 78, 344. Notes the influence of *NS* on Aaron Henry and quotes from *TMBV.*

2933. Litwack, Leon F. "Hellhound on My Trail: Race Relations in the South from Reconstruction to the Civil Rights Movement," in *Opening Doors: Perspectives on Race Relations in Comtemporary America.* Eds. Harry J. Knopke, Robert J. Norrell, and Ronald W. Rogers. Tuscaloosa: The University of Alabama Press, pp. 3–25. Quotes *BB* on the threat of white violence and the rebellion it provoked in some blacks (pp. 17, 18–19).

2934. Longest, George C., et al. "A Checklist of Scholarship on Southern Literature for 1990." *The Mississippi Quarterly,* 44 (Supplement), 1–213. Lists twenty-nine items on W and cross-references to thirty-nine other items dealing partially with W.

2935. Lubiano, Wahneema. "Toni Morrison," in *African American Writers.* Ed. Valerie Smith. New York: Scribner's, pp. 321–333. Mentions W briefly (p. 321).

2936. Maekawa, Yuji. "A Study of Richard Wright: Cross Damon's Freedom" in *The Outsider,* 32 (December), 63–71. Observes that although he died at the end of the novel, Cross Damon was set free mentally and physically after his hard struggle with American society and the Communist Party.

2937. Marable, Manning. *Race, Reform and Rebellion: The Second Reconstruction in Black America, 1945–1982.* Second edition. Jackson: University Press of Mississippi, pp. 45–46, 48, 50, 251. Revised reprint of 1984.

2938. Márquez, Roberto. "One Boricua's Baldwin: A Memoir and Personal Remembrance," in *James Baldwin: His Place in American Literary History and His Reception in Europe.* Ed. Jakob Köllhofer. Frankfurt am Main: Peter Lang, pp. 57–78. Mentions briefly W, *NS, BB,* and *AH* (p. 66).

2939. Martin, Terence. "The Romance," in *The Columbia History of the American Novel.* Ed. Emory Elliott. New York: Columbia University Press, pp. 72–88. Mentions briefly *NS* and Bigger Thomas (p. 87).

2940. Masuda, Mitsuko. "Humor in 'Five Episodes': Richard Wright's Humoristic State of Mind." *Nihon Women's University Veritas,* 13 (December), 107–114. Notes humorous scenes in "Island of Hallucination."

2941. Maynard, John Arthur. *Venice West: The Beat Generation in Southern California.* New Brunswick: Rutgers University Press, pp. 26, 29. Notes that Lawrence Lipton was called "Jerusalem's Richard Wright" and compares his novel *Brother, the Laugh Is Bitter* to *NS.*

2942. McCarthy, B. Eugene. "Models of History in Richard Wright's *Uncle Tom's Children.*" *Black American Literature Forum,* 25 (Winter), 729–743. Analyzes the stories as W's effort to present black Southern history in order to "correct false views of received history ... and offer a paradigm for understanding the future processes of history" (p. 730). The emerging structure is a Marxist dialectic showing "modes of achieving political and social, thus economic, power" (p. 741).

2943. McDowell, Deborah E. "Foreword," in *Moses, Man of the Mountain* by Zora Neale Hurston. New York: HarperCollins, pp. vii-xxii. Includes comparison of Hurston's story "The Fire and the Cloud" (1934) and W's "Fire and Cloud" (pp. viii, x). Hurston rejected W's collectivism.

2944. _____. "In the First Place: Making Frederick Douglass and the Afro-American Narrative Tradition," in *Critical Essays on Frederick Douglass.* Ed. William L. Andrews.

Boston: Twayne, pp. 192–214. Quotes Arna Bontemps mentioning W (p. 207).

2945. McKay, Nellie. "Afro-American Literature," in *Benet's Reader's Encyclopedia of American Literature*. Eds. George Perkins, Barbara Perkins, and Phillip Leininger. New York: HarperCollins, pp. 9–15. Mentions briefly W, *UTC*, *NS*, and *BB*.

2946. McKay, Nellie Y. "The Girls Who Became the Women: Childhood Memories in the Autobiographies of Harriet Jacobs, Mary Church Terrell, and Anne Moody," in *Tradition and the Talents of Women*. Ed. Florence Howe. Urbana: University of Illinois Press, pp. 106–124. Includes comparisons of W and Anne Moody (pp. 109, 119, 121, 208–209).

2947. Mechling, Jay. "The Failure of Folklore in Richard Wright's *Black Boy*." *Journal of American Folklore*, 104 (Summer), 275–294. "A close, critical reading of *Black Boy* (1945) shows the extent to which Richard Wright drew upon African-American folklore for the content and aesthetic style of his autobiographical narrative. But the close reading also discovers ways in which the folk traditions failed Wright, especially in the intercultural encounter. These instances of the failure of the folklore draw our attention to larger issues about the double bind as a structural instrument of cultural hegemony and about the limitation of folklore as a resource for resisting the double bind" (Mechling's summary).

2948. Miller, Eugene E. "Some Black Thoughts on Don L. Lee's *Think Black!* Thunk by a Frustrated White Academic Thinker," in *Dictionary of Literary Biography: Documentary Series: An Illustrated Chronicle*. Vol. 8. *The Black Aesthetic Movement*. Ed. Jeffrey Louis Decker. Detroit: Gale, pp. 178–185. Reprint of 1973.

2949. Miller, James A. "MLA Volume: *Approaches to Teaching Native Son*." *The Richard Wright Newsletter*. 1 (Spring), 3. Call for contributions.

2950. Miller, James E., Jr. "The Age of Uncertainty: After the Second World War (1945–Present)," in his *Heritage of American Literature*. Vol. II: *Civil War to the Present*. San Diego: Harcourt Brace Jovanovich, pp. 1405–1427. Mentions W briefly (p. 1421).

2951. _____. "James Baldwin," in his *Heritage of American Literature*. Vol. II. San Diego: Harcourt Brace Jovanovich, pp. 1895–1897. Quotes Baldwin on W and notes their quarrel.

2952. _____. "The Modernist Revolution: Between the World Wars (1914–1945)," in his *Heritage of American Literature*. Vol. II: *Civil War to the Present*. San Diego: Harcourt Brace Jovanovich, pp. 751–778. Mentions W, *UTC*, *NS*, and *BB* (pp. 762, 773, 774).

2953. _____. "Ralph Ellison," in his *Heritage of American Literature*. Vol. II. San Diego: Harcourt Brace Jovanovich, pp. 1783–1785. Mentions W briefly.

2954. _____. "Richard Wright (1908–1960)," in his *Heritage of American Literature*. Vol. II: *Civil War to the Present*. San Diego: Harcourt Brace Jovanovich, pp. 1333–1335. Bio-bibliographical headnote to two selections from *BB*.

2955. Miller, R. Baxter. "*The Afro-American Novel and Its Tradition*. Bernard W. Bell." *MELUS* 17 (Fall), 128–130. Review mentioning W briefly.

2956. _____. "Charles T. Davis: Trace of Southern History." *The Mississippi Quarterly*, 44 (Spring), 151–158. Notes Davis's work on W (p. 155).

2957. _____. "The Southern Trace of Black Critical Theory." *Xavier Review*, 11, 1–53. The epigraph is Blyden Jackson on W. Miller quotes several times from *BB*.

2958. _____. "A Tribute to the Masque of George Bass." *CLA Journal*, 35 (September), 115–119. Mentions W briefly (p. 116).

2959. Mobley, Marilyn Sanders. "Ann Petry," in *African American Writers*. Ed. Valerie Smith. New York: Scribner's, pp. 347–359. Comments on critical distortion of viewing Petry solely in relation to W's naturalism (p. 351).

2960. Montgomery, Maxine L. "Racial Armageddon: The Image of Apocalypse in Richard Wright's *Native Son*." *CLA Journal*, 34 (June), 453–466. Treats *NS* as a secular Jeremiad prefiguring a racial and class war unless America redeems itself from racial injustice. Only by moving outside the present social system can Bigger achieve identity through violence. Reprinted in revised form: 1996.

2961. Mosley, Walter. "The Outsider Comes In." *New York Newsday* (8 December), FanFare sec., p. 37. Favorable review of the Library of America edition of W. Assesses W's major place in American literature for his powerful exposure of a "morally culpable society."

2962. Muller, Gilbert H. "Comprehension, Rhetoric, Writing," in his *The McGraw-Hill Reader*. Fourth edition. New York: McGraw-Hill, p. 161. Twelve study questions and writing topics to accompany an excerpt from *BB*. Reprinted: 1994.

2963. _____. "Comprehension, Rhetoric, Writing," in his *The McGraw-Hill Reader*. Fourth edition. New York: McGraw-Hill, pp. 228–229. Study aids for "The Psychological Reactions of Oppressed People."

2964. _____. "Richard Wright *The Library Card*," in his *Instructor's Manual to Accompany The McGraw Hill Reader: Themes in the Disciplines*. Fourth edition, pp. 78–81. Teacher's aids for a selection from *BB*.

2965. _____. "Richard Wright, The Library Card," in his *The McGraw-Hill Reader*. Fourth edition. New York: McGraw-Hill, p. 153. Headnote to an excerpt from *BB*. Reprinted: 1994.

2966. _____. "Richard Wright *The Library Card*," in his *The McGraw-Hill reader: Themes in the Disciplines*. Fourth edition. New York: McGraw-Hill, p. 153. Reprint of.

2967. _____. "Richard Wright, The Psychological Reactions of Oppressed People," in his *The McGraw-Hill Reader*. Fourth edition. New York: McGraw-Hill, pp. 224–225. Reprint of 1982.

2968. _____. "Richard Wright *The Psychological Reactions of Oppressed People*," in his *Instructor's Manual to Accompany The McGraw-Hill Reader: Themes in the Disciplines*. Fourth edition, pp. 111–114. Teacher's aids for the essay.

2969. _____. "Richard Wright *The Psychological Reactions of Oppressed People*," in his *The McGraw-Hill Reader: Themes in the Disciplines*. Fourth edition. New York: McGraw-Hill, pp. 224–225. Reprint of.

2970. _____. "Comprehension, Rhetoric, Writing," in his *The McGraw-Hill Reader: Themes in the Disciplines*. Fourth edition. New

York: McGraw-Hill, pp. 228–229. Reprint of.

2971. _____. "Comprehension, Rhetoric, Writing," in his *The Mc-Graw-Hill Reader: Themes in the Disciplines.* Fourth edition. New York: McGraw-Hill p. 161. Reprint of.

2972. Murphy, James F. *The Proletarian Moment: The Controversy Over Leftism in Literature.* Urbana: University of Illinois Press, pp. 3, 10–11. Mentions briefly W and "Between the World and Me." Quotes from 1977.293.

2973. Mzamane, Mbulelo Vizikhungo. "Apartheid Defines the Contours of American Literary Studies in Southern Africa," in *As Others Read Us: International Perspectives on American Literature.* Ed. Huck Gutman. Amherst: The University of Massachussetts Press, pp. 219–235. Notes that *NS* is included in a South African course on African American literature (p. 224) and quotes Don Mattera acknowledging W's influence (p. 232).

2974. Hakajima, Yoshinobu. "*Native Son*: The Western Literary Form and African Voices." *Bulletin of Shiraume Gakuen Junior College*, 27 (April), 53–61. Rejecting the views of Ellison and Baldwin, Nakajima places W in both the black and Western cultural traditions. Bigger's is a condensed sublimation of African American history based on Western literature through the African-centered blues [T.K., R.B., and Y.H.].

2975. Namekata, Hitoshi. "Richard Wright's 'Big Black Good Man,'" *Bulletin of Musashino College for Music*, 23, 81–88. Finds humor in this short story and notes its reversal of the relation between white and black people as depicted in his earlier fiction.

2976. Neal, Larry. "And Shine Swam On," in *Dictionary of Literary Biography: Documentary Series: An Illustrated Chronicle.* Vol. 8: *The Black Aesthetic Movement.* Ed. Jeffrey Louis Decker. Detroit: Gale, pp. 3–13. Reprint of 1968.171.

2977. Newby, James Edward. *Black Authors: A Selected Annotated Bibliography.* New York: Garland, pp. 52, 275, 462–463, 597. Contains entries, some annotated, for *BB, TMBV, AH, LT, LD, NS, O, UTC,* and *WML.*

2978. Nixon, Will. "Thunder's Mouth and Its Enthusiasm for Black Culture." *American Visions*, 6 (August), 34–36. Notes that this press has issued two books by W.

2979. Norris, Margot. "Modernist Eruptions," in *The Columbia History of the American Novel.* Ed. Emory Elliott. New York: Columbia University Press, pp. 311–330. Mentions W briefly (p. 326).

2980. Ogbaa, Kalu. "Protest and the Individual Talents of Three Black Novelists." *CLA Journal*, 35 (December), 159–184. Treats W, Baldwin, and Ellison. The section on W (pp. 163–170) treats style and, especially, characterization as well as the protest theme. Numerous comparisons of W with Baldwin and Ellison are made throughout the essay. Unlike the other two, W "tends to blame the problems of the black American almost entirely on the racist policies of whites" (p. 162).

2981. Okada, Seiichi. "Richard Wright's Illusory South." *Saitama University Heron*, 25 (20 March), 7–14. Survey of what the South means to W in *BB* [T.K., R.B., and Y.H.].

2982. Okpewho, Isidore. "From a Goat Path in Africa: An Approach to the Poetry of Jay Wright." *Callaloo*, 14 (Summer), 692–726. Comments upon W at the Conference of Black Writers and Artists in Paris and notes that Senghor called *BB* "one of the major *African* autobiographies" (p. 697).

2983. Olney, James. "The Autobiography of America." *American Literary History*, 3 (Summer), 376–395. Mentions W briefly (p. 384).

2984. O'Meally, Robert. "Ralph Ellison," in *African American Writers.* Ed. Valerie Smith. New York: Scribner's, pp. 103–127. Discusses Ellison's friendship with W and the story W asked him to write for *New Challenge* (p. 109).

2985. Oriard, Michael. *Sporting with the Gods: The Rhetoric of Play and Game in American Culture.* Cambridge: Cambridge University Press, pp. 254, 311, 313, 315–316, 317, 321. Contains two paragraphs on the "rhetoric of game playing" in *NS* (pp. 315–316) and mentions W briefly elsewhere.

2986. Painter, Nell Irvin. "Who Was Lynched?" *The Nation*, 253 (11 November), 577. Mentions briefly Bessie and Bigger.

2987. Parker, Jeffrey D. "Wright, Richard," in *St. James Guide to Biography.* Ed. Paul E. Schillinger. Chicago and London: St. James Press, pp. 845–846. Describes and evaluates books by David Bakish, Robert Bone, Michel Fabre, Robert Felgar, Addison Gayle, Keneth Kinnamon, Margaret Walker, Constance Webb, and John A. Williams.

2988. Patterson, Tiffany R. L. "*A History of Afro-American Literature.* Volume I: *The Long Beginning, 1746–1895.* By Blyden Jackson." *The Journal of Southern History*, 57 (May), 362–364. Review noting that Jackson calls the period from 1930 to 1960 the "Age of Richard Wright."

2989. Payne, James Robert. "Horace A. Porter. *Stealing the Fire: The Art and Protest of James Baldwin.*" *World Literature Today*, 65 (Winter), 119–120. Review praising Porter's treatment of the W-Baldwin relationship.

2990. Peterson, Linda. "From Egocentric Speech to Public Discourse: Richard Wright Composes His Thoughts on *Black Boy*," in *The Essay Connection: Readings for Writers.* Ed. Lynn Z. Bloom. Third edition. Lexington, MA: D.C. Heath, pp. 152–170. Reprint of 1985.139.

2991. Pettis, Joyce. "Margaret Walker: Black Woman Writer of the South," in *Southern Women Writers: The New Generation.* Ed. Tonette Bond Inge. Tuscaloosa: The University of Alabama Press, pp. 9–19. Mentions W briefly (p. 10) and lists *Richard Wright: Daemonic Genius* in the bibliography (p. 19).

2992. Pinsker, Sanford. "Is There an American Literary Tradition?" *The Virginia Quarterly Review*, 67 (Spring), 347–354. Review of Cushing Strout's *Making American Tradition* noting its treatment of *NS* and Ellison's relation to W (p. 353).

2993. [Prenshaw, Peggy Whitman, Thomas J. Richardson, Noel Polk, and Stephen Flinn Young]. "Introduction: The Natchez Literary Celebration." *The Southern Quarterly*, 29 (Summer), 5–7. Mentions briefly Margaret Walker Alexander's address on W.

2994. Prevost, Verbie Lovorn. "Theses and Dissertations for 1990." *South Atlantic Review*, 56 (November), 137–165. Lists a thesis by William Burton Roy, "Unity in Richard Wright's *Uncle Tom's Children*" (p. 154).

2995. Rabinowitz, Paula, *Labor and Desire: Women's Revolutionary Fiction in Depression America*. Chapel Hill: The University of North Carolina Press, pp. 11, 30, 37–38, 40. Notes W's criticism of *Their Eyes Were Watching God*, his defense of the John Reed Clubs and his "cynical memoir" *AH*.

2996. _____. *Labor and Desire: Women's Revolutionary Fiction in Depression America*. Chapel Hill: The University of North Carolina Press, pp. 11, 30, 37–38, 40. Quotes from W's review of *Their Eyes Were Watching God* and comments on W and the John Reed Club and *AH*.

2997. Rajiv, Sudhi. *Forms of Black Consciousness*. New Delhi: Jainsons Publications, i–189 pp. After sketching the history of slavery and racism, Rajiv examines W and intellectual consciousness, Malcolm X and Religious Consciousness, Eldrige Cleaver and political consciousness. The final chapter is entitled "Towards a Revolutionary Consciousness."

2998. _____. *Forms of Black Consciousness*. New Delhi: Jansons Publications, 189 pp. Discusses the autobiographies of W, Malcolm X, and Eldridge Cleaver against the background of American racism. The chapter on W is entitled "Richard Wright and Intellectual Consciousness" (pp. 45–81).

2999. Rampersad, Arnold. "*Adventures of Huckleberry Finn* and Afro-American Literature," in *Satire or Evasion?: Black Perspectives on "Huckleberry Finn."* Eds. James S. Leonard, Thomas A. Tenney, and Thadious M. Davis. Durham, NC: Duke University Press, pp. 216–227. Notes W's use of dialect and a child's perspective, his naturalism, and his treatment of moral inversion — all of which are anticipated by Twain. Mentions "Blueprint for Negro Writing," "Big Boy Leaves Home," "Almos' a Man," *UTC*, "Voodoo of Hell's Half-Acre," *LT*, *O*, and *NS*.

3000. _____. "Baldwin, James," in *The Reader's Companion to American History*. Eds. Eric Foner and John A Garraty. Boston: Houghton Mifflin, pp. 74–75. Mentions briefly W and *NS*.

3001. _____. "Too Honest for His Own Time." *The New York Times* (29 December), pp. 3, 17–18. Discussion of the Library of America edition of W, explaining its textual decisions for *LT*, *UTC*, *NS*, *BB*, and *O*. This edition gives readers "the opportunity ... to hear a great American writer speak with his own voice about matters that still resonate at the center of our lives." Reprinted: 1995.

3002. _____. "Wright, Richard," in *The Reader's Companion to American History*. Eds. Eric Foner and John A. Garraty. Boston: Houghton Mifflin, pp. 1181–1182. Biographical sketch.

3003. Rauch, Esther Nettles. "Paul Lawrence Dunbar," in *African American Writers*. Ed. Valerie Smith. New York: Scribner's, pp. 87–102. Contains a paragraph on W's evaluation of Dunbar in *WML* (p. 93).

3004. Redding, J. Saunders. "From *The American Negro Writer and His Roots*," in *The Calvacade: African American Writing from 1760 to the Present*. Eds. Arthur P. Davis, J. Saunders Redding, and Joyce Ann Joyce. Vol. 1. Washington, DC: Howard University Press, pp. 655–661. Partial reprint of 1960.222.

3005. Reddy, M. "Baker, Houston A. *Workings of the spirit; the poetics of Afro-American women's writing.*" *Choice*, 28 (June), 1635. Review mentioning W briefly.

3006. Reed, Ishmael. "Introduction to *19 Necromancers from Now*," in *Dictionary of Literary Biography: Documentary Series: An Illustrated Chronicle*. Vol. 8. *The Black Aesthetic Movement*. Ed. Jeffrey Louis Decker. Detroit: Gale, pp. 272–277. Reprint of 1970.297.

3007. [Reid, Calvin]. "Wright Bio Ruling Eases Fair Use Restrictions: Biography of a Biography." *Publishers Weekly*, 238 (20 December), 15. Traces the history of Margaret Walker's biography of W and explains the legal decision permitting her to use unpublished materials.

3008. Reid, Stephen. "*The Library Card* Richard Wright (1908–1960)," in his *Purpose and Process: A Reader for Writers: Annotated Instructor's Edition*. Englewood Cliffs, NJ: Prentice-Hall, pp. 33–45. Reprints an excerpt from *BB* with headnote, marginalia, and study questions.

3009. Reilly, John M. "Ellison, Ralph (Waldo)," in *Benet's Reader's Encyclopedia of American Literature*. Eds. George Perkins, Barbara Perkins, and Phillip Leininger. New York: HarperCollins, pp. 302–303. Biographical sketch mentioning the W connection.

3010. _____. "Michel Fabre. *Richard Wright: Books and Writers.*" *Modern Fiction Studies*, 37 (Winter), 773–774. Favorable review noting W's interest in aesthetic matters as well as social message.

3011. _____. "Wright, Richard [Nathaniel] (1908–1960)," in *Benet's Reader's Encyclopedia of American Literature*. Eds. George Perkins, Barbara Perkins, and Phillip Leininger. New York: Harper Collins, pp. 1165–1166. Biographical critical article stressing the relevance of W's author's note in *The New Caravan* and that of "The Ethics of Living Jim Crow. Comments on *NS*, *BB*, *AH*, *LD*, *WML*, *BP*, *CC*, and *PS*. Also lists four critical studies of W.

3012. Rexroth, Kenneth, and James Laughlin: *Selected Letters*. Ed. Lee Bartlett. New York: W.W. Norton, pp. 185–186. Rexroth mentions W briefly and Bartlett provides a very brief note on W.

3013. Ridgely, Joseph, and G[eorge] P[erkins]. "The Novel Before 1960" in *Benet's Reader's Encyclopedia of American Literature*. Eds. George Perkins, Barbara Perkins, and Phillip Leininger. New York: HarperCollins, pp. 784–792. Mentions briefly W and *NS*.

3014. Rigney, Barbara Hill. *The Voices of Toni Morrison*. Columbus: Ohio State University Press, p. 28. Mentions briefly the theme of flight in *NS*.

3015. Roberts, Steven V., with Jeannye Thornton and Ted Gest. "The Crowning Thomas Affair." *U.S. News & World Report*, 111 (16 September), 24–26, 28–30. Reports that reading W aroused in Clarence Thomas "feelings of anger and isolation [he] often had but suppressed." Includes a photograph of W.

3016. Rogal, Samuel J., ed. *Calendar of Literary Facts: A Daily and Yearly Guide to Noteworthy Events in World Literature from 1450 to the Present*. Detroit: Gale, pp. 90, 123. Lists W's date of birth (p. 90) and death (p. 123).

3017. Rogers, Mary F. *Novels, Novelists, and Readers: Toward a Phenomenological Sociology of Literature*. Albany: State University of New York Press, pp. 41, 223. Mentions W briefly.

3018. Rosen, Margery D. "How to Get Your Kids to Love Books." *Ladies Home Journal*, 108 (April),

73–74, 76, 78, 80, 82, 84, 86, 88, 90–91. Notes that Arthur Ashe's favorite childhood book was *NS* (p. 84).

3019. Rosenthal, M.L. "On the 'Dissidents' of the Thirties," in his *Our Life in Poetry: Selected Essays and Reviews*. New York: Persea Books, pp. 37–43. Reprint of 1951.

3020. Rout, Kathleen. *Eldridge Cleaver*. Boston: Twayne, pp. 12, 13, 28, 30, 47, 117. Discusses Cleaver's embrace of W and *NS* and his rejection of James Baldwin. Mentions briefly Julia Wright.

3021. Rowan, Carl T. *Breaking Barriers: A Memoir*. Boston: Little Brown, pp. 71, 105, 368. Mentions briefly *NS* and *BB*.

3022. Rowell, Charles H. "An Interview with Henry Louis Gates, Jr." *Callaloo*, 14 (Spring), 444–463. Gates notes the intertextual relation between *BB* and Claude Brown's *Manchild in the Promised Land* (p. 450).

3023. _____. "'Let Me Be with Ole Jazzbo': An Interview with Sterling Brown." *Callaloo*, 14 (Fall), 795–815. Brown comments on W and folk culture: "he was a very talented novelist, but Dick was not an authority on certain aspects of folk culture. I don't think he felt jazz, and I don't think he felt the blues" (p. 796). Mentions W elsewhere (pp. 800, 804, 809, 810).

3024. Royot, Daniel, Jean Béranger, Yves Carlet, and Kermit Vanderbilt. "Toni Morrison," in their *Anthologie de la litterature américaine*. Paris: Presses Universitaires de France, pp. 614–615. Mentions briefly *NS*.

3025. _____. "La foi en l'homme resurgit lors de la Grande Dépression," in their *Anthologie de la littérature américaine*. Paris: Presses Universitaires de France, pp. 397–398. Mentions W briefly.

3026. _____. "La Deuxiéme Guerre mondiale: interim littéraire," in their *Anthologie de la litterature Américaine*, Paris: Presses Universitaires de France, pp. 451–452. Mentions briefly *BB* and *NS*.

3027. _____. "Ralph Ellison," in their *Anthologie de la litterature américaine*. *Presses Universitaires* de France, pp. 477–478. Notes W's influence on Ellison.

3028. Rubin, Louis D., Jr. "The Dixie Special: William Faulkner and the Southern Literary Renascence,"

in his *The Mockingbird in the Gum Tree: A Literary Gallimaufry*. Baton Rouge: Louisiana State University Press, pp. 31–62. Reprint of 1982.

3029. _____. "The High Sheriff of Yoknapatawpha County: A Study in the Genius of Place," in his *The Mockingbird in the Gum Tree: A Literary Gallimaufry*. Baton Rouge: Louisiana State University Press, pp. 63–83. Reprint of 1990.

3030. _____. "Tory Formalists, New York Intellectuals, and the New Historical Science of Criticism," in his *The Mockingbird in the Gum Tree: A Literary Gallimaufry*. Baton Rouge: Louisiana State University Press, pp. 193–204. Reprint of 1980.

3031. Ruland, Richard, and Malcolm Bradbury. *From Puritanism to Postmodernism: A History of American Literature*. London: Routledge, pp. 159, 266, 268, 277, 279–280. Comments on W's attraction to Marxism and on *UTC, NS, BB*, and *O*. "Like the best fiction of the 1930s Wright's work was reaching toward a visionary distillation of an oppressed human condition" (p. 280).

3032. Rushdy, Ashraf H.A. "Fraternal Blues: John Edgar Wideman's Homewood Trilogy." *Contemporary Literature*, 32 (Fall), 312–345. Mentions briefly the curtain metaphor in *NS* (p. 339).

3033. Sadoff, Dianne F. "Gender and African-American Narrative." *American Quarterly*, 43 (March), 119–127. Includes a review of Valerie Smith's *Self-Discovery and Authority in Afro-American Narrative* quoting from it on W's self-narrators (pp. 120–121).

3034. Saldívar, José David. *The Dialectics of Our America: Genealogy, Cultural Critique, and Literary History*. Durham, NC: Duke University Press, p. 99. Mentions W briefly.

3035. Saunders, James Robert. "Breaking Out of the Cage: The Autobiographical Writings of Maya Angelou." *The Hollins Critic*, 28 (October), 1–11. Mentions briefly *BB* (p. 2).

3036. Savery, Pancho. "'Who Was That Masked Man?': Literary Criticism and the Teaching of African American Literature in Introductory Courses," in *Practicing Theory in Introductory College Literature Courses*. Eds. James M. Cahalan and David D. Downing. Urbana: National Council of Teachers of English, pp.

189–198. Mentions W briefly (pp. 191, 192).

3037. Schaub, Thomas Hill. *American Fiction in the Cold War*. Madison: The University of Wisconsin Press, pp. 69, 92, 115. Mentions W briefly.

3038. Schmidt, Peter. *The Heart of the Story: Eudora Welty's Short Fiction*. Jackson: University Press of Mississippi, p. xv. Mentions W briefly.

3039. Schmitz, Neil. "Neo-Hoo-Doo: The Experimental Fiction of Ishmael Reed," in *Dictionary of Literary Biography: Documentary Series: An Illustrated Chronicle*. Vol. 8. *The Black Aesthetic Movement*. Ed. Jeffrey Louis Decker. Detroit: Gale, pp. 292–301. Reprint of 1974.

3040. Scott, Joyce H. *Slavery and the Literary Imagination*. Eds. Deborah E. McDowell and Arnold Rampersad; *From Folklore to Fiction: A Study of Folk Heroes and Rituals in the Black American Novel*. By H. Nigel Thomas; *Richard B. Moore, Caribbean Militant in Harlem: Collected Writings 1920–1972*. Eds. W Burghardt Turner and Joyce Moore Turner." *American Literature*, 63 (December), 759–762. Review mentioning W briefly.

3041. Scott, Nathan A., Jr. "American Literature Since 1914," in *The Reader's Companion to American History*. Eds. Eric Foner and John A Garraty. Boston: Houghton Mifflin, pp. 674–677. Mentions W briefly.

3042. Seed, David. "American Literature: The Twentieth Century: Fiction: Individual Authors," in *The Year's Work in English Studies*. Vol. 69. Oxford: Basil Blackwell, pp. 624–651. Comments on work on W by David Bradley, Jack B. Moore, Alan W. France, and Tracy Webb (pp. 640–641).

3043. _____. "American Literature: The Twentieth Century: Fiction: Individual Authors," in *The Year's Work in English Studies*. Vol. 69. Oxford: Basil Blackwell, pp. 573–583. Comments on work on W by Edward D. Clark.

3044. Seidel, Kathryn Lee. "The Artist in the Kitchen: The Economics of Creativity in Hurston's 'Sweat,'" in *Zora in Florida*. Eds. Steven Glassman and Kathryn Lee Seidel. Orlando: University of Central Florida Press, pp. 110–120. Comments on W's narrative mode and compares it to Hurston's story.

3045. Seymour, Gene. "Mencken and 'Negroes.'" *The Nation*, 253 (14 October), 430. Letter to the editor noting that Mencken inspired W.

3046. Seymour-Smith, Martin. *The Dent Dictionary of Fictional Characters.* London: J.M. Dent, p. 477. Lists Bigger Thomas.

3047. Shifflett, Lee. *Bookman's Guide to Americana.* Tenth edition. Metuchen, NJ: The Scarecrow Press, p. 510. Lists *NS* at $50.

3048. Showalter, Elaine. *Sister's Choice: Tradition and Change in American Women's Writing.* Oxford: Clarendon Press, pp. 120, 123. Mentions W briefly.

3049. Shulman, Robert. "Realism," in *The Columbia History of the American Novel.* Ed. Emory Elliott. New York: Columbia University Press, pp. 160–188. Mentions briefly Bigger Thomas (p. 180).

3050. Simpson, Anne K. *A Gathering of Gaines: The Man and the Writer.* Lafayette: University of Southwestern Louisiana, pp. 23, 95, 113, 265. Includes reprints of 1969 and 1971.

3051. Singh, Amritjit. "Keeping Up with George." *The Langston Hughes Review*, 9/10, 117–119. Mentions W briefly.

3052. Skerrett, Joseph T., Jr. "James Weldon Johnson 1871–1938," in *African American Writers.* Ed. Valerie Smith. New York: Scribner's, pp. 219–233. Mentions W briefly (p. 230).

3053. Smith, David L. "The Black Arts Movement and Its Critics." *American Literary History*, 3 (Spring), 93–110. Mentions W briefly (pp. 96, 97, 102).

3054. Smith, Michelle. "Discovering the tomb of Victor Séjour...." *Afram Newsletter*, Nos. 33–34 (October), pp. 24–25. Mentions W briefly.

3055. Smith, Valerie. "Introduction," in her *African American Writers.* New York: Scribner's, pp. vii–xvii. Mentions W and his relation to Zora Neale Hurston, Ralph Ellison, and James Baldwin (pp. xiii, xiv).

3056. Snell, Susan. "African American Studies." *The Society for the Study of Southern Literature Newsletter*, 24 (April), 27–30. Lists Keneth Kinnamon's *New Essays on Native Son.*

3057. _____. "Winter 1991–1992 Conferences: A Look Ahead." *The Society for the Study of Southern Literature Newsletter*, 24 (April), 10. Contains an announcement of the 1992 conference on "African Americans and Europe." Mentions W's plaque.

3058. Southerland, Ellease. "Zora Neale Hurston: The Novelist-Anthropologist's Life/Works," in *Dictionary of Literary Biography: An Illustrated Chronicle.* Vol. 8. *The Black Aesthetic Movement.* Ed. Jeffrey Louis Decker. Detroit: Gale, pp. 338–343. Reprint of 1974.

3059. Spillers, Hortense J. "Introduction: Who Cuts the Border? Some Readings on 'America,'" in her *Comparative American Identities: Race, Sex, and Nationality in the Modern Text.* New York: Routledge, pp. 1–25. Mentions briefly Bigger Thomas (p. 8).

3060. Stepto, Robert B. "Afterword: Distrust of the Reader in Afro-American Narratives," in his *From Behind the Veil: A Study of Afro-American Narrative.* Second edition. Urbana: University of Illinois Press, pp. 195–215. Reprint of 1986.

3061. _____. *From Behind the Veil: A Study of Afro-American Narrative.* Second edition. Urbana: University of Illinois Press, pp. 24, 44, 96, 116, 124, 128–162, 163, 175, 176, 177, 179, 182, 196–198, 199. Reprint of 1979.243 and 1986 with mention of W, *NS*, and *BB* in the new preface.

3062. Sternglass, Marilyn S. *Reading, Writing, and Reasoning.* Second edition. New York: Macmillan, pp. 9–10. Quotes and comments on a passage from *BB* on the excitement of reading.

3063. Stich, Klaus P. "Timothy Dow Adams. *Telling Lies in Modern American Autobiography.*" *The Canadian Review of American Studies*, 22 (Summer), 132–133. Review mentioning W briefly.

3064. Stillinger, Jack. *Multiple Authorship and the Myth of Solitary Genius.* New York: Oxford University Press, pp. 156, 211, 236–237. Notes intervention by persons other than W in *BB* and *NS*, citing relevant articles by Janice Thaddeus and Keneth Kinnamon.

3065. Stone, Albert E. "Modern American Autobiography: Texts and Transactions," in *American Autobiography: Retrospect and Prospect.* Ed. Paul John Eakin. Madison: The University of Wisconsin Press, pp. 95–120. Uses *BB* to show how one can "read and exploit autobiographies as history" (p. 98) and mentions W elsewhere (pp. 95, 112, 120).

3066. Strauss, William, and Neil Howe. *Generations: The History of America's Future.* New York: William Morrow, p. 273. Mentions W briefly.

3067. Streitfeld, David. "Wright Unexpurgated." *The Washington Post Book World* (18 August), p. 15. In an interview Arnold Rampersad explains deletion of sexual material from *NS* and political material from *BB* by the Book-of-the-Month Club.

3068. Strout, Cushing. "To the Editor." *The Journal of American History*, 78 (September), 763–764. Mentions W briefly.

3069. Sullivan, Ronald. "Court Relaxes Curb on Biographers Use of Unpublished Data." *The New York Times* (28 November), p. 13. Reports the Federal Appeals Court's decision in favor of Margaret Walker on the use of unpublished W material.

3070. Sundquist, Eric J. "Red, White, Black and Blue: The Color of American Modernism." *Transition*, 70, p. 99. Notes that Langston Hughes introduced W to Ralph Ellison.

3071. Suzuki, Mikio. "Margaret Walker's 'Richard Wright: Daemonic Genius.'" *Waseda University General Studies*, 90 (31 March), 195–198. Favorable review of Walker's biography comparing it to those by Webb, Fabre, and Gayle [T.K., R.B., and Y.K.].

3072. Sweeney, Vince. "The Power of Literature." *Research*, 11 (March), 19–21. Notes that *BB* is one of the few books by minority authors taught in high schools.

3073. Taylor, Henry. "Gwendolyn Brooks: An Essential Sanity." *The Kenyon Review*, 13 (Fall), 115–131. Comments on W's evaluation of the manuscript of *A Street in Bronzeville* (p. 119).

3074. Thelen, David. "Becoming Martin Luther King, Jr.: An Introduction." *The Journal of American History*, 78 (June), pp. 11–22. Mentions W briefly (p. 22).

3075. _____. "Conversation Between S. Paul Schilling and David Thelen." *The Journal of American History*, 78 (June), 63–80. Mentions W briefly (p. 66).

3076. Thomas, Brook. *The New Historicism and Other Old-Fashioned Topics.* Princeton, NJ: Princeton University Press, p. 14. Mentions W briefly.

3077. Thomas, H. Nigel. "Alice Walker's Grange Copeland as a Trickster Figure." *Obsidian II*, 6 (Spring), 60–72. Notes W's rejection of the trickster figure (p. 62) and briefly compares Walker's character and Bigger Thomas (p. 63).

3078. Trzyna, Thomas, and Martin Abbott. "Grieving in the Ethnic Literature Classroom." *College Literature*, 18 (October), 1–14. Mentions briefly *BB* (p. 3).

3079. Van Leer, David. "James Baldwin," in *African American Writers.* Ed. Valerie Smith. New York: Scribner's, pp. 1–14. Includes discussion of Baldwin's relation to W (pp. 2–3, 4, 7).

3080. _____. "Society and Identity," in *The Columbia History of the American Novel.* Ed. Emory Elliott. New York: Columbia University Press, pp. 485–509. Mentions W briefly (pp. 489, 496, 497).

3081. Wagner-Martin, Linda. "James Barbour and Tom Quirk, eds. *Writing the American Classics.*" *Modern Fiction Studies*, 37 (Summer), 253. Review mentioning Kinnamon's essay on *NS*.

3082. Walker, Alice. "The Black Writer and the Southern Experience," in *A Writer's Reader.* Eds. Donald Hall and D.L. Emblem. Sixth edition. New York: HarperCollins. Reprint of 1983.

3083. _____. "In Search of Our Mothers' Gardens," in *Dictionary of Literary Biography: Documentary Series: An Illustrated Chronicle.* Vol. 8. *The Black Aesthetic Movement.* Ed. Jeffrey Louis Decker. Detroit: Gale, pp. 330–335. Reprint of 1974.

3084. Walker, Dan. "Teaching Critical Concepts with Our Own Writing." *English Journal*, 80 (November), 77–82. Uses "The Man Who Saw the Flood" in a writing exercise.

3085. Wall, Cheryl A. "Zora Neale Hurston," in *African American Writers.* Ed. Valerie Smith. New York: Scribner's, pp. 205–218. The bibliography lists W's review of *Their Eyes Were Watching God.*

3086. Ward, Jerry W., Jr. "Sterling D. Plumpp: A Son of the Blues." *The Southern Quarterly*, 29 (Summer), 5–36. Includes correspondence and interviews with Plumpp, who mentions W several times: "Wright was the author of existentialism for me" (p. 19). Plumpp acknowledges W's profound influence on him.

3087. _____. "Wright's Explicit Prose Restored." *The Richard Wright Newsletter*, 1 (Fall), 2. Discusses the Library of America edition of W.

3088. Ward, Nathan. "The Time Machine." *American Heritage*, 42 (May/June), pp. 38, 40–43. Mentions briefly the play *NS*.

3089. Washington, Mary Helen. "Acknowledgments," in her *Memory of Kin: Stories About Family by Black Writers* (New York: Doubleday), pp. vii–viii. Mentions briefly "Big Boy Leaves Home."

3090. Weissinger, Thomas. "Current Bibliography." *Black American Literature Forum*, 25 (Winter), 795–814. Lists books on W by Michel Fabre, Keneth Kinnamon, Eugene E. Miller, and Margaret Walker, as well as the second edition of Paul Oliver's *Blues Fell This Morning* with W's foreword.

3091. Werner, Craig. "Fabre, Michel. *Richard Wright: books & writers.*" *Choice*, 28 (May), 1484. Favorable notice of "an indispensable tool for any student of Wright or the intellectual contexts of black writing."

3092. _____. "The Framing of Charles W. Chesnutt: Practical Deconstruction in the Afro-American Tradition." *The University of Mississippi Studies in English*, New Series, 9, pp. 1–25. Mentions W briefly (p. 3). Reprinted 1994.

3093. _____. "*The Signifying Monkey: A Theory of Afro-American Literary Criticism.* By Henry Louis Gates, Jr." *Journal of English and Germanic Philology*, 90 (April), 267–269. Review mentioning W and *NS*.

3094. West, Cornel. "Nihilism in Black America." *Dissent*, 38 (Spring), 221–226. Quotes from *TMBV* as an epigraph. Reprinted: 1993, 1994.

3095. West, Hollie I. "The Black Bard of Revolution," in *Dictionary of Literary Biography: Documentary Series: An Illustrated Chronicle.* Vol. 8: *The Black Aesthetic Movement.* Ed. Jeffrey Louis Decker. Detroit: Gale, pp. 207–208. Reprint of 1971.

3096. Whitlock, Elizabeth. "Introduction," in *Mississippi Writers: An Anthology.* Ed. Dorothy Abbott. Johnson: University Press of Mississippi, pp. xv–xxvi. Comments briefly on W and *BB* (pp. xv, xviii).

3097. Whyte, Malcom Arthur. "James Baldwin–Two Views: A Review Essay." *The Black Scholar*, 21 (Summer 1990-Summer 1991), 43–45. Mentions Baldwin's quarrel with W as presented by W.J. Weatherby (p. 44).

3098. Wilentz, Gay. "Affirming Critical Difference: Reading Black Women's Texts." *The Kenyon Review*, 13 (Summer), 146–151. Mentions briefly *BB* (p. 148).

3099. Wiley, Ralph. "The Dark Side of Mencken," in his *Why Black People Tend to Shout: Cold Facts and Wry Views from a Black Man's World.* New York: Carol Lane, pp. 21–30. Compares W and Jack London for their visceral emotional power, but faults W for "apologizing for being a writer" by listing in *BB* works and authors he had read.

3100. _____. "What to See in the South," in his *Why Black People Tend to Shout: Cold Facts and Wry Views From a Black Man's World.* New York: Carol Lane, pp. 121–126. Mentions W briefly (p. 125).

3101. Williams, Sherley Anne. "Introduction," in *Their Eyes Were Watching God.* By Zora Neale Hurston. Urbana: University of Illinois Press, pp. xiii–xxix. Mentions briefly W and *NS* (pp.xv, xxi).

3102. Williams, Wilburn. "Melvin Tolson," in *African American Writers.* Ed. Valerie Smith. New York: Scribner's, pp. 413–427. Mentions briefly (p. 413) and quotes him on Tolson (p. 420).

3103. Wilson, Charles Reagan. "Expatriates and Exiles," in *The Reader's Companion to American History.* Eds. Eric Foner and John A. Garraty. Boston: Houghton Mifflin, pp. 369–372. Mentions W briefly.

3104. Wilson, Robert. "Treats for Lovers of Language and Literature." *USA Today* (9 December), p. 4D. Includes a notice of the Library of America edition of W emphasizing editorial intervention in the works as first published.

3105. Winchell, Mark Royden. *Neoconservative Criticism: Norman Podhoretz, Kenneth S. Lynn, and Joseph Epstein.* Boston: Twayne, p. 135. Notes Mencken's appeal to W.

3106. Winslow, Art. "Our Holiday List." *The Nation*, 253 (30 December), 863–864. Mentions the Library of America edition.

3107. Wright, Julia. "Letter from Julia Wright." *The Richard Wright Newsletter*, 1 (Spring), 1. Excerpt from a letter endorsing the formation of the Richard Wright Circle and urging it to expand its activities outside the academy.

3108. _____. "Richard Wright." *The London Times Literary Supplement*, No. 4586 (22 February), p. 13. Responds to James Campbell's essay "Black Boys and the FBI" defending her competence as an interviewer and expressing skepticism about the notion that W acted as an informer on former communists.

3109. Yin, Xiad-Huang Yin. "Progress and Problems: American Literary Studies in China During the Post-Mao Era," in *As Others Read Us: International Perspectives on American Literature*. Ed. Huck Gutman. Amherst: The University of Massachusetts Press, pp. 49–64. Notes that *NS* is available in a Chinese edition despite W's criticism of communism (p. 59).

3110. Young, Al. "Interview: Ishmael Reed," in *Dictionary of Literary Biography: Documentary Series: An Illustrated Chronicle*. Vol. 8. *The Black Aesthetic Movement*. Ed. Jeff-

rey Louis Decker. Detroit: Gale, pp. 301–308. Reprint of 1972.

3111. Youngs, Tim. "Dickson D. Bruce, Jr., *Black American Writing from the Nadir: The Evolution of a Literary Tradition, 1877–1915*; Robert Bone, *Down Home: Origins of the Afro-American Short Story*; Henry Louis Gates, Jr., *The Signifying Monkey: A Theory of Afro-American Literary Criticism*; Ronda Glikin, "*Black Americans* [sic] *Women in Literature: A Bibliography, 1976 through 1987*." *Journal of American Studies*, 25 (April), 142–143. Review mentioning W briefly.

1992

3112. Abe, Daisei. "On Bigger Thomas: Richard Wright and Racial Prejudices." *Journal of Gifu College for Economics*," 26 (April), 59–85. Survey of Bigger's characterization on the basis of "How 'Bigger's characterization on the basis of "How 'Bigger' Was Born" and *NS* [T.K., R.B., and Y.H.].

3113. Abramson, Doris. "Introduction," in *Deep Are the Roots: Memoirs of a Black Expatriate*. By Gordon Heath. Amherst: The University of Massachusetts Press, pp. 3–8. Mentions W briefly (p. 3).

3114. Abubakar, Tanimu. "Social Mobility and the Novel: A Comparative Analysis of Iyayi's *Violence* and Wright's *Black Boy*." *Nigerian Journal of American Studies*, 2, pp. 89–101. Although W's autobiography and Iyayi's novel are separated by many decades, they are linked by "the mediating role of consciousness," their concern for the relationship between individuals and groups, and impoverishment as a mode of oppression.

3115. Adamczyk, Alice, ed. *The Kaiser Index to Black Resources, 1948–1986*. Volume 5. Brooklyn: Carlson, pp. 404–406. Lists 188 items from the Schomburg Center.

3116. Ahmad, Aijaz. *In Theory: Classes, Nations, Literatures*. London: Verso, pp. 87, 110, 111. Comments on W's sympathetic attitude

toward the Third World and mentions briefly *NS*.

3117. Algeo, Ann M. "The Courtroom as Forum: Homicide Trials by Dreiser, Wright, Capote, and Mailer." *Dissertation Abstracts International*, 53 (November), 1516-A. Finds that the trial scenes in *NS* and three other novels are "effective because they are faithful to both the realities of the courtroom forum and the thematic possibilities of the literary form."

3118. Als, Hilton. "Word!" *The Nation*, 254 (18 May), 667–670. Review of Darryl Pinckney's *High Cotton* mentioning briefly W, *NS*, *BB*, and *EM*.

3119. Andreas, James R. "Othello's African American Progeny." *South Atlantic Review*, 57 (November), 39–58. Compares the uses of *Othello* by W in *NS*, Ellison in *Invisible Man*, and Baraka in *Dutchman*. "Wright restages and reinterprets the problematic relationship of Othello and Desdemona; Ellison represents it comically; and Baraka reverses or inverts it" (p. 39). Andreas also compares Emilia of the play and Mrs. Dalton.

3120. Andrews, William L. "The Slave Narrative Tradition in African American Literature and Culture." *African American Review*, 26 (Fall), 506. Announcement of a National Endowment for the Humanities

Summer Seminar mentioning briefly *BB*.

3121. Anon. "*ABBWA Journal's* New and Current Releases." *ABBWA Journal*, 4 (Winter/Spring), 20–28. Contains annotated entries for the Library of America edition of W and for Michel Fabre's *Richard Wright: Books and Writers* (pp. 27–28).

3122. Anon. "African Americans and Europe: Paris, France." *The Richard Wright Newsletter*, 2 (Fall), 6. Includes favorable comments on the W sessions at the Paris conference.

3123. Anon. "Announcements." *The Richard Wright Newsletter*, 2 (Fall), 7–8. Announces a session on W at MLA and proposed sessions at CLA and ALA. Includes also a notice of Michel Fabre's *Richard Wright: Books and Writers*.

3124. Anon. "At Last. Unexpurgated. Authoritative. Wright." *ABBWA Journal*, 4 (Winter/Spring), 18. Advertisement for the Library of American edition of W.

3125. Anon. "Banned Books Week Celebrates Our 'Freedom to Read.'" *American Civil Liberties Union of Arkansas Newsletter* (Fall), p. 4. Mentions W briefly.

3126. Anon. *Bibliographic Guide to Black Studies: 1991*. Boston: G.K. Hall, pp. 536–537. Lists twenty-one secondary items concerning W in the New York Public Library, supplementing the *Dictionary Catalog of the Schomburg Collection of Negro Literature and History*.

3127. Anon. "A Bibliography of Works by Darwin T. Turner." *The Langston Hughes Review*, 11 (Fall), 40–47. Lists several items by Turner with W in the title.

3128. Anon. "*Black Boy*," in *The Encyclopedia Americana*. Ed. Lawrence T. Lorimer. Danbury, CT: Grolier, vol. 4. pp. 29–30.

3129. Anon. "Book Notes." *The Journal of Southern History*, 58 (May), 399–401. Contains a review of Suzanne W. Jones's *Growing Up in the South: An Anthology of Modern Southern Literature* mentioning W briefly.

3130. Anon. "Books Received, 1991." *College Literature*, 19 (February), 165–187. Annotated list including Joyce A. Joyce's *Richard Wright's Art of Tragedy* (p. 176).

3131. Anon. "Brief Mention." *American Literature*, 64 (March), 203–212. Includes a brief notice of *Politics in the African-American Novel: James Weldon Johnson, W.E.B. Du Bois, Richard Wright, and Ralph Ellison* by Richard Kostelanetz.

3132. Anon. "France." *American Studies International Newsletter*, Summer, p. 1. Mentions W briefly in a report on the Paris conference on "African Americans and Europe."

3133. Anon. *Index to Black Periodicals: 1991*. Boston: G.K. Hall, p. 271. Lists five items on W.

3134. Anon. "Literature Unit Plans." *English Journal*, 81 (January), inside front cover.

3135. Anon. "Literature Unit Plans." *English Journal*, 81 (February), 14.

3136. Anon. "Literature Unit Plans." *English Journal*, 81 (March), 105.

3137. Anon. "Literature Unit Plans." *English Journal*, 81 (April), 6.

3138. Anon. "Literature Unit Plans." *English Journal*, 81 (October), 1.

3139. Anon. "Memorable Faces from Wisconsin." *The Black Scholar*, 22 (Fall), 47. Advertisement mentioning W briefly.

3140. Anon. "Milestones." *Time*, 139 (24 February), 68. Contains an obituary of Alex Haley mentioning briefly *NS*.

3141. Anon. "*Native Son*," in *October Films*. New York: October Films, p. 18. Description of the 1987 film in a "1993 non-theatrical film catalog."

3142. Anon. "New From Greenwood Press." *The Black Scholar*, 22 (September), 60. Lists Jean-François Gounard's *The Racial Problem in the Works of Richard Wright and James Baldwin*.

3143. Anon. "Publications Relating to Mississippi." *The Journal of Mississippi History*, 54 (February), 125–127. Lists an article on W by Jay Melching.

3144. Anon. *The Radical Novel in the United States, 1900–1954*; in *Columbia Fall 1992 Catalog*. New York: Columbia University Press, 1992, p. 28. Publisher's notice mentioning briefly W and *NS*.

3145. Anon. "Recent & Relevant." *American Visions*, 7 (April/May), 35. Contains a notice of Michel Fabre's *From Harlem to Paris* mentioning W briefly.

3146. Anon. "Repères bibliographiques: Traductions françaises de romans et nouvelles écrits par des auteurs noirs américain (1930–1984)." *Focus*, pp. [20–21].

3147. Anon. "Richard Wright and His Contemporaries," in *SSSL Program: April 23–25, 1992*. New Orleans: Society for the Study of Southern Literature, p. 3. Lists a session chaired by Blyden Jackson with papers by Harry L. Faggett, Maria Frias, and Trudier Harris.

3148. Anon. "Special Sessions." *MLA Newsletter*, 24 (Winter), 9–10. Includes notice of a proposed convention session using W and Zora Neale Hurston as an example of "companionable or oppositional styles."

3149. Anon. "A Suggested Reading List of Works by African American Authors." *The Council Chronicle*, 1 (February), 7. Includes *BB*.

3150. Anon. "Texas Schools to Receive Collections of American Literature." *This Is Just to Say: NCTE Assembly on American Literature*, 3 (May), [4]. Reports a grant to place sixty-volume sets of The Library of America, including W, in Texas high schools.

3151. Anon. "Unexpurgated, Authoritative New Texts." *PMLA*, 107 (January), 196. Full-page publisher's notice of the Library of America edition of W.

3152. Anon. "*The Unfinished Quest of Richard Wright*." *CLA Journal*, 36 (December), following p. 244. Publisher's notice of the second edition of Fabre's biography. Includes a photograph of W.

3153. Anon. "University of Illinois Press." *The Black Scholar*, 22 (Summer), 66. Contains a notice of the second edition of Michel Fabre's *The Unfinished Quest of Richard Wright* with a blurb by Chester Himes.

3154. Anon. Untitled blurb in *Writers on the Left: Episodes in American Literary Communism*. New York: Columbia University Press, back cover. Mentions W briefly.

3155. Anon. "Writers on the Left," in *Columbia Fall 1992 Catalog*. New York: Columbia University Press, p. 28. Publisher's notice mentioning W briefly.

3156. Asante, Molefi Kete. "Locating a Text: Implications of Afrocentric Theory," in *Language and Literature in the African American Imagination*. Ed. Carol Blackshire-Belay. Westport, CT: Greenwood Press, pp. 9–20. Mentions W briefly (pp. 13, 14).

3157. _____, and Mark T. Mattson. *The Historical and Cultural Atlas of African Americans*. New York: Macmillan, pp. 107, 114, 146. Paperbound reprint of 1991

3158. Awkward, Michael. "Afro-American Literary Studies and the Politics of Identity." *Voices of the African Diaspora*, 8 (Spring), 3–8. Mentions briefly W and *BB* (p. 8).

3159. _____. "The Politics of Positionality: A Reply to Kenneth Warren." *American Literary History*, 4 (Spring), 104–109. Mentions W briefly (p. 106).

3160. Bacigalupo, Massimo. "Foreign Scholarship: Italian Contributions," in *American Literary Scholarship: An Annual 1990*. Ed. Louis Owens. Durham, NC: Duke University Press, pp. 436–457. Mentions W briefly (p. 439).

3161. Baker, Richard Eugene. "The Dynamics of the Absurd in the Existentialist Novel." *Dissertation Abstracts International*, 53 (August), 488-A–489-A. Includes consideration of *NS*.

3162. Baker, William. "Recent Work in Critical Theory." *Style*, 26 (Winter), 640–677. Includes brief comment on Richard Kostelanetz's *Politics in the African-American Novel: James Weldon Johnson, W.E.B.*

Du Bois, Richard Wright, and Ralph Ellison.

3163. Bakish, David. "Wright, Richard," in *Encyclopedia of World Literature in the 20th Century*. Revised edition. Ed. Leonard S. Klein. Vol. 4. New York: Continuum, pp. 664–666. Biographical-critical sketch with a brief bibliography.

3164. Baldwin, James. "The Harlem Ghetto," in *Speech and Power: The African-American Essay and Its Cultural Content from Polemics to Pulpit*. Vol. I. Ed. Gerald Early. Hopewell, NJ: The Ecco Press, pp. 100–108.

3165. Banks, Thomas. "*Mumbo Jumbo*," in *Masterpieces of African-American Literature*. Ed. Frank N. Magill. New York: HarperCollins, pp. 313–317. Mentions W briefly (p. 316).

3166. Baraka, Amiri. "The Myth of a 'Negro Literature,'" in *The New Cavalcade: African American Writing from 1760 to the Present*. Vol. II. Eds. Arthur P. Davis, J. Saunders Redding, and Joyce Ann Joyce. Washington: Howard University Press, pp. 447–454.

3167. Barksdale, Richard. "Black America and the Mask of Comedy," in *Praisesong of Survival: Lectures and Essays, 1957–89*. Urbana: University of Illinois Press, pp. 85–94.

3168. _____. "Black Autobiography and the Comic Vision," in his *Praisesong of Survival: Lectures and Essays, 1957–89*. Urbana: University of Illinois Press, pp. 95–107.

3169. _____. "Critical Theory and Problems of Canonicity in African American Literature," in his *Praisesong of Survival: Lectures and Essays, 1957–89*. Urbana: University of Illinois Press, pp. 32–38. Mentions W briefly (p. 34).

3170. _____. "Ethical Invisibility and the New Humanism," in his *Praisesong of Survival: Lectures and Essays, 1957–89*. Urbana: University of Illinois Press, pp. 48–53. Comments on *O* and W's existentialism mentioning also *BB*, Bigger Thomas, and *UTC*.

3171. _____. "Hughes's Poetry of the 1930s: A New Song for an Old Hurt," in his *Praisesong of Survival: Lectures and Essays, 1957–89*. Urbana: University of Illinois Press, pp. 202–228.

3172. _____. "Hughes: Blues, Jazz, and Low-down Folks," in his *Praisesong of Survival: Lectures and*

Essays, 1957–89. Urbana: University of Illinois Press, pp. 183–201.

3173. _____. "The Humanities: The Eye of the Needle in the Black Experience," in his *Praisesong of Survival: Lectures and Essays, 1957–89*. Urbana: University of Illinois Press, pp. 54–60. Mentions W briefly (p. 54).

3174. _____. "Langston Hughes and James Baldwin: Some Observations on a Literary Relationship," in his *Praisesong of Survival: Lectures and Essays, 1957–89*. Urbana: University of Illinois Press, pp. 239–244. Discusses W as Baldwin's father surrogate (pp. 240–241).

3175. _____. "Margaret Walker: Folk Orature and Historical Prophecy," in his *Praisesong of Survival: Lectures and Essays, 1957–89*. Urbana: University of Illinois Press, pp. 134–147.

3176. Barrett, Lindon. "*The Street*," in *Masterpieces of African-American Literature*. Ed. Frank N. Magill. New York: HarperCollins, pp. 546–549. Compares and contrasts *The Street* and W's fiction (p. 549).

3177. Bawer, Bruce. "All That Jazz." *The New Criterion*, 10 (May), 10–17. Mentions W briefly (p. 13).

3178. Baym, Nina. "Creating a National Literature," in *Making America: The Society and Culture of the United States*. Ed. Luther S. Luedtke. Chapel Hill: The University of North Carolina Press, pp. 219–235. Contains a paragraph on *NS* and the question of national identity (p. 233).

3179. Beauvoir, Simone de. *Letters to Sartre*. Trans. and ed. Quintin Hare. New York: Arcade, pp. 417, 419, 420–421, 423, 425, 426, 430, 433, 455, 456. In letters written from January to May 1947, de Beauvoir relates fondly many pleasant meetings with W and his family.

3180. Beavers, Herman. "Dead Rocks and Sleeping Men: Aurality in the Aesthetic of Langston Hughes." *The Langston Hughes Review*, 11 (Spring), 5. Mentions briefly in an endnote "Richard Wrights Blues."

3181. Becknell, Thomas. "*Black Boy: A Record of Childhood and Youth*," in *Masterpieces of African-American Literature*. Ed. Frank N. Magill. New York: HarperCollins, pp. 53–56. Summarizes the work, analyzes its language and theme,

and places it in the context of the American literary tradition. Contrasts *BB* to *The Autobiography of Benjamin Franklin*.

3182. Beilenson, John, and Heidi Jackson, comps. *Voices of Struggle, Voices of Pride*. White Plains, NY: Peter Pauper Press, p. 27. Includes a quotation from *NS*.

3183. Bell, Bernard W. "The Contemporary Afro-American Novel, 1: Neorealism," in *A Turbulent Voyage: Readings in African American Studies*. Ed. Floyd W. Hayas III. San Diego: Collegiate Press, pp. 330–361.

3184. _____. "The Image of Africa in the Afro-American Novel," in *The New Cavalcade: African American Writing from 1760 to the Present*. Vol. II. Eds. Arthur P. Davis, J. Saunders Redding, and Joyce Ann Joyce. Washington: Howard University Press, pp. 591–606.

3185. Bendixen, Alfred. "Notes of a Native Son," in *Masterpieces of African-American Literature*. Ed. Frank N. Magill. New York: HarperCollins, pp. 329–332. Discusses Baldwin's essays about W (pp. 329, 330–331).

3186. Benoist, Mary Ann. "Bibliography: African American Studies: Literature." *Society for the Study of Southern Literature Newsletter*, 25 (April), 15. Lists Robert Butler's *Native Son: The Emergence of a New Black Hero* and Jean-François's *the Racial Problem in The Works of Richard Wright and James Baldwin*.

3187. _____. "African American Studies: Literature." *Society for the Study of Southern Literature Newsletter*, 25 (November), 12. Lists editions of *NS*, *BB*, and *UTC*.

3188. Berland, Alwyn. *Light in August: A Study in Black and White*. New York: Twayne, p. 9. Mentions W briefly.

3189. Berry, Faith. "Introduction," in her *A Scholar's Conscience: Selected Writings of J. Saunders Redding*. Lexington: The University Press of Kentucky, p. 4. Quotes from W's favorable introduction to Redding's *No Day of Triumph*.

3190. _____. "The American Writers' Congress," in her *Good Morning Revolution: Uncollected Writings of Social Protest by Langston Hughes*. New York: Carol Publishing Group, pp. 135–138. Mentions W briefly.

3191. Bess, R. "Butler, Robert.

Native Son: The Emergence of a New Black Hero." *Choice*, 20 (April), 1222. Favorable review: "highly recommended for all levels of academic libraries."

3192. Bigsby, C.W.E. *Modern American Drama, 1945–1990.* Cambridge: Cambridge University Press, pp. 272. Mentions briefly W's potent metaphor of the laboratory dogs in *AH* and the image of the cornered rat in *NS*.

3193. Birkerts, Sven. "The Art of Memory." *The New Republic*, 207 (13 and 20 July), 42–44, 48–49. Essay on John Edgar Wideman mentioning W briefly (p. 49).

3194. Blackshire-Belay, Carol Aisha. "Afrocentricity and Literary Theory: The Maturing Imagination," in her *Language and Literature in the African American Imagination.* Westport, CT: Greenwood Press, pp. 3–7. Mentions W briefly.

3195. Bloom, James D. *Left Letters: the Culture Wars of Mike Gold and Joseph Freeman.* New York: Columbia University Press, p. 37. Mentions briefly *BB*.

3196. Bloom, Lynn Z. "*Telling Lies in Modern American Autobiography.* By Timothy Dow Adams." *American Literature*, 64 (December), 852–853. Includes a brief summary of Adams's treatment of *BB*.

3197. Bonetti, Kay. "An Interview with Margaret Walker Alexander." *The Missouri Review*, 15, No. 1, 111–131. Walker acknowledges W's influence on her work, comments on their friendship, denies that they were lovers, claims that he was bisexual, notes Hurston's influence on him and his influence on subsequent writers, and discusses the law suit between herself and Ellen Wright.

3198. Bowen, Peter. "*The Nature and Context of Minority Discourse.* Eds. Abdul R. JanMohamed and David Lloyd." *American Literature*, 64 (March), 189–190. Mentions briefly JanMohamed's essay on W.

3199. Boyd, Melba Joyce. "Holding a Torch for the Black Statue of Liberty." *The Black Scholar*, 22 (Fall), 52–55. Report on the 1992 International Conference on African Americans and Europe mentioning events relating to W.

3200. _____. "Holding a Torch for the black Statue of Liberty." *The Black Scholar*, 22 (Fall), pp. 52–55. Reports on the international confer-

ence in Paris on African Americans and Europe, including comment of the place of W as the central figure.

3201. Bracy, William. "Wright, Richard Nathaniel," in *The Encyclopedia Americana*. Ed. Lawrence T. Lorimer. Danbury, CT: Grolier, pp. 555–556.

3202. Bradley, David. Untitled excerpt, in *Black Literature Criticism*. Ed. James P. Draper. Vol. 3. Detroit: Gale, pp. 2018–2020. Partial reprint of 1986.

3203. _____. "Novelist Alice Walker: Telling the Black Woman's Story," in *Speech and Power: The African-American Essay and Its Cultural Content from Polemics to Pulpit*. Vol. I. Ed. Gerald Early. Hopewell, NJ: The Ecco Press, pp. 325–337.

3204. Bremer, Sidney H. *Urban Intersections: Meetings of Life and Literature in United States Cities*. Urbana: University of Illinois Press, pp. xiv, 179, 186, 190. Mentions briefly *NS*, W, and "Long Black Song."

3205. Brooks, Roy L. *Rethinking the American Race Problem*. Berkeley: University of California Press, p. 146.

3206. Brown, Cecil. "Richard Wright's Complexes and Black Writing Today," in *Speech and Power: The African-American Essay and Its Cultural Content from Polemics to Pulpit*. Vol. I. Ed. Gerald Early. Hopewell, NJ: The Ecco Press, pp. 298–307.

3207. Brown, Dennis. *Shoptalk: Conversations About Theater and Film with Twelve Writers, One Producer, and Tennessee Williams' Mother*. New York: Newmarket Press, p. 211. Mentions W briefly.

3208. Brucker, Carl. "*The Outsider*," in *Masterpieces of African-American Literature*. Ed. Frank N. Magill. New York: HarperCollins, pp. 337–340. Describes the principal characters, summarizes the plot, analyzes the novel's ideology, identifies the central theme as the quest for freedom, and comments on reviews of *O* and its relation to W's previous works.

3209. Buhle, Paul. "Daily Worker (and Successors)," in *Encyclopedia of the American Left*. Eds. Mari Jo Buhle, Paul Buhle, and Dan Georgakas. Urbana: University of Illinois Press, pp. 178–182. Reprint of 1990

3210. Burns, Landon C., and Elizabeth Buckmaster. "The Eigh-

teenth (1991) Supplement to a Cross-Referenced Index of Short Fiction Anthologies and Author Title Listings." *Studies in Short Fiction*, 29 (Spring), 237–298. Lists the appearances of "Big Boy Leaves Home" in Abbott and Koppelman, *The Signet Classic Book of Short Stories* and of "The Man Who Was Almost a Man" in Barnet's *The Harper Anthology of Fiction* and in Jones's *Growing Up in the South: An Anthology of Modern Southern Literature*.

3211. Burroway, Janet. *Writing Fiction: A Guide to Narrative Craft*. Third edition. New York: HarperCollins, p. 216. Quotes from "Big Boy Leaves Home" and comments on W's use of voice.

3212. Butler, Robert James. "Answering the Call." *African American Review*, 26 (Winter), 683–685. Review of John F. Callahan's *In the African-American Grain* mentioning briefly *NS* (p. 685).

3213. _____. "Finding the Right Texts: The Library of America's New Editions of Richard Wright's Major Works." *PMLA*, 107 (November), 1427. Announces a conference session with Butler presiding and papers by Jerry Ward, Jr., Keneth Kinnamon, and Yoshinobu Hakutani.

3214. Byrd, Rudolph P. "Shared Orientation and Narrative Acts in *Cane, Their Eyes Were Watching God*, and *Meridian*." *MELUS*, 17 (Winter), 41–56. Mentions briefly "Blueprint for Negro Writing" (p. 44).

3215. Camp, Carolyn. "The Rhetoric of Catalogues in Richard Wright's *Black Boy*." *MELUS*, 17 (Winter), 29–39. Analysis of four catalogues in *BB* in relation to the work's theme and structure. Conveying W's idealism as well as the terror of life in the South, they make possible a more hopeful reading of the work than is afforded by emphasizing its social aspects.

3216. Campbell, James. "Alexander Trocchi: The Biggest Fiend of All." *The Antioch Review*, 50 (Summer), 458–471. Mentions W briefly (p. 461).

3217. Cary, Lorene. "Summer Reading." *American Visions*, 7 (June/July), 33. Hopes to reread W in the Library of American edition.

3218. Champion, Ernest A. "*Critical Essays on James Baldwin.* Fred L. Standley and Nancy V. Burt."

MELUS, 17 (Winter), 131–138. Mentions Baldwin's feud with W (pp. 132, 137).

3219. [Chant, Elizabeth M., ed.]. "Conference Sessions & Panels/Ateliers & Tables-Rondes," in her *African Americans and Europe*. Cambridge, MA: W.E.B. Du Bois Institute for Afro-American Research, Harvard University, pp. 21, 23, 25, 27–29, 32–33, 35, 37, 39, 41, 43, 45, 47–49, 51. Lists sessions on W chaired by Hanna M. Bercovitch (with papers by Robert Bone, Yoshinobu Hakutani, and Eugene Miller), Edward Margolies (with papers by Virginia Whatley Smith, Alexi Zverev, and John Lowe), Jack Moore (with papers by Eugenio Suarez-Galban, Lynn Weiss, and Amritjit Singh), Keneth Kinnamon (with papers by Bruce Dick, Paul Oliver, and Maryemma Graham), and a paper by Wallace Bullock in another session.

3220. [Chant, Elizabeth M., ed.]. "Programme Overview," in her *African Americans and Europe*. Cambridge, MA: W.E.B. Du Bois Institute for Afro-American Research, Harvard University, pp. 7, 9, 11, 13, 15. Lists Levi Frazier's "A Black Boy: Tribute to Richard Wright," and the homage to W at 14, rue Monsieur-le-Prince.

3221. Chauhan, P.S. "Afro-American 'Exiles' and the French Connection." *Callaloo*, 15 (Fall), 1087–1089. Review of Michel Fabre's *From Harlem to Paris* mentioning W briefly.

3222. Clark, Keith. "A Distaff Dream Deferred? Ann Petry and the Art of Subversion." *African American Review*, 26 (Fall), 495–505. Comments on Petry's relation to the Wrightian tradition of the protest novel and compares Link of *The Narrows* to Bigger Thomas (p. 495). Also quotes W. Lawrence Hogue on *NS* (p. 502) and the privileging of W's angry protest over the different modes of Petry and Hurston by Robert Bone and others (p. 504).

3223. Clay, William L. *Just Permanent Interests: Black Americans in Congress, 1870–1991*. New York: Amistad, p. 351. Mentions briefly W and *NS*.

3224. Cobb, James C. *The Most Southern Place on Earth: The Mississippi Delta and the Roots of Regional Identity*. New York: Oxford University Press, pp. 120, 123, 164, 240, 295–296, 311, 315. Quotes from *BB*, "The Ethics of Living Jim Crow," and "Long Black Song." Refers to "Down by the Riverside." Quotes Ellison on *BB*.

3225. Cockrell, Thomas D. "Green, Paul Eliot," in *Encyclopedia of African-American Civil Rights: From Emancipation to the Present*. Eds. Charles D. Lowery and John F. Marszalek. Westport, CT: Greenwood, p. 223. Mentions briefly Green's collaboration with W on the play *NS*.

3226. Collins, Patricia Hill. "Learning to Think for Ourselves: Malcolm X's Black Nationalism Reconsidered," in *Malcolm X: In Our Own Image*. Ed. Joe Wood. New York: St. Martin's Press, pp. 59–85. Mentions W briefly (p. 69).

3227. Conoley, Gillian. "Susan Howe and Sam Cornish: Two Poetries, Two Histories." *The Kenyon Review*, 14 (Spring), 176–183. In the review of Cornish's *1935: A Memoir*, Conoley quotes from a passage describing W's first arrival in Chicago (p. 177) and mentions W elsewhere (p. 179).

3228. Costanzo, Angelo. "*The Interesting Narrative of the Life of Olaudah Equiano, or Gustavus Vassa, the African*," in *Masterpieces of African-American Literature*. Ed. Frank N. Magill. New York: HarperCollins, pp. 230–232. Mentions briefly *BB* (p. 232).

3229. Costilow, Cecil. "*Lawd Today*," in *Masterpieces of African-American Literature*. Ed. Frank N. Magill. New York: HarperCollins, pp. 253–256. Describes the principal characters, summarizes the plot, analyzes Jake Jackson, and praises the work's use of the language of the ghetto and its compact structure.

3230. Crews, Frederick. "Faulkner Methodized," in his *The Critics Bear It Away: American Fiction and the Academy*. New York: Random House, pp. 113–142.

3231. Crosland, Margaret. *Simone de Beauvoir: The Woman and Her Work*. London: Heinemann, pp. 341, 345, 346, 347–348, 357. Comments on de Beauvoir's friendship with W and his family, especially during her trip to New York in 1947.

3232. Cupp, Jeff. "The Stories of Langston Hughes," in *Masterpieces of African-American Literature*. Ed. Frank N. Magill. New York: HarperCollins, pp. 539–542. Asserts that Hughes's story "Father and Son" foreshadows *UTC* (p. 540).

3233. Dance, Daryl. "'He's Long Gone': The Theme of Escape in Black Folklore and Literature," in *The New Cavalcade: African American Writing from 1760 to the Present*. Vol. II. Eds. Arthur P. Davis, J. Saunders Redding, and Joyce A. Joyce. Washington: Howard University Press, pp. 546–553.

3234. David, Jay. "Richard Wright (1909 [sic]–1960): From *Black Boy*," in his *Growing Up Black*. New York: Avon, p. 10.

3235. Davis, Arthur P., and Joyce A. Joyce. "Addison Gayle, Jr.," in their and J. Saunders Redding's *The New Cavalcade: African American Writing from 1760 to the Present*. Vol. II. Washington: Howard University Press, pp. 569–570. Mentions Gayle's biography of W and his donation of the Richard Wright-Amiri Baraka award under the auspices of *Black World*.

3236. _____. "The African American Literary Revival," in their and J. Saunders Redding's *The New Cavalcade: African American Writing from 1760 to the Present*. Vol. II. Washington: Howard University Press, pp. 455–461. Begins with a prophetic quotation from "The Literature of the Negro in the United States."

3237. _____. "Donald B. Gibson," in their and J. Saunders Redding's *The New Cavalcade: African American Writing from 1760 to the Present*. Vol. II. Washington: Howard University Press, p. 564. Mentions briefly an "essay by Gibson on W."

3238. _____. "George Kent," in their and J. Saunders Redding's *The New Cavalcade: African American Writing from 1760 to the Present*. Vol. II. Washington: Howard University Press, pp. 161–162. Mentions briefly Kent's work on W.

3239. _____. "James Baldwin," in their and J. Saunders Redding's *The New Cavalcade: African American Writing from 1760 to the Present*. Vol. II. Washington: Howard University Press, pp. 10–12. Mentions Baldwin's early support by W and his attack on "the protest fiction associated with Richard Wright."

3240. _____. "John A. Williams," in their and J. Saunders Redding's *The New Cavalcade: African American Writing from 1760 to the Present*.

Vol. II. Washington: Howard University Press, pp. 231–232. Mentions briefly Williams's book on W.

3241. _____. "Joyce Ann Joyce," in their and J. Saunders Redding's *The New Cavalcade: African American Writing from 1760 to the Present.* Vol. II. Washington: Howard University Press, pp. 868–869. Comments on Joyce's *Richard Wright's Art of Tragedy.*

3242. _____. "Robert B. Stepto," in their and J. Saunders Redding's *The New Cavalcade: African American Writing from 1760 to the Present.* Vol. II. Washington: Howard University Press, pp. 737–738. Mentions briefly an article by Stepto on W.

3243. _____. "Robert G. O'Meally," in their and J. Saunders Redding's *The New Cavalcade: African American Writing from 1760 to the Present.* Vol. II. Washington: Howard University Press, pp. 814–815. Mentions briefly a lecture by O'Meally on "The Wright-Ellison Debate."

3244. Davis, Charles. "From Experience to Eloquence: Richard Wright's *Black Boy* as Art," in *The New Cavalcade: African American Writing from 1760 to the Present.* Vol. II. Eds. Arthur P. Davis, J. Saunders Redding, and Joyce Ann Joyce. Washington: Howard University Press, pp. 81–95.

3245. Davis, Frank Marshall. *Livin' the Blues: Memoirs of a Black Journalist and Poet.* Ed. John Edgar Tidwell. Madison: The University of Wisconsin Press, pp. 239, 240, 242–243, 364. Davis discusses his friendship with W beginning in 1936 and ending in 1945, commenting on the South Side Writers Club, the galley proof of *NS,* photography, and W's relation to the Communist Party. Of W's personality, Davis states: "He was an extrovert, warm and outgoing with an often ribald sense of humor" (p. 240). Mentions *UTC,* "Big Boy Leaves Home," *TMBV,* and *BB* as well as *NS.*

3246. Deck, Alice A. "*Changing Our Own Words: Essays on Criticism, Theory, and Writing by Black Women.* Ed. Cheryl A. Wall; *Wild Women in the Whirlwind: Afra-American Culture and the Contemporary Literary Renaissance.* Ed. Joanne Braxton and Andree McLaughlin; *Black American Women*

Novelists: An Annotated Bibliography. By Craig Werner." *American Literature,* 64 (December), 849–851. Mentions W briefly.

3247. DeCosta-Willis, Miriam. "Introduction," in *Erotique Noire/Black Erotica.* Eds. Miriam DeCosta-Willis, Reginald Martin, and Roseann P. Bell. New York: Doubleday, pp. xxix–xl. Notes that Sandra Y. Govan's essay in this anthology treats W among others.

3248. DeGout, Yasmin Y. "Dividing the Mind: Contradictory Portraits of Homoerotic Love in *Giovanni's Room.*" *African American Review,* 26 (Fall), 425–435. Mentions briefly Baldwin's quarrel with W (p. 425) and compares both Giovanni and David to *NS* (p. 434).

3249. Delbanco, Andrew. "An American Hunger." *The New Republic,* 206 (30 March), 28–30, 32–33. Essay-review of the Library of American edition of *Native Son* in the context of W's life and other works. Delbanco emphasizes in *NS* "the imperatives of the body," self-hatred, and "the thematics of race."

3250. Demby, William. "From Love Story Black," in *The New Cavalcade: African American Writing from 1760 to the Present.* Vol. II. Eds. Arthur P. Davis, J. Saunders Redding, and Joyce Ann Joyce. Washington: Howard University Press, pp. 115–132.

3251. DelFattore, Joan. *What Johnny Shouldn't Read: Textbook Censorship in America.* New Haven: Yale University Press, pp. 145, 154, 156, 157. Mentions W briefly as a target of censors.

3252. De Weever, Jacqueline. *Mythmaking and Metaphor in Black Women's Fiction.* New York: St. Martin's Press, pp. 5, 96, 154. Mentions briefly "The Man Who Lived Underground" and comments on *NS.*

3253. Dick, Bruce. "Uniting Present and Past, French and American: Post-Conference Interview with Michel Fabre." *The Southern Register* (Spring), p. 10. Fabre states that at his conference on "African Americans and Europe" he "particularly enjoyed the Round Table discussion with Ellen and Julia Wright" and others.

3254. _____. "Fabre, Michel. *From Harlem to Paris: Black American Writers in France, 1840–1980.*" *Afram Newsletter,* 35 (June), 31–32. Fa-

vorable review containing a paragraph on W and Paris.

3255. Dickstein, Morris. *Double Agent: The Critic and Society.* New York: Oxford University Press, p. 72.

3256. Diggins, John Patrick. *The Rise and Fall of the American Left.* New York: Norton, pp. 170, 258. Mentions W briefly.

3257. Dillard, Pam. "African American Expatriates Honored at Paris Conference." *The Southern Register* (Spring), pp. 8–9. Mentions the dedication of the plaque honoring W at 14 rue Monsieur-le-Prince and quotes William Ferris on W's expatriation.

3258. Dixon, Melvin. "Climbing Montmartre." *Afram Newsletter,* No. 35 (February — Special Number), 34.

3259. _____. "Climbing Montmartre," in *African Americans and Europe.* Ed. Elizabeth M. Chant. Cambridge, MA: W.E.B. DuBois Institute for Afro-American Research, Harvard University, p. 22. Reprint of 1983

3260. _____. "Richard, Richard: American Fuel." *Afram Newsletter,* No. 35 (February — Special Number), 36.

3261. _____. "Richard, Richard: An American Hunger." *Afram Newsletter,* No. 35 (February — Special Number), 35.

3262. Doreski, C.K. "From News to History: Robert Abbott and Carl Sandburg Read the 1919 Chicago Riot." *African American Review,* 26 (Winter), 637–650. In a note claims that Henry Dalton of *NS* is a "fictional construct of just such assured liberals" as Sandburg in *The Chicago Race Riots, 1919.*

3263. _____. "Kinship and History in Sam Cornish's *Generations.*" *Contemporary Literature,* 33 (Winter), 665–687. Quotes lines from Cornish's poems mentioning W and Bigger Thomas (pp. 676, 683–684).

3264. _____. "*1935: A Memoir.* By Sam Cornish." *Southern Humanities Review,* 26 (Fall), 373–376. Review quoting a passage mentioning *NS.*

3265. Draper, James P. "Arna Bontemps 1902–1973," in his *Black Literature Criticism.* Vol. I. Detroit: Gale, pp. 207–209. Quotes from W's review of *Black Thunder.*

3266. _____. "James Baldwin 1924–1987," in his *Black Literature*

Criticism. Vol. 1. Detroit: Gale, pp. 75–78. Notes Baldwin's meeting with W and their subsequent quarrel.

3267. _____. "John A. Williams 1925–," in his *Black Literature Criticism*. Vol. 3. Detroit: Gale, pp. 1932–1933. Mentions briefly Williams's life of W.

3268. _____. "John Edgar Wideman 1941–," in his *Black Literature Criticism*. Vol. 3. Detroit: Gale, pp. 1917–1918. Mentions W briefly.

3269. _____. "Margaret Walker 1915–," in his *Black Literature Criticism*. Vol. 3. Detroit: Gale, pp. 1830–1831. Comments on the friendship of Walker and W and their estrangement. Mentions Walker's book on W.

3270. _____. "Ralph Ellison 1914–," in his *Black Literature Criticism*. Vol. 1. Detroit: Gale, pp. 673–675. Mentions W briefly.

3271. _____. "Richard Wright 1908–1960," in his *Black Literature Criticism*. Vol. 3. Detroit: Gale, pp. 1994–1997, 2020–2021. Biographical-critical sketch emphasizing *UTC*, *NS*, and *BB*. Includes an annotated list of "Further Reading."

3272. _____. "William Attaway 1911?–1986," in his *Black Literature Criticism*. Vol. I. Detroit: Gale, pp. 56–57. Mentions briefly W and *NS*.

3273. _____. "Zora Neale Hurston 1901?–1960," in his *Black Literature Criticism*. Vol. 2. Detroit: Gale, pp. 1068–1070. Refers to W's review of *Their Eyes Were Watching God* and quotes from June Jordan mentioning *NS*.

3274. Drylie, Bob. "Uncle Tom's Children." *City Paper* (11 February). Favorable review of the Library of America edition of *UTC* stressing the theme of racism.

3275. Du Bois, W.E.B. Untitled excerpt, in *Black Literature Criticism*. Ed. James P. Draper. Vol. 3. Detroit: Gale, pp. 2001–2002. Partial reprint of 1945.883.

3276. duCille, Ann. "'Who Reads Here?': Back Talking with Houston Baker." *Novel: A Forum on Fiction*, 26 (Fall), 97–105. Essay-review of *Workings of the Spirit: The Poetics of Afro-American Women's Writing* mentioning W briefly (p. 98) and commenting on Baker's treatment of W, mentioning *NS* and *TMBV* (pp. 102, 104).

3277. Dudley, David. "*New Essays on Native Son*. Ed. Keneth Kinna-

mon." *Journal of English and Germanic Philology*, 91 (October), 594–596. Favorable review discussing the editor's introduction and each of the essays by the four contributors: Houston Baker, John Reilly, Trudier Harris, and Craig Werner. "Those who want to see how contemporary scholarship illuminates a by-now classic American text will be rewarded by this volume."

3278. Duffy, Susan, comp. *The Political Left in the American Theatre of the 1930s: A Bibliographical Sourcebook*. Metuchen, N.s.: The Scarecrow Press, pp. 90, 170. Lists the published version of the play *NS* (p. 170) and W's essay on "Negro Tradition in the Theatre (p. 90).

3279. Durham, Michael S. "The Word Is 'Slaves': A Trip Into Black History." *American Heritage*, 47 (April), 89–99. Notes that Bluff Park in Natchez has a marker noting that W was born "near Natchez (p. 98).

3280. Eagles, Brenda M. "A Bibliography of Dissertations Relating to Mississippi—1991." *The Journal of Mississippi History*, 54 (February), 97–99. Lists a dissertation on W by LaVinia Delois Jennings.

3281. Eakin, Paul John. *Touching the World: Reference in Autobiography*. Princeton, NJ: Princeton University Press, p. 191. Mentions briefly *BB*.

3282. Early, Gerald. "Benjamin J. Davis, Jr.," in his *Speech and Power: The African-American Essay and Its Cultural Content from Polemics to Pulpit*. Vol. I. Hopewell, NJ: The Ecco Press, p. 111. Headnote commenting on Davis's support of W in the Communist Party.

3283. _____. "The Black Intellectual and the Sport of Prizefighting," in his *Speech and Power: The African-American Essay and Its Cultural Content from Polemics to Pulpit*. Vol. I. Hopewell, NJ: The Ecco Press, pp. 193–207. Discusses W's preoccupation with popular culture and boxing in *NS* as well as in three journalistic articles (pp. 201–202).

3284. _____. "Gnostic or Gnomic?" in his *Speech and Power: The African-American Essay and Its Cultural Content from Polemics to Pulpit*. Vol. I. Hopewell, NJ: The Ecco Press, pp. vii–xv. Contrasts the attitudes toward Mencken displayed by W and Langston Hughes in *BB* and *The Big Sea*. "Hughes wishes to es-

cape ... the life of the mind and the supremacy of intellect over experience, while W seeks his liberation from a provincial family and an oppressive political and social system through books" (p. viii).

3285. _____. "On Being Subversive," in his *Speech and Power: The African-American Essay and Its Cultural Content from Polemics to Pulpit*. Vol. I. Hopewell, NJ: The Ecco Press, pp. 109–110. Mentions W briefly.

3286. _____. "Richard Wright," in his *Speech and Power: The African-American Essay and Its Cultural Content from Polemics to Pulpit*. Vol. I. Hopewell, NJ: The Ecco Press, p. 153. Headnote to W's "High Tide in Harlem" sketching his career.

3287. Easingwood, Peter, and David Seed. "American Literature: The Twentieth Century: Prose Fiction," in *The Year's Work in English Studies*. Vol. 70. Oxford: Blackwell Publishers, pp. 645–672. Comments on each of the essays in *Richard Wright: Myths and Realities* (pp. 659–660).

3288. _____. "American Literature: The Twentieth Century: Reference and General Criticism," in *The Year's Work in English Studies*, Vol. 70. Oxford: Blackwell, pp. 601–609. Mentions W briefly (p. 602).

3289. Elder, Arlene. "*Sassafras, Cypress & Indigo*: Ntozake Shange's Neo-Slave Blues Narrative." *African American Review*, 26 (Spring), 99–107. Mentions W briefly (p. 106).

3290. Ellison, Ralph. "Richard Wright's Blues." *The Antioch Review*, 50 (Winter and Spring), 61–74.

3291. _____. Untitled excerpt, in *Black Literature Criticism*. Ed. James P. Draper. Vol. 3. Detroit: Gale, pp. 2002–2003.

3292. Erkilla, Betsy, *The Wicked Sisters: Women Poets, Literary History and Discord*. New York: Oxford University Press, p. 199. States W, reading the manuscript of *A Street in Bronzeville* for Harper's recommended that "The Mother" be dropped.

3293. Estes-Hicks, Onita. "Report from Paris: Colloque International-Les Noirs Americans." *The Crisis*, 99 (June-July), 44, 46. Includes an account of the closing ceremony on 9 February, when conferees gathered on Rue Monsieur-le-Prince below the plaque on the apartment building where W lived to honor the memory of the author.

3294. Etheridge, Sharynn O. "Langston Hughes: An Annotated Bibliography (1977–1986)." *The Langston Hughes Review*, 11 (Spring), 41–57. The annotation for an article by Sherley Anne Williams mentions W briefly.

3295. _____. "Langston Hughes: An Annotated Bibliography (1977–1986)." *The Langston Hughes Review*, 11 (Spring), 54. Mentions W briefly.

3296. Evans, Charlene Taylor. "*Go Tell It on the Mountain*," in *Masterpieces of African-American Literature*. Ed. Frank N. Magill. New York: HarperCollins, pp. 186–188. Mentions W briefly (p. 188).

3297. Evans, Faun Bernbach, Barbara Gleason, and Mark Wiley. "'The Library Card' Richard Wright," in their *Cultural Tapestry: Readings for a Pluralistic Society*. New York: HarperCollins, pp. 456–457. Biographical headnote to an excerpt from *BB*.

3298. [Fabre, Michel], "Activities du CETANLA." *Afram Newsletter*, No. 36 (November), pp. 2–4. Includes listing of items for sale, including a W poster and recorded interviews with him, as well as mention of M. Lynn Weiss's research on W and Stein.

3299. [Fabre, Michel]. "Hélène Christol et Sylvie Mathè. *American Fiction*." *Afram Newsletter*, 35 (June), 52. Notice mentioning W briefly.

3300. _____. "A Participants' Who's Who." *Afram Newsletter*, No. 35 (February — Special Number), pp. 54–105. Mentions W s.v. entries for Samuel Allen, Hanna Bercovitch, Robert Bone, Wallace Bullock, Sergei Chakovsky, Nina Kressner Cobb, Robert Coles, Benjamin Davis, Thadious M. Davis, Michel Fabre, Maryemma Graham, Yoshinobu Hakutani, Keneth Kinnamon, Madison D. Lacy, Jr., Edward Margolies, Eugene E. Miler, James Miller, Jack Moore, James Nagel, Patrick M. Ryan, Amritjit Singh, Virginia Whatley Smith, Eugenio Suarez-Galban, Lynn Weiss, John A. Williams, Ellen Wright, and Julia Wright.

3301. _____. "Programme." *Afram Newsletter*, No. 35 (February — Special Number), pp. 1–31. List of events in the conference booklet of "African Americans and Europe," held in Paris, 5–9 February. Includes a performance of Levi Fra-

zier's "A Black Boy: Tribute to Richard Wright"; a ceremony in honor of W and in observance of the commemorative plaque at 14 rue Monsieur-le-Prince; and sessions on W chaired by Hanna M. Bercovitch (with papers by Robert Bone, Yoshinobu Hakutani, and Eugene Miller and a response by Walter A. Jackson), Edward Margolies (with papers by Virginia Whatley Smith, John Lowe, and Wallace Bullock), Jack Moore (with papers by Eugenio Suarez-Galban, Lynn Weiss, and Amritjit Singh), and Keneth Kinnamon (with papers by Bruce Dick, Paul Oliver, and Maryemma Graham); and a panel discussion with Michel Fabre, Ellen Wright, Julia Wright, Lesley Himes, Bernard Hassell, Samuel Allen, Edward Clark, Herbert Gentry, Richard Gibson, and Verta Mae Grosvenor.

3302. _____. "Regards sur les contemporains." *Focus*, pp. 12–16.

3303. _____. "*Trois américains à Paris, Richard Wright, Chester Himes, James Baldwin*." *Afram Newsletter*, 35 (June), 46. Notice of a compact disc containing interviews with the three writers.

3304. _____., ed. "Welcome from the Writers." *Afram Newsletter*, No. 35 (February — Special Number), pp. 32–53. Notes that Ellen and Julia Wright presented a haiku by W (p. 32).

3305. Fabre, Michel, Robert E. Skinner, and Lester Sullivan. *Chester Himes: An Annotated Primary and Secondary Bibliography*. Westport, CT: Greenwood Press, pp. 44, 57. Contains items on W's review of *If He Hollers Let Him Go* and W's introduction to the French translation of *Lonely Crusade*.

3306. Felgar, Robert. "The Cultural Work of Time in *Native Son*." *Notes on Mississippi Writers*, 24 (July), 99–103. Identifies four kinds of time in the novel: "synchronic, biblical, linear (or diachronic), and modernist." Bigger rejects the first two, associated with racism and religion respectively, and embraces the second two, suggesting clock-regulated activity and subjective experience respectively.

3307. Ferris, William R. "Region as Art," in *Regional Studies: The Interplay of Land and People*. Ed. Glen E. Lich. College Station: Texas A&M University Press, pp. 3–7. Mentions W briefly (p. 5).

3308. Fine, Richard. *James M. Cain and the American Authors' Authority*. Austin: University of Texas Press, p. 174. Mentions W briefly.

3309. Fischer, Elise. "'Bessie' & Anita Hill." *The Nation*, 254 (3 February), 110. Letter to the editor commenting on the murders of Mary and Bessie in *NS*.

3310. Fleming, Robert E. "Introduction." *American Literary Realism 1870–1910*, 24 (Spring), 3–5. Includes a brief comparison of W and Sutton Griggs.

3311. _____. "One World: A New Imprint for All Cultures." *American Visions*, 7 (February-March), pp. 32–36. Mentions the good sale of *NS* in 1940.

3312. Foley, Barbara. "Subversion and Oppositionality in the Academy," in *Pedagogy Is Politics: Literary Theory and Critical Teaching*. Ed. Maria-Regina Kecht. Urbana: University of Illinois Press, pp. 70–89. Contrasts briefly *UTC* and *Absalom, Absalom!* (p. 81).

3313. Fonteneau, Yvonne. "George E. Kent. *A Life of Gwendolyn Brooks*." *World Literature Today*, 66 (Winter), 137. Review mentioning W briefly.

3314. Foster, Frances Smith. "Autobiography After Emancipation: The Example of Elizabeth Keckley," in *Multicultural Autobiography: American Lives*. Ed. James Robert Payne. Knoxville: The University of Tennessee Press, pp. 32–63. Mentions *BB* briefly (p. 347).

3315. Fowler, H. Ramsey, and Jane E. Aaron. *The Little, Brown Handbook*. New York: Harper-Collins, pp. 370–371. Uses a paragraph from *BB* for an exercise in sentence variety.

3316. Furnas, J.C. "Why Johnny Needn't Read." *The American Scholar*, 61 (Spring), 247–253. Mentions briefly *NS*.

3317. Garber, Marjorie. *Vested Interests: Cross-Dressing and Cultural Anxiety*. New York: Routledge, pp. 273, 292–295, 298, 303, 375. Analyzes "Man of All Work" emphasizing gender, sexual, and racial dimensions. Points out analogies between W's radio play and "Little Red Riding Hood." "How does a 'boy' become a 'man' in the eyes of these white men? By putting on a dress" (p. 295).

3318. Gates, Henry Louis, Jr. "African American Criticism," in

Redrawing the Boundaries: The Transformation of English and American Literary Studies. Eds. Stephen Greenblatt and Giles Gunn. New York: Modern Language Association, pp. 303–319. Mentions W briefly (pp. 304, 308, 316).

3319. _____. "African American Studies in the 21st Century." *The Black Scholar*, 22 (Summer), 3–9. Quotes from *WML* (p. 5) and mentions W elsewhere.

3320. _____. "African American Studies in the 21st Century." *The Black Scholar*, 22 (Summer), 3–9. Quotes from *WML* and comments on W's failure to resolve "his ambivalent relation to both the Western and non–Western cultures."

3321. _____. "The Black Man's Burden," in *Black Popular Culture*, a project by Michele Wallace. Ed. Gina Dent. Seattle: Bay Press, pp. 75–83. Mentions briefly Paul Gilroy on *O* (p. 82).

3322. _____. "Integrating the American Mind," in his *Loose Canons: Notes on the Culture Wars.* New York: Oxford University Press, pp. 105–120. Quotes *WML* on W's allegiance to Western "reactions and attitudes" (pp. 110–111).

3323. _____. "Songs of a Racial Self: On Sterling A. Brown," in *Speech and Power: The African-American Essay and Its Cultural Content from Polemics to Pulpit.* Vol. I. Ed. Gerald Early. Hopewell, NJ: The Ecco Press, pp. 308–314.

3324. _____. "Tell Me, Sir, ... What Is 'Black' Literature?" in his *Loose Canons: Notes on the Culture Wars.* New York: Oxford University Press, pp. 87–104.

3325. _____. "'What's in a Name?': Some Meanings of Blackness," in his *Loose Canons: Notes on the Culture Wars.* New York: Oxford University Press, pp. 131–151.

3326. _____., et al. "Discussion," in *Black Popular Culture*, a project by Michele Wallace. Ed. Gina Dent. Seattle: Bay Press, pp. 85–91. Mentions "delivering the Richard Wright lectures" at the University of Pennsylvania (p. 86).

3327. _____. "Zora Neale Hurston," in *The Norton Guide to Writing.* By Thomas Cooley. New York: Norton, pp. 283–284. Reprint of 1990.

3328. Gayle, Addison Jr. "Cultural Nationalism: The Black Novelist in America," in *The New Cav-*

alcade: African American Writing from 1760 to the Present. Vol. II. Eds. Arthur P. Davis, J. Saunders Redding, and Joyce Ann Joyce. Washington: Howard University Press, pp. 570–579.

3329. Georgakas, Dan, and Ernie Brill. "Proletarian and Radical Writers—1930s and 1940s," in *Encyclopedia of the American Left.* Eds. Mari Jo Buhle, Paul Buhle, and Dan Georgakas. Urbana: University of Illinois Press, pp. 601–606.

3330. George, Nelson. *Elevating the Game: Black Men and Basketball.* Lincoln: University of Nebraska Press, pp. 61, 252. Comments on *NS* and lists *NS* and *BB* in the bibliography.

3331. Gibson, Donald B. "From 'Individualism and Community in Black Fiction,'" in *The New Cavalcade: African American Writing from 1760 to the Present.* Vol. II. Eds. Arthur P. Davis, J. Saunders Redding, and Joyce Ann Joyce. Washington: Howard University Press, pp. 565–568.

3332. Gibson, Richard. "African Americans in Europe: Stocktaking in The City of Light." *West Africa*, No. 3891 (13–19 April), pp. 628–629. Report on the Paris conference on "African Americans and Europe," with comments on Michel Fabre's work on W, Ollie Harrington's suspicions about W's death, and Julia Wright's admonition not to believe that W maintained close relations with U.S. officials during the Cold War. Mentions *BB*.

3333. Giles, James R. Untitled excerpt, in *Black Literature Criticism.* Ed. James P. Draper. Vol. 3. Detroit: Gale, pp. 2014–2017. Partial reprint of 1973.157.

3334. Gilliland, Joan F., and Joan T. Mead. "First Draft," in her *Reasons for Writing.* Englewood Cliffs, NJ: Prentice Hall, pp. 149–150. Uses a student paper on "The Man Who Was Almost A Man" to illustrate the function of an introductory paragraph.

3335. Gitelman, Lisa. "Negotiating a Vocabulary for Urban Infrastructure, Or, The WPA Meets the Teenage Mutant Ninja Turtles." *Journal of American Studies*, 26 (August), 147–158. Contains a paragraph on "The Man Who Lived Underground," relating it to an unfinished New York Writers Project book, *Underneath New York.*

3336. Gladney, Gerald. "On Bearing Witness." *Emerge*, 3 (March), 51. Review of *Bearing Witness*, edited by Henry Louis Gates, Jr., mentioning W briefly.

3337. Gladsky, Thomas S. *Princes, Peasants, and Other Polish Selves: Ethnicity in American Literature.* Amherst: The University of Massachusetts Press, pp. 83, 143, 144. Mentions *UTC* and quotes from W's introduction to Nelson Algren's *Never Come Morning.*

3338. Gounard, Jean-François. *The Racial Problem in the Works of Richard Wright and James Baldwin.* Westport, CT: Greenwood Press, viii + 303pp.

3339. Govan, Sandra Y. "Forbidden Fruits and Unholy Lusts: Illicit Sex in Black American Literature," in *Erotique Noire/Black Erotica.* Eds. Miriam DeCosta-Willis, Reginald Martin, and Roseann P. Bell. New York: Doubleday, pp. 35–43. Contains paragraphs on the sexual theme in *NS*, "The Man Who Killed a Shadow," and "Man of All Work" (pp. 40–41).

3340. Greenspon, Joanna, ed. *Humanities Index: April 1991 to March 1992.* New York: H.W. Wilson, p. 1357. Lists eight items s.v. W.

3341. Griffin, Noah W. "Paying a Posthumous Debt," *The Crisis*, 99 (March), 8, 30. Favorable review of the Library of America edition of W. Surveys W's works through *O*, stressing his honesty in dealing with race and racism, especially its sexual component.

3342. Gruesser, John Cullen. *White on Black: Contemporary Literature About Africa.* Urbana: University of Illinois Press, p. 47. Mentions W briefly.

3343. Gustafason, Thomas. *Representative Words: Politics, Literature, and the American Language, 1776–1865.* Cambridge: Cambridge University Press, pp. 256, 297–298. Quotes from *TMBV* and "How 'Bigger' Was Born."

3344. Hadella, Charlotte. "Fiction: The 1930s to the 1960s," in *American Literary Scholarship: An Annual 1990.* Ed. Louis Owens. Durham, NC: Duke University Press, pp. 267–294. Contains a favorable review of *New Essays on Native Son*, treating the introduction by Keneth Kinnamon and essays by John M. Reilly, Trudier Harris,

Houston A. Baker, Jr., and Craig Werner. Also notes essays on W by Willene P. Taylor, Onita Estes-Hicks, and George Uba.

3345. Hall, James C. "Darwin Turner and the Teaching of African-American Literature." *The Langston Hughes Review*, 11 (Fall), 10–14. Quotes Turner mentioning W briefly (p. 11).

3346. _____. "Toward a Map of Mis(sed) Reading: The Presence of Absence in *The Color Purple*, *African American Review*, 26 (Spring), 89–97. Mentions W briefly (p. 95).

3347. Hall, Stuart. "C.L.R. James: A Portrait," in *C.L.R. James's Caribbean*. Eds. Paget Henry and Paul Buhle. Durham: Duke University Press, pp. 3–16. Mentions W briefly (p. 9).

3348. Hamalian, Linda. "*Richard Wright's Art of Tragedy*. By Joyce Ann Joyce." *American Literature*, 64 (March), 179–180. Generally favorable review emphasizing Joyce's New Critical approach. Praises the "finely tuned" argument and the treatment of imagery in *NS*.

3349. Hargrove, Claude. "*Soul on Ice*," in *Masterpieces of African-American Literature*. Ed. Frank N. Magill. New York: HarperCollins, pp. 517–519. Notes Cleaver's reading of W (p. 517).

3350. Harrington, Walt. *Crossings: A White Man's Journey Into Black America*. New York: Harper-Collins, pp. 125, 127, 233, 309, 326, 415, 428, 439. The author travels to Natchez as homage to W and *BB*, visiting a house where W is believed to have lived. Also mentions W's expatriation, James Alan McPherson quoting W, *NS*, and comment by black high-school students on *BB*.

3351. Harris, Trudier. "The Meaning of a Tradition," in *The New Cavalcade: African American Writing from 1760 to the Present*. Vol. II. Eds. Arthur P. Davis, J. Saunders Redding, and Joyce Ann Joyce. Washington: Howard University Press, pp. 832–844.

3352. Harrison, Alferdteen. "Looking Back: A Conversation with Margaret Walker," in *Margaret Walker's "For My People": A Tribute*. Jackson: University Press of Mississippi, pp. 9–12. Includes comments on her book on W.

3353. Hayes, Floyd W., III. "African American Expressive Culture: Music and Literature," in his *A Tur-*bulent Voyage: Readings in African American Studies*. San Diego: Collegiate Press, pp. 263–268. Comments on "Blueprint for Negro Writing" (included on pp. 322–329) and mentions briefly *UTC*, *NS*, *BB*, *O*, *BP*, *CC*, *PS*, *WML*, *EM*, *LT*, and *AH*.

3354. Haynes, Karima A. "Soul to Soul: How a Black/Jewish/Polish/Russian/African Woman Found Her Roots." *Ebony*, 48 (December), 44–46, 48, 50, 135. Notes that W was on the bookshelves of the Moscow apartment of the granddaughter of an interracial Communist couple who emigrated from New York to the Soviet Union in 1931.

3355. Henderson, Stephen. "The Question of Form and Judgment in Contemporary Black American Poetry: 1962–1977," in *The New Cavalcade: African American Writing from 1760 to the Present*. Vol. II. Eds. Arthur P. Davis, J. Saunders Redding, and Joyce Ann Joyce. Washington: Howard University Press, pp. 177–197. Abbreviated reprint of 1977.

3356. Hernton, Calvin. "Shining." *Field*, 47 (Autumn), 34–40. Mentions W briefly (p. 35).

3357. Hillmann, Michael Craig. "*I Know Why the Caged Bird Sings*," in *Masterpieces of African-American Literature*. Ed. Frank N. Magill. New York: HarperCollins, pp. 214–217. Mentions W briefly (p. 217).

3358. Hilfer, Tony. *American Fiction Since 1940*. London: Longman. pp. 2, 9, 14–15, 34–41, 45, 47–49, 51, 52, 230, 285. Includes discussion of *NS* emphasizing "the smothering world of Bigger Thomas," which is manifest in the novel's language as well as action. Also mentions *O* and "The Man Who Lived Underground" as well as W's relation to Ellison, Baldwin, and Petry.

3359. Holladay, Hilary. "*Native Son's* Guilty Man." *The CEA Critic*, 54 (Winter), 30–36. Analyzes Boris Max as an inept lawyer guilty of "generalizations, self-doubts, long-winded tangents, and logical fallacies" in his defense of Bigger. By failing to plead not guilty or insanity, Max forfeits any chance Bigger may have to escape execution.

3360. Holloway, Karla F.C. *Moorings & Metaphors: Figures of Culture and Gender in Black Women's Literature*. New Brunswick, NJ: Rutgers University Press, pp. 7, 137. Mentions W and claims an "elliptical reference" to "The Man Who Lived Underground" in Gloria Naylor's *Linden Hills*.

3361. Holmes, Carolyn L. "Reassessing African American Literature Through an Afrocentric Paradigm: Zora N. Hurston and James Baldwin," in *Language and Literature in the African American Imagination*. Ed. Carol Blackshire-Belay. Westport, CT: Greenwood Press, pp. 37–51. Mentions W briefly (p. 46).

3362. Homberger, Eric. "John Reed Clubs," in *Encyclopedia of the American Left*. Eds. Mari Jo Buhle, Paul Buhle, and Dan Georgakas. Urbana: University of Illinois Press, pp. 649–650. Reprint of 1990.

3363. Hooks, Bell. *Black Looks: Race and Representations*. Boston: South End Press, p. 200. Lists *NS* in the bibliography.

3364. Houston, Helen. "Margaret Walker," in *Notable Black American Women*. Ed. Jessie Carney Smith. Detroit: Gale, pp. 1193–1195. Mentions W's friendship with Walker (p. 1194).

3365. Howard, Gerald. "The Bonfire This Time." *The Nation*, 254 (1 June), 755–757. Review of Richard Price's *Clockers* mentioning briefly *NS*.

3366. Howe, Irving. Untitled excerpt, in *Black Literature Criticism*. Ed. James P. Draper. Vol. 3. Detroit: Gale, p. 2003.

3367. Howell, Charlene W. "Richard Wright's Landmark Works in Print Again." *The Dallas Morning News* (23 February), p. 7J. Favorable review of the Library of America edition of W with a sketch of his life and career. Attributes the break with Communism to a clash between the party's "commitment to ideology" and W's "instinctive naturalism."

3368. Hubbard, Dolan. "Symbolizing America in Langston Hughes's 'Father and Son.'" *The Langston Hughes Review*, 11 (Spring), 14–20. States that Bert in the story "anticipates Wright's nihilistic anti-hero, Bigger Thomas" (p. 18).

3369. Hughes, Langston. "Democracy and Me," in *Good Morning Revolution: Uncollected Writings of Social Protest by Langston Hughes*. Ed. Faith Berry. New York: Carol Publishing Group, pp. 138–141. Speech at the Third American Writers' Congress, June 1939 mentioning W as "an excellent craftsman."

3370. Hunt, Patricia. "*My Father's Shadow: Intergenerational Conflict in African American Men's Autobiography*. By David L. Dudley." *American Literature*, 64 (September), 630–631. Review mentioning W briefly.

3371. Hunter, Clarence. "Mississippi Artist in the Diaspora: A New Look at Richard Wright." *Mississippi Libraries*, 56 (Summer), 44–45. Reports on a two-day symposium on W in February at Tougaloo College. Principal speakers were Margaret Walker Alexander, Max Rudin, and Jerry Ward. Includes synopses of their lectures.

3372. _____. "Mississippi Artist in the Diaspora: A New Look at Richard Wright." *The Richard Wright Newsletter*, 2 (Fall), 5.

3373. Hurt, James. *Writing Illinois: The Prairie, Lincoln, and Chicago*. Urbana: University of Illinois Press, pp. 99, 100. Notes Henry Claridge's treatment of W and Chicago.

3374. Hyman, Stanley Edgar. Untitled excerpt, in *Black Literature Criticism*. Ed. James P. Draper. Vol. 3. Detroit: Gale, pp. 2010–2012.

3375. Ichiki, Jun, "A Study of *Native Son*: Bigger Thomas and Malcom X." *Literary Study Essays of the Graduate School of Seinan Gakuin University*, 11 (January), 17–26. Argues that Bigger's consciousness is inherited by Malcolm. Examines Mary's murder and the assassination of Malcolm [T.K., R.B., and Y.H.].

3376. Imaizumi, Yoko. "Feminism, Black People, and Criticism: A Report on the Meeting of the 51st English Institute Conference." *Rising Generation*, 138 (1 December), 17. Reports that among four seminars is one on black exiles such as W, conducted by Henry Louis Gates, Jr.

3377. Inge, M. Thomas. "Faulkner," in *American Literary Scholarship: An Annual 1990*. Ed. Louis Owens. Durham, NC: Duke University Press, pp. 151–165. Notes W's praise of Faulkner in "A Man of the South."

3378. _____. *Faulkner, Sut, and Other Southerners: Essays in Literary History*. West Cornwall, CT: Locust Hill Press, p. xxiii. Mentions W briefly.

3379. Ingram, Elwanda D. "Dorothy West," in *Notable Black American Women*. Ed. Jessie Carney Smith.

Detroit: Gale, pp. 1238–1240. Notes W's connection with *New Challenge* (p. 1239).

3380. Italie, Hillel. "First-time Novelist Finds Lyrical, Literary Voice." Fayetteville *Northwest Arkansas Times* (13 March), p. 5B. Associated Press interview of Darryl Pickney mentioning briefly his reading of W.

3381. J., G.Y. "The Cold Reality of Hot Water." *American Visions*, 7 (August/September), 32, 33. States that Gayle Pemberton "acknowledges her fondness for Richard Wright."

3382. Jackson, Jacquelyne L. "*If He Hollers Let Him Go*," in *Masterpieces of African-American Literature*. Ed. Frank N. Magill. New York: HarperCollins, pp. 218–221. Notes that many of the reviewers of the Himes novel compared it to *NS* (p. 221).

3383. _____. "*Uncle Tom's Children*," in *Encyclopedia of African-American Civil Rights: From Emancipation to the Present*. Eds. Charles D. Lowery and John F. Marszalik. Westport, CT: Greenwood, p. 536. Emphasizes the work's powerful realism. Includes a selected bibliography of four items.

3384. James, C.L.R. "Black Studies and the Contemporary Student," in *The C.L.R. James Reader*. Ed. Anna Grimshaw. Oxford: Blackwell, pp. 390–404.

3385. _____. "Letters to Constance Webb," in *The C.L.R. James Reader*. Ed. Anna Grimshaw. Oxford: Blackwell, pp. 127–152. Relates a visit with W in 1945 before the publication of *BB*. James finds great affinity between his views on racial matters and W's.

3386. _____. "The Revolutionary Answer to the Negro Problem in the USA," in *The C.L.R. James Reader*. Ed. Anna Grimshaw. Oxford: Blackwell, pp. 182–189.

3387. Jan Mohamed, Abdul R. "Sexuality on/of the Racial Border: Foucault, Wright, and the Articulation of 'Racialized Sexuality,'" in *Discourses of Sexuality: From Aristotle to Aids*. Ed. Domna C. Stanton. Ann Arbor: The University of Michigan Press, pp. 94–116. Corrects Foucault's failure to racialize sexuality, using *NS* as an example of the need to do so. Bigger commits three "rapes": Mary, Bessie, and, the first, Gus. In Bigger's attempt to

achieve power and freedom through rape, "*Native Son* turns out to be a profoundly specular novel; it holds up a mirror to the structure and economy of phallocratic society, but it is unable to escape or undermine them" (p. 111).

3388. _____. "Worldliness-Without-World, Homelessness-as-Home: Toward a Definition of the Specular Border Intellectual," in *Edward Said: A Critical Reader*. Ed. Michael Sprinkler. Cambridge: MA: Blackwell, pp. 96–120. Contains a paragraph on W's project "to deconstruct the received, manichean subjectivity" (p. 116).

3389. Jirran, Raymond J. "*The Shadow Within*. By P.J. Robinson." *The Journal of Negro History*, 77 (Summer), 108. Mentions briefly W and *NS*.

3390. Johns, Robert L. "Ann Petry," in *Notable Black American Women*. Ed. Jessie Carney Smith. Detroit: Gale, pp. 844–847. Notes that reviewers of *The Street* wrongly "placed Petry in the school of Richard Wright" (p. 845).

3391. Jones, Kirkland C. "*Adam Clayton Powell, Jr.: The Political Biography of an American Dilemma*." *The Crisis*, 99 (April-May), 14, 16. Mentions briefly Addison Gayle's biography of W.

3392. _____. *Renaissance Man from Louisiana: A Biography of Arna Wendell Bontemps*. Westport, CT: Greenwood Press, pp. 70, 82, 98, 122–123, 135, 139–140, 144–145, 169, 172. Discusses the visit of Bontemps with W and Ellen Wright in Paris in September 1960 and the plan of W and Bontemps to collaborate on a film scenario on the Fisk Jubilee Singers (pp. 144–145). Relates Lawrence Reddicks's account of being introduced to W by Bontemps, who also introduced W to Ulysses Keys (p. 169). Mentions W briefly elsewhere.

3393. Jones, Margaret C. *Prophets in Babylon: Five California Novelists in the 1930's*. New York: Peter Lang, pp. 114, 137. Mentions briefly *NS* and W's early stories.

3394. Jones, Suzanne W. "Teaching 'Race Relations in Southern Literature.'" *Xavier Review*, 12 (Autumn), 41–49. Includes "The Ethics of Living Jim Crow" in the course reading list.

3395. Jordan, June. "Finding the Haystack in the Needle, or, the

Whole World of America and the challenge of Higher Education," in her *Technical Difficulties*. New York: Random House, pp. 89–101. Mentions briefly *NS* (p. 99).

3396. _____. "From Technical Difficulties: Requiem for the Champ," in *I Know What the Red Clay Looks Like: The Voice and Vision of Black Women Writers* by Rebecca Carroll. New York: Carol Southern Books, pp. 152–157.

3397. _____. "Requiem for the Champ," in her *Technical Difficulties*. New York: Random House, pp. 221–226. Essay on Mike Tyson and his blighted environment, with comparisons to Bigger Thomas.

3398. Joyce, Donald Franklin. "Vivian Harsh," in *Notable Black American Women*. Ed. Jessie Carney Smith. Detroit: Gale, pp. 474–475. Mentions this Chicago librarian's friendship with W, who gave an autographed copy of *NS* and a manuscript of "Big Boy Leaves Home" to the George Cleveland Hall Branch Library, where she was director.

3399. Joyce, Joyce Ann. "Change, Chance, and God in Zora Neale Hurston's *Their Eyes Were Watching God*," in *The New Cavalcade: African American Writing from 1760 to the Present*. Vol. II. Eds. Arthur P. Davis, J. Saunders Redding, and Joyce Ann Joyce. Washington: Howard University Press, pp. 869–877. Reprint of 1982

3400. Julien, Claude. "Martin Staniland.—*American Intellectuals and African Nationalists, 1955–1970.*" *Revue français d'etudes américaines*, No. 52 (May), p. 213. Review noting that W is not treated.

3401. _____. "Michel Fabre.—*Richard Wright: Books and Writers.*" *Études Anglaises*, 45 (July-September), 365–366. Highly favorable review praising Fabre's bibliographical precision and comprehensiveness and his inclusion of W's blurbs and opinions on his reading.

3402. Kaiser, Ernest. *The Kaiser Index to Black Resources, 1948–1986*. Brooklyn: Carlson, 1992, Vol. 5, pp. 404–406. Lists numerous items on W, some with brief annotation.

3403. Kauffman, Bill. "Zora Neale Hurston and Clarence Thomas." *Lincoln Review*, 10 (Fall-Winter), 11–13. Mentions W briefly (p. 11).

3404. Kauffman, Linda S. *Special Delivery: Epistolary Modes in Modern Fiction*. Chicago: University of Chi-cago Press, pp. 217–218. Comments on the contrast in the "self-construction of W and Zora Neale Hurston."

3405. Kerr, Judith N. "*Blood on the Forge*," in *Encyclopedia of African-American Civil Rights: From Emancipation to the Present*. Eds. Charles D. Lowery and John F. Marszalek. Westport, CT: Greenwood, pp. 56–57. Mentions briefly *TMBV*.

3406. Kekeh, Andrée. "Lieux et stratégies de résistance dans le discours romanesque de Gayle Jones, Toni Morrison, Alice Walker et Sherley Anne Williams." *Afram Newsletter*, 35 (June), pp. 19–24. Mentions W briefly (p. 19).

3407. Kelley, Robin D.G. "Black Americans." in *The Encyclopedia Americana*. Ed. Lawrence T. Lorimer. Danbury, CT: Grolier, vol. 4, pp. 28a–29. Mentions *NS* as a working-class novel.

3408. Kesterson, David B. "*Making American Tradition: Visions and Revisions from Ben Franklin to Alice Walker*. By Cushing Strout." *American Literature*, 64 (June), 422–423. Mentions W briefly.

3409. Khanga, Yelena, with Susan Jacoby. *Soul to Soul: The Story of a Black Russian American Family, 1865–1992*. New York: Norton, p. 167. Notes that W was not included in university literature courses in the Soviet Union.

3410. Kilson, Martin. "African Americans and Africa: A Critical Nexus." *Dissent*, 39 (Summer), 361–369. Includes discussion of W's role in The First Congress of Black Writers and Artists and quotes from the paper he delivered on this occasion in 1956.

3411. King, Martin Luther, Jr. "My Trip to the Land of Gandhi," in his *I Have a Dream: Writings and Speeches That Changed the World*. San Francisco: HarperSan Francisco, pp. 39–48.

3412. King, Richard H. *Civil Rights and the Idea of Freedom*. New York: Oxford University Press, pp. 75–76, 186. Notes W's estrangement from his father and mentions briefly the violence of Bigger Thomas.

3413. Kinnamon, Keneth. "Addenda to *A Richard Wright Bibliography*." *The Richard Wright Newsletter: Bibliography Supplement*, 2 (Fall), 1–30. Includes 368 annotated items as addenda to the original volume, *A Richard Wright Bibliography: Fifty Years of Criticism and Commentary, 1933–1982*.

3414. Kirszner, Laurie G., and Stephen R. Mandell. "*The Library Card* Richard Wright," in their *The Blair Reader*. Englewood Cliffs, NJ: Prentice-Hall, p. 26. Headnote to a selection from *BB*.

3415. _____. "*The Library Card* Richard Wright," in their *The Blair Reader: Annotated Instructor's Edition*. Englewood Cliffs, NJ: Prentice Hall, pp. 26–34. Contains marginal notes and writing suggestions.

3416. _____. "Responding to Reading," in their *The Blair Reader*. Englewood Cliffs, NJ: Prentice Hall, p. 34. Endnote to a selection from *BB*.

3417. Kishi, Akio. "Black American Literature – on Wright's *Black Boy*: An aftereffect of Slavery in the Society of the 1920's." *Biblia*, 19 (July), 70–72. Comments briefly on *BB* as an index to the legacy of slavery.

3418. Kroeber, Karl, "Novel: 7. United States," in *The Encyclopedia Americana*. Ed. Lawrence T. Lorimer. Dunbury, CT: Golier, vol. 20, pp. 510–511b.

3419. Krueger, Ellen. "'What one book do you love to teach, and why?'" *The Council Chronicle*, 1 (February), 8. A white teacher in "an affluent, predominantly white high school" chooses *BB*.

3420. Kunkel, Glenn E. "*The Sport of the Gods*," in *Masterpieces of African-American Literature*. Ed. Frank N. Magill. New York: HarperCollins, pp. 527–530. Mentions briefly *NS* (p. 530).

3421. Lee, A. Robert. "*Invisible Man*," in *Masterpieces of African-American Literature*. Ed. Frank N. Magill. New York: HarperCollins, pp. 233–236. Mentions briefly *NS* (p. 530).

3422. Leininger, Theresa A. "Barbara Chase-Riboud," in *Notable Black American Women*. Ed. Jessie Carney Smith. Detroit: Gale, pp. 177–181. Mentions W briefly (p. 180).

3423. Leiter, Samuel L. "*Native Son*" in his *The Encyclopedia of the New York Stage, 1940–1950*. Westport, CT: Greenwood Press, pp. 445–446. Provides production details of the 1941 play and its "pared down" version the following year,

Includes excerpts from drama critics.

3424. Leonard, John. "Her Soul's High Song." *The Nation*, 254 (25 May), 706–708, 710, 712, 714–716, 718. Review of Toni Morrison's *Jazz* mentioning W briefly (p. 706).

3425. Levin, David. "James Baldwin's Autobiographical Essays: The Problem of Negro Identity," in *Forms of Uncertainty: Essays in Historical Criticism*. Charlottesville: University Press of Virginia, pp. 237–245.

3426. Levy, Helen Fiddyment. *Fiction of the Home Place: Jewett, Cather, Glasgow, Porter, Welty, and Naylor*. Jackson: University Press of Mississippi, pp. 215–216. Comments on Henry Louis Gates's treatment of W in *The Signifying Monkey*.

3427. Lewis, Barbara Brewster. "Women Crossing Boundaries: A Field Report on the Paris Conference 'African Americans and Paris.'" *African American Review*, 26 (Fall), 515–519. Mentions the considerable attention given to W at the conference.

3428. Lionnet, Françoise. "Houston A. Baker, Jr. *Workings of the Spirit: The Poetics of Afro-American Women's Writing*; Missy Dehn Kubitschek, *Claiming the Heritage: African-American Women Novelists and History*." *College Literature*, 19 (February), 155–160. Review mentioning W briefly (pp. 156, 158).

3429. Longest, George, ed. "A Checklist of Scholarship on Southern Literature for 1991." *The Mississippi Quarterly*, 45 (Supplement), 1–180. Lists twelve items on W and cross-lists references to twenty-six other items dealing partially with W.

3430. Lowery, Charles D. "Spingarn Medal," in *Encyclopedia of African-American Civil Rights: From Emancipation to the Present*. Eds. Charles D. Lowery and John F. Marszalek. Westport, CT: Greenwood, p. 497. Mentions W as a medalist.

3431. Lunsford, Andrea, and Robert Connors. *The St. Martin's Handbook*. Second edition. New York: St. Martin's Press, pp. 133, 448. Quotes and comments on passages from *BB*.

3432. Lynch, Michael F. "Beyond Guilt and Innocence: Redemptive Suffering and Love in Baldwin's *Another Country*." *Obsidian II*, 7 (Spring-Summer), 1–18. Mentions briefly *NS* (p. 1).

3433. Lyne, William. "The Signifying Modernist: Ralph Ellison and the Limits of the Double Consciousness." *PMLA*, 107 (March), 319–330. Notes that Ellison identifies Eliot, Joyce, and Dostoevsky, not W, as influences on *Invisible Man*; mentions Henry Louis Gates's contrast of Ellison and W; and concludes by claiming that the "underlying economic and social realities" of *NS* and *Invisible Man* are similar.

3434. Macieski, Robert. "American Writers Congress," in *Encyclopedia of the American Left*. Eds. Mari Jo Buhle, Paul Buhle, and Dan Georgakas. Urbana: University of Illinois Press, pp. 33–34.

3435. Madhubuti, Haki. "25 Years with TWP and the Black Literary Tradition." *Black Books Bulletin*, 1 (Spring), 3–4, 19. Mentions W briefly (p. 4).

3436. Magistrale, Tony. "Hard Times." *African American Review*, 26 (Summer), 355–357. Review of Wanda Coleman's *African Sleeping Sickness: Stories & Poems* mentioning W briefly.

3437. Marable, Manning. "Blueprint for Black Studies and Multiculturalism." *The Black Scholar*, 22 (September), 30–35. Mentions W briefly (p. 31).

3438. _____. "Blueprint for Black Studies and Multiculturalism." *The Black Scholar*, (Summer), 30–35. Mentions W briefly (p. 31).

3439. _____. "The Crisis in Western Culture," in his *The Crisis of Color and Democracy: Essays on Race, Class and Power*. Monroe, ME: Common Courage Press, pp. 94–96. Mentions W briefly.

3440. Margolies, Edward. "Black Literary History." *The Mississippi Quarterly*, 45 (Winter), 105–110. Review of Blyden Jackson's *A History of Afro-American Literature, Volume I: The Long Beginning, 1746–1895* mentioning W briefly.

3441. _____. "*Talking at the Gates: A Life of James Baldwin*. By James Campbell." *American Literature*, 64 (June), 415–416. Mentions W briefly.

3442. _____. Untitled excerpt, in *Black Literature Criticism*. Ed. James P. Draper. Vol. 3. Detroit: Gale, pp. 2006–2010.

3443. Mason, Jimmie. "Using *Native Son* to Explore Language and Stereotype," in *Social Issues in the English Classroom*. Eds. C. Mark Hurlbert and Samuel Totten. Urbana, IL: National Council of Teachers of English, pp. 231–245. A high-school teacher in Pasadena, California, explains her method of teaching *NS* in a racially mixed school. She emphasizes open discussion, the deleterious effect of racial and ethnic epithets, and questions designed to induce students to examine their own racial attitudes through reading the novel.

3444. Masuda, Mitsuko. "A Study of *American Hunger*. 14, 81–96. Assuming that *AH* is not protest but a humorous work of art in search of the inner self, Masuda analyzes the humor.

3445. Maxwell, William. "*Abstract*: 'Down Home to Chicago': The Richard Wright – Zora Neale Hurston Debate and the Literature of the Great Migration." *The Richard Wright Newsletter*, 2 (Fall), 6. Compares W and Hurston in relation to the Great Migration, focusing on "Long Black Song" and "The Gilded Six-Bits."

3446. McDonald, Sheila J. "*Native Son*," in *Masterpieces of African-American Literature*. Ed. Frank N. Magill. New York: HarperCollins, pp. 325–328. Describes the principal characters, summarizes the plot, and analyzes the novel's determinism, characterization, major theme of fear, symbolism, and final section. W's novel is both naturalistic and existential, qualities growing out of black life.

3447. McGrady, Broderick. "*The Man Who Cried I Am*," in *Masterpieces of African-American Literature*. Ed. Frank N. Magill. New York: HarperCollins, pp. 277–280. Notes that the character Harry Ames is based on W (p. 277).

3448. McKay, Nellie Y. "Introduction," in *The Third Door: The Autobiography of an American Negro Woman* by Ellen Tarry. Tuscaloosa: The University of Alabama Press, pp. ix–xxvi. Includes contrast of Tarry's book and *BB* (pp. xiv–xvi, xxiv).

3449. McLeod, A.L. "Lamming, George. *In the castle of my skin*." *Choice*, 29 (July-August), 1678. Considers W's introduction to the orginal edition outmoded.

3450. Meese, Elizabeth. *(Sem) Erotics: Theorizing Lesbian: Writing*. New York University Press, p. 143. Comments on the W – Gertrude Stein Relationship.

3451. Menand, Louis. "The Hammer and the Nail." *The New Yorker*, 68 (20 July), 79–84. Essay-review of the Library of America edition of W together with an appraisal of W's career and intellectual development. According to Menand, after rejecting religion, racist American society, and Marxism, W adapted a Nietzchean view of the world in which domination and submission are ingrained human characteristics. W's writing and thinking reflected his "own particular history of deprivation."

3452. Michaels, Walter Benn. "Race Into Culture: A Critical Genealogy of Cultural Identity." *Critical Inquiry*, 18 (Summer), 655–685. Quotes from "I Bite the Hand That Feeds Me" to show that Bigger is "bereft of a culture."

3453. Michener, James A. *The World Is My Home: A Memoir*. New York: Random House, p. 478. Mentions W briefly.

3454. Miller, Eugene E. "From Our Readers: An Open Letter to Jerry Ward, Keneth Kinnamon, Arnold Rampersad and the *Wright Circle*." *The Richard Wright Newsletter*, 2 (Fall), 7.

3455. _____. "Open Letter Concerning the Library of America Edition of *Native Son*." *Afram Newsletter*, 35 (June), 30. Criticizes sharply Keneth Kinnamon and Arnold Rampersad for overestimating the importance of the passages restored in the Library of America Edition. Reprinted: 1992

3456. Miller, R. Baxter. "Framing and Framed Languages in Hughes's *Ask Your Mama: 12 Moods for Jazz*." *MELUS*, 17 (Winter), 3–13. Mentions W briefly (pp. 10, 11).

3457. Minter, David. "*The Southern Writer in the Postmodern World*. By Fred Hobson; *The Texas Legacy of Katherine Anne Porter*. By James T.F. Tanner." *The Journal of Southern History*, 58 (November), 767–769. Review mentioning W briefly.

3458. Mitgang, Herbert. "Books of the Times: An American Master and New Discoveries." *The New York Times* (1 January), p. 18. Favorable review of the Library of American edition of W. Emphasizes the utility of Arnold Rampersad's notes.

3459. _____. "Richard Wright's Works." *The Louisville Courier Journal* (11 January), p. A11. Review of the Library of America edition surveying W's career, noting the restoration of expurgated material, and concluding that *NS* and *BB* "retain their vigor and their relevance."

3460. Moody, Joycelyn. "*Workings of the Spirit: The Poetics of Afro-American Women's Writing*. By Houston A. Baker, Jr." *Modern Language Quarterly*, 53 (December), 475–481. Review containing a paragraph on Baker's treatment of *TMBV* and W's attitude toward women (pp. 477–478).

3461. Moore, Steven. "Richard Wright. *Early Works*; *Later Works*." *Review of Contemporary Fiction*, 12 (Spring), 166. Mixed review of the Library of America edition of W applauding the new texts but complaining of the surprising failure to include *LD* and *EM*.

3462. Moorer, Frank Edward. "Creating the Uncreated Features of My Face: The Social Self and Transcendence in Selected Black American and South African Autobiographies." *Dissertation Abstracts International*, 52 (June), 4379-A. Includes consideration of *BB*.

3463. Morey, Ann-Janine. "Margaret Atwood and Toni Morrison: Reflections on Postmodernism and the Study of Religion and Literature." *Journal of the American Academy of Religion*, 60 (Fall), 493–513. Mentions W briefly (p. 501). Reprinted: 1997.

3464. Mori, Aoi. "Richard Wright's *Native Son* and *Black Boy*: Shocking Treatment and Soothing Lyricism." *Kyushu American Literature*, 33, 69–76. *NS*, based on fact, is shocking to hypocritical whites, *BB* is lyrical and soothing because it deals with escape from the south. W shows African American identity to both races [T.K., R.B., and Y.K.].

3465. Moses, Wilson J. "On Dr. Charles T. Davis." *Reconstruction*, 2, 75–77. Mentions W briefly.

3466. Mūgo, Mīcere Gīthae. "Mīcere Gīthae Mūgo," in *Talking with African Writers*. Ed. Jane Wickinson. London: James Currey/Portsmouth, NH: Heinemann, p. 119. The Kenyan writer notes her early interest in African American literature including *NS* and *BB*.

3467. Munger, David. "*Richard Wright* The Library Card," in his *80 Readings*. New York: HarperCollins, p. 25. Headnote to an excerpt from *BB*.

3468. Murphy, James F. *The Proletarian Moment: The Controversy Over Leftism in Literature*. Urbana: University of Illinois Press, pp. 3, 10, 159. Mentions W briefly. Quotes Alvin Starr on "Blueprint for Negro Writing."

3469. Murray, Timothy D. "*Twice a Year*," in *American Literary Magazines*. Ed. Edward E. Chielens. Westport, CT: Greenwood Press, pp. 373–378. Notes that W served as associate editor and contributor.

3470. Natanson, Nicholas. *The Black Image in the New Deal: The Politics of FSA Photography*. Knoxville: The University of Tennessee Press, pp. 15, 143, 154, 173, 244–255, 288. Quotes from W's introduction to *Black Metropolis* and Sterling North's review of *NS*. Chapter Six contains substantial treatment of *TMBV* with information on the W-Rosskam collaboration, some drawn from the Wright archive at Yale. Natanson sharply criticizes the book for its monolithic view of black life, its muckraking tone, and "tricks involving captioning and visual-textual juxtaposition" (p. 250). Comments also on the reception of *TMBV*.

3471. Nazareth, Peter. "James Campbell. *Talking at the Gates: A Life of James Baldwin*." *World Literature Today*, 66 (Summer), 521–522. Review mentioning W briefly.

3472. Nielsen, Aldon L. "Melvin B. Tolson and the Deterritorialization of Modernism." *African American Review*, 26 (Summer), 241–255. Quotes Black Boy passages from *Harlem Gallery* (pp. 248, 249).

3473. Nnaemeka, Obioma. "Richard Wright: Climate of Fear and Violence." *The Western Journal of Black Studies*, 16 (Spring), 14–20. Discusses *UTC* and *NS*, of which "the main thesis … is that violence is a consequence of living in excessive fear or stress situations" (p. 14). Collectivism is the key to social change.

3474. Oates, Joyce Carol. "Introduction," in her *The Oxford Book of American Short Stories*. New York: Oxford University Press, pp. 3–16. Comments briefly on "The Man Who Was Almost a Man" and *NS* (p. 14).

3475. _____. "Richard Wright," in her *The Oxford Book of American Short Stories*. New York: Oxford University Press, p. 31. Headnote to

"The Man Who Was Almost a Man" commenting on *NS* and mentioning *UTC, BB, O, LT,* and *EM.* W is "an artist of complexity and subtlety."

3476. O'Connor, Mary. "Zora Neale Hurston and Talking Between Cultures." *Canadian Review of American Studies,* Special Issue, 141–161. Discusses W's review of *Their Eyes Were Watching God* (pp. 144–145).

3477. _____. "Zora Neale Hurston and Talking Between Cultures." *Canadian Review of American Studies,* Special Issue, Part I, 141–161. Comments on W's review of *Their Eyes Were Watching God* (pp. 144–145), and Hurston's review of *UTC* (p. 155).

3478. Olsen, Stephen. "Reading as Believing." *ADE Bulletin,* No. 102 (Fall), pp. 17–19. Mentions the "enabling power" for W of reading Dreiser and Lewis.

3479. O'Meally, Robert G. "Le Roman invisible de Ralph Ellison." *Focus,* pp. 9–11.

3480. Owens, Louis. *Other Destinies: Understanding the American Indian Novel.* Norman: University of Oklahoma Press, p. 44. Mentions W briefly.

3481. Pace, Barbara G. "The Textbook Canon: Genre, Gender, and Race in US Literature Anthologies." *English Journal,* 81 (September), 33–38. Lists W as a canonical author in high school textbooks s.v. Story/Novel Excerpt and Poetry (p. 34). Comments on "The Man Who Saw the Flood" (pp. 35, 37).

3482. Pearson, Norman Holmes. "American Literature," in *The Encyclopedia Americana.* Ed. Lawrence T. Lorimer. Danbury, CT: Grolier, 1992, vol. 1, pp. 691–709. Reprint of 1986.

3483. _____. "American Literature: The 20th Centrury," in *The Encyclopedia Americana.* Ed. Lawrence T. Lorimer. Danbury CT: Grolier, pp. 703–709.

3484. Peck, David R. *American Ethnic Literatures: Native American, African American, Chicano/Latino,* and *Asian American Writers and Their Backgrounds.* Pasadena, CA: Salem Press, pp. 10, 34, 43, 46, 73, 76, 80, 103, 105, 110, 111, 113–115, 120, 121, 122–126. Contains a list of W's books (p. 103) and mentions W briefly elsewhere.

3485. Peck, David. "New Masses," in *Encyclopedia of the American Left.*

Eds. Mari Jo Buhle, Paul Buhle, and Dan Georgakas. Urbana: University of Illinois Press, pp. 526–527. Reprint of 1990.

3486. Pemberton, Gayle. "The Hottest Water in Chicago," in her *The Hottest Water in Chicago: On Family, Race, Time, and American Culture.* Boston: Faber and Faber, pp. 3–12.

3487. _____. "The Koan of Nana," in her *The Hottest Water in Chicago: On Family, Race, Time, and American Culture.* Boston: Faber and Faber, pp. 88–107.

3488. _____. "Professor Dearest," in her *The Hottest Water in Chicago: On Family, Race, Time, and American Culture.* Boston: Faber and Faber, pp. 151–161. Quotes Simone de Beauvoir quoting W on the constant consciousness of being black in a racist society (pp. 153–154).

3489. _____. "Waiting for Godot on Jeffery Boulevard," in her *The Hottest Water in Chicago: On Family, Race, Time, and American Culture.* Boston: Faber and Faber, pp. 176–193. Mentions W and her doctoral thesis.

3490. _____. "The Zen of Bigger Thomas," in her *The Hottest Water in Chicago: On Family, Race, Time, and American Culture.* Boston: Faber and Faber, pp. 162–175. Discusses Bigger Thomas in the context of continuing black violence. Compares *NS,* "a comic tragedy," to *Invisible Man,* "a tragic comedy" (p. 172).

3491. Perreault, Donna Marie. "Questioning Authorship in Twentieth Century Literary Autobiography." *Dissertation Abstracts International,* 53 (August), 499-A. Includes a chapter on W.

3492. Perry, Margaret. "Gwendolyn Brooks," in *Notable Black American Women.* Ed. Jessie Carney Smith. Detroit: Gale, pp. 105–109. Mentions W briefly (p. 106).

3493. Peterson, Beverly. "*Home Ground: Southern Autobiography.* Edited by J. Bill Berry." *The Journal of Mississippi History,* 54 (August), 307–308. Review mentioning W briefly.

3494. Pétillon, Pierre-Yves. *Histoire de la littérature américaine: notre demi-siècle, 1939–1989.* Paris: Fayard, pp. 10, 15–17, 71, 75, 109, 110, 127, 144, 161, 163, 164, 357, 462, 491, 494, 569, 571, 572, 591, 592, 649, 650, 654, 700, 705, 710, 713,

714, 720, 723. The entry on W provides biographical information, comments on *NS,* and notes his influence on subsequent black writers, especially Ellison and Baldwin (pp. 15–17). Mentions W briefly elsewhere.

3495. Pettis, Joyce. "Talk as Defensive Artifice: Merle Kinbona in *The Chosen Place, The Timeless People.*" *African American Review,* 26 (Spring), 109–117. Mentions briefly "Big Boy Leaves Home" (p. 117).

3496. Pinckney, Darryl. "Trickster Tales," in *Speech and Power: The African-American Essay and Its Cultural Content from Polemics to Pulpit.* Vol. I. Ed. Gerald Early. Hopewell, NJ: The Ecco Press, pp. 315–324.

3497. Ploski, Harry A., and James Williams. *Reference Library of Black America.* Detroit: Gale, 1021–1022.

3498. Poirier, Richard. *Poetry and Pragmatism.* Cambridge, MA: Harvard University Press pp. 92, 201. Quotes Constance Webb quoting a statement by Gertrude Stein to W that "William James taught me all I Know."

3499. Portelli, Alessandro. *Il testo e la voce: Oralità, letteratura e democrazia in America.* Rome: Manifestolibri, pp. 93, 114, 126, 213, 214, 215, 225, 230, 246. Contains several references to *BB,* Bigger and *NS* (especially its dialogue), and one reference to *TMBV.*

3500. _____. "Introduzione," in *Narrazione della Vita di Frederick Douglass, Uno schiavo Americano, scritta da lui stesso.* Rome: Manifestolibri, pp. 7–42. Mentions W briefly (p. 7).

3501. Pratt, Mary Louise. *Imperial Eyes: Travel Writing and Transculturation.* London: Routledge, pp. 213, 221–223, 224. Discusses *BP,* emphasizing how it differs from the disparaging travel writing of Albert Moravia and Paul Theroux.

3502. Prevost, Verbie Lovorn. "Theses and Dissertations for 1991." *South Atlantic Review,* 57 (November), 169–199. Lists a thesis by Curtis Richard Scott, "The Dramatization of *Native Son:* How 'Bigger' Was Reborn."

3503. Rabinowitz, Paula. "*The Proletarian Moment: The Controversy over Leftism in Literature.* By James F. Murphy." *The Journal of American History,* 79 (December), 1227. Review mentioning W.

3504. Rabinowitz, Peter J. "Against

Close Reading," in *Pedagogy Is Politics: Literary Theory and Critical Teaching*. Ed. Maria-Regina Kecht. Urbana: University of Illinois Press, pp. 230–243. Mentions briefly *NS* (p. 233).

3505. Rajiv, Sudhi. *Forms of Black Consciousness*. New York: Advent Books, pp. i, ii, iii, 1–2, 5, 20–22, 23, 31, 39–40, 43–80, 81, 83, 91, 104, 120, 151, 152, 154–155, 156, 160, 164, 167, 168, 172, 174, 175, 176, 177, 183, 184, 195. The chapter on W, "Richard Wright and Intellectual Consciousness," consists mainly of summary of *BB* and *AH* emphasizing his racial consciousness, individualism, and alienation from his country. Mentions W and his works elsewhere with comparisons to Malcolm X and Eldridge Cleaver.

3506. Rampersad, Arnold. "*Adventures of Huckleberry Finn* and Afro-American Literature," in *Satire or Evasion? Black Perspectives on Huckleberry Finn*. Eds. James S. Leonard, Thomas A. Tenney, and Thadious M. Davis. Durham, NC: Duke University Press, pp. 216–227. Reprint of 1984.

3507. _____. "Design and Truth in Biography." *South Central Review*, 9 (Summer), 1–18. Discusses Michel Fabre's treatment in *The Unfinished Quest of Richard Wright* of "The Voodoo of Hell's Half-Acre" as a misuse of an interview source.

3508. _____. "The Fall of a Titan," in *The New Cavalcade: African American Writing from 1760 to the Present*. Eds. Arthur P. Davis, J. Saunders Redding, and Joyce Ann Joyce. Washington: Howard University Press, pp. 709–729.

3509. _____. "Too Honest for His Own Time." *The Richard Wright Newsletter*, 2 (Fall), 1–4.

3510. Raper, Julius Rowan. *Narcissus from Rubble: Competing Models of Character in Contemporary British and American Fiction*. Baton Rouge: Louisiana State University Press, pp. xi, xii, 9, 10, 154. Mentions briefly Bigger Thomas and W's reading of Sartre and Camus in the context of the theme of self-transcendence through creative violence.

3511. Redding, J. Saunders. "The Black Arts Movement, A Modest Dissent," in *A Scholar's Conscience: Selected Writings of J. Saunders Redding*. Ed. Faith Berry. Lexington:

University Press of Kentucky, pp. 212–218. Reprint of 1977.

3512. _____. "From 'The Meaning of Bandung,'" in *A Scholar's Conscience: Selected Writings of J. Saunders Redding*. Ed. Faith Berry. Lexington: University Press of Kentucky, pp. 131–134.

3513. _____. "The Negro Author, His Publisher, His Public, and His Purse," in *A Scholar's Conscience: Selected Writings of J. Saunders Redding*. Ed. Faith Berry. Lexington: University Press of Kentucky, pp. 140–146.

3514. _____. "Of Men and the Writing of Books," in his *A Scholar's Conscience: Selected Writings of J. Saunders Redding*. Ed. Faith Berry. Lexington: University Press of Kentucky, pp. 175–181.

3515. _____. "Review of *White Man, Listen!* by Richard Wright," in *A Scholar's Conscience: Selected Writings of J. Saunders Redding*. Ed. Faith Berry. Lexington: University Press of Kentucky, pp. 153–154.

3516. _____. "Richard Wright: An Evaluation," in *A Scholar's Conscience: Selected Writings of J. Saunders Redding*. Ed. Faith Berry. Lexington: University Press of Kentucky, pp. 155–161.

3517. Reilly, John M. "Afterword," in *Black Boy: A Record of Childhood and Youth*. New York: Harper & Row, pp. 286–288.

3518. _____. "*A Richard Wright Bibliography: Fifty Years of Criticism and Commentary, 1933–1982*. Compiled by Keneth Kinnamon with the help of Joseph Benson, Michel Fabre, and Craig Werner." *Resources for American Literary Study*, 18 (Fall), 269–272. Favorable review placing Kinnamon in the context of the academic legitimation of the study of African American literature. Comments on Kinnamon's early work on W before describing fully the *Bibliography* with emphasis on its expansive notion of literary reputation.

3519. Richardson, Mark. "Richard Wright." *The London Times Literary Supplement* (24 January), p. 15. The principal researcher of the Library of American edition of W rebuts James Campbell's criticism of it. W would not have revised *NS* and *BB*, Richardson asserts, if the Book-of-the-Month Club had not intervened.

3520. Ridley, Chauncey A. "Sethe's

'Big, Bad' Love," in *Understanding Others: Cultural and Cross-Cultural Studies and the Teaching of Literature*. Eds. Joseph Trimmer and Tilly Warnock. Urbana, Illinois: National Council of Teachers of English, pp. 153–164. Mentions briefly Bigger Thomas (p. 158).

3521. Rivlin, Gary. *Fire on the Prairie: Chicago's Harold Washington and the Politics of Race*. New York: Holt, p. 6. Mentions *NS* briefly in the context of its crowded Chicago setting.

3522. Robins, Natalie. *Alien Ink: The FBI's War on Freedom of Expression*. New York: William Morrow, pp. 282, 284–287, 345, 402. Discusses and quotes from W's 181-page FBI file. Quotes also from Addison Gayle, Cartha DeLoach, and Amiri Baraka on W's death.

3523. Robinson, Joyce Russell. "The Shadow Within: Du Boisian Double Consciousness in Five African-American Novels." *Dissertation Abstracts International*, 52 (June), 4332-A–4333-A. Includes consideration of *O*.

3524. Rodgers, Lawrence R. "Dorothy West's *The Living Is Easy* and the Ideal of Southern Folk Community." *African American Review*, 26 (Spring), 161–172. Includes discussion of West's conflict with W (p. 163) and mentions W elsewhere (p. 164).

3525. _____. "Lawrence Dunbar's *The Sport of the Gods:* The Doubly Conscious World of Plantation Fiction, Migration and Ascent." *American Literary Realism 1870–1910*, 24 (Spring), 42–57. Mentions W briefly (p. 44).

3526. Roget, Gwendoline L. "The Chester Himes Mystique." *African American Review*, 26 (Fall), 521–522. Comments on the profound effect on Himes of W's death.

3527. Rogin, Michael. "Black Masks, White Skin: Consciousness of Class and American National Culture." *Radical History Review*, 54 (Fall), 141–152. Mentions W in the dispute between Ellison and Irving Howe (p. 150).

3528. Rohrberger, Mary. "*Another Country*," in *Masterpieces of African-American Literature*. Ed. Frank N. Magill. New York: HarperCollins, pp. 5–8. Mentions W briefly (p. 8).

3529. Romine, Scott. "History and Poetry in Richard Wright's

Black Boy." Hypotheses: A Neo-Aristotelian Analysis 2, pp. 2–3. Argues that W changes history — his own — to art in *BB*.

3530. Rosenbaum, Jonathan. "Welles' Career: A Chronology," in his *This Is Orson Welles*. New York: HarperCollins, pp. 323–453. Includes entries for the opening of the Broadway and roadshow versions of the play *NS*. Includes a photograph from a rehearsal.

3531. Rowan, Carl T. *Breaking Barriers: A Memoir*. New York: HarperCollins, pp. 71, 105, 368. Reprint of 1991

3532. Rushdy, Ashraf H.A. "The Phenomenology of the Allmuseri: Charles Johnson and the Subject of the Narrative of Slavery." *African American Review*, 26 (Fall), 373–394. Mentions W briefly (p. 374) and quotes from and comments on his account of the Joe Louis-Max Baer fight (p. 389).

3533. Russell, Kathy, Midge Wilson, and Ronald Hall. *The Color Complex: The Politics of Skin Color Among African Americans*. New York: Harcourt Brace Jovanovich, p. 117. Notes that W's wives were white.

3534. Samuels, Wilfred D. "Soothsayer and Interpreter: Darwin T. Turner and African-American Literary Criticism." *The Langston Hughes Review*, 11 (Fall), 15–27. Mentions briefly W, *NS*, and *BB* (p. 15).

3535. Sanders, Ronald. Untitled excerpt, in *Black Literature Criticism*. Ed. James P. Draper. Vol. 3. Detroit: Gale, pp. 2003–2006.

3536. Saporta, Marc. "L'histoire de la littérature romanesque afro-américaine." *Focus*, pp. 1–8.

3537. Sasaki, Seiji. "Richard Wright's 'Long Black Song.'" *Newsletter of the Black Studies Association of Japan*, 34 (12 March), 2–3. Brief comment on the story focusing on the relation of sound to emotion.

3538. Saunders, James Robert. "Exorcising the Demons: John Edgar Wideman's Literary Response." *The Hollins Critic*, 29 (December), 1–10. Mentions briefly Ellison's "Richard Wright's Blues" (p. 8).

3539. Savery, Pancho. "Baldwin, Bebop, and 'Sonny's Blues,'" in *Understanding Others: Cultural and Cross-Cultural Studies and the Teaching of Literature*. Eds. Joseph Trimmer and Tilly Warnock. Urbana, IL: National Council of Teachers of English, pp. 165–176. Mentions

briefly and quotes from "Blueprint for Negro Writing" (p. 166).

3540. Sawyer-Lauçanno, Christopher. *The Continual Pilgrimage: American Writers in Paris, 1944–1960*. New York: Grove Press, pp. 4, 7–8, 9, 67–98, 99–102, 103, 109, 117, 123, 128, 151, 182, 183, 184, 185–186, 187–188, 189, 190, 191, 192, 203. The chapter on W treats his exile in Paris, emphasizing his welcome by French intellectuals, his quarrel with Baldwin, his commitment to political issues, and his decline.

3541. Schueller, Malini Johar. *The Politics of Voice: Liberalism and Social Criticism from Franklin to Kingston*. Albany: State University of New York Press, p. 166. Quotes from Russell J. Reising on W (1986).

3542. Schwarz, Daniel. "Review Essay: Canonicity, Culture, and Pluralism — A Humanistic Perspective on Professing English." *Texas Studies in Literature and Language*, 34 (Spring), 149–175. Mentions W briefly (p. 160).

3543. Scott, Curtis R. "The Dramatization of *Native Son*: How 'Bigger' Was Reborn." *The Journal of American Drama and Theatre*, 4, no. 3, pp. 5–41. Detailed treatment of the composition of the play, in which W, Paul Green, and, to a lesser degree, John Houseman and Orson Welles participated. Draws on the unpublished papers of Green as well as recollections and writings of the five men. Emphasizes Green's emphasis on some personal responsibility for Bigger in contrast to W's and Houseman's emphasis on social forces."

3544. Scruggs, Charles. "The Invisible City in Toni Morrison's *Beloved*." *Arizona Quarterly*, 48 (Autumn), 95–132. Mentions W briefly (pp. 94–95).

3545. Setterberg, Fred. "Zora Neale Hurston in the Land of 1,000 Dances." *The Georgia Review*, 46 (Winter), 627–643. Comments on W's assesment of Hurston (p. 631).

3546. Sharpe, Patricia. "*Their Eyes Were Watching God*," in *Masterpieces of African-American Literature*. Ed. Frank N. Magill. New York: HarperCollins, pp. 569–572. Notes and quotes from W's unfavorable assessment of Hurston's novel (p. 572).

3547. Shrodes, Caroline, Harry Finestone, and Michael Shugrue.

"Richard Wright: The Ethics of Living Jim Crow," in their *The Conscious Reader*. Fifth edition. New York: Macmillan, pp. 717, 725.

3548. _____. "Richard Wright: The Ethics of Living Jim Crow," in their *The Conscious Reader*. Fifth edition. New York: Macmillan, p. 717.

3549. _____. "Suggestions for Discussion, Suggestions for Writing," in their *The Conscious Reader*. Fifth edition. New York: Macmillan, p. 725.

3550. Shuman, R. Baird. "*The Long Dream*," in *Masterpieces of African-American Literature*. Ed. Frank N. Magill. New York: HarperCollins, pp. 265–269. Describes the principal characters, summarizes the plot, and analyzes characterization, particularly in relation to the castration metaphor. Relates W's protest in *LD* to his previous works and to the black literature of the 1960s.

3551. Singh, A[mritjit]. "Fabre, Michel. *From Harlem to Paris: Black American writers in France, 1840–1980*." *Choice*, 29 (June), 1540. Mentions W briefly.

3552. [Skerrett, Joseph T., Jr.]. "Preliminaries." *MELUS*, 17 (Winter), 1–2. Contains a prècis of Carolyn Camp's essay in this issue.

3553. Smith, Robert C. "'Politics' Is Not Enough: The Institutionalization of the African American Freedom Movement," in *From Exclusion to Inclusion: The Long Struggle for African American Political Power*. Eds. Ralph C. Gomes and Linda Faye Williams. Westport, CT: Greenwood Press, pp. 97–126. Mentions briefly F.B.I. surveillance of W and others.

3554. Smith, Thaddeus. "Communist Party," in *Encyclopedia of African-American Civil Rights: From Emancipation to the Present*. Eds. Charles D. Lowery and John F. Marszalik. Westport, CT: Greenwood, pp. 122–123. Mentions W briefly.

3555. Smith, Tom. "Public Radio Book Show: Nikki Giovanni," in *Conversations with Nikki Giovanni*. Ed. Virginia C. Fowler. Jackson: University Press of Mississippi, pp. 188–197. Transcript of a 1990 interview in which Smith mentions W briefly.

3556. Smith, Valerie. "The Documentary Impulse in Contemporary

African-American Film," in *Black Popular Culture*, a project by Michele Wallace. Ed. Gina Dent. Seattle: Bay Press, pp. 56–64. Mentions W briefly (p. 56).

3557. Sollors, Werner. "*People Who Led to My Plays:* Adrienne Kennedy's Autobiography," in *Intersecting Boundaries: The Theatre of Adrienne Kennedy*. Eds. Paul K. Bryant-Jackson and Lois More Overbeck. Minneapolis: University of Minnesota Press, pp. 13–20. Mentions W briefly (p. 14).

3558. Sowinska, Suzanne, *American Women Writers and the Radical Agenda, 1925–1940*. Ann Arbor: UMI, pp. 11, 110, 115, 118–122, 125, 127, 128, 143, 152, 224–225. Includes comment on the leftward movement of W and Langston Hughes (pp. 118–122). Also compares "Bright and Morning Star" and Grace Lampkins's *A Sign for Cain* (pp. 224–225) and mentions W elsewhere.

3559. Spears, Monroe. "*The History of Southern Literature,*" in *his Countries of the Mind*. Columbia: University of Missouri Press, pp. 291–294.

3560. Stanford, Ann Folwell. "Dialectics of Desire: War and the Resistive Voice in Gwendolyn Brooks's 'Negro Hero' and 'Gay Chaps at the Bar.'" *African American Review*, 26 (Summer), 197–211. Mentions in a note Mrs. Dalton in *NS*.

3561. Stephens, Martha. Untitled excerpt, in *Black Literature Criticism*. Ed. James P. Draper. Vol. 3. Detroit: Gale, pp. 2012–2014.

3562. Stepto, Robert B. "L'épanouissement d'une littérature." *Focus*, pp. 17–20.

3563. _____. "Teaching Afro-American Literature: Survey or Tradition: The Reconstruction of Instruction," in *The New Cavalcade: Afro-American Writing from 1760 to the Present*. Vol. II. Eds. Arthur P. Davis, J. Saunders Redding, and Joyce Ann Joyce. Washington: Howard University Press, pp. 738–750.

3564. Stone, Albert E. *The Return of Nat Turner: History, Literature, and Cultural Politics in Sixties America*. Athens: The University of Georgia Press, pp. 40, 194, 197, 296. Mentions W briefly and comments on his relation to *Black Thunder* by Arna Bontemps.

3565. [Suárez-Galban, Eugenio].

Catalogo General Origenes 1992. Madrid: Origenes, 23 pp. Publisher's catalog listing the Spanish translation of *PS*.

3566. Summerfield, Judith. "Consider This," in her *Negotiations: A Reader for Writers*. New York: McGraw-Hill, p. 559. Study aid for a selection from *BB*.

3567. _____. "Consider This, "in her *Negotiations: A Reader for Writers.*" New York: McGraw-Hill, p. 559. Comments on the passage in *BB* in which W borrows a white man's library card and becomes aware of serious literature.

3568. Tarry, Ellen. *The Third Door: The Autobiography of an American Negro Woman*. With intro. by Nellie Y. McKay. Tuscaloosa: The University of Alabama Press, p. 149.

3569. Tate, Claudia. "Conversations with Nikki Giovanni," in *Conversations with Nikki Giovanni*. Ed. Virginia C. Fowler. Jackson: University Press of Mississippi, pp. 133–150. Reprint of 1983.36

3570. _____. *Domestic Allegories of Political Desire: The Black Heroine's Text at the Turn of the Century*. New York: Oxford University Press, pp. 70–79, 88, 89, 249. Compares *BB* and *Their Eyes Were Watching God* "interrogating gender constructions and discourses of racial and sexual desire." The discussion focuses on gender differences in attitudes toward marriage and personal autonomy. Tate also comments on W as the central figure in protest fiction and the black aesthetic.

3571. Tate, Greg. "White Magic: Don DeLillo's Intelligence Newworks," in his *Flyboy in the Buttermilk: Essays on Contemporary America*. New York: Simon and Schuster, pp. 220–228. Mentions W briefly (p. 220).

3572. _____. "Yo! Hermeneutics!: Henry Louis Gates, Houston Baker, and David Toop," in his *Flyboy in the Buttermilk: Essays on Contemporary America*. New York: Simon and Schuster, pp. 145–158. Mentions W briefly (pp. 150, 153). Also mentions *TMBV* (p. 153).

3573. _____. "You Look Fabulist: Steve Erickson's Wild Kingdom," in his *Flyboy in the Buttermilk: Essays on Contemporary America*. New York: Simon and Schuster, pp. 214–219. Mentions W briefly (p. 215).

3574. Taylor, Jared. *Paved with*

Good Intentions: The Failure of Race Relations in Contemporary America. New York: Carroll & Graf, p. 125. Notes that *NS* was a Book-of-the-Month Club selection.

3575. Terrell, Angela. "Nikki Giovanni: 'Vision and Space,'" in *Conversations with Nikki Giovanni*. Ed. Virginia C. Fowler. Jackson: University Press of Mississippi, pp. 43–48.

3576. Thomas, Lorenzo. "The Poetry of Sonia Sanchez," in *Masterpieces of African-American Literature*. Ed. Frank N. Magill. New York: HarperCollins, pp. 439–442. Comments briefly on W's haiku (p. 440).

3577. Tidwell, John Edgar. "Introduction," in his edition of *Livin' the Blues: Memoirs of a Black Journalist and Poet* by Frank Marshall Davis. Madison: The University of Wisconsin Press, p. xix. Compares Davis to Bigger Thomas.

3578. Tillery, Tyrone. *Claude McKay: A Black Poet's Struggle for Identity*. Amherst: The University of Massachusetts Press, pp. 155–156. Quotes from "Blueprint for Negro Writing."

3579. _____. *Claude McKay: A Black Poet's Struggle for Ideality*. Amherst: The University of Massachusetts Press, pp. 155–156. Quotations from 1978.232.

3580. Toch, Hans. *Violent Man: An Inquiry Into the Psychology of Violence*. Revised edition. Washington, DC: American Psychological Association, pp. 182–183.

3581. Totten, Samuel. "Educating for the Development of Social Consciousness and Social Responsibility," in his and C. Mark Hurlbert's *Social Issues in the English Classroom*. Urbana, IL: National Council of Teachers of English, pp. 9–55. Mentions briefly *NS* (p. 34).

3582. Turner, Darwin. "Afro-American Literary Critics: An Introduction," in *The New Cavalcade: African American Writing from 1760 to the Present*. Vol. II. Eds. Arthur P. Davis, J. Saunders Redding, and Joyce Ann Joyce. Washington: Howard University Press, pp. 255–269. Reprint of 1971.298.

3583. _____. "Zora Neale Hurston: One More Time." *The Langston Hughes Review*, 11 (Fall), 34–37. Mentions growing up in a home with W on the bookshelves.

3584. Tuttleton, James W. "The

Problematic Texts of Richard Wright." *The Hudson Review*, 45 (Summer), 261–271. General overview of W's career occasioned by the publication of the Library of America edition. At the end of the essay Tuttleton rejects the restored texts of *BB* (with *AH*) and *NS* because they do not represent W's final intentions, for he never asked for restored editions.

3585. Van Deburg, William. *New Day in Babylon: The Black Power Movement and American Culture*. Chicago: The University of Chicago Press, p. 34. Mentions briefly W and *BP* (pp. 34, 314).

3586. Virtue, Hope McKay. "Haiku." *Afram*, No. 35 (February—Special Number), 32. Five haiku "in homage to Richard Wright."

3587. Wald, Alan. "In Retrospect: *On Native Grounds*." *Reviews in American History*, 20 (June), 276–288. Includes comments on Kazin's unfavorable treatment of W (pp. 279, 280, 285) while ignoring an important area of W's literary activity (p. 279).

3588. _____. "Introduction: The History of a Literary Radical: From Old Left to New" in his *The Responsibility of Intellectuals: Selected Essays on Marxist Traditions in Cultural Commitment*. Atlantic Highlands, NJ: Humanities Press, p. xii. Mentions W briefly.

3589. _____. "Introduction to the Morningside Books Edition," in *Writers on the Left: Episodes in American Literary Communism* by Daniel Aaron. New York: Columbia University Press, pp. xiii–xxxi. Mentions Michel Fabre's biography of W, reprints of W's work, Aaron's essay on W, and *LT*.

3590. _____. "Introduction," in his *The Responsibility of Intellectuals: Selected Essays on Marxist Traditions in Cultural Commitment*. Atlantic Highlands, NJ: Humanities Press, p. xii. Recalls studying W at Antioch College.

3591. _____. "Remembering the Answers," in his *The Responsibility of the Intellectuals: Selected Essays on Marxist Traditions in Cultural Commitment*. Atlantic Highlands, NJ: Humanities Press, pp. 85–91.

3592. _____. "The Subaltern Speaks." *Monthly Review*, 43 (April), 17–29. Mentions briefly *NS* (p. 28).

3593. _____. "The Subaltern Speaks." *Monthly Review*, 43 (1 April), pp. 17–29. Mentions W briefly (p. 18).

3594. _____. "Theorizing Cultural Difference: A Critique of the 'Ethnicity School,'" in his *The Responsibility of Intellectuals: Selected Essays on Marxist Traditions in Cultural Commitment*. Atlantic Highlands, NJ: Humanities Press, pp. 168–180.

3595. Walker, Alice. "The Unglamorous But Worthwhile Duties of the Black Revolutionary Artist, or of the Black Writer Who Simply Works and Writes," in *The Rhetoric of Struggle: Public Address by African American Women*. Ed. Robbie Jean Walker. New York: Garland, pp. 343–351.

3596. Walker, Warren S. "Bibliography." *Studies in Short Fiction*, 29 (Summer), 413–469. Lists a 1991 article by Myles R. Hurd.

3597. Ward, Jerry. "Ellison, Ralph," in *Encyclopedia of African-American Civil Rights: From Emancipation to the Present*. Eds. Charles D. Lowery and John F. Marszalek. Westport, CT: Greenwood, pp. 165–166. Mentions W briefly.

3598. _____. "*Native Son*," in *Encyclopedia of African-American Civil Rights: From Emancipation to the Present*. Eds. Charles D. Lowery and John F. Marszalek. Westport, CT: Greenwood, p. 391. Emphasizes the work's "fictional treatment of the sociology of racism." Includes a selected bibliography of six books.

3599. _____. "*Black Boy*," in *Encyclopedia of African-American Civil Rights: From Emancipation to the Present*. Eds. Charles D. Lowery and John F. Marszalek. Westport, CT: Greenwood, pp. 49. Entry praising the achievement of "yoking the pattern of slave narrative with perceptive social analysis. Includes a selected bibliography of four items.

3600. Ward, Jerry W., Jr. "Minutes of the Richard Wright Circle American Literature Association." *The Richard Wright Newsletter*, 2 (Fall), 4. Includes discussion of future W sessions.

3601. _____, and Maryemma Graham. "Letter from the Editors." *The Richard Wright Newsletter*, 2 (Fall), 1. Comments on the interest in W generated by the Library of America edition and notes Keneth Kinnamon's continuing bibliographical work.

3602. [Ward, Jerry W.] "Richard Wright," in his and John Oliver Killens's *Black Southern Voices: An Anthology of Fiction, Poetry, Drama, Nonfiction, and Critical Essays*. New York: Penguin Books, p. 34. Headnote to "The Man Who Saw the Flood commenting on W's stature and the formation of The Richard Wright Circle. Mentions a few secondary works as well as most of W's own books

3603. Warren, Nagueyalti. "Paule Burke Marshall," in *Notable Black American Women*. Ed. Jessie Carney Smith. Detroit: Gale, pp. 728–731. Mentions W briefly (p. 728).

3604. Washington, Gladys J. "*The Narrows*," in *Masterpieces of African-American Literature*. Ed. Frank N. Magill. New York: HarperCollins, pp. 321–324. Mentions briefly W and *NS* (p. 324).

3605. Watts, Jill. *God, Harlem U.S.A.: The Father Divine Story*. Berkeley: University of California Press, p. 119. Quotes W expressing hostility to Father Divine's movement.

3606. Webb, Constance. "Wright, Richard (1908–60)," in *Encyclopedia of the American Left*. Eds. Mari Jo Buhle, Paul Buhle, and Dan Georgakas. Urbana: University of Illinois Press, pp. 860–861.

3607. Weber, Ronald. *The Midwestern Ascendancy in American Writing*. Bloomington: Indiana University Press, p. 222. Mentions W briefly.

3608. Weinstein, Philip M. *Faulkner's Subject: A Cosmos No One Owns*. Cambridge: Cambridge University Press, p. 64. Mentions briefly "Big Boy leaves home."

3609. Weiss, Mary Lynn. "Two in France: Expatriation and Identity in Selected Works of Gertrude Stein and Richard Wright." *Dissertation Abstracts International*, 53 (November), 1521-A–1522-A, Includes consideration of *PS*, *BP*, and *WML*.

3610. Weixlmann, Joe. "African American Deconstruction of the Novel in the Work of Ishmael Reed and Clarence Major." *MELUS*, 17 (Winter), 57–79. Mentions W briefly (p. 76).

3611. West, Cornel. "Malcolm X and Black Rage," in *Malcolm X in Our Own Image*. Ed. Joe Wood. New York: St. Martin's Press, pp. 48–58. States that Malcolm X was closer to Bigger Thomas than to the protagonist of *Invisible Man*. Reprinted: 1994.

3612. West, Cornel, and Michael Lerner. "A Conversation Between Cornel West and Michael Lerner," in *Bridget and Boundaries: African Americans and American Jews*. Ed. Jack Salzman. New York: George Braziller, pp. 141–151. West cites W's comments on black anti–Semitism in *BB* (p. 149).

3613. Whitehead, Fred. "Conroy, Jack (1899–)," in *Encyclopedia of the American Left*. Eds. Mari Jo Buhle, Paul Buhle, and Dan Georgakas. Urbana: University of Illinois Press, pp. 163–164.

3614. Wideman, John Edgar. "Malcolm X: The Art of Autobiography," in *Malcolm X: In Our Own Image*. Ed. Joe Wood. New York: St. Martin's Press, pp. 101–116. Compares *BB* and *The Autobiography of Malcolm X*, the protagonists of which are racially "representative men" (p. 109).

3615. Williams, John A. "Richard Wright: The Legacy of a Native Son." *The Washington Post Book World* (22 September), pp. 1, 10. Review of the Library of America edition of W with emphasis on *NS*, *BB*, and *LT*. Williams also praises W's "power with language" and his social vision, but points out differences between W's childhood in the South and his own rearing in Syracuse.

3616. Winchell, Donna Haisty, *Alice Walker*, New York: Twayne, pp. 8, 15. Mentions W briefly.

3617. Wixson, Douglas C. "*The Rebel Poet, The Anvil, The New Anvil*," in *American Literary Magazines: The Twentieth Century*. Ed. Edward E. Chielens. Westport, CT: Greenwood Press, pp. 281–288. States that W first published in *The Anvil*.

3618. Wolfe, Charles, and Rip Lornell. *The Life and Legend of Leadbelly*. New York: HarperCollins, pp. 200–202, 207–208. Quotes extensively from W's *Daily Worker* article on Leadbelly and states that they were good friends—"drinking buddies" (p. 200). Also notes W's approval of Leadbelly's song "Bourgeois Blues."

3619. [Wright, Ellen and Julia]. La Famille de Richard Wright vous invite cordialement à assister à la pose d'une Plaque Commémorative le Dimanche 9 Fevrier 1992 de 10 à 12 heures au 14, rue Monsieur-le-Prince, 75006 Paris où il a vécu de 1948 à 1959. Printed invitation.

3620. Wright, Ellen, and Julia Wright. "Richard Wright." *The London Times Literary Supplement*, (31 January), p. 17. Rebuts James Campbell's criticism and upholds the authority of the Library of America edition of W.

3621. Yoshioka, Shizuyo. "In Re-

sponse to the Riddle of the Sphinx: James Baldwin's *Go Tell It on the Mountain*." *Seto Junior College of Kobe Women's College Studies Report*, 3 (March), 1–8. Discusses the W-Baldwin relationship, in which the latter must solve the riddle of the former. Baldwin charges that W ignores the black community, which he will provide, but he goes too far in his criticism of W.

3622. Young, Elizabeth, and Graham Caveney. *Shopping in Space: Essays on America's Black Generation Fiction*. New York: The Atlantic Monthly Press, p. 134. Mentions W briefly.

3623. Young, Stephen Flinn. "1992 SSSL Program: Schedule of Sessions." *Society for the Study of Southern Literature Newsletter*, 25 (April), 4. Lists a session on "Richard Wright and His Contemporaries" with papers by Harry L. Faggett, Maria Frias, and Trudier Harris. The Chair is Blyden Jackson.

3624. Zuckert, Catherine H. "The novel as a Form of American Political Thought," in *Reading Political Stories: Representations of Politics in Novels and Pictures*. Ed. Maureen Whitebrook. Lanham, MD: Rowan & Littlefield, pp. 121–148. Mentions W briefly (p. 123).

1993

3625. Aaron, Abe. "Abe Aaron to Jack Conroy, 13 January 1934 [excerpts]," in *American Proletarian Culture: The Twenties and the Thirties*. Vol. II of *Dictionary of Literary Biography Documentary Series: An Illustrated Chronicle*. Ed. Jon Christian Suggs. Detroit: Gale, p. 215. The first paragraph is on W, whom Aaron met in 1930. States that he writes fiction as well as poetry and calls him "swell."

3626. Abbandonato, Linda. "Rewriting the Heroine's Story in *The Color Purple*," in *Alice Walker: Critical Perspectives Past and Present*. Eds.

Henry Louis Gates, Jr., and K.A. Appiah. New York: Amistad, pp. 296–308.

3627. _____. "Rewriting the Heroine's Story in *The Color Purple*," in *Alice Walker: Critical Perspectives Past and Present*. Eds. Henry Louis Gates, Jr., and K.A. Appiah. New York: Amistad, pp. 296–308.

3628. Abe, Daisei. "On Bigger Thomas, II Richard Wright and Racial Prejudices." *Journal of Gifu College for Economics*, 27 (June), 109–136. Analyzes Bigger's psychology at Mary's bedside, concluding

that he does not hate her and has no reason for killing her.

3629. Adams, Timothy Dow. "'I Do Believe Him Though I Know He Lied': Lying as Genre and Metaphor in *Black Boy*," in *Richard Wright: Critical Perspectives Past and Present*. Eds. Henry Louis Gates, Jr., and K.A. Appiah. New York: Amistad, pp. 302–315.

3630. _____. Richard Wright *Black Boy*, in *Contemporary Literary Criticism*. Ed. Thomas Votteler. Detroit: Gale, pp. 389–296.

3631. Adero, Mailaika. "Richard Wright," in her *Up South: Stories,*

Studies, and Letters of This Century's African-American Migrations. New York: The New Press, p. 136. Brief biographical note following an excerpt from *AH.*

3632. Affleck, Joan, and Shawn E. Carleton. "Comparative Studies — Two or More Authors." *Journal of Modern Literature,* 18 (Spring), 208–211. Lists an article by William A. Proefriedt on W and others.

3633. Andrews, William L. "Chronology of Important Dates," in his *African American Autobiography: A Collection of Critical Essays.* Englewood Cliffs, NJ: Prentice Hall, pp. 224–225. Lists *BB.*

3634. _____. "Introduction," in his *African American Autobiography: A Collection of Critical Essays.* Englewood Cliffs, NJ: Prentice-Hall, pp. 1–7. Comments briefly on treatments of *BB* by Charles Davis and James Olney.

3635. _____. "*My Father's Shadow: American Men's Autobiography.* By David L. Dudley." *Journal of English and Germanic Philology,* 92 (April), 265–267. Review mentioning W and *BB.*

3636. _____. "Richard Wright and the African-American Autobiographical Tradition." *Style,* 27 (Summer), 271–284. Discusses the autobiographical dilemma of self-restraint for plausibility vs. total candor, which might be disbelieved by whites. W rejected the dilemma by opting for self-authentication, ignoring white or black approval. His alienation from both communities certified his integrity.

3637. Angyal, Andrew J. "The 'Complex Fate' of Being an American: The African-American Essayist and the Quest for Identity." *CLA Journal,* 37 (September), 64–80. Mentions briefly James Baldwin's friendship with W (p. 77).

3638. Anon. "American Literature," in *The Columbia Encyclopedia.* Eds. Barbara A. Chernow and George A. Vallasi. Fifth Edition. New York: Columbia University Press, pp. 84–85.

3639. Anon. "Baldwin, James Arthur," in *The African American Encyclopedia.* Ed. Michael W. Williams. Vol. 1. New York: Marshall Cavendish, pp. 109–112. Comments on Baldwin's relation to W.

3640. Anon. *Bibliographic Guide to Black Studies: 1992.* Boston: G.K. Hall, p. 355. Lists one secondary item concerning W in the New York Public Library, supplementing the *Dictionary Catalog of the Schomburg Collection of Negro Literature and History.*

3641. Anon. "Bishop, Shelton Hale," in *Encyclopedia of African American Religions.* New York: Garland, pp. 86–87. Mentions W, Frederic Wortham, and the Laforgue Clinic.

3642. Anon. "*The Black Atlantic: Modernity and Double Consciousness* (Harvard University Press)." *Richard Wright Newsletter,* 3 (Fall/Winter), 5. Notice pointing out that the chapter on W argues that he both affirms and negates western civilization.

3643. Anon. "Black Boy," in *The African American Encyclopedia.* Ed. Michael W. Williams. Vol. 1. New York: Marshall, p. 158. Entry on W's autobiography noting that he struggled against black submission as well as white racism.

3644. Anon. "Brief Mention." *American Literature,* 65 (September), 615–624. Contains a notice of Jean-François Gounard's *The Racial Problem in the Works of Richard Wright and James Baldwin.*

3645. Anon. "Call for an American Writers' Congress," in *American Proletarian Culture: The Twenties and the Thirties.* Vol. 11 of *Dictionary of Literary Biography Documentary Series: An Illustrated Chronicle.* Ed. Jon Christian Suggs. Detroit: Gale, pp. 296–297.

3646. Anon. "Canon Formation," in *The African American Encyclopedia.* Ed. Michael W. Williams. Vol. 1. New York: Marshall Cavendish, pp. 270–271. Mentions W briefly.

3647. Anon. *Chelsea Curriculum Publications.* Yeadon, PA: Chelsea, pp. 3, 4, 6, 9, 10, 12. Publisher's brochure listing collections of criticism on *NS,* Bigger Thomas, and W edited by Harold Bloom.

3648. Anon. "Claude Brown," in *The African American Encyclopedia.* Ed. Michael W. Williams. Vol. 1. New York: Marshall Cavendish, pp. 220–221. Mentions W briefly.

3649. Anon. *Comprehensive Dissertation Index 1992 Supplement. Volume 4.* Ann Arbor: Bell and Howell, p. 518. Lists dissertations treating W by Donna Marie Perreault, Ann M. Algeo, Richard Eugene Baker, Joyce Russell Robinson, and Mary Lynn Weiss.

3650. Anon. "Contributors," *The Langston Hughes Review* 12 (Fall), pp. 51, 52. Mentions Keneth Kinamon's work on W and notes that Jerry W. Ward, Jr. was a founder of the Richard Wright Circle.

3651. Anon. "*Conversations with Richard Wright* (University Press of Mississippi), edited by Keneth Kinnamon and Michel Fabre." *Richard Wright Newsletter,* 3 (Fall/Winter), 5. Notice of a work containing "interviews with Wright on his life in Paris and his views on race and America."

3652. Anon. "Davis, Charles Twitchell," in *The African American Encyclopedia.* Ed. Michael W. Williams. Vol. 2. New York: Marshall Cavendish, p. 419. Biographical entry mentioning Davis's work on W.

3653. Anon. "Detailed Schedule of Events." *South Atlantic Review,* 58 (September), 15–52. Lists a session on "Richard Wright's Travel Books" chaired by Virginia Whatley Smith with papers by Joyce Chadwick-Joshua, Yoshinobu Hakutani, and Keneth Kinnamon.

3654. Anon. "Detective Fiction by African Americans," in *The African American Encyclopedia.* Ed. Michael W. Williams. Vol. 2. New York: Marshall Cavendish, pp. 448–450. Mentions briefly W's "extensive collection of detective magazines" (p. 450).

3655. Anon. "Ellison, Ralph," in *The African American Encyclopedia.* Ed. Michael W. Williams. Vol. 2. New York: Marshall Cavendish, pp. 526–527. Mentions W briefly.

3656. Anon. "Film Biography of Richard Wright Nearly Complete." *Richard Wright Newsletter,* 3 (Fall/Winter), 2. Quotes producer Madison Davis Lacy on his film entitled *Black Boy,* notes locales and interviewees, and sketches Lacy's career.

3657. Anon. "*From Harlem to Paris: Black American Writers in France, 1840–1980.*" *Afram Newsletter,* No. 37 (May), p. 65. Publisher's advertisement mentioning W briefly.

3658. Anon. "History of American Literature," in *English Language: Specialized High-Technology Media Catalog for Grades 7 thru College.* Paradise, CA: Projected Learning Programs, p. 42. Describes a video in which W is included with Hemingway, Faulkner, Wolfe, Steinbeck,

O'Neill, Hellman, Stevens, and W.C. Williams s.v. "The Lost Generation's Many Voices."

3659. Anon. "Hurston, Zora Neale," in *The African American Encyclopedia*. Ed. Michael W. Williams. Vol. 3. New York: Marshall Cavendish, pp. 793–796. Notes W's criticism of *Their Eyes Were Watching God.*

3660. Anon. *Index to Black Periodicals: 1991.* Boston: G.K. Hall, p. 271. Lists five items on W.

3661. Anon. "John Reed Club Artists-Writers Midwest Club News," in *American Proletarian Culture: The Twenties and Thirties*. Vol. 11 of *Dictionary of Literary Biography Documentary Series: An Illustrated Chronicle*. Ed. Jon Christian Suggs. Detroit: Gale, pp. 217–219. Reprint partially from 1934.2, reporting that poems by W had appeared in *The Anvil* and that he spoke on "Revolutionary Negro Poetry" at the Indianapolis John Reed Club.

3662. Anon. *Languages and Literature 1993.* New York: Harper-Collins, p. 19. Publisher's notice of paperback editions of *NS, O, UTC,* and *BB* in the Library of America texts.

3663. Anon. "Lee, Canada," in *The African American Encyclopedia*. Ed. Michael W. Williams. Vol. 4. New York: Marshall Cavendish, pp. 950–951. Notes Lee's role as Bigger in the film *NS.*

3664. Anon. "Literature," in *The African American Encyclopedia*. Ed. Michael W. Williams. Vol. 4. New York: Marshall Cavendish, pp. 971–982. Contains a paragraph on W (pp. 978–979) and mentions him and *NS* elsewhere.

3665. Anon. "Literature Unit Plans." *English Journal*, 82 (January), 98.

3666. Anon. "Literature Unit Plans." *English Journal*, 82 (February), 105.

3667. Anon. "Literature Unit Plans." *English Journal*, 82 (March), 104.

3668. Anon. "Literature Unit Plans." *English Journal*, 82 (April), 14.

3669. Anon. "Literature Unit Plans." *English Journal*, 82 (September), 128.

3670. Anon. "Literature Unit Plans." *English Journal*, 82 (November), 1. Reprint of 1991.

3671. Anon. "Marxism and Afri-

can Americans," in *The African American Encyclopedia*. Ed. Michael W. Williams. Vol. 4. New York: Marshall Cavendish, pp. 1036–1039. Mentions briefly W's membership in the Communist Party.

3672. Anon. "Mississippi." *South Atlantic Review*, 58 (September), 192–193. Publisher's advertisement listing *Conversations with Richard Wright*, edited by Keneth Kinnamon and Michel Fabre.

3673. Anon. "National John Reed Club Conference," in *American Proletarian Culture: The Twenties and Thirties*. Vol. 11 of *Dictionary of Literary Biography Documentary Series: An Illustrated Chronicle*. Ed. Jon Christian Suggs. Detroit: Gale, pp. 262–263.

3674. Anon. "*Native Son*," in *The African American Encyclopedia*. Ed. Michael W. Williams. Vol. 4. New York: Marshall Cavendish, p. 1148. Brief entry with a photograph of Canada Lee as Bigger Thomas.

3675. Anon. "New American Fiction." *American Literature*, 65 (September), 631. Publisher's advertisement containing a blurb on Albert French's *Billy* by John Edgar Wideman mentioning W's "stark naturalism."

3676. Anon. "New from GPG." *American Literature*, 65 (March), [218]. Greenwood Press advertisement containing a notice of Jean-François Gounard's *The Racial Problem in the Works of Richard Wright and James Baldwin*.

3677. Anon. "New from GPG." *PMLA*, 108 (March), 389.

3678. Anon. "New from Penn State Press." *PMLA*, 108 (October), 1201. Contains a notice of Peter A. Dorsey's *Sacred Estrangement* mentioning W briefly.

3679. Anon. "*Notes of a Native Son*," in *The African American Encyclopedia*. Ed. Michael W. Williams. Vol. 4. New York: Marshall Cavendish, p. 1172. Mentions briefly *NS.*

3680. Anon. "Now Available from Duke." *Modern Language Quarterly*, 55 (December), [476]. Publisher's notice of Angelyn Mitchell's *Within the Circle* mentioning W briefly.

3681. Anon. "The *Outsider*," in *The African American Encyclopedia*. Ed. Michael W. Williams. Vol. 4 New York: Marshall Cavendish, p. 1194. Entry describing the plot very briefly.

3682. Anon. "Photograph of Mis-

sissippi Writers Featured in Calendar." *The Southern Register* (Fall), p. 5. W is one of those included in the calendar.

3683. Anon. "Professional Notes and Comment." *PMLA*, 108 (March), 356, 358, 360, 362, 364, 366. Contains a call for articles on *BP, CC,* and *PS* for a book to be edited by Virginia Whatley Smith (p. 358).

3684. Anon. "Recent Scholarship." *The Journal of American History*, 80 (December) 1217–1275. Lists Yoshinobu Hakutani's "Racial Oppression and Alienation in Richard Wright's 'Down by the Riverside' and 'Long Black Song.'"

3685. Anon. "Richard Wright." *The Richard Wright Newsletter*, 2 (Spring/Summer), 8. Harper Collins advertisement for paperback editions of *NS, BB, O,* and *UTC.*

3686. Anon. "Richard Wright *Black Boy*," in *Contemporary Literary Criticism*. Volume 74. Ed. Thomas Votteler. Detroit: Gale, pp. 354–397. After five introductory paragraphs, this entry reprints criticism of *BB* by Howard Mumford Jones (1945.971), W.E.B. DuBois (1945.883), Ralph Ellison (1945.890), Arthur P. Davis (1945.867), Rebecca Chalmers Barton (1948.129), Sidonie Ann Smith (1972.184), Claudia C. Tate (1976.186), Janice Thaddeus (1985), Yoshinobu Hakutani (1985), John O. Hodges (1985), and Timothy Dow Adams (1985). This entry also contains excerpts from *BB* and a brief annotated bibliography.

3687. Anon. "*Spiritual Empowerment in Afro-American Literature* by James H. Evans." *Women and Language*, 16 (Spring), pp. 62–63 Review mentioning W briefly.

3688. Anon. "Washington Weekend." *Cadenza* (19 February), pp. 2, 9. Announces a symposium on "Richard Wright and the 1950s" at Washington University in St. Louis. Listed participants are Julia Wright, Gerald Early, Amritjit Singh, Lynn Weiss, and Ollie Harrington. For reasons of health, Harrington was not able to attend. Keneth Kinnamon took his place.

3689. Anon. "The Round Table: Dealing with Sexually Explicit Language or Subject Matter in Literature." *English Journal*, 82 (April), 83–85. Contains a photograph of a paperback edition of *NS.*

3690. Anon. "Wisconsin." *The American Scholar*, 62 (Winter), 13.

Publisher's announcement of Frank Marshall Davis's *Livin' the Blues* mentioning W briefly.

3691. Anon. "Wright, Richard," in *The African American Encyclopedia*. Ed. Michael W. Williams. Vol. 6. New York: Marshall Cavendish, pp. 1752–1755. Substantial biographical entry with a full-page photograph.

3692. Anon. "Wright, Richard," in *The New Encyclopedia Britannica*. Chicago: Encyclopedia, pp. 773–774.

3693. Anon. "Wright, Richard," in *The Columbia Encyclopedia*. Eds. Barbara A. Chernow and George A. Vallasi. Fifth edition, New York: Columbia University Press, p. 3006.

3694. Anon. "Wright to Be Focus of 1994 Natchez Literary Celebration." *The Richard Wright Newsletter*, 3 (Fall/Winter), 6. Outlines numerous activities concerning W, including the presentation by Julia Wright of the first Richard Wright Literary Excellence Award, showing of the 1951 film *NS* with discussion, premiere of the film *Richard Wright— Black Boy* with commentary by Julia Wright, and a visit to the Natchez neighborhood where W's parents lived.

3695. Anon. "*Writing Chicago: Modernism, Ethnography, and the Novel* (Columbia University Press) by Carla Cappetti." *Richard Wright Newsletter*, 3 (Fall/Winter), 5. Notice mentioning the two chapters on W.

3696. Anon. "*Writing Chicago: Modernism, Ethography, and the Novel* by Carla Cappetti." *The Chronicle of Higher Education* (8 September), p. 14. Favorable review emphasizing Cappetti's treatment of W.

3697. Aptheker, Herbert. "*White Man, Listen*" (1957), in his *A Documentary History of the Negro People in the United States, 1951–1959*. New York: Citadel press, pp. 371–374. Headnote to two selections from *WML*.

3698. Aptheker, Herbert. "*White Man, Listen!* by Richard Wright," in his *A Documentary History of the Negro People in the United States*. Vol. 6. New York: Citadel Press, p. 371. Headnote to two excerpts from *WML*.

3699. ____. "*White Man, Listen!* (1957) by Richard Wright," in his *A Documentary History of the Negro People in the United States*. Vol. 6:

From the Korean War to the Emergence of Martin Luther King, Jr. New York: Citadel Press, p. 371. Brief headnote to two selections.

3700. Arvin, Newton. "A Letter on Proletarian Literature," in *American Proletarian Culture: The Twenties and the Thirties*. Vol. 11 of *Dictionary of Literary Biography Documentary Series: An Illustrated Chronicle*. Ed. Jon Christian Suggs. Detroit: Gale, pp. 339–343. Reprint of 1936.9.

3701. Asante, Moleti Kete. "African Interaction in the Americas," in his *Malcolm X as Cultural Hero and Other Afrocentric Essays*. Trenton, NJ: Africa World Press, pp. 143–152. Mentions W briefly (p. 144).

3702. Awkward, Michael. "Authorial Dreams of Wholeness: (Dis)unity, (Literary) Parentage, and *The Women of Brewster Place*," in *Gloria Naylor: Critical Perspectives Past and Present*. Eds. Henry Louis Gates, Jr., and K.A. Appiah. New York: Amistad Press, pp. 37–70.

3703. ____. "'The Evil of Fulfillment': Scapegoating and Narration in *The Bluest Eye*," in *Toni Morrison: Critical Perspectives Past and Present*. New York: Amistad, pp. 175–209.

3704. Baker, Houston A., Jr. *Black Studies, Rap, and the Academy*. Chicago: University of Chicago Press, p. 57. Quotes W as saying to a favorable reviewer, "Man, you went way beyond the book!"

3705. ____. "Harlem Renaissance," in *The New Princeton Encyclopedia of Poetry and Poetics*. Eds. Alex Preminger and T.V.F. Brogan. Princeton, NJ: Princeton University Press, pp. 495–496. Mentions W briefly.

3706. ____. "On Knowing Our Place," in *Richard Wright: Critical Perspectives Past and Present*. Eds. Henry Louis Gates, Jr., and K.A. Appiah. New York: Amistad, pp. 200–225. Revised reprint of 1990.

3707. ____. "When Lindbergh Sleeps with Bessie Smith: The Writing of Place in *Sula*," in *Toni Morrison: Critical Perspectives Past and Present*. Eds. Henry Louis Gates, Jr., and K.A. Appiah. New York: Amistad, pp. 236–260. Mentions briefly W (pp. 236, 244) and *NS* (p. 237).

3708. Baldwin, James. "Alas, Poor Richard," in *Major Writers of Short Fiction: Stories and Commentaries*. Ed. Ann Charters. Boston: St. Martin's Press, pp. 1394–1398.

3709. Banks, Toni. "From the Dust Jacket." *Quarterly Black Review of Books*, 1 (Winter), 31. Mentions W briefly.

3710. Barnett, Louise K. *Authority of Speech: Language, Society, and Self in the American Novel*. Athens: The University of Georgia Press, p. 261. Mentions W's review of *Their Eyes Were Watching God*.

3711. Bawer, Bruce. "Race and Art: James Baldwin," in his *The Aspect of Eternity*. Saint Paul: Graywolf Press, pp. 17–35.

3712. ____. "Race and Art: James Baldwin," in his *The Aspect of Eternity*. Saint Paul: Greywolf Press, pp. 17–35. Review of James Campbell's *Talking at the Gates: A Life of James Baldwin* including discussion of Baldwin's attitude toward W (pp. 18–20).

3713. Bearden, Romare, and Harry Henderson. *A History of African-American Artists from 1792 to the Present*. New York: Pantheon Books, pp. 234, 407. Notes W's contacts with artists meeting in Charles Alston's apartment in Harlem and Katherine Dunham's apartment in Chicago.

3714. Bell, Michael Davitt. *The Problem of American Realism: Studies in the Cultural History of a Literary Idea*. Chicago: The University of Chicago Press, pp. 164–165. Comments on the quotes from "How 'Bigger' Was Born."

3715. Bellow, Saul. "Writers, Intellectuals, Politics: Mainly Reminiscence." *The National Interest*, No. 31 (Spring), 124–134. Reports a conversation in Paris with W, who advised him to read Husserl (p. 129).

3716. Benston, Kimberly W. "The Veil of Black: (Un)Masking the Subject of African-American Modernism's 'Native Son.'" *Human Studies*, 16 (April), 69–99. The first half of this article examines the autobiographical stance of Benjamin Franklin, the racism of Thomas Jefferson, and the *Narrative* of Briton Hammon. Against this background the second half analyzes *NS* as a modernist version of "the slave narrator's drama of self-realization" (p. 81). Bigger is the author of his story, not Boris Max or Jan Erlone. The article concludes with a comparison of *NS* and *Narrative of the Life of Frederick Douglass*. Throughout Benston's approach is poststructuralist.

3717. Blake, Susan L. "Old John

in Harlem: The Urban Folktales of Langston Hughes," in *Langston Hughes: Critical Perspectives Past and Present*. Eds. Henry Louis Gates, Jr., and K.A. Appiah. New York: Amistad, pp. 205–212.

3718. Blair, Walter, and James R. Giles. "American Literature," in *The New Encyclopedia Britannica*. Chicago: Encyclopedia, Vol. 13, pp. 301–311.

3719. Blum, John, M., William S. McFeely, Edmund S. Morgan, Arthur M. Schlesinger, Jr., Kenneth M. Stampp, and C. Vann Woodward. *The National Experience: A History of the United States*. Eighth edition. Fort Worth: Harcourt Brace Jovanovich, p. 941. Mentions briefly *NS*, a "powerful portrayal."

3720. Bold, Christine. "Nicholas Natanson. *The Black Image in the New Deal: The Politics of FSA Photography*." *Canadian Review of American Studies*, 23 (Spring), 261–263. Mentions briefly *TMBV*.

3721. Bond, Cynthia. "Language, Speech, and Difference in *Their Eyes Were Watching God*," in *Zora Neale Hurston: Critical Perspectives: Past and Present*. Eds. Henry Louis Gates, Jr., and K.A. Appiah. New York: Amistad, pp. 204–217. Mentions W briefly (pp. 204, 213).

3722. _____. "Language, Speech, and Difference in *Their Eyes Were Watching God*, in Henry Louis Gates and R.A. Appiah's *Zora Neale Hurston: Critical Essays Past and Present*. New York: Amistad, pp. 204–217. Mentions W briefly.

3723. _____. "Language, Speech, And Difference in *Their Eyes Were Watching God*, in *Zora Neale Hurston: Critical Perspectives Past and Present*, ed. Henry Louis Gates, Jr., and K.A. Appiah. New York: Amistad, pp. 204–217. Mentions W briefly (pp. 204, 213).

3724. Bordo, Susan. "'Material Girl': The Effacements of Postmodern Culture," in *The Madonna Connection: Representational Politics, Subcultural Identities*, and *Cultural Theory*. Ed. Cathy Schwichtenberg. Boulder: Westview Press, pp. 265–290. Reports that Ice T compares himself to W (p. 288).

3725. Bradley, David. "*American Hunger (1977)*," in *Richard Wright: Critical Perspectives Past and Present*. Eds. Henry Louis Gates, Jr., and K.A. Appiah. New York: Amistad, pp. 69–71.

3726. Brantley, Will. *Feminine Sense in Southern Memoir: Smith, Glasgow, Welty, Hellman, Porter, and Hurston*. Jackson: University Press of Mississippi, pp. 19, 25, 31–32, 218, 224, 228, 236, 249. Mentions W briefly, comments on James Olney's comparison of *BB* and Eudora Welty's *One Writer's Beginning* (pp. 31–32), and contrasts W and Hurston (pp. 218, 224, 228, 236).

3727. Brodhead, Richard H. *Cultures of Letters: Scenes of Reading and Writing in Nineteenth-Century America*. Chicago: The University of Chicago Press, pp. 112–113, 226. Discusses W's difficult literary initiation in Jackson, Mississippi, in contrast to Eudora Welty's privileged one. Quotes from *BB* and cites Keneth Kinnamon's *The Emergence of Richard Wright*.

3728. Brown, Sterling A. "Athletics and the Arts (1951)," in *A Documentary History of the Negro People in the United States, 1951–1959*. Ed. Herbert Aptheker. New York: Citadel Press, pp. 17–54. Mentions briefly W (pp. 40, 45, 53), and the play *NS* (p. 40).

3729. Brown-Guillory, Elizabeth. "Bonner, Marita (1899–1971)," in *Black Women in America: An Historical Encyclopedia*. Vol. I. Ed. Darlene Clark Hine. Brooklyn: Carlson, pp. 148–149. Suggests a putative influence of Bonner on W.

3730. Bryant, Earle V. "Sexual Initiation and Survival in *The Long Dream*," in *Richard Wright: Critical Perspectives Past and Present*. Eds. Henry Louis Gates, Jr. and K.A. Appiah. New York: Amistad, pp. 424–432.

3731. Bullins, Ed. "Chester Himes: *Protest and Autobiographic Novels: A Personalized Reader Response*." *Afram Newsletter*, No. 37 (May), pp. 55–63. Bullins states that he was "psychologically traumatized" by reading *BB* at the age of thirteen.

3732. Burks, Ruth Elizabeth. "The effects of censorship and criticism on the film adaptations of Richard Wright's '*Native Son*.'" *Dissertation Abstracts International*, 53 (June), 4111A. A University of California, Los Angeles dissertation "using a methodological approach informed by such multiple theoretical perspectives as Marxism, poststructuralism, and tropological revision."

3733. Burns, Landon C., Eliza-

beth Buckmaster, and Jane E. Cooper. "The Nineteenth (1992) Supplement to a Cross-Referenced Index of Short Fiction Anthologies and Author-Title Listings." *Studies in Short Fiction*, 30 (Spring), 211–305. Lists the appearance of "Bright and Morning Star" in the fourth edition of *The Heath Introduction to Fiction*.

3734. Burrison, William. "*Lawd Today*: Wright's Tricky Apprenticeship," in *Richard Wright: Critical Perspectives Past and Present*. Eds. Henry Louis Gates, Jr., and K.A. Appiah. New York: Amistad, pp. 98–109.

3735. Butler, Robert James. "Alice Walker's Vision of the South in *The Third Life of Grange Copeland*." *African American Review*, 27 (Summer), 195–204. Compares the episode of the drowning of the white woman in Walker's novel to Bigger's killing of Mary Dalton (p. 202).

3736. Butler, Robert. "Farrell's Ethnic Neighborhood and Wright's Urban Ghetto: Two Visions of Chicago's South Side." *MELUS*, 18 (Spring), 103–111. Contrasts W's Gothic imagery and surrealistic description of the South Side, reflecting Bigger's subjective reality of alienation, and Farrell's more mimetic, fully rendered environment, reflecting a sense of possibility for Studs Lonigan denied to W's protagonist.

3737. Butler, Robert. "Visions of Southern Life and Religion in O'Connor's *Wise Blood* and *The Third Life of Grange Copeland*." *CLA Journal*, 36 (June), 349–370. Mentions briefly Bigger Thomas (p. 354).

3738. Callahan, John F. "'A Long Way from Home': The Art and Protest of Claude McKay and James Baldwin." *Contemporary Literature*, 34 (Winter), 767–776. Mentions W (pp. 767, 774–775) in a review of books by Tyrone Tillery and Horace A. Porter.

3739. Calmer, Alan. "A New Period in American Left-wing Literature," in *American Proletarian Culture: The Twenties and the Thirties*. Vol. 11 of *Dictionary of Literary Biography Documentary Series: An Illustrated Chronicle*. Ed. Jon Christian Suggs. Detroit: Gale, pp. 315–320.

3740. C[ampbell], J[ames]. "Michel Fabre: *The Unfinished Quest of*

Richard Wright, Second Edition," *TLS* (25 June), 32. Favorable review, but states that "it's probably time for a new biography of Wright."

3741. Cappetti, Carla. "Sociology of an Existence: Wright and the Chicago School," in *Richard Wright: Critical Perspectives Past and Present.* Eds. Henry Louis Gates, Jr., and K.A. Appiah. New York: Amistad, pp. 255–271. Reprint of 1985.38.

3742. _____. *Writing Chicago: Modernism, Ethnography, and the Novel.* New York: Columbia University Press, 282 pp. Revised and expanded version of the 1989 dissertation (see 1990). The last two chapters focus on W, especially *BB-AH*.

3743. Carey-Webb, Allen. "Racism and *Huckleberry Finn*: Censorship, Dialogue, and Change." *English Journal*, 82 (November), 22–34. Mentions W briefly (p. 26).

3744. Carmean, Karen. *Toni Morrison's World of Fiction*, Troy, NY: Whitson, p. 5 Mentions briefly *NS* as a selection of the Book-of-the-Month Club.

3745. Carter, Purvis M. "The Negro in Periodical Literature-1992." *The Journal of Negro History*, 78 (Summer), 196–206. Lists an article by Bill Kauffman mentioning W.

3746. Cary, Joyce. "*Black Power* (1954)," in *Richard Wright: Critical Perspectives Past and Present.* Eds. Henry Louis Gates, Jr., and K.A. Appiah. New York: Amistad, pp. 49–52.

3747. Caveney, Graham. "A City on the Hill: Joel Rose's Lower East Side," in *Shopping in Space: Essays on America's Black Generation Fiction.* Eds. Elizabeth Young and Graham Caveney. New York: Atlantic Monthly Press with Serpent's Tail, pp. 130–141. Mentions W briefly (p. 134).

3748. Cayton, Horace R. "*12 Million Black Voices* (1941)," in *Richard Wright: Critical Perspectives Past and Present.* Eds. Henry Louis Gates, Jr., and K.A. Appiah. New York: Amistad, pp. 26–27. Reprint of 1941.680.

3749. Chamberlin, J. Edward. *Come Back to Me My Language: Poetry and the West Indies.* Urbana: University of Illinois Press, p. 52. Mentions briefly W's skeptical attitude toward *negritude*.

3750. Charters, Ann. "Richard Wright," in her *Major Writers of Short Fiction: Stories and Commentaries.* Boston: St. Martin's Press, pp. 1372–1375. Headnote to "Big Black Good Man" and "The Man Who Was Almost a Man." Quotes from W, including a comment on the influence of Hemingway.

3751. _____. "Richard Wright: 'Big Black Good Man,'" in her *Resources for Teaching Major Writers of Short Fiction.* Boston: Bedford Books of St. Martin's Press, pp. 175–177. Critical analysis of the story emphasizing "multiculturalism and racial diversity." Also includes "Questions for Discussion," "Topics for Writing," and a brief bibliography.

3752. _____. "The Man Who Was Almost a Man," in her *Resources for Teaching Major Writers of Short Fiction.* Boston: Bedford Books of St. Martin's Press, pp. 176–177. Critical analysis arguing that W builds a serious story from a comic anecdote. Also includes "Topics for Writing" and a brief bibliography.

3753. Chay, Deborah G. "Rereading Barbara Smith: Black Feminist Criticism and the Category of Experience." *New Literary History*, 24 (Summer), 635–652. Quotes Deborah McDowell Mentioning W briefly.(see 1980. 160).

3754. Christian, Barbara T. "Layered Rhythms: Virginia Woolf and Toni Morrison." *Modern Fiction Studies*, 39 (Fall/Winter), 483–500. Mentions briefly "the Richard Wright era" (p. 485).

3755. Ciancio, Ralph A. "Richard Wright, Eugene O'Neill, and the Beast in the Skull." *Modern Language Studies*, 23 (Summer 1993), 45–59. Compares *The Hairy Ape* and *NS*, drawing on W's interest in the theater and O'Neill's interest in racial issues as well as showing specific parallels. Unlike Robert Fleming (1985), Ciancio believes that both works endorse leftist politics.

3756. Claridge, Henry. "American Literature to 1900: General," in *The Year's Work in English Studies*, Vol. 72. Oxford: Blackwell, pp. 422–429. Mentions briefly *BB*.

3757. Clark, S.L., et al. "Wright, Richard (1908–1960)," in *1992 M.L.A. International Bibliography of Books and Articles on the Modern Languages and Literatures Vol. 1: British and Irish, Commonwealth, English Caribbean, and American Literature.* Ed. Terence Ford. New York: the Modern Language Association of America, p. 276. Lists four items.

3758. Clarke, John Henrik. "Introduction," in his *Black American Short Stories: One Hundred Years of the Best.* New York: Hill and Wang, pp. xv–xxi.

3759. Colaiaco, James A. *Martin Luther King, Jr.: Apostle of Militant Nonviolence.* New York: St. Martin's Press, p. 162.

3760. Collins, Charles M., and David Cohen, eds. *The African Americans.* New York: Viking Penguin, p. 132. Mentions briefly *NS*.

3761. Cook, William W. "Writing in the Spaces Left." *College Composition and Communication*, 44 (February), 9–25. Includes discussion of *BB*, "the record of his transformation from objectified other to self-defining subjectivity" (p. 17). Focuses on W's encounter with Mencken and compares W to Frederick Douglass.

3762. Copage, Eric V. *Black Pearls: Daily Meditations, Affirmations, and Inspirations for African-Americans.* New York: William Morrow, p. April 25. Quotes briefly from *NS*.

3763. Cooper, Jan. "Zora Neale Hurston Was Always a Southerner Too," in *The Female Tradition in Southern Literature.* Ed. Carol S. Manning. Urbana: University of Illinois Press, pp. 58, 61, 65. Mentions W briefly.

3764. Cowley, Malcolm. "*Native Son* (1940)," in *Richard Wright: Critical Perspectives Past and Present.* Eds. Henry Louis Gates, Jr., and K.A. Appiah. New York: Amistad, pp. 9–11. Reprint of 1940.614.

3765. Cuevas, Sue Lonoff de. "Richard Wright *The Library Card*," in her *The College Reader: Linking Reading to Writing.* New York: HarperCollins, p. 25. Headnote to an excerpt from *BB*.

3766. Dalsgård, Katrine. "Alive and Well and Living on the Island of Martha's Vineyard: An Interview with Dorothy West, October 29, 1988." *The Langston Hughes Review*, 12 (Fall), 28–44. Dalsgård notes and West discusses W's association with *New Challenge*. West claims that W wanted to marry Marian Minus. She also expresses her belief that Ellison spied on W for the Communist Party (pp. 38–39).

3767. Dasher, Elaine. "*Generations*

in Black and White." Athens: The University of Georgia Press, 3 pp. Press release quoting Rudolph P. Byrd, editor of this collection of photographs by Carl Van Vechten: "Richard Wright had the look of an astonished child, an innocent ... I found the image startling given the nature of his fiction, such as *Native Son.*"

3768. Davie, Sharon. "Free Mules, Talking Buzzards, and Cracked Plates: The Politics of Dislocation in *Their Eyes Were Watching God.*" *PMLA*, 108 (May), 446–459. Quotes briefly from W's review of the Hurston novel (p. 448).

3769. Davis, Charles T. "From Experience to Eloquence: Richard Wright's *Black Boy* as Art," in *African American Autobiography: A Collection of Critical Essays.* Ed. William L. Andrews. Englewood Cliffs, NJ: Prentice-Hall, pp. 138–150. Reprint of 1979.76.

3770. Davis, Cynthia J. "Speaking the Body's Pain: Harriet Wilson's *Our Nig.*" *African American Review*, 27 (Fall), 391–404. Calls Bigger "a body which is nonetheless voiceless and powerless" (p. 401) and refers to Henry Louis Gates's treatment of the body in W's writing (p. 403).

3771. Davis, Thadious M. "Reading the Woman's Face in Langston Hughes's and Roy De Carava's *Sweet Flypaper of Life.*" *The Langston Hughes Review*, 12 (Spring), 22–28. Includes comparison of *TMBV* with the Hughes book.

3772. Dery, Mark. "Black to the Future: Interviews with Samuel R. Delany, Greg Tate, and Tricia Rose." *South Atlantic Quarterly*, 92 (Fall), 735–778. Tate mentions W briefly (p. 763).

3773. Diawara, Manthia. "*Noir by Noirs*: Towards a New Realism in Black Cinema." *African American Review*, 27 (Winter), 525–537. Mentions *NS* briefly (p. 528).

3774. Dick, Bruce. "*Daddy Goodness*: Richard Wright's Last Lampoon." *The Richard Wright Newsletter*, 2 (Spring/Summer), 2. Abstract of a paper presented at the Paris Conference of February 1992.

3775. Divakaruni, Chitra B. "'The Library Card' Richard Wright," in her *Multitude: Cross-Cultural Readings for Writers.* New York: McGraw-Hill, p. 338. Headnote to an excerpt from *BB*.

3776. Doctorow, E.L. "The Beliefs of Writers," in *Jack London, Hemingway, and the Constitution: Selected Essays, 1977–1992.* New York: Random House, pp. 103–116. Mentions W briefly (p. 114).

3777. Doreski, C.K. "Chicago, Race, and the Rhetoric of the 1919 Riot." *Prospects*, 18, 283–309. Mentions briefly *NS* (p. 301).

3778. Dorsey, Peter A. *Sacred Estrangement: The Rhetoric of Conversion in Modern American Autobiography.* University Park: The Pennsylvania State University Press, pp. 8, 10, 11–12, 13, 14, 15, 85, 165–167, 177, 179–188, 195, 196. In a chapter entitled "The Varieties of Black Experience: Zora Neale Hurston's *Dust Tracks on a Road* and the Autobiography of Richard Wright," Dorsey argues that though the two authors are different in many respects, they both are extreme individualists and they both subvert the conversion narrative common to American autobiography. Discusses W's distaste for religion and his feigned conversion. He "flirts with conversion discourse only in the end to delay its value as an epistemological model" (p. 185). W was always rebellious.

3779. duCille, Ann. *The Coupling Convention: Sex, Text, and Tradition in Black Women's Fiction.* New York: Oxford University Press, pp. 19, 80, 145, 167. Mentions briefly W and *NS*. Quotes from W's review of *Their Eyes Were Watching God.*

3780. _____. "Phallus(ies)of Interpretation: Toward Engendering the Black Critical 'I.'" *Callaloo*, 16 (Summer), 559–573. Mentions briefly *NS* (p. 567).

3781. Dungy, Gwen. "Pemberton, Gayle. *The Hottest Water in Chicago.*" *Obsidian II*, 8 (Fall-Winter), 131–135. Review commenting on Pemberton's treatment of *NS*.

3782. Durdin, Tillman. "*The Color Curtain* (1956)," in *Richard Wright: Critical Perspectives Past and Present.* Eds. Henry Louis Gates, Jr., and K.A. Appiah. New York: Amistad, pp. 53–55.

3783. Early, Gerald. "Introduction," in his *Lure and Loathing: Essays on Race, Identity, and the Ambivalence of Assimilation.* New York: Allen Lane/The Penguin Press, pp. xi–xxiv. Mentions W briefly (p. xiii).

3784. _____. "Margaret Walker," in his *Speech and Power: The Afri-*

can-American Essay and Its Cultural Context from Polemics to Pulpit. Vol. 2. Hopewell, NJ: The Ecco Press, p. 495. Headnote mentioning Walker's book on W.

3785. _____. "Richard Wright," in his *Speech and Power: The African-American Essay and Its Cultural Context from Polemics to Pulpit.* Vol. 2. Hopewell, NJ: The Ecco Press, p. 427. Headnote to W's "Tradition and Industrialization."

3786. Eastman, Max. "*The Outsider* (1953)," in *Richard Wright: Critical Perspectives Past and Present.* Eds. Henry Louis Gates, Jr., and K.A. Appiah. New York: Amistad, pp. 46–48. Reprint of 1953.119.

3787. Ellis, Grace. "Richard Wright 'Discovering Books,'" in her *Textures: Strategies for Reading and Writing.* Fort Worth: Harcourt Brace Jovanovich, pp. 55–61. Includes headnote and explanatory notes to an excerpt from *BB*.

3788. Ellison, Mary. "*Workings of the Spirit: The Poetics of Afro-American Women's Writings.* By Houston A. Baker." *The Modern Language Review*, 88 (April), 443–444. Review mentioning W briefly.

3789. Ellison, Ralph. "*Native Son* (1940)," in *Richard Wright: Critical Perspectives Past and Present.* Eds. Henry Louis Gates, Jr., and K.A. Appiah. New York: Amistad, pp. 11–18.

3790. Elshtain, Jean Bethke. "The Alchemy of Race." *Salmagundi*, No. 98–99 (Spring-Summer), 180–192. Review of Patricia J. Williams's *The Alchemy of Race and Rights* commenting on Bigger Thomas in the first paragraph.

3791. Estes-Hicks, Onita. "The Way We Were: Precious Memories of the Black Segregated South." *African American Review*, 27 (Spring), 5–18. Discusses *BB* as an archetypal autobiography of the black South emphasizing the "pattern of bondage-flight-freedom," then examines less negative views in autobiographical writing by Angelou, Alice Walker, Anne Moody, Leslie Alexander Lacy, Clifton R. Taulbert, and Dorothy Spruill Redford. The last three emphasize return and reconciliation, in contrast to *BB*. Also mentions *NS* (p. 10).

3792. Fabre, Michel. "Bibliographical Essay," in his *The Unfinished Quest of Richard Wright.* Second edition. Urbana: University of Illinois Press, pp. 625–631.

Discusses work on W with biographical relevance since 1973.

3793. [Fabre, Michel]. "*Conversations with Richard Wright*, ed. Kenneth [sic] Kinnamon and Michel Fabre." *Afram Newsletter*, No. 38 (December), 26. Notice of the collection of interviews with W.

3794. [Fabre, Michel]. "Ernest Gaines. *A Lesson Before Dying*." *Afram Newsletter*, No. 38 (December), pp. 22–23. Favorable review noting the similarity of the character Jefferson in Gaines's novel to Bigger Thomas.

3795. Fabre, Michel. *From Harlem to Paris: Black American Writers in France, 1840–1980.* Urbana: University of Illinois Press, Illini Books edition.

3796. _____. "Nouvelles du Centre," *Afram Newsletter*, No. 37 (May), pp. 1–2. Mentions W briefly.

3797. _____. "Preface to the Second Edition," in his *The Unfinished Quest of Richard Wright.* Second edition. Urbana: University of Illinois Press, pp. vii–xix. Fabre reviews his engagement with W's life and works, concedes the shortcomings and mistakes of his biography, amplifies his earlier treatment of W's relations with women, and discusses speculation about the circumstances and cause of W's death.

3798. _____. "Sawyer-Laucanno, Christopher. *A Continual Pilgrimage: American Writers in Paris, 1944–1960*." *Afram Newsletter*, No. 37 (May), 41. Review mentioning W briefly.

3799. _____. "*The Unfinished Quest of Richard Wright*, 2nd edition, by Michel Fabre." *Afram Newsletter*, No. 37 (May), p. 46. Favorable review focusing on Fabre's preface.

3800. Fadiman, Clifton. "*Native Son* (1940)," in *Richard Wright: Critical Perspectives Past and Present.* Eds. Henry Louis Gates, Jr., and K.A. Appiah. New York: Amistad, pp. 6–8.

3801. _____. "Foreword," in *Keeping Fires Night and Day: Selected Letters of Dorothy Canfield Fisher.* Columbia: University of Missouri Press, pp. ix–x. Mentions W briefly.

3802. Farrell, James T. "*Uncle Tom's Children* (1938)," in *Richard Wright: Critical Perspectives Past and Present.* Eds. Henry Louis Gates, Jr., and K.A. Appiah. New York: Amistad, pp. 4–5.

3803. Farrell, Walter C., Jr. "*Black

Like Me: In Defense of a Racial Reality," in *Censored Books: Critical Viewpoints.* Eds. Nicholas J. Karolides, Lee Burress, and John M. Kean. Metuchen, NJ: The Scarecrow Press, pp. 117–124. Mentions the social impact of *NS* (p. 117).

3804. Ferraro, Thomas J. *Ethnic Passages: Literary Immigrants in Twentieth-Century America.* Chicago: The University of Chicago Press, p. 197. Mentions W briefly.

3805. Ferreira, Patricia. "The Triple Duty of a Black Woman Filmmaker: An Interview with Carmen Coustaut." *African American Review*, 27 (Fall), 433–442. Coustaut acknowledges the influence of W (p. 434).

3806. Ferris, William. "Director's Column." *The Southern Register* (Fall), p. 2. Mentions W briefly.

3807. Fisher, Dorothy Canfield. "To Richard Wright, July 23 [1944]," in *Keeping Fires Night and Day: Selected Letters of Dorothy Canfield Fisher.* Columbia: University of Missouri Press, pp. 236–237. Fisher expresses satisfaction with the changes made by W in the ending of *BB*.

3808. _____. "To Richard Wright, August 23 [1944]," in *Keeping Fires Night and Day: Selected Letters of Dorothy Canfield Fisher.* Columbia: University of Missouri Press, pp. 238–239. Fisher reports that in response to other members of the Book-of-the-Month Club Committee she has toned down the criticism of southern whites in her review of *BB*.

3809. _____. "To Richard Wright, July 1 [1944]," in *Keeping Fires Night and Day: Selected Letters of Dorothy Canfield Fisher.* Ed. Mark J. Madigan. Columbia: University of Missouri Press, pp. 231–233. Fisher suggests that W alter the conclusion of *BB* to acknowledge the "men of good will" in America who have opposed racial discrimination.

3810. _____. "To J.W. Lane, 3 November 1945," in *Keeping Fires Night and Day: Selected Letters of Dorothy Canfield Fisher.* Ed. Mark J. Madigan. Columbia: University of Missouri Press, pp. 247–248. Fisher defends *BB* in response to a critical letter from a Chicago physician.

3811. _____. "To Harry Scherman, July 27, 1944," in *Keeping Fires Night and Day: Selected Letters of Dorothy Canfield Fisher.* Ed. Mark J.

Madigan. Columbia: University of Missouri Press, pp. 237–238. Fisher thinks W's comparison of Southern whites to Nazis is excessive and may cost Book-of-the-Month Club subscribers. Madigan here supplies an excerpt from Fisher's review in the Book-of-the-Month Club News.

3812. Fischer[sic], Dorothy Canfield, in *Black Boy = Jeunesse noire.* Paris: Gallimard.

3813. Fishkin, Shelley Fisher. *Was Huck Black?: Mark Twain and African-American Voices.* New York: Oxford University Press, pp. 4, 136–137, 139, 140–141, 213, 214, 217, 218. Notes that W found Twain's work "strangely familiar" and mentions *NS* and *O*.

3814. Fitch, Noël Riley. *Anaïs: The Erotic Life of Anaïs Nin.* Boston: Little, Brown, pp. 258, 286, 324. Mentions a party Nin gave for W and Canada Lee in 1943, a dinner for W in 1946, and a meeting with W in Paris.

3815. Flug, Michael. "Harsh, Vivian Gordon (1890–1960)," in *Black Women in America: An Historical Encyclopedia.* Vol. I. Ed. Darlene Clark Hine. Brooklyn: Carlson, pp. 542–543. Mentions W's speaking at the Hall branch of the Chicago Public Library, of which Harsh was librarian, and his presentation to Harsh of an inscribed copy of *NS*.

3816. Foley, Barbara. "The Politics of Poetics: Ideology and Narrative Form in *An American Tragedy* and *Native Son*," in *Richard Wright: Critical Perspectives Past and Present.* Eds. Henry Louis Gates, Jr., and K.A. Appiah. New York: Amistad, pp. 188–199.

3817. _____. *Radical Representations: Politics and Form in U.S. Proletarian Fiction, 1929–1941.* Durham, NC: Duke University Press, pp. 21, 26, 88, 105, 115, 171, 179, 187, 188, 189–190, 192, 203, 205, 206–212, 257, 328, 334, 359, 395, 405, 425. Discusses *UTC, NS,* and "How 'Bigger' Was Born" in the context of Marxist fiction (pp. 206–212), comments on *New Challenge* and "Blueprint for Negro Writing" (pp. 188–190), and quotes from *TMBV* elsewhere. Foley defends Max's courtroom speech and believes that *NS* is an antibildungsroman because Bigger does not achieve revolutionary class consciousness.

3818. Folks, Jeffrey J. *Southern Writers and the Machine: Faulkner to

Percy. New York: Peter Lang, pp. 5–6, 124. Comments briefly on *NS* and reprints 1991.

3819. Ford, Nick Aaron. "*The Long Dream* (1958)," in *Richard Wright: Critical Perspectives Past and Present.* Eds. Henry Louis Gates, Jr., and K.A. Appiah. New York: Amistad, pp. 59–60. Reprint of 1958.122.

3820. Gates, Henry Louis, Jr. "Preface," in his and K.A. Appiah's *Alice Walker: Critical Perspectives Past and Present.* New York: Amistad, pp. ix–xiii. Mentions briefly "the naturalist art" of W (p. ix).

3821. _____. "Preface," in his and K.A. Appiah's *Gloria Naylor: Critical Perspectives Past and Present.* New York: Amistad Press, pp. ix–x. Mentions briefly *NS* and *BB.*

3822. _____. "Preface," in his and K.A. Appiah's *Toni Morrison: Critical Perspectives Past and Present.* New York: Amistad, pp. ix–xiii. Mentions briefly W's "existential naturalist experimentation" (p. ix).

3823. _____. "Preface," in his and K.A. Appiah's *Alice Walker: Critical Perspectives Past and Present.* New York: Amistad, pp. ix–xiii. Mentions W briefly (p. ix).

3824. _____. "Preface: Langston Hughes," in his and K.A. Appiah's *Langston Hughes: Critical Perspectives Past and Present.* New York: Amistad, pp. ix–xii. Mentions briefly Maryemma Graham's comparison of W and Hughes. The collection includes W's review of *The Big Sea* (pp. 21–23).

3825. _____. "Preface: Richard Wright (1908–1960)," in his and K.A. Appiah's *Richard Wright: Critical Perspectives Past and Present.* New York: Amistad, pp. xi–xvi. Considers W as a naturalist writer, *NS* being "the single most influential shaping force in modern Black literary history." Comments on each of the twenty-two critical essays in the collection.

3826. _____. "*Their Eyes Were Watching God*: Hurston and the Speakerly Text," in his and K.A. Appiah's *Zora Neale Hurston: Critical Perspectives Past and Present.* New York: Amistad, pp. 154–203.

3827. _____. "The Welcome Table," in *Lure and Loathing: Essays on Race, Identity, and the Ambivalence of Assimilation.* Ed. Gerald Early. New York: Allen Lane/The Penguin Group, pp. 144–162. Mentions W briefly (p. 157).

3828. _____. "Zora Neale Hurston (1891–1960)," in his and K.A. Appiah's *Zora Neale Hurston: Critical Perspectives Past and Present.* New York: Amistad, pp. xi–xv. Mentions W briefly (p. xii). W's review of *Their Eyes Were Watching God* is included in this collection (pp. 16–18).

3829. Gates, Henry Louis, Jr. "Langston Hughes (1902–1967)," in his and K.A. Appiah's *Langston Hughes: Critical Perspectives Past and Present.* New York: Amistad, pp. ix–xii. Mentions W briefly.

3830. _____. "Preface," in his and K.A. Appiah's *Zora Neale Hurston: Critical Perspectives Past and Present.* New York: Amistad, pp. xi–xv. Notes that Hurston's "lyrical symbolism" was dismissed by W.

3831. _____. "The Welcome Table," in *Lure and Loathing: Essays on Race, Identity, and the Ambivalence of Assimilation.* Ed. Gerald Early. New York: The Penguin Press, pp. 144–162.

3832. _____. "*Their Eyes Were Watching God*: Hurston and the Speakerly Text," in his and K.A. Appiah's *Zora Neale Hurston's: Critical Perspectives Past and Present.* New York: Amistad, pp. 154–203.

3833. _____. "*Their Eyes Were Watching God*: Hurston and the Speakerly Text," in his and K.A. Appiah's *Zora Neale Hurston: Cultural Perspectives Past and Present.* New York: Amistad, pp. 154–203. Reprint of chapter 5 of 1987.

3834. Gates, Henry Louis and K.A. Appiah, eds. *Richard Wright: Critical Perspectives Past and Present.* New York: Amistad, pp. xvi + 476 pp. Contains a preface by Gates, twenty reprinted reviews, twenty-two reprinted essays, one original essay, notes on contributors, a chronology, and a bibliography of 245 items.

3835. _____. "Preface," in their *Zora Neale Hurston: Critical Perspectives Past and Present.* New York: Amistad, pp. xi–xv. Mentions W briefly (p. xii).

3836. Gavins, Raymond. *The Perils and Prospects of Southern Black Leadership: Gordon Blaine Hancock, 1884–1970.* Durham, NC: Duke University Press, pp. 87, 91.

3837. Gayle, Addison, Jr. "Cultural Strangulation: Black Literature and the White Aesthetic," in *Speech and Power: The African-American*

Essay and Its Cultural Content from Polemics to Pulpit. Vol. 2. Ed. Gerald Early. Hopewell, NJ: The Ecco Press, pp. 142–147.

3838. Gibson, Donald B. "Text and Countertext in *The Bluest Eye,*" in *Toni Morrison: Critical Perspectives Past and Present.* Eds. Henry Louis Gates, Jr., and K.A. Appiah. New York: Amistad, pp. 159–174. Mentions briefly *UTC* and "The Ethics of Living Jim Crow" (p. 160).

3839. Gillespie, Sheena, and Robert Singleton. "Discovering Books Richard Wright," in their *Across Cultures: A Reader for Writers.* Second edition. Boston: Allyn and Bacon, p. 216. Headnote to an excerpt from *BB.*

3840. Gilroy, Paul. *The Black Atlantic: Modernity and Double Consciousness.* Cambridge, MA: Harvard University Press, pp. 18, 30, 51, 69, 70, 92, 115, 146–186, 192, 195, 203. The long chapter on W, "Without the Consolation of Tears': 'Richard Wright, France, and the Ambivalence of Community," discusses his philosophical interests, his alleged misogyny, and the relation between his racial experience and his modernism. All of W's books are discussed, but emphasis falls on *O, EM,* and *LD.* Elsewhere W is mentioned and quoted.

3841. Goodwin, James. *Autobiography: The Self Made Text.* New York: Twayne, pp. 61–63. Summarizes episodes from *BB* and *AH.*

3842. Gould, Philip. "Ralph Ellison's 'Time-Haunted' Novel." *Arizona Quarterly,* 49 (Spring), 117–140. Quotes from *The God That Failed* (pp. 127–128) and quotes Mark Naison mentioning W.

3843. Graham, Maryemma, and Jerry Ward. "Announcements." *The Richard Wright Newsletter,* 2 (Spring/ Summer), 6–7. Announces the publication of *RP,* Jean-Francois Gounard's *The Racial Problem in the Works of Richard Wright and James Baldwin,* Henry Louis Gates, Jr. and K.A. Appiah's *Richard Wright: Critical Perspectives Past and Present, Richard Wright in the 1950's: A Symposium,* a grant of $650,000 to Mississippi Educational Television for a documentary on W.

3844. _____. "Letter from the Editors." *The Richard Wright Newsletter,* 2 (Spring/ Summer, 1. Reports the premier of the stage version of "The Man Who Lived Underground" and the discovery of the manuscript of *RP*.

3845. Graham, Maryemma. "The Fusion of Ideas: An Interview with Margaret Walker Alexander." *African American Review*, 27 (Summer), 279–286. Walker mentions her biography of W (pp. 279, 285).

3846. _____. "An Interview with Don Marshall." *The Richard Wright Newsletter*, 2 (Spring/Summer), 5–6. The actor-adapter of stage version of *The Man Who Lived Underground* reviews his career and emphasizes W's importance, especially for youth.

3847. _____. "Introduction to the Harper Perennial Edition," in *The Outsider* by Richard Wright. New York: HarperCollins, pp. xi–xxix. Arguing against a nonracial, existentialist reading of *O*, Graham places it in the contexts of W's intellectual development and world history, especially the struggles against fascism, racism, and colonialism. In this reading the novel is "a cautionary tale about the excesses of individuality and the dangers of human alienation." Thus, *O* has autobiographical as well as social and political importance.

3848. _____. "The Practice of a Social Art," in *Langston Hughes: Critical Perspectives Past and Present*. Eds. Henry Louis Gates, Jr., and K.A. Appiah. New York: Amistad, pp. 213–235. Quotes from W's review of *The Big Sea* (p. 214) and contrasts the views of Hughes and W on the issues of identity and alienation (p. 230).

3849. _____. "Richard Wright Circle." *Afram Newsletter*, No. 38 (December), p. 44. Description of the organization and membership application form.

3850. _____, and Jerry W. Ward, Jr. "*Black Boy (American Hunger)*: Freedom to Remember," in *Censored Books: Critical Viewpoints*. Eds. Nicholas J. Karolides, Lee Burress, John M. Kean. Metuchen, NJ: The Scarecrow Press, pp. 109–116. Defends *BB* as an authentic personal document and a trenchant social critique. It is essentially affirmative, which "the racism of the radical right and the political correctness of the conservative left" (p. 115) cannot validly dispute.

3851. _____, and Jerry W. Ward, Jr. "Letter from the Editors." *Richard Wright Newsletter*, 3 (Fall/Win-

ter), 2. Anticipates a good year for W studies in 1994 and urges renewal of subscriptions.

3852. _____, and Jerry Ward. "Rave Reviews!: *The Man Who Lived Underground*." *The Richard Wright Newsletter*, 2 (Spring/Summer), 4. Reprints favorable evaluations from Pittsburgh newspapers.

3853. _____, and Jerry Ward. "Report from the College Language Association Convention, April 1–3, 1993." *The Richard Wright Newsletter*, 2 (Spring/Summer), 3–4. Reports on papers at a special session on "Richard Wright: His Language, His Literature." The papers were as follows: "The Multicultural Background of *Native Son*" by Robert Butler, "Image, Text and Voice in the Wright-Rosskam Photographic Text," by Virginia Whatley Smith, and "*Black Power* Revisited: A Dialectical Analysis of Wright's African Vision" by Jocelyn Chadwick-Joshua.

3854. _____, and Jerry Ward. "World Premier of Richard Wright's *The Man Who Lived Underground*." *The Richard Wright Newsletter*, 2 (Spring/Summer), 4. Reports the stage adaptation of W's story running from 26 May to 20 June 1993 at the City Theatre in Pittsburgh. Don Marshall played the lead.

3855. Greenspon, Joanna, ed. *Humanities Index: April 1992 to March 1993*. New York: H.W. Wilson, p. 1235. Lists four items s. v. W.

3856. Grimshaw, Anna, and Keith Hart. "*American Civilization*: An Introduction," in their edition of *American Civilization* by C.L.R. James. Oxford: Blackwell, pp. 1–25. Mentions W briefly (p. 22).

3857. Guerrero, Ed. *Framing Blackness: The African American Image In Film*. Philidelphia: Temple University Press, pp. 174, 184. Mentions briefly "The Man Who Lived Underground" and Bigger Thomas.

3858. Guillory, John. *Cultural Capital: The Problem of Literary Canon Formation*. Chicago: The University of Chicago Press, p. 32. Mentions W briefly.

3859. Gwynn, R.S. "Richard Wright (1908–1960)," in his *Fiction: A HarperCollins Pocket Anthology*. New York: HarperCollins, p. 175. Headnote to "The Man Who Was Almost a Man."

3860. Hakutani, Yoshinobu. "Racial Oppression and Alienation in Richard Wright's 'Down by the Riverside' and 'Long Black Song.'" *The Mississippi Quarterly*, 46 (Spring), 231–239. Analyzes the two stories, arguing that W's treatment of the male protagonists is existential even though he had not yet been exposed to French existentialism. His characterization of Sarah, however, is "reminiscent of a version of transcendentalism and pantheism" as expressed by Whitman.

3861. Hall, Joan Wylie, *Shirley Jackson: A Study of the Short Fiction*. New York: Twayne, p. 83. Mentions W briefly.

3862. Ham, Debra Newman. *The African-American Mosaic: A Library of Congress Resource Guide for the Study of Black History and Culture*. Washington: Library of Congress, pp. 190, 244. Mentions briefly *TMBV* and *NS*.

3863. Handlin, Oscar. "*White Man, Listen!* (1957)," in *Richard Wright: Critical Perspectives Past and Present*. Eds. Henry Louis Gates, Jr., and K.A. Appiah. New York: Amistad, pp. 57–58.

3864. Hanke, Leone S. "The Power of Naming: Women and Law in Twentieth Century American Fiction." *Dissertation Abstracts International*, 53 (March), p. 3212A–3213A. Includes consideration of W.

3865. Harrington, Oliver. "The Last Days of Richard Wright," in his *Why I Left America and Other Essays*. Jackson: University Press of Mississippi, pp. 3–19.

3866. _____. "Look Homeward, Baby," in his *Why I Left America and Other Essays*. Jackson: University Press of Mississippi, pp. 44–77.

3867. _____. "The Mysterious Death of Richard Wright," in his *Why I Left America and Other Essays*. Jackson: University Press of Mississippi, pp. 20–25.

3868. _____. "Why I Left America," in *Why I Left America and Other Essays*. Ed. M. Thomas Inge. University Press of Mississippi, pp. 96–109.

3869. _____. *Why I Left America and Other Essays*. Jackson: University Press of Mississippi, pp. 96–109. Includes discussion of Harrington's close friendship with W.

3870. Hart, Jamie, and Elsa Barkley Brown. "Black Women in the United States: A Chronology," in

Black Women in America: An Historical Encyclopedia. Ed. Darlene Clark Hine. Vol. 2. Brooklyn: Carlson, pp. 1309–1332. Mentions briefly *NS* (p. 1330).

3871. Haskins, James S. *Always Movin' On: The Life of Langston Hughes.* Trenton, NJ: Africa World Press, p. 119. Mentions W briefly.

3872. Henderson, Mae. "Drama and Denial in *The Outsider,*" in *Richard Wright: Critical Perspectives Past and Present.* Eds. Henry Louis Gates, Jr., and K.A. Appiah. New York: Amistad, pp. 388–408. Transcending race and nationalism, *O* attempts to explore the human condition in a universal sense. Cross Damon's "radical individualism" is carried to a nihilistic extreme. Henderson shows how W uses drama, naturalism, and existentialism to indicate that "the process by which Cross shapes and directs his life duplicates the artistic or creative process by which the writer creates his fictional character and the world in which he lives" (p. 392).

3873. Hickey, Dennis, and Kenneth C. Wylie. *An Enchanting Darkness: The American Vision of Africa in the Twentieth Century.* East Lansing: Michigan State University Press, p. 344. List *BP* in the bibliography.

3874. Hicks, Granville. "*Lawd Today* (1963)," in *Richard Wright: Critical Perspectives Past and Present.* Eds. Henry Louis Gates, Jr., and K.A. Appiah. New York: Amistad, pp. 66–68.

3875. Hill, Robert A. "Literary Executor's Afterword," in *American Civilization* by C.L.R. James. Eds. Anna Grimshaw and Keith Hart. Oxford: Blackwell, pp. 293–366. Mentions W briefly (p. 325) and notes the "powerful intellectual stimulus" W gave to James (p. 349).

3876. Horne, Gerald. "The Red and the Black: The Communist Party and African-Americans in Historical Perspective," in *New Studies in the Politics and Culture of U.S. Communism.* Eds. Michael E. Brown, Randy Martin, Frank Rosengarten, and George Snedeker. New York: Monthly Review Press, pp. 149–237. Includes discussion of the W-Ben Davis relationship, stating that W "had once been a member of Davis's party cell, and still supported him in 1943" (p. 211). Also discusses Davis's public responses to W's works.

3877. _____. "Trends of Multiculturalism in Opposition." *The Black Scholar,* 23 (Summer/Fall), 58–61. Mentions Lorraine Hansberry's criticism of W's naturalism (p. 61).

3878. Hornsby, Alton, Jr. *Milestones in 20th-Century African-American History.* Detroit: Visible Ink Press, p. 35. Notes the publication of *NS.*

3879. Houser, George M. "Freedom's Struggle Crosses Oceans and Mountains: Martin Luther King, Jr., and the Liberation Struggles in Africa and America," in *We Shall Overcome: Martin Luther King, Jr., and the Black Freedom Struggle.* Eds. Peter J. Albert and Ronald Hoffman. New York: Da Capo Press, pp. 169–196.

3880. Howe, Irving. "*Eight Men* (1961)," in *Richard Wright: Critical Perspectives Past and Present.* Eds. Henry Louis Gates, Jr., and K.A. Appiah. New York: Amistad, pp. 62–65.

3881. Hughes, Langston. "Prelude to Our Age," in *The Collected Poems of Langston Hughes.* Eds. Arnold Rampersad and David Roessel. New York: Alfred A. Knopf, pp. 379–384.

3882. _____. "Where's the Horse for a Kid That's Black?" in *A Documentary History of the Negro People in the United States, 1951–1959.* New York: Citadel Press, pp. 391–393.

3883. Hurston, Zora Neale. "*Uncle Tom's Children* (1938)," in *Richard Wright: Critical Perspectives Past and Present.* Eds. Henry Louis Gates, Jr., and K.A. Appiah. New York: Amistad, pp. 3–4.

3884. Hynes, Joseph. "*Native Son* Fifty Years Later." *Cimarron Review,* No. 102 (January), 91–97. General essay on the novel emphasizing the racial theme and its persistence. Argues that at the end Bigger feels that like white capitalists he is willing to kill for what he wants. Without adopting Max's point of view, Hynes urges readers of *NS* to become less materialistic and selfish.

3885. Hynum, Rickey. "International Scholars Visit Ole Miss, Study Southern Culture." *The Southern Register* (Summer), p. 16. Mentions that the group studied W and other Southern writers at the University of Mississippi.

3886. Inge, M. Thomas, ed. *Dark Laughter: The Satiric Art of Oliver*

W. Harrington. Jackson: University Press of Mississippi, pp. xxiv–xxvi, xxxvi–xxxvii. Discusses the serialization of *NS* illustrated by Harrington in *The People's Voice,* aborted because of reader objections to profanity. Also treats Harrington's friendship with W in Paris as well as the Richard Gibson affair, quoting from Addison Gayle's account, and notes Harrington's suspicions concerning W's death.

3887. _____. "Introduction," in *Why I Left America and Other Essays* by Oliver W. Harrington. Jackson: University Press of Mississippi, pp. xvii–xxix. Includes discussion of Harrington's friendship with W beginning in 1951 in Paris.

3888. Inscoe, John C. "*Home Ground: Southern Autobiography.* Edited by J. Bill Berry." *The Journal of Southern History,* 59 (May), 430–431. Reviews James M. Cox's essay comparing Bigger Thomas and Joe Christmas of *Light in August.*

3889. James, C.L.R. *American Civilization.* Eds. Anna Grimshaw and Keith Hart. Oxford: Blackwell, pp. 37, 211, 234. Comments on W's attack on "Russian communism and its satellite parties from the left" and his attraction to existentialism.

3890. Janken, Kenneth Robert. *Rayford W. Logan and the Dilemma of the African-American Intellectual.* Amherst: The University of Massachusetts Press, pp. 147, 157. Mentions briefly W and *NS.*

3891. Jan Mohamed, Abdul R. "Negating the Negation: The Construction of Richard Wright," in *Richard Wright: Critical Perspectives Past and Present.* Eds. Henry Louis Gates, Jr., and K.A. Appiah. New York: Amistad, pp. 285–301.

3892. Jay, Gregory. "*Double Agent: The Critic and Society.* By Morris Dickstein." *The Journal of American History,* 80 (December), 1127–1128. Review mentioning W briefly.

3893. Jemie, Onwuchekwa. "Or Does It Explode?" in *Langston Hughes: Critical Perspectives Past and Present.* Eds. Henry Louis Gates, Jr., and K.A. Appiah. New York: Amistad, pp. 135–171.

3894. Johnson, Barbara. "The Re(a)d and the Black," in *Richard Wright: Critical Perspectives Past and Present.* Eds. Henry Louis Gates, Jr., and K.A. Appiah. New York: Amistad, pp. 149–155.

3895. Johnson, Charles. "A Phenomenology of the Black Body." *Michigan Quarterly Review*, 32 (Fall), 599–614. Comments on and quotes from *O*, calling Damon "a black existential hero (p. 608).

3896. Johnson, Charles. "Philosophy and Black Fiction," in *Speech and Power: The African-American Essay and Its Cultural Content from Polemics to Pulpit*. Vol. 2. Ed. Gerald Early. Hopewell, NJ: The Ecco Press, pp. 166–172.

3897. Johnson, Linck C. "Compositional History and the Composition of the Canon." *Resources for American Literary Study*, 19, No. 2, 301–308. Review of *Writing the American Classics* commenting on Keneth Kinnamon's essay "How *Native Son* Was Born" (pp. 304–305).

3898. Jones, Gayl. "Breaking Out of the Conventions of Dialect," in *Zora Neale Hurston: Critical Perspectives Past and Present*. New York: Amistad, pp. 141–153.

3899. _____. "Breaking Out of the Conventions of Dialect," in Henry Louis Gates and K.A Appiah's *Zora Neale Hurston: Critical Perspectives Past and Present*. New York: Amistad, pp. 141–153.

3900. _____. "Breaking Out of the Conventions of Dialect," in *Zora Neale Hurston: Critical Perspectives Past and Present*. Eds. Henry Louis Gates, Jr., and K.A. Appiah. New York: Amistad, pp. 141–153. Mentions briefly W's criticism of Hurston (p. 141).

3901. Joyce, Joyce Ann. "The Figurative Web of *Native Son*," in *Richard Wright: Critical Perspectives Past and Present*. Eds. Henry Louis Gates, Jr., and K.A. Appiah. New York: Amistad, pp. 171–187.

3902. Karenga, Maulana. *Introduction to Black Studies*. Second ed. Los Angeles: The University of Sankore Press, pp. 395, 421. Quotes Addison Gayle on W and mentions briefly *NS* and *BB*.

3903. Keegan, Michael. "Course Nurtures Teachers of Black Writings." *The Northeastern* [University] *Voice* (22 July), pp. 4, 8. Mentions W briefly.

3904. Kelly, Lionel. "American Literature: The Twentieth Century: Poetry," in *The Year's Work in English Studies*. Vol. 71. Oxford: Blackwell, pp. 560–600. Contains a lengthy paragraph describing Michel Fabre's *Richard Wright: Books and Writers* (p. 599).

3905. _____. "American Literature: The Twentieth Century: Twentieth Century American Poetry," in *The Year's Work in English Studies*. Vol. 72. Oxford: Blackwell Publishers, pp. 454–484. Contains a paragraph on Michel Fabre's *From Harlem to Paris* mentioning W briefly (pp. 456–457).

3906. Kent, George E. "Maya Angelou's *I Know Why the Caged Bird Sings* and Black Autobiographical Tradition," in *African American Autobiography: A Collection of Critical Essays*. Ed. William L. Andrews. Englewood Cliffs, NJ: Prentice-Hall, pp. 162–170.

3907. Kidd, Stuart. "*The Black Image in the New Deal: The Politics of FSA Photography*. By Nicholas Natanson." *The Southern Quarterly*, 31 (Winter), 201–203. Review mentioning briefly *TMBV*.

3908. Kiely, Robert. *Reverse Tradition: Postmodern Fictions and the Nineteenth Century Novel*. Cambridge: Harvard University Press, p. 234. Quotes Kate Millett on *BB*.

3909. Kinnamon, Keneth. "How *Native Son* Was Born," in *Richard Wright: Critical Perspectives Past and Present*. Eds. Henry Louis Gates, Jr., and K.A. Appiah. New York: Amistad, pp. 110–131.

3910. _____. "*Praisesong of Survival: Lectures and Essays, 1957–89*. By Richard K. Barksdale." *The Langston Hughes Review*, 12 (Fall), 23–26. Mentions W briefly (p. 26).

3911. _____. "*A Richard Wright Bibliography: 1983*." *The Richard Wright Newsletter: Bibliography Supplement*, 2 (Spring/Summer), 1–10. Contains 92 annotated items and an introduction explaining that this "is the first installment of a projected updating of *A Richard Wright Bibliography*."

3912. _____. "*Richard Wright: Daemonic Genius*. By Margaret Walker." *Resources for American Literary Study*, 19, 151–155. Unfavorable review complaining of poor writing, inaccuracy, subjectivity, lack of organization, and crude psychologizing.

3913. Kinnamon, Keneth, and Michel Fabre, eds. *Conversations with Richard Wright*. Jackson: University Press of Mississippi, 274 pp. An introduction and chronology precede sixty-three interviews and discussions constituting "a representative record of conversations with

Richard Wright that were printed or broadcast" (p. xv) from 1938 to 1960. The tone is usually serious, but interviewers were frequently struck by what one of them, Maurice Nadeau, called "the congenial aura his persona exudes" (p. xiv).

3914. Kinnard, Arthur H., Jr. "*Growing Up Black in Rural Mississippi: Memories of a Family, Heritage of a Place*. By Chalmers Archer, Jr." *The Journal of Mississippi History*, 55 (November), 322–323. Review mentioning briefly *BB*.

3915. Kirk, Ersye. *The Black Experience in Books for Children and Young Adults*. Ardmore, Oklahoma: Positive Impact, pp. 5, 68. Lists *BB* and *NS*.

3916. Kishi, Akio. "Black Literature: Richard Wright's *Black Boy* Reconsidered." *Biblia*, 20 (January), 64–66. Brief note on *BB* summarizing the life of the author.

3917. _____. "Black Literature: "Richard Wright's Autobiographical Novel, *Black Boy, a Sequel*, Reconsidered." *Biblia*, 21 (July), 43–47. Brief note on *AH*, which moves beyond protest.

3918. Kiuchi, Toru. "The Library of America's Edition of *Native Son*." *Nihon University Industrial Engineering Faculty Report B.*, 26 (20 June), 13–23. Clarifies the difference between the original edition of *NS* and The Library of America edition. The latter is more powerful and insightful, creating Bigger's personality more strongly.

3919. Klevar, Harvey L. *Erskine Caldwell: A Biography*. Knoxville: The University of Tennessee Press, p. 231. Comments on W's favorable review of *Trouble in July*.

3920. Klostermann, Berthold. *Blue Notes — Black Fiction: Schwarze Musik in der afroamerikanischen Erzählliteratur der zwanziger* und *dreißiger Jahre*. Trier: Wissenschaftlicher Verlag, pp. 3, 26, 205, 208–269, 271, 272–274, 275, 277, 281, 282, 283, 289, 303, 304, 305, 306, 309, 310, 311, 312, 313, 314, 316. After reviewing W's career in the thirties under the rubric "Black Culture in the Class Struggle," Klostermann analyzes the role of black music in W's early poetry, in each of the five stories of *UTC*, and, more briefly, in *NS*. Gives special attention to the influence of blues and oral sermons on the prose rhythm of *UTC*. Mentions W frequently throughout.

3921. Kowalewski, Michael. *Deadly Musings: Violence and Verbal Form in American Fiction.* Princeton, NJ: Princeton University Press, pp. 39, 40–41, 58. Examines W's realistic depiction of violence in *NS*, especially the furnace scene with the decapitation of Mary. Author and narrator seem to disappear as W employs "only that language which will prompt us to see right through it to imagined events and feel their imaginative palpability" (p. 41).

3922. Knopf, Marcy. "Dorothy West (1912–)," in her *The Sleeper Awakes: Harlem Renaissance Stories by Women.* New Brunswick: Rutgers University Press, p. 272. Mentions W and *New Challenge.*

3923. Kutzinski, Vera M. *Sugar's Secrets: Race and the Erotics of Cuban Nationalism.* Charlottesville: University Press of Virginia, p. 205. Mentions briefly *SH.*

3924. Lambert, Craig. "*The Paris Review* Interviewed." *Harvard Magazine,* 96 (November-December), 68–73. Contains a photograph of W in Paris with Peter Matthiessen and Max Steele.

3925. Leibowitz, Herbert. "'Arise, Ye Pris'ners of Starvation': Richard Wright's *Black Boy* and *American Hunger,*" in *Richard Wright: Critical Perspectives Past and Present.* Eds. Henry Louis Gates, Jr., and K.A. Appiah. New York: Amistad, pp. 328–358.

3926. Leitch, Thomas M. *Lionel Trilling: An Annotated Bibliography.* New York: Garland, pp. 210–211, 284–285, 286, 527, 542. Lists six items in which W figures.

3927. Leonard, John. "Jazz (1992)," in *Toni Morrison: Critical Perspectives Past and Present.* Eds. Henry Louis Gates, Jr., and K.A. Appiah. New York: Amistad, pp. 36–49.

3928. Levenson, Leah, and Jerry Notterstad. *Granville Hicks: The Intellectual in Mass Society.* Philadelphia: Temple University Press, pp. 89, 201, 217. Mentions W and the American Writers Congress, *O,* and *NS.*

3929. Levine, Ellen. *Freedom's Children.* New York: Putnam, p. 94. Quotes Thelma Eubanks on reading W in a Freedom School in Mississippi in the summer of 1964.

3930. Levy, Helen Fiddyment. "Lead on with Light," in *Gloria Naylor: Critical Perspectives Past and Present.* Eds. Henry Louis Gates, Jr.,

and K.A. Appiah. New York: Amistad, pp. 263–284.

3931. Lewis, R.W.B. "Robert Penn Warren's Canon of Precursors," in his *Literary Reflections: A Shoring of Images, 1960–1993.* Boston: Northeastern University Press, pp. 259–291. Mentions W briefly (p. 277).

3932. Lewis, Sinclair. "*Black Boy* (1945)," in *Richard Wright: Critical Perspectives Past and Present.* Eds. Henry Louis Gates, Jr., and K.A. Appiah. New York: Amistad, pp. 30–34.

3933. Lindberg, Kathryne V. "Mass Circulation versus *The Masses*: Covering the Modern Magazine Scene." *Boundary 2,* 20 (Summer), 51–83. Includes a discussion of W's "Joe Louis Uncovers Dynamite" in contrast to coverage by Paul Gallico in *The Saturday Evening Post* (pp. 67–69). W's "unabashedly communist" point of view celebrates the "revolutionary potential of the coupling of race and class struggle."

3934. Lindsey, Byron. "Michael F. Lynch. *Creative Revolt: A Study of Wright, Ellison and Dostoevsky.*" *Slavic and East European Journal,* 37 (Winter), 577. Mixed review of a book that includes analysis of *O.*

3935. Lock, Helen. "'A Man's Story is His Gris-gris': Ishmael Reed's Neo-HooDoo Aesthetic and the African-American Tradition." *South Central Review,* 10 (Spring), 67–77. Mentions briefly *UTC* and *NS* (p. 75).

3936. Locke, Alain. "*Native Son* (1940)," in *Richard Wright: Critical Perspectives Past and Present.* Eds. Henry Louis Gates, Jr., and K.A. Appiah. New York: Amistad, pp. 19–25.

3937. Longest, George C., et al. "A Checklist of Scholarship on Southern Literature for 1992." *The Mississippi Quarterly,* 46 (Supplement), 1–158. Lists four annotated items on W and cross-references to sixteen other items dealing partially with W.

3938. Lowance, Mason. "Slave Narratives," in *Black Women in America: An Historical Encyclopedia.* Vol. II. Ed. Darlene Clark Hine. Brooklyn: Carlson, pp. 1043–1045. Mentions briefly *BB.*

3939. Lowe, John. "'At Last Somewhere at Home': The European Refiguaration of Mississippi in *The Long Dream.*" *The Richard Wright Newsletter,* 2 (Spring/Summer), 2.

Abstract of a paper presented at the Paris Conference of February 1992.

3940. Lynch, Acklyn. *Nightmare Overhanging Darkly: Essays on Black Culture and Resistance.* Chicago: Third World Press, pp. 10, 12, 20–21, 25, 38, 43, 53–54, 72–73, 76, 235, 255. Quotes from *BB* (pp. 10, 53–54), *UTC* (pp. 20–21) and *NS* (pp. 72–73). Mentions *O, NS,* and Bigger Thomas elsewhere, always in relation to black resistance to white racism.

3941. Lynch, Michael F. "The Everlasting Father: Mythic Quest and Rebellion in Baldwin's *Go Tell It on the Mountain.*" *CLA Journal,* 37 (December), 156–175. Mentions briefly *NS* (p. 156) and W (p. 158).

3942. MacFarlane, Fenella. "Ellis, Evelyn (1894–1958)," in *Black Women in America: An Historical Encyclopedia.* Vol. I. Ed. Darlene Clark Hine. Brooklyn: Carlson, p. 392. Mentions Ellis's role as Mrs. Thomas in the play *NS.*

3943. _____. "West, Dorothy (1907–)," in *Black Women in America: An Historical Encyclopedia.* Vol. II. Ed. Darlene Clark Hine. Brooklyn: Carlson, pp. 1248–1249. Notes W's association with *New Challenge.*

3944. Mackey, Nathaniel. *Discrepant Engagement: Dissonance, Cross-Culturality, and Experimental Writing.* Cambridge: Cambridge University Press, p. 65. Quotes Clarence Major on W.

3945. Madhubuti, Haki R. "Black Critic," in *Speech and Power: The African-American Essay and Its Cultural Content from Polemics to Pulpit.* Vol. 2. Ed. Gerald Early. Hopewell, NJ: The Ecco Press, pp. 173–178.

3946. Madigan, Mark J., ed. *Keeping Fires Night and Day: Selected Letters of Dorothy Canfield Fisher.* Columbia: University of Missouri Press, pp. 6, 15, 18, 19, 231–239, 247–248, 349. Includes letters from Fisher to W dated 1, 12, 21, and 23 July and 23 August 1944 concerning the conclusion of *BB.* Fisher makes several suggestions for revision, one of which is to include some acknowledgment of white American racial liberalism. Fisher is gracious when W declines to do so. Another letter, to a Chicago physician, defends the selection of *BB* by the Book-of-the-Month Club. Madigan supplies a biographical note on W in an appendix.

3947. _____. "Chronology," in

his *Keeping Fires Night and Day: Selected Letters of Dorothy Canfield Fisher*. Columbia: The University of Missouri Press, pp. xvii–xx. Mentions briefly W and *BB* (p. xx).

3948. _____. "Introduction," in his *Keeping Fires Night and Day: Selected Letters of Dorothy Canfield Fisher*. Columbia: The University of Missouri Press, pp. 1–22. Comments on the "key role" of Fisher in W's career (pp. 18–19), mentioning *NS* and *BB*.

3949. Madsen, Deborah L. "American Literature: The Twentieth Century: Fiction: Post-1945," in *The Year's Work in English Studies*. Vol. 71. Oxford: Blackwell, pp. 615–654. Comments briefly on an essay on W by Blyden Jackson (p. 619) and more extensively on books on W by Michael F. Lynch (p. 630), Keneth Kinnamon (p. 653), and Harold Bloom (pp. 653–654).

3950. Major, Clarence. "Introduction," in his *Calling the Wind: Twentieth-Century African-American Short Stories*. New York: HarperCollins, pp. xiii–xxvi. Mentions W, *NS*, and Ellison's "Remembering Richard Wright." Quotes from "Blueprint for Negro Writing." "Bright and Morning Star" is included in this anthology.

3951. _____. "Necessary Distance: Afterthoughts on Becoming a Writer," in *Speech and Power: The African-American Essay and Its Cultural Context from Polemics to Pulpit*. Vol. 2. Ed. Gerald Early. Hopewell, NJ: The Ecco Press, pp. 148–159.

3952. Marcus, Steven. "*The Outsider* (1953)," in *Richard Wright: Critical Perspectives Past and Present*. Eds. Henry Louis Gates, Jr., and K.A. Appiah. New York: Amistad, pp. 35–45.

3953. Margolies, Edward. "Wright's Craft: The Short Stories," in *Richard Wright: Perspectives Past and Present*. Eds. Henry Louis Gates, Jr., and K.A. Appiah. New York: Amistad, pp. 75–97.

3954. Marshall, Timothy. "Booktalk." *Quarterly Black Review of Books*, 1 (Winter), 17–18. Quotes Haki Madhubuti mentioning W briefly.

3955. Masilela, Ntongela. "The Los Angeles School of Black Filmmakers," in *Black American Cinema*. Ed. Manthia Diawara. New York: Routledge, pp. 109, 113. Mentions briefly *AH* and *NS*.

3956. Mason, Theodore, Jr. "The Dynamics of Enclosure," in *Alice Walker: Critical Perspectives Past and Present*. Eds. Henry Louis Gates, Jr., and K.A. Appiah. New York: Amistad, pp. 126–139.

3957. _____. "The Dynamics of Enclosure," in *Alice Walker: Critical Perspectives Past and Present*. Eds. Henry Louis Gates, Jr., and K.A. Appiah. New York: Amistad, pp. 126–139.

3958. McCall, Dan. "Wright's American Hunger," in *Richard Wright: Critical Perspectives Past and Present*. Eds. Henry Louis Gates, Jr., and K.A. Appiah. New York: Amistad, pp. 359–368.

3959. McDowell, Deborah E. "In the First Place: Making Frederick Douglass and the Afro-American Narrative Tradition," in *African American Autobiography: A Collection of Critical Essays*. Ed. William L. Andrews. Englewood Cliffs, NJ: Prentice Hall, pp. 36–58.

3960. _____. "Lines of Descent/Dissenting Lines," in *Zora Neale Hurston: Critical Perspectives Past and Present*. Eds. Henry Louis Gates, Jr., and K.A. Appiah. New York: Amistad, pp. 230–240. Reprint of 1991.

3961. _____. "Lines of Descent/Dissenting Lives," in Henry Louis Gates and K.A. Appiah's *Zora Neale Hurston: Critical Perspectives Past and Present*. New York: Amistad, pp. 230–240. Notes Ellison's praise of W for *NS* and *UTC* (p. 231) and mentions W's view of Hurston's work as to folklorie.

3962. McKnight, Lynn. "Impressions of an Elusive South." *The Southern Register* (Fall), 1, 11. Review of Lisa Howarth's *The South: A Treasury of Art and Literature* noting that it contains excerpts from W.

3963. McLaughlin, Andree Nicola. "Introduction," in *Nightmare Overhanging Darkly: Essays on Black Culture and Resistance*. By Acklyn Lynch. Chicago: Third World Press, pp. xi–xiv. Mentions W briefly.

3964. McMichael, George. "James Baldwin 1924–1987," in his *Concise Anthology of American Literature*. Third edition. New York: Macmillan, pp. 2359–2360.

3965. _____. "James Baldwin 1924–1987," in his *Concise Anthology of American Literature*. Third edition. New York: Macmillan, pp. 2359–2360.

3966. _____. "Ralph Ellison 1914–," in his *Concise Anthology of American Literature*. Third edition. New York: Macmillan, p. 2099.

3967. _____, et al. "Richard Wright," in their *Anthology of American Literature*. Fifth edition. Vol. 2. New York: Macmillan, pp. 1564–1565. Biographical-bibliographical headnote to "The Man Who Was Almost a Man."

3968. _____. "Richard Wright 1908–1960," in his *Concise Anthology of American Literature*. Third edition. New York: Macmillan, pp. 2089–2090. Reprint of 1974.128 with an expanded bibliography.

3969. Merrill, Robert. "*Writing the American Classics*, Edited by James Barbour and Tom Quirk." *Modern Philology*, 90 (February), 448–451. Review commenting favorably on Keneth Kinnamon's essay on *NS* included in the collection.

3970. Michaels, Walter Benn. "Anti-Imperial Americanism," in *Cultures of United States Imperialism*. Eds. Amy Kaplan and Donald E. Pease. Durham: Duke University Press, pp. 365–391. Includes discussion of W and *NS* in relation to the thought of Melville Herskovits.

3971. Miller, Donald L. "The White City." *American Heritage*, 44 (July/August), 70–78, 80, 82–87. Mentions briefly W and Bigger Thomas (p. 86).

3972. Miller, Eugene E. "Authority, Gender, and Fiction." *African American Review*, 27 (Winter), 687–691. Review of the Library of America edition of *NS* disputing the view of Arnold Rampersad, Keneth Kinnamon, and Jerry Ward that it presents a more sexual Bigger. Rejecting such an intentional fallacy, Miller argues that it suggests an androgynous Bigger and places W "at least on the edges of the radical prefeminist camp."

3973. Miller, James A. "Gounard, Jean François. *The Racial Problem in the Works of Richard Wright and James Baldwin*." *Choice*, 30 (June), 1625. Unfavorable review. Gounard's treatment has been superseded.

3974. Miller, R. Baxter. "The Performance of African-American Autobiography." *Style*, 27 (Summer), 285–299. Mentions W briefly (p. 286).

3975. Minter, David. "Richard Wright 1908–1960," in *The Harper*

American Literature. Ed. Donald McQuade et al. Second edition. Vol. 2. New York: HarperCollins, pp. 1202–1205.

3976. Mobley, Marilyn Sanders. "The Mellow Moods and Difficult Truths of Toni Morrison." *The Southern Review*, 29 (July), 614–628. Mentions W briefly (p. 625).

3977. Monroe, Doreen E. "Contributors." *The Langston Hughes Review*, 12 (Fall), p. 51. Mentions W briefly s.v. Keneth Kinnamon.

3978. Morris, Willie. *New York Days.* Boston: Little, Brown, pp. 178, 180. Comments on discussions with James Baldwin and Margaret Walker about W.

3979. Moses, Wilson J. "Ambivalent Maybe," in *Lure and Loathing: Essays on Race, Identity, and the Ambivalence of Assimilation.* Ed. Gerald Early. New York: Allen Lane/The Penguin Group, pp. 274–290. Finds *O* "a far more satisfying and truthful depiction of the mind of the black man" than *NS* (p. 285).

3980. _____. *Black Messiahs and Uncle Toms: Social and Literary Manipulations of a Religious Myth.* Revised edition. University Park: The Pennsylvania State University Press, p. 144. Mentions *O* briefly.

3981. Muckley, Peter A. "Black American author-biography: From politics to myth and beyond." *Dissertation Abstracts International*, 53 (February), 2816-A. The dissertation includes consideration of W's "amendments to *Black Boy*, and his radical interpolations in *American Hunger*.

3982. Mullane, Deirdre. "Eldridge Cleaver 1935–," in her *Crossing the Danger Water: Three Hundred Years of African American Writing.* New York: Doubleday, pp. 670–671. Notes that while in prison Cleaver read W.

3983. _____. "Introduction," in her *Crossing the Danger Water: Three Hundred Years of African-American Writing.* New York: Doubleday, pp. xix–xxii. Mentions briefly W and *UTC*.

3984. _____. "Jack Johnson (1878–1946)," in her *Crossing the Danger Water: Three Hundred Years of African-American Writing.* New York: Doubleday, pp. 438–439. Mentions W briefly.

3985. _____. "James Baldwin (1924–1987)," in her *Crossing the Danger Water: Three Hundred Years*

of African-American Writing. New York: Doubleday, pp. 601–602. Notes Baldwin's sharp criticism of W.

3986. _____. "Joe Louis (1914–1981)," in her *Crossing the Danger Water: Three Hundred Years of African-American Writing.* New York: Doubleday, pp. 538–539. Headnote mentioning W briefly and his "Joe Louis Uncovers Dynamite."

3987. _____. "Langston Hughes (1902–1967)," in her *Crossing the Danger Water: Three Hundred Years of African-American Writing.* New York: Doubleday, pp. 499–500. Mentions W briefly.

3988. _____. "Ralph Ellison (1914–)," in her *Crossing the Danger Water: Three Hundred Years of African-American Writing.* New York: Doubleday, pp. 587–588. Comments on W's friendship with Ellison.

3989. _____. "Richard Wright (1908–1960)," in her *Crossing the Danger Water: Three Hundred Years of African-American Writing.* New York: Doubleday, pp. 554–556. Biographical headnote to "The Ethics of Living Jim Crow" with emphasis on W's early career. Contains two paragraphs on *NS*.

3990. Murray, Albert. "Identity, Diversity, and the Mainstream," in *Speech and Power: The African-American Essay and Its Cultural Content from Polemics to Pulpit.* Vol. 2. Ed. Gerald Early. Hopewell, NJ: The Ecco Press, pp. 340–341.

3991. Nagel, James. "*From Harlem to Paris: Black American Writers in France 1840–1980.* By Michel Fabre." *American Literature*, 65 (March), 185–186. Review mentioning W briefly.

3992. Naison, Mark. "Remaking America: Communists and Liberals in the Popular Front," in *New Studies in the Politics and Culture of U.S. Communism.* Eds. Michael E. Brown, Randy Martin, Frank Rosengarten, and George Snedeker. New York: Monthly Review Press, pp. 45–73. Mentions W briefly (p. 62).

3993. Nakajima, Yoshinobu. "On *Uncle Tom's Children*: Escape from the Southern Hegemony." *Bulletin of Shiraume Gakuen Junior College*, 29 (March), 129–137. Argues that *UTC* when published was mistakenly considered a protest novel against white racism, but it also protests the cultural hegemony of the white South.

3994. Namekata, Hitoshi. "Richard Wright's 'Big Black Good Man'" *Bulletin of Musashino College for Music*, 23 (February). Plot summary of the story with a psychoanalytical study of its central character's impact on the white hotel clerk [T.K., R.B., and Y.H.].

3995. Nash, Evelyn M. "*Why Black People Tend to Shout: Cold Facts and Wry Views from a Black Man's World.* By Ralph Wiley." *The Journal of Negro History*, 78 (Spring), 133–135. Mentions W briefly.

3996. Northouse, Cameron. *Ishmael Reed: An Interview.* Dallas: Contemporary Research Press, p. 50. Reed states he has an article on W forthcoming in the first issue of *The American Book Review*.

3997. Norton, Anne-Lucie, ed. *The Hutchinson Dictionary of Biography.* Oxford: Helicon, p. 703. Contains a very brief biographical sketch of W.

3998. _____. *The HarperCollins Dictionary of Biography.* New York: HarperCollins, p. 707.

3999. O'Brien, John. "Alice Walker: An Interview," in *Alice Walker: Critical Perspectives Past and Present.* Eds. Henry Louis Gates, Jr., and K.A. Appiah. New York: Amistad, pp. 326–346.

4000. _____. "Alice Walker: An Interview," in *Alice Walker: Critical Perspectives Past and Present.* Eds. Henry Louis Gates, Jr., and K.A. Appiah. New York: Amistad, pp. 326–346.

4001. Olney, James E. "The Value of Autobiography for Comparative Studies: African vs. Western Autobiography," in *African American Autobiography: A Collection of Critical Essays.* Ed. William L. Andrews. Englewood Cliffs, NJ: Prentice Hall, pp. 212–223.

4002. Ostrom, Hans. *Langston Hughes: A Study of the Short Fiction.* New York: Twayne, pp. 14, 60, 71. Mentions briefly W, his expatriation, and *NS*.

4003. Ottley, Roi. "*Pagan Spain* (1957)," in *Richard Wright: Critical Perspectives Past and Present.* Eds. Henry Louis Gates, Jr., and K.A. Appiah. New York: Amistad, p. 56.

4004. Parker, Robert Dale. "Material Choices: American Fictions, the Classroom, and the Post-Canon." *American Literary History*, 5 (Spring), 89–110. Suggests that *NS* may be considered racist in its portrayal of Bigger.

4005. Patrick, Barbara. "Gayl Jones (1949–)," in *Contemporary Fiction Writers of the South: A Bibliographical Sourcebook.* Eds. Joseph M. Flora and Robert Bain. Westport, CT: Greenwood Press, pp. 255–260. Mentions briefly *NS.* (p. 257).

4006. Patterson, Randy. "Cultural Diversity in the Capital City: Jackson and the Work of Eudora Welty, Richard Wright, and Samuel Beadle." *Richard Wright Newsletter,* 3 (Fall/Winter), 2. Abstract of a paper at a meeting of the Mississippi Council of Teachers of English, 24–25 September 1993. Contrasts W not only to Welty but also to Beadle, a black attorney and writer at the turn of the century.

4007. Patterson, Tiffany R.L. "Hurston, Zora Neale (1891–1960)," in *Black Women in America: A Historical Encyclopedia.* Vol. I. Ed. Darlene Clark Hine. Brooklyn: Carlson, pp. 598–603. Mentions W briefly (p. 599).

4008. Payne, Johnny. "Letters from Nowhere: Fanny Howe's *Forty Whacks* and Feminine Identity," in *Anxious Power: Reading, Writing, and Ambivalence in Narrative by Women.* Eds. Carol J. Singley and Susan Elizabeth Sweeney. Albany: State University of New York Press, pp. 329–347. Mentions W briefly (p. 346).

4009. Pfaff, Françoise. *Entretiens avec Maryse Condé.* Paris: Editions Karthala, pp. 144, 167. Mentions W briefly. Condé expresses dislike of W's didacticism.

4010. Pickering, James H. "Biographical Notes," in his *Fiction 50: An Introduction to the Short Story.* New York: Macmillan. pp. 747–767.

4011. _____. "Questions for Study," in his *Fiction 50: An Introduction to the Short Story.* New York: Macmillan, p. 695. For "The Man Who Was Almost a Man."

4012. Plum, Jay. "Blues, History, and the Dramaturgy of August Wilson." *African American Review,* 27 (Winter), 561–567. Mentions W briefly.

4013. Poirier, Suzanne. "Petry, Ann Lane (1908–)," in *Black Women in America: An Historical Encyclopedia.* Vol. II. Ed. Darlene Clark Hine. Brooklyn: Carlson, pp. 917–918. Notes that some critics place Petry in the "'Richard Wright school' of urban realism."

4014. Porter, Carolyn. "Getting Gendered," in *Changing Subjects: The Making of Feminist Literary Criticism.* Eds. Gayle Greene and Coppélia Kahn. London: Routledge, pp. 168–179. Mentions W briefly (p. 176).

4015. Porter, Horace A. "The Horror and the Glory: Richard Wright's Portrait of the Artist in *Black Boy* and *American Hunger,*" in *Richard Wright: Critical Perspectives Past and Present.* Eds. Henry Louis Gates, Jr., and K.A. Appiah. New York: Amistad, pp. 316–327.

4016. Pudaloff, Ross. "Celebrity as Identity: *Native Son* and Mass Culture," in *Richard Wright: Critical Perspectives Past and Present.* Eds. Henry Louis Gates, Jr., and K.A. Appiah. New York: Amistad, pp. 156–170.

4017. Rackham, Jeff, and Olivia Bertagnolli. "Out of Darkness," in their *Windows: Exploring Personal Values Through Reading and Writing.* New York: HarperCollins, pp. 534–536. Mentions W briefly.

4018. _____. "Reflections," in their *Windows: Exploring Personal Values Through Reading and Writing.* New York: HarperCollins, p. 543. Study questions for an excerpt from *BB.*

4019. Rampersad, Arnold. "Foreword," in *Lawd Today!* by Richard Wright. Boston: Northeastern University Press, pp. v–xi.

4020. _____. "Hughes's *Fine Clothes to the Jew,*" in *Langston Hughes: Critical Perspectives Past and Present.* Eds. Henry Louis Gates, Jr., and K.A. Appiah. New York: Amistad, pp. 53–68.

4021. _____. "A Note on the Edition," in *Lawd Today!* by Richard Wright. Boston: Northeastern University Press, pp. xiii–xv. Outlines briefly the textual history of the novel noting W's modernist experimentations in punctuation, capitalization, and usage "regularized by the first publisher of the novel and restored in this edition."

4022. _____. "*Rite of Passage* by Richard Wright: Excerpt from the 'Afterword' by Arnold Rampersad." *Richard Wright Newsletter,* 3 (Fall/Winter), 1. Partial reprint of 1993.

4023. _____. "Introduction to the Harper Perenial Edition," in *Native Son and How 'Bigger' Was Born.* Cutchogue, New York: Buccaneer Books, pp. xi–xxviii.

4024. _____. "Introduction to the Harper Perennial Edition," in *Native Son and How 'Bigger' Was Born.* New York: Harper Perennial, pp. xi–xxviii. Places *NS* in its social, historical and literary context, discusses Bigger's characterization and its social meaning, comments on the novel's reception, and places it high in the African American literary tradition. Also comments on W's fiction prior to *NS.*

4025. _____. "Chronology," in *Native Son and How 'Bigger' Was Born.* New York: Harper Perennial, pp. 541–572.

4026. _____. "Notes," in *Native Son and How 'Bigger' Was Born.* New York: Harper Perennial, pp. 578–594. Explanatory and historical notes on *NS.* Also mentions a few of the relevant biographical and bibliographical works on *NS.*

4027. _____. "Note on the Texts," in *Native Son and How 'Bigger' Was Born.* New York: Harper Perennial, pp. 573–577. Discusses the genesis of the two works.

4028. Ramsay, John G. "Toward Literary Citizenship: Reply to January Editorial." *English Journal,* 82 (September), 25–26. Mentions W and *BB.*

4029. Rankovic, Catherine. "Washington University Conference: Richard Wright in the 1950's, February 20, 1993." *The Richard Wright Newsletter,* 2 (Spring/Summer), 2. Reports presentations by Gerald Early on W's interest in existentalism and third world issues, by Lynn Weiss on *BP,* by Keneth Kinnamon on interviews with W, by Ollie Harrington, by videotape, on his friendship with W in Paris, by Guy Land on his video biography of W, by Amrijet Singh on W's increasing identification with the Third World, and by Julia Wright on the idea of exile in her father's thought.

4030. Rao, E. Raja. *Beyond Protest: A Critical Examination of Contemporary African American Fiction.* Delhi: Academic Foundation, pp. 29, 30, 32–34. Discusses W and the protest tradition.

4031. Redding, Saunders. "*The Long Dream* (1958)," in *Richard Wright: Critical Perspectives Past and Present.* Eds. Henry Louis Gates, Jr., and K.A. Appiah. New York: Amistad, pp. 60–61.

4032. Reed, Brian Keith. "An illusion of order: An analysis of Richard Wright's 'Native Son' and 'The Outsider,' and Ralph Ellison's 'Invisible Man.'" *Dissertation Abstracts International*, 53 (February), 2817-A. The protagonists of all three novels struggle with the question of good and evil, "frightened that the world is random and chaotic."

4033. Reed, Ishmael. "Beyond Los Angeles," in his *Airing Dirty Laundry*. Reading, MA: Addison Wesley, pp. 43–52. Mentions W briefly (p. 48).

4034. _____. "Bill Gunn — Director," in his *Airing Dirty Laundry*. Reading, MA: Addison-Wesley, pp. 112–119. Mentions briefly "a maimed version of Richard Wright's *Native Son*" produced by PBS (p. 116).

4035. _____. "Gwendolyn Brooks — Poet," in his *Airing Dirty Laundry*. Reading, MA: Addison-Wesley, pp. 104–111. Mentions W briefly (p. 104).

4036. _____. "Jess Mowry — Writer," in his *Airing Dirty Laundry*. Reading, MA: Addison-Wesley, pp. 157–164. Mentions W briefly (p. 160).

4037. _____. "Reginald Martin, Toni Cade Bambara — Writers," in his *Airing Dirty Laundry*. Reading, MA: Addison-Wesley, pp. 165–171. Mentions W briefly (p. 167).

4038. _____. "Zora Neale Hurston, Writer," in his *Airing Dirty Laundry*, Reading, MA: Addison-Wesley, pp. 146–151.

4039. Reilly, John M. "Richard Wright and the Art of Non-Fiction: Stepping Out on the Stage of the World," in *Richard Wright: Critical Perspectives Past and Present*. Eds. Henry Louis Gates, Jr., and K.A. Appiah. New York: Amistad, pp. 409–423.

4040. Riley, Dorthy Winbush, ed. *My Soul Looks Back, Less I Forget: A Collection of Quotations by People of Color*. New York: HarperCollins, pp. 11, 22, 36–37, 42, 48, 51, 57, 60, 74, 76, 87, 99, 103, 107, 119, 132, 143, 144, 176, 182, 197, 208, 213, 242, 248, 257, 260, 302, 325, 338, 346, 355, 365, 369, 375, 386, 387, 392, 396, 406, 412, 426, 432, 439, 443, 450, 453 s.v. alcohol, art/artist, blues, burden, change, Chicago, church, civilization, control, courage, death, dignity, dream, duality, end, face, fear, feeling, happiness, heart, hunger, imagination, injustice, life, loneliness, madness, man/manhood, peace, prison, reading, responsibility, roots, silence, slavery, South, stranger, strength, suffer, symbol, time, travel, vote, warming, woman, words, writing/writer, youth.

4041. Rogers, Michael. "Book Reviews: Classic Returns." *Library Journal*, 118 (15 March), 118. Includes a listing of paperback editions of *BB, NS, O,* and *UTC*.

4042. Roses, Lorraine Elena. "Harlem Renaissance," in *Black Women in America: An Historical Encyclopedia*. Vol. I. Ed. Darlene Clark Hine. Brooklyn: Carlson, pp. 529–532. Mentions "Blueprint for Negro Writing" and notes W's dismissal of *Their Eyes Were Watching God*.

4043. Roper, Gene, Jr. "At Ole Miss: Faulkner on Writers and Writing." *The Faulkner Newsletter and Yoknapatawpha Review*, 13 (April–June), 1,3. Reports a talk by Faulkner at the University of Mississippi in April 1947. In response to questions he "classified *Native Son* as a very good book while putting *Black Boy* in the propaganda category" (p. 3).

4044. Rowden, Terry. "A Play of Abstractions: Race, Sexuality, and Community in James Baldwin's *Another Country.*" *The Southern Review*, 29 (January), 41–50. Compare Baldwin's Rufus to Bigger Thomas (p. 42).

4045. _____. "A Play of Abstractions: Race, Sexuality, and Community in James Baldwin's *Another Country.*" *The Southern Review*, 29 (January), 41–50. Quotes a comment on W in Irving Howe's "James Baldwin: At Ease in Apocalypse."

4046. Russell, Kathy, Midge Wilson, and Ronald Hall. *The Color Complex: The Politics of Skin Color Among African Americans*. New York: Anchor Books/Doubleday, p. 117. Mentions briefly *NS* and W's white wives.

4047. Sallis, James. "In America's Black Heartland: The Achievement of Chester Himes." *Western Humanities Review*, 37 (Autumn), 191–206. Notes that Himes's early work is reminiscent of Richard Wright and proletarian work of the Forties" (p. 192).

4048. Sasamoto, Seiji. "Richard Wright's 'Long Black Song': An Effect of Sounds." *Bulletin of College for Vocational Training*, 22 (March), Survey of the sounds used in "Long Black Song." The baby's cry symbolizes Sarah's emotional reaction to the white salesman [T.K., R.B., and Y.H.].

4049. Saunders, James Robert. "The Ornamentation of Old Ideas: Naylor's First Three Novels," in *Gloria Naylor: Critical Perspectives Past and Present*. Eds. Henry Louis Gates, Jr., and K.A. Appiah. New York: Amistad, pp. 249–262.

4050. Schor, Edith. *Visible Ellison: A Study of Ralph Ellison's Fiction*. Westport, CT: Greenwood Press, p. 4. Mentions briefly W and *New Challenge*.

4051. Scruggs, Charles. "John F. Bassett. *Harlem in Review: Critical Reactions to Black American Writers, 1917–1939.*" *Modern Fiction Studies*, 39 (Summer), 374–375. Review noting coverage of *UTC*.

4052. _____. *Sweet Home: Invisible Cities in the Afro-American Novel*. Baltimore: The Johns Hopkins University Press, pp. 2, 4, 5, 8, 14–15, 21, 31, 32, 36–37, 38, 41, 50, 53–54, 55, 61–62, 64, 65, 68–69, 70, 71–73, 74, 75–77, 78, 84, 89–90, 92–94, 95, 97–99, 100, 101–102, 125, 129–131, 136, 137, 138–140, 145–146, 154, 155–156, 159, 160, 163–165, 168, 169, 176, 214–215, 206, 209, 212, 219, 254, 267, 269, 273, 285. Relates W to such topics as Baldwin, Ellison, Hurston, Mencken, Morrison, Louis Wirth, black popular culture and class division and other matters. Mentions or comments on *NS, AH, BB, TMBV, O*, "Blueprint for Negro Writing," *LT*, and "How Bigger Was Born."

4053. Shields, John C. "Introduction: African-American Poetics." *Style*, 27 (Summer), 167–171. Comments on the treatments of W by William L. Andrews and R. Baxter Miller in this issue.

4054. Shipman, Charles. *It Had to Be Revolution: Memoirs of an American Radical*. Ithaca: Cornell University Press, p. 186. Mentions W briefly.

4055. Shapiro, Herbert. "Racism," in *Encyclopedia of American Social History*. Eds. Mary Kupiec Cayton, Elliott J. Garn, and Peter W. Williams. Vol. II. New York: Scribner's, p. 2097. Mentions W. briefly.

4056. Silverman, Debra B. "Nella Larsen's *Quicksand*: Entangling the

Webs of Exoticism." *African American Review*, 27 (Winter), 599–614. Quotes John Malcolm Brinnin on Gertrude Stein's influence on W (p. 605).

4057. [Singh, Amritjit]. "Books Received." *MELUS*, 18 (Winter), 135–138. Lists *The Racial Problem in the Works of Richard Wright and James Baldwin* by Jean-Francois Gounard.

4058. Singh, Amritjit. "Julia Wright Visits Rhode Island College." *Richard Wright Newsletter*, 3 (Fall/Winter), 3. Reports a visit on 2 April 1993 with a full account of her speech entitled "Writing About Richard Wright: Reflections of a Daughter." Her method as a biographer is to bring out "the psychological, artistic, and political complexity of Wright's personality and work."

4059. Sitkoff, Harvard. *The Struggle for Black Equality 1954–1992*. Revised edition. New York: Harper-Collins, p. 199. Notes W's early use of the term "black power."

4060. [Skerrett, Joseph T., Jr.] "Preliminaries." *MELUS*, 18 (Spring), 1–3. Includes comments on Robert Butler's essay in this issue.

4061. Smith, Gary. "Fifth Avenue Uptown: James Baldwin, 1924–1987." *African American Review*, 27 (Winter), 635–638. Poem mentioning briefly Baldwin's quarrel with W.

4062. Smith, Lillian. *How Am I to Be Heard?: Letters of Lillian Smith*. Ed. Margaret Rose Gladney. Chapel Hill: The University of North Carolina Press, pp. 49, 62, 84–85. In a letter of 1942 to Glenn Rainey, Smith mentions W. In a letter to W dated 12 June 1944 Smith expresses her desire to "have a good talk [with W] about the responsibility of writers to their culture and its problems … free of any ideological ties."

4063. Smith, Valerie. "Alienation and Creativity in the Fiction of Richard Wright," in *Richard Wright: Critical Perspectives Past and Present*. Eds. Henry Louis Gates, Jr., and K.A. Appiah. New York: Amistad, pp. 433–447.

4064. [Smith, Virginia Whatley]. "Call for Papers!" *Afram Newsletter*, No. 38 (December), 28. For a collection on W's travel books.

4065. [Smith, Virginia Whatley]. "Call for Papers!" *Richard Wright Newsletter*, 3 (Fall/Winter), 7. For a

collection of essays on *BP, CC*, and *PS*.

4066. Smith, Virginia Whatley. "Image, Text, and Voice: Oppositions of Meanings in the Wright-Rosskam Photographic Text." *Obsidian II: Black Literature in Review*, 8 (Fall/Winter), 1–27. Analyzes *TMBV* as "an epistemological and semantic study about image, text, and voice, and their contradictory and hidden meanings" (p. 23), arguing that W and Rosskam worked together. Smith relies on Barthes for her theoretical framework.

4067. Smith, William Gardner. "The Negro Writer: Pitfalls and Compensations," in *Speech and Power: The African-American Essay and Its Cultural Content, from Polemics to Pulpit*. Vol. 2. Ed. Gerald Early. Hopewell, NJ: The Ecco Press, pp. 123–128.

4068. Spencer, Camille. "The Black Scholar Books Received." *The Black Scholar*, (Winter/Spring), 57, 59–63. Contains a notice of the second edition of Michel Fabre's *The Unfinished Quest of Richard Wright*.

4069. Stepto, Robert. "Literacy and Ascent: *Black Boy*," in *Richard Wright: Critical Perspectives Past and Present*. Eds. Henry Louis Gates, Jr., and K.A. Appiah. New York: Amistad, pp. 226–254.

4070. S[tevick], P[hilip] T. "Adams, Timothy Dow. *Telling Lies in Modern American Autobiography*." *Journal of Modern Literature*, 18 (Spring), 170–171. Notice mentioning W briefly.

4071. Stone, Albert E. "After *Black Boy* and *Dusk of Dawn*: Patterns in Recent Black Autobiography," in *African American Autobiography: A Collection of Critical Essays*. Ed. William L. Andrews. Englewood Cliffs, NJ: Prentice Hall, pp. 171–195.

4072. Stone, Albert E. "Postscript: Looking Back in 1992," in *African American Autobiography: A Collection of Critical Essays*. Ed. William L. Andrews. Englewood Cliffs, NJ: Prentice Hall, pp. 186–195. Mentions W briefly (p. 189).

4073. Stubbs, Mary Frances. "Walker, Margaret," in *African American Women: A Biographical Dictionary*. Ed. Dorothy C. Salem. New York: Garland, pp. 553–555. Discusses the friendship between W and Walker and its rupture.

4074. Suggs, Jon Christian. "Article: Richard Wright, Blueprint for

Negro Writing," in his *American Proletarian Culture: The Twenties and the Thirties*. Vol. 11 of *Dictionary of Literary Biography: An Illustrated Chronicle*. Detroit: Gale, p. 362. Headnote identifying *New Challenge* and asserting that "manuscript evidence suggests that other hands than Wright's may have been involved in the composition of this article." Includes a photograph of W.

4075. _____. "Historical Overview," in his *American Proletarian Culture: The Twenties and the Thirties*. Vol. 11 of *Dictionary of Literary Biography Documentary Series: An Illustrated Chronicle*. Detroit: Gale, pp. 3–16. Mentions W briefly (pp. 13, 16).

4076. _____. "Letters," in his *American Proletarian Culture: The Twenties and the Thirties*. Vol. 11 of *Dictionary of Literary Biography Series: An Illustrated Chronicle*. Detroit: Gale, pp. 214–215. Introduces letters from Abe Aaron to Jack Conroy, one of them (13 January 1934) containing a paragraph on W.

4077. Sundquist, Eric J. *To Wake the Nations: Race in the Making of American Literature*. Cambridge, MA: Harvard University Press, pp. 27, 29, 52, 423–424, 442. The first epigraph to Part I is from *TMBV*. Mentions *NS* and Bigger Thomas.

4078. Tanner, Laura E. "Uncovering the Magical Disguise of Language: The Narrative Presence in Richard Wright's *Native Son*," in *Richard Wright: Critical Perspectives Past and Present*. Eds. Henry Louis Gates, Jr., and K.A. Appiah. New York: Amistad, pp. 132–148.

4079. Tate, Claudia C. "Christian Existentialism in *The Outsider*," in *Richard Wright: Critical Perspectives Past and Present*. Eds. Henry Louis Gates, Jr., and K.A. Appiah. New York: Amistad, pp. 369–387.

4080. Teachout, Terry. "Notebook: Another Sun Person Heard From." *The New Criterion*, 12 (September), 91–96. Comments briefly on W (pp. 94, 96).

4081. Thaddeus, Janice. "The Metamorphosis of *Black Boy*," in *Richard Wright: Critical Perspectives Past and Present*. Eds. Henry Louis Gates, Jr., and K.A. Appiah. pp. 272–284.

4082. Thiong'o, Ngũgĩ wa. *Moving the Centre: The Struggle for Cultural Freedoms*. London: James Currey, pp. 7, 13. Mentions W briefly.

4083. Thompson, Julius E. *The Black Press in Mississippi, 1865–1985.* Gainesville: The University Press of Florida, pp. 23, 61. Mentions W briefly.

4084. Thompson, Kathleen. "Walker, Margaret Abigail," in *Black Women in America: An Historical Encyclopedia.* Vol. II. Ed. Darlene Clark Hine. Brooklyn: Carlson, pp. 1219–1220. Mentions briefly W and Walker's book on him.

4085. Tiryak, Mary. "Kent, George E. *A Life of Gwendolyn Brooks.*" *Journal of Modern Literature,* 18 (Spring), 251. Review mentioning W briefly.

4086. Toombs, Charles P. "The Confluence of Food and Identity in Gloria Naylor's *Linden Hills*: 'What We Eat Is Who We Is.'" *CLA Journal,* 37 (September), 1–18. Mentions briefly *NS* (p. 2).

4087. Towner, Theresa M. "Spirit Scripts." *The Mississippi Quarterly,* 46 (Fall), 601–615. Mentions briefly *BB* (p. 606).

4088. Traylor, Eleanor. "Naming the UnNamed: African American Criticism and African American Letters." *Black Books Bulletin: WordsWork,* 16 (Winter 1993/1994), 64–75. Mentions briefly *NS*.

4089. Trilling, Lionel. "*Black Boy* (1945)," in *Richard Wright: Critical Perspectives Past and Present.* Eds. Henry Louis Gates, Jr., and K.A. Appiah. New York: Amistad, pp. 28–30.

4090. Trimnell, Angus. *Conversations with Richard Wright.* Ed. by Keneth Kinnamon and Michel Fabre. Chicago: The Booklist, p. 1937. Favorable notice. Mentions briefly *NS, BB,* and *UTC.*

4091. Tulles, Allen. "Long Journey Home." *Southern Exposure,* 21 (Spring/Summer), 32–34. Mentions W briefly.

4092. TuSmith, Bonnie. *All My Relatives: Community in Contemporary Ethnic American Literatures.* Ann Arbor: The University of Michigan Press, pp. 184, 211. States that *BB* was misread by white reviewers as proof that "black people have no culture."

4093. Updike, John. "Exile on Main Street." *The New Yorker,* 69 (17 May), 91–97, Essay on Sinclair Lewis mentioning briefly the Library of America edition of W (p. 91).

4094. Vesterman, William. "Account: John E. Loftis on 'The Man Who Was Almost a Man' as a Parody of the Hunt Tradition," in his *Literature: An Introduction to Critical Reading.* Fort Worth: Harcourt Brace College, pp. 132–134. Commentary on 1986.

4095. _____. "A Brief Introduction to Racial and Ethnic Criticism," in his *Literature: An Introduction to Critical Reading.* Fort Worth: Harcourt Brace College, pp. 119–122. Includes comments on an essay on "The Man Who Was Almost a Man" by John Loftis.

4096. _____. Richard Wright (1908–1960), in his *Literature: An Introduction to Critical Reading.* Fort Worth: Harcourt Brace College, p. 122. Biographical headnote to "The Man Who Was Almost a Man."

4097. _____. "Suggestions for Discussion and Writing," in his *Literature: An Introduction to Critical Reading.* Fort Worth: Harcourt Brace College, pp. 134–135. To accompany "The Man Who Was Almost a Man."

4098. Vidal, Gore. "The Fourth Diary of Anaïs Nin," in his *United States: Essays, 1952–1992.* New York: Random House, pp. 1149–1154.

4099. Wald, Alan. "Culture and Commitment: U.S. Communist Writers Reconsidered," in *New Studies in the Politics and Culture of U.S. Communism.* Eds. Michael E. Brown, Randy Martin, Frank Rosengarten, and George Snedeker. New York: Monthly Review Press, pp. 281–305. Mentions W briefly (pp. 297, 302).

4100. Walker, Nancy A. *Telling Lies in Modern American Biography by Timothy Dow Adams. American Studies,* 34 (Fall) 152–153. Review praising Adam's treatment of W, whose dissembling was a survival technique.

4101. Wall, Cheryl A. "A Sure Attention to Voice." *Novel: A Forum on Fiction,* 26 (Winter), 223–225. Review of Gayl Jones's *Liberating Voices: Oral Tradition in African American Literature* mentioning W briefly.

4102. _____. "Zora Neale Hurston: Changing Her Own Words," in Henry Louis Gates and K.A. Appiah's *Zora Neale Hurston: Critical Perspectives Past and Present.* New York: Amistad, pp. 76–97. Mentions W briefly in a footnote (p. 97).

4103. _____. "Zora Neale Hurston: Changing Her Own Words," in *Zora Neale Hurston: Cultural Perspectives Past and Present.* Eds. Henry Louis Gates, Jr., and K.A. Appiah. New York: Amistad, pp. 76–97. Mentions briefly June Jordan's essay on W. and Hurston (pp. 77, 97).

4104. Ward, Jerry W., Jr. "Black South Literature: Before Day Annotations (for Blyden Jackson)." *African American Review,* 27 (Summer), 315–326. Comments on the intertextuality of *UTC, Their Eyes Were Watching God,* and Booker T. Washington's Cotton States Exposition speech (pp. 315–316). Also includes a favorable assessment of Margaret Walker's *Richard Wright: Daemonic Genuis* as an intellectual biography (pp. 318–319).

4105. _____. "Introduction to the HarperPerennial Edition," in *Black Boy (American Hunger).* By Richard Wright. New York: HarperCollins, pp. xi–xxi. Examines the publishing history of the work, notes its congruence with the tradition of the fugitive slave narrative, places it in the context of W's other works, and analyzes its themes. Emphasizes hunger as the dominant metaphor of W's life and work.

4106. _____. "Race and Gender in Richard Wright's *Black Boy.*" *Richard Wright Newsletter,* 3 (Fall/Winter), 2. Abstract of a paper at a meeting of the Mississippi Council of Teachers of English, 24–25 September 1993. Advocates using gender as well as race in teaching *BB.*

4107. Ward, Jerry. "Wright, Richard," in *Encyclopedia of African-American Civil Rights: From Emancipation to the Present.* Eds. Charles D. Lowery and John F. Marzalek. Westport, CT: Greenwood, pp. 593–594. Biographical sketch mentioning all of W's works except those published posthumously. Includes a selected bibliography of seven works.

4108. Warren, Kenneth W. "Appeals for (Mis) recognition: Theorizing the Diaspora," in *Cultures of United States Imperialism.* Eds. Amy Kaplan and Donald E. Pease. Durham: Duke University Press, pp. 392–406. Includes comment on *TMBV* (pp. 396–397)

4109. _____. *Black and White Strangers: Race and American Literary Realism.* Chicago: The University of Chicago Press, p. 6. Quotes Leslie Fiedler mentioning W briefly.

4110. _____. "The Mythic City:

An Interview with Leon Forrest." *Callaloo*, 16 (Spring), 392–408. Both Warren (p. 394) and Forrest (p. 405) mention W briefly. Reprinted: 1997.

4111. Weinstein, Philip M. *Faulkner's Subject: A Cosmos No One Owns.* Cambridge: Cambridge University Press, p. 64. Mentions briefly W and "Big Boy Leaves Home."

4112. Werner, Craig. "Gaines, Ernest J. *A Lesson Before Dying."* *Choice*, 31 (October), 287–288. Favorable notice stating that the "novel can be seen as a 'rewriting' of Richard Wright's *Native Son.*"

4113. _____. "Leon Forrest, the AACM and the Legacy of the Chicago Renaissance." *The Black Scholar*, 23 (Summer/Fall), 10–23. Comments on W's role in the Chicago Renaissance (pp. 11, 12, 13).

4114. West, Cornel. "Black Critics and the Pitfalls of Canon Formation," in his *Keeping Faith: Philosophy and Race in America.* New York: Routledge, pp. 32–43. Mentions W briefly (p. 39).

4115. _____. "Black Sexuality: The Taboo Subject," in his *Race Matters.* Boston: Beacon Press, p. 83. Cites Bigger Thomas as one stereotype of black sexuality.

4116. _____. "Horace Pippin's Challenge to Art Criticism," in *I Tell My Heart: The Art of Horace Pippin.* Ed. Judith E. Stein. New York: Universe, pp. 44–53. Mentions *NS* as the exemplar of black art as protest (p. 51).

4117. _____. "Horace Pippin's Challenge to Art Criticism," in his *Keeping Faith: Philosophy and Race in America.* New York: Routledge, pp. 55–66. Contrasts W's protest art, "preoccupied with the white normative game," with Pippin's painting, which is a "kind of redemptive culturalism."

4118. _____. *Keeping Faith: Philosophy and Race in America.* New York: Routledge, p. 65. Mentions briefly *NS*.

4119. _____. "Nihilism in Black America," in his *Race Matters.* Boston: Beacon Press, pp.

4120. Whaley, Liz and Liz Dodge. *Weaving in the Women: Transforming the High School English Curriculum.* Portsmouth, NH: Boynton/Cook, pp. 122, 196, 209, 227. Mentions briefly W and *BB*.

4121. White, Edmund. *Genet: A Biography.* New York: Knopf, p. 352.

Quotes from W's blurb for *Our Lady of the Flowers.* Mentions briefly *NS* and *BB*.

4122. Wiegman, Robyn. "The Anatomy of Lynching." *Journal of the History of Sexuality*, 3 (January), 445–467. Discusses the "rape mythos" in *NS*, which "captures Bigger in the definitional nexus of race, sexuality, and gender..." (p. 463).

4123. Wiley, Ralph. "It's Greek to Me," in his *What Black People Should Do Now.* New York: Ballantine Books, pp. 22–37. Notes that Allan Bloom did not include W in the canon (pp. 25–26).

4124. _____. "Mister Justice Thomas," in his *What Black People Should Do Now.* New York: Ballantine Books, pp. 103–125. Quotes from *BB* (pp. 114–115).

4125. _____. "On the A-Train to Venus with Isis," in his *What Black People Should Do Now.* New York: Ballantine Books, pp. 309–320. Mentions W briefly (p. 315).

4126. _____. "Some of My Best Friends," in his *What Black People Should Do Now.* New York: Ballantine Books, pp. 126–144. Mentions W briefly (p. 126).

4127. _____. "Why Black People Sing the Blues," in his *What Black People Should Do Now.* New York: Ballantine Books, pp. 257–284. Mentions W briefly (p. 273).

4128. Williams, Delores. *Sisters in the Wilderness: The Challenge of Womanist God-Talk.* Maryknoll, NY: Orbis Books, pp. 45, 46–49, 51, 56, 245. Discusses W's questioning of divine justice in *LD* and *NS* and mentions W elsewhere.

4129. Williams, John A. "Blackballing," in *Censored Books: Critical Viewpoints.* Eds. Nicholas J. Karolides, Lee Burress, and John M. Kean. Metuchen, NJ: The Scarecrow Press, pp. 11–18. Comments on black parental resistance to *BB* and *NS* because they are not "positive" (p. 12) and on W's FBI file (p. 15) and mentions W elsewhere. Also mentions a recent article on W and Baldwin by James Campbell in the *London Independent.*

4130. Williams, Sherley Anne. "Linden Hills," in *Gloria Naylor: Critical Perspectives Past and Present.* Eds. Henry Louis Gates, Jr., and K.A. Appiah. New York: Amistad Press, pp. 9–12.

4131. Wixson, Douglas. "'Through

Me Many Long Dumb Voices': Jack Conroy and the Illinois Writers Project, 1938–1942," in *Exploring the Midwestern Literary Imagination: Essays in Honor of David D. Anderson.* Troy, NY: Whitston, pp. 42–56. Mentions W's admiration of Conroy, "The Ethics of Living Jim Crow," and W's involvement with *American Stuff.*

4132. Woodward, Daniel. "Intramuralia: Twentieth-Century Fiction in the Huntington Library." *The Huntington Library Quarterly*, 56 (Spring), 213–227. Lists s.v. W "substantial holdings [of printed works] that lack some significant texts."

4133. Work, John W. *What Every CEO Already Knows About Managing Diversity.* Highland City, FL: Rainbow Books, p. 92. Mentions briefly *NS* and *BB*.

4134. Worley, Demetrice A., and Jesse Perry, Jr. "A Historical Overview of the African American Literary Tradition," in their *African American Literature: An Anthology of Nonfiction, Fiction, Poetry and Drama.* Lincolnwood, IL: National Textbook Company, pp. xvii–xxiv. Comments briefly on W and *NS* (p. xxi).

4135. _____. "Richard Wright," in their *African American Literature: An Anthology of Nonfiction, Fiction, Poetry and Drama.* Lincolnwood, IL: National Textbook Company, p. 80. Biographical headnote to "The Man Who Was Almost a Man."

4136. _____. "Thinking About the Story, Reading/Writing Connections," in *African American Literature: An Anthology of Nonfiction, Fiction, Poetry and Drama.* Lincolnwood, IL: National Textbook Company, p. 91. Study aids for "The Man Who Was Almost a Man."

4137. Wright, Julia. "Foreword: A Friendship Revisited," in *Why I Left America and Other Essays* by Oliver W. Harrington. Jackson: University Press of Mississippi, pp. ix + xv. Evaluates the friendship of W with George Padmore and Ollie Harrington, especially the latter. Utilizing a character in Island of Hallucination based on Harrington, Julia Wright emphasizes the closeness of her father's friendship with Harrington.

4138. _____. "Of Writers and Rewards: As They Lay Dying..." *International Herald Tribune* (4 November), p. 5. Argues that W should have received more honors during his lifetime, including the Nobel Prize.

4139. ____. "Of Writers and Rewards: As They Lay Dying..." *Richard Wright Newsletter*, 3 (Fall/Winter), 4–6.

4140. ____. "Rite of Passage Comes Out of the Shadows." *The Richard Wright Newsletter*, 2 (Spring/Summer) 1–2. Critique of the novella, relating it to biographical sources in W's life, especially his yearning for the black mother. Also comments on W's efforts to have it and another story included in a volume to be entitled *Ten Men*.

4141. Wyatt, Jean. "Giving Body to the Word: The Maternal Symbolic in Toni Morrison's *Beloved*." *PMLA*, 108 (May), 474–488. Quotes briefly from *TMBV* (p. 480).

4142. Wyatt-Brown, Bertram. "*The Return of Nat Turner: History, Literature, and Cultural Politics in Sixties America*. By Albert E. Stone." *The Journal of Southern History*, 59 (August), 587–589. Review mentioning W briefly.

4143. Wyrick, Jean, and Beverly J. Slaughter. "*Discovering Books* Richard Wright," in their *The Rinehart Reader*. Second edition. Fort Worth: Harcourt Brace Jovanovich, p. 35.

4144. ____. *The Rinehart Reader*. Fort Worth: Harcourt Brace Jovanovich, pp. 13, 42. Brief mention of W and a headnote to an excerpt from *BB*.

4145. ____. "Writers on Reading," in their *The Rinehart Reader*. Second edition. Fort Worth: Harcourt Brace Jovanovich, p. 13.

4146. Yarborough, Richard. "Introduction to the Harper Perennial Edition," in *Uncle Tom's Children* by Richard Wright." San Bernadino, California, pp. ix–xxix. Substantial critique of *UTC* placing it in the context of W's life and his experience in the John Reed Club, the Communist Party, the Federal Writer's Project, and W's rejection of the Harlem Renaissance. Each of the stories is examined. Concludes that "the real strength of this book resides in its" fierce determination to break the silence surrounding racism in the United States ... ya Salaam, Kalamu. "Enriching the Paper Trail: An Interview with Tom Dent." *African American Review*, 27 (Summer), 327–344. Mentions briefly W (p. 336) and *BB* (p. 343).

4147. Yoder, Edwin M., Jr. "An Eccentric Selection from the Nobel Folks." *International Herald Tribune* (13 October), p. 9. Mentions briefly W, *NS*, and Bigger Thomas.

4148. ____. "An Eccentric Selection from the Nobel Folks." *Richard Wright Newsletter*, 3 (Fall/Winter), 4.

4149. Young, Stephen. "African American Studies: Literature." *The Society for the Study of Southern Literature Newsletter* (November), 10–11. Lists Michel Fabre's *From Harlem to Paris: Black American Writers in France, 1840–1980*.

4150. ____. "General Criticism and Reference Works." *The Society for the Study of Southern Literature* (April), 14. Lists *Conversations with Richard Wright*, edited by Keneth Kinnamon and Michel Fabre.

4151. ____. "Major Authors." *The Society for the Study of Southern Literature Newsletter* (November), 20–21. Lists *Conversations with Richard Wright*, ed. Keneth Kinnamon and Michel Fabre, and Margaret Walker's *Richard Wright: Daemonic Genius*.

4152. ____. "Teaching Southern Literature." *Society for the Study of Southern Literature* (April), 5–6. Reports that Susan Snell teaches an honors composition class with readings from W and others.

1994

4153. Aaron, Daniel. "The Hyphenate Writer and American Letters," in his *American Notes: Selected Essays*. Boston: Northeastern University Press, pp. 69–83.

4154. ____. "Richard Wright and the Communist Party," in his *American Notes: Selected Essays*. Boston: Northeastern University Press, pp. 91–101.

4155. Abarry, Abu Shardow. "*Forms of Black Consciousness*. By Sudhi Rajiv." *Journal of Black Studies*, 24 (March), 368–370. Favorable review of a work treating *BB* and *AH* as well as writings by Malcolm X and Eldridge Cleaver.

4156. Adell, Sandra. *Double-Consciousness /Double Bind: Theoretical Issues in Twentieth-Century Black Literature*. Urbana: University of Illinois Press, pp. 51–56, 59–60, 65, 68–69, 71, 138, 139. Discusses the role of W and Baldwin in the 1956 Congress of Black Writers and Artists and in the third chapter analyzes double-consciousness in *BB* and Maya Angelou's *I Know Why the Caged Bird Sings*.

4157. ____. 'The Big E(llison)'s Texts and Intertexts: Eliot, Burke, and the Underground Man." *CLA Journal*, 37 (June 1994), 377–401. Compares and contrasts *Invisible Man* and "The Man Who Lived Underground." W influenced Elli-

son, but is closer than Ellison to Dostoevsky (pp. 398–400) and mentions W elsewhere (pp. 379, 382).

4158. Adisa, Opal Palmer. "*Workings of the Spirit: The Poetics of Afro-American Women's Writing*. Houston A. Baker, Jr." *MELUS*, 19 (Summer), 147–149. Review mentioning W, *NS*, and *TMBV*.

4159. Ajchenbaum, Yves-Marc. *A la vie, a la mort: L'histoire du journal Combat, 1941–1974*. Paris: Monde-Editions, p. 303. Mentions W briefly in connection with Garry Davis and the movement he started.

4160. Alsen, Eberhard. "'Toward the Living Sun': Richard Wright's

Change of Heart from *The Outsider* to *The Long Dream*." *CLA Journal*, 38 (December), 211–227. Argues that in *LD* W rejects the existentialism of his previous works in favor of individual autonomy and a search for spiritual essence. Alsen supports this thesis by comparing *O* and *LD* with respect to narrative structure, plot patterns, character changes and figurative language.

4161. Annas, Pamela J., and Robert C. Rosen. "Richard Wright (1908–1960)," in their *Literature and Society: An Introduction to Fiction, Poetry, Drama, Nonfiction*. Second edition. Englewood Cliffs, NJ: Prentice-Hall, p. 858. Headnote to "The Man Who Went to Chicago."

4162. _____. "Richard Wright 'The Man Who Went to Chicago,'" in their *Literature and Society: An Introduction to Fiction, Poetry, Drama, Nonfiction*. Second edition. Englewood Cliffs, NJ: Prentice-Hall, p. 858.

4163. _____. "Study and Discussion Questions, Writing Exercises," in their *Literature and Society: An Introduction to Fiction, Poetry, Drama, Nonfiction*. Second edition. Englewood Cliffs, NJ: Prentice-Hall, p. 883.

4164. Anon. "Almos' a Man by Richard Wright," in *Media Catalog*. Little Rock: Arkansas Humanities Resource Center, p. 34. Description of the dramatized video version of W's story.

4165. Anon. "Announcements." *The Richard Wright Newsletter*, 3 (December), 8. Notes the appearance of new editions of *CC* and *SH* from the University Press of Mississippi and announces a 1995 Mississippi Writers calendar featuring W and others.

4166. Anon. "*Black Boy*: A 50th Anniversary Retrospective." *The Richard Wright Newsletter*, 3 (December), 7. Includes a chronology from 1940 to 1991 and comments on *BB* and *AH* by Du Bois, Lionel Trilling, Irving Howe, Thomas A. Johnson, and Andrew Delbanco.

4167. Anon. "Books Received, 1993." *College Literature*, 21 (June), 180–194. Annotated list including Carla Cappetti's *Writing Chicago* with brief mention of W (p. 182) and Charles Scruggs's *Sweet Home* with brief mention of W (p. 191).

4168. Anon. "Bookshelf." *The New York Times Book Review* (13 Febru-

ary), p. 27. Includes a favorable notice of *RP*.

4169. Anon. *Comprehensive Dissertation Index 1993 Volume 4*. Ann Arbor: UMI, pp. 600–601. Lists dissertations treating W by Brian Keith Reed, Peter Mackley, and Vincent Perez.

4170. Anon. "*Emerge*'s Recommended Reading." *Emerge*, 5 (February), 110. Contains a brief notice of *RP*.

4171. Anon. "Fresh Perspectives." *The Nation*, 259 (26 September), 318. Contains a publisher's announcement of Jerry Gafio Watts's *Heroism and the Black Intellectual* with a blurb by Werner Sollors mentioning W briefly.

4172. Anon. "From NTC ... an African American Anthology That Is Both Manageable and Authoritative!" *English Journal*, 83 (February) back cover. Publisher's advertisement listing W as one of the authors included.

4173. Anon. "Hot Type." *The Chronicle of Higher Education* (13 July), p. A10. Reports on a survey of journals in social science indicating that W was cited sixty-two times in 1993.

4174. Anon. "Literature Unit Plans: Second Editions." *English Journal*, 83 (November), 1. Lists *BB* and *NS*.

4175. Anon. "Mississippi." *South Atlantic Review*, 59 (September), 198–199. University Press of Mississippi advertisement listing paperback reprints of *SH* with an introduction by Gerald Early and *CC* with an introduction by Amritjit Singh.

4176. Anon. "Mississippi." *The Black Scholar*, 24 (Summer 1994), 72. Publisher's advertisement listing *SH*, *CC*, and *Conversations with Richard Wright*.

4177. Anon. "*Native Son*,"in *The Reader's Companion to the Twentieth-Century Novel*. Ed. Peter Parker. London: Fourth Estate Limited, 1994, pp. 238–239. Plot summary and brief critical comment: "Wright's greatest achievements in the novel are its structure and the creation of the main character."

4178. Anon. "New York City Bookshops in the 1930s and 1940s: The Recollections of Walter Goldwater," in *Dictionary of Literary Biography Yearbook: 1993*. Detroit: Gale, pp. 139–172. Includes a page

from a 1961–1962 catalog of the University Place Book Shop listing four items by W (p. 159).

4179. Anon. "Award in Honor of Richard Wright." *The Black Scholar*, 24 (Winter), 78. Notes W's central role in the fifth annual Natchez Literary Celebration, at which Julia Wright will present an award and the Madison Lacy documentary film will be shown.

4180. Anon. "Professional Notes." *SAMLA News*, 15 (January), 7. Contains a notice inviting contributions to Virginia Whatley Smith's projected *New Reflections: Essays on Richard Wright's Travel Books*.

4181. Anon. "Publications Relating to Mississippi." *The Journal of Mississippi History*, 56 (February), 85–86. Lists an article on W and Eugene O'Neill by Richard A. Ciancio.

4182. Anon. "Ralph Ellison," in *Invisible Man* by Ralph Ellison. New York: The Modern Library, pp. v–vi. Mentions Ellison's early friendship with W (p. v).

4183. Anon. "Recent Scholarship." *The Journal of American History*, 81 (December), 1437–1493. Lists the article "Social Mobility and the Novel: A Comparative Analysis of Iyayi's *Violence* and Wright's *Black Boy*" by Tanimu Abubakar.

4184. Anon. "*Rite of Passage* Published." *Richard Wright Newsletter*, 3 (Spring/Summer), 2. Notice of publication of the novella with a facsimile of the dust jacket.

4185. Anon. "Southern California Voices/A Forum for Community Issues: Today's Topic." *Los Angeles Times* (9 May), Part B, p. 5. Introduction to Julia Wright's response to Ventura County censors (see 1994). Discusses censorship in general and notes that *BB* has frequently been a target.

4186. Anon. "*Worker-Writer in America: Jack Conroy and the Tradition of Midwestern Literary Radicalism, 1898–1900*," in *Sale*. Urbana: University of Illinois Press, p. 29. Publisher's notice containing W's statement that Conroy was "the old daddy of rebel writing."

4187. Anon. "Wright Film Biography Released." *Richard Wright Newsletter*, 3 (December), 1. Announces the early showings of *Richard Wright-Black Boy* in Jackson, San Diego, Baton Rouge, Boston, and on Mississippi Educational Television.

4188. Anon. "Wright, Richard," in *The Concise Columbia Encyclopedia*. Third edition. New York: Columbia University Press, p. 959.

4189. Anon. "Wright, Richard Nathaniel," in *Brockhaus Enzyklopädie* Mannheim: F.A. Brockhaus, 1994, p. 356. Brief biographical sketch with photograph.

4190. Anon, Albert Murray, Charles Johnson, Amiri Baraka, Leon Forrest, and Gwendolyn Brooks. "Remembering Ralph Ellison." *American Visions*, 9 (August/September), 34–38. Introduction states that W "sponsored Ellison's initial writing and introduced him to the world of the Communist Party." Brooks recalls a luncheon in New York with the Wrights and the Ellisons (pp. 37–38).

4191. Ashmore, Harry S. *Civil Rights and Wrongs: A Memoir of Race and Politics*. New York: Pantheon Books, pp. 193, 396–397. Mentions *NS* and quotes from *TMBV* and *WML*.

4192. Avery, Laurence G. "Introduction," in his *A Southern Life: Letters of Paul Green, 1916–1981*. Chapel Hill: University of North Carolina Press, p. xxiii. Mentions the dramatization of *NS*.

4193. Aycock, Wendell. "Bibliography." *Studies in Short Fiction*, 31 (Summer), 535–591. Lists a 1993 article by Yoshinobu Hakutani.

4194. Bacharan, Nicole. *Histoire des Noirs américains au XXe siècle*. Brussels: Editions Complexe, pp. 77, 87, 91, 190. Mentions briefly W, *UTC*, and *NS*.

4195. Bain, Robert, and Joseph Flora. "Contributors," in their *Contemporary Poets, Dramatists, Essayists, and Novelists of the South*. Westport CT: Greenwood Press, pp. 635–642. Notes that Hilary Holladay has published on W (p. 638).

4196. Baker, Houston A., Jr. "Generational Shifts and the Recent Criticism of Afro-American Literature," in *Within the Circle: An Anthology of African American Literary Criticism from the Harlem Renaissance to the Present*. Ed. Angelyn Mitchell. Durham, NC: Duke University Press, pp. 282–328.

4197. Baldwin, James. "Critical Extract," in *Black American Prose Writers of the Harlem Renaissance*. Ed. Harold Bloom. New York: Chelsea House, pp. 164–166.

4198. _____. "Everybody's Protest Novel," in *Within the Circle: An Anthology of African American Literary Criticism from the Harlem Renaissance to the Present*. Ed. Angelyn Mitchell. Durham, NC: Duke University Press, pp. 149–155.

4199. _____. "Critical Extract" in *Black American Prose Writers of the Harlem Renaissance*. Ed. Harold Bloom. New York: Chelsea House, pp. 164–166.

4200. Bancroft, Michael A. "Why Literature in the High School Curriculum?" *English Journal*, 83 (December), 23–25. Includes comment on teaching *NS*.

4201. Banner-Haley, Charles T. *The Fruits of Integration: Black Middle-Class Ideology and Culture, 1960–1990*. Jackson: University Press of Mississippi, pp. 99–102, 103, 108, 153. Discusses themes of "individualism versus collectivism and art versus politics" in *AH*, *NS*, and "Bright and Morning Star." Mentions W also in connection with Baldwin and John A. Williams.

4202. Barnwell, Thomas, and Leah McCraney. "The Man Who Was Almost a Man," in their *An Introduction to Critical Reading*. Second edition. Fort Worth: Harcourt Brace Jovanovich, pp. 51–59. Includes explanatory notes.

4203. Bass, Margaret Kent. "'Whirling Out of the Dance...' Three Autobiographies Written in Exile." *The Griot*, 13 (Fall), 42–46. Compares *BB*, *Down Second Avenue*, and *In the Castle of My Skin*. W, Lamming, and Mphahele all experience colonialism and an absent father, but W is the most embittered of the three. All overcome adverse circumstances to become authors.

4204. Baym, Nina. "Richard Wright, 1908–1960," in *The Norton Anthology of American Literature*. Eds. Baym, Wayne Franklin, Ronald Gottesman, Laurence B. Holland, David Kalstone, Arnold Krupat, Francis Murphy, Hershel Parker, William H. Pritchard, and Patricia B. Wallace. Fourth edition. Vol. 2. New York: W.W. Norton, pp. 1741–1742.

4205. _____. "Richard Wright," in *The Norton Anthology of American Literature*. Eds. Baym, Wayne Franklin, Ronald Gottesman, Laurence B. Holland, David Kalstone, Arnold Krupat, Francis Murphy, Hershel Parker, William H. Pritchard, and Patricia B. Wallace. Fourth edition.

Vol. 2. New York: W.W. Norton, p. 2846.

4206. Baym, Nina, and Laurence B. Holland. "American Literature Between the Wars, 1914–1945," in *The Norton Anthology of American Literature*. Eds. Baym, Wayne Franklin, Ronald Gottesman, Laurence B. Holland, David Kalstone, Arnold Krupat, Francis Murphy, Hershel Parker, William H. Pritchard, and Patricia B. Wallace. Fourth edition. Vol. 2. New York: W.W. Norton, pp. 939–950.

4207. Beaumont, Eric. "The Nathan Heard Interviews." *African American Review*, 28 (Fall), 395–410. Both Beaumont and Heard mention having read W (pp. 395, 396, 402).

4208. Beidler, Philip D. *Scriptures for a Generation: What We Were Reading in the '60s*. Athens: The University of Georgia Press, p. 46. Mentions W briefly.

4209. _____. *Scriptures for a Generation: What We Were Reading in the '60s*. Athens: The University of Georgia Press, p. 46. Mentions W briefly s.v. Brown, Claude.

4210. Bekale, Marc Mve. "Kowalewski, Michael. *Deadly Musings: Violence and Verbal Form in American Fiction*." *Afram Newsletter*, No. 40 (December), p. 42. Review mentioning W briefly.

4211. Bell, Bernard W. "Introduction: Clarence Major's Double Consciousness as a Black Postmodernist Artist." *African American Review*, 28 (Spring), 5–9. Mentions briefly Major's reading of W (p. 5).

4212. Bell, Vereen. "Early Twentieth-Century American Literature," in *The Reader's Adviser*. 14th Edition. New Providence, NJ: R.R. Bowker, pp. 791–907. Contains a paragraph on Bigger Thomas (pp. 802–803) and a biographical-critical sketch followed an annotated list of books about W (pp. 905–1907).

4213. Bellow, Saul. *It All Adds Up: From the Dim Past to the Uncertain Future*. New York: Viking, pp. 98–114.

4214. _____. "Writers, Intellectuals, Politics: Mainly Reminiscence," in his *It All Adds Up: From the Dim Past to the Uncertain Future: a Nonfiction Collection*. New York: Viking Penguin, pp 99–114.

4215. Benesch, Klaus. "From a Thing Into an *I Am*: Autobiographical Narrative and Metahistorical

Discourse in Contemporary African American Fiction," in *Historiographic Metafiction in Modern American and Canadian Literature*. Eds. Bernd Engler and Kurt Müller. Paderborn: Ferdinand Schöningh, pp. 253–265. Mentions W briefly (p. 254).

4216. Benoist, Mary Anne. "African American Studies: General." *Society for the Study of Southern Literature Newsletter*, 28 (November), 10. Lists the new edition of *CC*.

4217. _____. "African American Studies: Literature." *Society for the Study of Southern Literature Newsletter*, 28 (November), 10. Lists James Campbell's *Exiles in Paris*.

4218. Berman, Paul. "Introduction: The Other and the Almost the Same," in his *Blacks and Jews: Alliances and Arguments*. New York: Delacorte, pp. 1–28. Notes that W depicted Jews in *BB* (p. 11).

4219. Bernstein, Richard. *Dictatorship of Virtue: Multiculturalism and the Battle for America's Future*. New York: Alfred A. Knoff, pp. 50. 302 Mentions briefly W and "The Ethics of Living Jim Crow."

4220. Berthoff, Warner. "Continuity in Discontinuity: Literature in the American Situation," in his *American Trajectories: Authors and Readings, 1790–1970*. University Park: The Pennsylvania State University Press, pp. 3–18.

4221. Birch, Eva Lennox. *Black American Women's Writing: A Quilt of Many Colours*. New York: Harvester Wheatsheaf, pp. 10, 86, 123, 125. Mentions briefly W, *BB*, and *NS*.

4222. Blanton, Charles Daniel. "Carla Cappetti. *Writing Chicago: Modernism, Ethnography, and the Novel*." *Modern Fiction Studies*, 40 (Summer), 430–432. Favorable review noting that Cappetti relates the fiction of W, Algren, and Farrell to Chicago urban sociology.

4223. Bloom, Harold. "Introduction," in his *Black American Prose Writers of the Harlem Renaissance*. New York: Chelsea House, pp. xi–xii. Stresses the importance of biographical criticism in the study of W and Zora Neale Hurston.

4224. _____, ed. *Black American Prose Writers of the Harlem Renaissance*. New York: Chelsea House, pp. xi–xii, 3–4, 8–9. Contains introductions by Bloom and reprinted items by James Baldwin, Robert

Bone, Russell Brignano, St. Clair Drake, Ralph Ellison, Michel Fabre, Jean-François Gounard, Zora Neale Hurston, Alfred Kazin, Edward Margolies, Margaret Marshall, Paul Newlin, Arnold Rampersad, John Reilly, and Margaret Walker.

4225. _____. "Richard Wright 1908–1960," in his *Black American Prose Writers of the Harlem Renaissance*. New York: Chelsea House, pp. 159–160. Biographical sketch.

4226. Bloom, Lynn Z., and Ning Yu. "American Autobiography: The Changing Critical Canon." *A/B: Auto/Biography Studies*, 9 (Fall), 167–180. Using a statistical approach, the authors determine that W is a canonical autobiographer.

4227. Blount, Roy, Jr. "There's More to Southern Humor Than Foot-Long Pecan Rolls." *The New York Times Book Review* (11 December), pp. 3, 37. Mentions W briefly.

4228. Bohner, Charles H. "Biographical Notes," in his *Short Fiction: Classic and Contemporary*. Third edition. Englewood Cliffs, NJ: Prentice-Hall, pp. 1158–1177. Contains a note on W (p. 177).

4229. _____. "Questions," in his *Short Fiction: Classic and Contemporary*. Third edition. Englewood Cliffs, NJ: Prentice-Hall, p. 1095.

4230. Bone, Robert. "Arna Bontemps 1902–1973," in *Black American Prose Writers of the Harlem Renaissance*. New York: Chelsea House, pp. 8–9.

4231. _____. "Critical Extract," in *Black American Writers of the Harlem Renaissance*. Ed. Harold Bloom. New York: Chelsea House, pp. 83–84.

4232. Bontemps, Arna. "Critical Extract," in *Black American Women Poets and Dramatists*. Ed. Harold Bloom. New York: Chelsea House, pp. 92–93.

4233. Bowles, Paul. *In Touch: The Letters of Paul Bowles*. Ed. Jeffrey Miller. New York: Farrar, Straus, and Giroux, pp. 363. In a letter to Oliver Evans dated 13 January 1964, Bowles recalls the residency of W and family at the house in Brooklyn Heights.

4234. Boyd, Melba Joyce. *Discarded Legacy: Politics and Poetics in the Life of Frances E.W. Harper, 1825–1911*. Detroit: Wayne State University Press, p. 253. Lists *WML* in the bibliography.

4235. Bracy, William. "Wright,

Richard Nathaniel," in *The Encyclopedia Americana*. Ed. Lawrence T. Lorimer. Danbury, CT: Grolier Incorporated, pp. 55–556.

4236. Bradford, Adnee M. "Principles and Methods of Teaching Wright in Multicultural Contexts." *Richard Wright Newsletter*, 3 (Spring/Summer), 6–7. Report of a survey of teachers and ninth and eleventh grade students in North Carolina. There was strong interest in W, but he was not included in the anthology used in the eleventh-grade American literature course.

4237. Bray, Howard. "A Story of Redemption." *American Journalism Review*, 16 (April), 51–52. Review of Nathan McCall's *Makes Me Want to Holler* noting the impact on McCall of reading *NS*.

4238. Brewer, Jeutonne P. *The Federal Writers' Project: A Bibliography*. Methuen, NJ: Scarecrow, pp. 3, 5, 31, 37, 47, 50, 58–59, 66, 69–70. Annotated bibliography mentioning W and the Project.

4239. Brignano, Russell Carl. "Richard Wright 1908–1960," in *Black American Prose Writers of the Harlem Renaissance*. Ed. Harold Bloom. New York: Chelsea House, p. 167.

4240. Brookhart, Mary Hughes. "Margaret Walker," in *Contemporary Poets Dramatists, Essayists, and Novelists of the South: A Bio-Bibliographical Sourcebook*. Eds. Robert Bain and Joseph Flora. Westport, CT: Greenwood Press, pp. 504–514. Includes discussion of the Walker-W relationship, noting that Walker believes that W was more its literary beneficiary than she was. (pp. 505–506).

4241. Budick, Emily Miller. *Engendering Romance: Women Writers and the Hawthorne Tradition, 1950–1990*. New Haven: Yale University Press, pp. 112,146,186, 188, 192, 209. Relates *UTC* to Stowe, notes W's view of Communist exploitation of race, and mentions "Long Black Song," and the influence of Poe on *NS*.

4242. Buelens, Gert, and Ernst Rudin. "Introduction," in their *Deferring a Dream: Literary Sub-Versions of the American Columbiad*. Basel: Birkhäusen Verlag, pp. ix–xv. Comments on Robert Shulman's treatment of W in their collection.

4243. Buhle, Paul. "Marxism in the USA," in *C.L.R. James and*

Revolutionary Marxism: Selected Writings of C.L.R. James 1939–1949. Eds. Scott McLemee and Paul Le Blanc. Atlantic Highlands, NJ: Humanities Press, pp. 55–74. Mentions W briefly (p. 69).

4244. Burns, Landon C., Elizabeth Buckmaster, and Jane E. Cooper. "The Twentieth (1993) Supplement to a Cross-Referenced Index of Short Fiction Anthologies and Author-Title Listings." *Studies in Short Fiction,* 31 (Spring), 287–380. Lists the appearance of "Big Black Good Man" and "The Man Who Was Almost a Man" in Charters, *Major Writers of Short Fiction: Stories and Commentaries* (with *Manual*); the appearance of "Big Boy Leaves Home" in Schechter and Semeiks, *Discoveries: Fifty Stories of the Quest* (second edition); the appearance of "Bright and Morning Star" in Clarke, *A Century of the Best Black American Short Stories* and Major, *Calling the Wind: Twentieth-Century African-American Short Stories*; and the appearance of "The Man Who Was Almost a Man" in Oates, *The Oxford Book of American Short Stories,* Pickering, *Fiction 50: An Introduction to the Short Story,* and Roberts and Jacobs, *Fiction: An Introduction to Reading and Writing* (third edition).

4245. Butler, Robert J. "Mapping Ralph Ellison's Territory." *African American Review,* 28 (Summer), 321–325. Review of Mark Busby's *Ralph Ellison* praising its treatment of the Ellison-W relationship.

4246. Byerman, Keith E. *"Livin' the Blues: Memoirs of a Black Journalist and Poet.* By Frank Marshall Davis. Ed. John Edgar Tidwell." *The Journal of American History,* 80 (March), 1520–1521. Review mentioning W briefly.

4247. Calloway, Catherine. "Fiction: The 1930s to the 1960s," in *American Literary Scholarship: An Annual/1992.* Ed. David J. Nordloh. Durham, NC: Duke University Press, pp. 249–272. Comments on essays by James W. Tuttleton, Hilary Holladay, and James R. Andreas (pp. 255–256).

4248. Campbell, James. *Paris Interzone: Richard Wright, Lolita, Boris Vian and Others on the Left Bank, 1946–60.* London: Martin Secker and Warburg, xiii + 305 pp. Account of the Left Bank literary scene after World War II, beginning with

W's expatriation and ending with his mysterious death. Chapters three and six deal with the distrust rampant among black expatriates because of U.S. and French government surveillance of their political activities, aided by informers.

4249. Caponi, Gena Dagel. *Paul Bowles: Romantic Savage.* Carbondale: Southern Illinois University Press, p. 88. Mentions the residency of W and family in the house on Middagh Street in Brooklyn Heights, stating that "the black superintendant refused to tend the furnace for another black man."

4250. Carby, Hazel. "The Politics of Fiction, Anthropology, and the Folk: Zora Neale Hurston," in *History and Memory in African-American Culture.* Eds. Geneviève Fabre and Robert O'Meally. New York: Oxford University Press, pp. 28–44.

4251. Carr, Pat. "Black Like Them." *Texas Monthly,* 22 (May), 138, 153–157. Notes W's absence from academic textbooks in the fifties (p. 154), and mentions teaching W's fiction twenty years later (p. 157).

4252. Cargill, Oscar. "American Literature," in *Collier's Encyclopedia.* Ed. William D. Halsey. New York: Macmillan Educational Company, vol. 2, pp. 42–72. Mentions briefly W, *UTC,* and *NS* s.v. "Literature of Social Protest."

4253. Carter-Sigglow, Janet. *Making Her Way with Thunder: A Reappraisal of Zora Neale Hurston's Narrative Art.* Frankfurt am Main: Peter Lang, pp. 73, 74, 75, 82, 83. Comments with quotations on W's review of Hurston and Hurston's review of W.

4254. Castronovo, David. "Novel," in *Collier's Encyclopedia.* Ed. Lauren S. Bahr. New York: P.F. Collier, Vol. 17, pp. 697–718. Comments briefly on *NS* (p. 704).

4255. Charney, Mark J. "Voice and Perspective in the Film Adaptations of Gaines's Fiction," in *Critical Reflections on the Fiction of Ernest J. Gaines.* Ed. David C. Estes. Athens: The University of Georgia Press, pp. 124–138. Contrasts *NS* with Jerold Freedman's film version, which de-emphasizes Bigger's effort to achieve self-understanding (p. 137).

4256. Christian, Barbara. "But What Do We Think We're Doing Anyway: The State of Black Feminist Criticism(s) or My Version of a

Little Bit of History," in *Within the Circle: An Anthology of African American Literary Criticism from the Harlem Renaissance to the Present.* Ed. Angelyn Mitchell. Durham, NC: Duke University Press, pp. 499–514.

4257. _____. "The Race for Theory," in *Within the Circle: An Anthology of African American Literary Criticism from the Harlem Renaissance to the Present.* Ed. Angelyn Mitchell. Durham, NC: Duke University Press, pp. 348–359.

4258. Clark, VéVé. "Restaging Langston Hughes' *Scottsboro Limited,"* in *Conversations with Amiri Baraka.* Ed. Charlie Reilly. Jackson: University Press of Mississippi, 157–167.

4259. Clary, Françoise. "Carla Capetti. *Writing Chicago. Modernism, Ethnology and the Novel." Afram Newsletter,* 39 (June), 12–13. Review mentioning briefly W and *NS.*

4260. _____. "Sandra Addell [sic]. *Double Consciousness/Double Bind. Theoretical Issues in Twentieth Century Black Literature." Afram Newsletter,* No. 40 (December), pp. 27–29. Review noting the work's treatment of W and *BB.*

4261. Clinton, Catherine. "'With a Whip in His Hand': Rape, Memory, and African-American Women," in *History and Memory in African-American Culture.* Eds. Geneviève Fabre and Robert O'Meally. New York: Oxford University Press, pp. 205–218. Contains a treatment of the "rape" scene in "Long Black Song" (p. 213).

4262. Coleman, James W. "Clarence Major's *All-Night Visitors:* Calabanic [sic] Discourse and Black Male Expression." *African American Review,* 28 (Spring), 95–108. Quotes from 1989.

4263. Collins, Mary B. *Native Son: A Unit Plan.* Second Edition. Berlin, MD: Teacher's Pet Publications, 157 pp. Includes a biographical sketch and extensive outlines, vocabulary reviews, and other learning aids.

4264. Collins, Patricia Hill. "Learning to Think for Ourselves: Malcolm X's Black Nationalism Reconsidered," in *Malcolm X: In Our Own Image.* New York: Anchor/Doubleday, pp. 59–85.

4265. Cormier-Hamilton, Patrice. "Black Naturalism and Toni Morrison: The Journey Away from

Self-Love in *The Bluest Eye*." *MELUS*, 19 (Winter), 109–127. Quotes Max in *NS* (p. 110).

4266. Costanzo, Angelo. "*Sweet Home: Invisible Cities in the Afro-American Novel*. By Charles Scruggs." *American Literature*, 66 (September), 618–619. Review containing a paragraph on the work's chapter on W.

4267. Cowan, Tom, and Jack McGuire. *Timelines of African-American History*. New York: Roundtable Press, pp. 141, 188, 190, 194, 197, 205, 224, 230, 237, 290. Dates important events in W's career.

4268. Cowell, Pattie, et al. "Wright, Richard (1908–1960)," in *1993 MLA International Bibliography of Books and Articles on the Modern Languages and Literatures, Volume 1: British and Irish, Commonwealth, English Caribbean, and American Literatures*. Ed. Terence Ford. New York: The Modern Language Association of America, pp. 305, A420. Lists eleven items.

4269. Crouch, Stanley. "The Oklahoma Kid." *The New Republic*, 210 (9 May), 23–25. Mentions W briefly (p. 23).

4270. Crunden, Robert M. *A Brief History of American Culture*. New York: Paragon House, p. 281. Mentions briefly *NS* and W's early tutelage of Ellison.

4271. Cunningham, Lawrence, and John Reich. *Culture and Values: A Survey of the Western Humanities*. Second edition. Volume 2. Fort Worth: Harcourt Brace, p. 477. Mentions briefly *NS*.

4272. Crystal, David, ed. *The Cambridge Factfinder*. Cambridge: Cambridge University Press, p. 541. Lists W and *NS*.

4273. _____. *The Cambridge Factfinder*. Cambridge: Cambridge University Press, 1994, p. 541. Lists years of W's birth and death and mentions *NS*.

4274. Curry, Renée R. "Paul Gilroy. *The Black Atlantic: Modernity and Double Consciousness*." *Canadian Review of American Studies*, 24 (Spring), 158–161. Review containing a paragraph on Gilroy's treatment of W.

4275. Dace, Karen L. "Dissonance in European-American and African-American Communication." *The Western Journal of Black Studies*, 18 (Spring), 18–26. Using a passage from *NS* as a point of departure,

Dace discusses faulty interracial communication, especially the naive expressions of good will by whites such as Jan and Mary perceived by blacks as condescending and intrusive.

4276. Dathorne, O.R. *In Europe's Image: The Need for American Multiculturalism*. Westport, CT: Bergin & Garvey, p. 149. Comments briefly on W's condescending attitude in *BP*.

4277. Davis, Arthur P. "Integration and Race Literature," in *Within the Circle: An Anthology of African American Literary Criticism from the Harlem Renaissance to the Present*. Ed. Angelyn Mitchell. Durham, NC: Duke University Press, pp. 156–161.

4278. Davis, Bonnie M. "A Cultural Safari: Dispelling Myths and Creating Connections." *English Journal*, 83 (February), 24–26. Mentions W briefly.

4279. Davis, Rodney O. "*Writing Illinois: The Prairie, Lincoln, and Chicago*. By James Hurt." *Journal of English and Germanic Philology*, 93 (April), 279–281. Review mentioning W briefly (p. 281).

4280. Davis, Thadious M. *Nella Larsen, Novelist of the Harlem Renaissance: A Women's Life Unveiled*. Baton Rouge: Louisiana State University Press, pp. 442, 463. Claims that W's prominence in the thirties hindered prospects for Larsen's type of fiction.

4281. Dawson, Michael C. *Behind the Mule: Race and Class in African-American Politics*. Princeton, NJ: Princeton University Press, p. 51. Cites W's account of the murder of his uncle in *BB*.

4282. _____. *Behind the Mule: Race and Class in African-American Politics*. Princeton: Princeton University Press, p. 51. Makes reference to the account in *BB* of the murder of W's uncle by whites.

4283. Deena, Seodial. "The Irrationality of Bigger Thomas's World: A Frightening View for the Twenty-First Century Urban Population." *CLA Journal*, 38 (September), 20–30. Interprets the novel in terms of environmental determinism. Bigger's irrational world "twists him and makes him a killer." Includes much plot summary.

4284. De Santis, Christopher C. "The Content of a Distinguished Career." *African American Review*,

28 (Spring), 147–150. Review of Richard K. Barksdale's *Praisesong of Survival* commenting on his views about the "philosophical despair" of *O*.

4285. _____. "Representations of the Great Migration: A Review Essay." *The Southern Quarterly*, 32 (Summer), 149–156. Mentions W briefly (p. 156).

4286. Dick, Bruce. "*From Harlem to Paris: Black American Writers in France, 1840–1980* by Michel Fabre." *MELUS*, 19 (Spring), 133–135. Review commenting on W's expatriation.

4287. _____. "Kenneth [sic] Kinnamon and Michel Fabre, eds. *Conversations with Richard Wright*." *Afram Newsletter*, 39 (June), 9–10. Favorable review praising the publication of hitherto unavailable interviews. Notes W's efforts to counter racism and racial definitions.

4288. _____. "Michel Fabre.— *The Unfinished Quest of Richard Wright*. 2nd edition." *Études Anglaises*, 47 (October–December), 493. Favorable review commenting on Fabre's new preface and his bibliographical essay on W scholarship since 1973.

4289. _____. "Reed on Wright." *Richard Wright Newsletter*, 3 (Spring/Summer), 3. Reports a 1993 interview with Ishmael Reed, who praises W highly and criticizes attacks on him, especially at the 1992 Paris Conference on African Americans in Europe.

4290. Diggs, Anita Doreen. *The African American Resource Guide*. New York: Barricade Books, p. 27. Contains a briefly annotated entry on *BB*.

4291. Dittmer, John. *Local People: The Struggle for Civil Rights in Mississippi*. Urbana: University of Illinois Press, p. 54. Mentions W briefly.

4292. Doreski, C.K. "'Living Through History': Sam Cornish's *Generations*." *CLA Journal*, 38 (December), 193–210. Mentions Houston Baker on W (p. 195) and quotes from Cornish's poem "Bigger Thomas Says Some Bad Niggers Is Over Thirty" (p. 208).

4293. Dowell, Peter W. "Invisible Cities." *Callaloo*, 17 (Summer), 656–658. Review of *Sweet Home: Invisible Cities in the Afro-American Novel* by Charles Scruggs with favorable comment on its treatment of *NS*.

4294. Dowling, Colette. "The Song of Toni Morrison," in *Conversations with Toni Morrison*. Ed. Danielle Taylor-Guthrie. Jackson: University Press of Mississippi, pp. 48–59.

4295. _____. "Critical Extract," in *Black American Writers of the Harlem Renaissance*. Ed. Harold Bloom. New York: Chelsea House, pp. 112–114.

4296. Dubey, Madhu. *Black Women Novelists and the Nationalist Aesthetic*. Bloomington: Indiana University Press, pp. 122, 133. Mentions briefly W and Bigger Thomas.

4297. duCille, Ann. "The Occult of True Black Womanhood." *Signs*, 19 (Spring), 591–629. Mentions briefly "Big Boy Leaves Home" (p. 617).

4298. _____. "Postcolonialism and Afrocentricity: Discourse and Dat Course," in *The Black Columbiad: Defining Moments in African American Literature and Culture*. Eds. Werner Sollors and Maria Diedrich. Cambridge, MA: Harvard University Press, 28–41. Quotes W on the Negro as "America's metaphor" (p. 30).

4299. Dudziak, Mary L. "Josephine Baker, Racial Protest, and the Cold War." *The Journal of American History*, 81 (September), 543–570. Mentions W briefly (p. 568).

4300. Eagles, Brenda M. "A Bibliography of Dissertations Relating to Mississippi—1993." *The Journal of Mississippi History*, 56 (February), 61–67. Lists dissertations on W, Dreiser, Capote, and Mailer by Ann M. Algeo; on the film *NS* by Ruth Elizabeth Burks; and on W and Gertrude Stein by Lynn Weiss.

4301. Early, Gerald. "Afterword," in *Savage Holiday*. By Richard Wright. Jackson: University Press of Mississippi, pp. 223–235. Places *SH* in the context of W's intellectual development, stressing his belief in rationalism and his fascination with the atavistic and irrational. The novel addresses the question: "What is freedom and what is desire?" (p. 225). Quotes from interviews with W and uses Frederic Wertham and Erik Erikson to elucidate Erskine Fowler's psyche.

4302. _____. "The Black Intellectual and the Sport of Prizefighting," in his *The Culture of Bruising: Essays on Prizefighting, Literature, and Modern American Culture.*

Hopewell, NJ: The Ecco Press, pp. 5–45.

4303. _____. "Speak, Memory." *The New Republic*, 211 (4 July), 33–36. Review of Henry Louis Gates, Jr.'s *Colored People* quoting from *BB*.

4304. Edelman, Lee. *Homographesis: Essays in Gay Literary and Cultural Theory*. New York: Routledge, p. 51 Quotes from Baldwin's "Everybody's Protest Novel."

4305. Ellison, Ralph. "Critical Extract," in *Black American Prose Writers of the Harlem Renaissance*. Ed. Harold Bloom. New York: Chelsea House, pp. 163–164.

4306. _____. "Richard Wright 1908–1960," in *Black American Prose Writers of the Harlem Renaissance*. Ed. Harold Bloom. New York: Chelsea House, pp. 163–164.

4307. Enekwe, Ossie Onuora. "An Interview with Amiri Baraka," in *Conversations with Amiri Baraka*. Ed. Charlie Reilly. Jackson: University Press of Mississippi, pp. 118–129.

4308. Estes, David C. "Introduction," in his *Critical Reflections on the Fiction of Ernest J. Gaines*. Athens: The University of Georgia Press, pp. 1–11. Mentions W briefly (p. 11).

4309. Fabio, Sarah Webster. "Tripping with Black Writing," in *Within the Circle: An Anthology of African American Literary Criticism from the Harlem Renaissance to the Present*. Ed. Angelyn Mitchell. Durham, NC: Duke University Press, pp. 224–231.

4310. Fabre, Geneviève, and Robert O'Meally. "Introduction," in their *History and Memory in African American Culture*. New York: Oxford University Press, pp. 3–17. Quotes from *WML* (p. 4).

4311. [Fabre, Michel]. "Activité à venir." *Afram Newsletter*, No. 40 (December), pp. 2–3. Contains an announcement of a public showing of the film *Richard Wright—Black Boy* in Paris, probably in February 1995.

4312. Fabre, Michel. "Berthold Klostermann. *Blue Notes—Black Fiction. Schwarze Musik in der afroamerikanischen Erzählliteratur der zwanziger und dreissiger Jahre*." *Afram Newsletter*, 39 (June), 11–12. Review noting that Klostermann shows that W made extensive use of black music in his fiction.

4313. _____. "*Dark Laughter. The Satiric Art of Ollie W. Harrington*. Edited, with an introduction by W. [sic] Thomas Inge; Ollie W. Harrington. *Why I Left America and Other Essays*. With an introduction by M. Thomas Inge." *Afram Newsletter*, 39 (June), 8–9. Mentions Harrington's illustrations in the serialized *NS*, his friendship with W, and his essays on W.

4314. F[abre], [Michel]. "John A. Williams. *L'homme qui criait je suis*." *Afram Newsletter*, No. 40 (December), pp. 30–31. Review of the French translation of *The Man Who Cried I Am* mentioning W.

4315. Fabre, Michel. "Nouvelles du Centre." *Afram Newsletter*, 39 (June), 1–4. Mentions research on W and Gertrude Stein by Lynn Weiss and on W and Simone du Beauvoir by Margaret Simons.

4316. _____. "Paris as a Moment in African American Consciousness," in *The Black Columbiad: Defining Moments in African American Literature and Culture*. Eds. Werner Sollors and Maria Diedrich. Harvard English Studies 19. Cambridge, MA: Harvard University Press, pp. 123–138. Like many other African Americans, W responded favorably to the beauty and freedom of Paris. Fabre quotes from several previously unpublished sources to illustrate this response.

4317. _____. "Richard Wright 1908–1960," in *Black American Prose Writers of the Harlem Renaissance*. Ed. Harold Bloom. New York: Chelsea House, p. 169.

4318. _____. "Richard Wright. *Rite of Passage*. Afterword by Arnold Rampersad." *Afram Newsletter*, 39 (June), 15. Review comparing this unfinished novel to *Go Tell It on the Mountain* and concluding that more than a documentary or thesis novel, it is a psychological novel concerned with the relation between the individual and social authority, between delinquency and freedom.

4319. _____. "Critical Extract," in *Black American Prose Writers of the Harlem Renaissance*. Ed. Harold Bloom. New York: Chelsea House, p. 169

4320. Ferrante, Marco. "Sulle Ali: l'autobiografia di Malcolm X e *Native Son* di Richard Wright," in *Dialogo su Malcolm X*. Rome: Manifestolibri, pp. 113–118. Compares and contrasts Malcolm X and Bigger.

Both dream of flying, but only Malcolm does so. Bigger is isolated and inarticulate, Malcolm mastered the written and spoken word.

4321. Filreis, Alan, *Modernism from Right to Left: Wallace Stevens, the Thirties, & Literary Radicalism.* Cambridge: Cambridge University Press, pp. 186–283. Brief mentions of W.

4322. Finkenstaedt, Rose L.H. *Face-to-Face: Blacks in America: White Perceptions and Black Realities.* New York: William Morrow, pp. 185, 211–215, 248, 272, 276, 295. Discusses *NS*, *O*, and *WML*, quoting several critics, in a chapter on "The Black Dialectic with Respect to the Stereotype of the Black Beast" (pp. 211–215). Comments elsewhere on *NS* and *LD*.

4323. Fiol-Matta, Liza, and Miriam K. Chamberlain, eds. *Women of Color and the Multicultural Curriculum: Transforming the College Classroom.* New York: The Feminist Press, pp. 224, 227. Robert Combs of George Washington University includes "The Man Who was Almost a Man" in an American literature survey course.

4324. Fitzpatrick, Vincent. "Large in Scope and Sympathy: The Correspondence of Paul Green." *The Southern Literary Journal*, 27 (Fall), 104–108. Mentions briefly the play *NS* (p. 105).

4325. Flower, Dean. "Desegregating the Syllabus." *The Hudson Review*, 46 (Winter), 683–693. Notes that *NS* "drove a wedge into the solid block of white indifference to black writers" (p. 683).

4326. Fohlen, Claude. *Les Noirs aux Etats-Unis.* Paris: Presses Universitaires de France, pp. 37–38, 126.

4327. Foley, Barbara. "Subversion and Oppositionality in the Academy," in *Margins in the Classroom: Teaching Literature.* Eds. Kostas Myrsiades and Linda S. Myrsiades. Minneapolis: University of Minnesota Press, pp. 137–152. Suggests juxtaposing *UTC* with *Absalom, Absalom!*

4328. Folks, Jeffrey J. "'Last Call to the West': Richard Wright's *The Color Curtain*." *South Atlantic Review*, 59 (November), 77–88. Analyzes *CC* as an expression of W's "impulse ... toward a broadening of community and a search for cultural connection" (pp. 77, 78). Distrust-

ing sectarian and nationalist appeals, W affirmed "those values of reason, progress, and humanity he believed could be shared by all cultures" (p. 87).

4329. Folsom, Franklin. *Days of Anger, Days of Hope: A Memoir of the League of American Writers, 1937–1942.* Niwot: University Press of Colorado, pp. 74–75, 90, 93–94, 146, 158, 197–204, 208, 226, 238, 253–254. Discusses his friendship with W and its end with the dispute over eviction of tenants from the apartment W had bought in Greenwich Village, correcting Fabre on this matter. Comments on W's activities in the League of American Writers, quoting most of his opening address at the Fourth American Writers Congress on 6 June 1941. Quotes also from "the FB Eye Blues."

4330. _____. "The League of American Writers as I Found It." *The CEA Critic*, 56 (Winter), 8–19. Mentions W's objection to the closure of the John Reed Clubs (p. 12).

4331. Forrest, Leon. "Character Behind the Walls of Residential Segregation," in his *Relocations of the Spirit.* Wakefield, RI: Asphodel Press, pp. 49–65. Contains a paragraph on *NS* as a portrayal of Chicago ghetto life.

4332. _____. "Elijah," in his *Relocations of the Spirit.* Wakefield, RI: Asphodel Press, pp. 66–116. Discusses the scene in which the protagonist of "The Man Who Lived Underground" enters a black church (pp. 70–71).

4333. _____. "Evidences of Jimmy Baldwin," in his *Relocations of the Spirit.* Wakefield, RI: Asphodel Press, pp. 267–275. Mentions briefly Baldwin's argument with W (p. 270).

4334. _____. "Forged in Injustice," in his *Relocations of the Spirit.* Wakefield, RI: Asphodel Press, pp. 244–253.

4335. _____. "Gardner's Final Will and Testament to Writers," in his *Relocations of the Spirit.* Wakefield, RI: Asphodel Press, pp. 284–287. Mentions W briefly (p. 286).

4336. _____. "In the Light of the Likeness–Transformed," in his *Relocations of the Spirit.* Wakefield, RI: Asphodel Press, pp. 3–30.

4337. _____. "Michael's Mandate," in his *Relocations of the Spirit.* Wakefield, RI: Asphodel Press, pp. 301–323. Quotes from Ellison's

"Remembering Richard Wright" (pp. 301–302).

4338. _____. "Spiritual Flight of Female Fire," in his *Relocations of the Spirit.* Wakefield, RI: Asphodel Press, pp. 292–298. Mentions W briefly (p. 296).

4339. _____. "The Transformation of Grief," in his *Relocations of the Spirit.* Wakefield, RI: Asphodel Press, pp. 189–216. Comments on "Fire and Cloud" (p. 209).

4340. _____. *Relocations of the Spirit.* Wakefield, RI: Asphodel Press, pp. 27, 39–40, 56, 58, 108, 150, 209, 244, 251–253, 270, 286, 302. Comments on *NS* (pp. 39–40), discusses Allison Davis's psychobiography of W (pp. 251–253), and mentions W and his works elsewhere.

4341. Fraden, Rena. *Blueprints for a Black Federal Theatre, 1935–1939.* Cambridge: Cambridge University Press, pp. 17, 113–117, 135, 187, 223, 227, 228. Quotes extensively from *AH* on Federal Theatre in Chicago and discusses W's support of *Hymn to the Rising Sun* and Theodore Ward's *Big White Fog.* Mentions W elsewhere.

4342. Franklin, Jimmie Lewis. "Black Southerners, Shared Experience, and Place: A Reflection." *The Journal of Southern History*, 60 (February), 3–18. Recounts the meeting of W and Willie Morris in Paris and quotes from the conclusion of *BB* (p. 14).

4343. Franklin, John Hope, and Alfred A. Moss, Jr. *From Slavery to Freedom: A History of African Americans.* Seventh ed. New York: Knopf, pp. 421, 422, 555.

4344. Freeman, Mary Cecilia. "About the Authors: Biographical Notes," in her *The Writer's Perspective: Voices from American Cultures.* Englewood Cliffs, NJ: Prentice-Hall, pp. xxi–xxxii. Contains a note on W (pp. xxxi–xxxii).

4345. _____. "*American Hunger* Richard Wright," in her *The Writer's Perspective: Voices from American Cultures.* Englewood Cliffs, NJ: Prentice-Hall, p. 373. Headnote to a selection.

4346. _____. "*Black Boy* Richard Wright," in her *The Writer's Perspective: Voices from American Cultures.* Englewood Cliffs, NJ: Prentice-Hall, p. 364. Headnote to a selection.

4347. _____. "Response," in her *The Writer's Perspective: Voices from*

American Cultures. Englewood Cliffs, NJ: Prentice-Hall, p. 372. Study questions for an excerpt from *BB.*

4348. _____. "Response," in her *The Writer's Perspective: Voices from American Cultures.* Englewood Cliffs, NJ: Prentice-Hall, pp. 391–392. Study questions for an excerpt from *AH.*

4349. _____. "Topics Across Sections," in her *The Writer's Perspective: Voices from American Cultures.* Englewood Cliffs, NJ: Prentice-Hall, pp. 404–413. Contains a suggested writing topic on W (p. 407).

4350. Fullbrook, Kate, and Edward Fullbrook. *Simone de Beauvoir and Jean-Paul Sartre: The Remaking of a Twentieth-Century Legend.* New York: Basic Books, pp. 166, 178. Mentions W's friendship with de Beauvoir and his death.

4351. Gabbin, Joanne V. *Sterling A. Brown: Building the Black Aesthetic Tradition.* Charlottesville: University Press of Virginia, pp. 13, 71, 103, 108, 109.

4352. Gates, Henry Louis, Jr. "Blackness Without Blood," in *Legacy of Dissent: 40 Years of Writing from Dissent Magazine.* Ed. Nicolaus Mills. New York: Simon and Schuster, pp. 259–275.

4353. _____. "Foreword," in *Harlem on My Mind: Cultural Capital of Black America, 1900–1968.* Ed. Allon Schoener. New York: The New Press, p. [v]. Begins as follows: "If 'The Negro,' as Richard Wright famously observed, is America's metaphor, then Harlem … is the metaphor for African-American culture itself."

4354. _____. "Preface to Blackness: Text and Pretext," in *Within the Circle: An Anthology of African American Literary Criticism from the Harlem Renaissance to the Present.* Ed. Angelyn Mitchell. Durham: Duke University Press, pp. 235–255.

4355. Gayle, Addison, "Wright, Richard," in Academic *American Encyclopedia.* Ed. Bernard S. Cayne. Danbury, CT: Grolier, pp. 290–291.

4356. _____. "Wright, Richard," in *Academic American Encyclopedia.* Danbury, CT: Grolier, 1994, vol. 20, pp. 290–291.

4357. Gayle, Addison, Jr. "Cultural Strangulation: Black Literature and the White Aesthetic," in *Within the Circle: An Anthology of African American Literary Criticism from the*

Harlem Renaissance to the Present. Ed. Angelyn Mitchell. Durham, NC: Duke University Press, pp. 207–212.

4358. George, Nelson. *Blackface: Reflections on African-Americans and the Movies.* New York: HarperCollins, p. 21. Mentions W briefly.

4359. Gilbert, Sandra M., and Susan Gubar. *No Man's Land: The Place of the Woman Writer.* Vol. 3: *Letters from the Front.* New Haven: Yale University Press, p. 126. Mentions W briefly.

4360. Giles, James R. "*Writing Chicago: Modernism, Ethnography, and the Novel.* By Carla Cappetti." *American Literature,* 66 (June), 392–393. Favorable review commenting on Cappetti's treatment of W.

4361. Gillespie, Tim. "Why Literature Matters." *English Journal,* 83 (December), 16–21. Adduces W's example of the importance of reading, quoting from *BB* (p. 17).

4362. Giovanni, Nikki. *Shimmy Shimmy Shimmy Like My Sister Kate.* New York: Henry Holt, pp. 77–81, 173. Reprints "Between the World and Me," provides commentary on it and lynching in general, and includes a biographical note on W mentioning *UTC, NS,* "The Man Who Lived Underground," and *WML.*

4363. Goodman, Susan. "Jean Méral.—*Paris in American Literature.*" *Études Anglaises,* 47 (January–March), 109–110. Review mentioning W briefly.

4364. Goring, Rosemary. *Larousse Dictionary of Literary Characters.* Edinburgh: Larousse, p. 710. Contains a paragraph identifying Biggar [sic] Thomas.

4365. Gotera, Vince. *Radical Visions: Poetry by Vietnam Veterans.* Athens: The University of Georgia Press, p. 215. Mentions W briefly.

4366. Gounard, Jean-François. "Richard Wright 1908–1960," in *Black American Prose Writers of the Harlem Renaissance.* Ed. Harold Bloom. New York: Chelsea House, pp. 167–169.

4367. _____. "Critical Extract," in *Black American Prose Writers of the Harlem Renaissance.* Ed. Harold Bloom. New York: Chelsea House, pp. 167–169.

4368. Graham, Maryemma. "Margaret Walker b. 1915," in *The Heath Anthology of American Literature.*

Vol. 2. Ed. Paul Lauter. Lexington, MA: D.C. Heath, pp. 1897–1898. Mentions Walker's friendship with W.

4369. Graham, Maryemma, and Jerry W. Ward, Jr. "Letter from the Editors." *Richard Wright Newsletter,* 3 (Spring/Summer), 2. Urges that pedagogical, textual, and annotative material be sent to the publication.

4370. [Graham, Maryemma, and Jerry W. Ward, Jr.]. "Publication Notice." *Richard Wright Newsletter,* 3 (Spring/Summer), 8. Notice of Mark J. Madigan's edition of Dorothy Canfield Fisher's selected letters, including letters to and about W.

4371. _____. "Black Boy: A Fiftieth Anniversary Retrospective." *Richard Wright Newsletter,* 3 (December), 7. Provides a W chronology and excerpts from reviews of *BB* by W.E.B Du Bois, Lionel Trilling, Irving Howe, Thomas A. Johnson, and Andrew Delbanco.

4372. _____. "Wright Film Biography Released." *Richard Wright Newsletter,* 3 (December), 1. Announcement of *Richard Wright-Black Boy* reporting on the premier in Mississippi and plans for future showings. Also reports sources of funding and names the producers and directors of the film.

4373. Grattan, Mary C. "The American Library in Paris," in *Dictionary of Literary Biography Yearbook: 1993.* Detroit: Gale, pp. 226–233. Mentions briefly W as contributor to *The God That Failed* (p. 230).

4374. Gray, Jeffrey. "Essence and the Mulatto Traveler: Europe as Embodiment in Nella Larsen's *Quicksand.*" *Novel: A Forum on Fiction,* 27 (Spring), 257–270. Includes comments on W's initial reaction to Paris, comparing it to Larsen's response to Europe (pp. 260–261). Also mentions briefly W's introduction to *Black Metropolis.*

4375. Gray, Richard. *The Life of William Faulkner.* Oxford: Blackwell, p. 297. Mentions briefly *NS.*

4376. Green, Paul. *A Southern Life: Letters of Paul Green, 1916–1981.* Ed. Laurence G. Avery. Chapel Hill: University of North Carolina Press, pp. 261, 311, 318, 321–327, 395, 433, 549, 602–603, 662, 695. Includes comment by the editor on W's support of Green's play "Hymn to the Rising Sun"; a letter from

Green to Cass Canfield of Harper's expressing admiration for *NS* and requesting to dramatize it; excerpts from a letter from W to Green; a letter from Green to W.A. Stanbury about the dramatization; two letters from Green to W about the play; letters from Green to Orson Welles, Paul R. Reynolds, Jr., Frank J. Sheil, Abbott Van Nostrand, and Ellen Wright about the play and W's death; and an excerpt from a letter from Ellen Wright to Green about the play. Avery's ample notes provide a detailed context.

4377. Greenbaum, Vicky. "Expanding the Canon: Shaping Inclusive Reading Lists. *English Journal*, 83 (December), 36–39. Includes *BB* in "a list of fine writing and writers" praised by high-school students and teachers.

4378. Greenspon, Joanna, ed. *Humanities Index: April 1993 to March 1994*. New York: H.W. Wilson, p. 1264. Lists four items s.v. W.

4379. Griffith, Kelley. "Questions for Study," in her *Narrative Fiction: An Introduction and Anthology*. Fort Worth: Harcourt Brace College, pp. 468–469. To accompany "The Man Who Was Almost a Man."

4380. _____. "Richard Wright *The Man Who Was Almost a Man*," in her *Narrative Fiction: An Introduction and Anthology*. Fort Worth: Harcourt Brace College, pp. 459–460. Biographical headnote.

4381. _____. *Writing Essays About Literature: A Guide and Style Sheet*. Fourth edition. Fort Worth: Harcourt Brace, p. 37. Contains a paragraph on *NS*.

4382. Gysin, Fritz. "Predicaments of Skin: Boundaries in Recent African American Fiction," in *The Black Columbiad: Defining Moments in African American Literature and Culture*. Eds. Werner Sollors and Maria Diedrich. Harvard English Studies 19. Cambridge, MA: Harvard University Press, pp. 286–297. Notes W's emphasis on "the frightening aspects of whiteness" in his fiction" (p. 295).

4383. Hakutani, Yoshinobu. "Richard Wright's *The Man Who Lived Underground*, Nihilism, and Zen." *The Mississippi Quarterly*, 47 (Spring), 201–213. Argues that although the racial theme is emphatically present in W's novella, there is also a more generalized view of the human condition, one of passivity in an indifferent universe. His method here relies more on metaphor and symbol than accumulation of detail. The protagonist's achievement of enlightenment is analogous to that of Zen, which was an important concern in the haiku written at the end of W's life.

4384. Hall, Donald, and D.L. Emblen. "Considerations," in their *A Writer's Reader*. Seventh edition. New York: Harper Collins, p. 589.

4385. _____. "Richard Wright, *The Library Card*," in their *A Writer's Reader*. Seventh edition. New York: Harper Collins, p. 581. Reprint of 1976 with a photograph of W.

4386. Harris, Susan K. "*Domestic Allegories of Political Desire: The Black Heroine's Text at the Turn of the Century*. By Claudia Tate." *Journal of English and Germanic Philology*, 93 (January), 146–148. Comments on a debate with a black male critic on W's portrayal of women in *BB*.

4387. Harris, Trudier. "Toni Morrison: Solo Flight Through Literature Into History." *World Literature Today*, No. 68 (Winter), pp. 9–14. Mentions W and quotes briefly from *NS*.

4388. Harris, Will. "Early Black Women Playwrights and the Dual Liberation Motif." *African American Review*, 28 (Summer), 205–221. Mentions briefly *NS* (pp. 219, 221).

4389. Harris, William J. "An Interview with Amiri Baraka," in *Conversations with Amiri Baraka*. Ed. Charlie Reilly. Jackson: University Press of Mississippi, pp. 168–180.

4390. [Harrison, Nelson E.]. "Richard Wright Touring Theatre Heads Out This Fall." *Richard Wright Newsletter*, 3 (Spring/Summer), 7. Mentions productions of a dramatic version of "The Man Who Lived Underground" in Pittsburgh and Cleveland and plans for a production of "Man of All Work."

4391. Hart, James D., with Phillip W. Leininger. *The Oxford Companion to American Literature*. Sixth edition. New York: Oxford University Press, p. 741.

4392. Hayashi, Tetsumaro, and Beverly K. Simpson. *John Steinbeck: Dissertation Abstracts and Research Opportunities*. Metuchen, NJ: Scarecrow, pp. 95, 113, 118, 121. Lists dissertations involving W as well as Steinbeck by Michael Barry, Roger Neal Casey, and Leslie Pollard.

4393. Henderson, Gloria, William Day, and Sandra Waller. "Richard Wright (1908–1960)," in their *Literature and Ourselves: A Thematic Introduction for Readers and Writers*. New York: HarperCollins, pp. 691–692. Brief headnote to "The Man Who Was Almost a Man."

4394. Henderson, Mae G. "Where, by the way, is this train going?': A Case for (Re)Framing Black Cultural Studies." *The Journal of the Midwest Modern Language Association*, 27 (Spring), 42–50. Mentions W briefly (p. 46).

4395. Hitchens, Christopher. "Critic of the Booboisie." *Dissent*, 41 (Summer), 415–420. Mentions W briefly in a review of Fred Hobson's *Mencken: A Biography*.

4396. Hobson, Christopher Z. "Richard Wright's Communisms: Textual Variance, Intentionality, and Socialization, in *American Hunger*, 'I Tried to Be a Communist,' and *The God That Failed*. Text: *Transactions of the Society for Textual Scholarship*, 6, 307–344. Examines W's autobiographical writings after *BB* in an effort to trace W's attitudes toward Communism through a study of textual variations. *American Hunger* offers moderate criticism of Communism, acknowledging its appeal; "I Tried to Be a Communist" is polemical and "harshly negative" (p. 309). By authorizing the reprinting of "I Tried to Be a Communist" rather than the milder version in *American Hunger* when asked to contribute to *The God That Failed* indicates further estrangement from the Party, and *The Outsider* denounces Communism in much harsher terms. In his textual analysis Hobson uses W as a test case for the opposed textual theories of Greg and Bowers on the one hand and Hans Zeller on the other, utilizing the latter's notion of extratextual influence.

4397. Hobson, Fred. *Mencken: A Life*. New York: Random House, p. 250. Relates Mencken's early influence on W.

4398. Hogue, W. Lawrence. "Literary Production: A Silence in Afro-American Literary Practice," in *Within the Circle: An Anthology of African American Literary Criticism from the Harlem Renaissance to the Present*. Ed. Angelyn Mitchell. Durham, NC: Duke University Press, pp. 329–347.

4399. Holloway, Karla F.C. "Image, Act, and Identity in *In My Father's House*," in *Critical Reflections on the Fiction of Ernest J. Gaines*. Athens: The University of Georgia Press, pp. 180–194. Mentions W briefly (p. 192).

4400. Howe, Irving. "Naturalism and Taste," in his *A Critic's Notebook*. New York: Harcourt Brace, pp. 216–228. Mentions W briefly (p. 223).

4401. Hubbard, Dolan. *The Sermon and the African American Literary Imagination*. Columbia: University of Missouri Press, pp. 23, 147, 148. Quotes from "The Literature of the Negro in the United States" (p. 23) and mentions W briefly.

4402. Hurston, Zora Neale. "Critical Extract," in *Black American Writers of the Harlem Renaissance*. Ed. Harold Bloom. New York: Chelsea House, p. 160.

4403. _____. "Richard Wright 1908–1960," in *Black American Prose Writers of the Harlem Renaissance*. Ed. Harold Bloom. New York: Chelsea House, p. 160.

4404. Ingersoll, Earl G. "Gounard, Jean-François. *The Racial Problem in the Works of Richard Wright and James Baldwin*." *The Literary Griot*, 6 (Spring), 74–75. Unfavorable review pointing out outdated scholarship, excessive plot summary, and mechanical structure.

4405. Jablon, Madelyn. "Race and Sex in African-American Literature." *The Literary Griot*, 6 (Spring), 1–10. Comments on *NS* in light of Eldridge Cleaver's theory of "Primeval Mitosis" (pp. 8–9).

4406. Jacobson, Marcia. *Being a Boy Again: Autobiography and the American Boy Book*. Tuscaloosa: The University of Alabama Press, p. 158. Mentions *NS* as a "coming-of-age book.

4407. James, C.L.R. "Native Son and Revolution: A Review of *Native Son* by Richard Wright," in *C.L.R. James and Revolutionary Marxism: Selected Writings of C.L.R. James 1939–1949*. Eds. Scott McLemee and Paul Le Blanc. Atlantic Highlands, NJ: Humanities Press, pp. 88–91.

4408. _____. "On *Native Son* by Richard Wright (1940), in *C.L.R. James on the 'Negro Question*." Ed. Scott McLemee. Jackson: University Press of Mississippi, pp. 55–58.

4409. _____. "The Revolutionary Answer to the Negro Problem in the United States," in *C.L.R. James and Revolutionary Marxism: Selected Writings of C.L.R. James 1939–1949*. Eds. Scott McLemee and Paul Le Blanc. Atlanta Highlands, NJ: Humanities Press, pp. 179–187.

4410. Jarāb, Josef. "Black Stars, the Red Star, and the Blues," in *The Black Columbiad: Defining Moments in African American Literature and Culture*. Eds. Werner Sollors and Maria Diedrich. Harvard English Studies 19. Cambridge, MA: Harvard University Press, pp. 167–173. Notes that in 1954 Jaroslav Bouček published a brochure in Czechoslovakia denouncing W, "a writer who was not only a disgrace to the black proletariat but who made it his abominable task to depict blacks as beasts" (p. 171).

4411. Jaye, James R. "Richard Wright's Freedom: The Existentialism of *Uncle Tom's Children*." *The Midwest Quarterly*, 35 (Summer), 420–434. Argues that W's naturalism exists in tension with "the motifs of revolt, personal choice, and free will to combat a seemingly deterministic world" (p. 433). In support of this thesis Jaye analyzes "Down by the Riverside" and "Fire and Cloud."

4412. Jennings, C.A. "African-American Contributors to American Society," *in Black American Culture and Society: An Annotated Bibliography*. Ed. S.T. Rustavo. Commack, NY: Nova Science, pp. 1–31. Contains an entry on W (p. 9).

4413. Johnson, Abby Arthur, and Ronald Johnson. "Charting a New Course: African American Literary Politics Since 1976,"in *The Black Columbiad: Defining Moments in African American Literature and Culture*. Eds. Werner Sollors and Maria Diedrich. Harvard English Studies 19. Cambridge, MA: Harvard University Press, pp. 369–381. Cites Harry Neal's 1965 essay on W (p. 371) and mentions briefly the special W issue of *Callaloo* (p. 377).

4414. Johnson, Charles. "The Singular Vision of Ralph Ellison," in *Invisible Man* by Ralph Ellison. New York: The Modern Library, pp. vii–xii. Mentions W briefly (p. ix).

4415. Johnson-Cooper, Glendora. "Strengthening the African American Community Through Information Literacy," in *The Black Librarian in America Revisited*. Metuchen, NJ: Scarecrow, pp. 181–

192. Quotes Haki R. Madhubuti mentioning W briefly (p. 188).

4416. Joly, Claire. "Richard Wright: Ideal Reader, Real Audiences, and the Personalist Aesthetic of Social Protest." *Richard Wright Newsletter*, 3 (Spring/Summer), 8. Abstract of an MLA paper relating W's essay "Personalism" to his effort to elicit strong emotional response from his readers.

4417. Jones, LeRoi (Amiri Baraka). "The Myth of a 'Negro Literature,'" in *Within the Circle: An Anthology of African American Literary Criticism from the Harlem Renaissance to the Present*. Ed. Angelyn Mitchell. Durham, NC: Duke University Press, pp. 165–171.

4418. Jones, Lisa. "How I Invented Multiculturalism," in her *Bulletproof Diva: Tales of Race, Sex, and Hair*. New York: Doubleday, pp. 7–10. Notes that her high-school yearbook lists *NS* as one of her two favorite books.

4419. _____. "My Slave Name," in her *Bulletproof Diva: Tales of Race, Sex, and Hair*. New York: Doubleday, pp. 16–20. Mentions Bigger Thomas as an example of "names as metaphor."

4420. Jones, Michael D. "Information Needs of African Americans in the Prison System," in *The Black Librarian in America Revisited*. Metuchen, NJ: Scarecrow Press, pp. 338–343. Mentions W briefly (p. 340).

4421. Jordan, Elaine. "Susan Wolstenholme, *Gothic (Re)Visions: Writing Women as Readers*." *Journal of American Studies*, 28 (April 1994), 123–125. Mentions W briefly (p. 124).

4422. Jordan, June. "Finding the Haystack in the Needle, or, The Whole World of America and the Challenge of Higher Education," in her *Technical Difficulties*. New York: Vintage Books, pp. 89–101.

4423. _____. "Requiem for the Champ," in her *Technical Difficulties*. New York: Vintage Books, p. 89–101.

4424. Joyce, Joyce Ann. *Warriors, Conjurers and Priests: Defining African-centered Literary Criticism*. Chicago: Third World Press, pp. 13, 19, 30, 32, 34, 44, 49–72, 87, 91, 94, 97–99, 130, 200, 201, 219, 220, 227–228, 252, 287, 289. The second chapter analyzes *NS* as a romance in the symbolic tradition and

LD as a realistic novel. W's language in both works enhances his social message. Elsewhere Joyce discusses W in relation to Petry and Hurston. Quotes from "How 'Bigger' Was Born" (pp. 50–51), "Blueprint for Negro Writing" (p. 71), and "The Literature of the Negro in the United States" (p. 287).

4425. Justus, James H. "Southern Modernism and the Battle of Literary Succession." *The Southern Literary Journal*, 27 (Fall), 6–17. Mentions briefly *NS* (p. 11) and W (p. 15).

4426. Kael, Pauline. *For Keeps*. New York: Dutton, p. 271. Mentions the stage adaptation of *NS*.

4427. Kazin, Alfred. "Critical Extract," in *Black American Prose Writers of the Harlem Renaissance*. Ed. Harold Bloom. New York: Chelsea House, p. 173.

4428. Kelley, Robin D.G. "Black Americans," in *The Encyclopedia Americana*. Ed. Lawrence T. Lorimer. Danbury, CT: Grolier, pp. 28A, 29.

4429. Kinnamon, Keneth. "Three Black Writers and the Anthologized Canon," in *American Realism and the Canon*. Eds. Tom Quirk and Gary Scharnharst. Newark: University of Delaware Press, pp. 143–153. Mentions W briefly (pp. 148, 149, 150, 151).

4430. Kiuchi, Toru. "On Richard Wright's *Pagan Spain,*" *Nihon University Industrial Engineering Faculty Report B*, 27 (20 June), 25–44. Explains the background and making of W's Spanish travelogue and then analyzes its structure. The main themes are Hemingway's influence, Spanish society after the Civil War, bullfighting, religion and society, sex, and W's own racial consciousness. *PS* is not simply a record, but also an indication of the author's entry into the outside world thereafter.

4431. Lee, A. Robert. "State of the Art: Afro-America, The Before Columbus Foundation and the Literary Multiculturization of America." *Journal of American Studies*, 28 (April 1994), 433–450. Mentions briefly W and *NS* (pp. 437, 438, 444).

4432. Lindberg, Kathryne. "W.E.B. Du Bois's *Dusk of Dawn* and James Yates's *Mississippi to Madrid* or 'What Goes Around Comes Around and Around and Around'" in Autobiography." *The Massachusetts Review*, 35 (Summer), 283–308. Mentions *UTC* (p. 291) and W (p. 296).

4433. Kalaidjian, Walter, *American Culture Between the Wars: Revisionary Modernism and Postmodern Critique*. New York: Columbia University Press, pp. 61–63. Discusses W's relation to the Chicago John Reed Club, quoting extensively from *The God That Failed*.

4434. Kazin, Alfred. "Richard Wright 1908–1960," in *Black American Prose Writers of the Harlem Renaissance*. Ed. Harold Bloom. New York: Chelsea House, p. 173.

4435. Kelley, Robin D.G. *Race Rebels: Culture, Politics, and the Black Working Class*. New York: The Free Press, pp. 12, 35–36, 104, 128, 146. Mentions briefly W. and Bigger Thomas. Quotes from *TMBV*.

4436. Kenan, Randall. "From the Mountain Top." *The Nation*, 258 (2 May), 596, 598–599. Review of David Leeming's biography of James Baldwin mentioning W briefly.

4437. Kenny, W.P. "Killens, John Oliver," in *Encyclopedia of World Literature in the 20th Century*. Ed. Steven R. Serafin. Vol. 5. New York: Continuum, pp. 358–359. Mentions W briefly.

4438. ____. "Wilson, August," in *Encyclopedia of World Literature in the 20th Century*. Ed. Steven R. Serafin. Vol. 5. New York: Continuum, pp. 637–638. Mentions W briefly.

4439. Kent, George E. "Ethnic Impact in American Literature: Reflections on a Course," in *Within the Circle: An Anthology of African American Literary Criticism from the Harlem Renaissance to the Present*. Ed. Angelyn Mitchell. Durham, NC: Duke University Press, pp. 172–183.

4440. Kerley, Gary. "Fishkin, Shelly Fisher. *Was Huck Black?: Mark Twain and African-American Voices*." *Studies in American Fiction*, 22 (Spring), 254–255. Mentions W briefly.

4441. Ketchin, Susan. *The Christ-Haunted Landscape: Faith and Doubt in Southern Fiction*. Jackson: University Press of Mississippi, p. xiii. Mentions W briefly.

4442. King, Laurie. *Hear My Voice Bibliography: An Annotated Guide to Multicultural Literature from the United States*. Menlo Park, CA: Addison-Wesley, pp. 67–68. Contains an entry on *EM* emphasizing "The Man Who Went to Chicago."

4443. King, Tamara. "Southern Students Choose from Diverse Courses." *The Southern Register*, Winter, p. 10. Announces an undergraduate course entitled "Survey of the Major Works of Richard Wright" taught at the University of Mississippi in the spring semester of 1994.

4444. [Kinnamon, Keneth]. "Books Briefly Mentioned." *African American Review*, 28 (Fall), 495–496. Includes a notice of the reprint of the Library of America edition of *LT* noting the importance of Arnold Rampersad's foreword.

4445. ____. "Calls for Papers." *Richard Wright Newsletter*, 3 (Spring/Summer), 9. Announces *Critical Essays on Native Son*, describes the series in which it will appear, and invites submissions of original essays.

4446. ____. "Charles Scruggs. *Sweet Home: Invisible Cities in the Afro-American* Novel." *Modern Fiction Studies*, 40 (Summer), 364–365. Favorable review noting the treatment of *NS*.

4447. ____. "Foreword," in *Modern African American Writers*. New York: Facts on File, pp. vii–x. Comments briefly on W mentioning *NS* and *BB* (p. ix).

4448. ____. "Keneth Kinnamon Advises PBS Documentary About Richard Wright." *Arkansas English* (Fall), p. 2. Comments on Kinnamon's contributions to African American literary study and discusses his advisory role in Madison D. Lacy's film *Richard Wright-Black Boy*.

4449. ____. "A Richard Wright Bibliography: 1984." *Richard Wright Newsletter*, 3 (Spring/Summer) Supplement, 15pp. Includes 156 annotated items and a commentary on W studies in 1984.

4450. ____. "Richard Wright," in *Modern African American Writers*. Eds. Matthew J. Bruccoli and Judith S. Baughman. New York: Facts on File, pp. 63–73. Bibliography of W's book-length works together with a headnote and a selective secondary bibliography.

4451. Kirszner, Laurie G., and Stephen R. Mandell. "Reading and Reacting," in their *Literature: Reading, Reacting, Writing*, 2nd edition. Fort Worth: Harcourt Brace, p. 784.

4452. Klawans, Stuart. "'I was a weird example of Art': *My Amputations* as Cubist Confession." *African American Review*, 28 (Spring), 77–87. Mentions briefly *O* and Cross Damon.

4453. Knippling, Jim. "Censorship and African American Literature," in *Preserving Intellectual Freedom: Fighting Censorship in Our Schools*. Ed. Jean E. Brown. Urbana, IL: National Council of Teachers of English, pp. 73–80. Discusses W, "How 'Bigger' Was Born," in relation overt censorship, editorial changes, and W's own "mental censor."

4454. Kriegel, Leonard. "Forgive Me, Mrs. Reilly: or, How a New York Jew Learned to Love the South." *The Kenyon Review*, 16 (Summer), 45–54. Mentions W briefly (p. 48).

4455. Kubitschek, Missy Dehn. "Re-Viewing *Their Eyes*." *African American Review*, 28 (Summer), 305–309. Mentions W and *NS*. Comments on Hazel Carby's discussion of the disagreement between W and Hurston.

4456. Lauret, Maria. *Liberating Literature: Feminist Fiction in America*. London: Routledge. pp. 36, 40, 142, 143, 192, 207. Comments on Petry's *The Street*, emphasizing its difference from W. Also mentions *WML* and *NS*.

4457. Lawrence-Lightfoot, Sara. *I've Known Rivers: Lives of Loss and Liberation*. Reading, MA: Addison-Wesley, p. 540. Mentions W briefly.

4458. Lee, A. Robert. "Afro-America, the Before Columbus Foundation and the Literary Multiculturalization of America." *Journal of American Studies*, 28 (December), 433–450. Mentions briefly W and *NS* (pp. 437, 438).

4459. Leeming, David. *James Baldwin: A Biography*. New York: Holt, pp. 18, 36, 49–50, 52, 54, 56, 57, 62, 64–66, 73, 75, 93, 101, 120, 121, 180–182, 186, 187, 207, 290, 300, 308, 324, 366. Discusses Baldwin's first meeting with W, the example of W's exile, their friendship and subsequent quarrel in Paris, Baldwin's writings on W, his response to W's death, and other matters.

4460. Lennon, Peter. *Foreign Correspondent: Paris in the Sixties*. London: Picador, pp. 30–32. A journalist for the *Irish Times*, Lennon interviewed W in Paris in 1960. Excerpts are included here.

4461. _____. *Foreign Correspondent: Paris in the Sixties*. London: pp. 30–32. Discusses his interview with W for the *Irish Times*. Naive about racial matters, his questions were often gauche.

4462. Levine, George. "Introduction: Reclaiming the Aesthetic," in his *Aesthetics and Ideology*. New Brunswick, NJ: Rutgers University Press, pp. 1–28. Mentions W briefly.

4463. Lewis, David Levering. "Richard Wright," in his *The Portable Harlem Renaissance Reader*. New York: Viking Press. Headnote to "Blueprint for Negro Writing."

4464. Lindberg, Kathryne. "W.E.B. DuBois's *Dusk of Dawn* and James Yates's *Mississippi to Madrid* or 'What Goes Around Comes Around and Around and Around' in Autobiography." *The Massachusetts Review*, 35 (Summer), 283–308. Mentions *UTC* (p. 291) and W (p. 296).

4465. Lindsey, Howard O. *A History of Black America*. Secaucus, NJ: Chartwell Books, pp. 108, 109. Mentions "the powerful writings of W. Includes a photograph of W with Count Basie.

4466. Litz, A. Walton. "A National Art Form," in his *Major American Short Stories*. Third edition. New York: Oxford University Press, pp. 327–347.

4467. _____. "Richard Wright (1908–1960), in his *Major American Short Stories*. Third edition. New York: Oxford University Press, pp. 879–880.

4468. Lock, Helen. *A Case of Mistaken Identity: Detective Undercurrents in Recent African American Fiction*. New York: Peter Lang, p. 122. Mentions W briefly in a discussion of *Invisible Man*.

4469. Longest, George C., et al., "A Checklist of Scholarship on Southern Literature for 1993." *The Mississippi Quarterly*, 47 (Supplement), 1–219. Lists seven annotated items on W and cross-references to sixteen other items dealing partially with W.

4470. Lott, Eric. "Cornel West in the Hour of Chaos: Culture and Politics in *Race Matters*." *Social Text*, No. 40 (Fall), pp. 39–50. Comments on W and the Communist Party (p. 44).

4471. _____. "Routes." *The Nation*, 258 (2 May), 602–604. Review of Paul Gilroy's *The Black Atlantic* commenting on his treatment of W.

4472. Lupiano, Vincent dePaul, and Ken W. Sayers. *It Was a Very Good Year: A Cultural History of the United States from 1776 to the Present*. Holbrook, MA: Bob Adams, p. 323. Mentions *NS* briefly.

4473. Luscher, Robert M. "The Pulse of *Bloodline*," in *Critical Reflections on the Fiction of Ernest J. Gaines*. Ed. David C. Estes. Athens: The University of Georgia Press, pp. 62–88. Comments that *UTC* "thematically anticipates" *Bloodline* (p. 65).

4474. Lynch, Michael F. "Haunted by Innocence: The Debate with Dostoevsky in Wright's 'Other' Novel, *The Outsider*." *Richard Wright Newsletter*, 3 (Spring/Summer), 8. Abstract of a CLA paper emphasizing the indebtedness of *O* to *Crime and Punishment*, but showing that W plays "variations on his mentor's theme."

4475. Lyons, Richard D. "Ralph Ellison, Author of 'Invisible Man,' Is Dead at 80." *The New York Times* (17 April), p. 16. Notes Ellison's friendship with W.

4476. Madhubuti, Haki R. "Race, Rage, and Intellectual Development: A Personal Journey," in his *Claiming Earth: Race, Rage, Rape, Redemption; Blacks Seeking a Culture of Enlightened Empowerment*. Chicago: Third World Press, pp. 3–4. Includes discussion of the impact of reading *BB* at the age of thirteen, followed by *NS*, *UTC*, and *TMBV*.

4477. Madigan, Mark T. "'As True and Direct as a Birth or Death': Richard Wright on Jim Thompson's *Now and on Earth*." *Studies in American Fiction*, 22 (Spring), 105–110. Examines W's favorable blurb for the Thompson novel in relation to "some parallels in the authors' lives and careers" (p. 105).

4478. Major, Clarence. "Necessary Distance: Afterthoughts on Becoming a Writer." *African American Review*, 28 (Spring), 37–47.

4479. _____. "The Slave Trade: View from the Middle Passage." *African American Review*, 28 (Spring), 11–22. Poem mentioning Richard [W] briefly (p. 21).

4480. Mallon, William T. "Voicing Manhood: Masculinity and Dialogue in Ernest J. Gaines's 'The Sky Is Gray,' 'Three Men,' and *A Gathering of Old Men*." *Southern Studies*,

5 (Fall & Winter), 49–67. Quotes from *BB* to illustrate Southern racism (p. 51).

4481. Margolies, Edward. "Richard Wright 1908–1960," in *Black American Prose Writers of the Harlem Renaissance*. Ed. Harold Bloom. New York: Chelsea House, pp. 166–167.

4482. _____. "Critical Extract," in *Black American Prose Writers of the Harlem Renaissance*. Ed. Harold Bloom. New York: Chelsea House, pp. 166–167.

4483. Mariani, Paul. *Lost Puritan: A Life of Robert Lowell*. New York: W.W. Norton, p. 272. Records that Lowell preferred Baldwin's essays to W's "blarney."

4484. Mark, Rebecca. *The Dragon's Blood: Feminist Intertextuality in Eudora Welty's The Golden Apples*. Jackson: University Press of Mississippi, p. 96. Claims that"necrophilia is a central phenomenon" in *NS*.

4485. Marshall, Margaret. "Richard Wright 1908–1960," in *Black American Prose Writers of the Harlem Renaissance*. Ed. Harold Bloom. New York: Chelsea House, pp. 161–162.

4486. _____. "Critical Extract," in *Black American Prose Writers of the Harlem Renaissance*. Ed. Harold Bloom. New York: Chelsea House, pp. 161–162. Partial reprint of 1940. 784.

4487. Mason, Theodore O., Jr. "African-American Theory and Criticism: 1. Harlem Renaissance to the Black Arts Movement," in *The Johns Hopkins Guide to Literary Theory and Criticism*. Eds. Michael Groden and Martin Kreiswirth. Baltimore: The Johns Hopkins University Press, pp. 9–15. Discusses "Blueprint for Negro Writing" (pp. 11–12), especially its black nationalist implications, and mentions W elsewhere (pp. 10, 13, 14, 15) in relation to Baldwin and Ellison.

4488. _____. "African-American Theory and Criticism: 2. 1977 and After," in *The Johns Hopkins Guide to Literary Theory and Criticism*. Eds. Michael Groden and Martin Kreiswirth. Baltimore: The Johns Hopkins University Press, pp. 15–20. Mentions W briefly (pp. 15, 17).

4489. Masuda, Mitsuko. "The Articulateness of Bigger Thomas: A Rereading of *Native Son*. *Nikon Women's University Studies in English and American Literature*, 29 (March), 129–138. Asserts that Bigger is more articulate in the unexpurgated Library of America edition than in the 1940 first edition.

4490. Maxwell, William Joseph. "Dialectical Engagements: The 'New Negro' and the "Old Left,' 1918–1940." *Dissertation Abstracts International*, 55 (September), 567-A. Includes consideration of the W-Hurston dispute and the W-Algren friendship in relation to *UTC* and *NS*.

4491. McCaffery, Larry, and Jerzy Kutnik. "'I Follow My Eyes': An Interview with Clarence Major." *African American Review*, 28 (Spring), 121–138. Major mentions W and acknowledges his influence (pp. 124, 132).

4492. McCall, Nathan. "'It's Me Against the World.'" *The Washington Post Magazine* (30 January), pp. 6–13, 20–27.

4493. McConnell, Frank D. "Black American Literature," in *Collier's Encyclopedia*. Ed. William D. Halsey. New York: Macmillan Educational Company, vol. 2, pp. 72–74. Contains two paragraphs on W emphasizing *NS* and *BB*.

4494. McCoy, Adrian. "Dark Message of Play Finds Way from City Theatre to Hearts of Students." *Pittsburgh Post-Gazette* (4 September), p. K3. Reports that the script of the 1993 Pittsburgh City Theatre's dramatization of "The Man Who Lived Underground" was successfully taught in a high school in Florida to a highly responsive class of "African American, Haitian, Jamaican, and Creole students." Student comments are quoted. Julia and Ellen Wright were pleased with the student response.

4495. McDowell, Deborah E. "New Directions for Black Feminist Criticism," in *Within the Circle: An Anthology of African American Literary Criticism from the Harlem Renaissance to the Present*. Ed. Angelyn Mitchell. Durham, NC: Duke University Press, pp. 428–441.

4496. McKay, Nellie Y. "The Journals of Charlotte L. Forten-Grimké: Les Lieux de Mémoire in African-American Women's Autobiography," in *History and Memory in African-American Culture*. Eds. Geneviève Fabre and Robert O'Meally. New York: Oxford University Press, pp. 261–271. Quotes from comments made by James Olney in a discussion of *BB* (p. 264).

4497. McKnight, Reginald, ed. *African American Wisdom*. San Rafael, CA: New World Library, pp. 28, 52, 111–112. Contains two quotations by W and an identifying note.

4498. McLemee, Scott. "Afterword," in *C.L.R. James and Revolutionary Marxism: Selected Writing of C.L.R. James 1939–1949*. Eds. Scott McLemee and Paul Le Blanc. Atlantic Highlands, NJ: Humanities Press, pp. 209–238. Mentions briefly W (pp. 215, 230), *NS* (p. 220), and *BB* (p. 226).

4499. Mellen, Joan. *Kay Boyle: Author of Herself*. New York: Farrar, Straus & Giroux, pp. 310, 401. Notes that in 1949 W was prevented from speaking at Amerika Haus in 1949 because he was "politically undesireable." Also relates that Boyle accused W of "working with the State Department" as an informant so that he could keep his passport.

4500. Mercer, Kobena. *Welcome to the Jungle: New Positions in Black Cultural Studies*. New York: Routledge, pp. 246–248. Uses a conversation between W and C.L.R. James as a point of departure to explore the issue of "populist modernism."

4501. Middleton, JoAnn. "Fiction: 1900 to the 1930s," in *American Literary Scholarship: An Annual/1992*. Ed. David J. Nordloh. Durham, NC: Duke University Press, pp. 211–247. Mentions W briefly (p. 245).

4502. Miller, J.[ames] A. "*Richard Wright: critical perspectives past and present*, ed. Henry Louis Gates and K.A. Appiah." *Choice*, 31 (January), 782–783. Favorable review praising the selections, especially the "22 probing and illuminating essays by contemporary scholars," and the editing.

4503. Mills, Nicolaus. "White Man-Listen! 1957," in his *Legacy of Dissent: 40 Years of Writing from Dissent Magazine*. New York: Simon and Schuster, p. 229. Introductory note on W mentioning 5 of his books, but not *NS*.

4504. Minter, David. *A Cultural History of the American Novel: Henry James to William Faulkner*. Cambridge: Cambridge University Press, pp. 83, 152, 159, 160, 195, 196, 197, 202, 207. Mentions briefly W, *TMBV*, and *UTC*.

4505. Mitchell, Angelyn. "About the Critics," in her *Within the Circle: An Anthology of African American Literary Criticism from the Harlem Renaissance to the Present*. Durham, NC: Duke University Press pp. 528–530. Identifies W.

4506. _____. "Introduction: Voices Within the Circle: A Historical Overview of African American Literary Criticism," in her *Within the Circle: An Anthology of African American Literary Criticism from the Harlem Renaissance to the Present*. Durham, NC: Duke University Press, pp. 1–18. Comments on and quotes from "Blueprint for Negro Writing," relating it to *NS* (pp. 6–7).

4507. _____. "Useful Sources for Related Reading," in her *Within the Circle: An Anthology of African American Literary Criticism from the Harlem Renaissance to the Present*. Durham, NC: Duke University Press, pp. 523–525. Lists "How 'Bigger' Was Born."

4508. Moore, Jack B. "Bigger Thomas: Free at Last?" *The Mississippi Quarterly*, 47 (Winter), 151–156. Mainly favorable essay-review of Robert Butler's *Native Son*, but notes that the format of the series in which the book appears is constrictive. Perhaps, too, Butler's emphasis on the heroic Bigger, whose growth the novel traces, underestimates the character's frightening brutality. But the book is highly useful to W students and scholars at all levels.

4509. _____. "Calls for Papers." *Richard Wright Newsletter*, 3 (Spring/Summer), 9. Announces an issue of *Mississippi Quarterly* on "International perspectives on Richard Wright."

4510. _____. "The *Mississippi Quarterly* is planning to publish its second special issue on Richard Wright, focusing on 'International Perspectives on Richard Wright.'" *Afram Newsletter*, 39 (June), 26. Announcement and call for papers.

4511. _____. "*The Mississippi Quarterly* is planning to publish its second special issue on Richard Wright, focusing on 'International Perspectives on Richard Wright.'" *Amerikastudien*, 39 (Summer), 283. Invites contributions.

4512. _____. "*Native Son*: Novel by Richard Wright," in *Reference Guide to American Literature*. Third edition. Ed. Jim Kamp. Detroit: St.

James Press, pp. 1020–1021. Critical examination of *NS* commenting on its structure and theme. Though flawed, it reveals "what can happen when the human spirit is trapped."

4513. Morris, Willie, and William Ferris. "The Water in Which You Swim." *American Heritage*, 45 (July/August), 70–77. Interview of Ferris by Morris mentioning W's expatriation in Paris and Julia Wright's visit to Mississippi. Ferris also mentions the W symposium in Russia.

4514. Morrison, Toni, and Judith Wilson. "A Conversation with Toni Morrison," in *Conversations with Toni Morrison*. Ed. Danille Taylor-Guthrie. Jackson: University Press of Mississippi, pp. 129–137.

4515. Morton, Brian. "Writing One-handed." *New Statesman and Society*. 7 (September), 38. Includes an unfavorable review of James Campbell's *Paris Interzone: Richard Wright, Lolita, Boris Vian and Others on the Left Bank, 1946–1960*. Calls W "a man in whom the creative fire has gone out" and accuses him of "political ineptitude."

4516. Muckley, Peter A. *Black American Author-Biography: From Politics to Myths and Beyond*. London: Minerva Press, pp. vii, 20–21, 25, 32–33, 35, 41–42, 43–44, 62, 63, 67, 68, 78, 86–110, 111, 113, 117–118, 128, 132, 133, 135, 136, 152–156. Chapter Five, "Richard Wright and the Gods That Wailed," mediates between Fabre's view of *AH* as a movement toward existentialism and Reilly's belief that it commits the author to political engagement from his alienated perspective. Muckley studies ten passages in *AH* not appearing in *The God That Failed*, concluding that they result in three voices — "the ingénue; the prophetic; the worldly-wise" — together affirming the collective African American experience. Muckley also discusses *BB* and "The Man Who Lived Underground."

4517. Muller, Gilbert H. "Comprehension, Rhetoric, Writing," in his *The McGraw-Hill Reader*. Fifth edition. New York: McGraw-Hill, p. 184.

4518. _____. "Richard Wright" in his *The McGraw-Hill Reader: Themes in the Disciplines*. Fifth edition. New York: McGraw-Hill, p. 177.

4519. _____, and John A. Williams. "Questions," in their *Bridges: Literature Across Cultures*. New

York: McGraw-Hill, p. 524. Study aids for "The Man Who Was Almost a Man."

4520. _____. "Questions," in their *Bridges: Literature Across Cultures*. New York: McGraw-Hill, p. 524. Four study questions on "The Man Who Was Almost a Man."

4521. Müller-Hartmann, Andreas. "'The Nigger in the Woodpile': The Southern Literary Discourse of Race." *Amerikastudien*, 39 (Winter), 537–549. Quotes W on Zora Neale Hurston (p. 548).

4522. Nagel, James. "*Studies in American Fiction* at Twenty Years: A Farewell Retrospective." *Studies in American Fiction*, 22 (Spring), 111–118. Mentions the publication of an essay about W in the journal.

4523. Nagle, Richard W. "Wright's 'Black Boy.'" *Los Angeles Times* (12 April), Sec. B, p. 6. Letter to the editor supporting the use of *BB* in Ventura County schools.

4524. Nelson, E.S. "Scruggs, Charles. *Sweet Home: invisible cities in the Afro-American novel*." *Choice*, 31 (January), 783. Favorable notice mentioning W briefly.

4525. Newlin, Paul. "Richard Wright 1908–1960," in *Black American Prose Writers of the Harlem Renaissance*. Ed. Harold Bloom. New York: Chelsea House, pp. 169–170.

4526. _____. "Critical Abstract," in *Black American Prose Writers of the Harlem Renaissance*. Ed. Harold Bloom. New York: Chelsea House, pp. 169–170.

4527. Nielsen, Aldon L. *Writing Between the Lines: Race and Intertextuality*. Athens: The University of Georgia Press, pp. 4–5, 6, 98, 293. Quotes from *TMBV* the passage on English language acquisition by newly imported African slaves. Mentions "The Man Who Lived Underground."

4528. Noll, Elizabeth. "The Ripple Effect of Censorship: Silencing in the Classroom." *English Journal*, 83 (December), 59–64. Notes that *BB* has been censored in high schools (pp. 60, 62).

4529. Norman, Kelley. "Filming Wright: Making *Richard Wright: Black Boy*: An Interview with Madison Davis Lacy." *The Richard Wright Newsletter*, 3 (December), 4–7. Lacy discusses his preparation for the film, his use of archival footage, the process of selecting from a mass of material, use of the two film versions of *NS*, the Wright family, the need for emotional intensity in a film, and his hopes for what viewers will take away from the film. "I hope this film places Richard back at last in the public consciousness in a stronger position."

4530. Nossiter, Adam. "*Of Long Memory: Mississippi and the Murder of Medgar Evers*. Reading, MA: Addison-Wesley, p. 81. Mentions briefly *BB*.

4531. North, Michael. *The Dialect of Modernism: Race, Language, and Twentieth-Century Literature*. New York: Oxford Universtiy Press, pp. 76, 176, 193. Comments on W's opinions of Gertrude Stein and Zora Neale Hurston.

4532. Oates, Stephen B. *Let the Trumpet Sound: A Life of Martin Luter King, Jr.* New York: Harper Perennial, pp. 128, 426.

4533. Oliver, Eileen Iscoff. *Crossing the Mainstream: Multicultural Perspectives in Teaching Literature*. Urbana, IL: National Council of Teachers of English, pp. 9, 33, 35, 39–40, 54, 56, 57, 70, 82, 84, 89, 139, 141, 172, 191, 205, 233. Pedagogical comments, mostly on *BB* and *NS*.

4534. Olney, James. "Richard Wright in the Library of America." *Partisan Review*, 61 (Summer), 518–528. Essay-review of the Library of America edition of W. Olney argues that W in his fiction as in his autobiography was always "writing the story of himself as a writer even as he wrote the stories of his various protagonists" (p. 521). And he did so with unexcelled masculine power. Olney endorses the new version of *NS*, but objects to combining *BB* and *AH*, for the former is "a book that is as central and as important as any in the whole of American literature" (p. 528).

4535. Otfinoski, Steven. "Charles Waddell Chesnutt: Father of Black American Fiction," in his *Great Black Writers*. New York: Facts on File, pp. 12–20. States that Chesnutt's "The Web of Circumstance" prefigured W "in its stark realism ... and tragic fatalism" (p. 16).

4536. _____. "Introduction," in his *Great Black Writers*. New York: Facts on File, pp. vii–ix. Mentions W and *NS*.

4537. _____. "James Baldwin: Keeper of America's Conscience," in his *Great Black Writers*. New York:

Facts on File, pp. 79–88. Biographical sketch mentioning W briefly.

4538. _____. "Langston Hughes: Dean of Black Writers," in his *Great Black Writers*. New York: Facts on File, pp. 32–43. Mentions W briefly.

4539. _____. "Richard Wright: Native Son and Novelist," in his *Great Black Writers*. New York: Facts on File, pp. 12–20. Biographical sketch emphasizing *BB* and *NS*. Claims that in the fifties Ellison and Baldwin "were quickly eclipsing Wright" (p. 74). Includes a chronology and brief bibliography.

4540. Over, William. "Hurston, Zora Neale," in *Encyclopedia of World Literature in the 20th Century*. Ed. Steven R. Serafin. Vol. 5. New York: Continuum, pp. 299–300. Mentions W briefly.

4541. Ozick, Cynthia. "Literary Blacks and Jews," in *Blacks and Jews: Alliances and Arguments*. New York: Delacorte, pp. 42–66.

4542. Parini, Jay. *John Steinbeck: A Biography*. London: Heinemann, p. 203. Mentions W briefly.

4543. Pearson, Norman Holmes. "American Literature: The 20th Century," in *The Encyclopedia Americana*. Ed. Lawrence T. Lorimer. Danbury, CT: Grolier, pp. 703–709.

4544. _____. "American Literature: The Twentieth Century," in *The Encyclopedia Americana*. Ed. Lawrence T. Lorimer. Danbury, CT: Grolier, pp. 703–709.

4545. Pedersen, Carl. "Sea Change: The Middle Passage and the Transatlantic Imagination," in *The Black Columbiad: Defining Moments in African American Literature and Culture*. Eds. Werner Sollors and Maria Diedrich. Harvard English Studies 19. Cambridge, MA: Harvard University Press, pp. 42–51. Mentions briefly W's response to Africa (p. 50).

4546. Perez, Vincent A. "'Islands of Hallucinations': Race and Popular Culture in Three Novels by Richard Wright." *Dissertation Abstracts International*, 54 (March), 3438-A. Study of popular culture in relation to race in *LT*, *NS*, and *O*.

4547. Perkins, Barbara, Robyn Warhol, and George Perkins. "Zora Neale Hurston (1891–1960)," in their *Women's Work: An Anthology of American Literature*. New York: McGraw-Hill, p. 818. Notes W's dismissal of *Their Eyes Were Watching God*.

4548. Perkins, George, and Barbara Perkins. "After the Second World War," in their *The American Tradition in Literature*. Eighth edition. Vol. II. New York: McGraw-Hill, pp. 1343–1352.

4549. _____. "Richard Wright (1908–1960)," in their *The American Tradition in Literature*. Eighth edition. Vol. II. New York: McGraw-Hill, p. 1334.

4550. _____. "Richard Wright (1908–1960)," in their *The American Tradition in Literature*. Eighth edition. Short edition. New York: McGraw-Hill, p. 1635.

4551. Peterson, Dale E. "Richard Wright's Long Journey from Gorky to Dostoevsky." *African American Review*, 28 (Fall), 375–387. Argues the strong influence of Gorky and Dostoevsky on W, first comparing *BB* to Gorky's *Childhood*, then *NS* and "The Man Who Lived Underground" to *Crime and Punishment*. With childhood experiences quite similar to Gorky's, W came to share his "faith in collectivist culture and social engineering," but Bigger's anguish, like Raskolnikov's, "is experienced as a human conundrum, not as a sociological formula."

4552. Portelli, Alessandro. "Appunti per un'introduzione," in his *La Linea del colore: saggi sulla cultura afroamericana*. Rome: Manifestolibri, pp. 7–10. Mentions briefly W and *NS* (pp. 7, 8).

4553. _____. "C'è sempre una fine: memoria storica, dialogo e racconto collettivo," in his *La linea del colore: saggi sulla cultura afroamericana*. Rome: Manifestolibri, pp. 41–55. Mentions briefly *NS*, W, Bigger Thomas, and Mary Dalton (p. 53).

4554. _____. "History-Telling and Time: An Example from Kentucky," in *History and Memory in African-American Culture*. Eds. Geneviève Fabre and Robert O'Meally. New York: Oxford University Press, pp. 164–177. Mentions briefly Mary Dalton (p. 175).

4555. _____. "Introduzione alla letterature Afro-Americana," in *Altri lati del mondo*. Ed. Maria Antonietta Saracino. Rome: Sensibili alle foglie, pp. 31–72. Topical treatment of African American literature. Mentions W and *NS* frequently and quotes from "The Ethics of Living Jim Crow" and "The Man Who Was Almost a Man."

4556. _____. "Lo sguardo, lo specchio e la maschera," in his *La linea del colore: saggi sulla cultura afroamericana*. Rome: Manifestolibri, pp. 13–25. Mentions briefly W and Bigger Thomas, and quotes briefly from "The Ethics of Living Jim Crow" (pp. 13, 15, 24).

4557. _____. "Malcolm X e l'uso della storia," in his *La linea del colore: saggi sulla cultura afroamericana*. Rome: Manifestolibri, pp. 121–131. Includes a brief comparison of Bigger Thomas and Malcolm X (p. 122).

4558. _____. "Narrazione della vita di Frederick Douglass, schiavo americano, scritta da lui stesso: un classico americano," in his *La linea del colore: saggi sulla cultura afroamericana*. Rome: Manifestolibri, pp. 77–97.

4559. _____. "The Power of Blackness:gli afroamericani, le machine e l'energia del sottosuolo." *Arcma*, 2 (Summer-Fall 1994), 22–34. Examines the concept and actuality of enclosure, blackness, machines vs. human beings, underground chambers, the black hole, etc. in African American culture, and applies these ideas to W, especially *NS*, "The Man Who Lived Underground," and "Big Boy Leaves Home."

4560. _____. "Risanamento e rivolta: destino e contesto critico di *Native Son*," in his *La linea del colore: saggi sulla cultura afroamericana*, pp. 231–241. Examines the issue of Bigger's self-empowerment at the end of *NS*. Valerie Smith countered the Baldwin-Ellison view that Bigger is only a victim by arguing that Bigger achieves an understanding of his life and death. Portelli believes that Bigger's self-knowledge is tentative and does not alter social circumstances. Portelli compares W's treatment of this issue with similar themes in Gerald Vizenor, N. Scott Momaday, Leslie Silko, James Welch, Harriet Jacobs, and Zora Neale Hurston.

4561. _____. "The Sky's the Limit: dove comincia e dove finiace l'America." *Acoma*, 1, no. 1. Includes a discussion of the imagery of walls in *NS*.

4562. _____. "Suono e senso in *Native Son* di Richard Wright," in his *La linea del colore: saggi sulla cultura afroamericana*. Rome: Manifestolibri, pp. 195–229. A stylistic and linguistic analysis of sound and

sense in *NS*, treating such categories as critical clusters onomatopoeia, articulation, lexicon, rhetoric, syntax, distribution, and liminality. Throughout Portelli argues that W's conscious artistry makes sound reinforce sense in *NS*. Translated with revisions: 1997.

4563. _____. *The Text and the Voice: Writing, Speaking, and Democracy in American Literature*. New York: Columbia University Press, pp. 89, 108, 109, 220, 222, 225, 247, 259, 332, 343, 354, 356.

4564. _____. This speech is very vital: Studiare il rap," in his *La linea del colore: saggi sulla cultura afroamericana*, pp. 175–182. Revised and expanded version of 1989.

4565. _____. Toni Morrison: il fantasma e la città," in *La linea del colore: saggi sulla cultura afroamericana*, pp. 167–174.

4566. _____. "Malcolm X e la Storia," in *Dialogo su Malcolm X*. Rome: Manifestolibri, pp. 7–18. Includes comments on the opening scene of *NS*.

4567. Potter, Joan. *African-American Firsts: Famous, Little-Known and Unsung Triumphs of Blacks in America*. Elizabethtown, NY: Pinto Press, pp. 152, 153, 156. Contains a biographical sketch and a photograph of W. Also mentions his friendship with Ellison.

4568. Powell, Richard J. "Art History and Black Memory: Toward a 'Blues Aesthetic,'" in *History and Memory in African-American Culture*. Eds. Geneviève Fabre and Robert O'Meally. New York: Oxford University Press, pp. 228–243. Mentions briefly "Big Boy Leaves Home" (p. 238).

4569. Pratt, Louis Hill. *"Ann Petry: A Bio-Bibliography*. By Hazel Arnett Ervin." *CLA Journal*, 38 (December), 261–264. Mentions W as one of Petry's favorite authors (p. 263).

4570. Pritchard, William H. "James Baldwin, 1924–1987," in *The Norton Anthology of American Literature*. Eds. Nina Baym, Wayne Franklin, Ronald Gottesman, Laurence B. Holland, David Kalstone, Arnold Krupat, Francis Murphy, Hershel Parker, Patricia B. Wallace, and Pritchard. Fourth edition, Volume 2. New York: W.W. Norton, pp. 2080–2081.

4571. _____. "Ralph Ellison, 1914–," in *The Norton Anthology of*

American Literature. Eds. Nina Baym, Wayne Franklin, Ronald Gottesman, Laurence B. Holland, David Kalstone, Arnold Krupat, Frances Murphy, Hershel Parker, Patricia B. Wallace, and Pritchard. Fourth edition. Vol.2. New York: W.W. Norton, pp. 1901–1903.

4572. _____. "Ralph Ellison, 1914–1994" in *The Norton Anthology of American Literature*. Eds. Nina Baym, Wayne Franklin, Ronald Gottesman, Laurence B. Holland, David Kalstone, Arnold Krupat, Francis Murphy, Hershel Parker, Patricia B. Wallace, and Pritchard. Shorter fourth edition. New York: W.W. Norton, pp. 2217–2218.

4573. Pryse, Marjorie. *Teaching with the Norton Anthology of American Literature, Fourth Edition: A Guide for Instructors*. New York: Norton, pp. 35, 37, 41, 58, 72, 223, 228, 285, 295, 296. Places W in various syllabi and literary traditions.

4574. Rabinowitz, Paula. "Barbara Foley. *Radical Representations: Politics and Form in U.S. Proletarian Fiction, 1929–1941*." *Modern Fiction Studies*, 40 (Summer), 365–367. Review mentioning W briefly.

4575. _____. "Langston Hughes 1902–1967," in *Black American Prose Writers of the Harlem Renaissance*. Ed. Harold Bloom. New York: Chelsea House, pp. 72–73.

4576. _____. "Melville and Race," in *Herman Melville: A Collection of Critical Essays*. Ed. Myra Jehlen. Englewood Cliffs, NJ: Prentice-Hall, pp. 160–173. Mentions W and *NS* in relation to Baldwin, Ellison, and LeRoi Jones (pp. 162, 163, 167, 168, and 171).

4577. Rampersad, Arnold. "Afterword," in *Rite of Passage* by Richard Wright. New York: Harper Collins, pp. 117–142. Relates the novella to W's prior works *NS, O, UTC, BB*, and *EM*,— as well as to W's interest in politics and psychology. Unlike his other worlds, *RP* includes "a black woman standing for the finest human qualities...." Also includes a brief chronology of W's life.

4578. Rampson, Nancy. "Literature," in *African America: Portrait of a People*. Ed. Kenneth Estell. Detroit: Visible Ink, pp. 257–302. Includes a biographical sketch of W (pp. 301–302). Comments on W and *NS* (pp. 260–261, with photograph). Mentions W briefly (pp. 266, 278, 297, 400).

4579. Ramsey, William M. "The Compelling Ambivalence of Zora Neale Hurston's *Their Eyes Were Watching God.*" *The Southern Literary Journal*, 27 (Fall), 36–50. Mentions W's unfavorable review of the novel (p. 46).

4580. Raper, Julius Rowan. "Willie Morris (1934) in *Contemporary Poets, Dramatists, Essayists, and Novelists of the South: A Bio-Bibliographical Sourcebook.* Eds. Robert Bain and Joseph M. Flora. Westport CT: Greenwood Press, pp. 377–387. Comments on Morris's friendship with W (pp. 381, 384–385).

4581. Redding, J. Saunders. "American Negro Literature," in *Within the Circle: An Anthology of African American Literary Criticism from the Harlem Renaissance to the Present.* Ed. Angelyn Mitchell. Durham, NC: Duke University Press, pp. 106–116.

4582. Reilly, Charlie. *Conversations with Amiri Baraka.* Jackson: University Press of Mississippi, pp. 118–129, 157–180.

4583. Reilly, John M. "Richard Wright 1908–1960," in *Black American Prose Writers of the Harlem Renaissance.* Ed. Harold Bloom. New York: Chelsea House, pp. 171–172.

4584. _____. "Critical Abstract," in *Black American Prose Writers of the Harlem Renaissance.* Ed. Harold Bloom. New York: Chelsea House, pp. 171–172.

4585. _____. "Wright, Richard (Nathaniel)," in *Reference Guide to American Literature.* Third edition. Ed. Jim Kamp. Detroit, St. James Press, pp. 936–937.

4586. Remnick, David. "Visible Man." *The New Yorker*, 70 (14 March), 34–38. Mentions W as a friend and mentor of Ellison (p. 36).

4587. Ro, Sigmund. "Coming of Age: The Modernity of Postwar Black American Writing," in *The Black Columbiad: Defining Moments in African American Literature and Culture.* Eds. Werner Sollors and Maria Diedrich. Harvard English Studies 19. Cambridge, MA: Harvard University Press, pp. 226–233. Emphasizes the intellectual legacy of Du Bois and W: "'double consciousness' and ... native sonship" (p. 226). W developed the perpective of a sensibility divided between Westerness and blackness.

4588. Roark, Chris. "Hamlet, Malcolm X, and the Examined Ed-

ucation." *The CEA Critic*, 57 (Fall), 111–122. Quotes from *O* (p. 118).

4589. Roberts, Diane. *Faulkner and Southern Womanhood.* Athens: The University of Georgia Press, p. 96. Quotes Marjorie Garber quoting from "Man of All Work."

4590. Robinson, Lillian S. "John A. Williams," in *Encyclopedia of World Literature in the 20th Century.* Ed. Steven R. Serafin. Vol. 5. New York: Continuum, pp. 636–637. Mentions briefly Williams's biography of W.

4591. Roe, T.G. "Black History and Culture: Selected References," in *Black American Culture and Society: An Annotated Bibliography.* Ed. S.T. Rustavo. Commack, NY: Nova Science, pp. 33–83. Lists the Library of America edition of W (p. 41).

4592. Roget, Gwendolyn Lewis. "Chester Himes — The Ethics of Ambiguity: An Interview with Joseph Sandy Himes, Jr." *Xavier Review*, 14 (Spring 1994), 1–18. Mentions W briefly (pp. 16, 17).

4593. Romine, Scott. "Framing Southern Rhetoric: Lillian Smith's Narrative Persona in *Killers of the Dream.*" *South Atlantic Review*, 59 (May), 95–111. Mentions briefly *BB* (pp. 109, 111).

4594. Rosenblatt, Roger. "Black Autobiography," in his *The Man in the Water: Essays and Stories.* New York: Random House, pp. 59–70. Includes discussion of *BB* and *NS*.

4595. _____. "Portrait of a Prisoner," in his *The Man in the Water: Essays and Stories.* New York: Random House, pp. 52–58. Discusses an inmate at Attica Prison who reads W.

4596. Rosenfelt, Deborah. "From the Thirties: Tillie Olsen and the Radical Tradition," in *The Critical Response to Tillie Olsen.* Eds. Kay Hoyle Nelson and Nancy Huse. Westport, CT: Greenwood Press, pp. 54–89.

4597. Rowell, Charles H., and Sterling Brown. "Critical Extract," in *Black American Prose Writers of the Harlem Renaissance.* Ed. Harold Bloom. New York: Chelsea House, pp. 22–23.

4598. Ruas, Charles. "Toni Morrison," in *Conversations with Toni Morrison.* Ed. Danille Taylor-Guthrie. Jackson: University Press of Mississippi, pp. 93–118.

4599. Rubeo, Ugo. "Voice as Life-

saver: Defining the Function of Orality in Etheridge Knight's Poetry," in *The Black Columbiad: Defining Moments in African American Literature and Culture.* Eds. Werner Sollors and Maria Diedrich. Harvard English Studies 19. Cambridge, MA: Harvard University Press, pp. 275–285. Quotes Knight speaking about W in an interview.

4600. Russell-Robinson, Joyce. "Renaissance Manqué: Black WPA Artists in Chicago." *The Western Journal of Black Studies*, 18 (Spring), 36–43. Examines W's leading role in the Chicago Renaissance, a literary, musical, and artistic movement closely associated with the WPA and also the Communist Party.

4601. Ryon, Roderick. "*Cities of the Heartland: The Rise and Fall of the Industrial Midwest.* By Jon C. Teaford." *The Journal of Negro History*, 79 (Summer), 306–307. Mentions briefly W and *NS*.

4602. Sánchez, Jesús Benito. "Amor, odio y violencia en la narrativa de James Baldwin," in *Amor, odio, y violencia en la literatura norteamericana.* Ed. José Antonio Gurpegui. Alcalá de Henares: Universidad de Alcalá de Henares, pp. 41–47. Includes discussion of Baldwin's attitude toward W's violence, with special reference to *Another Country* and *NS*.

4603. Sanders, Mark A. "Literary Art and Marxist Doctrine: Sustained Tensions in *Uncle Tom's Children.*" *Richard Wright Newsletter*, 3 (Spring/Summer), 8. Abstract of a CLA paper arguing that in *UTC* W both "advances and celebrates Marxist ideology" and simultaneously strives for an artistic freedom that subverts it.

4604. Sayre, Robert F. "Experimental Lives, 1920–1960," in his *American Lives: An Anthology of Autobiographical Writing.* Madison: University of Wisconsin Press, pp. 535–543. Includes comments on *BB* and *AH* (pp. 541–542) and a brief comparison of W and James Agee (p. 542).

4605. _____. "James Baldwin (1924–1990) *The Discovery of What It Means to Be an American,*" in his *American Lives: An Anthology of Autobiographical Writing.* Madison: University of Wisconsin Press, pp. 621–622. Headnote mentioning W briefly.

4606. _____. "Note on the Selection of Texts," in his *American Lives: An Anthology of Autobiographical Writing*. Madison: University of Wisconsin Press, pp. xi–xii. Mentions briefly *BB*.

4607. _____. "Richard Wright (1908–1960) from *The God That Failed*,"in his *Anthology of Autobiographical Writing*. Madison: University of Wisconsin Press, pp. 571–572. Headnote on W's autobiographical writing in general.

4608. Scharnhorst, Gary. "19th-Century Literature," in *American Literary Scholarship: An Annual/ 1992*. Ed. David J. Nordloh. Durham, NC: Duke University Press, pp. 177–209. Mentions W briefly (p. 209).

4609. Schmidt, Klaus. "*The Outsider's Vision:" Die Marginalitatsthematik in ausgewahlten Prosatexten der afro-amerikanischen Erzahltradition Richard Wrights Native Son, Toni Morrisons Sula and John Edgar Widemans Reuben*. Frankfurt am Main: Peter Lang, pp. 17, 43–44, 47, 48–49, 50, 51, 57–164, 165, 179, 182, 211, 213, 214, 215, 227, 253, 259, 298, 312, 323, 324. The long section on *NS* treats Bigger as a "destructive rebel in search of social integration." After reviewing relevant scholarship, Schmidt considers such topics as double consciousness, psychosocial marginalizing, the underground motif, the urban wasteland, the Job story, Bigger as absurd hero, marginality and sexuality, and others.

4610. Scholes, Robert, Nancy R. Comley, and Janice Peritz. *The Practice of Writing and Instructor's Manual to Accompany The Practice of Writing*. Fourth edition. New York: St. Martin's Press, pp. 24–25, 96–97. Quotes and comments on the first four paragraphs of "The Man Who Lived Underground" in a discussion of narration.

4611. Sekora, John. "The Legacy of Frederick Douglass." *African American Review*, 28 (Fall), 473–479. Mentions W briefly (p. 478).

4612. _____. "Lonne Elder III (1931–), in *Contemporary Poets, Dramatists, Essayists, and Novelists of the South: A Bio-Bibliographical Sourcebook*. Eds. Robert Bain and Joseph M. Flora. Westport, CT: Greenwood Press, pp. 152–160). Mentions briefly the screen version of *NS* (p. 156).

4613. Shankar, Subramanian.

"From hearts of darkness to temples of doom: The discursive economy of the travel narrative in the colonial context." *Dissertation Abstracts International*, 54 (February), 3021-A. Includes consideration of *BP*.

4614. Shanley, J. Lyndon. "Willa Cather's Fierce Necessity." *The Sewanee Review*, 102 (Fall), 620–630. Mentions W briefly (p. 621).

4615. Shannon, Sandra G. "Strong Men Getting Stronger: Gaines's Defense of the Elderly Black Male in *A Gathering of Old Men*," in *Critical Reflections on the Fiction of Ernest Gaines*. Athens: The University of Georgia Press, pp. 195–214. Mentions briefly Mary and Bigger among other "love-hate relationships between the white female and the black male" (p. 208).

4616. Shelton, Frank W. "Of Machines and Men: Pastoralism in Gaines's Fiction," in *Critical Reflections on the Fiction of Ernest J. Gaines*. Ed. David C. Estes. Athens: The University of Georgia Press, pp. 12–29. Compares treatments of W and Hurston by Werner Sollors and Hazel Carby before discussing *Their Eyes Were Watching God* and *UTC*. The latter emphasizes the negative qualities of black life in the South (pp. 16–19).

4617. Shibata, Noriko. "A Study of *Native Son*: Richard Wright's artificial reality." Literary Studies of the Graduate School at Seinan Gakuin University," 13 (January), 1–15. Observes that W was successful in making two worlds in *NS*: African American and White.

4618. Shohat, Ella, and Robert Stam. *Unthinking Eurocentrism: Multiculturalism and the Media*. London: Routledge, p. 234. Mentions briefly *NS*.

4619. Shulman, Robert. "Subverting and Reconstructing the Dream: The Radical Voices of Le Sueur, Herbst, and Wright," in *Deferring a Dream: Literary Sub-Versions of the American Columbiad*. Eds. Gert Buelens and Ernst Rudin. Basel: Birkhäuser Verlag, pp. 24–36. After brief consideration of *LT*, Shulman offers a full analysis of "Fire and Cloud" (pp. 29–36), showing how W reconciles black nationalism, the American Dream, and Popular Front ideology.

4620. Singh, Amritjit. "Afterword," in *The Color Curtain: A Report on the Bandung Conference*.

Jackson: University Press of Mississippi, pp. 223–245. Emphasizes the continuing relevance of W's insights on East-West relations, anticipating the work of Frantz Fanon and Edward Said. Places *CC* in the context of W's entire career, noting W's early curiosity about international matters and his other nonfiction of the 1950s.

4621. Smith, David Lionel. "Chicago Poets, OBAC, and the Black Arts Movement," in *The Black Columbiad: Defining Moments in African American Literature and Culture*. Eds. Werner Sollors and Maria Diedrich. Harvard English Studies 19. Cambridge, MA: Harvard University Press, pp. 253–264. Mentions W briefly (pp. 260, 262).

4622. Smith, Robert P., Jr. "*Richard Wright, Daemonic Genius, A Portrait of the Man: A Critical Look at His Work*. By Margaret Walker." *CLA Journal*, 38 (September), 115–120. Extremely favorable review.

4623. Smith Sidonie, "Critical Extract," in *Black America Women Fiction Writers*. Ed. Harold Bloom. New York: Chelsea House, pp. 5–6.

4624. Smith, Susan Belasco. *American Literature Association: Conference on American Literature, June 1–5*. Los Angeles: California State University, Los Angeles, p. 5. Lists a session on "Richard Wright in Theory and Practice: 21st Century Directions," chaired by Maryemma Graham with papers by Yvonne Robinson Jones, David Bradley, Donald I. Marshall, and Nelson Harrison.

4625. Smith, Valerie. "Gender and Afro-Americanist Literary Theory and Criticism," in *Within the Circle: An Anthology of African American Literary Criticism from the Harlem Renaissance to the Present*. Ed. Angelyn Mitchell. Durham, NC: Duke University Press, pp. 482–498.

4626. Solomon, Charlotte D. "*Native Son*," in *Academic American Encyclopedia*. Ed. Bernard S. Cayne. Danbury, CT: Grolier, vol. 14, p. 47.

4627. Sollors, Werner. "National Identity and Ethnic Diversity: 'Of Plymouth Rock and Jamestown and Ellis Island'; Redefinitions of 'America,'" in *History and Memory in African-American Culture*. Eds. Geneviève Fabre and Robert O'Meally. New York: Oxford University Press, pp. 92–121. Quotes from *TMBV* and comments on "Transcontinental" and *NS* affirming the American idea in contrast to his anti-American attitude beginning when he chose exile (pp. 112, 113–114).

4628. _____, and Maria Diedrich. "Conceiving Blackness," in their *The Black Columbiad: Defining Moments in African American Literature and Culture*. Harvard English Studies 19. Cambridge, MA: Harvard University Press, pp. 11–14. Notes that Michel Fabre is W's biographer.

4629. _____. "Introduction," in their *The Black Columbiad: Defining Moments in African American Literature and Culture*. Harvard English Studies 19. Cambridge, MA: Harvard University Press, pp. 1–8. Mentions W briefly (p. 7).

4630. _____. "Sources of Modern African American Cultural Authority," in their *The Black Columbiad: Defining Moments in African American Literature and Culture*. Harvard English Studies 19. Cambridge, MA: Harvard University Press, pp. 141–143. Comments on M. Lynn Weiss's article on *PS*.

4631. Solomon, Charlotte, D. "*Native Son*," in *Academic American Encyclopedia*. Danbury, CT: Grolier, 1994, Vol. 14, p. 47.

4632. Sommer, Constance. "Class Split by Uproar Over Reading Assignment." *Los Angeles Times* (4 April), Sec. A, pp. 3, 21. Reports a controversy over the assignment of *BB* in a Ventura County, California, high school honors class. Of sixty eight students in two sections, eleven are reading an alternative because of parental objections. Quotes parents on both sides of the issue, as well as Richard Yarborough.

4633. _____. "Passages in 'Black Boy' Raise Furor in Fillmore; Education: Some Parents Contend That Richard Wright's Book Contains Amoral, Violent Messages. Others Defend the Autobiography." *Los Angeles Times* (28 March), Metro Sec., Part B, p. 1. Quotes parents, the teacher Andrea Allen (who thinks "the book is wonderful"), Richard Yarborough, and *BB* itself. The episode concerning the killing of the kitten elicited strong objections. Eleven students objecting to *BB* are excused from class to read *My Antonia* in the school library.

4634. Spillers, Hortense J. "*The Crisis of the Negro Intellectual*: A Post-Date." *Boundary 2*, 21 (Fall), 64–116. Mentions W briefly (p. 67).

4635. _____. "*The Crisis of the Negro Intellectual: A Post-Date*. *Boundary 2*, 21 (Fall), 65–116. Mentions W briefly (p. 67).

4636. Stepto, Robert. "Intimate Things in Place: A Conversation with Toni Morrison," in *Conversations with Toni Morrison*. Ed. Danille Taylor-Guthrie. Jackson: University Press of Mississippi, pp. 10–29.

4637. Sterne, Richard Clark. *Dark Mirror: The Sense of Injustice in Modern European and American Literature*. New York: Fordham University Press, pp. 245, 247. Comments on an "uncertainty about ethical standards" in *NS*.

4638. Stewart, R. "McCall, Nathan. *Makes Me Wanna Holler: A Young Black Man in America*." *Choice*, 32 (September), 216. Review stating that "the book belongs to the same genre as Richard Wright's *Native Son*."

4639. Stuttaford, Genevieve. "*Exiled in Paris: Richard Wright, James Baldwin, Samuel Beckett and Their Circle on the Left Bank* by James Campbell." *Publishers Weekly*, 241 (12 December), 54. Review noting that the work deals with the quarrel between W and Baldwin.

4640. Tate, Linda. *A Southern Weave of Women: Fiction of the Contemporary South*. Athens: The University of Georgia Press, pp. 116, 118, 121, 129. Mentions briefly *NS* and *BB*.

4641. _____. *A Southern Weave of Women: Fiction of the Contemporary South*. Athens: The University of Georgia Press, pp. 116, 118, 121, 129. Comments on *NS* in contrast to *The Color Purple*.

4642. Taylor, John. "Exiled on the Left Bank." *TLS: The Times Literary Supplement*, No. 4775 (7 October), pp. 36–37. Favorable review of James Campbell's *Paris Interzone* including discussion of W.

4643. Travis, Molly Abel. "*Beloved* and *Middle Passage*: Race, Narrative and the Critic's Essentialism." *Narrative*, 2 (October), 180, 196. Comments on the Ellison-Howe controversy on W and W's unfavorable assessment of Hurston.

4644. Traylor, Eleanor. "Naming the UnNamed: African American Criticism and African American Letters." *Black Books Bulletin: WordsWork*, 16 (Winter 1993/1994), 64–75) Mentions briefly *NS*.

4645. Trimmer, Joseph F., and C. Wade Jennings, eds. "Richard Wright, 'The Man Who Was Almost a Man,'" in their *Fictions*, 3rd edition. Fort Worth: Harcourt Brace, p. 1226. Biographical headnote.

4646. Tuleja, Tad. *The New York Public Library Book of Popular Americana*. New York: Macmillan, p. 439. Brief biographical entry mentioning *NS*, *UTC*, *BB*, and *WML*.

4647. Turner, Patricia A. *Ceramic Uncles and Celluloid Mammies*. New York: Doubleday, pp. 85, 87. Mentions briefly W and *UTC*.

4648. Twombly, Robert C. "Harlem Renaissance," in *Collier's Encyclopedia*. Ed. Lauren S. Bahr. New York: P.F. Collier, vol. 11, pp. 654–655.

4649. Vahlkamp, Charles G. "An Overview of Two Film Versions of the Famous Novel *Native Son*." *Richard Wright Newsletter*, 3 (Spring/Summer), 7. Abstract of a Natchez Literary Celebration paper noting differences between the versions to illustrate "how social attitudes and aesthetic sensibilities change over time."

4650. Wald, Alan M. "Alfred Kazin in Retrospect," in his *Writing from the Left: New Essays on Radical Culture and Politics*. London: Verso, pp. 28–39.

4651. _____. "Belief and Ideology in the Work of Robert Hayden," in his *Writing from the Left: New Essays on Radical Culture and Politics*. London: Verso, pp. 192–198. Mentions W briefly (p. 192).

4652. _____. "Communist Writers Fight Back in Cold War Amerika," in his *Writing from the Left: New Essays on Radical Culture and Politics*. London: Verso, pp. 85–99. Mentions W briefly (p. 92).

4653. _____. "Communist Writers Fight Back in Cold War America," in *Styles of Cultural Activism: From Theory and Pedagogy to Women, Indians, and Communism*. Ed. Philip Goldstein. Newark: University of Delaware Press, pp.

4654. _____. "Culture and Commitment: U.S. Communist Writers Reconsidered," in his *Writing from the Left: New Essays on Radical Culture and Politics*. London: Verso, pp. 67–84.

4655. _____. "Foreword to the New Edition," in *Iron City*. By Lloyd L. Brown. Boston: Northeastern University Press, pp. vii–xxxviii.

4656. _____. "Introduction: The Marxist Literary Tradition in the United States," in his *Writing from the Left: New Essays on Radical Culture and Politics*. London: Verso, pp. 1–10. Mentions W briefly (pp. 2, 4, 9).

4657. _____. "John Sanford and 'America Smith,'" in his *Writing from the Left: New Essays on Radical Culture and Politics*. London: Verso, pp. 199–211. Mentions briefly *UTC*, (p. 202) and comments on *TMBV* (pp. 203, 210).

4658. _____. "The Legacy of Daniel Aaron," in his *Writing from the Left: New Essays on Radical Culture and Politics*. London: Verso, pp. 13–27.

4659. _____. "Literary 'Leftism' Reconsidered." *Science & Society*, 57 (Summer), 214–222. Mentions W briefly (p. 215).

4660. _____. "Literary 'Leftism' Reconsidered," in his *Writing from the Left: New Essays on Radical Culture and Politics*. London: Verso, pp. 144–151.

4661. _____. "Lloyd Brown and the African-American Left," in his *Writing from the Left: New Essays on Radical Culture and Politics*. London: Verso, pp. 212–232. Contains numerous references to W and Communism, mentioning "Bright and Morning Star," *AH*, *UTC*, and Margaret Walker's biography of W. Discusses "Blueprint for Negro Writing," *NS*, and "How Bigger Was Born."

4662. _____. "*Radical Representations: Politics and Form in U.S. Proletarian Fiction, 1929–1941*. By Barbara Foley." *American Literature*, 66 (December), 856–857. Mentions W briefly.

4663. _____. "The Subaltern Speaks," in his *Writing from the Left: New Essays on Radical Culture and Politics*. London: Verso, pp. 178–186.

4664. _____. "The 1930s Left in US Literature Reconsidered," in his *Writing from the Left: New Essays on Radical Culture and Politics*. London: Verso, pp. 100–113. Mentions W briefly (p. 102). Reprinted in revised form.

4665. Walker, Alice. "The Black Writer and the Southern Experience," in *A Writer's Reader*. Eds. Donald Hall and D.L. Emblen. Seventh edition. New York: HarperCollins, pp. 539–544.

4666. _____. "In Search of Our Mothers' Gardens," in *Within the Circle: An Anthology of African American Literary Criticism from the Harlem Renaissance to the Present*. Ed. Angelyn Mitchell. Durham, NC: Duke University Press, pp. 401–409.

4667. Walker, Margaret. "Richard Wright 1908–1960," in *Black American Prose Writers of the Harlem Renaissance*. Ed. Harold Bloom. New York: Chelsea House, pp. 170–171.

4668. Wall, Cheryl. "On Freedom and the Will to Adorn: Debating Aesthetics and/as Ideology in African American Literature," in *Aesthetics and Ideology*. Ed. George Levine. New Brunswick, NJ: Rutgers University Press, pp. 283–303. Analyzes W, especially in "Blueprint for Negro Literature [sic]," as an exponent of ideology and political struggle, in contrast to the aesthetic emphasis of Zora Neale Hurston. Alice Walker reconciles and subsumes both agendas, especially in her essays.

4669. Walther, Malin Lavon. "Re-Wrighting *Native Son*: Gwendolyn Brooks's Domestic Aesthetic in *Maud Martha*." *Tulsa Studies in Women's Literature*, 13 (Spring), 143–145. Contrasts W's violent treatment of the rat scene which opens *NS* to the soft treatment of the release of the mouse in chapter 17 of the Brooks novel.

4670. Ward, Jerry W., Jr. "Cinematic Ironies: *Native Son* on Literature and Film." *Richard Wright Newsletter*, 3 (Spring/Summer), 7. Abstract of a Natchez Literary Celebration paper calling *NS* a "hypertextual phenomenon" appearing in fictional, dramatic, and cinematic versions. "Our effort to understand *Native Son* becomes richly ironic as the cinema on the screen intersects with the cinema in our minds."

4671. _____. "Ishmael Reed (1938)," in *Contemporary Poets, Dramatists, Essayists, and Novelists of the South: A bio–Bibliographical Sourcebook*. Eds. Robert Bain and Joseph Flora. Westport, CT: Greenwood Press, pp. 407–417. Mentions W briefly (pp. 408–409, 412). Mentions W stressing Reed's difference.

4672. _____. "Report from Natchez Literary Celebration, June 2–4, 1994." *Richard Wright Newsletter*, 3 (Spring/Summer), 1. Emphasizes events with a W emphasis: lectures on the film *NS* and a showing of the 1987 film and clips from the 1951 version, a talk on his film *Black Boy* by Madison David Lacy, Jr., videotape of Governor William Winter presenting the first Richard Wright Literary Excellence Award to Eudora Welty, and Julia Wright's talk about "Black Boy's Children," noting that her father's "love made childhood a treasured period in her life."

4673. _____. "Voices: Racial Reading." *Southern Exposure*, 22 (Summer), 47–49. Includes photographs of W and Faulkner with the following caption: "Why do so many Southern conversations resemble debates between Richard Wright and William Faulkner?"

4674. Washington, Mary Helen. "'The Darkened Eye Restored': Notes Toward a Literary History of Black Women," in *Within the Circle: An Anthology of African American Literary Criticism from the Harlem Renaissance to the Present*. Ed. Angelyn Mitchell. Durham, NC: Duke University Press, pp. 442–453.

4675. Watkins, Mel. *On the Real Side: Laughing, Lying, and Signifying — the Underground Tradition of African-American Humor*. New York: Simon & Schuster, pp. 34, 402, 419, 424–426. Quotes from *BB*, notes W's criticism of Hurston, and quotes "genuine examples of African-American ghetto humor" from *NS* and *LT*.

4676. _____. "Talk with Toni Morrison," in *Conversations with Toni Morrison*. Ed. Danille Taylor-Guthrie. Jackson: University Press of Mississippi, pp. 43–47.

4677. _____. "The Relentless Prophet." *The New York Times Book Review* (15 May), p. 30. Review of David Leeming's *James Baldwin: A Biography* mentioning his early friendship with W.

4678. Watts, Jerry Gafio. *Heroism and the Black Intellectual: Ralph Ellison, Politics, and Afro-American Intellectual Life*. Chapel Hill: The University of North Carolina Press, pp. xi, 12, 16, 19, 26, 29, 38–45, 52, 54–55, 57–59, 66–71, 74, 86, 89–93, 107–108, 110, 119, 123, 129, 137, 138. Extended discussion of W as Ellison's early intellectual mentor, their disagreement over the function of literature, Ellison's "Richard Wright's Blues," W and the intellectual exchange between W and Ellison on freedom and oppression in black life, and other topics. A self-designated "Wright-man," Watts usually favors W's side on the issues raised.

4679. Webb, Constance. "Wright, Richard Nathaniel," in *Colliers Encyclopedia*. Ed. Lauren S. Bahr. New York: P.F. Collier, vol. 23, p. 638.

4680. Weiss, M. Lynn. "*Para Usted*: Richard Wright's *Pagan Spain*," in *The Black Columbiad: Defining Moments in African American Literature and Culture*. Eds. Werner Sollors and Maria Diedrich. Harvard English Studies 19. Cambridge, MA: Harvard University Press, pp. 212–225. Discusses the origin, reception, and meaning of *PS*. Notes W's poor Spanish and his perspective as a protest writer. Although an expatriate writing on a "pagan" European country, W places himself in American literary traditions, that of Washington Irving and Hemingway as a writer on Spain and that of Emerson and Whitman in asserting his freedom, his lack of inhibiting traditions, and his orientation toward the future.

4681. Werner, Craig Hansen. "Bigger's Blues: Native Son and the Articulation of Afro-American Modernism," in his *Playing the Changes: From Afro-Modernism to the Jazz Impulse*. Urbana: University of Illinois Press, pp. 183–211.

4682. _____. Black Blues in the City: The Voices of Gwendolyn Brooks," in his *Playing the Changes: From Afro-Modernism to the Jazz Impulse*. Urbana: University of Illinois Press, pp. 142–161. Quotes George Kent comparing *In the Mecca* and *NS* (p. 142).

4683. _____. Endurance and Excavation: Afro-American Responses to Faulkner," in his *Playing the Changes: From Afro-Modernism to the Jazz Impulse*. Urbana: University of Illinois Press, pp. 27–62.

4684. _____. James Baldwin: Politics and the Gospel Impulse," in his *Playing the Changes: From Afro-Modernism to the Jazz Impulse*. Urbana: University of Illinois Press, pp. 213–240.

4685. _____. "*Langston Hughes: critical perspectives past and present*,

ed. Henry Louis Gates and K.A. Appiah." *Choice*, 31 (January), 780. Review noting a contribution by W.

4686. _____. Leon Forrest and the AACM: The Jazz Impulse and the Chicago Renaissance," in his *Playing the Changes: From Afro-Modernism to the Jazz Impulse*. Urbana: University of Illinois Press, pp. 241–262. Includes comment on "The School of Wright," *NS*, the John Reed Club, the Southside Writers Group, and W's preface to *Black Metropolis*.

4687. _____. "On the Ends of Afro-Modernist Autobiography," in his *Playing the Changes: From Afro-Modernism to the Jazz Impulse*. Urbana: University of Illinois Press, pp. 84–100.

4688. West, Cornel. "Black Sexuality: The Taboo Subject," in his *Race Matters*. New York: Vintage/Random House, pp. 117–131.

4689. _____. "Horace Pippen's Challenge to Art Criticism," in his *Keeping Faith: Philosophy and Race in America*. New York: Routledge, pp. 55–66.

4690. _____. "Malcolm X and Black Rage," in his *Race Matters*. New York: Vintage/Random House, pp. 133–151.

4691. _____. "Malcolm X and Black Rage," in *Malcolm X: In Our Own Image*. Ed. Joe Wood. New York: Anchor/Doubleday, pp. 59–85.

4692. _____. "Nihilism in Black America," in his *Race Matters*. New York: Vintage/Random House, pp.

4693. Weston, Ruth D. *Gothic Traditions and Narrative Techniques in the Fiction of Eudora Welty*. Baton Rouge: Louisiana State University Press, p. 5. Briefly places *NS* in the Gothic tradition.

4694. White, Jack E. "The Beauty of Black Art." *Time*, 144 (10 October), 66–73. Mentions W briefly (p. 69).

4695. _____. "Between Two Worlds." *Time*, 143 (7 March), 68. Review of Nathan McCall's *Makes Me Want to Holler* and Brent Staples's *Parallel Time* mentioning W briefly.

4696. Whitehead, John W. "*Sacred Estrangement: The Rhetoric of Conversion in Modern American Autobiography*. By Peter A. Dorsey." *Christianity and Literature*, 43 (Winter), 251–252. Review mentioning briefly W and *BB*.

4697. Wideman, John Edgar. "Malcolm X: The Art of Autobiography," in *Malcolm X: In Our Own Image*. Ed. Joe Woods. New York: Anchor/Doubleday, pp. 101–116. Reprint of 1992.

4698. Wilentz, Gay. "Gayl Jones's Oraliterary Explorations." *African American Review*, 28 (Spring), 141–145. Quotes Jones mentioning W.

4699. Williams, John A. "John A. Williams interviews von Wolfgang Binder," in *Facing America: Multikulturelle Literatur der heutigen USA in Texten und Interviews: Ein Lesebuch*. Zurich: Rotpunktverlag, pp. 394–413. Mentions W briefly (pp. 395, 405, 409).

4700. Williams, Sherley Anne. "Some Implications of Womanist Theory," in *Within the Circle: An Anthology of African American Literary Criticism from the Harlem Renaissance to the Present*. Ed. Angelyn Mitchell. Durham, NC: Duke University Press, pp. 515–521.

4701. Williams, Ted. "In Memoriam: Ralph Ellison 1914–1994." *Richard Wright Newsletter*, 3 (Spring/Summer), 4. Notes Ellison's meeting W in New York and his relation to the *Richard Wright Newsletter*.

4702. Wills, Garry. "Sons and Daughters of Chicago." *The New York Review of Books*, 41 (9 June), 52–59. Includes a review of Carla Cappetti's *Writing Chicago* with a paragraph on W and sociology.

4703. Wixson, Douglas. *Worker-Writer in America: Jack Conroy and the Tradition of Midwestern Literary Radicalism, 1898–1990*. Urbana: University of Illinois Press, pp. 3, 72, 102, 177, 245, 300, 351, 355, 359, 360–361, 365, 378, 379, 380–381, 395, 397, 415, 422, 425, 440, 443, 454, 471, 477, 483, 486, 489, 530, 540, 552, 553, 574. The numerous mentions of W include previously unreported facts and opinions.

4704. Woodford, John. "The Pleasure of His Company: Two New Books Afford a Reappreciation of Richard Wright." *The Black Scholar*, 24 (Summer), pp. 51–56. Favorable review of *Conversations with Richard Wright* and *Rite of Passage*. The former demonstrates cogency, prescience, and persistence in analyzing social and racial issues. The latter is "a funky gruel, so foul and vibrant, hideous and humorous" (p. 56)."

4705. Wright, Julia. "*Black Boy—*

A Literary Cleansing?" *Richard Wright Newsletter*, 3 (Spring/Summer), 4–6. Comments on an effort to censor *BB* by religious fundamentalists in Ventura County, California. Because the effort centered on the cat-killing episode, Julia Wright explains its psychology as purgative (comparing *BB* to *Adventures of Huckleberry Finn* and to fairy tales), and notes her father's mature love of cats.

4706. _____. "Comment: Out of 'Blind Anger, Insight.'" *Los Angeles Times* (9 May), Sec. B, p. 4.

4707. _____. "Richard Wright: A Cinematic Life." *The Richard Wright Newsletter*, 3 (December), 2–3. Discusses W's film version of *NS*, the suitability of his life for cinematic treatment, and her role as consultant. Her assessment of the film is favorable with some reservations. She would have liked to see more comments by people who knew Wright personally.

4708. Wurst, Gayle. "Ben Franklin in Harlem: The Drama of De-ferral in Ann Petry's *The Street*," in *Deferring a Dream: Literary Subversions of the American Columbiad*. Eds. Gert Buelens and Ernst Rudin. Basel: Birkhäuser Verlag, pp. 1–23. Mentions briefly *NS* and its relation to Petry's novel (pp. 2, 20).

4709. Young, Stephen. "African American Studies: Literature." *The Society for the Study of Southern Literature Newsletter* (April), 10. Lists Jean-Francois Gounard's *The Racial Problem in the Works of Richard Wright and James Baldwin* and W's *Rite of Passage* with an afterword by Arnold Rampersad.

4710. _____. "African American Studies: Literature." *Society for the Study of Southern Literature Newsletter* (November), 10–11. Lists James Campbell's *Exiles in Paris: Richard Wright, James Baldwin, Samuel Beckett and Their Circle on the Left Bank*.

4711. _____. "Conference Notes." *The Society for the Study of Southern Literature Newsletter* (April), 5–6. Reports on W conferences in Jackson and Natchez Mississippi.

4712. _____. "People and Projects." *The Society for the Study of Southern Literature Newsletter* (April), 1–2. Reports that Jerry W. Ward, Jr., "wrote the introduction for the Harper Perennial edition (1993) of *Black Boy* (*American Hunger*).

4713. Young, Stephen Flinn. "African American Studies: Literature." *The Society for the Study of Southern Literature Newsletter*. 27 (April), 10. Lists *RP*.

4714. _____. "Conference Notes." *The Society for the Study of Southern Literature Newsletter*, 27 (April), 5–6. Announces W at the Natchez Literary Celebration, 2–4 June 1994, and plans for a research conference on W autobiography and biography in Jackson, Mississippi, in June 1995.

4715. Zinn, Howard. *You Can't Be Neutral on a Moving Train: A Personal History of Our Times*. Boston: Beacon Press, pp. 178, 199. Mentions briefly W and *BB*.

1995

4716. Abbott, Ruth, and Ira Simmons. "An Interview with Ishmael Reed," in *Conversations with Ishmael Reed*. Eds. Bruce Dicks and Amritjit Singh. Jackson: University Press of Mississippi, pp. 74–95.

4717. Adams, Janus. "July 27," in his *Glory Days: 365 Inspired Moments in African-American History*. New York: Harper Collins, p. [203]. A full-page commemoration of the WPA mentioning W briefly.

4718. Adams, Timothy Dow. "I Do Believe Him Though I Know He Lies: Lying as Genre and Metaphor in Richard Wright's *Black Boy*," in *Richard Wright: A Collection of Critical Essays*. Ed. Arnold Rampersad. Englewood Cliffs, NJ: Prentice-Hall, pp. 83–97.

4719. Adelson, Roger. "Interview with Darlene Clark Hine." *The Historian*, 57 (Winter), 259–274. Speaks of a "reading list" at Roosevelt University including W.

4720. Allen, Caffilene. "The World as Possibility: The Significance of Freud's *Totem and Taboo* in Ellison's *Invisible Man*." *Literature and Psychology*, 41 (Spring/Summer), 1–18. Mentions W briefly (p. 1).

4721. Anatol, Giselle. "*Ernest Gaines*. Valerie Melissa Babb." *MELUS*, 20 (Spring), 127–129. Mentions briefly *NS*.

4722. Andrews, Larry. "The Sensory Assault of the City in Ann Petry's *The Street*," in *The City in African-American Literature*. Eds. Yoshinobu Hakutani and Robert Butler. Madison/Teaneck, NJ: Fairleigh Dickinson University Press, pp. 196–211. Mentions briefly W and Bigger Thomas (pp. 197, 199).

4723. Anon. "Addison Gayle, Jr.," in *The Schomburg Center Guide to Black Literature from the Eighteenth Century to the Present*. Ed. Roger M. Valade III. Detroit: Gale Research,

p. 176. Mentions Gayle's biography of W.

4724. Anon. "Announcements." *Richard Wright Newsletter*, 4 (Spring/Summer), 3. Reports that Madison D. Lacy's *Richard Wright–Black Boy* won an Emmy for the Southeast Region in 1994, that *Rite of Passage* was "included on the Notable Children's Trade Books in the Field of Social Sciences for 1995 list," and that the Natchez Literary Celebration was held on 1–3 June 1995.

4725. Anon. *Bibliographic Guide to Black Studies: 1994*. New York: G.K. Hall, p. 390. Lists four primary items concerning W in the New York Public Library, supplementing the *Dictionary Catalog of the Schomburg Collection of Negro Literature and History*.

4726. Anon. "*Black Boy*," in *Merriam-Webster's Encyclopedia of Literature*. Ed. Kathleen Kuiper. Springfield, MA: Merriam-Webster, p.

144. Entry stating that the work is sometimes considered a fictionalized autobiography or an autobiographical novel because of its use of novelistic techniques.

4727. Anon. "*Black Boy: A Record of Childhood and Youth*, in *The Schomburg Center Guide to Black Literature from the Eighteenth Century to the Present*. Ed. Roger Valade. Detroit: Gale Research, p. 47. Emphasizes that *BB* is a record of "Southern black despair," but notes that Fabre suspects that it is "not entirely truthful."

4728. Anon. "*Black Boy: A Record of Childhood and Youth*," in *The Essential Black Literature Guide*. Ed. Roger M. Valade III. Detroit: Visible Ink Press, p. 39.

4729. Anon. "*The Black Columbiad*." *Collegium for African American Research Newsletter*, 4 (Winter), 10. Review listing the table of contents, including an essay on *PS* by M. Lynn Weiss.

4730. Anon. "*Black Fire*," in *The Schomburg Center Guide to Black Literature from the Eighteenth Century to the Present*. Ed. Roger M. Valade III. Detroit: Gale Research, pp. 47–48. Mentions W briefly.

4731. Anon. "*Black Fire*," in *The Essential Black Literature Guide*. Ed. Roger M. Valade III. Detroit: Visible Ink Press, pp. 39–40.

4732. Anon. "*The Book of Negro Folklore*," in *The Schomburg Center Guide to Black Literature from the Eighteenth Century to the Present*. Ed. Roger M. Valade III. Detroit: Gale Research, p. 59. Mentions W briefly as a contributor to the book.

4733. Anon. "*The Book of Negro Folklore*," in *The Essential Black Literature Guide*. Ed. Roger Valade III. Detroit: Visible Ink Press, p. 51.

4734. Anon. "Brief Mention." *American Literature*, 67 (September), 623–635. Includes notices of *The Black Columbiad* and *The City in African American Literature* mentioning W briefly (p. 632).

4735. Anon. "Brief Mention." *American Literature*, 67 (December), 897–907. Mentions *UTC* in a review of J. Gerald Kennedy's *Modern American Short Story Sequences: Composite Fictions and Fictive Communities* (p. 902) and contains notices of reprint editions of *SH* and *CC* (pp. 904–905).

4736. Anon. "*Brotherman—The Odyssey of Black Men in America*

edited by Herb Boyd and Robert L. Allen." *The Black Scholar*, 25 (Winter), 56. Favorable review mentioning W briefly.

4737. Anon. "Calls for Papers for 1995 Convention in Chicago." *MLA Newsletter*, 27 (Spring), 8–27. Mentions W as a possible topic for a session on "Black Literary and Cultural Nationalism(s)" (p. 8) and proposes a session on "Down South, Up South: Richard Wright and the South" (p. 16).

4738. Anon. "Chronology," in *The Schomburg Center Guide to Black Literature from the Eighteenth Century to the Present*. Ed. Roger M. Valade III. Detroit: Gale Research, pp. xv–xxvi. Lists W's birth and death, as well as the publication of *NS* and *BB*.

4739. Anon. *Comprehensive Dissertation Index 1994 Supplement, Volume 4*. Ann Arbor: UMI, p. 491. Lists dissertations treating W by William Maxwell, Subramaniam Shankhar.

4740. Anon. "LIT." *Contemporary Literature*, 36 (Fall), following p. 569. Advertisement for the journal LIT mentioning an article on W and Morrison by Kimberly Drake.

4741. Anon. "*Dark Symphony: Negro Literature in America*," in *The Schomburg Center Guide to Black Literature from the Eighteenth Century to the Present*. Ed. Roger M. Valade III. Detroit: Gale Research, p. 120. Notes that W is included in a section of "Major Authors."

4742. Anon. "*Dark Symphony: Negro Literature in America*," in *The Essential Black Literature Guide*. Ed. Roger M. Valade III. Detroit: Visible Ink Press, p. 103.

4743. Anon. "Detailed Schedule of Events." *South Atlantic Review*, 60 (September), 15–67. South Atlantic Modern Language Association program including a session on "Down South, Up South: Richard Wright and the South" chaired by Virginia Whatley Smith with papers by Mary Kemp Davis and Warren Carson.

4744. Anon. "Dorothy West," in *The Schomburg Center Guide to Black Literature from the Eighteenth Century to the Present*. Ed. Roger M. Valade. Detroit: Gale Research, p. 471. Mentions W briefly.

4745. Anon. "Dorothy West," in *The Essential Black Literature Guide*. Ed. Roger M. Valade III. Detroit: Visible Ink Press, pp. 375–376.

4746. Anon. "E. Ethelbert Miller," in *The Schomburg Center Guide to Black Literature from the Eighteenth Century to the Present*. Ed. Roger M. Valade III. Detroit: Gale Research, p. 295. Mentions Miller's *Voice of a Native Son: The Poetics of Richard Wright*, actually written by Eugene E. Miller.

4747. Anon. "Ellison, Ralph," in *Merriam-Webster's Encyclopedia of Literature*. Ed. Kathleen Kuiper. Springfield, MA: Merriam-Webster, p. 374. Mentions W briefly.

4748. Anon. "The God That Failed." *Performing Arts: Music Center of Los Angeles County*, November, p. 5. Quotes from W's contribution to the Crossman book.

4749. Anon. *Index to Black Periodicals: 1993*. New York: G.K. Hall, p. 377. Lists two items on W.

4750. Anon. "Invited One-Time-Only Session." *SAMLA News*, 16 (January), 10. Announcement of a session on "'Down South, Up South': Richard Wright and the South" at the annual convention of the South Atlantic Modern Language Association in Atlanta, 3–5 November. Chair is Virginia Whatley Smith.

4751. Anon. "John A. Williams," in *The Schomburg Center Guide to Black Literature from the Eighteenth Century to the Present*. Ed. Roger M. Valade III. Detroit: Gale Research, pp. 478–479. Mentions briefly Williams's biography of W.

4752. Anon. "John A. Williams," in *The Essential Black Literature Guide*. Ed. Roger Valade III. Detroit: Visible Ink Press, pp. 381–382.

4753. Anon. *Literature & Language: Books for Courses 1994/1995*. New York: Dutton/Signet, pp. 38, 40. Includes notices of *The Signet Classic Book of Southern Short Stories*, containing "Big Boy Leaves Home," and *Growing Up in the South: An Anthology of Modern Southern Literature*, containing "The Man Who Was Almost a Man."

4754. Anon. "LIT." *Contemporary Literature*, 36 (Fall), following p. 569. Advertisement for the journal LIT. Mentioning an article on W and Morrison by Kimberly Drake.

4755. Anon. *Literature & Theatre 1995*. Westport, CT: Greenwood, pp. 6, 17. Lists *The Critical Response to Richard Wright* and *The Racial Problem in the Works of Richard Wright and James Baldwin*.

4756. Anon. *"Living Our Stories, Telling Our Truths."* Callaloo, 18 (Spring), p. 416. Publisher's advertisement noting that W is treated in this book by V.P. Franklin.

4757. Anon. *"The Man Who Cried I Am,"* in *The Schomburg Center Guide to Black Literature from the Eighteenth Century to the Present.* Ed. Roger M. Valade III. Detroit: Gale Research, p. 281. Notes that the character Harry Ames is based on W.

4758. Anon. "Margaret Walker," in *The Schomburg Center Guide to Black Literature from the Eighteenth Century to the Present.* Ed. Roger M. Valade. Detroit: Gale Research, pp. 464–465. Mentions Walker's friendship with W and her book on him.

4759. Anon. "Margaret Walker," in *The Essential Black Literature Guide.* Ed. Roger M. Valade. Detroit: Visible Ink Press, pp. 371–372.

4760. Anon. "Mississippi." *American Literature,* 67 (March), [207]. Publisher's advertisement listing new editions of *Savage Holiday* and *The Color Curtain* with afterwords by Gerald Early and Amritjit Singh respectively.

4761. Anon. "Mississippi." *Contemporary Literature,* 36 (Summer), [397]. Advertisement for the University Press of Mississippi listing *SH* with an afterword by Gerald Early.

4762. Anon. "Mississippi." *The Southern Register* (Winter), p. 14. Contains a publisher's notice of new editions of *SH* and *CC.*

4763. Anon. *"Native Son,"* in *The Essential Black Literature Guide.* Ed. Roger M. Valade III. Detroit: Visible Ink Press, pp. 269–270.

4764. Anon. *"Native Son,"* in *A Reader's Guide to the Twentieth-Century Novel."* Ed. Peter Parker. New York: Oxford University Press, pp. 238–239. Plot summary followed by a critical note praising the structure and characterization of Bigger in the novel.

4765. Anon. *"Native Son,"* in *Merriam-Webster's Encyclopedia of Literature.* Ed. Kathleen Kuiper. Springfield, MA: Merriam-Webster, p. 799. Entry emphasizing the novel's violence.

4766. Anon. *"Native Son,"* in *The Schomburg Center Guide to Black Literature from the Eighteenth Century to the Present.* Ed. Roger M.

Valade III. Detroit: Gale Research, pp. 312–313. Plot summary of the book "considered by most critics to be Richard Wright's best work."

4767. Anon. *"Native Son* by Richard Wright." *Book-of-the-Month Club News,* September, p. 31. Notice consisting of a favorable judgment by James Baldwin.

4768. Anon. "New from Greenwood Press." *PMLA,* 110 (March), 326. Contains a publisher's notice of *The Critical Response to Richard Wright* edited by Robert J. Butler.

4769. Anon. *"Nobody Knows My Name,"* in *The Schomburg Center Guide to Black Literature from the Eighteenth Century to the Present.* Ed. Roger M. Valade III. Detroit: Gale Research, pp. 323–324. Mentions briefly Baldwin's essay on W, "Alas, Poor Richard."

4770. Anon. *"Nobody Knows My Name: More Notes of a Native Son,"* in *The Essential Black Literature Guide.* Ed. Roger M. Valade III. Detroit: Visible Ink Press, p. 277.

4771. Anon. *"Notes of a Native Son,"* in *The Schomburg Center Guide to Black Literature from the Eighteenth Century to the Present.* Ed. Roger M. Valade III. Detroit: Gale Research, p. 324. Mentions Baldwin's comparison of Wright and Harriet Beecher Stowe.

4772. Anon. *"Notes of a Native Son,"* in *The Essential Black Literature Guide.* Ed. Roger M. Valade. Detroit: Visible Ink Press, pp. 278–279.

4773. Anon. "Now in Paperback: *Sweet Home."* Callaloo, 18 (Spring), p. [540]. Publisher's advertisement for the book by Charles Scruggs. Mentions W briefly.

4774. Anon. "Publications Relating to Mississippi." *The Journal of Mississippi History,* 57 (February), 91–92. Lists an article on "The Man Who Lived Underground" by Yoshinobu Hakutani.

4775. Anon. "Publications Relating to Mississippi." *The Journal of Mississippi History,* 57 (Fall), 267–269. Lists an article on *The Color Curtain* by Jeffrey J. Folks.

4776. Anon. "Racism," in *The Essential Black Literature Guide.* Ed. Roger M. Valade III. Detroit: Visible Ink Press, pp. 304–305.

4777. Anon. "Racism," in *The Schomburg Center Guide to Black Literature from the Eighteenth Century to the Present.* Ed. Roger M.

Valade III. Detroit: Gale Research, pp. 378–379. Includes comments on *NS* and the protest tradition.

4778. Anon. "Ralph Ellison," in *The Essential Black Literature Guide.* Detroit: Visible Ink Press, pp. 129–130.

4779. Anon. "Ralph Ellison," in *The Schomburg Center Guide to Black Literature from the Eighteenth Century to the Present.* Ed. Roger M. Valade III. Detroit: Gale Research, pp. 150–151. Mentions W's early influence on Ellison.

4780. Anon. "Recent Publications." *Richard Wright Newsletter,* 4 (Spring/Summer), 4. Annotated listings of books edited by Robert J. Butler and Arnold Rampersad and articles by Mark J. Madigan and Christopher Z. Hobson.

4781. Anon. "Recent Scholarship: African Americans." *The Journal of American History,* 82 (June), 392–395. Lists an article by Roosevelt Williams treating W and others (p. 394).

4782. Anon. "Recent Scholarship: Intellectual and Cultural History." *The Journal of American History,* 82 (June), 409–413. Lists an article on *CC* by Jeffrey Folks (p. 410).

4783. Anon. "Regional Roundup." *Southern Register,* Summer, p. 22. Announces a special *Mississippi Quarterly* issue on "International Perspectives on Richard Wright" and solicits contributions.

4784. Anon. "Richard Wright," in *American Diversity, American Identity: The Lives and Works of 145 Writers Who Define the American Experience.* Ed. John D. Roth. New York: Henry Holt, pp. 353–357. Reference entry listing W's works, sketching his life, and analyzing *LT* and *NS.* W "gives American literature its strongest statement of the existential theme of alienated humanity defining itself. Includes a brief secondary bibliography.

4785. Anon. "Richard Wright," in *American Diversity, American Identity.* New York: Henry Holt, pp. 353–356. Provides biographical information and analyses of *LT* and *NS,* Assesses favorably W's literary achievement and the relentless integrity" of his vision. Also provides a brief bibliography.

4786. Anon. "Richard Wright," in *The Essential Black Literature Guide.* Ed. Roger M. Valade III. Detroit: Visible Ink Press, pp. 387–388.

4787. Anon. "Richard Wright," in *The Schomburg Center Guide to Black Literature from the Eighteenth Century to the Present.* Ed. Roger M. Valade III. Detroit: Gale Research, pp. 485–486. Biographical-critical sketch mentioning most of W's works. Calls W "an essential figure … one of the most powerful writers of the twentieth century."

4788. Anon. "'Richard Wright—Black Boy' National Teleconference." *English Journal*, 84 (October), 117. Announces the teleconference hosted by Jerry Ward on 4 October.

4789. Anon. "*Rite of Passage*," in *Daedalus Books Fall 1995* (Hyattsville, MD: Daedalus Books), p. 26. Bookseller's favorable notice.

4790. Anon. "Slave Narrative," in *The Essential Black Literature Guide.* Ed. Roger M. Valade III. Detroit: Visible Ink Press, p. 336.

4791. Anon. "Slave Narrative," in *The Schomburg Center Guide to Black Literature from the Eighteenth Century to the Present.* Ed. Roger M. Valade III. Detroit: Gale Research, pp. 418–419. Mentions briefly the influence of the slave narrative on W. Reprinted: 1995.

4792. Anon. "*Soul on Ice*," in *The Essential Black Literature Guide.* Ed. Roger Valade III. Detroit: Visible Ink Press, pp. 341–342. Reprint of 1995.

4793. Anon. "*Soul on Ice*," in *The Schomburg Center Guide to Black Literature from the Eighteenth Century to the Present.* Ed. Roger M. Valade III. Detroit: Gale Research, pp. 423–424. Mentions briefly W's influence on Eldrige Cleaver. Reprinted: 1995.

4794. Anon. "Timeline," in *The Essential Black Literature Guide.* Ed. Roger M. Valade III. Detroit: Visible Ink Press, pp. 393–407. Reprint of 1995.

4795. Anon. "Toni Morrison." *The Georgia Review*, 49 (Spring), 315–317. Notes that *NS* was the main selection of the Book-of-the-Month Club in 1940.

4796. Anon. *Transatlantic Passages.* Tenerife, Spain: Universidad de la Laguna, p. [6]. Conference program of the Collegium for African American Research listing a plenary lecture by Michel Fabre on "'What Is Africa to Me': Richard Wright and the Gold Coast."

4797. Anon. "Toni Morrison." *The Georgia Review*, 49 (Spring), 315–317. Notes that *NS* was the main selection of the Book-of-the-Month Club in 1940.

4798. Anon. "Treasure Classics from Book-of-the-Month Club." *Book-of-the-Month Club News*, Holiday, p. 42. Contains a notice of *NS* with a quotation from James Baldwin.

4799. Anon. "*Uncle Tom's Children*," in *Merriam-Webster's Encyclopedia of Literature.* Ed. Kathleen Kuiper. Springfield, MA: Merriam-Webster, pp. 1147–1148. Entry mentioning each of the novellas and the additions to the 1940 edition.

4800. Anon. "WPA Federal Writers' Project," in *Merriam-Webster's Encyclopedia of Literature.* Ed. Kathleen Kuiper. Springfield, MA: Merriam-Webster, p. 1215. Mentions W briefly.

4801. Anon. "Wright, Richard (1908–1960)," in *A Reader's Guide to the Twentieth-Century Novel.* Ed. Peter Parker. New York: Oxford University Press, p. 723. Very brief biographical sketch.

4802. Anon. "Wright, Richard," in *Merriam-Webster's Encyclopedia of Literature.* Ed. Kathleen Kuiper. Springfield, MA: Merriam-Webster, p. 1216. Biographical entry mentioning *UTC, NS, EM, O, WML,* and *AH.*

4803. Appiah, Kwame Anthony. "A Long Way from Home: Wright in the Gold Coast," in *Richard Wright: A Collection of Critical Essays.* Ed. Arnold Rampersad. Englewood Cliffs, NJ: Prentice Hall, pp. 188–201.

4804. Asman, Kevin G. "Marxism and the Critique of Communism in Richard Wright's *Native Son*." *Research & Society*, 8, 2–13. Though critical of the Communist Party, W embraced Marxist thought in his early career. This essay explores the novel's "critique of Communism and its relationship to Marxist theory by explicating the course of Bigger's revolutionary development" (p. 4). Asman focuses on the planned robbery of Blum, Bigger's relation to Mary as a hired provider of labor, his relation to Bessie, and his inability to achieve self-determination because he is determined by social and, especially, economic forces.

4805. Atkinson, Michael. "Richard Wright's 'Big Boy Leaves Home' and a Tale from Ovid: A Metamor-phosis Transformed." *Richard Wright: A Collection of Critical Essays.* Ed. Arnold Rampersad. Englewood Cliffs, NJ: Prentice Hall, pp. 129–139.

4806. Awkward, Michael. "Authorial Dreams of Wholeness: (Dis) Unity, (Literary) Parentage, and *The Women of Brewster Place*," in *Gloria Naylor: Critical Perspectives Past and Present.* Eds. Henry Louis Gates, Jr., and K.A. Appiah. New York: Amistad, pp. 37–69.

4807. _____. *Negotiating Difference: Race, Gender, and the Politics of Positionality.* Chicago: University of Chicago Press, pp. 27, 67, 69, 217–218. Mentions W briefly. Comments on and quotes from *BB* (pp. 217–218).

4808. Badt, Karin Luisa. "The Roots of the Body in Toni Morrison: A *Mater* of 'Ancient Properties.'" *African American Review*, 29 (Winter), 567–577. Mentions W briefly (p. 576).

4809. Bair, Deirdre, *Anaïs Nin: A Biography.* New York: G.P. Putnam's Sons, pp. 268, 326, 382. Relates that Nin saw the play *NS* and played up to W at a dinner party. In her diary she wrote that W "wanted to take her to France with him."

4810. Baker, Houston, A., Jr. "Critical Memory and the Black Public Sphere," in *The Black Public Sphere.* Ed. The Black Public Sphere Collective. Chicago: The University of Chicago Press, pp. 5–38. Comments on *NS*, comparing Bigger to the Black Panther Leader Fred Hampton (p. 31).

4811. Baldwin, James. "Richard Wright, 1908–1960," in *Major Black American Writers Through the Harlem Renaissance.* Ed. Harold Bloom. New York: Chelsea House, pp. 175–177.

4812. Bandler, Michael J. "Portrait of a Man Reading," in *Conversations with Chester Himes.* Eds. Michel Fabre and Robert E. Skinner. Jackson: University Press of Mississippi, pp. 108–111.

4813. Baraka, Amiri. "In the Tradition," in his *Transbluency: The Selected Poems of Amiri Baraka/LeRoi Jones (1961–1995).* Ed. Paul Vangelisti. New York: Marsilio, pp. 199–210.

4814. *Barat Review.* "A Dialogue with His Audience," in *Conversations with Ralph Ellison.* Eds. Maryemma Graham and Amritjit Singh.

Jackson: University Press of Mississippi, pp. 136–140.

4815. Basie, Count. *Good Morning Blues: The Autobiography of Count Basie as Told to Albert Murray.* New York: Da Capo Press, pp. 250–251.

4816. Bass, Barbara K. "Balm in Gilead: A Jewish Woman Looks at Race and Gender." *The Zora Neale Hurston Forum,* 9 (Spring/Fall), 28–34. Mentions W briefly (p. 32).

4817. [Baym, Nina]. "American Literature Before the Wars, 1914–1945," in *The Norton Anthology of American Literature.* Shorter fourth edition. Eds. Nina Baym, Ronald Gottesman, Laurence B. Holland, David Kalstone, Arnold Krupat, Francis Murphy, Hershel Parker, William H. Pritchard, and Patricia B. Wallace. New York: W.W. Norton, pp. 1709–1720.

4818. _____. "Richard Wright, 1908–1960," in *The Norton Anthology of American Literature.* Eds. Baym, Wayne Franklin, Ronald Gottesman, Laurence B. Holland, David Kalstone, Arnold Krupat, Francis Murphy, Hershel Parker, William H. Pritchard, and Patricia B. Wallace. Shorter fourth edition. New York: W.W. Norton, pp. 1741–1742.

4819. Baym, Nina, and Laurence B. Holland. "American Literature Between the Wars, 1914–1945," in *The Norton Anthology of American Literature.* Eds. Nina Baym, Ronald Gottesman, Laurence B. Holland, Francis Murphy, Hershel Parker, William H. Pritchard, David Kalstone, and Patricia B. Wallace. Shorter fourth edition. New York: W.W. Norton, pp. 1709–1720.

4820. Beauford, Fred. "A Conversation with Ernest J. Gaines," in *Conversations with Ernest Gaines.* Ed. John Lowe. Jackson: University Press of Mississippi, pp. 16–24.

4821. Beavers, Herman. *Wrestling Angels Into Song: The Fictions of Ernest J. Gaines and James Alan McPherson.* Philadelphia: University of Pennsylvania Press, pp. 15, 20, 22, 29, 40–41, 42, 130, 171–172, 178, 221, 222, 229, 239, 245, 248, 253. Comments on Ellison's attitudes toward W, notes that Gaines distances himself from W, and suggests that "A Sense of Story" may be McPherson's rewriting of the "Fate" secton of *NS* and that Gaines does the same in *A Lesson Before Dying.* Mentions

"The Man Who Lived Underground," "The Ethics of Living Jim Crow," *BB, UTC,* Bigger, Cross Damon, and "Fire and Cloud."

4822. Beckner, Chrisanne. *1000 African-Americans Who Shaped American History.* San Francisco: Bluewood Books, pp. 7, 76, 92. Includes a biographical sketch of W (p. 76) and mentions W elsewhere.

4823. _____. "Richard Wright, 1908–1960," in her *100 African Americans Who Shaped American History.* San Francisco: Bluewood Books, p. 76. Biographical sketch.

4824. Bellow, Saul. "Preface," in *The Collected Essays of Ralph Ellison.* Ed. John F. Callahan. New York: The Modern Library, pp. ix–xii. Mentions W briefly (p. x).

4825. Belton, Don. "Our father's thoughts come shining down," in *Speak My Name: Black Men on Masculinity and the American Dream.* Boston: Beacon Press, p. [v]. Dedication to W and numerous others.

4826. Benoist, Mary Anne, "Major Authors and Poets." *The Society for the Study of Southern Literature Newsletter,* 29 (November), 10. Lists a book on W by Robert J. Butler and new editions of *PS* and *WML.*

4827. Benoist, Mary Anne. "Paperbacks and Reprints." *The Society for the Study of Southern Literature Newsletter,* 29 (November), 19. Lists *CC.*

4828. Bergland, Betty. "*Domestic Allegories of Political Desire: The Black Heroine's Texts at the Turn of the Century.* Claudia Tate." *MELUS,* 20 (Summer), 152–157. Mentions briefly *BB* (p. 155).

4829. Bernstein, Richard. "Ralph Ellison Essays Receive Elegant attention." *Omaha Sunday World Herald* (31 December). Review discussing the Howe-Ellison debate over W.

4830. Berry, Faith. "Introduction to the Harper Perennial Edition," in *Pagan Spain.* By Richard Wright. New York: HarperCollins, pp. ix–xxvii. Praises W's venturesome spirit in *PS,* but notes numerous errors of fact and interpretation.

4831. Bérubé, Michael. "Public Academy." *The New Yorker,* 70 (9 January), 73–80. Mentions W briefly (p. 74)

4832. Binder, Wolfgang, and John A. Williams. "John A. Williams," in *American Contradictions: Interviews with Nine American Writers.* Eds.

Wolfgang Binder and Helmbrecht Breinig. Hanover, NH: University Press of New England, pp. 166–184. In this interview Williams compares the antipathy to books in his own family to that in W's (pp. 169–170) and mentions W elsewhere.

4833. Bloom, Harold, "Richard Wright, 1908–1960," in his *Major Black American Writers Through the Harlem Renaissance.* New York: Chelsea House, pp. 170–171. Biographical and bibliographical sketch.

4834. Bobo, Jacqueline. *Black Women as Cultural Readers.* New York: Columbia University Press, p. 194. Mentions briefly *O.*

4835. Bogarad, Carley Rees, and Jan Zlatnik Schmidt. "Explorations of the Text," Journal Entries, Ideas for Writing," in their *Legacies:* Fiction, Poetry, Drama, *Nonfiction.* Fort Worth: Harcourt Brace, p. 106. Study aids for The Man Who Was Almost a Man."

4836. _____. "*The Man Who Was Almost a Man* Richard Wright," in their *Legacies: Fiction, Poetry, Drama, Nonfiction.* Fort Worth: Harcourt Brace College, p. 96. Headnote to "The Man Who Was Almost a Man."

4837. _____. "Richard Wright," in their *Legacies: Fiction, Poetry, Drama, Nonfiction.* Fort Worth: Harcourt Brace College, p. 96. Biographical headnote to "The Man Who Was Almost a Man."

4838. Boggs, Grace Lee. "C.L.R. James: Organizing in the U.S.A., 1938–1953," in *C.L.R. James: His Intellectual Legacies.* Eds. Selwyn R. Cudjoe and William E. Cain. Amherst: University of Massachusetts Press, pp. 163–172. Mentions briefly Constance Webb and her book on W (p. 164).

4839. Bondi, Victor, Darren Harris-Fain, and James W. Hipp. "Media," in *American Decades: 1930–1939.* Ed. Victor Bondi. Detroit: Gale Research, pp. 339–380. Mentions W briefly (p. 346).

4840. Bone, Robert [Critical Extract], in *Black American Women Fiction Writers.* Ed. Harold Bloom. New York: Chelsea House, pp. 62–63.

4841. Bonnemère, Yves. "*The African Americans,* edited by David Cohen and Charles M. Collins." *Afram Newsletter,* No. 41 (June), pp. 28–29. Mentions briefly *NS.*

4842. Bontemps, Arna. "Review

of *The Outsider*," in *The Critical Response to Richard Wright*. Ed. Robert J. Butler. Westport, CT: Greenwood, Press, pp. 105–107.

4843. Borus, Daniel H. "*Writing Chicago: Modernism, Ethnography, and the Novel*." By Carla Capetti. *The Journal of American History*, 81 (March 1995, 1796–1797. Mixed review of a book "by turns smart and frustrating." Claims that "demonstrating the sociological of W's work does not completely negate the "Anti-African Americanist" interpretation."

4844. Bower, Anne L. "Sharing Responsibility for American Lit: 'A Spectacular and Dangerous World of Choice,'" in *The Canon in the Classroom: The Pedagogical Implications of Canon Revision in American Literature*. Ed. John Alberti. New York: Garland, pp. 221–240. Mentions briefly "The Man Who Was Almost a Man" (p. 228).

4845. Bowman, John S., ed. *The Cambridge Dictionary of American Biography*. Cambridge: Cambridge University Press, p. 221. Contains an entry on Ellison mentioning W briefly.

4846. _____, ed. *The Cambridge Dictionary of American Biography*. Cambridge: Cambridge University Press, p. 815. Contains an entry on W.

4847. Boyd, Herb, and Robert L. Allen. "About the Contributors," in their *Brotherman: The Odyssey of Black Men in America—An Anthology*. New York: Ballantine Books, pp. 887–915. Contains a biographical note on W (p. 915).

4848. _____. "Introduction," in their *Brotherman: The Odyssey of Black Men in American—An Anthology*. New York: Ballantine Books, pp. xxi–xxxiv. Mentions W briefly (p. xxii, xxiv).

4849. _____. "Bigger, Bird, and the Man From Cat Island," in his *Down the Glory Road*. New York: Avon, pp. 123–132. Includes a sketch of W's career emphasizing the autobiographical source of his writing. Mentions *UTC*, *BB*, and *PS*, and provides a paragraph on *NS*. Also mentions briefly *O* (p. 14).

4850. Boyd, Melba Joyce. "Envisioning Freedom: Jazz, Film, Writing and the Reconstruction of American Thought," in *The Canon in the Classroom: The Pedagogical Implications of Canon Revision in*

American Literature. Ed. John Alberti. New York: Garland, pp. 261–281. Contains a paragraph on the film version of "Almost a Man" (p. 269) and mentions Boyd's essay on *NS* (pp. 279, 280).

4851. Boynton, Robert S. "The New Intellectuals." *The Atlantic Monthly*, 275 (March), 53–56, 60–62, 64–68, 70. Mentions W briefly (p. 70).

4852. Bradbury, Malcolm. *Dangerous Pilgrimages: Trans-Atlantic Mythologies and the Novel*. London: Secker and Warburg, pp. 219, 420–421, 422. Mentions *NS*, *BB*, and W's connections with Chicago, Communism, and existentialism. Notes that Saul Bellow observed W reading Husserl in Paris cafes.

4853. Bradley, David. "Layers of Paradox." *Dissent*, 42 (Winter), 112–120. Review of Henry Louis Gates, Jr.'s *Colored People* with comparisons to *BB*.

4854. _____. "David Bradley," in *Swing Low: Black Men Writing* by Rebecca Carroll. New York: Carol Southern Books. pp. 3–12. Mentions briefly Bigger Thomas.

4855. Breit, Harvey. "Talk with Ralph Ellison," in *Conversations with Ralph Ellison*. Eds. Maryemma Graham and Amritjit Singh. Jackson: University Press of Mississippi, pp. 3–5.

4856. Brièrre, Annie. "Conversation with Chester Himes," in *Conversations with Chester Himes*. Eds. Michel Fabre and Robert E. Skinner. Jackson: University Press of Mississippi, pp. 1–4.

4857. Brignano, Russell Carl. "Richard Wright, 1908–1960," in *Major Black American Writers Through the Harlem Renaissance*. Ed. Harold Bloom. New York: Chelsea House, p. 180.

4858. Brooks, Neil. "On Becoming an Ex-Man: Postmodern Irony and the Extinguishing of Certainties in *The Autobiography of an Ex-Colored Man*." *College Literature*, 22 (October), 17–29. Mentions briefly *BB* (p. 25).

4859. Browder, Laura, and David McLean. "The Arts," in *American Decades: 1930–1939*. Ed. Victor Bondi. Detroit: Gale, pp. 25–90. Lists and comments on *UTC* (pp. 39, 44, 53, 54) and mentions the play *NS* (p. 72).

4860. Brown, Cecil. "Interview with Toni Morrison." *The Massa-*

chusetts Review, 36 (Autumn), 455–473. Includes discussion of W, who "does action practically better than anybody" (p. 455) according to Morrison, but black women are less interested in confrontation. Both Brown and Morrison make other comments about W.

4861. _____. "Cecil Brown," in *Swing Low: Black Men Writing* by Rebecca Carroll. New York: Carol Southern Books. pp. 22–28. Mentions W briefly (p. 25).

4862. Brown, Claude. "Introduction," in *Swing Low: Black Men Writing* by Rebecca Carroll. New York: Carol Southern Books. pp. xi–xvi. Mentions W briefly (p. xiv).

4863. Brown, Elsa Barkley. "Imaging Lynching: African American Women, Communities of Struggle, and Collective Memory," in *African American Women Speak Out on Anita Hill-Clarence Thomas*. Ed. Geneva Smitherman. Detroit: Wayne State University Press, pp. 100–124. Compares Bigger and Bessie in *NS* (p. 113).

4864. Brown, Martha H. "*Up South: Stories, Studies, and Letters of This Century's Black Migrations*. Edited by Malaika Adero." *The Journal of Southern History*, 61 (November), 835–836. Quotes briefly from *AH*.

4865. Brozan, Nadine. "Chronicle." *The New York Times* (16 November), p. D26. Contains a telephone interview with Julia Wright, who came from Paris to celebrate the fiftieth anniversary of *BB*. She comments on *BB*, *NS*, and W's efforts on behalf of Clinton Brewer.

4866. Bryant, Jerry H. "The Violence of *Native Son*," in *Richard Wright: A Collection of Critical Essays*. Ed. Arnold Rampersad. Englewood Cliffs, NJ: Prentice-Hall, pp. 12–25.

4867. Brüning, Eberhard. "*Stadtluft macht frei!*: African American Writers and Berlin (1892–1932)," in *The City in African-American Literature*. Eds. Yoshinobu Hakutani and Robert Butler: Madison/Teaneck, NJ: Fairleigh Dickinson University Press, pp. 79–95. Mentions W briefly (p. 93).

4868. Buckner, Dilla. "Spirituality, Sexuality, and Creativity: A Conversation with Margaret Walker-Alexander," in *My Soul is a Witness: African-American Women's Spirituality*. Ed. Gloria Wade-Gayles.

Boston: Beacon Press, pp. 224–228. Walker mentions teaching a seminar on W.

4869. Budd, Louis J. "The American Background," in *The Cambridge Companion to American Realism and Naturalism.* Ed. Donald Pizer. Cambridge: Cambridge University Press, pp. 21–46. Mentions W briefly(p. 43).

4870. Buhle, Paul M. *A Dreamer's Paradise Lost: Louis C. Fraina/Lewis Corey (1892–1953) and the Decline of Radicalism in the United States.* New Jersey: Humanities Press, pp. 155, 167. Mentions W briefly.

4871. _____. "The 1950s and 1960s: Open and Hidden Relations." *Prospects: An Annual of American Cultural Studies*, 20, 467–478. Mentions W briefly (pp. 475, 488).

4872. Butler, Robert J. "Chronology," in his *The Critical Response to Richard Wright.* Westport, CT: Greenwood Press, pp. xix–xxiii. Fairly detailed W chronology but does not mention his move to New York, his vacation in Mexico, or his trips to Spain and the resulting *Pagan Spain.*

4873. _____. "The City as Liberating Space in *Life and Times of Frederick Douglass*," in his and Yoshinobu Hakutani's *The City in African-American Literature.* Madison/Teaneck, NJ: Fairleigh Dickinson University Press, pp. 21–36. Mentions briefly *BB* (p. 34).

4874. _____. "The City as Psychological Frontier in Ralph Ellison's *Invisible Man* and Charles Johnson's *Faith and the Good Thing*," in his and Yoshinobu Hakutani's *The City in African-American Literature.* Madison/Teaneck, NJ: Fairleigh Dickinson University Press, pp. 123–137. Mentions W briefly (p. 124).

4875. _____. "Introduction," in his *The Critical Response to Richard Wright.* Westport, CT: Greenwood Press, pp. xxv–xxxix. Reviews the critical response to *UTC, BB, O,* and *EM,* considering selected contemporary reviews, the period "from the midsixties to the late seventies [when] Wright's reputation as a writer and thinker was restored," the emphasis on W's artistry and his relation to various literary traditions during the eighties and nineties, and the debate over the Library of America edition. Butler concludes

by relating the contents of this volume to his outline of the development of W criticism.

4876. _____. "The Invisible Woman in Wright's *Rite of Passage*," in his *The Critical Response to Richard Wright.* Westport, CT: Greenwood Press, pp. 185–189. Analysis and favorable evaluation of the posthumously published *RP* (1994) emphasizing its connection with W's other work, stressing "the existential fragility of its protagonists's identity with a narrative that describes how his life is completely transformed by a single dramatic event" (p. 185). The juvenile male protagonist is torn between masculine and feminine values, but it is clear that W favors the latter.

4877. _____. "Keneth Kinnamon and Michel Fabre, eds. *Conversations with Richard Wright.*" *African American Review*, 29 (Spring), 131–134. Favorable review praising the editors' recovery of obscure items. The collection shows W's pleasant personality, his interest in religion, his Americaness, his attention to craft, and his balanced, humanistic perspective.

4878. _____. "Thematic and Formal Unity in Richard Wright's *Eight Men*," in his *The Critical Response to Richard Wright.* Westport, CT: Greenwood Press, pp. 151–160. Argues that *EM* comprises "a carefully arranged sequence of thematically related stories which are also unified by strong patterns of imagery and symbol" (p. 152). Thematically, the protagonists move from victimization through stages of consciousness to a capacity for accurate vision and positive action. Formal unity is achieved through recurring patterns of imagery involving entrapment, fire, and sight.

4879. _____. "Wright's *Native Son* and Two Novels by Zola: A Comparative Study," in his *The Critical Response to Richard Wright.* Westport, CT: Greenwood Press, pp. 51–59.

4880. Caesar, Terry P. "Pieties and Theories: The Heath in the Survey, the Survey in the Discipline." *Arizona Quarterly*, 51 (Winter), 109–140. Asserts that in "The Man Who Was Almost a Man" the main issue is class not race.

4881. Callahan, John F. "Introduction," in his *The Collected Essays of Ralph Ellison.* New York: The

Modern Library, pp. xvii–xxix. Mentions briefly W and Ellison's essay "Remembering Richard Wright," pp. xxi, xxii.

4882. [_____]. "Ralph Ellison," in his *The Collected Essays of Ralph Ellison.* New York: The Modern Library, pp. v–vi. Mentions briefly Ellison's friendship with W.

4883. Calloway, Catherine. "Fiction: The 1930s to the 1960s," in *American Literary Scholarship: An Annual/1993.* Ed. Gary Scharnhorst. Durham: Duke University Press, pp. 233–254. Comments on books on W by Keneth Kinnamon and Michel Fabre, by Henry Louis Gates, Jr., and K.A. Appiah, and by Margaret Walker. Also notes treatment of W in *Sweet Home* by Charles Scruggs.

4884. Campbell, James. *Exiled in Paris: Richard Wright, James Baldwin, Samuel Beckett, and Others on the Left Bank.* New York: Scribner, xi + 271 pp. Account of the Left Bank literary scene after World War II, beginning with W's expatriation and ending with his mysterious death. Chapter Three and Six deal with the distrust rampant among black expatriates because of U.S. and French government surveillance of their political activities, aided by informers.

4885. _____. *Exiled in Paris: Richard Wright, James Baldwin, Samuel Beckett, and Others on the Left Bank.* New York: Scribner, xi + 271 pp.

4886. Campbell, Jane. "Walker, Margaret," in *The Oxford Companion to Women's Writing in the United States.* Eds. Cathy N. Davidson and Linda Wagner-Martin. New York: Oxford University Press, pp. 904–905. Mentions W briefly.

4887. Canby, Henry Seidel. "Review of *Native Son*," in *The Critical Response to Richard Wright.* Ed. Robert J. Butler. Westport, CT: Greenwood Press, pp. 23–24.

4888. Cannon, Steve. "Reminisin' in C: Remembering Ralph Waldo Emerson." *Callaloo*, 18 (Spring), 288–297. Cannon recalls his admiration of W (p. 288) and his impatience with Ellison in an interview because he was not more forthcoming about W (p. 289). Cannon also mentions briefly *NS* and *O* (p. 295).

4889. Cannon, Steve, Lennox Raphael, and James Thompson. "A Very Stern Discipline: An Interview with Ralph Ellison," in *Conversations*

with Ralph Ellison. Eds. Maryemma Graham and Amritjit Singh. Jackson: University Press of Mississippi, pp. 109–135.

4890. _____."A Very Stern Discipline: An Interview with Ralph Ellison," in *Conversations with Ralph Ellison.* Jackson: University Press of Mississippi, pp. 109–135.

4891. Cappetti, Carla. "Sociology of an Existence: Richard Wright and the Chicago School," in *The Critical Response to Richard Wright.* Ed. Robert J. Butler. Westport, CT: Greenwood Press, pp. 81–93.

4892. Carey-Webb, Allen. "Teaching to the Contemporary Crisis: Notes on English 223-Prison, Race, and Social Justice." *College Literature,* 22 (October), 1–16. Discusses a topical course on "Prison, Race, and Social Justice" in African American literature in which *NS* was a major text, quite applicable to the 1990s.

4893. _____. "Youth Violence and the Language Arts: A Topic for the Classroom." *English Journal,* 84 (September), 29–37. Reports a Michigan teacher's use of *NS* as "one of the most important and powerful texts for exploring the causes of violence…" (p. 29).

4894. Caron, Timothy Paul. "'Ragtag and bob-ends of old stories': Biblical intertextuality in Faulkner, Hurston, Wright, and O'Connor." *Dissertation Abstracts International,* 55 (March), 2828-A. The dissertation examines religion and political action in *UTC.*

4895. Carter, Tom. "Ernest Gaines," in *Conversations with Ernest Gaines.* Ed. John Lowe. Jackson: University Press of Mississippi, pp. 80–85.

4896. Casement, William. "Some Myths About the Great Books." *The Midwest Quarterly,* 36 (Winter), 203–218. Mentions briefly W as "moving toward canonization" (p. 207).

4897. Cassimere, Raphael, Jr. "Flashback: 80 Years Ago: The Spingarn Medal." *The Crisis,* 102 (July), 10. Mentions W briefly as a recipient of the medal.

4898. Cataliotti, Robert H. *The Music in African American Fiction.* New York: Garland, pp. 125–138, 147, 176, 178, 180, 211, 229. Admitting that W's representation of music in his fiction was minimal, Cataliotti, goes on to discuss "Blue-

print for Negro Writing," *UTC, NS,* and the influence of Marxism. Also mentions *BB.*

4899. Chaka, Malik M. "Anthology of Black American Men Is a Living Mosaic." *The Crisis,* 102 (October), 8. Review of *Brotherman* mentioning W. briefly.

4900. Champion, Ernest A. *Mr. Baldwin, I Presume: James Baldwin-Chinua Achebe, A Meeting of Minds.* Lanham, Maryland: University Press of America, pp. 38–40, 75, 100, 101, 102, 105–106. Relates that in his class at Bowling Green State University, Baldwin required his students to read *Uncle Tom's Cabin, NS, Things Fall Apart,* and *Go Tell It on the Mountain.* He also reopened to his class the W-Baldwin quarrel (pp. 38–40). Elsewhere Champion discusses *NS.*

4901. Charters, Ann. "Richard Wright," in her *The Story and Its Writer: An Introduction to Short Fiction.* Fourth edition. Boston: Bedford Books, p. 1350.

4902. _____. "Richard Wright," in her *The Story and Its Writers: An Introduction to Short Fiction.* Compact fourth edition. Boston: Bedford Books, p. 723.

4903. _____. "Richard Wright," in her *The Story and Its Writer: An Introduction to Short Fiction.* Fourth edition. Boston: Bedford Books, pp. 1515–1517. Mentions that W took his epigraph to *BB* from the Book of Job and then quotes from the autobiography.

4904. Charters, Ann. "Richard Wright," in her *The Story and Its Writer: An Introduction to Short Fiction.* Compact fourth edition. Boston: Bedford Books, pp. 838–840.

4905. Chester, Alfred, and Vilma Howard. "The Art of Fiction: An Interview," in *Conversations with Ralph Ellison.* Eds. Maryemma Graham and Amritjit Singh. Jackson: University Press of Mississippi, pp. 6–19.

4906. Christian, Barbara. "A Rough Terrain: The Case of Shaping an Anthology of Caribbean Women Writers," in *The Ethnic Canon: Histories, Institutions, and Interventions.* Ed. David Palumbo-Liu. Minneapolis: University of Minnesota Press, pp. 241–259. Mentions briefly W's analysis of racism and colonialism in *WML* (p. 245).

4907. _____. "A Rough Terrain: The Case of Shaping an Anthology

of Caribbean Women Writers," in *The Ethnic Canon: Histories, Institutions, and Interventions.* Ed. David Palumbo-Liu. Minneapolis: University of Minnesota Press, p. 245. Mentions briefly *WML.*

4908. Christian, Charles M., with the assistance of Sari J. Bennett. *Black Saga: The African American Experience.* Boston: Houghton Mifflin, pp. 352, 361. Mentions briefly W and *NS.*

4909. Clark, Keith [Critical Extract], in *Black American Women Fiction Writers,* Ed. Harold Bloom. New York: Chelsea House, pp. 191–193. Mentions W briefly.

4910. Clary, Françoise. "Joyce Ann Joyce. *Warriors, Conjurers and Priests: Defining African-centered Literary Criticism.*" *Afram Newsletter,* No. 41 (June), pp. 26–27. Comments on "Richard Wright: A Romantic and a Realist."

4911. Coiner, Constance. *Better Red: The Writing and Resistance of Tillie Olsen and Meridel Le Sueur.* New York: Oxford University Press, pp. 27, 94–95, 155. Quotes W on the Chicago John Reed Club, compares W and Le Sueur on their attitudes to the Communist Party, and mentions W briefly.

4912. _____. "*Worker-Writer in America: Jack Conroy and the Tradition of Midwestern Literary Radicalism, 1898–1990.* By Douglas Wixson." *The Journal of American History,* 82 (December), 1267–1268. Notes that Conroy published the early W, who called him "the old daddy of rebel writing."

4913. Cobb, James C. "'Damn Brother, I Don't Believe I'd A-Told That!' Humor and the Cultural Identity of the American South." *Southern Cultures,* 1 (Summer), 481–492. Quotes briefly from *BB* (p. 482).

4914. _____. "Editor's Afterword: The Rounded Man as Writer," in his *The Mississippi Delta and the World: The Memoirs of David L. Cohn.* Baton Rouge: Louisiana State University Press, pp. 183–213. Includes discussion of Cohn's review of *NS* (p. 187).

4915. Cologne-Brookes, Gavin. "Jerry Gafio Watts, *Heroism and the Black Intellectual: Ralph Ellison, Politics, and Afro-American Intellectual Life.*" *The Journal of American Studies,* 29 (August), 321–322. Review mentioning W briefly.

4916. _____. *The Novels of William Styron: From Harmony to History*. Baton Rouge: Louisiana State University Press, p. 144. Mentions W briefly.

4917. Conger, Lesley. "Jimmy on East 15th Street." *African American Review*. 29 (Winter), 557–566. Memoir of an early friendship with James Baldwin mentioning his first meeting with W through Esther Carlson (pp. 561, 564, 565). Also mentions a literary group, Hammer & Tongs, which included Carlson and W but excluded Baldwin "because of his 'psychological record'" (p. 563).

4918. Copage, Eric V. *Black Pearls for Parents: Meditations, Affirmations, and Inspirations for African-American Parents*. New York: William Morrow, p. September 14. Quotes briefly from *BB*.

4919. Corry, John. "An American Novelist Who Sometimes Teaches," in *Conversations with Ralph Ellison*. Eds. Maryemma Graham and Amritjit Singh. Jackson: University Press of Mississippi, pp. 98–108.

4920. Cronin, Gloria. *American Literature Association: Conference on American Literature, May 26–28, 1985*. Los Angeles: California State University, Los Angeles, p. 26. Lists a session on "Film Biography and the 50th Anniversary Symposium of Richard Wright's *Black Boy*," chaired by Robert J. Butler with papers by Keneth Kinnamon, Yoshinobu Hakutani, and John Reilly, and a partial showing of the film *Richard Wright— Black Boy*.

4921. Crooks, Robert. "From the Far Side of the Urban Frontier: The Detective Fiction of Chester Himes and Walter Mosley." *College Literature*, 22 (October), 68–90. The epigraph of this article is from *NS*

4922. Crouch, Stanley. "Beyond American Tribalism," in his *The All-American Skin Game, or, The Decoy of Race: The Long and the Short of It, 1990–1994*. New York: Pantheon Books, pp. 112–118. Mentions briefly *AH* and *BB* (p. 116).

4923. _____. "Beyond American Tribalism," in his *The All-American Skin Game, or, The Decoy of Race*. New York: Vintage Books, pp. 113–118.

4924. _____. "The Measure of the Oklahoma Kid," in his *The All-American Skin Game, or, The Decoy of Race: The Long and the Short of It,*

1990–1994. New York: Pantheon Books, pp. 85–92.

4925. Cudjoe, Selwyn R. "'As Ever, Darling, All My Love, Nello': The Love Letters of C.L.R. James," in *C.L.R. James: His Intellectual Legacies*. Eds. Selwyn R. Cudjoe and William E. Cain. Amherst: University of Massachusetts Press, pp. 215–243. Notes that James wrote of W in his letters to Constance Webb (p. 223).

4926. _____, and William E. Cain. "Introduction," in their *C.L.R. James: His Intellectual Legacies*. Amherst: University of Massachusetts Press, pp. 1–19. Mentions W briefly (pp. 5, 7).

4927. Cupp, Jeffrey. "Consider Me: Bearers of the African American Tradition," in *American Diversity, American Identity: The Lives and Works of 145 Writers Who Define the American Experience*. Ed. John K. Roth. New York: Henry Holt, pp. 280–282. Includes a paragraph on *NS* and mention of *BB* and *AH*.

4928. Curren, Erik D. "Should Their Eyes Have Been Watching God?: Hurston's Use of Religious Experience and Gothic Horror." *African American Review*, 29 (Spring), 17–25. Compares W and Hurston, noting that the former embraced and the latter rejected Western rationalism (pp. 19–20).

4929. Damon, Maria. "*American Culture Between the Wars: Revisionary Modernism and Postmodern Critique*. By Walter Kalaidjian." *Journal of English and Germanic Philology*, 94 (July), 393–396. Review mentioning W briefly (pp. 392, 395).

4930. Davenport-Hines, Richard. *Auden*. New York: Pantheon Books, p. 207. Mentions briefly W and family in the house on Middagh.

4931. Davis, Thadious. "Reading the Woman's Face in Langston Hughes and Roy DeCarava's *Sweet Flypaper of Life*, in *Langston Hughes: The Man, His Art, and His Continuing Influence*. Ed. C. James Trotman. New York: Garland, pp. 100, 149–150. Includes comments by David Bradley on *TMBV*.

4932. Davis-Adeshotè, Jeanette. *Black Survival in White America: From Past History to the Next Century*. Orange, NJ: Bryant and Dillon, p. 63. Mentions briefly *NS*.

4933. Dawahare, Anthony. "*Radical Representations: Politics and Form in U.S. Proletarian Fiction,*

1929–1941. Barbara Foley." *MELUS*, 20 (Fall), 148–150. Favorable review praising Foley's discussion of *UTC* and *NS*.

4934. DeCosta-Willis, Miriam. "Southern Folk Roots in the Slave Poetry of Elma Stuckey." *CLA Journal*, 38 (June), 390–403. Mentions W briefly (pp. 391, 397).

4935. De Genova, Nick. "Gangster Rap and Nihilism in Black America: Some Questions of Life and Death." *Social Text*, 43 (Fall), 89–132. Discusses "the ways that Richard Wright's exploration of the themes of nihilism enables an appreciation of the complexities of gangster rap as a creative form of African American cultural production and cultural politics" (p. 89). Cites *TMBV, UTC*, "How 'Bigger' Was Born," *NS, O*, "The Man Who Lived Underground," and *WML*.

4936. Delbanco, Andrew. *The Death of Satan: How Americans Have Lost the Sense of Evil*. New York: Farrar, Straus and Giroux, p. 194. Mentions briefly *NS*.

4937. _____. "The Mark of Zora." *The New Republic*, 213 (3 July), 30–32, 34–35. Review of the Library of America edition of Zora Neale Hurston quoting briefly from W's review of *Their Eyes Were Watching God* (p. 34).

4938. Denniston, Dorothy Hamer. *The Fiction of Paule Marshall: Reconstructions of History, Culture, and Gender*. Knoxville: The University of Tennessee Press, p. 15. Mentions W briefly.

4939. DeSantis, Christopher C. "*Playing the Changes: From Afro-Modernism to the Jazz impulse*. By Craig Hansen Werner." *The Southern Quarterly*, 34 (Fall), 125–128. Review commenting favorably on Werner's treatment of W (pp. 126, 127).

4940. Deutsch, Leonard J. "Ralph Waldo Ellison (1 March 1914–16 April 1994)," in *Dictionary of Literary Biography: 1994*. E. James W. Hipp. Detroit: Gale, pp. 261–265. Mentions Ellison's friendship with W, (p. 262) who published his first piece in *New Challenge*.

4941. Dews, Carlos. "McCullers recalls W" *The Richard Wright Newsletter*, 4 no. 1 (Spring/Summer), 5–7, Quoting unpublished material, Dews discusses W's friendship with McCullers in New York and Paris." Dick and I often discussed the

South." W commiserated with her after her stroke, comparing it to his mother's.

4942. Dick, Bruce. "Kenneth [sic] Kinnamon and Michel Fabre, eds.— *Conversations with Richard Wright.*" *Études Anglaises*, 48 (January–March), 114–115. Favorable review with special praise for the inclusion of "major statements" by W toward the end of his life "nearly unavailable to the American reader."

4943. _____. "Ishmael Reed: An Interview." in his and Amritjit Singh's *Conversations with Ishmael Reed.* Jackson: University Press of Mississippi, pp. 344–356. Reed praises W highly as "a giant. *BB* and *UTC* "are flawless books. Reed also mentions favorably W's haiku.

4944. Diggs, Anita Doreen. *Talking Drums: An African-American Quote Collection.* New York: St. Martin's Press, pp. 22, 49, 94. Includes two quotations from *BB* and one from *NS*.

4945. Dilg, Mary A. "The Opening of the American Mind: Challenges in the Cross-Cultural Teaching of Literature." *English Journal*, 84 (March), 18–25. Mentions briefly *NS* (pp. 23, 25).

4946. Dillard, Annie, and Cort Conley. "Richard Wright (1908–1960)," in their *Modern American Memoirs.* New York: HarperCollins, p. 178. Biographical headnote to an excerpt from *BB.*

4947. Domini, John. "Ishmael Reed: A Conversation with John Domini," in *Conversations with Ishmael Reed.* Eds. Bruce Dick and Amritjit Singh. Jackson: Mississippi, pp. 128–143.

4948. Dorsey, Peter A. "De-Authorizing Slavery: Realism in Stowe's *Uncle Tom's Cabin* and Brown's *Clotel.*" *ESQ: A Journal of the American Renaissance*, 41 (Fourth Quarter), 257–288. Mentions briefly Baldwin's treatment of W in "Everybody's Protest Novel."

4949. Dow, William. "Report from the Other Academy: Non-American Voices and American Literature." *Revue Française d'Études Américaines*, No. 65 (July), 484–495. Praises Michel Fabre's work on W (p. 490).

4950. D'Souza, Dinesh, *The End of Racism: Principles for a Multiracial Society.* New York: The Free Press, pp. 99, 175, 245. Cites "How 'Bigger' Was Born" and *WML.*

4951. Douglas, Ann. *Terrible Honesty: Mongrel Manhattan in the 1920s.* New York: Farrar, Straus and Giroux, pp. 468, 480, 535–536, 551, 552. In addition to brief mentions of W, Douglas comments on his friendship with Frederic Wertham (pp. 535–536).

4952. Doyle, Mary Ellen, S.C.N. "A MELUS Interview: Ernest J. Gaines — 'Other Things to Write About,'" in *Conversations with Ernest Gaines.* Ed. John Lowe. Jackson: University Press of Mississippi, pp. 149–171.

4953. [Drake, Kimberly]. "'The Dismal Swamp of Race Hatred': Protest Literature and the Politics of Representation," in *American Literature Section of the Modern Language Association.* Ed. Paul Sorrentino. Blacksburg: Virginia Polytechnic Institute and State University, p. 42. Abstract of a paper on W and Hurston.

4954. _____. "Rape and Resignation: Silencing the Victim in the Novels of Morrison and Wright." *Lit: Literature Interpretation Theory.* 6 (Winter), 63–72. Argues that in *NS* and *The Bluest Eye* W and Morrison use "coercive narration" to focus on the social determinism that engage the reader's attention on Bigger and Cholly as victims. By doing so, the authors "missed the opportunity to develop a more complete amount of African American experiences of sexual violence."

4955. Du Bois, W.E. Burghardt. "Richard Wright Looks Back," in *The Critical Response to Richard Wright.* Ed. Robert J. Butler. Westport, CT: Greenwood Press, pp. 67–68.

4956. Eady, Cornelius. "Cornelius Eady,"in *Swing Low: Black Men Writing* by Rebecca Carroll. New York: Carol Southern Books, pp. 55–65. Mentions W briefly (p. 60).

4957. Eagles, Brenda M. "A Bibliography of Dissertations Relating to Mississippi." *The Journal of Mississippi History*, 57 (February), 67–71. Lists a dissertation on W by Vincent Anthony Perez.

4958. Ellison, Ralph. "A Dialogue with His Audience," in *Conversations with Ralph Ellison.* Eds. Maryemma Graham and Amritjit Singh. Jackson: University Press of Mississippi, pp. 136–140.

4959. _____. "The Art of Fiction: An Interview," in *The Collected Es-*

says of Ralph Ellison. Ed. John F. Callahan. New York: The Modern Library, pp. 210–223.

4960. _____. "Beating That Boy," in *The Collected Essays of Ralph Ellison.* Ed. John F. Callahan. New York: The Modern Library, pp. 145–150.

4961. _____. "Change the Joke and Slip the Yoke," in *The Collected Essays of Ralph Ellison.* Ed. John F. Callahan. New York: The Modern Library, pp. 100–112.

4962. _____. "Hidden Name and Complex Fate: A Writer's Experience in the United States," in *The Collected Essays of Ralph Ellison.* Ed. John F. Callahan. New York: The Modern Library, pp. 189–209.

4963. _____. "On Initiation Rites and Power: A Lecture at West Point," in *The Collected Essays of Ralph Ellison.* Ed. John F. Callahan. New York: The Modern Library, pp. 520–541.

4964. _____. "Remembering Richard Wright," in *The Collected Essays of Ralph Ellison.* Ed. John F. Callahan. New York: The Modern Library, pp. 659–675.

4965. _____. "Richard Wright's Blues," in *The Collected Essays of Ralph Ellison.* Ed. John F. Callahan. New York: The Modern Library, pp. 128–144.

4966. _____. "Richard Wright, 1908–1960." in *Major Black American Writers Through the Harlem Renaissance.* Ed. Harold Bloom. New York: Chelsea House, pp. 174–175.

4967. _____. "That Same Pain, That Same Pleasure: An Interview, in *The Collected Essays of Ralph Ellison.* Ed. John F. Callahan. New York: The Modern Library, pp. 63–80.

4968. _____. "Twentieth-Century Fiction and the Black Mask of Humanity," in *The Collected Essays of Ralph Ellison.* Ed. John F. Callahan. New York: The Modern Library, pp. 81–99.

4969. _____. "The World and the Jug," in *The Collected Essays of Ralph Ellison.* Ed. John F. Callahan. New York: The Modern Library, pp. 155–188.

4970. _____, and James Alan McPherson. "Indivisible Man," in *The Collected Essays of Ralph Ellison.* Ed. John F. Callahan. New York: The Modern Library, pp. 353–395.

4971. Ellison, Ralph, and John Hersey. "'A Completion of Personality': A Talk with Ralph Ellison," in *The Collected Essays of Ralph Ellison*. Ed. John F. Callahan. New York: The Modern Library, pp. 783–817.

4972. Ellison, Ralph, James Thompson, Lennox Raphael, and Steve Cannon. "'A Very Stern Discipline,'" in *The Collected Essays of Richard Wright*. Ed. John F. Callahan. New York: The Modern Library, pp. 726–754.

4973. Fabre, Geneviève. "Craig Hansen Werner. *Playing the Changes From Afro-Modernism to the Jazz Impulse*." *Afram Newsletter*, No. 41 (June), pp. 4–5. Praises "Bigger's Blues."

4974. [Fabre, Michel]. "Activités et Annonces." *Afram Newsletter*, No. 42 (December), pp. 1–4. Mentions briefly a lecture by Julia Wright on her biography of her father at the American Church in Paris on 13 November 1996. Notes also that W is treated by James Campbell in *Paris Interzone*.

4975. _____. "Autres nouvelles." *Afram Newsletter*, No. 42 (December), p. 4. Announces a special issue of *Mississippi Quarterly* on international perspectives on W.

4976. _____. "Chester Himes Direct," in *Conversations with Chester Himes*. Eds. Michel Fabre and Robert E. Skinner. Jackson: University Press of Mississippi, pp. 125–142.

4977. _____. "Expatriation," in *A Companion to American Thought*. Eds. Richard Wightman Fox and James T. Kloppenberg. Cambridge, MA: Blackwell, pp. 224, 225. Mentions W briefly.

4978. _____. "Interview with Chester Himes," in *Conversations with Chester Himes*. Eds. Michel Fabre and Robert E. Skinner. Jackson: University Press of Mississippi, pp. 5–8. The subject of this 1963 interview is W. Himes discusses W and the Communist Party, Ellen Wright, W's generosity, his expatriation, his relation to Baldwin, Ellison, and Himes himself. W was an original, "one of the great writers of this century," leaving "a legacy of honest protest against injustice" (p. 8).

4979. _____. "Nouvelles du Centre." *Afram Newsletter*, No. 41, pp. 1–3. Notes the presentation in Paris of David Lacy's documentary film *Black Boy* and mentions Bruce Dick's research on W's theater.

4980. _____. "Richard Wright and the French Existentialists," in *The Critical Response to Richard Wright*. Ed. Robert J. Butler. Westport, CT: Greenwood Press, pp. 111–121.

4981. _____. "Richard Wright, 1908–1960," in *Major Black American Writers of Through the Harlem Renaissance*. Ed. Harold Bloom. New York: Chelsea House, p. 182.

4982. _____. "Richard Wright's Paris," in *The City in African-American Literature*. Eds. Yoshinobu Hakutani and Robert Butler. Madison/Teaneck, NJ: Fairleigh Dickinson University Press, pp. 96–109. Treats W's use and image of Paris in his creative writing," commenting on *O* and discussing "Island of Hallucination," both the parts published in *Soon, One Morning* and the unpublished parts. Fishbelly's adventures in Paris are not autobiographical, but like his protagonist W "lived *in* Paris but he was not really *of* it" (p. 109). His literary treatment of Paris excels that of William Gardner Smith or Chester Himes, but falls short of Baldwin's.

4983. _____. "Wright, Richard," in *A Companion to American Thought*. Eds. Richard Wightman Fox and James T. Kloppenberg. Cambridge, MA: Blackwell, pp. 755–756. Sketches W's life and reviews his work with emphasis on Marxism and racial protest.

4984. _____, and Robert E. Skinner. "Introduction," in their *Conversations with Chester Himes*. Jackson: University Press of Mississippi, pp. ix–xiv. Mentions briefly W and the first film version of *NS* (pp. ix, xi).

4985. Fanou, Luc. "Images of Africa in African-American Literature in the sixties." *Dissertation Abstracts International*, 56 (August), 541–A. Includes consideration of *LD*.

4986. Ferguson, SallyAnn H. "West, Dorothy," in *The Oxford Companion to Women's Writing in the United States*. Eds. Cathy N. Davidson and Linda Wagner-Martin. New York: Oxford University Press, pp. 913–914. Mentions W briefly.

4987. Ferris, William. "Director's Column." *The Southern Register* (Winter), p. 2. Mentions briefly the film *Richard Wright— Black Boy*.

4988. Fikes, Robert, Jr. "Escaping the Literary Ghetto: African American Authors of White Life Novels, 1946–1994." *The Western Journal of Black Studies*, 19 (Spring), 105–112. Includes a discussion of *SH* with some attention to responses by critics (p. 108).

4989. Fishkin, Shelley Fisher. "Interrogating 'Whiteness,' Complicating 'Blackness': Remapping American Culture." *American Quarterly*, 47 (September), 428–466. Mentions briefly the 1994 republication of *SH* (p. 449) with an introduction by Gerald Early. Fishkin also comments on Fabre's study of W's reading (p. 450).

4990. Floyd, Samuel A., Jr. *The Power of Black Music: Interpreting Its History from Africa to the United States*. New York: Oxford University Press, p. 129. Comments on Bessie and the blues in *NS*.

4991. Foley, Barbara. "Renarrating the Thirties in the Forties and Fifties." *Prospects: An Annual of American Cultural Studies*, 20, 455–466. Mentions W briefly (p. 457).

4992. _____. "Satire or Evasion? Black Perspectives on *Huckleberry Finn*. Edited by *James S. Leonard*, *Thomas A. Tenny*, and *Thadious Davis*. The Word in Black and White: Reading "Race" in American Literature. 1638–1867. *Dana D. Nelson*." *Modern Philology*, 92 (February), 379–385. Review mentioning W briefly.

4993. Franklin, V.P. *Living Our Stories, Telling Our Truths: Autobiography and the Making of the African-American Intellectual Tradition*. New York: Scribner, pp. 11, 16–17, 137, 187–222, 275, 279–292, 300, 308, 311, 316, 349, 350, 354–357, 365, 366, 389. Contains a chapter on W and Hurston, comparing especially the course of their careers and their attitudes toward folk culture (pp. 187–22). Also includes an extended treatment of the W-Baldwin relationship (pp. 279–282). The epigraph to the "Introduction" is a quotation from W, and Franklin frequently mentions W and his works elsewhere.

4994. Friedman, Murray, with the assistance of Peter Binzen. *What Went Wrong?: The Creation and Collapse of the Black-Jewish Alliance*. New York: The Free Press, pp. 28, 119, 121, 217. Quotes from *BB* on black anti–Semitism, notes W's association with Jewish fellow-communists, and mentions briefly NS.

4995. _____. *What Went Wrong?*: The Creation and Collapse of the *Black-Jewish Alliance*. New York: The Free Press, pp. 28, 119, 121, 217. Quotes from *BB*, mentions W's attraction to communism, mentions *BB*, and comments on Boris Max in *NS*.

4996. Gaga [Mark S. Johnson]. "Interview with Ishmael Reed," in *Conversations with Ishmael Reed*. Eds. Bruce Dick and Amritjit Singh. Jackson: University Press of Mississippi, pp. 51–58.

4997. Gaines, Kevin K. *Uplifting the Race: Black Leadership, Politics, and Culture in the Twentieth Century*. Chapel Hill: The University of North Carolina Press, pp. 1, 52–53, 249. Quotes from and comments on "The Ethics of Living Jim Crow" and mentions W briefly.

4998. Gardner, Laurel J. "The Progression of Meaning in the Images of Violence in Richard Wright's *Uncle Tom's Children* and *Native Son*." *CLA Journal*, 38 (June), 420–440. Discusses the use of violence both to confer dignity through self-assertion on his protagonists and to shock readers into an awareness of racism. Notes that W "examines Bigger's acts of violence in much more psychological depth" (p. 433) than those of the protagonists of *UTC*.

4999. Gates, Henry Louis, Jr. "Foreword," in *Harlem on My Mind: Cultural Capital of Black America, 1900–1968*. Ed. Allon Schoener. New York: The New Press, p. [v]. Begins as follows: "If 'The Negro,' as Richard Wright famously observed, is America's metaphor, then Harlem … is the metaphor for African-American culture itself."

5000. _____. "Henry Louis Gates, Jr.," in *Swing Low: Black Men Writing* by Rebecca Carroll. New York: Carol Southern Books. pp. 98–112. Mentions briefly *NS* (p. 102).

5001. Gaudet, Marcia, and Carl Wooton. "Talking with Ernest Gaines," in *Conversations with Ernest Gaines*. Ed. John Lowe. Jackson: University Press of Mississippi, pp. 221–240.

5002. Geller, Allen. "An Interview with Ralph Ellison, in *Conversations with Ralph Ellison*. Eds. Maryemma Graham and Amritjit Singh. Jackson: University Press of Mississippi, pp. 70–86.

5003. Gibson, Donald B. "The Harlem Renaissance City: Its Multi-Illusionary Dimension," in *The City in African-American Literature*. Madison, Teaneck, NJ: Fairleigh Dickinson University Press, p. 42. Mentions W briefly.

5004. Gibson, Donald B. "Wright's Invisible Native Son," in *The Critical Response to Richard Wright*. Ed. Robert J. Butler. Westport, CT: Greenwood Press, pp. 35–42.

5005. Giles, James R. "The Fat Man Finds His Voice, Part 2: Richard Wright's *Native Son*," in his *The Naturalistic Inner-City Novel in America: Encounters with the Fat Man*. Columbia: University of South Carolina Press, pp. 71–95. Argues that W was unable to reconcile the political and racial themes of *NS*, the latter predominating. Similarly, the failure to maintain narrative distance after the "Fear" section results in "artistic confusion." Giles also discusses Bigger's life as "masturbatory" and notes the existential themes in the novel. W is frequently mentioned elsewhere in the book (pp. 5, 11, 12, 13, 33, 43, 116, 117, 122, 167, 169, 172, 185–186, 197).

5006. Gilroy, Paul. "Roots and Routes: Black Identity as an Outernational Project," in *Racial and Ethnic Identity: Psychological Development and Creative Expression*. Eds. Herbert W. Harris, Howard C. Blue, and Ezra E.H. Griffith. New York: Routledge, pp. 15–30. Comments on W's debt to Marx, Nietzsche, and Freud in *The Long Dream* and "On the Psychological Reactions of Oppressed People" (pp. 23–24) and mentions W elsewhere (p. 29).

5007. Ginsberg, Allen. *Journals Mid-Fifties 1954–1958*. Ed. Gordon Ball. New York: Harper Collins, p. 339. Records meeting W in Paris in 1958. Ginsberg had seen the Broadway production of *NS*.

5008. Glisson, Susan. "Center Publishes Literary Guide to Mississippi." *The Southern Register*, Summer, p. 15. Mentions W briefly.

5009. Goudie, S.X. "'Leavin' a Mark on the Wor(l)d': Marksmen and Marked Men in *Middle Passage*." *African American Review*, 29 (Spring), 109–122. Quotes Johnson mentioning W briefly (p. 117).

5010. Gounard, Jean-François, "Richard Wright, 1908–1960," in *Major Black American Writers Through the Harlem Renaissance*. Ed. Harold Bloom. New York: Chelsea House, pp. 180–182.

5011. Graham, Lawrence Otis. *Member of the Club: Reflections on Life in a Racially Polarized World*. New York: HarperCollins, p. 39. Mentions briefly W and *NS*. Reprinted: 1996.

5012. Graham, Maryemma. "Walker, Margaret," in *Encyclopedia of African-American Culture and History*. Eds. Jack Salzman, David Lionel Smith, and Cornel West. Vol. 5. New York: Macmillan, pp. 2767–2768. Mentions Walker's friendship with W and her biography, *Richard Wright: Daemonic Genius*.

5013. Graham, Maryemma and Amritjit Singh. "Chronology," in their *Conversations with Ralph Ellison*. Jackson: University Press of Mississippi, pp. xvii–xx. Mentions briefly W and Ellison's review of *BB*.

5014. _____. "Introduction," in their *Conversations with Ralph Ellison*. Jackson: University Press of Mississippi, pp. vii–xv. Mentions W briefly (p. ix).

5015. Graham, Maryemma, and Jerry W. Ward, Jr. "Letter from the Editors." *Richard Wright Newsletter*, 4 (Spring/Summer), 2. Comments on the contents of this issue, relating the tension between the personal and the political to W's own art.

5016. Gregory, Ross. *Modern America 1914 to 1945*. New York: Facts on File, pp. 55, 263, 299, 353, 402. Records the publication of *NS*, W as a "famous native" of Mississippi, connects W with "a golden age of American literature, provides a profile of W's life, and quotes from *TMBV*.

5017. Guerrero, Ed. "The Black Man on Our Screens and the Empty Space in Representation." *Callaloo*, 18 (Spring), 395–400. Mentions briefly W (pp. 397–398) and his idea of "double vision" (p. 399).

5018. Griffin, Farah Jasmine. *"Who Set You Flowin'?: The African-American Migration Narrative*. New York: Oxford University Press, pp. 7–8, 10, 27–37, 46, 51, 69–83, 105, 123–130, 160–165. Includes discussion of *BB, TMBV, LT, NS* in relation to the Great Migration and the Northern urban experience. Also compares and contrasts W's treatment to works on similar themes by Toomer, Baldwin, Petry, Ellison, and others.

5019. Gutiérrez-Jones. *Rethinking*

the Borderlands: Between Chicano Culture and Legal Discourse. Berkely: University of California Press, pp. 84, 185. Mentions briefly Ellison's continuing dialogue with W.

5020. Hakutani, Yoshinobu. "The City and Richard Wright's Quest for Freedom," in his and Robert Butler's *The City in African-American Literature.* Madison/Teaneck, NJ: Fairleigh Dickinson University Press, pp. 50–63. Surveys W's theme of the city as a site of freedom and self-creation, focusing on *NS* and *O,* but treating or mentioning *BB, TMBV, LD, LT, AH,* "The Man Who Lived Underground," "Fire and Cloud," and "Bright and Morning Star." Both Bigger Thomas and Cross Damon seek freedom: Bigger achieves it psychologically; Cross is defeated in his quest but "ends his life as a failed humanist rather than a nihilist" (p. 60).

5021. _____. "Creation of the Self in Richard Wright's *Black Boy,*" in *The Critical Response to Richard Wright.* Ed. Robert J. Butler. Westport, CT: Greenwood Press, pp. 71–79.

5022. _____. "Henry Louis Gates, Jr., and K.A. Appiah, eds. *Richard Wright: Critical Perspectives Past and Present." African American Review,* 29 (Winter), 683–687. Favorable review with extended comment on Gates's preface and essays by Keneth Kinnamon, Laura Tanner, Joyce Ann Joyce, Barbara Johnson, Houston Baker, Ross Pudaloff, Robert Stepto, Carla Cappetti, Abdul Jan-Mohamed, Janice Thaddeus, William Burrison, Claudia Tate, and Earle V. Bryant.

5023. _____. "If the Street Could Talk: James Baldwin's Search for Love and Understanding," in his and Robert Butler's *The City in African-American Literature.* Madison/Teaneck, NJ: Fairleigh Dickinson University Press, pp. 150–167. Includes a comparison of *NS* and *If Beale Street Could Talk.* Although the situations are similar, W's novel stresses self-liberation through violence, whereas Baldwin's emphasizes the importance of love, intraracial as well as personal. Hakutani also comments on *O,* mentions W elsewhere, and refers to *TMBV.*

5024. _____. "The Library of America Edition of *The Outsider,*" in *The Critical Response to Richard Wright.* Ed. Robert J. Butler. West-

port, CT: Greenwood Press, pp. 177–180. Argues that changes W made in the typescript of *O* were designed "to express a version of existentialism in which human action is taken as the result of an individual's choice and will," but Cross Damon remains an outsider with yearnings to be an insider. Hakutani does not deal with W's changes as a response to suggestions for revision and compression made by Jack Fischer at Harper.

5025. _____. "Richard Wright's *The Outsider* and Albert Camus's *The Stranger,*" in *Richard Wright: A Collection of Critical Essays.* Ed. Arnold Rampersad. Englewood Cliffs, NJ: Prentice Hall, pp. 162–173.

5026. _____, and Robert Butler. "Introduction," in their *The City in African-American Literature.* Madison/Teaneck, NJ: Fairleigh Dickinson University Press, pp. 9–18. Comments on W's Chicago, mentioning Bigger Thomas, *BB,* and *AH* (pp. 10, 12). Comments also on essays on W by Hakutani, Jack B. Moore, and Michel Fabre included in this collection (pp. 13, 14).

5027. Hall, B.C., and C.T. Wood. *The South.* New York: Scribner, p. 189. Mentions W briefly.

5028. Hansberry, Lorraine. "Review of *The Outsider,*" in *The Critical Response to Richard Wright.* Ed. Robert J. Butler. Westport, CT: Greenwood Press, p. 109.

5029. Hapke, Laura. *Daughters of the Great Depression: Women, Work, and Fiction in the American 1930s.* Athens: The University of Georgia Press, pp. 62–64, 134, 138, 140, 222. Discusses *NS,* comparing it to the work of Langston Hughes and emphasizing Bigger's hatred of women. Also notes W's disapproval of Hurston (p. 134) and comments on his portrayal of Bessie Mears.

5030. Hardack, Richard. "'A Music Seeking Its Words': Double-Timing and Double-Consciousness in Toni Morrison's *Jazz." Callaloo,* 18 (Spring), 451–471. Includes discussion of Bigger's double-consciousness in *NS* (pp. 453, 454). Mentions Bigger elsewhere (pp. 461, 468).

5031. Harding, Vincent. "You've Taken My Nat and Gone," in *The Critical Responses to William Styron.* Ed. Daniel W. Ross. Westport CT: Greenwood Press, pp. 133–139. Reprint of 1968.

5032. Harley, Sharon. *The Timetables of African-American History: A Chronology of the Most Important People and Events in African-American History.* New York: Simon & Schuster, pp. 245, 247, 257. Includes entries for *UTC, NS,* and *BB.* Contains a photograph of W. Reprinted: 1996.

5033. Harmon, Charles C. "The human element: Styles of subjectivity in the United States, 1900–1940." *Dissertation Abstracts International,* 56 (July), 241-A Includes consideration of *NS* and *BB.*

5034. Harris, Trudier. "Adventures in a 'Foreign Country': African American Humor and the South." *Southern Cultures,* 1 (Summer), 457–465. Mentions briefly *UTC,* "How 'Bigger' Was Born," and *NS.*

5035. _____. "Taboos, Literary," in *The Oxford Companion to Women's Writing in the United States.* Eds. Cathy N. Davidson and Linda Wagner-Martin. New York: Oxford University Press, pp. 867–868. Mentions briefly Aunt Sue of "Bright and Morning Star."

5036. Harris-Fain, Darren. "The Arts," in *American Decades: 1960–1969.* Ed. Richard Layman. Detroit: Gale, pp. 23–68. Notes W's death (p. 66).

5037. Hart, James D. "Wright, Richard {Nathaniel}" in his *The Oxford Companion to American Literature.* Sixth Edition. New York: Oxford University Press, p. 741.

5038. Hersey, John. "'A Completion of Personality: A Talk with Ralph Ellison." in *Conversations with Ralph Ellison.* Eds. Maryemma Graham and Amritjit Singh. Jackson: University Press of Mississippi, pp. 272–301.

5039. _____. "'A Completion of Personality': A Talk with Ralph Ellison," in *Conversations with Ralph Ellison.* Eds. Maryemma Graham and Amritjit Singh. Jackson: University Press of Mississippi, pp. 272–301.

5040. Hill, Michael E. "'Black Boy' Follows Author's Rise and Fall." Austin *American Statesman* (3 September), p. 11. Summarizes W's life as depicted in Madison Davis Lacy's film *Richard Wright— Black Boy.*

5041. _____. "One Man's Struggle, Triumph and Exile." *The Washington Post* (3 September), p. Y06 (TV Week). Favorable review of the documentary *Richard Wright: Black Boy*.

5042. [Holland, Laurence B., and Nina Baym]. "Richard Wright 1908–1960," in *The Norton Anthology of American Literature*. Shorter fourth edition. Eds. Nina Baym, Ronald Gottesman, Laurence B. Holland, David Kalstone, Arnold Krupat, Francis Murphy, Hershel Parker, William H. Pritchard, and Patricia B. Wallace. New York: Norton, pp. 2120–2121, 2694.

5043. Holloway, Karla F.C. *Codes of Conduct: Race, Ethics, and the Color of Our Character*. New Brunswick, NJ: Rutgers University Press, pp. 182, 183, 189. Comments on and quotes from *BB* in a chapter on "The Moral Lives of Children."

5044. Horne, Gerald. *Fire This Time: The Watts Uprising and the 1960s*. Charlottesville: University Press of Virginia, p. 21. Mentions W briefly.

5045. Howe, Irving. "Richard Wright: A Word of Farewell," in *The Critical Response to Richard Wright*. Ed. Robert J. Butler. Westport, CT: Greenwood Press, pp. 137–139.

5046. Howland, Jonathan. "Attentive Reading in the Age of Canon Clamor." *English Journal*, 84 (March), 35–38. Mentions briefly *BB*.

5047. Hubbard, Dolan. *The Sermon and the African American Literary Imagination*. Columbia: University of Missouri Press, pp. 23, 147, 148, 167. Mentions W briefly and refers to "The Literature of the Negro in the United States" and *TMBV*.

5048. Hudson, Robert J., and Robert P. Smith, Jr. "Publications by CLA Members: 1994–95." *CLA Journal*, 39 (December), 243–250. Lists Robert Butler's review of *Conversations with Richard Wright* (p. 245).

5049. Huggins, Nathan Irvin. "'Here to Stay,'" in his *Revelations: American History, American Myths*. Ed. Brenda Smith Huggins. New York: Oxford University Press, pp. 115–120.

5050. _____. "Modernism and the Harlem Renaissance," in his *Revelations: American History, American Myths*. Ed. Brenda Smith Huggins. New York: Oxford University Press, pp. 158–165.

5051. Hughes, Langston. *Ask Your Mama*, in *The Collected Poems of Langston Hughes*. Eds. Arnold Rampersad and David Roessel. New York: Knopf, pp. 472–531.

5052. _____. *Ask Your Mama: 12 Moods for Jazz*, in *The Collected Poems of Langston Hughes*. Eds. Arnold Rampersad and David Roessel. New York: Knopf, pp. 472–531.

5053. _____. "Prelude to Our Age: A Negro History Poem," in *The Collected Poems of Langston Hughes*. Eds. Arnold Rampersad and David Roessel. New York: Knopf, 379–384.

5054. _____, Milton Meltzer, C. Eric Lincoln, and Jon Michael Spencer. *A Pictorial History of African Americans*. Sixth edition. New York: Crown Publishers, pp. 281, 186, 352.

5055. Hughes, Langston. "Art and the Heart," in *Langston Hughes and the Chicago Defender*. Ed. Christopher De Santis. Urbana: University of Illinois Press, pp. 202–203.

5056. _____. "Horn of Plenty," in *The Collected Poems of Langston Hughes*. Eds. Arnold Rampersad and David Roessel, pp. 497–531.

5057. _____. "Old Customs Die Young," in *Langston Hughes and the Chicago Defender*. Ed. Christopher C. De Santis. Urbana: University of Illinois Press, pp. 67–69.

5058. _____. "The See-Saw of Race," in *Langston Hughes and the Chicago Defender: Essays on Race, Politics, and Culture, 1942–1962*. Ed. Christopher C. De Santes. Urbana: University of Illinois Press, pp. 31–32.

5059. _____. "Theaters, Clubs and Negroes," in *Langston Hughes and the Chicago Defender*. Ed. Christopher C. De Santis. Urbana: University of Illinois Press, pp. 53–54.

5060. Hunter, Clarence. "Reflections on the Black Male of the Twenties and Thirties. *The Richard Wright Newsletter*, 4, no. 1 (Spring/Summer), 6–7. A talk at Tougaloo at a symposium to honor the fiftieth anniversary of *BB*. W "captures the frustration, hardship, toil and fears of the black male during this period," but Hunter praises black survival during this period.

5061. Hurston, Zora Neale. "Richard Wright, 1908–1960," in *Major Black American Writers Through the Harlem Renaissance*. Ed. Harold Bloom. New York: Chelsea House, p. 171.

5062. Hutchinson, Earl Ofari. *Blacks and Reds: Race and Class in Conflict, 1919–1990*. East Lansing: Michigan State University Press, pp. 3, 149–151, 155, 162–163. Discusses W's membership in the Communist Party, "a mixture of storm and euphoria" (p. 149). W found the John Reed Club beneficial and enjoyed his tenure at the *Daily Worker*, but became concerned when he was accused of "petty bourgeois nationalism" and when the Party tried to interfere with his writing. Mentions *NS* and "Blueprint for Negro Writing" and quotes from an interview with Carlton Moss, a friend of W in the thirties.

5063. Hutchinson, George. *The Harlem Renaissance in Black and White*. Cambridge, MA: Harvard University Press, pp. 58, 273, 274–277. Mentions W briefly and comments on his relation to radical politics (e.g., in *NS*), and the influence of Mencken.

5064. Idahosa, Paul. "James and Fanon and the Problem of the Intelligentsia in Popular Organizations," in *C.L.R. James: His Intellectual Legacies*. Eds. Selwyn R. Cudjoe and William E. Cain. Amherst: University of Massachusetts Press, pp. 388–404. Mentions W briefly (p. 392).

5065. Isaacs, Harold. "Five Writers and Their African Ancestors," in *Conversations with Ralph Ellison*. Eds. Maryemma Graham and Amritjit Singh. Jackson: University Press of Mississippi, pp. 63–69.

5066. Jackson, Blyden. "Richard Wright: Black Boy from America's Black Belt and Urban Ghettos," in *The Critical Response to Richard Wright*. Ed. Robert J. Butler. Westport, CT: Greenwood Press, pp. 3–14.

5067. James, Judith. Giblin Wunderkind: The Reputation of Carson McCullers, 1940–1990. Columbia, SC: Camden House, pp. 1, 3, 10–12, 13, 153. Discusses W's perceptive and favorable review of *The Heart Is a Lonely Hunter*. Also notes his residence in Brooklyn.

5068. JanMohamed, Abdul R. "Negating the Negation as a Form of Affirmation in Minority Discourse: The Construction of Richard Wright as Subject," in *Richard Wright: A Collection of Critical Essays*. Ed. Arnold Rampersad. Englewood Cliffs, NJ: Prentice-Hall, pp. 107–123.

5069. Jennings, La Vinia Delois. *Alice Childress*, New York: Twayne, p. 17. Mentions the stage version of *NS* by W and Paul Green.

5070. Johnson, Charles. "Charles Johnson," in *Swing Low: Black Men Writing* by Rebecca Carroll. New York: Carol Southern Books. pp. 113–127. Mentions briefly W's Marxism (p. 118).

5071. Johnson, Venice, ed. *Heart Full of Grace: A Thousand Years of Black Wisdom.* New York: Simon & Schuster, pp. 39, 43, 70, 104, 127, 242, 257, 273, 283, 302. Quotes W on the blues, brotherhood, dignity, equality, God, shame, the South, truth, violence, and youth.

5072. Joiner, Robert L. "The Merits of Autobiography." *Emerge*, 6 (March), 62. Review of V.P. Franklin's *Living Our Stories, Telling Our Truths* mentioning W briefly.

5073. Joly, Claire Helene. "A Bridge of Words: The American Critical Reception of Richard Wright, 1938–1945." *Dissertation Abstracts International*, 55 (April), 3189-A. Focuses on art, protest, and idealogy in the response to *UTC, NS,* and *BB.*

5074. Jones, Howard Mumford. "Uneven Effect," in *The Critical Response to Richard Wright*. Ed. Robert J. Butler. Westport, CT: Greenwood Press, pp. 27–28.

5075. Jones, Olaive Burrowes. "On Going Home," in *My Soul Is a Witness: African-American Women's Spirituality*. E. Gloria Wade-Gayles. Boston: Beacon Press, pp. 209–214. Mentions reading W as a student at Texas Southern University (p. 211).

5076. Jones, Quincy, and Alex Haley. "Playboy Interview: Quincy Jones (July 1990)," in *Brotherman: The Odyssey of Black Men in America*. Eds. Herb Boyd and Robert L. Allen. New York: Ballantine Books, pp. 667–676.

5077. Jordan, June [Critical Extract], in *Black American Women Fiction Writers*. Ed. Harold Bloom. New York: Chelsea House, pp. 17–18.

5078. Joyce, Joyce Ann. "Race, Culture, and Gender in Langston Hughes's *The Ways of White Folks,*" in *Langston Hughes: The Man, His Art, and His Continuing Influence*. Ed. C. James Trotman. New York: Garland, p. 100. Compares briefly W's and Hughes's short stories.

5079. _____. "Race, Culture, and Gender in Langston Hughes's *The Ways of White Folks,*" in *Langston Hughes: The Man, His Art, and His Continuing Influence*. New York: Garland. Includes a brief comment on *UTC.*

5080. Kaname, Hiroshi. "'The Man Who Lived Underground' and the Thought of 'Reversal.'" *Osaka Prefectural University Studies in British and American Language and Culture*, 43 (March), 155–156. Examines the influence of existentialism on this novella.

5081. Kanwar, Asha S. "Zora: An Indian Perspective." *The Zora Neale Hurston Forum*, 9 (Fall), 1–12. Mentions W briefly (p. 7).

5082. Kaplan, Cora. "Baldwin, James," in *A Companion to American Thought*. Eds. Richard Wightman Fox and James T. Kloppenberg. Cambridge, MA: Blackwell, pp. 54–55. Mentions W briefly.

5083. Kaufman, Jonathan. *Broken Alliance: The Turbulent Times Between Blacks and Jews in America.* New York: Tombstone, pp. 36–37.

5084. Kaufmann, Michael. "*Up from Communism: Conservative Odysseys in American Intellectual Development*. By John P. Diggins." *American Literature*, 67 (March), 168–169. Mentions W briefly.

5085. Kazemek, Francis E. "African Literature in the Secondary English Language Arts Classroom." *English Journal*, 84 (October), 95–102. Mentions W briefly (p. 95).

5086. Kazin, Alfred. *Writing Was Everything*. Cambridge, MA: Harvard University Press, pp. 38–47. Comments on W and the Communist Party, *BB*, and, at greater length, *NS*. Kazin considers W, with whom he was slightly acquainted, "the strongest and most enduring black talent in twentieth-century American writing" (pp. 3839), especially because of his emphasis on the *deed*, not the interpretation.

5087. _____. "Richard Wright, 1908–1960," in *Major Black American Writers Through the Harlem Renaissance*. Ed. Harold Bloom. New York: Chelsea House, p. 186.

5088. Keady, Sylvia. "Richard Wright's Women Characters and Inequality," in *The Critical Response to Richard Wright*. Ed. Robert J. Butler. Westport, CT: Greenwood Press, pp. 43–49.

5089. Keller, Jürg. *The American Dream Gone Astray: Critical Realism in American Fiction, 1920–1940.* Bern: Peter Lang, p. 188. Includes *NS* in a checklist of novels of critical realism 1920–1940.

5090. Kelly, James R. "Theses and Dissertations for 1994." *South Atlantic Review*, 60 (November), 191–236. Lists a thesis by Cindy H. Tipton, "Read All About It: The Media in Richard Wright's *Native Son* and Theodore Dreiser's *An American Tragedy*," a thesis by Henry A. Nejako, "Richard Wright and Ralph Ellison: Conflicting Masculinities," and a thesis by Dorothy Parry Thompson, "The Presence of Democratic Socialism in Richard Wright's *Native Son.*"

5091. Kelley, Robin D.G. "Confessions of a Nice Negro, or Why I Shaved My Head," in *Speak My Name: Black Men on Masculinity and the American Dream*. Ed. Don Belton. Boston: Beacon Press, pp. 12–22. Mentions briefly Bigger Thomas (p. 16).

5092. Kennedy, J. Gerald. "Introduction: The American Short Story Sequence — Definitions and Implications," in his *Modern American Short Story Sequences: Composite Fictions and Fictive Communities*. New York: Cambridge University Press, pp. vii–xv. Includes comments on John Lowe's essay on *UTC.*

5093. Kennedy, X.J., and Dana Gioia. "Reading Long Stories and Novels," in their *An Introduction to Fiction*. Sixth edition. New York: HarperCollins, pp. 264–269. Mentions briefly *BB.*

5094. Keppel, Ben. *The Work of Democracy: Ralph Bunche, Kenneth B. Clark, Lorraine Hansberry, and the Cultural Politics of Race*. Cambridge, MA: Harvard University Press, pp. 1, 3, 186, 204. The epigraph is a quotation from *TMBV.* Elsewhere Keppel mentions briefly W, *TMBV* [calling it *Ten Million Black Voices*], and *BB.*

5095. Kester, Gunilla Theander. *Writing the Subject: Bildung and the African American Text*. New York: Peter Lang, pp. 33, 111. Mentions briefly W and "The Man Who Lived Underground."

5096. Kilson, Martin. "Paradoxes of Black American Leadership." *Dissent*, 42 (Summer), 368–372. Mentions W briefly (p. 368).

5097. Kim, Michelle Har. "*The Black Album*. By Hanif Kureishi." *The Nation*, 261 (11 September), pp.

245–246. Review mentioning W briefly.

5098. King, Joyce Elaine, and Carolyn Ann Mitchell. *Black Mothers to Sons: Juxtaposing African American Literature with Social Practice.* Revised edition. New York: Peter Lang, pp. 9–11, 44.

5099. Kinnamon, Keneth. "A Richard Wright Bibliography: 1985." *Richard Wright Newsletter,* 4 (Spring/Summer), Supplement, 18pp. Includes 184 annotated items and a commentary on W studies in 1985.

5100. _____. "Call and Response: Intertextuality in Two Autobiographical Works by Richard Wright and Maya Angelou," in *Richard Wright: A Collection of Critical Essays.* Ed. Arnold Rampersad. Englewood Cliffs, NJ: Prentice Hall, pp. 98–106.

5101. _____. "Ellison in Urbana: Memories and an Interview." *Callaloo,* 18 (Spring), 273–279. Recalls discussing W with Ellison (p. 274).

5102. _____. "The Library of America Edition of *Native Son,*" in *The Critical Response to Richard Wright.* Ed. Robert J. Butler. Westport, CT: Greenwood Press, pp. 173–176. Discusses textual issues in *NS,* considering his own work and that of Arnold Rampersad and Mark Richardson. Examines the debate over the restoration in the 1991 edition of sexual passages cut from the proofs of the 1940 edition, noting that most reviewers approved the new edition. Expresses a preference for an edition restoring the sexual cuts but retaining other changes made before publication of the 1940 edition.

5103. _____. "*Native Son*: The Personal, Social, and Political Background," in *The Critical Response to Richard Wright.* Ed. Robert J. Butler. Westport, CT: Greenwood Press, pp. 15–20.

5104. Kiuchi, Toru. "On Richard Wright's *Rite of Passage.*" *Nihon University Industrial Engineering Faculty Report B.* 28 (June), 31–38. Contends that *Rite of Passage* shifts W's emphasis from mere realism to the psychological analysis of a teenage boy.

5105. Kostelanetz, Richard. "An Interview with Ralph Ellison," in *Conversations with Ralph Ellison.* Eds. Maryemma Graham and Amritjit Singh. Jackson: University Press of Mississippi, pp. 87–97.

5106. Kutulas, Judy. *The Long War: The Intellectual People's Front and Anti-Stalinism.* Durham, NC: pp. 37, 40, 85, 90. Quotes from *AH* on the Communist Party and the John Reed Clubs.

5107. Ladner, Joyce A. *Tomorrow's Tomorrow: The Black Woman.* Lincoln: University of Nebraska Press, p. 47. Reprint of 1971.

5108. LaGuardia, Dolores, and Hans P. Guth. "The Responsive Reader; Thinking, Talking, Writing, Collaborative Projects," in their *American Visions: Multicultural Literature for Writers.* Mountain View, CA: Mayfield, pp. 198–199. Study aids for an excerpt from *BB.*

5109. _____. "A Separate Road Richard Wright," in their *American Visions: Multicultural Literature for Writers.* Mountain View, CA: Mayfield, p. 189. Headnote to an excerpt from *BB* with an epigraph by John Reilly.

5110. Lasch, Christopher. *The Revolt of the Elites and the Betrayal of Democracy.* New York: Norton, p. 185. Mentions W briefly.

5111. Lauter, Paul. "Proletarianism," in *A Companion to American Thought.* Eds. Richard Wightman Fox and James T. Kloppenberg. Cambridge, MA: Blackwell, pp. 551–552. Mentions W briefly.

5112. Lawrence-Lightfoot, Sara. *I've Known Rivers: Lives of Loss and Liberation.* New York: Penguin Books, p. 540.

5113. Lee, A. Robert. "Imamu Amiri Baraka," in *American Drama.* Ed Clive Bloom. New York: St. Martin's Press, pp. 97–116. Mentions briefly the play *NS* (p. 98), *NS* (p. 102) and "The Man Who Lived Underground" (p. 104).

5114. Lee, Charles. "Black Hunger," in *The Critical Response to Richard Wright.* Ed. Robert J. Butler. Westport, CT: Greenwood Press, pp. 65–66.

5115. Leeming, David. *James Baldwin: A Biography.* New York: Holt, pp. 18, 36, 49–50, 52, 54, 56, 57, 62, 64–66, 73, 75, 93, 101, 120, 121, 180–182, 186, 187, 207, 290, 300, 308, 324, 366.

5116. _____. *James Baldwin: A Biography.* New York: Holt, pp. 18, 36, 49–50, 52, 54, 56, 57, 62, 64–66, 73, 75, 93, 101, 120, 121, 180–182, 186, 187, 207, 290, 300, 308, 324, 366. Paperback reprint of 1994.

5117. Leonard, John. "Book Watch." *The Nation,* 261 (10 July), 67–68. Review of Mary Lee Settle's *Choices* mentioning W briefly.

5118. LeSeur, Geta. *Ten Is the Age of Darkness: The Black Bildungsroman.* Columbia: University of Missouri Press, pp. 6, 12, 13, 19, 24, 26, 73, 74, 85, 92, 95, 98, 99, 194, 196. Comments on W and *BB* in the third chapter, "His Great Struggle Beginning: African American Male Initiation," and mentions W elsewhere. Also mentions *O* and *NS.*

5119. Lester, Cheryl. "Racial Awareness and Arrested Development: *The Sound and the Fury* and the Great Migration (1915–1928)," in *The Cambridge Companion to William Faulkner.* Ed. Philip M. Weinstein. Cambridge: Cambridge University Press, pp. 131–132. Quotes and comments on a passage concerning racial awareness from *AH.*

5120. Levin, David. "Ralph Ellison." *Callaloo,* 18 (Spring), 272. The epigraph to this poem is a quotation from *Shadow and Act* on W, and the poem itself mentions W.

5121. Lewis, David Levering. "Introduction," in his *The Portable Harlem Renaissance Reader.* New York: Penguin Books, pp. xiii–xli. Mentions briefly W's connection to the WPA and to the Communist Party (p. xl).

5122. Lewis, Earl. "Connecting Memory, Self, and the Power of Place in African American Urban History." *Journal of Urban History,* 21 (March), 347–371. Quotes from *BB* and comments briefly.

5123. Lindfors, Bernth. "Achebe and the Indians," in his *Long Drums and Canons: Teaching and Researching African Literatures.* Trenton, NJ: Africa World Press, pp. 77–86. Mentions W briefly (p. 82).

5124. _____. *Black African Literature in English, 1987–1991.* London: Hans Zell, pp. 292, 304, 427, 517. Lists items on W by Robert Philipson, Khalizquzzaman, M. Elias, Jairus Adagba Ede (master's thesis), and Tayo Olafioye.

5125. Linett, Deena. "A Comment on 'Through the Looking-Glass: A Response.'" *College English,* 57 (December), 963–965. Quotes Jane Peterson mentioning *BB.*

5126. Linkon, Sherry, and Bill Mullen. "Gender, Race, and Place: Teaching Working-Class Students in Youngstown." *Radical Teacher*, 46, pp. 27–32. Includes Mullen's account of teaching *NS* at Youngstown State. White students were responsive to the novel's critique of class, but not to its emphasis on racism. Also treats the complex student reaction to the "intersection of gender and sexuality … with race and class" (p. 30).

5127. Lipsitz, George. "The Possessive Investment in Whiteness: Racialized Social Democracy and the 'White' Problem in American Studies." *American Quarterly*, 47 (September), 369–387. Includes comment on W's statement: "There isn't any Negro problem; there is only a white problem" (p. 369).

5128. Long, Richard, and Eugenia W. Collier. "Ralph Ellison (b. 1914)" in their *Afro-American Writing: An Anthology of Prose and Poetry*. University Park: The Pennsylania State University Press, p. 495. Headnote mentions W's early encouragement of Ellison. Also mentions briefly *NS*.

5129. Loury, Glenn C. "Black Dignity and the Common Good," in his *One by One from the Inside Out: Essays and Reviews on Race and Responsibility in America*. New York: The Free Press, pp. 13–31.

5130. _____. *One By One from the Inside out: Essays and Reviews on Race and Responsibility in America*. New York: The Free Press.

5131. Lowe, John. "An Interview with Ernest Gaines," in his *Conversations with Ernest Gaines*. Jackson: University Press of Mississippi, pp. 297–328. Lowe mentions W several times, and Gaines comments on W and Dostoevsky (p. 318).

5132. _____. "Wright Writing Reading: Narrative Strategies in *Uncle Tom's Children*," in *Modern American Short Story Sequences: Composite Fictions and Fictive Communities*. Ed. J. Gerald Kennedy. New York: Cambridge University Press, pp. 52–75.

5133. _____. "An Interview with Ernest Gaines," in his *Conversations with Ernest Gaines*. Jackson: University Press of Mississippi, pp. 297–328. Lowe refers to "Down by the Riverside" (p. 313), mentions W briefly (p. 315), and comments on the W-Hurston contrast (pp. 315, 316, 317), and the conclusion of *NS*. Gaines notes Dostoevsky's influence on W, but states that he himself was

more influenced by Turgenev, Tolstoy and Gogol (p. 318).

5134. Lynch, Michael F. "The Wall and the Mirror in the Promised Land: The City in the Novels of Gloria Naylor," in *The City in African-American Literature*. Eds. Yoshinobu Hakutani and Robert Butler. Madison/Teaneck, NJ: Fairleigh Dickinson University Press, pp. 181–195. Quotes from "How 'Bigger' Was Born" (p. 183), comments on *NS*, "The Man Who Lived Underground," and *O* (pp. 183–184), and mentions W elsewhere.

5135. Maddock, Mary. "Paul Green (1894–1981)," in *American Playwrights, 1880–1945: A Research and Production Sourcebook*. Westport, CT: Greenwood Press, pp. 121–131. Mentions briefly the play *NS* (p. 122).

5136. Madhubuti, Haki R. "Race, Rage, and Intellectual Development: A Personal Journey," in *Speak My Name: Black Men on Masculinity and the American Dream*. Ed. Don Belton. Boston: Beacon Press, pp. 246–256.

5137. Magistrale, Tony. "From St. Petersburg to Chicago: Wright's *Crime and Punishment*," in *Richard Wright: A Collection of Critical Essays*. Ed. Arnold Rampersad. Englewood Cliffs, NJ: Prentice Hall, pp. 53–62. Reprint of 1986.

5138. Marcus, Greil. *The Dustbin of History*. Cambridge, MA: Harvard University Press, p. 144. Refers briefly to *BB*.

5139. Margolies, Edward. " *The Unfinished Quest of Richard Wright* by Michel Fabre." *African American Review*, 29 (Fall), 525–527. Essay-review of the second edition of Fabre's biography. Margolies esteems Fabre's work, using it as an opportunity for his own reassessment of W's career. He emphasizes the evolving nature of W's thought.

5140. _____. "Richard Wright, 1908–1960," in *Major Black American Writers Through the Harlem Renaissance*. Ed. Harold Bloom. New York: Chelsea House, p. 179.

5141. Marrengane, Ntombi. "Butler, Robert J (editor), *The Critical Response to Richard Wright*." *The Black Scholar*, 25 (Spring), 67. Brief notice mentioning that the work draws from two generations of W scholarship.

5142. _____. " *The Black Scholar Books Received.*" *The Black Scholar*,

25 (Spring), 67–74. Contains a notice of Robert J. Butler's *The Critical Response to Richard Wright* and Sandra Adell's *Double Consciousness/Double Bind* mentioning W briefly.

5143. Marshall, Margaret. "Richard Wright, 1908–1960," in *Major Black American Writers Through the Harlem Renaissance*. Ed. Harold Bloom. New York: Chelsea House, pp. 172–173.

5144. Martin, Reginald. "Black Aesthetic," in *The Oxford Companion to Women's Writing in the United States*. Eds. Cathy N. Davidson and Linda Wagner-Martin. New York: Oxford University Press, pp. 117–119. Comments on W as "the exemplar of what a black writer should be and do" for critics of the black aesthetic movement.

5145. Martin, Terence. *Parables of Possibility: The American Need for Beginnings*. New York: Columbia University Press, pp. 200–201. Comments on *NS* stressing Bigger's final self-creation in a social situation of constricted space.

5146. Martine, James J. "Drama," in *American Literary Scholarship: An Annual/1993*. Ed. Gary Scharnhorst. Durham: Duke University Press, pp. 313–339. Mentions Ralph Ciancio's article "Richard Wright, Eugene O'Neill, and the Beast in the Skull" (p. 326).

5147. Mayberry, Susan Neal. "Ask Your Mama: Women in Langston Hughes's *The Ways of White Folks*." *The Langston Hughes Review*, 13 (Winter/Summer), 12–25. Notes briefly W's unfavorable portrayals of women and his criticism of Hurston (p. 13).

5148. McBride, Dwight. "Paul Gilroy. *The Black Atlantic: Modernity and Double Consciousness*." *Modern Fiction Studies*, 41 (Summer), 388–391. Favorable review noting that the chapter on W takes "seriously the depth of W's philosophical interests."

5149. McCall, Dan. "Richard Wright, 1908–1960," in *Major Black American Writers Through the Harlem Renaissance*. Ed. Harold Bloom. New York: Chelsea House, pp. 177–178.

5150. McCall, Nathan. "From Makes Me Wanna Holler: *Native Son*," in *Swing Low: Black Men Writing* by Rebecca Carroll. New York: Carol Southern Books. pp. 152–160.

5151. McDowell, Deborah E. *"The Changing Same": Black Women's Literature, Criticism, and Theory.* Bloomington: Indiana University Press, pp. 6, 14, 122–123, 182. Mentions *BB* and "The Man Who Lived Underground," and comments on *NS* in relation to an essay by Mel Watkins.

5152. McLean, David. "The Arts," in *American Decades: 1940–1949.* Ed. Victor Bondi. Detroit: Gale, pp. 27–92. Lists and comments on *NS* (pp. 28, 40, 53) and *BB* (p. 34, 53). A biographical entry (pp. 82–83), based on Addison Gayle's biography has the following rubrics: Going North, First Fiction, Black Boy, To Paris, To Africa, and Final Work. Photographs of W appear on pp. 52, 82.

5153. McLendon, Jacquelyn Y. *The Politics of Color in the Fiction of Jessie Fauset and Nella Larsen.* Charlottesville: University Press of Virginia, p. 109. Comments on *NS* in a discussion of Fauset's *Passing.*

5154. Meiser, Mary. "'The Kitten' Richard Wright," in her *Good Writing!.* Boston: Allyn and Bacon, p. 61. Brief headnote to an excerpt from *BB.*

5155. _____. "Thinking About Content, Thinking About Writing, Personal Connections," in her *Good Writing!.* Boston: Allyn and Bacon, p. 65. Study aids for an excerpt from *BB.*

5156. Metzger, Mary Janell. "A Journey Defined by Place: Anti-Racism in the College Classroom," in *Teaching a "New Canon"?: Students, Teachers, and Texts in the College Literature Classroom.* Urbana, IL: National Council of Teachers of English, pp. 67–80. Mentions W briefly (p. 75).

5157. Meyerowitz, Rael, *Transferring to America: Jewish Interpretations of American Dreams.* Albany: State University of New York Press, p. 24. Notes that Marcus Klein treats W in *Foreigners.*

5158. Michaels, Walter Benn. *Our America: Nationism, Modernism, and Pluralism.* Durham, NC: Duke University Press, pp. 124–126, 168, 175–176. Comments on W's view of the African past in *NS* and "I Bite the Hand That Feeds Me" in relation to Melville J. Herskovits's *The Myth of the Negro Past.*

5159. _____. "Race Into Culture: a Critical Genealogy of Cultural

Identity," in *Identities.* Eds. Kwame Anthony Appiah and Henry Louis Gates, Jr. Chicago: The University of Chicago Press, pp. 32–62.

5160. Miller, Dan B. *Erskine Caldwell: The Journey from Tobacco Road.* New York: Knopf, pp. 271, 276, 280, 309. Comments on W's favorable review of *Trouble in July* (pp. 271, 276) and mentions W elsewhere.

5161. Miller, Eugene E. "Richard Wright, Community, and the French Connection." *Twentieth Century Literature,* 41 (Fall), 265–280. Argues for the influence of Jean-Richard Bloch and, especially, Henri Barbusse on *Native Son* and, especially, "The Man Who Lived Underground." Miller draws on unpublished material by W and parallel passages from W and Barbusse's *Under Fire,* and *The Inferno* in presenting his case, noting that both writers were fascinated by "the mysterious power of language" (p. 275).

5162. _____. "Authority, Gender, and Fiction," in *The Critical Response to Richard Wright.* Ed. Robert J. Butler. Westport, CT: Greenwood Press, pp. 181–184.

5163. Miller, Jeanetta. "Battle Hymn of American Studies." *English Journal,* 84 (January), 88–92. Mentions briefly *BB* (p. 91).

5164. Miller, Nina. "*Liberating Literature: Feminist Fiction in America.* By Maria Lauret." *American Literature,* 67 (December), 876–878. Mentions briefly the "Richard Wright School."

5165. Mixon, Wayne. *The People's Writer: Erskine Caldwell and the South.* Charlottesville: University Press of Virginia, p. 81. Comments on W's favorable review of *Trouble in July* and mentions "The Ethics of Living Jim Crow."

5166. Mobley, Marilyn Sanders. "Call and Response: Voice, Community, and Dialogic Structures in Toni Morrison's *Song of Solomon,*" in *New Essays on Song of Solomon.* Ed. Valerie Smith. Cambridge: Cambridge University Press, pp. 41–68. Mentions briefly W and *NS* (pp. 56, 67).

5167. Moody, Joycelyn K. "*Domestic Allegories of Political Desire: The Black Heroine's Text at the Turn of the Century.* By Claudia Tate." *Modern Language Quarterly,* 56 (June), 241–245. Mentions briefly W and *BB* (p. 244).

5168. Moore, Jack B. "'No Street Numbers in Accra': Richard Wright's African Cities," in *The City in African-American Literature.* Eds. Yoshinobu Hakutani and Robert Butler. Madison/Teaneck, NJ: Fairleigh Dickinson University Press, pp. 64–78. Describes and evaluates W's response to Accra and Kumasi in *BP.* Accustomed to the amenities of Paris, W registers culture shock at what he considers the confusion, filth, and oppressive climate of the Gold Coast cities, but he also found London and Liverpool depressing. Includes a comparison of *BP* and Aky Kewi Armah's *The Beautyful Ones Are Not Yet Born.*

5169. Moore, Jack B. "The Voice in *12 Million Black Voices,*" in *Richard Wright: A Collection of Critical Essays.* Ed. Arnold Rampersad. Englewood Cliffs, NJ: Prentice Hall, pp. 140–147.

5170. Moreland, Richard C. "'Rag-tag and bob-ends of old stories': Biblical intertextuality in Faulkner, Hurston, Wright, and O'Connor." *Dissertation Abstracts International,* 55 (March), p. 2828-A. Includes a chapter on *UTC.*

5171. Muckley, Peter A. *Black American Author-Biography: From Politics to Myth and Beyond.* London: Minerva Press, pp. vii, 20–21, 25, 32–33, 35, 41–42, 43–44, 62, 63, 67, 68, 78, 86–110, 111, 113, 117–118, 128, 132, 133, 135, 136, 152–156. Chapter Five, "Richard Wright and the Gods That Wailed," mediates between Fabre's view of *AH* as a movement toward existentialism and Reilly's belief that it commits the author to political engagement from his alienated perspective. Muckley studies ten passages in *AH* not appearing in *The God That Failed,* concluding that they result in three voices — "the ingénue; the prophetic; the worldly-wise" — together affirming the collective African American experience. Mulkey also discusses *BB* and "The Man Who Lived Underground."

5172. Mullane, Deirdre, ed. "Richard Wright (1908–1960)," in her *Words to Make My Dream Children Live: A Book of African American Quotations.* New York: Doubleday, pp. 490–492. Brief headnote and fifteen quotations.

5173. Mullen, Edward. "Afro-Hispanic and Afro-American Literary Historiography: Comments on

Generational Shifts." *CLA Journal*, 38 (June), 371–389. Mentions W briefly (p. 375).

5174. Muller, Gilbert H., and John A. Williams. "Biographical Profiles," in their *The McGraw-Hill Introduction to Literature*. Second edition. New York: McGraw-Hill, pp. 1079–1108.

5175. _____. "Questions," in their *The McGraw-Hill Introduction to Literature*. Second edition. New York: McGraw-Hill, p. 259.

5176. _____. "Understanding Fiction," in their *The McGraw Hill Introduction to Literature*. Second edition. New York: McGraw-Hill, pp. 3–7.

5177. Nadel, Alan. *Containment Culture: American Narratives, Postmodernism, and the Atomic Age*. Durham, NC: Duke University Press, pp. 229, 253. Mentions briefly Bigger Thomas and W.

5178. Nakagomi, Kazumasa. "A Study of R. Wright's Alienation in *The Long Dream*." *Nihon University Studies in English Language and Literature*, 17 (September), 37–61. Argues that W's assertion in *LD* is that African Americans will never be free from racial prejudice and their American Dream will never come true despite their efforts.

5179. Nazareth, Peter. "Joyce Ann Joyce. *Warriors, Conjurers, and Priests: Defining African-Centered Literary Criticism*." *World Literature Today*, 69 (Autumn), pp. 802–803. Favorable review mentioning Joyce's section on W.

5180. Newlin, Paul. "Richard Wright, 1908–1960," in *Major Black American Writers Through the Harlem Renaissance*. Ed. Harold Bloom. New York: Chelsea House, pp. 182–183.

5181. Newton, Adam Zachary. "Call Me/It Ishmael: The Sound of Recognition in *Call It Sleep* and *Invisible Man*." *Prospects: An Annual of American Cultural Studies*, 20, 361–385. Mentions W briefly (p. 366).

5182. _____. *Narrative Ethics*. Cambridge: Harvard University Press, pp. 32, 185, 195, 222–238, 292, 322–324. Discusses the intertextuality of *NS* with *Benito Cereno*, Stephen Crane's "The Monster," and *Cane*; selected reader response to *NS*; and the face imagery that helps to define the "representational ethics" of the novel.

5183. Nielsen, Aldon L. "Reading James Reading," in *C.L.R. James: His Intellectual Legacies*. Eds. Selwyn R. Cudjoe and William E. Cain. Amherst: University of Massachusetts Press, pp. 348–355. Comments on James's reading on Heidegger at W's suggestion and then passing on Heidegger to Wilson Harris (pp. 349–350).

5184. Norman, Kelly. "*Richard Wright-Black Boy* Rounds Scholarly Conference Circuit." *Richard Wright Newsletter*, 4 (Spring/Summer), 1–2. Reports showings of the film and panel discussions at the annual conference of the Modern Language Association, the Louisville Conference on Twentieth Century Literature, the plenary session of the National Association of Humanities Education conference, the Boston premiére at the Museum of Fine Arts with an audience of 400, two screenings at Providence, the annual conference of the American Literature Association in Baltimore, and the annual meeting of the College Language Association in Baton Rouge. Panelists at the various screenings were Madison D. Lacy, Guy Land, Keneth Kinnamon, Trudier Harris, Danille Taylor-Guthrie, John Reilly, Maryemma Graham, Julia Wright, Amritjit Singh, Yoshinobu Hakutani, and Jerry Ward.

5185. Nussbaum, Martha C. *Poetic Justice: The Literary Imagination and Public Life*. Boston: Beacon Press, pp. vii, 2–10, 11, 93–97, 98, 119. Discusses *NS*, concluding that "engaging the [white] reader in this tragedy of social helplessness, the novel constructs a [white] reader who is a judicious and neutral judge of Bigger Thomas... The stigma of racial hate and shame emerges as fundamentally deforming of human personality and community, and the novel-reading stance calls out for political and social equality..." (pp. 96–97). One of Nussbaum's epigraphs is from *NS*.

5186. O'Brien, John. "Interview with Ralph Ellison," in *Conversations with Ralph Ellison*. Eds. Maryemma Graham and Amritjit Singh. Jackson: University Press of Mississippi, pp. 222–234.

5187. O'Connell, Shaun. *Remarkable, Unspeakable New York: A Literary History*. Boston: Beacon Press, pp. 187, 193, 195. Comments on W in relation to Petry, Baldwin, and Ellison.

5188. Oppenheimer, Evelyn. *A Book Lover in Texas*. Denton: University of North Texas Press, pp. 31, 119, 137. Mentions W and *NS* (p. 119) briefly.

5189. Osteen, Mark. "Re-Seeing Reds." *Novel: A Forum on Fiction*, 28 (Spring), 348–351. Review of Barbara Foley's *Radical Representations: Politics and Form in U.S. Proletarian Fiction, 1929–1941* mentioning W briefly (p. 349).

5190. Otero, Rosalie. *Guide to American Drama Explication*. New York: G.K. Hall, p. 406. Lists Morgan Himmelstein's *Drama Was a Weapon*, Sievers's *Freud on Broadway*, Young's *Immortal Shadows*, and Isaacs's "Five Writers and Their African Ancestors" s.v. W.

5191. Ownby, Ted. "The Snopes Trilogy and the Emergence of Consumer Culture," in *Faulkner and Ideology: Faulkner and Yoknapatawpha*. Jackson: University Press of Mississippi, pp. 95–128. Includes discussion of W's negative attitude toward consumer culture (pp. 101–103).

5192. Owomoyela, Oyekan. "John Cullen Gruesser. *White on Black: Contemporary Literature About Africa*; Dennis Hickey and Kenneth C. Wylie. *An Enchanting Darkness: The American Vision of Africa in the Twentieth Century*." *African American Review*, 29 (Spring), 137–140. Review mentioning briefly W's ambivalence toward Africa (p. 139).

5193. Page, Lisa. "High Yellow White Trash," in *Skin Deep: Black Women and White Women Write About Race*. Eds. Marita Golden and Susan Richards Shreve. New York: Nan A. Talese/Doubleday, pp. 13–23. Mentions W briefly (p. 18).

5194. Page, Philip. *Dangerous Freedom: Fusion and Fragmentation in Toni Morrison's Novels*. Jackson: University Press of Mississippi, p. 80. Mentions briefly *EM* and *NS*.

5195. Parrill, William. "An Interview with Ernest Gaines," in *Conversations with Ernest Gaines*. Ed. John Lowe. Jackson: University Press of Mississippi, pp. 172–199.

5196. Payne, Charles M. *I've Got the Light of Freedom: The Organizing Tradition and the Mississippi Freedom Struggle*. Berkeley: University of California Press, pp. 427, 455. Mentions W briefly.

5197. Peterson, Jane. "Through the Looking-Glass: A Response."

College English, 57 (March), 310–318. Mentions briefly *BB* (p. 311).

5198. Pinckney, Darryl. "Darryl Pinckney," in *Swing Low: Black Men Writing* by Rebecca Carroll. New York: Carol Southern Books. pp. 177–186. Mentions W briefly (p. 179).

5199. Pinn, Anthony B. *Why, Lord?: Suffering and Evil in Black Theology*. New York: Continuum Books, pp. 102, 121, 150, 153. Includes discussion of *BB* and *NS* in relation to religion. W "rejects Christian solace."

5200. Pinsker, Sanford. "Black Rage/White Guilt: Act II." *The Georgia Review*, 49 (Fall), 732–739. Review of two books by Derrick Bell including a discussion of the influence of the rage of *NS* on subsequent black writing. Also discusses the Howe-Ellison exchange and Baldwin's response to W's protest fiction (pp. 732–733).

5201. _____. "Black Rage/White Guilt: Act II." *The Georgia Review*, 49 (Fall), 732–739. Calling *NS* "the Negro novel that successive generations of black writers ... would struggle against but never quite supplant," Pinsker considers the Howe-Ellison exchange, Baldwin's response to W, and two books by Derrick Bell.

5202. Pizer, Donald. "Introduction: The Problem of Definition," in his *The Cambridge Companion to American Realism and Naturalism*. Cambridge: Cambridge University Press, pp. 1–18. Mentions W briefly (p. 14).

5203. Plant, Deborah G. *Every Tub Must Sit on Its Own Bottom: The Philosophy and Politics of Zora Neale Hurston*. Urbana: University of Illinois Press, pp. 67–68, 191. Comments on and quotes from "Blueprint for Negro Writing."

5204. Poore, Charles. "Review of *Native Son*," in *The Critical Response to Richard Wright*. Ed. Robert J. Butler. Westport, CT: Greenwood Press, pp. 25–26.

5205. Popkin, Michael, ed. *Modern Black Writers*. New York: Continuum.

5206. Prescott, Orville. "Review of *Black Boy*," in *The Critical Response to Richard Wright*. Ed. Robert J. Butler. Westport, CT: Greenwood Press, pp. 63–64.

5207. _____. "Review of *The Outsider*," in *The Critical Response to*

Richard Wright. Ed. Robert J. Butler. Westport, CT: Greenwood Press, pp. 103–104.

5208. Rampersad, Arnold. "A Chronology of the Life of Langston Hughes," in his *The Collected Poems of Langston Hughes*. New York: Knopf, pp. 3–20. Mentions a reception for W and Hughes sponsored by *New Anvil*, *NS*, and a visit to W in Paris shortly before his death (pp. 12, 17).

5209. _____. "Introduction," in his *Richard Wright: A Collection of Critical Essays*. Englewood Cliffs, NJ: Prentice Hall, pp. 1–11. Surveys W's career and assesses his standing. "In African American fiction, he was perhaps the most significant and influential author of this century. Certainly few later writers have matched Wright in the fearless and uncompromising nature of his essential vision, or created works of art as decisive in defining what history has made of the African American character" (p. 11).

5210. _____, ed. *Richard Wright: A Collection of Critical Essays*. Englewood Cliffs, NJ: Prentice Hall, iv + 211 pp. Contains an introduction, chronology, notes on contributors, and bibliography, as well as previously published essays by Timothy Dow Adams, Kwame Anthony Appiah, Michael Atkinson, Jerry H. Bryant, Yoshinobu Hakutani, Abdul R. JanMohamed, Keneth Kinnamon, Tony Magistrale, Jack B. Moore, Arnold Rampersad, John M. Reilly, Joseph T. Skerrett, Jr., Louis Tremaine, Patricia D. Watkins, and Sherley Anne Williams.

5211. _____. "*Lawd Today!*" in his *Richard Wright: A Collection of Critical Essays*. Englewood Cliffs, NJ: Prentice Hall, pp. 124–128.

5212. _____. "Too Honest for His Own Good," in *The Critical Response to Richard Wright*. Ed. Robert J. Butler. Westport, CT: Greenwood Press, pp. 163–166.

5213. _____, and David Roessel. "A Chronology of the Life of Langston Hughes," in their *The Collected Poems of Langston Hughes*. New York: Alfred A. Knopf, pp. 8–20. Includes comments on Hughes's response to *NS* in 1940 (p. 12) and notes his visit with W in Paris in 1960 (p. 17).

5214. _____. "Notes to the Poems," in their *The Collected Poems of Langston Hughes*. New York:

Knopf, pp. 611–687. Mentions W's description of Beale Street in *BB* (p. 623), Canada Lee's role as Bigger in the play *NS* (p. 653), the novel *NS* (p. 663), and, glossing line 52 of *Ask Your Mama*, W, *NS*, and *BB* (p. 676).

5215. Ramsey, Priscilla R. "John A. Williams: The Black American Narrative and the City," in *The City in African-American Literature*. Eds. Yoshinobu Hakutani and Robert Butler. Madison/Teaneck, NJ: Fairleigh Dickinson University Press, pp. 212–226. Mentions briefly W as the prototype for Harry Ames in *The Man Who Cried I Am* (p. 216).

5216. [David L. Ransel]. "Contributors." *The American Historical Review*, 100 (June), iii–xiii. Mentions briefly work on W by Thomas Cripps (p. xi).

5217. Redding, Saunders. "Review of *Eight Men*," in *The Critical Response to Richard Wright*. Ed. Robert J. Butler. Westport, CT: Greenwood Press, pp. 135–136.

5218. Reed, Ishmael, Quincy Troupe, and Steve Cannon. "The Essential Ellison," in *Conversations with Ralph Ellison*. Eds. Maryemma Graham and Amritjit Singh. Jackson: University Press of Mississippi, pp. 342–377.

5219. _____, Quincy Troupe, and Steve Cannon. "The Essential Ellison," in *Conversations with Ralph Ellison*. Eds. Maryemma Graham and Amritjit Singh. Jackson: University Press of Mississippi, pp. 342–377.

5220. _____, and John O'Brian/1971," in *Conversations with Ishmael Reed*. Eds. Bruce Dick and Amritjit Singh. Jackson: University Press of Mississippi, pp. 14–40.

5221. Reilly, John M. "Richard Wright and the Art of Non-Fiction: Stepping Out on the Stage of the World," in *Richard Wright: A Collection of Critical Essays*. Ed. Arnold Rampersad. Englewood Cliffs, NJ: Prentice Hall, pp. 174–187.

5222. _____. "Richard Wright, 1908–1960," in *Major Black American Writers Through the Harlem Renaissance*. Ed. Harold Bloom. New York Chelsea House, pp. 184–185.

5223. Reineke, Yvonne. "Practicing Theory." *American Quarterly*, 47 (December), 727–734. Quotes T.V. Reed mentioning W (p. 731).

5224. Remnick, David. "Visible Man," in *Conversations with Ralph*

Ellison. Eds. Maryemma Graham and Amritjit Singh. Jackson: University Press of Mississippi, pp. 392–401.

5225. Rico, Barbara, and Sandra Mano. "New 'Theme(s) for English B': Reimagining Contexts for Learning in Multiethnic Writing Classes," in *The Canon in the Classroom: The Pedagogical Implications of Canon Revision in American Literature*. Ed. John Alberti. New York: Garland, pp. 99–116. Mentions briefly "The Man Who Was Almost a Man" (p. 102).

5226. Robeson, Elizabeth. "The Ambiguity of Julia Peterkin." *The Journal of Southern History*, 61 (November), 761–786. Mentions W briefly (p. 770).

5227. Robinson, Cedric. "Introduction," in *White Man Listen!* New York: Harper Perennial, pp. xiii–xxv. Summarizes W's life and career in the U.S. and France, explains his relation to Marxism and to the Third World, and explicates his "analytical skills and political wisdom." Also notes the importance of the revival of interest in W.

5228. Romanet, Jerome de. "A Conversation with Melvin Dixon, New York City, January 6, 1992." *Afram Newsletter*, No. 42 (December), pp. 19–32. Dixon comments on the Library of America edition of W.

5229. Rose, Mike. "Chicago Hope: Comets in the Classroom." *The Nation*, 261 (16 October), 424–428. Mentions briefly W and *NS* (p. 424).

5230. Rosen, Steven J. "African American Anti-Semitism and Himes's *Lonely Crusade*." *MELUS*, 20 (Summer), 47–68. Mentions briefly W's criticism of black Communists in *AH* (p. 51).

5231. Royot, Daniel. "Foreign Scholarship: French Contributions," in *American Literary Scholarship: An Annual/1993*. Ed. Gary Scharnhorst. Durham: Duke University Press, pp. 355–367. Mentions Corinne Duboin's "Segregation and the Representation of Urban Space in Richard Wright's *Native Son*" (p. 365).

5232. Rubin, Louis D., Jr. *A Writer's Companion*. Baton Rouge: Louisiana State University Press, p. 555. Lists *NS* and its primary characters s.v. Some Famous Novels.

5233. Rubin, Rachel. "Ellison, Ralph," in *A Companion to American*

Thought. Eds. Richard Wightman Fox and James T. Kloppenberg. Cambridge, MA: Blackwell, pp. 203–204. Mentions W briefly.

5234. Saeta, Elsa, and Izora Skinner. "Interview with Ernest Gaines," in *Conversations with Ernest Gaines*. Ed. John Lowe. Jackson: University Press of Mississippi, pp. 16–24.

5235. Saunders, James Robert. *The Wayward Preacher in the Literature of African American Women*. Jefferson, NC: McFarland, p. 48. Comments on the folkloric use of trains in W and Hurston.

5236. Schoener, Allon, ed. *Harlem on My Mind: Cultural Capital of Black America, 1900–1968*. New York: The New Press, p. 163.

5237. Segal, Ronald. *The Black Diaspora*. New York: Farrar, Straus & Giroux, p. 418. Comments briefly on W and *NS*.

5238. Shannon, Sandra. *The Dramatic Vision of August Wilson*. Washington, DC: Howard UP, pp. 18, 23, 39, 122. Notes Wilson's early reading of W and mentions *TMBV*.

5239. Shaw, Harry B. "The Historical Pragmatism of Richard K. Barksdale." *The Langston Hughes Review*, 13 (Fall/Spring), 1–20. Mentions W briefly (p. 10).

5240. Shrodes, Caroline, Harry Finestone, Michael Shugrue, and Fontaine Maury Belford. "Richard Wright '*The Ethics of Living Jim Crow*,'" in their *The Conscious Reader*. Sixth edition. New York: Macmillan, p. 749. Reprint of 1985.

5241. _____. "Suggestions for Discussion, Suggestions for Writing," in their *The Conscious Reader*. Sixth edition. New York: Macmillan, p. 757.

5242. Sillen, Samuel. "Review of *Native Son*," in *The Critical Response to Richard Wright*. Ed. Robert J. Butler. Westport, CT: Greenwood Press, pp. 31–33.

5243. Simons, Margaret A. "Introduction," in her *Feminist Interpretations of Simone de Beauvoir*. University Park: The Pennsylvania State University Press, pp. 1–28. Briefly notes W's influence on de Beauvoir (pp. 4–5).

5244. _____. "*The Second Sex*: From Marxism to Radical Feminism," in her *Feminist Interpretations of Simone de Beauvoir*. University Park: The Pennsylvania State University Press, pp. 243–262.

5245. Simons, Margaret A. "*The*

Second Sex: From Marxism to Radical Feminism," in her *Feminist Interpretations of Simone de Beauvoir*. University Park: The Pennsylvania State University Press, pp. 243–262. Notes that de Beauvoir read and published W (p. 246).

5246. Singh, Amritjit. "Introduction to the Harper Perennial Edition," in *Black Power: A Record of Reactions in a Land of Pathos*. By Richard Wright. New York: Harper Perennial, pp. xi–xxxiv. Substantial treatment of *BP* and the issues it raises concerning the West and Africa. It is "one of the richest texts in the tradition of travel literature." W was grappling with new definitions of community and individual empowerment that would allow a more encompassing humanity."

5247. _____. "Richard Wright's *The Outsider*: Existentialist Exemplar or Critique?," in *The Critical Response to Richard Wright*. Ed. Robert J. Butler. Westport, CT: Greenwood Press, pp. 123–129.

5248. Skerrett, Joseph T., Jr. "Composing Bigger: Wright and the Making of *Native Son*," in *Richard Wright: A Collection of Critical Essays*. Ed. Arnold Rampersad. Englewood Cliffs, NJ: Prentice Hall, pp. 26–39.

5249. Skinner, Robert E. "Streets of Fear: The Los Angeles Novels of Chester Himes," in *Los Angeles in Fiction: A Collection of Essays*. Ed. David Fine. Revised edition. Albuquerque: University of New Mexico Press, pp. 227–238. Mentions W briefly (p. 235).

5250. Skow, John. "The Second Time Around." *Time*, 146 (24 July), 67. Article on Dorothy West mentioning W briefly.

5251. Smagorinsky, Peter. "New Canons, New Problems: The Challenge of Promoting a Sense of Kinship Among Students of Diversity," in *Teaching a "New Canon"?: Students, Teachers, and Texts in the College Literature Classroom*. Urbana, Ill." National Council of Teachers of English, pp. 48–64. Includes discussion of pedagogical problems in teaching *NS* and *BB* (pp. 51, 55–56, 57–58, 62).

5252. Smith, Charles M. "'Richard Wright: Black Boy,' Sept. 4, 10 p.m., Channel 13." *The New York Amsterdam News* (2 September), p. 28. Announces and discusses Madison D. Lacy's documentary film.

5253. Smith, Lillian. "Richard Wright Adds a Chapter to Our Bitter Chronicle," in *The Critical Response to Richard Wright*. Ed. Robert J. Butler. Westport, CT: Greenwood Press, p. 69.

5254. Smith, Sidonie Ann [citical extract], in *Black American Women Fiction Writers*. Ed. Harold Bloom. New York: Chelsea House, pp. 5–6.

5255. Smitherman, Geneva. "'Students' Right to Their Own Language': A Retrospective." *English Journal*, 84 (January), 21–27. Mentions briefly *BP* (p. 21).

5256. Snyder, Robert E. "*A Southern Life: Letters of Paul Green, 1916–1981*. Edited by Lawrence G. Avery." *The Journal of Southern History*, 61 (August), 633–634. Review mentioning W briefly as a correspondent of Green.

5257. Sporn, Paul. *Against Itself: The Federal Theater and Writers' Project in the Midwest*. Detroit: Wayne State University Press, pp. 138, 225, 276, 281, 313. Mentions W briefly.

5258. Stam, Robert. "Orson Welles, Brazil, and the Power of Blackness," in *Perspectives on Orson Welles*. Ed. Morris Beja. New York: G.K. Hall, pp. 219–244.

5259. Starr, John R. "Racial Discrimination's Roots." *Little Rock Arkansas Democrat Gazette* (5 September), p. 5B. Autobiographical account of the white columnist's racist childhood and youth in Lake Village and Pine Bluff. In high school reading *BB* put "the first chinks in [his] armor of racism."

5260. Steinberg, Stephen. *Turning Back: The Retreat from Racial Justice in American Thought and Policy*. Boston: Beacon Press, pp. x, 17, 71–72. Mentions W with brief quotations.

5261. Stephens, Henrietta. "Richard Wright Lectures." *csblac*, June, p. 1. Describes a lecture series at the Center for the Study of Black Literature and Culture of the University of Pennsylvania. The 1995 lecturer was Arnold Rampersad, one of whose lectures, on 21 March, was "Hurston, Hughes, Wright, and the Quest for Identity."

5262. Stepto, Michele. "Richard Wright," in her *African American Voices*. Brookfield, Connecticut: The Milbrook Press, pp. 120–121. Headnote to a selection from *BB* concerning W's Uncle Hoskins. Also lists 4 of W's books (p. 156).

5263. Stepto, Robert B., and Michael S. Harper. "Study and Experience: an Interview with Ralph Ellison," in *Conversations with Ralph Ellison*. Eds. Maryemma Graham and Amritjit Singh. Jackson: University Press of Mississippi, pp. 319–341.

5264. ____, and Michael S. Harper. "Study and Experience: an Interview with Ralph Ellison," in *Conversations with Ralph Ellison*. Eds. Maryemma Graham and Amritjit Singh. Jackson: University Press of Mississippi, pp. 319–341.

5265. Stern, Richard. "Ralph Ellison." *The Antioch Review*, 53 (Winter), pp. 107–110. Mentions Nathan Scott's piece on W.

5266. Stern, Richard. "Ralph Ellison." *Callaloo*, 18 (Spring), 284–287.

5267. Stonum, Gary Lee. "Themes, Topics, Criticism," in *American Literary Scholarship: An Annual/1993*: Ed. Gary Scharnhorst. Durham: Duke University Press, pp. 341–354. Notes treatment of W in Peter A. Dorsey's *Sacred Estrangement* (p. 348) and in Paul Gilroy's *The Black Atlantic* (p. 352).

5268. Storhoff, Gary. "*Chester Himes: An Annotated Primary and Secondary Bibliography*. Compiled by Michel Fabre, Robert E. Skinner, and Lester Sullivan." *MELUS*, 20 (Fall), 137–139. Review mentioning W briefly.

5269. Strout, Cushing. "In Memoriam: Ralph Ellison 1914–1994." *The Sewanee Review*, 103 (Spring), 295–299. Includes commentary contrasting W and Ellison.

5270. Sullivan, Richard. "Lives of More Than Quiet Desperation," in *The Critical Response to Richard Wright*. Ed. Robert J. Butler. Westport, CT: Greenwood Press, pp. 133–134.

5271. Sundquist, Eric J. "Bibliography," in his *Cultural Contexts for Ralph Ellison's Invisible Man*. Boston: Bedford/St. Martin's, pp. 249–255. Lists "Blueprint for Negro Writing," "I Tried to Be a Communist," and *TMBV*.

5272. ____. "Introduction," in his *Cultural Contexts for Ralph Ellison's Invisible Man*. Boston: Bedford/St. Martin's, pp. 1–28. Comments on W's influence on Ellison, mentioning *NS*, *UTC*, W's disillusionment with the Communist Party, and *TMBV* (pp. 2, 8, 13, 18).

5273. ____. "Preface," in his *Cultural Contexts for Ralph Ellison's Invisible Man*. Boston: Bedford/St. Martin's, pp. v–vii. Mentions W briefly.

5274. ____. "Richard Wright *Twelve Million Black Voices*," in his *Cultural Contexts for Ralph Ellison's Invisible Man*. Boston: Bedford/St. Martin's, pp. 104–106. Headnote to an excerpt from *TMBV*, reviewing W's career and noting Ellison's strongly favorable response to *TMBV*.

5275. ____. "Street Market Song, *De Sweet Pertater Man*; Leo Gurley, *Sweet-the-Monkey*," in his *Cultural Contexts for Ralph Ellison's Invisible Man*. Boston: Bedford/St. Martin's, pp. 132–135. Mentions W briefly.

5276. ____. "The Literature of Slavery and African American Culture," in *The Cambridge History of American Literature*, Vol. 2. Ed. Sacvan Bercovitch. Cambridge: Cambridge University Press, pp. 239–328. Mentions briefly *UTC* (p. 292).

5277. Tarshis, Jerome. "The Other 300 Years: a Conversation with Ernest J. Gaines, Author of *The Autobiography of Miss Jane Pittman*," in *Conversations with Ernest J. Gaines*. Ed. John Lowe. Jackson: University Press of Mississippi, pp. 72–79.

5278. Tate, Greg. "Greg Tate," in *Swing Low: Black Men Writing* by Rebecca Carroll. New York: Carol Southern Books. pp. 206–218. Mentions briefly *NS* (p. 215).

5279. Thomas, H. Nigel. "The Bad Nigger Figure in Selected Works of Richard Wright, William Melvin Kelley, and Ernest Gaines." *CLA Journal*, 39 (December), 143–164. Includes examination of Bigger Thomas, Big Boy, Dan Taylor, Silas, and Aunt Sue. Bigger "is the quintessential Bad Nigger of American literature" (p. 150).

5280. Timmerman, John H. "Introduction to *The Man Who Was Almost a Man*," in his *A Nation's Voice: An Anthology of American Short Fiction*. Fort Worth: Harcourt Brace College, pp. 533–534. Critical-biographical headnote.

5281. ____. "Introduction: Understanding American Literature Through Context," in his *A Nation's Voice: An Anthology of Short Fiction*. Fort Worth: Harcourt Brace College, pp. 1–8. Mentions W briefly (p. 5).

5282. ____. "Ways of Understanding the Text," in his *A Nation's Voice: An Anthology of Short Fiction.* Fort Worth: Harcourt Brace College, pp. 839–855. Comments briefly on "The Man Who Was Almost a Man" (p. 855).

5283. _____. "Introduction to 'The Man Who Was Almost a Man,'" in his *A Nation's Voice: An Anthology of American Short Fiction.* Fort Worth: Harcourt Brace, pp. 533–534. Critical headnote.

5284. _____. "Introduction: Understanding American Literature Through Context," in his *A Nation's Voice: An Anthology of American Short Fiction.* Fort Worth: Harcourt Brace, pp. 1–8. Mentions W briefly (p. 5).

5285. _____. "Way of Understanding the Text," in his *A Nation's Voice: An Anthology of American Short Fiction.* Fort Worth: Harcourt Brace, pp. 839–855. Comments on W's Marxism in relation to "The Man Who Was Almost a Man" (p. 855).

5286. Tooker, Dan, and Roger Hofheins. "Ernest J. Gaines," in *Conversations with Ernest Gaines.* Ed. John Lowe. Jackson: University Press of Mississippi, pp. 99–111.

5287. Tremaine, Louis. "The Dissociated Sensibility of Bigger Thomas in Wright's *Native Son,*" in *Richard Wright: A Collection of Critical Essays.* Ed. Arnold Rampersad. Englewood Cliffs, NJ: Prentice-Hall, pp. 40–52.

5288. Trilling, Lionel. "A Tragic Situation." *The Nation,* 260 (15 May), 684.

5289. Tuttleton, James W. "The Achievement of Ralph Ellison." *The New Criterion,* 14 (December), 5–10. Mentions W briefly (pp. 5, 6) and comments on the Howe-Ellison exchange in relation to W (pp. 8–9).

5290. _____. "The Problematic Texts of Richard Wright," in *The Critical Response to Richard Wright.* Ed. Robert J. Butler. Westport, CT: Greenwood Press, pp. 167–172.

5291. Underwood, Thomas A. "Mencken, H[enry] L[ouis]," in *A Companion to American Thought.* Eds. Richard Wightman Fox and James T. Kloppenberg. Cambridge, MA: Blackwell, pp. 447–449. Notes Mencken's influence on W, quoting from *BB.*

5292. Unger, Douglas. "Trying to Break Away," in *An Unsentimental Education: Writers and Chicago.* Ed.

Molly McQuade. Chicago: The University of Chicago Press, p. 219. Mentions "the crazed flight of Richard Wright's Bigger Thomas."

5293. Valade, Roger M., III. "*Native Son,*" in *The Essential Black Literature Guide.* Detroit: Visible Ink Press, pp. 269–270. Plot summary with critical comments.

5294. Valentine, Victoria. "Not Without Langston." *Emerge,* 6 (May), 58–59. Article on Hughes mentioning W briefly.

5295. _____. "Wright Angles." *Emerge,* 6 (September), 76. Review of paperback editions of *BP, PS,* and *WML.* Also mentions the film *Richard Wright-Black Boy.*

5296. Van Leer, David. "The Fire Last Time." *The New Republic,* 212 (13 February), 36–39. Review of David Leeming's *James Baldwin: A Biography* mentioning his association with W.

5297. Wald, Alan. "Introduction," in *The People From Heaven* by John Sanford. Urbana: University of Illinois Press, pp. xi–xxxvi. Mentions W, *UTC* (p. xvi), *TMBV* (p. xviii), and *AH* (p. xxxii).

5298. _____. "Introduction," in *The People From Heaven* by John Sanford. Urbana: University of Illinois Press, pp. xi–xxxvi. Mentions W, *UTC,* and *TMBV* (p. xviii), and notes W's dedication to the Communist Party in the 1930s.

5299. _____. "Marxist Literary Resistance to the Cold War." *Prospects: An Annual of American Cultural Studies,* 20, 479–492. Mentions W briefly (pp. 484, 485, 487, 492).

5300. Wald, Priscilla. "Hurston, Zora Neale," in *A Companion to American Thought.* Eds. Richard Wightman Fox and James T. Kloppenberg. Cambridge, MA: Blackwell, pp. 322–323. Mentions W briefly.

5301. Walker, Margaret. "Richard Wright, 1908–1960," in *Major Black American Writers Through the Harlem Renaissance.* Eds. Harold Bloom. New York: Chelsea House, pp. 183–184.

5302. Walker, Pierre A. "Racial Protest, Identity, Words, and Form in Maya Angelou's *I Know Why the Caged Bird Sings.*" *College Literature,* 22 (October), 91–108. Includes comparison of Angelou's autobiography and *BB.*

5303. Wall, Cheryl A. *Women of*

the Harlem Renaissance. Bloomington: Indiana University Press, pp. 10, 196, 197, 208. Mentions *NS* and Zora Neale Hurston's review of *UTC.*

5304. Wallace, Margaret. "A Powerful Novel About a Boy from Chicago's Black Belt," in *The Critical Response to Richard Wright.* Ed. Robert J. Butler. Westport, CT: Greenwood Press, pp. 29–30.

5305. Wallace, Maurice. "Constructing the Black Masculine: Frederick Douglass, Booker T. Washington, and the Sublimits of African American Autobiography," in *Subjects and Citizens: Nation, Race, and Gender from Oroonoko to Anita Hill.* Eds. Michael Moon and Cathy N. Davidson. Durham, NC: Duke University Press, pp. 245–270. Mentions W briefly (p. 246).

5306. Ward, Douglas Turner. "Foreword," in *Classic Plays from the Negro Ensemble Company.* Ed. Paul Carter Harrison and Gus Edwards. Pittsburgh: University of Pittsburgh Press, pp. xi–xxiv. Relates obtaining the script of *Daddy Goodness* from Robert Hooks and then producing and directing the play in 1968.

5307. Ward, Jerry W., Jr. "Introduction to the Harper Perennial Edition of *Black Boy (American Hunger),*" in *The Critical Response to Richard Wright.* Ed. Robert J. Butler. Westport, CT: Greenwood Press, pp. 95–99.

5308. _____. *Richard Wright: Black Boy: A Teacher's Guide for Secondary and Post Secondary Educators.* Jackson: Mississippi Educational Television, 25 pp. Designed to accompany the film documentary of W's life, this guide contains an overview; questions and activities before and after viewing under the rubrics of history, education, literature, psychology, sociology, and political science/cultural studies; and a bibliography.

5309. Washington, Bryan R. *The Politics of Exile: Ideology in Henry James, F. Scott Fitzgerald, and James Baldwin.* Boston: Northeastern University Press, pp. 7, 17, 20, 72–73, 97, 136. Compares Baldwin and W with respect to protest fiction, quotes from "How 'Bigger' Was Born," mentions *NS* and *UTC,* and mentions W elsewhere.

5310. Watkins, Mel. *On the Real Side: Laughing, Lying, and Signifying—the Underground Tradition of*

African-American Humor. New York: Touchstone, pp. 34, 402, 419, 424–426.

5311. Watkins, Patricia D. "The Paradoxical Structure of Richard Wright's 'The Man Who Lived Underground," in *Richard Wright: A Collection of Critical Essays.* Ed. Arnold Rampersad. Englewood Cliffs, NJ: Prentice Hall, pp. 148–161.

5312. _____. "The Paradoxical Structure of Richard Wright's 'The Man Who Lived Underground,'" in *The Critical Response to Richard Wright.* Ed. Robert J. Butler. Westport, CT: Greenwood Press, pp. 141–150.

5313. Watts, Jill. *God, Harlem U.S.A.: The Father Divine Story.* Berkeley: University of California Press, p. 119.

5314. Weaver, Bruce L. *Novel Openings: First Sentences of 11,000 Fictional Works, Topically Arranged with Subject, Keyword, Author and Title Indexing.* Jefferson, NC: McFarland, pp. 116, 157, 364, 430. Quotes first sentences of *LT, LD, O,* and *NS.*

5315. Welch, Linda Latham. "Reading Lists Still Spark Controversy." Austin *American-Statesman* (18 September) p. A1. Article on parental censorship efforts in Texas public schools. One objected to *BB.*

5316. Werner, Craig. "Chicago Renaissance," in *The Oxford Companion to Women's Writing in the United States.* Eds. Cathy N. Davidson and Linda Wagner-Martin. New York: Oxford University Press, pp. 165–167. Comments on W's place in this literary movement, mentioning his introduction to *Black Metropolis, NS, New Challenge,* "Blueprint for Negro Writing," and *AH.*

5317. _____. *Gold Bugs and the Powers of Blackness: Re-reading Poe.* Baltimore: The Edgar Allen Poe Society, pp. 4, 9, 12, 13, 25, 27. Mentions W several times and quotes his dictum: "If Poe were alive, he would not have to invent horror; horror would invent him" (p. 4).

5318. Wiegman, Robyn. *American Anatomies: Theorizing Race and Gender.* Durham, NC: University of North Carolina Press, pp. 14, 100–104, 223, 259. Analyzes *NS* as "our literature's most compelling story of the black man caught in the mythology of the rapist" (p. 100).

Wiegman shows how sexual metaphors allow a gendered reading of several scenes.

5319. Wilentz, Sean. "Socialism," in *A Companion to American Thought.* Eds. Richard Wightman Fox and James T. Kloppenberg. Cambridge, MA: Blackwell, pp. 637–641. Mentions W briefly (p. 637).

5320. Wiley, Ralph. "On the A-Train to Venus with Isis," in *Brotherman: The Odyssey of Black Men in America.* Eds. Herb Boyd and Robert L. Allen. New York: Ballantine Books, pp. 278–285.

5321. Williams, Harry McKinley. "Understanding the Bag the Cat Is In: Father and Son in Richard Wright's *Black Boy.*" *Journal of African American Men,* 1 (Summer), 92–98. Argues that W's depiction of his father is unfair because he does not take into account all the social factors operating in his life.

5322. Williams, John A. "My Man Himes: An Interview with Chester Himes," in *Conversations with Chester Himes.* Eds. Michel Fabre and Robert E. Skinner. Jackson: University Press of Mississippi, pp. 29–82.

5323. Williams, Sherley Anne. "Papa Dick and Sister-Woman: Reflections on Women in the Fiction of Richard Wright," in *Richard Wright: A Collection of Critical Essays.* Ed. Arnold Rampersad. Englewood Cliffs, NJ: Prentice Hall, pp. 63–82.

5324. Wilson, Sondra Kathryn. "Introduction," in her *The Selected Writings of James Weldon Johnson.* Vol. II. New York: Oxford University Press, pp. 3–5. Briefly compares Johnson and W, mentioning *UTC* and *NS.*

5325. Wood, Ruth Pirsig, *Lolita in Peyton Place: Highbrow, Middlebrow, and Lowbrow Novels of the 1950s.* New York: Garland, p. 119. Includes comments on *O.*

5326. Woods, Paula L. "Appendix: Mystery Chronology," in her *Spooks, Spies, and Private Eyes: Black Mystery, Crime, and Suspense Fiction.* New York: Doubleday, pp. 343–350. Includes entries for W's birth and for *NS* (pp. 345, 348).

5327. _____. "Introduction," in her *Spooks, Spies, and Private Eyes: Black Mystery, Crime, and Suspense Fiction.* New York: Doubleday, pp. xiii–xviii. Mentions briefly "The Man Who Killed a Shadow" and *NS* (p. xvi).

5328. _____. "Richard Wright, 'The Man Who Killed a Shadow,'" in her *Spooks, Spies, and Private Eyes: Black Mystery, Crime, and Suspense Fiction.* New York: Doubleday, p. 89. Headnote to the story.

5329. Worcester, Kent. "C.L.R. James and the American Century," in *C.L.R. James: His Intellectual Legacies.* Eds. Selwyn R. Cudjoe and William E. Cain. Amherst: University of Massachusetts Press, pp. 173–190. Mentions W briefly (p. 178).

5330. Wright, Julia. "For Mumia Abu-Jamal." *Richard Wright Newsletter,* 4 (Spring/Summer), 3. Relates Bigger Thomas to the writer journalist Abu-Jamal, condemned to death in the electric chair. Julia Wright states that her father would have supported Abu-Jamal as he did Clinton Brewer.

5331. Wright, Lee Alfred. *Identity, Family, and Folklore in African American Literature.* New York: Garland, pp. x, 75, 92, 95, 102, 129, 130. Comments on *NS, BB,* and Houston Baker and Henry Louis Gates on W.

5332. Young, Al. "Interview: Ishmael Reed," in *Conversations with Ishmael Reed.* Eds. Bruce Dick and Amritjit Singh. Jackson: University Press of Mississippi, pp. 41–50.

5333. Young, Stephen. "Articles Published by SSSL Members." *Society for the Study of Southern Literature Newsletter* (April), 8–9. Lists an article by William L. Andrews on W and autobiographical tradition.

5334. _____. "Audio & Video Cassettes & CDs." *Society for the Study of Southern Literature Newsletter* (April), 20. Lists *Richard Wright: Black Boy.*

5335. _____. "Major Authors and Poets." *Society for the Study of Southern Literature* (November), 10. Lists Robert Butler's *The Critical Response to Richard Wright* and paperback editions of *PS* and *WML.*

5336. Zamir, Shamoon. *Dark Voices: W.E.B. Du Bois and American Thought 1888–1903.* Chicago: The University of Chicago Press, p. 208. Comments on Fanon's use of *NS* in *Black Skin, White Masks.*

5337. Zimmerman, Raymond Samuel. "Masculinity and violence in 20th century American literature." *Dissertation Abstracts International,* 55 (April), 3194-A–3195-A. Compares Hemingway's *Death in the Afternoon, LT,* and Gustav

Hasford's *The Short-Timers* as portraying the ideology of masculinism. *LT* is an exposure of the ideology, not an endorsement.

5338. Zhang Yan. "I Wish I Had Met Richard Wright at Bandung in 1955." *China Today*, 44 (November), 25–27. Analyzes the Bandung

Conference, comparing his conclusions to W's in *CC*. Both emphasize the baneful role of colonialism and the conciliatory stance of Zhou Enlai.

5339. Zinn, Howard. *A People's History of the United States: 1492 to Present.* New York: Harper Perennial, pp. 437–438.

5340. Zrimsek, James. "The Arts," in *American Decades: 1980–1989.* Ed. Victor Bondi. Detroit: Gale, pp. 23–138. Mentions August Wilson's reading W (p. 123).

1996

5341. Alexander, Harriet Semmes, comp. *American and British Poetry: A Guide to the Criticism.* Athens: Ohio University Press/Swallow Press, pp. 447. Lists items on W's poetry by John McCluskey, Jr., Robert A Coles, and Bruce Dick.

5342. Algeo, Ann M. *The Courtroom as Forum: Homicide Trials by Dreiser, Wright, Capote, and Mailer.* New York: Peter Lang, pp. 2, 4, 43–69, 75, 84, 89, 118, 120, 141–143, 145, 148–150. The chapter on *NS* treats the sources and background of the novel, but focuses on the coroner's inquest and the courtroom procedures. Algeo concludes that W's "themes of the effect of class and race remain fresh, and we still struggle to correct the flaws he highlighted in a legal process influenced by racism, politics, and greed" (p. 69).

5343. Als, Hilton. *The Women.* New York: Farrar, Straus, Giroux, p. 130. Quotes Baldwin on W.

5344. Ambrose, D. Lena. "Encouraging Black Writers." *The Chronicle of Higher Education* (14 June), p. A45. Describes the establishment by Marita Golden of the Zora Neale Hurston/Richard Wright Foundation to encourage black writers in college by awarding literary prizes.

5345. Anon. *African American Perspectives, 1996–1997.* San Francisco: Resolution/California Newsreel, p. 13. Catalog notice of the video *Richard Wright—Black Boy* including blurbs by Henry Louis Gates, Jr., John Edgar Wideman, and Charles Johnson.

5346. Anon. "ALA 1996: Session 70: Richard Wright and Theoreti-

cal Illumination," *Richard Wright Newsletter*, 5 (Fall), 7. Contains abstracts of papers by J. Lee Greene on *SH*, Mark A Sanders on *UTC*, and Michael F. Lynch on *O*.

5347. Anon. "America's Dream." *People Weekly*, 45 (12 February), p. 18. Praises Danny Glover's performance in a television version of "Long Black Song."

5348. Anon. "America's Dream." *People Magazine*, 45 (12 February), 17. Notice of the video version of "Long Black Song."

5349. Anon. "Announcements." *Richard Wright Newsletter*, 4 (Spring), 2. Reports a showing of the film *Richard Wright: Black Boy* with comments by Jerry Ward at the Natchez Literary Celebration, 1–2 June, and announces an open meeting of the Richard Wright Circle at the American Literature Association conference in San Diego, 30 May–2 June 1996.

5350. Anon. *Bibliographic Guide to Black Studies: 1995.* New York: G.K. Hall, 337. Lists three primary and two secondary items concerning W in the New York Public Library, supplementing the *Dictionary Catalog of the Schomburg Collection of Negro Literature and History.*

5351. Anon. "*Black Boy,*" in *The Encyclopedia Americana.* Ed. Lawrence T. Lorimer. Danbury, CT: Grolier, pp. 29–30. Brief summary of *BB*, an important document in the struggle for equal rights in the United States.

5352. Anon. "*Black Writers and Latin America: Cross-Cultural Affinities* by Richard Jackson," in *Howard University Press 1997.* Washington: Howard University Press, p. 1. Pub-

lisher's announcement noting that Jackson treats W among other authors.

5353. Anon. "*Critical Essays on Richard Wright's Native Son,*" in *Twayne-G.K. Hall & Co. 1997 Literature Catalog.* New York: Twayne, p. 15. Publisher's announcement calling this compilation by Keneth Kinnamon "The most comprehensive gathering of essays on Richard Wright's famous novel."

5354. Anon. "Dissertations." *Journal of Modern Literature*, 19 (Spring), 374–876. Lists a dissertation by Donna Marie Perreault treating W and others.

5355. Anon. "Dissertations." *Journal of Modern Literature*, 19 (Spring), 391–392. Lists a dissertation by Marc Jeffrey Abernathy treating W and others.

5356. Anon. "Garland Publishing." *PMLA*, 111 (November), 1570. Contains a notice of *The Harlem Renaissance 1920–1940* mentioning W briefly.

5357. Anon. "HarperCollins Publishers." *PMLA*, 111 (October), 1228. Includes a publisher's notice of a paperback reprint of *EM* with an introduction by Paul Gilroy.

5358. Anon. "HarperCollins Publishers." *PMLA*, 111 (November), 1444. Publisher's advertisement listing a paperback edition of *EM* with an introduction by Paul Gilroy.

5359. Anon. "Illinois History from the Trail of Tears to the Paths of Greatness," in *Illinois: 1996 Visitors Guide.* Springfield: Illinois Department of Commerce and Community Affairs, Bureau of Tourism, pp. 6–8. Mentions W briefly.

5360. Anon. *Index to Black Peri-*

odicals: 1994. New York: G.K. Hall, p. 322. Lists five items on W.

5361. Anon. *Index to Black Periodicals: 1995.* New York: G.K. Hall, p. 376. Lists three items on W.

5362. Anon. "Literature Unit Plans." *English Journal,* 85 (January), 16. Advertisement listing *BB* and *NS.*

5363. Anon. "Literature Unit Plans." *English Journal,* 85 (February), 14.

5364. Anon. "Literature Unit Plans." *English Journal,* 85 (March), 120.

5365. Anon. "Margaret Walker. *Richard Wright: Daemonic Genius,*" in *Literature Catalog 1996.* New York: Penguin USA, p. 24. Publisher's announcement.

5366. Anon. "*The Mid-Century American Novel, 1935–1965: A Critical History,*" in *Twayne-G.K. Hall & Co. 1997 Literature Catalog.* New York: Twayne, p. 6. Publisher's announcement noting that this book by Linda Wagner-Martin covers "such canonical figures as Steinbeck and Wright" as well as others.

5367. Anon. "The Modern Language Association Promoting Excellence in Teaching and Scholarship." *American Literature,* 68 (September) [688–689]. Announces that a volume on *NS* is in production in the MLA Approaches to Teaching World Literature series.

5368. Anon. "*Native Son* (1940) Richard (Nathaniel) Wright (1908–1960), in *The New York Public Library's Books of the Century.* New York: Oxford University Press, p. 23. Includes comments on *NS* by Irving Howe and David Bradley.

5369. Anon. "News From Natchez: Two Writers Win '96 Richard Wright Literary Awards." *Richard Wright Newsletter,* 5 (Fall), 3. Announcement of the winners of the annual Richard Wright Literary Excellence Award: Ellen Douglas for fiction and Willie Morris for nonfiction.

5370. Anon. "*Pinktoes* by Chester Himes," in *University Press of Mississippi, March Through August 1996.* Jackson: University Press of Mississippi, p. 5. Publisher's announcement mentioning briefly W as a friend of Himes.

5371. Anon. "Program." *PMLA,* 111 (November), 1298–1410. Lists the following papers: "Richard Wright's *Black Power* as Political and Cultural Discourse" by Yoshinobu Hakutani (p. 1324), "Unmaking the Male Body: Richard Wright and the Politics of Black Masculinity" (p. 1354), and "Richard Wright's Outsider: Exorcising Demons" by Maryemma Graham, "Misogyny and Homophobia in *The Long Dream*" by Loretta S. Burns, and "The All-White World of *Savage Holiday*" by Xavier Nicholas (p. 1393).

5372. Anon. "Rediscover These Classics!" *PMLA* 111 (September), 1008. Publisher's advertisement for a reissue of *EM* with an introduction by Paul Gilroy.

5373. Anon. "*Richard Wright and Racial Discourse* Yoshinobu Hakutani." *American Literature,* 68 (June), [512]. Publisher's announcement.

5374. Anon. "Richard Wright and Racial Discourse." *Reference and Research Book News,* 11, p. 73. Brief notice of Hakutani's book.

5375. Anon. "RWC Minutes from the American Literature Association." *Richard Wright Newsletter,* 5 (Fall), 8. Business meeting with Jerry Ward, Mary Kemp Davis, Donald Gibson, Alfonso Hoskins, Yoshinob Hakatuni, Mark A. Sanders, and Virginia Whatley Smith in attendance.

5376. Anon. "Southern Women: 300 Years of Influence." Natchez, MS: Natchez Convention & Visitors Bureau, p. 2. Convention brochure listing a paper by Maryemma Graham on "Margaret Walker and Richard Wright's Mississippi" to be delivered on 31 May.

5377. Anon. "Wright National Teleconference." *Richard Wright Newsletter,* 4 (Spring), 15. Reports a televised symposium sponsored by Mississippi Educational Television on 4 October 1995. Participants were Julia Wright, Joyce Ann Joyce, Margaret Walker Alexander, Keneth Kinnamon, Maryemma Graham, and Madison Davis Lacy.

5378. Anon. "Wright, Richard," in *The New Webster's International Encyclopedia.* Ed. Michael Harkavy. Naples, FL: Trident Press, p. 1205. Brief biographical note.

5379. Anon. "Wright, Richard (Nathaniel)," in *The Oxford Companion to Twentieth-Century Literature in English.* Ed. Jenny Stringer. Oxford: Oxford University Press, pp. 737–738. Biographical sketch.

5380. Anon. "Wright, Richard (Nathaniel [1908–60])," in *The Ox-ford Companion to Twentieth-Century Literature in English.* Ed. Jenny Stringer. Oxford: Oxford University Press, pp. 737–738. Biographical sketch mentioning W's books through *EM.*

5381. Anon. *The Young Oxford History of African Americans.* New York: Oxford University Press, p. 5. Publisher's brochure including a brief quotation from *TMBV.*

5382. Anstendig, Linda, and David Hicks. "Probing the Work, Identifying Issues," in their *Writing Through Literature.* Upper Saddle River, NJ: Prentice-Hall, p. 103. Study questions for "The Man Who Was Almost a Man."

5383. _____. "Richard Wright 'The Man Who Was Almost a Man,'" in their *Writing Through Literature.* Upper Saddle River, NJ: Prentice-Hall, pp. 93–94. Brief headnote.

5384. Applebome, Peter. *Dixie Rising: How the South Is Shaping American Values, Politics, and Culture.* New York: Random House, pp. 11, 140, 292, 309. Mentions briefly W and *BB.*

5385. Arac, Jonathan. "Putting the River on New Maps: Nation, Race, and Beyond in Reading *Huckleberry Finn.*" *American Literary History,* 8 (Spring), 110–129. Mentions briefly *BB* (p. 121).

5386. Baker, Christina Looper. *In a Generous Spirit: A First-Person Biography of Myra Page.* Urbana: University of Illinois Press, pp. 100, 147. Mentions W briefly.

5387. Baker, Houston A. "From 'The Florescence of Nationalism in the 1960s and 1970s,'" in *On Gwendolyn Brooks: Reliant Contemplation.* Ed. Stephen Caldwell Wright. Ann Arbor: The University of Michigan Press, pp. 116–123.

5388. _____. "There Is No More Beautiful Way," in *Cornerstones: An Anthology of African American Literature.* Ed. Melvin Donalson. New York: St. Martin's Press, pp. 856–863.

5389. Bambara, Toni Cade. "Reading the Signs, Empowering the Eye," in *Deep Sightings and Rescue Missions: Fiction, Essays, and Conversations.* Ed. Toni Morrison. New York: Pantheon Books, pp. 89–138. Mentions briefly Bigger Thomas (p. 90).

5390. Banks, William M. *Black Intellectuals: Race and Responsibility* *in American Life.* New York: Norton, pp. 101, 109–110, 130, 132, 178, 198, 200, 207, 235. Comments briefly on W in relation to the Chicago group and the Writers' Project (pp. 109–110), quotes from "Blueprint for Negro Writing" (p. 198), and mentions W elsewhere.

5391. Baraka, Amiri. "Critical Extract," in *Black American Women Poets and Dramatists.* Ed. Harold Bloom. New York: Chelsea House, pp. 99–100. Mentions W briefly.

5392. _____. "Jimmy!" in his *Eulogies.* New York: Marsilio, pp. 91–98. Eulogy of James Baldwin mentioning W briefly (p. 94).

5393. Barnes, Deborah. "'I'd Rather Be a Lamppost in Chicago': Richard Wright and the Chicago Renaissance of African American Literature." *The Langston Hughes Review,* 14 (Spring/Fall), 52–61. Traces the social background and literary development of the Chicago Renaissance, contrasting it to its Harlem antecedent and emphasizing W's central role. Discusses *TMBV* and comments on *LT, O,* and *NS.*

5394. Barrett, Lindon. "*Double-Consciousness/Double Bind: Theoretical Issues in Twentieth-Century Black Literature.* By Sandra Adell." *American Literature,* 68 (June), 476–477. Mentions briefly *BB.*

5395. Basu, Biman. "Public and Private Discourses and the Black Female Subject: Gayl Jones' *Eva's Man.*" *Callaloo,* 19 (Winter), 193–208. Mentions W briefly (p. 195).

5396. Bell, Bernard W. "Genealogical Shifts in Du Bois's Discourse on Double Consciousness as the Sign of African American Difference," in *W.E.B. Du Bois on Race and Culture: Philosophy, Politics, and Poetics.* Eds. Bernard W. Bell, Emily R. Grosholz, and James B. Stewart. New York: Routledge, pp. 87–108. Mentions briefly *NS* (p. 96).

5397. Bell, Janet Cheatham. "My Country, But Not My Kind," in her *Victory of the Spirit: Meditations on Black Quotations.* New York: Warner Books, p. 96. Quotes from *AH.*

5398. _____. "No Man Around the House," in her *Victory of the Spirit: Meditations on Black Quotations.* New York: Warner Books, p. 67. Mentions W briefly.

5399. Benoist, Mary Anne. "Major Authors." *Society for the Study of Southern Literature Newsletter,* 30 (April), 14. Lists Adam Zachary

Newton's *Narrative Ethics,* which discusses *NS.*

5400. Benson, Jackson, J. *Wallace Stegner: His Life and Work.* New York: Viking, p. 106. Mentions briefly Bigger and *NS.*

5401. Berman, Paul. "The Romantic Revolutionary." *The New Yorker,* 72 (29 July), 68–72. Review of books by and about C.L.R. James mentioning his friendship with W (p. 68).

5402. _____. "The Romantic Revolutionary." *The New Yorker,* 72 (July), 68–72. Article on C.L.R. James commenting on his friendship with W.

5403. Best, Stephen Michael. "'Stand by Your Man': Richard Wright, Lynch Pedagogy, and Rethinking Black Male Agency," in *Representing Black Men.* Eds. Marcellus Blount and George P. Cunningham. New York: Routledge, pp. 111–130. Discusses *BB* in an effort to "map the protocols for recognizing and subjecting to resignification the discursive sign of the ostensibly 'weak' black man in the interest of marking it as a site of resistance. "In doing so Best enlists the aid of Gramsci, Laclau, Mouffe, and Lacan. Also comments on"The Ethics of Living Jim Crow."

5404. Blight, David W. "*Terrible Honesty: Mongrel Manhattan in the 1920s.* By Ann Douglas." *The Journal of American History,* 82 (March), 1614–1616. Quotes Ellison mentioning W as a "relative."

5405. Bloom, James D. "Political Incorrectness: The 1930s Legacy for Literary Studies," in *Radical Revisions: Rereading 1930s Culture.* Eds. Bill Mullen and Sherry Linkon. Urbana: University of Illinois Press, pp. 264–275. Mentions and quotes from W (pp. 265, 266, 267, 268).

5406. Bloom, Harold."Margaret Walker b. 1915," in his *Black American Women Poets and Dramatists,* New York: Chelsea House, pp 219–220, 223. Comments on the W-Walker friendship, noting her research for him when he was writing *NS* and lists her W biography.

5407. Blount, Marcellus, and George P. Cunningham. "Introduction," in their *Representing Black Men.* New York: Routledge, pp. ix–xv. Comments on Stephen M. Best's article on W in this collection.

5408. Boccia, Michael. "An Inter-

view with Charles Johnson." *African American Review,* 30 (Winter), 611–618. Johnson states that "only three black writers qualified (for me) as philosophically engaging: Jean Toomer, Richard Wright, and Ralph Ellison." He also warns against missing "the treatment of temporal experience" in *NS* by reading the novel merely as a social tract (p. 615).

5409. Bockting, Ineke. "Reconstructing the 'Necessary' World: Southern Defensive Narrative and the Childhood Autobiography," in '*Writing' Nation and 'Writing' Region in America.* Eds. Theo D'haen and Hans Bertens. Amsterdam: VU University Press, pp. 145–155. Quotes a passage from *BB* and compares it to Anne Moody's *Coming of Age in Mississippi* (pp. 153–154).

5410. Bontemps, Arna. "Negro Poets, Then and Now," in *The Harlem Renaissance, 1920–1940.* Vol. 5. Ed. Cary D. Wintz. New York: Garland, pp. 147–152.

5411. Boyd, Herb, and Robert L. Allen. "About the Contributors," in their *Brotherman: The Odyssey of Black Men in America–An Anthology.* New York: Ballantine Books, pp. 887–915.

5412. _____. "Introduction," in their *Brotherman: The Odyssey of Black Men in America–An Anthology.* New York: Ballantine Books, pp. xxi–xxxiv.

5413. Boyd, Herb. "Richard Wright's Daughter Reveals the Real 'Native Son.'" *New York Amsterdam News,* 1 June, pp. 23, 25. Reports on a lecture by Julia Wright at the Studio Museum in Harlem on 27 May 1996. She comments on *BB, NS,* and *WML,* and relates an incident in which she was denied use of the restroom facilities in Bergdoff Goodman department store in New York. "My father was furious, and this was probably the straw the broke the camel's back," hastening W's expatriation.

5414. _____. "Ollie Harrington: In Memoriam." *The Black Scholar,* (Winter/Spring), 74. Notes Harrington's friendship with W.

5415. Bracy, William. "Wright, Richard Nathaniel," in *The Encyclopedia Americana.* Ed. Lawrence T. Lorimer. Vol. 29. Danbury, CT: Grolier, pp. 555–556.

5416. _____. "Wright, Richard Nathaniel," in *The Encyclopedia*

Americana. Ed. Lawrence T. Lorimer. Vol. 29. Danbury, CT: Grolier, pp. 555–556.

5417. Bredeson, Carmen. *American Writers of the Twentieth Century.* Springfield. NJ: Enslow, p. 71. Comments on W's help to James Baldwin.

5418. Brinkley, Douglas. "Caution: I Brake for History." *American Heritage,* 47 (April), 62–64, 66, 68, 70, 72, 74. Notes that W is buried in the Père Lachaise Cemetery in Paris (p. 63).

5419. Brinkmeyer, Robert. "Why Finland?" *The Southern Register* (Spring), pp. 12–13. Notes interest in W in Finland and elsewhere in Europe. Mentions briefly *UTC.*

5420. Brown, John L. "Alfred Kazin. *Writing Was Everything.*" *World Literature Today,* 70 (Spring), 410–411. Review quoting Kazin calling W "the most enduring talent of 20th century American writing" (p. 411).

5421. Brown, Sterling A. "The Negro Author and His Publisher," in *The Harlem Renaissance, 1920–1940.* Vol. 5. Ed. Cary D. Wintz. New York: Garland, pp. 399–412.

5422. _____. "The New Negro in Literature (1925–1955)," in *The Harlem Renaissance, 1920–1940.* Vol. 5. Ed. Cary D. Wintz. New York: Garland, pp. 203–218.

5423. Bruner, Edward M. "Tourism in Ghana: The Representation of Slavery and the Return of the Black Diaspora." *American Anthropologist,* 98 (June), 290–304. Comments on and quotes from *BP* (pp. 291–292).

5424. Bryer, Jackson, and Neil Simon. "Neil Simon," in *Speaking on Stage: Interviews with Contemporary Playwrights.* Tuscaloosa: The University of Alabama Press, pp. 58–81. Simon recalls seeing his first play, *NS.* He was "mesmerized by what the theatre could do" (p. 61).

5425. Bucci, Richard. Maxnotes for *Native Son.* Piscataway, N.J., 86 pp. Contains a biographical sketch of W, information on the historical background, a list of characters in the novel, a plot summary, analysis of themes and influences, study questions and answers, paper topics, a chapter on "How 'Bigger' Was Born, and a brief bibliography.

5426. Burns, Ben. *Nitty Gritty: A White Editor in Black Journalism.* Jackson: University Press of Mississippi, pp. 35, 56, 79–82, 149, 166, 168–174, 177, 191. Recounts his interview with Gertrude Stein about W and devotes a chapter to "The Richard Wright Squabble" (pp. 167–182). Burns contests the accounts by Gayle and Fabre of his role in the dispute over W's "The Shame of Chicago," placing blame on *Ebony* publisher John H. Johnson. Afterwards Burns and his family had cordial relations with the Wrights in Paris.

5427. Bus, Heiner. "Asiatische Literatur," in *Amerikanische Literaturgeschichte.* Ed. Hubert Zapf. Stuttgart: Metzler, pp. 455–464 Briefly compares *NS* and Carlos Bulosan's *America Is in the Heart* (p. 456.)

5428. Butler, Robert. "*Richard Wright and Racial Discourse.*" *Richard Wright Newsletter,* 5 (Fall), 1, 6. Highly favorable review of Yoshinobu Hakutani's critical study, praising especially its treatment of *BP, CC,* and *PS.*

5429. _____. "RWC Notes from the College Language Association." *Richard Wright Newsletter,* 5 (Fall), 8. Report on a panel on *RP* with contributions by Jerry Ward, Adnee Bradford, and Onita Estes Hicks.

5430. Butler, Robert James. "Richard Wright. *Rite of Passage.*" *African American Review,* 30 (Summer), 315–320.

5431. Byrd, Rudolph P. "*Oxherding Tale* and *Siddhartha*: Philosophy, Fiction, and the Emergence of a Hidden Tradition." *African American Review,* 30 (Winter), 549–558. Mentions briefly "The Man Who Lived Underground" and *O* (p. 557).

5432. Callahan, John. "Introduction," in Ralph Ellison's *Flying Home and Other Stories.* New York: Random House, pp. ix–xxxviii. Includes comments on Ellison's early friendship with W and quotes from letters to him (pp. x, xi, xiii).

5433. Callahan, John F. "The Unpublished Ellison." *The New Yorker,* 72 (29 April & 6 May), 110. Mentions Ellison's early friendship with W and his review of *BB.*

5434. Callow, Simon. *Orson Welles: The Road to Xanadu.* New York: Viking, pp. 540–548, 550–554. Discusses the Welles-Houseman-Wright collaboration in bringing *NS* to the stage. Includes frequent quotations from the W-Houseman correspondence. Details various stage effects and cites reactions from critics praising the production. Callow concludes that "*Native Son* represented two important things, not necessarily serving each other: Wright's vision, and Welles's talent" (p. 553).

5435. Calloway, Catherine. "Fiction: The 1930s to the 1960s," in *American Literary Scholarship: An Annual/1994.* Ed. David J. Nordloh. Durham, NC: Duke University Press, pp. 279–302. Reviews articles on W by Jeffrey J. Folks, Mark J. Madigan, Yoshinobu Hakutani, James A. Jaye, Dale E. Peterson, Eberhard Alsen, Joyce A. Joyce, M. Lynn Weiss, and Sandra Adell (pp. 381–282, 283).

5436. Carafiol, Peter. "The Nationalist Model for American Ethnic Narrative," in '*Writing' Nation and 'Writing' Region in America.* Eds. Theo D'haen and Hans Bertens. Amsterdam: VU University Press, pp. 166–185. After discussing *Up from Slavery* and *Ragged Dick* as expressions of the myth of self-creation in America, Carafiol provides a substantial treatment of *NS* (pp. 178–185) as a refutation of the dream of success. W's novel "can be read as unmasking the interpretive assumptions that stand behind both the discourse of 'America' and ethnic discourses" (p. 184).

5437. _____. "'Who I Was': Ethnic Identity and American Literary Ethnocentrism," in *Criticism and the Color Line: Desegregating American Literary Studies.* Ed. Henry B. Wonham. New Brunswick, NJ: Rutgers University Press, pp. 43–62. Includes a discussion (pp. 54–61) of *NS* as a "composition of individual identity and of a specifically 'ethnic' identity" (p. 44). Bigger has no real options in his society. *NS* is a subversive novel departing from the usual ethnic narrative, indeed breaking out of all frames of interpretation.

5438. Carlin, Deborah. "African-American Writers: General," in *Reader's Guide to Literature in English.* Ed. Mark Hawkins-Dady. Chicago: Fitzgray Dearborn, pp. 9–14. Mentions W in comments on Robert A. Bone, Houston Baker, Melvin Dixon, Keith Byerman, C.W.E. Bigsby, and A. Robert Lee.

5439. Caron, Timothy P. "'The Reds Are in the Bible Room': Political Activism and the Bible in

Richard Wright's *Uncle Tom's Children*." *Studies in American Fiction*, 24 (Spring), 45–64. Examines religious and political themes in *UTC*. Imbued with the black religious experience of the South and committed to Communism, W reconciles them in his short story collection. Communism allows him to see "revolutionary potential" in biblical faith and "the victorious results of a Christian praxis driven by a Marxist demand for social justice." Each of the five stories is analyzed from this perspective.

5440. Cart, Michael. *From Romance to Realism: 50 Years of Growing and Change in Young Adult Literature*. New York: Harper Collins, p. 35. Mentions W briefly.

5441. Chapman, Abraham. "The Harlem Renaissance in Literary History," in *Analysis and Assessment, 1940–1979*. Vol. 6 of *The Harlem Renaissance, 1920–1940*. Ed. Cary D. Wintz. New York: Garland, pp. 2–22.

5442. Chénetier, Marc. *Beyond Suspicion: New American Fiction Since 1960*. Trans. Elizabeth A. Houlding. Philadelphia: University of Pennsylvania Press, pp. 11, 13. Mentions W briefly.

5443. Christian, Barbara T. "Metafore duttili: il racconto afroamericano," in *Volo di ritorno: antologia di racconti afroamericani* (1859–1977). Florence: Le Lettere, pp. 11–26. Comments on W's Marxism, *UTC*, and *NS*.

5444. Chude-Sokei, Louis. "The Black Atlantic Paradigm: Paul Gilroy and the Fractured Landscape of 'Race.'" *American Quarterly*, 48 (December), 740–745. Review of *The Black Atlantic* commenting on Gilroy's chapter on W (p. 741).

5445. Claridge, Henry. "Fiction: American-20th Century: Before World War II," in *Reader's Guide to Literature in English*. Chicago: Fitzroy Dearborn, pp. 278–281. Mentions W in a comment on Brian Lee.

5446. Clark, Edward. *Dictionary Catalog of the Collection of African American Literature in the Mildred F. Sawyer Library of Suffolk University*. Boston: Suffolk University, pp. 205–206. Includes twenty-five items s.v. "Wright, Richard."

5447. Clark, James W., Jr. "Getting Dick Prosser Right." *The Thomas Wolfe Review*, 20 (Fall), 21–33. Quotes from W's review of *Black Thunder*.

5448. Cobb, James C. "Community and Identity: Redefining Southern Culture." *The Georgia Review*, 50 (Spring), 9–24. Mentions W briefly (p. 11).

5449. _____. "Community and Identity: Redefining Southern Culture." *The Georgia Review*, 50 (Spring), 9–24. Mentions W briefly (pp. 11, 12).

5450. Coles, Robert. "Then & Now." *Commonweal*, 123 (17 May), 20–22. Review of Anthony Walton's *Mississippi: An American Journey* mentioning W briefly.

5451. Cochran, David. "So Much Nonsense Must Make Sense: The Black Vision of Chester Himes." *The Midwest Quarterly*, 38 (Autumn), 11–30. Mentions W briefly (p. 17).

5452. Conn, Peter. *Pearl S. Buck: A Cultural Biography*. Cambridge: Cambridge University Press, pp. 232, 261. Quotes from a letter to Buck from Eugene Kinckle of the Urban League praising her "magnanimity and contrasting it to W's "misanthropy and cynicism." Also mentions that W was under scrutiny by the F.B.I.

5453. Cooper, Wayne F. *Claude McKay: Rebel Sojourner in the Harlem Renaissance: A Biography*. Baton Rouge: Louisiana State University Press, pp. 82, 259, 320, 338, 361.

5454. Corkin, Stanley, and Phyllis Frus. "An Ex-centric Approach to American Cultural Studies: The Interesting Case of Zora Neale Hurston as a Noncanonical Writer." *Prospects*, 21, 193–228. Cites "Blueprint for Negro Writing" (p. 217, 228) and W's review of *Their Eyes Were Watching God* (pp. 200, 228).

5455. Cose, Ellis. "Color Blind." *Newsweek*, (25 November), 51, 53, 56. The first paragraph relates W's effort to advance in his job at the optical firm in Jackson, as related in "The Ethics of Living Jim Crow." The effort was doomed by racism. Mentions *UTC*.

5456. Crawford, Colin. *Uproar at Dancing Rabbit Creek: Battling Over Race, Class, and the Environment*. Reading, MA: Addison-Wesley, pp. xviii–xix. Quotes from "The Ethics of Living Jim Crow."

5457. Curry, Barbara K., and James Michael Brodie. *Sweet Words So Brave: The Story of African American Literature*. Madison, WI: Zino Press, pp. 27–28, 36, 47, 64. Con-

tains a biographical sketch of W with photograph. Also mentions his friendship with Ellison and Baldwin.

5458. Curtis, Nancy C. *Black Heritage Sites: An African American Odyssey and Finder's Guide*. Chicago: American Library Association, p. 150. An entry on the Smith Robertson Elementary School notes that W was a graduate.

5459. _____. "Smith Robertson Elementary School," in her *Black Heritage Sites*. Chicago: American Library Association, p. 150. Historical sketch mentioning W as "a distinguished graduate."

5460. Davenport-Hines, Richard. *Auden*. New York: Pantheon Books, p. 207. Mentions W briefly.

5461. Davis, Arthur P. "Integration and Race Literature," in *Analysis and Assessment, 1940–1979*. Vol. 6 of *The Harlem Renaissance, 1920–1940*. Ed. Cary D. Wintz. New York: Garland, pp. 275–280.

5462. Davis, Lennard J. "Are Novels Good for Us?" *The Nation*, 263 (15/22), 40–42. Review of Martha C. Nussbaum's *Poetic Justice: The Literary Imagination and Public Life* mentioning briefly *NS*.

5463. Davis, Thadious M. "Erasing the 'We of Me' and Rewriting the Racial Script: Carson McCullers's Two *Member[s] of the Wedding*, in *Critical Essays on Carson McCullers*. Eds. Beverly Lyon Clark and Melvin J. Friedman. New York: G.K. Hall, pp. 206–219. Quotes Richard Cook quoting W on McCullers.

5464. _____. Erasing the 'We of 'Me' and Rewriting the Racial Script: Carson McCullers's Two *Member[s] of the Wedding*, in *Critical Essays on Carson McCullers*. Eds. Melvin J. Friedman and Beverly Lyon Clark. New York: G.K. Hall, p. 218. Quotes Richard M. Cook Quoting W's praise of McCullers.

5465. Deena, Seodial. "Colonial and Canonical Marginalization and Oppression on the Basis of Gender." *CLA Journal*, 40 (September), 46–59. Includes criticism of W as a sexist black male writer (pp. 51–52, 55).

5466. Demirturk, Lale. "Teaching Richard Wright in Ankara, Turkey." *Richard Wright Newsletter*, 5 (Fall), 4–5. Relates the difficulties in teaching *NS* owing to cross-cultural differences. At first Turkish students were hostile to Bigger, but became more sympathetic as they learned more about American racism.

5467. Denning, Michael. *The Cultural Front: The Laboring of American Culture in the Twentieth Century.* London and New York: Verso, pp. 15, 26, 55, 60–61, 70, 93, 113, 119, 124, 131, 155, 157, 168, 201, 209–211, 217, 223–229, 232, 234, 237–240, 242–243, 247, 251–254, 264, 273, 328, 316, 331–332, 335, 340, 347, 350, 357, 360, 365, 372, 373, 397, 398–399, 400, 445, 471, 484. Mentions W frequently as a member of the cultural front in the Thirties and Forties. Comments on *AH* (pp. 55, 60–61, 209–211), *TMBV* (p. 119), *NS* (pp. 155, 316, 365, 372–373), *UTC* (p. 124), and *LT* (pp. 234, 242–243, 251–254). Comments also on W's relation to the John Reed Club and his friendship with Ellison (pp. 331–332.)

5468. Diawara, Manthia. "The Absent One: The Avant-Garde and the Black Imaginary in *Looking for Langston*," in *Representing Black Men.* Eds. Marcellus Blount and George P. Cunningham. New York: Routledge, pp. 205–224. Mentions W briefly (p. 219).

5469. Dickerson, Debra. "She's Gotta Have It." *The New Republic,* 214 (6 May), 12–14. Mentions briefly *NS.*

5470. Diedrich, Maria. "Afroamerikanische Literatur," in *Amerikanische Literaturgeschichte.* Ed. Hubert Zapf. Stuttgart: Metzler, pp. 402–426. Contains two paragraphs on W mentioning *UTC*," "Bright and Morning Star," *O,* and "Blueprint for Negro Writing," and especially, *NS.* Also comments on the Wright School (p. 417).

5471. Diedrich, Maria. "Lloyd L. Brown. *Iron City.*" *African American Review,* 30 (Summer), 320–322. The first paragraph of this review discusses the ambivalent Communist reception of *NS;* Diedrich then points out that Brown thought it "a vicious caricature of black life." W, *NS,* and "I Have Seen Black Hands" are also mentioned subsequently.

5472. Diefendorf, Elizabeth, ed. *The New York Public Library's Books of the Century.* New York: Oxford University Press, p. 221. Lists *NS.*

5473. Dietrich, Julia. *The Old Left in History and Literature.* New York: Twayne, pp. 88, 150–154, 178,

187. Discusses W's relationship to the Communist Party, drawing mainly on his contribution to *The God That Failed.* Mentions briefly *NS, BB,* and *O.*

5474. Dimock, Wai Chee. *Residues of Justice: Literature, Law, Philosophy.* Berkeley: University of California Press, p. 222. Quotes from "How 'Bigger' Was Born," comparing W's protagonist to Robert Charles of New Orleans, who killed seven people in 1900.

5475. Dolan, Marc. *Modern Lives: A Cultural Re-reading of "The Lost Generation."* West Lafayette, IN: Purdue University Press, pp. 56–57, 194–195. Comments on *BB,* especially as it presents both public and private history.

5476. Donalson, Melvin. "Fiction: Overview," in his *Cornerstones: An Anthology of African American Literature.* New York: St. Martin's Press, pp. 199–207. Includes comments on W's protest writing, mentioning *NS,* "The Man Who Killed a Shadow," and *UTC* (pp. 201–202).

5477. _____. "Henry Louis Gates, Jr.," in his *Cornerstones: An Anthology of African American Literature.* New York: St. Martin's Press, pp. 880–881. Mentions the W volume in the Critical Perspectives Past and Present series.

5478. _____. "James Baldwin (1924–1987)," in his *Cornerstones: An Anthology of African American Literature.* New York: St. Martin's Press, pp. 344–345. Headnote mentioning W briefly.

5479. _____. "John A. Williams (1925–)," in his *Cornerstones: An Anthology of African American Literature.* New York: St. Martin's Press, pp. 355–356. Headnote mentioning *The Most Native of Sons: A Biography of Richard Wright.*

5480. _____. "Literary Criticism and Theory: Overview," in his *Cornerstones: An Anthology of African American Literature.* New York: St. Martin's Press, pp. 847–855. Mentions briefly W and naturalism (p. 848).

5481. _____. "Nonfiction: Overview," in his *Cornerstones: An Anthology of African American Literature.* New York: St. Martin's Press, pp. 547–555. Mentions briefly W and *BB* (pp. 552, 554).

5482. _____. "Preface" to his *Cornerstones: An Anthology of African American Literature.* New York:

St. Martin's Press, pp. xiii–xix. Mentions W briefly (p. xv).

5483. _____. "Ralph Ellison (1914–94)," in his *Cornerstones: An Anthology of African American Literature.* New York: St. Martin's Press, pp. 736–737. Headnote mentioning W briefly.

5484. _____. "Richard Wright (1908–1960)," in his *Cornerstones: An Anthology of African American Literature.* New York: St. Martin's Press, pp. 317–318. Biographical-critical headnote to "The Man Who Killed a Shadow."

5485. _____. "Samuel W. Allen (1917–)," in his *Cornerstones: An Anthology of African American Literature.* New York: St. Martin's Press, pp. 152–153. Headnote mentioning W briefly.

5486. Donoghue, Denis. "What Literature Does." *Partisan Review,* 63 (Fall), 406–419. Includes a refutation of Martha Nussbaum's argument for the salutary effect of reading *NS* as part of "an education for public rationality." Far from being socially representative, *NS* "is mere cartoon, a bizarre fantasy."

5487. Douglas, Ann. *Terrible Honesty: Mongrel Manhattan in the 1920s.* New York: Noonday Press, pp. 468, 480, 535–536, 551, 552.

5488. Duberman, Martin. *Paul Robeson.* New York: The New Press, pp. 197, 225, 243, 626, 633, 643, 692.

5489. Dubey, Madhu. "Joyce Ann Joyce. *Warriors, Conjurers and Priests: Defining African-Centered Literary Criticism.*" *African American Review,* 30 (Fall), 464–467. Mentions W briefly.

5490. _____. "The Mythos of Gumbo: Leon Forrest Talks About *Divine Days.*" *Callaloo,* 19 (Summer), pp. 588–602. Forrest asserts that W "was really on to something about Bigger (p. 596). He likes to teach W, but disavows his influence. Praises "Fire and Cloud" as "just an amazing story" (p. 600).

5491. duCille, Ann. "The Occult of True Black Womanhood," in her *Skin Trade.* Cambridge, MA: Harvard University Press, pp. 81–119.

5492. _____. "Postcolonialism and Afrocentricity: Discourse and Dat Course," in her *Skin Trade.* Cambridge, MA: Harvard University Press, pp. 120–135.

5493. Du Plessis, Rachel Blau. "Baker, Houston, Jr. *Workings of the*

Spirit: The Poetics of African American Women's Writing." *Journal of Modern Literature*, 19 (Spring), 377–378. Notice mentioning W briefly.

5494. Eagles, Brenda M. "A Bibliography of Dissertations Relating to Mississippi—1995." *The Journal of Negro History*, 58 (Spring), 91–93. Lists a dissertation by Timothy Caron on W and others.

5495. Ellison, Ralph. "Remembering Richard Wright," in *African American Literature: A Brief Introduction and Anthology.* Ed. Al Young. New York: HarperCollins, pp. 47–58.

5496. Estes-Hicks, Onita. "Jean Toomer and the Politics and Poetics of National Identity," in *Analysis and Assessment, 1980–1994.* Vol. 7 of *The Harlem Renaissance, 1920–1940.* Ed. Cary D. Wintz. New York: Garland, pp. 298–320.

5497. Evans, Oliver. "The Case of Carson McCullers," in *Critical Essays on Carson McCullers.* Eds. Beverly Lyon Clark and Marvin J. Friedman. New York: G.K. Hall, pp. 124–128. Notes W's "enthusiastic criticism of McCullers.

5498. Ezenwa-Ohaeto. "Notions and Nuances: Africa in the Works of James Baldwin," in *Of Dreams Deferred, Dead or Alive: Perspectives on African-American Writers.* Ed. Femi Ojo-Ade. Westport, CT: Greenwood, pp. 107–114. Mentions W briefly (pp. 107, 110–111).

5499. Fabi, M. Giulia. "Introduzione," in *Volo di ritorno: Antologia di racconti afroamericani (1859–1977)* Florence: Le Lettere, pp. 27–36. Mentions W briefly (pp. 34, 35). The anthology includes an Italian translation of "Bright and Morning Star" (pp. 197–239).

5500. Fabi, M. Giulia. "Profili Bibliografici," in *Volo di ritorno: Antologia di raconti afroamericani (1859–1977).* Florence: Le Lettere, pp. 409–482. The W entry (pp. 477–482) consists of a biographical sketch, a list of Italian translations of W's work, and a bibliography of secondary sources.

5501. Fabre, Michel. "M. Thomas Inge, ed. *Dark Laughter: The Satiric Art of Oliver W. Harrington*; Ollie W. Harrington. *Why I Left America and Other Essays.*" *African American Review*, 30 (Summer), 305–306. Mentions Harrington's illustrations for the serialization of *NS* and his close friendship with W in Paris.

Discusses at some length the question of the cause of W's death.

5502. [_____]. "Melvin Donaldson. *Cornerstones. An Anthology of African American Literature.*" *Revue AFRAM Review*, No. 44 (December), 13–14. Review comparing *Cornerstones* to *The Norton Anthology of African American Literature* and mentioning W briefly.

5503. _____. "Yoshinobu Hakutani. *Richard Wright and Racial Discourse.*" *Revue AFRAM Review*, No. 44 (December), 22–23. Favorable review emphasizing Hakutani's comparison of W to other writers and cultures.

5504. Ferris, William. "Director's Column." *The Southern Register* (Summer/Fall), p. 2. Mentions W briefly.

5505. Fisher, Benjamin F. "Poe," in *American Literary Scholarship: An Annual/1994.* Ed. David J. Nordloh. Durham, NC: Duke University Press, pp. 39–47. Mentions W briefly (p. 46).

5506. Fishkin, Shelley Fisher. "Break Dancing in the Drawing Room: Mark Twain and African-American Voices," in *Literary Influence and African-American Writers: Collected Essays.* Ed. Tracy Mishkin. New York: Garland, pp. 65–127.

5507. _____. "Interrogating 'Whiteness,' Complicating 'Blackness': Remapping American Culture," in *Criticism and the Color Line: Desegregating American Literary Studies.* Ed. Henry B. Wonham. New Brunswick, NJ: Rutgers University Press, pp. 251–290. Mentions briefly *SH* (p. 270) and Michel Fabre's *Richard Wright: Books and Writers* (p. 272).

5508. Fleischner, Jennifer. *Mastering Slavery: Memory, Family, and Identity in Women's Slave Narratives.* New York: New York University Press, p. 35. Mentions briefly *The Man Who Lived Underground.*

5509. Fleming, Robert. "Preface," in his *The Wisdom of the Elders.* New York: Ballantine Books, pp. xv–xxii. Mentions W's statement that African Americans are "America's Metaphor" (pp. xx). This book includes a quotation from *TMBV* (p. 244).

5510. _____, ed. *The Wisdom of the Elders.* New York: Ballantine Books, p. 244. Quotes from *TMBV* on the black church.

5511. Fodde, Luisanna, and Paola Boi. "Zora Neale Hurston, The

Black Woman Writer in the Thirties and Forties (Part 1); Moses, Man of Power, Man of Knowledge (Part 2)," in *Analysis and Assessment, 1980–1994.* Vol. 7 of *The Harlem Renaissance, 1920–1940.* Ed. Cary D. Wintz. New York: Garland, pp. 241–249.

5512. Foley, Barbara. "Writing Chicago: Modernism, Ethnicity, and the Novel. *Carla Cappetti.*" *Modern Philology*, 94 (August), 129–132. Review summarizing Cappetti's account of the influence of sociology on W.

5513. Fordham, Signithia. *Blacked Out: Dilemmas of Race, Identity, and Success at Capital High.* Chicago: The University of Chicago Press, p. 367. Mentions W briefly.

5514. Fowler, Virginia C. *Gloria Naylor: In Search of Sanctuary.* New York: Twayne, pp. 136, 168. Mentions W briefly and relates Carl in "Man of All Work" to a Naylor character.

5515. Franklin, V.P., and Bettye Collier-Thomas. "Biography, Race Vindication, and African-American Intellectuals: Introductory Essay." *The Journal of Negro History*, 81 (Spring, Summer, Winter, Fall), 1–16. Mentions W briefly (p. 2).

5516. Fredrickson, Robert S. "Robert Stone's Decadent Leftists." *Papers on Language and Literature*, 32 (Summer), 315–334. Mentions briefly Bigger Thomas (p. 320).

5517. Friedman, Melvin J. "*The Mortgaged Heart:* The Workshop of Carson McCullers," in his and Beverly Lyon Clark's *Critical Essays on Carson McCullers.* New York: G.K. Hall, pp. 67–77.

5518. Gaines, Kevin K. *Uplifting the Race: Black Leadership, Politics, and Culture in the Twentieth Century.* Chapel Hill: The University of North Carolina Press, pp. 1, 52–53, 249. Includes an epigraph from "The Ethics of Living Jim Crow" and mentions it and W subsequently.

5519. Gallagher, Brian. "About Us, For Us, Near Us: The Irish and Harlem Renaissances," in *Analysis and Assessment, 1980–1994.* Vol. 7 of *The Harlem Renaissance, 1920–1940.* Ed. Cary D. Wintz. New York: Garland, pp. 228–240.

5520. _____. "'About Us, For Us, Near Us': The Irish and Harlem Renaissances," in *Literary Influence and African-American Writers: Collected*

Essays. Ed. Tracy Mishkin. New York: Garland, pp. 157–170.

5521. Gardaphé, Fred L. "Left-Out: Three Italian-American Writers of the 1930s," in *Radical Revisions: Rereading 1930s Culture.* Eds. Bill Mullen and Sherry Linkon. Urbana: University of Illinois Press, pp. 60–77. Mentions briefly W, *AH*, *NS*, and "I Tried to Be a Communist" (pp. 62, 73, 77).

5522. Gardner, Hannah. "Crow Nation: The Black Belt of Pryor." *Richard Wright Newsletter,* 4 (Spring), 11–13. Essay by a twelfth-grade student at the Noble and Greenough School in Dedham, Massachusetts. Applies Max's view in *NS* that whites want to perceive blacks as criminals to justify their racism to the student's visit to a Crow Indian ceremony, where she felt superior to the drunken men but awed by the dancers.

5523. Gates, Henry Louis, Jr. "The Blackness of Blackness: A Critique of the Sign and the Signifying Monkey," in *Cornerstone: An Anthology of African American Literature.* Ed. Melvin Donalson. New York: St. Martin's Press, pp. 881–913.

5524. _____. "Foreword," in *Harlem on My Mind: Cultural Capital of Black America, 1900–1968.* Ed. Allon Schoener. New York: The New Press, p. [1]. Begins by quoting W's statement that the Negro is America's metaphor.

5525. _____, and Nellie Y. McKay. "Preface: Talking Books," in their *The Norton Anthology of African American Literature.* New York: Norton, pp. xxvii–xli. Mentions briefly "Blueprint for Negro Writing" (pp. xxvii–xli), *BB* (p. xxxvi), *NS* (p. xxxviii), and "The Man Who Lived Underground" (p. xxxix).

5526. _____. "King of Cats." *The New Yorker,* 72 (8 April), 70–81. Article on Albert Murray noting his disapproval of W's sociological fiction (p. 72).

5527. Giddings, Paula. *When and Where I Enter: The Impact of Black Women on Race and Sex in America.* New York: William Morrow, pp. 239, 322.

5528. Gillespie, Sheena, and Robert Singleton. "Discovering Books *Richard Wright,*" in their *Across Cultures: A Reader for Writers.* Boston: Allyn and Bacon, p. 201. Headnote to an excerpt from *BB*.

5529. _____. "Interpretations, Correspondences, Applications," in their *Across Cultures: A Reader for Writers.* Boston: Allyn and Bacon, pp. 208–209. Study aids for an excerpt from *BB*.

5530. Gilroy, Paul. "Introduction" to the Harper Perennial edition of *Eight Men.* New York: Harper Collins, pp. xi–xxi. Analyzes the collection favorably in terms of the crisis of black masculinity, connecting "the social and economic with the psychological and cultural" (p. xxi).

5531. Gilyard, Keith. *Let's Flip the Script: An African American Discourse on Language, Literature, and Learning.* Detroit: Wayne State University Press, 24, 50, 105. Mentions briefly W, Fred Daniels, and "Bigger Thomas."

5532. Glantz, Shelley. "Richard Wright: Writing Is His Weapon." *School Library Journal,* 42 (June), 80. Unfavorable review of a video on W.

5533. Glicksberg, Charles I. "The Alienation of Negro Literature," in *Analysis and Assessment, 1940–1979.* Vol. 6 of *The Harlem Renaissance, 1920–1940.* Ed. Cary D. Wintz. New York: Garland, pp. 347–356.

5534. _____. "Bias, Fiction, and the Negro," in *Analysis and Assessment, 1940–1979.* Vol. 6 of *The Harlem Renaissance, 1920–1940.* Ed. Cary D. Wintz. New York: Garland, pp. 55–63.

5535. _____. "Negro Fiction in America," in *Analysis and Assessment, 1940–1979.* Vol. 6 of *The Harlem Renaissance, 1920–1940.* Ed. Cary D. Wintz. New York: Garland, pp. 43–54.

5536. _____. "Race and Revolution in Negro Literature," in *Analysis and Assessment, 1940–1979.* Vol. 6 of *The Harlem Renaissance, 1920–1940.* Ed. Cary D. Wintz. New York: Garland, pp. 266–274.

5537. Glissant, Edouard. *Faulkner, Mississippi.* Paris: Éditions Stock, pp. 83. 90–91, 224. Mentions briefly W (pp. 83, 224) and *NS* and *BB* (pp. 90–91).

5538. Goldfield, David R. "The South," in *Encyclopedia of the United States in the Twentieth Century.* Ed. Stanley I. Kutler. New York: Scribner's. Vol. 1, pp. 61–79. Mentions W briefly (p. 68).

5539. Gomes, Peter J. *The Good Book: Reading the Bible with Mind*

and Heart. New York: William Morrow, p. 240. Mentions W briefly.

5540. Graham, Lawrence Otis. *Member of the Club: Reflections on Life in a Racially Polarized World.* New York: HarperPerennial, p. 39. Reprint of 1995.

5541. Graham, Maryemma, and Jerry W. Ward, Jr. "From the Editors." *Richard Wright Newsletter.* 5 (Fall), 10. On the fifth anniversary of the Richard Wright Circle, the editors call for "more information on the global reception of Wright."

5542. Grant, William E. "*Native Son,*" in *Masterplots.* Revised Second Edition. Ed. Frank N. Magill. Pasadena: Salem Press, pp. 4415–4419.

5543. Greene, J. Lee. *Blacks in Eden: The African American Novel's First Century.* Charlottesville: University Press of Virginia, pp. 5, 9–10, 143, 167, 172–188, 189, 223–259. Analyzes "Big Boy Leaves Home" and *NS* in a chapter entitled "Black Adams." As a rebellious Adam, Big Boy goes through the Biblical stages of "the temptation, transgression, judgment, ejection (punishment)," and the postlapsarian condition. The analysis of *NS* also emphasizes Biblical connections. The thematic and structural pattern of *NS* revolves around Bigger's birth-death-rebirth. Greene mentions W frequently elsewhere.

5544. Griffiths, Frederick T. "'Sorcery Is Dialectical': Plato and Jean Toomer in Charles Johnson's *The Sorcerer's Apprentice.*" *African American Review,* 30 (Winter), 527–538. Mentions briefly "Wright's Underground Man" (p. 536) and mentions W elsewhere (p. 538).

5545. Grimshaw, Anna. "Glossary," in her *Special Delivery: The Letters of C.L.R. James to Constance Webb, 1939–1948.* Oxford: Blackwell, pp. 383–388. Includes an entry on W (p. 388).

5546. _____. "Introduction," in her *Special Delivery: The Letters of C.L.R. James to Constance Webb, 1939–1948.* Oxford: Blackwell, pp. 1–35. Mentions W briefly (p. 12), discusses a letter James wrote to Webb following his first meeting W (p. 27), and comments on Webb's decision to write a critical essay on W (p. 29).

5547. _____. "Special Delivery: The Letters of C.L.R. James to Constance Webb, 1939–1948," in *Rethinking C.L.R. James.* Ed. Grant

Farred. Oxford: Blackwell, pp. 45–73. Discusses James on W (p. 63) and mentions Webb's writing on W (p. 66).

5548. Gunning, Sandra. *Race, Rape, and Lynching: The Red Record of American Literature, 1890–1912.* New York: Oxford University Press, pp. 9, 151. Quotes from Robyn Wiegman and Trudier Harris on W.

5549. _____. *Race, Rape, and Lynching: The Red Record of American Literature,* 1890–1912. New York: Oxford University Press, p. 9. Comments on and quotes from Robyn Wiegman's treatment of *NS*.

5550. Guy-Sheftall, Beverly. "The Women of Bronzeville," in *On Gwendolyn Brooks: Reliant Contemplation.* Ed. Stephen Caldwell Wright. Ann Arbor: The University of Michigan Press, pp. 233–245.

5551. Hakutani, Yoshinobu. "*The Color Curtain Revisited*: A Review Essay." *Richard Wright Newsletter,* 4 (Spring), 3–5. Occasioned by the University Press of Mississippi edition, this essay emphasizes the work's multiculturalism, which is unified by nonwhite racialism. Hakutani relates *CC* to *BP* and mentions also "Long Black Song," *O,* and *WML.*

5552. _____. "Racial Discourse and Self-Creation: Richard Wright's *Black Boy,*" in *Teaching American Ethnic Literatures: Nineteen Essays.* Eds. John R. Maitino and David R. Peck. Albuquerque: University of New Mexico Press, pp. 119–132. Revised reprint of 1985 with an added section on teaching the work emphasizing style or themes or historical context. Includes an annotated bibliography.

5553. _____. *Richard Wright and Racial Discourse.* Columbia: University of Missouri Press, 325 pp. After an "Introduction" reviewing W scholarship, Hakutani provides chapters on *LT, UTC, NS,* the city (*BB, O, BP, CC, PS, EM* and a final chapter on W's haiku, comparing them to the Japanese practice and noting their conformity with respect to style and nature as a subject matter.

5554. _____. "Richard Wright's *The Long Dream* as Racial and Sexual Discourse." *African American Review,* 30 (Summer), 267–280. Argues that *LD* is a novel about sex and race, in that order: "While Wright's description of racial tur-

moil constitutes the surface structure … the deep structure consists of Fishbelly's initiation into manhood, which Wright portrays in personal, psychological, and sexual terms." To achieve manhood, the protagonist must violate the taboo against miscegenation of a black male and a white female. Thus the sexual and racial themes come together.

5555. Hale, Anthony R. "Framing the Folk: Zora Neale Hurston, John Millington Synge, and the Politics of Aesthetic Ethnography." *The Comparatist,* 20 (May), 50–59. Quotes briefly *TMBV* and notes W criticism of Hurston (p. 57).

5556. Hanchard, Michael. "Marx, Trinidad, Cricket." *The Nation,* 262 (27 May), 29–31. Review of Kent Worcester's *C.L.R. James: A Political Biography* mentioning W briefly (p. 29).

5557. Hardack, Richard. "Swing to the White, Back to the Black: Writing and 'Sourcery' in Ishmael Reed's *Mumbo Jumbo,*" in *Literary Influence and African-American Writers: Collected Essays.* Ed. Tracy Mishkin. New York: Garland, pp. 271–300. Mentions W briefly (p. 293).

5558. Harley, Sharon. *The Timetables of African-American History: A Chronology of the Most Important People and Events in African-American History.* New York: Simon & Schuster, pp. 245, 247, 257.

5559. Hart, Robert C. "Black-White Literary Relations in the Harlem Renaissance," in *Analysis and Assessment, 1940–1979.* Vol. 6 of *The Harlem Renaissance, 1920–1940.* Ed. Cary D. Wintz. New York: Garland, pp. 234–250.

5560. Hatch, James V., and Ted Shine. "*Native Son*" 1941. New York: The Free Press, pp. 432–433.

5561. Hayden, Robert. "El-Hajj Malik El-Shabazz," in his *Collected Poems.* Ed. Frederick Glaysher. New York: Liveright, pp. 86–100.

5562. Henderson, Mae G. "Introduction." *Callaloo,* 19 (Winter), 57–59. Recalls reading W on her own as an undergraduate student at Carleton College.

5563. _____. "'Where, by the way, is this train going?': A Case for Black (Cultural) Studies." *Callaloo,* 19 (Winter), 60–67. Mentions W briefly (p. 64).

5564. Hernton, Calvin. "Chattanooga Black Boy: Identity and

Racism," in *Names We Call Home: Autobiography on Racial Identity.* Eds. Becky Thompson and Sangeeta Tyagi. New York: Routledge, pp. 139–152. Mentions briefly W and "the ethics of living Jim Crow" (p. 149).

5565. Hersch, Charles. "'Let Freedom Ring!': Free Jazz and African-American Politics." *Cultural Critique,* 32 (Winter), 97–123. Quotes W on the blues (pp. 104–105).

5566. Hicks, Heather J. "*The Naturalistic Inner-City Novel in America: Encounters with the Fat Man.* By James R. Giles." *American Literature,* 68 (September), 648–649. Review mentioning W briefly.

5567. Higginbotham, A. Leon, Jr. *Shades of Freedom: Racial Politics and Presumptions of the American Legal Process.* New York: Oxford University Press, pp. 12–13, 168, 190. Quotes from *TMBV* and the introduction to *Black Metropolis.*

5568. Hill, Lynda Marion. *Social Rituals and the Verbal Art of Zora Neale Hurston.* Washington: Howard University Press, pp. xxx, 3, 32, 115, 189, 195. Mentions briefly W, "Down by the Riverside" (p. 115), and *UTC* (p. 195).

5569. Hine, Darlene Clark. "Divine Obsessions: History and Culture of Miles Davis, in her *Speak Truth to Power: Black Professional Class in United States History.* Brooklyn: Carlson, pp. 115–125. Mentions W briefly (p. 120).

5570. _____. "Introduction," in her *Speak Truth to Power: Black Professional Class in United States History.* Brooklyn: Carlson, pp. xvii–xxxiii. Mentions briefly W (p. xxx) and *NS* (p. xli).

5571. _____. *Speak Truth to Power: Black Professional Class in United States History.* Brooklyn: Carlson, pp. xxx, xli, 120. Brief mentions of W and *NS*.

5572. Hobson, Fred. "Of Canons and Cultural Wars," in *The Future of Southern Letters.* Eds. Jefferson Humphries and John Lowe. New York: Oxford University Press, pp. 72–86. Mentions W briefly (pp. 80–86).

5573. Hodges, Graham. "Literature,"in *Dictionary of American History: Supplement.* Eds. Robert H. Ferrell and Joan Hoff. Part 1. New York: Scribner's, pp. 369–372. Mentions W briefly (p. 370).

5574. Holladay, Hilary. *Ann Petry.* New York: Twayne, pp. 12–13, 21,

38, 45, 63. Compares Petry's autobiographical statement about writing *The Street* to "How 'Bigger' Was Born" and compares Petry's novel to *NS* (pp. 12–13, 45). Mentions Bigger and *NS* elsewhere.

5575. Hollinger, David A. "Literary Culture," in *Encyclopedia of the United States in the Twentieth Century*. Ed. Stanley I. Kutler. New York: Scribner's, Vol. IV, pp. 1435–1460. Mentions briefly *NS* and W's expatriation (p. 1450).

5576. Holloway, David. "Fiction: American-General," in *Reader's Guide to Literature in English*. Ed. Mark Hawkins-Dady. Chicago: Fitzroy Dearborn, pp. 273–276. Mentions W in a comment on Michael Cooke.

5577. Holtz, Daniel J. "History on the Margins and in the Mainstream: Teaching *The Sound and the Fury* in Its Southern Historical Context," in *Approaches to Teaching Faulkner's The Sound and the Fury*. Eds. Stephen Hahn and Arthur F. Kinney. New York: The Modern Language Association of America, pp. 96–100. Mentions briefly W's term for lynching: "white death."

5578. Hopkins, Larry. "Inventing Self: Parallels in the African-German and African-American Experience," in *The African-German Experience: Critical Essays*. Ed. Carol Aisha Blackshire-Belay. Westport, CT: Praeger, p. 49. Mentions W briefly.

5579. Hotek, Adam. "Eyes on the Horizon." *Center for the Study of Black Literature and Culture* (Summer), pp. 6–7. Essay on Ellison mentioning briefly his "Richard Wright's Blues."

5580. House, Elizabeth B. "*Who Set You Flowin'?*": The African-American Migration Narrative. By Farah Jasmine Griffin." *American Literature*, 68 (March), 271–272. Notes Griffin's treatment of W.

5581. Howard, H. Wendell. "Paul Robeson Remembered." *The Midwest Quarterly*, 38 (Autumn), 102–115. Mentions W briefly (p. 110).

5582. Hubbard, Dolan. "Slipping Into Darkness: CLA and Black Intellectual Formation." *CLA Journal*, 40 (September), 1–20. Mentions briefly the special W issue of *CLA Journal* (p. 5).

5583. Hudgins, Andrew. "An Autobiographer's Lies." *The American Scholar*, 65 (Autumn), 541–553. States that *BB* is "in the service of Marxism" (p. 551).

5584. Huggins, Nathan I. "Introduction," in *Analysis and Assessment, 1940–1979*. Vol. 6 of *The Harlem Renaissance, 1920–1940*. Ed. Cary D. Wintz. New York: Garland, pp. 65–73.

5585. Hughes, Langston. "The Twenties: Harlem and Its Negritude," in *Analysis and Assessment, 1940–1979*. Vol. 6 of *The Harlem Renaissance, 1920–1940*. Ed. Cary D. Wintz. New York: Garland, pp. 403–412.

5586. _____, Mozell C. Hill, and M. Carl Holman. "Some Practical Observations: A Colloquy," in *The Harlem Renaissance, 1920–1940*. Vol. 5. Ed. Cary D. Wintz. New York: Garland, pp. 131–135.

5587. Hutchinson, Earl Ofari. *The Assassination of the Black Male Image*. New York: Simon & Schuster, p. 86. Quotes from "The Ethics of Living Jim Crow."

5588. _____. *Beyond O.J.: Race, Sex, and Class Lessons for America*. Montreal: Black Rose Books, pp. 5–6, 76. Chapter One opens with a comparison of Bigger Thomas and O.J. Simpson. A later reference comments on the scene between Bigger and Gus.

5589. Ickstadt, Heinz. "Die Amerikanische Moderne," in *Amerikanische Literaturgeschichte*. Ed. Hubert Zapf. Stuttgart: Metzler, pp. 218–280. Mentions briefly W (p. 226), *LT* (pp. 229, 233, 276), and *NS* (p. 227).

5590. Inman. James A. "Love and Awareness in "Hurston's Janie: An Archetypal Connection." *The Zora Neale Hurston Forum*, 10 (Spring/Fall), 1–5. Mentions briefly W's social protest (p. 5).

5591. Jack, Belinda Elizabeth. *Negritude and Literary Criticism: The History and Theory of "Negro-African" Literature in French*. Westport, CT: Greenwood Press, p. 58. Mentions W briefly.

5592. Jack, Peter Monro. "Crime and Punishment and Explanation in Full." *The New York Times Book Review* (6 October), p. 56.

5593. Jackson, Blyden. "The Negro's Image of the Universe as Reflected in His Fiction," in *Analysis and Assessment, 1940–1979*. Vol. 6 of *The Harlem Renaissance, 1920–1940*. Ed. Cary D. Wintz. New York: Garland, pp. 80–89.

5594. _____. "The Negro's Negro in Negro Literature," in *Analysis and*

Assessment, 1940–1979. Vol. 6 of *The Harlem Renaissance, 1920–1940*. Ed. Cary D. Wintz. New York: Garland, pp. 74–79.

5595. Jackson, Kennell. *American Is Me: 170 Fresh Questions and Answers on Black American History*. New York: HarperCollins, pp. 280–282, 292. Comments on *NS* in a biographical context. Mentions also W's expatriation.

5596. Jackson, Walter A. "White Liberal Intellectuals, Civil Rights and Gradualism, 1954–60," in *The Making of Martin Luther King and the Civil Rights Movement*. Eds. Brian Ward and Tony Badger. New York: New York University Press, pp. 96–114. Mentions W briefly (p. 96).

5597. James, C.L.R. "The Revolutionary Answer to the Negro Problem in the United States," in *C.L.R. James on the 'Negro Question.'* Ed. Scott McLemee. Jackson: University Press of Mississippi, pp. 138–147.

5598. _____. *Special Delivery: The Letters of C.L.R. James to Constance Webb, 1939–1948*. Ed. Anna Grimshaw. Oxford: Blackwell, pp. 124, 148, 155, 160, 162, 184, 189–190, 194, 196, 208–209, 214–222, 226, 228, 231, 236–237, 239, 245–246, 248, 251–252, 256, 282, 301, 304–305, 313, 315, 319, 321, 339, 351, 360–362, 375. Comments on W and communism (pp. 124, 148, 160, 162, 237), discusses Webb's writing on W (pp. 221, 226, 245, 251–252), 255–256, 282, 301, 305, 319, 321, 339, 351, 360–362, 375), comments on W and the "Negro question" (pp. 189–190, 194, 313), and mentions W, *NS*, and *BB* elsewhere.

5599. _____. *C.L.R. James on the "Negro Question,"* Ed. Scott McLemee. Jackson: University Press of Mississippi, pp. xxiii, xxv–xxvii. Notes James's essays on W and comments on their friendship despite their political differences. Reprints James's "On Native Son" and his "Public awareness of the Negro Question," which mentions *BB*.

5600. Jardine, Gail. "To Be Black, Male, and Conscious: Race, Rage, and Manhood in America." *American Quarterly*, 48 (June), 385–393. Review of *Makes Me Want to Holler* mentioning the powerful effect of *NS* on Nathan McCall (p. 389).

5601. Jarvis, Brian. "Ellison, Ralph," in *Reader's Guide to Literature in English*. Ed. Mark Hawkins-

Dady. Chicago: Fitzroy Dearborn, pp. 246–248. Mentions W in comments on Michael F. Lynch and John Hersey.

5602. Jaskoski, Helen. "Carlos Bulosan's Literary Debt to Richard Wright," in *Literary Influence and African-American Writers: Collected Essays.* Ed. Tracy Mishkin. New York: Garland, pp. 231–243 Compares *BB* and Bulosan's America *Is in the Heart,* finding direct influence and general similarities in the social conditions of African Americans in the South and Filipinos in California. Also discusses the issue of whether the books are autobiography or fictionalized autobiography.

5603. Jay, Gregory. "The Discipline of the Syllabus," in *Reconceptualizing American Literary/Cultural Studies: Rhetoric, History, and Politics in the Humanities.* Ed. William E. Cain. New York: Garland, pp. 101–116. Mentions W briefly (p. 104).

5604. Jeffreys, Mark. "Irony Without Condescension: Sterling A. Brown's Nod to Robert Frost and Race," in *Literary Influence and African-American Writers: Collected Essays.* Ed. Tracy Mishkin. New York: Garland, pp. 211–229. Mentions W briefly (p. 211).

5605. Jenkins, McKay Bradley. "'A Strange and Bitter Crop: Metaphors of Race, Sex, and Segregation in the 1940's American South." *Dissertation Abstracts International-A,* 57/04 (October), p. 1618. Mentions W. briefly in relation to Lillian Smith's *Strange Fruit* and *Killers of the Dream.*

5606. Johgart, Steve, and Leigh Magnuson, eds. *Comprehensive Dissertation Index 1995 Supplement, Volume 4.* Ann Arbor: UMI, p. 545. Lists dissertations treating W by Luc Fanou, Raymond Samuel Zimmerman, and Timothy Paul Caron.

5607. Johnson, Abby Arthur. "Literary Midwife: Jessie Redmon Fauset and the Harlem Renaissance," in *Analysis and Assessment, 1940–1979.* Vol. 6 of *The Harlem Renaissance, 1920–1940.* Ed. Cary D. Wintz. New York: Garland, pp. 313–323.

5608. Johnson, Charles. "Being and Race," in *Cornerstones: An Anthology of African American Literature.* Ed. Melvin Donalson. New York: St. Martin's Press, pp. 938–957.

5609. Johnson, Charles S. "The Negro Renaissance and Its Significance," in *The Harlem Renaissance, 1920–1940.* Vol. 5. Ed. Cary D. Wintz. New York: Garland, pp. 226–234.

5610. Jones, Quincy, and Alex Haley. "Playboy Interview: Quincy Jones (July 1990)," in *Brotherman: The Odyssey of Black Men in America.* Eds. Herb Boyd and Robert L. Allen. New York: Ballantine Books, pp. 667–676.

5611. Jones, Robert B. "Kostelanetz, Richard. *Politics in the African-American Novel." Journal of Modern Literature,* 19 (Spring), 385. Notice mentioning briefly W and *NS.*

5612. Joyce, Joyce Ann. *Ijala: Sonia Sanchez and the African Poetic Tradition.* Chicago: Third World P, pp. 35, 41, 79. Mentions briefly W, *NS* (p. 44), and Bigger Thomas and Cross Damon (p. 79).

5613. Kaname, Hiroshi. "Richard Wright and Escape: With an Emphasis on Two Short Stories." *Osaka Prefectural University Studies in British and American Language and Culture,* 44, 57–71. Compares "Big Boy Leaves Home" with "The Man Who Was Almost a Man" to clarify why the conclusions are different despite the common theme of flight.

5614. Kaplan, Carla. *The Erotics of Talk: Women's Writing and Feminist Paradigms.* New York: Oxford University Press, pp. 112, 119. Mentions W's criticism of Hurston.

5615. Kazin, Alfred. *A Lifetime Burning in Every Moment.* New York: Harper Collins, p. 209. Mentions briefly *BB.*

5616. Kelly, James R. "Theses and Dissertations for 1995." *South Atlantic Review,* 61 (Fall), 165–190. Lists a thesis by Mark Grimm Lamson, "Transporting and Transforming the Self: Imagination in the Early Autobiographies of Frederick Douglass, Richard Wright, and Maya Angelou."

5617. Kelley, Robin D.G. *Race Rebels: Culture, Politics, and the Black Working Class.* New York: The Free Press, pp. 12, 35–36, 104, 128, 146.

5618. Keyes, Ben. "Redemption With, Redemption Without." *Richard Wright Newsletter,* 4 (Spring), 9–12. Essay by a twelfth-grade student at the Noble and Greenough School in Dedham, Massachusetts. Analyzes Bigger's rejection of Rev-

erend Hammond's version of Christianity in *NS.* Perhaps Bigger's disbelief could have been overcome if Hammond had emphasized divine punishments for whites as well as the hope of heaven for blacks.

5619. Kinder, Donald R., and Lynn M. Sanders. *Divided by Color: Racial Politics and Democratic Ideals.* Chicago: The University of Chicago Press, p. 96. Mentions W briefly.

5620. Kinney, Arthur F. *Go Down, Moses: The Miscegenation of Time.* New York: Twayne, pp. 15–16, 126, 160. Comments on *BB* and W as a racial writer.

5621. Kinnamon, Keneth. "A Richard Wright Bibliography: 1986." *Richard Wright Newsletter,* 5 (Spring/Summer), Supplement, 20 pp. Includes 183 annotated items and a commentary on W studies in 1996.

5622. Kinnamon, Keneth. "Keneth Kinnamon on Angelou's Celebration of Black Culture," in *Maya Angelou's I Know Why the Caged Bird Sings.* Ed. Harold Bloom. Broomall, PA: Chelsea House, pp. 39–40.

5623. Kirszner, Laurie G., and Stephen R. Mandell. "'The Library Card' Richard Wright," in their *The Blair Reader.* Second edition. Upper Saddle River, NJ: Prentice-Hall, p. 406.

5624. _____. "Responding to Reading," in their *The Blair Reader.* Second edition. Upper Saddle River, NJ: Prentice-Hall, pp. 413–414. Reprint of 1992.

5625. Klawans, Stuart. "Orson Welles Hollowed Out." *The Nation,* 262 (8/15 January), 28–30. Review of Simon Callow's *Orson Welles: The Road to Xanadu.* Mentions the stage production of *NS.*

5626. Klein, Marcus. "Douglas Wixson. *Worker-Writer in America: Jack Conroy and the Tradition of Midwestern Literary Radicalism, 1898–1990." Modern Fiction Studies,* 42 (Spring), 138–140. Review mentioning W briefly.

5627. Klinkowitz, Jerome. "Fiction: The 1960s to the Present," *American Literary Scholarship: An Annual/1994.* Ed. David J. Nordloh. Durham, NC: Duke University Press, pp. 303–323. Mentions W briefly (p. 309).

5628. [Korshin, Paul]. "New Appointments." *Penn English,* Fall, p. 2. Contains a sketch of Christopher Looby mentioning his research project on W and mass culture.

5629. Knight, Brenda. *Women of the Beat Generation.* Berkeley: Conari Press, p. 20. Mentions the Wrights living among other writers in Brooklyn Heights.

5630. Kroeber, Karl. "Novel," in *The Encyclopedia Americana.* Ed. Lawrence T. Lorimer. Vol. 20. Danbury, CT: Grolier, pp. 505–511b.

5631. _____. "Novel," in *Encyclopedia Americana.* Ed. Lawrence T. Lorimer. Danbury, CT: Grolier, vol. 20, pp. 505–511b. Notes indebtedness of Ellison and Baldwin to W, "whose novel *Native Son* and autobiography *Black Boy* remain classics of black writing," Reprinted: 2000.

5632. Kutenplon, Deborah, and Ellen Olmstead. "*Rite of Passage*," in their *Young Adult Fiction by African American Writers, 1968–1993.* New York: Garland, 328–330. Plot summary and critique of the novella. Readers will find it dated, but it has emotional immediacy and provides an opportunity for urban youth to reflect on their own situation.

5633. Laryea, Doris Lucas. "The Open Eye of Lenard Duane Moore: An Interview." *Obsidian II: Black Literature in Review,* 11 (Spring-Summer, Fall-Winter), 159–184. Moore comments briefly on W's haiku (p. 169) and his fiction (p. 179).

5634. Lattin, Patricia H., and Vernon E. Lattin. "Dual Vision in Gwendolyn Brooks's *Maud Martha*," in *On Gwendolyn Brooks: Reliant Contemplation.* Ed. Stephen Caldwell Wright. Ann Arbor: The University of Michigan Press, pp. 136–145.

5635. Lauter, Paul. "Race and Gender in the Shaping of the American Literary Canon: A Case Study from the Twenties," in *Analysis and Assessment, 1940–1979.* Vol. 7 of *The Harlem Renaissance, 1920–1940.* Ed. Cary D. Wintz. New York: Garland, pp. 103–131.

5636. Lee, Kun Jong. "Ellison's Racial Variations on American Themes." *African American Review,* 30 (Fall), 421–440. Discusses Ellison's writings on W, early and late (pp. 425–427, 430, 433–434). Mentions *BB* and *NS.*

5637. Lee, Ulysses. "Criticism at Mid-Century," in *The Harlem Renaissance, 1920–1940.* Vol. 5. Ed. Cary D. Wintz. New York: Garland, pp. 136–145.

5638. Lee, Valerie. *Granny Midwives and Black Women Writers: Double-Dutched Readings.* New York: Routledge, p. 142. Recalls "hearing Margaret Walker say that only someone who understood racism in Mississippi could write a credible biography of Richard Wright, who was born in the Mississippi Woods, "a veritable hell" (p. 142).

5639. Lemann, Nicholas. "The End of Racism?" *American Heritage,* 47 (February/March), 93–103, 105. In an interview with Dinesh D'-Souza, Lemann mentions briefly W's novels and *TMBV.*

5640. Lester, Cheryl. "A Response to Lawrence Rodgers." *The Langston Hughes Review,* 14 (Spring/Fall), 13–15. Mentions W briefly and contrasts him to Zora Neale Hurston.

5641. Lester, Cheryl and John Edgar Tidwell. "Frank Marshall Davis and The Chicago Black Renaissance: An Introduction." *The Langston Hughes Review,* 14 nos. 1 and 2 (Spring-Fall), 1–64. Reports on Midwest Modern Language Association meeting with papers by Lawrence R. Rodgers, John Gennari, Lisa Wooley, Deborah Barnes, and John Tidwell.

5642. _____. "Frank Marshall Davis and the Chicago Black renaissance: An Introduction." *The Langston Hughes Review,* (Spring/Fall), 1–3. Comments on Alain Locke's early response to W and Marshall, Lawrence W. Rodgers later response, Robert Bone's essay on W and the Chicago Renaissance, and Deborah Barnes's article on the same theme.

5643. Lewis, Earl. "Race," in *Encyclopedia of the United States in the Twentieth Century.* Ed. Stanley I. Kutler. New York: Scribners'. Vol. 1, pp. 129–160. Mentions briefly *NS* (p. 154).

5644. Lincoln, C. Eric. *Coming Through the Fire: Surviving Race and Place in America.* Durham, NC: Duke University Press, p. 58. Mentions W briefly.

5645. Locke, Alain. "God Save Reality!" in *The Harlem Renaissance, 1920–1940.* Vol. 4. Ed. Cary D. Wintz. New York: Garland, pp. 296–306.

5646. _____. "Jingo, Counter-Jingo and Us," in *The Harlem Renaissance, 1920–1940.* Vol. 4. Ed. Cary D. Wintz. New York: Garland, pp. 307–316.

5647. _____. "The Negro: 'New' or Newer," in *The Harlem Renaissance, 1920–1940.* Vol. 4. Ed. Cary D. Wintz. New York: Garland, pp. 318–331.

5648. _____. "Self-Criticism: The Third Dimension in Culture," in *The Harlem Renaissance, 1920–1940.* Vol. 5. Ed. Cary D. Wintz. New York: Garland, pp. 165–168.

5649. Lockyer, Judith. "Southern United States Literature: 20th Century," in *Reader's Guide to Literature in English.* Chicago: Fitzroy and Dearborn, pp. 744–746. Mentions W in a comment on J. Bill Berry.

5650. Logan, Lisa, "Introduction," in *Critical Essays on Carson McCullers.* Eds. Beverly Lyon Clark and Melvin J. Friedman. New York: G.K. Hall, pp. 1–14. Includes comments by W on *The Heart Is a Lonely Hunter* (p. 2) His review of their work is represented from *The New Republic* (pp. 17–18).

5651. Lord, James. *Some Remarkable Men.* New York: Farrar, Straus Giroux, p. 281. Mentions W briefly.

5652. Love, Spencie. *One Blood: The Death and Resurrection of Charles R. Drew.* Chapel Hill: The University of North Carolina Press, p. 176. Quotes from *BB.*

5653. Lowe, John. "An Interview with Brenda Marie Osbey," in *The Future of Southern Letters.* Eds. Jefferson Humphries and John Lowe. New York: Oxford University Press, pp. 93–118. Lowe mentions W briefly (p. 116).

5654. _____. "Introduction," in *The Future of Southern Letters.* Eds. Jefferson Humphries and John Lowe. New York: Oxford University Press, pp. 3–19. Comments on W and quotes from *TMBV* (pp. 14, 16–17, 18).

5655. _____. "Craig Werner. *Playing the Changes: From Afro-Modernism to the Jazz Impulse.*" *African American Review,* 30 (Winter), 678–681. Comments on Werner's treatment of W, especially *NS* (p. 680).

5656. Lubiano, Wahneema. "Constructing and Reconstructing Afro-American Texts: The Critic as Ambassador and Referee," in *Analysis and Assessment, 1940–1979.* Vol. 7 of *The Harlem Renaissance, 1920–1940.* Ed. Cary D. Wintz. New York: Garland, pp. 58–73.

5657. Lynch, Michael F. "Haunted by Innocence: The Debate with Dostoevsky in Wright's 'Other

Novel,' *The Outsider." African American Review*, 30 (Summer), 255–266. Argues for the superiority of *O* over *NS*: "More consistent ideologically and better structured ... it includes a more complex treatment of the themes of freedom and identity." Borrowing heavily from Dostoevsky, especially *Crime and Punishment*, W rebuts his view of the guilt-ridden criminal, presenting instead in Cross Damon an "innocent" criminal who embraces both the danger and the exultation of existential freedom.

5658. Lyne, William. "Tiger Teeth Around Their Neck: The Cultural Logic of the Canonization of African American Literature." *Arizona Quarterly*, 52 (Autumn), 99–125.

5659. MacLeod, Christine. "Yoshinobu Hakutani and Robert Butler (eds.), *The City in African American Literature" Journal of American Studies*. 30 (April), 159–160. Unfavorable review complaining about the three essays on W.

5660. Madhubuti, Haki R. "Gwendolyn Brooks: Beyond the Wordmaker–The Making of an African Poet," in *On Gwendolyn Brooks: Reliant Contemplation*. Ed. Stephen Caldwell Wright. Ann Arbor: The University of Michigan Press, pp. 81–96.

5661. _____. "Introduction," in his *Ground Work: New and Selected Poems of Don L. Lee/Haki R. Madhubuti from 1966–1996*. Chicago: Third World Press, pp. xxiii + xxv. Mentions W briefly.

5662. Madsen, Deborah L. "Fiction: American-20th Century," in *Reader's Guide to Literature in English*. Chicago: Fitzroy Dearborn, pp. 277–278. Mentions W in a comment on Thomas Daniel Young.

5663. Maitino, John R., and David R. Peck. "African American Literature: Preface," in their *Teaching American Ethnic Literatures: Nineteen Essays*. Albuquerque: University of New Mexico Press, pp. 101–104. Mentions briefly *BB* and *UTC*.

5664. _____, and David R. Peck. "Introduction," in their *Teaching American Ethnic Literatures: Nineteen Essays*. Albuquerque: University of New Mexico Press, pp. 3–16. Includes a discussion of teaching *BB* (pp. 5–6) and mentions W elsewhere (pp. 10, 11, 12, 103).

5665. Margolies, Edward. "Afterword to the 1996 Edition," in *Pink-*

toes. By Chester Himes. Jackson: University Press of Mississippi, pp. 257–264. Notes that Molly Moon, prototype of the protagonist of *Pinktoes*, was a friend of W.

5666. _____. "The Image of the Primitive in Black Letters," in *Analysis and Assessment, 1940–1979*. Vol. 6 of *The Harlem Renaissance, 1920–1940*. Ed. Cary D. Wintz. New York: Garland, pp. 325–377.

5667. Mason, Theodore O., Jr. "'Mapping' Richard Wright: A Response to Deborah Barnes' 'I'd Rather Be a Lamppost in Chicago': Richard Wright and the Chicago Renaissance of African American Literature." *The Langston Hughes Review*, 14 (Spring/Fall), 62–64. Emphasizes the evolution of W's career, his tendency to criticize naturalism and social science, "unpacking the very assumptions" that inform his early work.

5668. Matsumoto, Noboru. "Richard Wright's 'Big Boy Leaves Home': A Railroad and the Dream of a Black Boy," in *Rereading American Short Stories: Woman, Family and Ethnicity*. Tokyo: Hokuseido, pp. 195–208. Maintains that "Big Boy Leaves Home" should not be read as protest, but instead with a focus on the effective use of spirituals and railroad folklore.

5669. Maud, Ralph. *Charles Olson's Reading: A Biography*. Carbondale: Southern Illinois University Press, pp. 7, 242. Relates that Olson, sympathetic with the underdog, had a fight with his best friend over *BB*. In a letter to Waldo Franks in 1939, also stated that he likes *UTC*.

5670. Maxwell, William J. "Black and White, Unite and Write: New Integrationist Criticism of U.S. Literary Modernism." *Minnesota Review*, no. 47, pp. 205–215. Mentions W briefly (pp. 208, 209, 213).

5671. _____. "The Proletarian as New Negro: Mike Gold's Harlem Renaissance," in *Radical Revisions: Rereading 1930s Culture*. Eds. Bill Mullen and Sherry Linkon. Urbana: University of Illinois Press, pp. 91–119. Mentions W and the Communist Party (p. 94) and Gold's treatment of W in *The Hollow Men* (p. 113).

5672. McCaffery, Larry, and Jerzy Kutnik. "Beneath a Precipice: An Interview with Clarence Major," in McCaffery's *Some Other Frequency: Interviews with Innovative American*

Authors. Philadelphia: University of Pennsylvania Press, pp. 241–264. Mentions W briefly (pp. 248, 257).

5673. McCluskey, John, Jr. "*Not So Simple: The 'Simple' Stories by Langston Hughes*. By Donna Akiba Sullivan Harper." *American Literature*, 68 (June), 478–479. Mentions W briefly and alludes to "How 'Bigger' Was Born."

5674. McKay, Nellie Y. "Wright, Richard," in *The World Book Encyclopedia*, Chicago: World Book, vol. 21, p. 510. Critical sketch mentioning *UTC*, *NS*, *TMBV*, *BB*, *WML*, and *AH*.

5675. McLemee, Scott. "Introduction: The Enigma of Arrival," in *C.L.R. James on the 'Negro Question.'* Jackson: University Press of Mississippi, pp. xxiii, xxvii. Mentions two pieces by James on W and quotes from another essay by James.

5676. McMahan, Elizabeth, Susan X. Day, and Robert Funk. "Biographical Notes," in their *Literature and the Writing Process*. Fourth edition. Upper Saddle River, NJ: Prentice-Hall, pp. 1119–1144.

5677. Meehan, Kevin. "Imagining Revolutionary Communities: Narrative and Social Change in George Jackson's *Soledad Brother*, Jean-Bertrand Aristide's *In the Parish of the Poor*, and Merle Collins's *Angel*." *In Process*, 1 (Fall), 20–35. Quotes from *BB* the passage about W's last meeting with his father, comparing it to a similar passage in *Soledad Brother*.

5678. Meier, August. "Some Reflections on the Negro Novel," in *Analysis and Assessment, 1940–1979*. Vol. 6 of *The Harlem Renaissance, 1920–1940*. Ed. Cary D. Wintz. New York: Garland, pp. 124–133.

5679. Meisenhelder, Susan. "Ethnic and Gender Identity in Zora Neale Hurston's *Their Eyes Were Watching God*," in *Teaching American Ethnic Literatures: Nineteen Essays*. Eds. John R. Maitino and David Peck. Albuquerque: University of New Mexico Press, pp. 105–117. Contrasts *UTC* and Hurston's novel, quoting W's review of it (p. 113).

5680. Mellen, Joan. *Hellman and Hammett: The Legendary Passion of Lillian Hellman and Dashiell Hammett*. New York: HarperCollins, p. 110. Quotes an unfavorable comment on W by Hammett.

5681. Middleton, Jo Ann. "Fiction: 1900 to the 1930s," in *American*

Literary Scholarship: An Annual/ 1994. Ed. David J. Nordloh. Durham, NC: Duke University Press, pp. 241–278. Mentions briefly an article treating W by Robert Shulman (p. 276).

5682. Miller, James A. "African-American Writing of the 1930s: A Prologue,"in *Radical Revisions: Rereading 1930s Culture.* Eds. Bill Mullen and Sherry Linkon. Urbana: University of Illinois Press, pp. 78–90. Comments on and quotes from "Blueprint for Negro Writing" and mentions *UTC* (pp. 79, 80, 89, 90).

5683. _____. "Wright, Richard," in *Reader's Guide to Literature in English.* Ed. Mark Hawkins-Dady. Chicago: Fitzroy Dearborn, pp. 880–881. Provides a well-informed review of books on W by Michel Fabre, Constance Webb, Addison Gayle, Dan McCall, Keneth Kinnamon, Margaret Walker, Henry Louis Gates, Jr., and K.A. Appiah.

5684. Miller, Jeanne-Marie. "'Measure Him Right': An Analysis of Lorraine Hansberry's *Raisin in the Sun,*" in *Teaching American Ethnic Literatures: Nineteen Essays.* Eds. John R. Maitino and David R. Peck. Albuquerque: University of New Mexico Press, pp. 133–145. Includes the play *NS* in a bibliography of related works.

5685. Mills, Jerry Leath. "Equine Gothic: The Dead Mule as Generic Signifier in Southern Literature of the Twentieth Century." *The Southern Literary Journal,* 29 (Fall), 2–17. Includes consideration of "The Man Who Was Almost a Man," pp. 8–9, 16.

5686. Mishkin, Tracy. "Theorizing Literary Influence and African American Writers," in her *Literary Influence and African-American Writers: Collected Essays.* New York: Garland, pp. 3–20. Comments on the influence of W on Ellison and Carlos Bulosan (pp. 10, 11–12, 13, 17).

5687. Mondadori, Alberto. *Lettere di una vita, 1922–1975.* Ed. Gian Carlo Ferretti. Milan: Arnoldo Mondadori Editore, pp. 332, 695–696. In a letter dated 17 March 1949 to Gianni Cortese, his agent in Paris, Mondadori details business matters concerning publication of Italian translations of W and suggests that W be dealt with diplomatically because he is not an easy person to deal with ("non è una persona facile da trattarsi"). In a letter dated 17 July Mondadore mentions W's "La letteratura negra negli USA."

5688. Montgomery, Maxine Lavon. *The Apocalypse in African-American Fiction.* Gainesville: University Press of Florida, pp. 3–4, 13–14, 28–39, 56. Contains a revised reprint of 1991, treats apocalyptic fire imagery in both *NS* and *UTC,* and quotes from "Blueprint for Negro Literature."

5689. Moore, Opal. "The Problem of (Black) Art," in *Blurred Boundaries: Critical Essays on American Literature, Language, and Culture.* Frankfurt am Main: Peter Lang, pp. 177–193. Contains a paragraph on the second film version of *NS* and the questions it raised (p. 181). Also refers to W's review of *Their Eyes Were Watching God* (p. 182).

5690. Morace, Robert A. "The Facts in Black and White: Cheever's *Falconer,* Wideman's *Philadelphia Fire,*" in *Powerless Fictions? Ethics, Cultural Critique, and American Fiction in the Age of Postmodernism.* Ed. Ricardo Miguel Alfonso. Amsterdam: Rodopi, pp. 85–112. Mentions W briefly (p. 100).

5691. Moses, Wilson. "V.P. Franklin. *Living Our Stories, Telling Our Truths: Autobiography and the Making of the African-American Intellectual Tradition.*" *American Historical Review,* 10 (October), 1270. Mentions favorably Franklin's essay on Richard Wright and Zora Neale Hurston.

5692. Mullen, Bill. "Popular Fronts: *Negro Story* Magazine and the African American Literary Response to World War II." *African American Review,* 30 (Spring), 5–15. Notes Fern Gayden's association in the South Side Writers' Group with W, whose "Almos' a Man" she published in the first issue of *Negro Story.* Also comments on W's defection from the left, anticipated in *NS,* to which Ann Petry's *The Street* is a corrective.

5693. _____, and Sherry Linkon. "Introduction: Rereading 1930s Culture," in their *Radical Revisions: Rereading 1930s Culture.* Urbana: University of Illinois Press, pp. 1–12. Mentions W briefly (p. 11).

5694. Mulvey, Christopher. "Harlem: Entrance and Initiation," in *Analysis and Assessment, 1980–1994.* Vol. 7 of *The Harlem Renaissance, 1920–1940.* Ed. Cary D. Wintz. New York: Garland, pp. 210–220.

5695. Müller, Kurt. "Die Reihe 'The American Novel: New Essays' (General Editor: Emory Elliott): Neuere Veröffentlichungen." *Amerikastudien,* No. 41, 705–711. Mentions briefly *NS* (p. 706).

5696. Murphy, Geraldine. "Subversive Anti-Stalinism: Race and Sexuality in the Early Essays of James Baldwin." *ELH,* 63 (Winter), 1021–1046. Includes discussion of Baldwin's critique of *NS* (pp. 1025, 1027–1030) and W and Baldwin in Paris (pp. 1032, 1034), especially in relation to Cold War politics.

5697. Murray, Albert. *The Blue Devils of Nada: A Contemporary American Approach to Aesthetic Statement.* New York: Pantheon, pp. 202–203. Claims that W misunderstood the blues, hearing the words but ignoring the music.

5698. Myrdal, Gunnar. *An American Dilemma: The Negro Problem and Modern Democracy.* 2 vols. New Brunswick, NJ: Transaction, pp. 656, 734, 735, 936, 989, 992.

5699. Nagel, James, "General Editor's Note," in *"Critical Essays on Carson McCullers.* Eds. Beverly Lyon Clark and Melvin J. Friedman. New York: G.K. Hall, p. xi.

5700. Nair, Supriya. *Caliban's Curse: George Lamming and the Revisioning of History.* Ann Arbor: The University of Michigan Press, p. 6. Mentions W's comments on *In the Castle of My Skin.*

5701. Nakagomi, Kazumasa. "A Study of Bigger's Alienation in *Native Son.*" *Nihon University Studies in English Language and Literature,* 44 (March), 153–172. States that the alienation of Bigger is caused by his own destructive nature and pressure from other characters in the novel.

5702. Nash, Peter Adam. "Mob Rule and the Teaching of Literature." *English Journal,* 85 (April), 16–18. Reports teaching *BB* by allowing students to develop their own interpretations without intervention by the teacher.

5703. Nash, William R. "Illuminating Zora Neale Hurston's Laughter." *The Southern Literary Journal,* 28 (Spring), 124–127. Review of John Lowe's *Jump at the Sun: Zora Neale Hurston's Cosmic Comedy* noting its treatment of W's disparagement of Hurston's folk humor.

5704. Neiva, Aurora Maria Soares.

"'Native Son' in Brazilian Portuguese with a study on dialects and translation: A nonlogocentric approach." *Dissertations Abstracts International*, 56 (April), 3933-A. A Northern Illinois University dissertation including a discussion of W's use of dialect and an annotated translation of *NS* into Brazilian Portuguese.

5705. Nellen, Ted. "Teaching Richard Wright in New York City." *Richard Wright Newsletter*, 5 (Fall), 5–6. Teaching "The Fight" (an excerpt from *BB*) in New York. Nellen stresses nonviolent conflict resolution.

5706. Nelson, Cary. "Poetry Chorus: Dialogic Politics in 1930s Poetry," in *Radical Revisions: Rereading 1930s Culture*. Eds. Bill Mullen and Sherry Linkon. Urbana: University of Illinois Press, pp. 29–59. Comments briefly on W's proletarian poetry and quotes a few lines (pp. 46, 50, 54).

5707 Neri, Algerina. "Foreign Scholarship: Italian Contributions," in *American Literary Scholarship: An Annual/1994*. Ed. David J. Nordloh. Durham, NC: Duke University Press, pp. 433–449. Comments on work on W by Sandro Portelli.

5708. Newman, Richard. "Books and Writers of the Harlem Renaissance," in his *Words Like Freedom: Essays on African-American Culture and History*. West Cornwall, CT: Locust Hill Press, pp. 171–179. Mentions W briefly (p. 176).

5709. _____. "Religion," in His *Words Like Freedom: Essays on African-American Culture and History*. West Cornwall, CT: Locust Hill Press, p. 99. Quotes W on black religion.

5710. _____. "Words Like Freedom: Afro-American Books and Manuscripts in the Henry W. and Albert A. Berg Collection of English and American Literature of the New York Public Library," in His *Words Like Freedom: Essays on African-American Culture and History*. West Cornwall, CT: Locust Hill Press. Notes that Carl Van Vechten photographed W. Comments on W items in the Berg Collection (pp. 24–25).

5711. Nwankwo, Chimalum. "Richard Wright: A Dubious Legacy," in *Of Dreams Deferred, Dead, or Alive: Perspectives on African-American Writers*. Ed. Femi Ojo-

Ade. Westport, CT: Greenwood, pp. 53–64. Strong attack on W's work, personality, and character. Escape and disloyalty to race and family are the salient qualities. Nwankwo treats *BP* and *BB* at some length, but also comments on *NS*, *LD*, *SH*, *TMBV*, *AH*, *PS*, and *UTC*.

5712. Nyamtukudza, S. *Richard Wright's Native Son*. Harare: College Press, 104 pp. Study guide for African readers discussing both literary, and historical aspects of the novel. Also contains a plot summary and a glossary.

5713. Ogunyemi, Chikwenye Okonjo. *Africa Wo/Man Palava: The Nigerian Novel by Women*. Chicago: The University of Chicago Press, pp. 66, 204–205, 234. Mentions W briefly and compares *NS* to novels by Adaora Lily Ulasi and Buchi Emecheta.

5714. Ojo-Ade, Femi. "Africa and America: A Question of Continuities, Cleavage, and Dreams Deferred," in his *Of Dreams Deferred, Dead or Alive: African Perspectives on African-American Writers*. Westport, CT: Greenwood, pp. 1–27. Notes W's anti–Garveyism (p. 6), comments on *LT*, *BB*, *O*, and *BP* (pp. 15–16), and compares W's attitude toward Africa to Baldwin's (pp. 16–17).

5715. Olney, James. "Autobiographical Traditions Black and White," in *The Future of Southern Letters*. Eds. Jefferson Humphries and John Lowe. New York: Oxford University Press, pp. 134–142.

5716. Ostendorf, Berndt. "Judith Kelleher Schafer, *Slavery, the Civil Law, and the Supreme Court* of Louisiana; Reid Mitchell, *All on a Mardi Gras Day*; Craig Hansen Werner, *Playing the Changes*" *Amerikastudien*, 41, No. 3, 516–519. The review of the Werner book mentions W briefly (p. 518).

5717. Painter, Nell Irvin. "A Different Sense of Time." *The Nation*, 262 (6 May), 38, 42–43. Review of *The Future of the Race* by Henry Louis Gates, Jr., and Cornel West mentioning W briefly (p. 42).

5718. _____, with revision by Robin D.G. Kelley. "Black Americans," in *The Encyclopedia Americana*. Ed. Lawrence T. Lorimer. Vol. 4. Danbury, CT: Grolier, pp. 28A–29.

5719. Pavlić, Edward. "Syndetic Redemption: Above-Underground

Emergence in David Bradley's *The Chaneysville Incident*." *African American Review*, 30 (Summer) 165–184. One of three epigraphs to this article is a quotation from "The Man Who Lived Underground."

5720. Payne, Charles M. *I've Got the Light of Freedom: The Organizing Tradition and the Mississippi Freedom Struggle*. Berkeley: University of California Press, pp. 427, 455.

5721. Payne, James Robert. "David Leeming. *James Baldwin: A Biography*." *World Literature Today*, No. 70 (Winter), p. 194. Mentions W briefly.

5722. Pearson, Norman Holmes. "American Literature: The Twentieth Century," in *The Encyclopedia Americana*. Ed. Lawrence T. Lorimer. Danbury, CT: Grolier, pp. 703–709.

5723. _____. "American Literature," in *The Encyclopedia Americana*. Ed. Lawrence T. Lorimer. Vol. 1. Danbury, CT: Grolier, pp. 691–709.

5724. Pereira, Malin Walther. "Werner Sollors and Maria Diedrich, eds. *The Black Columbiad: Defining Moments in African American Literature and Culture*." *Modern Fiction Studies*, 42 (Winter), 831–833. Review mentioning W briefly.

5725. Peters, Renate. "Sartre, White America, and the Black Problem." *Canadian Review of American Studies*, 27, no. 1, 21–41. Contrasts Sartre's simplistic view of American racial issues to W's knowledgeable view (pp. 29, 37, 39). But Sartre finally came to W's position that the racial problem was a *white* problem (p. 41).

5726. Pfaff, Françoise. *Conversations with Maryse Condé*. Lincoln: University of Nebraska Press, pp. 99, 116.

5727. Phillips, Caryl. "Mariner, Renegade and Castaway." *The New Republic*, 215 (5 August), 32–39. Review of Kent Worcester's *C.L.R. James: A Political Biography* commenting on his relation to W.

5728. Phillips, Roberta. "Bigger and Me." *Richard Wright Newsletter*, 4 (Spring), 6–8. Essay by an eleventh-grade student at the Noble and Greenough School in Dedham, Massachusetts. Phillips notes the difference between Bigger's situation and hers, especially with respect to educational opportunity, but demonstrates the persistence of white racism through an autobiographical account of school experiences.

5729. Pinsker, Sanford. "Albert Murray: The Black Intellectuals' Maverick Patriarch." *The Virginia Quarterly Review*, 72 (Autumn), 678–684. Mentions briefly *NS* (p. 681).

5730. _____. "Black Rage/White Guilt: Act II," in his *Worrying About Race: Reflections During a Troubled Time*. Troy, NY: Whitson, pp. 131–140. Comments of the influence of *NS* on subsequent black writing.

5731. _____. "Black Rage/White Guilt: Act II," in *Worrying About Race, 1985–1995: Reflections During a Troubled Time*. Troy, NY: Whitston, pp. 131–140.

5732. _____. "Home Boys Between Hard Covers," in his *Worrying About Race: Reflections During a Troubled Time*. Troy, NY: Whitson, pp. 106–119. Review of Nathan McCall's *Makes Me Wanna Holler* commenting on *BB* and *NS*, quoting from the latter.

5733. _____. "Irving Howe's Negro Problem–and Ours," in his *Worrying About Race 1985–1995: Reflections During a Troubled Time*. Troy, NY: Whitson, pp. 31–45. Discusses Howe's racial attitudes and his preference for W over Ellison and Baldwin.

5734. _____. "Leibowitz, Herbert. *Fabricating Lives: Explorations in American Autobiography*." *Journal of Modern Literature*, 19 (Spring), 369. Notice mentioning W briefly.

5735. _____. "Spike Lee: Protest, Literary Tradition, and the Individual Filmmaker," in his *Worrying About Race 1985–1995: Reflections During a Troubled Time*. Troy, NY: Whitston, pp. 46–56. Includes comments on W, the protest tradition, and the Howe-Ellison exchange. Mentions briefly *NS* (p. 46).

5736. _____. "Spike Lee: Protest, Literary Tradition, and the Individual Filmmaker," in his *Worrying About Race 1985–1995: Reflections During a Troubled Time*. Troy, NY: Whitson, pp. 46–56. Includes comment on Howe's "Black Boys and Native Sons," p. 46.

5737. Pinson, Hermine D. "Geography and Identity in Melvin Dixson's *Change of Territory*." *MELUS*, 21 (Spring), 99–111. Mentions briefly *AH* and discusses Dixson's poems on W (pp. 105, 109).

5738. Plummer, Brenda Gayle. *Rising Wind: Black Americans and U.S. Foreign Affairs, 1935–1960*. Chapel Hill: University of North Carolina Press, pp. 64, 254. Mentions W's support of the Loyalists in the Spanish Civil War and his involvement with the Paris Conference of Black Writers and Artists.

5739. Portelli, Alessandro. "*Savage Holiday*: Nakedness, Whiteness: Defining the Social Self." *Richard Wright Newsletter*, 4 (Spring), 1–2. Favorable review of the University of Mississippi edition. "*Savage Holiday* is a book about nakedness, literal and metaphorical." The novel is valuable in itself and in its intertextuality with *NS*.

5740. Presley, Delma Eugene, "Carson McCullers and the South," in *Critical Essays on Carson McCullers*, Eds. Beverly Lyon Clark and Melvin J. Friedman. New York: G.K. Hall, pp. 99–110.

5741. _____. "Carson McCullers and the South," in *Critical Essays on Carson McCullers*. Eds. Melvin J. Friedman and Beverly Lyon Clark. New York: G.K. Hall, pp. 99–110.

5742. Quarles, Benjamin. *The Negro in the Making of America*. Third edition. New York: Touchstone, pp. 289–290.

5743. Quirk, Tom. "Introduction," in his and James Barbour's *Biographies of Books: The Compositional Histories of Notable American Writings*. Columbia: University of Missouri Press, pp. 1–10. Mentions briefly *NS* (p. 3).

5744. Rampersad, Arnold. "Du Bois's Passage to India: *Dark Princess*," in *W.E.B. Du Bois on Race and Culture*. Eds. Bernard W. Bell, Emily R. Grosholz, and James B. Stewart. New York: Routledge, pp. 161–176. Quotes from *WML* on the Negro as "America's metaphor" (p. 173).

5745. Redding, Saunders, "American Negro Literature," in *Analysis and Assessment, 1940–1979*. Vol. 6 of *The Harlem Renaissance, 1920–1940*. Ed. Cary D. Wintz. New York: Garland, pp. 149–160.

5746. _____. "The Negro Author: His Publisher, His Public, and His Purse," in *The Harlem Renaissance, 1920–1940*. Vol. 5. Ed. Cary D. Wintz. New York: Garland, pp. 414–418.

5747. _____. "The Problems of the Negro Writer," in *Analysis and Assessment, 1940–1979*. Vol. 6 of *The Harlem Renaissance, 1920–1940*. Ed.

Cary D. Wintz. New York: Garland, pp. 135–148.

5748. Reddy, Maureen T. "*African American Autobiography: A Collection of Critical Essays*. Edited by William L. Andrews." *MELUS*, 21 (Summer), 179–181. Review mentioning briefly W and *BB*.

5749. Rediger, Pat. *Great African Americans in Literature*. New York: Crabtree, pp. 12, 18, 61–63. Contains a biographical sketch of W with photograph. W is also mentioned in biographical sketches of Baldwin and Ellison.

5750. Reed, Bill. "Van Vechten's Eye." *The New York Times* (12 December), p. A36. Letter to the editor mentioning W briefly.

5751. Reilly, John M. "Founding a Literature." *Resources for American Literary Study*, 22, No. 2, pp. 250–254. Mentions briefly *A Richard Wright Bibliography* and Himes in relation to W.

5752. Reins, Keith M. "A Target on the Blackboard." *English Journal*, 85 (September), 19–23. Recalls reading and teaching *BB*.

5753. Remnick, David. "Profiles: Dr. Wilson's Neighborhood." *The New Yorker*, 72 (April 29 and May 6), 96–102, 104–107. Remnick begins his article on the sociologist William Julius Wilson by noting that the neighborhood he studies is that about which W learned so much from previous Chicago sociologists. Mentions briefly *UTC, NS*, and *BB*.

5754. Rice, Herbert William. *Toni Morrison and the American Tradition: A Rhetorical Reading*. New York: Peter Lang, p. 67. Comments on the airplane scene in *NS*.

5755. Richards, Phillip. "Model Minorities." *The Massachusetts Review*, 37 (Spring), 137–147. Mentions "the rage of Bigger Thomas."

5756. Richter, David H. "Richard Wright," in his *Narrative/Theory*. White Plains, NY: Longman Publishers, pp. 62–63. Biographical headnote to a reprint of "Blueprint for Negro Writing."

5757. Robbins, Louise S. "Racism and Censorship in Cold War Oklahoma: The Case of Ruth W. Brown and the Bartlesville Public Library." *Southwestern Historical Quarterly*, 100, 19–46. Mentions the library incident in *BB*, (p. 25).

5758. Roberts, Nora Ruth. *Three Radical Women Writers: Class and*

Gender in Meridel Le Sueur, Tillie Olsen, and Josephine Herbst. New York: Garland, p. 32. Mentions W briefly.

5759/5760. Rodgers, Lawrence R. "Richard Wright, Frank Marshall Davis and the Chicago Renaissance." *The Langston Hughes Review,* 14 (Spring/Fall), 4–12. Compares the lives and early careers of W and Davis. Also compares the Harlem Renaissance and the Chicago Renaissance, noting the dissimilarities.

5761. Rogers, Kenneth Scott. "The Literary Study of Non-Fiction: An Analysis of Selected Works by George Orwell, Richard Wright, Zora Neale Hurston, and Virginia Woolf." *Dissertation Abstracts International,* A, 57/03 (September), p. 1153. Includes treatment of *TMBV.*

5762. Rohlehr, Gordon. "West Indian Poetry: Some Problems of Assessment II," in *The Routledge Reader in Caribbean Literature.* Eds. Alison Donnell and Sarah Lawson Welsh. London: Routledge, pp. 321–326.

5763. Room, Adrian. *Literally Entitled: A Dictionary of the Origins of the Titles of Over 1300 Major Literary Works of the Nineteenth and Twentieth Centuries.* Jefferson, NC: McFarland, p. 150. Mentions briefly *NS.*

5764. Rorty, Richard. "Fraternity Reigns." *The New York Times Magazine* (29 September), 155. Mentions W briefly.

5765. Roseboro, Anna J. Small. *Autobiography Guide for Black Boy by Richard Wright.* Glenview, IL: Scott Foresman. Teacher's study guide with lesson plans, plot summary, biographical information, and other study aides.

5766. Ross, Andrew. "Civilization in One Country? The American James," in *Rethinking C.L.R. James.* Ed. Grant Farred. Oxford: Blackwell, pp. 76–84. Mentions W briefly (p. 77).

5767. Rowell, Charles H. "An Interview with John McCluskey, Jr." *Callaloo,* 19 (Fall), pp. 911–928. McCluskey admires W "as a man fiercely loyal to ideas," especially in *BP* (p. 923). Mentions Bigger and W elsewhere (p. 921, 926).

5768. Ruff, Shawn Stewart. "Introduction," in his *Go the Way Your Blood Beats: An Anthology of Lesbian and Gay Fiction by African-American Writers.* New York: Henry Holt,

pp. xxi–xxix. Includes comments on W's "desperate crossdresser in 'Man of All Work'" (pp. xxii, xxiii) and mentions W elsewhere (p. xxvi). "Man of All Work" is reprinted on pp. 278–315, and W is briefly identified on p. 54.

5769. Sasamoto, Seiji, "The Objectified Structure of Nature in Richard Wright's *Uncle Tom's Children,*" in *Rereading American Short Stories: Woman, Family,* and Ethnicity, pp. 307–320. States that *UTC* contrasts human violence with the rich natural order of the South.

5770. Scherman, Tony. "The Omni-American." *American Heritage,* 47 (September), 68–77. Review with Albert Murray, who comments unfavorably on W. *NS* is "based on Marxist ideology" (p. 72).

5771. Scruggs, Charles. "'All Dressed Up But No Place to Go': The Black Writer and Audience During the Harlem Renaissance," in *Analysis and Assessment, 1940–1979.* Vol 6 of *The Harlem Renaissance, 1920–1940.* Ed. Cary D. Wintz. New York: Garland, pp. 281–301.

5772. _____. "Craig Hansen Werner. *Playing the Changes: From Afro-Modernism to the Jazz Impulse.*" *Modern Fiction Studies,* 42 (Spring), 142–145. Favorable review focusing on Werner's treatment of *NS.*

5773. _____. "*James Baldwin: A Biography.* By David Leeming." *American Literature,* 68 (June), 479–480. Comments on "obtuse criticism" of W.

5774. Seaton, James. *Cultural Conservatism, Political Liberalism: From Criticism to Cultural Studies.* Ann Arbor: The University of Michigan Press, pp. 97–98, 244–245. Quotes Ellison on W and quotes from *BB* on the liberating effect of reading Mencken.

5775. _____. *Cultural Conservatism, Political Liberalism: From Criticism to Cultural Studies.* Ann Arbor: University of Michigan Press, pp. 97–98, 244–245. Discusses Ellison's critique of W in response to Irving Howe and comments on the stimulus Mencken gave to W, quoting from *BB.*

5776. Segal, Ronald. *The Black Diaspora.* New York: The Noonday Press, p. 418. Mentions briefly W and *NS.*

5777. _____. *The Black Diaspora.* New York: Farrar, Straus and Giroux, p. 418.

5778. Shannon, Sandra G. "The Role of Memory in August Wilson's Four-Hundred-Year Autobiography," in *Memory and Cultural Politics: New Approaches to American Ethnic Literatures.* Eds. Amritjit Singh, Joseph T. Skerrett, Jr. Boston: Northeastern University Press, pp. 175–193. Comments briefly on *TMBV* (p. 183).

5779. Shteir, Rachel. "Everybody Slept Here." *The New York Times Book Review* (10 November), p. 71. Article on the house at 7. Middagh Street, Brooklyn, noting that W and his family lived there.

5780. Simmonds, Roy. *John Steinbeck: The War Years, 1939–1945.* Lewisburg, PA: Bucknell University Press, p. 44. Comments on W's acquaintance with Steinbeck in Mexico and his friendship with Herbert Kline.

5781. Singh, Amritjit, Joseph T. Skerrett, Jr., and Robert E. Hogan. "Introduction," in their *Memory and Cultural Politics: New Approaches to American Ethnic Literatures.* Boston: Northeastern University Press, pp. 3–18. Mentions W briefly (p. 9).

5782. Smelstor, Marjorie. "*Black Boy: A Record of Childhood and Youth,*" in *Masterplots.* Revised Second Edition. Ed. Frank N. Magill. Pasadena, CA: Salem Press, pp. 669–672. Summarizes the autobiography and provides a critique and a brief bibliography.

5783. Smith, Virginia Whatley. "Contributors Notes." *Obsidian II: Black Literature in Review,* 11 (Spring-Summer, Fall-Winter), 283. Mentions her work on W.

5784. _____. "Sorcery, Double-Consciousness, and Warring Souls: An Intertextual Reading of *Middle Passage* and *Captain Blackman.*" *African American Review,* 30 (Winter), 659–674. Quotes a comment from Johnson's *Being & Race* mentioning W briefly (p. 659).

5785. Smith, William Gardner. "The Negro Writer: Pitfalls and Compensations," in *The Harlem Renaissance, 1920–1940.* Vol. 5. Ed. Cary D. Wintz. New York: Garland, pp. 169–175.

5786. Soitos, Stephen F. *The Blues Detective: A Study of African American Detective Fiction.* Amherst: The University of Massachusetts Press, pp. x, 134. Comments on W's interest in detective fiction and mentions briefly W in Paris.

5787. Stange, Maren. "'Illusion Complete Within Itself': Ray De-Carava's Photography." *The Yale Journal of Criticism*, 9 (Spring), 63–92. Mentions briefly *TMBV*, *NS*, and *BB* (pp. 79, 81, 91).

5788. Staples, Brent. "*The Collected Essays of Ralph Ellison*. Edited by John F. Callahan." *The New York Times Book Review* (12 May), 6–7. Includes comment on the Ellison-Howe debate over W.

5789. Steele, Jeffrey. "The Politics of Mourning: Cultural Grief-Work from Frederick Douglass to Fanny Fern," in *Criticism and the Color Line: Desegregating American Literary Studies*. Ed. Henry B. Wonham. New Brunswick, NJ: Rutgers University Press, pp. 95–111. Contains two paragraphs on *BB*, which forces the reader "to share with him the liberating work of mourning the ontological loss structured into the lives of the oppressed" (p. 98).

5790. Stephens, Henrietta. "The Richard Wright Lectures." *Center for the Study of Black Literature & Culture* (Summer), p. 1. Announces Manthia Diawara as the lecturer for annual series at the University of Pennsylvania. One of the lectures was on "Richard Wright and African Modernity."

5791. Stevens, Bonnie Klomp, and Larry L. Stewart. *A Guide to Literary Criticism and Research*. Third edition, Fort Worth: Harcourt Brace College, p. 98. Mentions W briefly.

5792. Stewart, Jeffrey C. *1001 Things Everyone Should Know About African American History*. New York: Doubleday, pp. 281–282, 293. Includes a paragraph on *NS* along with a photograph of W.

5793. _____. *1001 Things Everyone Should Know About African American History*. New York: Doubleday, 281–282, 293. A paragraph on *NS* and a brief mention of W.

5794. Storhoff, Gary. "Slaying the Fathers: The Autobiography of Chester Himes." *a/b: Auto/Biography Studies*, 11 (Spring), 38–55. W is treated extensively in this Oedipal reading of Himes's life and autobiography, especially on pp. 43–46. His rage against W, his benefactor, involves literary jealousy, gender suspicions, and a slaying of *BB* and *AH*, works that influenced Himes.

5795. Story, Ralph D. "Gender and Ambition: Zora Neale Hurston in the Harlem Renaissance," in *Analysis and Assessment, 1980–1994*.

Vol. 7 of *The Harlem Renaissance, 1920–1940*. Ed. Cary D. Wintz. New York: Garland, pp. 353–359.

5796. Stovall, Tyler. *Paris Noir: African Americans in the City of Light*. Boston: Houghton Mifflin, xi + 366 pp. Contains a substantial treatment of W's expatriation: his motives for going to Paris, the milieu of the Tournon and the Monaco, his circle of friends, his political and racial activities, and his trip to Africa. Also treats briefly W's early literary career.

5797. Suggs, Henry Lewis. "Democracy on Trial: The Black Press, Black Migration and the Evolution of Culture and Community in Minnesota, 1865–1970," in his *The Black Press in the Middle West, 1865–1985*. Westport, CT: Greenwood Press, pp. 165–211. Notes a "spirited debate" on *NS* in the Minneapolis *Spokesman* (pp. 182–183).

5798. Takara, Kathryn Waddell. "Rage and Passion in the Poetry of Frank Marshall Davis." *The Black Scholar*, 26 (Summer), 17–26. Mentions W briefly (p. 20).

5799. Tate, Claudia. "The Inevitability of the Present." *PMLA*, 111 (October), 1147–1148. Mentions her Ph.D. thesis on "The Act of Rebellious Creation: The Novels of Richard Wright."

5800. Taylor, Clyde. "Film." in *The Oxford Companion to African American Literature*. Eds. William L. Andrews, Frances Smith Foster, and Trudier Harris. New York: Oxford University Press, pp. 275–279. Includes favorable comment on the film version of *NS* (p. 276).

5801. Teres, Harvey. *Renewing the Left: Politics, Imagination, and the New York Intellectuals*. New York: Oxford University Press, pp. 41, 148, 159, 206–208, 211, 212, 213–214, 216, 220, 223, 227. Discusses and mentions responses to W by the New York Intellectuals, as well as his relations to Ellison and Baldwin.

5802. Thelwell, Michael. "Toward a Collective Vision: Issues in International Literary Criticism," in *Cornerstones: An Anthology of African American Literature*. Ed. Melvin Donalson. New York: St. Martin's Press, pp. 914–925. Quotes W in response to Faulkner: "Literature is a struggle over the nature of reality."

5803. Thomas, Lorenzo. "Poetry: The 1940s to the Present," in *American Literary Scholarship: An An-*

nual/1994. Ed. David J. Nordloh. Durham, NC: Duke University Press, pp. 345–362. Mentions W briefly (p. 346).

5804. Thomson, David. *Rosebud: The Story of Orson Welles*. New York: Knopf, pp. 189–190. Discusses briefly the part of Welles in the play *NS*.

5805. Tidwell, John Edgar. "'I Was a Weaver of Jagged Words': Social Function in the Poetry of Frank Marshall Davis." *The Langston Hughes Review*, 14 (Spring/Fall), 65–78. Mentions W briefly (p. 70).

5806/5807. Tindall, George B., and David E. Shi. *America: A Narrative History*. New York: Norton, pp. 1194, 1195–1196, 1336. Reprint of 1984 plus a brief mention of W (p. 1194) and a quotation from *TMBV*.

5808. Touré. "Dick and James." *VLS: Voice Literary Supplement*, No. 142 (February), 15. Mentions W briefly.

5809. Ture, Kwame. "Kwame Ture (Stokley Carmichael): Political Activist, Organizer, Author," in *First Word: Black Scholars, Thinkers, Warriors: Knowledge, Wisdom, Mental Liberation*. Ed. Kwaku Person-Lynn. New York: Harlem River Press, pp. 197–213. Mentions briefly *BP* (p. 207).

5810. Tuttleton, James W. "Jacques et moi," in his *Vital Signs: Essays on American Literature and Criticism*. Chicago: Ivan R. Dee, pp. 312–333. Mentions W briefly (p. 316).

5811. Valade, Roger M., III. *The Essential Black Literature Guide*. Detroit: Visible Ink, pp. xi, 39, 51, 103, 131, 269–270, 277–278, 305, 336, 341, 371, 375, 382, 386–388, 397, 400, 402. The main biographical entry on W (pp. 386–388) has a photograph, the full-page version of which serves as the frontspiece. There are also entries on *BB* (p. 39) and *NS* (pp. 269–270), and W appears in the chronology and elsewhere.

5812. Van Ness, Gordon, ed. *Striking In: The Early Notebooks of James Dickey*. Columbia: University of Missouri Press, p. 190. Dickey includes *NS* in a book list.

5813. Vecoli, Rudolph J. "Ethnicity and Immigration," in *Encyclopedia of the United States in the Twentieth Century*. Ed. Stanley I. Kutler. New York: Scribner's, Vol. 1, pp. 161–193. Mentions W briefly as a working-class writer (p. 176).

5814. Wagner-Martin, Linda. "'Closer to the Edge': Toni Morrison's *Song of Solomon*," in *Teaching American Ethnic Literatures: Nineteen Essays*. Eds. John R. Maitino and David R. Peck. Albuquerque: University of New Mexico Press, pp. 147–157. Includes *UTC* in a bibliography of related works.

5815. Wald, Alan M. "The 1930s Left in U.S. Literature Reconsidered," in *Radical Revisions: Rereading 1930s Culture*. Eds. Bill Mullen and Sherry Linkon. Urbana: University of Illinois Press, pp. 13–28. Mentions W briefly (p. 15).

5816. Wald, Gayle. "'A Most Disagreeable Mirror': Reflections on White Identitiy in *Black Like Me*," in *Passing and the Fictions of Identity*. Ed. Elaine K. Ginsberg. Durham: Duke University Press, pp. 151–177. Mentions briefly "The Ethics of Living Jim Crow" (p. 152).

5817. Walker, Pierre A. "Theoretical Dimensions of *Invisible Man*," in *Literary Influence and African-American Writers: Collected Essays*. Ed. Tracy Mishkin. New York: Garland, pp. 245–268. Applies Bloom's anxiety of influence, Foucault, and cultural studies to Ellison's novel, with extensive discussion on Ellison and W. Mentions *BB*, *NS*, and *TMBV*.

5818. Walther, Malvin Lavon. "*Playing the Changes: From Afro-Modernism to the Jazz Impulse*." *CLA Journal*, 39 (March), 349–398. Mentions briefly W (p. 395) and *NS* (p. 397).

5819. _____. "Sandra Adell. *Double-Consciousness/Double-Bind: Theoretical Issues in Twentieth-Century Black Literature*." *Modern Fiction Studies*, 42 Spring, 136–138. Review noting Adell's treatment of *BB*.

5820. Walton, Anthony. *Mississippi: An American Journey*. New York: Knopf, pp. 6, 28–32, 213. Discusses W's Mississippi experience and his "incredible" emergence. Notes his immense achievement and influence. Mentions *NS* and quotes from *BB*.

5821. Warren, Kenneth W. "African American Cultural Movements," in *Encyclopedia of the United States in the Twentieth Century*. Ed. Stanley Kutler. New York: Scribners', pp. 1593–1607. Comments on W and the Left, mentioning "Blueprint for Negro Writing," *UTC*, and *NS*.

5822. Webster, Harvey Curtis.

"Pity the Giants," in *On Gwendolyn Brooks: Reliant Contemplation*. Ed. Stephen Caldwell Wright. Ann Arbor: The University of Michigan Press, pp. 19–22.

5823. Weinstein, Randy F. *Against the Tide: Commentaries on a Collection of African Americana, 1711–1987*. New York: Glen Horowitz Booksetter, pp. 182–183, 185–186, 190, 191. Contains annotated listing of *UTC* (presentation copy to Martha Foley), *NS* (Amiri Baraka's copy), *BB* (Eslanda Robeson's copy), and an entry on "Richard Wright's Blues" noting the W-Ellison relation.

5824. Wenke, John. "Melville," in *American Literary Scholarship: An Annual/1994*. Ed. David J. Nordloh. Durham, NC: Duke University Press, pp. 49–62. Notes that Arnold Rampersad "links Babo and Richard Wright's Bigger Thomas" (p. 50).

5825. Werner, Craig. "Barbara Foley. *Radical Representations: Politics and Form in U.S. Proletarian Fiction, 1929–1941*, Walter Kalaidjian. *American Culture Between the Wars: Revisionary Modernism & Postmodern Critique*." *African American Review*, 30 (Spring), 119–121. Review mentioning W and "Blueprint for Negro Writing."

5826. _____. "Barbara Foley. *Radical Representations: Politics and Form in U.S. Proletarian Fiction, 1929–1941*; Walter Kalaidjian. *American Culture Between the Wars: Revisionary Modernism & Postmodern Critique*." *African American Review*, 30 (Spring), 119–121. Mentions briefly W, "Blueprint for Negro Writing," and *NS*.

5827. _____. "*Heroism & the Black Intellectual: Ralph Ellison, Politics, and Afro-American Intellectual Life*. By Jerry Gafio Watts." *Journal of English and Germanic Philology*, 95 (April), 280–281. Mentions briefly W and "Blueprint for Negro Writing."

5828. West, Clarissa N. "Essays with an Attitude." *English Journal*, 85 (January), 93–94. Review of Ralph Wiley's *Why Black People Tend to Shout* mentioning W briefly.

5829. West, Cornel, Jorge Klor de Alva, and Earl Shorris. "Our Next Race Question." *Harper's Magazine*, 292 (April), 55–63. Quotes W that "the Negro is America's metaphor."

5830. Wheat, John. "Lightnin' Hopkins: Blues Bard of the Third Ward," in *Juneteenth Texas: Essays in*

African-American Folklore. Eds. Francis E. Abernethy, Patrick B. Mullen, and Alan B. Govenar. Denton: University of North Texas Press, pp. 255–271. Refers to the introduction to *Blues Fell This Morning*, calling W a "black scholar."

5831. Whitfield, Stephen J. "A Critical Cicerone." *The Virginia Quarterly Review*, 72 (Spring), 351–355. Review of Daniel Aaron's *American Notes: Selected Essays* mentioning W briefly.

5832. Wiley, Ralph. "On the A-Train to Venus with Isis," in *Brotherman: The Odyssey of Black Men in America*. Eds. Herb Boyd and Robert L. Allen. New York: Ballantine Books, pp. 278–285.

5833. Wilhelmus, Tom. "Without Color: Zora Neale Hurston." *The Hudson Review*, 48 (Winter), 672–678. Mentions W briefly (p. 673).

5834. Williams, John A. "Chester Himes. *Plan B*. Eds. Michel Fabre and Robert E. Skinner." *African American Review*, 30 (Fall), 492–494. Mentions W briefly.

5835. Williams, Patricia J. "Meditations on Masculinity." *Callaloo* 19 (Fall), pp. 814–822. Notes John Edgar Wideman's assessment of W's rejection of his father.

5836. Winchell, Mark Royden. *Cleanth Brooks and the Rise of Modern Criticism*. Charlottesville: University Press of Virginia, p. 370. Mentions W briefly.

5837. Winslow, Henry F., Sr. "Two Black Poets and Their Legacy," in *Analysis and Assessment, 1980–1994*. Vol. 7 of *The Harlem Renaissance*. Ed. Cary D. Wintz. New York: Garland, pp. 397–403.

5838. Wirth-Nesher, Hana. *City Codes: Reading the Modern Urban Novel*. Cambridge: Cambridge University Press, pp. 11, 89, 92–93. Comments on "The Man Who Lived Underground," and its influence on Ellison.

5839. Wise, Christopher, and Cora Agatucci. "Historical Review of African-American Literature," in *English Postcoloniality: Literatures from Around the World*. Eds. Radhika Mohanran and Gita Rajan. Westport, CT: Greenwood Press, p. 138. Comments on W's politics, his naturalistic mode, and his relation to Hurston, Ellison, and Baldwin.

5840. Wonham, Henry B. "Introduction," in his *Criticism and the Color Line: Desegregating American*

Literary Studies. New Brunswick, NJ: Rutgers University Press, pp. 1–15. Mentions briefly W (pp. 4, 5, 9) and *NS* (p. 7).

5841. Wood, Joe. "The Soloist: Albert Murray's Blues People." *VLS: The Village Voice Literary Supplement.* No. 142 (February), 17–22. Interview with Albert Murray, who considers *NS* unrepresentative of black life (p. 19).

5842. _____. "The Soloist: Albert Murray's Blues People." *VLS*, no. 142 (February 1996), pp. 17–22. Mentions W briefly (p. 20).

5843. Woods, Tim. "James R. Giles, *The Naturalistic Inner-City Novel in America: Encounters with the Fat Man.*" *Journal of American Studies*, 30 (December 1996), 474–475. Review mentioning W briefly.

5844. Woolley, Lisa. "From Chicago to Chicago Renaissance: The Poetry of Fenton Johnson." *The Langston Hughes Review*, 14 (Spring/Fall), 36–48. Mentions W briefly (pp. 37, 44, 46).

5845. Worcester, Kent. *C.L.R. James: A Political Biography.* Albany: State University of New York Press, pp. xiii, 68, 74–77, 101, 106, 185. Discusses W's friendship with James and Constance Webb, as well as her biographical work on W (pp. 74–77). As a Trotskyist, James was critical of W's politics until he left the Communist Party. Mentions W and *NS* elsewhere.

5846. Wright, Esmond. *The American Dream: From Reconstruction to Reagan.* Cambridge, MA: Blackwell, pp. 27, 256, 408, 554. Mentions briefly W, *NS*, *UTC*, and *BP*.

5847. Yaakov, Juliette, and John Greenfieldt, eds. *Fiction Catalog.* 13th edition. New York: Wilson, pp. 714–715. Annotated entry includes *EM*, *LT*, *NS*, *O*, *UTC*, and the Library of America edition.

5848. Yaeger, Patricia. *Flannery O'Connor and the Aesthetics of Torture.* Athens: The University of Georgia Press, pp. 190, 205. Comments on and quotes from "Big Boy Leaves Home" and mentions "Richard Wright's humble homes."

5849. Yarborough, Richard. "Strategies of Black Characterization in *Uncle Tom's Cabin* and the Early Afro-American Novel," in *Literary Influence and African-American Writers: Collected Essays.* Ed. Tracy Mishkin. New York: Garland, pp. 23–64.

5850. Youga, Jan, Mark H. Withrow, and Janis Flint-Ferguson. "Conquering the Streets of Memphis *Richard Wright*," in their *Readings Are Writings: A Guide to Reading and Writing Well.* Upper Saddle River, NJ: Prentice Hall, pp. 54–55, 60. Study notes and questions for a selection from *BB*.

5851. _____. "Discovering Books *Richard Wright*," in their *Readings Are Writings: A Guide to Reading and Writing Well.* Upper Saddle River, NJ: Prentice Hall, pp. 391–396. Study notes and questions for a selection from *BB*.

5852. Young, Al. "Margaret Walker (b. 1915)," in his *African American Literature: A Brief Introduction and Anthology.* New York: HarperCollins, p. 402. Mentions W and Walker's biography of W.

5853. _____. "John A. Williams (b. 1925)," in his *African American Literature: A Brief Introduction and Anthology.* New York: HarperCollins, p. 184. Headnote mentioning Williams's biography of W.

5854. _____. "Ralph Ellison (1914–1994)," in his *African American Literature: A Brief Introduction and Anthology.* New York: HarperCollins, p. 47. Headnote to "Remembering Richard Wright" mentioning W as Ellison's friend.

5855. _____. "Richard Wright (1908–1960)," in his *African American Literature: A Brief Introduction and Anthology.* New York: HarperCollins, p. 115. Biographical headnote to "Almos' a Man."

5856. _____. "Selected Bibliography," in his *African American Literature: A Brief Introduction and Anthology.* New York: HarperCollins, pp. 544–552. Lists books on W by Houston Baker, Jr., Michel Fabre, Jean-François Gounard, and Keneth Kinnamon.

5857. _____. "Zora Neale Hurston (1881–1960)," in his *African American Literature: A Brief Introduction and Anthology.* New York: HarperCollins, p. 99. Headnote mentioning W briefly.

5858. Young, Andrew. *An Easy Burden: The Civil Rights Movement and the Transformation of America.* New York: HarperCollins, pp. 17–18. Discusses his reading of *BB* and the discomfort his parents and their friends felt about W's revelations.

5859. Young, Reggie. "On Stepping Into Footprints Which Feel Like Your Own: Literacy, Empowerment, and the African-American Literary Tradition," in *Literary Influence and Afro-American Writers: Collected Essays.* Ed. Tracy Mishkin. New York: Garland, pp. 359–389. Mentions briefly W and *NS* (pp. 370, 381).

5860. Young, Stephen. "Major Authors." *Society for the Study of Southern Literature Newsletter* (November), 6. Lists James A. Miller's *Approaches to Teaching Wright's Native Son.*

5861. _____. "Nominees for SSSL Executive Council." *Society for the Study of Southern Literature Newsletter* (November), 1. Notes Jerry Ward's interest in W.

5862. _____. "African American: Literature." *Society for the Study of Southern Literature Newsletter* (November), 6. Lists James A. Miller's *Approaches to Teaching Wright's Native Son.*

5863. _____. "Major Authors." *Society for the Study of Southern Literature Newsletter* (April), 14. Lists s.v. W Adam Zachary Newton's *Narrative Ethics.*

5864. _____. "Recent Papers and Conference Panels by SSSL Members" *Society for the Study of Southern Literature Newsletter* (April), 5–6. Lists a paper on *UTC* delivered by John Lowe at the University of Erlangen-Nuremburg.

5865. Youssef, Sitamon Mubarak. "'Southern Nights' and the Angry Voice of Richard Wright." *The Marjorie Kinnan Rawlings Journal of Florida Literature*, 7, 85–98. Surveys W's life in the South emphasizing his difficult and traumatic relations with his mother and grandmother. Examines the first three stories of *UTC* in this context.

5866. Zaller, Robert. "Black, White, Red All Over." *The Nation*, 262 (17 June), 30, 32–33. Review of Ben Burns's *Nitty Gritty: A White Editor in Black Journalism* mentioning W and referring to W's "The Shame of Chicago" (pp. 30, 32).

5867. Zunz, Olivier. "Class," in *Encyclopedia of the United States in the Twentieth Century.* Ed. Stanley I. Kutler. New York: Scribners', Vol. 1, pp. 195–220. Mentions W briefly (p. 213).

1997

5868. Abe, Daisei. "On Bigger Thomas III: Richard Wright and Racial Prejudices." *Journal of Gifu College for Economics*, 31 (November), 355–387. Contends that *NS* is not totally fictional, for it is based on W's own experiences in Chicago. The social cause of Bigger's crime is understandable in the context of white racism.

5869. Accomando, Christina. "Attaway, William," in *The Oxford Companion to African American Literature*. Eds. William L. Andrews, Frances Smith Foster, and Trudier Harris. New York: Oxford University Press, pp. 30–31. Comments on the Attaway-W friendship, including W's visit to the University of Illinois.

5870. Adair, Vivyan Campbell. "From 'goodma' to 'welfare queen': A 'Genealogy' of the Poor Women in 20th Century American Literature, Photography, and Culture," *Dissertation Abstracts International—A*, 57/12 (June), p 5197. Dissertation including comment on W.

5871. Ahmad, Aijaz. "From *In Theory: Classes, Nations, Literatures*," in *Postcolonial Criticism*. Eds. Bart Moore-Gilbert, Gareth Stanton, and Willy Maley. London: Longman, pp. 248–272.

5872. Ailey, Alvin, James Baldwin, Romare Bearden, and Albert Murray. "To Hear Another Language," in *Conversations With Albert Murray*. Ed. Roberta S. Maguire. Jackson: University Press of Mississippi, pp. 25–45.

5873. Albright, Angela. "Zora Neale Hurston's *Their Eyes Were Watching God* as a Blueprint for Negro Writing." *Publications of the Arkansas Philological Association*, 23 (Spring), 2–11. Argues that despite W's objections to *Their Eyes Were Watching God*, Hurston's novel "meets many of the criteria [W] sets … embodying the values and elements of black culture that he finds so positive."

5874. Altman, Susan. *The Encyclopedia of African-American Heritage*. New York: Facts on File, pp.

21, 279. Mentions W s.v. Baldwin and includes a biographical sketch and a photograph of W as Bigger in the film *NS*.

5875. Anderson, Jervis. *Bayard Rustin: Troubles I've Seen: A Biography*. New York: HarperCollins, pp. 104, 157. Mentions briefly *BB* and W.

5876. Andrews, William L. "Autobiography: Overview," in *The Oxford Companion to African American Literature*. Eds. William L. Andrews, Frances Smith Foster, and Trudier Harris. New York: Oxford University Press, p. 34. Mentions W briefly.

5877. _____. "Autobiography: Secular Autobiography," in *The Oxford Companion to African American Literature*. Eds. William L. Andrews, Frances Smith Foster, and Trudier Harris. New York: Oxford University Press, pp. 34–37. Includes brief discussion of *BB*, a "grim portrayal of a southern black youth's evolution into the quintessentially alienated modernist writer dedicated to speaking the truth for no one but himself" (p. 37).

5878. _____. "Victor Séjour (1817–1874)," in *The Norton Anthology of African American Literature*. Eds. Henry Louis Gates, Jr., and Nellie Y. McKay. New York: Norton, pp. 286–287. Mentions W's expatriation and notes that Séjour's story "The Mulatto" anticipates W's social and psychological themes.

5879. Anon. "African American Perspectives: The Classic Video Collection," in *Shattering the Silences: Video for a Diverse Campus*. San Francisco: Resolution/California Newsreel, p. 14. Includes a producer's notice of "Richard Wright: Black Boy."

5880. Anon. "African Americans in the Land of Lincoln." Edwardsville: Southern Illinois University. Program of a conference listing a paper by Margaret A. Simons entitled "Richard Wright: From *Black Metropolis* to the City of Lights," 18 April.

5881. Anon. *American Literature*. New York: Oxford University Press,

p. 11. Contains a publisher's notice of Claudia Tate's *Desire and the Protocols of Race* mentioning W briefly.

5882. Anon. "*Approaches to Teaching Wright's Native Son*." *College English*, 59 (October), following p. 727. Publisher's notice including a list of contributors.

5883. Anon. "Births," in *The Literary Almanac*. Kansas City: Andrews McMeel, p. 18. Notes W's birth in 1908.

5884. Anon. "Book News: Approaches Volume on Wright's *Native Son* Published." *MLA Newsletter*, 29 (Fall), 14. Publisher's notice of *Approaches to Teaching Wright's Native Son*, edited by James A. Miller.

5885. Anon. *Carroll & Graf Publishers College Catalog 1997–1998*. New York: Carroll Graf, p. 43. Contains a publisher's notice of the paperback edition of *TMBV*.

5886. Anon. "Chelsea Literary Series," in *Literature from The Scholar's Bookshelf*. Cranbury, NJ: The Scholar's Bookshelf, pp. 64–65. Lists the volume on W and the volume on *NS* in series edited by Harold Bloom.

5887. Anon. "Conservative Trends in Literary Study." *PMLA*, 112 (November), 1277. Announces a paper by Patricia Carter entitled "When the Critics Read (W)Right: Critical Discourse and the Rhetoric of Anti-Communism in *Black Boy (American Hunger)*" to be delivered at the Modern Language Association Convention on 28 December.

5888. Anon. "Controversial Books," in *The Literary Almanac*. Kansas City: McMeel, p. 269. Lists *NS* as one of the dozen books "most frequently challenged" in 1995–1996 by school and library censors.

5889. Anon. "Critical Responses in Arts and Letters from Greenwood Press." *PMLA*, 112 (March), 41. Lists *The Critical Response to Richard Wright* edited by Robert J. Butler.

5890. Anon. "Cross-Generational Connections I: New Black American Male Narratives." *PMLA*, 112 (November), 1335. Announces a paper by Aimé Jero Ellis entitled "Mapping Black American Identity in the Narratives of Nathan McCall, Malcolm X, Ralph Ellison, and Richard Wright" to be delivered at the Modern Language Association Convention on 29 December.

5891. Anon. "The Eighth Annual Natchez Literary Celebration Presents Famous Southern Families in Fiction and Fact." Natchez, MS: Copiah-Lincoln Community College. Brochure listing the "presentation of the Richard Wright Literary Excellence Awards to Ms. Elizabeth Spencer and Mr. Shelby Foote" on 31 May.

5892. Anon. "Ellison, Ralph [Waldo]," in *The Dictionary of Global Culture*. Eds. Kwame Anthony Appiah and Henry Louis Gates, Jr. New York: Knopf, pp. 205–206. Biographical sketch mentioning W briefly.

5893. Anon. "*Emerge's* Recommended Reading." *Emerge*, 9 (November), 103. Mentions W briefly in a notice of *Generations of Black and White Photographs*.

5894. Anon. "HarperCollins Publishers." *PMLA*, 112 (March), 330. Lists the paperback edition of *EM* with an introduction by Paul Gilroy.

5895. Anon. "James Baldwin," in *The Literary Almanac*. Kansas City: Andrews McMeel, p. 224. Mentions W's early support of Baldwin.

5896. Anon. "Just Published," in *New and Selected Titles: Summer 1997*. New York: Modern Language Association, p. 4. Publisher's notice of *Approaches to Teaching Wright's Native Son*, edited by James A. Miller.

5897. Anon. "Life in Harlem," in *Langston Hughes: The Contemporary Reviews*. Ed. Tish Dace. Cambridge: Cambridge University Press, p. 439.

5898. Anon. "Life of a Black Man," in *Langston Hughes: The Contemporary Reviews*. Ed. Tish Dace. Cambridge: Cambridge University Press, pp. 245–246.

5899. Anon. "The Literature of Upheaval." *American Literature*, 69 (September), tenth unnumbered page following page 664. Contains a publisher's notice of Lawrence Rodgers's *Canaan Bound* mentioning W briefly.

5900. Anon. "Native Son," in *Multicultural Literature*. Princeton, NJ: *Films for the Humanities & Sci-*

ences, p. [2]. Distributor's announcement of the video.

5901. Anon. "The New Selections in the Third Edition." *The Heath Anthology of American Literature Newsletter*, No. 16 (Fall), 3. Notes the inclusion of "Bright and Morning Star."

5902. Anon. "A New Volume in the Approaches to Teaching World Literature Series." *American Literature*, 69 (December), following 905. Publisher's notice of *Approaches to Teaching Wright's Native Son* edited by James A. Miller. Contains a blurb by Susan L. Blake.

5903. Anon. "A New Volume in the Approaches to Teaching World Literature Series." *American Quarterly*, 49 (December), following p. 397. Publisher's notice of James A. Miller's *Approaches to Teaching Wright's Native Son*. Includes a list of contributors.

5904. Anon. *Novels for Students: "Invisible Man" Ralph Ellison, 1952.* Detroit: Gale Research, pp. 153–173. Pamphlet mentioning W's invitation to Ellison to write a book review (p. 154). Also mentions briefly *NS* (p. 166).

5905. Anon. *Novels for Students: Black Boy* Richard Wright 1945. Detroit: Gale Research, pp. 43–65. Pamplet providing a detailed summary of *BB*, calling it "a masterful recording of his own life in the form of the novel." Also contains a biographical sketch of W., comments on the "characters" appearing in the books, discussion of themes, brief analysis of style and structure, information about historical context, critical extracts from commentary on *BB*, and a brief bibliography.

5906. Anon. *Novels for Students: Presenting Analysis, Context, and Criticism*. Detroit: Gale Research, pp. 43–65. Consists of a brief biography of W, followed by a detailed plot summary, a discussion of the people portrayed in the work, explanation of themes, "topics for further study," individualism as the meaning of life, prose style, structure, historical context with comparison to the present, a critical overview with comments by Ellison, Lionel Trilling, Sinclair Lewis, Ronald Sanders, Edward Margolies, Roger Whitlow, Maryemma Graham, Jerry Ward, Jr., Timothy Dow Adams, and Robert J. Butler. Also mentions Bigger Thomas, Fred Dan-

iels, Cross Damon, Big Boy, and "The Man Who Was Almost a Man." Includes a bibliography of fourteen items.

5907. Anon. *On Being Female, Black, and Free: Essays by Margaret Walker, 1932–1992*. Ed. Maryemma Graham. Knoxville: University of Tennessee Press, p. 1. Publishers notice mentioning W briefly.

5908. Anon. "Oxford University Press." *PMLA*, 112 (October), 1189. Contains a notice of Claudia Tate's *Desire and the Protocols of Race: Black Novels and Psychoanalysis* mentioning W briefly.

5909. Anon. "Read All About It!: Postage Stamps for World Literacy." *Negro History Bulletin*, 60 (July–September), 2. W is one of twelve African American writers honored by a postage stamp in Ghana or Uganda.

5910. Anon. "Recent Scholarship." *The Journal of American History*, 84 (December), 1195–1265. Lists a 1996 Penn State dissertation entitled "The Discourse on Slavery and Race in American Fiction: From Harriet Beecher Stowe's *Uncle Tom's Cabin* to Richard Wright's *Uncle Tom's Children*" (p. 1197).

5911. Anon. "*Richard Wright and the Library Card*," in *Lee & Low Books Fall 1997*. New York: Lee & Low, p. 5. Publisher's notice of a juvenile written by William Miller and illustrated by Gregory Christie.

5912. Anon. "*Richard Wright-Black Boy*," in *African American Perspectives, 1996–1997*. San Francisco: Resolution/California Newsreel, p. 13.

5913. Anon. "Spring Paperbacks from Da Capo Press." *The New York Review of Books*, 44 (15 May), 39. Includes an announcement of a reprint of *Richard Wright Reader*.

5914. Anon. "1960," *The Literary Almanac*. Kansas City: Andrews McMeel, pp. 124–125. Includes a notice of W's death with a biographical sketch and a photograph. Mentions *UTC*, *NS*, and *BB*.

5915. Anon. Untitled note. *Richard Wright Newsletter*, 5 (Spring/Summer), 9. Notes that Mary Kemp Davis gave a talk on *BB* and *Kaffir Boy* at the annual meeting of the College Language Association.

5916. Anon. "Widow Upset Over Minister's Plot to Ban Book." Fayetteville *Northwest Arkansas Times* (18 May), p. C11. Associated Press report that Ellen Wright wrote a letter to the Jacksonville *Florida Times Union* protesting an effort to ban *BB* from schools "because it uses racially derogatory language."

5917. Anon. "Wright, Richard," in *The Dictionary of Global Culture*. Eds. Kwame Anthony Appiah and Henry Louis Gates, Jr. New York: Knopf, pp. 701–702. Biographical sketch.

5918. Archibald, Rev. Chestina Mitchell. "Lord, Here We Is, Maybe for the Last Time," in her *Say Amen! The African American Family's Book of Prayers*. New York: Dutton Signet, p. 287. Biographical footnote to a quotation from *NS*.

5919. Arensberg, Liliane K. "Death as a Metaphor of Self in *I Know Why the Caged Bird Sings*," in *Readings on Maya Angelou*. Ed. Mary E. Williams. San Diego: Greenhaven Press, pp. 115–119.

5920. Ashwill, Gary, Chris Kromm, and Jordan Green. "Writing from the Bottom Up: A Southern Tradition." *Southern Exposure*, 25 (Fall/Winter), 12–15. Mentions W briefly (p. 15).

5921. Auger, Philip. *Native Sons in No Man's Land*: Rewriting Afro-American Manhood in the *Novels of Baldwin, Walker, Wideman, and Gaines*. New York: Garland, 2000, ix + 79 pp. Calling Bigger "a modern codification of black manhood inscribed as powerless, animalistic, and inarticulate" (p. 1) because he is victimized by racist discourse (in the Foucauldian sense), Auger proceeds in subsequent chapters to discuss novels by Baldwin, Walker, Wideman, and Gaines that address the issue of black manhood, especially in relation to W.

5922. Ayers, David. "Craig Hansen Werner. *Playing the Changes: From Afro-Modernism to the Jazz Impulse*." *Journal of American Studies*, 31 (April), 116–117. Mentions W briefly.

5923. Ayers, Edward L., and Bradley C. Mittendorf. "From *Black Boy*: Richard Wright (1908–1960)," in their *The Oxford Book of the American South: Testimony, Memory, and Fiction*. New York: Oxford University Press, p. 335. Headnote to an excerpt.

5924. ____." Preface," in their *The Oxford Book of the American South: Testimony, Memory, and Fiction*. New York: Oxford Uni-

versity Press, pp. ix–x. Mentions W briefly.

5925. ____. "Preface," in their *The Oxford Book of the American South: Testimony, Memory, and Fiction*. New York: Oxford University Press, pp. ix–x. Mentions W briefly.

5926. Azoulay, Katya Gibel. *Black, Jewish, and Interracial: It's Not the Color of Your Skin, But the Race of Your Kin, and Other Myths of Identity*. Durham: Duke University Press, p. 76. Quotes W's statement that "There was no agency in the world so capable of making men feel the earth and the people upon it as the Communist Party."

5927. Baker, Houston A. Jr. "The Black Arts Movement 1960–1970," in *The Norton Anthology of African American Literature*. Eds. Henry Louis Gates, Jr., and Nellie Y. McKay. New York: W.W. Norton, pp. 1791–2010. Includes brief but favorable mention of W as relevant to the Sixties (p. 1804).

5928. ____. "John Alfred Williams," in *The Norton Anthology of African American Literature*. Eds. Henry Louis Gates, Jr., and Nellie McKay. New York: W.W. Norton, pp. 1883–1834. Biographical-critical sketch noting Williams's admiration of W, who is the prototype of the character Harry Ames in *The Man Who Cried I Am*.

5929. Baldwin, James. "Everybody's Protest Novel," in *Call and Response: The Riverside Anthology of the African American Literary Tradition*. Eds. Patricia Liggins Hill, Bernard W. Bell, Trudier Harris, William J. Harris, R. Baxter Miller, and Sondra A. O'Neale. Boston: Houghton Mifflin, pp. 1316–1320.

5930. ____. "Everybody's Protest Novel," in *The Norton Anthology of African American Literature*. Eds. Henry Louis Gates, Jr., and Nellie McKay. New York: W.W. Norton, pp. 1654–1659.

5931. ____. "Many Thousands Gone," in *The Norton Anthology of African American Literature*. Eds. Henry Louis Gates, Jr., and Nellie McKay. New York: W.W. Norton, pp. 1659–1670.

5932. Banks, Marva O. "Heard, Nathan C.," in *The Oxford Companion to African American Literature*. Eds. William L. Andrews, Frances Smith Foster, and Trudier Harris. New York: Oxford University Press, pp. 350–351. Quotes

Richard Yarborough calling Heard "a latter-day Richard Wright" (p. 351).

5933. Barker, Deborah E. "Visual Markers: Art and Mass Media in Alice Walker's *Meridian*." *African American Review*, 31 (Fall), 463–479. Mentions briefly *TMBV* (p. 478).

5934. Bassett, John E. "Introduction," in his *Defining Southern Literature: Perspectives and Assessments, 1831–1952*. Madison-Teaneck, NJ: Fairleigh Dickinson University Press, pp. 33, 35. Mentions W briefly.

5935. Bateman, Beverly. "Albert Murray: Up Tempo or 'The Velocity of Celebration,'" in *Conversations with Albert Murray* ed. Roberta Maguire. Jackson: University Press of Mississippi, pp. 16–24.

5936. Bates, Beth Tompkins. "A New Crowd Challenges the Agenda of the Old Guard in the NAACP, 1933–1941." *The American Historical Review*, 102 (April), 340–377. Mentions briefly W's essay "Two Million Black Voices" (p. 360).

5937. Bell, Bernard W. "Nails, Snails, and Puppy-Dog Tails: Black Male Stereotypes in the Diasporic Fiction of Toni Morrison, Alice Walker, and Terry McMillan," in *Contemporary Literature in the African Diaspora*. Eds. Olga Barrios and Bernard W. Bell. Salamanca: Universidad de Salamanca, pp. 67–74. Mentions briefly W and *NS* (pp. 69, 70, 71).

5938. Bell, Bernard W., Patricia Liggins Hill, and Horace A. Porter. "Call: Integrationist Poetics or Black Poetics?" in *Call and Response: The Riverside Anthology of the African American Literary Tradition*. Eds. Patricia Liggins Hill, Bernard W. Bell, Trudier Harris, William J. Harris, R. Baxter Miller, and Sondra A. O'Neale. Boston: Houghton Mifflin, pp. 1078–1080. Comments on Baldwin's criticism of W and quotes Richard Barksdale on Bigger Thomas.

5939. ____. "Dorothy West (1907–)," in *Call and Response: The Riverside Anthology of the African American Literary Tradition*. Eds. Patricia Liggins Hill, Bernard W. Bell, Trudier Harris, William J. Harris, R. Baxter Miller, and Sondra A. O'Neale. Boston: Houghton Mifflin, pp. 1267–1272. Mentions W briefly as an associate editor of *New Challenge* (p. 1269).

5940. _____. "James Baldwin (1924–1987)," in *Call and Response: The Riverside Anthology of the African American Literary Tradition*. Eds. Patricia Liggins Hill, Bernard W. Bell, Trudier Harris, William J. Harris, R. Baxter Miller, and Sondra A. O'Neale. Boston: Houghton Mifflin, pp. 1295–1298. Mentions briefly W and *NS*.

5941. _____. "John Oliver Killens (1916–1987)," in *Call and Response: The Riverside Anthology of The African American Literary Tradition*. Eds. Patricia Liggins Hill, Bernard W. Bell, Trudier Harris, William J. Harris, R. Baxter Miller, and Sondra A. O'Neale. Boston: Houghton Mifflin, pp. 1290–1293. Mentions W briefly.

5942. _____. "Margaret Esse Danner (1915–1988)," in *Call and Response: The Riverside Anthology of the African American Literary Tradition*. Eds. Patricia Liggins Hill, Bernard W. Bell, Trudier Harris, William J. Harris, R. Baxter Miller, and Sondra A. O'Neale. Boston: Houghton Mifflin, pp. 1151–1153. Mentions briefly W, *O*, *LD*, *BP*, and *PS*.

5943. _____. "Margaret Walker (1915–)," in *Call and Response: The Riverside Anthology of The African American Literary Tradition*. Eds. Patricia Liggins Hill, Bernard W. Bell, Trudier Harris, William J. Harris, R. Baxter Miller, and Sondra A. O'Neale. Boston: Houghton Mifflin, pp. 1157–1159. Contains a paragraph on the W-Walker "collaboration" in the thirties.

5944. _____. "Owen Dodson (1914–1983)," in *Call and Response: The Riverside Anthology of the African American Literary Tradition*. Eds. Patricia Liggins Hill, Bernard W. Bell, Trudier Harris, William J. Harris, R. Baxter Miller, and Sondra A. O'Neale. Boston: Houghton Mifflin, pp. 1146–1149. Mentions W briefly.

5945. _____. "Ralph Ellison (1914–1994), in *Call and Response: The Riverside Anthology of the African American Literary Tradition*. Eds. Patricia Liggins Hill, Bernard W. Bell, Trudier Harris, William J. Harris, R. Baxter Miller, and Sondra A. O'Neale. Boston: Houghton Mifflin, pp. 1274–1278. Contains a paragraph on Ellison's relation to W (pp. 1275–1276).

5946. _____. "Win the War Blues: African American History and Culture, 1945–1960: 'Does It Dry Up Like a Raisin in the Sun?': Post-Renaissance and Post-Reformation," in *Call and Response: The Riverside Anthology of the African American Literary Tradition*. Eds. Patricia Liggins Hill, Bernard W. Bell, Trudier Harris, William J. Harris, R. Baxter Miller, and Sondra A. O'Neale. Boston: Houghton Mifflin, pp. 1065–1073. Comments on W's existentialism (p. 1068).

5947. _____. "The Writers' Response," in *Call and Response: The Riverside Anthology of the African American Literary Tradition*. Eds. Patricia Liggins Hill, Bernard W. Bell, Trudier Harris, William J. Harris, R. Baxter Miller, and Sondra A. O'Neale. Boston: Houghton Mifflin, pp. 1080–1090. Comments on *O*, *SH*, *LD*, and *BP* in relation to existentialism (p. 1087) and mentions W elsewhere (p. 1089).

5948. Benoist, Mary Anne. "African American: Literature." *Society for the Study of Southern Literature Newsletter*. 31 (November), 8. Lists the re-issue of *Richard Wright Reader*.

5949. Berger, Roger A. "*Soul on Ice*," in *The Oxford Companion to African American Literature*. Eds. William L. Andrews, Frances Smith Foster, and Trudier Harris. New York: Oxford University Press, p. 680. Notes Cleaver's high opinion of W.

5950. Berk, Stephen E. *A Time to Heal: John Perkins, Community Development, and Racial Reconciliation*. Grand Rapids, MI: Baker Books, p. 140. Mentions W briefly.

5951. Bernard, Louise. "The Musicality of Language: Redefining History in Suzan-Lori Parks's *The Death of the Last Black Man in the Whole Entire World*." *African American Review*, 31 (Winter), 687–698. Mentions briefly *NS* and Bigger Thomas in relation to a character in the Parks play named And Bigger And Bigger And Bigger (p. 696).

5952. Berry, Abner. "Not So Simple," in *Langston Hughes: The Contemporary Reviews*. Ed. Tish Dace. Cambridge: Cambridge University Press, pp. 452–454.

5953. Bérubé, Michael. "Max, Media, and Mimesis: Bigger's Representation in *Native Son*," in *Approaches to Teaching Wright's Native Son*. Ed. James A. Miller. New York: The Modern Language Association of America, pp. 112–119. Announcing at the beginning that his argument "is that *Native Son* is about African American representation in the legal and in the mimetic sense, and that the novel enacts its concerns with representation partly by representing itself in its own narrative machinery," Bérubé focuses on Max and Buckley, the press, and the recapitulation of the narrative in the Fate section. He finds the novel "is less concerned with Bigger's representativeness than with Bigger's multiple representations, and what these tell us about the processes by which blackness is constructed and consumed" (p. 117).

5954. Bess, R. "Hakutani, Yoshinobu. *Richard Wright and Racial Discourse*." *Choice*, 34 (February), pp. 965–966. Favorable notice setting forth the steps of Hakutani's discussion of W.

5955. Bickley, R. Bruce, Jr., and Hugh T. Keeman. *Joel Chandler Harris: An Annotated Bibliography of Criticism, 1977–1996 with Supplement, 1892–1976*. Westport, CT: Greenwood Press, pp. 25, 72, 137, 138. Mentions briefly W and "Big Boy Leaves Home"; quotes W on the Uncle Remus stories (p. 138).

5956. Birt, Robert. "Existence, Identity, and Liberation," in *Existence in Black: An Anthology of Black Existential Philosophy*. Ed. Lewis R. Gordon. New York: Routledge, pp. 205–213. Mentions W and quotes from *AH* (p. 207).

5957. Blake, Susan L. "Linden Peach. *Toni Morrison*," *African American Review*, 31 (Fall), 533–535. Mentions W briefly.

5958. Boehnlein, James M. "*Worker-Writer in America: Jack Conroy and the Tradition of Midwestern Literary Radicalism, 1898–1990*, by Douglas Wixson." *The Midwest Quarterly*, 38 (Spring), 338–339. Review mentioning W briefly.

5959. Bogus, Diane A. "Lessons in Truth: Teaching Ourselves and Our Students *Native Son*," in *Approaches to Teaching Wright's Native Son*. Ed. James A. Miller. New York: The Modern Language Association of America, pp. 102–111. Writing from a Christian point of view, Bogus emphasizes Bigger's spiritual conversion in the Fate section. Bigger's effort to believe is important because "it suggests a moral or spiritual reading that can serve the moral and spiritual lives of students and teach them the importance of taking responsibility for themselves" (p. 109).

5960. B[onnoitt], M[urray] duQ. "Under the Covers," in *Langston Hughes: The Contemporary Reviews*. Ed. Tish Dace. Cambridge: Cambridge University Press, p. 256.

5961. Bordelon, Pam. "New Tracks on *Dust Tracks*: Toward a Reassessment of the Life of Zora Neale Hurston." *African American Review*, 31 (Spring), 5–21. Mentions W briefly (pp. 12, 15).

5962. Boudreau, Kristin. "*The Apocalypse in African-American Fiction*. By Maxine Lavon Montgomery." *American Literature*, 69 (March), 223–224. Briefly mentions *NS*.

5963. Boyd, Melba Joyce. "Literacy and the Liberation of Bigger Thomas," in *Approaches to Teaching Wright's Native Son*. Ed. James A. Miller. New York: The Modern Language Association of America, pp. 35–41. Emphasizes the importance of social issues in the novel by analyzing the role of movies, black-white imagery, the persistence of racism, and the 1986 film version of *NS*.

5964. Boyd, Todd. *Am I Black Enough for You?: Popular Culture from the 'Hood and Beyond*. Bloomington: Indiana University Press, p. 75. Mentions W briefly.

5965. Bradley, David. "Our Crowd, Their Crowd: Race, Reader, and *Moby-Dick*," in *Melville's Everlasting Dawn*. Eds. John Bryant and Robert Milder. Kent, OH: The Kent State University Press, pp. 119–146. Mentions W checking out books from a segregated library (p. 125) and comments on the problem of cultural illiteracy as exemplified by Mary Dalton (pp. 136–137).

5966. Brodhead, Richard H. "Melville; or Aggression," in *Melville's Evermoving Dawn: Centennial Essays*. Eds. John Bryant and Robert Milder. Kent, OH: The Kent State University Press, pp. 181–191. Mentions W briefly (p. 191).

5967. Brookhart, Mary Hughes. "Allen, Samuel W.," in *The Oxford Companion to African American Literature*. Eds. William L. Andrews, Frances Smith Foster, and Trudier Harris. New York: Oxford University Press, pp. 12–13. Notes W's help to Allen as a young poet in Paris (p. 12).

5968. Brown, Bill. "Global Bod-ies/Postnationalities: Charles Johnson's Consumer Culture." *Representations*, No. 58 (Spring), 24–48. Mentions briefly W, *NS*, and the movie *Trader Horn* (p. 28).

5969. Brown, John L. "Ralph Ellison. *Flying Home and Other Stories*. John F. Callahan, ed. *The Collected Essays*." *World Literature Today*. No. 71 (Autumn), p. 786. Mentions W briefly.

5970. Brown, Lloyd L. "Not So Simple," in *Langston Hughes: The Contemporary Reviews*. Ed. Tish Dace. Cambridge: Cambridge University Press, pp. 363–365.

5971. Brown, Sterling A. "Insight, Courage, and Craftsmanship," in *Critical Essays on Richard Wright's Native Son*. Ed. Keneth Kinnamon. New York: G.K. Hall, pp. 53–55. Reprint of 1940.572.

5972. Bruce, Dickson D., Jr. "Protest Literature," in *The Oxford Companion to African American Literature*. Eds. William L. Andrews, Frances Smith Foster, and Trudier Harris. New York: Oxford University Press, pp. 600–604. Contains a paragraph on W as a protest writer, mentioning *UTC*, *NS*, and *BB* (p. 603).

5973. Brundage, W. Fitzhugh. "Introduction," in his *Under Sentence of Death: Lynching in the South*. Chapel Hill: University of North Carolina Press, pp. 1, 15. Mentions W briefly.

5974. Bryant, Cedric Gael. "Criticism from 1920 to 1964," in *The Oxford Companion to African American Literature*. Eds. William L. Andrews, Frances Smith Foster, and Trudier Harris. New York: Oxford University Press, pp. 187–190. Mentions briefly "Blueprint for Negro Writing," *NS*, and W in the debate between Ellison and Irving Howe.

5975. Bryant, J.A., Jr. *Twentieth-Century Southern Literature*. Lexington: The University Press of Kentucky, pp. 6, 155–159. Biographical-critical sketch of W, emphasizing racial protest. Includes a contrast of W and Ellison.

5976. Bryant, Jerry H. *Victims and Heroes: Racial Violence in the African American Novel*. Amherst: The University of Massachusetts Press, pp. 2, 33, 124, 127, 159, 194, 197–210, 211, 212, 213, 214, 216, 220, 223, 227, 230, 276, 278, 339, 341–344, 345. Chapter 8, "Richard Wright and Bigger Thomas: Grace

in Damnation," analyzes *NS* and *BB*. Both emphasize black revolt against white racism, but W shows the clash of value systems, both flawed, in this conflict. Bryant mentions W and his works frequently outside of this chapter (pp. 197–210).

5977. Bryant, John. "The Persistence of Melville: Representative Writer for a Multicultural Age," in *Melville's Evermoving Dawn: Centennial Essays*. Eds. John Bryant and Robert Milder. Kent, OH: The Kent State University Press, pp. 1–28. Mentions W briefly (pp. 5, 15).

5978. Burgum, Edwin Berry. "The Promise of Democracy and the Fiction of Richard Wright," in *Critical Essays on Richard Wright's Native Son*. Ed. Keneth Kinnamon. New York: G.K. Hall, pp. 63–74.

5979. Burke, Kathleen. "Notable Books for Children." *Smithsonian*, 28 (November), 163–164, 166–175. Contains a brief review of William Miller's *Richard Wright and the Library Card* (p. 172).

5980. Burkholder, Robert E. "Early-19th Century American Literature," in *American Literary Scholarship: An Annual 1995*. Ed. Gary Scharnhorst. Durham, NC: Duke University Press, pp. 207–233. Mentions W briefly (p. 224).

5981. Bus, Heiner. "Asiatisch-amerikanische Literatur," in *Amerikanische Literaturgeschichte*. Ed. Hubert Zapf. Stuttgart: J.B. Metzler, pp. 455–464. Mentions briefly *NS* as an influence on Carlos Bulosan (p. 456).

5982. Butler, Robert J. "Seeing *Native Son*," in *Approaches to Teaching Wright's Native Son*. Ed. James A. Miller. New York: The Modern Language Association, pp. 22–27. Having taught *NS* over three decades, Butler finds that its power grips all kinds of students. Without sacrificing the validity of this impact of the work, Butler tries to explore its artistic complexities with his students, especially those related to structure and imagery.

5983. _____. "Tone in *Native Son*," in *Critical Essays on Richard Wright's Native Son*. Ed. Keneth Kinnamon. New York: G.K. Hall, pp. 126–137.

5984. Callahan, John F. "Lynching," in *The Oxford Companion to African American Literature*. Eds.

William L. Andrews, Frances Smith Foster, and Trudier Harris. New York: Oxford University Press, pp. 465–467. Discusses "Big Boy Leaves Home" (p. 466).

5985. Calloway, Catherine. "Fiction: The 1930s to the 1960s," in *American Literary Scholarship: An Annual 1995.* Ed. Gary Scharnhorst. Durham, NC: Duke University Press, pp. 303–329. Comments on work treating W by Laura Hapke, Yoshinobu Hakutani, Jack B. Moore, Eugene E. Miller, Michel Fabre, James R. Giles, Kimberly Drake, John Lowe, and H. Nigel Thomas (pp. 303, 305, 307, 308).

5986. Callahan, John F. *In the African-American Grain: Call-and-Response in Twentieth-Century Black Fiction.* Urbana: University of Illinois Press, pp. 113, 165, 187, 256, 264.

5987. Campbell, Clarice T. *Civil Rights Chronicle: Letters from the South.* Jackson: University Press of Mississippi, p. 38. Mentions briefly *BB.*

5988. Caruth, Gorton. *The Encyclopedia of American Facts and Dates.* Tenth Edition. New York: Harper Collins, pp. 500, Notes the publication of *UTC* (p. 500), *NS* (p. 506), *BB* (p. 528), *O* (p. 558), and records W's death (p. 592).

5989. Carroll, Pamela Sissi. "Today's Teens, Their Problems, and Their Literature: Revisiting G. Robert Carlsen's *Books and the Teenage Reader* Thirty Years Later." *English Journal,* 86 (March), 25–34. Mentions briefly *RP* (pp. 31,34).

5990. Cassuto, Leonard. "The Covert Psychoanalysis of *Native Son,*" in *Approaches to Teaching Wright's Native Son.* Ed. James A. Miller. New York: The Modern Language Association of America, pp. 89–94. Argues that since "Bigger Thomas is pure desire, desire practically unmediated by reason," he "cries out for psychoanalysis" (pp. 90, 91). Without referring to Freud, Cassuto leads his students to consider Bigger's unconscious. In this way he merges the psychological and the social aspects of the novel.

5991. _____. *The Inhuman Race: The Racial Grotesque in American Literature.* New York: Columbia University Press, p. 29. Quotes from the last sentence of "How 'Bigger' Was Born."

5992. Cawelti, John G. "Leon Forrest: The Labyrinth of Luminos-

ity: An Introduction," in his *Leon Forrest: Introductions and Interpretations.* Bowling Green, OH: Bowling Green State University Popular Press, pp. 1–74. The first epigraph is a quotation from W's introduction to *Black Metropolis.* Also mentions briefly *NS* and Bigger Thomas (p. 2).

5993. _____. "Leon Forrest: The Labrinth of Luminosity: An Introduction," in his *Leon Forrest: Introductions and Interpretations.* Bowling Green: Bowling Green State University Popular Press, pp. 1–74. Comments on the Chicago neighborhood of Bigger Thomas (p. 2).

5994. _____. "Appendix 2: Leon Forrest at the University of Kentucky," in his *Leon Forrest: Introductions and Interpretations.* Bowling Green, OH: Bowling Green State University Popular Press, pp. 286–313. The editor mentions briefly W and *NS* in a headnote (p. 286). Forrest states that W's characters are not complex, serving mainly as symbols (p. 309).

5995. Challener, Daniel D. *Stories of Resilience in Maxine Hong Kingston, Richard Rodriguez, John Edgar Wideman, and Tobias Wolff.* New York: Garland, pp. 44, 67, 130. Contains brief mentions of *BB.*

5996. Chametzky, Jules. "*Writing From the Left: New Essays on Radical Culture and Politics.* Alan M. Wald." *MELUS,* 22 (Summer), 133–136. Review mentioning W briefly (p. 134).

5997. Chancy, Myriam J.A. "*Criticism and the Color Line: Desegregating American Literary Studies.* Ed. Henry B. Wonham." *American Literature,* 69 (June), 431–432. Review mentioning W briefly.

5998. Chiwengo, Ngwarsungu. "Writing the Self Through Homer: Peter Abrahams' *Tell, Freedom* Mirroring Richard Wright's *Black Boy.*" *Richard Wright Newsletter,* 5 (Spring/Summer), 9, 11. Abstract of a 1997 CLA convention paper. States that Abrahams differs from W's treatment of his people by emphasizing "the humanness and generosity of Africans, but nevertheless his "subjectivity comes into being ... solely in his relationship to Wright's experience and being."

5999. Christian, Barbara T. "Layered Rhythms: Virginia Woolf and Toni Morrison," in *Toni Morrison: Critical and Theoretical Approaches.*

Ed. Nancy J. Peterson. Baltimore: The Johns Hopkins University Press, pp. 19–36.

6000. _____. "Clarence Major," in *The Norton Anthology of African American Literature.* Eds. Henry Louis Gates, Jr., and Nellie Y. McKay. New York: W.W. Norton, pp. 2241–2242. Mentions briefly W as an influence on Major.

6001. _____. "Ernest J. Gaines," in *The Norton Anthology of African American Literature.* Eds. Henry Louis Gates, Jr., and Nelly Y. McKay. New York: W.W. Norton, pp. 2180–2182. Notes that Gaines disavowed W's influence.

6002. _____. "Toni Morrison," in *The Norton Anthology of African American Literature.* Eds. Henry Louis Gates, Jr., and Nellie Y. McKay. New York: W.W. Norton, pp. 2094–2098. Mentions briefly W and *NS,* pp. 2095, 2096.

6003. _____. "Paule Marshall," in *The Norton Anthology of African American Literature.* Eds. Henry Louis Gates, Jr., and Nellie Y. McKay. New York: W.W. Norton, pp. 2050–2052. Mentions W briefly.

6004. Claridge, Henry. "American Literature: The Twentieth Century: Fiction 1940–45," in *The Year's Work in English Studies.* Vol. 75. Oxford: Blackwell, pp. 631–640. Contains a review of Carla Cappetti's *Writing Chicago* mentioning W.

6005. Cochran, Robert. "Ride It Like You're Flyin': The Story of 'The Rock Island Line.'" *Arkansas Historical Quarterly,* 56 (Summer), 201–229. Quotes from and comments on W's article on Leadbelly in the *Daily Worker.*

6006. Cohn, David L. "The Negro Novel: Richard Wright," in *Critical Essays on Richard Wright's Native Son.* Ed. Keneth Kinnamon. New York: G.K. Hall, pp. 45–48.

6007. Collins, Michael. "History," in *The Oxford Companion to African American Literature.* Eds. William L. Andrews, Frances Smith Foster, Trudier Harris. New York: Oxford University Press, pp. 359–363. Notes that W coined the term "Black Power" (p. 361).

6008. Cone, James H. *Black Theology and Black Power.* Maryknoll, NY: Orbis Books, pp. 20–21, 23.

6009. _____. *God of the Oppressed.* Revised edition. Maryknoll, NY: Orbis Books, pp. 3, 172.

6010. Conner, Kimberly Rae. "Spirituals," in *The Oxford Companion to African American Literature*. Eds. William L. Andrews, Frances Smith Foster, and Trudier Harris. New York: Oxford University Press, pp. 693–696. Notes W's interest in the spirituals.

6011. Corbin, Raymond M. *1,999 Facts About Blacks: A Sourcebook of African-American Achievement*. Second edition. Lanham, MD: Madison *Books*, pp. 94, 95, 113, 118, 214.

6012. Cornwell, JoAnne. "African Literature," in *The Oxford Companion to African American Literature*. Eds. William L. Andrews, Frances Smith Foster, and Trudier Harris. New York: Oxford University Press, pp. 5–7. Notes that W "became hugely popular among Negritude writers and activists abroad."

6013. Corse, Sarah M., and Monica D. Griffin. "Cultural Valorization and African American Literary History." *Sociological Forum*, 12 (June), 173–203. Includes comment on and quotations from W's review of *Their Eyes Were Watching God* (pp. 176, 177, 178, 181, 184, 202).

6014. Cose, Ellis. *Color-Blind: Seeing Beyond Race in a Race-Obsessed World*. New York: HarperCollins, pp. 161–162. Quotes from "The Ethics of Living Jim Crow" and provides a brief commentary.

6015. Cowart, David. "Faulkner and Joyce in Morrison's *Song of Solomon*," in *Toni Morrison's Fiction: Contemporary Criticism*. Ed. David L. Middleton. New York: Garland, pp. 95–108.

6016. Cowley, Malcolm. "The Case of Bigger Thomas," in *Critical Essays on Richard Wright's Native Son*. Ed. Keneth Kinnamon. New York: G.K. Hall, pp. 37–39.

6017. Crane, Gregg D. "The Path of Law and Literature." *American Literary History*, 9 (Winter), 758–775. Mentions briefly *NS* (p. 760).

6018. Crouch, Stanley. "Beyond American Tribalism: Leon Forrest's *Divine Days*," in *Leon Forrest: Introductions and Interpretations*. Ed. John G. Cawelti. Bowling Green, OH: Bowling Green State University Popular Press, pp. 263–268.

6019. ____. "Beyond American Tribalism: Leon Forrest's *Divine Days*," in *Leon Forrest: Introductions and Interpretations*. Ed. John G. Cawelti. Bowling Green: Bowling Green State University Poplar Press,

pp. 263–268. Claims that *Invisible Man* "was built upon Richard Wright's *AH* and *BB*" (p. 266).

6020. Crunden, Robert M. "*A Companion to American Thought*. Ed. by Richard Wightman and James T. Kloppenberg." *The Journal of American History*, 83 (March), 1364–1365. Mentions W briefly.

6021. Curnutt, Kirk, "Richard Wright: Free Indirect Discourse, Dialect, and Empathy in 'Almos' a Man," in his *Wise Economics: Brevity and Storytelling in American Short Stories*. Moscow: University of Idaho Press, pp. 187–202. Uses analysis of discourse and style to argue that W is sympathetic, not ironic in presenting the effort of Dave Saunders to achieve manhood.

6022. Current-Garcia, Eugene, and Bert Hitchcock. "Richard Wright, 1908–1960," in their *American Short Stories*. Sixth edition. New York: Longman, pp. 421–422.

6023. ____. "Suggestions for Discussion and Writing," in their *American Short Stories*. Sixth edition. New York: Longman, p. 553. The last discussion question mentions W, whose "Big Black Good Men" is included on pp. 422–431.

6024. Dace, Tish. "Checklist of Additional Reviews," in her *Langston Hughes: The Contemporary Reviews*. Cambridge: Cambridge University Press, pp. 1–46. Lists W's "As Richard Wright Sees Autobiographies of Langston Hughes and W.E.B. DuBois."

6025. ____. "Introduction," in her *Langston Hughes: The Contemporary Reviews*. Cambridge: Cambridge University Press, pp. 1–46. Notes that some reviewers preferred *The Big Sea* to *NS* (p. 14).

6026. Davis, Jane. *South Africa: A Botched Civilization?: Racial Conflict and Identity in Selected South African Novels*. Lanham, MD: University Press of America, pp. 50–51, 64, 108–109, 128–132, 134–140. Quotes *AH* in relation to Alex La Guma's *Time of the Butcherbird* and compares Athol Fugard's *Tsotsi* to *NS*, emphasizing characterization, protest, existentialism, and the role of women.

6027. Davis, Rose Parkman. *Zora Neale Hurston: An Annotated Bibliography and Reference Guide*. Westport, CT: Greenwood Press, pp. 3, 9, 12, 16, 27–28, 36, 48, 65–66, 98, 106, 107, 111. Lists a review by W and a reprinting of it as well as items

on Hurston involving W, including dissertations, a master's thesis, essays and book chapters, and periodical articles.

6028. Davis, Thadious M. "Erasing the 'We of Me' and Rewriting the Racial Script: Carson McCullers Two *Member[s] of the Wedding*," in *Critical Essays on Carson McCullers*. Eds. Beverly Lyon Clark and Melvin J. Friedman. New York: G.K. Hall, pp. 206–219. Quotes W praising McCullers (p. 218).

6029. de Jongh, James. "Places," in *The Oxford Companion to African American Literature*. Eds. William L. Andrews, Frances Smith Foster, and Trudier Harris. New York: Oxford University Press, pp. 575–579.

6030. Delbanco, Andrew. "An American Hunger," in *Critical Essays on Richard Wright's Native Son*. Ed. Keneth Kinnamon. New York: G.K. Hall, pp. 138–146.

6031. ____. *Required Reading: Why Our American Classics Matter Now*. New York: Farrar, Straus, and Giroux, pp. 173–187.

6032. Demiturk, Lale. "Mastering the Master's Tongue: Bigger as Oppressor in Richard Wright's *Native Son*. "*The Mississippi Quarterly*, 50 (Spring), 267–276. Argues that Bigger changes from victim of racist "Image-formation of the Other" to a manipulator of racist images, thus controlling his own self-image "in an attempt to alleviate his marginal role in the oppressive definitional framework."

6033. De Santis, Christopher C. "Badman," in *The Oxford Companion to African American Literature*. Eds. William L. Andrews, Frances Smith Foster, and Trudier Harris. New York: Oxford University Press, p. 42. Cites Bigger Thomas as an example of "Badman."

6034. Denissova, Tamara. "Richard Wright: The Problem of Self-Identification." *The Mississippi Quarterly*, 50 (Spring), 239–253. Discusses *BB, AH,* and *O* in relation to W's effort to establish a personal identity, a task that Russians and Ukrainians are now facing. Includes a prefatory survey of the publication of W's works in Russian translation and Russian responses.

6035. Diedrich, Maria. "Afroamerikanische Literatur," in *Amerikanische Literaturgeschichte*. Ed. Hubert Zapf. Stuttgart: Verlag J.B. Metzler, pp. 402–426. Contains three paragraphs on W (p. 417) discussing *LT, UTC, NS*, and, more briefly, *BB* and *O*. Notes W's early Marxism, his subsequent existentialism, and his extensive influence on African American literature. W is mentioned briefly elsewhere in the chapter.

6036. Dodge, Georgina. "Recovering Acts in American Im/migrant Autobiography." Dissertation *Abstracts International—* A, 57/07 (January), p. 3017. Treats the "autobiographical strategies" of W and three others.

6037. Donaldson, Susan V. "Gender, Race, and Allen Tate's Profession of Letters in the South," in her and Anne Goodwyn Jones's *Haunted Bodies: Gender and Southern Texts*. Charlottesville: University Press of Virginia, pp. 492–518. Mentions W briefly (p. 508).

6038. _____, and Anne Goodwyn Jones. "Haunted Bodies: Rethinking the South Through Gender," in their *Haunted Bodies: Gender and Southern Texts*. Charlottesville: University Press of Virginia, pp. 1–19. Mentions briefly *BB* (p. 3).

6039. Dorsey, Brian. *Who Stole the Soul?: Blaxploitation Echoed in the Harlem Renaissance*. Ed. James Hogg. Salzburg: Institut für Anglistik und Amerikanistik, pp. 23, 129. Quotes from "Blueprint for Negro Writing" and lists it in the bibliography.

6040. Dorsey, David. "*Of Dreams Deferred, Dead or Alive: African Perspectives on African-American Writers*. Ed. Femi Ojo-Ade." *CLA Journal*, 41 (December), 229–241. Includes comment on an essay on W (especially *BP*) by Chimalum Nwankwo (p. 233) and mentions W elsewhere (p. 239).

6041. Drake, Kimberly. "Rewriting the American Self: Race, Gender, and Identity in the Autobiographies of Frederick Douglass and Harriet Jacobs." *MELUS*, 22 (Winter), 91–108. Mentions W briefly (p. 107).

6042. duCille, Ann. "The Occult of True Black Womanhood: Critical Demeanor and Black Feminist Studies," in *Female Subjects in Black and White: Race Psychoanalysis in Black and White*. Eds. Elizabeth Abel, Barbara Christian, and Helene Moglen. Berkeley: University of California Press, pp. 21–56. Mentions Missy Kubitschek mentioning "Big Boy Leaves Home" and notes

that Houston Baker treats W in *Workings of the Spirit* (pp. 44, 46).

6043. Early, Gerald. "Decoding Ralph Ellison." *Dissent*, 44 (Summer), 114–118. Review of three books by or about Ellison including a substantial comparison of Ellison and W. "Neither writer is more successfully modernist than the other" (p. 117). Both are "staunch individualists ... wary of the harshness of conformity and anti-intellectualism in black life" (p. 117).

6044. _____. "Essay," in *The Oxford Companion to African American Literature*. Eds. William L. Andrews, Frances Smith Foster, and Trudier Harris. New York: Oxford University Press, p. 259. Mentions *WML*.

6045. Ellison, Ralph. "Book Reviews: *Native Son*, by Richard Wright," in *Critical Essays on Richard Wright's Native Son*. Ed. Keneth Kinnamon. New York: G.K. Hall, pp. 43–44.

6046. _____. "The World and the Jug," in *The Norton Anthology of African American Literature*. Eds. Henry Louis Gates, Jr., and Nellie Y. McKay. New York: W.W. Norton, pp. 1549–1571.

6047. Ensslen, Klaus. "Bryan R. Washington, *The Politics of Exile: Ideology in Henry James, F. Scott Fitzgerald and James Baldwin*; John E. Bassett, *Harlem in Review: Critical Reactions to Black American Writers, 1917–1939*." *Amerikastudien*, 42, No. 2, 287–289. Review mentioning briefly *NS* (p. 289).

6048. _____. "Werner Sollors and Maria Diedrich, eds. *The Black Columbiad: Defining Moments in African American Literature and Culture*." *Amerikastudien*, 42, No. 2, 284–287. Review mentioning briefly M. Lynn Weiss's essay on *PS*.

6049. Erickson, Peter. "Paul Gilroy. *The Black Atlantic: Modernity and Double Consciousness*." *African American Review*, 31 (Fall), 506–508. Review praising Gilroy's "remarkably fresh perspective on Wright's career."

6050. Evans, Nicholas. "*Langston Hughes: Critical Perspectives Past and Present*. Edited by Henry Louis Gates, Jr., and K.A. Appiah." *MELUS*, 22 (Spring), 147–149. Mentions W briefly (pp. 147, 148).

6051. Evans, Oliver. "The Case of Carson McCullers," in *Critical Essays on Carson McCullers*. Eds. Bev-

erly Lyon Clark and Melvin J. Friedman. New York: G.K. Hall, pp. 124–128.

6052. Fabre, Michel. "Richard Wright's Critical Reception in France — Censors Right and Left, Negritude Intellectuals, the Literary Set, and the General Public." *The Mississippi Quarterly*, 50 (Spring), 307–325. Comprehensive survey of the French response to W, especially in relation to the political context. Praised by left-wing existentialists, he was denounced by Communists as a renegade. W was well received by French speaking Africans even though he had reservations about Negritude. Fabre includes a previously unpublished obituary of W by Jean Wagner, calling it "a fair summary of the French critical assessment of Richard Wright at the time of his death, by casting him as a powerful and universal winter, a race-conscious black intellectual, and a tragic figure" (p. 323). Although French interest in American literary naturalism has declined in recent years and Ellison and Morrison are more popular now than W, his relevance as a social critic continues as racial and social problems become more apparent in France itself.

6053. _____. "Introduction," in his and Ellen Wright's *A Richard Wright Reader*. New York: DaCapo Press, pp. vii–xxiv.

6054. Fanon, Frantz. "On National Culture," in *Postcolonial Criticism*. Eds. Bart Moore-Gilbert, Gareth Stanton, and Willy Maley. London: Longman, pp. 91–111.

6055. Fast, Robin Riley. "*Brothers and Keepers* and the Tradition of the Slave Narrative." *MELUS*, 22 (Winter), 3–20. Mentions briefly *BB* (p. 15).

6056. Felgar, Robert. "*Native Son* and Its Readers," in *Approaches to Teaching Wright's Native Son*. Ed. James A. Miller. New York: The Modern Language Association of America, pp. 67–74. Instead of lecturing, Felgar combines reader-response and cultural criticism to enliven his class and stimulate discussion. In this way, students become "aware of their racial, gender-based, social, cultural, and allochronic assumptions" (p. 73).

6057. Felton, Sharon, and Michelle C. Loris. "Introduction," in their *The Critical Response to Gloria Naylor*. Westport, CT: Greenwood

Press, pp. 1–11. Mentions W briefly (p. 3).

6058. [Ferraro, Thomas J.]. "Brief Mention." *American Literature*, 69 (September), 647–658. Includes a notice of *Critical Essays on Carson McCullers* mentioning W briefly (p. 654).

6059. Fishkin, Shelley Fisher. *Lighting Out for the Territory: Reflections on Mark Twain and American Culture*. New York: Oxford University Press, pp. 90, 111, 191. Mentions W briefly.

6060. Fishburn, Katherine. *The Problem of Embodiment in Early African American Narrative*. Westport, CT: Greenwood Press, p. 26. Mentions briefly W and existentialism.

6061. Foley, Barbara. "The Rhetoric of Anticommunism in Invisible Man." *College English*, 59 (September), 530–547. Mentions W's unfavorable portrayal of Communism in *AH* (p. 536) and "I Tried to Be a Communist" (p. 538) and quotes from Ellison's letters to W in the Beineke collection (p. 541).

6062. Fontenot, Chester J., Jr. "Churches," in *The Oxford Companion to African American Literature*. Eds. William L. Andrews, Frances Smith Foster, and Trudier Harris. New York: Oxford University Press, pp. 143–147. Comments on W's "radical critique of Christianity," especially in *NS* (pp. 145–146).

6063. Ford, Karen J. "These Old Writing Paper Blues: The Blues Stanza and Literary Poetry." *College Literature*, 24 (October), 84–103. Quotes W on the blues (p. 95).

6064. Ford, Nick Aaron. "A Blueprint for Negro Authors," in *Call and Response: The Riverside Anthology of the African American Literary Tradition*. Eds. Patricia Liggins Hill, Bernard W. Bell, Trudier Harris, William J. Harris, R. Baxter Miller, and Sondra A. O'Neale. Boston: Houghton Mifflin, pp.

6065. Forman, James. *The Making of Black Revolutionaries*. Illustrated edition. Seattle: University of Washington Press, pp. 4, 35, 75.

6066. Forrest, Leon. "Appendix 2: Leon Forrest at the University of Kentucky: Two Interviews," in *Leon Forrest: Introductions and Interpretations*. Ed. John G. Cawelti. Bowling Green, OH: Bowling Green State University Popular Press, pp. 286–

313. To students in a course on Faulkner and African-American literature (including *NS*), Forrest comments on W's characterization.

6067. Foster, Frances Smith. "But, Is It Good Enough to Teach?" in *Rethinking American Literature*. Eds. Lil Brannon and Brenda M. Greene. Urbana, IL: National Council of Teachers of English, pp. 193–202. Mentions briefly W and *NS* (pp. 193, 195).

6068. _____. "Canonization," in *The Oxford Companion to African American Literature*. Eds. William L. Andrews, Frances Smith Foster, and Trudier Harris. New York: Oxford University Press, pp. 119–120. Mentions W briefly.

6069. _____. "Diasporic Literature," in *The Oxford Companion to African American Literature*. Eds. William L. Andrews, Frances Scott Foster, and Trudier Harris. New York: Oxford University Press, pp. 218–222. Comments on *BP* (pp. 221).

6070. _____. "Mosley, Walter," in *The Oxford Companion to African American Literature*. Eds. William L. Andrews, Frances Smith Foster, and Trudier Harris. New York: Oxford University Press, pp. 510–511. Mentions W briefly.

6071. _____. "Leon Forrest at the University of Kentucky: Two Interviews," in *Leon Forrest: Introductions and Interpretations*. Ed. John G. Cawelti. Bowling Green: Bowling Green State University Poplar Press, pp. 286–313. Forrest criticizes W's characterization.

6072. Foster, Frances Smith, and Claudia May. "Class," in *The Oxford Companion to African American Literature*. Eds. William L. Andrews, Frances Smith Foster, and Trudier Harris. New York: Oxford University Press, pp. 153–156. Contains a paragraph on *NS* and mentions briefly *UTC* and "I Tried to Be a Communist."

6073. Fraden, Rena, "Paul Sporn. *Against Itself: The Federal Theater and Writers' Projects in the Midwest*." *American Historical Review*, 102 (April), 557–558. Review mentioning W briefly.

6074. Franklin, H. Bruce. "*Sentenced to Death: The American Novel and Capital Punishment*. By David Guest." *American Literature*, 69 (December), 865–866. Review commenting briefly on the work's treatment of *NS*.

6075. Franko, Mark. "Nation, Class, and Ethnicities in Modern Dance of the 1930s." *Theatre Journal*, 49 (December), 475–491. Mentions briefly *BB-AH*, p. 490.

6076. Friedman, Melvin. "*The Mortgage of Heart: The Workshop of Carson McCullers*," in *Critical Essays on Carson McCullers*. Eds. Beverly Lyon Clark and Melvin J. Friedman. New York: G.K. Hall, pp. 67–77.

6077. Gammage, Jeff. "Baltimore's Great Blacks in Wax Museum Aims to Make Impression." *Houston Chronicle* (25 May), 8. A statue of W is included.

6078. Gates, Henry Louis, Jr. "Going Back." *The New Republic*, 216 (16 June), 19–22. Mentions W briefly (p. 20).

6079. _____. "Harlem on Our Minds." *Critical Inquiry*, 24 (Autumn), 1–12. Quotes Cornel West mentioning W (p. 5); quotes from *WML* (p. 8); mentions Bigger, Bessie, and *NS* (pp. 9, 11, 12); and contrasts W's naturalism to the "lyrical modernism" of Hurston, Toomer, and Ellison.

6080. Gates, Henry, Louis Jr. and Nellie Y. McKay. "Preface: Talking Books," in their *The Norton Anthology of African American Literature*. New York: W.W. Norton, pp. xxvii–xliv. Comments on and quotes from "Blueprint for Negro Writing" (p. xxxiv). Also mentions briefly *The Man Who Lived Underground* (p. xxxix).

6081. _____. "The Vernacular Traditions," in their *The Norton Anthology of African American Literature*. New York: W.W. Norton, pp. 1–125. Mentions briefly *LT* (p. 117).

6082. _____. "African American Literature in Context," in their *The Norton Anthology of African American Literature*, pp. 2612-2623. Chronology including *UTC, NS* and *BB*.

6083. _____. "Selected Bibliographies," in their *The Norton Anthology of African American Literature*. New York: W.W. Norton, pp. 2625-2648. The entry for W includes most of his books as well as work on him by Michel Fabre, Constance Webb, Margaret Walker, James Baldwin, Irving Howe, Ralph Ellison, Robert Stepto, Sherley Ann Williams, Houston Baker, Joyce Ann Joyce, Keneth Kinnamon, Yoshinobu Hakutami and Harold Bloom.

6084. Gayle, Addison, "The Black

Aesthetic," in *The Norton Anthology of African American Literature*. Eds. Henry Louis Gates, Jr., and Nellie Y. McKay. New York: W.W. Norton, pp. 1870–1877.

6085/6. Gelfand, Marvin. "Taking a Leap: A Talk with Albert Murray," in *Conversations with Albert Murray*. Ed. Roberta S. Maguire. Jackson: University Press of Mississippi, pp. 8–11.

6087. George, Stephen K. "The Horror of Bigger Thomas: The Perception of Form Without Face in Richard Wright's *Native Son*." *African American Review*, 31 (Fall), 497–504. Applies the ethical philosophy of Emmanuel Levinas to *NS*. Eliciting both sympathy for his oppression and horror at his reactive violence, W shows that Bigger initially responds to "the face of the other" with the requisite respect for human dignity that is the basis of ethical behavior. When Jan recognizes Bigger's human face in Book Three, Bigger begins to reciprocate and so to begin his moral evolution, finally becoming "someone who ultimately sees others as human beings like himself" (p. 503).

6088. Gibboney, Roberta K. "Philanthropy in *Invisible Man*." *MELUS*, 22 (Fall), 183–194. Mentions briefly Mr. Dalton in *NS*.

6089. Gibson, Donald B. "*Black Boy*," in *The Oxford Companion to African American Literature*. New York: Oxford University Press, pp. 74–75. Entry on *BB* stressing its relation to the tradition of black autobiography of presenting the particulars of one life as exemplifying the general racial plight. Also notes that white racism affects black family relations, especially the way mother treats son.

6090. _____. "*Native Son*," in *The Oxford Companion to African American Literature*. Eds. William L. Andrews, Frances Smith Foster, and Trudier Harris. New York: Oxford University Press, p. 527. Plot summary of the novel.

6091. _____. "*Uncle Tom's Children*," in *The Oxford Companion to African American Literature*. Eds. William L. Andrews, Frances Smith Foster, and Trudier Harris. New York: Oxford University Press, pp. 741–742. Entry describing the 1938 and 1940 editions and providing a precis of each of the three stories.

6092. _____. "Wright, Richard," in *The Oxford Companion to African American Literature*. Eds. William L. Andrews, Frances Smith Foster, and Trudier Harris. New York: Oxford University Press, pp. 793–795. Critical-biographical entry mentioning all his works except *Rite of Passage*. Comments on his youth in Mississippi, his relation to the Communist Party, and his expatriation. W "changed the landscape of possibility for African American writers" (p. 793). Includes a bibliographical note listing eleven books on W.

6093. _____. "Wright's Invisible Native Son," in *Critical Essays on Richard Wright's Native Son*. Ed. Keneth Kinnamon. New York: G.K. Hall, pp. 75–85.

6094. Gloster, Hugh M. "Race and the Negro Writer," in *Call and Response: The Riverside Anthology of the African American Literary Tradition*. Eds. Patricia Liggins Hill, Bernard W. Bell, Trudier Harris, William J. Harris, R. Baxter Miller, and Sondra A. O'Neale. Boston: Houghton Mifflin, pp. 1109–1111.

6095. _____. "The Negro Writer and the Southern Scene," in *Defining Southern Literature: Perspectives and Assessments, 1831–1952*. Madison-Teaneck, New Jersey, pp. 430–433.

6096. Goddu, Teresa A. *Gothic America: Narrative, History, and Nation*. New York: Columbia University Press, pp. 1–3, 12, 131–132, 153, 184, 217. The point of departure of this study is the account in *BB* of reading the "thrilling horror stories" in the magazine supplement of a racist newspaper. Comments also on W's connection in "How 'Bigger' Was Born of the gothic mode and black experience.

6097. Gold, Mike. "Change the World: Dick Wright Gives America a Significant Picture in 'Native Son,'" in *Critical Essays on Richard Wright's Native Son*. Ed. Keneth Kinnamon. New York: G.K. Hall, pp. 40–42.

6098. Goldfield, David. "A Sense of Place: Jews, Blacks, and White Gentiles in the American South." *Southern Cultures*, 3, no. 1, 58–79. Quotes W on black anti-Semitism (p. 73).

6099. Gordon, Lewis R. "Existential Dynamics of Theorizing Black Invisibility," in his *Existence in Black: An Anthology of Existential*

Philosophy. New York: Routledge, pp. 69–79. Mentions W briefly (p. 78).

6100. _____. "Introduction: Black Existential Philosophy," in his *Existence in Black: An Anthology of Black Existential Philosophy*. New York: Routledge, pp. 1–9. Contains brief mentions of W (pp. 7, 8, 9).

6101. _____. *Her Majesty's Other Children: Sketches of Racism from a Neocolonial Age*. Lanham, Maryland: Rowman & Littlefield, pp. 94, 152, 170, 183–184. Mentions W briefly.

6102. _____. "Introduction: Black Existential Philosophy," in his *Existence in Black: An Anthology of Existential Philosophy*. New York: Routledge, pp. 1–9. Mentions W briefly.

6103. Graham, Maryemma. "Biographical Note," in her *On Being Female, Black, and Free: Essays by Margaret Walker*. Knoxville: The University of Tennessee Press, pp. xxi–xxiii. Mentions Walker's friendship with W and her book on him.

6104. _____. "Introduction," in her *On Being Female, Black, and Free: Essays by Margaret Walker, 1932–1992*. Knoxville: The University of Tennessee Press, pp. xxi–xxii. Mentions the W-Walker friendship.

6105. _____. "Introduction," in her *On Being Female, Black, and Free: Essays by Margaret Walker*. Knoxville: The University of Tennessee Press, pp. xi–xii. Mentions W briefly (pp. xi, xii).

6106. _____. "Novel," in *The Oxford Companion to African American Literature*. Eds. William L. Andrews, Frances Smith Foster, and Trudier Harris. New York: Oxford University Press, pp. 541–548. Discusses W's place in the development of the African American novel and mentions his followers in protest fiction (p. 543).

6107. Graham, Maryemma, and Jerry W. Ward, Jr. "From the Editors." *Richard Wright Newsletter*, 5 (Spring/Summer), 2–3. Proposes various possibilities for celebrating the centenary of W's birth in 2008, mentions new works including or treating W, and requests letters endorsing a U.S. postage stamp honoring W.

6108. _____. "RWC Sponsored Session: Richard Wright: Teaching His Work." *Richard Wright Newslet-*

ter*, 5 (Spring/Summer), 10. Announced a session at the American Literature Session chaired by Yoshinobu Hakutani with panel members Linda Wagner-Martin, Robert Butler, Trudier Harris, and Donald B. Gibson.

6109. Grant, Nathan. "Innocence and Ambiguity in the Films of Charles Burnett," in *Representing Blackness: Issues in Film and Video*. Ed. Valerie Smith. New Brunswick, NJ: Rutgers University Press, pp. 135–155. Mentions briefly *NS* (p. 154).

6110. Grewal, Gurleen. "'Laundering the Head of Whitewash': Mimicry and Resistance in *The Bluest Eye*," in *Approaches to Teaching the Novels of Toni Morrison*. Eds. Nellie Y. McKay and Kathryn Earle. New York: The Modern Language Association of America, pp. 118–126. Comments briefly on W's misogyny (p. 120).

6111. Griffin, Farah Jasmine. "On Women, Teaching, and *Native Son*," in *Approaches to Teaching Wright's Native Son*. Ed. James A. Miller. New York: The Modern Language Association of America, pp. 75–80. Although Farah Griffin's white students view Bigger as a social victim of racism, her black female students react strongly to Bigger's treatment of women. But "if there is no escaping his sexism, there is also no escaping the value Wright has rendered in the creation of Bigger and Bigger's fictional landscape" (p. 80).

6112. _____. "West, Dorothy," in *The Oxford Companion to African American Literature*. Eds. William L. Andrews, Frances Smith Foster, and Trudier Harris. New York: Oxford University Press, pp. 766–767. Comments on W's role in *New Challenge*.

6113. Grimes-Williams, Johanna L. "Character Types," in *The Oxford Companion to African American Literature*. Eds. William L. Andrews, Frances Smith Foster, and Trudier Harris. New York: Oxford University Press, pp. 127–130. Classifies Bigger Thomas as "the brute for whom the violent response seems to be the only form of communication" (p. 129).

6114. Gruesser, John C. "Travel Writing," in *The Oxford Companion to African American Literature*. Eds. William L. Andrews, Frances Smith Foster, and Trudier Harris. New York: Oxford University Press, pp.

735–736. Calls W "the single most important African American literary traveler" and comments on *BP*, *CC*, and *PS*.

6115. Gubar, Susan. *Racechanges: White Skin, Black Face in American Culture*. New York: Oxford University Press, pp. 31, 260. Quotes W's "The Negro is America's metaphor" and mentions W's treatment of Pushkin and Dumas in *WML*.

6116. Guerrero, Ed. "Tracking 'The Look' in the Novels of Toni Morrison," in *Toni Morrison's Fiction: Contemporary Criticism*. Ed. David L. Middleton. New York: Garland, pp. 27–41.

6117. Guest, David. *Sentenced to Death: The American Novel and Capital Punishment*. Jackson: University Press of Mississippi, pp. 75–103, 104, 169. Includes a substantial treatment of *NS*, comparing it to *An American Tragedy* and emphasizing its "rhetorical determinism" even more than its environmental determinism. Explains the influence of the Leopold and Loeb case and the Scottsboro Boys on W's novel.

6118. Gwynn, R.S. "Richard Wright 1908–1960," in his *Fiction: A Longman Pocket Anthology*, Second Edition, p. 124. Headnote to "The Man Who Was Almost a Man" providing a brief biography mentioning *NS* and *BB*.

6119. Hagen, Lyman B. *Heart of a Woman, Mind of a Writer, and Soul of a Poet: A Critical Analysis of the Writings of Maya Angelou*. Lanham, MD: University Press of America, pp. 5, 9. Mentions briefly *BB* and W.

6120. Hakutani, Yoshinobu. "Native Son, Pudd'nhead Wilson, and Racial Discourse," in *Critical Essays on Richard Wright's Native Son*. Ed. Keneth Kinnamon. New York: Twayne, pp. 183–195.

6121. Hall, James C. "Brown, Frank London," in *The Oxford Companion to African American Literature*. Eds. William L. Andrews, Frances Smith Foster, and Trudier Harris. New York: Oxford University Press, pp. 101–102. Notes W's influence on Brown.

6122. _____. "Teaching Interculturalism: Symbiosis, Interpretation, and *Native Son*," in *Approaches to Teaching Native Son*. Ed. James A. Miller. New York: The Modern Language Association of America,

pp. 81–88. Advocates "interculturalism as an aesthetic and an ethic, a hermeneutic that demands of students recognition of the ways that Wright's text implicates all readers" (p. 81). Hall draws on theories of Kisho Kurokawa and Henry Giroux in emphasizing the importance of cultural criticism, "border crossings," and cultural geography.

6123. Hamalian, Linda. "*Richard Wright and Racial Discourse*. By Yoshinobu Hakutani." *American Literature*, 69 (September), 638–639. Mixed review praising Hakutani's treatment of specific works but asking for "a clearer definition … of racial discourse."

6124. Hamilton, Sharon. "Wright's *Native Son*." *The Explicator*, 55 (Summer), 227–229. Discusses W's use of Poe, especially "The Black Cat," in *NS*. She is professedly unaware of previous scholarly work on Poe and W.

6125. Hammond, Thomas N. "Paris–New York: Venues of migration and the Exportation of African-American Culture." *CLA Journal*, 41 (December), 135–146. Includes discussion of W in Paris, where his "passion and social consciousness were heightened by the more politicized environment in France" (p. 143).

6126. Hannon, Charles. "Teaching the Conflicts as a Temporary Instructor." *College Literature*, 24 (June), 126–141. Includes a discussion of "The Man Who Was Almost a Man" comparing Dave's economic bondage to the lot of temporary college teachers. Hannon's students emphasize free agency; Hannon stresses exploitative determinism.

6127. Harding, Desmond. "The Power of Place: Richard Wright's *Native Son*." *CLA Journal*, 40 (March), 367–379. Examines the effect on *NS* of architectural determinism, a sense of "conscious history" (Houston Baker's term), and psychosexual violence against both Gus and Bessie.

6128. Hardy, Lyda Mary. "Who's New in Multicultural Literature Part One." *English Journal*, 86 (November), 104–106. Mentions W briefly.

6129. Harris, Paul. *Black Rage Confronts the Law*. New York: New York University Press, pp. 3–4, 183, 273. Discusses and quotes from *NS* (pp. 3–4, 183), and quotes from *TMBV* (p. 273).

6130. Harris, Trudier. "Baldwin, James," in *The Oxford Companion to African American Literature*. Eds. William L. Andrews, Frances Smith Foster, and Trudier Harris. New York: Oxford University Press, pp. 44–46. Mentions Baldwin's acquaintance with W.

6131. _____. "Folk Literature," in *The Oxford Companion to African American Literature*. Eds. William L. Andrews, Frances Smith Foster, and Trudier Harris. New York: Oxford University Press, pp. 282–286. Notes W's use of folklore in *UTC* and *NS* (p. 284).

6132. _____. "Speech and Dialect," in *The Oxford Companion to African American Literature*. Eds. William L. Andrews, Frances Smith Foster, and Trudier Harris. New York: Oxford University Press, pp. 687–691. Comments on W's use of dialect (p. 689).

6133. Harris, William J. "Black Aesthetic," in *The Oxford Companion to African American Literature*. Eds. William L. Andrews, Frances Smith Foster, and Trudier Harris. New York: Oxford University Press, pp. 67–70. Contains a paragraph on "Blueprint for Negro Writing" stressing W's fusion of Marxism and the black folk tradition.

6134. _____. "Call for Social Revolution and Political Strategies," in *Call and Response: The Riverside Anthology of the African American Literary Tradition*. Eds. Patricia Liggins Hill, Bernard W. Bell, Trudier Harris, William J. Harris, R. Baxter Miller, and Sondra A. O'Neale. Boston: Houghton Mifflin, pp. 1345–1354. Mentions Stokely Carmichael's use of W's term "Black Power" (p. 1347).

6135. _____. "Critical Theory and Debate: The Black Aesthetic or Black Poststructuralism?" in *Call and Response: The Riverside Anthology of the African American Literary Tradition*. Boston: Houghton Mifflin, 1977, pp. 1365–1370. Mentions W briefly (p. 1366).

6136. _____. "Charles Johnson (1948–)," in *Call and Response: The Riverside Anthology of the African American Literary Tradition*. Eds. Patricia Liggins Hill, Bernard W. Bell, Trudier Harris, William J. Harris, R. Baxter Miller, and Sondra A. O'Neale. Boston: Houghton Mifflin, pp. 1927–1931. Mentions W briefly (p. 1928).

6137. _____. "Joyce Ann Joyce (1949–)," in *Call and Response: The Riverside Anthology of the African American Literary Tradition*. Eds. Patricia Liggins Hill, Bernard W. Bell, Trudier Harris, William J. Harris, R. Baxter Miller, and Sondra A. O'Neale. Boston: Houghton Mifflin, pp. 1458–1459. Comments on Joyce's book on W.

6138. _____. "Melvin Dixon (1950–1992)," in *Call and Response: The Riverside Anthology of the African American Literary Tradition*. Eds. Patricia Liggins Hill, Bernard W. Bell, Trudier Harris, William J. Harris, R. Baxter Miller, and Sondra A. O'Neale. Boston: Houghton Mifflin, pp. 1943–1944. Mentions Dixon's research on W in Paris.

6139. _____. "Toni Morrison (Chloe Anthony Wofford) (1931–)," in *Call and Response: The Riverside Anthology of the African American Literary Tradition*. Eds. Patricia Liggins Hill, Bernard W. Bell, Trudier Harris, William J. Harris, R. Baxter Miller, and Sondra A. O'Neale. Boston: Houghton Mifflin, pp. 1694–1699. Refers briefly to the Richard Wright Circle (p. 1698).

6140. Hayes, Floyd W., III. "The Concept of Double Vision in Richard Wright's *The Outsider*: Fragmented Blackness in the Age of Nihilism," in *Existence in Black: An Anthology of Existential Philosophy*. Ed. Lewis R. Gordon. New York: Routledge, pp. 173–183. As an existential nihilist, W presents Cross Damon as representative of "black subjective alienation in a society experiencing change and challenge" (p. 173). Du Boisian double consciousness becomes the "double vision" of Cross Damon (and W) as outsider moving beyond modernism toward the postmodern.

6141. Henderson, Gloria Mason, Bill Day, and Sandra Stevenson Miller. "Richard Wright (1908–1960), in their *Literature and Ourselves: A Thematic Introduction for Readers and Writers*. Second edition. New York: Longman, p. 774. Brief headnote to "The Man Who Was Almost a Man."

6142. Herman, David. "Scripts, Sequences, and Stories: Elements of a Postclassical Narratology." *PMLA*, 112 (October), 1046–1047. Quotes and comments on a passage from the scene in Mary's bedroom in *NS* (p. 1047).

6143. Hill, Ernest. *Satisfied with Nothin'*. New York: Scribner Paperback Fiction, front cover. Quotes Joan Mellen in The *Baltimore Sun* stating that "Hill has created a long-awaited incarnation of Richard Wright's Bigger Thomas."

6144. Hill, Patricia Liggins, Bernard W. Bell, Trudier Harris, William J. Harris, R. Baxter Miller, and Sondra A. O'Neale. "Preface," in their *Call and Response: The Riverside Anthology of the African American Literary Tradition*. Boston: Houghton Mifflin, pp. xxxiii–xxxviii. Mentions briefly "Long Black Song" (p. xxxv).

6145. Hoberman, John. *Darwin's Athletes: How Sport Has Damaged Black America and Preserved the Myth of Race*. Boston: Houghton Mifflin, pp. 21, 82, 215. Mentions briefly *BB* and *NS*. Quotes Gerald Early quoting W.

6146. Holloway, Karla F.C. "Cultural Narratives Passed On: African American Mourning Stories." *College English*, 59 (January), 32–40. Comments on *NS* and *LD* in the contexts of the Emmett Till lynching and the gang murder of eleven-year old Robert Sandifer in Chicago. All represent mourning as cultural narrative.

6147. _____. "Gender," in *The Oxford Companion to African American Literature*. Eds. William L. Andrews, Frances Smith Foster, and Trudier Harris. New York: Oxford University Press, pp. 312–315. Mentions W briefly (pp. 313, 315).

6148. Hongo, Garrett. "Gardens We Have Left." *Profession 1997*, pp. 18–23. Mentions W briefly (p. 21).

6149. Horne, Gerald. *Fire This Time: The Watts Uprising and the 1960s*. New York: Da Capo Press, p. 21.

6150. Hornsby, Alton, Jr. *Chronology of African American History from 1492 to the Present*. Detroit: Gale, pp. 145–146.

6151. Hubbard, Dolan. "Sermons and Preaching," in *The Oxford Companion to African American Literature*. Eds. William L. Andrews, Frances Smith Foster, and Trudier Harris. New York: Oxford University Press, pp. 648–652. Notes W's subversion of the traditional black sermon in *NS* "by placing it in the mouth of attorney Boris Max" (p. 651).

6152. _____. "Introduction: Can I Get a Witness?" in his *Recovered Writers/Recovered Texts: Race, Class, and Gender in Black Women's Literature.* Knoxville: The University of Tennessee Press, pp. xi–xxiii. Mentions briefly *NS* (p. xv) and W (p. xix).

6153. Hunter, T.K. "Explorations in the City of Light: African-American Artists in Paris, 1945–1965 at the Studio Museum of Harlem." *Race and Reason*, 3, pp. 70–71. Mentions briefly W's expatriation.

6154. Ickstadt, Heinz. "Die Amerikanische Moderne," in *Amerikanische Literaturgeschichte.* Ed. Herbert Zapf. Stuttgart: Verlag J. Metzler, pp. 218–281. Mentions W briefly in relation to Gertrude Stein (p. 226), and James Agee (p. 276). Also contains brief mentions of *LT* (pp. 229, 233) and *NS* (p. 277).

6155. Irr, Caren. "The Politics of Spatial Phobias in *Native Son*," in *Critical Essays on Richard Wright's Native Son.* Ed. Keneth Kinnamon. New York: G.K. Hall, pp. 196–212. Argues that *NS*, far from being a simple proletarian novel, is a "revisionist critique" of that form, effected by emphasis on Bigger's spatial phobias. Constricted and confined by urban capitalism, he cannot reach a stage of revolutionary awareness without evolving from a feudal past.

6156. Jablon, Madelyn. *Black Metafiction: Self-Consciousness in African American Literature.* Iowa City: University of Iowa Press, pp. 17–18, 82, 86–97, 184–186. Discusses Larry Neal on W and Ellison (pp. 17–18), mentions briefly *NS* (p. 82), and argues for W's influence on Ernest Gaines despite the latter's disavowal.

6157. Jack, Peter Monro. "*Native Son,*" in *The Literary Almanac.* Kansas City: Andrews McMeel, p. 76. Quotes from Jack's review of the novel and includes a photograph of the second edition of the novel.

6158. Jackson, Agnes Moreland. "Religion," in *The Oxford Companion to African American Literature.* Eds. William L. Andrews, Frances Smith Foster, and Trudier Harris. New York: Oxford University Press, pp. 626–631. Discusses W's use of religion and religious music in *UTC* and *NS* (pp. 629–630).

6159. Jackson, Kennell. *America Is Me: 170 Fresh Questions and Answers on Black American History.*

New York: HarperPerennial, pp. 280–282, 292.

6160. James, Charles L. "*Black Thunder,*" in *The Oxford Companion to African American Literature.* Eds. William L. Andrews, Frances Smith Foster, and Trudier Harris. New York: Oxford University Press, pp. 82–83. Notes W's favorable review of the Bontemps novel.

6161. Janken, Kenneth R. "Expatriatism," in *The Oxford Companion to African American Literature.* Eds. William L. Andrews, Frances Smith Foster, and Trudier Harris. New York: Oxford University Press, pp. 262–264.

6162. Jarrett, Robert L. *Cormac McCarthy.* New York: Twayne, p. 35. Mentions briefly W and the "underground man."

6163. Jay, Gregory. "Jewish Writers in a Multicultural Literature Class." *The Heath Anthology of American Literature Newsletter.* No. 16 (Fall), pp. 8–9, 11. Mentions W briefly (p. 9).

6164. Jay, Gregory S. *American Literature and the Culture Wars.* Ithaca: Cornell University Press, pp. 92, 149. Mentions W briefly.

6165. _____. "Not Born on the Fourth of July: Cultural Differences and American Studies," in *Rethinking American Literature.* Eds. Lil Brannon and Brenda M. Greene. Urbana, IL: National Council of Teachers of English, pp. 3–31. Mentions W briefly (p. 24).

6166. Johgart, Steve, Leigh Magnuson, and David Panian, eds. *Comprehensive Dissertation Index 1996 Supplement, Volume 4.* Ann Arbor: UMI, p. 662. Lists dissertations treating W by David Nicholls and Philip Auger.

6167. Johnson, Abby Arthur, and Ronald Maberry Johnson. "Scholarly Journals and Literary Magazines," in *The Oxford Companion to African American Literature.* Eds. William L. Andrews, Frances Smith Foster, and Trudier Harris. New York: Oxford University Press, pp. 567–569. Mentions briefly W and "Blueprint for Negro Writing."

6168. Johnson, J.R. [C.L.R. James]. "Native Son and Revolution," in *Critical Essays on Richard Wright's Native Son.* Ed. Keneth Kinnamon. New York: G.K. Hall, pp. 49–52.

6169. Jones, Gayl. "Breaking Out of the Conventions of Dialect," in

"*Sweat.*" Ed. Cheryl A. Wall. New Brunswick: Rutgers University Press, pp. 153–168.

6170. Jones, LeRoi. "Reviews: Books: Langston Hughes' *Tambourines to Glory,*" in *Langston Hughes: The Contemporary Reviews.* Ed. Tish Dace. Cambridge: Cambridge University Press, pp. 598–602.

6171. Jones, Sharon L. "*Conjuring Culture: Biblical Formations of Black America.* Theophus H. Smith. *MELUS*, 22 (Fall), 203–205. Review asking for "an examination of the influence of the King James Bible in the fiction of writers such as Richard Wright..." (p. 205).

6172. Jones, Yvonne Robinson. "Censorship," in *The Oxford Companion to African American Literature.* Eds. William L. Andrews, Francis Smith Foster, and Trudier Harris. New York: Oxford University Press, pp. 122–126. Quotes *BB* on Mencken, comments on F.B.I. and State Department surveillance of W, and discusses the quarrel between W and Baldwin.

6173. Joyce, Joyce Ann. "The Black Canon: Reconstructing Black American Literary Criticism," in *Call and Response: The Riverside Anthology of the African American Literary Tradition.* Eds. Patricia Liggins Hill, Bernard W. Bell, Trudier Harris, William J. Harris, R. Baxter Miller, and Sondra A. O'Neale. Boston: Houghton Mifflin, pp. 1459–1465.

6174. _____. "Madhubuti, Haki R.," in *The Oxford Companion to African American Literature.* Eds. William L. Andrews, Frances Smith Foster, and Trudier Harris. New York: Oxford University Press, pp. 469–471.

6175. Kershner, R.B. *The Twentieth-Century Novel: An Introduction.* Boston: Bedford Books, pp. 47, 67, 80, 82. Notes Gertrude Stein's praise of W. Also mentions *UTC*, *NS*, and *BB*.

6176. Kim, Daniel Y. "Invisible Desires: Homoerotic Racism and Its Homophobic Critique in Ralph Ellison's *Invisible Man.*" *Novel: A Forum on Fiction*, 30 (Spring), 309–328. Mentions briefly "Richard Wright's Blues" (p. 312).

6177. King, Nicole R. "Anna Grimshaw, ed. *Special Delivery: The Letters of C.L.R. James to Constance Webb, 1939–1948*; Grant Farred, ed.

Rethinking C.L.R. James." African American Review, 31 (Fall), 535–537. Mentions W briefly.

6178. Kinnamon, Keneth. "Anthologies of African-American Literature from 1845 to 1994." *Callaloo*, 20 (Spring), 461–481. Mentions W briefly (p. 464).

6179. ____. "A Richard Wright Bibliography: 1987." *Richard Wright Newsletter*, 6 (Spring/Summer), Supplement, 31 pp. Includes 285 annotated items and a commentary on W studies in 1987.

6180. ____. "*Black and White Strangers: Race and American Literary Realism.* By Kenneth W. Warren." *Journal of English and Germanic Philology*, 96 (January), 150–152. Review mentioning W briefly (p. 152).

6181. ____. "Books Briefly Mentioned." *African American Review*, 31 (Spring), 184. Contains a notice of Peter Parker and Frank Kermode's *A Reader's Guide to the Twentieth-Century Novel* mentioning W briefly.

6182. ____. "Books Briefly Mentioned." *African American Review*, 31 (Fall), 558. Includes a notice of *The French Critical Reception of African-American Literature from the Beginnings to 1970: An Annotated Bibliography* mentioning W briefly.

6183. ____. *Critical Essays on Richard Wright's Native Son.* New York: G.K. Hall, xi + 258 pp. Contains a lengthy introduction by the editor; reprints of 1940.614, 1940.674, 1940.639, 1940.608, 1940.732, 1940.572, 1940.858, 1943.23, 1969.109, 1969.180, 1974.158, 1986, 1987, 1991, 1992, 1993; and original essays by Yoshinobu Hakutani, Caren Irr, and Alessandro Portelli.

6184. ____. "Introduction," in his *Critical Essays on Richard Wright's Native Son.* New York: G.K. Hall, pp. 1–34. Descriptive and evaluative review of responses to the novel from publication to 1997.

6185. ____. "Richard Wright," in *Prospects for the Study of American Literature: A Guide for Scholars and Students.* Ed. Richard Kopley. New York: New York University Press, pp. 315–330. Reviews W criticism and scholarship up to the mid nineties, then calls for further work, emphasizing biography, textual scholarship, editing of correspondence and unpublished work, W's international importance, and other approaches.

6186. Kirszner, Laurie G., and Stephen R. Mandell. "Reading and

Reacting," in their *Literature: Reading, Reacting, Writing.* Third edition. Fort Worth: Harcourt Brace College, pp. 207–208. Study aids for "Big Black Good Man."

6187. ____. "Reading and Reacting," in their *Literature: Reading, Reacting, Writing.* Third edition. Fort Worth: Harcourt Brace College, p. 845.

6188. ____. "Reading and Reacting," in their *Literature: Reading, Reacting, Writing.* Compact third edition, p. 716.

6189. ____. "Richard Wright," in their *Literature: Reading, Reacting, Writing.* Compact third edition. Fort Worth: Harcourt Brace College, pp. 174–175.

6190. ____. "Reading and Reacting," in their Literature: *Reading, Reacting, Writing.* Compact third edition, pp. 185–186.

6191. ____. "Richard Wright," in their *Literature: Reading, Reacting, Writing.* Third edition. Fort Worth: Harcourt Brace College, pp. 196–197. Biographical headnote to "Big Black Good Man."

6192. Kiuchi, Toru, and Yoshinobu Hakutani. "The Critical Response in Japan to Richard Wright." *The Mississippi Quarterly*, 50 (Spring), 353–364. Surveys W's reception in Japan from 1940, when *NS* was translated, to 1992, when *BB* reached its eighteenth impression, having sold over 126,000 copies. The early interest in W was centered in the Communist Party. In the fifties *BB*, *UTC*, and *O* were translated, and academic interest in W was strong, but Ellison and Baldwin, followed by Morrison and Walker, began to receive more attention in the seventies and thereafter. Almost fifty books and articles on W are cited dealing with almost all his works.

6193. ____. "Richard Wright and Black Music." *Nihon University Industrial Engineering Faculty Report B*, 30 (20 June), 11–20. Maintains that W changed his view of black music after be began his French exile.

6194. Klinkowitz, Jerome. "Fiction: The 1960s to the Present," in *American Literary Scholarship: An Annual 1995.* Ed. Gary Scharnhorst. Durham, NC: Duke University Press, 331–360. Mentions Fabre's essay on W in Paris (p. 341).

6195. Kodat, Catherine Gunther.

"Biting the Head That Writes You: Southern African-American Folk Narrative and the Place of Women in *Their Eyes Were Watching God*," in *Haunted Bodies: Gender and Southern Texts.* Eds. Anne Goodwyn Jones and Susan V. Donaldson. Charlottesville: University Press of Virginia, pp. 319–342. Comments on Henry Louis Gates's comparison of W and Hurston, mentioning *BB* and *NS* (pp. 324–325).

6196. Kreyling, Michael. "Old Lights, New Lights." *The Mississippi Quarterly*, 50 (Winter), 151–157. Review of *The Future of Southern Letters* mentioning briefly *BB* (p. 154).

6197. Kritzberg, Barry. "Teaching Richard Wright in Chicago, Illinois: Let Them Read All About It in the 'World's Greatest Newspaper!'" *Richard Wright Newsletter*, 5 (Spring/ Summer), 4–5. Includes quotations on the Nixon Case from the Chicago *Daily News* and *American* as well as the *Chicago Tribune.* Contrasts the Leopold-Loeb case to those of Nixon and Bigger.

6198. Kuenz, Jane. "American Racial Discourse, 1900–1930: Schuyler's *Black No More.*" *Novel: A Forum on Fiction*, 30 (Winter), 170–192. Mentions briefly *NS* (p. 172).

6199. Laughlin, James S. "Beyond *Beyond the Culture Wars*: Students Teaching Themselves the Conflicts," in *Rethinking American Literature.* Eds. Lil Brannon and Brenda M. Greene. Urbana, IL: National Council of Teachers of English, pp. 231–248.

6200. Lauter, Paul. "The New Selections in the Third Edition." *The Heath Anthology of American Literature Newsletter* (Fall), p. 3. "Bright and Morning Star" is the new addition to the W selections.

6201. Lee, A. Robert. "Black Periodical Press," in *The Oxford Companion to African American Literature.* Eds. William L. Andrews, Frances Smith Foster, and Trudier Harris. New York: Oxford University Press, pp. 565–567. Notes W's connection to *New Challenge.*

6202. ____. "'Equilibrium out of their chaos': Ordered Unorder in the Witherspoon-Bloodworth Trilogy of Leon Forrest," in *Leon Forrest: Introductions and Interpretations.* Ed. John G. Cawelti. Bowling Green, OH: Bowling Green State University Popular Press, pp. 97–

114. Mentions briefly *NS* (p. 98) and "The Man Who Lived Underground" (p. 101).

6203. Lester, Neal A. "Hair," in *The Oxford Companion to African American Literature*. Eds. William L. Andrews, Frances Smith Foster, and Trudier Harris. New York: Oxford University Press, pp. 333–335. Notes that W uses the term "wooly" in an affectionate sense in "The Ethics of Living Jim Crow."

6204. Leuchtenmüller, Thomas. *Die Macht der Vergangenheit: Einführung in Leben und Werk August Wilsons*. Würzburg: Könighausen und Neumann, p. 14. Mentions W briefly.

6205. Levinsohn, Florence Hamlish. *Looking for Farrakhan*. Chicago: Ivan R. Dee, p. 162. Quotes W on black anti-Semitism.

6206. Lypsyte, Robert. "The Rights to the Streets of Memphis by Richard Wright," in his *The Contender and Related Readings*. Evanston, IL: McDougal Littell, pp. 227. Headnote to an excerpt from *BB*.

6207. Little, Jonathan. *Charles Johnson's Spiritual Imagination*. Columbia: University of Missouri Press, pp. 12, 14, 44, 54–55, 58–65, 76–79, 98, 114, 168. The second chapter compares *NS* and Johnson's unpublished novel "Faith and the Good Thing." The protagonists, Bigger and Faith, are overwhelmed by the Chicago environment. In his novel Johnson borrows W's naturalism and his "integrationist aesthetics." Mentions "Blueprint for Negro Writing," "How 'Bigger' Was Born," and "The Literature of the Negro in the United States."

6208. Livingston, Michael E., ed. *The African-American Book of Lists*. New York: Berkley, pp. 119, 120, 122. Lists *NS* and W.

6209. Loeb, Jeff. "MIA: African American Autobiography of the Vietnam War." *African American Review*, 31 (Spring), 105–123. Mentions briefly *BB* (p. 116).

6210. Logan, Lisa. "Introduction," in *Critical Essays on Carson McCullers*. Eds. Beverly Lyon Clark and Melvin J. Friedman. New York: G.K. Hall, pp. 1–14. Mentions W briefly (pp. 2, 6, 7, 12).

6211. Lowe, John. "Humor," in *The Oxford Companion to African American Literature*. Eds. William L. Andrews, Frances Smith Foster, and Trudier Harris. New York: Ox-

ford University Press, pp. 370–375. Includes comments on "Man of All Work" and "The Man Who Lived Underground" (p. 374).

6212. Lowery, Raymond. "Sometimes Bitter but More Often Humorous," in *Langston Hughes: The Contemporary Reviews*. Ed. Tish Dace. Cambridge: Cambridge University Press, pp. 570–571.

6213. Lyne, Bill. "Maryemma Graham and Amritjit Singh, eds. *Conversations with Ralph Ellison*." *African American Review*, 31 (Fall), 531–533. Comments on Ellison's attitude toward W as revealed in interviews.

6214. Madhubuti, Haki R. "A Personal Journey: Race, Rage, and Intellectual Development," in *In Praise of Our Fathers and Our Mothers: A Black Family Treasury by Outstanding Authors and Artists*. Eds. Wade Hudson and Cheryl Willis Hudson. East Orange, New Jersey, pp. 63–69. Includes an account of reading *BB*, *NS*, *UTC*, and *TMBV*, thereby changing his life.

6215. Major, Clarence. "Caryl Phillips. *Crossing the River*." *African American Review*, 31 (Spring), 172–174. Mentions briefly *BP*.

6216. Major, John S. "Richard Wright," in *The New Lifetime Reading Plan* by Clifton Fadiman and John S. Major. Fourth edition. New York: Harper Collins, pp. 100–101. Brief biographical sketch mentioning *NS* and *BB*.

6217. Malvasi, Mark G. *The Unregenerate South: The Agrarian Thought of John Crowe Ransom, Allen Tate, and Donald Davidson*. Baton Rouge: Louisiana State University Press, p. 1. Mentions W briefly.

6218. Margolies, Edward, and Michel Fabre. *The Several Lives of Chester Himes*. Jackson: University Press of Mississippi, pp. 43, 46, 54–55, 57, 64, 67, 77, 79, 80–81, 87, 92, 110, 116, 117–118, 132, 142, 150, 162, 184, 185, 188. Biography including numerous references to the W-Himes friendship. Himes and Ellison "found Wright both dazzlingly impressive and relatively unsophisticated" (p. 55). Himes and W met in July 1945, resulting in a friendship that was a "peculiar mix of admiration, amusement, and envy" (p. 54). Discusses W's death and funeral.

6219. Marquez, Antonio C.

"Voices of Caliban: From Curse to Discourse." *Confluencia*, 13 (Fall), 159–160. Contains a paragraph on W's discovery as recorded in *BB* that words could be weapons.

6220. Marx, Christoph. "'History comes full circle': Nkrumah, Kenyatta, Mandela über Nation und Ethnizität in Afrika." *Historische Zeitschrift*, 265 (October), 373–393. Contains two footnote references to *BP* (pp. 374, 377).

6221. Maxwell, William J. "Black and White, Unite and Write: New Integrationist Criticism of U.S. Literary Modernism." *The Minnesota Review*, 47 (May), 205–215. Mentions W briefly (p. 213).

6222. _____. "'Is It True What They Say About Dixie?': Richard Wright, Zora Neale Hurston, and Rural/Urban Exchange in Modern African-American Literature," in *Knowing Your Place: Rural Identity and Cultural Hierarchy*. Eds. Barbara Ching and Gerald W. Creed. New York: Routledge, pp. 71–104. Intervenes in the Hurston vs. W debate by arguing that W affirmed the black folk South and had reservations about the Great Migration. Includes comparisons of the influence of social science on both writers and of "The Gilded Six-Bits" and "Long Black Song." Also discusses "Fire and Cloud" and Hurston's "The Fire and the Cloud."

6223. McCoy, Beth. "Cheryl Wall. *Women of the Harlem Renaissance*; Deborah G. Plant. *Every Tub Must Sit on Its Own Bottom*; Farah Jasmine Griffin. '*Who set you flowin'?': The African American Migration Narrative*." *Modern Fiction Studies*, 43 (Winter), 993–1001. The review of the Griffin book mentions W briefly (pp. 998, 999).

6224. McDowell, Deborah E. "Conversations with Dorothy West," in *Harlem Renaissance Re-examined: A Revised and Expanded Edition*. Eds. Victor A. Kramer and Robert A. Russ. Troy, New York: Whitston, pp. 285–303.

6225. _____. "Reading Family Matters," in *Haunted Bodies: Gender and Southern Texts*. Eds. Anne Goodwyn Jones and Susan V. Donaldson. Charlottesville: University of Virginia Press, pp. 389–415. Cites and comments on Bigger's treatment of Bessie in *NS* (p. 394).

6226. McDowell, Deborah E., and Hortense Spillers. "Ann Petry," in *The Norton Anthology of African American Literature*. Eds. Henry Louis Gates Jr., and Nellie McKay. New York: W.W. Norton, pp. 1476–1478. Compares Petry and W, but insists on the difference between "the sexual politics of race and the racial politics of gender" (p. 1477).

6227. _____. "Chester B. Himes," in *The Norton Anthology of African American Literature*. Eds. Henry Louis Gates, Jr., and Nellie Y. McKay. New York: W.W. Norton, pp. 1467–1468. Mentions W briefly (p. 1468).

6228. _____. "Dorothy West," in *The Norton Anthology of African American Literature*. Eds. Henry Louis Gates, Jr., and Nellie Y. McKay. New York: W.W. Norton, pp. 1358–1359. Mentions W and *New Challenge*.

6229. _____. "James Baldwin," in *The Norton Anthology of African American Literature*. Eds. Henry Louis Gates, Jr., and Nellie McKay. New York: W.W. Norton, pp. 1650–1654. Includes comment on the W-Baldwin relationship.

6230. _____. "Richard Wright," in *The Norton Anthology of African American Literature*. Eds. Henry Louis Gates, Jr., and Nellie Y. McKay, New York: W.W. Norton, pp. 1376–1380. Biographical-critical essay emphasizing the influence of Mencken as well as Communism. Discusses *NS, BB, TMBV* and mentions *O, BP, WML*, and *AH*. "Blueprint for Negro Writing," "The Ethics of Living Jim Crow," "Long Black Song," "The Man Who Lived Underground," and portions of *BB* are reprinted on pp. 1380–1467.

6231. _____. "Lorraine Hansberry," in *The Norton Anthology of African American Literature*. Eds. Henry Louis Gates, Jr., and Nellie Y. McKay. New York: W.W. Norton, pp. 1725–1728. Notes that some critics have compared *A Raisin in the Sun* to *NS* (p. 1725).

6232. _____. "Ralph Ellison," in *The Norton Anthology of African American Literature*. Eds. Henry Louis Gates, Jr., and Nellie Y. McKay. New York: W.W. Norton, pp. 1515–1518. Notes W's role as a friend and "informal teacher and mentor" to Ellison.

6233. _____. "Realism, Naturalism, Modernism: 1940–1960," in *The Norton Anthology of African American Literature*. Eds. Henry Louis

Gates, Jr., and Nellie Y. McKay. New York: W.W. Norton, pp. 1319–1328. Discusses W and the Wright School emphasizing urban realism and stressing the impact of *NS* on subsequent black fiction. Mentions "Blueprint for Negro Writing," "How Bigger Was Born," *TMBV*, and the W-Ellison relationship.

6234. _____. "Margaret Walker," in *The Norton Anthology of African American Literature*. Eds. Henry Louis Gates, Jr., and Nellie McKay. New York: W.W. Norton, pp. 1571–1572. Includes discussion of the W-Walker friendship and "literary collaboration" (p. 1572).

6235. McGee, Patrick. *Ishmael Reed and the Ends of Race*. New York: St. Martin's Press, pp. 53, 89, 106, 114–115. Mentions Bigger Thomas, *NS*, and W, and comments on the favorable estimates of W by Houston Baker and Ishmael Reed.

6236. McGilligan, Patrick. "John (Jack) Berry," in his and Paul Buhle's *Tender Comrades: A Backstory of the Hollywood Blacklist*. New York: St. Martin's Press, pp. 55–89. Berry describes his relation to the play *NS* as actor and as director of the road show version.

6237. McLaren, Joseph. *Langston Hughes: Folk Dramatist in the Protest Tradition*. Westport, CT: Greenwood Press, pp. 7, 35, 41, 160, 165, 171. Comments on W and the Left (p. 7) and mentions W and *NS* elsewhere. Notes that Hughes wrote a skit about W called "*Native Son: The Boogie Woogie Man*" (p. 167).

6238. McLaurin, Melton. "Rituals of Initiation and Rebellion: Adolescent Responses to Segregation in Southern Autobiography." *Southern Cultures*, 3, No. 2, 5–24. Contains a paragraph on *BB* emphasizing W's early sensitivity to the white threat (pp. 7–8). Also relates W's refusal to read the graduation speech written by his principal (pp. 14–15), and narrates W's recollection of the story of a black woman who avenges her husband's murder by a white mob (p. 22).

6239. McMahon, Frank. "Rereading *The Outsider*: Double-Consciousnes and the Divided Self." *Mississippi Quarterly*, 50 (Fall), 289–305. Drawing on work by Paul Gilroy, Fanon, DuBois, and R.D. Laing, McMahon analyzes the social, psychological, and autobiographical, as well as political, sources

of Cross Damon's ordeal. He compares *O* to *NS*, mentioning also Douglass, Toni Morrison, *WML*, and "The Ethics of Living Jim Crow."

6240. McMichael, George. "James Baldwin 1924–1987," in his *Anthology of American Literature*, Sixth edition, Vol. II. Upper Saddle River, NJ: Prentice-Hall, pp. 1906–1907.

6241. _____. "Ralph Ellison 1914–1994," in his *Anthology of American Literature*, Sixth edition, Vol. II. Upper Saddle River, NJ: Prentice-Hall, pp. 1530–1531.

6242. _____. "Richard Wright 1908–1960," in his *Anthology of American Literature*, Sixth edition, Vol. II, pp. 1521–1522.

6243. _____. 'Richard Wright," in his *Anthology of American Literature*. Vol. II. Upper Saddle River, NJ: Prentice Hall, pp. 1521–1530. Revised reprint of 1974.128.

6244. _____. "Twentieth-Century Literature," in his *Anthology of American Literature*, Sixth edition, Vol. II. Upper Saddle River, NJ: Prentice-Hall, 985–991.

6245. Melnick, Jeffrey. "*Double-Consciousness/Double Bind: Theoretical Issues in Twentieth-Century Black Literature. By Sandra Adell.*" *Journal of English and Germanic Philology*, 96 (January), 152–154. Review mentioning W briefly (p. 153).

6246. Meehan, Kevin. "Spiking Canons." *The Nation*, 264 (12 May), 42–44, 46. Review of *The Norton Anthology of African American Literature* mentioning briefly W and "The Man Who Lived Underground."

6247. Meyer, Adam. "Jews," in *The Oxford Companion to African American Literature*. Eds. William L. Andrews, Frances Smith Foster, and Trudier Harris. New York: Oxford University Press, p. 398.

6248. Miller, Andrew Thompson. "Black Power," in *Reader's Guide to American History*. Chicago: Fitzroy Dearborn, pp. 64–66. Notes that W used the term before it became current in the sixties.

6249. Miller, James A. "Bigger Thomas's Quest for Voice and Audience in Richard Wright's *Native Son*," in *Critical Essays on Richard Wright's Native Son*. Ed. Keneth Kinnamon. New York: G.K. Hall, pp. 119–125.

6250. _____. "Communism," in *The Oxford Companion to African*

American Literature. Eds. William L. Andrews, Frances Smith Foster, and Trudier Harris. New York: Oxford University Press, pp. 165–167. Comments on W's affiliation with the John Reed Club and the Communist Party early in his career and mentions his critique of Communists in *O*.

6251. _____. "Introduction," in his *Approaches to Teaching Wright's Native Son*. New York: The Modern Language Association of America, pp. 11–15. Comments on each of the fifteen essays in the collection, noting how they address the major issues, social and literary, raised by *NS*.

6252. _____. "Materials," in his *Approaches to Teaching Wright's Native Son*. New York: The Modern Language Association of America, pp. 1–8. Reviews W scholarship, especially as it relates to the teaching of *NS*.

6253. _____. "Preface to the Volume," in his *Approaches to Teaching Wright's Native Son*. New York: The Modern Language Association of America, pp. ix–x. Reports that a survey of teachers resulting in this book addressed such questions as the following: "Why do teachers teach *Native Son*? What assumptions do they make about the novel? What aspects do they emphasize and why? Is it possible to strike a balance between the literary and extraliterary values of the novel?"

6254. Miller, R. Baxter, and Patricia Liggins Hill. "Ann Petry (1908–)," in *Call and Response: The Riverside Anthology of the African American Literary Tradition*. Eds. Patricia Liggins Hill, Bernard W. Bell, Trudier Harris, William J. Harris, R. Baxter Miller, and Sondra A. O'Neale. Boston: Houghton Mifflin, pp. 1028–1031. The bibliographical note mentions "critical works that equate Petry's work with that of Richard Wright" (p. 1031).

6255. _____. "'Bound No'th Blues': African American History and Culture, 1915–1945: 'What Happens to a Dream Deferred?': Renaissance and Reformation," in *Call and Response: The Riverside Anthology of the African American Literary Tradition*. Eds. Patricia Liggins Hill, Bernard W. Bell, Trudier Harris, William J. Harris, R. Baxter Miller, and Sondra A. O'Neale. Boston: Houghton Mifflin, pp. 766–

795. Quotes from "Blueprint for Negro Writing" (p. 791), discusses *BB* and *NS* (p. 794), and mentions W elsewhere (pp. 792, 793, 795).

6256. _____. "Chester Himes (1909–1984)," in *Call and Response: The Riverside Anthology of the African American Literary Tradition*. Eds. Patricia Liggins Hill, Bernard W. Bell, Trudier Harris, William J. Harris, R. Baxter Miller, and Sondra A. O'Neale. Boston: Houghton Mifflin, pp. 1060–1062. Mentions briefly W and Bigger Thomas.

6257. _____. "Frank Marshall Davis (1905–1987)," in *Call and Response: The Riverside Anthology of the African American Literary Tradition*. Eds. Patricia Liggins Hill, Bernard W. Bell, Trudier Harris, William J. Harris, R. Baxter Miller, and Sondra A. O'Neale. Boston: Houghton Mifflin, pp. 1005–1009. Discusses the W-Davis friendship and mentions briefly *BB*, *NS*, and *UTC* (p. 1006).

6258. _____. "Richard Wright (1908–1960)," in *Call and Response: The Riverside Anthology of the African American Literary Tradition*. Eds. Patricia Liggins Hill, Bernard W. Bell, Trudier Harris, William J. Harris, R. Baxter Miller, and Sondra A. O'Neale. Boston: Houghton Mifflin, pp. 1011–1015. Biographical-critical essay ranking W "among the foremost authors of fiction during the nineteenth and twentieth centuries" (p. 1011). Mentions all of W's books except *AH* and *RP* and comments substantially on *UTC* and *NS*. Includes a bibliographical note citing books by Fabre, Webb, Walker, Williams, Kinnamon, and Joyce. The selection reprinted is "Long Black Song."

6259. Miller, William. *Richard Wright and the Library Card*. Illustrated by Gregory Christie. New York: Lee & Law Books, 30 pp. Children's book recounting episodes from Chapters XIII and XIV of *BB*. Miller takes liberties with W's text, but the illustrations are attractive.

6260. Moon, Michael. "Brief Mention." *American Literature*, 69 (March), 247–258. Contains a notice of Femi Ojo-Ade's *Of Dreams Deferred, Dead or Alive: African Perspectives on African-American Writers* mentioning W briefly (p. 253).

6261. Moore, Deborah Dash. "Separate Paths: Blacks and Jews in the Twentieth-Century South," in

Struggles in the Promised Land: Toward a History of Black-Jewish Relations in the United States. Eds. Jack Salzman and Cornel West. New York: Oxford University Press, pp. 275–293. Quotes from *BB* (p. 285).

6262. Moore, Jack B. "Editor's Comments." *The Mississippi Quarterly*, 50 (Spring), 237. Introductory to a special W issue. Includes a dedication to Michel Fabre, the co-editor.

6263. _____. "A Personal Appreciation of Richard Wright's Universality." *The Mississippi Quarterly*, 50 (Spring), 365–374. Argues for the universality of W's individualism, discussing *BB* (*AH*) and *NS*, mentioning other works by W, and citing such scholars as John M. Reilly, Robert Butler, Michel Fabre, Jerry Ward, Keneth Kinnamon, Carla Capetti, Donald Gibson, Amritjit Singh, Yoshinobu Hakutani, Abdul Jan Mohamed, and Frank McMahon.

6264. Moore-Gilbert, Bart, Gareth Stanton, and Willy Maley. "Introduction," in their *Postcolonial Criticism*. London: Longman, pp. 1–72. Mentions W briefly and quotes from Abdul JanMohamed on W (pp. 10, 50).

6265. Mpoyi-Buatu, Thomas. "1947–1997: Cinquantenaire de *Présence Africaine*." *Présence Africaine*, No. 156, pp. 5–10. Mentions W as one of the founders of the journal.

6266. _____. "1947–1997: Fiftieth Anniversary of *Présence Africaine*, No. 156, pp. 11–15. Translation of 1997.

6267. Morey, Ann-Janine. "Margaret Atwood and Toni Morrison: Reflections on Postmodernism and the Study of Religion and Literature," in *Toni Morrison's Fiction: Contemporary Criticism*. Ed. David L. Middleton. New York: Garland, pp. 247–268.

6268. Mostern, Kenneth. "Double Consciousness/Double Bind: *Theoretical Issues in Twentieth Century Black Literature*. Sandra Adell." *MELUS*, 22 (Winter), 193–197. Mentions briefly *BB* (p. 196).

6269. Munton, Alan. "Misreading Morrison, Mishearing Jazz: A Response to Toni Morrison's Jazz Critics." *Journal of American Studies*, 31 (August), 235–251. Mentions W briefly (p. 251).

6270. Nagel, James. "General Editor's Note," in *Critical Essays on Richard Wright's Native Son.* Ed. Keneth Kinnamon. New York: G.K. Hall, p. ix. Describes the collection.

6271. _____. "General Editor's Note," in *Critical Essays on Carson McCullers.* Eds. Beverly Lyon Clark and Melvin J. Friedman. New York: G.K. Hall, p. xi. Mentions W briefly.

6272. _____. "Images of 'Vision' in *Native Son*," in *Critical Essays on Richard Wright's Native Son.* Ed. Keneth Kinnamon. New York: G.K. Hall, pp. 86–93.

6273. Nakagomi, Kazumasa. "A Study of the Relationship Between Terror and Alienation Seen in *Native Son.*" *Nihon University Studies in English Language and Literature*, 18 (January), 1–9. Contends that the main reason why Bigger is alienated is his fear of whites.

6274. Nakatani, Takashi. "Richard Wright's *Native Son* and the Modernism Age." *Yokohama City University Treatises: Humanities*, 48 (March), 77–100. Deals with two questions: the effect of *NS* on the relation between literature and politics and why the novel shows W's interest in fascism.

6275. Namekata, Hitoshi. "The 1930's and Wright." *Bulletin of Musashino College for Music*, 29, 133–142. Argues that *UTC* did not advocate communism because W thought that the African American Community in the South was more important.

6276. Nash, William R. "The Dream Defined: *Bailey's Café* and the Reconstruction of American Cultural Identities," in *The Critical Response to Gloria Naylor.* Westport, CT: Greenwood Press, pp. 211–225. Mentions W's use of snow imagery in *NS*, relating it to a scene in the Naylor work.

6277. Nelson, Jill. "Black Americans in Paris." *The Nation*, 264 (13/20 January), 31–32. Review of Tyler Stovall's *Paris Noir: African Americans in the City of Light* mentioning W briefly.

6278. Neri, Algerina. "Scholarship in Languages Other Than English: Italian Contributions," in *American Literary Scholarship: An Annual 1995.* Durham, NC: Duke University Press, pp. 467–484. Mentions an essay by Alessandro Portelli mentioning W and others.

6279. Nickerson, Catherine. "Murder as Social Criticism." *Amer-* *ican Literary History*; 9 (Winter), 744–757. Mentions W briefly (p. 754).

6280. Nielsen, Aldon Lynn. *Black Chant: Languages of African-American Postmodernism.* Cambridge: Cambridge University Press, p. 135. Mentions W briefly.

6281. _____. *C.L.R. James: A Critical Introduction.* Jackson: University Press of Mississippi, pp. xiii, xviii, 35–37, 160. Discusses James's friendship with W, his review of *NS*, and their plans for other publications (pp. 35–37). Elsewhere Nielsen mentions "The Man Who Lived Underground" and comments on James's response to *BB*.

6282. Noble, Marianne. "The Ecstasies of Sentimental Wounding in *Uncle Tom's Cabin*," *Journal of Criticism*, 10, no. 2, pp. 295–320. Mentions briefly *NS* (p. 318).

6283. Okada, Seiichi. "A Study of Richard Wright: On Bigger Thomas's Various Phases of Hate." *Saitama University Bulletin*, 33, 155–168. States that Bigger hated not only white people but also his family and friends. Varieties of hate are stated in "How 'Bigger' Was Born."

6284. Olson, Barbara K. "'Come-to-Jesus Stuff' in James Baldwin's *Go Tell It on the Mountain* and *The Amen Corner.*" *African American Review*, 31 (Summer), 295–301. Quotes Baldwin on *NS* (p. 300).

6285. Olson, Ted. "Folklore," in *The Oxford Companion to African American Literature.* Eds. William L. Andrews, Frances Smith Foster, and Trudier Harris. New York: Oxford University Press, pp. 286–290. Mentions *NS* as a treatment of the badman figure (p. 286).

6286. _____. "Jim Crow," in *The Oxford Companion to African American Literature.* Eds. William L. Andrews, Frances Smith Foster, and Trudier Harris. New York: Oxford University Press, pp. 398–399.

6287. O'Meally, Robert G. "The Vernacular Tradition," in *The Norton Anthology of African American Literature.* Eds. Henry Louis Gates, Jr., and Nellie Y. McKay. New York: Norton, pp. 2, 23, 117. Mentions briefly W, *BB*, and *LT*.

6288. O'Neale, Sondra A. "'Go Down, Moses, Way Down in Egypt's Land': African American History and Culture, 1619–1808: The Description of the Conditions of Slavery and Oppression," in *Call and* *Response: The Riverside Anthology of the African American Literary Tradition.* Eds. Patricia Hill Liggins, Bernard W. Bell, Trudier Harris, William J. Harris, R. Baxter Miller, and Sondra A. O'Neale. Boston: Houghton Mifflin, pp. 1–27. Mentions briefly W, Bigger Thomas, and *NS* (pp. 3, 23).

6289. Orr, Elaine Neil. *Subject to Negotiation: Reading Feminist Criticism and American Women's Fictions.* Charlottesville: University Press of Virginia, pp. 3, 51. Mentions W in relation to Hurston.

6290. Parker, Robert Dale. "Who Shot the Sheriff: Storytelling, Indian Identity, and the Marketplace of Masculinity in D'Arcy McNickle's *The Surrounded.*" *Modern Fiction Studies*, 43 (Winter), 898–932. Mentions briefly *NS* and *BB* (pp. 919, 932).

6291. Passaro, Vince. "Black Letters on a White Page." *Harper's*, 295 (July), 70–75. Mentions W briefly (p. 74).

6292. Peters, Pearlie. "Masking," in *The Oxford Companion to African American Literature.* Eds. William L. Andrews, Frances Smith Foster, and Trudier Harris. New York: Oxford University Press, p. 483. Mentions briefly *UTC*.

6293. Peters, Renate. "Sartre, White America, and the Black Problem." *Canadian Review of American Studies*, 27, No. 1, pp. 21–41. Includes comments on W by Sartre in *What Is Literature?* and *Anti-Semite and Jew* and quotes W in his interview with Michel Gordey.

6294. Peterson, Bernard L., Jr. *The African American Theatre Directory, 1816–1960: A Comprehensive Guide to Early Black Theatre Organizations, Companies, Theatres, and Performing Groups.* Westport, CT: Greenwood Press, pp. 122, 149, 170. Mentions Melvin B. Tolson's dramatization of *BB*, W's membership in Negro Playwrights Company, and scenes from *NS* directed by Arthur Clifton Lamb at Prairie View A. & M.

6295. _____. "Drama," in *The Oxford Companion to African American Literature.* Eds. William L. Andrews, Frances Smith Foster, and Trudier Harris. New York: Oxford University Press, pp. 228–234. Mentions briefly the play *NS*.

6296. Peterson, Nancy J. "'Say Make Me, Remake Me': Toni Morrison and the Reconstruction of

African-American History," in her *Toni Morrison: Critical and Theoretical Approaches*. Baltimore: The Johns Hopkins University Press, pp. 201–221. Mentions W briefly (p. 210).

6297. Pettis, Joyce. "Reading Ann Petry's *The Narrows* into Black Literary Tradition," in Recovered *Writers/Recovered Texts: Race, Class, and Gender in Black Women's Literature*. Ed. Dolan Hubbard. Knoxville: The University of Tennessee Press, 116–128. Mentions W briefly (p. 117).

6298. Pierpont, Claudia Roth. "A Society of One: Zora Neale Hurston, American Contrarian." *The New Yorker*, 73 (17 February), 80–86, 88–91. Begins with an account of the Hurston–W quarrel and mentions W near the end (pp. 90, 91).

6299. Pinckney, Darryl. "The Drama of Ralph Ellison." *The New York Review of Books*, 44 (15 May), 52–56, 58–60. Contains a substantial discussion of the W-Ellison relation, both personal and literary. Includes a caricature of W by David Levine.

6300. Pinsker, Sanford. "'The Bluesteel, Rawhide, Patent-Leather Implications of Fairy Tales': A Conversation with Albert Murray." *The Georgia Review*, 51 (Summer), 205–221. Mentions W briefly (p. 219).

6301. Polk, Noel, *Outside the Southern Myth*. Jackson: University Press of Mississippi, pp. 98, 103, 122. Mentions reading *BB* and *NS*.

6302. Portelli, Alessandro. "Everybody's Healing Novel: *Native Son* and Its Contemporary Critical Context." *The Mississippi Quarterly*, 50 (Spring), 255–265. Argues that the corrective to *NS* as social protest has overemphasized Bigger's psychological healing and tranquility at the end of the novel. Such a development in Bigger is at most tentative and incipient, for the closing doors of his cell and his impending execution foreclose further growth.

6303. _____. "On the Lower Frequencies: Sound and Meaning in *Native Son*," in *Critical Essays on Richard Wright's Native Son*. Ed. Keneth Kinnamon. New York: G.K. Hall, pp. 213–249. Exhaustive linguistic analysis of "the grammar of sounds" in *NS*. W's deliberate use of various sound patterns joins sound and sense in a hitherto unexplored aspect of the novel's style.

6304. Posner, Richard A. "Against Ethical Criticism." *Philosophy and Literature*, 21 (April), 1–27. Refuting Martha Nussbaum (see 1995) and endorsing Harold Bloom, Posner considers *NS* to be a badly written period piece (pp. 15–16).

6305. Posnock, Ross. "How It Feels to Be a Problem: Du Bois, Fanon, and the 'Impossible Life' of the Black Intellectual." *Critical Inquiry*, 23 (Winter), 323–348. Quotes from W's preface to *WML* and quotes from Fanon's letter to W dated 3 January 1953 (p. 348).

6306. Powell, Richard J. *Black Art and Culture in the 20th Century*. London: Thames and Hudson, pp. 69, 90. Mentions briefly W and *LT*.

6307. Poulos, Jennifer H. "'Shouting Curses': The Politics of 'Bad' Language in Richard Wright's *Black Boy*." *The Journal of Negro History*, 82 (Winter), 54–66. Examines the use of "bad" and "good" language in *NS*, emphasizing the role of language use in self realization. Comments also on *NS* and "How 'Bigger' Was Born."

6308. Powell, Timothy B. "Toni Morrison: The Struggle to Depict the Black Figure on the White Page," in *Toni Morrison's Fiction: Contemporary Criticism*. Ed. David L. Middleton. New York: Garland, pp. 47–60.

6309. Presley, Delma Eugene. "Carson McCullers and the South," in *Critical Essays on Carson McCullers*. Eds. Beverly Lyon Clark and Melvin J. Friedman. New York: G.K. Hall, pp. 99–110.

6310. Pryse, Marjorie. "Teaching American Literature as Cultural Encounter: Models for Organizing the Introductory Course," in *Rethinking American Literature*. Eds. Lil Brannon and Brenda M. Greene. Urbana, IL: National Council of Teachers of English, pp. 175–192. Mentions W briefly (p. 183).

6311. Putnam, Diane. "Introducing ... the Assistant Editor." *Richard Wright Newsletter*, 5 (Spring/Summer), 3. Expresses gratitude for her tenure on the *Richard Wright Newsletter*.

6312. Qualls, Youra. "The Bookshelf: Simple — New Observer of U.S. Scene," in *Langston Hughes: The Contemporary Reviews*. Ed. Tish Dace. Cambridge: Cambridge University Press, p. 375.

6313. Quinn, Laura L. "*Native Son* as Project," in *Approaches to Teaching Wright's Native Son*. Ed. James A. Miller. New York: The Modern Language Association of America, pp. 42–47. Discusses student enthusiasm for and resistance to *NS* "in a small, expensive liberal arts college." Teachers should mediate such responses "by having students interact with the historical complexities of the novel's production and reception" (p. 43).

6314. Radway, Janice A. *A Feeling for Books: The Book-of-the-Month Club, Literary Taste, and Middle-Class Desire*. Chapel Hill: The University of North Carolina Press, pp. 286–287, 297, 392. Discusses the revisions of *NS* and *BB* required by the club. Includes information from unpublished correspondence between W and Dorothy Canfield Fisher.

6315. Rampersad, Arnold. "Biography," in *The Oxford Companion to African American Literature*. Eds. William L. Andrews, Frances Smith Foster, and Trudier Harris. New York: Oxford University Press, pp. 65–67. Mentions favorably Michel Fabre's *The Unfinished Quest of Richard Wright*.

6316. _____. "Shadow and Veil: Melville and Modern Black Consciousness," in *Melville's Evermoving Dawn: Centennial Essays*. Eds. John Bryant and Robert Milder. Kent, OH: The Kent State University Press, pp. 162–177. Comments on Baldwin's mistaken attack on W, calls Babo in "Benito Cereno" a "kind of prediction of *Native Son* (p. 166), and mentions W elsewhere (pp. 171, 174).

6317. Raper, Julius Rowan. "*Culture of Horror: The Psychology of Violence in the South* by Richard E. Nisbett and Dov Cohen." *Southern Cultures*, 3, no. 1, 80–83. Review mentioning W briefly (p. 82).

6318. Rascoe, Burton. "Negro Novel and White Reviewers," in *Critical Essays on Richard Wright's Native Son*. Ed. Keneth Kinnamon. New York: G.K. Hall, pp. 56–59.

6319. Rath, Richard Cullen. "Echo and Narcissus: The Afrocentric Pragmatism of W.E.B. DuBois." *The Journal of American History*, 84 (September), 461–495. Mentions briefly *BB* (p. 462).

6320. Reckley, Ralph, Sr. "Ellison, Ralph," in *The Oxford Companion to African American Literature*. Eds. William L. Andrews,

Frances Smith Foster, and Trudier Harris. New York: Oxford University Press, pp. 252–254.

6321. _____. "*Invisible Man*," in *The Oxford Companion to African American Literature*. Eds. William L. Andrews, Frances Smith Foster, and Trudier Harris. New York: Oxford University Press, pp. 388–389.

6322. Redfield, Terrica. "Reading Wright in Tougaloo, Mississippi: *Lawd Today! Versus The Outsider*: Realistic Representation of the Afro-American Male." *Richard Wright Newsletter*, 5 (Spring/Summer), 5–7. Argues that Jake's rude descriptions of desire and women's bodies are more realistic than Cross's more intellectualized discourse.

6323. Reed, Ishmael. "Bigger and O.J.," in *Birth of a Nation'hood*. Eds. Toni Morrison and Claudia Brodsky Lacour. New York: Random House, pp. 169–195. Examines similarities between Bigger and O.J. Simpson and their biased treatment by white media and the white system of justice. Praises *NS* as "a classic novel, as it was when it was published on March 1, 1940."

6324. Reilly, John M. "Eric J. Sundquist. *Cultural Contexts for Ralph Ellison's Invisible Man*." *African American Review*, 31 (Summer), 342–343. Notes that Sundquist includes material from *TMBV*.

6325. Richards, Gary Neal. "Another Southern Renaissance: Sexual Otherness in Mid-Twentieth-Century Southern Fiction." *Dissertation Abstracts International—*A, 57/08 (February), p. 3499. Devotes a chapter to *LD* arguing that it shows W's understanding of a racialized South's inhibition of compulsory heterosexuality in African American men.

6326. Robbins, Anthony, and Joseph McClendon III. *Unlimited Power: A Black Choice*. New York: Simon & Schuster, p. 413. Quotes from *BB*.

6327. Robbins, Sarah. "Gendering the History of the Antislavery Narrative: Juxtaposing *Uncle Tom's Cabin* and *Benito Cereno*, *Beloved* and *Middle Passage*." *American Quarterly*, 49 (September), 531–573. Quotes Richard Yarborough quoting from "How Bigger Was Born" the passage in which W expresses his disappointment in the sentimentalism with which *UTC* was received (pp. 546–547).

6328. Robinson, Lillian S. *In the*

Canon's Mouth: Dispatches from the Culture Wars. Bloomington: Indiana University Press, p. 141. Mentions W briefly.

6329. Rodgers, Lawrence R. *Canaan Bound: The African-American Great Migration Novel*. Urbana: University of Illinois Press, pp. 6, 8, 11, 18, 28, 38, 40, 42, 54, 67, 74, 96, 98–109, 110–112, 113, 124, 133, 134, 135, 136, 140, 144, 147, 164, 166, 173, 181, 182, 196. Chapter 3, "The Fugitive Migrant Novel's Critique of Ascent," contains a substantial treatment of the context of *NS* in the Chicago Renaissance, the Chicago School of sociology, and W's own life experiences. Mentions W frequently elsewhere.

6330. Romanet, Jerome de. "*Revisiting Madeleine* and 'The Outing': James Baldwin's Revision of Gide's Sexual Politics." *MELUS*, 22 (Spring), 3–14. Mentions W briefly (p. 3).

6331. Romine, Scott. "*The Christ-Haunted Landscape: Faith and Doubt in Southern Fiction*, by Susan Ketchin." *The Mississippi Quarterly*, 50 (Winter), 177–179. Mentions briefly *BB* (p. 177).

6332. Roper, John Herbert. "On Richard Wright and Paul Eliot Green." *Richard Wright Newsletter*, 5 (Spring/Summer), 1, 7–8. Recounts the W-Green relationship in 1936 during W's work in the Federal Theatre Project on production of Green's *Hymn to the Rising Sun* and in 1940 during their collaboration on the play *NS*. Notes also that the play was produced in Chapel Hill, N.C., in 1978.

6333. Rowden, Terry. "*Sweet Home: Invisible Cities in the Afro-American Novel*. Charles Scruggs." *MELUS*, 22 (Summer), 137–139. Mixed review praising Scruggs's treatment of *NS*.

6334. Rowell, Charles H. "'An All-Purpose, All-American Literary Intellectual': An Interview with Albert Murray." *Callaloo*, 20 (Spring), 319–414. Murray states that he "was searching for a way to write affirmative books," unlike W and Baldwin (p. 412).

6335. _____. "'Beyond the Hard Work and Discipline': An Interview with Leon Forrest." *Callaloo*, 20 (Spring), 342–356. Forrest states that he read W in grade school (p. 348).

6336. _____. "An Interview with Charles Johnson." *Callaloo*, 20 (Sum-

mer), 531–547. Johnson acknowledges the early stylistic influence of W (p. 534) and found interesting "the existential moves he makes within naturalism" (p. 536).

6337. _____. "An Interview with Clarence Major." *Callaloo*, 20 (Summer), 667–678. Major recalls reading W in Chicago, encouraged by a bookseller who had known him (p. 668).

6338. _____. "An Interview with Gloria Naylor." *Callaloo*, 20 (Winter), 179–192. Naylor recalls reading W as an undergraduate at Brooklyn College (p. 190) and mentions W elsewhere (p. 197).

6339. Russ, Robert A. "Chronology of the Harlem Renaissance," in *Harlem Renaissance Re-examined*. Eds. Victor A. Kramer and Robert A. Russ. Troy, NY: Whitston, pp. 25–42. Mentions briefly *NS* (p. 25).

6340. Ruth, Kent. "Breaking Out of the 'Cage' of Negro Writing," in *Langston Hughes: The Contemporary Reviews*. Ed. Tish Dace. Cambridge: Cambridge University Press, p. 444.

6341. Salaam, Kalamu ya. "Black Arts Movement," in *The Oxford Companion to African American Literature*. Eds. William L. Andrews, Frances Smith Foster, and Trudier Harris. New York: Oxford University Press, pp. 70–74. Mentions W briefly (p. 70).

6342. Salzman, Jack. "Introduction," in his and Cornel West's *Struggles in the Promised Land: Toward a History of Black-Jewish Relations in the United States*. New York: Oxford University Press, pp. 1–19. Quotes from *BB* (p. 13).

6343. Satz, Martha. "A Missionary to 'Her People' Teaches *Native Son*," in *Approaches to Teaching Wright's Native Son*. Ed. James A. Miller. New York: The Modern Language Association of America, pp. 54–66. Most of this essay is concerned with Satz's approach to racial sensitivity training. The last four pages deal with the responses of her students at S.M.U. to the novel.

6344. Saunders, James Robert. *Tightrope Walk: Identity, Survival and the Corporate World in African American Literature*. Jefferson, NC: McFarland, pp. 77, 92, 109, 112, 117) Mentions W briefly in chapters on Ishmael Reed, Jill Nelson, and Bebe Moore. Campbell. Also mentions or comments briefly on *NS* (pp. 112, 122–123) and *LT* (p. 112).

6345. Schaller, Barry R. *A Vision of American Law, Literature, and the Stories We Tell.* Westport, CT: Praeger, pp. 13, 23. Mentions briefly *NS* and compares it to *Invisible Man.*

6346. Scherman, Tony. "The Omni-American," in *Conversations with Albert Murray.* Ed. Roberta S. Maguire. Jackson: University Press of Mississippi, pp. 123–136.

6347. Schmidt, Klaus. "Teaching *Native Son* in a German Undergraduate Literature Class," in *Approaches to Teaching Wright's Native Son.* Ed. James A. Miller. New York: The Modern Language Association of America, pp. 28–34. Emphasizes the importance and complexity of the theme of marginality in the novel, discussing "the protagonist's double consciousness ... the mirror function of women's marginalization, the male outsider's process of articulation encoded by an intricate blues syntax, and the deictic relativity of inside and outside" (p. 28).

6348. Scott, Daryl Michael. *Social Policy and the Image of the Damaged Black Psyche, 1880–1996.* Chapel Hill: The University of North Carolina Press, pp. 98–102, 103, 165, 167, 168–169. Discusses W as a "fiction writer posing as social psychiatrist," and analyzes *NS* as the origin of "black rage imagery."

6349. Scruggs, Charles. "The City Without Maps in Richard Wright's *Native Son,*" in *Critical Essays on Richard Wright's Native Son.* Ed. Keneth Kinnamon. New York: G.K. Hall, pp. 147–179.

6350. Sekora, John. "Freedom," in *The Oxford Companion to African American Literature.* Eds. William L. Andrews, Frances Smith Foster, and Trudier Harris. New York: Oxford University Press, pp. 297–301.

6351. _____. "Libraries and Research Centers," in *The Oxford Companion to African American Literature.* Eds. William L. Andrews, Frances Smith Foster, and Trudier Harris. New York: Oxford University Press, pp. 437–440. Mentions W briefly (p. 438).

6352. _____. "Slavery," in *The Oxford Companion to African American Literature.* Eds. William L. Andrews, Frances Smith Foster, and Trudier Harris. New York: Oxford University Press, pp. 670–673. Relates W's autobiographical writing to that of Frederick Douglass. Men-

tions also "Big Boy Leaves Home" and "The Man Who Lived Underground."

6353. Sengova, Joko. "Native Identity and Alienation in Richard Wright's *Native Son* and Chinua Achebe's *Things Fall Apart:* A Cross-Cultural Analysis." *The Mississippi Quarterly,* 50 (Spring), 329–351. Applies the formula of fear-flight-fate to each novel, especially in relation to the themes of native identity and alienation." Bigger is both representative of a universal type of alienation and a character involved in the specific situation of American racism. Sengova analyzes Bigger's speech patterns, comparing them to those of creole languages.

6354. Sernett, Milton C. *Bound for the Promised Land: African Americans and the Great Migration.* Durham: Duke University Press, pp. 123, 180–181, 188, 227. Mentions Farah Jasmine Griffin on *AH,* quotes from *TMBV,* and notes W's literary naturalism.

6355. Shatz, Adam. "Bebop and Stalinist Kitsch." *The Nation,* 264 (10 March), 25–28. Review of Michael Denning's *The Cultural Front: The Laboring of American Culture in the Twentieth Century* mentioning W briefly (p. 26).

6356. Shields, Johanna Nicol. *"Southern Writers and Their Worlds.* By Christopher Morris, Susan A. Eacker, Anne Goodwyn Jones, Bertram Wyatt-Brown, and Charles Joyner." *The Journal of Southern History,* 63 (August), 665–666. Mentions briefly W's influence on William Styron.

6357. Shields, John C. "Short Story," in *The Oxford Companion to African American Literature.* Eds. William L. Andrews, Frances Smith Foster, and Trudier Harris. New York: Oxford University Press, pp. 660–665.

6358. Shipler, David K. *A Country of Strangers: Blacks and Whites in America.* New York: Knopf, pp. 55, 205. Mentions W briefly and relates an anecdote about Haki Madhubuti reading *BB.*

6359. Siegel, Paul N. "The Conclusion of Richard Wright's *Native Son,*" in *Critical Essays on Richard Wright's Native Son.* Ed. Keneth Kinnamon. New York: G.K. Hall, pp. 94–103.

6360. Silk, John. "Racist and Antiracist Ideology in Films of the Amer-

ican South," in, *Race and Racism: Essays in Social Geography.* Ed. Peter Jackson. London: Allen S. Unwin, pp. 326–344. Mentions briefly W's racism.

6361. Sims-Wood, Janet. "Bibliography," in *The Oxford Companion to African American Literature.* Eds. William L. Andrews, Frances Smith Foster, and Trudier Harris. New York: Oxford University Press, pp. 62–63. Mentions *A Richard Wright Bibliography* and notes coverage of W in *Black American Writers, Bibliographical Essays.*

6362. Singh, Amritjit. "Harlem Renaissance," in *The Oxford Companion to African American Literature.* Eds. William L. Andrews, Frances Smith Foster, and Trudier Harris. New York: Oxford University Press, pp. 340–342.

6363. _____. "Toward an Effective Antiracism." *Race and Reason,* 3, pp. 62–70. Includes favorable discussion of W's "profound and devastating critique of the ascendancy of antiracist universalism available from within the confines of Cold War America" (p. 65).

6364. _____."The Possibilities of a Radical Consciousness: African Americans and New Immigrants," in *Multi-America: Essays on Cultural Wars and Cultural Peace.* New York: Viking, pp. 218–237. Mentions briefly *BB* (p. 224).

6365. Singh, Nikhil Pal. "Toward an Effective Antiracism." *Race and Reason,* 3, pp. 62–70. Includes commentary on W's insistence during the Cold War on the "double vision" of African Americans and the importance of antiracism. Quotes from *WML.*

6366. Skerrett, Joseph T., Jr. "Composing Bigger: Wright and the Making of *Native Son,*" in *Critical Essays on Richard Wright's Native Son.* Ed. Keneth Kinnamon. New York: G.K. Hall, pp. 104–118.

6367. Sleeper, Jim. *Liberal Racism.* New York: Viking, pp. 104, 176. Mentions W briefly.

6368. Smethurst, James. "Bill Mullen and Sherry Linkon, eds. *Radical Revisions: Rereading 1930s Culture.*" *African American Literature,* 31 (Fall), 518–520. Mentions W briefly.

6369. Smith, Barbara. "Toward a Black Feminist Criticism," in *Call and Response: The Riverside Anthology of the African American Literary Tradition.* Eds. Patricia Liggins Hill,

Bernard W. Bell, Trudier Harris, William J. Harris, R. Baxter Miller, and Sondra A. O'Neale. Boston: Houghton Mifflin, pp. 1815–1827.

6370. Smith, Sidonie Ann. "The Quest for Self-Acceptance in *I Know Why the Caged Bird Sings*," in *Readings on Maya Angelou*. Ed. Mary E. Williams. San Diego: Greenhaven Press, pp. 120–127.

6371. Smith, Valerie. "Late Twentieth Century," in *The Oxford Companion to African American Literature*. Eds. William L. Andrews, Frances Smith Foster, and Trudier Harris. New York: Oxford University Press, pp. 456–459. Mentions all of W's work except *UTC* and. Discusses W's relation with Ellison and Baldwin.

6372. Smith, Virginia Whatley. "Arnold Rampersad, ed. *Richard Wright: A Collection of Critical Essays*." *African American Review*, 31 (Spring), 148–151. Comments on each of the fifteen essays collected in this volume, finding Abdul Jan Mohammed's "The Construction of Richard Wright as Subject" to be "the most profound." Also discusses restrictions on the use of W manuscripts material at Yale.

6373. _____. "*Native Son* as a Depiction of a Carceral Society," in *Approaches to Teaching Wright's Native Son*. Ed. James A. Miller. New York: The Modern Language Association of America, pp. 95–101. Uses Foucault's *Discipline and Punish: The Birth of the Prison* as a tool for the interpretation of *NS*. W's novel preceded Foucault's work, but the latter helps students to "deepen their understanding of Wright's critique of America" (p. 101).

6374. _____. "The Search for Richard Wright: Horace Cayton's Unfinished Quest." *Richard Wright Newsletter*, 5 (Spring/Summer), 9, 11. Abstract of a 1997 CLA convention paper proclaiming the importance of Cayton's projected biography of W. "An archival biography" by Cayton "exists," she maintains.

6375. Snipes, Katherine (revised by Thomas J. Cassidy), "Richard Wright," in *Short Story Writers*, vol. 3, Ed. Frank N. Magill. Pasadena: Salem Press, pp. 985–992. In addition to analyses of "Fire and Cloud" and "The Man Who Lived Underground," Snipes provides biographical information, a statement of W's

achievements, and primary and secondary bibliographies.

6376. Snodgrass, Mary Ellen. "The Mississippi River," in her *Encyclopedia of Southern Literature*. Santa Barbara, CA: ABC-CLIO, pp. 214–225. Mentions briefly *BB* (p. 214).

6377. _____. "*Native Son*," in her *Encyclopedia of Southern Literature*. Santa Barbara, CA: ABC-CLIO, pp. 227–233. Plot summary of the novel that made its author "an internationally revered literary lion and spokesman for oppressed blacks. Includes a photograph of Bigger and Mary in the stage version.

6378. _____. "Preface," in her *Encyclopedia of Southern Literature*. Santa Barbara, CA: ABC-CLIO, pp. ix–xi. Mentions briefly W, *BB*, and *NS*.

6379. _____. "Protest Literature," in her *Encyclopedia of Southern Literature*. Santa Barbara, CA: ABC-CLIO, pp. 262–270. Includes comment on "Between the World and Me" (p. 265).

6380. _____. "Religious Fundamentalism," in her *Encyclopedia of Southern Literature*. Santa Barbara, CA: ABC-CLIO, pp. 287–290. Comments on W's family's fundamentalism as recounted in *BB* (p. 289).

6381. _____. "Wright, Richard," in her *Encyclopedia of Southern Writing*. Santa Barbara, CA: ABC-CLIO, 381–385. Biographical sketch of "a brilliant iconoclast, realist, and literary touchstone ... the sire of African American realism." Includes a photograph of W.

6382. Sollors, Werner. *Neither Black Nor White Yet Both: Thematic Explorations of Interracial Literature*. New York: Oxford University Press, pp. 55, 270, 284, 314, 412, 435, 451. Passing mention of W and *WML*, "Down by the Riverside," *NS*, *BB*, The Ethics of Living Jim Crow," and "Long Black Song." Also notes that W opposed the mulatto tradition in literature.

6383. Spack, Ruth. "The (In)Visibility of the Person(al) in Academe." *College English*, 59 (January), 9–31. Comments on a passage from *BB* that might encourage anti–Semitism (p. 23).

6384. Spencer, Jon Michael. *The New Negroes and Their Music*. Knoxville: The University of Tennessee Press, pp. 99, 137. Mentions W briefly.

6385. Spilka, Mark. *Eight Lessons in Love: A Domestic Violence Reader*. Columbia: University of Missouri Press, pp. 8, 18, 33, 269, 271. Criticizes W's Criticism of *Their Eyes Were Watching God* and accuses W of sexism in *NS*.

6386. Standley, Fred L. "David Leeming. *James Baldwin: A Biography*." *African American Review*, 31 (Summer), 339–341. Mentions W briefly (p. 340).

6387. Storhoff, Gary. "Doing the (W)right Thing: Approaching Wright and Lee," in *Approaches to Teaching Wright's Native Son*. Ed. James A. Miller. New York: The Modern Language Association of America, pp. 120–126. Arguing that "the central issue of *Native Son* [is] the enforcement of restricted space" (p. 121), Storhoff compares *NS* and Spike Lee's film, which he teaches together.

6388. Stuhr-Rommereim, Rebecca. *Autobiographies by Americans of Color: An Annotated Bibliography*. Troy, NY: Whitston, pp. 238–239. Contains an entry on *BB-AH* with some details about its publication.

6389. Takeuchi, Mikako. "In Quest of Words Toward Wakefulness: Richard Wright's *Black Boy and American Hunger*." *Hiyoshi Campus Bulletin of Keio Gijuku University: English Language and British and American Literature*, 30 (March), 95–115. Notes that W's autobiographical writings showed how language ability empowered efforts to achieve freedom.

6390. Taylor, Clyde. "Fear and Black Genius." *Black Renaissance/Renaissance Noire*, 1 (Summer/Fall), 6–7. Mentions W briefly.

6391. Terry-Morgan, Elmo. "*Noise/Funk*: Fo' Real Black Theatre on 'Da Great White Way." *African American Review*, 31 (Winter), 677–686. Mentions briefly the play *NS* (pp. 678, 681).

6392. Thernstrom, Stephan and Abigail Thernstrom. *America in Black and White: One Nation, Indivisible*. New York: Simon and Schuster, pp. 16, 43, 51–56, 121, 373. Draws on *BB-AH* for material illustrative of Jim Crow and the Great Migration. Also notes W's favorable reaction to *An American Dilemma*.

6393. Thomas, Lorenzo. "Blues Aesthetic," in *The Oxford Companion to African American Literature*.

Eds. William L. Andrews, Frances Smith Foster, and Trudier Harris. New York: Oxford University Press, pp. 87–89. Comments on W's statement of the relation of folk to literary expression in *WML*.

6394. Thompson, Julius E. "The Black Poet in Mississippi, 1900–1980," in *Africana Studies: A Disciplinary Quest for Both Theory and Method*. Ed. James L. Conyers, Jr. Jefferson, NC: McFarland, pp. 208–228. Contains a paragraph on W's early poetry (p. 212), brief mention of his haiku (p. 217), and bibliographical information (p. 225).

6395. Thompson, Julius E. "The Black Poet in Mississippi, 1900–1980," in *Africana Studies: A Disciplinary Quest for Both Theory and Method*. Ed. James L. Conyers, Jr. Jefferson, NC: McFarland, pp. 208–228. Contains a paragraph on W, noting the Marxist element in his poetry (p. 212), but also mentions his haiku (p. 214). An endnote lists some secondary sources.

6396. Toombs, Charles P. "The Confluence of Food and Identity in Gloria Naylor's *Linden Hills*: 'What We Eat Is Who We Is,'" in *The Critical Response to Gloria Naylor*. Westport, CT: Greenwood Press, pp. 88–98.

6397. Towner, Theresa M. "Black Mothers on the Dixie Limited: *As I Lay Dying* and *The Bluest Eye*," in *Unflinching Gaze: Morrison and Faulkner Re-Envisioned*. Eds. Carol A. Kolmarten, Stephen M. Ross, and Judith Bryant Wittenberg. Jackson: University Press of Mississippi, pp. 115–127. Mentions briefly Faulkner's criticism of W for being too "political" (p. 125).

6398. Tretzer, Annette. "'Let Us All Be Kissing Friends?': Zora Neale Hurston and Race Politics in Dixie." *Journal of American Studies*, 31 (April), 69–78. Mentions briefly *NS* (p. 75).

6399. Trimmer, Joseph F. "Teaching Others: A Cautionary Tale," in *Rethinking American Literature*. Eds. Lil Brannon and Brenda M. Greene. Urbana, IL: National Council of Teachers of English, pp. 249–256. Mentions briefly W and *NS* (p. 252).

6400. Tyson, Timothy B. "Civil Rights Movement," in *The Oxford Companion to African American Literature*. Eds. William L. Andrews, Frances Smith Foster, and Trudier

Harris. New York: Oxford University Press, pp. 147–152. Mentions W briefly (p. 149).

6401. Von Eschen, Penny M. *Race Against Empire: Black Americans and Anticolonialsim, 1937–1957*. Ithaca: Cornell University Press, pp. 169, 175. Quotes *CC*, notes that W was impressed by Chou En-lai, and mentions W's attendance at the artists and writers conference in Paris in 1956.

6402. Wagner, Wendy. "Stowe, Harriet Beecher," in *The Oxford Companion to African American Literature*. Eds. William L. Andrews, Frances Smith Foster, and Trudier Harris. New York: Oxford University Press, pp. 704–705. Notes that W alludes to *Uncle Tom's Cabin* in both *UTC* and *NS*.

6403. Wagner-Martin, Linda. "Richard Wright's *Uncle Tom's Children* of the Great Depression." *Richard Wright Newsletter*, 5 (Spring/Summer), 10, 11. Abstract of a 1997 American Literature Association convention paper placing W in the thirties tradition of proletarian fiction, of which he had a close knowledge. *UTC* and its protagonist are "true children of the Great Depression."

6404. _____, *The Mid-Century American Novel*. New York: Twayne, pp. 1, 17, 21, 24, 33–34, 41, 48–49, 51, 92–97, 102. In addition to brief mentions of W, Wagner-Martin praises *NS* and *BB*, but views *SH* unfavorably.

6405. Wald, Gayle. "'A Most Disagreeable Mirror': Reflections on White Identity in *Black Like Me*," in *Passing and the Fictions of Identity*. Ed. Elaine K. Ginsberg. Durham, NC: Duke University Press, pp. 151–177. Mentions briefly "The Ethics of Living Jim Crow" (p. 152).

6406. Walker, Alice. "In Search of Our Mother's Gardens," in *Literature and Ourselves: A Thematic Introduction for Readers and Writers*. Eds. Gloria Mason Henderson, Bill Day, and Sandra Stevenson Waller. Second edition. New York: Longman, pp. 1103–1110.

6407. _____. "In Search of Our Mothers' Gardens," in *The Norton Anthology of African American Literature*. Eds. Henry Louis Gates, Jr., and Nellie Y. McKay. New York: W.W. Norton, pp. 2380–2386. Reprint of 1974.

6408. Walker, F. Patton. "The

Narrator's Editorialist Voice in *The Autobiography of an Ex-Coloured Man*." *CLA Journal*, 41 (September), 70–92. Quotes Linda MacKethan mentioning W briefly (p. 91).

6409. Walker, Margaret. "Black Culture," in her *On Being Female, Black, and Free: Essays by Margaret Walker, 1932–1992*. Ed. Maryemma Graham. Knoxville: The University of Tennessee Press, pp. 64–78. Mentions W briefly (p. 68).

6410. _____. "Black Culure," in her *On Being Female, Black, and Free: Essays by Margaret Walker, 1932–1992*. Knoxville: The University of Tennessee Press, pp. 64–85. Mentions W as a recipient of the Spingarn Medal (p. 68).

6411. _____. "Discovering Our Connections: Africa Heritage, Southern Culture, and the American Experience," in her *On Being Female, Black, and Free: Essays by Margaret Walker, 1932–1992*. Ed. Maryemma Graham. Knoxville: The University of Tennessee Press, pp. 57–63. Mentions W and claims that Zora Neale Hurston influenced "Big Boy Leaves Home" (pp. 59,61).

6412. _____. "Epilogue: Race, Gender, and the Law," in her *On Being Female, Black, and Free: Essays by Margaret Walker, 1932–1992*. Ed. Maryemma Graham. Knoxville: The University of Tennessee Press, pp. 232–236. Comments on the legal process involving her biography of W (p. 235).

6413. _____. "Epilogue: Race, Gender, and the Law," in her *On Being Female, Black, and Free: Essays by Margaret Walker, 1932–1992*. Knoxville: The University of Tennessee Press, pp. 232–236. Mentions her biography of W (p. 235).

6414. _____. "Mississippi and the Nation," in her *On Being Female, Black, and Free: Essays by Margaret Walker, 1932–1992*. Ed. Maryemma Graham. Knoxville: The University of Tennessee Press, pp. 145–150. Mentions W briefly (p. 146–149).

6415. _____. "Mississippi and the Nation," in her *On Being Female, Black, and Free: Essays by Margaret Walker, 1932–1992*. Knoxville: The University of Tennessee Press, pp. 145–150. Mentions W briefly (p. 149).

6416. _____. "Natchez and Richard Wright in Southern American Literature," in her *On Being Female, Black, and Free: Essays by Margaret*

Walker, 1932–1992. Ed. Maryemma Graham. Knoxville: The University of Tennessee Press, pp. 118–122.

6417. _____. "Natchez and Richard Wright in Southern American Literature," in *On Being Female, Black and Free: Essays by Margaret Walker, 1932–1992.* Knoxville: The University of Tennessee Press, pp. 118–122. Contrasts the romantic vision of the South propagated by the New Critics to W's view of the South as "a racial hell."

6418. _____. "Of Tennessee and the River." in *On Being Female, Black, and Free: Essays by Margaret Walker, 1932–1992.* Knoxville: The University of Tennessee Press, pp. 108–117. Commenting on W's Memphis, calls him perhaps the most important black writer of the twentieth century" (p. 113).

6419. _____. "On Being Female, Black, and Free," in her *On Being Female, Black, and Free: Essays by Margaret Walker, 1932–1992.* Ed. Maryemma Graham. Knoxville: The University of Tennessee Press, pp. 3–25. Mentions W briefly (p. 5).

6420. _____. "On Being Female, Black and Free," in her *On Being Female, Black and Free.* Ed. Maryemma Graham. Knoxville: The University of Tennessee Press, pp. 3–11. States that W's salary in the WPA was $125 per month while hers was $85 per month (p. 5).

6421. _____. "Reflections on Black Women Writers," in her *On Being Female, Black, and Free: Essays by Margaret Walker, 1932–1992.* Ed. Maryemma Graham. Knoxville: The University of Tennessee Press, pp. 41–53. Claims that Zora Neale Hurston "had a profound influence" on W (p. 45) and mentions the "school of Richard Wright" (p. 46).

6422. _____. "Symbol, Myth, and Legend: Folk Elements in African American Literature," in her *On Being Female, Black, and Free: Essays by Margaret Walker, 1932–1992.* Knoxville: The University of Tennessee Press, pp. 58–63. Mentions briefly W and "Big Boy Leaves Home" (pp. 59, 61).

6423. Wall, Cheryl A. "Chronology," in her *"Sweat."* New Brunswick: Rutgers University Press, pp. 21–22. Notes W's unfavorable review of *Their Eyes Were Watching God.*

6424. _____. "Hurston, Zora

Neale," in *The Oxford Companion to African American Literature.* Eds. William L. Andrews, Frances Smith Foster, and Trudier Harris. New York: Oxford University Press, pp. 376–378. Mentions briefly W and *NS* (p. 377).

6425. _____. *"Their Eyes Were Watching God,"* in *The Oxford Companion to African American Literature.* Eds. William L. Andrews, Frances Smith Foster, and Trudier Harris. New York: Oxford University Press, p. 724. Mentions W's unfavorable review of the Hurston novel.

6426. Walton, Hanes, Jr. *African American Power and Politics: The Political Context Variable.* New York: Columbia University Press, p. 90. Mentions W briefly.

6427. Ward, Jerry W., Jr. *"Native Son:* Six Versions Seeking Interpretation," in *Approaches to Teaching Wright's Native Son.* Ed. James A. Miller. New York: The Modern Language Association of America, pp. 16–21. Compares the versions of *NS* represented in the 1939 proofs (published in the 1991 text), the 1940 text, Paul Green's 1941 dramatization and its 1968 revision, and the 1950 and 1986 film versions.

6428. _____. "Walker, Margaret," in *The Oxford Companion to African American Literature.* Eds. William L. Andrews, Francis Smith Foster, and Trudier Harris. New York: Oxford University Press, pp. 752–753. Discusses Walker's friendship with W and mentions her biography *Richard Wright: Daemonic Genius.*

6429. _____. "Wright, Richard (1908–1960," in his *Trouble the Water: 250 Years of African-American Poetry.* New York: Mentor, p. 559. Brief note emphasizing W's poetry.

6430. Warren, Kenneth W. 'The Mythic City: An Interview with Leon Forrest," in *Leon Forrest: Introductions and Interpretations.* Ed. John G. Cawelti. Bowling Green, OH: Bowling Green State University Popular Press, pp. 75–96.

6431. _____. "The Mythic City: An Interview with Leon Forrest," in *Leon Forrest: Introduction and Interpretations.* Ed. John G. Cawelti. Bowling Green: Bowling Green State University Popular Press, pp. 75–96. Forrest, unlike W, attests to the viable folk tradition in Chicago (pp. 77–78).

6432. Watson, Charles S. *The History of Southern Drama.* Lexington: The University Press of Kentucky, pp. 107, 111, 112. Mentions W, Bigger Thomas, and the play *NS* in a chapter on Paul Green.

6433. Weiss, M. Lynn. "Robert J. Butler, ed. *The Critical Response to Richard Wright." African American Review,* 31 (Summer), 337–339. Generally unfavorable review stating that the collection does not break new ground; specifically, it does not address the works of W's expatriation.

6434. Werner, Craig. "Chicago Renaissance," in *The Oxford Companion to African American Literature.* Eds. William L. Andrews, Frances Smith Foster, and Trudier Harris. New York: Oxford University Press, pp. 132–133. Notes W's key role.

6435. _____. "Gerald Early. *Daughters: On Family and Fatherhood." African American Review,* 31 (Spring), 168–169. Mentions *O* briefly.

6436. _____. *"Jazz:* Morrison and the Music of Tradition," in *Approaches to Teaching the Novels of Toni Morrison.* Eds. Nellie Y. McKay and Kathryn Earle. New York: The Modern Language Association of America, pp. 86–92. Mentions W briefly (p. 87).

6437. _____. "Leon Forrest and the AACM: The Jazz Impulse and the Legacy of the Chicago Renaissance," in *Leon Forrest: Introductions and Interpretations.* Ed. John G. Cawelti. Bowling Green, OH: Bowling Green State University Popular Press, pp. 127–151.

6438. West, Elizabeth J. "Black Nationalism," in *The Oxford Companion to African American Literature.* Eds. William L. Andrews, Frances Smith Foster, and Trudier Harris. New York: Oxford University Press, pp. 75–79. Mentions W briefly (p. 79).

6439. West, Woody. "In Defense of American Classics" *The Washington Times* (28 September), Section B, p. 7. Book review of Andrew Delbanco's *Required Reading* mentioning its essay on W.

6440. White, Craig Howard. "Federal Writers' Project," in *The Oxford Companion to African American Literature.* Eds. William L. Andrews, Frances Smith Foster, and Trudier Harris. New York: Oxford University

Press, pp. 270–271. Notes that W left his job at the Chicago Post Office to join the Federal Writers Project, allowing him time to write *NS*.

6441. White, Garrett H. "Race and the Teaching of *Native Son*," in *Approaches to Teaching Wright's Native Son*. Ed. James A. Miller. New York: The Modern Language Association of America, pp. 48–53. Advocates an emphasis on race as the central issue of the novel, utilizing a Du Boisian double-consciousness but avoiding any form of white authentication.

6442. Wiggins, William H., Jr. "Performances and Pageants," in *The Oxford Companion to African American Literature*. Eds. William L. Andrews, Frances Smith Foster, and Trudier Harris. New York: Oxford University Press, pp. 564–565. Mentions the dozens in "Big Boy Leaves Home" and notes that the title of *BB* is from a blues singer's signature.

6443. Williams, Mary E. "Maya Angelou: A Biography," in her *Readings on Maya Angelou*." San Diego: Greenhaven Press, pp. 14–29. Mentions briefly W's influence on Angelou.

6444. Williams, Patricia Robinson. "Garvey, Marcus," in *The Oxford Companion to African American Literature*. Eds. William L. Andrews, Frances Smith Foster, and Trudier Harris. New York: Oxford University Press, p. 309. Comments on W and Bigger Thomas.

6445. Williamson, Joel. "Wounds, Not Scars: Lynching, the National Conscience, and the American Historian." *The Journal of American History*, 83 (March), 1221–1253. Mentions W briefly (p. 1244).

6446. Wood, Joe. "The Soloist: Albert Murray's Blues People," in *Conversations with Albert Murray*. Ed. Roberta S. Maguire. Jackson: University Press of Mississippi, pp. 94–109.

6447. Woodson, Carter G. "Book Reviews," in *Langston Hughes: The Contemporary Reviews*. Ed. Tish Dace. Cambridge: Cambridge University Press, p. 266.

6448. Worley, Demetrice A., and Jesse Perry, Jr. "Discussion Questions; Writing Topics," in their *African American Literature: An Anthology*. Second edition. Lincolnwood, IL: National Textbook Company, p. 414. Study aids for "The Man Who Was Almost a Man."

6449. _____. "Richard Wright," in their *African American Literature: An Anthology*. Second edition. Lincolnwood, IL: National Textbook Company, p. 404. Biographical headnote to "The Man Who Was Almost a Man."

6450. Wright, W.D. *Black Intellectuals, Black Cognition, and a Black Aesthetic*. Westport, CT: Praeger, pp. 145, 152, 153, 168. Quotes from "Blueprint for Negro Writing" (p. 152) and mentions *O* and *SH*.

6451. Wyatt-Brown, Bertram. "The Mask of Obedience: Male Slave Psychology in the Old South," in *Haunted Bodies: Gender and Southern Texts*. Eds. Anne Goodwyn Jones and Susan V. Donaldson. Charlottesville: University Press of Virginia, pp. 23–55. Comments briefly on W and *BB* (pp. 44, 54).

6452. Yaeger, Patricia. "Beyond the Hummingbird: Southern Women Writers and the Southern Gargantua," in *Haunted Bodies: Gender and Southern Texts*. Eds. Anne Goodwyn Jones and Susan V. Donaldson. Charlottesville: University of Virginia Press, pp. 287–318. Mentions W briefly (p. 287).

6453. Yan, Zhang. "I Wish I Had Met Richard Wright at Bandung in 1955 (Reflections on a Conference Attended by Both Wright and the Author)." *The Mississippi Quarterly*, 50 (Spring), 277–287. A Chinese journalist who attended the Bandung Conference, Zhang Yan presents an account closely parallel to W's in *CC*, which he did not read until 1995. He agrees with W's assessment of the importance of the conference and of Zhou Enlai's successful efforts at pacification and conciliation.

6454. Young, Reggie. "Black Stereotypes," in *The Oxford Companion to African American Literature*. Eds. William L. Andrews, Frances Smith Foster, and Trudier Harris. New York: Oxford University Press, pp. 698–701. Contains a paragraph on Bigger Thomas, "inscribed in violence, hatred, and revolt" (p. 700).

6455. Young, Stephen. "African American: Literature." *Society for the Study of Southern Literature* (November), 8. Lists *A Richard Wright Reader*.

6456. _____. "Requests for Information." *Society for the Study of Southern Literature Newsletter* (April), 4. Relays a request from Jerry Ward for information about W projects for the *Richard Wright* Newsletter.

6457. Zimmerman, Brett. "A Catalogue of Rhetorical Terms from American Literature and Oratory." *Style*, 31 (Winter), 730–759. Uses examples from *NS* to illustrate *Adynata* (p. 736), *Enthymeme* (p. 749), and *Polysyndeton* (pp. 755–756). Also analyzes Buckley's "devious use of rhetorical devices" in Book III.

1998

6458. Ailey, Alvin, James Baldwin, Romare Bearden, and Albert Murray. "To Hear Another Language," in *Conversations with Albert Murray*. Ed. Roberta S. Maguire.

Jackson: University Press of Mississippi, pp. 25–45.

6459. Albright, Angela. "*Native Son* by Richard Wright," in *Encyclopedia of the Novel*. Ed. Paul Schel-

linger. Chicago: Fitzroy Dearborn, pp. 911–912. Discusses the reception of the novel as well as its background. Includes a brief biography.

6460. Alexander, Allen. "The

Fourth Face: The Image of God in Toni Morrison's *The Bluest Eye*." *African American Review*, 32 (Summer), 293–303. Mentions briefly W and *BB* (p. 293).

6461. Alexander, Edward. *Irving Howe: Socialist, Critic, Jew.* Bloomington: Indiana University Press, pp. xiv, 121–122, 124, 125. Discusses the controversy with Ellison over Howe's essay "Black Boys and Native Sons." Also notes that Howe made W a contributing editor of *Dissent* in 1959.

6462. Allen, Carol. *Black Women Intellectuals: Strategies of Nation, Family, and Neighborhood in the Works of Pauline Hopkins, Jessie Fauset, and Marita Bonner.* New York: Garland, pp. 13, 77, 94. Mentions briefly W, *NS*, and Bigger Thomas.

6463. Als, Hilton. "The Enemy Within: The Making and Unmaking of James Baldwin." *The New Yorker*, 74 (16 February), 72–80. Includes discussion of W's relation to Baldwin.

6464. Anderson, Jervis. *Bayard Rustin: Troubles I've Seen.* Berkeley: University of California Press, pp. 104, 157.

6465. Andrews, William L. "Narrating Slavery," in *Teaching African American Literature: Theory and Practice.* Eds. Maryemma Graham, Sharon Pineault-Burke, and Marianna White Davis. New York: Routledge, pp. 12–30. Includes commentary on *BB*, especially in relation to Douglass and Angelou (pp. 13, 20, 24–29).

6466. Anon. "Abraham Chapman, editor. *Black Voices: An Anthology of Afro-American Literature*," in *Literature and Language: Books for Courses 1998–1999.* New York: Penguin Putnam, p. 10. Publisher's listing mentioning W briefly.

6467. Anon. *African American Literature.* New York: Harper Collins, 8 pp. Publisher's brochure with annotated listings of paperback editions of *EM, PS, O, UTC, NS,* and *BB.* Blurbs are included for *EM, UTC, NS,* and *BB.*

6468. Anon. "*The American Short Story*," in *The Short Story: Collections for Spring 1999 Courses.* New York: Bantam Doubleday Dell, p. [5]. Publisher's notice of a collection edited by Calvin Skaggs including "Almos' a Man."

6469. Anon. "*The Apocalypse in African-American Fiction*," in *American Literature from University Press of Florida.* Gainesville. University Press of Florida, pp. 4–5. Mentions briefly *NS*.

6470. Anon. "Approaches to Teaching World Literature." *PMLA*, 113 (September), 1036–1037. Lists the volume on *NS* edited by James A. Miller.

6471. Anon. "*Approaches to Teaching Wright's Native Son*," in *Approaches to Teaching World Literature.* New York: The Modern Language Association of America, p. 53. Publisher's announcement. The cover of this catalog contains a photograph of W as Bigger in the film *NS*.

6472. Anon. *Bibliographic Guide to Black Studies 1997.* New York: G.K. Hall, p. 484. Lists seven items s.v. Wright, Richard, 1908–1960.

6473. Anon. "The Black Scholar Book Reviews." *The Black Scholar*, 28 (Spring), 82–87. Includes a review of Lloyd L Brown's *Iron City* mentioning W's brutal yet popular realism."

6474. Anon. "Brief Mention." *American Literature*, 70 (September), 691–702. Includes a notice of *A Place Called Mississippi* mentioning W briefly (p. 700).

6475. Anon. "Brief Mention." *American Literature*, 70 (December), 921–933. Lists James A. Miller's *Approaches to Teaching Wright's Native Son* (p. 927).

6476. Anon. "Chronology," in *James Baldwin: Collected Essays.* New York: The Library of America, pp. 845–859. Records meeting W and seeing him in France.

6477. Anon. "Classics Are Perennial." *English Journal*, 88 (September), 5. Publisher's advertisement including *BB* and *NS*.

6478. Anon. "Classics Are Perennial." *PMLA*, 113 (November), 1546. Publisher's advertisement listing *BB* and *NS*.

6479. Anon. "Contributors." *MELUS*, 23 (Fall), 245–247. Mentions a forthcoming article on W by Anthony Dawahare.

6480. Anon. "Cumulative Indexes," in *Drama Criticism.* Ed. Lawrence Trudeau. Detroit: Gale, 413–530. Includes a listing of reference books treating W published by Gale (p. 510).

6481. Anon. "Doctoral Dissertations in American Studies, 1996–1997." *American Quarterly*, 50 (June), 447–469. Includes an abstract of a doctoral dissertation by Amy Elizabeth Carreiro treating W and others.

6482. Anon. "Dorothy Abbott and Susan Koppelman, editors. *The Signet Classic Book of Southern Short Stories*," in *Literature and Language: Books for Courses 1998–1999.* New York: Penguin Putnam, p. 39. Publisher's listing mentioning briefly "Big Boy Leaves Home."

6483. Anon. "Dorothy West, Writer of the Harlem Renaissance Era, Dies in Boston at Age 91." *Jet*, 94 (7 September), 53. Obituary mentioning W briefly.

6484. Anon. "Felgar, Robert. 'Understanding Richard Wright's *Black Boy*,'" *The Black Scholar*, 28 (Fall/Winter), 56 Brief notice emphasizing the work's pedagogical purpose.

6485. Anon. "*Emerge's* Recommended Reading." *Emerge*, 9 (January), 83. Includes a brief notice of *Richard Wright and the Library Card.*

6486. Anon. "Greenwood Press." *English Journal*, 88 (November), 105. Contains a publisher's notice of Robert Felgar's *Understanding Richard Wright's Black Boy.*

6487. Anon. "Hurston/Wright Foundation Program." *Richard Wright Newsletter*, 6 (Fall/Winter), 3. Reports a 15 November 1997 screening of *Richard Wright-Black Boy* at the Virginia Museum of Fine Arts in Richmond followed by a panel discussion with Julia Wright, Madison Lacy, and Jerry Ward. The event was sponsored by the foundation begun by Marita Golden.

6488. Anon. "*In Search of Africa* Manthia Diawara," in *Harvard University Press Fall/Winter 1998.* Cambridge, MA: Harvard University Press, p. 20. Mentions W briefly.

6489. Anon. "Kids' Books That Tell Our Story." *Essence*, 29 (May), 182. Includes a brief notice of William Miller's *Richard Wright and the Library Card.*

6490. Anon. "More Volumes in the Approaches to Teaching World Literature Series," in *New Titles Winter-Spring 1998.* New York: Modern Language Association, pp. 7–9. Lists James A. Miller's volume on *NS*.

6491. Anon. "Native Son," in *Films for the Humanities & Sciences.* Princeton, NJ: Films for the Humanities & Sciences, p. 28. Catalog notice of a video on *NS*.

6492. Anon. "Native Son," in *Films for the Humanities & Sciences: American Literature*. Princeton, NJ: Films for the Humanities & Sciences, p. 7. Video catalog entry.

6493. Anon. "*New*: Africa to America to Paris: The Migration of Black Writers," in *Films for the Humanities & Sciences: American Literature*. Princeton, NJ: Films for the Humanities & Sciences, p. 6. Video catalog entry mentioning W briefly.

6494. Anon. "*New*: Native Son," in *Films for the Humanities & Sciences*. Princeton, NJ: Films for the Humanities & Sciences, p. 33. Distributor's notice.

6495. Anon. "Notes on Publications." *Richard Wright Newsletter*, 6 (Fall/Winter), 3. Notice of *Approaches to Teaching Wright's Native Son* edited by James A. Miller.

6496. Anon. "Novelist Dies." *USA Today* (18 August), p. 1.D. Obituary of Dorothy West mentioning W briefly.

6497. Anon. "Wright Richard," in *The Cambridge Biographical Encyclopedia*. Second edition. Ed. David Crystal. Cambridge: Cambridge University Press, p. 1011. Biographical sketch mentioning *NS*, *BB*, and "The Man Who Lived Underground."

6498. Anon. "The originals of Hemingway, Fitzgerald, Faulkner, Steinbeck and more … are available again." *The Atlantic Monthly*, 281 (February), 23. Advertisement for facsimiles of first editions, including *NS*.

6499. Anon. "Oxford University Press." *American Literature*, 70 (September), end matter. Contains a publisher's notice of Claudia Tate's *Psychoanalysis and Black Novels* mentioning W briefly.

6500. Anon. "Postage Stamps for World Literacy." *Richard Wright Newsletter*, 6 (Fall/Winter), 3. Notes that Ghana and Uganda issued stamps honoring six African American writers, including W.

6501. Anon. "Preliminaries." *MELUS*, 23 (Fall), 1–2. Includes comment on Floyd Ogburn's essay on W's haiku.

6502. Anon. "*Psychoanalysis and Black Novels: Desire and the Protocols of Race*, by Claudia Tate." *Virginia Quarterly Review*, 74 (Autumn), 122. Favorable notice mentioning W briefly.

6503. Anon. "Recent Scholarship." *The Journal of American History*, 85 (September), 776–844. Lists articles on W by Michel Fabre (p. 796) and Zhang Han (p. 799).

6504. Anon. "*Richard Wright, Daemonic Genius: A Portrait of the Man, a Critical Look at His Work*," in *Daedalus Books Early Summer 1998*. Hyattsville, MD: *Daedalus Books*, p. 16. Remainder catalog notice.

6505. Anon. *The South: Its Land and Its Literature*. Natchez: Copiah-Lincoln Community College, 5 pp. Flyer of the ninth annual Natchez Literary Celebration listing papers on "From the Mississippi Earth: The Autobiographical Voices of Hollis Watkins, Endesha Ida Mae Holland, Richard Wright, and Anne Moody" by Jerry W. Ward Jr. and "Blues Language in the Works of the Mississippi Writers Richard, Muddy Waters, and Sterling Plumpp" by Sterling Plumpp on 6 June.

6506. Anon. "*The Suburb of Dissent: Cultural Politics in the United States and Canada During the 1930s. Caren Irr*," in *Duke University Press: Books & Journals Fall & Winter 1998*. Durham, NC: Duke University Press, pp. 26–27. Publisher's announcement noting that Irr "highlights works by Richard Wright" and others.

6507. Anon. "Suzanne Jones. *Growing Up in the South: An Anthology of Modern Southern Literature*," in *Literature and Language: Books for Courses 1998–1999*. New York: Penguin Putnam, p. 40. Publisher's listing mentioning briefly "The Man Who Was Almost a Man."

6508. Anon. "Tate, Claudia. *Psychoanalysis and Black Novels*." *The Black Scholar*, 28 (Summer), 64. Brief review noting that W is among the authors discussed.

6509. Anon. *Teacher's Video Company: English 1999*. Scottsdale, AZ: Teacher's Video, p. 65. Catalog entries for four videos on W: *Writing Is His Weapon, Almos' a Man, America's Dream*, and *Native Son*.

6510. Anon. "*The Black Scholar* Book Reviews." *The Black Scholar*, 28 (Spring), 82–87. Includes a review of Lloyd L. Brown's *Iron City* mentioning W's brutal yet popular realism and *BB* (p. 83).

6511. Anon. "Three Books by Black Authors Among 100 Best English-Language Novels of the 20th Century." *Jet*, 94 (10 August), pp. 35–36. Reports that *NS* placed twentieth in the Modern Library poll.

6512. Anon. "University Press of Mississippi." *African American Review*, 32 (Winter), [719]. Publisher's list including *Gertude Stein and Richard Wright: The Poetics and Politics of Modernism* by M. Lynn Weiss.

6513. Anon. "University Press of Mississippi." *PMLA*, 113 (November), 1613. Publisher's advertisement listing *Gertrude Stein and Richard Wright: The Poetics and Politics of Modernism* by M. Lynn Weiss.

6514. Anon. "Wright News: New Marker for Richard Wright in Natchez." *Richard Wright Newsletter*, 6 (Spring/Summer), 3. Announces the marker unveiled on 20 February 1998 at the house at 20 E. Woodlawn Street, where W lived briefly with his maternal grandparents.

6515. Anon. "Wright, Richard," in *The American Desk Encyclopedia*. New York: Oxford University Press, pp. 877–878. Brief entry mentioning *NS* and *BB*.

6516. Anon. "Wright, Richard," in *The Cambridge Biographical Encyclopedia*. Ed. David Crystal. Cambridge University Press, p. 101) Biographical sketch mentioning *NS*, *BB* and "The Man Who Lived Underground."

6517. Anon. "Young Adult Literature." *English Journal*, 87 (January), 102–107. Includes a brief statement of the theme of *BB* (p. 104).

6518. Applebome, Peter. "Beating a Dead Mule, Partly in Fun." *The New York Times* (13 June), pp. B7, B9. Mentions W briefly (p. B7).

6519. Arensberg, Liliane. "Death as a Metaphor of Self in *I Know Why the Caged Bird Sings*," in *Maya Angelou's I Know Why the Caged Bird Sings*. Ed. Harold Bloom. Philadelphia: Chelsea House, pp. 31–46.

6520. Aronson, Marilyn Carlson. "Black Portraits in African-American Literature: A Perspective from 1920–1996, Including the Midwest." *Social Science Journal*, 35, no. 4, 635–644. Includes a paragraph on W commenting on "Fire and Cloud," and "Black [sic] Boy Leaves Home" (p. 638). Also mentions *NS*, *UTC*, and *BB*.

6521. Asante, Molefi K., and Mark J. Matson. *The African-American Atlas: Black History and Culture—An Illustrated Reference*. New York: Macmillan, p. 148.

6522. Atkinson, Yvonne, and Philip Page. "'I Been Worried Sick

About You Too, Macon': Toni Morrison, the South, and the Oral Tradition." *Studies in the Literary Imagination*, 31 (Fall), 97–107. Mentions briefly *BB* (pp. 106, 107).

6523. Ayers, Edward L. "When the North Is the South: Life in the Netherlands." *Southern Cultures*, 4, no. 4, 45–49. Mentions the availability of books by W in Groningen (p. 47).

6524. Baker, Houston A., Jr. "Modernism and the Harlem Renaissance," in *Locating American Studies: The Evolution of a Discipline*. Ed. Lucy Maddox. Baltimore: The Johns Hopkins University Press, pp. 261–274. Mentions W briefly (p. 272).

6525. _____. "Yes, Virginia, There Is an Answer." *College Literature*, 25 (Winter), 184–189. Mentions briefly W and *NS* (p. 185).

6526. Baker, Lee D. *From Savage to Negro: Anthropology and the Construction of Race, 1896–1954.* Berkeley: University of California Press, pp. 236, 310. Lists *NS* in a chronology and in the bibliography.

6527. Baldwin, James. "Alas, Poor Richard," in his *Collected Essays*. New York: The Library of America, pp. 247–268.

6528. _____. "Everybody's Protest Novel," in his *Collected Essays*. New York: The Library of America, pp. 11–18.

6529. _____. "History as Nightmare," in his *Collected Essays*. New York: The Library of America, pp. 579–581.

6530. _____. "Many Thousands Gone," in his *Collected Essays*. New York: The Library of America, pp. 19–35.

6531. _____. "Notes for a Hypothetical Novel: An Address" in his *Collected Essays*. New York: The Library of America, pp. 221–223.

6532. _____. "*Notes of a Native Son*," in his *Collected Essays*. New York: Library of America, pp. 63–87.

6533. _____. "Princes and Powers," in his *Collected Essays*. New York: The Library of America, pp. 143–169.

6534. _____. *The Devil Finds Work*," in his *Collected Essays*. The Library of America, pp. 478–572.

6535. Balfour, Lawrie. "A Most Disagreeable Mirror: Race Consciousness as Double Consciousness." *Political Theory*, 26 (June),

346–369. Includes discussion of James Baldwin's discussion of Bigger Thomas in "Many Thousands Gone" (pp. 355, 357, 359, 367).

6536. Banks, Michelle. "Oprah Winfrey, 1954– , Talk Show Host, Actress, Producer, Entrepreneur," in *Black Heroes of the 20th Century*, Ed. Jessie Carney Smith. Detroit: Visible Ink, pp. 673–679. Mentions briefly Winfrey's role in the second film version of *NS* (p. 678).

6537. Baraka, Amiri. "Paul Robeson and the Theater." *Black Renaissance/Renaissance Noire*, 2 (Fall/Winter), 12–34. Mentions W briefly (p. 23).

6538. Barnes, Deborah H. "'The Elephant and the Race Problem': Sterling A. Brown and Arthur P. Davis as Cultural Conservators." *Callaloo*, 21 (Winter), 985–997. Mentions W briefly (p. 989).

6539. Baym, Nina. "American Literature Between the Wars, 1914–1945," in *The Norton Anthology of American Literature* Eds. Baym, Wayne Franklin, Ronald Gottesman, Laurence B. Holland, David Kalstone, Jerome Klinkowitz, Arnold Krupat, Francis Murphy, Hershel Parker, William H. Pritchard, and Patricia B. Holland. Fifth edition. Vol. 2. New York: W.W. Norton, pp. 911–921.

6540. _____. "Richard Wright," in *The Norton Anthology of American Literature*. Eds. Baym, Wayne Franklin, Ronald Gottesman, Laurence B. Holland, David Kalstone, Jerome Klinkowitz, Arnold Krupat, Francis Murphy, Hershel Parker, William H. Pritchard, and Patricia B. Wallace. Fifth edition. Vol. 2. New York: W.W. Norton, p. 2878.

6541. _____. "Richard Wright, 1908–1960," in *The Norton Anthology of American Literature*. Eds. Baym, Wayne Franklin, Ronald Gottesman, Laurence B. Holland, David Kalstone, Jerome Klinkowitz, Arnold Krupat, Francis Murphy, Hershel Parker, William H. Pritchard, and Patricia B. Wallace. New York: W.W. Norton, pp. 1756–1757.

6542. Beauvoir, Simone de. *A Transatlantic Love Affair: Letter to Nelson Algren*. New York: The New Press, pp. 28, 31, 74, 84, 149, 161, 168, 173, 176, 178, 191, 198–199, 212, 248, 250, 260, 289, 295, 311, 325, 360, 375, 376, 390, 398, 399–400, 417, 421, 423, 439, 454, 463, 465, 467, 479, 495, 501, 523, 529, 540,

543. Letters from February 1947 to November 1964 contain numerous references to W, his writing, his activities, and his family. Sartre and de Beauvoir dined with W and Ellen frequently, and Ellen and de Beauvoir were close friends. De Beauvoir comments on *NS*, *BB*, the film *NS* (which she liked), *O* (meaningless, crazy, stupid story"), the RDR and W's participation, and other political matters.

6543. Bell, Bernard W. "Voices of Double Consciousness in African American Fiction: Charles W. Chesnutt, Zora Neale Hurston, Dorothy West, and Richard Wright," in *Teaching African American Literature: Theory and Practice*. Eds. Maryemma Graham, Sharon Pineault-Burke, and Marianna White Davis. New York: Routledge, pp. 132–140. Includes a brief analysis of "Bright and Morning Star," in which "the voices of race, gender, and class are most dramatically and dialectically balanced" (p. 139). Mentions W elsewhere (pp. 133, 134, 135, 138).

6544. Bellow, Saul. "Ralph Ellison in Tivoli." *Partisan Review*, 65 (Fall), 524–528. Bellow recalls discussing W with Ellison (p. 525).

6545. Berlant, Lauren. "Poor Eliza." *American Literature*, 70 (September), 635–668. Comments briefly on James Baldwin's attitude toward *NS* (p. 658).

6546. Bernstein, David N. *Teacher's Video Company: English 1998*. Scottsdale, AZ: Teacher's Video, p. 65. Includes distributor's catalog notices of four videos on W together with reproductions of their jackets: the 1986 film of *NS*, "Richard Wright: Writing Is His Weapon," "America's Dream" with Snipes and Glover acting out "several short stories," and the 1976 dramatization of "Almos' a Man."

6547. Birkerts, Sven. Untitled excerpt, in *John Edgar Wideman: A Study of the Short Fiction*. Ed. Keith E. Byerman. New York: Twayne, pp. 106–110.

6548. Blockson, Charles L. *Damn Rare: The Memoirs of an African-American Bibliophile*. Tracy, CA: Quantum Leap, pp. 35, 187, 188, 194, 195, 200, 201, 269, 320, 321. Mentions W frequently in the long section on "Black Paris: The African Americans in Europe Writers Conference (pp. 185–198). Also mentions or lists *NS* and *BB*.

6549. Bone, Robert. "Richard Wright's Phototext: *Twelve Million Black Voices.*" *Richard Wright Newsletter*, 6 (Fall/Winter), 16. Abstract of a paper arguing that *TMBV* "is the central document of the Chicago Renaissance," heavily indebted to the Chicago School of Sociology.

6550. Bonetti, Kay. "Interview with John Edgar Wideman," in *Conversations with John Edgar Wideman*. Ed. Bonnie TuSmith. Jackson: University Press of Mississippi, pp. 42–61.

6551. Bongie, Chris. *Islands and Exiles: The Creole Identities of Post/Colonial Literature*. Stanford, CA: Stanford University Press, p. 19. Quotes Paul Gilroy quoting W.

6552. Booker, M. Keith. "Proletarian Novel: Socialist Realism in the United States and Great Britain," in *Encyclopedia of the Novel*. Ed. Paul Schellinger. Chicago: Fitzroy Dearborn, pp. 1042–1045. Mentions briefly *NS*.

6553. Boris, Eileen. "'You Wouldn't Want One of 'Em Dancing with Your Wife': Racialized Bodies on the Job in World War II." *American Quarterly*, 50 (March), 77–108. Mentions briefly *NS* (p. 100).

6554. Bourne, Stephen. *Black in the British Frame: Black People in British Film and Television 1896–1996*. London: Cassell. Mentions briefly a West End production of the play *NS* in 1948.

6555. Bracken, James K. *Reference Works in British and American Literature*. Englewood, CO: Libraries Unlimited, p. 579. Describes *Richard Wright: A Primary Bibliography* by Charles T. Davis and Michel Fabre and *A Richard Wright Bibliography: Fifty Years of Criticism and Commentary* by Keneth Kinnamon.

6556. Bradley, David, and Shelley Fisher Fishkin. *The Encyclopedia of Civil Rights in America*. Vol. 2 Armonk, NY: M.E. Sharpe, p. 541. Mentions briefly *NS*.

6557. Brainard, Dulcy. "*Haiku: This Other World.*" *Publisher's Weekly*, 245 (27 July), p. 71. Review, generally favorable, of the collection by "one of our all-time great writers."

6558. Braxton, Joanne M. "A Song of Transcendence: Maya Angelou," in *Maya Angelou's I Know Why the Caged Bird Sings*. Ed. Harold Bloom. Philadelphia: Chelsea House, pp. 93–110.

6559. Bray, Rosemary L. "An Elo-quent, Pitiless Prophet." *The American Scholar*, 67 (Spring), 162–164. Mentions briefly Baldwin's "bitter challenge to Richard Wright in 'Everybody's Protest Novel'" (p. 162).

6560. Brown, Mary Ellen, and Bruce A. Rosenberg, eds. *Encyclopedia of Folklore and Literature*. Santa Barbara, CA: ABC-CLIO, p. 676. Mentions briefly *BB*.

6561. Brucker, Carl. "*The Outsider*," in *Cyclopedia of Literary Characters*. Ed. A.J. Sobczak. Pasadena, CA: Salem Press, pp. 1441–1442. Lists and Identifies ten of the characters of the novel.

6562. Budick, Emily Miller. *Blacks and Jews in Literary Conversation*. New York: Cambridge University Press, pp. 21, 23, 25, 27, 28, 30, 31, 33, 34, 41, 42–43, 44, 46, 47, 52, 168, 169, 233. Mentions W and *NS* as they figure in literary disputes among Ralph Ellison, Irving Howe, Stanley Edgar Hyman, James Baldwin, and Cynthia Ozick. Declines to treat Boris Max because W's treatment of him does "not lift Jewish-black relations, off the social axis into the realm of myth, and psychohistory (p. 169).

6563. Buell, Lawrence. "Circling the Spheres: A Dialogue." *American Literature*, 70 (September), 465–490. Comments briefly on the mutual admiration of W and Gertrude Stein (p. 468) and on *NS*, *O*, and "The Man Who Lived Underground" (pp. 470–471).

6564. Butler, Johnnella E. "African American Studies and the 'Warring Ideals': The Color Line Meets the Borderlands," in *Race and Reason*, 4, pp. 30–35. Quotes Henry Louis Gates, Jr. on W's identification with the West (see 1992).

6565. Butler, Robert. *Contemporary African American Fiction: The Open Journey*. Cranbury, NJ: Fairleigh Dickinson University Press, pp. 13, 16, 18–19, 22, 23–40, 41, 72, 135, 150. In a chapter on *Their Eyes Were Watching God* and *NS*, Butler calls them both "stunted narratives" because American social conditions prevent their protagonists from the "open motion" they desire. But Bigger does achieve psychological freedom in "the open spaces of the self" (p. 40) at the end of the novel. Comments also on *BB*.

6566. _____. "Ralph Ellison. *Flying Home and Other Stories.*" *African American Review*, 32 (Spring), 164–167. Review emphasizing W's influence on Ellison's early fiction.

6567. _____. "Teaching *Native Son* in Prison." *Richard Wright Newsletter*, 6 (Fall/Winter), 4–5. Relates teaching *Native Son* and three other novels in a freshman composition course at Wyoming Correctional Facility in Western New York in 1997, citing strong and perceptive student responses to the novel, especially on the issue of free will vs. determinism.

6568. _____. "Ralph Ellison. *Flying Home and Other Stories.* Ed. John F. Callahan." *African American Review*, 32 (Spring), 164–167. Review mentioning W briefly.

6569. Byerman, Keith E. *John Edgar Wideman: A Study of the Short Fiction*. New York: Twayne, p. ix. Mentions W briefly.

6570. Calloway, Catherine. "Fiction: The 1930's to the 1960's," in *American Literary Scholarship: An Annual:* Ed. David J. Nordloh. Durham: Duke University Press, pp. 305–334. Includes comments on work on W by Peter Carafiol, Yoshinobu Hakutani, Sitamon Mubaraka, Timothy Caron, Chimalum Nwanko, Helen Jaskowski, James Olney (pp. 309, 311).

6571. Campbell, James. "Very Poor Pilgrims." *The Times Literary Supplement*, No. 5027 (6 August), p. 34. Review of *I Was Born a Slave* mentioning W briefly.

6572. Carmichael, Jacqueline Miller. *Trumpeting a Fiery Sound: History and Folklore in Margaret Walker's Jubilee*. Athens: The University of Georgia Press, pp. 9, 10, 33, 46, 72, 110, 111, 117, 122, 132. Mentions briefly W and the Chicago literary scene (p. 9), calls him a male chauvinist, coments on Ellen Wright's suit, and discusses the making of *Richard Wright: Daemonic Genius*.

6573. Carter, Linda M. "August Wilson, 1945– , Playwright, Poet," in *Black Heroes of the 20th Century*. Ed. Jessie Carney Smith. Detroit: Visible Ink, pp. 667–673. Biographical sketch mentioning W briefly (p. 668).

6574. Castillo, Susan. "Yoshinobu Hakutani, *Richard Wright and Racial Discourse.*" *Journal of American Studies*, 32 (August), 340–341. Mixed review praising Hakutani's comparative perspective but criticizing his failure to show that W himself was "a product of ... discursive practices." Also, Hakutani uncritically identifies with his subject.

6575. Chadwick-Joshua, Jocelyn. *The Jim Dilemma: Reading Race in Huckleberry Finn.* Jackson: University Press of Mississippi, p. 25. Mentions briefly *NS.*

6576. Champion, Laurie, and Bruce A. Glasrud. "African Americans in the West: A Short Story Tradition." *The Journal of Big Bend Studies,* 10, 221–242. Mentions briefly *UTC* (p. 227), Ellison's comment that he and W were "divided by geography" (p. 229), *NS* and "How 'Bigger' Was Born" (p. 242).

6577. Ciraulo, Dina. "Narrative Style in Oscar Micheaux's *Within Our Gates.*" *Wide Angle,* 20 (October), 75–91. Quotes Cornel West quoting from *TMBV.*

6578. Clarence, Judy. "Wright, Richard. *Haiku: This Other World.*" *Library Journal,* 123 (15 September), 84. Favorable notice pointing out the collection's "melancholy air," perhaps a reflection of Wright's failing health and expatriate status.

6579. Clarke, George Elliott. "Contesting a Model Blackness: A Meditation on African-Canadian African Americanism, or The Structures of African Canadianité." *Essays on Canadian Writing.* No. 63 (Spring), pp. 12–13, 29, 44–45. Quotes from Margolies's "The Letters of Richard Wright": "The Western World must make up its mind whether it hates colored people more than it hates Communists, or does it hate Communists more than it hates colored people.

6580. Cliff, Michelle. "Telling It on the Mountain." *The Nation,* 266 (11 May), 24, 26–30. Review of James Baldwin's *Collected Essays* and *Early Novels and Stories* mentioning W, Bigger, and *NS.*

6581. Coleman, James W. Untitled excerpt, in *John Edgar Wideman: A Study of the Short Fiction.* Ed. Keith E. Byerman. New York: Twayne, pp. 105–106.

6582. _____. "Interview with John Edgar Wideman," in *Conversations with John Edgar Wideman.* Ed. Bonnie TuSmith. Jackson: University Press of Mississippi, pp. 62–80.

6583. Coles, Yolanda Robinson. "Books." *American Visions,* 12 (December–January), 34. Includes a brief notice of *Richard Wright and the Library Card* by William Miller.

6584. Collier, Eugenia. "Sterling's Way." *Callaloo,* 21 (Winter), 884–887. Mentions W briefly (p. 884).

6585. Collins, Patricia Hill. *Fighting Words: Black Women and the Search for Justice.* Minneapolis: University of Minnesota Press, pp. 176–177. Contrasts briefly the work of W and Zora Neale Hurston.

6586. Coon, Katherine Driscoll. "'A Rip in the Tent': Teaching (African) American Literature," in *Teaching African American Literature: Theory and Practice.* Eds. Maryemma Graham, Sharon Pineault-Burke, and Marianna White Davis. New York: Routledge, pp. 31–51. Discusses teaching "Bright and Morning Star" and *NS* in a private high school (pp. 37–38) and mentions W elsewhere (p. 34).

6587. Cowley, Malcolm. "'Not Men': A Natural History of American Naturalism," in *Documents of American Realism and Naturalism.* Ed. Donald Pizer. Carbondale: Southern Illinois University Press, pp. 225–238.

6588. Cronin, Gloria L. "Introduction: Going to the Far Horizon," in her *Critical Essays on Zora Neale Hurston.* New York: G.K. Hall, pp. 1–29. Mentions briefly W's "painful naturalism" (p. 6) and his review of *Their Eyes Were Watching God* (p. 9), and reprints "Between Laughter and Tears" (pp. 75–76).

6589. Crouch, Stanley, "Some Words about Albert Murray," in his *Always in Pursuit: Fresh American Perspectives, 1995–1997.* New York: Pantheon Books, pp. 132–178. Mentions W briefly (p. 135).

6590. _____. "Two on the Money," in his *Always in Pursuit: Fresh American Perspectives, 1995–1997.* New York: Pantheon Books, pp. 114–116. Favorable review of *BB/AH* and Ellison's *Shadow and Act.* Praises W's criticism of Communists.

6591. Davidson, Cathy N. "Preface: No More Separate Spheres!" *American Literature,* 70 (September), 443–463. Mentions the treatment of W, Baldwin, and the theme of sentimentality in Lauren Berlant's essay in this special issue (p. 455).

6592. Davis, Angela Y. "Art on the Frontline: Mandate for a People's Culture," in her *The Angela Y. Davis Reader.* Ed. Joy James. Malden, MA: Blackwell, pp. 235–247.

6593. _____. "Art on the Frontline: Mandate for a People's Culture," in *The Angela Y. Davis Reader.* Ed. Joy James. Malden, MA: Blackwell, pp. 235–247.

6594. Davis, Lennard J. "Journalism and the novel. Ed. Paul Schellinger. Chicago: Fitzray Dearborn, pp. 850–851.

6595. Davis, Thadious M. "A Female Face: Or, Masking the Masculine in African American Fiction Before Richard Wright," in *Teaching African American Literature: Theory and Practice.* Eds. Maryemma Graham, Sharon Pineault–Burke, and Marianna White Davis. New York: Routledge, pp. 98–131. Explains "Wright's impact on African American fiction … not by a direct examination of his texts, but rather by presenting one formulation of a female face and an unmasking of the male in selected texts before the advent of Wright, who … retains a 'Black-Southern-Male-in-the-Age-of-Jim-Crow writerly perspective'" (p. 99). Also compares *TMBV* and Langston Hughes's and Roy De Carava's *The Sweet Flypaper of Life* (pp. 115–118) and mentions *BB, NS,* and *O.*

6596. DeCoste, Damon Marcel. "To Blot It All Out: The Politics of Realism in Richard Wright's *Native Son.*" *Style,* 32 (Spring), 127–147. Arguing against the view that literary realism is inherently conservative because it affirms prevailing social myths. DeCoste analyzes *NS* to show that its realism is an oppositional force, effectively critiquing "class and race relations" (p. 130). Bigger's desire for "a wholesale erasure of reality (p. 132), himself included, is a denial of reality that has dire consequences. W's alternative to Bigger's denial is "a discourse of disclosure" (p. 142) of oppression, which is what *NS* is.

6597. DeFazio, Albert J., III. "Fitzgerald and Hemingway," in *American Literary Scholarship: An Annual 1996.* Ed. David J. Nordloh. Durham: Duke University Press, pp. 179–197. Includes comment on an article comparing Fitzgerald and W (p. 183).

6598. DeLamotte, Eugenia C. *Places of Silence, Journeys of Freedom: The Fiction of Paule Marshall.* Philadelphia: University of Pennsylvania Press, p. 174. Quotes from 1979.77A on W's influence on Marshall.

6599. Diawara, Manthia. "Act One," in *Soul: Black Power, Politics,* *and Pleasure*. Eds. Monique Guillory and Richard C. Green. New York: New York University Press, pp. 289–299. Mentions W briefly (p. 293).

6600. _____. *In Search of Africa*. Cambridge, MA: Harvard University Press, pp. 5, 44, 55, 59–60, 63–65, 67–77, 163–164, 219. The section on "Richard Wright and Modern Africa" (pp. 59–76) is a sympathetic and admiring account of "Tradition and Industrialization" and *BP*, affirming W's view that Africa needs secularization, modernization, and democracy. Also discusses Baldwin's account of W at the 1956 Paris congress and mentions W elsewhere.

6601. Dodge, Georgina. "Henry B. Wonham, ed. *Criticism and the Color Line: Desegregating American Literary Studies*." *African American Review*, 32 (Summer), 331–332. Review mentioning W briefly.

6602. Domina, Lynn. *Understanding a Raisin in the Sun: A Student Casebook to Issues, Sources, and Historical Documents*. Westport, CT, pp. 104–106. Contains an excerpt from *NS* and two paragraphs comparing the novel to Hansberry's play. The works are similar in "thematic concerns," but *NS* is naturalistic and *A Raisin in the Sun* is realistic.

6603. Doreski, C.K. *Writing America Black: Race Rhetoric in the Public Sphere*. New York: Cambridge University Press, pp. 57, 218, 226. Mentions briefly *NS* and Mr. Dalton. Also quotes Melvin B. Tolson on white acceptance of W.

6604. Douglas, Ann. "Periodizing the American Century: Modernism, Postmodernism, and Postcolonialism in the Cold War Context." *Modernism/Modernity*, 5 (September), 71–98. Contains several mentions of W (pp. 81, 84, 85, 90, 92, 96). Also mentions *WML*. Douglas considers W one of "the major intellectuals of the 1940s and 1950s" (p. 85).

6605. Doyle, Robert P. *Banned Books: 1998 Resource Book*. Chicago: Jade, p. 108. Reports that *BB* was banned or challenged in Island Trees, New York, Lincoln, Nebraska, Round Rock, Texas and Jacksonville, Florida. *NS* received similar treatment in Goffstown, New Hampshire, Elmwood Park, New Jersey, North Adams, Massachusetts, Berrien Springs, Michigan, Yakima,

Washington, and High Point, North Carolina.

6606. Drake, Kimberly. "Ann Petry's Contribution to American Literature." *MLA Newsletter*, 30 (Spring), 24. A call for papers mentioning W's influence on Petry as a possible topic.

6607. Drew, Bettina. "Love Between the Lines." *The Nation*, 267 (26 October), 28–31. Review of Simone de Beauvoir's *A Transatlantic Love Affair: Letters to Nelson Algren* mentioning W briefly (p. 29).

6608. Dubey, Madhu. "Narration and Migration: *Jazz* and Vernacular Theories of Black Women's Fiction." *American Literary History*, 10 (Summer), 291–316. Mentions W briefly (p. 292).

6609. Dunn, Lois, and Michelle Banks. "Oprah Winfrey, 1954– , Talk Show Host, Actress, Entrepreneur," in *Black Heroes of the 20th Century*. Ed. Jessie Carney Smith. Detroit: Visible Ink, pp. 673–679. Biographical sketch mentioning her appearance in the film *NS*.

6610. Eagles, Brenda M. "A Bibliography of Dissertations Relating to Mississippi —1997." *The Journal of Mississippi History*, 60 (Spring), 75–79. Lists a dissertation treating W by Kenneth Scott Rogers (p. 78).

6611. Earle, Scott. "*The Grapes of Wrath* by John Steinbeck," in *Encyclopedia of the Novel*. Ed. Paul Schellinger. Chicago: Fitzroy Dearborn, pp. 504–505 Mentions briefly Mike Gold's praise of *NS*.

6612. Early, Gerald. "Pulp and Circumstance: The Story of Jazz in High Places," in *The Jazz Cadence of American Culture*. Ed. Robert G. O'Meally. New York: Columbia University Press, pp. 393–430. Mentions briefly *LT* (p. 401).

6613. Easingwood, Peter, Lionel Kelly, and David Seed. "American Literature: The Twentieth Century," in *A Critical Bibliography of American Literature Studies*. Vol. IV. Oxford: Blackwell, pp. 25–116. Mentions W briefly (p. 26) and comments on work on W by C. James Trotman, Robbie Jean Walker, Stephen Soitos, Joseph Bodziock, Michael Atkinson, Nagueyalti Warren, Robert L. Douglas, Marjorie Smelstor, Allison Rieke, Elizabeth J. Ciner, Paul Newlin, and Thomas Larson (pp. 83–84).

6614. Edwards, Brent. "The Seem-

ingly Eclipsed Window of Form: James Weldon Johnson's Prefaces," in *The Jazz Cadence of American Culture*. Ed. Robert G. O'Meally. New York: Columbia University Press, pp. 580–601. Mentions briefly W's phrase "The Form of Things Unknown" (pp. 581, 599).

6615. _____. "The Seemingly Eclipsed Window of Form: James Weldon Johnson's Prefaces," in *The Jazz Cadence of American Culture*. Ed. Robert G. O'Meally. New York: Columbia University Press, pp. 580–601. Quotes W's phrase "Form of Things Unknown" and mentions W in a footnote.

6616. Edwards, Jonathan. "Bigger Is Revealed to Himself." *Richard Wright Newsletter*, 6 (Fall/Winter), 7–8. Argues that Bigger's murders of Mary and Bessie were not determined by external forces but are manifestations of "what is truly inside of himself...."

6617. Ellison, Ralph. "Richard Wright's Blues," in *The Jazz Cadence of American Culture*. Ed. Robert G. O'Meally. New York: Columbia University Press, pp. 552–562.

6618. Elmer, Jonathan. "Spectacle and Event in *Native Son*." *American Literature*, 70 (December), 767–798. Adduces trauma theory to explain the novel, especially the scene in Mary's bedroom, where her suffocation by Bigger is both inevitable and accidental. Elmer also relates television as a medium to his perception of the novel. Among the theoretical perspectives he presents as a gloss on *NS* are Claude Lanzmann, Jean-François Lyotard, Lacan, Abdul JanMohamed, Foucault, and Gilles Deleuze. He concludes that *NS* "continues to pressure us toward conflicting conclusions that share only their unacceptability" (p. 792).

6619. English, Daylanne K. "Somebody Else's Foremother: David Haynes and Zora Neale Hurston." *African American Review*, 33 (Summer), 283–297 Notes Ellison's disavowal of W as a literary ancestor (p. 285) and mentions W's "infamous" review of *Their Eyes Were Watching God* (p. 292).

6620. The English Association. *A Critical Bibliography of American Literature Studies*. Oxford: Blackwell. Four volumes, The index contains 107 items pertaining to W.

6621. [Fabre, Michel]. "En Bref-

Short Notices." *Revue AFRAM Review*, no. 47, June, pp. 31–32. Includes notices of a new edition of *CC*.

6622. _____. "Leon Litwack. *Trouble in Mind: Black Southerners in the Age of Jim Crow.*" *Revue AFRAM Review*, no. 47, June, pp. 30–31. Favorable review mentioning briefly *TMBV* and *BB*.

6623. Farley, Christopher John. "Smiling Amid Corpses." *Time*, 152 (7 September), 78. Review of Edwidge Danticat's *The Farming of Bones* mentioning W briefly.

6624. Felgar, Robert. *Understanding Richard Wright's Black Boy: A Student Casebook to Issues, Sources, and Historical Documents.* Westport, CT: Greenwood Press, 178 pp. Designed for high-school students, this guide provides social and historical background to *BB* as well as some literary analysis. Sources include Benjamin Franklin, Douglass, Du Bois, Washington, and others.

6625. [Ferraro, Thomas J.]. "Brief Mention." *American Literature*, 70 (June), 427–438. Includes a notice of *Writers for the Nation: American Literary Modernism.* By Barry Chabot mentioning W briefly.

6626. Fisher, Benjamin F. "Poe," in *American Literary Scholarship: An Annual 1996.* Ed. David J. Nordloh. Durham: Duke University Press, pp. 43–52. Mentions treatment of W in Craig Werner's *Goldbugs and the Powers of Blackness.*

6627. _____. "Poe," in *American Literary Scholarship: An Annual 1996.* Ed. David J. Nordloh. Durham: Duke University Press, pp. 43–52. Mentions W briefly (p. 44).

6628. Fisher, Vivian Njeri. "Richard Wright, 1908–1960, Writer," in *Black Heroes of the Twentieth Century.* Ed. Jessie Carney Smith. Detroit: Visible Ink, pp. 690–698. Substantial biographical essay with two photographs of W.

6629. Foldy, Kate. "Felgar, Robert. *Understanding Richard Wright's Black Boy: A Student Casebook to Issues, Sources, and Historical Documents.*" *School Library Journal*, 44 (September), 216. Praises this work as "a detailed and insightful complement to Wright's book, but finds Felgar's first chapter "somewhat confused."

6630. Foley, Barbara. "Ralph Ellison as Proletarian Journalist." *Science and Society*, 62 (Winter 1998–

1999) pp. 537–556. Mentions W several times.

6631. Foley, Barbara Clare. "333A. The Red and the Black." *PMLA*, 113 (November), 1364. Lists a paper entitled "Getting It Right: Richard Wright's Communism and Black Communists in Context" by Anthony D. Dawahare.

6632. Forman, Seth. *Blacks in the Jewish Mind: A Crisis of Liberalism.* New York: New York University Press, pp. 114, 123, 124, 125. Comments on Baldwin's criticism of W and Howe's support of W in "'Black Boys and *Native Sons.*" Mentions W elsewhere.

6633. Frank, Leonard Roy. *Random House Webster's Quotationary.* New York: Random House, pp. 17, 773. Includes two quotations from *NS*.

6634. Franklin, Phyllis. "Report of the Executive Director." *PMLA*, 113 (May), 456–469. Lists James A. Miller's *Approaches to Teaching Wright's Native Son* (p. 461).

6635. Franklin, V.P. "The Portrayal of Jews in *The Autobiography of Malcolm X*," in *African Americans and Jews in the Twentieth Century: Studies in Convergence and Conflict.* Eds. V.P. Franklin, Nancy L. Grant, Harold M. Kletnick, and Genna Rae McNeil. Columbia: University of Missouri Press, pp. 293–308. Mentions briefly *BB* (p. 297).

6636. [Frick, Judie]. "The Department of English Invites You to Hear." Fayetteville, Arkansas. Flyer announcing a lecture by Michael Awkward on "'A Yearning for Identification': Reading the Mother in Richard Wright's *Black Boy*" at the University of Arkansas on 30 March.

6637. Füredi, Frank. *The Silent War: Imperialism and the Changing Perception of Race.* New Brunswick: Rutgers University Press, pp. 104–105. Discusses Malcolm Cowley's discussion of *UTC*.

6638. Fultz, Lucille P. "Southern Ethos/Black Ethics in Toni Morrison's Fiction." *Studies in the Literary Imagination*, 31 (Fall), 79–95. Comments on "Black Ethics" as described by W in *BB* and "The Ethics of Living Jim Crow" (p. 84).

6639. Gabler-Hover, Janet. "*Blacks in Eden: The African American Novel's First Century.* By J. Lee Greene." *American Literature*, 70 (March), 200–201. Review mentioning W and *NS*.

6640. García Gómez, Emilio. "La autobiografía de Chester Himes o la razón del absurdo," in his *Lengua, etnia y comunicación.* Zaragoza: Libros Pórtico, pp. 252–260. Includes comments on W's expatriation (pp. 252, 253) and his two white wives (p. 258).

6641. _____. "Cultura, individuo y nacionalidad," in his *Lengua, etnia y comunicación.* Zaragoza: Libros Pórtico, pp. 96–99. Notes that W was the product of factors other than formal education.

6642. _____. "Intercambios conversacionales y fallos comunicativos," in his *Lengua, etnia y comunicación.* Zaragoza: Libros Pórtico, pp. 169–181. Uses extracts from "Big Boy Leaves Home" and *BB* to illustrate failures of communication.

6643. _____. "Richard Wright: la voz del Mississipi [sic]" in his *Lengua, etnia y comunicación.* Zaragoza: Libros Pórtico, pp. 265–272. Review of W's career from the John Reed Club of Chicago to his death in exile. Emphasizes his estrangement from his race. Comments on *UTC, NS, BB, O, SH, LD,* and the haiku, with brief reference also to *PS, BP,* and *EM.*

6644. Gates, Anita. "Theater Review: Rediscovering a Writer Through Her Own Words." *The New York Times*, 3 November, p. E6. Mentions W briefly.

6645. Geiger, Jeffrey. "Unmaking the Male Body: The Politics of Masculinity in *The Long Dream.*" *African American Review*, 33 (Summer), 197–207. Drawing on theoretical perspectives of Elaine Scarry, Michel Foucault, and Trudier Harris, Geiger focuses on the lynched Chris's body in Tyree Tucker's funeral home as the key passage in the novel, for its "negative lesson ... serves to deconstruct–or 'unmake'–the evolving masculine identity" of Fishbelly (p. 197). White racism directly or indirectly emasculates black males in the South.

6646. Gilbert, Susan. "Maya Angelou's *I Know Why the Caged Bird Sings*: Paths to Escape," in *Maya Angelou's I Know Why the Caged Bird Sings.* Ed. Harold Bloom. Philadelphia: Chelsea House, pp. 81–91.

6647. Glick, Nathan. "The Socialist Who Loved Keats." *The Atlantic Monthly*, 281 (January), 99–105. Article on Irving Howe including discussion of his dispute with

Ellison about W and protest literature (pp. 101–102).

6648. Glitsch, Catherine. *American Novel Explication*. North Haven, CT: Shoe String Press, pp. 274–276. Lists two items on *LT*, four items on *LD*, twenty-four items on *NS*, and seven items on *O*.

6649. Glueck, Grace. "Colorful Patchwork Tales of Black and White, Life and Death." *The New York Times*, 20 October, p. E35. Mentions W briefly.

6650. Goldberg, Elizabeth Swanson. "The Way We Do the Things We Do: Enunciation and Effect in the Multicultural Classroom," in *Teaching African American Literature: Theory and Practice*. Eds. Maryemma Graham, Sharon Pineault-Burke, and Marianna White Davis. New York: Routledge, pp. 151–177. Comments on analytical and stereotypical student responses to Bigger (p. 161).

6651. Goodwin, James. "The Depression Era in Black and White: Four American Photo-Texts." *Criticism*, 40 (Spring), 273–307. Considers *TMBV* along with *You Have Seen Their Faces*, Dorothea Lange and Paul Schuster Taylor's *An American Exodus*, and *Let Us Now Praise Famous Men*. W emphasizes the oral more than the pictoral. Goodwin also comments on *NS*, *BB*, and W's introduction to *Black Metropolis*.

6652. Graham, Maryemma. "Hazel Rowley." *Richard Wright Newsletter*, 6 (Spring/Summer), 6–8. Interview in which Rowley discusses her biography of W to be completed in June 2000 and her qualifications as a biographer.

6653. _____. "Introduction: When Teaching Matters," in *Teaching African American Literature: Theory and Practice*. Eds. Maryemma Graham, Sharon Pineault-Burke, and Marianna White Davis. New York: Routledge, pp. 1–11. Mentions W briefly (pp. 7, 9).

6654. _____. "Michel Fabre." *Richard Wright Newsletter*, 6 (Spring/Summer), 1, 4–5. Interview in which Fabre discusses his biography of W, comments on books by Margaret Walker and Eugene E. Miller, Hazel Rowley's work on a W biography and other works-in-progress, and his own interest in Louisiana Afro-Creoles in the nineteenth century.

6655. Graham, Maryemma, and Jerry W. Ward, Jr. "From the Edi-

tors." *Richard Wright Newsletter*, 6 (Fall/Winter 1997-1998), 2. Comments on the contents of this issue.

6656. Graham, Maryemma, Jerry W. Ward, and Diana Putnam. "From the Editors." *Richard Wright Newsletter*, 6 (Spring/Summer), 2. Announcement that James A. Miller will become the new editor. Putnam reviews the current issue, which she assembled.

6657. Grant, Nathan L. "Notes of a Prodigal Son: James Baldwin and the Apostasy of Soul," in *Soul: Black Power, Politics, and Pleasure*. Eds. Monique Guillory and Richard C. Green. New York: New York University Press, pp. 32–44. Includes discussion of Baldwin's attitudes toward W, whose Bigger Thomas was the "most enduring literary prototype of soul" (pp. 33–35). Notes also Iceberg Slim's relation to W.

6658. Gretlund, Jan Nordby. *Frames of Southern Mind: Reflections on the Stoic, Bi-Racial & Existential South*. Odense: Odense University Press, pp. 112, 270. Mentions W briefly.

6659. _____. "Component Parts: The Novelist as Autobiographer," in his and Karl-Heinz Westarp's *The Late Novels of Eudora Welty*." Columbia: University of South Carolina Press, p. 168. Mentions briefly *BB*.

6660. Grewal, Gurleen. *Circles of Sorrow, Lines of Struggle: The Novels of Toni Morrison*. Baton Rouge: Louisiana State University Press, pp. 33, 124, 127. Comments on W's "apparent disregard for how ... Bessie was killed" (p. 33) and quotes from *TMBV*.

6661. Griffin, Farah J., and Cheryl J. Fish. "Richard Wright," in their *A Stranger in the Village: Two Centuries of African-American Travel Writing*. Boston: Beacon Press, p. 150. Headnote to an excerpt from *BP*.

6662. Grimes-Williams, Johanna L. "Haki Madhubuti, 1942– , Poet, Essayist, Educator, Publisher," in *Black Heroes of the 20th Century*. Ed. Jessie Carney Smith. Detroit: Visible Ink, pp. 455–459. Biographical sketch mentioning the influence of *BB* on Madhubuti (p. 456).

6663. Gubar, Susan. "What Ails Feminist Criticism?" *Critical Inquiry*, 24 (Summer), 878–902. Mentions briefly *WML* (p. 889).

6664. Guerrero, Ed. "Black Stars in Exile: Paul Robeson, O.J. Simp-

son, and Othello," in *Paul Robeson: Artist and Citizen*. Ed. Jeffrey C. Stewart. New Brunswick, NJ: Rutgers University Press and the Paul Robeson Cultural Center, pp. 275–288. Mentions W briefly (p. 277).

6665. Haggard-Gilson, Nancy. "Against the Grain: Black Conservatives and Jewish Neoconservatives," in *African Americans and Jews in the Twentieth Century: Studies in Convergence and Conflict*. Eds. V.P. Franklin, Nancy L. Grant, Harold M. Kletnick, and Genna Rae McNeil. Columbia: University of Missouri Press, pp. 165–190. Mentions W briefly (p. 190).

6666. Hakutani, Yoshinobu, and Robert L. Tener. "Afterword," in their *Haiku: This Other World* by Richard Wright. New York: Arcade, pp. 245–304. After a history of Japanese haiku (pp. 245–265), Hakutani and Tener discuss W's interest in nature, trace his interest in the form in 1959 and 1960, and evaluate his practice of the art.

6667. Hakutani, Yoshinobu, and Robert L. Tener. "Notes on the Haiku," in their *Haiku: This Other World* by Richard Wright. New York: Arcade, pp. 207–244. Consists of notes on 127 of the 817 haiku included in the collection.

6668. Hale, Grace Elizabeth. *Making Whiteness: The Culture of Segregation in the South, 1890–1940*. New York: Pantheon Books, pp. 204, 228. Quotes W. on the "white death" and its effect on black males.

6669. Hanke, Michael. "Einleitung," in his *Amerikanische Short Stories des 20 Jahrhunderts*. Stuttgart: Phillip Reclam jun., pp. 9–17. Comments on "The Man Who Was Almost a Man" as an initiation story and includes it in this collection.

6670. Hapgood, Lynne. "Politics and the Novel," in *Encyclopedia of the Novel*. Ed. Paul Schellinger. Chicago: Fitzroy Dearborn, p. 1022. Mentions briefly W and *NS*.

6671. Hare, Nathan. "Introduction," in *Somethin' Proper*. By Marvin X (Jackmon). Castro Valley, California: Black Bird Press, p. v. Quotes from *BB* and mentions *NS* briefly.

6672. Harris, Trudier. "Lying Through Our Teeth?: The Quagmire of Cultural Diversity," in *Teaching African American Literature: Theory and Practice*. Eds. Maryemma Graham, Sharon Pineault-

Burke, and Marianna White Davis. New York: Routledge, pp. 210–222. Mentions briefly *UTC* (p. 211).

6673. _____. "Margaret Walker b. 1915," in *The Literature of the American South*. Ed. William L. Andrews. New York: W.W. Norton, pp 721–723. Comments on Walker's friendship with W and her biography of him.

6674. _____. "Ralph Ellison 1914–1994," in *The Literature of the American South*. Ed. William L. Andrews. New York: W.W. Norton, pp. 698–700. Notes Ellison's literary disagreements with W.

6675. [_____]. "Richard Wright 1908–1960." in *The Literature of the American South*. Ed. William L. Andrews. New York: W.W. Norton, pp. 545–548. Substantial biographical sketch, calling W the most important voice in black American Literature for the first half of the twentieth century.

6676. Hasegawa, Midori. "Poetic Description in *Uncle Tom's Children* and *Native Son*." *Toetsu College for Education Graduate School Studies*, 13, 155–167. Shows that *UTC* and *NS* have numerous scenes with poetic descriptions that relate to themes and enrich the works themselves.

6677. Hauke, Kathleen A. *Ted Poston: Pioneer American Journalist*. Athens: The University of Georgia Press, pp. 70–71, 99, 130. Comments briefly on W in the Federal Writers Project and quotes from Poston's review of *O*.

6678. Heaman, Patricia B. "*Every Tub Must Sit on Its Own Bottom: The Philosophy and Politics of Zora Neale Hurston*. Deborah G. Plant." *MELUS*, 23 (Summer), 219–221. Mentions W briefly (p. 221).

6679. Hechtkopf, Jackie. "Miller, William. *Richard Wright and the Library Card*." *School Library Journal*, 44 (February), 88–89. Review of a children's book based on an episode in *BB*. The reviewer cites two other books that "describe a love of learning hindered by racism in a more inspiring way."

6680. Helton, Tena L. "'What Was Said and What Was Left Unsaid': *Black Boy* as Survival Guide for a Black Man and Artist." *CLA Journal*, 42 (December), 147–163. Discusses the influence of family and gang (mistakenly called "Memphis gang" instead of Jackson gang

(i.e., Dick Wright Clan). From both family and gang W learned survival skills. His family's efforts to stifle his voice only increased his need for expression. Helton supports her argument with references to such sociologists as Waln K. Brown, Andrew Billingsly, and Teresa Labov.

6681. Herrington, Joan. "*I Ain't Sorry for Nothin' I Done": August Wilson's Process of Playwrighting*. New York: Limelight Editions, p. 11. Mentions W briefly.

6682. Hersch, Charles. *Democratic Artworks: Politics and the Arts from Trilling to Dylan*. Albany: State University of New York Press, pp. 110–111. Quotes W on the blues.

6683. Hiett, John. "*Native Son* by Richard Wright." *Library Journal*, 123 (15 October) 114. Review of an audio tape of *NS*. James Earl Jones is an excellent reader, but the novel is so drastically abridged as to be quite unsatisfactory.

6684. Hoagwood, Terence Allan. "*On Gwendolyn Brooks: Reliant Contemplation*. Edited by Stephen Caldwell Wright." *MELUS*, 23 (Fall), 212–215. Mentions W briefly (p. 214).

6685. Hoberek, Andrew. "Race Man, Organization Man, Invisible Man." *Modern Language Quarterly*, 59 (March), 99–108. Mentions briefly "the militant example of Richard Wright" (p. 99) and Bigger Thomas (p. 108).

6686. Hobson, Fred. "The Depression and Southern Writing," in *The Literature of the American South*. Ed. William L. Andrews. New York: W.W. Norton, pp. 251–253. Includes comment on W mentioning *UTC*, *NS*, and *BB*, and contrasting Hurston to W.

6687. _____. "Zora Neale Hurston, in 'The New South 1880–1940,'" in *The Literature of the American South*. Ed. William L. Andrews. New York: W.W. Norton, pp. 405–407. Notes W's disagreement with Hurston.

6688. Hoffman, Edwin D. "Being White in Black/White Relations: A Professor's Singular Life Journey." *Monthly Review*, 49 (March), 35–49. Mentions W briefly (p. 37).

6689. Horne, Gerald. "Comrades and Friends: The Personal/Political World of Paul Robeson," in *Paul Robeson: Artist and Citizen*. Ed. Jeffrey C. Stewart. New Brunswick, NJ: Rutgers University Press and

The Paul Robeson Cultural Center, pp. 197–215. Mentions W briefly (p. 200).

6690. Howe, Stephen. *Afrocentrism: Mythical Pasts and Imagined Homes*. London: Verso, p. 112. Mentions briefly *BP*.

6691. Ichiki, Jun. "Richard Wright and His Reception of What It Is Like to Be an African American." *College Treatise Institute of International Culture*, 9 (July), 123–137. Examining *BB* clarifies W's notion of what it means to be black, which is applied in *NS*.

6692. Irr, Caren. *The Suburb of Dissent: Cultural Politics in the United States and Canada During the 1930's*. Durham: Duke University Press, pp. 20, 106, 121–141, 145.

6693. Isaeff, Kristi M. "The Hunger of Existence: Class and Race Dimensions in Richard Wright's *Black Boy (American Hunger)*," in *The Image of Class in Literature, Media, and Society*. Eds. Will Wright and Steven Kaplan. Pueblo, CO: The Society for the Interdisciplinary Study of Social Imagery, pp 183–187. Summarizes W's autobiography emphasizing class and race. Disillusioned by his experiences in both the South and the North, he concludes in a state of alienated "existence awareness."

6694. Jarrett, David, and Mary Jarrett. "American Literature: The Twentieth Century," in *Critical Bibliography of American Literature Studies*. Vol. II. Oxford: Blackwell, pp. 380–411. Comments on work on W by Yoshinobu Hakutani and Fritz Gysin (pp. 410 and 411).

6695. Jenkins, Everett, Jr. *Pan-African Chronology II: A Comprehensive Reference to the Black Quest for Freedom in Africa, the Americas, Europe and Asia, 1865–1915*. Jefferson, NC: McFarland, pp. 400–434, 449. Includes a biographical sketch (p. 400), and brief mentions of W in sketches of Willard Motley and Ralph Ellison.

6696. Jenkins, Robert L. "*Mississippi: An American Journey*. By Anthony Walton." *The Journal of Southern History*, 64 (November), 785–786. Mentions W briefly.

6697. Johnson, Barbara. "Euphemism, Understatement, and the Passive Voice: Genealogy of African-American Poetry," in her *The Feminist Difference: Literature, Psychoanalysis, Race, and Gender*. Cambridge, MA: Harvard University Press, pp. 91–100.

6698. _____. "The Re(a)d and the Black: Richard Wright's Blueprint," in her *The Feminist Difference: Literature, Psychoanalysis, Race, and Gender.* Cambridge, MA: Harvard University Press, pp. 61–73.

6699. Johnson, Charles. "Thinking in Public: A Forum." *American Literary History,* 10 (Spring), 34–40. Mentions briefly *NS* (p. 37).

6700. Joly, Claire. "*Native Son* and the Book-of-the-Month Club." *Richard Wright Newsletter,* 6 (Spring/Summer), 8–11. Relying on unpublished as well as published sources, Joly documents the debate within the Book-of-the-Month Club over the selection of *NS.* William Allen White objected strongly, but Dorothy Canfield Fisher and Henry Seidel Canby prevailed, though not without serious misgivings.

6701. Jones, Anne Goodwyn. "Sushi South: Teaching Southern Culture in Japan." *Southern Cultures,* 4, no. 4, 20–30. Mentions W briefly (pp. 25, 29).

6702. Jones, Clara B., and Matthew V. Johnson. "*Psychoanalysis and Black Novels: Desire and the Protocols of Race.* Author: Claudia Tate." *The Western Journal of Black Studies,* 22 (Fall), 205–206. Review containing a paragraph on Tate's treatment of *SH.*

6703. Jones, Jacqueline. *American Work: Four Centuries of Black and White Labor.* New York: W.W. Norton, p. 341. Mentions W briefly on the Federal Writers Project.

6704. Jong, Erica. "I've Got a Little List." *The Nation,* 267 (16 November), 32, 34–35. Includes the Modern Library list of the best novels of the twentieth century with *NS* as twentieth (p. 33). W is mentioned elsewhere (p. 34).

6705. Kanneh, Kadiatu. *African Identities: Race, Nation and Culture in Ethnography, Pan-Africanism and Black Literatures.* London: Routledge, p. 64. Mentions briefly "Richard Wright's notion of 'Double Vision'" and discusses Paul Gilroy.

6706. Kato, Makiko. "From Spiritual Liberation to Physical Death." *Nagoya College and Junior College for Formative Arts Bulletin* (March), 43–49. Explains Bigger's statement: "What I killed for I am." Spiritually dead at the beginning of *NS,* Bigger revives spiritually after killing Mary.

6707. Kazin, Michael. "Left with the Arts." *Dissent,* 45 (Winter), 139–142. Review of Michael Denning's *The Cultural Front* mentioning briefly W and *NS* (p. 140).

6708. Kelly, Lionel, Pat Righelato, and Deborah Madsen. "American Literature: The Twentieth Century," in *A Critical Bibliography of American Literature Studies.* Vol. IV. Oxford: Blackwell, pp. 290–345. Comments on work on W by Michel Fabre, pp. 292–293.

6709. _____. "American Literature: The Twentieth Century," in *A Critcal Bibliography of American Literature Studies.* Vol. IV. Oxford: Blackwell, pp. 146–257. Comments on work on W by Michael F. Lynch (p. 215), William Cain (p. 222), Timothy Dow Adams (p. 238), Harold Bloom (p. 238), Keneth Kinnamon (p. 238,) John M. Reilly (p. 238), Trudier Harris (p. 238), Houston A. Baker (p. 238), Craig Werner (p. 238), James Baldwin (p. 238), Ross Pudaloff (pp. 238–239), Robert J. Butler (p. 239), Tony Magistrale (p. 239), Valerie Smith (p. 239), Alan W. France (p. 239), Edward Watson (p. 239), Keneth Kinnamon (p. 239), and Dorothy Redden (p. 239).

6710. Kelly, Lionel, Pat Righelato, Henry Claridge, Deborah Parsons, Peter Vernon, and Steven Price. "American Literature: The Twentieth Century," in *A Critical Bibliography of American Literature Studies.* Vol. IV. Oxford: Blackwell, pp. 557–661. Comments on work on W by Carla Cappetti (p. 602).

6711. Kelley, Robin D.G. "Integration: What's Left?" *The Nation,* 267 (14 December), pp. 17–19. Mentions W briefly (p. 18).

6712. Kent, George E. "Maya Angelou's *I Know Why the Caged Bird Sings* and Black Autobiographical Tradition," in *Maya Angelou's I Know Why the Caged Bird Sings.* Ed. Harold Bloom. Philadelphia: Chelsea House, pp. 15–24. Reprint of 1993.

6713. Kershner, R. Brandon. "Modernism: The Modern Novel," in *Encyclopedia of the Novel.* Ed. Paul Schellinger. Chicago: Fitzroy Dearborn, pp. 854–861. Mentions W briefly (p. 858).

6714. King, Adele. "*Mission to Kala* by Mongo Beti," in *Encyclopedia of the Novel.* Ed. Paul Schellinger. Chicago: Fitzroy Dearborn,

pp. 850–851. Notes that Beti acknowledges Wright's influence on his fiction.

6715. King, Debra Walker. *Deep Talk: Reading African-American Literary Names.* Charlottesville: University Press of Virginia, pp. 31, 51, 191–195, 201. Discusses W's grandfather in *BB,* who was misnamed Richard Vinson instead of Richard Wilson when he was mustered out of the Union Army. This event "dispossesses and silences his grandfather's public identity" (p. 191).

6716. King, Martin Luther, Jr. *The Autobiography of Martin Luther King, Jr.* Ed. Clayborne Carson. New York: Warner Books, pp. 122, 320. King relates meeting W in Paris and notes that W had used the term *black power* before it was used in the civil rights movement.

6717. King, Richard H. "*Not Like Us: How Europeans Have Loved, Hated, and Transformed American Culture Since World War II* by Richard Pells." *Southern Cultures,* 4, no. 4, 80–83. Mentions briefly W's expatriation (p. 82).

6718. Kinnamon, Keneth. "A Richard Wright Bibliography: 1988." *Richard Wright Newsletter,* (Fall Winter), Supplement, 31 pp. Includes 351 annotated items and a commentary on W studies in 1988.

6719. _____. "*A Richard Wright Bibliography: 1989.*" *Richard Wright Newsletter,* (Spring/Summer), supplement. Lists 293 annotated items and provides a critical review of W scholarships in 1989.

6720. [Kinnamon, Keneth]. "Books Briefly Mentioned." *African American Review,* 32 (Summer), 366. Includes a notice of William Miller's children's book *Richard Wright and the Library Card* and notices of books by Richard Kopley and Charles Scruggs mentioning briefly W and *NS.*

6721. _____. "Call and Response: Intertextuality in Two Autobiographical Works by Richard Wright and Maya Angelou," in *Maya Angelou's I Know Why the Caged Bird Sings,* Ed. Harold Bloom. Philadelphia: Chelsea House, pp. 69–79.

6722. Kiuchi, Toru. "Richard Wright and Black Music." *Richard Wright Newsletter,* 6 (Fall/Winter), 1, 11–15. Traces W's ideas about black music throughout his career, finding that they became more inclusive and more objective after his expatriation.

6723. _____. "Richard Wright's *Black Power*: From Black Liberation in America to Third World Liberation." *Nihon University Industrial Engineering Faculty Report B*, 31 (20 June), 15–27. States that *BP* is not merely a strong message to Nkrumah, but also an expansion of W's call for liberation from America to the Third World.

6724. Klinkowitz, Jerome."Fiction: The 1960's to the Present," in *American Literary Scholarship: An Annual 1996*. Durham: Duke University Press, pp. 335–356. Includes comment on a article comparing David Bradley and W (p. 344).

6725. _____. *Keeping Literary Company: Working with Writers Since the Sixties*. Albany: State University of New York Press, pp. 178, 185. Mentions W briefly.

6726. Kohn, Howard. *We Had a Dream: A Tale of the Struggle for Integration in America*. New York: Simon & Schuster, pp. 270–271. Quotes from *NS*.

6727. Kolocotroni, Vassiliki, Jane Goldman, and Olga Taxidou. "Introduction," in their *Modernism: An Anthology of Sources and Documents*. Chicago: The University of Chicago Press, pp. xvii–xx. Mentions W's admonitions on racial violence and his thoughts on Poe (p. xix).

6728. _____. "Richard Wright (1908–60): From How 'Bigger' Was Born 1940," in their *Modernism: An Anthology of Sources and Documents*. Chicago: The University of Chicago Press, p. 617. Headnote to an excerpt from the essay.

6729. Konzett, Delia Caparoso. "*Their Eyes Were Watching God* by Zora Neale Hurston," in *Encyclopedia of the Novel*. Ed. Paul Schelling. Chicago: Fitzroy Dearborn, pp. 1327–1328. Comments on W's unfavorable review of the Hurston novel.

6730. Kreyling, Michael. *Inventing Southern Literature*. Jackson: University Press of Mississippi, pp. 35, 46, 49–50, 78–81, 82, 84–86, 88–91, 94, 98. Discusses Louis Rubin's unfavorable opinion of W (pp. 49–50); W's emphasis on race and his rejection of the Southern literary tradition in "The Ethics of Living Jim Crow," "Big Boy Leaves Home," *NS*, and *BB* (pp. 78–81); and Ellison's disagreements with W (pp. 84–85). Mentions W briefly elsewhere.

6731. [Lacy, Madison D.]. "Richard Wright–Black Boy," in *African American Perspectives*. San Francisco: California Newsreel, p. 13. Publisher's notice of a video with blurbs by Charles Johnson and Houston A. Baker, Jr.

6732. Leak, Jeffrey B. "An Interview with Brent Wade." *African American Review*, 32 (Fall), 427–433. Wade acknowledges W as a literary ancestor (p. 427) and mentions Bigger Thomas as an example of alienation (p. 430).

6733. Latortue, Régine. "En quête d'une image indigéniste: Les romancières noires Americaines." *Présence Africaine*, No. 158, pp. 80–85. Includes comment on W's treatment of his women characters (pp. 81–82).

6734. Lauter, Paul. "An Alternative to the Modern *Library's Top 100*." *The Heath Anthology of American Literature Newsletter*, No. 18 (Fall), 10. Mentions W briefly.

6735. Lee, Gary. "Black Americans in Paris." Little Rock *Arkansas-Gazette* (5 July), Sec. H, p. 6. Includes comments on W in Paris and a photograph of W.

6736. Lee, A. Robert. *Designs of Blackness: Mappings in the Literature and Culture of Afro-America*. London: Pluto Press, pp. 4, 5, 8, 9, 14, 16, 30, 36–38, 41, 60, 90–106, 113, 117, 118, 154, 165, 176. Chapter 5, "Richard Wright's Inside Narratives," insists on W's eclectic imagination and his "inside narratives," which combine treatment of overt racial oppression with a bluesy "visceral underground sediment of black American history. In these terms Lee discusses *UTC*, *EM*, *LT*, *NS*, and *LD*. Mentions W briefly elsewhere.

6737. Leeming, David. *Amazing Grace: A Life of Beauford Delaney*. New York: Oxford University Press, pp. 47, 81, 95, 103, 111, 115. Mentions W briefly, especially in relation to Baldwin, and describes W at the Café Tournon as favoring "a permanent break with racist America" and feeling "uncomfortable with homosexuals" (p. 115).

6738. _____. "The African American Novel," in *African American Literature: Voices in a Tradition*. Ed. Fannie Safier. Austin: Holt, Rinehart and Winston, pp. 572–582. Includes discussion of W, who established "the great tradition" as "the

first universally recognized 'giant' of African American Literature."

6739. Leland, John. "*Blacks in Eden: The African American Novel's First Century* by J. Lee Greene." *Southern Cultures*, 4, no. 4, 101–103. Review commenting on "Big Boy Leaves Home" and *NS*.

6740. Lemke, Sieglinde. *Primitivist Modernism: Black Culture and the Origins of Transatlantic Modernism*. New York: Oxford University Press, pp. 10, 80, 143. Mentions briefly W and *NS*. Quotes from W's preface to *Blues Fell This Morning*.

6741. Leonard, Florence. "Miller, William. *Richard Wright and the Library Card*." *Childhood Education*, 74, no. 5, 326. Favorable notice.

6742. Levitt, Morton P. "1995-1996 Annual Review Double Issue." *Journal of Modern Literature*, 21 (Spring), 345–492. Lists two books (Butler and Hakutani) and one article (Caron) s.v. W.

6743. Lewis, Randolph. "Resistance to Theory: American Studies and the Challenge of Critical Studies." *Canadian Review of American Studies*, 28, No. 2, 1–36. Mentions briefly *NS* (p. 31).

6744. Lewis, R.W.B. "Afterword," in *Cleanth Brooks and Robert Penn Warren: A Literary Correspondence*. Ed. James A. Grimshaw, Jr. Columbia: University of Missouri Press, pp. 417–424. Mentions W briefly (p. 419).

6745. _____. "Afterword, "in *Cleanth Brooks and Robert Penn Warren a Literary Correspondence*. Ed. James Grimshaw, Jr. Columbia: University of Missouri Press, p. 419. Mentions W briefly.

6746. Lind, Michael. "Where Have You Gone, Louis Sullivan?" *Harper's Magazine*, 296 (February), 53–59. Mentions W briefly (p. 57).

6747. Lionnet, Françoise. "Con Artists and Storytellers: Maya Angelou's Problematic Sense of Audience," in *Maya Angelou's I Know Why the Caged Bird Sings*. Ed. Harold Bloom. Philadelphia: Chelsea House, pp. 111–140.

6748. Lipsitz, George. "'Sent for You Yesterday, Here You Come Today:' American Studies Scholarship and the New Social Movements." *Cultural Critique*, 40, pp. 203–232. Mentions W briefly (p. 212).

6749. Litwack, Leon F. *Trouble in Mind: Black Southerners in the Age of*

Jim Crow. New York: Alfred A. Knopf, pp. 9, 11–12, 14, 19, 21–22, 23, 26–27, 29, 34, 38, 39, 41–42, 50, 71, 72–73, 91, 111–112, 114, 142, 154, 164, 175, 350, 361–362, 380–381, 400, 414, 415–416, 421, 422, 432, 433, 439, 441, 446–447, 478, 483, 493, 494–495, 552. Quotes *BB* frequently on racist attitudes and practices and their effects on Black Southerners. Also quotes from *How Bigger Was Born* and mentions "Bright and Morning Star."

6750. Love, Candice M. "The Southern Tradition: Representation of Race in the Work of William Faulkner and Richard Wright." *Richard Wright Newsletter*, 6 (Spring/Summer), 12. Abstract of a paper presented at the College Language Association conference in 1998. Her work-in-progress deals with *NS, O,* and *LD* as well as *The Sound and the Fury, Light in August,* and *Go Down, Moses.*

6751. Lupton, Mary Jane. *Maya Angelou: A Critical Companion.* Westport, CT: Greenwood Press, pp. 33, 41, 68, 102. Includes discussion of *BB.* Mentions *BP* and "The Man Who Lived Underground."

6752. MacEwan, Mary. *Richard Wright's Black Boy.* New York: Barnes and Noble, 57 pp. A Monarch Notes Study Guide with the following rubrics: A Note about the Work, Introduction to Richard Wright, The Author's Works, Historical Perspectives, Detailed Summary, Critical Commentary, Character Analysis, Essay Questions and Answers, and Bibliography.

6753. Macieski, Robert. "American Writers Congress," in *Encyclopedia of the American Left.* New York: Oxford University Press, pp. 43–44. Mentions W briefly.

6754. Margraf, Sarah and Joline Tibbtts. "*Native Son* (1940)" in *The Encyclopedia of Novels into Films,* edited by John C. Tibbetts and James M. Welsh. New York: Facts on File, pp. 295–297 Provides a plot summary of the novel and an unfavorable critique of the two film versions.

6755. Mason, Theodore O., Jr. "The African-American Anthology: Mapping the Territory, Taking the National Census, Building the Museum." *American Literary History,* 10 (Spring), 185–198. Mentions W briefly (p. 198).

6756. [McCray, Judith]. "For My

People: The Life and Writing of Margaret Walker," in *African American Perspectives.* San Francisco: California Newsreel, p. 12. Notice of a video mentioning Walker's friendship with W.

6757. McKissack, Patricia, and Fredrick L. McKissack. *Young, Black, and Determined: A Biography of Lorraine Hansberry.* New York: Holiday House, pp. 60–61, 77, 112. Discusses Hansberry's review of *O* and includes a photograph of W (p. 61).

6758. Miller, James A. "From the New Editor." *Richard Wright Newsletter,* 6 (Spring/Summer), 3. Praises the achievements of the *Richard Wright Newsletter.*

6759. Mills, Charles W. *Blackness Visible: Essays on Philosophy and Race.* Ithaca: Cornell University Press, pp. 15, 111–112, 203. Mentions "The Ethics of Living Jim Crow" and *NS.*

6760. Mishkin, Tracy. *The Harlem and Irish Renaissances: Language, Identity, and Representation.* Gainesville: University Press of Florida, p. 65. Quotes from W's review of *Their Eyes Were Watching God* (p. 64).

6761. Mitchell, Angelyn. "Cary D. Wintz, ed. *The Harlem Renaissance, 1920–1940: The Critics and the Harlem Renaissance.*" *African American Review,* 32 (Fall), 495–497. Mentions W briefly (p. 496).

6762. Modleski, Tania. *Old Wives' Tales and Other Women's Stories.* New York: New York University Press, p. 19. Includes comments of W, *Uncle Tom's Cabin* and the Clarence Thomas Anita Hill hearings.

6763. Moin, Gulfishaan. "The Twenties in Black and White: A Comparative Study of Fitzgerald's *The Great Gatsby* and Wright's *Black Boy* and *American Hunger,*" in *F. Scott Fitzgerald: Centenary Essays from India.* New Delhi: Prestige Books, pp. 110–115. Both critiques of the American Dream, Fitzgerald's novel and W's autobiography, depict aspiration denied, but W has a deeper social responsibility.

6764. Monroe, William. *Power to Hurt: The Virtues of Alienation.* Urbana: University of Illinois Press, p. 103. Mentions W briefly.

6765. Montgomery-Crawford, Maxine. "African American Novel," in *Encyclopedia of the Novel.* Ed. Paul Schellinger. Chicago: Fitzroy Dearborn, pp. 12–16. Includes a critique of *NS,* "signaling the triumph of

naturalism." Selfhood through violence 'was a powerful counterbalance to the myth of the American dream (p. 14).

6766. Moore, G.H., and T.R. Arp. "American literature," in *A Critical Bibliography of American Literature Studies,* Vol. I. Oxford: Blackwell, pp. 211, 308, 347, 348, 479, 495, 511. Comments on works on W by Herbert Hill, Walter Allen, David Littlejohn, Seymour L. Gross, and John Edward Hardy.

6767. Mostern, Kenneth. "Review Essay: Social Marginality/Blackness: Subjects of Postmodernity." *MELUS,* 23 (Winter), 167–187. Mentions W briefly (p. 174).

6768. Mullen, Edward J. *Afro-Cuban Literature: Critical Junctures.* Westport, CT: Greenwood Press, p. 30. Mentions W briefly.

6769. Murray, Pauli. "Can These Bones Live Again?," in *Daughters of Thunder: Black Women Preachers and Their Sermons, 1850–1979.* Ed. Bettye Collier-Thomas. San Francisco: Jossey-Bass, pp. 270–276. Mentions W briefly (p. 274).

6770. Mvebekale, Marc. "Richard Wright, le jeu du decepteur et la phenomenologie Hegelienne." *Revue AFRAM Review,* No. 47 (June), pp. 5–13. Analyzes Bigger's role as signifying trickster in *NS,* drawing on existential and Hegelian philosophy as well as the black folk tradition. He moves from a defensive role to self-affirmation. Also compares briefly Bigger and Cross Damon in *O.*

6771. Nakagomi, Kazumasa. "A Study of R. Wright's Alienation as Seen in *Black Boy.*" *Nihon University Studies in English Language and Literature,* 19 (March), 1–12. Contends that *BB* shows W's alienation from the American black and white worlds because he became aware of the larger world outside the South.

6772. Neal, Mark Anthony. "'It Be's That Way Sometimes 'Cause I Can't Control the Rhyme': Notes from the Post-Soul Intelligentsia." *Black Renaissance/Renaissance Noire,* 1 (Spring/Summer), 8–24. Discusses briefly W as protest writer, mentioning *NS* and *TMBV* (p. 13).

6773. Nussbaum, Martha. "Thinking in Public: A Forum." *American Literary History,* 10 (Spring), 52–61. Mentions briefly *NS* (p. 58).

6774. O'Brien, John. "John Wideman," in *Conversations with John Edgar Wideman*. Ed. Bonnie Tu-Smith. Jackson: University Press of Mississippi, pp. 5–13. Reprint of 1973.309.

6775. ____. "John Edgar Wideman," in *Conversations with John Wideman*. Ed. Bonnie TuSmith. Jackson: University Press of Mississippi, pp. 5–13.

6776. O'Brien, Michael. "The Apprehension of the South in Modern Culture." *Southern Cultures*, 4, no. 4, 3–18. Mentions briefly W's expatriation (p. 14).

6777. Ogburn, Floyd, Jr. "Richard Wright's Unpublished Haiku: A World Elsewhere." *MELUS*, 23 (Fall), 57–81. Argues that W's haiku is not a departure at the end of his career but the realization of his poetics stated in portions of "Blueprint for Negro Writing" and *BB*. Examines W's study of haiku poems at Yale, maintaining that he departed from Japanese tradition by organizing them conceptually rather that seasonally.

6778. Oitate, Magatsugu. "The Symbolic Style in Richard Wright's 'Down by the Riverside.'" *Okinawa International University Foreign Language Studies* 2 (March), 91–113. Clarifies the symbolic meaning of the protagonist's name (Mann) and the scene with boat, light, and water.

6779. Okafor-Newsum, Ikechukwu. "*Canaan Bound: The African-American Great Migration Novel*, by Lawrence R. Rodgers." *Research in African Literatures*, 29 (Winter), 204–206. Review mentioning W.

6780. Olney, James. *Memory and Narrative: The Weave of Life-Writing*. Chicago: The University of Chicago Press, pp. 230, 239–243, 263, 297. Argues that the *I* in *BB* "is clearly *he*, and compares W's "autobiographical" writing to that of Gertrude Stein and Samuel Beckett. Also mentions *UTC* and *NS*.

6781. Olson, Gary A. "Literature," in *The Encyclopedia of Civil Rights in America*. Armonk, NY: Sharpe Reference, pp. 537–545. Comments briefly on W and his "bitter novel," *Native Son*.

6782. Olson, Ray. "Wright, Richard. *Haiku: This Other World*. Eds. by Yoshinobu Hakutani and Robert L. Tener." *Booklist*, 95 (1 September), 58. Favorable notice emphasizing W's "capacity for a deep communion with nature."

6783. O'Meally, Robert G. "Introduction," in his *The Jazz Cadence of American Culture*. New York: Columbia University Press, pp. 117–119. Quotes W's statement that "the Negro is America's metaphor" (p. 118).

6784. ____. "Part 2: One Nation Under a Groove, or the United State of Jazzocracy: Introduction," in his *The Jazz Cadence of American Culture*. New York: Columbia University Press, pp. 17–19. Quotes W that the Negro is America's metaphor.

6785. ____. "Preface," in his *The Jazz Cadence of American Culture*. New York: Columbia University Press, pp. ix–xvi. Mentions W briefly (p. xiii).

6786. ____. "Sterling A. Brown's Literary Essays: The Black Reader in the Text." *Callaloo*, 21 (Winter), 1013–1022. Mentions *UTC* and quotes from Brown's review of *NS* (p. 1017).

6787. Ouellet, Nelson. "L'exclusion de la 'porte ouverte' les préférences raciales des patrons et la chronologie de la Grande Migration, 1865–1925." *Canadian Review of American Studies*, 28, No. 3, 87–128. Includes *BB* in the bibliography (p. 128).

6788. Patterson, Orlando. *Rituals of Blood: Consequences of Slavery in Two American Centuries*, Washington: Civitas/Counterpoint, p. 174. Notes the ritualistic aspect of lynching in "Big Boy Leaves Home."

6789. Payne, Les, "Is Mencken Relevant to Blacks? Was He Ever?" *Menckeniana*, No. 147, pp. 1–9. Argues that despite his racism, Mencken was a stimulus to black writers, especially W.

6790. Pemberton, William E. "*Lawd Today*," in *Cyclopedia of Literary Characters*. Revised Edition. Ed. A.J. Sobczak. Pasadena: Salem Press, pp. 1058–1059. Identifies Jake, his wife, his cronies, Doc Higgins, and Duke.

6791. ____. "*The Long Dream*" in *Cyclopedia of Literary Characters*. Ed. A.J. Sobczak. Pasadena, CA: Salem Press, pp. 1114–1115. Lists and identifies eight of the characters of the novel.

6792. Perkins, Margo V. "The Achievement and Failure of *Nigger Heaven*: Carl Van Vechten and the Harlem Renaissance." *CLA Journal*, (September), 1–23. Mentions W briefly (p. 20).

6793. Petrie, Phil W. "Milestones." *The Crisis*, 105 (September/October), 6. Contains an obituary of Dorothy West mentioning W briefly.

6794. Phillips, Elizabeth C. *Richard Wright's Native Son*. New York: Barnes & Noble, pp. 95. A *Monarch Notes* study guide with the following Rubrics: Introduction to Richard Wright, Introduction to *Native Son*, Detailed Analysis, Character Analysis, Themes, Stylistic Qualities, Survey of Criticism, Essay Questions and Answers, and Bibliography.

6795. Pinckney, Darryl. "The Magic of James Baldwin." *The New York Review of Books*, 45 (19 November), 64–74. Includes discussion of Baldwin's essays on W (pp. 64–65, 68, 69, 70) and a caricature of W by David Levine (p. 68).

6796. Pineault-Burke, Sharon, and Jennifer R. Novak. "Selected Bibliography for Teaching African American Literature," in *Teaching African American Literature: Theory and Practice*. Eds. Maryemma Graham, Sharon Pineault-Burke, and Marianna White Davis. New York: Routledge, pp. 223–240. Lists eight works by W (pp. 232, 234).

6797. Pinsker, Sanford. "Stanley Crouch, Our Black American Mencken." *The Virginia Quarterly Review*, 74 (Summer), 426–433. Begins with a discussion of W's indebtedness to Mencken, citing *BB* and *NS* (pp. 426–427). Mentions W elsewhere (pp. 428, 429).

6798. ____. "Literary Culture and Its Watchdogs." *The Georgia Review*, 52 (Spring), 130–141. Includes discussion of the deletions in *NS* dictated by the Book-of-the-Month Club (p. 137).

6799. Podhoretz, Norman. "Why *The God That Failed Failed*," in his *The Bloody Crossroads: Where Literature and Politics Meet*. New York: Simon and Schuster, pp. 17–32. Mentions W briefly (p. 20).

6800. Posnock, Ross. *Color and Culture*. Cambridge, MA: Harvard University Press, pp. 1, 6, 10, 61–64. 69, 70, 77–78, 80, 214, 308, 321. This study of black writers as intellectuals includes discussion of *BB* (pp. 61–64) and *O* (pp. 77–78) as well as quotations from these works and from *WML*. Posnock emphasizes W's estrangement from racial and political identification or limitation.

6801. Powell, Richard J. "Art History and Black Memory: Toward a 'Blues Aesthetic,'" in *The Jazz Cadence of American Culture*. Ed. Robert G. O'Meally. New York: Columbia University Press, pp. 182–195. Mentions briefly "Big Boy Leaves Home" (p. 188).

6802. Preston, Rohan B. "The Furious Flower." *Emerge*, 9 (July/August), 50–53. Quotes Gwendolyn Brooks mentioning W briefly (p. 53).

6803. Pritchard, William H. "James Baldwin, 1924–1987," in *The Norton Anthology of American Literature*. Eds. Nina Baym, Wayne Franklin, Ronald Gottesman, Laurence B. Holland, David Kalstone, Jerome Klinkowitz, Arnold Krupat, Francis Murphy, Hershel Parker, William H. Pritchard, and Patricia B. Holland. Fifth edition. Vol. 2. New York: W.W. Norton, p. 1999.

6804. _____. "Ralph Ellison, 1914–1994," in *The Norton Anthology of American Literature*. Eds. Nina Baym, Wayne Franklin, Ronald Gottesman, Laurence B. Holland, David Kalstone, Jerome Klinkowitz, Arnold Krupat, Francis Murphy, Hershel Parker, William H. Pritchard, and Patricia B. Holland.

6805. Putnam, "Reading Jazz: Book Review." *Richard Wright Newsletter*, 6 (Fall/Winter), 8–10. Review of *The Color of Jazz: Race and Representation in Postwar American Culture* by John Panish, mentioning W briefly.

6806. Rambsy, Howard II. "Repressed Potentials: Do Cross Damons Walk Amongst Us?" *Richard Wright Newsletter*, 6 (Fall/Winter), 6. Relates Bigger Thomas, Jake Jackson, and Cross Damon to present stereotypes of young black males. Bigger and Jake fit, but Cross the intellectual does not.

6807. Rampersad, Arnold. "Contemporary African American Literature," in *African American Literature: Voices in a Tradition*. Ed. Fannie Safier. Austin: Holt, Rinehart and Winston, pp. 453–797. Includes comment on W and *NS* (pp. 453–454), and *BB* (456).

6808. Reed, Ishmael. "John Edgar Wideman," in *Conversations with John Edgar Wideman*. Ed. Bonnie TuSmith. Jackson: University Press of Mississippi, pp. 126–138. Interview in which Wideman mentions W briefly (p. 127).

6809. _____. "John Edgar Wide-

man," in *Conversations with John Edgar Wideman*. Ed. Bonnie TuSmith. Jackson: University Press of Mississippi, pp. 126–138.

6810. Reisman, Rosemary M., and Suzanne Booker-Canfield. *Contemporary Southern Men Fiction Writers: An Annotated Bibliography*. Lanham, MD: Scarecrow, pp. 187, 369. Provides annotated entries for articles treating W by H. Nigel Thomas and Charles Joyner.

6811. Richards, Larry. "*Native Son*," in his *African American Films Through 1959: A Comprehensive, Illustrated Filmography*. Jefferson, NC: McFarland, pp. 121–122. Lists cast members and others involved in the 1951 film and summarizes briefly the plot. Reproduces a poster advertising the film.

6812. Richards, Phillip M. "A Stranger in the Village: Coming of Age in a White College." *Dissent*, 45 (Summer), 75–80. Mentions W briefly (p. 77).

6813. Roediger, David R. "On White Women Workers: Richard Wright," in his *Black on White: Black Writers on What It Means to Be White*. New York: Schocken Books, p. 295. Headnote to an excerpt from *BB*. Mentions *NS*, *UTC*, *SH*, and *BB*.

6814. _____. "Speech: Robert Hayden," in his *Black on White: Black Writers on What It Means to Be White*. New York: Schocken Books, p. 122. Mentions briefly "I Have Seen Black Hands."

6815. _____. "White Terrors," in his *Black on White: Black Writers on What It Means to Be White*. New York: Schocken Books, pp. 317–319. One of the eight epigraphs to this final section of the book is a quotation from W.

6816. _____. "On White Women Workers: Richard Wright," in his *Black on White: Black Writers on What It Means to Be White*. New York: Schocken Books, p. 295. Headnote to an excerpt from *BB* on white working women.

6817. Rogin, Michael. *Blackface, White Noise: Jewish Immigrants in the Hollywood Melting Pot*. Berkeley: University of California Press, pp. 26, 274, 290. Quotes from "How 'Bigger' Was Born" and mentions the Howe-Ellison dispute about social protest fiction.

6818. Rotella, Carlo. *October Cities: The Redevelopment of Urban*

Literature. Berkeley: University of California Press, pp. 1–2, 19–20, 33, 34, 49–50, 61, 68, 80, 84–85, 92, 96–98, 101, 143, 144, 152, 157, 171, 244, 294, 313, 323. Frequent mention of W's relation with or influence on such writers as Nelson Algren, Claude Brown, and William Gardner Smith. *NS* is mentioned frequently.

6819. Rowell, Charles H. "An Interview with John Edgar Wideman," in *Conversations with John Edgar Wideman*. Ed. Bonnie TuSmith. Jackson: University Press of Mississippi, pp. 86–104.

6820. _____. "An Interview with John Edgar Wideman," in *John Edgar Wideman: A Study of the Short Fiction*. Ed. Keith E. Byerman. New York: Twayne, pp. 90–100.

6821. _____. "An Interview with Kevin Young." *Callaloo*, 21 (Winter), 43–54. Young recalls buying a first edition of *NS* in San Francisco (p. 51).

6822. _____. "An Interview with Randall Kenan." *Callaloo*, 21 (Winter), 133–148. Kenan prefers *UTC* and *BB* to *NS*, which is more political than personal (p. 143).

6823. _____. "'Let Me Be with Ole Jazzbo': An Interview with Sterling Brown." *Callaloo*, 21 (Fall), 789–809.

6824. _____. "An Interview with Clarence Major," *Callaloo*, 20, pp. 667–678. Major mentions an old man in Chicago who had known W. "He talked about Wright a lot and got me started reading ... Wright and Chester Himes."

6825. Rowley, Hazel. "Richard Wright: Intellectual Exile," in *Writing the Lives of Writers*. Eds. Warwick Gould and Thomas F. Staley. New York: St. Martin's Press, pp. 302–312. Discusses W's career as a dissenting public intellectual both in the United States and abroad. His "hybrid identity, his homelessness, and the range of his intellectual inquiry make him a figure who transcends national and cultural boundaries" (p. 311).

6826. Russell, Dick. *Black Genius and the American Experience*. New York: Carroll and Graf, pp. 39, 103, 147–148, 150–151, 210, 223, 239. Mentions W in relation to Ellison, Harlem, Gordon Parks (with W's conversation), and Cornel West.

6827. Samuels, Wilfred D. "Going Home: A Conversation with

John Edgar Wideman," in *Conversations with John Edgar Wideman*. Ed. Bonnie TuSmith. Jackson: University Press of Mississippi, pp. 14–31.

6828. _____. "Going Home: A Conversation with John Edgar Wideman," in *John Edgar Wideman: A Study of the Short Fiction*. Ed. Keith E. Byerman. New York: Twayne, pp. 83–89.

6829. Sartwell, Crispin. *Act Like You Know: African-American Autobiography and White Identity*. Chicago: University of Chicago Press, pp. 9, 92–93, 94, 105–106, 112–114, 127, 137, 139, 143, 148–150, 152, 153. Discusses *NS* as example of black-white ambivalence: yearning and fear for the other (pp. 112–114). Discusses W and Hurston and their contrasting responses to racial issues (pp. 148–150). Mentions *BB* frequently.

6830. Saxton, Ruth O. *The Girl: Constructions of the Girl in Contemporary Fiction by Women*. New York: St. Martin's Press, p. xiv. Mentions reading W.

6831. Schafer, Elizabeth. "'I'm Gonna Glory in Learnin': Academic Aspirations of African American Characters in Children's Literature." *African American Review*, 32 (Spring), 57–66. Mentions briefly *Rite of Passage* (pp. 63, 66).

6832. Scruggs, Charles. "Farah Jasmine Griffin. '*Who Set You Flowin'?: The African-American Migration Narrative*." *African American Review*, 32 (Spring), 161–164. Review taking issue with Griffin's treatment of W. Mentions "Big Boy Leaves Home," *AH*, "Long Black Song," and "Man of All Work."

6833. _____. "Yoshinobu Hakutani and Robert Butler, eds. *The City in African-American Literature*." *African American Review*, 32 (Summer), 340–342. Review praising Fabre's treatment of "Island of Hallucination."

6834. Scruggs, Charles, and Lee Vandemarr. *Jean Toomer and the Terrors of American History*. Philadelphia: University of Pennsylvania Press, pp. 198, 214, 223. Mentions briefly W, *BB*, and *NS*.

6835. Seed, David. "The City and the Novel," in *Encyclopedia of the Novel*. Ed. Paul Schellinger. Chicago: Fitzroy Dearborn, pp. 218–221. Mentions *NS* in which the city denies the promise of success to blacks.

6836. Seed, David, and Ian Bell. "American Literature: The Twentieth Century," in *A Critical Bibliography of American Literature Studies*. Vol. III. Oxford: Blackwell, pp. 189–285. Comments on work on W by Lewis A. Lawson (p. 197), Michel Fabre (pp. 262–263), Mary F. Disney (p. 263), Alice B. Toklas (p. 270), and James Baldwin (p. 273).

6837. _____. "American Literature: The Twentieth Century," in *A Critical Bibliography of American Literature Studies*. Vol. III. Oxford: Blackwell, pp. 327–420. Comments on work on W by Margaret Walker (p. 337), Arnold Rampersad (p. 407), and Harold Hellenbrand (p. 408).

6838. Seed, David, and Lionel Kelly. "American Literature: The Twentieth Century," in *A Critical Bibliography of American Literature Studies* Vol. III. Oxford: Blackwell, pp. 456–550. Comments on work on W by Brian Lee (p. 504), Joyce Ann Joyce (pp. 504–505), Lynda Hungerford (p. 505), Laura E. Tanner (p. 505), and Michael Atkinson (p. 505).

6839. _____. "American Literature: The Twentieth Century," in *A Critical Bibliography of American Literature Studies*. Vol. III. Oxford: Blackwell, pp. 575–678. Comments on work on W by Edward D. Clark (p. 576), and Dorothy Abbott (p. 608).

6840. Shatz, Adam. "Up from Tuskegee." *The Nation*, 266 (12/19 January), 25–28. Review of Adolph L. Reed Jr.'s *W.E.B. Du Bois and American Political Thought* mentioning W briefly (p. 28).

6841. Shaw, Harry B. "Stephen Caldwell Wright, ed. *On Gwendolyn Brooks: Reliant Contemplation*." *African American Review*, 32 (Fall), 499–500. Quotes a review of Brooks by Harvey Curtis Webster mentioning W briefly.

6842. Shin, Andrew, and Barbara Judson. "Beneath the Black Aesthetic: James Baldwin's Primer of Black American Masculinity." *African American Review*, 32 (Summer), 247–261. Includes discussion of W's dominant position ("masculinist enterprise") in African American literature from the forties to the seventies and Baldwin's reaction to it.

6843. Silverblatt, Michael. "Interview with John Edgar Wideman About *Fatheralong*," in *Conversations*

with John Wideman. Ed. Bonnie Tu-Smith. Jackson: University Press of Mississippi, pp. 158–164. Mentions W in relation to his actual father and as a literary father (p. 159).

6844. Singh, Nikhil Pal. "Culture/Wars: Recoding Empire in an Age of Democracy." *American Quarterly*, 50 (September), 471–522. Mentions W briefly (pp. 487, 505).

6845. Sizaire, Philippe. "Sur l'ocean de l'histoire. Derive des ideaux et metamorphose de l'être dans *Speranza* de Sven Delbanc et *Middle Passage* de Charles Johnson." *Revue AFRAM Review*, No. 47 (June), pp. 13–22. Mentions W briefly (p. 14).

6846. Smallwood, David. "Richard Wright," in *Profiles of Great African Americans*. Lincolnwood, IL: Publications International, pp. 367–370. Biographical sketch commenting on *NS* and mentioning *UTC*, *BB*, *O*, and *WML*.

6847. Smith, Barbara. "Sexual Politics and the Fiction of Zora Neale Hurston," in her *The Truth That Never Hurts: Writings on Race, Gender, and Freedom*. New Brunswick, NJ: Rutgers University Press, pp. 28–38.

6848. _____. "Toward a Black Feminist Criticism," in her *The Truth That Never Hurts: Writings on Race, Gender, and Freedom*. New Brunswick, NJ: Rutgers University Press, pp. 4–21.

6849. Smith, Dinita. "Jean Hutson, Schomburg Chief, Dies at 83." *The New York Times* (7 February), p. B18. Notes her friendship with W.

6850. Smith, Felipe. *American Body Politics: Race, Gender, and Black Literary Renaissance*. Athens: The University of Georgia Press, p. 413. Mentions briefly *BB*.

6851. Smith, Jessie Carney. "Arna Bontemps, 1902–1973, Writer, Librarian, Teacher," in her *Black Heroes of the 20th Century*. Detroit: Visible Ink, pp. 77–82. Biographical sketch mentioning his friendship with W (p. 79).

6852. Smith, Sidonie Ann. "The Song of a Caged Bird: Maya Angelou's Quest After Self-Acceptance," in *Maya Angelou's I Know Why the Caged Bird Sings*. Ed. Harold Bloom. Philadelphia: Chelsea House, pp. 3–13.

6853. Solomon, Mark. *The Cry Was Unity: Communists and African Americans, 1917–1936*. Jackson: University Press of Mississippi, pp, 88, 160, 269, 277, 281. Quotes from Max's courtroom speech in *NS* (p. 88), quotes from "I Have Seen Black Hands" (p. 277), and mentions W elsewhere in relation to the Communist Party.

6854. Spiegel, Alan, *James Agee and the Legend of Himself: A Critical Study*. Columbia: University of Missouri Press, p. 15. Mentions W briefly.

6855. Splawn, P. Jane. "'Change the Joke[r] and Slip the Yoke': Boal's 'Joker' System in Mtozake Shange's *for colored* girls and spell #7." *Modern Drama*, 41 (Fall), 386–398. Quotes from *TMBV* on manipulation of language by African Americans.

6856. [Stephens, Henrietta]. "Minutes, October 22, 1997: Seminar Presenter: Dr. Claudia Tate." *Center for the Study of Black Literature and Culture* (Fall), pp. 8–9. Summary of a paper on *SH* extracted from Tate's *Psychoanalysis and Black Novels* and presented at the University of Pennsylvania.

6857. Steward, Douglas. "Saint's Progeny: Assotto Saint, Gay Black Poets, and Poetic Agency in the Field of the Queer Symbolic." *African American Review*, 33 (Fall), 507–518. Comments briefly on Bigger and *NS* (p. 517).

6858. Story, Ralph D. "Gender and Ambition: Zora Neale Hurston in the Harlem Renaissance," in *Critical Essays on Zora Neale Hurston*. Ed. Gloria L. Cronin. New York: G.K. Hall, pp. 128–138.

6859. Stout, Janis P. *Through the Window, Out the Door: Women's Narratives of Departure, from Austin and Cather to Tyler, Morrison, and Didion*. Tuscaloosa: The University of Alabama Press, p. 154. Mentions briefly *UTC* and *TMBV*.

6860. Strouf, Judie L.H. *Literature Lover's Book of Lists: Serious Trivia for the Bibliophile*. Paramus, NJ: Prentice Hall Press, pp. 66, 73, 79, 140, 253, 254, 256, 257, 333, 378. W and his works appear in lists of high school "Oldies, but Goodies, fiction, biography, the American novel masters, black writers, major American writers, and titles taken from previous work.

6861. Sutcliffe, Ann. "*The Third Life of Grange Copeland*: Alice Walker's Debate with Richard Wright's *Native Son* in the Creation of an Imaginative Path to Masculinity."

Richard Wright Newsletter, 6 (Spring/Summer), 12. Abstract of a paper delivered at the Conference of the Society for the Study of Southern Literature in 1998. Sutcliffe rejects any anxiety of influence in Walker's response to W's novel.

6862. Takeuchi, Mikako. "*Native Son*: The Incarnation of a Lost Language." *Hiyoshi Campus English Language and Literature Bulletin of Keio Gijuku University*, 33 (September), 251–268. Argues that Bigger's statement that "What I Killed for I Am" is not a regression but an expression of his tenacity for life and his unvocalized potential.

6863. _____. "*The Outsider* and Richard Wright's Apocalyptic Creation." *Keio Gijuku University Literary Studies*, 75 (December), 188–203. Argues that although *NS* is successful in presenting a troubled youth in a Chicago slum, it can also be read as W's autobiography for the modern age, moving from the Deep South through the North to Escape.

6864. Tangum, Marion, and Marjorie Smelstor. "Hurston's and Angelou's Visual Art: The Distancing Vision and the Beckoning Gaze." *The Southern Literary Journal*, 31 (Fall), 80–97. Mentions W briefly (pp. 80, 95).

6865. Tanner, Tony. "The Good Manners of Andrew Delbanco." *Raritan*, 17 (Winter), 137–150. Review of Delbanco's *Required Reading* mentioning favorably its essay on W.

6866. Tate, Claudia. *Psychoanalysis and Black Novels: Desire and the Protocols of Race*. New York: Oxford University Press, pp. 4–6, 7–8, 9, 10–11, 19–20, 56, 86–118, 123, 140, 162, 163, 180, 181–182, 189, 191, 205, 206–207. Divided into sections on Decentering the Racial Plot in *The Outsider* and *Savage Holiday*, Wright's Compulsive Plot of Violence and Its Critics, Reproducing the Primal Trauma in *Savage Holiday*, The Bad Mother, Wright's Urtext of Matricidal Impulse, and Textual Traces of Repressed Rage at the Mother, the chapter on *SH* provides a detailed Freudian-Kleinian reading of the novel. Arguing that by making explicit the psychological compulsion to violence and locating it primarily in hostility to the mother and only secondarily in racial rage, Tate claims that W was able to overcome misogynist violence in *LD*. Elsewhere Tate discusses or comments

on "Long Black Song," "Big Boy Leaves Home," *EM*, *LT*, "Blueprint for Negro Writing," *O*, and some unpublished writings by W.

6867. Tavernier, Linda. "Felgar, Robert. *Understanding Richard Wright's Black Boy*." *The Black Scholar*, 28 (Fall/Winter), 56. Review emphasizing the work's pedagogical purpose in providing the context of *BB*.

6868. Taylor, Clyde R. *The Mask of Art: Breaking the Aesthetic Contract–Film and Literature*. Bloomington: Indiana University Press, pp. 180, 231, 250, 262. Quotes from "Blueprint for Negro Writing," comments on the movie scene in *NS*, mentions W briefly, and notes that W "broke the aesthetic contract" in writing *NS* after *UTC*.

6869. Thomas, Lorenzo. "Poetry: The 1940's to the Present," in *American Literary Scholarship: An Annual 1996*. Durham: Duke University Press, pp. 379–403. Includes comment on an article on Melvin Dixon that identifies allusions to W.

6870. _____, "Poetry: The 1940s to the Present," in *American Literary Scholarship: An Annual* 1996. Ed. David J. Nordloh. Durham, NC: Duke University Press, pp. 379–403. Mentions W briefly in relation to Melvin Dixon (p. 398).

6871. Thompson, Clifford. "Black & American: What Does It Mean?" *Commonweal*, 125 (13 February), 15–17. Mentions W briefly.

6872. Tidwell, John Edgar, and John S. Wright. "'Steady and Unaccusing': An Interview with Sterling A. Brown." *Callaloo*, 21 (Winter), 811–821. Brown recognizes W's stature but disparages his interest in existentialism (pp. 819–820).

6873. _____. "From Renaissance to Mid-Forties," in *African American Literature: Voices in a Tradition*. Ed. Fannie Safier. Austin: Holt Rinehart and Winston, pp. 379–451. Contains a biographical sketch of W with photograph (p. 410), comment on his naturalism and his influence. These are followed by an account of his schooling from *BB* as well as study questions. "The Man Who Was Almost a Man" is reprinted (pp. 420–430) with study aids. Similar material follows for Margaret Walker, mentioning her connection with W.

6874. Tomkins, Calvin. "Profiles: Putting Something Over Something

Else," in *The Jazz Cadence of American Culture*. Ed. Robert G. O'Meally. New York: Columbia University Press, pp. 224–242. Mentions briefly W in Paris (p. 232).

6875. Travis, Molly Abel. *Reading Cultures: The Construction of Readers in the Twentieth Century*. Carbondale: Southern Illinois University Press, pp. 69, 146. Mentions W briefly and contrasts him to Hurston.

6876. Tuttleton, James W. *A Fine Silver Thread: Essays on American Writing and Criticism*. Chicago: Ivan R. Dee, p. xiii. Mentions the disagreement between W and Baldwin about protest fiction.

6877. Valentine, Victoria. "Noteworthy." *Emerge*, 9 (March), 58. Review of the Library of America edition of James Baldwin mentioning W briefly.

6878. Vickery, John B. "American Literature to 1900," in *Critical Bibliography of American Literature Studies*. Vol. II. Oxford: Blackwell, pp. 639–655. Comments on work on W by Ladell Payne (pp. 649–650). And Marcus Klein (p. 659).

6879. _____. "American Literature to 1900." in *Critical Bibliography of American Literature Studies*. Vol. II. Oxford: Blackwell, pp. 529–550. Comments on work on W by Yoshinobu Hakutani (p. 550).

6880. _____. "American Literature: The Twentieth Century," in *Critical Bibliography of American Literature Studies*. Vol. II. Oxford: Blackwell, pp. 604–638. Comments on work on W by A. Robert Lee (p. 607).

6881. _____. "American Literature: The Twentieth Century," in *A Critical Bibliography of American Literature Studies*. Vol. III. Oxford: Blackwell, pp. 22–45. Comments on work on W by Ralph Bogardus and Fred Hobson (pp. 22–223) and Raymond Hedin (p. 35).

6882. _____. "American Literature to 1900," in *A Critical Bibliography of American Literature Studies*. Vol. III. Oxford: Blackwell, pp. 1–21. Comments on work on W by Fritz Fleischmann (p. 4).

6883. _____. "American Literature to 1900," in *A Critical Bibliography of American Literature Studies*. Vol. III. Oxford: Blackwell, pp. 46–70. Comments on work on W by A. Robert Lee (p. 47).

6884. Wacquant, Loic. "'A Black City Within the White': Revisiting America's Dark Ghetto." *Black Renaissance/Renaissance Noire*, 2 (Fall/Winter), 141–151. The epigraph is a quotation from W's preface to *Black Metropolis*.

6885. Walcott, Rinaldo. "Deceived: The Unreadability of the O.J. Simpson Case." *Canadian Review of American Studies*, 28, no. 2, 177–188. Review of *Birth of a Nation 'Hood: Gaze, Script, and Spectacle in the O.J. Simpson Case* containing a discussion of Ishmael Reed's contribution comparing O.J. and Bigger Thomas (p. 181).

6886. _____. "Deceived: The Unreliability of the O.J. Simpson Case." *Canadian Review of American Studies*, 28, no. 2, pp. 177–188. Includes discussion of Ishmael Reed's comparison of O.J. Simpson and W. (p. 181).

6887. Wald, Priscilla. "*The Power of the Porch: The Storyteller's Craft in Zora Neale Hurston, Gloria Naylor, and Randall Kenan*. By Trudier Harris." *American Literature*, 70 (March), 202–203. Review mentioning W's review of *Their Eyes Were Watching God*.

6888. Walrond, Ann. *Eudora Welty: A Writer's Life*. New York: Doubleday, pp. 13, 15–17, 30, 95, 112, 160–161, 164, 204. This biography begins with a comparison of the young Welty and the young W. "Nothing would illuminate the horror and the stupidity of the segregated south more vividly than the fact that W and Eudora Welty never met, although they were the same age, had similar interests…." Mentions *UTC, NS, TMBV,* and *BB*. Notes that Welty declined to interview *BB* (pp. 160–161). Also relates a story about Mississippi racism in Paris.

6889. Walker, Pierre A. "Zora Neale Hurston and the Post-Modern Self in *Dust Tracks on a Road*." *African American Review*, 32 (Fall), 387–399. Mentions W briefly (p. 393).

6890. Walrond, Eric. "Review of *Twelve Million Black Voices* by Richard Wright," in "*Winds Can Wake Up the Dead*": *An Eric Walrond Reader*. Ed. Louis J. Parassandola. Detroit: Wayne State University Press, pp. 292–293.

6891. Ward, Brian. *Just My Soul Responding: Rhythm and Blues, Black Consciousness, and Relations*. Berkeley: University of California Press, p. 239. Quotes from *BB*.

6892. Ward, Jerry W., Jr. Untitled statement, back cover of *Scripts: Sketches and Tales of Urban Mississippi*. By C. Liegh McInnis. Jackson: MS: Psychedelic Press. Compares the first story in this collection to W.

6893. Washington, Mary Helen. "Foreword," in *Their Eyes Were Watching God*. New York: Harper Perennial Classics, 1998, pp. ix–xvii. Comments on W's unfavorable evaluation of the Hurston novel.

6894. Wasserman, Jerry. "Where the Soul Still Dances: The Blues and Canadian Drama." *Essays on Canadian Writing*, 65 (Fall), 56–75. Quotes Paul Oliver quoting W on the blues.

6895. Watkins, James H. "Introduction," in his *Southern Selves: From Mark Twain and Eudora Welty to Maya Angelou and Kaye Gibbons: A Collection of Autobiographical Writing*. New York: Random House, pp. xiii–xvii. Mentions briefly W and *BB*.

6896. _____. "Richard Wright (1908–1960)," in his *Southern Selves: From Mark Twain and Eudora Welty to Maya Angelou and Kaye Gibbons: A Collection of Autobiographical Writing*. New York: Random House, pp. 366–367. Biographical headnote to an excerpt from *BB*.

6897. Watkins, Mel. *Dancing with Strangers: A Memoir*. New York: Simon & Schuster, pp. 275, 280, 310. Mentions reading W.

6898. Webb, Constance. "Wright, Richard," in *Encyclopedia of the American Left*. Second edition, pp. 908–909. Biographical-critical sketch by W's first biographer. Contains a brief bibliography.

6899. Weiss, M. Lynn. *Gertrude Stein and Richard Wright: The Poetics and Politics of Modernism*. Jackson: University Press of Mississippi, xiii + 150 pp. After an opening chapter establishing the biographical nexus of the two writers and their connection to literary modernism, Weiss provides three chapters comparing a pair of works by the two authors: *Paris France* and *Pagan Spain*, *Black Power* and *Everybody's Autobiography*, and *Lectures in America* and *White Man, Listen!* Living in exile, Stein and Wright offered as outsiders insight into issues of both personal identity and social and political matters.

6900. White, Shane, and Graham

White. *Stylin': African American Expressive Culture from Its Beginnings to the Zoot Suit*. Ithaca: Cornell University Press, pp. 4, 156, 158–159, 261. Mentions W briefly, discusses and quotes from *BB*, and quotes Horace Cayton mentioning Bigger Thomas.

6901. Wilkerson, Isabel. "A Great Escape, A Dwindling Legacy." *The New York Times* (15 February), Section 5, p. 8. Article on the Great Migration to Chicago mentioning W briefly.

6902. Wood, Joe. "Up from Brownsville." *Dissent*, 45 (Fall), 119–127. Review of Alfred Kazin's memoirs mentioning W briefly (p. 123).

6903. Woods, Clyde. *Development Arrested: The Blues and Plantation Power in the Mississippi Delta*. London, New York: Verso, pp. 25, 29, 32–33, 106, 119, 129–130, 147–148. Attributes to W the development of a "blues epistemology," quoting from "Blueprint to Negro Literature," the introduction to the album "Southern Exposure: The Blues of Josh White, *BB*, "Down by the Riverside," and "Fire and Cloud." Woods also comments on W's use of the blues in relation to the Chicago School of Sociology.

6904. Wright, Julia. "Introduction," in *Haiku: This Other World* by Richard Wright. Eds. Yoshinobu Hakutani and Robert L. Tener. New York: Arcade, pp. vii + xiv. Describes the biographical background of W's haiku written during the last months of his life. In poor health, under surveillance for political reasons, grieving over the loss of his mother and some close friends, W wrote this poetry of loss and retrieval, of temperate joy and wistful humor, of exile and fragments of a dreamed return" (p. xii).

6905. Wyatt, Jean. "Giving Body to the Word: The Maternal Symbolic in Toni Morrison's Beloved," in *Critical Essays on Toni Morrison's Beloved*. New York: G.K. Hall, pp. 211–232.

6906. Young, Stephen. "Literary Studies." *Society for the Study of Southern Literature* (April), 22–26. Notes that *Prospects for the Study of American Literature* treats W.

6907. _____. "Southern Author Societies." *Society for the Study of Southern Literature*, 32 (November), 6. Lists the Richard Wright Circle.

6908. X, Marvin (Jackmon). *Somethin' Proper: The Life and Times of a North American African Poet*. Castro Valley, CA: Black Bird Press, pp. 106, 171, 172. Comments briefly on Baldwin and W. Includes a photograph of W (p. 107).

1999

6909. Abe, Daisei. "On Bigger Thomas, IV: Richard Wright and Racial Prejudices." *Journal of Gifu College for Economics*, 33 (June), 143–168. Argues for the folkloric base of W's work, especially the two streams of African American culture: folk and church.

6910. Adams, Timothy Dow. "Autobiography," in *Encyclopedia of American Literature*. Eds. Steven R. Serafin and Alfred Bendixen. New York: Continuum, pp. 61–64. Mentions briefly *BB* (p. 64).

6911. Adeleke, Tunde. "Who Are We?: Africa and the Problem of Black American Identity." *Canadian Review of American Studies*, 29, no. 1, p. 86. Cites *WML*.

6912. Albrecht, James M. "Saying Yes and Saying No: Individualist Ethics in Ellison, Burke, and Emerson." *PMLA*, 114 (January), 46–63. Mentions W briefly (p. 46).

6913. Alexander, Margaret Walker, and Joanne V. Gabbin. "Conversation," in *The Furious Flowering of African American Poetry*. Ed. Joanne V. Gabbin. Charlottesville: University Press of Virginia, pp. 239–251. Mentions reading W (p. 241)and *UTC* (p. 242). Also claims that Hurston influenced W (p. 244).

6914. Allen, Marlene D. "Ann Petry (1908–1997)," in *Contemporary African American Novelists: A Bio-Bibliographical Critical Sourcebook*. Ed. Emmanuel S. Nelson. Westport, CT: Greenwood Press, pp. 377–383. Notes that many critics compared Petry's *The Street* to *NS* (p. 381).

6915. Ames, Russell. "Social Realism in Charles W. Chesnutt," in *Critical Essays on Charles W. Chesnutt*. Ed. Joseph R. McElrath, Jr. New York: G.K. Hall, pp. 147–154.

6916. Anderson, Edith. *Love in Exile: An American Writer's Memoir of Life in Divided Berlin*. South Royalton, VT: Steerforth Press, pp. 27, 30–39, 43–46, 48, 251–255. Recounts a friendship with W, close but apparently not physical, in Paris beginning in 1947. W gave her money and invited her to accompany him to Monte Carlo, but she declined. The book includes letters from W dated 29 July 1949 and April 1952, another when Gide won the Nobel Prize. She calls W "a spiritually wounded man, lost on earth."

6917. Anderson, Marilyn. "Begin in the Middle," in her *Keys to Successful Writing: Unlocking the Writer Within*. New York: Longman, p. 99. Uses W as an example of a writer who wrote the body of a work (*NS*) before the introductory pages.

6918. Anon. "Abraham Chapman, editor. *Black Voices*," in *Literature & Language*. New York: Penguin Putnam, p. 10. Catalog entry mentioning W briefly.

6919. Anon. "Activités Prevues." *Revue AFRAM Review*, No. 48 (January), p. 1. Announces a forthcoming round-table discussion with Bruce Dick speaking on "Richard Wright's Tragic Vision."

6920. Anon. "Activités du 1er semestre 1999." *Revue AFRAM Review*, No. 49 (June), pp. 3–4. Includes announcement of a conference at the University of Paris VII on 16 January with a paper on "Richard Wright's Tragic Vision" by Bruce Dick.

6921. Anon. *"Africa to America to Paris: The Migration of Black Writers,"* in *American Literature.* Princeton, NJ: Films for the Humanities & Sciences, p. 9. Catalog entry mentioning W briefly.

6922. Anon. "Africa to America to Paris: The Migration of Black Writers," in *English: Video & CD-ROM Programs 1999–2000.* Princeton, NJ: Films for the Humanities & Sciences, p. 28. Catalog entry with a photograph and brief mention of W.

6923. Anon. *"African American Literary Criticism, 1773 to 2000,"* in *New from Twayne Publishers.* Old Tappan, NJ: Twayne. Publisher's flyer for an anthology by Hazel Arnett Ervin. Mentions W briefly.

6924. Anon. "African American Studies." Levittown, PA: Garland, p. [3]. Publisher's notice of Philip Auger's *Native Sons in No Man's Land* mentioning briefly *NS* and Bigger Thomas.

6925. Anon. *All Things English: Prentice Hall 2000.* Upper Saddle River, NJ: Prentice Hall, pp. 73, 79, 90, 93, 98, 125. Lists the following anthologies with selections by W: *Literature and Society: An Introduction to Fiction, Poetry, Drama, Nonfiction* ("The Man Who Went to Chicago"), *Literature and the Writing Process* ("The Man Who Was Almost a Man"), *Anthology of American Literature* ("The Man Who Was Almost a Man"), *The Prentice Hall Anthology of African American Literature* (excerpt from *NS*, "The Man Who Lived Underground," excerpt from *BB*, "The Man Who Was Almost a Man"), *Literature of the Western World* ("Big Boy Leaves Home"), and *The American Short Story Video Series* ("Almos' a Man").

6926. Anon. *"American Dreams in Mississippi: Consumers, Poverty, and Culture, 1830–1998* by Ted Ownby," in *The University of North Carolina Press: Spring and Summer 1999.* Chapel Hill: The University of North Carolina Press, p. 20. Publisher's notice mentioning W briefly.

6927. Anon. "Audiocassettes," in *English 1999B.* New York: Educational Frontiers, pp. 13–14. Lists an audiocassette of *BB* read by Brock Peters.

6928. Anon. "Dorothy Abbott and Susan Kopelman, editors. *The Signet Classic Book of Southern Short Stories,"* in *Literature & Language.* New York: Penguin Putnam, p. 39. Catalog entry mentioning briefly "Big Boy Leaves Home."

6929. Anon. "Ebony Bookshelf." *Ebony,* 55 (December), 20–23. Lists *NS* and *BB* among the most important books in English by black writers. Includes a photograph of W (p. 23).

6930. Anon. "En bref … Livres reçus." *Revue AFRAM Review,* No. 49 (June), pp. 30–31. Mentions W briefly in a notice of the French translation of *The Man Who Cried I Am.*

6931. Anon. "Emilio Garcia Gomez; *Lengua, etnia y comunicacion."* *Revue AFRAM Review,* No. 48 (January), pp. 40–41. Notes that this collection contains an essay on "Richard Wright, Voice of Mississippi."

6932. Anon. *"English: Video & CD-ROM Programs 1999."* Princeton, NJ: Films for the Humanities & Sciences, p. 32. Includes an annotated listing of the video *Africa to America to Paris: The Migration of Black Writers.*

6933. Anon. *"For My People: Margaret Walker,"* in *African American Perspectives 2000.* San Francisco: California Newsreel/Resolution, p. 12. Catalog notice of a video mentioning W briefly.

6934. Anon. "Four Giants of American Literature." *The Crisis,* 106 (January/February), 59. Includes a biographical sketch of W.

6935. Anon. "Four Giants of American Literature." *The New Crisis,* 106 (January–February) 59–60. Brief profiles of Hurston, W, Ellison and Baldwin. W was "the African American who changed the face of American Literature," p. 60.

6936. Anon. "From Producer/Director Judith McCray, a New Documentary Film Commemorating the Illustrious Margaret Walker," *Richard Wright Newsletter,* 7 (Fall/Winter), 4. Mentions Walker's friendship with W.

6937. Anon. "In Memoriam: Margaret Walker Alexander 1915–1998." *The Southern Register* (Winter), p. 21. Mentions briefly her book on W.

6938. Anon. "Literature and Language," in *The New York Public Library African American Desk Reference.* New York: John Wiley, pp. 335–366. Mentions *NS* (pp. 337,

340) and includes a brief biographical note on W (p. 363).

6939. Anon. "Make Literature Come Alive for Your Students." *English Journal,* 88 (May), following p. 36. Publisher's advertisement including Robert Felgar's *Understanding Richard Wright's Black Boy.*

6940. Anon. "Native Son," in *Films for the Humanities & Sciences: Multicultural Literature.* Princeton, NJ: *Films for the Humanities & Sciences,* p. 2. Notice of the film on W emphasizing his attack on racism.

6941. Anon. "Native Son: The Life and Work of Richard Wright," in *American Literature."* Princeton, NJ: Films for the Humanities & Sciences, p. 10. Catalog notice of a video with commentary by John Edgar Wideman and Bebe Moore Campbell.

6942. Anon. *"Native Sons in 'No Man's Land,'"* in *Garland Publishing: Literature 2000.* Levittown, PA: Garland, p. 40. Publisher's notice mentioning briefly Bigger Thomas.

6943. Anon. *"New Letters."* *African American Review,* 33 (Fall), following p. 546. Advertisement listing W as one of the authors published in the journal.

6944. Anon. "100 Most Important Blacks in the 20th Century." *Ebony,* 55 (December), 44–48, 50, 54, 56, 58, 60. Photograph of W with caption: "Author whose powerful work captured the rage coursing through Black America" (p. 60).

6945. Anon. "Over 100 years of creative and vital American Poetry in one volume." New York: Oxford University Press, p. [3]. Publisher's brochure listing "We of the Streets" in the table of contents of Cary Nelson's *Anthology of Modern American Poetry.*

6946. Anon. "Oxford University Press." *PMLA,* 114 (May), 423. Publisher's advertisement containing a notice of Claudia Tate's *Psychoanalysis and Black Novels* mentioning W briefly.

6947. Anon. "Preliminaries." *MELUS,* 24 (Spring), 1–3. Includes comment on Lâle Demirtürk's article on *SH.*

6948. Anon. "Professional Notes and Comments." *PMLA,* 114 (October), 1136. Contains a call for essays on American literary naturalism mentioning W briefly.

6949. Anon. "Recent Scholarship." *The Journal of American History,* 86

(December), 1474. Lists a dissertation by Michael Stephen Collins on W and three others.

6950. Anon. *"Richard Wright and the Library Card* by William Miller," in *Lee & Low Books: Annual Catalog 1999–2000*. New York: Lee & Low Books, p. 6. Publisher's notice.

6951. Anon. *"Richard Wright-Black Boy,"* in *African American Perspectives 2000*. San Francisco: California Newsreel/Resolution, p. 12. Catalog notice of the 1994 video.

6952. Anon. "Richard Wright *Writing Is His Weapon*; Almos' a Man *Richard Wright*; Native Son *Richard Wright,"* in *Teacher's Video Company*: Scottsdale, AZ: Teacher's Video, p. 65. Catalog items.

6953. Anon. *"Southern Selves: From Mark Twain and Eudora Welty to Maya Angelou and Kaye Gibbons,* edited with an introduction by James H. Watkins." *The Virginia Quarterly Review*, 75 (Spring), 50, 52. Mentions W's "searing portrait of life under Jim Crow."

6954. Anon. "Suzanne Jones, editor. *Growing Up in the South,"* in *Literature & Language*. New York: Penguin Putnam, p. 40. Catalog entry mentioning briefly "The Man Who Was Almost a Man."

6955. Anon. *Teacher's Video Company: English 1998–1999*. Scottsdale, AZ: Teacher's Video, p. 65. Catalog containing brief descriptions of *Writing Is His Weapon*, the 1986 film *NS*, *Almos' a Man*, and *America's Dream* (dramatized short stories by W and Maya Angelou).

6956. Anon. "Time Line of African American History," in *The New York Public Library African American Desk Reference*. New York: John Wiley, pp. 2–23. Notes the publication of *NS*.

6957. Anon. "When You Want the Best Literature Resource Publications, Call on Teacher's Pet Publications." *English Journal*, 88 (March), 103. *BB* and *NS* are among titles listed.

6958. Anon. "Wordsworth, Wouk, Wright, Wyss, & Yeats," in *Teacher's Video Company: English 2001*. Scottsdale, AZ: Teacher's Video, 2000, p. 65. Catalog listing of *America's Dream*, a video including "Maya Angelou's and Richard Wright's most moving stories" narrated by Wesley Snipes and Danny Glover.

6959. Applebome, Peter. "Willie Morris, 64, Writer on the Southern Experience." *The New York Times* (3 August), Sec. A, p. 13. Quotes W saying "I got out of the South, but I never got the South out of me."

6960. Arensberg, Liliane K. "Death as Metaphor of Self," in *Maya Angelou's I Know Why the Caged Bird Sings: A Casebook*. New York: Oxford University Press, pp. 111–127.

6961. Asim, Jabari. "What Is This New Thing?" in *The Furious Flowering of African American Poetry*. Ed. Joanne Gabbin. Charlottesville: University Press of Virginia, pp. 310–316. Comments on the strong impact of reading "Between the World and Me" (p. 313).

6962. Avery, Laurence G. "Green, Paul," in *American National Biography*. Eds. John A. Garraty and Mark C. Carnes. Vol. 9. New York: Oxford University Press, pp. 504–506. Mentions briefly the play *NS*.

6963. Awkward, Michael. *Scenes of Instruction: A Memoir*. Durham: Duke University Press, pp. 1–2, 9, 186–196. In the context of his own life, Awkward examines *BB*, especially those parts treating W's relationship with his father and, especially, his mother. One of the five epigraphs is from *BB*, and Awkward recalls reading *NS* as a sophomore at Brandeis.

6964. Bailey, Frankie Y., and Alice P. Green. *"Law Never Here": A Social History of African American Responses to Issues of Crime and Justice*. Westport, CT: Praeger, pp. 80, 115, 116–117. Includes discussion of "Man of All Work," *UTC*, "The Man Who Killed a Shadow," and *NS*.

6965. Baker, Houston. "Introduction to *Blues, Ideology, and Afro-American Literature,"* in *Write Me a Few of Your Lines: A Blues Reader*. Ed. Steven C. Tracy. Amherst: University of Massachusetts Press, pp. 456–469.

6966. Baker, Houston A., Jr. "From 'Toward a Critical Prospect for the Future,' in *The Journey Back: Issues in Black Literature and Criticism* (1980)," in *African American Literary Criticism, 1773 to 2000*. Ed. Hazel Arnett Ervin. New York: Twayne, pp. 192–197.

6967. Bakish, David. "Wright, Richard," in *Encyclopedia of World Literature in the 20th Century*, Third Edition, Vol. 4. Farmington Hills, MI, pp. 537–538. Biographical-critical sketch mentioning most of W's major works. "He is now remembered as a prophet of racial turbulence, a master at describing individuals psychologically struggling … and a skillful blender of poetic beauty with harsh reality."

6968. Baldwin, James. "From 'Everybody's Protest Novel' (1949)," in *African American Literary Criticism, 1773 to 2000*. Ed. Hazel Arnett Ervin. New York: Twayne, pp. 91–102.

6969. _____. "From 'Many Thousand Gone' (1951)," in *African American Literary Criticism, 1773 to 2000*. Ed. Hazel Arnett Ervin. New York: Twayne, pp. 99–102.

6970. Baldwin, Richard E. "The Art of *The Conjure Woman*," in *Critical Essays on Charles W. Chesnutt*. Ed. Joseph R. McElrath, Jr. New York: G.K. Hall, pp. 170–180.

6971. Balfour, Lawrie. "Finding the Words: Baldwin, Race Consciousness, and Democratic Theory," in *James Baldwin Now*. New York: New York University Press, pp. 75–99. Comments briefly on the W-Baldwin relationship (p. 95).

6972. Baraka, Amiri. "Margaret Walker Alexander." *The Nation*, 268 (4 January), 32–33. After Langston Hughes and Sterling Brown, "the twin headlines of literary divinity were Richard Wright and Margaret Walker Alexander," but W at the end of his career turned away from the mass experience of his people.

6973. _____. "Margaret Walker Alexander, 1915–1998: A Tribute to Her Life and Work." *Richard Wright Newsletter*, 7 (Fall/Winter), 1, 3, 6.

6974. Barrett, Lindon. *Blackness and Value: Seeing Double*. New York: Cambridge University Press, pp. 125–126, 267. Compares Ann Petry's *The Street* and *NS*, especially with respect to violence. Quotes from "How 'Bigger' Was Born."

6975. Bascom, Lionel C. "Visible Men," in his *A Renaissance in Harlem: Lost Voices of an American Community*. New York: Avon Books, pp. 33–35. Mentions W briefly.

6976. Baskin, Barbara. *"Dreamer/ The Men of Brewster Place/Native Son/Native Son." The Booklist*, 95 (1 January–15 January), 95. 900. Review of four audio recordings, including two of *NS* by James Earl Jones and Peter Francis James.

6977. Bascom, Lionel C. "Visible Men," in his *A Renaissance in*

Harlem: Lost Essays of the WPA, by Ralph Ellison, Dorothy West, and Other Voices of the Lost Generation. New York: Amistad, pp. 33–35. Notes Ellison's early connection with W.

6978. Beauford, Fred. *The Rejected American.* Irvington, NJ: Morton Books, p. 116. Mentions W briefly.

6979. Beauvoir, Simone de. *America Day by Day.* Berkeley: University of California Press, 390 pp.

6980. Bekale, Marc Mve. "La Figuration de l'indicible *Heart of Darkness* et *The Outsider.*" *Revue AFRAM Review,* No. 49 (June), p. 14. Compares the two novels with respect to their use of "a poetic of the unutterable" resulting in a metaphysical impasse.

6981. Berben-Masi, Jacqueline. "From *Brothers and Keepers* to *Two Cities*: Social and Cultural Consciousness, Art and Imagination: An Interview with John Edgar Wideman." *Callaloo,* 22 (Summer), 568–584. Mentions briefly the quarrel between W and Baldwin (p. 568).

6982. Berger, Maurice. *White Lies: Race and the Myths of Whiteness.* New York: Farrar, Straus and Giroux, p. 126. Mentions W briefly.

6983. Bigsby, Christopher. *Contemporary American Playwrights.* Cambridge: Cambridge University Press, p. 41. Mentions W briefly.

6984. Bloom, James D. "Political Incorrectness: The 1930s Legacy for Literary Studies," in *Radical Revisions: Rereading 1930s Culture.* Eds. Bill Mullen and Sherry Linkon. Urbana: University of Illinois Press, pp. 264–275. Comments on W and Communism (pp. 266, 267, 268).

6985. Blumenthal, Ralph. "Edith Anderson, 83, Chronicler of Life in East Germany, Dies," *The New York Times* (18 April), p. 46. Obituary mentioning briefly Anderson's encounters with W.

6986. _____. "John Berry, 82, Stage and Film Director Who Exiled Himself During Blacklisting of 1950's." *The New York Times* 1 (December), p. 31. Obituary noting that Berry "played in and helped direct Welles's production of *NS* and later took it on the road.

6987. Boerman-Cornell, William. "The Five Humors." *English Journal,* 88 (March), 66–69. Mentions briefly the use of dialect in *NS* (pp. 68, 69).

6988. Boesenberg, Eva. *Gender-Voice-Vernacular: The Formation of Female Subjectivity in Zora Neale Hurston, Toni Morrison and Alice Walker.* Heidelberg: Universitätsverlag C. Winter, p. 60. Cites in a footnote June Jordan's essay on W and Hurston.

6989. Boggs, Nicholas. "Of Mimicry and (*Little Man Little*) Man: Toward a Queersighted Theory of Black Childhood," in *James Baldwin Now.* Ed. Dwight A. McBride. New York: New York University Press, pp. 122–160. Agrees that Baldwin signifies on W, especially *BB*, in his children's book. Baldwin revises "the black masculinist canon with the critical signifying difference of queerness" (p. 124).

6990. Bold, Christine. *The WPA Guides: Mapping America.* Jackson: University Press of Mississippi, pp. 93, 195, 113.

6991. Bolden, Tonya. *Strong Men Keep Coming: The Book of African American Men.* New York: John Wiley & Sons, p. 210. Calls W Chester Himes's "idol."

6992. Bonomo, Joe. "Pursuing the Self." *The Georgia Review,* 53 (Fall), 580–590. Review of James Olney's *Memory & Narrative: The Weave of Life Writing* mentioning W briefly.

6993. Booker, M. Keith. *Film and the American Left: A Research Guide.* Westport, CT: Greenwood Press, pp. 178–179. Contains plot summaries with bibliographical references to the film versions of *NS* (1951 and 1986). Notes that neither film emphasizes the novel's leftist point of view.

6994. _____. "The Great Unmentionable: Class, Race, and Gender in American Leftist Culture and Contemporary Literary Studies." *Working Paper Series in Cultural Studies, Ethnicity, and Race Relations.* No. 7, pp. 2, 5–6, 8, 9. Discusses W, especially *NS*, in relation to communism, anticommunism, and existentialism.

6995. _____. *The Modern American Novel of the Left: A Research Guide.* Westport, CT: Greenwood Press, pp. 4, 33, 48, 52, 165, 221, 222, 223, 310, 338, 351–355, 357. Provides a plot summary and highly favorable critique of *NS* (pp. 351–357). Elsewhere Booker mentions W briefly in entries on William Attaway, Arna Bontemps, Lloyd Brown,

Chester Himes, Toni Morrison, Willard Motley, William Gardner Smith, Margaret Walker, and Anzia Yezierska.

6996. Bordelon, Pamela. "Foreword," in her *Go Gator and Muddy the Water: Writings by Zora Neale Hurston from the Federal Writers' Project.* New York: Norton, p. ix. Mentions W briefly.

6997. _____. "Zora Neale Hurston: A Biographical Essay," in her *Go Gator and Muddy the Water: Writings by Zora Neale Hurston from the Federal Writers' Project.* New York: Norton, pp. 8, 14, 31, 32. Mentions W briefly and discusses his review of *Their Eyes Were Watching God.*

6998. Branham, Harold. "Henry Louis Gates, Jr." in *Literary Critics and Criticism.* Ed. Chris Murray. Chicago: Fitzroy Dearborn, pp. 426–428. Mentions W. briefly.

6999. Braxton, Joanne. "Selected Bibliography," in her *Maya Angelou's I Know Why the Caged Bird Sings.* New York: Oxford University Press, pp. 160–162. Lists Keneth Kinnamon's essay on Angelou and W.

7000. Brevard, Lisa Pertillar. "'Branches Without Roots'—but Full Flowers," *Black Issues in Higher Education,* 16 (8 July), 74. Review of W's *Haiku: This Other World* praising W's poems but regretting that they are not contextualized with works by other African American writers such as Toomer, Hurston, Hughes, and Bontemps.

7001. Brown, Kimberly N. "Gayl Jones (1949–)," in *Contemporary African American Novelists: A Bio-Bibliographical Critical Sourcebook.* Ed. Emmanuel S. Nelson. Westport, CT: Greenwood Press, pp. 227–232. Compares *Eva's Man* and *NS* (p. 230).

7002. Brown, Lloyd. "The Expatriate Consciousness in Black American Literature (1972)," in *African American Literary Criticism, 1773 to 2000.* Ed. Hazel Arnett Ervin. New York: Twayne, pp. 135–140. Reprint of 1972.37 with a footnote by Ervin.

7003. Bryant, Earle V. "Johnny's American Hunger: Metaphor and Meaning in Richard Wright's *Rite of Passage.*" *CLA Journal,* 43 (December), 181–193. Identifies hunger as the controlling fact and metaphor of the novella, relating it to *BB, NS,* and "The Man Who Lived Underground." The deprivation leading to hunger results in rebellion against an unjust society.

7004. Bush, Rod. *We Are Not What We Seem: Black Nationalism and Class Struggle in the American Century.* New York: New York University Press, pp. 1, 55, 133. Quotes from and comments on *TMBV* and mentions W briefly.

7005. Butler, Robert. "*The Dialect of Modernism: Race, Language, and Twentieth-Century Literature.* By Michael North." *American Studies*, 40 (Spring), pp. 145–146. Mentions W briefly.

7006. _____. "Farrell, James [Thomas]," in *Encyclopedia of American Literature.* Eds. Steven R. Serafin and Alfred Bendixen. New York: Continuum, pp. 349–350. Biographical sketch noting briefly Farrell's influence on W.

7007. Byerman, Keith. "Angularity: An Interview with Leon Forrest." *African American Review*, 33 (Fall), 439–450. Forrest mentions W briefly (p. 440).

7008. Byrd, Rudolph P. "It Rests by Changing: Process in *The Sorcerer's Apprentice*, in his *I Call Myself an Artist: Writings by and About Charles Johnson.* Bloomington: Indiana University Press, pp. 333–352. Notes Johnson's interest in the philosophical aspects of W's works, mentioning *UTC* and "Blueprint for Negro Writing."

7009. _____. "Preface," in *I Call Myself an Artist: Writings by and About Charles Johnson.* Bloomington: Indiana University Press, pp. xi–xiv. Notes that in 1997 Ghana issued a postage stamp honoring W.

7010. Cady, Jack. *The American Writer: Shaping a Nation's Mind.* New York: St. Martin's Press, pp. 59, 152–153, 171, 176–179, 220–221, 223, 265–266. Comments on W's life and career, *NS*, and reactions to that novel. Elsewhere Cady mentions W briefly.

7011. Calder Angus. "Chester Himes and the Art of Fiction," in *The Critical Response to Chester Himes.* Westport, CT: Greenwood Press, pp. 101–116. Includes comparison of *NS* to *Crime and Punishment* and mentions Himes's friendship with W in France.

7012. Callahan, John E. "Introduction." *The New Republic*, 220 (1 March), 34–35. Mentions W and "The Man Who Lived Under-

ground" briefly while introducing a selection of Ellison's letters.

7013. Calloway, Catherine. "Fiction: The 1930s to the 1960s," in *American Literary Scholarship: An Annual 1997.* Ed. Gary Scharnhorst. Durham: Duke University Press, pp. 281–312. Reviews briefly James A. Miller's *Approaches to Teaching Wright's Native Son*, a special W issue of *Mississippi Quarterly*, and essays by Sharon Hamilton, Desmond Harding, Stephen K. George, Keneth Kinnamon, Angela Albright, and William J. Maxwell. Also mentions briefly treatment of W in a book by Joseph A. Bryant (pp. 285–287, 289, 296, 297).

7014. Campbell, James. "Kerouac's Blues." *The Antioch Review*, 57 (Summer), 363–370. Mentions briefly W and *NS* (p. 368).

7015. _____. *This Is the Beat Generation: New York–San Francisco–Paris.* London: Decker & Warburg, pp. 83, 140–141. Notes that the Beat Generation did not read W.

7016. Carby, Hazel V. *Cultures in Babylon: Black Britain and African America.* London: Verso, 282 pp.

7017. Carlson, Thomas M. "Timeline of Southern Literary History," in his *Contemporary Southern Writers.* Detroit: St. James Press, pp. xi–xix. Notes the publication of *UTC*, *NS*, and *BB*.

7018. Carreiro, Amy E. "Ghosts of the Harlem Renaissance: 'Negrotarians' in Richard Wright's *Native Son.*" *Journal of Negro History*, 84 (Winter), 247. Reads *NS* as a critique of white liberals and white Communists who overlook racism as the basic cause of the plight of black people, emphasizing instead class as the main factor.

7019. Chander, Harish. "Ralph Waldo Ellison (1914–1994)," in *Contemporary African American Novelists: A Bio-Bibliographical Critical Sourcebook.* Ed. Emmanuel S. Nelson. Westport, CT: Greenwood Press, pp. 142–153. Comments on Ellison's review of *UTC* and notes his departure from W's "social realism" (p. 144). Mentions the dispute between Ellison and Irving Howe over W (p. 151).

7020. Chiwengo, Ngwarsungu. "Exile, Knowledge, and Self: Home in Peter Abrahams's Work." *The South Atlantic Quarterly* (Winter/Spring), pp. 163–175.

7021. Christensen, Peter G. "Wil-

liam Demby (1922–)," in *Contemporary African American Novelists: A Bio-Bibliographical Critical Sourcebook.* Ed. Emmanuel S. Nelson. Westport, CT: Greenwood Press, pp. 122–128.

7022. Christol, Hélène. "The African American Concept of the Fantastic as Middle Passage," in *Black Imagination and the Middle Passage.* Eds. Maria Diedrich, Henry Louis Gates, Jr. and Carl Pedersen. New York: Oxford University Press, pp. 164–173. Mentions W briefly (p. 177).

7023. Claridge, Henry, and Deborah Parsons. "American Literature: The Twentieth Century: Fiction 1900–1945," in *The Year's Work in English Studies.* Vol. 77. Oxford: Blackwell, pp. 727–739. Comments on an article on W and Scott Fitzgerald (p. 738).

7024. Clark, Keith. "Black Male Subjectivity Deferred?: The Quest for Voice in Lorraine Hansberry's *A Raisin in the Sun*," in *Black Women Playwrights: Visions on the American Stage.* Ed. Carol P. Marsh-Lockett. New York: Garland, p. 88. Mentions W briefly.

7025. _____. "Re(W)righting Black Male Subjectivity: The Communal Poetics of Ernest Gaines's *A Gathering of Old Men.*" *Callaloo*, 21 (Winter), 195–207. Rejecting the Wrightian protest tradition, Gaines's "protagonists depart substantially from "the psychologically and culturally mutilated Bigger Thomas" (p. 195). The old men in the Gaines novel emphasize voice and community rather than violence.

7026. Clarke-Hazlett, Christopher. "Of the People." *American Quarterly*, 51 (June), 426–436. Mentions W briefly (p. 433).

7027. Clayton, Bruce, "Southern Intellectuals," in his and John Salmond's *Debating Southern History: Ideas and Action in the Twentieth Century.* Lanham, MD: Rowman and Littlefield, pp. 3–81. Includes discussion of W's career, focusing on *NS*, *BB*, and *AH* (pp. 47–48) and mentions W elsewhere (pp. 12, 19, 37).

7028. Clegg, Roger. "The Black List." *The American Enterprise*, 10 (January–February), 84–88. Compares and contrasts *NS*, *Invisible Man*, and *Go Tell It on the Mountain.* The plots of the first two are similar, but Bigger is a "super predator," whereas Ellison's protagonist is introspective and Baldwin's is religious. For the conservative Clegg religious faith is the solution for blacks.

7029. Cohen, Philip, and Joseph R. Urgo. "Faulkner," in *American Literary Scholarship: An Annual 1997*. Ed. Gary Scharnhorst. Durham: Duke University Press, pp. 151–181. Mentions briefly W (p. 162) and *BB* (p. 175).

7030. Coleman, Wanda. "Letters to E. Ethelbert Miller." *Callaloo*, 22 (Winter), 99–106. Coleman mentions W briefly in a letter dated 14 April 1997 (p. 105).

7031. Coles, Robert. *Black Writers Abroad: A Study of Black American Writers in Europe and Africa*. New York: Garland, pp. 6, 8, 10, 101, 102, 105–116, 127–128. Includes discussion of W's alienation, despite his commercial and critical success, that led him to exile (pp. 105–106), describes W's life in Paris and his relations with Baldwin and Himes (pp. 107–116).

7032. Conrad, Peter. *Modern Times, Modern Places*. New York: Alfred A. Knopf, pp. 468–469, 647, 658. Comments on Bigger at the movies and his use of "the same nominalist weapons that have been used against him.

7033. Cox, Linda. "Expatriates," in *Encyclopedia of American Literature*. Eds. Steven R. Serafin and Alfred Bendixen. New York: Continuum, pp. 343–348. Mentions briefly *NS*, W's expatriation, *O*, and *BP* (pp. 347–348).

7034. Crow, Charles L. "Under the Upas Tree: Charles W. Chesnutt's Gothic," in *Critical Essays on Charles W. Chesnutt*. Ed. Joseph R. McElrath, Jr. New York: G.K. Hall, pp. 261–270. Mentions W briefly (p. 260).

7035. Darsey, James. "Baldwin's Cosmopolitan Loneliness," in *James Baldwin Now*. New York: New York University Press, pp. 187–207. Mentions "Everybody's Protest Novel" and Baldwin's break with W (p. 189).

7036. Davey, Elizabeth. "The Souths of Sterling A. Brown." *Southern Cultures*, 5 (Summer), 20–45. Mentions briefly *TMBV* (p. 39).

7037. Davis, Mary Kemp. "Being Southern and Southern Being: Geography and Ontology in Southern Writing." *PMLA*, 114 (November),

1233. Lists a paper by Virginia Whatley Smith on "Confronting Whiteness, Confronting Death: Ritual Space in 'Almos' a Man' and *A Gathering of Old Men*."

7038. _____. *Nat Turner Before the Bar of Justice: Fictional Treatments of the Southampton Slave Insurrection*. Baton Rouge: Louisiana State University Press, p. 46. Comments on Book Three of *NS*.

7039. Dawahare, Anthony. "From No Man's Land to Mother-land: Emasculation and Nationalism in Richard Wright's Depression Era Urban Novels." *African American Review*, 33 (Fall), 451–466. Discusses psychological and political aspects of *LT*, "A Blueprint for Negro Writing," *TMBV*, and *NS*. In his *Daily Worker* articles W points to the solution of the sexual and racial frustration of such characters as Bigger and Jake: "the thirties' Communists' ideal of socialism, as well as the very struggle for the ideal — a social order without sexism, classes, and racism."

7040. Dearborn, Mary V. *Mailer: A Biography*. Boston: Houghton Mifflin, p. 127. Mentions briefly W and *BB*.

7041. Debo, Annette. "Margaret Walker (1915–)," in *Contemporary African American Novelists: A Bio-Bibliographical Critical Sourcebook*. Ed. Emmanuel S. Nelson. Westport, CT: Greenwood Press, pp. 469–474. The bibliography of this entry lists Walker's biography of W (p. 473).

7042. Demirtürk, Lâle. "Mapping the Terrain of Whiteness: Richard Wright's *Savage Holiday*." *MELUS*, 24 (Spring), 129–140. Argues that W's "dealing with white people's problem of freedom is a strategy that enables him to make an effective political statement on the positionality of whiteness as an ideology in America that inevitably raises the issue of freedom for black people" (p. 130). More implicit than open conflict between the races, the point of white racism is raised by the portrayal of the psychologically damaged Erskine Fowler's attitude toward his victim Mabel, who, though white, represents the Other.

7043. De Romanet, Jerome. "A Conversation with Melvin Dixon (New York City, January 6, 1992)." *Revue AFRAM Review*, No. 48 (January), pp. 9–22. Dixon mentions W

briefly (p. 21).

7044. Deutsch, Leonard. "*Representing Black Men*. Eds. Marcellus Blount and George P. Cunningham." *MELUS*, 24 (Spring), 255–258. Review noting that this collection contains an essay on *NS* by Stephen Michael Best.

7045. Devine, Michael J. "Algren, Nelson," in *American National Biography*. Eds. John A. Garraty and Mark C. Carnes. Vol. 1. New York: Oxford University Press, pp. 290–291. Mentions W briefly.

7046. Diawara, Manthia. "The 'I' Narrator in Black Diaspora Documentary," in *Struggles for Representation: African American Documentary Film and Video*. Eds. Phyllis R. Klotman, and Janet K. Cutler. Bloomington: Indiana University Press, p. 321. Mentions *BP*.

7047. Dick, Bruce Allen. "A Conversation with Ishmael Reed," in his *The Critical Response to Ishmael Reed*. Westport, CT: Greenwood Press, pp. 228–249. Reed mentions W four times, always favorably.

7048. _____. "Edward Margolies et Michel Fabre. *The Several Lives of Chester Himes*." *Revue AFRAM Review*, No. 49 (June), pp. 25–26. Review mentioning W briefly.

7049. Dickson-Carr, Darryl B. "African American Literature," in *Encyclopedia of American Literature*. Eds. Steven R. Serafin and Alfred Bendixen. New York: Continuum, pp. 15–22. Comments briefly on "The Ethics of Living Jim Crow," *UTC*, and *NS* (p. 18).

7050. Dickstein, Morris. "Fiction and Society, 1940–1970," in *The Cambridge History of American Literature*. Vol. 7. Ed. Sacvan Bercovitch. Cambridge: Cambridge University Press, pp. 103–310. Mentions briefly W (pp. 111, 137, 142, 175, 249, 268); *AH* (pp. 147, 263, 287; *BB* (pp. 107, 147, 263, 287); 289; "The Man Who Lived Underground" (p. 138), and *NS* (p. 107). The latter references to W pertain to his rejection by Ellison and Baldwin.

7051. Diedrich, Maria, Henry Louis Gates, Jr., and Carl Pedersen. "Part III: 'In Africa, There Are No Niggers' (*Vernon Reid*)," in their *Black Imaginations and the Middle Passage*. New York: Oxford University Press, pp. 175–182. Mentions W briefly (p. 177).

7052. Dievler, James A. "Sexual

Exiles: James Baldwin and *Another Country*, in *James Baldwin Now*. Ed. Dwight A. McBride. New York: New York University Press, pp. 161–183. Comments briefly on Baldwin as "the successor to Richard Wright" (p. 180).

7053. Dinerstein, Joel. "Lester Young and the Birth of Cool," in *Signifyin(g), Sanctifyin', and Slam Dunking: A Reader in African American Expressive Culture*. Ed. Gena Dagel Caponi. Amherst: The University of Massachusetts Press, pp. 239–276. Mentions briefly *UTC* (p. 260).

7054. Dudley, David L. "Teaching Douglass's *Narrative* in the World Literature Survey," in *Approaches to Teaching Narrative of the Life of Frederick Douglass*. New York: The Modern Language Association, pp. 133–138. Mentions W briefly (p. 137).

7055. Durham, Joyce. "Dorothy West and the Importance of Black 'Little' Magazines of the 1930s: *Challenge and New Challenge*." *The Langston Hughes Review*, 16 (Fall/Spring 1999/2001), 19–31. Includes discussion of W's role in *New Challenge*.

7056. Eagles, Brenda M. "A Bibliography of Dissertations Relating to Mississippi—1998." *The Journal of Mississippi History*, 61 (Spring), 77–82. Lists a dissertation by Amy Elizabeth Carreiro treating W and others.

7057. Echeruo, Michael J.C. "An African Diaspora: The Ontological Project," in *The African Diaspora: African Origins and New World Identities*. Eds. Isidore Okpewho, Carole Boyce Davies, and Ali A. Mazrui, Bloomington: Indiana University Press, pp. 3–18. Mentions W briefly (p. 13).

7058. Edmondson, Belinda. *Making Men: Gender, Literary Authority, and Women's Writing in Caribbean Narrative*. Durham, NC: Duke University Press, p. 195. Mentions briefly W and *NS*.

7059. Ellison, Ralph. "'American Culture Is of a Whole': From the Letters of Ralph Ellison." *The New Republic*, 220 (1 March), 35–49. Includes a letter to W dated 27 October 1937 discussing his mother's death, his relation to his brother, the lack of the *Daily Worker* and *New Masses*, and referring to *New Challenge*. Also includes a letter to *Time*

claiming that "Wright wrote better in Chicago and Brooklyn than he has in Paris" (p. 39), as well as a long letter to Stanley Edgar Hyman in 1970 discussing "The Man Who Lived Underground" and denying that it influenced *Invisible Man*.

7060. _____. "Richard Wright's Blues." *The Antioch Review*, 57 (Summer), 263–276.

7061. English, Daylanne K. "Somebody Else's Foremother: David Haynes and Zora Neale Hurston." *African American Review*, 33 (Summer), 283–297. Mentions W briefly (p. 285).

7062. _____. "Selecting the Harlem Renaissance." *Critical Inquiry*, 25 (Summer), 807–821. Mentions briefly W and Bigger Thomas (p. 810).

7063. Ervin, Hazel Arnett. "Introduction," in her *African American Literary Criticism, 1773 to 2000*. New York: Twayne, pp. 1–20. Quotes from "How 'Bigger' Was Born" (pp. 3–4) and "Blueprint for Negro Writing" (p. 12) and mentions W elsewhere.

7064. _____. "Lloyd W. Brown, 'The Expatriate Consciousness in Black American Literature (1972),'" in her *African American Literary Criticism 1773–2000*. New York: Twayne, p. 135. Headnote mentioning W briefly.

7065. _____. "Richard Wright, 'Blueprint for Negro Writing,'" in her *African American Literary Criticism, 1773 to 2000*. New York: Twayne, p. 82. Headnote to a reprint of W's essay, raising questions about W's relation to the African American critical tradition.

7066. _____. "Suggested Reading with Similar Theme," in her *African American Literary Criticism, 1773 to 2000*. New York: Twayne, p. 112. Suggests reading "How 'Bigger' Was Born."

7067. Fabre, Michel. "A Case of Rape," in *The Critical Response to Chester Himes*. Ed. Charles L.P. Silet. Westport, CT: Greenwood Press, pp. 25–32.

7068. Fabre, Michel. "Lynn Weiss. *Gertrude Stein and Richard Wright: The Poetics and Politics of Modernism*." *Revue AFRAM Review*, No. 48 (January), 32–33. Review noting that Weiss moves beyond the biographical convergence of the two writers to a comparison of specific works.

7069. _____. "Richard Wright. *Haiku. This Other World*. Edited with Notes and an Afterword by Yoshinobu Hakutani and Robert L. Tener." *Revue AFRAM Review*," No. 49 (June), p. 28. Highly favorable review praising Julia Wright's introduction and Hakutani's editing. Fabre makes high claims for W as poet on the basis of his haiku, which expand his canon and demonstrate his diversity as a writer.

7070. _____. "A Case of Rape," in *The Critical Response to Chester Himes*. Ed. Charles L.P. Silet. Westport, CT: Greenwood Press, pp. 25–32.

7071. Favor, J. Martin. *Authentic Blackness: The Folk in the New Negro Renaissance*. Durham: Duke UP, p. 155. Notes critical attention to the folk element in *BB* and *AH*.

7072. Ferguson, Roderick A. "The Parvenue Baldwin and the Other Side of Redemption: Modernity, Race, Sexuality, and the Cold War," in *James Baldwin Now*. Ed. Dwight A. McBride. New York: New York University Press, pp. 233–261. Includes discussion of "Everybody's Protest Novel," with quotations. Also mentions *TMBV* (p. 245) and W's interest in sociology.

7073. Fishburn, Katherine. "The Delinquent's Sabbath; or, The Return of the Repressed: The Matter of Bodies in *Native Son*." *Studies in the Novel*, 32 (Summer), 202–221. Analyzes the role of body in the novel, where it is even more important than voice. Drawing on such theorists as Elaine Scarry, Gadamer, Foucault and others, Fishburn examines Bigger's first visit to the Dalton mansion, his night with Mary and Jan, the bedroom scene, the murder of Bessie, and other episodes in which consciousness of the body is paramount. She also relates his consciousness of body to the exploitation of black bodies in slavery and to twentieth-century racism.

7074. Fogarty, Robert S. "Jazz, Jazz, Jazz." *The Antioch Review*, 57 (Summer), 260–262. Mentions briefly Ellison's "Richard Wright's Blues."

7075. Foley, Barbara. "Reading Redness: Politics and Audience in Ralph Ellison's Early Short Fiction." *Journal of Narrative Theory*, 29 (Fall), 323–339. Includes references to Ellison's early correspondence with W.

7076. Ford, Douglas. "Crossroads and Cross-Currents in *Invisible Man*." *Modern Fiction Studies*, 45 (Winter), 887–904. Mentions briefly Ellison's "Richard Wright's Blues."

7077. Forman, Seth. "On Howe, Ellison, and the Black Intellectuals." *Partisan Review*, 66 (Fall), 587–595. The point of departure is the Howe-Ellison debate over W.

7078. Fort, Charles, and Charles A. Peek. "African American," in their *A William Faulkner Encyclopedia*. Westport, CT: Greenwood Press, pp. 6–9. Mentions briefly Faulkner's correspondence with W.

7079. Fortescue, John. "Chronology 1940–1990," in *The Cambridge History of American Literature*. Vol. 7. Ed. Sacvan Bercovitch. Cambridge: Cambridge University Press, pp. 716–761. Mentions briefly W and *NS* (p. 718), *BB* (p. 270), *AH*, and *EM* (p. 732).

7080. Fox, Robert Elliot. "Diasporacentrism and Black Aural Texts," in *The African Diaspora: African Origins and New World Identities*. Eds. Isidore Okpewho, Carole Boyce Davies, and Ali A. Mazrui. Bloomington: Indiana University Press, pp. 367–378. Comments on W's phrase "the forms of things unknown (p. 373).

7081. Franke, Astrid. *Keys to Controversies: Stereotypes in Modern American Novels*. New York: St. Martin's Press, p. 283. Mentions W briefly.

7082. Gabbin, Joanne V. "Blooming in the Whirlwind: The Early Poetry of Gwendolyn Brooks," in her *The Furious Flowering of African American Poetry*. Charlottesville: University Press of Virginia, pp. 252–273. Compares briefly Bigger Thomas and Brooks's Satin Legs Smith" (p. 255).

7083. _____. "Joyce A. Joyce," in her *The Furious Flowering of African American Poetry*. Charlottesville: University Press of Virginia, pp. 319–320. Mentions briefly Joyce's work on W.

7084. _____. "Margaret Walker Alexander: A Mirrored Pool of Brilliance." *Callaloo*, 22 (Winter), v–vii. Mentions Walker's biography of W.

7085. Gale, Robert L. "Conroy, Jack," in *American National Biography*. Eds. John A. Garraty and Mark C. Carnes. Vol. 5. New York: Oxford University Press, pp. 356–357. Mentions W briefly.

7086. Gartner, Carol B. "Charles W. Chesnutt: Novelist of a Cause," in *Critical Essays on Charles W. Chesnutt*. Ed. Joseph R. McElrath, Jr. New York: G.K. Hall, pp. 155–169.

7087. Gates, Henry Louis, Jr. "*Flight to Canada*," in *The Critical Response to Ishmael Reed*. Ed. Bruce Allen Dick with the assistence of Pavel Zemliansky. Westport, CT: Greenwood Press, pp. 119–122. Reprint of 1978.108.

7088. _____. "The Last Sublime Rifts of a Literary Jazzman." *Time*, 153 (28 June), 66, 67. Review of Ralph Ellison's *Juneteenth* mentioning briefly *NS*.

7089. _____. *Wonders of the African World*. New York: Knopf, p. 12. Quotes from *BP* to illustrate W's estrangement from Africa, characteristic of many African Americans.

7090. Geiger, Jeffrey. "Unmaking the Male Body: The Politics of Masculinity in *The Long Dream*." *African American Review*, 33 (Summer), 197–207. Drawing on work by Michel Foucault, Elaine Scarry, and Trudier Harris on the societal significance of torture, Geiger analyzes the role of lynching in "Between the World and Me" and, more extensively, *LD*, focusing on Dr. Bruce's examination of Chris's body and the resulting psychological damage sustained by Fishbelly.

7091. Gilbert, Jenifer W. "Ellison, Ralph Waldo," in *American National Biography*. Eds. John A. Garraty and Mark C. Carnes. Vol. 7. New York: Oxford University Press, pp. 448–450. Includes comments on the W-Ellison relationship and Ellison's writings on W.

7092. Gilbert, Susan. "Paths to Escape," in *Maya Angelou's I Know Why the Caged Bird Sings: A Casebook*. Ed. Joanne Braxton. New York: Oxford University Press, pp. 99–110. Mentions *NS* briefly (p. 105) and contrasts *BB* and Angelou's autobiography (pp. 106–107).

7093. Glasrud, Bruce A., and Laurie Champion. "Chester B. Himes (1909–1984)," in *Contemporary African American Novelists: A Bio-Bibliographical Critical Sourcebook*. Ed. Emmanuel S. Nelson. Westport, CT: Greenwood Press, pp. 203–210. Mentions W briefly (p. 204).

7094. Gleason, William A. *The Leisure Ethic: Work and Play in American Literature, 1840–1940*. Stanford: Stanford University Press, pp. viii, xi, 259–262, 287–288, 290–303, 341, 348, 402, 403–404. Includes a substantial comparison of *NS* and *An American Tragedy*. Both attack early twentieth-century theories about work and play, but W's social criticism is sharper than Dreiser's. Also mentions "Big Boy Leaves Home," "How 'Bigger' Was Born," *TMBV*, and *UTC*.

7095. Glenn, Karen. "Richard Wright's Surprising Secret." *Literary Cavalcade*, 51 (February), 20. Review of *This Other World* contrasting these quiet haiku to the militancy of his earlier work. Includes a biographical sketch of W and an assessment of *This Other World* and its origins by Julia Wright.

7096. Glissant, Edouard. "In Black and White." *The Oxford American*, No. 35 (January/February), 50–53. Mentions briefly *NS* and *BB*.

7097. _____. *Faulkner, Mississippi*. New York: Farrar, Straus and Giroux, pp. 57, 63, 163.

7098. Glover, David. "Teresa A. Goddu, *Gothic America: Narrative, History, and Nation*." *Journal of American Studies*, 33 (April), 198–199. Mentions briefly *BB*.

7099. Goldie, Terry. "Saint Fanon and 'Homosexual Territory,'" in *Frantz Fanon: Critical Perspectives*. Ed. Anthony C. Alessandrini. London: Routledge, pp. 75–86. Mentions briefly W's "extreme homophobia" (p. 77).

7100. Goddu, Teresa A. "Vampire Gothic." *American Literary History*, 11 (Spring), 125–141. Mentions briefly W's use of the gothic (pp. 137, 138).

7101. Gordon, Jacob U. *The African-American Male: An Annotated Bibliography*. Westport, CT, p. 79. Mentions W briefly.

7102. Gosse, Van. "Mickey Mouse and Chain Gangs, Hot Jazz and the CIO." *American Quarterly*, 51 (December), 931–939. Review of Michael Denning's *The Cultural Front: The Laboring of American Culture in the Twentieth Century* mentioning W as an ex–Communist who remained with the Popular Front.

7103. Graham, Maryemma. "Margaret Walker: Fully a Poet, Fully a Woman (1915–1998)." *The Black Scholar*, 29 (Summer/Fall), 37–47. Includes comment on W and the South Side Writers Group.

7104. Gray, Christine Rauchfuss, *Willis Richardson, Forgotten Pioneer of African-American Drama*. Westport: CT, Greenwood Press, p. 55.

Quotes from "Blueprint for Negro Writing."

7105. Griffin, Barbara L.J. *"The Apocalypse in African-American Fiction.* Maxine Lavon Montgomery." *MELUS,* 24 (Spring), 249–251. Review commenting on Montgomery's treatment of *NS.*

7106. _____. "Attaway, William [Alexander]," in *Encyclopedia of American Literature.* Eds. Steven R. Serafin and Alfred Bendixen. New York: Continuum, pp. 56–57. Mentions briefly W and *NS.*

7107. Gross, Ernie, *The American Years: A Chronology of United States History.* New York: Charles Scribner's, pp. 342, 401. Records publication year of *NS* and year of W's death.

7108. Hairston, Loyle. "Chester Himes–'Alien' in Exile," in *The Critical Response to Chester Himes.* Ed. Charles L.P. Silet. Westport, CT: Greenwood Press, pp. 21–24.

7109. Hakutani, Yoshinobu. "Baldwin, James," in *Encyclopedia of American Literature.* Eds. Steven R. Serafin and Alfred Bendixen. New York: Continuum, pp. 66–67. Notes Baldwin's esteem for *BB* and criticism of *NS.*

7110. Halio, Jay L., and Ben Siegel. "Introduction," in their *American Literary Dimensions: Poems and Essays in Honor of Melvin J. Friedman.* Newark: University of Delaware Press, pp. 21–26. Mentions Mark Krupnick's high opinion of *BB* (p. 25).

7111. Hall, Perry A. *In the Vineyard: Working in African American Studies.* Knoxville: The University of Tennessee Press, p. 28. Refers briefly to W's later novels.

7112. Hansom, Paul. *"Political Fiction and the American Self.* By John Whalen-Bridge." *American Literature,* 71 (September), 603–604. Review mentioning W briefly.

7113. Hapke, Laura. "A Labor Studies Approach to Douglass's *Narrative,*" in *Approaches to Teaching Narrative of the Life of Frederick Douglass.* New York: The Modern Language Association of America, pp. 88–94. Mentions briefly *NS* (p. 93).

7114. Hardack, Richard. "Black Skin, White Tissues: Local Color and Universal Solvents in the Novels of Charles Johnson." *Callaloo,* 22 (Fall), 1028–1053. Mentions briefly *NS* (p. 1043).

7115. Harper, Michael S., and Aldon Lynn Nielsen. "Conversation," in *The Furious Flowering of African American Poetry.* Ed. Joanne V. Gabbin. Charlottesville: University Press of Virginia, pp. 77–85. Harper mentions reading W (p. 83).

7116. Harris, Trudier. "Before the Strength, the Pain: Portraits of Elderly Black Women in Early Twentieth-Century Anti-Lynching Plays," in *Black Women Playwrights: Visions on the American Stage.* Ed. Carol P. Marsh-Lockett. New York: Garland, p. 27. Comments on "Between the World and Me" and "Big Boy Leaves Home."

7117. Harrison, Naomi. "Dorothy West: A Bibliography." *Bulletin of Bibliography,* 56 (December 1999), 181–187. Mentions W and *New Challenge* (p. 181).

7118. Hathaway, Heather. *Caribbean Waves: Relocating Claude McKay and Paule Marshall.* Bloomington: Indiana University Press, p. 67. Mentions briefly W and *BB.*

7119. Hellwig, David J. "Black Images of Jews From Reconstruction to Depression," in *Strangers and Neighbors: Relations Between Blacks and Jews.* Eds. Maurianne Adams and John Bracey. Amherst: University of Massachusetts Press, pp. 300–315. Notes the passages in *BB* about black anti-semitism (pp. 300, 308).

7120. Hernton, Calvin. "Postscript: *A Case of Rape,*" in *The Critical Response to Chester Himes.* Ed. Charles L.P. Silet. Westport, CT: Greenwood Press, pp. 139–153.

7121. Hertzberg, Steven. "Jews and Blacks," in *Strangers and Neighbors: Relations Between Blacks and Jews.* Eds. Maurianne Adams and John Bracey. Amherst: University of Massachusetts Press, pp. 245–260. Comments on the passage in *BB* on black anti-semitism (p. 253).

7122. [Hill, Cason L. Hill]. "Contributors." *CLA Journal,* 43 (December), ii. The entry for Earle V. Bryant mentions his work on W.

7123. Hoff, Vickie, and Shelley Glantz. *"Understanding Richard Wright's Black Boy."* *Book Report,* 17 (January/February), 76. Favorable review of the Robert Felgar book emphasizing its pedagogical utility.

7124. Holloway, Karla F.C. "The Death of Culture." *The Massachusetts Review,* 40 (Spring), 31–43. Includes comments on *LD* (pp. 34–40)

7125. Holton, Robert. *On the Road: Kerouac's Ragged American Journey.* New York: Twayne, pp. 35, 91. Mentions briefly *NS* and W.

7126. Honey, Michael Keith. *Black Workers Remember: An Oral History of Segregation, Unionism, and the Freedom Struggle.* Berkeley: University of California Press, pp. 123, 130, 370. Quotes a passage from *TMBV* and mentions briefly *BB.*

7127. Hopkins, Dwight N. *Introducing Black Theology of Liberation.* Maryknoll, NY: Orbis Books, p. 70. Mentions W briefly.

7128. Hoyrd, André. "Melvin Dixon (1950–1992)," in *Contemporary African American Novelists: A Bio-Bibliographical Critical Sourcebook.* Ed. Emmanuel S. Nelson. Westport, CT: Greenwood Press, pp. 129–136. Comments on W's "profound" influence on Dixon (p. 130) and mentions his use of W in his writing (pp. 130, 133).

7129. Hull, Mary E. *Censorship in America: A Reference Handbook.* Santa Barbara, CA: ABC-CLIO, p. 10. Notes that African Americans have protested the inclusion in schools of works by W, Hughes, and Angelou because they contain racial stereotypes.

7130. Hutchinson, George. "Cary D. Wintz, ed. *The Harlem Renaissance, 1920–1940.* Vol. 6–*Analysis and Assessment, 1940–1979,* and Vol. 7–*Analysis and Assessment, 1980–1994.*" *African American Review,* 33 (Fall), 529–530. Mentions W briefly (p. 529).

7131. Igo, J.N., Jr. "Weiss, M. Lynn. *Gertrude Stein and Richard Wright: The Poetics and Politics of Modernism.*" *Choice,* 36 (July/August), pp. 1949–1950. Review stating that the book is more suitable for undergraduates than for the specialist.

7132. Jackson, John P. "Cayton, Horace Roscoe," in *American National Biography.* Eds. John Garraty and Mark C. Carnes. New York: Oxford University Press, Vol. 4, pp. 596–597. Biographical sketch mentioning W briefly.

7133. Jackson, Lawrence P. "Ralph Ellison, Sharpies, Rinehart, and Politics in *Invisible Man.*" *The Massachusetts Review,* 40 (Spring), pp. 71–95. Argues that Ellison moved away from his militant leftism supporting Bigger's revolutionary potential toward endorsement of zoot-suiters.

Quotes from Ellison to W in Mexico.

7134. James, Caryn. "Black Artists Grappling with Profound Questions of Art and Race," *New York Times* 1 (February), p. E8. Mentions W's criticism of Hurston and Baldwin's criticism of W.

7135. Jenkins, McKay. *The South in Black and White: Race, Sex, and Literature in the 1940s*. Chapel Hill: The University of North Carolina Press, pp. 4, 96, 141, 142, 155. Mentions W briefly (p. 4), comments on and quotes from "Down by the Riverside" (p. 96), mentions *BB* (p. 141) and *NS* (p. 142), and quotes from W's review of *The Heart Is a Lonely Hunter* (p. 155).

7136. Jenkins, Robert L. "*All Shook: Up: Mississippi Roots of American Popular Music*. By Christine Wilson." *The Journal of Mississippi History*, 61 (Spring), 108–109. Review mentioning W briefly.

7137. Jimoh, Yemisi. "Cary D. Wintz, ed. *The Harlem Renaissance, 1920–1940*. Vol. 5–*Remembering the Harlem Renaissance*." *African American Review*, 33 (Fall), 526–530. Mentions briefly W and *WML* (pp. 527–528).

7138. Johnson, Charles. "A Capsule History of Blacks in Comics," in *I Call Myself an Artist: Writings by and About Charles Johnson*. Ed. Rudolph P. Byrd. Bloomington: Indiana University Press, pp. 203–213. Includes discussion of Ollie Harrington and his friendship with W p. 205.

7139. _____. "I Call Myself an Artist," in *I Call Myself an Artist: Writings by and About Charles Johnson*. Ed. Rudolph P. Byrd. Bloomington: Indiana University Press, pp. 3–30. Mentions Bigger Thomas, W and W's existential stories" (p. 22).

7140. _____. "Novelists of Memory," in *I Call Myself an Artist: Writings by and About Charles Johnson*. Ed. Rudolph P. Byrd. Bloomington: Indiana University Press, pp. 97–107.

7141. _____. "A Phenomenology of the Black Body," in *I Call Myself an Artist: Writings by and About Charles Johnson*. Ed. Rudolph P. Byrd. Bloomington: Indiana University Press, pp. 109–122.

7142. _____. "Philosophy and Black Fiction," in *I Call Myself an Artist: Writings by and About Charles Johnson*. Ed. Rudolph P. Byrd. Bloomington: Indiana University Press, pp. 79–84.

7143. _____. "Review of *Richard Wright: Works*," in *I Call Myself an Artist: Writings by and About Charles Johnson*. Ed. Rudolph Byrd. Bloomington: Indiana University Press, pp. 175–179.

7144. _____. "Selected Cartoons," in *I Call Myself an Artist: Writings by and About Charles Johnson*. Ed. Rudolph P. Byrd. Bloomington: Indiana University Press, pp. 215–221. The first cartoon features W sitting before a publisher with the manuscript of *NS* in his hand. The publisher tells him that "a book about black anger will simply never sell."

7145. _____. "Where Philosophy and Fiction Meet," in *I Call Myself an Artist: Writings By and About Charles Johnson*. Ed. Rudolph Byrd. Bloomington: Indiana University Press, pp. 91–95.

7146. _____. "Whole Sight: Notes on New Black Fiction," in *I Call Myself an Artist: Writings By and About Charles Johnson*. Ed. Rudolph P. Byrd. Bloomington: Indiana University Press, pp. 85–90.

7147. Johnson-Roullier, Cyraina. "(An) Other Modernism: James Baldwin, *Giovanni's Room*, and the Rhetoric of Flight." *Modern Fiction Studies*, 45 (Winter), 932–956. Mentions briefly *NS* (pp. 938, 952).

7148. Jones, Anne Goodwyn. "'I Was Telling It': Race, Gender, and the Puzzle of the Storyteller." *Southern Cultures*, 5, No. 1, 29–43. Mentions "Big Boy Leaves Home" (p. 39).

7149. Jones, Gwendolyn S. "Blyden Jackson (1910–)," in *Contemporary African American Novelists: A Bio-Bibliographical Critical Sourcebook*. Ed. Emmanuel S. Nelson. Westport, CT: Greenwood Press, pp. 215–219. Mentions W briefly (p. 216).

7150. Jones, Jacqueline C. "Finding a Way to Listen: The Emergence of the Hero as an Artist in James Baldwin's 'Sonny's Blues.'" *CLA Journal*, 42 (June), 462–482. Mentions briefly Ellison's essay "Richard Wright's Blues."

7151. Joyce, Donald Franklin, comp. *Rooted in the Chants of Slaves, Blacks in the Humanities, 1985–1997: A Selected Annotated Bibliography*. Westport, CT: Greenwood Press, pp. 112, 119, 120, 122,

123. Contains entries on W or mentioning W.

7152. Joyce, Joyce A. "*Bantu, Nkodi, Ndungu*, and *Nganga*: Language, Politics, Music, and Religion African American Poetry," in *The Furious Flowering of African American Poetry*. Ed. Joanne V. Gabbin. Charlottesville: University Press of Virginia, pp. 49–117. Mentions W briefly (p. 100).

7153. [Julien, Claude]. "Contributors." *Callaloo*, 22 (Summer), 759–761. Includes a note on Michel Fabre mentioning *Conversations with Richard Wright* (p. 759).

7154. Julien, Claude. "Introduction." *Callaloo* 22 (Summer), 537–546. Introduction to a collection of essays on John Wideman. Mentions W and comments on "How 'Bigger' Was Born" (pp. 538, 543).

7155. Karanja, Ayana I. *Zora Neale Hurston: The Breath of Her Voice*. New York: Peter Lang, p. 17. Quotes Langston Hughes mentioning W briefly in a letter to Arna Bontemps.

7156. Kay, Roy. "Albert Murray (1916–)," in *Contemporary African American Novelists: A Bio-Bibliographical Critical Sourcebook*. Ed. Emmanuel S. Nelson. Westport, CT: Greenwood Press, pp. 355–359. Mentions W briefly (p. 358).

7157. Kelley, Robin D.G. "A Poetics of Anticolonialism." *The Monthly Review* 51 (November), 1–21. Mentions briefly *WML* (p. 2).

7158. Kenan, Randall. *Walking on Water: Black American Lives at the Turn of the Twenty-First Century*. New York: Knopf, pp. 42, 153, 159, 412, 615. Comments on W's relation to Chicago and expresses dislike for *NS*, admiration for *UTC* and *BB* (p. 153). Mentions W elsewhere, including his influence on Haki Madhubuti (p. 159).

7159. Kenison, Katrina. "Foreword," in her and John Updike's *The Best American Short Stories of the Century*. Boston: Houghton Mifflin, pp. viii–xiv. Mentions W briefly (p. viii).

7160. Kent, George. "Rhythms of Black Experience," in *The Critical Response to Chester Himes*. Ed. Charles L.P. Silet. Westport, CT: Greenwood Press, pp. 17–19.

7161. Kesterson, David B. "*Conversations with John Edgar Wideman*, edited by Bonnie TuSmith." *The Mississippi Quarterly*, 52 (Winter),

203–205. Mentions W briefly (p. 205).

7162. Ketner, Carla. "Richard Wright and the Library Card." *Book Links*, 8 (May), 17. Review of a children's book by William Miller retelling an episode in *BB*: "fictionalized but not sentimentalized."

7163. Kilson, Martin. "Stranger in His Own House: A Reply to Phillip Richards." *Dissent*, 46 (Spring), 87–90. Quotes Richards mentioning W briefly.

7164. Kinnamon, Keneth. "A Richard Wright Bibliography: 1989." *Richard Wright Newsletter*, 6 (Spring/Summer), Supplement, 27pp. Includes 293 annotated items and a commentary on W studies in 1989.

7165. _____. "A Richard Wright Bibliography: 1990." *Richard Wright Newsletter*, 6 (Spring/Summer), Supplement, 33pp. Includes 374 annotated items and a commentary on W studies in 1990.

7166. _____. "A Richard Wright Bibliography: 1991." *Richard Wright Newsletter*, 7 (Spring/Summer), Supplement, 33pp. Includes 374 annotated items and a commentary on W studies in 1991.

7167. Kinugasa, Seiji. "On Richard Wright's *Lawd Today!*" *Seiwa College Theses: Humanities*, 27 (December, 57–68. Summarizes W's life. Provides a plot summary and publishing history of *LT*, "a fine description of an African American's experiences.

7168. Kirby, David. "What Is a Book?" *The Virginia Quarterly Review*, 75 (Spring), 292–304. Two groups responded to the following question: "What 10 books would you like your own children to have read by the time they finish college?" Twenty-five advanced placement English high school students ranked *BB* seventh. Ten faculty in English and modern languages ranked *NS* tenth.

7169. Klinkowitz, Jerome. "*City Codes: Reading the Modern Urban Novel*; *The Naturalistic Inner-City Novel in America*." *American Studies*, 40 (Spring), 149–150. Review mentioning briefly W and Bigger Thomas (p. 150).

7170. Koslow, Philip, ed. *The New York Public Library African American Desk Reference*. New York: John Wiley, pp. 15, 337, 340, 363. Mentions briefly *Native Son*, *BB*, *BP*, *CC*, *PS*, and *WML*.

7171. Kranz, Rachel, and Philip J. Koslow. *The Biographical Dictionary of African Americans*. New York: Checkmark Books, pp. 15, 74, 150, 251, 273–276. Contains a biographical sketch of W with a brief bibliography (pp. 273–276). Mentions W in sketches of James Baldwin (p. 15), Ralph Ellison (p. 74), Canada Lee (p. 150), and Margaret Walker (p. 251).

7172. Krupnick, Mark. "Jewish Autobiographies and the Counter-Example of Philip Roth," in *American Literary Dimensions: Poems and Essays in Honor of Melvin J. Friedman*. Eds. Jay L. Halio and Ben Siegel. Newark: University of Delaware Press, pp. 155–167. Briefly compares favorably *BB* to Jewish autobiographical writing (pp. 156–157).

7173. Lamothe, Daphne. "Vodou Imagery, African-American Tradition and Cultural Transformation" in Zora Neale Hurston's *Their Eyes Were Watching God*, 22 (Winter), 157–175. Quotes from W's unfavorable review of the Hurston novel (p. 168).

7174. Lauter, Paul. "The Heath Top 100." *The Heath Anthology Newsletter*, No. 19 (Spring), pp. 1–5. In a poll conducted by Lauter on "the most significant twentieth-century books of fiction in English," *NS* ranked eighth with sixteen votes.

7175. Lee, A. Robert. "Violence Real and Imagined: The Novels of Chester Himes," in *The Critical Response to Chester Himes*. Ed. Charles L.P. Silet. Westport, CT: Greenwood Press, pp. 65–81.

7176. Leonard, John. "Emancipation Proclamation." *The Nation*, 268 (14 June), 36–40. Mentions W briefly (pp. 36, 39).

7177. Lepschy, Wolfgang. "A *MELUS* Interview: Ernest J. Gaines." *MELUS*, 24 (Spring), 197–208. Gaines mentions briefly W's papers (p. 197).

7178. Lessig, Matthew. "Class, Character, and 'Croppers: Faulkner's Snopeses and the Plight of the Sharecropper." *Arizona Quarterly*, 55 (Winter), 79–113. Mentions briefly *UTC* (p. 84).

7179. Lester, Neal A. "'Find Out If They's White or Black': Race Relations," in his *Understanding Zora Neale Hurston's Their Eyes Were Watching God: A Student Casebook to Issues, Sources, and Historical Documents*. Westport, CT: Greenwood Press, pp. 89–150. Quotes from "The Ethics of Living Jim Crow."

7180. _____. "Literary Analysis," in his *Understanding Zora Neale Hurston's Their Eyes Were Watching God: A Student Casebook to Issues, Sources, and Historical Documents*. Westport, CT: Greenwood Press, pp. 1–19. Quotes from W's review of the Hurston novel (p. 3).

7181. Levine, Daniel. *Bayard Rustin and the Civil Rights Movement*. New Brunswick: Rutgers University Press, pp. 12, 43. Mentions briefly W and *BB*.

7182. Levitt, Morton P. "1997–1998 Double Issue." *Journal of Modern Literature*, 22 (Spring), 411–547. Lists a book by M. Lynn Weiss (p. 458), a special W issue of *Mississippi Quarterly* (p. 543) and an article by Damon Marcel DeCoste (p. 543).

7183. Liston, Maureen. "Chester Himes: 'A Nigger,'" in *The Critical Response to Chester Himes*. Ed. Charles L.P. Silet. Westport, CT: Greenwood Press, pp. 83–92.

7184. _____. "Chester Himes: 'A Nigger,'" in *The Critical Response to Chester Himes*. Ed. Charles L.P. Silet. Westport, CT: Greenwood Press, pp. 83–92.

7185. Lock, Graham. *Blutopia: Visions of the Future and Revisions of the Past in the Work of Sun Ra, Duke Ellington, and Anthony Braxton*. Durham, NC: Duke University Press, pp. 65–66. Quotes a long passage from *O* to illustrate the affinity between W and Sun Ra.

7186. MacLeod, Christine. "American Literature: The Twentieth Century: Black American Literature," in *The Year's Work in English Studies*. Vol. 77. Oxford: Blackwell, pp. 794–811. Comments on articles on W by Stephen Best, Yoshinobu Hakutani, Michael Lynch, and Timothy Caron, and books by Maxine Lavon Montgomery and Yoshinobu Hakutani (pp. 800, 811).

7187. Madhubuti, Haki. "As Serious as First Love,'" in *Black Genius: African American Solutions to African American Problems*. Eds. Walter Mosley, Manthia Diawara, Clyde Taylor, and Regina Austin. New York: W.W. Norton, pp. 53–86. Recalls his experience of reading *BB*, *NS*, and *TMBV*.

7188. Martin, Charles. "Optic Black: Implied Texts and the Colors of Photography," in *The African Diaspora: African Origins and New*

World Identities. Bloomington: Indiana University Press, pp. 452–468. Refers briefly to *BB* (p. 453).

7189. Masilela, Ntongela. "New Negroism and New Africanism: The Influence of United States Modernity on the Construction of South African Modernity." *Black Renaissance/Renaissance Noire,* 2 (Summer), 46–59. Mentions briefly *UTC* and *NS* (p. 58).

7190. Masuda, Mitsuko. "The Other as Formative of the Self in Richard Wright's *The Outsider.*" *Nihon Women's University Studies in English and American Literature,* 34 (March), 61–75. Maintains that clarifying W's notion of "the Other" is a key to analyzing his view of existentialism because he was born in Mississippi, which is "the Other" to W.

7191. Maxwell, William J. *New Negro, Old Left: African-American Writing and Communism Between the Wars.* New York: Columbia University Press, pp. 2, 3–4, 7, 8, 88, 92, 98, 121, 131, 133, 151, 154, 156–169, 160–176, 179–182, 183–189, 191–193, 195, 197, 198, 200–201, 205, 216–217, 218. Arguing the mutual benefits of the close association of African American writers and Communism, Maxwell treats W extensively, especially in relation to Zora Neale Hurston and Nelson Algren. W and Hurston agreed more than they disagreed on the value of black folk culture, and W was influenced by Algren's *Somebody in Boots* when he wrote *NS.*

7192. McBride, Dwight A. "Introduction: 'How Much Time Do You Want for Your Progress?': New Approaches to James Baldwin," in his *James Baldwin Now.* New York: New York University Press, pp. 1–9. Mentions W briefly (p. 9).

7193. McCullers, Carson. *Illumination and Night Glare: The Unfinished Autobiography of Carson McCullers.* Ed. with an introduction by Carlos L. Dews. Madison: The University of Wisconsin Press, pp. 23, 43, 62, 64. Mentions W in Brooklyn Heights and a visit to the Wrights in Paris. "Another writer who was particularly dear to me was Richard Wright … Dick and I often discussed the South.

7194. McGovern, Terence J. "Steven Corbin (1953–1999)," in *Contemporary African American Novelists: A Bio-Bibliographical Crit-*

ical Sourcebook. Ed. Emmanuel S. Nelson. Westport, CT: Greenwood Press, pp. 108–114. Mentions Corbin's reading W (p. 108).

7195. McGowan, Todd. "Liberation and Domination: *Their Eyes Were Watching God* and the Evolution of Capitalism." *MELUS,* 24 (Spring), 109–128. Mentions and quotes from "Between Laughter and Tears."

7196. McKay, Nellie Y. "Introduction," in *Toni Morrison's Beloved: A Casebook.* Eds. William L. Andrews and Nellie Y. McKay. New York: Oxford University Press, pp. 3–19. Mentions briefly *NS* (p. 6).

7197. McLaren, Joseph. "Alice Walker and the Legacy of African American Discourse on Africa," in *The African Diaspora: African Origins and New World Identities.* Eds. Isidore Okpewho, Carole Boyce Davies, and Ali A. Mazrui. Bloomington: Indiana University Press, pp. 525–537. Includes discussion of *BP* emphasizing W's criticism of African religion and ritual (pp. 528–529).

7198. McQuail, Josephine A. "Counterculture and Literature," in *Encyclopedia of American Literature.* Eds. Steven R. Serafin and Alfred Bendixen. New York: Continuum, pp. 223–228. Mentions W briefly (p. 225).

7199. Mebane, Mary E. *Mary, Wayfarer.* Chapel Hill: The University of North Carolina Press, pp. 16, 68, 92–93.

7200. Meisenhelder, Susan Edwards. *Hitting a Straight Lick with a Crooked Stick: Race and Gender in the Work of Zora Neale Hurston.* Tuscaloosa: The University of Alabama Press, pp. 1–2. Mentions W briefly.

7201. Mercer, Kobena. "Busy in the Ruins of a Wretched Phantasia," in *Frantz Fanon: Critical Perspectives.* Ed. Anthony C. Alessandrini. London: Routledge, pp. 195–218. Mentions W briefly (p. 206).

7202. Miller, E. Ethelbert. "My Language, My Imagination: The Politics of Poetry." *Arts & Letters Journal of Contemporary Culture,* 1 (Spring), 90–100. Mentions W briefly (p. 96).

7203. Miller, James A. "A Message from the New Editor." *Richard Wright Newsletter,* 7 (Fall/Winter), 2. Statement of publishing policy.

7204. Miller, Joshua L. "The Discovery of What It Means to Be a

Witness: James Baldwin's Dialectics of Difference," in *James Baldwin Now.* Ed. Dwight A. McBride. New York: New York University Press, pp. 331–359. Comments on W's influence on Baldwin and discusses W's "exilic perspective," to which Baldwin reacted. Mentions "I Choose Exile, *O, CC, PS, NS,* and *TMBV.*

7205. Miller, Nina. *Making Love Modern: The Intimate Public Worlds of New York's Literary Women.* New York: Oxford University Press, p. 212. Mentions W briefly.

7206. Mills, Jerry Leath. "Is There a Dead Mule in It?" *Harper's Magazine,* 299 (November), 33–34, 36.

7207. Moraru, Christian. "Charles Johnson (1948–)," in *Contemporary African American Novelists: A Bio-Bibliographical Critical Sourcebook.* Ed. Westport, CT: Greenwood Press, pp. 220–226. Mentions briefly W and *O* (p. 222).

7208. Mostern, Kenneth. *Autobiography and Black Identity Politics: Racialization in Twentieth-Century America.* Cambridge: Cambridge University Press, pp. 104, 107, 112, 114, 118, 128. Suggests that W's dislike of Hurston was political rather than misogynist, praising William Maxwell's account of the dispute; quotes from *O,* comments on W and the John Reed Club, and comments on *AH.*

7209. Mullen, Bill V. *Popular Fronts: Chicago and African American Cultural Politics, 1935–46.* Urbana: University of Illinois Press, pp. 5, 9, 13, 14, 19–43, 57, 63, 106–107, 130, 134–135, 137, 158, 165–168, 170, 185, 186, 233. Chapter 1, "Chicago and the Politics of Reputation: Richard Wright's "Long Black Shadow" analyzes W's troubled relationship with the left during his early career, especially in relation to Chicago's Popular Front and Negro People's Front politics. Elsewhere Mullen examines W's relationship to *Negro Story* (pp. 106–107, 134–135), Gwendolyn Brooks's imaginative response to W) (pp. 158, 165–166, 168, 170), and the end of W's friendship with Ben Burns (pp. 185–186).

7210. Muller, Gilbert H. "Himes, Chester Bomar," in *American National Biography.* Eds. John Garraty and Mark C. Carnes. New York: Oxford University Press, Vol. 10, pp. 832–833. Mentions briefly Himes's association with W in Paris.

7211. Mumford, Kevin. "*Color & Culture: Black Writers and the Making of the Modern Intellectual.* By Ross Posnock." *The Journal of American History*, 86 (December) pp. 1357–1358. Review mentioning W briefly.

7212. Murphy, Brenda. "Plays and Playwrights: 1915–1945," in *The Cambridge History of American Theatre.* Vol. 2: 1870–1945. Eds. Don B. Wilmeth and Christopher Bigsby. Cambridge University Press, pp. 289–342. Mentions briefly the play *NS* (p. 328).

7213. Mvuyekure, Pierre-Damien. "Ishmael Reed (1938–)," in *Contemporary African American Novelists: A Bio-Bibliographical Critical Sourcebook.* Ed. Emmanuel S. Nelson. Westport, CT: Greenwood Press, pp. 391–400. Mentions briefly *NS* (p. 395).

7214. Nadel, Alan. "Ellison, Ralph [Waldo]," in *Encyclopedia of American Literature.* Eds. Steven R. Serafin and Alfred Bendixen. New York: Continuum, pp. 327–328. Mentions W briefly.

7215. Nakagomi, Kazumasa. "A Study of the Tragic Contradictory Nature of Rex Tucker." *Nihon University Studies in English Language and Literature*, 20 (April), 1–10. Analyzes the character of Fishbelly in *LD*.

7216. Namekata, Hitoshi. "Memory: 'Long Black Song' as a Transformed story of 'Bluebeard'" 3 (February), 41–49. Compares W's story to Perrault's, both of which deal with sexual misconduct. "Long Black Song" resembles a fairy tale in which the number three is important: hat, pencil, and handkerchief are evidence of adultery.

7217. Neal, Larry. "Any Day Now: Black Art and Black Liberation," in *Write Me a Few of Your Lines: A Blues Reader.* Ed. Steven C. Tracy. Amherst: University of Massachusetts Press, pp. 422–433.

7218. Nelson, Raymond. "Domestic Harlem: The Detective Fiction of Chester Himes," in *The Critical Response to Chester Himes.* Ed. Charles L.P. Silet. Westport, CT: Greenwood Press, pp. 53–63.

7219. Newton, Adam Zachary. *Facing Black and Jew: Literature as Public Space in Twentieth-Century America.* Cambridge: Cambridge University Press, pp. 32, 74. Mentions briefly W and *NS.*

7220. Nicholson, Philip Yale. *Who Do We Think We Are? Race and Nation in the Modern World.* London: M.E. Sharpe, p. 161. Comments briefly on W and the Communist Party.

7221. Nielsen, Aldon, and Michael S. Harper. "Conversation," in *The Furious Flowering of African American Poetry.* Ed. Joanne V. Gabbin. Charlottesville: University Press of Virginia, p. 83. Harper mentions reading W.

7222. Nolan, Tom. *Ross Macdonald: A Biography,* New York: Scribner, p. 61. Mentions Ken Millar (a.k.a. Ross Macdonald) singing "King Joe" while wheeling his daughter across the University of Michigan campus.

7223. Nowlin, Michael E. "Tate, Claudia. *Psychoanalysis and Black Novels: Desire and the Protocols of Race.*" *Studies in the Novel*, 31 (Summer), 255–257. Review commenting on Tate's treatment of *SH.*

7224. Okada, Seiichi. "A Study of Richard Wright: A Black Writer in Exile." *Saitama University Bulletin*, 35 (November) 57–76. Summarizes W's biography from his first trip to France until his death, analyzing his life and environment in Europe and his works.

7225. Okpewho, Isidore. "Introduction," in *The African Diaspora: African Origins and New World Identities.* Eds. Isidore Okpewho, Carole Boyce Davies, and Ali A. Mazuri. Bloomington: Indiana University Press, pp. xi–xxviii. Quotes Paul Gilroy quoting W saying to Ellison: "Really, Ralph, after I broke with the Communist Party I had nowhere else to go" (p. xxiii), but Ntongela Masilela states that W's travels "were a search for the historical meaning of Africa" (p. xxvi).

7226. Owen, John. "*Native Son* by Richard Wright." *Library Journal*, 124 (1 March), 127. Review of an unabridged audio tape of *NS.* "Peter Francis James's narration is thoughtful but lacks intensity."

7227. Ownby, Ted. *American Dreams in Mississippi: Consumers, Poverty, and Culture, 1830–1998.* Chapel Hill: The University of North Carolina Press, pp. 4, 130, 132–135, 145–146, 148, 161. Contrasts the conservative William Alexander Percy and the radical W. Both rejected consumer culture, but

for quite different reasons. Also contrasts W and Eudora Welty.

7228. Padgett, Tim. "In the Company of Man." *Time*, 154 (25 October), 26. Mentions briefly *BB.*

7229. Page, Tim, ed. *Selected Letters of Dawn Powell 1913–1965.* New York: Henry Holt, p. 196. In a letter to Joseph Gousha dated 11 December 1950, Powell writes about attending a reception for Louis Fischer and Sartre. She remembers W from the Davis house in Brooklyn. She describes W as a "nice fellow."

7230. Palattella, John. "How to Make a Rhyme of a Mystery?" *Dissent*, 46 (Fall), 112–115. Review of Ellison's *Juneteenth* mentioning briefly Irving Howe's criticism of Ellison "for not writing protest novels like Richard Wright's" (p. 115).

7231. Patterson, Orlando. *Rituals of Blood: Consequences of Slavery in Two American Centuries.* Washington: Civitas/Counterpoint, p. 174. Mentions briefly "Big Boy Leaves Home."

7232. Pfeil, Fred. "Policiers Noirs," in *The Critical Response to Chester Himes.* Ed. Charles L.P. Silet. Westport, CT: Greenwood Press, pp. 37–40.

7233. Plant, Deborah. "Introduction," in *Contemporary African American Novelists: A Bio-Bibliographical Critical Sourcebook.* Ed. Emanuel S. Nelson. Westport, CT: Greenwood Press, pp. xv–xx. Mentions briefly W, *NS*, and Bigger Thomas (pp. xvii–xviii).

7234. Podhoretz, Norman. *Ex-Friends: Falling Out with Allen Ginsberg, Lionel & Diana Trilling, Lillian Hellman, Hannah Arendt, and Norman Mailer.* New York: The Free Press, p. 105. Mentions W briefly.

7235. Portelli, Alessandro. "Mediterranean Passage: The Beginnings of an African American Example," in *Black Imagination and the Middle Passage.* Eds. Maria Diedrich, Henry Louis Gates, Jr., and Carl Pedersen. New York: Oxford University Press, pp. 282–304. Mentions briefly W and *AH* (pp. 294–299).

7236. _____. "Yoshinobu Hakutani, *Richard Wright and Racial Discourse.*" *African American Review*, 33 (Fall). pp. 539–541). Essay-Review noting Hakutani's use of genre analysis in his comparative reading of W and Dreiser, Twain, Dostevski, and Camus. Portelli praises Hakutani's consideration of W's non-fiction, but wishes the book had given more consideration to language and historical context and questions whether Bigger and Cross Damon "uphold the concept of what it means to be human in America."

7237. Porter, Horace. "Jazz Beginnings: Ralph Ellison and Charlie Christian in Oklahoma City." *The Antioch Review*, 57 (Summer), 277–295. Mentions briefly *BB* (p. 279) and W (p. 284).

7238. Postlewait, Thomas. "The Hieroglyphic Stage: American Theatre and Society, Post Civil-War to 1945," in *The Cambridge History of American Theatre*. Vol. 2: 1870–1945. Eds. Don B. Wilmeth and Christopher Bigsby. Cambridge University Press, pp. 107–195. Contains an account of the play *NS*, its origin, the role of Orson Welles and John Housman, its Broadway production, and its critical reception. It was "drama of the highest calibre."

7239. Radway, Janice A. *A Feeling for Books: The Book-of-the-Month Club, Literary Taste, and Middle-Class Desire*. Chapel Hill: The University of North Carolina Press, pp. 286–287, 297, 392.

7240. ____. "Mediterranean Passage: The Beginnings of an African Italian Literature and the African American Example," in *Black Imagination and the Middle Passage*. Eds. Maria Diedrich, Henry Louis Gates, Jr., and Carl Pedersen. New York: Oxford University Press, pp. 282–304. Mentions briefly W (p. 294) and *AH* (p. 299).

7241. Ramsey, Kwasi. "About the Author," in his *Notes from the New Chitlin Circuit*. Jamaica, NY: Black Alchemist Press, p. 119. Ramsey acknowledges W's influence on his work.

7242. Rayson, Ann. "Baldwin, James," in *American National Biography*. Eds. John A. Garraty and Mark C. Carnes. Vol. 2. New York: Oxford University Press, pp. 49–51. Contains a paragraph on the W-Baldwin relationship.

7243. ____. "Wright, Richard," in *American National Biography*. Eds. John A. Garraty and Mark C. Carnes, Vol. 24. New York: Oxford University Press, pp. 47–50. Substantial biographical sketch with an appended bibliographical note.

7244. Raynaud, Claudine. "'Mask to Mask.' The Real Joke": Surfiction/Autofiction, or the Tale of the Purloined Watermelon." *Callaloo*, 22 (Summer), 695–712. Mentions briefly "the school of Richard Wright (p. 711).

7245. Reckley, Ralph. "The Use of the Doppelganger or Double in Chester Himes' *Lonely Crusade*," in *The Critical Response to Chester Himes*. Ed. Charles L.P. Silet. Westport, CT: Greenwood Press, pp. 93–100.

7246. Rhoden, William C. "Just Ranting and Raving Doesn't Win." *The New York Times* (30 December) p. D1. Includes comparison of basketball player Latrell Sprewell to Bigger Thomas.

7247. Richard, Jean-Pierre. "Du negrier zu bateau ivre: figures et rythmes du temps dans l'oeuvre de John Edgar Wideman." *Revue AFRAM Review*, No. 49 (June), pp. 3–4. Precis of a University of Paris doctoral dissertation mentioning W briefly.

7248. ____. "John Edgar Wideman: A Bibliography of Primary and Secondary Sources." *Callaloo*, 22 (Summer), 750–758. Lists Wideman's review of *"Native Son": A Richard Wright Reader*.

7249. Robinson, Greg. "Ralph Ellison, Albert Murray, Stanley Crouch, and Modern Black Cultural Conservatism," in *Black Conservatism: Essays in Intellectual and Political History*. New York: Garland, pp. 151–167. Includes comment on the Howe-Ellison controversy over W.

7250. Rochi, Jean-Paul. "'In the Darkening Gleam of the Window'-Pane: La Parole homosexuelle face au signe noir dans *Giovanni's Room* de James Baldwin." *Revue AFRAM Review*, No. 49 (June), pp. 4–9. Mentions W briefly (p. 4).

7251. Rodgers, Lawrence. "*Victims and Heroes: Racial Violence in the African American Novel*. By Jerry H. Bryant." *American Studies*, 40 (Spring), 152–153. Review mentioning briefly W and *NS*.

7252. Rodriguez, Barbara. *Autobiographical Inscriptions: Form, Personhood, and the American Woman Writer of Color*. New York: Oxford University Press, pp. 25–26. Comments on the views of Hazel Carby and Henry Louis Gates, Jr., concerning the different perspectives of W and Zora Neale Hurston.

7253. Roediger, David. "*Color and Culture*. By Ross Posnock."

American Literature, 7 (September), 599–600. Review mentioning W briefly.

7254. Roget, Gwendoline Lewis. "The Chester Himes Mystique," in *The Critical Response to Chester Himes*. Ed. Charles L.P. Silet. Westport, CT: Greenwood Press, pp. 31–35.

7255. ____. "The Chester Himes Mystique," in *The Critical Response to Chester Himes*. Ed. Charles L.P. Silet. Westport, CT: Greenwood Press, pp. 33–35.

7256. ____. "Chester Himes—The Ethics of Ambiguity: An Interview with Joseph Sandy Himes, Jr.," in *The Critical Response to Chester Himes*. Ed. Charles L.P. Silet. Westport, CT: Greenwood Press, pp. 259–272.

7257. Romine, Scott. *The Narrative Forms of Southern Community*. Baton Rouge: Louisiana State University Press, pp. 22, 142. Mentions briefly and quotes from *BB*.

7258. ____. *The Narrative Forms of Southern Community*. Baton Rouge: Louisiana State University Press, pp. 22, 142. Refers to and quotes from *BB*.

7259. Rorty, Richard. *Philosophy and Social Hope*. London: Penguin Books, p. 250. Mentions W briefly.

7260. Rosen, Steven J. "African American Anti-Semitism and Himes's *Lonely Crusade*," in *The Critical Response to Chester Himes*. Ed. Charles L.P. Silet. Westport, CT: Greenwood Press, pp. 221–239. Reprint of 1995.

7261. Rosenblum, Trudi Miller. "*Native Son*." *Billboard*, 111 (March), 27. Favorable review of the audio recording of James Earl Jones reading *NS*.

7262. Ross, Marlon B. "White Fantasies of Desire: Baldwin and the Racial Identities of Sexuality," in *James Baldwin Now*. Ed. Dwight A. McBride. New York: New York University Press, pp. 13–55. Mentions W briefly (pp. 34, 46, 54).

7263. Rowell, Charles H. "An Interview with Brent Hayes Edwards." *Callaloo*, 22 (Fall), 784–797. Refers to W's response to a questionnaire from *Preuves*.

7264. ____. "An Interview with Farah Jasmine Griffin." *Callaloo*, 22 (Fall), 872–892. Mentions W briefly (p. 880) and quotes from Griffin's essay on W in *Approaches to Teaching Wright's Native Son*.

7265. Rowley, Hazel. "Backstage and Onstage: The Drama of *Native Son*," 52 (Spring), 215–237. Detailed account of the genesis and development of the play *NS* and its book version, especially the roles of Paul Green and John Houseman. Draws heavily on papers, letters, and unpublished material by W and his collaborators, including Orson Welles.

7266. _____. "The Shadow of the White Woman: Richard Wright and the Book-of-the-Month Club." *Partisan Review*, 66 (Fall), 625–634. Discusses changes made by W in *NS* and *BB* under pressure from the Book-of-the-Month Club, especially from its dominant force, Dorothy Canfield Fisher. The effect was to soften W's message and compromise his artistic integrity.

7267. Rushdy, Ashraf H.A. "Madelyn Jablon. *Black Metafiction: Self-Consciousness in African American Literature.*" *Modern Fiction Studies*, 45 (Summer), 502–504. Mentions *NS* as a "predecessor text for Ernest Gaines's *A Lesson Before Dying.*

7268. _____. *Neo-Slave Narratives: Studies in the Social Logic of a Literary Form.* New York: Oxford University Press, pp. 70, 137, 181. Compares Lou-Ann Turner in William Styron's *Confessions of Nat Turner* to Bessie Mears in *NS* (p. 70). Mentions briefly W and *NS* elsewhere.

7269. _____. "The Phenomenology of Allmuseri: Charles Johnson and the Subject of the Narrative of Slavery," in *I Call Myself an Artist: Writings by and About Charles Johnson.* Ed. Rudolph P. Byrd. Bloomington: Indiana University Press, pp. 369–389. Reprint of 1992.

7270. Rusk, Lauren. "Selfhood and Strategy in *Notes of a Native Son*," in *James Baldwin Now.* Ed. Dwight A. McBride. New York: New York University Press, pp. 360–392. Mentions briefly W and *NS* (pp. 367, 370).

7271. Sallis, James. "In America's Black Heartland: The Achievement of Chester Himes," in *The Critical Response to Chester Himes.* Ed. Charles L.P. Silet. Westport, CT: Greenwood Press, pp. 127–137.

7272. Samson, John. "Melville," in *American Literary Scholarship: An Annual 1997.* Ed. Gary Scharnhorst. Durham: Duke University Press, pp. 45–60. Mentions W briefly (p. 45).

7273. Saunders, James Robert. "Claudia Tate. *Psychoanalysis and Black Novels: Desire and Protocols of Race.*" *Modern Fiction Studies*, 45 (Summer), 498–502. Calls Tate's treatment of W "absolutely brilliant" in showing that W's depiction of violence derives from his family and its responses to racism.

7274. _____. "Jerry H. Bryant. *Victims and Heroes: Racial Violence in the African American Novel.*" *Modern Fiction Studies*, 44 (Summer 1998), 402–404. Favorable review, but the chapter on W is weak because it offers little that is original.

7275. Savage, Barbara Dianne. *Broadcasting Freedom: Radio, War, and the Politics of Race, 1938–1948.* Chapel Hill: The University of North Carolina Press, pp. 16, 86, 217–222, 237, 241, 243, 263, 264, 341–342, 347. Contains a discussion containing new material about W's role in the broadcast on *Town Meeting* on the racial problem. Includes comment on the response of listeners, mostly outrage and protest (pp. 217–222, 341–342). Mentions W briefly elsewhere.

7276. Scharnhorst, Gary. "General Reference Books," in his *American Literary Scholarship: An Annual 1997.* Durham: Duke University Press, pp. 501–508. Mentions W briefly (p. 504).

7277. Schenk, Leslie. "Literary Biographies Today." *World Literature Today.* 73 (Winter), 88–92. Mentions W briefly.

7278. Schmitz, Neil. "Neo Hoodo: The Experimental Fiction of Ishmael Reed," in *The Critical Response to Ishmael Reed.* Ed. Bruce Allen Dick with the assistance of Pavel Zemliansky. Westport, CT: Greenwood Press, pp. 69–82.

7279. Schultz, Elizabeth. "The Power of Blackness: Richard Wright Re-Writes *Moby-Dick.*" *African American Review*, 33 (Winter), 639–654. Thorough treatment of W's use of the Melville novel in *NS* emphasizing Bigger as an epic hero: "By signifying on *Moby-Dick* ... Wright presents his readers simultaneously with a scathing exposé of American racism and a triumphant African-American epic:' Schultz documents W's knowledge of Melville and Lewis Mumford's biography, shows how he inflects the whiteness of the whale with racial

meanings, deals with the issue of free will vs. determinism, notes similar character traits in Ahab and Bigger and, in his expanding awareness of human solidarity, Bigger's similarity to Ishmael. Schultz also traces Melville's influence on the language and imagery of *NS*.

7280. Selzer, Linda Furgurson. "Reading the Painterly Text: Clarence Major's 'The Slave Trade: View from the Middle Passage.'" *African American Review*, 33 (Summer), 209–229. Refers to W's statement in *WML* that "the Negro is America's metaphor, showing that Major uses it in his poem.

7281. Sharpe, William Chapman. "The City and Literature," in *Encyclopedia of American Literature.* Eds. Steven R. Serafin and Alfred Bendixen. New York: Continuum, pp. 194–197. Mentions briefly "The Man Who Lived Underground" and *NS*.

7282. Silet, Charles L.P. "Introduction," in his *The Critical Response to Chester Himes.* Westport, CT: Greenwood Press, pp. xvii, xviii, xxi. Mentions W briefly.

7283. Simms-Burton, Michele Lisa. "The Chicago Renaissance: Revisiting a Literary Movement, 1920–30." *PMLA*, 114 (November), 1245. Lists a paper by James A. Miller on "Going Postal: Richard Wright's Anti-Renaissance Novel, *Lawd Today.*"

7284/5. Skinner, Robert. "The Black Man in the Literature of Labor: The Early Novels of Chester Himes," in *The Critical Response to Chester Himes.* Ed. Charles L.P. Silet. Westport, CT: Greenwood Press, pp. 187–200.

7286. Smethurst, James Edward. *The New Red Negro: The Literary Left and African American Poetry, 1930–1946.* New York: Oxford University Press, pp. 10, 22, 27, 32, 34, 37, 38–39, 40, 41, 42, 43–44, 45, 47, 48, 88, 89, 168–170, 179, 181, 204, 224, 238, 243, 246, 247, 248. Comments on "King Joe" (pp. 10, 32, 134, 157); *NS* (pp. 48, 89, 238, 247, 248); W and the Communist Party (pp. 38–39, 45, 48); South Side Writers Group (pp. 40, 224); "I Am a Red Slogan" (p. 42); and W and Gwendolyn Brooks' (pp. 168–170). Mentions W elsewhere.

7287. Smith, Barbara. "Recent Fiction: *The Last Days of Louisiana Red,*" in *The Critical Response to Ish-*

mael Reed. Ed. Bruce Allen Dick with the assistance of Pavel Zemliansky. Westport, CT: Greenwood Press, pp. 83–85.

7288. _____. "Toward a Black Feminist Criticism (1977)," in *African American Literary Criticism, 1773 to 2000*. Ed. Hazel Arnett Ervin. New York: Twayne, pp. 162–171.

7289. Stanley, Sandra K. "Black Literature, Desire and the Psychoanalytical Model." *Callaloo*, 21 (Winter), 253–254. Review of Claudia Tate's *Psychoanalysis and Black Novels* noting that it treats *SH*.

7290. Steele, Shelby. "The Content of His Character." *The New Republic*, 220 (1 March), 27–34. Review of *Flying Home and Other Stories* mentioning W briefly (p. 27).

7291. Steinberg, Stephen. "Occupational Apartheid in America: Race, Labor Market Segmentation, and Affirmative Action," in *Without Justice for All: The New Liberalism and Our Retreat from Racial Equality*. Ed. Adolph Reed Jr. New York: Westview Press, pp. 215–233. Quotes W on white and black resistance to exposing the magnitude of racism (p. 222).

7292. _____. "Occupational Apartheid in America: Race, Labor Market Segmentation, and Affirmative Action," in *Without Justice for All: The New Liberalism and Our Retreat from Racial Equality*. Ed. Adolph Reed Jr. Boulder: Westview Press, pp. 215–233. Quotes W on black and white reluctance to discuss the racial problem "in all of its hideous fullness" (p. 222).

7293. Steiner, Stanley, and Joy Steiner. "*Richard Wright and the Library Card* by William Miller." *Book Links*, 8 (March), 22. Brief notice.

7294. Steinhorn, Leonard, and Barbara Diggs-Brown. *By the Color of Our Skin: The Illusion of Integration and the Reality of Race*. New York: Dutton, pp. 45, 80. Mentions briefly *BB* and W.

7295. Stephens, Gregory. *On Racial Frontiers: The New Culture of Frederick Douglass, Ralph Ellison, and Bob Marley*. Cambridge: Cambridge University Press, pp. 95, 119, 120–121. Discusses W's relation to Ellison and mentions W briefly.

7296. Stevens, Norman D. "A Review Article: Librarians and Libraries for Children." *The Library Quarterly*, 69 (January), p. 90. Lists William Miller's *Richard Wright and the Library Card* and comments briefly.

7297. Stevens, Shane. "The Best Black American Novelist Writing Today," in *The Critical Response to Chester Himes*. Ed. Charles L.P. Silet. Westport, CT: Greenwood Press, pp. 13–15.

7298. Storhoff, Gary. "Slaying the Fathers: The Autobiography of Chester Himes," in *The Critical Response to Chester Himes*. Ed. Charles L.P. Silet. Westport, CT: Greenwood Press, pp. 241–255.

7299. Sundquist, Eric J. "The Business of Inventing the South." *Mississippi Quarterly*, 52 (Fall), 685–687. Mentions W briefly (p. 686).

7300. Takeuchi, Mikako. "Yoshinobu Hakutani, *Richard Wright and Racial Discourse*," *English Literature Studies*, 76 (September), 60–64. Review noting Hakutani's "consistent attitude to evaluate Wright's works positively."

7301. Tate, Claudia. "Maya Angelou: An Interview," in *Maya Angelou's I Know Why the Caged Bird Sings: A Casebook*. Ed. Joanne Braxton. New York: Oxford University Press, pp. 149–158.

7302. _____. "Introduction: Race and Psychoanalysis," in *Psychoanalysis and Black Novels, Desire and the Protocols of Race*," in *African American Literary Criticism, 1773 to 2000*. Ed. Hazel Arnett Ervin. New York: Twayne, pp. 481–486.

7303. _____. "Maya Angelou: An Interview," in *Maya Angelou's I Know Why the Caged Bird Sings: A Casebook*. New York: Oxford University Press, pp. 149–158.

7304. Thomas, Lorenzo. "Two Crowns of Thoth: A Study of Ishmael Reed's *The Last Days of Louisiana Red*," in *The Critical Response to Ishmael Reed*. Ed. Bruce Allen Dick with the assistance of Pavel Zemliansky. Westport, CT: Greenwood Press, pp. 85–104.

7305. Thompson, Julius E. *Dudley Randall, Broadside Press, and the Black Arts Movement in Detroit, 1960–1995*. Jefferson, NC: McFarland, p. 15. Mentions W briefly.

7306. Titon, Jeff Todd. "From 'The Songs: Formulaic Structure and Meaning in Early Downhome Blues,'" in *Write Me a Few of Your Lines: A Blues Reader*. Ed. Steven C. Tracy. Amherst: University of Mass-

achusetts Press, pp. 361–363.

7307. Tolbert, Blake. "*Dudley Randall, Broadside Press, and the Black Arts Movement in Detroit, 1960–1995*." *Western Journal of Black Studies*, 23 (Winter), 257–258. Review mentioning W briefly.

7308. Tomlinson, Robert. "'Paying One's Dues': Expatriation as Personal Experience and Paradigm in the Works of James Baldwin." *African American Review*, 33 (Spring), 135–148. Quotes Baldwin's essay "Alas, Poor Richard" and comments on his quarrel with W (pp. 140, 142, 145, 147).

7309. Tracy, Steven C. "Defining the Blues–Useful/Interesting/Provocative Definitions," in his *Write Me a Few of Your Lines: A Blues Reader*. Amherst: University of Massachusetts Press, pp. 10–12. Includes a comment by W.

7310. _____. "Hughes, Langston," in *American National Biography*. Eds. John Garraty and Mark C. Carnes. New York: Oxford University Press, Vol. II, pp. 429–432. Mentions briefly *NS* (p. 431).

7311. _____. "A Note on the Readings," in his *Write Me a Few of Your Lines: A Blues Reader*. Amherst: University of Massachusetts Press, pp. 8–9. Mentions W briefly.

7312. Traylor, Eleanor W. "A Blues View of Life (Literature and the Blues Vision)," in *The Blues Aesthetic: Black Culture and Modernism*. Ed. Richard J. Powell. Washington, DC: Washington Project for the Arts, pp. 43–44. Mentions briefly *UTC*.

7313. _____. "A Blues View of Life (Literature and the Blues Vision) (1989)," in *African American Literary Criticism 1773–2000*. Ed. Hazel Arnett Ervin. New York: Twayne, pp. 285–288.

7314. Trombold, John. "The Minstrel Show Goes to the Great War: Zora Neale Hurston's Mass Cultural Other." *MELUS*, 24 (Spring), 85–107. Includes comments on "Almos' a Man" (pp. 88, 90) and *NS* (p. 99).

7315. Tuhkanen, Mikko Juhani. "'A [B]igger's Place': Lynching and Specularity in Richard Wright's 'Fire and Cloud' and *Native Son*." *African American Review*, 33 (Spring), 125–133. Drawing on theoretical perspectives of Robin Wiegman and Foucauld, Tuhkanen argues that Taylor's corporal punishment is less restrictive than the humiliation of "enforced visibility" that Bigger experiences.

7316. Updike, John. "Introduction," in his and Katrina Kenison's *The Best American Short Stories of the Century*. Boston: Houghton Mifflin, p. xviii. Calls "Bright and Morning Star" "a painful relic of a time when American blacks could see their lone friend and best hope in the Communist party."

7317. Valentine, Victoria. "Noteworthy." *Emerge*, 10 (March), 68. A review of Margaret Walker's *Jubilee* mentioning W briefly.

7318. Wachtel, Paul L. *Race in the Mind of America: Breaking the Vicious Circle Between Blacks and Whites*. New York: Routledge, p. 147. Mentions W briefly.

7319. Walden, Daniel. "Abraham Cahan and Richard Wright: The American Dream and the Dream of America?" *The Mid-Atlantic Almanack*, 8, 101–113. Reviews the lives careers, and politics of the two writers, arguing that by compromise Cahan achieved the dream, but W, focusing unblinkingly on the integrity of his vision, did not.

7320. Walker, Pierre A. "Racial Protest, Identity, Words, and Form," in *Maya Angelou's I Know Why the Caged Bird Sings: A Casebook*. Ed. Joanne M. Braxton. New York: Oxford University Press, pp. 77–97.

7321. Wallace, Maurice. "'I'm Not Entirely What I Look Like': Richard Wright, James Baldwin, and the Hegemony of Vision; or Jimmy's FBEye Blues," in *James Baldwin Now*. Ed. Dwight A. McBride. New York: New York University Press, pp. 289–306. The first half of this essay discusses the role of "the ekphrastic menace to black male subjecthood" in *NS*. The "racial glare" of whites debilitates Bigger, even paralyzes him. In making his case Wallace adduces theoretical perspectives of W.J.T. Mitchell and Martin Heidegger.

7322. Wallace, Michele. "Female Troubles: Ishmael Reed's Tunnel Vision," in *The Critical Response to Ishmael Reed*. Ed. Bruce Allen Dick with the assistance of Pavel Zemliansky. Westport, CT: Greenwood Press, pp. 183–191.

7323. Walton, Anthony. "Plugging Into the Mythic Past." *The Oxford American*, No. 35 (January/

February), 88–90. Mentions W briefly.

7324. Ward, Jerry W., Jr. "Foreword in *Black Southern Voices: An Anthology* (1992)," in *African American Literary Criticism, 1773 to 2000*. Ed. Hazel Arnett Ervin. New York: Twayne, pp. 353–358.

7325. _____. "*In Search of Africa*." *Richard Wright Newsletter*, 7 (Fall/Winter), 3. Review emphasizing Manthia Diawara's favorable treatment of *BP*. Ward urges more consideration of W's nonfiction of the 1950s.

7326. Watermeier, Daniel J. "Actors and Acting," in *The Cambridge History of American Theatre*. Vol 2: 1870–1945. Eds. Don B. Wilmeth and Christopher Bigsby. Cambridge: Cambridge University Press, pp. 446–486. Mentions briefly the play *NS* (p. 481).

7327. Weaks, Mary Louise. "The Gendered South." *Mississippi Quarterly*, 52 (Winter), 163–170. Review of *Haunted Bodies: Gender and Southern Texts*, edited by Anne Goodwyn Jones and Susan V. Donaldson, mentioning briefly *BB* (p. 165) and W (p. 169).

7328. Weiner, Lois. "Teaching in Urban Public Schools *Is* Different." *English Journal*, 88 (May), 21–25. Comments on teaching *BB* with emphasis on hunger as a metaphor (pp. 22–23).

7329. _____. "To Teach or Not to Teach in an Urban School?" *English Journal*, 88 (May), 21–23. Mentions briefly hunger "as a compelling metaphor" in *BB*.

7330. Werner, Craig. *A Change Is Gonna Come: Music, Race & the Soul of America*. New York: Penguin Putnam, pp. 24, 63. Mentions briefly W, *NS*, and *BB*.

7331. West, Cornel. "Black Strivings in Twilight Civilization," in *The Cornel West Reader*. New York: Basic Books, pp. 87–118. Includes discussion of Bigger Thomas as exemplification of self-hatred of others (pp. 109–113).

7332. _____. "The Dilemma of the Black Intellectual," in his *The Cornel West Reader*. New York: Basic Books, pp. 302–315.

7333. _____. "Horace Pippin's Challenge to Art Criticism," in *The Cornel West Reader*. New York: Basic Books, pp. 447–455.

7334. West, Cornel, Jorge Klor de Alva, and Earl Shorris. "On Black-

Brown Relations," in West's *The Cornel West Reader*. New York: Basic Books, pp. 499–513.

7335. West, Elizabeth J. "*African American Literary Criticism, 1773 to 2000*. By Hazel Arnett Ervin." *CLA Journal*, 43 (December), 254–258. Includes brief comment on W as critic (p. 256).

7336. White, Deborah Gray. *Too Heavy a Load: Black Women in Defense of Themselves, 1894–1994*. New York: Norton, p. 76. Mentions W briefly.

7337. White, Joseph L., and James H. Cones III. *Black Man Emerging: Facing the Past and Seizing the Future*. New York: Routledge, pp. 57, 143, 181, 236, 259. Mentions briefly W, *NS*, and *BB*.

7338. Willard, Carla. "*The Leisure Ethic: Work and Play in American Literature, 1840–1940*. By William A. Gleason." *American Literature*, 71 (December), 830–831. Review containing a paragraph contesting Gleason's treatment of *An American Tragedy* and *NS*.

7339. Williams, Adebayo. "Femi Ojo-Ade, ed. *Of Dreams Deferred, Dead or Alive: African Perspectives on African-American Writers*." *African American Review*, 33 (Fall), 530–533. Review criticizing Chimalum Nwanko's "Richard Wright: A Dubious Legacy."

7340. Williams, Roland L., Jr. "Dewayne Wickham. *Woodholme: A Black Man's Story of Growing Up Alone*." *African American Review*, 33 (Spring), 174–176. Mentions briefly W and *BB* (pp. 175, 176).

7341. Williams, Sherley Anne. "from Meditations on History (1980)," in *Callaloo*, 22 (Fall), 768–770.

7342. Wolfe, Peter. *August Wilson*. New York: Twayne, p. 2. Notes that Wilson read W while a teenager.

7343. Woller, Joel. "First-Person Plural: The Voice of the Masses' in Farm Security Administration Documentary." *Journal of Narrative Theory*, 29 (Fall), 340–366. Compares and contrasts *TMBV* and Pare Lorentz's *The River*. W's book is racial and radical; Lorentz's is nationalistic and liberal. Woller also comments on *NS*.

7344. _____. "Introduction" *Journal of Narrative Theory*, 29 (Fall), 241–250. Comments on his article treating *TMBV* in this issue of the journal.

7345. Wood, Irene. "Richard Wright — Black Boy." *The Booklist*, 95 (15 February), 1081. Notice of the Lacy video.

7346. Wood, James. "The Writer and the Preacher." *The New Republic*, 220 (28 June), 38–42. Review of Ralph Ellison's *Juneteenth* mentioning briefly "Richard Wright's Blues" (p. 40).

7347. Woodard, Komozi. "Preface," in his *A Nation Within a Nation: Amiri Baraka (LeRoi Jones) and Black Power Politics*. Chapel Hill: The University of North Carolina Press, pp. xi, xii. Mentions W briefly.

7348. Woodard, Loretta G. "Barry Beckham (1944–)," in *Contemporary African American Novelists: A Bio-Bibliographical Critical Sourcebook*. Ed. Emmanuel S. Nelson. Westport, CT: Greenwood Press, pp. 29–35. Mentions Beckham's reading W in high school (p. 29).

7349. _____. "Marita Golden (1950–)," in *Contemporary African American Novelists: A Bio-Bibliographical Critical Sourcebook*. Ed. Emmanuel S. Nelson. Westport, CT: Greenwood Press, pp. 177–184. States that Golden "started the Zora Neale Hurston/Richard Wright Foundation in 1990" (p. 178).

7350. Wright, David. "No Hiding Place: Exile 'Underground' in James Baldwin's 'This Morning, This Evening, So Soon.'" *CLA Journal*, 42 (June), 445–461. Compares Baldwin's story to "The Man Who Lived Underground" and *Invisible Man*. More optimistic than W or Ellison, Baldwin holds out hope that alienation can be overcome, especially in the hopeful days of the Civil Rights Movement.

7351. Wright, Michelle. "Alas Poor Richard'!": Transatlantic Baldwin, the Politics of Forgetting, and the Project of Modernity," in *James Baldwin Now*. Ed. Dwight A. McBride. New York: New York University Press, pp. 208–232. Includes discussion of Baldwin's attack on W and the experience of both as expatriates.

7352. Wright, Richard. "I Have Seen Black Hands." *The Crisis*, 106 (July/August), 68–69. Reprint of W's poem with a very brief biographical note.

7353. Young, Stephen. "Southern Author Societies." *Society for the Study of Southern Literature Newsletter*, 33 (November), 7. Lists the Richard Wright Circle.

7354. _____. "Nominees for the SSSL Executive Council." *The Society for the Study of Southern Literature Newsletter*, 33 (November), p. 2. Notes briefly Mary Kemp Davis's work on W.

7355. Zafar, Rafia. "'Going to Chicago': Ethnic Lives in the Windy City." *PMLA*, 114 (November), 1341. Lists a paper by Timothy B. Spears on "Going to Smash in Chicago: Richard Wright, *Native Son*, and the Erotic Violence of Migration."

2000

7356. Abrahams, Peter. *The Black Experience in the 20th Century: An Autobiography and Meditation*. Bloomington: Indiana University Press, pp. 82–85, 87–88, 92, 94, 132–133, 146. Includes discussion of his friendship with W in London and Paris, W's existentialism, and his quarrel with Baldwin. Also comments on W's interest in women, his trip to Bandung, and the shock of his death: "like a loss in the family: a dear, difficult, complex, at times, trying member of the family, but family nonetheless."

7357. Adams, Timothy Dow. "Autobiography," in *The Continuum Encyclopedia of American Literature*. Ed. Steven R. Serafin. New York: Continuum, pp. 61–64. Mentions briefly *BB* (p. 64).

7358. _____. "Lies in *Black Boy*," in *Readings on Black Boy*. Ed. Hayley Mitchell. San Diego: Greenhaven Press, pp. 80–90. Includes a headnote by Mitchell.

7359. _____. "Lies in *Black Boy*," in *Readings on Black Boy*. Ed. Hayley Mitchel. San Diego: Greenhaven Press, pp. 80–90. Partial reprint of 1985.

7360. Alsen, Eberhard. "Richard Wright (1908–1960), in *African American Authors, 1745–1945: A Bio-Bibliographical Sourcebook*. Ed. Emmanuel S. Nelson. Westport, CT: Greenwood Press, pp. 488–507. Biographical-critical sketch including a section on W's critical reception and a brief bibliography which includes nothing more recent than 1988.

7361. Ammons, Elizabeth, and Susan Belasco. "Critical Commentary on *Uncle Tom's Cabin*," in their *Approaches to Teaching Stowe's Uncle Tom's Cabin*. New York: The Modern Language Association, pp. 12–14. Mentions W briefly.

7362. Andrews, William L. "Richard Wright: The Self and the South," in *Readings on Black Boy*. Ed. Hayley Mitchell. San Diego: Greenhaven Press, pp. 103–108. Partial reprint of 1988. Includes a headnote by Mitchell.

7363. _____. "Richard Wright: The Self and the South," in *Readings on Black Boy*. Ed. Hayley Mitchell, San Diego: Greenhaven Press, pp. 103–108.

7364. Annas, Pamela, and Robert C. Rosen. "Richard Wright (1908–1960)," in their *Literature and Society: An Introduction to Fiction, Poetry, Drama, Nonfiction*. Third edition. Upper Saddle River, NJ: Prentice Hall, p. 857.

7365. _____. "Study and Discussion Questions, Suggestions for Writing," in their *Literature and Society: An Introduction to Fiction, Poetry, Drama, Nonfiction*. Third edition. Upper Saddle River, NJ: Prentice Hall, p. 881.

7366. Anon. "Africa to America to Paris. The Migration of Black Writers," in *Films for the Humanities & Sciences: American Literature*. Princeton, NJ: Films for the Humanities & Sciences, p. 11. Catalog notice of a video treating W and Baldwin.

7367. Anon. "Africa to America to Paris: The Migration of Black Writers," in *Films for the Sciences and Humanities*. Princeton, NJ: Films for the Sciences and Humanities, p. 29. Producers' notice mentioning W briefly.

7368. Anon. "Africa to America to Paris: The Migration of Black Writers," in *American Literature*. Princeton, NJ: Films for the Humanities & Sciences, p. 10.

7369. Anon. *"Black on Black: Twentieth-Century African American Writing About Africa,"* in *The University Press of Kentucky: Spring and Summer 2000*. Lexington: University Press of Kentucky, p. 11. Publisher's announcement mentioning W briefly.

7370. Anon. *"Black Boy,"* *The Encyclopedia Americana*. Ed. Mark Cummings. Danbury, CT: Grolier, pp. 29–30.

7371. Anon. "A Conversation with Connie Porter," in *All-Bright Court* by Connie Porter. Boston: Houghton Mifflin, pp. 229–230. Porter mentions reading W as a teenager.

7372. Anon. "Contributors." *MELUS*, 25 (Fall, Winter) [329–332]. Mentions work on W by Kimberly Drake and Keith Danner (p. [230]).

7373. Anon. "Faculty News." *Morgan State University Blackboard*, 2 (Winter-Spring), pp. 2–3, 12. Department of English Newsletter reporting that Minnie Washington gave a lecture entitled "Happy Birthday, Bigger!"

7374. Anon. "Give America's Best." *The New Republic,* 223 (4 December), 41 Advertisement for The Library of America mentioning W briefly.

7375. Anon. "Guides for Teachers," in *Modern Language Association Fall-Winter*. New York: Modern Language Association, pp. 8–9. Lists *Approaches to Teaching Richard Wright's Native Son* edited by James A. Miller.

7376. Anon. "The Hurston/Wright Foundation Announces the 11th Annual Hurston/Wright Awards." *Richard Wright Newsletter*, 7 (Spring/Summer), 10. Provides information on this award for previously unpublished fiction established by Marita Golden.

7377. Anon. *"James Baldwin Now.*

Ed. Dwight McBride." *American Literature*, 72 (September), 685. Notice mentioning Maurice Wallace's essay on W and Baldwin.

7378. Anon. "More volumes in the Approaches to Teaching World Literature series," in *Modern Language Association Publications*. New York: Modern Language Association, p. 11. Lists James A. Miller's volume on *NS*.

7379. Anon. "The Natchez Literary Celebration Presents the Sacred South: Writings from the Bible Belt." Natchez: Copiah-Lincoln Community College, p. [4]. Brochure including announcement of an award ceremony presenting Richard Wright Literary Excellence Awards to Beth Henley and David G. Sansing.

7380. Anon. *"Nation of Letters: A Concise Anthology of American Literature,"* in *Anthologies and Textbooks for All Seasons."* Waterbury, CT: Brandywine Press, p. [2]. Publisher's brochure listing W among the authors represented in the anthology.

7381. Anon. "Native Son: The Life and Work of Richard Wright," in *American Literature*. Princeton, NJ: Films for the Humanities & Sciences, p. 10. Publisher's catalog notice of a video featuring John Edgar Wideman and Bebe Moore Campbell.

7382. Anon. "Native Son: The Life and Work of Richard Wright," in *Films for the Humanities & Sciences: American Literature*. Princeton, NJ: Films for the Humanities & Sciences, p. 11. Catalog notice of a video.

7383. Anon. *"New Deal Modernism: American Literature and the Invention of the Welfare State* Michael Szalay," in *Duke University Press*. Durham, NC: Duke University Press, p. 29. Publisher's notice stating that W is treated extensively.

7384. Anon. "New Titles from Northeastern." *American Quarterly*, 52 (June), [412]. Publisher's advertisement listing the new edition of *LD* with a foreword by Keneth Kinnamon. Includes a photograph of W.

7385. Anon. "Random House, Inc." *PMLA*, 115 [November], 1632–1633. Publisher's list including W's *Haiku: This Other World*.

7386. Anon. "Recent Scholarship,"

The Journal of American History, 87 (December), 1184–1237. Lists articles on W and Ellison (p. 1185), an article on *SH* (p. 1220), and a dissertation on "The Politics of Community in the Work of Richard Wright" (p. 1203).

7387. Anon. "Richard Wright: Writing Is His Weapon," in *The Cinema Guild's Video Collection: Literature and Language Arts*. New York: The Cinema Guild, p. [3]. Announcement of the film by Rex Barnett.

7388. Anon. "Southern History in Periodicals, 1999: A Selected Bibliography." *The Journal of Southern History*, 66 (May), 321–371. Lists a reprint of Ellison's "Richard Wright's Blues" (p. 325, 357) and an article on *BB* by Tena Helton.

7389. Anon. *"Up from Bondage: The Literature of Russian and African American Soul*. Dale E. Peterson," in *Duke University Press*. Durham, NC: Duke University Press, p. 31. Publisher's notice mentioning W briefly.

7390. Anon. "What Can You Do at HarperCollins?" *PMLA*, 115 (November), 1677. Publisher's advertisement mentioning briefly *BB*.

7391. Anon. "Wright, Richard," in *The Columbia Encyclopedia*, sixth edition. New York: Columbia University Press, 2000, p. 3114. Biographical sketch with a brief secondary bibliography.

7392. Anon. "Wright, Richard," in *Encyclopedia of American History: The Great Depression and World War II*. New York: Facts on File, pp. 399–400. Biographical sketch mentioning Rowley's biography.

7393. Ansbro, John J. *Martin Luther King, Jr.: Nonviolent Strategies and Tactics for Social Change*. Lanham, MD: Madison Books, pp. 211, 226.

7394/5. Appel, Jacob M. "McKay, Claude (1890–1948)," in *St. James Encyclopedia of Popular Culture*. Eds. Tom Pendergast and Sara Pendergast. Vol. 3. Detroit: St. James Press, p. 327. Mentions W briefly.

7396. Armstrong, Julie Buckner. *"Illumination and Night Glare: The Unfinished Autobiography of Carson McCullers."* *The Southern Quarterly*, 38 (Winter), pp. 165–166. Review mentioning W briefly.

7397. Arnold, David L.G. "Seven Guitars: August Wilson's Economy of Blues," in *August Wilson: A Casebook.* Ed. Marilyn Elkins. New York: Garland, pp. 199–225. Quotes Ellison's definition of the blues, mistakenly locating it in "his essay on Richard Wright's *Native Son* (p. 202).

7398. Atlas, James. *Bellow.* New York: Random House, pp. 63, 142, 145, 170. Mentions W on the Writers' Project (p. 63), at the Café Roquet and hosting Bellow and Capote in his apartment (p. 142).

7399. Auciello, Joseph. "Chronicle of a Battle Foretold: Curriculum and Social Change." *English Journal,* 89 (March), 89–96. Mentions briefly *NS* and *BB* (p. 94).

7400. Auger, Philip. *Native Sons in No Man's Land: Rewriting Afro-American Manhood* in the Novels of *Baldwin, Walker, Wideman, and Gaines.* New York: Garland, pp. 1–14, 17, 18, 19, 24–25, 30–32, 35, 39, 41, 46, 58, 69. Argues that *NS* depicted in Bigger a protagonist unable to achieve manhood because he cannot control discourse even though W controls discourse by writing the novel. Auger examines Baldwin, Alice Walker, John Wideman, and Ernest Gaines to show that they rewrite W's narrative in such a way as to achieve discursive space.

7401. Badikian, Beatriz. "Baldwin, James (1924–1987)," in *St. James Encyclopedia of Popular Culture.* Eds. Tom Pendergast and Sara Pendergast. Vol. 1. Detroit: St. James Press, pp. 161–163. Mentions W briefly.

7402. _____. "Baldwin, James (1924–1987)." in *St. James Encyclopedia of Popular Culture.* Detroit: St. James Press, Vol. 1, 161–162. Mentions Baldwin meeting W.

7403. Baker, Houston A., Jr. "Preface: Unsettling Blackness." *American Literature,* 72 (June), 243–247. Notes that Lawrence Jackson's essay in this special issue of *American Literature* treats "The vexed 'racial romance'" between W and Ellison.

7404. Bandler, Michael. J "The Good Old Boy's Taste in Books," in *Conversations with Willie Morris.* Ed. Jack Bales. Jackson: University Press of Mississippi, pp. 112–115.

7405. Banks, Russell. "John Brown's Body: James Baldwin and Frank Shatz in Conversation." *Transition,* 9, nos. 1 and 2, pp. 250–266. Baldwin speaks briefly but admiringly of W (p. 263).

7406. Barrett, William. "Black and Blue: A Negro Céline," in *The Critical Response to Ralph Ellison.* Ed. Robert J. Butler. Westport, CT: Greenwood Press, pp. 23–25.

7407. _____. "Black and Blue: A Negro Alive," in *The Critical Responses to Ralph Ellison.* Ed. Robert J. Butler. Westport, CT: Greenwood Press, pp. 23–25.

7408. Bell, Vikki. "Owned Suffering: Thinking the Feminist Political Imagination with Simone de Beauvoir and Richard Wright," in *Thinking Through Feminism.* Eds. Sarah Ahmed, Jane Kilby, Celia Lury, Maureen McNeill, and Beverly Skeggs, New York: Routledge, pp. 61–76. Bell "reads the work of de Beauvoir and Wright intertextually with a view to understanding the rhetorical figures that operate within the political positions that are drawn there, and the maneuvers and conflicts that arise through these figures." She discusses also W's interest in women's issues, *NS.* Mentions *TMBV.*

7409. Berger, Maurice. *White Lies: Race and the Myths of Whiteness.* New York: Farrar, Straus and Giroux, p. 126.

7410. Bigsby, C.W.E. *Modern American Drama, 1945–2000.* Cambridge: Cambridge University Press, pp. 1, 278. Mentions briefly *AH* and *NS.*

7411. Birnbaum, Jonathan, and Clarence Taylor, eds. *Civil Rights Since 1787: A Reader on the Black Struggle.* New York: New York University Press, pp. 195–196. Quotes from *BB* and comments on W's reaction to racism.

7412. Black, Joel. "The Genealogy of Violence in African-American Literature: Non-Native Sources of *Native Son,*" in *The Conscience of Humankind: Literature and Traumatic Experiences.* Ed. Elrod Ibsch. Amsterdam: pp. 325–335. Relates *NS* to W's early Gothic efforts, to his setting his grandmother's house on fire, to the Luddites, and to the Badass figure.

7413. Bland, Sterling Bland, Jr. *Voices of the Fugitives: Runaway Slave Stories and Their Fictions of Self-Creation.* Westport, CT: Greenwood Press, pp. 13, 25, 26. Mentions *BB* and quotes from *TMBV.*

7414. Bloom, Alexander. "*The Suburb of Dissent: Cultural Politics in the United States and Canada dur-*

ing the 1930s. By Caren Irr." *The Journal of American History,* 87 (June), 270–271. Review noting that Irr treats *NS.*

7415. Boggs, Nicholas. "Queer Black Studies: An Annotated Bibliography, 1994–1999." *Callaloo,* 23 (Winter), 479–494. Lists an article on W by Stephen Best (p. 486).

7416. Bolden, Tonya. "Johnson, Charles," in *African-American Writers: A Dictionary.* Eds. Shari Dorantes Hatch and Michael R. Strickland. Santa Barbara: ABC-CLIO, p. 194. Mentions briefly W, whom Johnson admired.

7417. Bone, Robert. "*Terrible Honesty: Mongrel Manhattan in the 1920's.* Ann Douglas. *MELUS,* 25 (Fall/Winter), 278–286. Review mentioning W briefly (p. 284).

7418. Booker, Christopher B. "I Will Wear *No Chain*": A Social History of *African American Males,* Westport, CT: Greenwood Press, pp. 170, 244. Quotes from "The Ethics of Living Jim Crow" to exemplify difficulties with white co-workers, who demanded deference.

7419. Bowser, Pearl, and Louise Spence. *Writing Himself Into History*: Oscar Micheaux, *His Silent Films, and His Audiences.* New Brunswick, NJ: Rutgers University Press, pp. 110, 128, 215–216, 219. Discusses Micheaux's unfavorable portrayal in his novel *The Story of Dorothy Stanfield* of Frank Night, a character closely based on W.

7420. Boyd, Herb. "Foreword," in his *Three Centuries of African American History Told by Those Who Lived It.* New York: Doubleday, p. xviii. Mentions W briefly.

7421. Bracks, Leantin LaVerne, and Jessie Carney Smith, "Chronology," in their *Reference Library of Black America.* Vol. I. Farmington Hills, MI: Gale Group, pp. 1–84. Notes that in 1937 W becomes editor of *Challenge,* urging "social realism" (p. 24).

7422. _____. "Chronology," in their *Reference Library of Black America.* Vol. I. Farmington Hills, MI: Gale Group, pp. 1–84. Notes that in 1937 W becomes editor of *Challenge,* urging "social realism" (p. 24).

7423. _____. "Literature," in *Reference Library of Black America,* Vol. III. Farmington Hills, MI: Gale

Group, pp. 711–712, 747–748. Notes that *NS* signaled the transition from the Harlem Renaissance to the anti-racism that followed. Also provides a biographical sketch of W (pp. 747–748).

7424. _____. "Literature," in *Reference Library of Black America*, Vol. III. Farmington Hills, MI: Gale Group, pp. 711–712, 747–748. Notes that *NS* signaled the transition from the Harlem Renaissance to the anti-racism that followed. Also provides a biographical sketch of W (pp. 747–748).

7425. Bracy, William. "Wright, Richard Nathaniel," in *The Encyclopedia Americana*. Ed. Mark Cummings. Danbury, CT: Grolier, pp. 555–556.

7426. _____. "Wright, Richard Nathaniel," in *The Encyclopedia Americana*. Ed. Mark Cummings. Danbury, CT: Grolier, pp. 555–556.

7427. Brinkmeyer, Robert H., Jr. "*Inventing Southern Literature*: A Review Essay." *The Southern Quarterly*, 38 (Spring), pp. 206–212. Review mentioning W briefly (pp. 208, 209).

7428. Browder, Laura. *Slippery Characters: Ethnic Impersonators and American Identities*. Chapel Hill: University of North Carolina Press, p. 5. Comments briefly on *BB*.

7429. Brown, John L. "Ralph Ellison. *Juneteenth*." *World Literature Today*. 74 (Winter) 156–157. Mentions W briefly.

7430. Brown, Lloyd L. "The Deep Pit," in *The Critical Response to Ralph Ellison*. Ed. Robert J. Butler. Westport, CT: The Greenwood Press, pp. 31–33.

7431. _____. "The Deep Pit," in *The Critical Response to Richard Wright*. Ed. Robert J. Butler. Westport, CT: Greenwood Press, pp. 31–33.

7432. Brucker, Carl. "Ishmael Reed," in *Notable American Novelists*. Pasadena, CA: Salem Press, Vol. 3, pp. 894–903. Mentions briefly *NS* and *BB*.

7433. Bryant, Jerry H. "Explaining the Violence of *Native Son*," in *Readings on Native Son*. Ed. Hayley R. Mitchell. San Diego: Greenhaven Press, pp. 157–163.

7434. Burg, Barbara A., Richard Newman, and Elizabeth E. Sandager. *Guide to African American and African Primary Sources at Har-*

vard University. Phoenix: Oryx Press, p. 60. Lists a 1938 letter from W to Lewis Stiles Gannett.

7435. Butler, Johnnella E. "African American Studies and the 'Warring Ideals': The Color Line Meets the Borderlands," in *Dispatches from the Ebony Tower: Intellectuals Confront the African American Experience*. Ed. Manning Marable. New York: Columbia University Press, pp. 141–152. Comments briefly on W's identification with the West.

7436. _____. "African American Studies and the 'Warring Ideals': The Color Line Meets the Borderlands," in *Dispatches from the Ebony Tower: Intellectuals Confront the African American Experience*. Ed. Manning Marable. New York: Columbia University Press, pp. 144–152.

7437. Busby, Mark. "Ralph Ellison (1 March 1914–16 April 1994)," in *American Novelists Since World War II, Sixth Series*. Eds. James R. Giles and Wanda H. Giles. Detroit: Gale, pp. 128–140. Includes discussion of W's friendship with Ellison.

7438. Butler, Robert. "Native Son Is Set in a Gothic Ghetto," in *Readings on Native Son*. Ed. Hayley R. Mitchell. San Diego: Greenhaven Press, pp. 120–124.

7439. _____. "Urban Frontiers, Neighborhoods and Traps: The City in Dreiser's *Sister Carrie*, Farrell's *Studs Lonigan*, and Wright's *Native Son*," in *Theodore Dreiser and American Culture: New Readings*. Ed. Yoshinobu Hakutani. Newark: University of Delaware Press, pp. 274–290. Compares the three urban novels, all of which use the metaphor of a window on the city out of which the protagonist gazes. Bigger Thomas sees only a black urban nightmare, not the arena of meaningful human action available to Carrie and Studs.

7440. _____. "Wright, Richard [Nathaniel]," in *The Continuum Encyclopedia of American Literature*. Ed. Steven R. Serafin. New York: Continuum, pp. 1269–1270. Biographical-critical sketch praising highly W's role in changing literary traditions and racial consciousness. Butler does not treat W's travel books.

7441. Butler, Robert J. "Chronology," in his *The Critical Response to Ralph Ellison*. Westport, CT: Greenwood Press, pp. xli–xlv. Mentions W briefly.

7442. _____. "Introduction," in his *The Critical Response to Ralph Ellison*. Westport, CT: Greenwood Press, pp. xix–xl. Mentions briefly W, *NS*, and Bigger Thomas.

7443. _____. "The Metaphor of the Journey in *Black Boy*," in *Readings on Black Boy*. Ed. Hayley Mitchell. San Diego: Greenhaven Press, pp. 131–140. Includes a headnote by Mitchell.

7444. _____. "Introduction," in his *The Critical Response to Ralph Ellison*. Westport, CT: Greenwood Press, pp. xix–xl. Contains numerous references to W, mentioning Bigger, *NS*, Howe vs. Ellison in relation to W, and other critics views on W and Ellison.

7445. Butler, Robert James, "Violence Is Bigger's Automatic Response," in *Readings on Native Son*. Ed. Hayley R. Mitchell. San Diego: Greenhaven Press, p. 159.

7446. Callahan, John F., ed. *Trading Twelves: The Selected Letters of Ralph Ellison and Albert Murray*. New York: The Modern Library, pp. xxii, 4, 20, 29, 31, 43, 47, 79, 142–143, 152, 157. Ellison claims that W "could never bring himself to conceive a character as complicated as himself" (p. 29), criticizes W's expatriation (p. 43) and his association with French existentialists, expresses annoyance with W's "self importance" but concedes the importance of *BP* (p. 79), claims that W is "interested in racial approaches to culture" (p. 143), and notes W's interest in *Presence African* (p. 157).

7447. Calloway, Catherine. "Fiction: The 1930s to the 1960s," in *American Literary Scholarship: An Annual 1998*. Durham: Duke University Press, pp. 287–314. Includes comments on work on W by M. Lynn Weiss, Robert Felgar, Barbara Johnson, Jonathan Elmer, Damon Marcel DeCoste, Emily Miller Budick, and Robert Butler (pp. 285, 288–289, 290, 295).

7448. Carby, Hazel V. "The Politics of Fiction, Anthropology, and the Folk," in *Their Eyes Were Watching God: A Casebook*. Ed. Cheryl A. Wall. New York: Oxford University Press, pp. 117–136.

7449. Caron, Timothy P. *Struggles Over the Word: Race and Religion in O'Connor, Faulkner, Hurston, and Wright*. Macon, Georgia: Mercer University Press, pp. 2, 5, 6–7, 8, 19, 233, 29, 79, 112–140, 143, 144,

145. The chapter on W, "'The Reds Are in the Bible Room': The Bible and Political Activism in Richard Wright's *Uncle Tom's Children*," examines biblical intertextuality in *UTC*, especially "Fire and Cloud" and "Bright and Morning Star." Caron also draws on "Blueprint for Negro Writing," *BB*, and *AH* to explain how W transformed black religious tradition to serve radical political ends.

7450. Carson, Sharon. "Africana Constellations: African American Studies and *Uncle Tom's Children*," in *Approaches to Teaching Stowe's Uncle Tom's Cabin*. Eds. Elizabeth Ammons and Susan Belasco. New York: The Modern Language Association, pp. 162–171. Mentions briefly *UTC* (p. 167).

7451. Chafe, William H. "'The Gods Bring Threads to Webs Begun.'" *The Journal of American History*, 86 (March), 1531–1551. An article on African American life in the Jim Crow South with quotations from *BB* (pp. 1533, 1535, 1538).

7452. Champion, Laurie. "*Gayl Jones. Mosquito.*" *African American Review*, 34 (Summer), 366–368. Mentions W briefly (p. 367).

7453. _____, and Bruce A. Glasrud. "Zora Neale Hurston (1891–1960)," in *African American Authors, 1745–1945: A Bio-Bibliographical Sourcebook*. Ed. Emmanuel S. Nelson. Westport, CT: Greenwood Press, pp. 259–269. Notes W's criticism of *Their Eyes Were Watching God* (pp. 263, 269).

7454. Chrisman, Laura. "Rethinking Black Atlanticism." *The Black Scholar*, 30 (Fall/Winter), p. 12. Quotes Paul Gilroy on W.

7455. Christian, Barbara. "The Race for Theory," in *The Black Feminist Reader*. Eds. Joy James and T. Denean Sharpley-Whiting. Malden, MA: Blackwell, pp. 12–23. Mentions W briefly (p. 14).

7456. Ciner, Elizabeth. "The Image of the Father in *Black Boy*," in *Readings on Black Boy*." Ed. Hayley Mitchell. San Diego: Greenhaven Press, pp. 141–151.

7457. Cockburn, Alexander. "Even Worse Than Orwell." *The Nation*, 270 (5 June), 10. Notes that W contributed to *The God That Failed*.

7458. Cohen, Philip, and Joseph R. Urgo. "Faulkner," in *American Literary Scholarship: An Annual 1998*. Durham: Duke University Press, pp. 149–178. Mentions briefly "The Man Who Was Almost a Man" (p. 154).

7459. Collins, Michael Steven. "Risk, Altruism and Universal Historiography in the Works and Days of Ralph Bunche, Sterling Brown, Richard Wright, and Robert Hayden." *Dissertation Abstracts International*, 60 (January), 7. Deals with risk and altruism in W and others.

7460. Conner, Marc C. "Introduction: Aesthetics and the African American Novel," in his *The Aesthetics of Toni Morrison: Speaking the Unspeakable*. Jackson: University Press of Mississippi, pp. ix–xxviii. Includes discussion of "Blueprint for Negro Writing" (p. xiv), quotation from W's review of *Their Eyes Were Watching God* (p. xv), comment on Ellison's difference from W (pp. xv–xvi), and mention of W elsewhere (pp. xviii, xx, xxi, xxviii).

7461. Conner, Kimberly Rae. *Imagining Grace: Liberating Theologies in the Slave Narrative Tradition*. Urbana: University of Illinois Press, pp. 12–13, 55, 56, 69–109, 110, 113, 116–117, 119, 144, 256, 262, 277, 289–290. The second chapter provides a thorough treatment of *BB-AH* in relation to slave narratives and to liberation theology. The work is a fictionalized autobiography comparable to Billie Holiday's "Strange Fruit." Conner gives ample treatment of W's attitude toward religion, treats "Between the World and Me," and comments on *TMBV*. She also mentions briefly W and *BB-AH* in relation to Ernest Gaines, Glenn Rigon, and Charlie Haden.

7462. Corbett, William. "Interview with Sam Cornish." *Obsidian III*, 1 (Fall/Winter), 71–84. Mentions W briefly (p. 72).

7463. Cornish, Sam. "The South Is My Home." *Obsidian III*, 1 (Fall/Winter), 67–68. Poem mentioning briefly Bigger Thomas.

7464. Crouch, Stanley. "The Oklahoma Kid," in *The Critical Response to Ralph Ellison*. Ed. Robert J. Butler. Westport, CT: Greenwood Press, pp. 195–198.

7465. Danner, Keith. "*Black Power: A Record of Reactions in a Land of Pathos*. Introduction by Amritjit Singh. *The Color Curtain*. Introduction by Amritjit Singh. *White Man, Listen*! Introduction by Cedric Robinson." *MELUS*, 25 (Fall/Winter), 295–303. Review summarizing the contents of the three books and pointing out some problems in W's analysis.

7466. _____. "The Politics of Community in the Work of Richard Wright." *Dissertation Abstracts International*, 60 (March), 3359. Treats *UTC* and *NS* in relation to community, racism, and communism.

7467. Davis, Charles T. "*Black Boy* as Art," in *Readings on Black Boy*. Ed. Hayley Mitchell. San Diego: Greenhaven Press, pp. 69–79. Partial reprint of 1979.76. Includes a headnote by Mitchell.

7468. _____. "*Black Boy* as Art," in *Readings on Black Boy*. Ed. Hayley Mitchell. San Diego: Greenhaven Press, pp. 69–79.

7469. Davis, Jane. *The White Image in the Black Mind: A Study of African American Literature* Westport, CT: Greenwood Press, pp. xv–xvl, 1–2, 4, 5, 6, 7, 8, 58, 69, 88, 89, 90, 93, 94, 195, 96–98, 105, 106, 109, 110, 112, 126, 128, 129, 130, 143–144. Quotes or refers to *AH, BB*, "How Bigger Was Born," *LT, LD, NS, O, SH*, and *TMBV*, all in relation to the title of the book.

7470. Deck, Alice. "*Psychoanalysis and Black Novels: Desire and the Protocols of Race*. By Claudia Tate." *Journal of English and Germanic Philology*, 99 (April), 280–282. Review mentioning favorably Tate's treatment of *SH*.

7471. Deena, Seodial. "Urban Racism Causes Bigger's Irrationality," in *Readings on Native Son*. Ed. Hayley R. Mitchell. San Diego: Greenhaven Press, pp. 133–141.

7472. DeFazio, Albert J., III. "Fitzgerald and Hemingway," in *American Literary Scholarship: An Annual/1998*. Ed. David J. Nordloh. Durham: Duke University Press, pp. 179–194. Mentions W briefly (p. 185).

7473. De Romanet, Jerome. "A Conversation with Melvin Dixon." *Callaloo*, 23 (Winter), 84–109. Dixon comments on the Library of America edition of W (p. 87) and De Romanet mentions W elsewhere (p. 106).

7474. De Santis, Christopher C. "'Some Cord of kinship stronger and deeper than blood': An Interview with John F. Callahan, Editor of Ralph Ellison's *Juneteenth*." *African American Review*, 34 (Winter), 601–620. Callahan mentions and quotes from Ellison's essay on *BB*, "Richard Wright's Blues."

7475. Dobbs, Cynthia. "Gurleen Grewal. *Circles of Sorrow, Lives of Struggle: The Novels of Toni Morrison.*" *African American Review*, 34 (Summer), 362–363. Mentions W briefly (p. 363).

7476. DeFazio, Albert III. "Fitzgerald and Hemingway," in *American Literary Scholarship: An Annual 1998.* Durham: Duke University Press, pp. 179–194. Mentions W briefly (p. 185).

7477. De Mott, Robert. "Novella," in *The Facts on File Companion to the American Short Story* by Abby Werlock. New York: Facts on File, pp. 317–320. Mentions W briefly (p. 318).

7478. Dickson, Darryl B. Dickson-Carr. "African American Literature," in *The Continuum Encyclopedia of American Literature.* Ed. Steven R. Serafin. New York: Continuum, pp. 15–22. Comments on W's protest fiction and its influence (pp. 18–19).

7479. Dix, Andrew. "William A. Gleason, *The Leisure Ethic.*" *Journal of American Studies*, 34 (April), 168–169. Review mentioning briefly *NS*.

7480. Dodson, Howard, Christopher Moore, and Roberta Yaney. *The Black New Yorkers: The Schomburg Illustrated Chronology.* New York: John Wiley, pp. 241, 248, 255, 264. Quotes from "High Tide in Harlem." Mentions *NS* and the play *NS*. Notes W's move to Greenwich Village and then to Paris.

7481. Douglas, Robert L. "*Native Son* Is a Novel of Religious Skepticism," in *Readings on Native Son.* Ed. Hayley R. Mitchell. San Diego. Greenhaven Press, pp. 143–147.

7482. Doyle, Kegan. "Joe Louis in Black and White." *Aethlon*, 18 (Fall), pp. 112–133. Includes extensive discussion of W's ambivalent attitude toward Louis as a social symbol. Bigger's story resembles Louis's in various ways, and boxing imagery is pervasive in *NS*. Also discusses each of W's articles on Louis as well as *LT* and *PS*.

7483. Drake, Kimberly. "'Big Boy Leaves Home' Richard Wright," in *The Facts on File Companion to the American Short Story* by Abby Werlock. New York: Facts on File, pp. 57–58 Provides a synopis of the story, a favorable evaluation, and a brief bibliography.

7484. _____. "'Fire and Cloud' Richard Wright," in *The Facts on File Companion to the American Short Story* by Abby Werlock. New York: Facts on File, p. 163. Plot summary with a critique and brief bibliography of secondary sources.

7485. _____. "The Man Who Was Almost a Man," in *The Facts on File Companion to the American Short Story* by Abby Werlock. New York: Facts on File, p. 287. Explains the genesis of the story as an adaptation from "Tarbaby's Dawn" and provides a plot summary.

7486. _____. "Wright, Richard (1908–1960)," in *The Facts on File Companion to the American Short Story* by Abby Werlock. New York: Facts on File, pp. 453–455. Biographical-critical sketch together with a primary and secondary bibliography of twenty-six books, calls W "the single most influential author in African American literary history."

7487. Drowne, Kathleen N. "'An Irrevocable Condition': Constructions of Home and the Writing of Place in *Giovanni's Room*," in *Re-Viewing James Baldwin: Things Not Seen.* Ed. D. Quentin Miller. Philadelphia: Temple University Press, pp. 72–87. Mentions W briefly (p. 72).

7488. duCille, Ann. "Where in the World Is William Wells Brown? Thomas Jefferson, Sally Hemings, and the DNA of African-American Literary History." *American Literary History*, 12 (Fall), 443–462. Mentions briefly *NS* (p. 451).

7489. Duvall, John N. *The Identifying Fictions of Toni Morrison: Modernist Authenticity and Postmodern Blackness.* New York: Palgrave, pp. 25, 97. Mentions briefly W and *NS*.

7490. Eagles, Brenda M. "A Bibliography of Dissertations Relating to Mississippi —1999." *The Journal of Mississippi History*, 62 (Spring), 64–67. Lists dissertations treating W by Michael Stephen Collins, Stephen Michael Brauer, Valerie Renee Sweeney Prince, and Veronica Marie Toombs.

7491. _____. "Recent Manuscript Accessions at Mississippi Colleges and Universities." *The Journal of Mississippi History*, 62, pp. 60–61. W letter to a Mississippi magazine mentioning "race relations, South Africa, his work on *New Challenge*,

and his reading of *Absalom, Absalom!*

7492. Earle, Jonathan. *The Routledge Atlas of African American History.* New York: Routledge, p. 125. Mentions W briefly.

7493. Early, Gerald. "Black Voices: Themes in African-American Literature," in *Upon Theses Shores: Themes in the African-American Experience*, Eds. William R. Scott and William G. Shade. New York: Routledge, pp. 270–284. Early's point of departure is W's statement that "The Negro is America's metaphor, and he gives W more attention to W than to anyone else. Comments on *UTC*, *BB*, and, especially, *NS*.

7494. Effiong, Philip Uko. *In Search of a Model for African-American Drama: A Study of Selected Plays by Lorraine Hansberry, Amiri Baraka, and Ntozake Shange.* Lanham, MD, p. 132. Mentions W briefly.

7495. Ellis, Cassandra M. "The Black Boy Looks at the Silver Screen: Baldwin as Moviegoer," in *Re-Viewing James Baldwin: Things Not Seen.* Ed. D. Quentin Miller. Philadelphia: Temple University Press, pp. 190–214. Mentions briefly the stage and film versions of *NS* (pp. 199, 202).

7496. Ellison, Ralph. "From 'The Art of Fiction: An Interview' (1955)," in *African American Literary Criticism, 1773 to 2000.* Ed. Hazel Arnett Ervin. New York: Twayne, pp. 105–110.

7497. _____. "Richard Wright Sings the Blues," in *Readings on Black Boy.* Ed. Hayley Mitchell. San Diego: Greenhaven Press, pp. 55–57. Includes a headnote by Mitchell.

7498. Emanuel, James A. "The American Black Man's Experience Is Reflected Through Imagery in *Native Son*," in *Readings on Native Son.* Ed. Hayley R. Mitchell. San Diego: Greenhaven Press, pp. 52–61.

7499. Faulkner, Howard. "Richard Wright," in *Notable American Novelists.* Pasadena, CA: Salem Press, Vol. 3, pp. 1173–1182. Provides substantial critiques of *UTC*, *EM*, *BB*, *NS*, *AH*, *LD*, and *O*, Includes biographical sketches and a brief bibliography. At his best, W "gives American literature its strongest statement of the existential theme of a alienated people defining themselves.

7500. Feldman, Michael. "An Interview with Willie Morris," in *Conversations with Willie Morris.*

Ed. Jack Bales. Jackson: University Press of Mississippi, pp. 148–153. Transcript of a radio interview in which Morris mentions W briefly (p. 153).

7501. Felgar, Robert. "Putting Bigger Thomas on the Map." *Richard Wright Newsletter*, 7 (Spring/Summer), 1–4. Examines Bigger's resistance to totalizing means of control, whether the Marxist variety of Jan and Max or the capitalist variety of Mr. Dalton. The novel's "cartographic discourse" is the main mode of showing Bigger's rejection of efforts to place him on a "classificatory grid." He is determined to "be his own cartographer" (p. 4).

7502. _____. "The Violence of the Beast: Animal Imagery in *Native Son*," in *Readings on Native Son*. Ed. Hayley R. Mitchell. San Diego: Greenhaven Press, pp. 62–66.

7503. Fleming, Robert. *The African American Writer's Handbook*. New York: Ballantine, pp. 19, 28, 30, 106, 109, 111, 113, 116, 135, 170, 177, 180, 187, 198, 203, 208, 209, 211, 219, 265. Gives considerable attention to W, especially to *NS* and its influence and to his advice on writing. Mentions *LD, BB, O, TMBV*.

7504. Flynn, Richard. "'The Kindergarten of New Consciousness': Gwendolyn Brooks and the Social Construction of Childhood." *African American Review*, 34 (Fall), 483–499. Quotes from *TMBV*, a possible influence on Brooks's early poetry (p. 485). Also mentions briefly W's introduction to *Black Metropolis* (p. 496).

7505. Foner, Eric. "The Century: A *Nation's* Eye View." *The Nation*, 270 (10/17 January), pp. 5–53. Lists *NS* in the timeline.

7506. Foster, Frances Smith. "African American Literary Study, Now and Then and Again." *PMLA*, 115 (December), pp. 1965–1967. Mentions briefly *NS* (p. 1967).

7507. Fox, Robert. "James T. Farrell (1904–1979)." in *The Columbia Companion to the Twentieth-Century American Short Story*. Ed. Blanche Gelfant. New York: Columbia University Press, pp. 248–251. Mentions briefly Farrell's influence on W (p. 251).

7508. _____. "James T. Farrell (1904–1979)," in *The Columbia Companion to the Twentieth-Century Short Story*. Ed. Blanche Gelfant. New York: Columbia University

Press, pp. 248–251. Notes Farrell's influence on W (p. 251).

7509. Furukawa, Hiromi, and Kinugasa Seiji. "Translator's Afterword," in *Lawd Today!* [the Japanese translation, adding posthumous items including some haiku. Calls *LT* "a vivid description and valuable record of subculture."

7510. Gardner, Laurel J. "Violence in *Native Son* Shocks Readers Into Awareness of Oppression," in *Readings on Native Son*. Ed. Hayley R. Mitchell. San Diego: Greenhaven Press, pp. 164–171.

7511. Garrett, George. "A Summing Up at Century's End," in *Dictionary of Literary Biography Yearbook: 1999*. Ed. Matthew J. Bruccoli. Detroit: Gale, pp. 188–192. W is listed among the thirty "Best Twentieth-Century Novelists Writing in English" (p. 190).

7512. Gates, Henry Louis, Jr. "From 'Loose Canons: Notes on the Culture Wars'," in *The Prentice Hall Anthology of African American Literature*. Eds. Rochelle Smith and Sharon L. Jones. Upper Saddle River, NJ: Prentice Hall, pp. 1044.

7513. _____. "Zora Neale Hurston and the Speakerly Text," in *Their Eyes Were Watching God: A Casebook*. Ed. Cheryl A. Wall. New York: Oxford University Press, pp. 59–116.

7514. Gates, Henry Louis, Jr., and Cornel West. *The African American Century: How Black Americans Have Shaped Our Country*. New York: Simon and Schuster, pp. 94, 132, 190–193, 206. Notes W's disparagement of Houston and discusses W as an "Inside-Outsider."

7515. _____. "Bessie Coleman: Aviator (1892–1926)," in their *The African American Century: How Black Americans Have Shaped Our Country*. New York: The Free Press, pp. 90–94. Notes that W depicts "the frustration of African Americans with the racism of aviation."

7516. _____. "Ralph Ellison: The True Native Son," in their *The African American Century: How Black Americans Have Shaped Our Country*. New York: The Free Press, pp. 205–208. Comments on Ellison's friendship with W.

7517. _____. "Richard Wright: Insider-Outsider," in their *The African American Century: How Black Americans Have Shaped Our Country*. New York: The Free Press, pp.

190–193. Biographical sketch emphasizing W's internal conflict "marked both by success and excess. Mentions most of his works and contains a photograph.

7518. _____. "Robert Johnson: King of the Delta Blues," in their *The African American Century: How Black Americans Have Shaped Our Country*. New York: The Free Press, pp. 133–135. States that Johnson's "lyrics hold more existential agony that a Richard Wright novel."

7519. _____. "Zora Neale Hurston: The Anthropologist (1891–1960)," in their *The African American Century: How Black Americans Have Shaped Our Country*. New York: The Free Press, pp. 130–132. Mentions W briefly.

7520. _____. Robert Johnson: King of the Delta Blues," in their *The African-American Century: How Black Americans Have Shaped Our Country*. New York: The Free Press, pp. 133–135. Claims that Johnson's "lyrics hold more existential agony than a Richard Wright novel."

7521. _____. "Zora Neale Hurston," in their *The African-American Century: How Black Americans Have Shaped Our Country*. New York: The Free Press, pp. 130–132. Notes that W was dismissive of Hurston.

7522. _____. "Bessie Coleman, Aviator (1892–1926), in their *The African-American Century: How Black Americans Have Shaped Our Country*. New York: The Free Press, pp. 90–94. Notes that W depicts in his fiction the frustration of African Americans with the racism of aviation.

7523. _____. "Ralph Ellison," *The True Native Son (1914–1994)*," in their *The African-American Century: How Black Americans Have Shaped Our Country*. New York: The Free Press, pp. 205–208. Comments on the literary friendship of Ellison and W.

7524. _____. "Richard Wright: Inside-Outsider (1908–1960), in their *The African-American Century: How Black Americans Have Shaped Our Country*. New York: The Free Press, pp. 190–193. Biographical sketch emphasizing paradoxes: "Much of Wright's conflict was internal." But he achieved commercial and literary success, and "African-American literary history between 1940 and 1960 can be thought of as the age of Richard Wright" (p. 193).

7525. Gibson, Donald B. "The Strength of Individual Will," in *Readings on Black Boy.* Ed. Hayley Mitchell. San Diego: Greenhaven Press, pp. 109–112. Includes a headnote by Mitchell.

7526. _____. "The Strength of Individual Will," in *Readings on Black Boy.* Ed. Hayley Mitchell. San Diego: Greenhaven Press, pp. 109–112.

7527. Giles, James R. *Violence in the Contemporary American Novel: An End to Innocence.* Columbia: University of South Carolina Press, pp. 27, 45, 46, 54, 63. Mentions W and *NS* in comparison to fiction by Richard Price, John Edgar Wideman, Caleb Carr, and Nelson Algren.

7528. Gill, Glenda E. *No Surrender! No Retreat!: African American Pioneer Performers of Twentieth-Century American Theater.* New York: St. Martin's Press, pp. 15, 37, 116–118, 207. Contains a discussion of the play *NS* (pp. 116–118) and mentions W elsewhere. Quotes from reviews of the play.

7529. Gilroy, Paul, *Against Race: Imagining Political Culture Beyond the Color Line.* Cambridge, MA: Harvard University Press, pp. 167, 250, 284, 286, 340. Quotes from W's "The American Problem — Its Negro Phase" (p. 250) and *WML* (p. 340) and mentions W elsewhere.

7530. Glasrud, Bruce A., and Laurie Champion, eds. "Preface," in their *The African American West: A Century of Short Stories.* Boulder: University Press of Colorado, pp. ix–xi. A quotation from *BB* is the epigraph of the book. In commenting on it, the editors mention *NS*, *UTC*, and *BB*.

7531. _____. "Introduction: African Americans in the West, A Short Story Tradition," in their *The African American West: A Century of Short Stories.* Boulder: University Press of Colorado, pp. 1–28.

7532. Goffman, Ethan. "Tangled Roots: History, Theory, and African American Studies." *Modern Fiction Studies*, 46 (Winter), 1008–1016. Review of books by Lindon Barrett and William Maxwell mentioning W briefly (p. 1009) and commenting on Maxwell's "attempt to reconcile Richard Wright and Zora Neale Hurston (pp. 1011–1012)."

7533. _____. *Imaging Each Other: Blacks and Jews in Contemporary American Literature.* Albany: State University Press of New York, pp. 25–29, 30–36, 164. Notes W's favorable association of Jews and Communism, discusses *NS*, and states that Jay Neugeboren's 1966 novel *Big Man* is "a version of Richard Wright's *Native Son* transposed to a basketball setting."

7534. Gordon, Lewis R. *Existentia Africana: Understanding Africana Existential Thought.* New York: Routledge, pp. 9, 13, 16, 19–21, 38–39, 42, 45, 55–56. Mentions W in relation to Sartre and de Beauvoir, takes exception to Cedric Robinson on W, emphasizes W's "Promethean" importance to black existentialism, and mentions W briefly.

7535. _____. "Africana Thought and African Diasporic Studies." *The Black Scholar*, 30 (Fall), 25–31. Comments on Cross Damon and the conclusion of *O*.

7536. Graham, Maryemma, and Jerry W. Ward. "*Black Boy* Is Appropriate Reading for Young Adults," in *Readings on Black Boy.* Ed. Hayley Mitchell. San Diego: Greenhaven Press, pp. 162–166.

7537. Gray, Richard. *Southern Aberrations: Writers of the American South and the Problems of Regionalism.* Baton Rouge: Louisiana State University Press, pp. 102, 105–106, 109, 125, 126, 151, 170. Discusses the dismissal of W and *NS* by Louis Rubin and Robert Jacobs in *South* (pp. 102, 105–106, 109), compares the role of Buckley in *NS* to General Sherman in *So Red the Rose* (pp. 125, 126), and mentions briefly Bigger and *NS* (pp. 151, 170).

7538. Griffin, Barbara L.J. "Attaway, William," in *The Continuum Encyclopedia of American Literature.* Ed. Steven R. Serafin. New York: Continuum, pp. 56–57. Claims that in *Blood on the Forge* Attaway's "artistic genius views rivals that of Richard Wright in *Native Son.*"

7539. Griffin, Farah Jasmine. "Lawrence R. Rodgers. *Canaan Bound: The African-American Great Migration Novel.*" *African American Review*, 34 (Fall), 531–532. Review relating *NS* to other Chicago novels of "fugitive migrant fiction."

7540. Gross, Robert A. "The Transnational Turn: Rediscovering American Studies in a Wider World." *Journal of American Studies*, 34 (December), 373–393. Mentions W briefly (p. 383).

7541. Gross, Seymour. "Wright's Allusions to Color-Blindness in *Native Son*," in *Readings on Native Son.* Ed. Hayley R. Mitchell. San Diego: Greenhaven Press, pp. 67–69.

7542. Grossman, James R. "A Chance to Make Good: 1900–1929," in *To Make Our World Anew: A History of African Americans.* Eds. Robin D.G. Kelley and Earl Lewis. New York: Oxford University Press, pp. 345–408. Mentions W briefly (pp. 387, 388).

7543. _____. "A Chance to Make Good," in *To Make Our World Anew: A History of African Americans.* Eds. Robin D.G. Kelley and Earl Leurix. New York: Oxford University Press, pp. 345–408. Comments on W's arrival in Chicago (pp. 387, 388).

7544. Gruesser, John Cullen. *Black on Black: Twentieth-Century African American Writing About Africa.* Lexington: University Press of Kentucky, pp. 3, 47, 67, 77, 93, 137, 138–144, 146, 150, 151, 157. Discusses *BP* emphasizing W's attack on missionary activity, his evolutionary language, his critique of colonialism, and, especially his inability to divest himself of Western attitudes.

7545. Gunther, Michael A. "Critical Analysis of Literature: Making the Connection Between Reading and Writing." *English Journal*, 89 (March), 85–88. Mentions briefly *NS* (p. 86).

7546. Gutberlet, Joseph C. "Federal Writers Project," in *Encyclopedia of American History: The Great Depression and World War II.* New York: Facts on File, p. 121. Mentions W briefly.

7547. Hakutani, Yoshinobu. "Baldwin, James," in *The Continuum Encyclopedia of American Literature.* Ed. Steven R. Serafin. New York: Continuum, pp. 66–67. Notes Baldwin's high regard for *BB*, but contrasts his autobiographical writing to W's.

7548. _____. "Introduction," in his *Theodore Dreiser and American Culture: New Readings.* Newark: University of Delaware Press, pp. 13, 14, 18. Mentions W briefly and quotes from *BB*. Also summarizes the essays in the collection.

7549. _____. "*Sister Carrie*: Novel and Romance," in his *Theodore Dreiser and American Culture: New Readings.* Newark: University of Delaware Press, pp. 23–38. Comments on *NS*, noting that Bigger is a triumphant victim.

7550. _____. "Wright's Autobiography Becomes a Universal Story of Black Experience," in *Readings on Black Boy*. Ed. Hayley Mitchell. San Diego: Greenhaven Press, pp. 153–161. Includes a headnote by Mitchell.

7551. _____. "Wright, Dreiser, and Spatial Narrative," in his *Theodore Dreiser and American Culture: New Readings*. Newark: University of Delaware Press, pp. 248–273. Extensive treatment of the Dreiser-W relationship, showing the influence of "Nigger Jeff" (as well as the Acteon myth) on "Big Boy Leaves Home." W's esteem for Dreiser especially *Jennie Gerhardt*, is explained, but W was too subjective to be a naturalist. *An American Tragedy* influenced *NS*, but W is concerned less with the cause of Bigger's crime than with its result — a liberating self-knowledge. The two novels also differ stylistically and structurally.

7552. _____. "Introduction," in his *Theodore Dreiser and American Culture: New Readings*. Newark: University of Delaware Press, pp. 13–18. Mentions briefly W (pp. 14, 18).

7553. _____. "*Sister Carrie*: Novel and Romance," in his *Theodore Dreiser and American Culture: New Readings*. Newark: University of Delaware Press, pp. 23–38. Mentions briefly W, Bigger Thomas and *NS*.

7554. _____. "Bibliography," in his *Theodore Dreiser and American Culture*. Newark: University of Delaware Press, pp. 291–305. Includes items on W.

7555. _____. "Wright's Autobiography Becomes a Universal Story of Black Experience," in *Readings on Black Boy*. Ed. Hayley Mitchell. San Diego: Greenhaven Press, pp. 153–161. Partial reprint of 1996.

7556. Hamalian, Linda. "*The Suburb of Dissent: Cultural Politics in the United States and Canada During the 1930s*. By Caren Irr." *American Literature*, 72 (March), 208–209. Review noting that Irr "sharpens the debate over Richard Wright's loyalty, which was divided "between the masses and intellectuals [and] between African Americans or Communists."

7557. Hancuff, Richard. "M. Lynn

Weiss, *Gertrude Stein and Richard Wright: The Poetics and Politics of Modernism*." *Richard Wright Newsletter*, 7 (Fall/Winter), 4–5. Generally favorable review praising the two authors' effort to define their American identity by means of their foreign experiences, but criticizes Stein's work for the Petain government and W's misogyny.

7558. Hapke, Laura. *Labor's Text: The Worker in American Fiction*. New Brunswick, NJ: Rutgers University Press, pp. 11, 208, 213, 217, 220, 221, 236–239, 241, 265, 273, 274, 307, 386, 416. Discusses *NS* in relation to "Blacks without Money" and the inadequacy of New Deal relief programs. Also traces W's own work history. Mentions W and his works elsewhere.

7559. Harper, Michael S. "Bigger's Blues," in *Songlines in Michaeltree: New and Collected Poems*. Urbana: University of Illinois Press, p. 90.

7560. _____. "Afterword: A Film," in his *Songlines in Michaeltree: New and Collected Poems*. Urbana: University of Illinois Press, pp. 96–97.

7561. _____. "Calligraphy," in his *Songlines in Michaeltree: New and Collected Poems*. Urbana: University of Illinois Press, pp. 252–253. Mentions W and Michel [Fabre].

7562. _____. "Figments," in his *Songlines in Michaeltree: New and Collected Poems*. Urbana: University of Illinois Press, pp. 313–322. Includes lines rendering comments by Julia Wright on her father's life (pp. 320–321).

7563. _____. "History as Diabolical Materialism," in his *Songlines in Michaeltree: New and Collected Poems*. Urbana: University of Illinois Press, p. 92.

7564. _____. "The Meaning of Protest," in his *Songlines in Michaeltree: New and Collected Poems*. Urbana: University of Illinois Press, p. 88.

7565. _____. "Notes to the Poems," in his *Songs in Michaeltrees: New and Collected Poems*. Urbana: University of Illinois Press, pp. 375–386. Comments that the poem "Abe" was written for Abraham and Belle Chapman, who "gave Richard Wright room and board while he wrote *Black Boy*" (p. 380).

7566. _____. "Parable," in his *Songlines in Michaeltree: New and Collected Poems*. Urbana: University of Illinois Press, p. 91.

7567. _____. "Reading from Isherwood's Letter Circa 1959–63," in his *Songlines in Michaeltree: New and Collected Poems*. Urbana: University of Illinois Press, pp. 264–268. Mentions W briefly (p. 267).

7568. _____. "Tree Fever," in his *Songlines in Michaeltree: New and Collected Poems*. Urbana: University of Illinois Press, p. 89.

7569. Hatch, Shari Dorantes. "Allen, Samuel W.," in *African-American Writers: A Dictionary*. Eds. Shari Dorantes Hatch and Michael R. Strickland. Santa Barbara: ABC-CLIO, pp. 3–4. Notes that in Paris Allen met W, who helped him to publish poetry.

7570. _____. "Baker, Houston A." in *African-American Writers: A Dictionary*. Eds. Shari Dorantes Hatch and Michael R. Strickland. Santa Barbara: ABC-CLIO, p. 9. Mentions a book by Baker treating W and others.

7571. _____. "Baldwin, James," in *African-American Writers: A Dictionary*. Eds. Shari Dorantes Hatch and Michael R. Strickland. Santa Barbara: ABC-CLIO, pp. 10–13. Mentions Baldwin's early friendship with W and its rupture (p. 10) and mentions W and *NS* elsewhere (p. 13).

7572. _____. "Bonner, Marita," in *African-American Writers: A Dictionary*. Eds. Shari Dorantes Hatch and Michael R. Strickland. Santa Barbara: ABC-CLIO, pp. 25–26. Claims that Bonner's story "Tin Can" "may have inspired" *NS*.

7573. _____. "Ellison, Ralph," in *African-American Writers: A Dictionary*. Eds. Shari Dorantes Hatch and Michael R. Strickland. Santa Barbara: *ABC-CLIO*, pp. 103–107. Includes discussion of Ellison's relation to W (pp. 105–106).

7574. _____. "Gayle, Addison, Jr.," in *African-American Writers: A Dictionary*. Eds. Shari Dorantes Hatch and Michael R. Strickland. Santa Barbara: ABC-CLIO, pp. 137–138. Lists *Richard Wright: Ordeal of a Native Son*.

7575. _____. "Bontemps, Arna Wendell," in *African-American Writers: a Dictionary*. Eds. Shari Dorantes Hatch and Michael R. Strickland. Santa Barbara: ABC-CLIO, pp. 26–30. Mentions W briefly (p. 28).

7576. _____. "Marshall, Paule," in *African-American Writers*. Eds.

Shari Dorantes Hatch and Michael R. Strickland. Santa Barbara: ABC-CLIO, pp. 239–242. Mentions W briefly (p. 239).

7577. _____. "McMillan, Jerry," in *African-American Writers: A Dictionary*. Eds. Shari Dorantes Hatch and Michael R. Strickland. Santa Barbara: ABC-CLIO, pp. 247–251. Mentions McMillan's reading of W.

7578. _____. "Murray, Albert L.," in *African American Writers: A Dictionary*. Eds. Shari Dorantes Hatch and Michael R. Strickland. Santa Barbara: ABC-CLIO, pp. 262–263. Mentions W briefly.

7579. _____. "Oral Tradition," in *African-American Writers: A Dictionary*. Eds. Shari Dorantes Hatch and Michael R. Strickland. Santa Barbara: ABC-CLIO, pp. 273–276. Mentions briefly UTC (p. 275) and *NS* (p. 276).

7580. _____. "Rivers, Conrad Kent," in *African-American Writers: A Dictionary*. Eds. Shari Dorantes Hatch and Michael R. Strickland. Santa Barbara: ABC-CLIO, p. 302. Mentions briefly Rivers's *The Wright Poems*.

7581. _____. "Walker, Margaret," in *African-American Writers: A Dictionary*. Eds. Shari Dorantes Hatch and Michael R Strickland. Santa Barbara: ABC-CLIO, pp. 368–370. Includes comment on Walker's relation to W.

7582. _____. "West, Dorothy," in *African-American Writers: A Dictionary*. Eds. Shari Dorantes Hatch and Michael R. Strickland. Santa Barbara: ABC-CLIO, pp. 379–380. Notes W's connection to *New Challenge* and mentions "Blueprint for Negro Writing."

7583. _____. "Williams, John A." in *African-American Writers: A Dictionary*. Eds. Shari Dorantes Hatch and Michael R. Strickland. Santa Barbara: ABC-CLIO, pp. 388–389. Mentions briefly Williams's biography of W.

7584. _____. "Wilson, August," in *African-American Writers: A Dictionary*. Eds. Shari Dorantes Hatch and Michael R. Strickland. Santa Barbara: ABC-CLIO, pp. 391–395. Mentions that Wilson was reading W at an early age (p. 391).

7585. _____. "Wright, Richard," in *African-American Writers: A Biography* Eds. Shari Dorantes Hatch and Michael R. Strickland. Santa Barbara: ABC-CLIO, pp. 402–411.

Substantial biographical-critical essay covering all periods of W's life and works.

7586. Henderson, Carol E. "Freedom to Self-Create: Identity and the Politics of Movement in Contemporary African American Fiction." *Modern Fiction Studies*, 46 (Winter), 998–1003. Review of books by Robert Butler and Philip Page mentioning W briefly (p. 999).

7587. _____. "The 'Walking Wounded': Rethinking Black Women's Identity in Ann Petrey *The Street*," *Modern Fiction Studies*, 46 (Winter), 849–867. Mentions briefly *NS* (p. 850).

7588. Henderson, Mae G. "James Baldwin: Expatriation, Homosexual Panic, and Man's Estate." *Callaloo*, 23 (Winter), 313–327. Comments on and quotes from "Everybody's Protest Novel" (pp. 313, 314).

7589. Henry, Paget. *Caliban's Reason: Introducing Afro-Caribbean Philosophy*. New York: Routledge, p. 156. Mentions W briefly.

7590. Hodges, John O. "Narrative Structure of *Black Boy*," in *Readings on Black Boy*. Ed. Hayley Mitchell. San Diego: Greenhaven Press, pp. 43–54. Partial reprint of 1985. Includes a headnote by Mitchell.

7591. _____. "Narrative Structure of *Black Boy*," in Readings on *Black Boy*. Ed. Hayley Mitchell. San Diego: Greenhaven Press, pp. 43–54.

7592. Hoem, Sheri I. "'Shifting Spirits': Ancestral Constructs in the Postmodern Writing of John Edgar Wideman." *African American Review*, 34 (Summer), 249–262. Mentions W briefly (p. 249).

7593. Hogue, W. Lawrence. "Disrupting the White/Black Binary: William Melvin Kelley's *A Different Drummer*." *CLA Journal*, 44 (September), pp. 1–42. Quotes David Bradley mentioning W briefly (p. 41).

7594. Honey, Michael Keith. *Black Workers Remember: An Oral History of Segregation, Unionism, and the Freedom Struggle*. Berkeley: University of California Press, pp. 123, 130, 370. Quotes from *TMBV* and mentions *BB*.

7595. Horne, Gerald. *Race Woman: The Lives of Shirley Graham Du Bois*. New York: New York University Press, pp. 4, 18, 126–127, 129, 170, 171, 318. Cites Ollie Harington

on W's unpopularity with other black expatriates, notes that Graham was friendly with W and his wife (p. 18) but disliked *NS* (pp. 126–127), refers to a State Department memorandum, reputedly by W, claiming that Nkruma was a feminist (p. 170).

7596. Howard, Catherine. "*Inventing Southern Literature*. By Michael Kreyling." *The Journal of Southern History*, 66 (August), 670–671. Review mentioning W briefly.

7597. Hume, Kathryn. *American Dream, American Nightmare: Fiction Since 1960*. Urbana: University of Illinois Press, p. 297. Quotes William Lyne mentioning W briefly.

7598. Hussman, Lawrence, "Expansive and Unnameable Desire in American Fiction: From 'Naturalism' to Postmodernism," in *Theodore Dreiser and American Culture*. Ed. Yoshinobu Hakutani. Newark: University of Delaware Press. Mentions W briefly (p. 219) and comments on Bigger's fantasy life (p. 221).

7599. _____. "Expansive and Unnameable Desire in American Fiction: From 'Naturalism' to Postmodernism," in *Theodore Dreiser and American Culture: New Readings*. Newark: University of Delaware Press, pp. 214–233.

7600. Inouchi, Yushiro. "Richard Wright's Encounter with Haiku." *Waseda University English Literature*, 79 (10 March), 131–145. Summarizes the relationship between W and Haiku, citing *Haiku: This Other World*. At the end of his life W returned to nature in the American South.

7601. _____. "Richard Wright's Encounter with Haiku." *Waseda University English Literature*, 79 (10 March), 131–145. Summarizes the relation of W to Haiku, citing *This Other World*. At the end of his life he returned to the world of nature in his childhood.

7602. Inscoe, John C. "*Tell About the South: Voices in Black and White*. Part 2: *Prophets & Poets*." *The Journal of American History*, 87 (December), 1156–1157. Review of a film about Southern writers, including W in the role of Bigger Thomas. Also, "Margaret Walker and Nikki Giovanni recall their associations with Richard Wright during his years as a novice writer and as a Communist."

7603. Irr, Caren. "*The New Red Negro: The Literary Left and African*

American Poetry, 1930–1946. By James Edward Smethurst." *American Literature*, 72 (September), 645–646. Review mentioning W briefly.

7604. Iton, Richard. *Solidarity Blues: Race, Culture, and the American Left.* Chapel Hill: The University of North Carolina Press, pp. 67, 119–121, 200–201. Comments on W's attitude toward communism, quoting from "I Tried to Be a Communist" and *Presence Africaine*.

7605. Jackson, Lawrence P. "The Birth of the Critic: The Literary Friendship of Ralph Ellison and Richard Wright." *American Literature*, 72 (June), 321–355. Traces the W-Ellison relation from its beginning in 1937, drawing on archival as well as printed sources. Initially Ellison's close friend and mentor, W's differing political and literary agenda became less attractive to Ellison, especially after the success of *Invisible Man*. W's expatriation also further estranged the two men.

7606. _____. "An Interview with Edward P. Jones." *African American Review*, 34 (Spring), 95–103. Jones recalls his attraction to "emotional writing," citing *UTC*, especially "Fire and Cloud" (p. 98).

7607. _____. "The Last of the Old Negro." *Richard Wright Newsletter*, 7 (Spring/Summer), 6–9. Review of William J. Maxwell's *New Negro, Old Left: African American Writing and Communism Between the Wars* including treatment of the last two chapters comparing W and Hurston and W and Algren.

7608. Japtok, Martin, "Harper, Michael S[teven]," in *The Continuum Encyclopedia of American Literature.* Ed. Steven R. Serafin. New York: Continuum, pp. 485–486. Mentions briefly Michael Harper's treatment of W in *Debridement*.

7609. _____. "Petry, Ann," in *The Continuum Enclyopedia of American Literature.* Ed. Steven R. Serafin. New York: Continuum, pp. 882–883. Mentions W briefly.

7610. Jarrett, Gene. "'Couldn't Find Them Anywhere': Thomas Glave's *Whose Song?* (Post) Modernist Literary Queerings, and the Trauma of Witnessing, Memory, and Testimony." *Callaloo*, 23 (Fall), 1241–1258. Mentions briefly "Man of All Work" (p. 1246).

7611. _____. "'*Who Set You Flowin'?*': The African-American Migration Narrative, by Farah Jasmine Griffin." *The Black Scholar*, 30 (Summer), 47–49. Mentions briefly W and *TMBV* (pp. 47, 49)

7612. Jones, Gayl. "From Liberating Voices: Oral Tradition in African American Literature," in *The Prentice Hall Anthology of African American Literature.* Eds. Rochelle Smith and Sharon L. Jones. Upper Saddle River, NJ: Prentice Hall, pp. 1099–1110. Partial reprint of 1991, re W and *Their Eyes Were Watching God.*

7613. Jones, Suzanne W. "New Narratives of Southern Manhood: Race Masculinity, and Closure in Ernest Gaines's Fiction," in *The World Is Our Home: Society and Culture in Contemporary Southern Writing.* Eds. Jeffrey Folks and Nancy Summers Folks. Lexington: The University Press of Kentucky, pp. 29–52. Includes of brief comparison of W and Ernest Gaines (p. 51).

7614. Joseph, Peniel E. "Book Review: Dissidents in the Dark." *Social Identities*, 6 (March), 107–112. Review of Joy James's *Shadowboxing* mentioning W briefly (p. 110).

7615. Joyce, Joyce Ann. "Wright's Craft Is as Important as Content in *Native Son*," in *Readings on Native Son*, ed. Hayley R. Mitchell. San Diego: Greenhaven Press, pp. 45–51. Partial reprint of 1982.78.

7616. Julien, Eileen. "*Terrains de Rencontre*: Césaire, Fanon, and Wright on Culture and Decolonization." *Yale French Studies*, no. 98, pp. 149–166. Discusses W's speech at the First International Conference of Negro Writers and Artists, emphasizing his disagreement with the views of Césaire and Fanon. W hated colonialism but also rejected tribalism and religion.

7617. Kadlec, David. *Mosaic Modernism: Anarchism, Pragmatism, Culture.* Baltimore: The Johns Hopkins University Press, pp. 190, 211, 304. Notes W's criticism of Zora Neale Hurston and Hazel Carby's unfavorable comparison of Hurston to W.

7618. Kaname, Hiroshi. "Suffering of Self-Fulfullment: *The Outsider* Reconsidered." *Osaka Prefectural University Studies in British and American Language and Culture*, 48 (March), 107–126. Considers the technique of *O* and calls Cross Damon "a strong character suffering as a modern man.

7619. Kaplan, Carla. "The Erot-

ics of Talk: 'That Oldest Human Longing'" in *Their Eyes Were Watching God: A Casebook.* Ed. Cheryl A. Wall. New York: Oxford University Press, pp. 137–163.

7620. Keiler, Allan. *Marian Anderson: A Singer's Journey.* New York: Scribner, p. 229. Mentions W briefly.

7621. Kella, Elizabeth. *Beloved Communities: Solidarity and Difference in Fiction by Michael Ondaatje, Toni Morrison, and Joy Kogawa.* Uppsala: Acta Universitatis Upsaliensis, pp. 55, 58–59, 60, 121, 127. Comments on W and *NS.*

7622. Kelly, Jack. "I Thought I Was Writing Realism." *American Legacy*, 6 (Fall), 35–38, 40–42. Essay on Chester Himes mentioning W briefly (p. 42).

7623. Kelley Robin D.G. "Foreword," in Cedric J. Robinson's *Black Marxism.* Chapel Hill: The University of North Carolina Press, pp. xii–xxiii. Mentions W briefly (p. xv).

7624. Kelly, Susan, and Sonia Sanchez. "Discipline and Craft: An Interview with Sonia Sanchez." *African American Review*, 34 (Winter), 679–687. Sanchez mentions briefly teaching W (p. 685).

7625. Kelley, Robin D.G. "Foreword," in *Black Marxism: The Making of the Black Radical Tradition.* Chapel Hill: The University of North Carolina Press, pp. xi–xxvi. Mentions W briefly (pp. xv, xix).

7626. Kim, Sang-Yule. "The Postcolonial Wright: W/ri(gh)ting Violence in His Early Works." *Dissertation Abstracts International* 60, 2924. Treat's violence and W's relationship to colonialism.

7627. Kimball, Roger. *The Long March: How the Cultural Revolution of the 1960's Changed America.* San Francisco: Encounter Books, p. 215. Notes that Eldridge Cleaver read W.

7628. Kinnamon, Keneth. "Books Briefly Mentioned." *African American Review*, 34 (Spring), 183–184. Contains an unfavorable notice of Robert Felgar's *Understanding Richard Wright's Black Boy: A Student Casebook to Issues, Sources, and Historical Documents.*

7629. Kinnamon, Keneth. "Foreword," in *The Long Dream* by Richard Wright. Boston: Northeastern University Press, pp. vii–xiv. Considers contemporary reviews of the novel, explores the theme of sex in relation to racism, acknowledges stylistic lapses, and notes an excessively complicated plot. But characterization is strong, and the novel's "detailed, ample portrayal of life in the racist South" (p. xiii) is unmatched.

7630. Komunyakaa, Yusef. "Hotbeds and Crossing Over Poetic Traditions: An Interview with Kristin Naca," in his *Blue Notes: Essays, Interviews, and Commentaries*. Ed. Radiclani Clytus. Ann Arbor: The University of Michigan Press, pp. 85–92. Comments on the bellhop scene in *BB* and cites "that Richard Wright epigram 'It startled as no more than a blue vase or red rug'" (p. 89).

7631. Krell, David Farrell. "The Bodies of Black Folk: From Kant and Hegel to DuBois and Baldwin." *Boundary 2*, 27 (Fall), 103–134. Mentions W briefly (p. 107).

7632. Kroeber, Karl. "Novel," in *Encyclopedia Americana*. Ed. Mark Cummings. Danbury, CT: Grolier, pp. 505–511b.

7633. Kumar, Amitava. *Passport Photos*. Berkeley: University of California Press, pp. 55–56. Includes comment on *TMBV*.

7634. Kurosu, Kishiko. "The World of Richard Wright's Haiku." *Annual Proceedings of Saitama Junior College*, 9 (March), 31–38. Claims that W reached the Zen state of "Nothingness" by coming close to nature through his haiku.

7635. Lamothe, Daphne. "Voudu, African American Tradition, and Cultural Transformation in Zora Neale Hurston's *Their Eyes Were Watching God*," in *Their Eyes Were Watching God: A Casebook*. Ed. Cheryl A. Wall. New York: Oxford University Press, pp. 165–187.

7636. Lauret, Maria. *Alice Walker*. New York: St. Martin's Press, pp. 53, 55, 58, 203. Comments on the intertextuality of *The Third Life of Grange Copeland* and *NS*.

7637. Lee, D.T. "Hall of Fame Builds a Broad Pedestal for Black Writers." *Emerge*, 11 (February), 104. Mentions briefly John A. Williams's book on W.

7638. Lee, Kun Jong. "Ellison's Racial Variations on American Themes," in *The Critical Response to Ralph Ellison*. Ed. Robert J. Butler. Westport, CT: Greenwood Press, pp. 173–192.

7639. _____. "Ellison's Racial Variations on American Themes," in *The Critical Response to Ralph Ellison*. Ed. Robert J. Butler. Westport, CT: Greenwood Press, pp. 173–192.

7640. Leeming, David Adams. "Foreword," in *Re-Viewing James Baldwin: Things Not Seen*. Ed. D. Quentin Miller. Philadelphia: Temple University Press, pp. vii–ix. Mentions briefly Bigger Thomas (p. vii).

7641. LeSeur, Geta. *Not All Okies Are White: Black Cotton Pickers in Arizona*. Columbia: University of Missouri Press, p. 187. Mentions briefly *TMBV*.

7642. Lewis, David Levering. *W.E.B. Du Bois: The Fight for Equality and the American Century, 1919–1963*. New York: Henry Holt, pp. 471, 472. Mentions Du Bois meeting W in Chicago in 1940. He admired *NS*.

7643. Lewis, Sinclair. "A Negro Revolution of Letters," in *Readings on Black Boy*. Ed. Hayley Mitchell. San Diego: Greenhaven Press, p. 167. Partial reprint of 1945.997.

7644. Lively, Adam. *Masks: Blackness, Race, and the Imagination*. Oxford University Press, pp. 4, 203, 234, 249–257. Asserting that "Wright's world is one of unremitting violent conflict between black and white" (p. 251), Lively discusses *UTC*, *NS*, and the reaction of W to Ellison and Baldwin. Mentions also *BB*.

7645. Locke, Alain. "From *Native Son to Invisible Man*: A Review of the Literature of the Negro for 1952," in *The Critical Response to Invisible Man*. Ed. Robert J. Butler. Westport, CT: Greenwood Press, pp. 41–42.

7646. _____. "From *Native Son* to *Invisible Man*: A Review of the Literature of the Negro for 1952," in *The Critical Response to Ralph Ellison*. Ed. Robert J. Butler. Westport, CT: Greenwood Press, pp. 41–42.

7647. Lowe, John. "Transcendence in the House of the Dead: The Subversive Gaze of *A Lesson Before Dying*," in *The World Is Our Home: Society and Culture in Contemporary Southern Writing*. Eds. Jeffrey Folks and Nancy Summers Folks. Lexington: The University Press of Kentucky, p. 147. Mentions briefly the optical company episode in *BB*.

7648. Lynch, Michael F. "Staying Out of the Temple: Baldwin, the African American Church, and *The Amen Corner*," in *Re-Viewing James Baldwin: Things Not Seen*. Ed. D. Quentin Miller. Philadelphia: Temple University Press, pp. 33–71. Mentions W briefly (pp. 41, 43) and comments briefly on Baldwin's treatment of W in "Everybody's Protest Novel" (p. 48).

7649. Lyne, William. "No Accident: From Black Power to Black Box Office." *African American Review*, 34 (Spring), 40–59. Mentions briefly W (p. 41) and *BB* (p. 44).

7650. Mack, Tara. "Racisme déjà vu." *Emerge*, 11 (June), 48–52. Mentions W briefly (pp. 50, 52).

7651. Malcolmson, Scott L. *One Drop of Blood: The American Misadventure of Race*. New York: Farrar Straus Giroux, pp. 241–243. Quotes from and comments on "Blueprint for Negro Writing."

7652. Marable, Manning, and Leith Mullings, eds. *Let Nobody Turn Us Around: An African American Anthology*. Lanham, MD: Rowman & Littlefield, p. 367. Mentions W briefly.

7653. Marriott, David. "'The Derived Life of Fiction': Race, Childhood and Culture." *New Formations*, 42 (Winter), 31–46. Discussion of Frederic Wertham's *Dark Legend* and W's *Savage Holiday* from a psychoanalytical perspective, considering also *NS*. The main themes are matricide, racism, and fiction as reality.

7654. _____. *On Black Men*. New York: Columbia University Press, pp. vii, viii, x, xi, xiii, 5,6, 10–11, 86, 87–88, 101–104, 105–109. Quotes from *BP*, *NS*, "Between the World and Me," "How Jim Crow Feels," *TMBV*, and *BB*. Discusses "the dream of a different world," W's relation to his father, Fanon and W, W and Baldwin, and W and Ellison.

7655. Masiella, Diane, and Lisa Bahlinger. "Folktales," in *African-American Writers: A Dictionary*. Santa Barbara: ABC-CLIO, pp. 116–119. Mentions W briefly (p. 118).

7656. _____. "Spirituals," in *African-American Reviews: A Dictionary*. Eds. Shari Dorantes Hatch and Michael R. Strickland. Santa Barbara: ABC-CLIO, pp. 333–334. Notes W's knowledge of spirituals.

7657. McCann, Sean, *Gumshoe America: Hard-Boiled Crime Fiction and the Rise and Fall of New Deal Liberalism*. Durham: Duke University Press, pp. 262, 276–278, 280. Discusses the relation of Chester

Himes to W, and his reaction to Baldwin's attacks on W.

7658. McMillen, Neil R. "Jim Crow and the Limits of Freedom, 1890–1940," in *Civil Rights Since 1787*. Eds. Jonathan Birnbaum and Clarence Taylor. New York: New York University Press, pp. 190–202. Reprint of 1989.

7659. Meehan, Kevin. "Françoise Pfaff, ed. *Conversations with Maryse Condé.*" *African American Review*, 34 (Fall), 548–550. Mentions W briefly.

7660. Miles, Barry. *The Beat Hotel: Ginsberg, Burroughs, and Corso in Paris, 1958–1963.* New York: Grove Press, p. 4. Mentions W briefly as a refugee from racism.

7661. Miller, D. Quentin. "Introduction," in his *Re-Viewing James Baldwin: Things Not Seen.* Philadelphia: Temple University Press, pp. 1–11. Mentions W briefly (p. 4).

7662. _____. "James Baldwin, Poet," in his *Re-Viewing James Baldwin: Things Not Seen.* Philadelphia: Temple University Press, pp. 233–254. Quotes from *The Norton Anthology of African American Literature* a passage mentioning W briefly (p. 235).

7663. Miller, James A. "A Message from the Editor." *Richard Wright Newsletter*, 7 (Fall/Winter), 3. Announces changes in organization of the Richard Wright Circle and upcoming conference meetings on W.

7664. _____. "A Message From the Editor." *Richard Wright Newsletter*, 7 (Spring/Summer), 3. Notes the opening of a new stage version of *NS* at the Harlem School of the Arts on 6 October, cites suggestions by Jerry Ward and Maryemma Graham for celebrating the centennial of Wright's birth, and invites contributions to the *Newsletter*.

7665. _____. "Bigger Thomas Wants to Be Heard," in *Readings on Native Son.* Ed. Hayley R. Mitchell. San Diego: Greenhaven Press, pp. 107–114.

7666. Miller, Joshua. "'A Striking Addiction to Irreality': *Nothing Personal* and the Legacy of the Photo-Text Genre," in *Re-Viewing James Baldwin: Things Not Seen.* Ed. D. Quentin Miller. Philadelphia: Temple University Press, pp. 154–189). Includes an analysis of *TMBV* with comparisons to *The Sweet Flypaper of Life* by Langston Hughes and Roy

DeCavara and *Nothing Personal* by James Baldwin and Richard Avedon (pp. 163–172). Quotes Ellison's highly favorable opinion of *TMBV* (p. 170).

7667. Mitchell, Hayley. "Chronology," in her *Readings on Black Boy.* San Diego: Greenhaven Press, pp. 179–183. Notes important events and publications in W's life.

7668. _____. "For Further Research," in her *Readings on Black Boy.* Ed. Hayley Mitchell. San Diego: Greenhaven Press, pp. 184–185. Lists twenty-six books.

7669. _____. "For Further Research," in her *Readings on Black Boy.* San Diego: Greenhaven Press, pp. 184–185. Bibliography of twenty-six items.

7670. _____. "Introduction: Is *Black Boy* Really Autobiography?" in her *Readings on Black Boy.* San Diego: Greenhaven Press, pp. 11–12. Considers the mixture of fact and fiction in *BB*, quoting Hakutani, Margaret Walker, Du Bois, and Kinnamon.

7671. _____. "Introduction," in her *Readings on Native Son.* San Diego: Greenhaven Press, pp. 12–13. Discusses the early impact of *NS*, drawing mainly from Keneth Kinnamon's "How *Native Son* Was Born."

7672. _____. "Richard Wright: A Biography," in her *Readings on Black Boy.* San Diego: Greenhaven Press, pp. 13–32. Biographical essay with numerous quotations from Fabre, Gayle, and Kinnamon.

7673. _____. "Richard Wright: A Biography," in her *Readings on Black Boy.* San Diego: Greenhaven Press, pp. 15–32. Fairly detailed biographical account, with quotations from Michel Fabre, Keneth Kinnamon and Margaret Walker.

7674. Mitchell, Hayley R. "Characters and Plot," in her *Readings on Native Son.* San Diego: Greenhaven Press, pp. 36–41. Comments briefly on Bigger Thomas, Vera Thomas, Buddy Thomas, Bessie Mears, G.H., Gus, Jack, Mr. Dalton, Mrs. Dalton, Peggy, Jan Erlone, Britten, Buckley, and Boris Max, Also summarizes the plot.

7675. _____. "Chronology," in her *Readings on Native Son*," San Diego: Greenhaven Press, pp. 172–177. Somewhat detailed chronology from W's birth to his cremation in Paris.

7676. _____. "For Further Research," in her *Readings on Native Son.* San Diego: Greenhaven Press, pp. 178–180. Bibliography of thirty items.

7677. _____. "Richard Wright: A Biography," in her *Readings on Native Son*, San Diego: Greenhaven Press, pp. 14–35. Substantial biographical essay, drawing mainly from *BB*, *AH*, Keneth Kinnamon's *The Emergence of Richard Wright*, and Michel Fabre's *The Unfinished Quest of Richard Wright.*

7678. Montgomery, Maxine. "The Fire This Time: Apocalypse and the African American Novel Tradition," in *African Americans and the Bible: Sacred Texts and Social Textures.* Ed. Vincent L. Wimbush. New York: Continuum, pp. 489–500. Includes a discussion of *NS* as a "mature literary apocalypse-one relegating the American Dream to a bygone era" (p. 496). Also comments on *O* and "The Man Who Lived Underground" (p. 494).

7679. Moody, Joycelyn, and Caroline Chung Simpson. "Themes, Topics, Criticism," in *American Literary Scholarship: An Annual 1998.* Durham: Duke University Press, pp. 417–451. Includes comment on Claudia Tate's *Psychoanalysis and Black Novels* and Barbara Johnson's *The Feminist Difference*, both of which treat W.

7680. Moore, Rayburn S. "The South," in *The Continuum Encyclopedia of American Literature.* Ed. Steven R. Serafin. New York: Continuum, pp. 1066–1068. Mentions W briefly (p. 1067).

7681. Mootry, Maria K. "Wright's Male Heroes and Female Characters Are Archetypes," in *Readings on Native Son.* San Diego: Greenhaven Press, pp. 82–90.

7682. Murray, Albert. "Preface," in *Trading Twelves: The Selected Letters of Ralph Ellison and Albert Murray.* Ed. John F. Callahan. New York: The Modern Library, pp. xix–xxiv. Murray in New York in 1942 encountered Ellison, but did not foresee their lasting friendship: "I thought that he was as involved with Marxism as Richard Wright.... I also assumed that he regarded himself as a refugee from the South, much as Wright did (pp. xxii).

7683. Nadel, Alan. "Ellison, Ralph," in *The Continuum Encyclopedia of American Literature.* Ed.

Steven R. Serafin. New York: Continuum, pp. 327–328. Notes briefly the encouragement W gave to Ellison.

7684. Nagarkar, Shaashwat, and Jerry W. Ward, Jr. "An Email Exchange Between Jerry Ward and Shaashwat Nagarker Concerning *Black Boy*." *Richard Wright Newsletter*, 7 (Fall/Winter), 1, 3. A student in a Michigan high school queries Ward about censorship in the 1945 and 1991 editions of *BB*. Ward responds, emphasizing the first publisher's desire not to offend Northern readers.

7685. Nagel, James. "The American Short Story Cycle," in *The Columbia Companion to the Twentieth-Century American Short Story*. Ed. Blanche Gelfant. New York: Columbia University Press, pp. 9–14. Mentions *UTC*, "unified by themes of white oppression of black families" (p. 11).

7686. _____. "The American Short Story Cycle," in *The Columbia Companion to the Twentieth-Century American Short Story*. Ed. Blanche Gelfant. New York: Columbia University Press, pp. 9–14. Mentions briefly *UTC*, which is "unified by themes of white oppression of black families" (p. 11).

7687. Namekata, Hitoshi. "Behind the Laughter in "Man of All Work." *Tokyo Metropolitan Junior College International Studies of Culture*, 4 (February), 1–6. Claims that W's story derives from a Grimm fairy tale, as an exile look at American life with a cool eye.

7688. _____. "Richard Wright," in *Black Writers of the World*. Eds. Tsunehiko, Kitajima Gishin, and Shin Yamamoto. Tokyo: Takashobo Y Press, pp. 180–181. Summarizes W's career and provides a plot summary of *NS*, a bibliography, and a note for researchers.

7689. Naylor, Gloria, and Nikki Giovanni. "Conversation." *Callaloo*, 24 (Fall), 1395–1409. Includes comments on W's expatriation (pp. 1399, 1400).

7690. Nicholls, David G. *Conjuring the Folk: Forms of Modernity in African America*. Ann Arbor: The University of Michigan Press, pp. 15, 17, 24, 31, 32, 85–86, 111, 113–129, 132, 153, 154, 155. A substantial chapter on *TMBV* treats its narrative voice and its Marxist analysis of African American history from the Middle Passage to the Great Migration. Elsewhere Nicholls mentions "Red Clay Blues" and "Blueprint for Negro Writing and comments on "Long Black Song" (p. 85).

7691. Noble, Marianne K. "Masochistic Eroticism in *Uncle Tom's Cabin*," in *Approaches to Teaching Stowe's Uncle Tom's Cabin*. Eds. Elizabeth Ammons and Susan Belasco. New York: The Modern Language Association, pp. 150–161. Mentions briefly *NS* (p. 160).

7692. Oates, Joyce Carol, and Robert Atwan. "James Baldwin," in their *The Best American Essays of the Century*. Boston: Houghton Mifflin, pp. 570–571. Biographical note mentioning W's help to the young Baldwin.

7693. _____. "Richard Wright," in their *The Best American Essays of the Century*. Boston: Houghton Mifflin, p. 590. Biographical note mentioning *UTC*, *BB*, *NS*, *BP*, *CC*, *PS*, and *WML*.

7694. Ochshorn, Kathleen. "Wright's Minor Women Characters Are More Sympathetic Than the Men," in *Readings on Native Son*, Ed. Halley R. Mitchell. San Diego: Greenhaven Press, pp. 91–97.

7695. Orlans, Harold. "Selling Richard Wright." *Change*, 32 (May-June). Brief account of editorial interference with the manuscripts of *NS* and *BB*. Based on the Rowley biography.

7696. Patterson, Anita. "Jazz, Realism, and the Modernist Lyric: The Poetry of Langston Hughes." *Modern Language Quarterly*, 61 (December), pp. 651–682. Quotes from W's review of *The Big Sea* (p. 651).

7697. Peach, Linden. *Toni Morrison*. Second ed. New York: St. Martins Press, p. 12.

7698. Pearson, Norman Holmes. "American Literature: The Twentieth Century," in *The Encyclopedia Americana*. Ed. Mark Cummings. Danbury, CT: Grolier, pp. 703–709.

7699. Peck, Dale. "American Booty." *The New Republic*, 222 (22 May), pp. 36–41. Review of Stanley Crouch's *Don't the Moon Look Lonesome* mentioning W briefly (p. 39).

7700. Peterson, Dale E. *Up from Bondage: The Literatures of Russian and African American Soul*. Durham, NC: Duke University Press, pp. 10. 109, 125–132, 136–142. Discusses similarities between W and Maxim Gorky, especially in *BB* and Gorky's *Childhood*. Both writers rejected folk life and embraced Marxism. Also discusses W's quarrel with Hurston and mentions *AH*, "Blueprint for Negro Writing," and "The Man Who Lived Underground."

7701. Pettis, Joyce, "Qualities of Endurance: Paule Marshall's *Brown Girl, Brownstones,*" *The Black Scholar*, 30 (Summer), 15–20. Mentions W briefly (pp. 17, 18).

7702. Pfister, Joel. "Complicity Critiques." *American Literary History*, 12 (Fall), 610–632. Includes discussion of W's reading of escapist fiction and his quarrel with Zora Neale Hurston (pp. 620–623). Mentions *BB*, *NS*, and *UTC*.

7703. Philipson, Robert. *The Identity Question: Blacks and Jews in Europe and America*. Jackson: University Press of Mississippi, pp. 91–92, 112, 132, 138, 143, 152–153, 172–173, 118–123. Contains extensive treatment of W, often in comparison to Afred Kazin. W's relation to the left is emphasized. Among W's works consered or mentioned are *BB*, *AH*, "Blueprint for Negro Writing," and "The Literature of the Negro in the United States."

7704. Pierpont, Claudia Roth, *Passionate Minds: Women Rewriting the World*. New York: Alfred A. Knopf, pp. 34, 133–134, 135, 140, 152, 157, 163, 238. Mentions or comments on W in chapters on Gertrude Stein, Zora Neale Hurston, Eudora Welty, and Doris Lessing. Mentions *UTC*, *NS*, and *BB*. Notes that Welty refused to review *BB*.

7705/7706. Pinson, Hermine "*Haiku: This Other World* by Richard Wright." *Richard Wright Newsletter*, 7 (Spring/Summer), 4–6. Favorable review emphasizing the biographical context, praising the editorial work by Yoshinobu Hakutani and Robert L. Tener and the introduction by Julia Wright, and taking satisfaction in the spiritual repose W found in haiku at the end of his turbulent life and work.

7707. Plant, Deborah G. "Gloria L. Cronin. *Critical Essays: Zora Neale Hurston*." *African American Review*, 34 (Winter), 729–732. Review mentioning W briefly (p. 731).

7708. Porter, Horace A. "Black Boy Is a Metaphor for the Birth of an Artist," in *Readings on Black Boy*.

Ed. Hayley Mitchell. San Diego: Greenhaven Press, pp. 113–123. Includes headnote by Mitchell.

7709. _____. "James Baldwin (1924–1987)," in *The Columbia Companion to the Twentieth-Century American Short Story*. Ed. Blanche H. Gelfant. New York: Columbia University Press, pp. 114–117. Notes that a character in a Baldwin story "refuses to play Bigger Thomas in a movie version of" *NS* (p. 116).

7710. _____. "James Baldwin (1924–1987)," in The Columbia Companion to the *Twentieth-Century Short Story*. Ed. Blanche Gelfant. New York: Columbia University Press, pp. 114–117. States that Baldwin declined to play Bigger Thomas in a projected movie version of *NS* (p. 116).

7711. Posnock, Ross. "The Dream of Deracination": *American Literary History*, 12 (Winter), 802–818. Review of Manthia Diawara's *In Search of Africa* discussing its favorable view of BP (pp. 810, 812–813),

7712. Powers, Peter. "'The Singing Man Who Must Be Reckoned With' Private Desire and Public Responsibility in the Poetry of Countee Cullen." *African American Review*, 34 (Winter), 661–678. Mentions W briefly (p. 664).

7713. Prescott, Orville. "A Review of *Invisible Man*," in *The Critical Response to Ralph Ellison*. Ed. Robert J. Butler. Westport, CT: Greenwood Press, pp. 19–20.

7714. Primeau, Ronald R. "Imagination Transforms Wright's Racist World in *Black Boy*," in *Readings on Black Boy*. Ed. Hayley Mitchell. San Diego: Greenhaven Press, pp. 170–178. Includes a headnote by Mitchell.

7715. _____. "Imagination Transforms Wright's Racist World in *Black Boy*, in *Readings on Black Boy*. Ed. Hayley Mitchell. San Diego: Greenhaven Press, pp. 170–178.

7716. Proefriedt, William A. "The Theme of Education in *Black Boy*," in *Readings on Black Boy*. Ed. Hayley Mitchell. San Diego: Greenhaven Press, pp. 124–130. Includes a headnote by Mitchell.

7717. _____. "The Theme of Education in *Black Boy*, in *Readings on Black Boy*. Ed. Hayley Mitchell. San Diego: Greenhaven Press, pp. 124–130.

7718. Prono, Luca. "Wright, Richard (1908–1960)," in *St. James Encyclopedia of Popular Culture*, Eds. Toni Pendergast and Sara Pendergast. Vol. 5. Detroit: St. James Press, pp. 196–197. Biographical sketch with a brief, eccentrically selected bibliography. Includes a photograph of W.

7719. Propheter, Douglas. "Literature," in *Encyclopedia of American History: The Great Depression and World War II*. New York: Facts on File, pp. 190–193. Comments briefly on *NS* and *BB*.

7720. Pudaloff, Ross. "Bigger Thomas Is a Product of Mass Culture," in *Readings on Native Son*. Ed. Haley R. Mitchell. San Diego: Greenhaven Press, pp. 98–106.

7721. Rachleff, Peter. "Rethinking Cultural Politics and the Politics of Culture." *Callaloo*, 23 (Fall), 1516–1519. Review of Bill V. Mullen's *Popular Fronts: Chicago and African-American Cultural Politics, 1935–1946* including discussion of Mullen's treatment of *NS*. Also comments on W's relationship to the Communist Party.

7722. Rambsy, Howard, II. "(Re-) Introducing a Black Boy: Studying Richard Wright and His Writings in the 21st Century." *Richard Wright Newsletter*, 7 (Fall/Winter), pp. 1, 3. Response of a young black Mississippian to reading W, especially *BB*, moving from the personal to the scholarly.

7723. Rayapati, Jacob R. "Interview with poet Gerald [W.] Barrax." *Obsidian III*, 1 (Fall/Winter), 24–41. Barrax mentions reading *TMBV* (p. 35).

7724. Reed, Adolph, Jr. *Class Notes: Posing as Politics and Other Thoughts on the American Scene*. New York: The New Press, p. 74. Mentions briefly Bigger Thomas.

7725. Reed, Ishmael. "Bigger and O.J.," in his *The Reed Reader*, New York: Basic Books, pp. 247–265.

7726. _____. "Introduction," in his *The Reed Reader*. New York: Basic Books, pp. xi–xxx, xxiii. Refers to the use of W and *NS* in his novel *The Last Days of Louisiana Red*, notes Ellison's praise of W for being guided by Freud and Marx, and states that Henry Louis Gates, Jr., charged W with sexism.

7727. _____. "Soyinka Among the Monoculturalists," in his *The Reed Reader*. New York: Basic Books, pp. 267–271. Mentions W briefly (p. 270).

7728. _____. "Shrovetide in Old New Orleans," in his *The Reed Reader*. New York: Basic Books, pp. 305–326.

7729. _____. "300 Years of 1984," in his *The Reed Reader*. New York: Basic Books, pp. 235–246. Mentions briefly *SH* (p. 236).

7730. Reesman, Jeanne Campbell. "Fiction: 1900 to the 1930s," in *American Literary Scholarship: An Annual 1998*. Durham: Duke University Press, pp. 257–285. Includes comments on M. Lynn Weiss's book on Gertrude Stein and W (p. 258) and mentions W elsewhere, pp. 283, 285.

7731. Reilly, John M. "Robert Butler. *Contemporary African American Fiction: The Open Journey*." *African American Review*, 34 (Winter), 722–724. Review mentioning Butler's treatment of W.

7732. _____. "The Testament of Ralph Ellison," in *The Critical Response to Ralph Ellison*. Ed. Robert J. Butler. Westport, CT: Greenwood Press, pp. 161–171.

7733. _____. "The Testament of Ralph Ellison," in *The Critical Response to Ralph Ellison*. Ed. Robert J. Butler. Westport, CT: Greenwood Press, pp. 161–171.

7734. Reynolds, Guy. "'Sketches of Spain': Richard Wright's *Pagan Spain* and African-American Representations of the Hispanic." *Journal of American Studies*, 34 (December), 487–502. Locates *Pagan Spain* in the contexts of African American writing on Spain, the sociology of the Chicago School, the Spanish Civil War, and Catholicism. It yokes "together the generalizing & rhetoric of a social-scientific study with a travel journal's reliance on the telling vignette or cameo" (p. 499).

7735. Richards, Phillip M. "Robert Hayden (1913–1980): An Appreciation." *The Massachusetts Review*, 40 (Winter), 599–613. Mentions W briefly (p. 603).

7736. Richards, Phillip M., and Neil Schlager. "A Robert Lee, ed., *Black Fiction: New Studies in the Afro-American Novel Since 1945*," in their *Best Literature By and About Blacks*. Detroit: Gale Group, p. 295. Notes that W is treated

7737. _____. "Addison Gayle Jr., *Bondage, Freedom, and Beyond: The Prose of Black Americans*, in their *Best Literature by and About Blacks*." Detroit: Gale Group, p. 286. Notes that W is included.

7738. _____. "Addison Gayle, Jr., *Richard Wright: Ordeal of a Native Son*, in their *Best Literature by and About Blacks*." Detroit: Gale Group, p. 190. Comments on this biography of W "filtered through an African, rather than white European lens."

7739. _____. "Arthur Paul Davis," in their *Best Literature by and About Blacks*. Detroit: Gale Group, p. 175. Mentions W briefly.

7740. _____, "Claudia C. Tate, 'Psychoanalysis and Black Novels: Desire and the Protocols of Race,'" in their *Best Literature By and About Blacks*. Detroit: Gale Group, p. 303. Applies psychoanalysis to *SH*.

7741. _____. "Clarence Major, *The Dark and Feeling: Black American Writers and Their Work*," in their *Best Literature By and About Blacks*. Detroit: Gale Group, p. 296. Notes that W is treated.

7742. _____. "Henry B. Wonham, ed. *Criticism and the Color Line: Desegregating American Literary Studies*." in their *Best Literature By and About Blacks*. Detroit: Gale Group, p. 306. Includes examination of W.

7743. _____. "Blyden Jackson, *The Waiting Years: Essays on American Negro Literature*." in their *Best Literature By and About Blacks*. Detroit: Gale Group, p. 292. W is one of the authors treated.

7744. _____. "Michael S. Harper, 'Heartblow: Messages," in their *Best Literature By and About Blacks*. Detroit: Gale Group, p. 260. Notes that the Harper poem focuses on W. Mentions briefly *NS* and *BB*.

7745. _____. "Charles T. Davis and Henry Louis Gates, Jr., ed., *Black Is the Color of the Cosmos: Essays on Afro-American Literature and Culture, 1942–1981*, in their *Best Literature By and About Blacks*. Detroit: Gale Group, p. 283. Notes that one section of the book is entitled "On Wright, Ellison, and Baldwin."

7746. _____. "David Littlejohn, *Black on White: A Critical Survey of Writing By American Negroes*, in their *Best Literature by and About Blacks*." Detroit: Gale Group, p. 295. Notes that Littlejohn divides his study into two parts — before and after *NS*.

7747. _____. "Donald B. Gibson, ed. *Five Black Writers: Essays on Wright, Ellison, Baldwin, Hughes,* and *LeRoi Jones*," in their *Best Literature By and About Black Writers*. Detroit: Gale Group, p. 286. Treats *NS* with a political emphasis.

7748. _____. "Dolan Hubbard, *The Sermon and the African American Literary Imagination*," in their *Best Literature By and About Blacks*. Detroit: Gale Group, p. 290. Includes treatment of the sermon in W.

7749. _____. "Donald B. Gibson, ed. *The Politics of Literary Expression: A Study of Major Black Writers*," in their *Best Literature By and About Blacks*. Detroit: Gale Group, pp. 286–297. W is one of the writers treated.

7750. _____. "Farah Jasmine Griffin, '*Who Set You Flowin'?: The African American Migration Narrative*," in their *Best Literature By and About Blacks*." Detroit: Gale Group, p. 287. W is discussed in the Griffin book.

7751. _____. "George Wylie Henderson, *Ollie Miss: A Novel*," in their *Best Literature By and About Blacks*. Detroit: Gale Group, p. 39. Mentions W briefly.

7752. _____. "Herbert Hill, *Anger, and Beyond: The Negro Writer in the United States*," in their *Best Literature By and About Blacks*. Detroit: Gale Group, p. 289. Notes that the collection has a chapter on W.

7753. _____. "Houston A. Baker, Jr., *The Journey Back: Issues in Black Literature and Criticism*," in their *Best Literature By and About Blacks*. Detroit: Gale Group, p. 279. Notes that Baker examines W and others in this book.

7754. _____. "James H. Evans, Jr., *Spiritual Empowerment in Afro-American Literature: Frederick Douglass, Rebecca Jackson, Booker T. Washington, Richard Wright, Toni Morrison*," in their *Best Literature By and About Blacks*." Detroit: Gale Group, p. 285. Notes that *NS* is treated (p. 285).

7755. _____. "James O. Young, 'Black Writers of the Thirties,'" in their *Best Literature By and About Blacks*. Detroit: Gale Group, p. 306. Notes that Young examines W in the "intellectual and cultural context of the period.

7756. _____. "Joyce Ann Joyce, *Richard Wright's Art of Tragedy*," in their *Best Literature By and About Blacks*. Detroit: Gale Group, p. 293.

Notice emphasizing Joyce's treatment of W's craft.

7757. _____. "Michael S. Harper, 'The Meaning of Protest,'" in their *Best Literature By and About Blacks*. Detroit: Gale Group, p. 260. The poem mentions *PS*.

7758. _____. "Ladell Payne, *Black Novelists and the Southern Literary Traditions*,'" in their *Best Literature By and About Blacks*. Detroit: Gale Group, p. 298. Includes W, arguing for an "interconnection of black and white southern writers."

7759. _____. "Maxine Lavon Montgomery, '*The Apocalypse in African American Fiction*,'" in their *Best Literature By and About Blacks*. Detroit: Gale Group, p. 297. Notes that *NS* is analyzed.

7760. _____. "Richard Wright, *Fire and Cloud*," in *Best Literature By and About Blacks*. Detroit: Gale Group, pp. 277–278. Summarizes the radio play, based on "Fire and Cloud."

7761. _____. "Richard Wright, *The Long Dream: A Novel*," in their *Best Literature By and About Blacks*. Detroit: Gale Group, p. 148. Brief plot summary and evaluation.

7762. _____. "Richard Wright, *Native Son*," in their *Best Literature By and About Blacks*. Detroit: Gale Group, p. 241. Brief plot summary and evaluation.

7763. _____. "Richard Wright, *The Outsider*," in their *Best Literature By and About Blacks*. Detroit: Gale Group, p. 148. Emphasizes the existential origin of the novel and influence of Sartre.

7764. _____. "Richard Wright, Paul Green, *Native Son* (the Biography of a Young American): *A Play in Ten Scenes*" in their *Best Literature By and About Blacks*, Detroit: Gale Group, p. 278. Explains that the play is derived from the novel and mentions Orson Welles as director and Canada Lee as male lead.

7765. _____. "Richard Wright, *Savage Holiday*," in their *Best Literature By and About Blacks*. Detroit: Gale Group, p. 149. Unfavorable evaluation of the novel: "failure to integrate Freudian theory into an arguably weak plot."

7766. _____. "Richard Wright, *Uncle Tom's Children: Four Novellas*," in their *Best Literature By and About Blacks*. Detroit: Gale Group. Notes that *UTC* developed out of the Federal Writers Project and emphasizes their "striking portrayal of racism in America.

7767. _____. "Noel Schraufnagel, '*From Apology to Protest: The Black American Novel*'" in their *Best Literature By and About Blacks*. Detroit: Gale Group, pp. 301–302. This early (1973) study begins with *NS*.

7768. _____. "Seymour L. Gross and John Edward Hardy, *Images of the Negro in American Literature*," in their *Best Literature By and About Blacks*. Detroit: Gale Group, p. 287. W is one of the writers discussed.

7769. _____. "Trudier Harris, '*From Mammies to Militants: Domestics in Black American Literature*,'" in their *Best Literature By and About Blacks*. Detroit: Gale Group. Notes that Harris treats "Man of All Work."

7770. _____. "Valerie Smith, *Self-Discovery and Authority in Afro-American Narrative*," in their *Best Literature By and About Blacks*. Detroit: Gale Group, p. 302. Treats W as well as slave narratives.

7771. _____. "V.P. Franklin, *Living Our Stories, Telling Our Truths: Autobiography and Making of the African American Intellectual Tradition*," in their *Best Literature By and About Blacks*. Detroit: Gale Group, p. 187. Includes consideration of W.

7772. _____. "Victor Sejour, *The Brown Overcoat*." in their *Best Literature By and About Blacks*. Detroit: Gale Group, p. 12. Compares briefly Sejour's success in Paris to Wright's.

7773. Robinson, Cedric J. *Black Marxism: The Making of the Black Radical Tradition*. Chapel Hill: University of North Carolina Press, pp. 182–183, 184, 289–292, 294–305, 313, 315–316, 404, 406, 407. Contains a new preface and a foreword by Robin D.G. Kelley.

7774. _____. "Preface," in his *Black Marxism: The Making of the Black Radical Tradition*. Chapel Hill: University of North Carolina Press, pp. xxvii–xxxiii. Mentions W briefly (p. xxxi).

7775. Rohy, Valerie, *Impossible Women: Lesbian Figures and American Literature*. Ithaca: Cornell University Press, pp. 106–107. Includes comments on W's criticism of *Their Eyes Were Watching God*

7776. _____. *Impossible Women: Lesbian Figures and American Literature*. Ithaca: Cornell University Press, pp. 106–107. Paraphrases and quotes from W's criticism of *Their Eyes Were Watching God*.

7777. Rosenblatt, Roger. "Why Writers Attack Writers." *Time*, 155 (24 January), 86. Mentions briefly Baldwin's attack on W.

7778. Rotella, Carlo. "Realists and the Romance of Street Credentials." *PMLA*, 115 (November), 1453. Announcement of an MLA Convention session including a paper on W by Robert Carl Nowatski.

7779. Rubin, Louis D., Jr. "Blyden Jackson: A Memory." *CLA Journal*, 44 (September), 133–139. Mentions briefly a lecture by Jackson on "Richard Wright in a Moment of Truth" (p. 134).

7780. Rubin, Rachel. *Jewish Gangsters of Modern Literature*. Urbana: University of Illinois Press, p. 189. Mentions briefly *BB*.

7781. Rubin, Stevin J. "*Native Son* Is a Novel of Revolt," in *Readings on Native Son*. Ed. Hayley R. Mitchell. San Diego: Greenhaven Press, pp. 153–156.

7782. Rushdy, Ashraf H.A. "Bonnie TuSmith, ed. *Conversations with John Edgar Wideman*." *African American Review*, 34 (Fall), 544–546. Mentions W briefly.

7783. Ryan, Katy. "Revolutionary Suicide in Toni Morrison's Fiction." *African American Review*, 34 (Fall), 389–412. Quotes briefly *BB* (p. 407).

7784. Sallis, James. *Chester Himes: A Life*. New York: Walker, pp. 66, 68, 88, 93, 94–96, 110, 116, 122, 123, 139, 145, 183, 184, 189, 190, 191, 243, 245, 257, 266, 267, 283, 330–331. Mentions briefly *UTC, BB, NS, LD* "Islands of Hallucination" and discusses W's relation to Himes, with attention to Ellison and Baldwin as well.

7785. _____. *Chester Himes: A Life*. New York: Walker, pp. 66, 68, 88, 93, 94–96, 110, 116, 122, 123, 139, 145, 183, 184, 189, 190, 191, 243, 245, 257, 266, 267, 283, 330–331. Mentions briefly *UTC, BB, NS, LD*, "Islands of Hallucination" and discusses W's relation to Himes, with attention to Ellison and Baldwin as well.

7786. Samuels, Wilfred D. "African-American Short Fiction," in *The Facts on File Companion to the American Short Story*. Ed. Abby Werlock. New York: Facts on File, pp. 4–8. Includes discussion of W as a short story writer who "confirmed the 'universality' and legitimacy" of African American fiction." Mentions briefly *UTC*, and *EM*.

7787. Saunders, James Robert. "Bigger Thomas Represents the Social Plight of the Lower Classes," in *Readings on Native Son*. Ed. Hayley R. Mitchell. San Diego: Greenhaven Press, pp. 115–118.

7788. Savery, Pancho. "Maryemma Graham, Sharon Pineault-Burke, and Marianna White Davis, eds. *Teaching African American Literature: Theory and Practice*." *African American Review*, 34 (Fall), 525–527. Review mentioning W briefly (p. 527).

7789. Scott, William R., and William G. Shade. "Introduction: The Long Rugged Road," in their *Upon These Shores: Themes in the African American Experience, 1600 to the Present*. New York: Routledge, pp. 1–18. The epigraph is a quotation from *TMBV* and W is mentioned briefly (p. 11).

7790. Scruggs, Charles W. "Man's Need for Community: The Failure of the City in *Native Son*, in *Readings on Native Son*. Ed. Haley R. Mitchell. San Diego: Greenhaven Press, pp. 125–132.

7791. Sharpe, William Chapman. "City and Literature, The," in *The Continuum Encyclopedia of American Literature*. Ed. Steven R. Serafin. New York: Continuum, pp. 194–196. Comments briefly on *NS* (p. 196).

7792. Shulman, Robert. *The Power of Political Art: The 1930s Literary Left Reconsidered*. Chapel Hill: University of North Carolina Press, pp. 1, 2, 15, 17, 18, 19, 23, 28, 29, 31–33, 137–180, 183, 244, 277. Arguing for the literary quality as well as political relevance of Thirties literature, Shulman both sketches W's early career and reputation (pp. 31–33) and analyzes *NS* at length (pp. 137–180). Also mentions *AH, BB, BP, LT, O, TMBV, UTC*, and some of the poems.

7793. Siegel, Paul N. "The Conclusion of *Native Son* Is Often Misunderstood," in Readings on *Native Son*. Ed. Hayley R. Mitchell. San Diego: Greenhaven Press, pp. 70–80. Partial reprint of 1974.

7794. Singh, Nikhil Pal. "Toward an Effective Antiracism," in *Dispatches from the Ebony Tower: Intellectuals Confront the African American Experience*. Ed. Manning Marable. New York: Columbia University Press, pp. 31–51. Includes discussion of W's critique of "antiracist universalism" (pp. 37. 39, 48–49).

7795. Skeggs, Beverly. "Introduction," in *Transformations: Thinking Through Feminism*. Eds. Sara Ahmed, Jane Kilby, Celia Lury, Maureen McNeill, and Beverly Skeggs. New York: Routledge, pp. 1–23. Mentions W briefly (p. 30).

7796. Skerrett, Joseph T., Jr. "The Wright Interpretation: Ralph Ellison and the Anxiety of Influence," in *The Critical Response to Ralph Ellison*. Ed. Robert J. Butler. Westport, CT: Greenwood Press, pp. 149–159.

7797. _____. "Writing as Survival in *Black Boy*," in *Readings on Black Boy*. Ed. Hayley Mitchell. San Diego: Greenhaven Press, pp. 92–102. Partial reprint of 1979.237. Includes a headnote by Mitchell.

7798. _____. "The Wright Interpretation: Ralph Ellison and the Anxiety of Influence," in *The Critical Response to Ralph Ellison*. Ed. Robert J. Butler. Westport, CT: Greenwood Press, pp. 149–159.

7799. Skerrett, Joseph T., Jr. "Writing as Survival in Black Boy," in *Readings on Black Boy*. Ed. Hayley Mitchell. San Diego: Greenhaven Press, pp. 92–102.

7800. Smead, Howard. "African Americans," in *Encyclopedia of American History: The Great Depression and World War II*. New York: Facts on File, pp. 2–5. Mentions briefly *NS*.

7801. Smith, Barbara. "Toward a Black Feminist Criticism," in *The Prentice Hall Anthology of African American Literature*. Eds. Rochelle Smith and Sharon L. Jones. Upper Saddle River, NJ: Prentice Hall, pp. 1010–1023.

7802. Smith, David Lionel. "The African American Short Story," in *The Columbia Companion to the Twentieth-Century American Short Story*. Ed. Blanche H. Gelfant. New York: Columbia University Press, pp. 25–33. Considers briefly *UTC* and *EM* mentioning specifically only "Man of All Work" (pp. 28–29).

7803. _____. "The African American Short Story," in *The Columbia Companion to the Twentieth-Century American Short Story*. Ed. Blanche Gelfant. New York: Columbia University Press, pp. 25–33. Includes

discussion of *UTC* as protest fiction and mention of *EM* as experimental.

7804. _____. "Richard Wright (1908–1960). In *The Columbia Companion to the Twentieth-Century American Story*. Ed. Blanche Gelfant. New York: Columbia University Press, pp. 591–596. Contains a biographical sketch of W and comments on all the stories in *UTC* and *EM*, which "offer a broad representation of Wright's multifaceted art." Smith also lists four critical studies.

7805. _____. "Richard Wright," in *The Columbia Companion to the Twentieth-Century American Short Story*. Ed. Blanche H. Gelfant. New York: Columbia University Presss, pp. 591–596. Biographical essay together with analysis of the stories in *EM* as well as *UTC*. Gives special attention to "The Man Who Lived Underground" and "Big Black Good Man."

7806. _____. "The African American Short Story," in *The Columbia Companion to the Twentieth-Century Short Story*. New York: Columbia University Press, pp. 25–33. Includes a paragraph on W, noting his disagreement with Hurston and the expanding scope of his stories. Comments on *UTC* and *EM*.

7807. Smith, Felipe. "Prospects of AMERICA: Nation as Woman in the Poetry of DuBois, Johnson, and McKay," in *Reading Race in American Poetry: An Area of Act*. Ed. Aldon Lynn Nielsen. Urbana: University of Illinois Press, pp. 25–42. Mentions W briefly (p. 41).

7808. Smith, Newton. "Green, Paul [Eliot]," in *The Continuum Encyclopedia of American Literature*. Ed. Steven R. Serafin. New York: Continuum, pp. 458–459. Mentions briefly the play *NS*.

7809. Smith, Rochelle, and Sharon L. Jones. "Addison Gayle, Jr. (1932–1991)," in their *The Prentice Hall Anthology of African American Literature*. Upper Saddle River, NJ: Prentice Hall, p. 977. Headnote to "The Function of Black Literature at the Present Time," which quotes from "Blueprint for Negro Writing" (pp. 983, 984).

7810. _____. "African American Literary Criticism: Introduction," in their *The Prentice Hall Anthology of African American Literature*. Upper Saddle River, NJ: Prentice Hall, pp. 951–954. Mentions briefly W and

"Blueprint for Negro Writing" (pp. 952, 953). "Blueprint" is reprinted on pp. 965–973.

7811. _____. "African American Literary Criticism," in their *The Prentice Hall Anthology of African American Literature*. Upper Saddle River, NJ: Prentice Hall, pp. 951–116. Mentions W briefly (pp. 952, 983, 984, 1014, 1024, 1038, 1045, 1046, 1072.

7812. _____. "Introduction," in their *The Prentice Hall Anthology of African American Literature*. Upper Saddle River, NJ: Prentice Hall, pp. 1–4. Mentions W briefly (p. 2).

7813. _____. "Margaret Walker Alexander (1915–1998)," in their *The Prentice Hall Anthology of African American Literature*. Upper Saddle River, NJ: Prentice Hall, p. 473. Mentions briefly Walker's book on W.

7814. _____. "The Protest Movement 1940–1959," in their *The Prentice Hall Anthology of African American Literature*. Upper Saddle River, NJ: Prentice Hall, pp. 468–472. Contains a paragraph on W mentioning *NS* and *BB* (p. 471).

7815. _____. "Ralph Ellison (1914–1994)," in their *The Prentice Hall Anthology of African American Literature*. Upper Saddle River, NJ: Prentice Hall, p. 552. Headnote mentioning W briefly.

7816. _____. "Ralph Ellison (1914–1994), in their *The Prentice Hall Anthology of African American Literature*. Upper Saddle River, NJ: Prentice Hall, p. 552. Biographical sketch mentioning W briefly.

7817. _____. "Richard Wright (1908–1960)," in their *The Prentice Hall Anthology of African American Literature*. Upper Saddle River, NJ: Prentice Hall, p. 473. Biographical headnote to excerpts from *NS* and *BB* and to "The Man Who Lived Underground" and "The Man Who Was Almost a Man."

7818. _____. "Timeline," in their *The Prentice Hall Anthology of African American Literature*. Upper Saddle River, NJ: Prentice Hall, pp. 1117–1121. Lists the publication of *NS* and *BB*.

7819. _____. "Writing About African American Literature," in their *The Prentice Hall Anthology of African American Literature*. Upper Saddle River, NJ: Prentice Hall, pp. 112–116. Mentions briefly *NS* (p. 1115).

7820. Smith, Sidonie Ann. "Richard Wright's *Black Boy*: A Twentieth-Century Slave Narrative," in *Readings on Black Boy*. Ed. Hayley Mitchell. Readings on *Black Boy*. San Diego: Greenhaven Press, pp. 34–42.

7821. Smith, Virginia Whatley. "Richard Wright Reconsidered: Wright's Fictions of His Exile Years, 1946–60." *PMLA*, 115 (November), 1471. Announcement of an MLA Convention session with papers by Yoshinobu Hakutani, John M. Reilly, John Wharton Lowe, and Keith E. Byerman.

7822. St. Jean, Shawn. "Dreiser and American Literary Paganism: A Reading of the Trilogy of Desire," in *Theodore Dreiser and American Culture: New Readings*. Ed. Yoshinobu Hakutani. Newark: University of Delaware Press, pp. 203–213. Mentions W briefly (p. 204).

7823. _____. "Dreiser and American Literary Paganism: A Reading of the Trilogy of Desire," in *Theodore Dreiser and American Culture: New Readings*. Newark: University of Delaware Press, p. 203.

7824. Stepto, Robert B. "Wayne Miller's photographs capture a black Chicago of fifty years ago…," in *Chicago's South Side, 1946–1948*. By Wayne F. Miller. Berkeley: University of California Press, pp. xi + xii. Mentions briefly *NS*.

7825. _____, and Michael S. Harper. "Study and Experience: An Interview with Ralph Ellison," in *The Critical Response to Ralph Ellison*. Ed. Robert J. Butler. Westport, CT: Greenwood Press, pp. 3–16.

7826. _____. Study and Experience: An interview with Ralph Ellison," in *The Critical Response to Ralph Ellison*. Ed. Robert L. Butler. Westport, CT: Greenwood Press, pp. 3–16.

7827. Stille, Alexander. "The Spy Who Failed." *The New Yorker*, 76 (15 May), pp. 44–46, 48. Mentions W briefly as contributor to *The God That Failed*.

7828. Stoval, Tyler. "The Fire This Time: Black American Expatriates and the Algerian War." *Yale French Studies*, No. 98, pp. 182–200. Discusses W and his circle in Paris. Outspokenly anticolonialist, W nevertheless kept quiet about Algeria for fear of being expelled from France. Includes discussion of W's Parisian friends, black and white, and the Gibson affair.

7829. Strickland, Michael R. "Madhubuti: Haki." in *African American Writers: A Dictionary*. Eds. Shari Dorantes Hatch and Michael R. Strickland. Santa Barbara: ABC-CLIO, pp. 236–237. Discusses Lee reading *BB*.

7830. Suarez, Ernest. "Writing Southern Literary History." *The Southern Review*, 36 (Autumn), 881–892. Mentions W briefly (pp. 887–888).

7831. Suggs, Jon-Christian. *Whispered Consolations: Law and Narrative in African American Life*. Ann Arbor: The University of Michigan Press, pp. 3, 44, 235–245, 248, 260–261, 272, 287, 308. Chapter 8 includes a comparison of *NS* and *Knock on Any Door* as "novels in which the critique of American law is framed through a premodernist literary naturalism" (p. 236). Suggs also considers *Blood on the Forge, If He Hollers Let Him Go* and *Lonely Crusade* in relation to *NS*.

7832. Szalay, Michael. *New Deal Modernism: American Literature and the Invention of the Welfare State*. Durham: Duke University Press, pp. 2, 3, 5, 11, 18, 22, 37, 52, 62, 68, 70, 98, 146, 165, 208–212, 215–221, 225–227, 241, 244, 248, 252, 255, 321–325. Contains substantial treatment of W in relation to a personal and national search for security during the thirties, arguing that he moves from Communism toward the New Deal and the welfare state. Examines *NS, O, TMBV, LT* and *SH*.

7833. Tate, Claudia. "Barbara Johnson. *The Feminist Difference: Literature, Psychoanalysis, Race, and Gender*." *African American Review*, 34 (Spring), 159–162. Review containing a paragraph on Johnson's treatment of *NS* (p. 160).

7834. Thaddeus, Janice. "*Black Boy* Is Incomplete Without *American Hunger*," in *Readings on Black Boy*. Ed. Hayley Mitchell. San Diego: Greenhaven Press, pp. 58–68. Includes a headnote by Mitchell.

7835. _____. "*Black Boy* Is Incomplete Without *American Hunger*," in *Readings on Black Boy*. Ed. Hayley Mitchell. San Diego: Greenhaven Press, pp. 58–68.

7836. Thelwell, Ekwueme Michael. "The Professor and the Activists: A Memoir of Sterling Brown."

The Massachusetts Review, 40 (Winter), 617–638. Mentions W briefly (p. 632).

7837. Thomas, Lorenzo. *Extraordinary Measures: Afrocentric Modernism and Twentieth-Century American Poetry*. Tuscaloosa: The University of Alabama Press, pp. 2, 12, 80, 81, 91, 92, 215. Quotes W on Phillis Wheatley (p. 2), comments on "I Have Seen Black Hands" (p. 81), mentions *BB* (p. 91), quotes from "Blueprint for Negro Writing," and mentions *WML*.

7838. Tolentino, Cynthia. "The Road Out of the Black Belt: Sociology's Fictions and Black Subjectivity in *Native Son*." *Novel: A Forum on Fiction*; 33 (Summer), 377–405. Examines W's relation to the Communist Party, sociology, black literary development, black subjectivity and agency, racism, white liberalism, the historical context of the thirties, especially as all of these are embodied in *NS*.

7839. Towner, Theresa M. *Faulkner on the Color Line: The Later Novels*. Jackson: University Press of Mississippi, pp. 80, 156. Notes Faulkner's admonition to W to emphasize literary artistry, not race. Also mentions "Big Boy Leaves Home."

7840. Trefzer, Annette. "Possessing the Self: Caribbean Identities in Zora Neale Hurston's *Tell My Horse*." *African American Review*, 34 (Summer), 299–312. Mentions briefly W's membership in the Communist Party (pp. 299–312).

7841. _____. "Richard Gray, *Writing the South: Ideas of an American Region*." *South Central Review*, 17 (Summer), 104–106. Review mentioning W briefly.

7842. Trotter, Joe William, Jr. "From a Raw Deal to a New Deal?: 1929–1945," in *To Make Our World Anew: A History of African Americans*. Eds. Robin D.G. Kelley and Earl Lewis. New York: Oxford University Press, pp. 409–444. Mentions briefly W (p. 419), *UTC* (p. 433) and *NS* (pp. 433, 448).

7843. Tuttleton, James W. "The Achievement of Ralph Ellison," in *The Critical Response to Ralph Ellison*. Ed. Robert J. Butler. Westport, CT: Greenwood Press, pp. 211–216.

7844. Upshur-Ransome, Cora Lee. *A Comparison of the African Presence in Earlier and Later American History Textbooks*. Lanham, MD: University Press of America. Refers briefly to *BB* (p. 54) and comments on the W-Hurston conflict (pp. 56–57).

7845. Wagner-Martin, Linda. "Lost Generation Short Stories," in *The Facts on File Companion to the American Short Story* by Abby Werlock. New York: Facts on File, pp. 272–273. Mentions W briefly.

7846. Wald, Alan. "Mark Solomon. *The Cry Was Unity: Communists and African Americans, 1917–1936. African American Review*, 34 (Winter), 716–718. Review mentioning briefly *O* (p. 716) and W (p. 718).

7847. _____. "*New Negro, Old Left: African-American Writing and Communism Between the Wars*. By William J. Maxwell." *American Literature*, 72 (September), 644–645. Favorable review commenting on Maxwell's treatment of W.

7848. Wald, Gayle. *Crossing the Line: Racial passing in Twentieth-Century U.S. Literature and Culture.* Durham, NC: Duke University Press, p. 95. Mentions briefly W and *NS*.

7849. Wald, Elijah. *Josh White: Society Blues.* Amherst: University of Massachusetts Press, pp. 81–83, 88, 143. Comments on and quotes from W's liner notes to White's album *Southern Exposure*, noting the leftist slant.

7850. Wall, Cheryl A. "Introduction," in her *Their Eyes Were Watching God: A Casebook.* New York: Oxford University Press, pp. 3–16. Comments on W's response to Hurston's novel (pp. 9–10, 12, 14, 16).

7851. Walls, Doyle W. "A Missed Clue Proves the Existence of Racism in *Native Son*," in *Readings on Native Son.* Ed. Hayley R Mitchell. San Diego: Greenhaven Press, pp. 148–151.

7852. Walters, Ronald W., and Cedric Johnson. *Bibliography of African American Leadership: An Annotated Guide.* Westport, CT: Greenwood Press, pp. 9, 72, 265. Brief mentions of W in works by V.P. Franklin, Cedric Robinson, and Madison Davis Lacy.

7853. Walton, Anthony. "Richard Wright, Haiku Poet." *Utne Reader*, no. 98 (March–April), pp. 96–97. Comments on using a poetic form that allowed W "freedom from typecasting" but caused him to neglect "human issues."

7854. Ward, Cynthia. "From the Suwanee to Egypt, There's No Place Like Home." *PMLA*, 115 (January), 75–88. Quotes from and comments briefly on "Between Laughter and Tears" (pp. 76, 77, 88).

7855. Warren, Kenneth W. "As White as Anybody': Race and the Politics of Counting as Black." *New Literary History*, 31 (Autumn), 709–726. Includes discussion of Ellison's criticism of W (pp. 714–715).

7856. _____. "The End(s) of African American Studies." *American Literary History*, 12 (Fall), 637–655. Quotes from *TMBV*: "We are not what we seem" (p. 645).

7857. Weems, Robert E., Jr. "*American Dreams in Mississippi: Consumers, Poverty, and Culture, 1830–1998.*" *The Journal of American History*, 87 (September), 691–692. Review mentioning W briefly.

7858. Werlock, Abby. "Algren, Nelson (1909–1981)," in her *The Facts on File Companion to the American Short Story.* New York: Facts on File, pp. 12–13. Mentions W briefly.

7859. _____. "Appendix I: Winners of Selected Short Story Prizes," in *The Facts on File Companion to the American Short Story.* New York: Facts on File, pp. 463–511. Lists "Fire and Cloud" as a winner of an O. Henry Memorial Award in 1938 (p. 467) "Almos' a Man" in 1941 (p. 468).

7860. _____. "Appendix II: Suggested Readings by Theme and Topic," in her *The Facts on File Companion to the American Short Story.* New York: Facts on File, pp. 512–526. Lists "Almos' a Man," "Bright and Morning Star," "The Ethics of Living Jim Crow," "Long Black Song," "The Man Who Killed a Shadow, and "The Man Who Lived Underground" s.v. African Americans; "Almos' a Man" s.v. Family Life–Mothers, Sons and Daughters; "Long Black Song" s.v. Marriage and Divorce.

7861. _____. "'Big Black Good Man' Richard Wright," in her *The Facts on File Companion to the American Short Story.* New York: Facts on File, pp. 56–57. Provides a summary of the story and comments on Olaf as a personification of whiteness.

7862. _____. "Hughes, (James) Langston (1902–1976)," in her *The Facts on File Companion to the American Short Story.* New York: Facts on File, pp. 222–223.

7863. _____. "Hurston, Zora Neale (1891–1960)," in her *The Facts on File Companion to the American Short Story.* New York: Facts on File, pp. 223–224. Mentions W briefly.

7864. _____. "Introduction," in her *The Facts on File Companion to the American Short Story.* New York: Facts on File, pp. vii–viii. Mentions W briefly (pp. x, xi).

7865. _____. "John Henry," in her *The Facts on File Companion to the American Short Story.* New York: Facts on File, p. 240 Speculates that John Henry "may be the inspiration for ... "Big Black Good Man."

7866. Werner, Craig, "James Baldwin," in *Notable American Novelist.* Pasadena, CA: Salem Press, vol. 1, pp. 41, 42. Notes Baldwin's earlier friendship with W and their subsequent feud.

7867. West, Cornel. "The Dilemma of the Black Intellectual (1993)," in *The Prentice Hall Anthology of African American Literature.* Eds. Rochelle Smith and Sharon L. Jones. Upper Saddle River, NJ: Prentice Hall, pp. 1071–1083.

7868. Will, Barbara. "*Gertrude Stein and Richard Wright: The Poetics and Politics of Modernism.* By Lynn Weiss." *American Literature*, 72 (March), 206–207. Favorable review: "both Stein and Wright studies can benefit from this kind of comparative analysis."

7869. Williams, Roland L., Jr. *African American Autobiography and the Quest for Freedom.* Westport, CT: Greenwood Press, pp. 127, 134, 143. Quotes from *WML*, comments on *BB* with quotations, and mentions W briefly.

7870. Williams, Sherley Anne. "Encountering Zora Neale Hurston," in *Their Eyes Were Watching God: A Casebook.* Ed. Cheryl A. Wall. New York: Oxford University Press, pp. 19–25.

7871. Williams, Tennessee. *The Selected Letters of Tennessee Williams.* Vol. 1. Eds. Albert J. Devlin and Nancy M. Tischler. New York: New Directions, pp. 87, 340, 395. In a letter to Wilbur Schramm, Williams complains of the dullness of a meeting of the Chicago Writers group: W, Algren, and Conroy. Also mentions W as a contributor to *American Scenes* and his collaboration with Paul Green on the play *NS*.

7872. Wimbush, Vincent L. "Introduction: Reading Darkness, Reading Scriptures," in his *African Americans and the Bible: Sacred Texts and Social Textures*. New York: Continuum, pp. 1–43. Discusses Houston Baker's treatment of *BB* in *Blues, Ideology, and Afro-American Literature: A Vernacular Theory* (pp. 37–38).

7873. Wind, Astrid. "Adam Lively, *Masks: Blackness, Race, and the Imagination." Journal of American Studies*, 34 (June), 178–179. Review mentioning W briefly.

7874. Winter, Kari J. "Narrative Desire in Ann Petry's *The Street." Jx*, 4 (Spring), pp. 101–112. Comments on the theme of hunger in Petry and W (p. 105) and mentions briefly Bigger Thomas.

7875. Wolfe, Jessie. "'Ambivalent Man': Ellison's Rejection of Communism." *African American Review*, 34 (Winter), 621–637. Includes comparison to W's experience with Communism (pp. 630–637). Ellison's rejection was more complete, affirming in a Cold War context traditional American democratic ideals. W retained an ambivalent attitude,

asserting his own individualism but nostalgic toward his early experience in the Party and retaining some Marxist attitudes.

7876. Woodhul, Winifred. "Mohammed Dib and the French Question." *Yale French Studies*. No. 98: *The French Fifties*, pp. 66–78. Notes W's link with *Présence Africaine* and mentions the First International Congress of Black Writers and artists (pp. 68–69).

7877. Woodson, Jon. "Alpha and Omega: Expressive Form in Sam Cornish's Poetry." *Obsidian III*, 1 (Fall/Winter), 85–95. Mentions briefly W's revolutionary poetry (p. 90).

7878. Woolley, Lisa. *American Voices of the Chicago Renaissance*. DeKalb: Northern Illinois University Press, pp. 13, 122, 136, 139, 141, 144, 150. Focuses on the *first* Chicago Renaissance (Sandburg, Harriet Monroe, Masters, Fenton Johnson, et al.), but W is mentioned frequently.

7879. Yaeger, Patricia. *Dirt and Desire: Reconstructing Southern*

Women's Writing, 1930–1990. Chicago: The University of Chicago Press, pp. 14–15, 29, 45, 110, 173, 205, 207, 208, 241, 234–235. Comments on and quotes from *UTC* (pp. 14–15, 29, 45, 110) notes W's objection to Hurston (p. 205), comments on "Silt" (p. 208), refers to *BB* (p. 241), and comments on "The Ethics of Living Jim Crow" (pp. 234–235).

7880. Young, Reggie. "faith flight (from *Salvation Song*)." *African American Review*, 34 (Spring), 105–117. Excerpt from a novel manuscript mentioning *UTC* and W (pp. 110–111).

7881. _____. "Kimberly Rae Connor. *Imagining Grace: Liberating Theologies in the Slave Narrative Tradition." African American Review*, 34, pp. 710–712. Review mentioning W briefly (p. 711).

7882. Yow, Dede. "Bobbie Ann Mason (1940–)," in *The Columbia Companion to the Twentieth-Century American Short Story*. Ed. Blanche Gelfant. New York: Columbia University Press, pp. 358–360. Mentions W. briefly (p. 360).

2001

7883. [Abadie, Ann J.]. "2001 Oxford Conference for the Book." *The Southern Register* (Spring/Summer), 23–25. Includes comment on Jerry Ward's keynote address on "Richard Wright: The Enduring Challenge of His Legacy" and panel discussion by Michel Fabre, Geneviève Fabre, Keneth Kinnamon, Paul Oliver, and Hazel Rowley. The 2001 Conference was dedicated to W.

7884. Abbott, Charlotte, Sarah F. Gold, and Mark Rotell. "*Richard Wright: The Life and Times* by Hazel Rowley." *Publishers Weekly*, 248 (18 June), p. 68. Review praising Rowley's research but objecting to her "biographer's rapt psychologizing."

7885. Accomando, Christina. "Attaway, William," in *The Concise Oxford Companion to African American Literature*. Eds. William L. Andrews, Frances Smith Foster, and

Trudier Harris. New York: Oxford University Press, pp. 12–13.

7886. Ailey, Alvin, James Baldwin, Romare Bearden, and Albert Murray in conversation. "To Hear Another Language." *Callaloo*, 24 (Spring), 656–677.

7887. Albert, Stew. "White Radicals, Black Panthers, and a Sense of Fulfillment," in Kathleen Cleaver and George Katsiaficas's *Liberation, Imagination, and the Black Panther Party: A New Look at the Panthers and Their Legacy*. New York: Routledge, pp. 188–189. Mentions briefly W and Ellen Wright (p. 194).

7888. Allister, Mark. *Refiguring the Map of Sorrow: Nature Writing and Autobiography*. Charlottesville: University Press of Virginia, pp. 1, 14. Mentions briefly *BB*.

7889. Als, Hilton. "Unhappy Endings." *The New Yorker*, 77 (3 December), 94, 96–101. Article on

Carson McCullers quoting W on *The Heart Is a Lonely Hunter* (p. 96).

7890. Anderson, Michael. "A Native Son in Exile." *The New York Times Book Review* (26 August), pp. 11–12. Review of Hazel Rowley's *Richard Wright: The Life and Times* praising its research and documentation but criticizing its lack of analysis and its failure to bring W alive and convey his "tang of personality."

7891. Anderson, Paul Allen. *Deep River: Music and Memory in Harlem Renaissance Thought*. Durham: Duke University Press, pp. 74, 206. Mentions briefly *NS* and quotes disparaging comments on Zora Neale Hurston in her review of *UTC*.

7892. Andrews, William L., Frances Smith Foster, and Trudier Harris. "Introduction," in their *The Concise Oxford Companion to African American Literature*. New York:

Oxford University Press, pp. vii, ix.

7893. _____."Slave Narratives," in *Encyclopedia of American Studies*. Eds. George T. Curian, Miles Orvell, Johnnella E. Butler, and Jay Mechling. New York: Grolier Educational, pp. 119–121. Claims that *BB* is related to the antebellum slave narrative.

7894. Anon. "A Conversation with Emily Bernard." New York: Alfred A. Knopf, 6 pp. Publisher's publicity brochure for Bernard's collection of the Hughes-Van Vechten correspondence. Mentions W briefly (p. 2).

7895. Anon. "Blackness and Heterosexuality." *PMLA*, 116 (November), 1681. Announces a convention session including a paper by Robert Reid-Pharr entitled "Bodies, Business, and the Black Bourgeoisie: The Incomplete Heterosexual Project of Richard Wright's *The Long Dream*."

7896. Anon. "BMI Educational Services." *English Journal*, 90 (March), 124. Advertisement for Francine G. Wacht's *I Remember: An Autobiography Text*, which includes an excerpt from W.

7897. Anon. "Books in Brief." *The Crisis*, 108 (May/June). Notice of *Voices in Our Blood: America's Best on the Civil Rights Movement*, in which W is included.

7898. Anon. "Briefly Noted." *The New Yorker*, 77 (22 October), p. 77. Includes a favorable notice of Hazel Rowley's *Richard Wright: The Life and Times*.

7899. Anon. "Carson McCullers, Complete Novels," in *The Library of America Fall 2001*. New York: Literary Classics of the U.S., p. 5. Quotes W placing McCullers above Anderson, Faulkner, and Hemingway.

7900. Anon. "*Critical Memory: Public Spheres, African American Writing, and Black Fathers and Sons in America*," in *Georgia: Spring-Summer Books*. Athens: University of Georgia Press, p. 15. Publisher's notice of a book by Houston A. Baker, Jr. mentioning briefly *BB*.

7901. Anon. "Ellison and the *Wright* Stuff." *Wilson Quarterly*, 25 (Spring), 104. Review of Lawrence P. Jackson's *The Birth of the Critic*.

7902. Anon. "Five Favorite African American Authors." *Scholastic Action*, 24 (12 February), 1–15 pp. Rates W as one of the "top five Afri-

can American writers." Mentions briefly *BB*.

7903. Anon. "General Studies," in *The Harvard Guide to African American History*. Ed. Evelyn Brooks Higginbotham. Cambridge: Harvard University Press, pp. 211–213. Lists *TMBV* (p. 213).

7904. Anon. "Geographical Areas," in *The Harvard Guide to African American History*. Ed. Evelyn Brooks Higginbotham. Cambridge: Harvard University Press, pp 677–774. Lists W's 1977 article in *Dissent*.

7905. Anon. "Haiku as International Culture: Theories and Practices of a Cross-Cultural Poetic Genre." *PMLA*, 116 (November), 1681. Announces a convention session including a paper by Yoshinobu Hakutani entitled "Richard Wright's Haiku and 'The African Primal Outlook upon Life.'"

7906. Anon. "Harcourt/Harvest Books News." San Diego: Harvest/Harcourt. Flyer for Jeffrey Renard Allen's *Rails Under My Back* mentioning W briefly.

7907. Anon. *The Eighth Oxford Conference for the Book*. Oxford, Mississippi: The University of Mississippi Center for the Study of Southern Culture, 6pp. Brochure of a conference dedicated to W, 30 March–1 April, with a paper by Jerry W. Ward, Jr., on "Richard Wright: The Enduring Challenge of His Legacy," with comments by Geneviève and Michel Fabre, Paul Oliver, and Hazel Rowley.

7908. Anon. "Making the Classics Accessible." *English Journal*, 90 (March), 8. Publisher's advertisement listing Robert Felgar's *Student Companion to Richard Wright*.

7909. Anon. "New in Literature & Culture." *PMLA*, 116 (September), 1248. Contains a publisher's notice of *From Richard Wright to Toni Morrison: Ethics in Modern and Postmodern American Narrative* by Jeffrey J. Folks.

7910. Anon. "*New Letters*." *African American Review*, 35 (Winter), 650. Advertisement mentioning W briefly.

7911. Anon. "Note," in *Incidents in the Life of a Slave Girl* by Harriet Jacobs. Mineola, New York: Dover Publications, pp. v–vii.

7912. Anon. "*Rails Under My Back*," in *Harcourt Spring-Summer*. New York: Harcourt, p. 32. Publisher's review of a novel by Jeffery Renard Allen mentioning W briefly.

7913. Anon. "*Richard Wright*, by Hazel Rowley." *The Christian Science Monitor* (15 November), p. 14. Very brief notice.

7914. Anon. "*Richard Wright: The Life and Times*," *Kirkus Reviews* 69 (1 June), 790. Favorable review of a "fresh and realistic depiction of W. The reviewer emphasizes W's life before expatriation.

7915. Anon. "*Richard Wright: The Life and Times*, Hazel Rowley." *Publishers Weekly*, 248 (18 June), 68. Review praising Rowley's research but complaining about her "rapt psychologizing."

7916. Anon. "*Richard Wright's Travel Writings: New Reflections*," in *University Press of Mississippi Reading: Spring & Summer 2001*. Jackson: University Press of Mississippi, pp. 14–15. Publisher's review emphasizing W's innovations in the travel genre, anticipating postcolonial writing.

7917. Anon. "*Student Companion to Richard Wright*." *African American Review*, 35 (Fall), 500–501. Favorable notice of Robert Felgar's book. Laments the absence of treatment of *Rite of Passage* and the haiku poems, but praises Felgar's "cinematic reading" of *NS*.

7918. Anon. "12th Annual Hurston/Wright Award." Washington, DC: The Hurston/Wright Foundation. Announcement of the fiction award for 2002.

7919. Anon. "Writing Against the Odds." *Literary Cavalcade*, 53 (April), p. T2. Comments on W's scheme for securing library books in Memphis.

7920. Arnold, Martin. "Books by Black Writers Gather on Best-Seller Lists." Little Rock *Arkansas Democrat-Gazette* (5 August), p. 4H. Includes a comment by Henry Louis Gates:"Fifty years ago, white readers read Richard Wright to learn about the other...."

7921. Baker, Houston A., Jr. *Critical Memory: Public Spheres, African American Writing, and Black Fathers and Sons in America*. Athens: The University of Georgia Press, 75 pp. Discusses the episode of the cook spitting in the soup from *BB* (pp. 3–8), compares Ellison unfavorably to W (pp. 29–30, 40), and mentions elsewhere W, *BB*, and *TMBV*.

7922. _____. *Turning South Again: Re-Thinking Modernism/Re-Reading*

Booker T. Durham: Duke University Press, pp. 27, 51–52, 54. Quotes from "Between the World and Me" and mentions W briefly elsewhere.

7923. Balfour, Lawrie. *The Evidence of Things Not Said: James Baldwin and the Promise of American Democracy.* Ithaca: Cornell University Press, pp. 11, 14, 46–48, 60, 80, 113. Brief comments on W, *NS*, and Bigger Thomas.

7924. Balshaw, Maria. *Looking for Harlem: Urban Aesthetics in African American Literature.* London: Pluto Press, pp. 5, 6, 12, 13, 19, 92, 95, 98–100, 114–117, 144. Compares the reception of *NS* and *The Street*, and the novels themselves. *The Street* is a "counter-text" to *NS*, emphasizing gender as well as race.

7925. Barthelemy, Anthony G. "Hazel V. Carby. *Cultures in Babylon: Black Britain and African America.*" *African American Review*, 35 (Spring), 145–146. Review mentioning W briefly.

7926. Bass, Patrick Henry. "Bookmark." *Essence*, 32 (September), 84. Favorable notice of Hazel Rowley's *Richard Wright: The Life and Times.*

7927. Bell, Bernard W. "Introduction: Clarence Major's Transgressive Voice and Double Consciousness as an African American Postmodernist Artist," in his *Clarence Major and His Art: Portraits of an African American Postmodernist.* Chapel Hill: University of North Carolina Press, p. 1. Mentions W briefly.

7928. Berke, Nancy. *Women Poets on the Left: Lola Ridge, Genevieve Taggard, Margaret Walker.* Gainesville: University Press of Florida, pp. 15, 29, 116, 124, 125, 133–134, 138, 144, 146, 185. Discusses the W-Walker relationship, especially in relation to radical politics.

7929. Bernard, Emily. "Dramatis Personae," in her *Remember Me to Harlem: The Letters of Langston Hughes and Carl Van Vechten, 1925–1964.* New York: Alfred A. Knopf, pp. xxxi–xxxix. Mentions W briefly, s.v. "Chester Himes" (p. xxxiv).

7930. _____, ed. *Remember Me to Harlem: The Letters of Langston Hughes and Carl Van Vechten, 1925–1964.* New York: Alfred A. Knopf, pp. 142, 150, 161, 163, 172, 172n, 186n, 230, 285n, 308, 313–314. The first seven are from Hughes's letters and concern *NS*, the eighth is from a Van Vechten letter and mentions

"I Tried to Be a Communist," the ninth mentions Van Vechten's photograph of W, the headnote of the ninth mentions the dramatization of *LD*, and the last, 12 December 1960, mentions Hughes's visit to W just before he died.

7931. Berry, S. Torriano, and Venise T. Berry. *The 50 Most Influential Black Films: A Celebration of African American Talent, Determination, and Creativity.* New York: Citadel Press, p. 27. Mentions briefly *NS*, the novel and the first film.

7932. Biles, Roger. "Race and Housing in Chicago." *Journal of the Illinois State Historical Society*, 94 (Spring), 31–38. Notes that racial segregation in Chicago continued long after W exposed it in *NS*.

7933. _____. "Race and Housing in Chicago." *Journal of the Illinois State Historical Society*, 94 (Spring), 31–38. Begins with a quotation from Bigger: "Why they make us live in one corner of the city?"

7934. Blight, David W. *Race and Reunion: The Civil War and American Memory.* Cambridge: Harvard University Press, p. 315. Quotes from *TMBV*, calling it W's "proletarian manifesto of black history."

7935. Bloshteyn, Maria R. "Rage and Revolt: Dostoyevsky and Three African-American Writers." *Comparative Literature Studies*, 38 (Fall), 277–309. Substantial, fully researched examination of the relation of Dostoyevsky to W, Ellison, and Baldwin. Also discusses these writers' relation to each other as readers of Dostoyevsky and critics of each other.

7936. Boelhower, William. "No Free Gifts: Toomer's 'Fern' and the Harlem Renaissance," in *Temples for Tomorrow. Looking Back at the Harlem Renaissance.* Eds. Geneviève Fabre and Michel Feith. Bloomington: Indiana University Press, pp. 193–209. Quotes from "Blueprint for Negro Writing" (p. 198).

7937. Booker, M. Keith. "Dale E. Peterson. *Up from Bondage: The Literatures of Russian and African American Soul.*" *African American Review*, 35 (Winter), 657–658. Review commenting on the relation of Gorky and W.

7938. Boris, Eileen. "'Arm and Arm': Racialized Bodies and Color Lines." *Journal of American Studies*, 35 (April), 1–20. Noting the discussion of *NS* and *Strange Fruit* in *If*

He Hollers Let Him Go, Boris proceeds to compare W and Lillian Smith, emphasizing "racialized bodies."

7939. Bracey, John H., Adam Biggs, and Corey Walker. "1968–1999," in *The Harvard Guide to African-American History.* Ed. Evelyn Brooks Higginbotham. Cambridge, MA: Harvard University Press, pp. 595–633. Lists W's "With Black Radicals in Chicago."

7940. Bracken, James K., and Larry G. Hinman. "Richard (Nathaniel) Wright, 1908–1960," in their *The Undergraduate's Companion to American Writers and Their Web Sites.* Englewood, CO: Libraries Unlimited, pp. 209–210. Lists web sites, biographies, and bibliographies with brief annotation.

7941. Brady, Lenore L. "Clarence Major (1936–)," in *New Bones: Contemporary Black Writers in America.* Eds. Kevin Everod Quashie, Joyce Lausch, and Keith D. Miller. Upper Saddle River, NJ: Prentice-Hall, pp. 689–698. Mentions that Major read W (p. 689).

7942. Brinkmeyer, Robert H., Jr. "Members in the Spotlight." *The Society for the Study of Southern Literature Newsletter*, 35 (November), 8. Includes mention of Jerry Ward's address on W in Oxford, Mississippi.

7943. _____. "Members in the Spotlight." *The Society for the Study of Southern Literature Newsletter*, 35 (November), 8. Reports that Jerry W. Ward, Jr. spoke on "Richard Wright: The Enduring Challenge of His Legacy" at the 2001 Oxford Conference for the book.

7944. Brookhart, Mary Hughes. "Allen, Samuel W.," in *The Concise Oxford Companion to African American Literature.* Eds. William L. Andrews, Frances Smith Foster, and Trudier Harris. New York: Oxford University Press, pp. 3–4.

7945. Brown, Jeffrey A. *Black Superheroes, Milestone Comics and Their Fans.* Jackson: University Press of Mississippi, p. 44. Mentions W briefly.

7946. Brownell, Blaine A. "The South," in *The Oxford Companion to United States History.* Ed. Paul S. Boyer. New York: Oxford University Press, pp. 733–734. Mentions W briefly.

7947. Buell, Lawrence, *Writing*

for an Endangered World: Literature, Culture, and Environment in the U.S. and Beyond. Cambridge: Harvard University Press, pp. 28, 46, 138–142, 150, 153, 161, 230, 310, 311. Discusses *NS* in relation to urban ecology, with comparisons to Dreiser and Upton Sinclair, and the Chicago School of Sociology. Also mentions or quotes from "How 'Bigger' Was Born" and *TMBV*.

7948. Bunker, Nathaniel. "Primary Sources on Microform," in *The Harvard Guide to African-American History.* Ed. Evelyn Brooks Higginbotham. Cambridge, MA: Harvard University Press, pp. 67–75. Lists the Schomburg Collection's two microfilm reels about W (p. 75).

7949. Burkett, Randall K., Leon F. Litwack, and Richard Newman. "Autobiography and Biography," in *The Harvard Guide to African-American History.* Ed. Evelyn Brooks Higginbotham. Cambridge, MA: Harvard University Press, pp. 777–830. Includes an entry on W listing works by Michel Fabre, Robert M. Farnsworth and David Ray, Addison Gayle, Margaret Walker, Constance Webb, and John Williams as well as *AH* and *BB* (p. 829).

7950. Byerman, Keith. "Dale E. Peterson. *Up from Bondage: The Literatures of Russian and African American Soul." Modern Fiction Studies,* 47 (Winter), 1031–1033. Review mentioning W briefly. pp. 1031–1033.

7951. Cahan, Richard. "Another Native Son." *Chicago* (1 June), pp. 89–91, 124–130. Discusses the relation of the Nixon case to *NS*, providing more information on Nixon's trial and background than previous researchers. Emphasizes the role of white racism.

7952. Callahan, John F. "Ellison, Ralph," in *The Oxford Companion to United States History.* Ed. Paul S. Boyer. New York: Oxford University Press, pp. 222–223. Mentions Ellison's friendship with W.

7953. Calloway, Catherine. "Fiction: The 1930s to the 1960s," in *American Literary Scholarship: An Annual/1999.* Ed. Gary Scharnhorst. Durham: Duke University Press, pp. 313–335. Includes comments on articles on W by Earle V. Bryant, Hazel Rowley, Mikko Juhani, Tuhkanen, Katherine Fishburn, Elizabeth Schultz, Anthony Dawahare,

Lâle Demirtürk, and David Wright (pp. 314–317).

7954. Campbell, Josie P. *Student Companion to Zora Neale Hurston.* Westport, CT: Greenwood Press, pp. 152, 156. Lists W's review of *Their Eyes Were Watching God* and *NS*.

7955. Cappetti, Carla. "Black Orpheus: Richard Wright's 'The Man Who Lived Underground.'" *MELUS,* 26 (Winter), pp. 41–68. Substantial reading relating the novella to European literature and philosophy as well as to W's own works, especially, *O.* Although Fred Daniel's social values prove illusory, at the end he dies full of hope.

7956. Carmichael, Jacqueline Miller. "'Rumblings in Folk Traditions Served Southern Style,'" in Maryemma Graham's *Fields Watered with Blood,* pp. 241–268. Mentions W as treated by H. Nigel Thomas.

7957. Carrigan, Henry L., Jr. "Richard Wright." *Library Journal,* 126 (1 July), 91. Unfavorable review of Hazel Rowley's *Richard Wright: The Life and Times* calling it "an uninspired biographical pastiche."

7958. Carroll, Michael. "Al Young, Jazz Griot," in *African American Jazz and Rap: Social and Philosophical Examinations of Black Expressive Behavior.* Ed. James L. Conyers, Jr. Jefferson, NC: McFarland, p. 157. Mentions briefly *BB.*

7959. Carson, Clayborne. "1945–1968," in *The Harvard Guide to African-American History.* Ed. Evelyn Brooks Higginbotham. Cambridge, MA: Harvard University Press, pp. 559–593. Lists *CC* (p. 582).

7960. Champion, Laurie. "Socioeconomics in Selected Short Stories of Zora Neale Hurston," *The Southern Quarterly,* 40 (Fall), 79–92. Mentions W briefly (p. 79) and quotes June Jordan mentioning briefly *NS.*

7961. Cheng, Anne Anlin. *The Melancholy of Race: Psychoanalysis, Assimilation, and Hidden Grief.* New York: Oxford University Press, 2000, p. 14. Quotes briefly from *WML.*

7962. Chiwengo, Ngwarsungu. "Gazing Through the Screen: Richard Wright's Africa," in *Richard Wright's Travel Writings: New Reflections.* Ed. Virginia Whatley Smith. Jackson: University Press of Mississippi, pp. 20–44. Unfavorable evaluation of *BP* arguing that the sub-

ject is more W's African American identity than Africa itself. Intellectually he is thoroughly Western — rational and directed by linear time — while he finds the African to be static and sensuous. But W finds that a history of suffering, not racialistic bonds, links him with Africans. African progress, though, depends on its Westernization.

7963. Christian, Barbara. "But What Do We Think We're Doing Anyway: The State of Black Feminist Criticism(s) or My Version of a Little Bit of History," in *Black Feminist Cultural Criticism.* Ed. Jacqueline Bobo. Malden, MA: Blackwell, pp. 38–52.

7964. Clark, Keith. "Introduction," in his *Contemporary Black Men's Fiction and Drama.* Urbana: University of Illinois Press, pp. 1–13. Mentions briefly W's place "at the summit of the African-American male literary pantheon" (p. 3), compares his protest to Ellison's (p. 5), and notes his influence (p. 6).

7965. Cleaver, Kathleen Neal. "Mobilizing for Mumia Abu-Jamal in Paris," in her and George Katsiaficas's *Liberation, Imagination, and the Black Panther Party: A New Look at the Panthers and Their Legacy.* New York: Routledge, pp. 51–68. Includes mention of W, Julia Wright, and Ellen Wright (pp. 52–53, 68).

7966. Cobb, William Jelani. "Getting Richard Right." *The Crisis,* 108 (November/December), 62–63. Favorable review of Hazel Rowley's *Richard Wright: The Life and Times.*

7967. Coleman, James W. *Black Male Fiction and the Legacy of Caliban.* Lexington: The University Press of Kentucky, pp. 16, 129–130, 133, 176, 178. Comments on *NS* and its influence.

7968. Collier, Eugenia. "Fields Watered with Blood: Myth and Ritual in the Poetry of Margaret Walker," in Maryemma Graham's *Fields Watered with Blood,* pp. 98–109. Mentions W briefly (p. 101).

7969. Conyers, James L., Jr., ed. *African American Jazz and Rap: Social and Philosophical Examinations of Black Expressive Behavior.* Jefferson, NC: McFarland, pp. 21, 30, 157. Includes essays by Warren C. Swindell and Michael Carroll mentioning W and *BB.*

7970. Crouch, Stanley, "Blues for

America." *Partisan Review*, 68 (Winter), 79–88. Contains a substantial discussion of W as autobiographer. Compares him to Ellison, Hemingway, and Albert Murray, all of whom have a "blues sensibility."

7971. Daniel, Pete. "Carol Polsgrove. *Divided Minds: Intellectuals and the Civil Rights Movement.*" *The American Historical Review*, 106 (December), 1832. Review mentioning W briefly.

7972. Davis, Jack E. "Environmental Injustice: Introduction," in his *The Civil Rights Movement*. Malden, MA: Blackwell, pp. 257–258. Begins with a reference to the first scene of *NS*.

7973. _____. *Race Against Time: Culture and Separation in Natchez Since 1930*. Baton Rouge: Louisiana State University Press, pp. 3, 14, 19, 20, 267, 268. Mentions and quotes from W, "Natchez's most renowned native and historical figure," who was little known by whites in Natchez.

7974. Dawson, Michael. *Black Visions: The Roots of Contemporary African American Political Ideologies*. Chicago: The University of Chicago Press, pp. 18, 19, 26, 190, 285, 315, 318. Comments on W's Marxism, white violence, and his doubts about white America supporting racial quality.

7975. Delaney, Kate. "America Perceived," in *Encyclopedia of American Studies*. Eds. George T Curian, Miles Orvell, Johnnella E. Butler, and Jay Mechling. New York: Grolier Educational, pp. 92–96. Notes W's enthusiastic reception in Paris (p. 93).

7976. Demirtürk, E. Lâle. "The Making and Unmaking of Whiteness: Richard Wright's *Rite of Passage*." MELUS, 26 (Summer), 83–94. Argues that W's novella "unmasks whiteness as a mark of ideology and racial privilege." Compares the protagonist, Johnny Gibbs, to Bigger and Cross Damon.

7977. Diana, M. Casey. "African American Short Fiction," in *Critical Survey of Short Fiction*. Second Revised Edition. Ed. Charles E. May. Pasadena: Salem Press, pp. 2864–2870. Includes discussion of W's early career and achievements. Claims that he was deeply influenced in his short fiction by Chekhov.

7978. Dickson-Carr, Darryl. *African American Satire: The Sacredly Profane Novel*. Columbia: University of Missouri Press, pp. 29, 78, 84, 85, 86–87, 88–89, 98, 99, 100, 132–133. Mentions W and *NS* (pp. 84, 86), W and Hurston (p. 87). Mentions W and *NS* and comments on W's rejection of Hurston. Also discusses Cecil Brown's satiric treatment of Bigger in his *The Life and Loves of Mr. Jiveass Nigger*.

7979. Dimock, Wai Chee. "Deep Time: American Literature and World History." *American Literary History*, 13 (Winter), 755–775. Mentions W. briefly (p. 757).

7980. Dixon, Melvin. "Climbing Montmartre." *Callaloo*, 24 (Summer), 721.

7981. Donahoo, Robert. "McKay Jenkins, *The South in Black and White: Race, Sex and Literature in the 1940s*." *South Central Review*, 18 (Spring/Summer), 135–136. Mentions briefly *BB*.

7982. duCille, Ann. "The Occult of True Black Womanhood: Critical Demeanor and Black Feminist Studies," in *Feminism and 'Race'*. Ed. Kum-Kum Bhavani. Oxford: Oxford University Press, pp. 233–260.

7983. Duck, Leigh Anne. "'*Go there tuh know there*: Zora Neale Hurston and the Chronotope of the Folk." *American Literary History*, 13 (Summer), 265–294. Includes a brief analysis of "Long Black Song" to illustrate his view of the gap between folk consciousness and the "modern." Also cites the reunion of W with his father to make the same point. Cites *BB* and "Blueprint for Negro Writing."

7984. Dudley, David L. "Foreword," in *Critical Memory: Public Spheres, African American Writing, and Black Fathers and Sons in America*. Athens: The University of Georgia Press, pp. xi–xii. Mentions W briefly.

7985. Durham, Joyce. "Dorothy West and the Importance of Black 'Little' Magazines of the 1930s: *Challenge* and *New Challenge*." *The Langston Hughes Review*, 16 (Fall/Spring 1999/2001), 19–31. Includes discussion of W's role in *New Challenge*.

7986. Eagles, Brenda M. "A Bibliography of Dissertations Relating to Mississippi — 2000." *The Journal of Mississippi History*, 63 (Spring), 63–66. Lists dissertations treating W by Keith D. Danner, Paul Hanson, Charles Land, Dariek Bruce Scott, and Elizabeth Anne Yukius.

7987. Earl, Riggins R., Jr. *Dark Salutations: Ritual, God, and Greetings in the African American Community*. Harrisburg, PA: Trinity Press International, pp. 152–158, 185. Discusses *BB* and *NS* in the context of "racist salutatory paradigms." Comments also on W's rejection of religion.

7988. Early, Gerald. "Sammy Davis, Jr." in his *The Sammy Davis Jr. Reader*. New York: Farrar, Straus and Giroux, pp. 3–59. Quotes from an essay on W by Ellison.

7989. Eby, Clare. "Slouching Toward Beastliness: Richard Wright's Anatomy of Thomas Dixon." *African American Review*, 35 (Fall), pp. 439–458. Analyzes Dixon's popularization of the stereotype of the black man as rapist beast, then examines W's use of this racist fantasy in *NS*, which "needs to be seen as parodying the white supremacist vision." The issue of whether or not W actually read any Dixon is not addressed.

7990. Edgerton, Robert B. *Hidden Heroism: Black Soldiers in America's Wars*. Boulder, CO: Westview Press, pp. 124, 217. Mentions briefly *UTC*, *NS*, and *BB*, and quotes W's statement about freedom in Paris.

7991. Edwards, Tim. "Everything Is Eating Everything Else: The Naturalistic Impulse in Harry Crews's *A Feast of Snakes*," in *Perspectives on Harry Crews*. Ed. Erik Bledsoe. Jackson: University Press of Mississippi, pp. 63–77. Mentions briefly *NS* (p. 75).

7992. Erdim, Esin. "Jublilee, or Setting the Record Straight," in Maryemma Graham's *Fields Watered with Blood*, pp. 290–303. Mentions W briefly (p. 301).

7993. Evans, Dennis F. "The Good Women, Bad Women, Prostitutes and Slaves of *Pagan Spain*," in *Richard Wright's Travel Writings: New Reflections*. Ed. Virginia Whatley Smith. Jackson: University Press of Mississippi, pp. 165–175. Argues that in Kristevian terms Wright was a *foreigner* in his own land, but in Spain he was literally a foreigner and thus able to see the absurdity of male chauvinism and to identify with Spanish women as victims of unjust degradation.

7994. Evans, Gareth. "William J. Maxwell, *New Negro, Old Left*: African American *Writing and Commu-*

nism Between the Wars." Journal of American Studies, 35 (August), 366–367. Comments on Maxwell's treatment of W and Algren as well as W and Hurston.

7995. Eversley, Shelly. "The Lunatic's Fancy and the Work of Art." *American Literary History*, 13 (Fall), 445–468. Discusses the relation of W and Ellison to the Lafargue Clinic and its influence on their work. W turned from naturalism and social fiction to "the psychology of race and alienation." *RP* and *O* are treated in these terms.

7996. _____. "Twentieth-Century Literature in the New Century." *College English*, 64 (September), 20–22. Mentions W briefly.

7997. Eyerman, Ron. *Cultural Trauma: Slavery and the Formation of African American Identity*. Cambridge: Cambridge University Press, pp. 131, 145, 155–158. Mentions W's early encouragement of Ellison, a reading he gave from *NS*, and provides an account of his early life, and his involvement with the Communist Party. Mentions *UTC, TMBV*, and *BP*.

7998. Fabi, M. Giulia. *Passing and the Rise of the African American Novel*. Urbana: University of Illinois Press, pp. 69, 105, 118–119, 122, 125, 133, 143, 161. Mentions briefly W, *NS*, and *BB*. Does not mention "Man of All Work."

7999. Fabre, Genevieve, and Michel Feith. "Temples for Tomorrow: Introductory Essay," in their *Temples for Tomorrow: Looking Back at the Harlem Renaissance*. Bloomington: Indiana University Press, p. 26. Mentions W briefly.

8000. Fabre, Michel. "French American Fellowship," in *Organizing Black America: An Encyclopedia of African American Associations*. Ed. Nina Mjagkij. New York: Garland, p. 238. Describes the group W formed in December 1950 to "combat the extension of racist ideas and practices" and to support minorities and oppressed people in their search for freedom.

8001. _____. "The Harlem Renaissance Abroad: French Critics and the New Negro Literary Movement (1924–1964)," in *Temples for Tomorrow: Looking Back at the Harlem Renaissance*. Bloomington: Indiana University Press, pp. 314–332. Mentions briefly W and "I Have Seen Black Hands."

8002. _____. "The Reception of *Cane* in France," in *Jean Toomer and the Harlem Renaissance*. Eds. Geneviève Fabre and Michel Feith. New Brunswick: Rutgers University Press, pp. 202–214. Mentions W briefly (p. 211).

8003. Favor, J. Martin. "Bill V. Mullen. *Popular Fronts: Chicago and African-American Cultural Politics, 1935–46*." *American Historical Review*, 106 (February), pp. 202–203. Includes comment on W and Communism.

8004. Fleming, Robert. "*Richard Wright: The Life and Times*." Nashville *BookPage*, p. 1. Very favorable review of the Hazel Rowley biography, with mention of the biographies by Margaret Walker and Michel Fabre. Rowley's is a superb book from start to finish."

8005. Fletcher, Gilbert. "Painted Voices." *QBR: The Black Book Review* (November–December), 27–29. Includes comment on W's expatriation and reproduction of a portrait of W.

8006. Flota, Brian. "The 'Little Book' That Time Forgot: Richard Wright's *Savage Holiday*." *Richard Wright Newsletter*, 8 (Fall-Winter), 3, 7–12. Protests the neglect of *SH*, arguing that it has satiric power in its presentation of the "invisibility" of whiteness. Fowler's behavior exemplifies that "the viciousness of whiteness is that it is thoroughly invisible. Thus the novel has a social as well as psychological dimension.

8007. Foer, Franklin. "Anxiety of Influence." *The New Republic*, 224 (12 February), 50. Quotes Laura Bush stating that *BB* advances understanding of "the boiling rage and desperate yearning of those who were denied full membership in America's promise."

8008. Foley, Barbara. "Bill V. Mullen. *Popular Fronts: Chicago and African-American Cultural Politics, 1936–46*." *African American Review*, 35 (Spring), 140–141. Review noting that Mullen argues that W's estrangement from Communism "was anomalous rather than paradigmatic" (p. 141).

8009. _____. "Proletarian Literature," in *Encyclopedia of American Studies*. Eds. Miles Orwell and Jay Mechling. New York: Grolier Educational, pp. 417–419. Mentions briefly *UTC* and *NS* (pp. 418, 419).

8010. Folks, Jeffrey J. "Introduc-

tion," in his *From Richard Wright to Toni Morrison: Ethics in Modern and Postmodern American Narrative*. New York: Peter Long, pp. 1–18. Notes the importance of W's seminal influence, deriving especially from *NS*, and the reaction to it by Baldwin and others (pp. 9–10).

8011. _____. "'Last Call to the West': Richard Wright's *The Color Curtain*," in his *From Richard Wright to Toni Morrison: Ethics in Modern and Postmodern American Narrative*. New York: Peter Lang, pp. 19–38.

8012. Foster, Frances Smith. "Rivers, Conrad Kent," in *The Concise Oxford Companion to African American Literature*. Eds. William L. Andrews, Frances Smith Foster, and Trudier Harris. New York: Oxford University Press, p. 349.

8013. Fox, Robert. "James T. Farrell (1904–1979)," in *The Columbia Companion to the Twentieth-Century American Short Story*. Ed. Blanche H. Gelfant. New York: Columbia University Press, pp. 248–251. Mentions W. briefly (p. 251).

8014. Freeman, John. "Sorrow, Rage, Bitterness." *The American Scholar*, 70 (Autumn), 145–147. Mixed review of Hazel Rowley's *Richard Wright. The Life and Times*: calling it "competent, readable, but vexingly tepid."

8015. Fullbrook, Kate. "A. Robert Lee, *Designs of Blackness: Mappings in the Literature and Culture of Afro-America*." *Journal of American Studies*, 35 (August), 360. Notes that Lee treats W with "especial delight."

8016. Gerstle, Gary. *American Crucible: Race and Nation in the Twentieth Century*. Princeton: Princeton University Press, p. 248. Mentions W briefly.

8017. Gibson, Donald B. "*Black Boy*," in *The Concise Oxford Companion to African American Literature*. Eds. William L. Andrews, Frances Smith Foster, and Trudier Harris. New York: Oxford University Press, pp. 35–36.

8018. _____. "*Uncle Tom's Children*," in *The Concise Oxford Companion to African American Literature*. Eds. William L. Andrews, Frances Smith Foster, and Trudier Harris. New York: Oxford University Press, pp. 405–406.

8019. _____. "New Negro, Old Left: African-American Writing and Communism Between the Wars. By

William J. Maxwell; *The New Red Negro: The Literary Left and African American Poetry, 1930–1946*. By James Edward Smethurst." *The Journal of American History*, 88 (June), 249–250. Favorable review mentioning W briefly.

8020. _____. "Wright, Richard," in *The Concise Oxford Companion to African American Literature*. Eds. William L. Andrews, Frances Smith Foster, and Trudier Harris. New York: Oxford University Press, pp. 447–449.

8021. _____. "Wright, Richard," in *The Oxford Companion to United States History*. New York: Oxford University Press, pp. 851–852. Biographical-critical sketch with a brief bibliography of three items, Mentions and comments briefly on *UTC, NS, O* and *LD*.

8022. _____. "Wright, Richard, in *The Oxford Companion to United States History*. Ed. Paul S. Boyer. Oxford: Oxford University Press, 2001, pp. 851–852. Biographical sketch with a brief bibliography.

8023. Gilsdorf, Ethan. "The Expatriate Writer in Paris: Revising the Myth." *Poets & Writers*, 29 (May/June), 14–19. Mentions W briefly (p. 15).

8024. Graham, Maryemma. "Chronology," in her *Fields Watered with Blood: Critical Essays on Margaret Walker*. Athens: The University of Georgia Press, pp. xix–xxvii. Dates Walker's meeting W and joining the South Side Writers group, the end of the friendship with W, and her writing and speaking on W.

8025. _____. "'I Want to Write, I Want to Write the Songs of My People': The Emergence of Margaret Walker," in her *Fields Watered with Blood*, pp. 11–27. Discusses Walker's friendship with W and her relation to the other writers of the Chicago Group.

8026. _____, and Deborah Whaley. "Introduction: The Most Famous Person Nobody Knows," in Graham's *Fields Watered with Blood*, pp. 1–8. Notes the end of the W-Walker friendship (pp. 1–2).

8027. Grammer, John M. "Reconstructing Southern Literature." *American Literary History*, 13 (Spring) 126–140. Mentions W briefly (p. 127).

8028. Grantham, Dewey W. *The South in Modern America: A Region at Odds*. Fayetteville: The University of Arkansas Press, pp. 153, 192, 326. Brief mentions of W and *BB*.

8029. Grant, Nancy L., and Darlene Clark Hine. "1932–1945," in *The Harvard Guide to African-American History*. Ed. Evelyn Brooks Higginbotham. Cambridge, MA: Harvard University Press, pp. 529–558. Lists W's "With Black Radicals in Chicago" (p. 547) and "Blueprint for Negro Writing" (p. 548).

8030. Graulich, Melody, and Mara Witzling. "The Freedom to Say What She Pleases: A Conversation with Faith Ringgold," in *Black Feminist Cultural Criticism*. Ed. Jacqueline Bobo. Malden, MA: Blackwell, pp. 184–209. Mentions W briefly (pp. 196, 200).

8031. Green, Tara Tarnisha. "'That Preacher's Going to Eat All the Chicken!': Power and Religion in Richard Wright." *Dissertation Abstracts International*, 61 (April), 3996–3997. Abstract of a dissertation relating W to Hegel on master-slave relationships.

8032. Griffiths, Frederick T. "Ralph Ellison, Richard Wright, and the Case of Angelo Herndon." *African American Review*, 35 (Winter), 315–341. Detailed examination of W's use of the Angelo Herndon case and *Let Me Live*, with a briefer treatment of Ellison's debt to Herndon. In the case of W, Griffiths relates *AH* to Herndon's more committed communist activism. Numerous passages in *BB*, "The Ethics of Living Jim Crow," *UTC* (especially "Bright and Morning Star"), and *NS* are directly indebted to Herndon's autobiography, and *O* and *LD* satirize Herndon and the Communist Party. Adducing many parallel passages to support his case, Griffiths places his argument in the context of the role of the black intellectual in radical politics.

8033. Gurga, Lee. "Richard Wright's Place in American Haiku." *Richard Wright Newsletter*, 8 (Fall-Winter), 1–2, 4–7. After defining haiku as a poetic genre, not a form, Gurga assesses W's *TOW*. Too many of the poems rely on figurative language rather that "vivid literal images," but the focus on nature is laudable, and W deserves credit as pioneer in American haiku.

8034. Gussow, Adam. "'Make My Getaway': The Blues Lives of Black Minstrels in W.C. Handy's *Father of the Blues*." *African American Review*, 35 (Spring), 5–28. Contains numerous comparisons and contrasts between Handy's autobiography and such works by W as *NS, BB*, and "Big Boy Leaves Home" (pp. 5–6, 9, 14).

8035. Guttman, Sondra. "What Bigger Killed For: Rereading Violence Against Women in *Native Son*." *Texas Studies in Literature and Language*, 43 (Summer), 169–193. Examines the sexual scenes in *NS*, noting the connection between sexual and political desire. W is critical of both traditional and Marxist attitudes toward women. Guttman rejects the notion that *NS* reflects the misogyny in its author.

8036. Gwin, Minrose. "The Intricate Design' of Margaret Walker's Humanism," in Maryemma Graham's *Fields Watered with Blood*, pp. 66–77. Mentions W briefly (p. 68).

8037. Hakutani, Yoshinobu. "*The Color Curtain*: Richard Wright's Journey Into Asia," in *Richard Wright's Travel Writings: New Reflections*. Ed. Virginia Whatley Smith. Jackson: University Press of Mississippi, pp. 63–77. The first part of this essay concerns W's realization of the similarity of Zen Buddhism and the Akan religion of Ghana, both based on a primal, poetic vision of life. The second part (pp. 68–77) compares *BP* and *CC*, analyzing the result of W's trip to Bandung.

8038. _____. "James A. Emanuel. *Jazz from the Haiku King*." *African American Review*, 35 (Winter), 681–684. Review mentioning W's interest in both haiku and jazz.

8039. _____. "Richard Wright, Toni Morrison, and the African 'Primal Outlook upon Life." *The Southern Quarterly*, 40 (Fall), 39–53. Discusses similarities between *Beloved* and W's treatment of African life and values in *BP*. Emphasizes the communal nature of African Life and its relation to a circular notion of time. Hakutani also discusses briefly *PS*.

8040. Haley, Alex. "Alex Haley Interviews Sammy Davis, Jr." in *The Sammy Davis, Jr. Reader*. Ed. Gerald Early. New York: Farrar Straus and Giroux, pp. 452–499.

8041. Hall, James C. *Mercy, Mercy Me: African-American Culture and the American Sixties*. New York: Oxford University Press, pp. 12, 131, 36, 81, 82, 98, 99, 201. Comments on W's expatriation and mentions briefly *BP, CC, PS, WML,* and "Blueprint for Negro Writing."

8042. Hapke, Laura. *Labor's Text: The Worker in American Fiction.* New Brunswick: Rutgers University Press, pp. 11, 208, 213, 217, 220, 221, 236–239, 241, 265, 273, 274, 307, 387, 416. The most extensive treatment of W is a consideration of *NS* "as a radical treatment of work and race in the 1930s" (p. 236). Elsewhere Hapke mentions W, Bigger, *LT,* and W defending Van Vechten.

8043. Harper, Michael S. "The Meaning of Protest," in *New Bones: Contemporary Black Writers in America.* Eds. Kevin Everod Quashie, Joyce Lausch, and Keith D. Miller. Upper Saddle River, NJ: Prentice-Hall, pp. 387–388.

8044. Harris, Trudier. "Baldwin, James," in *The Concise Oxford Companion to African American Literature.* Eds. William L. Andrews, Frances Smith Foster, and Trudier Harris. New York: Oxford University Press, pp. 20–22. Reprint of 1997 with slightly expanded bibliography.

8045. _____. *Saints, Sinners, Saviors: Strong Black Women in African American Literature.* New York: Palgrave, p. 34. Mentions briefly *NS.*

8046. Higginbotham, Evelyn Brooks. "General Studies," in her *The Harvard Guide to African-American History.* Cambridge, MA: Harvard University Press, pp. 211–213. Lists *TMBV* (p. 213).

8047. Hogue, W. Lawrence. "Darryl Dickson-Carr. *African American Satire: The Sacredly Profane Novel.*" *Canadian Review of American Studies,* 31, no. 3, p. 201. Mentions briefly *BB* and *NS.*

8048. Holcomb, Gary E. "New Negroes, Black Communists, and the New Pluralism." *American Quarterly,* 53 (June), 367–376. Favorable review of William Maxwell's *New Negro, Old Left: African-American Writing and Communism Between the Wars* and Cedric Robinson's *Black Marxism,* both of which treat W as a central figure.

8049. Hönnighausen, Lothar, and Valeria Lerda: "Southern Writers," in *Encyclopedia of American Studies.* Eds. Miles Orwell and Jay Mechling. New York: Grolier, pp. 161–164. Claims that *BB* makes W a Southern Writer (p. 163).

8050. Horton, James Oliver, and Lois E. Horton. *Hard Road to Freedom: The Story of African America.* New Brunswick, New Jersey: Rutgers University Press, pp. 227–230. Uses the early W's case as a paradigm of the Great Migration. Notes his rejection of Garvey and the UNIA.

8051. Houtchens, Bobbi Ciriza, ed. "English in the News." *English Journal,* 90 (May), 117–122. Includes a report from *Ethnic News Watch* mentioning W briefly (p. 121).

8052. _____. "English in the News." *English Journal,* 90 (July), 105. Reprints from the *New York Times* a eulogy of Gwendolyn Brooks including high praise from W.

8053. Howorth, Richard. *The Eighth Oxford Conference for the Book.* Oxford, MS: Center for the Study of Southern Culture, 12 pp. Program brochure of a conference dedicated to W, the cover featuring Van Vechten's photograph of him. Howorth contributes a biographical sketch. The panel on W (30 March) consisted of Jerry W. Ward, Michel Fabre, Geneviève Fabre, Paul Oliver, and Hazel Rowley.

8054. Hudson-Weems, Clenora. "The African American Literary Tradition," in *The African American Experience: An Historiographical and Bibliographical Guide.* Eds. Arvarh E. Strickland and Robert E. Weems. Westport, CT: Greenwood Press, pp. 117–143. Includes a discussion of W's career and works, especially in the context of leftist and protest writing (pp. 128–131).

8055. Hughes, Langston. "*Ask Your Mama: 12 Moods for Jazz,*" in *The Poems: 1951–1967.* Ed. Arnold Rampersad. Vol. 3 of *The Collected Works of Langston Hughes.* Columbia: University of Missouri Press, pp. 79–125.

8056. _____. *Fight for Freedom and Other Writings on Civil Rights.* Ed. Christopher De Santis. Volume 10 of *The Collected Works of Langston Hughes.* Columbia: University of Missouri Press.

8057. _____. *Fight for Freedom and Other Writings on Civil Rights.* Volume 10 of *The Collected Works of Langston Hughes.* Ed. Christopher De Santis. Columbia: University of Missouri Press, pp. 23–205.

8058. _____. "The Need for Heroes," in *Fight for Freedom and Other Writings on Civil Rights.* Ed. Christopher De Santis. Volume 10 of *The*

Collected Works of Langston Hughes. Columbia: University of Missouri Press.

8059. James, Charles L. "*Black Thunder,*" in *The Concise Oxford Companion to African American Literature.* Eds. William L. Andrews, Frances Smith Foster, and Trudier Harris. New York: Oxford University Press, pp. 36–37.

8060. Jefferson, Robert F. "Segregation, Racial," in *The Oxford Companion to United States History.* Ed. Paul S. Boyer. New York: Oxford University Press, pp. 696–697. Mentions W briefly.

8061. Jeffries, Dexter. "Richard Wright and the 'Daily Worker': A Native Son's Journalistic Apprenticeship." *Dissertation Abstracts International,* 61 (March), 3567. Abstract of a dissertation treating W's work on *The Daily Worker,* 1936–1938.

8062. Jenkins, Everett, Jr. *Pan-African Chronology III: A Comprehensive Reference to the Black Quest for Freedom in Africa, the Americas, Europe and Asia, 1914–1929.* Jefferson, NC: McFarland, pp. 13, 156, 262, 319. Mentions briefly W's friendship with Ellison, his ties to the Communist Party, and *NS.*

8063. Johnson, Charles. "A Phenomenology of the Black Body," in *Traps: African American Men on Gender and Sexuality.* Eds. Rudolph P. Byrd and Beverly Guy-Sheftall. Bloomington: Indiana UP, pp. 223–235. Comments on and quotes from *O* (p. 231).

8064. Johnson, David R. *Conrad Richter: A Writer's Life.* University Park: The Pennsylvania State University Press, pp. 217–218. Reports that Richter was upset because his novel *The Trees* was paired by the Book-of-the-Month Club with *NS,* hurting sales. He wrote in his journal "that he resented deeply his being associated with a Negro writer of a sensationally lurid novel."

8065. Joiner, Lottie. "Books in Brief." *The Crisis,* 108 (May/June), 53. Includes a notice of James Meacham's *Voices in Our Blood: America's Best on the Civil Rights Movement* mentioning W briefly.

8066. Jones, Arthur C. "Upon This Rock: The Foundational Influence of the Spirituals," in his and Ferdinand Jones's *The Triumph of the Soul: Cultural and Psychological Aspects of African American Music.*

Westport, CT: Praeger, p. 16. Mentions briefly *BB*.

8067. Joseph, Peniel E. "Black Liberation Without Apology: Reconceptualizing the Black Power Movement." *The Black Scholar*, 31 (Fall/Winter), 2–19. Includes discussion of *BP*, *CC*, and *WML* (pp. 3–4).

8068. _____. "Review Essay: Beyond the Color Curtain: A Review of Radio Free Dixie: Robert F. Williams and the Roots of Black Power." *The Black Scholar*, 31 (Spring), 43–49. Mentions W briefly (p. 44).

8069. Jurca, Catherine. *White Diaspora: The Suburb and the Twentieth-Century American Novel*. Princeton University Press, pp. 7–8, 15, 99–100, 101–104, 105, 106–107, 109, 113, 115–119, 120, 121, 122, 123, 124, 125, 127–129, 130–131, 135, 210, 211, 215, 216. The chapter on *NS* (pp. 99–132, 208–213) suggests "that the principal site of racial contestations is less the white body of the landlord's daughter" than the affluent neighborhood of Hyde Park-Kenwood. Jurca's analysis draws on the sociology of Ernest W. Burgess and other social scientists. The final section of the chapter treats W in Paris.

8070. Karem, Jeff. "'I Could Never Really Leave the South': Regionalism and the Transformation of Richard Wright's *American Hunger*." *American Literary History*, 13 (Winter), 694–715. Discusses the publication history of *BB* (*AH*), treating W's response to the reception of *UTC* and *NS*, the roles of Edward Aswell, Paul Reynolds, and Dorothy Canfield Fisher in the revision of the work, its marketing by Harper's, and reviews.

8071. Karrer, Wolfgang. "Black Modernism?: The Early Poetry of Jean Toomer and Claude McKay," in *Jean Toomer and the Harlem Renaissance*. Eds. Geneviève Fabre and Michel Feith. New Brunswick: Rutgers University Press, pp. 128–141. Mentions W briefly (p. 141).

8072. Kato, Makiko. "A Hero Hankering After Love–Wright's *Native Son*," in *American Literature Reread Through Heroes*. Ed. Miyoko Sasaki. Tokyo: Keisoshobo, pp. 131–149. Notes that W predicted through *NS* that in the twenty-first century "a monster like Bigger who kills to show that he exists would appear again."

8073. Kerr-Ritchie, Jeffrey. "Ted Ownby. *American Dreams in Mississippi: Consumers, Poverty, and Culture, 1830–1998*." *American Historical Review*, 106 (February), pp. 199–200. Mentions W briefly.

8074. Kim, Sang-yule [The Politics of Racial Representation: A Discursive Warfare Between Wright's *Uncle Tom's Children* and Faulkner's *Go Down Moses*]. *Studies in Modern Fiction*, 8 (Winter), 41–64. Compares racial stereotypes in the two works. The article is in Korean with an English summary.

8075. King, Nicole. *C.L.R. James and Creolization: Circles of Influence*. Jackson: University Press of Mississippi, pp. xvi–xvii, 9–10, 19, 27, 76, 79–80, 82, 86–101, 109, 148, 149, 151. Chapter Four, "Factions and Fictions," compares James and W on "The Negro Question." Both were radicals, but James had more faith than W did in the revolutionary potential of the black masses. In this context King discusses *NS*, "Blueprint for Negro Writing," and "I Tried to Be a Communist." W is also mentioned elsewhere in this book.

8076. King, Richard H. "Richard Gray, *Southern Aberrations: Writers of the American South and the Problems of Regionalism*." *Journal of American Studies*, 35 (April), 153–155. Mentions W briefly (p. 154).

8077. King, Wilma. "African American Women," in *The African American Experience: An Historiographical and Bibliographical Guide*. Eds. Arvarh E. Strickland and Robert E. Weems, Jr. Westport, CT: Greenwood Press, pp. 71–92. Notes W's disapproval of Jessie Fauset's work (p. 82).

8078. King, Woodie, Jr. "No Identity Crisis: An Introduction to the Plays of Ron Milner," in *What the Wine-Sellers Buy Plus Three: Four Plays by Ron Milner*, Detroit: Wayne State University Press, pp. 11–19. Mentions W briefly.

8079. Kinnamon, Keneth. "*A Richard Wright Bibliography: 1992*." *Richard Wright Newsletter*, 8 (Fall/Winter). Contains 430 annotated items with a page of evaluation of the year's work.

8080. _____. "Books Briefly Mentioned." *African American Review*, 35 (Fall), 500–501. Contains a review of Robert Felgar's *Student Companion to Richard Wright* not-

ing that it is useful for its intended audience, but not for professional scholars.

8081. _____. "Wright, Hemingway, and the Bullfight: An Aficionado's View," in *Richard Wright's Travel Writings: New Reflections*. Ed. Virginia Whatley Smith. Jackson: University Press of Mississippi, pp. 157–164. Compares the bullfight sections of *PS* and *Death in the Afternoon*, concluding that although Hemingway is much more knowledgeable about the spectacle and its technical aspects, W complements Hemingway by emphasizing its mythic dimension involving sexuality and the religious impulse.

8082. Klawans, Stuart. "'I Was a Weird Example of Art': *My Amputations* as Cubist Confession," in *Clarence Major and His Art: Portraits of an African American Postmodernist*. Ed. Bernard W. Bell. Chapel Hill: University of North Carolina Press, pp. 207–218.

8083. Klotman, Phyllis. "'Oh Freedom': Women and History in Margaret Walker's *Jubilee*," in Maryemma Graham's *Fields Watered with Blood*, pp. 209–224. Mentions W briefly (p. 217).

8084. Koolish, Lynda. "John A. Williams," in her *African American Writers: Portraits and Visions*. Jackson: University Press of Mississippi, p. 114. Relates Williams to W as a protest writer.

8085. Kornegay, Jamie. "Off the Page." *662 Yoknapatawpha Arts Council* (Spring), pp. 2, 5. On the occasion of the eighth annual Oxford Conference of the Book, dedicated to W, Kornegay supplies a biographical paragraph and announces a panel on W with contributions by Jerry Ward, Michel and Geneviève Fabre, Paul Oliver, and Hazel Rowley. Contains the Van Vechten photograph of W.

8086. Kraut, B. "Philipson, Robert. 'The Identity Question: Blacks and Jews in Europe and America.'" *Choice*, 39 (September), 162. Review mentioning W briefly.

8087. Lamar, Jake. "The Outsider." *Washington Post Book World* (12 August), pp. 1, 3. Highly favorable review of Hazel Rowley's *Richard Wright: The Life and Times*, calling it the best biography since Fabre's. If it is occasionally short on analysis, it is "long on sheer narrative momentum ... thorough and engrossing from the first page to the last."

8088. Lansford, Tom M. "American Character," in *Encyclopedia of American Studies*. Eds. Miles Orwell and Jay Mechling. New York: Grolier Educational, pp. 97–98. Notes that W treats the denial of the American dream in *AH*.

8089. Lasch-Quinn, Elisabeth. *Race Experts: How Racial Etiquette, Sensitivity Training, and New Age Therapy Hijacked the Civil Rights Revolution*. New York: W.W. Norton, p. 25. Mentions briefly *NS*.

8090. Lauret, Maria. "African American Fiction," in *Beginning Ethnic American Literature*. Eds. Helena Grice, Candida Hepwarth, Maria Lauret, and Martin Padget. Manchester: Manchester University Press, pp. 77, 78, 79, 80, 85, 99, 115. Comments on W in relation to changing patterns of African American Fiction. Mentions "Blueprint for Negro Writing."

8091. Lausch, R. Joyce, with Kevin Everod Quashie, and Keith D. Miller. "Introduction," in their *New Bones: Contemporary Black Writers in America*. Upper Saddle River, NJ: Prentice-Hall, pp. 1–14. Mentions W briefly (pp. 7–8).

8092. Leak, Jeffrey. "Introduction," in his *Rac[e]ing to the Right: Selected Essays of George S. Schuyler*. Knoxville: The University of Tennessee Press, pp. xv–xlv. Mentions W briefly (pp. xx).

8093. Lee, A. Robert. "Dwight A. McBride, *James Baldwin Now*." *Journal of American Studies*. 35 (December), 514–516. Mentions W briefly (p. 515).

8094. Lehan, Richard. "*Sister Carrie*," in *Literary Masterpieces*, Volume 7. Detroit: Gale Group, p. 148. Mentions W briefly.

8095. Leininger-Miller, Theresa. "New Negro Artists," in *Paris: African American Painters and Sculptors in the City of Light, 1922–1934*. New Brunswick: Rutgers University Press, pp. 250, 274. Mentions briefly W and *NS*.

8096. Lester, Neal A. "Beyond 'Bitches and hoes' Sexual Violence, Violent Sex, and Sexual Fantasy as Black Masculinist Performance in Richard Wright's 'The Man Who Killed a Shadow.'" *Richard Wright Newsletter*, 8 (Spring-Summer), 1–12. Argues that Saul, an unreliable narrator, acts out masculine aggres-

sion on his victim without provocation from her. Cites numerous examples of similar behavior in rap music and hip-hop performance.

8097. Lindberg, Kathryne. "Depejorating 'Uplift' and Re-centering Race Poetry: Lorenzo Thomas's *Extraordinary Measures*." *Boundary 2*, 28 (Summer), 21–32. Mentions briefly W's 'Blue Print' [sic] (p. 26).

8098. Lokaisingh-Meighoo, Sean. "The Diasporic Mo(ve)ment: Indentureship and Indo-Caribbean Identity," in *Nation Dance: Religion, Identity, and Cultural Difference in the Caribbean*. Ed. Patrick Taylor. Bloomington: Indiana University Press, pp. 171–192. Quotes Paul Gilroy mentioning W briefly (p. 177).

8099. Lowe, John. "Richard Wright as Traveler/Ethnographer: The Conundrums of *Pagan Spain*," in *Richard Wright's Travel Writings: New Reflections*. Ed. Virginia Whatley Smith. Jackson: University Press of Mississippi, pp. 119–156. Compares W with Hurston as a literary ethnographer, then places *PS* in its political and religious context as well as in W's personal context, linking the two. The Chicago school of sociology is also applied. Lowe deals with the entirety of *PS*, but focuses on the plight of Spanish women, the connection between Spanish Catholicism and paganism, and the bullfight. He believes that W succeeds in connecting emotionally with his Spanish informants and with the readers of *PS*, a "therapeutic narrative."

8100. Mackey, Nathaniel. "To Define an Ultimate Dimness: The Poetry of Clarence Major," in *Clarence Major and His Art: Portraits of an African American Postmodernist*. Ed. Bernard W. Bell. Chapel Hill: University of North Carolina Press, pp. 133–149.

8101. _____. "Necessary Distance: Afterthoughts on Becoming a Writer," in *Clarence Major and His Art: Portraits of an African American Postmodernist*. Ed. Bernard W. Bell. Chapel Hill: University of North Carolina Press, pp. 63–76.

8102. Mason, Byron Douglas. "Beyond Primitivism: Richard Wright and the Chicago Renaissance." *Dissertation Abstracts International*, 61 (February), 3222. Abstract of a dissertation treating *NS*, W and the Chicago Renaissance as

compared to the Harlem Renaissance.

8103. Mason, Theodore A. "Rivers, Conrad Kent," in *The Concise Oxford Companion to African American Literature*. Eds. William L. Andrews, Frances Smith Foster, and Trudier Harris. New York: Oxford University Press, p. 349.

8104. Maxwell, William J. "James Edward Smethurst. *The New Red Negro: The Literary Left and African American Poetry*." *African American Review*, 35 (Spring), 143–145. Review mentioning briefly W and the Wright School.

8105. McCaffery, Larry, and Jerzy Kutnik. "'I Follow My Eyes': An Interview with Clarence Major," in *Clarence Major and His Art: Portraits of an African American Postmodernist*. Ed. Bernard W. Bell. Chapel Hill: University of North Carolina Press, pp. 77–98.

8106. McGowan, Todd. *The Feminine "No!": Psychoanalysis and the New Canon*. Albany: State University of New York Press, pp. 85–86. Notes W's disparagement of *Their Eyes Were Watching God*.

8107. McGurty, Eileen Maura. "From NIMBY to Civil Rights: The Origins of the Environmental Justice Movement," in *The Civil Rights Movement*. Ed. Jack E. Davis. Malden, MA: Blackwell Publishers, pp. 258–274. Cites the opening pages of *NS* as an early example of a squalid environment contributing to racial injustice.

8108. McKinley, Catherine, Nelson George, Kenji Jasper, Omar Tyree, Brian Keath Jackson, and E. Lynn Harris. "Black Male Fiction: Riding the Wake of the Female Writers?: A Harlem Book Fair Panel Discussion." *QBR: The Black Book Review* (November-December), 31–33. Tyree and McKinley mention W briefly.

8109. McLellan, Tyler, and Jill Yoe. "Book conference honors writers." *The Daily Mississippian* (30 March), pp. 1, 7. Reports the beginning of the eighth annual Oxford Conference for the Book at the University of Mississippi, dedicated to W. Jerry W. Ward will deliver the keynote lecture on "Richard Wright: The Enduring Challenge of his Legacy," to be followed by talks by Michel Fabre, Geneviève Fabre, Paul Oliver, and Hazel Rowley.

8110/8111. Meacham, Jon. "Before the Storm," in his *Voices in Our Blood: America's Best on the Civil Rights Movement*. New York: Random House, pp. 9–11. Comments on *NS* and the genesis of *TMBV* (p. 9). An extensive excerpt from *TMBV* appears on pp. 13–32.

8112. _____. "Into the Streets," in his *Voices in Our Blood: America's Best on the Civil Rights Movement*. New York: Random House, pp. 104–109. Notes that Langston Hughes introduced Ralph Ellison to W.

8113. _____. "Introduction in his *Voices in Our Blood: America's Best on the Civil Rights Movement*. New York: Random House, pp. 3–8. Relates the meeting of W and Willie Morris in 1957 and quotes from *BB* (p. 31).

8114. Miller, James A. "A Message from the Editor." *Richard Wright Newsletter*, 8 (Fall-Winter), 3. Announces the appointment of Howard Ramsby II and Virginia Whatley Smith to the Advisory Board of the *Richard Wright Newsletter*.

8115. _____, Susan D. Pennybacker, and Eve Rosenhaft. "Mother Ada Wright and the the International Campaign to Free the Scottsboro Boys, 1931–1934." *The American Historical Review*, 106 (April), 430. A note on the authors mentions Miller's *Approaches to Teaching Wright's "Native Son"* and his dissertation on W.

8116. _____. "William J. Maxwell. *New Negro, Old Left: African-American Writing and Communism Between the Wars*." *African American Review*, 35 (Spring), 142–143. Review commenting on Maxwell's treatment of W in relation to Hurston and Nelson Algren.

8117. Minter, David. *Faulkner's Questioning Narratives: Fiction of His Major Phase, 1929–42*. Urbana: University of Illinois Press, pp. 55, 132. Mentions W briefly.

8118. Miller, R. Baxter. "The 'Etched Flame' of Margaret Walker: Biblical and Literary Re-Creation in Southern History," in Maryemma Graham's *Fields Watered with Blood*, pp. 81–97. Notes Walker's biographical writings about W (p. 82).

8119. Mitchell, Carolyn. "'A Laying on of Hands': Transcending the City in Ntozake Shange's *for colored girls who have considered suicide/ when the rainbow is enuff*," in *Black Feminist Cultural Criticism*. Ed. Jacqueline Bobo. Malden, MA:

Blackwell, pp. 262–279. Includes comments on "The Man Who Lived Underground" (pp. 267, 277), and mentions W briefly (p. 276).

8120. Moore, Jack B. "'No Street Numbers in Accra': Richard Wright's African Cities," in *Richard Wright's Travel Writings: New Reflections*. Ed. Virginia Whatley Smith. Jackson: University Press of Mississippi, pp. 45–59.

8121. Morgan, Gordon D. "Aggression and Shootings." Fayetteville *Northwest Arkansas Times* (3 January), p. A4. Mentions briefly *NS*.

8122. Morgan, Stacy I. "Migration, Material Culture, and Identity in William Attaway's *Blood on the Forge* and Harriette Arnow's *The Dollmaker*." *College English*, 63 (July), 712–740. Mentions briefly *TMBV* (p. 721) and W (p. 723).

8123. Mullen, Bill V. "Breaking the Signifying Chain: A New Blueprint for African-American Literary Studies." *Modern Fiction Studies*, 47 (Spring), 145–163. Emphasizes the working class nature of much African American writing arguing that a similar critical perspective is needed. Mentions W and his "Blueprint for Negro Writing" (pp. 155, 156, 160).

8124. Mungazi, Dickson A. *The Journey to the Promised Land: The African American Struggle for Development Since the Civil War*. Westport, CT: Praeger, p. 94. Mentions W briefly.

8125. Murray, Albert. *From the Briarpatch File: On Context, Procedure, and American Identity*. New York: Pantheon Books. Mentions W briefly (pp. 163, 192).

8126. Nadel, Alan. "Ralph Ellison and the American Canon." *American Literary History*, 13 (Summer), 393–404. Quotes Ellison praising W (p. 397).

8127. Nagel, James. "The American Short Story Cycle," in *The Columbia Companion to the Twentieth-Century American Short Story*. Ed. Blanche H. Gelfant. New York: Columbia University Press, pp. 9–14. Notes that the stories in *UTC* are "unified by themes of white oppression of black families" (p. 11).

8128. _____. *The Contemporary American Short-Story Cycle: The Ethnic Resonance of Genre*. Baton Rouge: Louisiana State University Press, p. 7. Notes that *UTC* is "unified by themes of white oppression of black families."

8129. Nash, William R. "The Life and the Mind: A Reconciliation." *The Southern Literary Journal*, 34 (Fall), 133–135. Review of Claudia Tate's *Psychoanalysis and the Black Novel: The Protocols of Race* commenting on her treatment of W.

8130. Naylor, Gloria. "Bookshelf: A Few Choice Titles from My Library." *The Oprah Magazine*, 2 (August), 164. Includes an appreciative note on *NS*, one of "only two books in my life that have made me cry."

8131. Nebo, Annette. "Power, Destiny, and Individual Choice in Gloria Naylor's Naturalism." *CLA Journal*, 44 (June), 492–522. Argues that although influenced by W and Petry, Naylor developed "her own brand of naturalism, one responsive to the changing politics of the sixties and seventies.

8132. Nejako, Alexander. "Bigger's Choice: The Failure of African-American Masculinities in *Native Son*." *CLA Journal*, 44 (June), 423–440. Argues that W accepted the white male model derived from Chicago sociologists and the movies for black males, ignoring the sustaining power of black society. Bigger is explained in this framework. W was also mindful of his white audience.

8133. Nelson, Cary. *Revolutionary Memory: Recovering the Poetry of the American Left*. New York: Routledge, pp. 65, 167, 172, 177. Mentions W briefly and quotes from "We of the Streets," "I Have Seen Black Hands," and "I Am a Red Slogan."

8134. Nesmith, N. Graham. "*Living with Music: Ralph Ellison's Jazz Writings*. *The New York Times Book Review* (8 July), p. 20. Mentions W briefly.

8135. Newman, Richard. "Bibliography," in *The Harvard Guide to African-American History*. Ed. Evelyn Brooks Higginbotham. Cambridge, MA: Harvard University Press, pp. 3–22. Includes description of *A Richard Wright Bibliography: Fifty Years of Criticism and Commentary, 1933–1982*.

8136. Noe, Marcia, and Scott Dent. "Richard Wright," in *Dictionary of Midwestern Literature*. Bloomington: Indiana University Press, pp. 548–550. Biographical-critical sketch with bibliography of criticism.

8137. O'Brien, Anthony. *Against Normalization: Writing Radical*

Democracy in South Africa. Durham: Duke University Press, pp. 63, 247. Quotes from *AH* and mentions W's use of the trope of hunger.

8138. O'Dell, Darlene. *Sites of Southern Memory: The Autobiographies of Katherine Du Pre Lumpkin.* Charlottesville: University Press of Virginia, pp. 25, 158. Mentions briefly *NS*.

8139. Patterson, Troy. "*Richard Wright: The Life and Times.*" *Entertainment Weekly* (7 September), p. 158. Review of Hazel Rowley's biography, calling it "definitive on the life and times and indefinite about the thinker and his work." Includes a photograph of W.

8140. Peddie, Ian. "Poles Apart? Ethnicity, Race, Class, and Nelson Algren." *Modern Fiction Studies*, 47 (Spring), 119–144. Mentions W frequently (pp. 118, 120, 121, 126, 131, 135, 140). Quotes from a letter by W stating that "Nelson does for the Polish folk of Chicago what Faulkner does for the poor white folk of Mississippi (p. 126).

8141. Pedersen, Carl. "The Tropics in New York: Claude McKay and the New Negro Movement," in *Temples for Tomorrow, Looking Back at the Harlem Renaissance.* Eds. Geneviève Fabre and Michel Feith. Bloomington: Indiana University Press, pp. 259–269. Mentions briefly W's exile in Paris (p. 260).

8142. Perez, Vincent. "Movies, Marxism, and Jim Crow: Richard Wright's Cultural Criticism." *Texas Studies in Literature and Language.* 43 (Summer), pp. 142–168. Examines the influence of media culture and black folk culture, as well as Marxism, on *LT, NS, TMBV,* and *O,* concluding that "the belief that subordinated groups have the capacity to resist their ideology saturated environment tempers Wright's cultural pessimism."

8143. Perry, Carolyn Elaine. "The Augustan Confessional Tradition Transformed in '*Black Boy*' and 'Hunger of Memory.'" *Dissertation Abstracts International,* 62 (November), 2001. Abstract of a dissertation treating W and Richard Rodriguez.

8144. Peterson, Bernard L., Jr. *Profiles of African American Stage Performers and Theatre People, 1816–1960.* Westport, CT: Greenwood Press, pp. 164, 239–240, 278. Mentions W and the play *NS* in an entry for Canada Lee, notes that Melvin B. Tolson dramatized *BB,* and includes a biographical sketch of W emphasizing his dramatic works (p. 278).

8145. Pinckney, Darryl. "The Black American Tragedy." *The New York Review of Books,* 48 (1 November), 68–73. Essay-review of Hazel Rowley's *Richard Wright: The Life and Times* narrating the major phases of W's life. Pinckney calls Rowley's biography "excellent, entirely readable," pointing out that the author had access to information that Fabre could not use. Pinckney takes W's side in the dispute with Baldwin and Ellison over the role of the black writer. The title of the review and the concluding sentence emphasizes W's connection to Midwestern realists, especially Dreiser.

8146. Pinar, William R. *The Gender of Racial Politics and Violence in America: Lynching, Prison, Rape, and the Crisis of Masculinity.* New York: Peter Lang, pp. 19, 57, 80, 216, 221, 226, 227, 230–231, 859, 888. Quotes from *LD* and *NS,* discusses "Between the World and Me," "Big Boy Leaves Home," *NS,* and *LD,* drawing on such critics as Trudier Harris, Blyden Jackson, Noel Schraufnagel, and Robin Wiegman. Mentions W elsewhere (pp. 57, 216, 859).

8147. Pinn, Anthony. "*Black Boy: A Record of Childhood and Youth.* Richard Wright," in his *By These Hands: A Documentary History of African American Humanism.* New York: New York University Press, pp. 183–191. Includes a section of *BB* and commentary on W's rejection of religion. Also provides a brief bibliography.

8148. Pinsker, Sanford. "Contemporary American Fiction Through University Press Filters." *The Georgia Review,* 55 (Summer), 374–381. Mentions W briefly (p. 379).

8149. Polito, Robert. "*Chester Himes: A Life.*" *The New York Times Book Review* (18 March), p. 11. Review mentioning W's influence on Himes.

8150. Polk, Noel. "Engaging the Political in Our Texts, in Our Classrooms" in *Eudora Welty and Politics: Did the Writer Crusade?* Eds. Harriet Pollack and Suzanne Marrs. Baton Rouge: Louisiana State University Press, pp. 47–67. Mentions *NS* and *BB* (p. 53).

8151. Porter, Horace A. *Jazz Country: Ralph Ellison in America.* Iowa City: University of Iowa Press, pp. 2, 5, 6, 124, 125, 127, 128–129, 130–131, 142, 144. Includes discussion of Ellison's relations with W and his writings about him, including the exchange with Irving Howe.

8152. _____. "James Baldwin (1924–1987)," in *The Columbia Companion to the Twentieth-Century American Short Story.* Ed. Blanche H. Gelfant. New York: Columbia University Press, pp. 114–117. Notes that in "Previous Condition" the protagonist Peter, an actor, refuses to play Bigger Thomas in a movie (p. 116).

8153. Posner, Richard A. *Public Intellectuals: A Study of Decline.* Cambridge: Harvard University Press, pp. 10, 233. Mentions W briefly (p. 10). Calls *NS* a mediocre novel.

8154. Quirk, Tom. *Nothing Abstract: Investigations in the American Literary Imagination.* Columbia: University of Missouri Press, pp. 29, 30, 43. Comments on *NS,* the Nixon case, and Communist ideology vs. "the existential dilemma."

8155. Rabinowitz, Paula. "Domestic Labor, Film Noir, Proletarian Literature, and Black Women's Fiction." *Modern Fiction Studies,* 47 (Spring), 229–254. Mentions briefly W and *TMBV* (pp. 233, 243, 254)

8156. Rampersad, Arnold. "Racial Doubt and Racial Shame in the Harlem Renaissance," in *Temples for Tomorrow: Looking Back at the Harlem Renaissance.* Eds. Geneviève Fabre and Michel Feith. Bloomington: Indiana University Press, pp. 31–44. Includes discussion of "Blueprint for Negro Writing" and mentions *UTC, NS,* and *BB.*

8157. Rand, William E. "Chester Himes as a Naturalistic Writer in the Tradition of Richard Wright and Theodore Dreiser." *CLA Journal,* 44 (June), 442–450. Compares *If He Hollers Let Him Go* with *An American Tragedy and NS,* noting Himes's admiration of W.

8158. Raynor, Deirdre. "African American Literature," in *Encyclopedia of American Studies.* Eds. Miles Orwell and Jay Mechling. New York: Grolier Educational, pp. 22–27. Includes comments on W and protest literature (pp. 25, 26).

8159. Reckley, Ralph, Sr. "Ellison, Ralph," in *The Concise Oxford Companion to African American Literature.* Eds. William L. Andrews, Frances Smith Foster, and Trudier

Harris. New York: Oxford University Press, pp. 129–131. Reprint of 1997 with expanded bibliography.

8160. Reesman, Jeanne Campbell. "Fiction: 1900 to the 1930s," in *American Literary Scholarship: An Annual/1999*. Ed. Gary Scharnhorst. Durham: Duke University Press, pp. 289–311. Includes comments on an article by William A. Gleason on Dreiser and W (pp. 296–297).

8161. Reilly, John. "Virginia Whatley Smith, ed. *Richard Wright's Travel Writings: New Reflections*." Jackson: University Press of Mississippi, pp. 248. Favorable review with special praise for contributions by John Lowe, Keneth Kinnamon, and Smith herself.

8162. Renda, Mary A. *Taking Haiti: Military Occupation and the Culture of U.S. Imperialism, 1915–1940*. Chapel Hill: The University of North Carolina Press, p. 283. Notes W's praise of *Black Thunder*.

8163. Rhodes, Kate. "Robert Butler, *Contemporary African American Fiction: The Open Journey." Journal of American Studies*. 35 (April), 138. Mentions W briefly.

8164. Romine, Scott. "Race and Pollution in Southwestern Humor," in *The Humor of the Old South*. Eds. M. Thomas Inge and Edward J. Piacentino. Lexington: The University Press of Kentucky, pp. 70, 72. Mentions W briefly and quotes from *AH*.

8165. Rosenberg, Warren. *Legacy of Rage: Jewish Masculinity, Violence, and Culture*. Amherst: University of Massachusetts Press, pp. 25, 27, 128. Mentions W briefly.

8166. Rotella, Guy. "Szalay, Michael. *New Deal Modernism: American Literature and the Invention of the Welfare State." Studies in American Fiction*, 29 (Autumn), 253–255. Mentions W briefly.

8167. Rowell, Charles H. "An Interview with John Edgar Wideman," in *New Bones: Contemporary Black Writers in America*. Eds. Kevin Everod Quashie, Joyce Lausch, and Keith D. Miller. Upper Saddle River, NJ: Prentice-Hall, pp. 1026–1037.

8168. Rowley, Hazel. *Richard Wright: The Life and Times*. New York: Henry Holt, x + 626pp. Full-scale biography based on extensive research in archives, privately owned correspondence and notes, audiotapes, FBI files reluctantly de-

classified and released, State Department documents, interviews and correspondence with Ellen Wright, Constance Webb, Madison D. Lacy, Helènè Bokanowski, Manuel Cooke, Richard Gibson, and many other informants. In contrast to earlier biographers, Rowley focuses on W's personal life and sexual affairs with such partners as Edith Anderson, Naomi Replansky, Madylyn Jackson, Marion Sawyer, Jean Wallace, Vivian Werner, Celia Hornung, and others. The early years of his marriage to Ellen and the birth of his daughters were happy, however, as his journal attests. Rowley also treats extensively W's failing health and his relation to Dr. Schwarzmann, who may have inadvertently caused W's death by prescribing oral bismuth therapy, the toxicity of which was not known at the time. Rowley includes a selected bibliography of forty-seven items.

8169. _____. "London After Bloomsbury." *The Nation*, 273 (19 November), 28–29. Mentions briefly Rowley's *Richard Wright: The Life and Times*.

8170. Rushdy, Ashraf H.A. *Remembering Generations: Race and Family in Contemporary African American Fiction*. Chapel Hill: The University of North Carolina Press, p. 9. Mentions W briefly.

8171. Sallis, James. *Chester Himes: A Life*. New York: Walker, pp. 66, 88, 94–95, 110, 111, 116, 145, 176, 180, 183, 184, 189–190, 191, 193–195, 198–199, 243, 245, 257, 266, 267, 272, 283, 288, 330–331. Includes discussion of the triangle of friends: W, Himes and Ellison. Himes and W were very close. Also comments on W's expatriation and death. Mentions *UTC, NS, BB, O, LD*, and "Island of Hallucinations."

8172. Samson, John. "Melville," in *American Literary Scholarship: An Annual/1999*. Ed. Gary Scharnhorst. Durham: Duke University Press, pp. 53–69. Includes comment on Elizabeth Schultz's article on *NS* and Melville (p. 60).

8173. Savigneau, Josyane. *Carson McCullers: A Life*. Boston: Houghton Mifflin, pp. 66, 75, 99, 100, 167. Praises W's review of *The Heart Is a Lonely Hunter*, notes his residence in Brooklyn Heights, and comments on his concern about McCullers's health.

8174. Schaub, Thomas H. "Literature: Since World War I," in *The Oxford Companion to United States History*. Ed. Paul S. Boyer. New York: Oxford University Press, pp. 457–459. Mentions briefly W and *NS*.

8175. Schnack, Pat. "*Partners in Reading: A Community Reading/Writing Project*." *English Journal*, 90 (May), 95–101. Mentions briefly *NS* (pp. 97, 101).

8176. Schwetman, John D. "Ethnic Enclaves," in *Encyclopedia of American Studies*. Eds. Miles Orwell and Jay Mechling. New York: Grolier Educational, pp. 313–314. Comments on white violence against blacks in *UTC* (p. 313).

8177. Scruggs, Charles. "Jean Toomer and Kenneth Burke and the Persistence of the Past." *American Literary History*, 13 (Spring), 41–66. Mentions briefly W's interest in Burke.

8178. Seaman, Donna. "Rowley, Hazel. *Richard Wright: The Life and Times*." *Booklist*, 97 (July), 1969. Favorable review: "Wright's life story, so well told, illuminates crucial aspects of African American history and culture."

8179. Selzer, Linda Ferguson. "Reading the Painterly Text: Clarence Major's 'The Slave Trade': View from the Middle Passage," in *Clarence Major and His Art: Portraits of an African American Post Modernist*. Ed. Bernard W. Bell. Chapel Hill: University of North Carolina Press, pp. 101–131.

8180. Shankar, S. "Richard Wright's *Black Power*: Colonial Politics and the Travel Narrative," in *Richard Wright's Travel Writings: New Reflections*. Ed. Virginia Whatley Smith. Jackson: University Press of Mississippi, pp. 3–19.

8181. _____. *Textual Traffic: Colonialism, Modernity, and the Economy of the Text*. State University of New York Press, pp. 53, 83, 104, 119–147, 149, 150, 183, 197, 198. Treats W and *BP* extensively in a chapter entitled "Wright and Wrong in a Land of Pathos," considering from a postcolonial perspective such issues as tradition and modernity, black political power, racial estrangement, and kinship. Shankar also evaluates prior commentary on *BP* by Paul Gilroy, John M. Reilly, Anthony Appiah, and compares W's book to *Heart of Darkness*, Maya

Angelou's *All God's Children Need Traveling Shoes*, and C.L.R. James's *Nkrumah and the Ghana Revolution*. There is also comment on *BB* and *O*.

8182. Shulman, Robert. "Writers and Politics." in *Encyclopedia of American Studies*. Eds. Miles Orwell and Jay Mechling. New York: Grolier Educational, pp. 380–385. Mentions briefly *UTC* and *NS* (p. 383).

8183. Simms, L. Moody. "Federal Arts Projects," in *Encyclopedia of American Studies*. Eds. Miles Orwell and Jay Mechling. New York: Grolier Educational, Vol. 2, pp. 130–133. Mentions W briefly.

8184. Singh, Amritjit. "Harlem Renaissance," in *The Oxford Companion to United States History*. Ed. Paul S. Boyer. Oxford: Oxford University Press, 2001. Mentions briefly W and *NS*.

8185. Skurowski, Piotr. "U.S.– Eastern European Relations," in *Encyclopedia of American Studies*, Eds. Miles Orwell and Jay Mechling. New York: Grolier Educational, Vol. 2, pp. 263–266. Mentions W briefly.

8186. Smethurst, James. "Invented by Horror: The Gothic and African American Literary Ideology in *Native Son*." *African American Review*, 35 (Spring), 29–40. Explores W's use of gothic elements in the novel in relation to Southern folk culture and Northern mass culture. Using gothic themes, *NS* is anti-gothic because it rejects irrationalism and capitalism and affirms Communism.

8187. Smith, David Lionel. "The African American Short Story," in *The Columbia Companion to Twentieth-Century American Short Story*. Ed. Blanche H. Gelfant. New York: Columbia University Press, pp. 25–33. Notes that although *UTC* is protest fiction, W broadens his range in *EM* (pp. 28–29).

8188. _____. "Richard Wright (1908–1960)," in *The Columbia Companion to Twentieth-Century American Short Story*. Ed. Blanche H. Gelfant. New York: Columbia University Press, pp. 591–596. Comments on most of W's short stories, with special praise for "Big Boy Leaves Home," "Fire and Cloud," "The Man Who Was Almost a Man," and "The Man Who Lived Underground." Stresses the lighter tone of the later stories.

8189. Smith, Valerie. "Late Twen-tieth Century," in *The Concise Oxford Companion to African American Literature*. New York: Oxford University Press, pp. 469–472. Comments on W, mentioning ten of his books, and discusses his relation to Baldwin and Ellison (p. 470).

8190. Smith, Virginia Whatley. "'French West Africa': Behind the Scenes with Richard Wright, the Travel Writer," in her *Richard Wright's Travel Writings: New Reflections*. Jackson: University Press of Mississippi, pp. 179–214. Detailed account of W's conception of a book on French West Africa, his preparation for the project, its historical context, and its relation to his other travel books. Draws extensively on the unpublished manuscripts at Yale.

8191. _____. Introduction," in her *Richard Wright's Travel Writings: New Reflections*. Jackson: University Press of Mississippi, pp. xi + xv. Relates the book to the genre of travel writing, to the African American travel/slave narrative, and to W's interest in the Third World as a pioneer in postcolonialism. Smith also summarizes briefly the essays included in the collection by the following: S. Shankar Ngwarsungu Chiwengo, Jack B. Moore, Yoshinobu Hakutani, John Lowe, Keneth Kinnamon, Dennis F. Evans, and Smith herself (two essays).

8192. _____. "Richard Wright's Passage to Indonesia: The Travel Writer/Narrator as Participant/Observer of Anti-Colonial Imperatives in *The Color Curtain*," in her *Richard Wright's Travel Writings: New Reflections*. Jackson: University Press of Mississippi, pp. 78–115. In addition to an account of W's important role as "participant/observer" of the Bandung Conference, Smith provides information on the publication of the American and English editions of *CC*, centered mainly on issues concerning the genre of travel book, which W wished to expand from a touristic account to a sociopolitical ethnographic study.

8193. Snipes, Katherine, updated by Thomas J. Cassidy. "Richard Wright," in *Critical Survey of Short Fiction*. Second Revised Edition. Ed. Charles E. May. Pasadena: Saber Press, pp. 2560–2565.

8194. Sollors, Werner. "Jean Toomer's *Cane*: Modernism and Race in Interwar America," in *Jean Toomer and the Harlem Renaissance*.

Eds. Geneviève Fabre and Michel Feith. New Brunswick: Rutgers University Press, pp. 18–37. Mentions briefly *NS* (p. 34).

8195. Stange, Maren. "Documentary Photography and Photojournalism," in *Encyclopedia of American Studies*. Eds. Miles Orwell and Jay Mechling. New York: Grolier Educational, pp. 316–321. Mentions briefly *TMBV* (p. 318).

8196. Stange, Maren. "'Photographs Taken in Everday Life': *Ebony's* Photojournalistic Discourse," in *The Black Press: New Literary and Historical Essays*. Ed. Todd Vogel. New Brunswick: Rutgers University, pp. 207–227. Includes a discussion of W's "The Shame of Chicago" (pp. 220–224).

8197. Steffen, Therese. *Crossing Color: Transcultural Space and Place in Rita Dove's Poetry, Fiction, and Drama*. New York: Oxford University Press, pp. 26, 170, 174. Dove disavows influence of W on her work.

8198. Stepto, Robert B. "Michael Awkward. *Scenes of Instruction: A Memoir*." *African American Review*, 35 (Fall), 493–494. Mentions W briefly.

8199. St. Jean, Shawn. *Pagan Dreiser: Songs from American Mythology*. Madison-Teaneck, New Jersey: Fairleigh Dickinson University Press, pp. 28, 36. Brief mentions of W in relation to naturalism.

8200. Stockton, Kathryn Bond. "Review: Reading Details, Teaching Politics: Political Mantras and the Politics of Luxury." *College English*, 64 (September), 109–121. Contains a review of Claudia Tate's *Psychoanalysis and Black Novels* mentioning *SH* (p. 119).

8201. Swindell, Warren C. "The Role of Criticism in Black Popular Culture," in *African American Jazz and Rap: Social and Philosophical Examinations of Black Expressive Behavior*. Ed. James L. Conyers, Jr. Jefferson, NC, McFarland, pp. 20–32.

8202. Tate, Claudia, "*Black Women Writers at Work*: An Interview with Margaret Walker," in Maryemma Graham's *Fields Watered with Blood*, pp. 28–42.

8203. Tate, Greg. "Triple Threat." *The Village Voice* (16 October), 98–100. Review of Hazel Rowley's *Richard Wright: The Life and Times* as well as biographies of Baraka and

Fanon. Calls Rowley's book "traditional and gossipy" and notes the good use it makes of W's papers at Yale.

8204. Tavernier, Linda. "Abrahams, Peter. *The Black Experience in the 20th Century.*" *The Black Scholar*, 31 (Summer), 56. Mentions W briefly.

8205. ____. "*The Black Scholar* Books Received," *The Black Scholar*, 31 (Spring), 65–68. Contains a notice of David Marriott's *On Black Men* mentioning W briefly (p. 67.)

8206. ____. "*The Black Scholar* Books Received." *The Black Scholar*, 31 (Summer), 56–61. Mentions W briefly in a notice of *The Black Experience in the 20th Century* by Peter Abrahams (p. 56).

8207. Taylor, Clyde. "Oscar Micheaux and the Harlem Renaissance," in *Temples for Tomorrow: Looking Back at the Harlem Renaissance.* Eds. Geneviève Fabre and Michel Feith. Bloomington: Indiana University Press, p. 134. Notes that in *The Story of Dorothy Stanfield* Taylor is critical of a character that resembles W.

8208. Thurston, Michael. "'Bombed in Spain: Langston Hughes, the Black Press, and the Spanish Civil War," in *The Black Press: New Literary and Historical Essays.* Ed. Todd Vogel. New Brunswick: Rutgers University Press, pp. 140–158. Notes that W interviewed Louise Thompson on the Spanish Civil War for the *Daily Worker* (p. 154).

8209. Tolentino, Cynthia. "The Liberal, The Sociologist, and the Novelist: Narratives of Race and National Development in African American and Asian American Fiction of the 1940's" *American Quarterly*, 53 (December), 775–776. Abstract of a Brown University Dissertation treating *NS*.

8210. Traylor, Eleanor. "'Bolder Measures Crashing Through': Margaret Walker's Poem of the Century," in Maryemma Graham's *Fields Watered with Blood*, pp. 110–138. Mentions Walker's biography of W (p. 112) and W's challenge to black poets (p. 113).

8211. Trotter, Joe W., Jr. "African Americans," in *The Oxford Companion to United States History.* Ed. Paul S. Boyer. New York: Oxford University Press, pp. 11–15. Mentions briefly W and *NS* (p. 14)

8212. ____, Jr. "African Americans," in The Oxford Companion to *United States History.* Ed. Paul S. Boyer. Oxford University Press, 2001, pp. 11–15. Mentions briefly W and *NS* (p. 14).

8213. Tucker, Cynthia. "Introduction," in Lynda Koolish's *African American Writers: Portraits and Visions.* Jackson: University Press of Mississippi, pp. ix–x. Mentions W briefly.

8214. Tusa, Bobs M. "Introduction," in her and Herbert Randall's *Faces of Freedom Summer.* Tuscaloosa: The University of Alabama Press, pp. 1–28. Quotes teacher Sandra Adickes describing her Freedom School in Hattiesburg, where students were given paperbacks of *NS* and *BB* (p. 21).

8215. Washington, Robert E. *The Ideologies of African American Literature: From the Harlem Renaissance to the Black Nationalist Revolt.* Lanham, MD: Rowman & Littlefield, pp. 119–230, 249. Contains substantial treatments of W and his works in his Communist period and his existentialist phase. Treats or mentions *BB, BP, CC, EM, LT, LD, NS, O, PS, SH, TMBV, UTC,* and *WML.* Washington's approach is sociological and historical.

8216. Watkins, James H. "Autobiographical Authority and the Representation of 'Redneck' Masculinity in *A Childhood,*" in *Perspectives on Harry Crews.* Ed. Erik Bledsoe. Jackson: University Press of Mississippi, pp. 15–28. Refers to *BB* as having "canonical status."

8217. Watkins, Mel. "In Memoriam: Gwendolyn Brooks (1917–2000)." *The Black Scholar*, 31 (Spring), 51–54. Notes that W recommended Brooks to a publisher.

8218. Watts, Jerry Gafio. *Amiri Baraka: The Politics and Art of a Black Intellectual.* New York: New York University Press, pp. 116–117, 163–164, 198, 205, 379–380, 440–442, 460–461, 470, 472, 474, 482–483, 539. Comments on Baraka's shifting opinions on W on such topics as relation to black music, marriage to white women, African problems, Marxism, tradition in African American literature, the revolutionary tradition, politics, and others.

8219. ____. *Amiri Baraka: The Politics and Art of a Black Intellectual.* New York: New York University Press, pp. 116–117, 163–164, 198,

205, 379–380, 440–442, 460–461, 470, 474, 482, 483, 539. Comments on Baraka's view of W, Sartre on W, W on Africa, the attitude of the Black Arts Movement toward W, W and Baraka as Marxists, quotes from "How 'Bigger' Was Born," and mentions W elsewhere.

8220. Weixlmann, Joe. "Clarence Major's Singing Voice(s)," in *Clarence Major and His Art: Portraits of an African American Postmodernist.* Ed. Bernard W. Bell. Chapel Hill: University of North Carolina Press, pp. 243–263. Mentions *NS* (pp. 251, 253, 258) and "The Man Who Lived Underground" (pp. 251, 258) with brief comparisons to Major.

8221. Werner, Craig H. "Early Twentieth Century," in *The Concise Oxford Companion to African American Literature.* New York: Oxford University Press, pp. 466–469. Mentions W briefly (p. 466) and discusses W in relation to the Chicago Renaissance (p. 468).

8222. Wheeler, Elizabeth A. *Uncontained: Urban Fiction in Postwar America.* New Brunswick: Rutgers University Press, pp. 46, 104, 113. Comments on Himes's indebtedness to W.

8223. White, Craig Howard. "*Federal Writers' Project (FWP),*" in *The Concise Oxford Companion to African American Literature.* Eds. William L. Andrews, Frances Smith Foster, and Trudier Harris. New York: Oxford University Press, pp. 139–140.

8224. Willis, Deborah. "Photography," in *The Harvard Guide to African-American History.* Ed. Evelyn Brooks Higginbotham. Cambridge, MA: Harvard University Press, pp. 167–176. Lists *TMBV* (p. 176).

8225. Wilson, Charles E., Jr. *Gloria Naylor: A Critical Companion.* Westport, CT: Greenwood Press, pp. 16, 31, 34. Mentions briefly "Blueprint for Negro Writing," W's criticism of Hurston, and *NS.*

8226. Williams, Patricia Robinson. "Garvey, Marcus," in *The Concise Oxford Companion to African American Literature.* Eds. William L. Andrews, Frances Smith Foster, and Trudier Harris. New York: Oxford University Press, pp. 159–160.

8227. Wood, Jacqueline. "Sambo Subjects: 'Declining the Stereotype in Suzan-Lori Park's *The Death of the Last Black Man in the Whole En-*

tire World." *Studies in the Humanities*, 28 (June and December), 109–119.

8228. Woods, Paula L. "Decoding the History of Black Mysteries." *The Crisis*, 108 (September/October), 62–65. Mentions W briefly and includes a photograph of him smiling broadly.

8229. Wright, Richard. "*Black Boy.*" *Literary Cavalcade*, 53 (April), pp. 1–7. Contains quotations from *BB* biographical information on W, and a proposed essay topic.

8230. Wydeven, J.J. "*Theodore Dreiser and American Culture: New Readings*, ed. Yoshinobu Hakutani." *Choice*, 38 (January), 909. Notice mentioning W briefly.

8231. Ybarra, Michael J. "A Literary Sensation, a Precarious Existence." *Wall Street Journal* (4 September), A 20. Review of Hazel Rowley's *Richard Wright: The Life and Times.* Praises Rowley for good writing and prodigious research, but complains of the "odd absence of literary criticism."

8232. Young, Joseph A. "Phenomenology and Textual Power in Richard Wright's 'The Man Who Lived Underground.'" *MELUS*, 26 (Winter). Phenomenological reading of the novella, relating it to *NS* and *BB* and drawing on Edmund Husserl and Maurice Merleau-Ponty, as well as Robert Scholes's textual theory.

8233. Young, Robert. "The Linguistic Turn, Materialism and Race: Toward an Aesthetics of Crisis." *Callalloo*, 24 (Winter), pp. 334–344. Attempts to "reclaim a concept-based materialist understanding of race." Discusses *BB* as "an effective counter to 'narratives of specificity.'"

8234. Yow, Dede. "Bobbie Ann Mason (1940–)," in *The Columbia Companion to the Twentieth-Century American Short Story*. New York: Columbia University Press, pp. 358–360. Mentions W briefly.

2002

8235. Abbott, Megan E. *The Street Was Mine: White Masculinity in Hardboiled Fiction and Film Noir.* New York: Palgrave Macmillan, p. 223. Mentions W briefly.

8236. Allen, Jeffery Renard. "Courts and Cornerstones." *Poets & Writers Magazine*, 30 (January/February), 36–39. Mentions W briefly (p. 37).

8237. Als, Hilton. "More Harm Than Good." *The New Yorker*, 77 (11 February), 82–88. Mentions briefly *BB* (p. 88).

8238. Anon. "Africa to America to Paris: The Migration of Black Writers," in *Films for the Humanities and Social Sciences.* Princeton, NJ, p. 8. Distributor's notice mentioning W briefly.

8239. Anon. "America's Dream, *Richard Wright*," in *Teacher's Video Company English 2002.* Scottsdale, AZ: Teacher's Video Company, p. 16. Notice of a video of W's "most moving stories" featuring Wesley Snipes and Danny Glover.

8240. Anon. "Approaches to Teaching World Literature." *PMLA*, 117 (September), 1100. Lists James A. Miller's volume on *NS*.

8241. Anon. "*Black Manhood in James Baldwin, Ernest J. Gaines, and August Wilson* Keith Clark," *Illinois*

(Spring/Summer), p. 21. Mentions W briefly.

8242. Anon. "*Contemporary Black Men's Fiction and Drama.*" Ed. Keith Clark. *American Literature* 74 (June), 451. Review mentioning W briefly.

8243. Anon. "*Conversations with Margaret Walker.*" Ed. Maryemma Graham in *Mississippi.* Jackson: University Press of Mississippi (Fall/Winter) 2002-2003, p. 8. Catalog notice mentioning briefly Walker's friendship with W.

8244. Anon. "Edward M. Pavlić, *Crossroads Modernism: Descent and Emergence in African-American Literary Culture*," in *University of Minnesota Press Spring 2002 Titles.* Minneapolis: University of Minnesota Press, p. 31. Publisher's notice mentioning W briefly.

8245. Anon. "For My People: The Life and Writing of Margaret Walker," in *African American Perspectives 2002.* San Francisco: California Newsreel, p. 17 Video catalog notice mentioning her friendship with W.

8246. Anon. "Holtzbrinck Publishers." *PMLA*, 117 (November), 1686. Lists Hazel Rowley's biography of W.

8247. Anon. "Memoir, Biography, and Literature/Literary Criti-

cism," in *Mississippi.* Jackson: University Press of Mississippi, p. 26. Lists *Richard Wright's Travel Writings: New Reflections* with a reproduction of the front dust jacket.

8248. Anon. "Monday, 30 December." *PMLA*, 117 (November), 1538. Lists a convention paper by Crystal J. Lucky on "Liberation Theology in Richard Wright's 'Bright and Morning Star.'"

8249. Anon. "*Nationalism, Marxism, and African American Literature Between the Wars: A New Pandora's Box*," in *Mississippi*, Jackson: University Press of Mississippi (Fall Winter 2002-2003), p. 19. Catalog notice mentioning W briefly.

8250. Anon. "*Nationalism, Marxism, and African American Literature Between the Wars: A New Pandora's Box*," in *Mississippi*, Jackson: University Press of Mississippi (Fall-Winter 2002-2003), p. 19. Publisher's catalog notice mentioning W twice.

8251. Anon. "Native Son, *Richard Wright*," in *Teacher's Video Company English 2002.* Scottsdale, AZ: Teacher's Video Company, p. 69. Distributor's notice.

8252. Anon. "Native Son, *Richard Wright*," in *Teacher's Video Company English 2002.* Scottsdale, AZ: Teacher's Video Company, p. 69. Notice of a video of the 1986 film *NS*.

8253. Anon. "Native Son: The Life and Work of Richard Wright," in *Films for the Humanities and Social Sciences*. Princeton, NJ, p. 7. Distributor's notice of a video featuring commentary by Bebe Moore and John Wideman.

8254. Anon. "*Pagan Spain* by Richard Wright with an introductory essay by Faith Berry." *Mississippi* (Spring/Summer), pp. 18–19. Publisher's catalog review emphasizing W's effort to present "a sociological critique of a corrupt system of government."

8255. Anon. *Ralph Ellison: An American Journey*. San Francisco: California Newsreel, p. [3]. Video producer's brochure including a notice of Madison D. Lacy's 1994 video *Richard Wright: Black Boy* with blurbs by Charles Johnson and John Edgar Wideman.

8256. Anon. "Ralph Ellison: An American Journey." San Francisco: California Newsreel Resolution, p. [3]. Video producer's flyer containing a notice of Madison D. Lacy's *Richard Wright: Black Boy.*"

8257. Anon. "Ralph Ellison: An American Journey in *African American Perspectives 2002*. San Francisco: California Newsreel, p. 15. Video catalog notice calling the early Ellison W's protégée.

8258. Anon. "Recent Scholarship." *The Journal of American History*, 89 (June), 338–393. Lists Clare Eby's article "Slouching Toward Beastliness: Richard Wright's Anatomy of Thomas Dixon" (p. 338) and Jeff Karem's "'I Could Never Really Leave the South': Richard Wright's *American Hunger* (p. 339).

8259. Anon. "Recent Scholarship." *The Journal of American History*, 89 (December), 1190–1261. Lists a dissertation by Shawnrece on "Richard Wright and the Discourses of Race, Gender, and Religion" (p. 1192).

8260. Anon. "Richard Wright in Black Boy," in *African American Perspectives 2002*. San Francisco: California Newsreel, p. 19. Video catalog notice of the Madison D. Lacy film.

8261. Anon. "Richard Wright *Pagan Spain*," in *Mississippi*. Jackson: University Press of Mississippi (Fall/Winter 2002-2003) p. 23. Catalog listing.

8262. Anon. Wright, Richard," in *The New Encyclopaedia Britannica*. Chicago: Encyclopaedia Britannica, Vol. 12, p. 773. Biographical sketch mentioning *NS*, *BB*, *O*, *W*, *MS*, and *AH*.

8263. Anon. "*Richard Wright's Travel Writings: New Reflections*," in *Mississippi*. Jackson: University Press of Mississippi (Fall/Winter 2002-2003), p. 26. Catalog listing.

8264. Anon. "Richard Wright Video," in *Black History Month*. Plainview, NY: Great Events, p. 8. Catalog notice of Richard Wright: *Writing Is His Weapon.*

8265. Anon. "*Richard Wright's Travel Writing: New Reflections*," in *Mississippi*. Jackson: University Press of Mississippi (Fall/Winter 2002-2003), p. 26. Catalog listing.

8266. Anon. "Richard Wright: *Writings Is His Weapon*," in *Teacher's Vidio Company*. Scottsdale, AZ, p. 68. Catalog notice.

8267. Anon. "Richard Wright: *Writing Is His Weapon*." Scottsdale, AZ: *Teacher's Video Company*, p. 68. Distributor's notice.

8268. Anon. "Short Story Anthologies," in *Literature and Language 2002/2003*. Includes a notice of *The Signet Classic Book of Southern Short Stories* containing "Big Boy Leaves Home."

8269. Anon. "Sunday, 29 December." *PMLA*, 117 (November), 1517." Includes an announcement of a lecture by Julia Wright on "Richard Wright's Last Years: A Memoir."

8270. Anon. "'The Man Who Saw the Flood,' Richard Wright" *American Short Stories*. Boston: McDougal Littell, pp. 294–299. Reprints the story and includes photographs of W (pp. 294, 296).

8271. Anon. "*Touring Literary Mississippi* by Patti Carr Black and Marion Barnwell," in *Mississippi*. Jackson: University Press of Mississippi (Fall/Winter 2002-2003), p. 6. Catalog notice mentioning W briefly.

8272. Anon. "Voices of Diversity Poster Set," in *Black History Month*. Plainview, NY: Great Events, p. 38. Includes a reproduction of the W Poster.

8273. Anon. "2002 Zora Neale Hurston Richard Wright Award Winners." *The New York Review of Books*, 49 (21 November), 45. Announces Chinua Achebe for lifetime achievement and David Anthony Dawahare for debut in fiction.

8274. Applegate, E.C. "Ralph Ellison (1914–1994)," in his *American Naturalistic and Realistic Novelists: A Biographical Dictionary*. Westport, CT: Greenwood Press, pp. 127–130. Mentions W's invitation to Ellison to contribute to *New Challenge*.

8275. _____. "Richard Wright (1908–1960)," in his *American Naturalistic and Realistic Novelists: A Biographical Dictionary*. Westport, CT: Greenwood Press, pp. 403–406. Biographical sketch mentioning or summarizing *UTC*, *NS* (novel and play), *TMBV*, *BB*, *SH*, *BP*, *CC*, *LD*, and *EM*. Includes a bibliography of nine books about W.

8276. Ards, Angela. "Haki Madhubuti: The Measure of Man." *Black Issues Book Review*, 4 (March/April), pp. 1–5. Biographical sketch. Madhubuti recalls reading *BB* at an early age — "the first time I had been smacked in the face with the power of ideas."

8277. Asim, Jabari, "From Experience to Eloquence." *The Crisis*, 109 (May/June), 50–51. Quotes Charles T. Davis on *BB*.

8278. Baker, Barbara A. "Blues," in The *Companion to Southern Literature*. Eds. Joseph M. Flora and Lucinda MacKethan. Baton Rouge: Louisiana State University Press, pp. 112–113. Mentions W briefly.

8279. Baker, Houston A. Jr. "Blue Men, Black Writing, and Southern Revisions." *The South Atlantic Quarterly*, 101 (Winter), 7–17.

8280. Bashmakova, Louisa P. "Tom Quirk. *Nothing Abstract: Investigations in the American Literary Imagination*." *American Studies International*, 40 (October), 89–90. Review mentioning W briefly.

8281. Bates, Beth Tompkins. "The Migration's Legacy." *Footsteps*, 4, 38. Discusses W in relation to the Great Migration, drawing on and quoting from *BB*. Notes that the New Negro led to the Civil Rights Movement.

8282. Beppu, Keiko. "Japanese Contributions," in *American Literary Scholarships: An Annual 2000*. Ed. David Nordloh. Durham: Duke University Press, pp. 495–509. Mentions briefly a new journal entitled *Faulkner Studies*, which includes an article on W in its second issue.

8283. Berlant, Lauren. "Poor Eliza," in *No More Separate Spheres! A Next Wave American Studies Reader*. Eds. Cathy N. Davidson and Jessamyn Hatcher. Durham: Duke University Press, pp. 291–323. Mentions briefly *NS* and Bigger Thomas (p. 313).

8284. Berry, Faith, "Introduction," in *Pagan Spain* by Richard Wright. Jackson: University Press of Mississippi, pp. ix–xxvii. Treats the book as a turning point in W's career as he moves from racial issues to a study of Spain under Franco with its poverty and repression. Berry corrects W's numerous errors about Spain and its history, but admires his boldness in undertaking the work.

8285. Berry, Wes. "Toni Morrison's Revisionary 'Nature Writing': *Song of Solomon* and the Blasted Pastoral," in *South to a New Place: Region, Literature, Culture.* Eds. Suzanne W. Jones and Sharon Monteith. Baton Rouge: Louisiana State University Press, pp. 147–164. Mentions W briefly (pp. 148–150.)

8286. _____. "Toni Morrison's Revisionary 'Nature Writing': *Song of Solomon* and the Blasted Pastoral," in *South to a New Place: Region Literature, Culture.* Eds. Suzanne W. Jones and Sharon Monteith. Baton Rouge: Louisiana State University Press, pp. 147–164. Mentions W and *UTC* (p. 148, 150).

8287. Black, Patti Carr, and Marion Barwell. *Touring Literary Mississippi.* Jackson: University Press of Mississippi, pp. 36, 95, 105–106, 160, 172. Notes that Willie Morris sought out W in Paris, mentions Margaret Walker's friendship with W and her book on him, and provides a biographical sketch of W with photograph.

8288. Blair, Walter. "American Literature: The 20th Century," in *The New Encyclopedia Britannica.* Chicago: Encyclopedia Britannica, vol. 13, pp. 305–311. Calls *UTC*, *NS*, and *BB* "works of burning social protest, Dostoyevskyan in their intensity."

8289. Boan, Devon. *The Black "I": Author and Audience in African American Literature.* New York: Peter Lang, pp. 4, 7, 44. Mentions W's ideological realism and quotes from "Blueprint for Negro Writing" and from James A. Miller on Bigger Thomas.

8290. _____. *The Black "I": Author and Audience in African American Literature.* New York: Peter Lang, pp. 4, 7, 44. Mentions W's ideological realism as a new stage of African American Literature, quotes from "Blueprint for Negro Writing," and comments on James A. Miller's Bakhtinian view of *NS*.

8291. Bonetti, Kay. "An Interview with Margaret Walker Alexander," in *Conversations with Margaret Walker.* Ed. Maryemma Graham. Jackson: University Press of Mississippi, pp. 125–136. Reprint of 1992.

8292. Botto, Louis. "Majestic Theatre," in his *At This Theatre: 100 years of Broadway Shows, Stories and Stars.* Ed. Robert Viagas. New York: Applause Theatre & Cinema Books, pp. 252–260. Mentions the return engagement of the play *NS* in 1942.

8293. _____. "St. James Theatre," in his *At This Theatre: 100 Years of Broadway Shows, Stories, and Stars.* Ed. Robert Viagas. New York: Applause Theatre & Cinema Books, p. 260. Contains a paragraph on the play *NS*, "a dramatic Thunderbolt."

8294. Boyd, Molly. "Gothicism," in *The Companion to Southern Literature.* Eds. Joseph M. Flora and Lucinda MacKethan. Baton Rouge: Louisiana State University Press, pp. 311–316. Mentions the lynching of W's uncle.

8295. Brinkmeyer, Robert H., Jr. "*Peter Taylor: A Writer's Life.*" *The Southern Register* (Winter), 16–17. Review mentioning W briefly.

8296. _____. "Members in the Spotlight." *The Society for the Study of Southern Literature Newsletter*, 35 (May), pp. 6–7. Mentions a conference paper by John Lowe on "Southern Writers in Europe: The Examples of Richard Wright and Elizabeth Spencer."

8297. _____. "Recent or Forthcoming Member Publications." *The Society for the Study of Southern Literature Newsletter*, 35 (May), pp. 8–10. Lists Jeffrey J. Folks's *From Richard Wright to Toni Morrison* and John Lowe's "Richard Wright as Traveler/Ethnographer."

8298. Budd, Louis, J. "Twain, Mark," in The *Companion to Southern Literature.* Eds. Joseph M. Flora and Lucinda MacKethan. Baton Rouge: Louisiana State University Press, pp. 917–918. States that "while respecting *Huckleberry Finn*, Richard Wright took interest in Twain primarily as a mind and personality, deployed most engagingly in *The Innocents Abroad.*"

8299. Budick, Emily. "*The Identity Question: Blacks and Jews in Eu-rope and America.* By Robert Philipson." *American Studies*, 43 (Spring), 175. Review mentioning briefly *BB*.

8300. Burr, Zofia. *Of Women, Poetry and Power: Strategies of Address in Dickinson. Miles, Brooks, Lorde, and Angelou.* Urbana: University of Illinois Press, p. 116. Mentions W briefly.

8301. Butler, Robert. "Jeffery Renard Allen. *Rails Under My Back.*" *African American Review*, 36 (Spring), 170–171. Review mentioning briefly *NS*.

8302. Byerman, Keith E. "Race, Idea of," in *The Companion to Southern Literature.* Eds. Joseph M. Flora and Lucinda MacKethan. Baton Rouge: Louisiana State University Press, pp. 705–709. States that W "made his reputation by portraying the deep psychological effects of prejudice" (p. 709).

8303. Calloway, Catherine. "Fiction: The 1930s to the 1960s," in *American Literary Scholarship: An Annual 2000.* Durham: Duke University Press, pp. 307–331. Includes notices of the chapter on W in Philip Auger's *Native Sons in No Man's Land* (p. 309), Lawrence Jackson's essay on W and Ellison (p. 310), and Yoshinobu Hakutani's on W and Dreiser (p. 283).

8304. Campbell, Frank. "*Richard Wright: The Life and Times.*" *Biography: An Interdisciplinary Quarterly*, 25 (Winter), 273–274. Excerpt from 2001.

8305. Campbell, Ruth, "Interview with Margaret Walker," in *Conversations with Margaret Walker.* Maryemma Graham. Jackson: University Press of Mississippi, pp. 92–97.

8306. _____. "Interview with Margaret Walker," in *Conversations with Margaret Walker.* Jackson: University Press of Mississippi, pp. 92–97. Walker mentions W briefly as a great writer.

8307. Carmichael, Jacqueline Miller. "Margaret Walker's Reflections and Celebrations: An Interview," in *Conversations with Margaret Walker.* Ed. Maryemma Graham. Jackson: University Press of Mississippi, pp. 153–171.

8308. _____. "Margaret Walker's Reflections and Celebrations: An Interview," in *Conversations with Margaret Walker.* Jackson: University Press of Mississippi, pp. 153–171. Reprint of 1998.

8309. Carr, Brian, and Tova Cooper. "Zora Neale Hurston and Modernism at the Critical Limit." *Modern Fiction Studies*, 48 (Summer), 285–313. Includes comments on W's review of *Their Eyes Were Watching God* (pp. 291–292, 307–308).

8310. Carr, Robert. *Black Nationalism in the New World: Reading the African-American and West Indian*. Experience. Durham: Duke University Press, p. 15. Mentions W briefly.

8311. Cartwright, Keith. *Reading Africa Into American Literature: Epics, Fables, and Gothic Tales*. Lexington: The University Press of Kentucky, p. 69. Mentions W briefly.

8312. Chrisman, Robert. "Robert Hayden: The Transition Years, 1946–1948," in *Robert Hayden: Essays on the Poetry*. Eds. Laurence Goldstein and Robert Chrisman. The University of Michigan Press, pp. 129–154. Mentions W briefly (p. 132).

8313. Clark, Keith. *Black Manhood in James Baldwin, Ernest J. Gaines, and August Wilson*, Urbana: University of Illinois Press, pp. 3, 4,5, 6, 8, 13, 14, 16, 25, 27, 28, 31, 33, 38, 46, 47, 56, 58, 65, 66–68, 71–75, 78, 79, 81, 88, 89, 92, 110, 116, 128, 130, 134. Examines the response to W's masculinist model, especially in *NS* and *BB*, by the three writers. W's emphasis on "victimization isolation, and patriarchy has been replaced by stress on "community, camaraderie, and intimacy."

8314. Cobb, William Jelani. "Visible Man." *The Crisis*, 109 (September/October), 49. Review of Lawrence Jackson's biography of Ralph Ellison mentioning W briefly.

8315. Coleman, Wanda. "Book Reviewing, African-American Style." *The Nation*, 275 (16 September), 25–27, 29. Mentions W briefly (p. 26).

8316. _____. "On Reviewing Black Literature-African-American Style." *QBR: The Black Book Review* (October), 37. Mentions W briefly.

8317. Cook, Sylvia J. "Proletarian Novel," in *The Companion to Southern Literature*. Eds. Joseph Flora and Lucinda MacKethan. Baton Rouge: Louisiana State University Press, pp. 684–688. Mentions briefly W and *UTC* (pp. 686, 688).

8318. Croft, Robert W. *A Zora Neale Hurston Companion*. West-

port, CT: Greenwood Press, pp. xxvi, 156. Mentions W's unfavorable review of *Their Eyes Were Watching God*.

8319. Cromwell, Adelaide M. "Frazier's Background and an Overview," in *E. Franklin Frazier and the Black Bourgeoisie*. Columbia: University of Missouri Press, pp. 30–43. Mentions W briefly and quotes from his introduction to *Black Metropolis* (p. 34).

8320. Cruse, Harold. "Individualism and the 'Open Society,'" in *The Essential Harold Cruse: A Reader*. Ed. William Jelani Cobb. New York: Palgrave, pp. 49–56.

8321. _____. "Individualism and the 'Open Society,'" in *The Essential Harold Cruse: A Reader*. Ed. William Jelani Cobb. New York: Palgrave, pp. 49–56. Partial reprint of 1967.25.

8322. _____. "Letter to Ralph Story, "in *The Essential Harold Cruse: A Reader*. E. William Jelani Cobb, New York: Palgrave, pp. 238–243. Mentions briefly W and *NS* (pp. 239–240).

8323. _____. "Letter to Ralph Story," in *The Essential Harold Cruse: A Reader*." Ed. William Jelani Cobb. New York: Palgrave, pp. 238–243. Notes that *NS* was not well received by blacks and that W received career support from white women, not black women.

8324. _____. "Negroes and Jews — The Two Nationalisms and the Bloc(ked) Plurality" in *The Essential Harold Cruse: A Reader*. Ed. William Jelani Cobb. New York: Palgrave, pp. 71–90.

8325. Davies, Jude. "Yoshinobu Hakutani. *Theodore Dreiser and American Culture: New Readings*." *Journal of American Studies*, 36 (August), 360–361. Mentions W briefly.

8326. Davis, Eisa. "Lucille Clifton and Sonia Sanchez: A Conversation." *Callaloo*, 25 (Fall), 1038–1074. Mentions W briefly (p. 1061).

8327. Dawahare, Anthony. *Nationalism, Marxism and African American Literature Between the Wars: A New Pandora's Box*. Jackson: University Press of Mississippi, pp. 9, 12, 74, 105, 109, 111, 112, 113–115, 116, 117, 119–122, 124–130, 131, 132, 133. Argues that Marxism was more important than black nationalism in the twenties and thirties. The chapter "Richard Wright's Critique of Nationalist Desire uses a Marxist-

psychoanalytical approach to a reading of *LT* and *NS*. Also mentions "Blueprint for Negro Writing."

8328. Dickstein, Morris. *Leopards in the Temple: The Transforation of American Fiction 1945–1970*. Cambridge: Harvard University Press, pp. 4, 9, 29, 55, 60, 93, 181, 186, 189, 194–195, 204, 205–206, 209. Includes discussion of W and his relation to Himes, Ellison, and Baldwin. Mentions *NS*, *BB*, *AH*, and "The Man Who Lived Underground."

8329. Duck, Leigh Anne. "*Struggles Over the Word: Race and Religion in O'Connor, Faulkner, Hurston, and Wright.*" *Modern Fiction Studies*, 48 (Summer), 499–501. Review mentioning W's use of "biblical discourse" in *UTC*.

8330. Eagles, Brenda M. "A Bibliography of Dissertations Relating to Mississippi — 2001." *The Journal of Mississippi History*, 64 (Spring), 47–52. Lists dissertations treating W by Tara Tamisha Green, Dexter Jeffries, Frederick Jeffrey Karem, Jennifer Spungin, Byron Douglas Mason, Carolyn Elaine Perry, and Cynthia Hocson Tolentino.

8331. Ellis, Aimé J. "Where Is Bigger's Humanity? Black Male Community in Richard Wright's *Native Son*," *ANQ: A Quarterly Journal of Short Articles, Notes, and Reviews*, 15 (Summer), 23–30. Examines Bigger's relation to his black friends, finding elements of homosociality. His conversations with Gus, G.H., and Jack help "to purge the psychic pain of urban blight."

8332. Elliott, Michael A. *The Culture Concept: Writing and Difference in the Age of Realism*. Minneapolis: University of Minnesota Press, p. 183. Notes W's criticism of *Their Eyes Were Watching God*.

8333. "The Ethics of Living Jim Crow: An Autobiographical Sketch," in *Black Orpheus: Rhetoric and Readings*. Ed. Ruby M. Lewis. Boston: Person Custom Publishing, pp. 33–42. Reprints the essay and includes study questions.

8334. Evans, Gareth, and Robert Shulman. "*The Power of Political Art: The 1930s Literary Left*." *Journal of American Studies*, 36 (August), 377–378. Review mentioning Shulman's treatment of *NS*.

8335. Everett, Percival. "Foreword," in *Making Callaloo: 25 Years of Black Literature*. Ed. Charles

Henry Rowell. New York: St. Martin's Press, pp. xv–xvii. Mentions W briefly.

8336. Ewell, Barbara C., and Pamela Glenn Menke. "Introduction," in their *Southern Local Color: Stories of Region, Race, and Gender.* Athens: The University of Georgia Press, p. lxiv. Mentions W briefly.

8337. Eyerman, Ron. *Cultural Trauma: Slavery and the Formation of African American Identity.* Cambridge: Cambridge University Press, pp. 131, 145, 155–158. Discusses W's affiliation with the Left and the South Side Writers Group, Mentions *NS, UTC,* and *TMBV.* Also notes W's appearance on a radio program honoring Canada Lee in 1945.

8338. Fikes, Robert, Jr. "Adventures in Exoticism: The 'Black Life' Novels of White Writers." *The Western Journal of Black Studies,* 26 (Spring), 6–15. Mentions W briefly (p. 12).

8339. Fishkin, Shelley Fisher. "Desegregating American Literary Studies," in *Aesthetics in a Multicultural Age.* New York: Oxford University Press, pp. 121–134. Argues for more attention to works by black writers on white people and to works by white writers on black people. Includes a discussion of *SH* noting similarities of Erskine Fowler to Bigger Thomas (pp. 122–124).

8340. Fitzpatrick, Vincent. "Bibliographical Checklist." *Menckeniana,* No. 164 (Winter), II. Notes Arnold Rampersad's mention of W and Mencken in his chronology in W's *Early Works.*

8341. Fleming, Robert. "John A. Williams: A Writer Beyond 'isms." *Black Issues Book Review,* 4 (July/August) pp. 1–3. Quotes Williams saying that he was "bowled over by *NS,* "totally sympathizing with Bigger Thomas."

8342. _____. "*Richard Wright: The Life and Times* by Hazel Rowley." *Black Issues Book Review,* 4 (January-February). Favorable review praising Rowley's research and new insights into W's personality. The book "demonstrates that a biography can be relevant and entertaining without resorting to gossip, innuendo, or idle speculation."

8343. Flora, Joseph M. "Reconstruction," in *The Companion to Southern Literature.* Eds. Joseph M. Flora and Lucinda MacKethan, Baton Rouge: Louisiana State University Press, pp. 726–729. Notes that in *UTC* W dealt with sharecropping (p. 727).

8344. _____. "Sex and Sexuality," in *The Companion to Southern Literature.* Eds. Joseph M. Flora and Lucinda MacKethan. Baton Rouge: Louisiana State University Press, pp. 776–779. Notes that both Faulkner and W "portrayed the special plight of the black male as regards the white woman (p. 777).

8345. _____. "Short Story Cycles," in *The Companion to Southern Literature.* Eds. Joseph M. Flora and Lucinda MacKethan. Baton Rouge: Louisiana State University, pp. 796–799. Mentions briefly *UTC* (p. 799).

8346. Foley, Barbara. "New Historicism, Liberalism, and the Re-Marginalization of the Left." *The Minnesota Review* n.s. 55-7 (October), 302–318. Contains a substantial passage on Michael Szalay's *New Deal Modernism,* especially its treatment of W (pp. 310–311, 313), and also treats Catherine Jurca's view of *NS* in *White Diaspora* (pp. 315–317).

8347. Franklin, V.P., and Bettye Collier-Thomas. "Biography, Race Vindication, and African American Intellectuals." *The Journal of African American History,* 87 (Winter), 160–174. Mentions W briefly (p. 161).

8348. Freeburg, Christopher C. "*Imagining Grace: Liberating Theologies in the Slave Narrative Tradition.* By Kimberly Rae Connor." *American Literature,* 74 (September), 638–640. Mentions briefly *BB* (p. 639).

8349. Freibert, Lucy M. "Southern Song: An Interview with Margaret Walker," in *Conversations with Margaret Walker.* Ed. Maryemma Graham. Jackson: University Press of Mississippi, pp. 98–112.

8350. Fullen, Marilyn K. "James Baldwin," in her *Great Black Writers.* Greensboro, NC: Open Hand, pp. 43–51. Mentions briefly W's early encouragement of Baldwin (p. 46).

8351. Gabbin, Joanne V. "Conversation: Margaret Walker Alexander," in *Conversations With Margaret Walker.* Ed. Maryemma Graham. Jackson: University Press of Mississippi, pp. 176–187. Reprint of 1999.

8352. Gayle, Addison, Jr. "Cultural Strangulation: Black Literature and the White Aesthetic," in *Walkin' the Talk: An Anthology of African American Studies.* Upper Saddle River, NJ: Prentice Hall, pp. 538–543.

8353. Genter, Robert. "Toward a Theory of Rhetoric: Ralph Ellison, Kenneth Burke, and the Problem of Modernism." *Twentieth-Century Literature,* 48 (Summer), 191–214.

8354. Giles, Paul. *Virtual Americas: Transnational Fictions and the Transatlantic Imaginary.* Durham: Duke University Press, p. 270. Mentions Paul Gilroy's treatment of W.

8355. Gilmore, Brian. "Stand by the Man: Black America and the Dilemma of Patriotism." *The Progressive,* 66 (January), 24–27. Discusses the black reaction to the planes crashing into the Pentagon and to the issue of allegiance to the United States. Includes treatment of W's response to World War II.

8356. Giovani, Nikki. "Margaret Walker and Nikki Giovanni: Two Women, Two Views," in *Conversations with Margaret Walker.* Ed. Maryemma Graham. Jackson: University Press of Mississippi, pp. 3–18. Excerpt from 1974.80.

8357. Gordon, Lewis R. "Sociality and Community in Black: A Phenomenological Essay," in *Quest for Community and Identity: Critical Essays in Africana Social Philosophy* Ed. Robert E. Birt. Lanham, MD: Rowman Littlefield, pp. 105–123. Mentions briefly W, *NS,* and *O.*

8358. Graham, Maryemma. "Chronology," in her *Conversations with Margaret Walker.* Jackson: University Press of Mississippi, pp. xv–xiii. Mentions Walker's *Richard Wright: Daemonic Genius.*

8359. _____. *Conversations with Margaret Walker.* Jackson: University Press of Mississippi, p. xviii + 198. Contains interviews by Nikki Giovanni, Charles H. Rowell, Marcia Greenlee, Claudia Tate, John Griffin Jones, Ruth Campbell, Lucy M. Freibert, Jerry W. Ward, Kay Bonetti, Alferdteen Harrison, Maryemma Graham, Jacqueline Miller, Dilla Beukner, and Joanne V. Gabbin–most of them mentioning or discussing w.

8360. _____. "The Fusion of Ideas: An Interview with Margaret Walker Alexander," in her *Conversations with Margaret Walker.*" Jackson: University Press of Mississippi, pp. 143–152. Reprint of 1993.

8361. _____. "The Fusion of Ideas: An Interview with Margaret

Walker Alexander," in her *Conversations with Margaret Walker*. Jackson: University Press of Mississippi, pp. 143–152. Reprint of 1993.

8362. ____. "Introduction," in her *Conversations with Margaret Walker*. Jackson University of Mississippi Press, pp. vi–xiv. Mentions W's leadership of the Southside Writers Group (p. ix) and doubts that he was Walker's lover.

8363. ____. "The Fusion of Ideas: An Interview with Margaret Walker Alexander," in her *Conversations with Margaret Walker*. Jackson: University Press of Mississippi, pp. 143–153.

8364. Green, Tara T. "The Virgin Mary, Eve, and Mary Magdalene in Richard Wright's Novels." *CLA Journal*, 46 (December), 168–193. Analyzes the characterization of white women in W according to their biblical counterparts: Mary Dalton as Mary Magdalene, Eva Blount as the Virgin Mary, Gladys in *LD* and Mabel in *SH*. as Eve the temptress. "W's men may have ambiguous feelings about women, but they benefit from the white women's presence in their lives.

8365. Greenlee, Marcia. "Black Women and Oral History: Margaret Walker Alexander," in *Conversations with Margaret Walker*. Jackson: University Press of Mississippi, pp. 32–58. Reprint of 1990.

8366. ____. "Black Women and Oral History: Margaret Walker Alexander," in *Conversations with Margaret Walker*. Ed. Maryemma Graham. Jackson: University Press of Mississippi, pp. 32–58. Reprint of 1990.

8367. Griffin, Barbara L.J. "James Baldwin (1924–1987)," in *African American Autobiographers: A Sourcebook*. Ed. Emmanuel S. Nelson. Westport, CT: Greenwood Press, pp. 29–36. Comments on Baldwin's critique of W's protest fiction (pp. 30–32).

8368. Griffin, Barbara L.J. "James Baldwin (1924–1987)," in *African American Autobiographers: A Sourcebook*. Ed. Emmanuel S. Nelson. Westport, CT: Greenwood Press, pp. 29–36. Includes commentary on Baldwin's critique of *NS* and W's response (pp. 31–32, 34, 35).

8369. Griffith, Paul. "James Baldwin's Confrontation with Racist Terror in the American South: Sexual Mythology and Psychoneurosis in 'Going to Meet the Man.'" *Journal of Black Studies*, 32 (May), 506–527. Mentions briefly W and *NS* (p. 507).

8370. Griffiths, Frederick. "Copy Wright: What Is an (Invisible) Author?" *New Literary History*, 33 (Spring), 315–341. Analyzes issues of authorship, invisibility, and anonymity in *The Autobiography of an Ex-Colored Man*, *Invisible Man*, "The Ethics of Living Jim Crow," *BB*, "How 'Bigger Was Born," and black autobiographical narrative by unknown authors.

8371. Gussow, Adam. *Seems Like Murder Here: Southern Violence and the Blues Tradition*. Chicago: The University of Chicago Press, pp. 1, 32–33, 34, 44, 67, 68–69, 72, 79, 159, 168, 237, 244–245, 249, 278, 306. Comments on or quotes from *BB*, *Between the World and Me*, *NS*, "Big Boy Leaves Home," "The Ethics of Living Jim Crow," W's criticism of Hurston, and W's introduction to *Blues Fell This Morning*.

8372. Hakutani, Yoshinobu." Richard Wright's *Pagan Spain* and Cross-Cultural Discourse," in his *Postmodernity and Cross-Culturalism*, Madison-Teaneck, NJ: Fairleigh Dickinson UP, pp. 43–61.

8373. Hancuff, Rich. "William J. Maxwell. *New Negro, Old Left: African-American Writing and Communism Between the Wars*." *American Studies International*, 40 (October), 97. Review including comment on Maxwell's treatment of W.

8374. Harde, Roxanne. "'We will make our own future: Text': 'Allegory, Iconoclasm, and Reverence in Ishmael Reeds's *Mumbo Jumbo*." *Critique*, 43 (Summer), 361–377. Mentions briefly W (p. 362) and *NS* (p. 347)

8375. Harper, Donna Akiba Sullivan. "Langston's Simple Genius." *The Crisis*, 109 (January/February), 32–35. Mentions briefly W and *NS* (p. 32).

8376. Harper, Michael S. "Every Shut-Eye Aint Asleep/Every Goodbye Aint Gone: Robert Hayden (1913–1980), in *Robert Hayden: Essays on the Poetry*. Eds. Laurence Goldstein and Robert Chrisman. The University of Michigan Press, pp. 104–111. States that although Hayden never met W, they corresponded.

8377. Harris, James Henry. *The Courage to Lead Leadership in the African American Urban Church*. Lanham, MD: Rowman & Littlefield, p. 4. Mentions W briefly.

8378. Harris, Leonard. "Community: What Type of Entity and What Type of Moral Commitment?," in *The Quest for Community and Identity: Critical Essays in Africana Social Philosophy*. Ed. Robert E. Birt. Lanham, MD: Rowman & Littlefield, pp. 243–255.

8379. Harris-Lopez, Trudier. *South of Tradition: Essays on African American Literature*. Athens; The University of Georgia Press, pp. 33, 51, 63, 133. Comments on Bigger as "crazy nigger," finds an autobiographical element in *NS*, mentions Cross Damon, and notes that Bernice in August Wilson's *The Piano Lesson* echoes Sarah in "Long Black Dream."

8380. Harris, Trudier. "Lynching," in *The Companion to Southern Literature*. Eds. Joseph M. Flora and Lucinda MacKethan. Baton Rouge: Louisiana State University Press, pp. 462–464. Comments on lynching as a subject in W's work, especially concerning the sexual taboo.

8381. Harrison, Alferdteen. "Looking Back: A Conversation with Margaret Walker," in *Conversations with Margaret Walker*. Ed. Maryemma Graham. Jackson: University Press of Mississippi, pp. 137–142.

8382. Hayden, Robert. "An Interview with Dennis Gendron," in *Robert Hayden: Essays on the Poetry*. Eds. Laurence Goldstein and Robert Chrisman. Ann Arbor: The University of Michigan Press, pp. 15–29. Mentions briefly W (p. 20) and *NS* (p. 24).

8383. Heavilin, Barbara A. *John Steinbeck's The Grapes of Wrath: A Reference Guide*. Westport, CT: Greenwood Press, p. 77. Mentions briefly *UTC*.

8384. Hefferman, Lee. "*Richard Wright and the Library Card*." *Book Links* (February-March), 39. Favorable notice of William Miller's juvenile drawn from the library episode in *BB*.

8385. Henderson, Carol E. *Scarring the Black Body: Race and Representation in African American Literature*. Columbia: University of Missouri Press, pp. 113, 120–123, 138, 142–146, 149–151. Includes substantial discussion of physical and psychic scarring of the black male body in W and other writers. Treats *NS*, "Between the World and Me," and *EM* (especially "The Man Who Killed a Shadow").

8386. Herbert, T. Walter. *Sexual Violence and American Manhood.* Cambridge: Harvard University Press. Includes discussion of *NS* (pp. 25, 106–107, 116–128, 138), *SH* (pp. 107, 125–126), and *UTC* (p. 116). *NS* "explores the complex relationships that link white racism and economic oppression to the gender politics that encompasses white and black men."

8387. Hernton, Calvin. "Shining," in *Robert Hayden: Essays on the Poetry.* Eds. Laurence Goldstein and Robert Chrisman. The University of Michigan Press, pp. 322–327.

8388. Hertzberg, Hendrik. "Can You Forgive Him?" *The New Yorker,* 78 (11 March), 85–89. Mentions W briefly as a contributor to *The God That Failed* (p. 85).

8389. Hietala, Thomas R. *The Fight of the Century: Jack Johnson, Joe Louis, and the Struggle for Racial Equality.* Armonk, NY: M.E. Sharpe, pp. 3–5, 185, 200–201, 211, 350. Begins with an account of W's life in the South, recounting at length the episode of Shorty, the elevator operator. For W, his contemporaries Johnson and Louis had symbolic importance. Also comments on "Joe Louis Uncovers Dyaomite' and quotes from *TMBV* and mentions *TMBV*.

8390. [Hill, Cason L.] "Contributors." *CLA Journal,* 45 (March) p. ii. Notes that Eberhard Alsen has published on W.

8391. Hitchcock, Bert. "Deep South," in *The Companion to Southern Literature.* Eds. Joseph M. Flora and Lucinda MacKethan. Baton Rouge: Louisiana State University Press, pp. 200–202. Mentions W briefly.

8392. Hobbs, Richard S. *The Cayton Legacy: An African American Family.* Pullman: Washington State University press, pp. 110, 114, 119, 121–123, 127, 129–146, 183. Substantial coverage of the Cayton-W friendship, the Chicago scene, and Cayton's plans to write a biography of W.

8393. Hobson, Fred. "Southern Women's Autobiography," in *The History of Southern Women's Literature.* Eds. Carolyn Perry and Mary Louise Weaks. Baton Rouge: Louisiana State University Press, pp. 268–

274. Mentions W briefly (pp. 270, 273).

8394. _____. "Telling About the South," in *The Companion to Southern Literature.* Eds. Joseph M. Flora and Lucinda MacKethan. Baton Rouge: Louisiana State University Press, pp. 878–880. Mentions W briefly.

8395. Horton, James Oliver, and Lois E. Horton. *Hard Road to Freedom: The Story of African America.* New Brunswick: Rutgers University Press, Vol. Two, pp. 80–84. Begins with an account of W's early life as emblematic, especially in relation to the Great Migration.

8396. Horton-Stallings, LaMonda. "*Contemporary Black Men's Fiction and Drama: Author, Keith Clark.*" The Western Journal of *Black Studies,* 26 (Fall), 184–185. Review mentioning W briefly.

8397. _____. "*Contemporary Black Men's Fiction and Drama.*" *The Western Journal of Black Studies,* 26 (Fall), 184–185. Review mentioning W briefly.

8398. Howard, Jenifer. "*Richard Wright: The Life and Times,* by Hazel Rowley." *The Washington Post Book World* (4 August), p. 11. Highly favorable notice, It "is long on sheer narrative momentum."

8399. Hoye, Timothy. "Szalay, Michael. *New Deal Modernism: American Literature and the Invention of the Welfare State.*" *Studies in the Novel,* 34 (Summer), pp. 240–243. Review mentioning W briefly.

8400. Hubbard, Lee, "Out There: Mavericks of Black Literture." *Black Issues Book Review,* 4 (July-August), p. 1. Review mentioning W briefly.

8401. Hughes, Langston. "Black Writers in a Troubled World," in *Essays on Art, Race, Politics, and World Affairs,* volume 9 of *The Collected Works of Langston Hughes.* Ed. Christopher De Santis. Columbia: University of Columbia Press, pp. 474–479. Mentions briefly W and *NS*.

8402. _____." Culture Via the Back Door," in *The Collected Works of Langston Hughes.* Vol. 9: *Essays on Art, Race, Politics, and World Affairs.* Ed. Christopher C. De Santis. Columbia: University of Missouri Press, pp. 263–265.

8403. _____. "Democracy and Me," in *The Collected Works of Langston Hughes.* Vol. 9: *Essays on Art, Race, Politics, and World Affairs.*

Ed. Christopher C. De Santis. Columbia: University of Missouri Press, pp. 203–206. Speech at the Third Writers' Congress, calls W an "excellent craftsman."

8404. _____. "*Ebony's* Nativity: An Evaluation from Birth," in *The Collected Works of Langston Hughes.* Vol. 9: *Essays on Art, Race, Politics, and World Affairs.* Ed. Christopher C. De Santis. Columbia: University of Missouri Press, pp. 425–429.

8405. _____. "A Fine New Poet," in *Essays on Art, Race, Politics, and World Affairs,* volume 9 of *The Collected Works of Langston Hughes.* Ed. Christopher DeSantis. Columbia: University of Missouri Press, pp. 532–537. Mentions briefly W and *TMBV* (p. 532).

8406. _____. "From Harlem to Paris," in *Essays on Art, Race, Politics, and World Affairs,* volume 9 of *The Collected Works of Langston Hughes.* Ed. Christopher De Santis. Columbia: University of Missouri Press, pp. 541–542.

8407. _____. "The Future of Black America," in *The Collected Works of Langston Hughes.* Vol. 9: *Essays on Art, Race, Politics, and World Affairs.* Ed. Christopher C. De Santis. Columbia: University of Missouri Press, pp. 229–232. Reprint of 1943.43.

8408. _____. "Greetings, Good Neighbors," in *The Collected Works of Langston Hughes.* Vol. 9: *Essays on Art, Race, Politics, and World Affairs.* Ed. Christopher C. De Santis. Columbia: University of Missouri Press, pp. 251–253. Essay written in the mid forties noting the success of *NS* in Brazil and Argentina.

8409. _____. "Introduction," in his *The Best Short Stories by Negro Writers*: An *Anthology from 1899 to the Present,* in *Essays on Art, Race, Politics, and World Affairs,* Volume 9 of *The Collected Works of Langston Hughes.* Ed. Christopher De Santis. Columbia: University of Missouri Press, pp. 525–529.

8410. _____. "It's About Time," in *Essays on Art, Race, Politics, and World Affairs,* volume 9 of *The Collected Works of Langston Hughes.* Ed. Christopher De Santis. Columbia: University of Missouri Press, pp. 262–263. Mentions W briefly.

8411. _____. "Langston Hughes' Speech at the National Assembly of Authors and Dramatists Symposium: 'The Writer's Position in America,'" in *The Collected Works of*

Langston Hughes. Vol. 9: *Essays on Art, Race, Politics, and World Affairs.* Ed. Christopher De Santis. Columbia: University of Missouri Press, pp. 357–359. Reprint of 1957.

8412. _____. "The Negro and American Entertainment," in *Essays on Art, Race, Politics, and World Affairs,* Vol. 9: *The Collected Works of Langston Hughes.* Ed. Christopher C. De Santis. Columbia: University of Missouri Press, pp. 430–454.

8413. _____. "Negro Writers and the War," in *The Collected Works of Langston Hughes.* Vol. 9: *Essays on Art, Race, Politics, and World Affairs.* Ed. Christopher C. De Santis. Columbia: University of Missouri Press, pp. 215–219. Essay written in 1942 mentioning W briefly.

8414. _____. "Richard Wright's Last Guest," in *The Collected Works of Langston Hughes.* Vol. 9: *Essays on Art, Race, Politics, and World Affairs.* Ed. Christopher C. De Santis. Columbia: University of Missouri Press, pp. 384–385.

8415. _____. "Some Practical Observations: A Colloquy," *The Collected Works of Langston Hughes.* Vol. 9: Essays on Art, Race, Politics, and World Affairs. Ed. Christopher C. De Santis. Columbia: University of Missouri Press, pp. 306–310.

8416. _____. "The Streets of Chicago," in *Essays on Art, Race, Politics, and World Affairs,* volume 9 of *The Collected Works of Langston Hughes.* Ed. Christopher De Santis. Columbia: University of Missouri Press, pp. 327–331. Mentions briefly *NS* (p. 327).

8417. _____. "The Twenties: Harlem and Its Negritude," in *The Collected Works of Langston Hughes.* Vol. 9: *Essays on Art, Race, Politics, and World Affairs.* Ed. Christopher C. De Santis. Columbia: University of Missouri Press, pp. 465–474. Reprint of 1966.80.

8418. _____. "The Woes of a Writer," in *The Collected Works of Langston Hughes.* Vol. 9: *Essays on Art, Race, Politics, and World Affairs.* Ed. Christopher C. De Santis. Columbia: University of Missouri Press, pp. 390–392.

8419. Huisman, Leo I. "Richard Wright's Blue Prose." *Michigan Academician,* 34 (Spring), 57. Abstract of a conference paper on "Long Black Song." Sarah symbolizes non-violent hope.

8420. Idol, John L., Jr. "Com-munity," in *The Companion to Southern Literature.* Eds. Joseph M. Flora and Lucinda MacKethan. Baton Rouge: Louisiana State University Press, pp. 175–178.

8421. Ikard, David. "Love Jones: A Black Male Feminist Critique of Chester Himes's *If He Hollers Let Him Go.*" *African American Review,* 36 (Summer), pp. 299–310. Notes that several critics consider the protagonist of this Himes novel" a socially conscious Bigger Thomas" (p. 300).

8422. Irons, Susan H. "Anthologies of Southern Literature," in *The Companion to Southern Literature.* Eds. Joseph M. Flora and Lucinda MacKethan. Baton Rouge: Louisiana State University Press, pp. 35–39. Notes that *The Literature of the South* included W, the first anthology to do so.

8423. Ishizuka, Hideo. "Translator's Afterword," in the Japanese translation of *PS.* Summarizes W's career and states that W's nonfiction is an interpretation of Spanish culture among many others.

8424. Jackson, Lawrence. *Ralph Ellison: Emergence of Genius.* New York: Wiley, xiii + 498 pp. Contains extensive discussion of the W-Ellison relationship, drawing on abundant quotations from unpublished letters and diary entries by W, Ellison, Langston Hughes, and others. Emphasizes W's tutelage of Ellison, Baldwin and Himes. That of Ellison was political as well as literary. The book ends with the publication of *Invisible Man,* by which time the close, fraternal friendships had ended. The New York literary and political scene in the thirties and forties is fully evoked, including W's dealings with the Communist Party, his reading with Ellison of Unamuno, competition among black writers, and much else. *UTC, NS, BB, LT,* "Blueprint for Negro Writing," "I Tried to be a Communist," "The Man Who Lived Underground," *O, SH, TMBV,* and *WML,* are all mentioned or discussed.

8425. James, Charles L. "Arna Bontemps: Harlem Renaissance Writer, Librarian, and Family Man." *The Crisis,* 109 (September/October), 22–28. Mentions W briefly (p. 24).

8426. Jebb, John F. "Crimes and Criminals," in *The Companion to Southern Literature.* Eds. Joseph M. Flora and Lucinda MacKethan. Baton Rouge: Louisiana State University Press, pp. 192–194. Comments briefly on *UTC.*

8427. Jennings, Regina. "Cheikh Anta Diop, Malcolm X, and Haki Madhubuti: Claiming and Containing Continuity in Black Language and Institutions." *Journal of Black Studies,* 33 (November), 126–144. Notes that Madhubuiti read *BB* at an early age.

8428. Johnson, Charles. "Issues & Views." *The Crisis,* 109 (March/April), 17–20. Essay on Ralph Ellison's mentioning Larry Neal's 1965 essay on W (p. 19) and quoting from an Ellison letter to Albert Murray in 1952: "We've taken on in our first books a task of defining reality which none of the other boys had the equipment to handle — except Wright, and he could never bring himself to conceive a character as complicated as himself (p. 20).

8429. Johnson, Claudia Durst, and Vernon Johnson. "Introduction," in their *The Social Impact of the Novel.* Westport, CT: Greenwood Press, pp. vii–xvi. Mentions W briefly (p. x).

8430. _____. "Native Son, by Richard Wright (United States, 1940)," in their *The Social Impact of the Novel.* Westport, CT: Greenwood Press, pp. 299–300. Places the novel in its social and historical context and summarizes the plot.

8431. Johnson, Vernon Damani, and Bill Lyne. "Introduction," in their *Walkin' the Talk: An Anthology of African American Studies.* Upper Saddle River, NJ: Prentice Hall, pp. xv–xx. Mentions W briefly (p. xix).

8432. _____. "Preface," in their *Walkin' the Talk: An Anthology of African American Studies.* Upper Saddle River, NJ: Prentice Hall, pp. xiii–xiv. Mentions briefly *WML.*

8433. Jones, John Griffin. "A Mississippi Writer Talks," in *Conversations with Margaret Walker.* Jackson: University Press of Mississippi, pp. 72–91.

8434. _____. "A Mississippi Writer Talks," in *Conversations with Margaret Walker.* Ed. Maryemma Graham. Jackson: University Press of Mississippi, pp. 72–91.

8435. Jones, J. Sydney "Richard Wright," in *Authors and Artists for Young Adults.* Detroit: Gale Research, pp. 253–263. Provides summaries of W's biography, literary career, and writings, together with critical comments and a bibliography.

8436. Jones, Suzanne W. "I'll Take My Land: Contemporary Southern Agrarians," in *South to a New Place: Region, Literature, Culture.* Eds. Suzanne W. Jones and Sharon Monteith. Baton Rouge: Louisiana State University Press, pp. 121–146. Mentions W briefly (p. 121).

8437. _____. "Race Relations," in *The Companion to Southern Literature.* Eds. Joseph M. Flora and Lucinda MacKethan. Baton Rouge: Louisiana State University Press, pp. 709–714. Mentions briefly "Big Boy Leaves Home" (p. 714).

8438. Jordan, June." Requiem for the Champ." *The Progressive*, 66 (August), 14–15.

8439. Kaplan, Carla, "Introduction," in her *Zora Neale Hurston: A Life in Letters.* New York: Random House, pp. 15, 26. Notes that W accused Hurston of pandering to whites. In a letter to William Bradford Huie dated 6 September 1954, Hurston accuses W of "trashy writing" (p. 719).

8440. Katz, Alan. "Transition is Tugging at a Local Avant-Garde Author," in *Conversations with Clarence Major.* Ed. Nancy Bunge. Jackson: University Press of Mississippi, pp. 51–54.

8441. Kelley, Robin D.G. *Freedom Dreams: The Black Radical Imagination.* Boston: Beacon Press, pp. 38, 50, 54, 174, 181–184, 186, 187. Argues for W's use of surrealism and comments on W and Communism.

8442. King, Kimbal. "Drama, 1900 to Present," in *The Companion to Southern Literature.* Eds. Joseph M. Flora and Lucinda MacKethan. Baton Rouge: Louisiana State University Press, pp. 225–229. Mentions briefly the play *NS*.

8443. King, Richard H. "Racism," in *The Companion to Southern Literature.* Eds. Joseph M. Flora and Linda MacKethan. Baton Rouge Louisiana State University Press, pp. 714–716. Comments on *NS* and *BB* as narratives of escape from racism.

8444. Kirby, David. *What Is a Book?* Athens: The University of Georgia Press, pp. 190, 194. Reports placement of *BB* and *NS* on various reading lists. Mentions *BB* and *NS* in a discussion of the literary canon.

8445. Knadler, Stephen P. *The Fugitive Race: Minority Writers Resisting Whiteness.* Jackson: University Press of Mississippi, pp. xiii, xxvii, 146–158. In a chapter on "Reembodying the 'Savage' State: Wright's *Savage Holiday*, Knadler argues that the work involves gender anxiety–even homosexual panic–as well as Freudian psychology and social criticism. He also notes W's uneasiness about men dancing with men in *BP*.

8446. _____. "Transition is Tugging at a Local Avant-Garde Author," in *Conversations with Clarence Major.* Ed. Nancy Bunge. Jackson: University Press of Mississippi, pp.

8447. Kreyling, Michael. "Biography," in *The Companion to Southern Literature.* Eds. Joseph M. Flora and Lucinda MacKethan. Baton Rouge: Louisiana State University Press, pp. 100–103. Includes comment on *BB* and on biographies of W by Constance Webb, Michel Fabre, and Margaret Walker.

8448. "Las estrellas son negras' Irra: Two Post-Colonial Subjects of Literature of the African Diaspora." *CLA Journal*, 46 (December), 207–225. Compares *NS* and a novel by Arnoldo Palacios. Relies on Post-Colonial Theory.

8449. Lee, Kun Jong. "The African-American Presence in Younghill Kang's *East Goes West.*" *CLA Journal*, 45 (March), 329–359. Mentions W briefly (p. 342).

8450. Lee, Lester P., Jr. "*Richard Wright: The Life and Times.*" *Harvard Review*, No. 22 (Spring), 210–212. Favorable review praising Rowley's "keen eye for historical detail, accuracy, and context" (p. 210).

8451. Lee, A. Robert. "Dwight A. McBride, *James Baldwin Now.*" *Journal of American Studies*, 36 (December), 540–541. Mentions W briefly.

8452. Leonard, John. "Ralph Ellison, Sort of (Plus Hemingway and Salinger)," in his *Lonesome Rangers: Homeless Minds, Promised Lands, Fugitive Cultures.* New York: The New Press, pp. 134–146. Mentions W briefly (pp. 135, 145).

8453. Lewis, Nghana. "'We Must Speak with the Same Weapons': Reinscribing Resistance in Zora Neale Hurston's *Dust Tracks on a Road.*" *CLA Journal*, 45 (March), 311–328. Quotes briefly from "Blueprint for Negro Writing (p. 313).

8454. Lewis, Ruby M., ed. "The Ethics of Living Jim Crow: An Autobiographical Sketch," in *Black Orpheus: Rhetoric and Readings.* Boston: Pearson Custom, pp. 33–42. Reprints the essay and includes study questions.

8455. Lingeman, Richard R. *Sinclair Lewis: Rebel from Main Street.* New York: Random House, p. 494. Mentions Lewis's favorable response to *BB*.

8456. Link, Katherine. "'Illuminating the Darkened Corridors': An Interview with Alexs Pate." *African American Review*, 36 (Winter), 597–609. Pate mentions W briefly (p. 607).

8457. Lisker, Donna. "'Controversy Only Means Disagreement': Alice Childress's Activist Drama," in *Southern Women Playwrights: New Essays in Literary History and Criticism.* Eds. Robert L. McDonald and Linda Rohrer Paige. Tuscaloosa: The University of Alabama Press, pp. 73–88. Mentions W briefly (p. 73).

8458. Logan, Shirley Wilson. "'What Are We Worth': Anna Julia Cooper Defines Black Women's Work at the Dawn of the Twentieth Century," in *Sister Circle: Black Women and Work.* Eds. Sharon Harley and The Black Women and Work Collective. New Brunswick: Rutgers University Press, pp. 146–163. Comments on the issue of the commencement speech in *BB* (p. 147).

8459. Lowe, John. "'Let the People Sing!': Zora Neale Hurston and the Dream of a Negro Theater," in *Southern Women Playwrights: New Essays in Literary History and Criticism.* Eds. Robert L. McDonald and Linda Rohrer Paige. Tuscaloosa: The University of Alabama Press, pp. 11–26. Mentions W briefly (p. 14).

8460. Lucy, Robin Jane. "Chester Bomar Himes (1909–1984)," in *African American Autobiographers: A Sourcebook.* Ed. Emmanuel S. Nelson. Westport, CT: Greenwood Press, pp. 185–191. Comments on Himes's break with W in France.

8461. Maccarone. "Adapting *Native Son.*" *Stage Directions* (June), 34–35. Describes an adaptation of the play by Christopher McElroen with the approval of Ellen Wright for the classical theatre of Harlem. This version emphasizes W's dialogue and restores elements that Paul Green cut.

8462. MacKethan, Lucinda. "African American Spirituals," in *The Companion to Southern Literature.* Eds. Joseph M. Flora and Lucinda MacKethan. Baton Rouge: Louisiana State University Press, pp. 19–21. Notes W's use of spirituals in *UTC.*

8463. _____. "Hurston, Zora Neale, in *The Companion to Southern Literature.* Eds. Joseph M. Flora and Lucinda MacKethan. Baton Rouge: Louisiana State University Press, pp. 363–364. Mentions briefly W's "scathing review" of *Their Eyes Were Watching God.*

8464. _____. "The Modern Novel," in *The History of Southern Women's Literature.* Eds. Carolyn Perry and Mary Louise Weaks. Baton Rouge: Louisiana State University Press, pp. 251–268. Mentions W briefly (p. 252).

8465. _____. "Wright, Richard," in *The Companion to Southern Literature.* Eds. Joseph M. Flora and Lucinda MacKethan. Baton Rouge: Louisiana State University Press, pp. 1003–1104. Biographical sketch emphasizing W's early career and his protest against racism.

8466. Marcus, Jane. "Suptionpremises." *Modernism/Modernity,* 9 (September), 490–502. Includes a photograph of *TMBV* (p. 490) and mentions W briefly (p. 495).

8467. Martin, Herbert Woodward, and Ronald Primeau. "Introduction to the Short Stories," in their *In His Own Voice: The Dramatic and Other Uncollected Works of Paul Lawrence Dunbar.* Athens: Ohio University Press, pp. 215–219. Mentions W briefly (p. 215).

8468. Martin, Herbert Woodward. "Marilyn Nelson, *Carver: A Life in Poems." African American Review,* 36 (Summer), pp. 345–349. Mentions briefly "Between the World and Me" (p. 347).

8469. Martin, Philip. "A Deep Song Voice." Little Rock *Arkansas Democrat Gazette* (27 January), Section E, pp. 1–2. Mentions W briefly.

8470. Martin, Tony. "John Cullen Gruesser. *Black on Black: Twentieth-Century African American Writing About Africa." African American Review,* 36 (Spring), 147–149. Review mentioning briefly *BP.*

8471. Mason, Theodore O., and Gary Lee Stonum. "Themes, Topics,

Criticism," in *American Literary Scholarship: An Annual 2000.* Ed. David J. Nordloh. Durham: Duke University Press, pp. 435–449. Mentions W briefly (p. 449).

8472. _____. "Themes, Topics, Criticism," in *American Literary Schoarship: An Annual 2000.* Durham: Duke University Press, pp. 435–449. Contains a review of Dale Peterson's *Up from Bondage* mentioning W briefly (p. 448).

8473. May, Charles E. "Short Story, 1900 to World War II," in *The Companion to Southern Literature.* Eds. Joseph M. Flora and Lucinda MacKethan. Baton Rouge: Louisiana State University Press, pp. 787–790. Comments on "Bright and Morning Star," "Big Boy Leaves Home," and "The Man Who Lived Underground."

8474. Maxwell, William J. "Richard Iton. *Solidarity Blues: Race Culture, and the American Left." African American Review,* 36 (Winter), 687–689. Mentions W briefly.

8475. McCaffery, Larry, and Jerzy Kutnik. "Beneath a Precipice: An Interview with Clarence Major," in *Conversations with Clarence Major.* Ed. Nancy Bunge. Jackson: University Press of Mississippi, pp. 70–92.

8476. McCluskey, John, Jr. "Jerry Bryant. *Victims and Heroes: Racial Violence in the African American Novel." African American Review,* 36 (Spring), 143–144. Review with favorable comments on Bryant's treatment of Bigger as an existential hero.

8477. McGowan, Todd. *The Feminine "No!" Psychoanalysis and the New Canon.* Albany: State University of New York Press, pp. 85–86. Notes W's disparagement of *Their Eyes Were Watching God.*

8478. Meer, Sarah. "Claudia Tate, *Psychoanalysis and Black Novels: Desire and the Protocol of Race." Journal of American Studies,* 36 (April), 184–185. Favorable review, especially on Tate's treatment of *SH.*

8479. Meriwether, James H. *Proudly We Can Be Africans: Black Americans and Africa 1935–1961.* Chapel Hill: The University of North Carolina Press, pp. 155–156, 171, 178. Discusses *BP,* noting that W shifted his focus from politics to unsuccessful efforts to identify with Africans. Also mentions W's role in the Paris Conference for Negro Writers and Artists.

8480. Miller, Ivor L. *Aerosol Kingdom: Subway Painters of New York City.* Jackson: University Press of Mississippi, p. 101. Comments on W's use of trains in "Big Boy Leaves Home."

8481. Millichap, Joseph R. *Dixie Limited: Railroads, Culture, and the Southern Renaissance.* Lexington: The University Press of Kentucky, pp. 20, 50, 74, 88, 90–91, 94. Discusses the influence of railroads & trains in W's early fiction. Mentions *NS* as well as "Big Boy Leaves Home."

8482. Mills, Jerry Leath. "Guns," in *The Companion to Southern Literature.* Eds. Joseph M. Flora and Lucinda MacKethan. Baton Rouge: Louisiana State University Press, pp. 325–326. Mentions briefly the pistol in "The Man Who Was Almost a Man."

8483. _____. "The Mule," in *The Companion to Southern Literature.* Eds. Joseph M. Flora and Lucinda MacKethan. Baton Rouge: Louisiana State University Press, pp. 517–518. Mentions briefly "The Man Who Was Almost a Man."

8484. Mitchell, Douglas L. "Caves," in *The Companion to Southern Literature.* Eds. Joseph M. Flora and Lucinda MacKethan. Baton Rouge: Louisiana State University Press, pp. 133–135. Mentions briefly "The Man Who Lived Underground."

8485. Mixon, Wayne. "Jim Crow," in *The Companion to Southern Literature.* Eds. Joseph M. Flora and Lucinda MacKethan. Baton Rouge: Louisiana State University Press, pp. 389–390. Calls "The Ethics of Living Jim Crow" a "definitive statement on the subject."

8486. Monteith, Sharon, and Suzanne W. Jones. "Introduction: South to New Places," in their *South to a New Place: Region, Literature, Culture*: Baton Rouge: Louisiana State University Press, pp. 1–19. Mentions W briefly (p. 2).

8487. Moore, Lorrie. "The Long Voyage Home." *The New York Review of Books,* 49 (10 October), 33–35. Review of Darryl Pinckney's *Out There: Mavericks of Black Literature.* Mentions W briefly (p. 33).

8488. Morris, Willie. "Despair in Mississippi," Hope in Texas," in his *Shifting Interludes: Selected Essays.* Ed. Jack Bales. Jackson: University Press of Mississippi, pp. 102–110. Recalls meeting W in Paris.

8489. Mullen, Bill V. "Discovering Postcolonialism." *American Quarterly*, 54 (December), 701–707 Highly favorable review of Virginia Whatley Smith's *Richard Wright's Travel Writings: New Reflections* emphasizing W's major role in initiating postcolonial studies.

8490. _____. "*The Power of Political Art: The 1930's Literary Left Reconsidered.* By Robert Shulman." *Modern Language Quarterly*, 63 (June), 269–273. Review critical of Shulman's treatment of W (p. 272).

8491. Neal, Mark Anthony. *Soul Babies: Black Popular Culture and the Post-Soul Aesthetic*. New York: Routledge, pp. 2, 106–107. Comments on W's relation to French existentialists and his attitude toward African American academics. Mentions *NS* and *TMBV*.

8492. Nejako, Alexander. "Bigger's Choice: The Failure of African-American masculinities in *Native Son.*" *CLA Journal*, 44 (June), 423–441. Argues that without black paternal role models, W believes that black youths must turn to rich white males, but these are racist. These views, derived mainly from the Chicago School of Sociology, are applied by W not only in *NS* but also in *EM*.

8493. Nelson, Emmanuel S. "Anne Moody (1940–)," in *African American Autobiographers: A Sourcebook*. Ed. Emmanuel S. Nelson. Westport, CT: Greenwood Press, pp. 280–285. Includes brief comparison of *Coming of Age in Mississippi* with *BB* (pp. 281, 283).

8494. Nelson, Emmanuel. "Preface," in his *African American Autobiographers: A Sourcebook*. Westport, CT, pp. iii–xv. Mentions W briefly (p. xiv).

8495. Neubauer, Alexander. "Clarence Major," in *Conversations with Clarence Major*. Ed. Nancy Bunge. Jackson: University Press of Mississippi, pp. 93–104. Reprint of 1994.

8496. Nugent, Richard, Bruce. *Gay Rebel of the Harlem Renaissance: Selections from the Work of Richard Bruce Nugent*. Ed. Thomas H. Wirth. Durham: Duke University Press, p. 32. Mentions briefly W and *New Challenge*.

8497. O'Connor, Margaret Anne. "Sometime Southerner," in *The Companion to Southern Literature*. Eds. Joseph M. Flora and Lucinda MacKethan. Baton Rouge, Louis-

iana State University Press, pp. 814–815. Mentions W briefly.

8498. Oliver, Lawrence J. "The Current Dialogue on Whiteness Studies." *Callaloo*, 25 (Fall), 1277. Mentions W briefly.

8499. _____. "*New Deal Modernism: American Literature and the Invention of the Welfare State*. By Michael Szalay." *The Journal of American History*. 89 (June), 273–274. Review noting that Szalay treats W.

8500. Olubunmi Smith, Pamela, and Daniel P. Kunene, eds. *Tongue and Mother Tongue: African Literature and the Perpetual Quest for Identity*. Trenton, NJ: Africa World Press, pp. 205. Includes articles on W and Alex La Guma.

8501. Ostrom, Hans. "'Banquet in Honor,'" in his *A Langston Hughes Encyclopedia*. Westport, CT: Greenwood Press, p. 29. Mentions W briefly as co-editor of *Negro Quarterly*.

8502. _____. "*The Best Short Stories by Negro Writers: An Anthology from 1899 to the Present*" in his *A Langston Hughes Encyclopedia*. Westport, CT: Greenwood Press, p. 33. Notes that W is included in the collection.

8503. _____. "*The Book of Negro Folklore,*" in his *A Langston Hughes Encyclopedia*. Westport, CT: Greenwood Press, p. 56. Notes that W is included in the collection.

8504. _____. "Ellison, Ralph (1914–1994)," in his *A Langston Hughes Encyclopedia*. Westport, CT: Greenwood Press, pp. 112–113. Mentions W briefly.

8505. _____. "I Wonder as I Wander," in his *A Langston Hughes Encyclopedia.*" Westport, CT: Greenwood Press, pp. 171–172. Mentions W briefly.

8506. _____. "Preface," in his *A Langston Hughes Encyclopedia*. Westport, CT: Greenwood Press, pp. vii–xii. Mentions W briefly (p. x).

8507. _____. "Wright, Richard (1908–1960)," in his *A Langston Hughes Encyclopedia*. Westport, CT: Greenwood Press, p. 430. Biographical sketch with emphasis on Hughes's attitude toward W.

8508. Page, Philip. "Jeffrey J. Folks. *From Richard Wright to Toni Morrison: Ethics in Modern and Postmodern American Narrative*." *African American Review*, 36 (Summer), pp. 332–333. Unfavorable review

noting Folks's treatment of *CC* (p. 332).

8509. Painter, Nell Irvin. "Social Equality and Rape in the Fin de Siècle South," in her *Southern History Across the Color Line*. Chapel Hill: The University of North Carolina Press, pp. 112–133.

8510. Paquet, Sandra Pouchet. *Caribbean Autobiography: Cultural Identity and Self-Representation*. Madison: University of Wisconsin Press, pp. 83, 105, 116–117, 122, 285–286, 288. Includes discussion of *BB* in relation to autobiographies by Claude McKay and George Lamming.

8511. Park, Yow-Me, and Gayle Wald. "Native Daughters in the Promised Land, Gender, Race, and the Question of Separate Spheres," in *No More Separate Spheres! A Next Wave American Studies Reader*. Eds. Cathy N. Davidson and Jessamyn Hatcher. Durham: Duke University Press, pp. 263–287. Mentions briefly *NS* (p, 273).

8512. Pavlić, Edward M. *Crossroads Modernism: Descent and Emergence in African-American Literary Culture*. Minneapolis: University of Minnesota Press, pp. xxix, xx, xxiii, 26, 28, 86, 93–112, 179, 205. Includes a substantial treatment of "The Man Who Lived Underground," which "intertwines the nationalist and existentialist levels of experience, thus dramatizing" the violent tension between above — and underground realities and visions.

8513. Pencak, William. "Paul Robeson and Classical Music," in *Paul Robeson: Essays on His Life and Legacy*. Eds. Joseph Dorinson and William Pencak. Jefferson, NC: McFarland, pp. 152–159.

8514. Peniel, E. Joseph. "All Power to the People!: Teaching Black Nationalism in the Post-Civil Rights Era," in *Teaching the American Civil Rights Movement: Freedom's Bittersweet Song*. Eds. Julie Buckner Armstrong, Susan Hult Edwards, Houston Bryan Roberson, and Rhonda Y. Williams. New York: Routledge, pp. 147–158. Mentions W's radicalism (pp. 149–150).

8515. Pettis, Joyce. "Margaret Walker," in *The History of Southern Women's Literature*. Eds. Carolyn Perry and Mary Louise Weaks. Baton Rouge: Louisiana State University Press, pp. 498–502. Mentions briefly Walker's biography of W (p. 50).

8516. Pinckney, Darryl. "Caryl Phillips," in his *Out There: Mavericks of Black Literature*, New York: Basic Civitas Books, pp. 107–157. Notes the strong impact of *NS* on Phillips's desire to be a writer (pp. 117–118) and mentions W elsewhere (p. 147).

8517. _____. "*Richard Wright: The Life and Times.*" *Biography: An Interdisciplinary Quarterly*, 25 (Winter) 373–274. Brief excerpt from 2001.

8518. _____. "Vincent O. Carter," in his "*Out There: Mavericks of Black Literature.*" New York: Basic Civitas Books, pp. 55–105. Mentions briefly *NS* (p. 99) and W (p. 101).

8519. Pond, Susan Evans. "Nathan J. McCall (1954–)," in *African American Autobiographers: A Sourcebook.* Ed. Emmanuel S. Nelson. Westport, CT: Greenwood Press, pp. 264–269. Mentions McCall's reading of *NS* (p. 265).

8520. Powell, Tara F. "Intellectual," in *The Companion to Southern Literature.* Eds. Joseph M. Flora and Lucinda MacKethan. Baton Rouge: Louisiana State University Press, pp. 375–377. Notes that Cross Damon in *O* is similar to Rayber in Flannery O'Connor's *The Violent Bear It Away.*

8521. Rabinowitz, Paula. "*New Deal Modernism: American Literature and the Invention of the Welfare State.* By Michael Szalay." *Modern Language Quarterly*, 63 (December), 552–555. Review commenting on Szalay's treatment of W and *O*.

8522. _____. "*New Deal Modernism: American Literature and the Invention of the Welfare State.* By Michael Szalay." *Modern Language Quarterly*, 63 (December) Review noting W's treatment in the book, especially in relation to Ayn Rand and to *O*.

8523. Rahming, Melvin B. "'Goodbye to All That!' Engaging the Shift of Sensibility Between John Webster's *The White Devil* and Amiri Baraka's *Dutchman.*" *CLA Journal*, 46 (September), 72–97. Mentions briefly *NS* (p. 95).

8524. Rampersad, Arnold. *The Life of Langston Hughes* Vol. 2: *1941–1967. I Dream a World.* New York: Oxford University Press.

8525. _____. "The Life & Times of Langston Hughes." *The Crisis,*

109 (January/February), 22–28. Mentions W briefly (p. 27).

8526. Raper, Julius Rowan. "Modernism," in *The Companion to Southern Literature.* Eds. Joseph M. Flora and Lucinda MacKethan. Baton Rouge: Louisiana State University Press, pp. 514–516. Mentions briefly W's "spare" writing.

8527. Regester, Charlene B. *Black Entertainers in African American Newspaper Articles. Vol. 1: An Annotated Bibliography of the Chicago Defender, the Afro-American (Baltimore), the Los Angeles Sentinel, and the New York Amsterdam News, 1910–1950.* Jefferson, NC: McFarland, pp. 380, 382, 383, 384, 385, 385–386, 387, 389, 391, 391–392, 392, 398, 399, 400, 401, 402, 408, 411, 416, 421, 422, 425, 438, 447, 452, 468, 472, 473, 516, 600, 606, 619, 631, 632, 644, 655, 661, 665. Lists articles on reader response to *NS*, on the play *NS*, the Negro Playwright's Company benefit, the film *NS*, "Joe Louis Blues," juvenile delinquency, and freedom in France.

8528. Regosin, Elizabeth. *Freedom's Promise: Ex-Slave Families and Citizenship in the Age of Emancipation.* Charlottesville: UP of Virginia, pp. 60–61. Cites the account in *BB* of W's grandfather's difficulty with regards to his name.

8529. Reilly, John M. "*Richard Wright's Travel Writings: New Reflections.*" *African American Review*, 36 (Fall), 503–505. Favorable review of the collection of essays edited by Virginia Whatley Smith. Discusses each contribution, with special praise for essays by Keneth Kinnamon, Yoshinobu Hakutani, Jack B. Moore, and Smith herself.

8530. Reynolds, Clarence V. "Ann Lane Petry," *Black Issues Book Review*, 4 (July/August), pp. 79–80. Biographical-critical sketch noting that Petry "was most often compared to Richard Wright."

8531. Richardson, Thomas J. "Yankee," in *The Companion to Southern Literature.* Eds. Joseph M. Flora and Lucinda MacKethan. Baton Rouge: Louisiana State University Press, pp. 1006–1008. Mentions W briefly (p. 1007).

8532. Ritterhouse, Jennifer. "*Divided Minds: Intellectuals and the Civil Rights Movement.* By Carol Polsgrove.*" *The Journal of Southern History*, 68 (November), 1005–1006. Mentions W briefly.

8533. Roazen, Paul. "Literary Politics in the Cold War." *The Sewanee Review*, 110 (Fall), cxii–cxv. Mentions W briefly (p. cxiv).

8534. Roediger, David R. *Colored White: Transcending the Racial Past.* Berkeley: University of California Press, p. 173. Quotes briefly from *WML*.

8535. Rohrbach, Augusta. *Truth Stronger Than Fiction: Race, Realism, and the U.S. Literary Marketplace.* New York: Palgrave, pp. 117–118. Mentions W. as a best-selling novelist.

8536. Romine, Scott. "Where Is Southern Literature?: The Practice of Place in a Postsouthern Age," in *South to a New Place: Region, Literature, Culture.* Eds. Suzanne W. Jones and Sharon Monteith. Baton Rouge: Louisiana State University Press, pp. 23–43. Includes discussion of W and his absence from the Southern canon (pp. 32, 41).

8537. _____. "Where Is Southern Literature?: The Practice of Place in a Postsouthern Age," in *South to a New Place: Region, Literature, Culture.* Eds. Suzanne W. Jones and Sharon Monteith. Baton Rouge: Louisiana State University Press, pp. 23–43. Mentions W briefly (p. 41) and comments on *BB*.

8538. Rowe, Anne E. "Northern Audiences," in *The Companion to Southern Literature.* Eds. Joseph M. Flora and Lucinda MacKethan. Baton Rouge: Louisiana State University Press, pp. 568–571. Mentions W briefly (p. 570).

8539. Rowell, Charles H. "An Interview with Clarence Major," in *Conversations with Clarence Major.* Jackson: University Press of Mississippi, pp. 128–141.

8540. _____. "An Interview with Clarence Major," in *Conversations with Clarence Major.* Jackson: University Press of Mississippi, pp. 128–141. Reprint of 1997.

8541. _____. "Poetry, History, and Humanism: An Interview with Margaret Walker," in *Conversations with Margaret Walker.* Ed. Maryemma Graham. Jackson: University Press of Mississippi, pp. 19–31. Reprint of 1975.162.

8542. Samway, Patrick, S.J. "Short Story, World War II to Present," in *The Companion to Southern Literature.* Eds. Joseph M. Flora and Lucinda MacKethan. Baton Rouge: Louisiana State University Press, pp.

790–796. Mentions briefly W, *NS*, *BB*, and *EM* (pp. 791–792).

8543. San Juan, Epifanio. *Racism and Cultural Studies: Critiques of Multiculturalist Ideology and the Politics of Difference.* Durham: Duke University Press, pp. 1, 23, 52. Quotes from *WML.*

8544. Savage, Barbara. "Radio and the Political Discourse of Racial Equality," in *Radio Reader: Essays in the Cultural History of Radio.* Eds. Michele Hilmes and Jason Loviglio. New York: Routledge, pp. 231–255. Reports W's militant views expressed in May 1945 on the *Town Meeting* program and the response from racist whites and supportive blacks (pp. 236–241, 245, 250).

8545. Schneider, Mark Robert. *We Return Fighting: The Civil Rights Movement in the Jazz Age.* Boston: Northeastern University Press, p. 400. Mentions briefly W and Bigger Thomas.

8546. Scott, Lynn Orilla. *James Baldwin's Later Fiction: Witness to the Journey.* East Lansing: Michigan State University Press, pp. xiii, xviii, xviii–xix, xxiii, xxviii–xxx, 5, 6, 8–10, 13, 26–30, 33, 35, 51, 75, 92, 97, 112–114, 123, 144, 183, 201. Includes comment on Baldwin's critique of W and Horace Porter and Houston Baker comparing W and Baldwin. Also discusses the signifying of *If Beale Street Could Talk* on *NS* (pp. 112–113). Elsewhere mentions briefly *BB* and "Big Boy Leaves Home."

8547. Scott, R. Neil. *Flannery O'Connor: An Annotated Reference Guide to Criticism.* Milledgeville, GA: Timberlane Books, pp. 243, 319, 491. Includes items relevant to W by Jeffrey J. Folks, Fred Hobson, John Orr, Ladell Payne, William Joseph Barnette, Timothy Paul Caron, Michael John Kowalewski, Anthony Samuel Magistrale and Richard May.

8548. Scott, Lynn Orilla. *James Baldwin's Later Fiction: Witness to the Journey.* East Lansing: Michigan State University Press, pp. xxiii, xviii, xviii–xix, xxiii, xviii, xxiii, xxviii, 5, 6, 8–10, 13, 26–30, 33, 35, 51, 75, 92, 97, 112–114, 123, 144, 183, 201. Includes comment on Baldwin's critique of W and Horace Porter and Houston Baker comparing W and Baldwin. Also discusses the signifying of *If Beale Street Could Talk* on *NS* (pp. 112–113). Elsewhere

mentions briefly *BB* and "Big Boy Leaves Home."

8549. Shepperd, Walt, "Work with the Universe: An Interview with Clarence Major and Victor Hernandez Cruz," in *Conversations with Clarence Major.* Ed. Nancy Bunge. Jackson: University Press of Mississippi, pp. 3–9. Mentions W briefly

8550. Sherman, Scott. "*Amiri Baraka: The Politics and Art of a Black Intellectual.* By Jerry Gafio Watts." *Dissent* (Spring), pp. 107–108. Quotes Arnold Rampersad commenting on W (p. 107) notes that Baraka read *BB* at the age of thirteen (p. 108), and quotes Baraka mentioning W (p. 108).

8551. Shinn, Christopher A. "Masquerade, *Magic,* and Carnival in Ralph Ellison's *Invisible Man.*" *African American Review,* 36 (Summer), pp. 243–261. Comments on the Ellison-Howe debate on W and protest fiction (pp. 257–258).

8552. Sielke, Sabine. *Reading Rape: The Rhetoric of Sexual Violence in American Literature and Culture, 1790–1990.* Princeton: Princeton University Press, pp. 9, 27, 55, 57, 76, 77, 102–116, 117, 124, 125, 143, 145, 147, 148, 158, 176, 207. Includes a substantial analysis of the meaning of rape in *NS* s.v. "'Not What One Did to Women': Enacting Projections and Constructing the Racial Border." Also compares *NS* and *Sanctuary.*

8553. Singer, D. Liam. "Michael Szalay. *New Deal Modernism: American Literature and the Invention of the Welfare State.*" *American Studies International,* 40 (October), 103–104. Review mentioning W briefly.

8554. _____. "Michael Szalay, *New Deal Modernism: American Literature and the Invention of the Welfare State. American Studies International,* 40 (October), 103–104. Review mentioning W briefly.

8555. Singer, Marc. "'Black Skins' and White Masks: Comic Books and the Secret of Race." *African American Review,* 36 (Spring), 107–119. Mentions W briefly (p. 118).

8556. Sklaroff, Lauren Rebecca. "Constructing G.I. Joe Louis: Cultural Solutions to the 'Negro Problem' During World War II." *The Journal of American History,* 89 (December), 458–983. Quotes from W's "Joe Louis Uncovers Dynamite," p. 970.

8557. Smith, Judith E. "Radio's

'Cultural Front,' 1938–1978," in *Radio Reader: Essays in the Cultural History of Radio.* Eds. Michele Hilmes and Jason Loviglio. New York: Routledge, pp. 209–230. Reports that the program *New World A-Coming* in February 1945 celebrated Canada Lee and the play *NS,* including "on-air congratulations" from W (p. 223).

8558. Smith, Virginia Whatley. "African American Literature, 1919 to Present," in *The Companion to Southern Literature.* Eds. Joseph M. Flora and Lucinda MacKethan. Baton Rouge: Louisiana State University Press, pp. 15–19. Contains a paragraph on W's influence (p. 17).

8559. Solomon, William. *Literature, Amusement, and Technology in the Great Depression.* Cambridge: Cambridge University Press, pp. 123, 228, 252. Discusses "How 'Bigger' Was Born," comparing W's depiction of the proletariat to Dahlberg and Algren.

8560. Steele, Shelby. "The Age of White Guilt and the Disappearance of the Black Individual." *Harper's,* 305 (November), 33–42. Mentions W briefly (pp. 37, 42).

8561. Stout, Jeffrey. "Theses on Black Nationalism," in *Is It Nation Time?: Contemporary Essays on Black Power and Black Nationalism.* Chicago: The University of Chicago Press, pp. 234–256. Comments on Ellison's critique of W and compares W and Malcolm X (pp. 247–248).

8562. Stoval, Taressa. "Literary Renaissance at Hurston/Wright Awards." *The Crisis,* 109 (November/December), 8. Reports on an awards ceremony.

8563. Takara, Kathryn. "Frank Marshall Davis: A Forgotten Voice in the Chicago Black Renaissance." *The Western Journal of Black Studies,* 26 (Winter), 215–227. Mentions W and the South Side Writers Group (p. 217).

8564. Tate, Claudia. "Interview with Margaret Walker," in *Conversations with Margaret Walker.* Ed. Maryemma Graham. Jackson: University Press of Mississippi, pp. 59–71. Reprint of 1983.

8565. Tavernier, Linda. "Lopez-Harris, Trudier. *South of Tradition: Essays on African American Literature.*" *The Black Scholar,* 32 (Fall/Winter), 59. Mentions W briefly.

8566. _____. "Pinn, Anthony B.

(ed.) *By These Hands: A Documentary History of African American Humanism." The Black Scholar*, 32 (Spring), 62. Mentions W briefly.

8567. _____. "Rowley, Hazel. *Richard Wright: The Life and Times." The Black Scholar*, 32 (Fall/Winter), 61. Brief descriptive review.

8568. _____. "Wald, Alan. *Exiles from a Future Time: The Forging of the Mid-Twentieth-Century Literary Left." The Black Scholar*, 32 (Summer), 57. Mentions W briefly.

8569. Taylor, Helen. "The South and Britain: Celtic Cultural Connections," in *South to a New Place: Region, Literature, Culture*. Eds. Suzanne M. Jones and Sharon Monteith. Baton Rouge: Louisiana State University Press, pp. 340–362. Refers briefly to *BB* (p. 345).

8570. Taylor, Ula Yvette. *The Veiled Garvey: The Life and Times of Amy Jacques Garvey*. Chapel Hill: The University of North Carolina Press, p. 216. Mentions briefly W's "sense of dislocation in Ghana."

8571. Thomas, H. Nigel. "Richard Wright (1908–1960)," in *African American Autobiographers: A Sourcebook*. Ed. Emmanuel S. Nelson. Westport, CT: Greenwood Press, pp. 391–406. Includes a detailed biographical sketch, a section on autobiographical works and themes, critical reception and a bibliography of fifty-six items.

8572. _____. "Richard Wright (1908–1960), in *African American Autobiographers: A Sourcebook*. Westport, CT: Greenwood Press, pp. 391–406. After a substantial summary of W's life, Thomas discusses "autobiographical works and themes in *TMBV, BP, CC, PS*, and *WML*, as well as in *BB*. The final section of the essay traces the critical response to *BB-AH*.

8573. Thompson, Carlyle V. "From a Hog to a Black Man: Black Male Subjectivity and Ritualistic Lynching in Ernest J. Gaines's *A Lesson Before Dying." CLA Journal*. 45 (March), 295–310. Quotes from *TMBV* (p. 295).

8574. Thurston, Michael. "Gumshoe America: *Hard-Boiled Crime Fiction and the Rise and Fall of New Deal Liberalism*. By Sean McCann; *New Deal Modernism: American Literature and the Invention of the Welfare State*. By Michael Szalay. "*American Literature*, 74 (June), 421–423. Mentions W briefly.

8575. Tidwell, John Edgar. "Introduction: Wearing Jagged Words Into Song," in his *Black Moods: Collected Poems/Frank Marshall Davis*. Urbana: University of Illinois Press, pp. xxi–lxv. Mentions W briefly (p. xxix).

8576. Tillis, Antonio D. "*Native Son's* Bigger and *Las Estrellas Son Negras*' Irra: Two Post-Colonial Subjects of Literature of the African Diaspora." *CLA Journal*, 46 (December), 207–225. Compares *NS* and a novel by an Afro-Columbian writer, Arnoldo Palacios. The perspective and methodology are Post-Colonial Theory. Both clearly exemplify "the social and psychological struggles of socially marginalized people of African descent" (p. 224).

8577. Tilly, Nancy. "Storytelling," in *The Companion to Southern Literature* Eds. Joseph M. Flora and Lucinda MacKethan. Baton Rouge: Louisiana State University Press, pp. 862–864. Mentions briefly W, who redeems "brutal stories with art."

8578. *Tongue and Mother Tongue: African Literature and the Perpetual Quest for Identity*. Eds. Pamela Olubunmi Smith and Danial P. Kunene, Trenton, NJ: Africa World Press, 205 pp. Includes articles on W and Alex La Guma.

8579. Turner, Darwin T. "Robert Hayden Remembered," in *Robert Hayden: Essays on the Poetry*. Eds. Laurence Goldstein and Robert Chrisman. Ann Arbor: The University of Michigan Press, pp. 87–103. Comments on *NS* and W's domination of the literary scene in the 1940s (p. 89).

8580. Vogel, Amber. "Ellison, Ralph Waldo," in *The Companion to Southern Literature*. Eds. Joseph M. Flora and Lucinda MacKethan. Baton Rouge: Louisiana State University Press, pp. 230–231. Comments on the W-Ellison friendship, including Ellison's writings about W.

8581. _____. "Novel, 1900 to World War II," in *The Companion to Southern Literature*. Eds. Joseph M. Flora and Lucinda MacKethan. Baton Rouge: Louisiana State University Press, pp. 582–592. Note's W's unfavorable opinion of Hurston.

8582. Wald, Alan M. *Exiled from a Future Time: The Forging of the Mid-Twentieth-Century Literary*

Left. Chapel Hill: The University of North Carolina Press, pp. 7, 36, 68, 69, 79, 84, 90–93, 132, 265, 266, 269, 270, 272, 273, 274, 275, 276, 277, 278, 279, 281, 282, 284, 285–287, 288, 289, 294, 295, 296, 297, 314, 319, 321. In addition to a biographical sketch of W (pp. 90–93), Wald comments on his political activities and allegiances during all phases of his literary life and discusses or mentions *BB, UTC*, "The Ethics of Living Jim Crow," and "Blueprint for Negro Writing."

8583. Walker, Margaret, and Nikki Giovanni: "Two Women, Two Views," in *Conversations with Margaret Walker*. Ed. Maryemma Graham. Jackson: University Press of Mississippi, pp. 3–18. Reprint of 1974.80.

8584. Wallace, Maurice O. *Constructing the Black Masculine: Identity and Ideality in African American Men's Literature and Culture, 1775–1995*. Durham: Duke University Press, pp. 7–8, 34–46. Considers *NS* "as the urtext for the ekphrastic threat to black male representation and the private life of the black masculine." Discusses from this perspective the bedroom scene in the Dalton house, the inquest, and the relation of Bigger and Max.

8585. Wallace, Maurice. "Constructing the Black Masculine: Frederick Douglass, *Booker T. Washington, and the sublimits of African American Autobiography*," in *No More Separate Spheres!: A Next Wave American Studies Reader*. Eds. Cathy N. Davidson and Jessamyn Hatcher. Durham: Duke University Press, pp. 237–262. Mentions W briefly (p. 238).

8586. Ward, Jerry W., Jr. "A Writer for Her People," in *Conversations with Margaret Walker*. Ed. Maryemma Graham. Jackson: University Press of Mississippi, pp. 113–124. Reprint of 1991.

8587. Ward, Selena, and Ross Naughton. *Black Boy*: Richard Wright. New York: Sparknotes, 89 pp. Study guide with plot summary and analysis, comment on the main characters, historical context, essay topics, themes, motifs, symbols, and a review quiz.

8588. Weinstein, Philip. "Postmodern Intimations: Musing on Invisibility: William Faulkner, Richard Wright, and Ralph Ellison," in *Faulkner and Postmodernism*. Jackson: University Press of Mississippi, pp. 19–38. Includes discussion of *NS* and "The Man Who Lived Underground," emphasizing their indebtedness to Dostoevsky and Faulkner.

8589. Wells, Monique Y. "Four Traced Steps of *Native Son*: Richard Wright's Paris." Little Rock *Arkansas Democrat-Gazette* (21 April), p. 2H. Comments on places associated with W in Paris, mainly on the Left Bank, and includes a map marking the route of a walking tour. Source is the Cox News Source.

8590. Wilcox, Hilda Mader. "Wright On." *The Crisis*, 109 (May/June), 4. Letter to the editor praising Hazel Rowley's *Richard Wright: His Life and Times*.

8591. Wilson, Bobby M. "*Critically Understanding Race-Connected Practices: A Reading of W.E.B. Du-Bois and Richard Wright*." *Professional Geographer*, 54 (February), pp. 31–42. Argues that although race must be understood in historical and geographical context, a study of W and DuBois suggests that it is fundamentally "beyond text, located in space and time."

8592. Wilson, Charles E., Jr. "Black Migrations," in *The Companion to Southern Literature*. Eds. Joseph M. Flora and Lucinda MacKethan. Baton Rouge: Louisiana State University Press, pp. 107–108. Mentions briefly W's autobiography.

8593. Wong, Hertha D. Sweet. "Taking Place: African-Native American Subjectivity in *A Yellow Raft in Blue Water*," in *Mixed Race Literature*. Stanford: Stanford University Press, pp. 165–176. Mentions W briefly (p. 168).

8594. Yaffe, David. "Ellison Unbound." *The Nation*, 274 (4 March), 34–35. Mentions W briefly.

8595. Yates, Gayle Graham. "Mississippi, Literature of," in *The Companion to Southern Literature*. Eds. Joseph M. Flora and Lucinda MacKethan. Baton Rouge: Louisiana State University Press, pp. 499–505. Names W among the "literary giants of the twentieth century" who were Mississippians (p. 499).

8596. Zender, Karl F. *Faulkner and the Politics of Reading*. Baton Rouge: Louisiana State University Press, p. 92. Mentions W briefly.

8597. Zhang, Aimin. *The Origins of the African American Civil Rights Movements, 1865–1956*. New York: Routledge, p. 67. Mentions briefly *UTC* and *NS*.

8598. _____. *The Origins of the African American Civil Rights Movements, 1865–1956*. New York: Routledge, p. 67. Mentions briefly *UTC* and *NS*.

2003

8599. Abrahams, Roger D. "Commentary," in *Slavery and the American South*. Ed. Winthrop D. Jordan. Jackson: University Press of Mississippi, pp. 169–176. Comments on the view of W and others that the blues contain "metaphors for ... alienated states of being" (p. 169).

8600. Andrews, William L., and Douglas Taylor, eds. *Richard Wright's Black Boy (American Hunger): A Casebook*. Oxford: Oxford University Press, pp. 210. After a substantial introduction the editors present eleven essays and reviews of *BB*, followed by a list of twenty-six titles s.v. suggested reading.

8601. Anon. "Painted Voices: An Artist's Journey Into the World of Black Writers." *Black Issues Book Review*, 5 (May/June) p. 32. Reproduces a painting of W.

8602. Anon. "*The Souls of Black Folk: One Hundred Years Later*. Ed. Doland Hubbard." *American Literature*, 75 (December), p. 917. Notice mentioning W briefly.

8603. Arnold, Edwin T. "Unruly Ghost: Erskine Caldwell at 100." *The Southern Review*, 39 (Autumn), pp. 851–868. Notes that W admired Caldwell's work.

8604. Bell, Bernard W. "Percival L. Everett. *Erasure*." *African American Review*, 37 (Summer/Fall), 474–476. Review mentioning briefly W's naturalism.

8605. Birnbaum, Michele. *Race, Work, and Desire in American Literature, 1860–1930*. New York: Cambridge University Press, pp. 24, 96, 143, 144. Comments on the Bigger-Mary, situation in *NS*.

8606. Booker, M. Keith. "Baldwin, James," in his *The Chinua Achebe Encyclopedia*. Westport, CT: Greenwood Press, p. 39. Mentions W briefly.

8607. Boyd, Herb. "The Writing Process; Scissors and Glue: Reflections of an Anthologist." *Black Issues Book Review*, 5 (May/June), p. 1. Quotes W that "all you need to compile an anthology is a pair of scissors and a pot of glue."

8608. Braziel, Jana Evans. "Trans-American Constructions of Black Masculinity: Dany Laferrière, le Nègre and the Late Capitalist American *machine-dèsirante.*" *Callaloo*, 26 (Summer), pp. 867–900. Laferrière aspires to become the best black witer: Meilleur que Dick Wright" (p. 879).

8609. Breu, Christopher. "Freudian knot or Gordian Knot?: The Contradictions of Racialized Masculinity in Chester Himes' *If He Hollers Let Him Go*." *Callaloo*, 26 (Summer), pp. 776–795. Calls the Himes novel "the privileged ligature between Wright's social realism and Ellison's psychological emphasis."

8610. Brinkley, Douglas. "Unmasking Writers of the W.P.A." *The New York Times* (2 August) pp. BT. B9. Notes W's participation and includes a photograph of him.

8611. Briones, Matthew M. "Call-and-Response: Tracing the Ideological shifts of Richard Wright through His Correspondence with Friends and Fellow Literati." *African American Review*, 37 (Spring), pp. 53–65. Quotes extensively from W's unpublished journals and his correspondence with Ellison, Cayton,

Aswell, Joe Brown. W comments on his writing prospects, on communism, on his French connections, and on his literary ambition.

8612. Brister, Rose Ann. "The Last Regionalist?: An Interview with Ernest J. Gaines." *Callaloo*, 26 (Summer), pp. 549–564. Gaines regrets that "too many of our writers emulated Richard Wright's *Native Son* and *Black Boy*."

8613. Brooks, Shanesha R.F. Brooks. "*The Black Scholar* Books Received." *The Black Scholar*, 33 (Fall-Winter), p. 56. Contains a brief notice of *Richard Wright's Black Boy (American Hunger)*, p. 56.

8614. Byerman, Keith E. "*Ralph Ellison: An American Journey*." *The Journal of American History*, 90 1133–1134. Review of a film on Ellison. Mentions briefly W and his influence on the young Ellison.

8615. Carby, Hazel. "African America Intellectuals Symposium." *The Journal of African American History*, 88 (Winter), 78–82. Mentions briefly *Savage Holiday* and W.

8616. Cobb, Michael L. "Different Authority: Religious Apostrophe and the Fiction of Blackness in Paule Marshall's *Brown Girl, Brownstones*." *University of Toronto Quarterly*, 72 (Spring), pp. 631–648. Mentions briefly *BB* (p. 632).

8617. Dawahare, Anthony. *Nationalism, Marxism, and African American Literature Between the Wars: A New Pandora's Box*. Jackson: University Press of Mississippi, Contains a chapter entitled "Richard Wright's Critique of Nationalist Desire" emphasizing his "Marxist psychoanalytic perspective." considers *LT*, *NS*, *UTC*, and *TMBV*.

8618. Delton, Jennifer. "Before the White Negro: Sin and Salvation in *Kingsblood Royal*" *American Literary History*, 15 (Spring) pp. 311–335. Comments on *NS* in an essay on Sinclair Lewis's novel and mentions "How Bigger Was Born."

8619. Dinerstein, Joel. *Swinging the Machine: Modernity, Technology, and African American Culture Between the World Wars*. Amherst: University of Massachusetts Press, p. 256. Quotes briefly from *TMBV*.

8620. Donalson, Melvin. *Black Directors in Hollywood*. Austin: University of Texas Press, p. 9. Mentions W briefly.

8621. Dubey, Madhu. *Signs and Cities: Black Literary Postmodernism*.

Chicago: The University of Chicago Press, pp. 284. Contains numerous brief mentions of W.

8622. Egèjuru, Phanuel Akubueze, eds. "*Tongue and Mother Tongue: African Literature and the Perpetual Quest for Identity*." *The Black Scholar*, 33 (Fall-Winter), pp. 51–53. Mentions an article on Wand La Guma (p. 53).

8623. Foley, Barbara. *Spectres of 1919: Class and Nation in the Making of the New Nation*. Urbana: University of Illinois Press, pp. 13, 102. Mentions W's phrase "the ethics of living Jim Crow."

8624. Garrett, Daniel. "Hazel Rowley. *Richard Wright: The Life and Times*." *World Literature Today*, 77 (April-June), pp. 109–110. Review of Hazel Rowley's biography focusing on the diversity of W's writing. "His legacy is complex — at once aesthetic, intellectual, and political.

8625. Gayles, Gloria Wade, ed. *Conversations with Gwendolyn Brooks*. Jackson: University Press of Mississippi, pp. 5, 32, 117. Notes W's early support of Brooks and compares Brooks's "I love Those Little Booths at Bevnenuti's" to the episode in *NS* when Bigger must take Mary and Jan to a black café.

8626. Gondóla, Ch. Didier. "'But I Ain't African, I'm American!" in *Blackening Europe: The African American Presence*. New York: Routledge, pp. 201–205. Includes discussion of W's affinity for France and his expatriation.

8627. Gussow, Adam. "'Fingering the Jagged Grain': Ellison's Wright and the Southern Blues Violences." *Boundary 2: An International Journal of Literature and Culture*, 30 (Summer), pp. 137–55.

8628. Harris, Shanette M. "Constructing a Psychological Perspective: The Observer and the observed in *The Souls of Black Folk*, in *The Souls of Black Folk One Hundred Years Later*. Ed. Dolan Hubbard. Columbia: University of Missouri Press, pp. 218–250. Comments on Allison Davis's *Leadership, Love and Aggression* as it treats W.

8629. Hicks, Heather. "'This Strange Communion': Surveillance and the Spectatorship in Ann Petry's *The Street*." *African American Review*, 37 (Spring), pp. 21–37. Compares Petry's *The Street* to *NS* with respect to "the dynamics of spectatorship and surveillance that ani-

mate the racist social formation of Harlem."

8630. Higashida, Cheryl. "Aunt Sue's Children: Re-Viewing the Gender(ed) Politics of Richard Wright's Radicalism." *American Literature*, 75 (June), pp. 396–425. Focuses on *UTC* to dispute black feminist rejection of W, asserting that "African Americans are centered to his "literary synthesis of Marxism and black cultural nationalism."

8631. Jordan, Winthrop D. "Introduction," in his *Slavery and the American South*. Jackson: University Press of Mississippi, pp. ix–xx. Mentions W briefly.

8632. Kiuchi, Toru "The Schomburg Center for Research in Black Culture, ed. *Jubilee: The Emergence of African-American Culture*," *African American Review*, 37 (Winter), 649–651. Mentions briefly *BP* (p. 648).

8633. Knadler, Stephen. "*Black Manhood in James Baldwin, Ernest J. Gaines, and August Wilson* by Keith Clark." *American Literature*, 75 (March), pp. 201–202. Review mentioning briefly W and Bigger.

8634. Marable, Manning. "*Black Boy: A Record of Childhood and Youth*," in his *Freedom on My Mind: The Columbia Documentary History of the African American Experience*. New York: Columbia University Press, pp. 470–481. Biographical headnote and a substantial excerpt from *BB*.

8635. _____. "High Tide in Harlem," in his *The Columbia Documentary History of the African American Experience*. New York: Columbia University Press, pp. 608–613. Biographical headnote and a reprint of "High Tide in Harlem."

8636. _____. "Introduction," in his *Freedom on My Mind: The Columbia Documentary History of the African American Experience*. New York: Columbia University Press, p. xvi alludes to *BB* and comments on "High Tide in Harlem."

8637. Mattox, Jake. "*Black Nationalism in the New World: Reading the African American and West Indian Experience, by Robert Carr*." *The Mississippi Quarterly*, 56 (Spring), pp. 445–446.

8638. Miklódy, Éva "A.R.T., Klikk, K.A.O.S. and the Rest: Hungarian youth Rapping," in *Blackening Europe: The African American Presence*. New York: Routledge, pp. 187–200.

8639. Miller, James A. "Frank Marshall Davis. *Black Moods: Collected Poems*." Urbana: University of Illinois Press), pp. 466–467. Favorable review with special praise for editor Edgar Tidwell. Mentions W briefly (p. 466). Mentions W briefly (p. 188).

8640. Painter, Nell Irvin. "Introduction: Claudia Tate and the Protocols of Black Literature and Scholarship." *The Journal of African American History*, 88 (Winter), 60–65.

8641. Pereira, Malin. *Rita Dove's Cosmopolitanism*. Urbana: University of Illinois Press, pp. 76–78, 89. Comments on the Howe-Ellison dispute and mentions W briefly.

8642. Perkinson, James W. "Rap as Wrap and Rapture: North American Poplar Culture and the Denial of Death," in Anthony B. Pinn's *Noise and Spirit: The Religious and Spiritual Sensibilities of Rap Music*. New York: New York University Press, pp. 131–153. Quotes from *WML* (p. 131) and mentions W briefly elsewhere (p. 140).

8643. Pettinger, Alasdair. "'At heart One Negro Everywhere' African American Travel Writing," in *Beyond the Borders: American Literature and Post-Colonial Theory*. Ed. Deborah L. Madsen. London: Pluto Press, pp. 81, 88. Notes that W was denied a passport and alludes to *BP*.

8644. Pinn, Anthony B. "'Handlin' My Business: Exploring Rap's Humanist Sensibilities." in his *Noise and Spirit: The Religious and Spiritual Sensibilities of Rap Music*. New York: New York University Press, pp. 85–104. Refers to W's "existential leanings" and to Cross Damon.

8645. Ramadanoric, Petar, "*Native Son's* Tragedy: Traversing the Death Drive with Bigger Thomas." *Arizona Quarterly*, 59 (Summer), pp. 81–105. Treats NS as a Sophoclean tragedy, drawing on Laconian theory. Since Bigger "assumes a singular fate that is realized at the moment of his ultimate demise," *NS* is not a protest novel.

8646. Raphael-Hernandez, Heike. "'Niggas' and 'Skins,'" in *Blackening Europe: The African-American Presence*. New York: Routledge, pp. 287–291. Quotes from W's introduction to *Black Metropolis*.

8647. Reed, Ishmael. *Another Day at the Front: Dispatches from the Race War*. New York: Basic Books, pp. 13, 19, 22, 43. Brief mentions of W in relation to curricular, canonical, and feminist issues.

8648. Reilly, John M. "Michael K. Jackson. *Black Masculinity and the Frontier Myth in American Literature*," *African American Review*, 37 (Winter), 647–649. Review commenting on Johnson's treatment of "The Man Who Was Almost a Man" and "Big Boy Leaves Home."

8649. Robinson, Owen. "Maria Balshaw, *Looking for Harlem: Urban Aesthetics in African American Literature*." Journal of American Studies, *37*, 455–456. Review mentioning briefly W and *NS*.

8650. Sharmayne, Jiton. "Sometimes Funny, but Most Times Deadly Serious: Amiri Baraka as a Political Saterist." *African American Review*, 7 (Summer/Fall) pp. 399–405. Mentions briefly Bigger Thomas (p. 402).

8651. Smethurst, James. "'Pat Your Foot and Turn the Corner': Amiri Baraka, the Black Arts Movement, and the Poetics of a Popular Avant-Garde." *African American Review*, 37 (Summer/Fall, pp. 261–270. Mentions briefly W's "King Joe."

8652. Smith, Virginia Whatley. "They Sing the Song of Slavery: Frederick Douglass's Narrative and W.E.B DuBois's *The Souls of Black Folk* as Intertexts of Richard Wright's *12 Million Black Voices*," in *The Souls of Black Folk One Hundred Years Later*. Ed. with Introduction by Doland Hubbard. Columbia: University of Missouri Press, pp. 85–129. Analyzes *TMBV* in relation to Douglass's *Narrative* and DuBois's *The Souls of Black Folk*. Prefers the militant ex-slave to the cultivated DuBois. Smith draws on Barthes and W.J.T. Mitchell for theoretical perspectives as she develops her case. Also treats the rhetoric of photographic image in W's work.

8653. Steele, Max. "Richard Wright: The Visible Man." *The Paris Review*, No. 167 (Fall). Reminiscences of Steele about W and Ellen in the Fifties in Paris. Also comments on W's visit to Chapel Hill and threats on his life there.

8654. Stewart, Jacqueline. "Negroes Laughing at Themselves? Black Spectatorship and the Performance of Urban Modernity." *Critical Inquiry*, 29 (Summer), pp. 650–677. Includes substantial discussion of Bigger at the movies as well as the Chicago background.

8655. Stuckey, Sterling. "Paul Robeson, and Richard Wright on the Arts and Slave Culture," in *Slavery and the American South*. Ed. Winthrop D. Jordan. Jackson: University Press of Mississippi, pp. 146–168. Contrasts W's rejection of African influence on African American culture to Robeson's opposite view, but notes than in *BP* W modified this view.

8656. Sundquist, Eric J. "In the Lion's Mouth." *American Literary History*, 15 (Spring), pp. 34–38. Includes comment on *LD*, "whose utter saturation in racial violence and death made it at once anachronistic and paradigmatic as a novel of Jim Crow."

8657. Tavernier-Almada, Linda. "*The Black Scholar* Books Received." The Black Scholar, 33 (Summer), pp. 55–61. Contains a brief notice of Hazel Rowley's *Richard Wright: The Life and Times* (p. 60).

8658. Thomas, Lorenzo. "The Characters of Consciousness." *African American Review*, 37 (Summer/Fall), pp. 189–190. Mentions briefly *LT*.

8659. Webb, Constance. *Not Without Love: Memoirs*. Hanover, New Hampshire: University Press of New England, vii + 290 pp. Autobiography with extensive comment on W and his circle: C.L.R. James, Ellison, and Himes. Includes discussion of visits with W and Ellen in Brooklyn Heights and Wading River as well as discussion of her literary tutelage by W and her reading *BB* in proof.

8660. Yukins, Elizabeth. "The Business of Patriarchy: Black Paternity and Illegitimate Economics in Richard Wright's *The Long Dream*. *Modern Fiction Studies*, 49 (Winter), pp. 746–779. Argues that the novel "should be a key text in the canon, for it illustrates his mature vision of how race and economics combine to shape the psychosexual dynamics of masculinity."

Addenda 1934–1982

8661. Anon. "National John Reed Club Conference." *Partisan Review*, 1 (November-December 1934), 60–61. Notes that W is on the new national committee. Reprinted: 1993.

8662. The Editors of *The New Masses*. "Is Roosevelt Backing the Terror?" *New Masses*, 12 (31 July 1934), 7. W is one of 125 signers of a letter to Roosevelt protesting "a series of illegal raids on workers' organizations on the Pacific Coast."

8663. Anon. "Letters in Brief." *New Masses*, 17 (22 October 1935), p. 22. Notes that Isaac Horwitz commends Richard Wright's article "Joe Louis Uncovers Dynamite," though another finds that it "does harm to the Negro people."

8664. Anon. "Letters in Brief." *New Masses*, 17 (29 October 1935), 19. Reports that Creighton J. Hill of Wellesley Hills, MA, admires "Joe Louis Uncovers Dynamite," but that Oril Brown of Evanston, IL, disliked the "moral-pointing foreword" and E. Colman of New York disliked the piece itself.

8665. Anon. "Mid-West Writers Conference." *New Masses*, 19 (16 June 1936), 4. Includes W among the thirteen writers calling for the conference, 13–14 June 1936.

8666. Anon. "Who's Who." *New Masses*, 21 (15 December 1936), 3. Notes on contributors to the twenty-fifth anniversary edition. W is "a young Negro poet living in Chicago who has contributed frequently to our pages."

8667. Alsberg, Henry G. "Notes on the Contributors," in his *American Stuff*. New York: The Viking Press, 1937, pp. 293–301. Includes a brief note on W, whose "The Ethics of Living Jim Crow" is included in this volume.

8668. Anon. "Between Ourselves." *New Masses*, 29 (20 December 1938), 2. Quotes a reader's favorable comment on "Bright and Morning Star."

8669. Anon. "Christmas Book Sale." *New Masses*, 30 (27 December 1938), 22. Offers James Allen's *The Negro Question* and *UTC* for a combined price of $2.98.

8670. Anon. "Sale Now On." *New Masses*, 29 (20 December 1938), 25. Worker's Book Shop advertisement listing *UTC*.

8671. Anon. "Who's Who." *New Masses*, 26 (8 March 1938), 2. Announces that W has won "first prize of $500 in a nationwide contest among W.P.A. writers."

8672. Anon. "Who's Who." *New Masses*, 27 (10 May 1938), 2. Notes the publication of *UTC* and the award of $500 to W in the W.P.A. contest.

8673. Calverton, V.F. "The Negro," in *America Now: An Inquiry Into Civilization in the United States*. New York: Scribner's, 1938, pp. 484–502. States that *UTC* "has about it the unquestioned stamp of genius" (p. 500).

8674. Ford, James W. *The Negro and the Democratic Front*. New York: International, 1938, pp. 192, 193, 206. Mentions W briefly.

8675. Sillen, Samuel. "The Negro and the Democratic Front." *New Masses*, 29 (6 December 1939), 20–23. Mentions W briefly (p. 22).

8676. Anon. "Between Ourselves." *New Masses*, 31 (16 May 1939), 2. Announces a lecture by W on 12 May.

8677. Anon. "Dinner Reception to Be Given Haitian by Writers and Artists." *The New York Age* (4 November 1939). Lists W as a guest of honor at the event held for Jacques Roumain.

8678. Anon. "Haitian Scribe to Be Honored." *The New York Amsterdam News* (11 November 1939), p. 7. Lists W as a guest of honor at a banquet reception for Jacques Roumain.

8679. Anon. "*New Masses* Lecture Bureau." *New Masses*, 30 (14 March 1939), 24. Advertisement listing W as one of thirteen lecturers available.

8680. Anon. "The New York City Project." *Direction*, 2 (May-June 1939), 14. Mentions W briefly.

8681. O'Brien, Edward J. "Biographical Notes," in his *50 Best American Short Stories 1915-1939*. Boston: Houghton Mifflin, 1939, p. 868. Brief biographical note. "Bright and Morning Star" is included in this volume (pp. 810–850).

8682. _____. *The Best Short Stories 1939*. Boston: Houghton Mifflin, 1939. The volume is dedicated to W and Jessie Stuart and includes "Bright and Morning Star."

8683. Sillen, Samuel. "The People, Yes." *New Masses*, 31 (6 June 1939), 22–23. Mentions briefly *UTC*.

8684. Anon. "Book Notes: Richard Wright's New Novel Praised." *Minneapolis Spokesman* (26 January 1940), p. 3. Quotes Henry Seidel Canby on *NS*.

8685. Anon. "Life of a Black Man." *Newsweek*, 46 (26 August 1940), 44. Review of Langston Hughes's *The Big Sea* mentioning W briefly. Reprinted: 1997.

8686. Anon. "Looks at Books." *The Pittsburgh Courier* (28 December 1940) p. 11. Review of Len Zinberg's *Walk Hard, Talk Loud* comparing it favorably to *NS*.

8687. Anon. "'Native Son' and Its Implications Forum Discussion." *Minneapolis Spokesman* (24 May 1940), p. 1. Reports a vigorous discussion of the novel by the panel and the audience at the Minneapolis Sunday Forum on 19 May.

8688. Anon. "'Native Son,' Much Discussed Novel, Forum Topic." *Minneapolis Spokesman* (17 May 1940), p. 1. Announces a review and panel discussion of the novel at the Sunday Evening Book Review Club.

8689. Anon. "The Negro Playwright's Company." *Equality*, 2 (October-November 1940), 19. Mentions W and *NS*.

8690. Anon. "R. Wright Explains." *The Pittsburgh Courier* (28 December 1940), p. 11. Notice of *How Bigger Was Born* calling W "confused and bewildered."

8691. Illinois Writers' Project. *Cavalcade of the American Negro.* Chicago: Diamond Jubilee Exposition Authority, 1940, p. 44. Notes the great popularity of *NS*.

8692. Jones, Claudia. "The Story of Bigger Thomas." *The Review* (April 1940). Review of *NS* in the organ of the Young Communist League of the United States. Jones's mixed response praises the novel's power, calling it "a major contribution to Negro culture," but criticizes W's treatment of Mary and Jan and his greater emphasis on psychology than on economics.

8693. Luccock, Halford E. *American Mirror: Social, Ethical, and Religious Aspects of American Literature 1930–1940.* New York: Macmillan, 1940, pp. 79–81, 83, 84, 135, 246. Speaks of W's "sullen, straight, bitter realism" and discusses favorably *NS*. Also mentions "Fire and Cloud," a "powerful story."

8694. Newman, Cecil E. "The Lesson of Native Son." *Minneapolis Spokesman* (26 April 1940), p. 2. Editorial defending the novel against charges of unfavorable characterization of the black minister and the role of social uplift organizations. Emphasizes W's message of environmental determinism resulting from racism.

8695. Newman, De Velma. "Every Negro Has Felt Like 'Native Son,'

Staff Writer Says." *Minneapolis Spokesman* (24 May 1940), p. 4. Contests prevailing view as expressed at the Sunday Forum that Bigger is not representative of his race. Newman emphasizes black fear in the presence of whites.

8696. Schuyler, George S. "Views and Reviews." *The Pittsburgh Courier* (5 October 1940), p. 6. Mentions W briefly and unfavorably.

8697. _____. "Views and Reviews." *The Pittsburgh Courier* (7 December 1940), p. 6. Recommends *NS* as a Christmas present despite its "many flaws."

8698. Sutherland, Robert L., and Julian L. Woodward. *Introductory Sociology.* Second ed. Chicago: J.B. Lippincott, 1940, p. 394. Mentions briefly *NS*.

8699. Woodson, Carter G. "*The Big Sea, an Autobiography.* By Langston Hughes." *Journal of Negro History*, 25 (October 1940), 567–568. Mentions W briefly. Reprinted: 1997.

8700. Anon. "'Citizen Kane' Brings Some Fine New Actors to the Screen" *PM* (2 May 1941), p. 5. Notes that Everett Sloane played in *NS*.

8701. Anon. "Historical News and Notices." *The Journal of Mississippi History*, 3 (January 1941), 61–67. Contains a notice of *O. Henry Memorial Award: Prize Stories of 1940* mentioning "Almos' a Man," "Fire and Cloud," *NS*, and W's Mississippi birth (pp. 63–64). Mentions also David Cohn's "The Negro Novel: Richard Wright" and W's rebuttal (p. 66).

8702. Anon. "Historical News and Notices." *The Journal of Mississippi History*, 3 (July 1941), 252–255. Contains a brief notice of the play *NS*.

8703. Anon. "Negro Leaders Issue Protest." *PM* (27 March 1941), p. 19. Notes that W is among the signers of a protest against Jim Crow.

8704. Anon. "Negro Youth to Weigh War-Time responsibilities." *PM* (31 October 1941). Announces a November Washington conference at which W and others will speak.

8705. Anon. "News of the Theater." *New York Herald Tribune* (24 March 1941), p. 8. Announces the premiere on this date of the play *NS*.

8706. Anon. "Rehearsals of 'Native Son' Go On Amid Apparent Confusion." *New York Herald Tribune* (16 March 1941), Sec. IV, p. 1.

Sketch of a scene in rehearsal of the play *NS*.

8707. Anon. "This World." *Minneapolis Spokesman* (25 April 1941), p. 2. Notes that *NS* is still running on Broadway.

8708. Brickell, Herschel. "American Literature," in *1941 Britannica Book of the Year.* Chicago: Encyclopedia Britannica, pp. 43–46. Includes favorable comment on *NS* and, especially, *UTC*.

8709. Claxton, Oliver. "*Native Son* (Paul Green and Richard Wright, St. James Theatre, March 24, 1941)." *Cue* 10 (29 March 1941), p. 30. The play's strong message comes through, but "Mr. Weller's production gives the play a strength and a value it does not intrinsically hold." Reprinted: 1986.

8710. Coan, Otis W., and Richard G. Lillard. *America in Fiction: An Annotated List of Novels That Interpret Aspects of Life in the United States.* Stanford, CA: Stanford University Press, 1941, p. 149. Contains entries for *UTC* and *NS*. Reprinted: 1945, 1949, 1956, 1967.

8711. Foley, Martha. "Foreword," in *The Best Short Stories 1941.* Ed. Edward J. O'Brien. Boston: Houghton Mifflin, 1941, pp. xiii–xvii. Mentions W briefly.

8712. Inglis, Rewey Belle, John Gehlmann, Mary Rives Bowman, and Norman Foerster, eds. *Adventures in American Literature.* Third ed. New York: Harcourt, Brace, 1941, p. 1210. Mentions W briefly as "a rising young novelist and short-story writer."

8713. Kozlenko, William. "Richard Wright," in his *American Scenes.* New York: John Day, 1941, p. 52. Biographical sketch. A radio adaptation of "Fire and Cloud" by Charles K. O'Neill is included in this volume (pp. 51, 53–71).

8714. Lindsay, David. "Folk History." *PM* (2 November, 1941) p. 56. Favorable notice of *TMBV*, "a study of Negro life from the inside."

8715. Newman, Cecil E. "Richard Wright Wins 1940 Spingarn Medal." *Minneapolis Spokesman* (7 February 1941), p. 1. Includes an excerpt from the selection committee citation as well as W's complete acceptance statement.

8716. _____. "This World." *Minneapolis Spokesman* (19 December 1941), p. 1. Notes favorable reception of *TMBV*.

8717. O'Brien, Edward J. "Distinctive Short Stories in American Magazines," in his *The Best Short Stories 1941*. Boston: Houghton Mifflin, pp. 401–407. Lists "Almos' a Man" (p. 406).

8718. Rapport, Samuel. "Literature," in *The American Annual: An Encyclopedia of Current Events*. Ed. A.H. McDannald. New York: Americana, 1941, pp. 409–417. Mentions *NS*, "the novel which probably created the greatest controversy during 1940" (p. 410).

8719. Schuyler, George S. "Views and Reviews." *The Pittsburgh Courier* (18 January 1941), p. 6. Rebuts a letter taking issue with Schuyler's unfavorable comparison of *NS* to Len Zinberg's *Walk Hard-Talk Loud*. Complains of "indignation, Communistic meandering, and pointless psychology in *NS*.

8720. Seaver, Edwin. "Readers and Writers." New York. Typescript of a radio interview with W on 23 December 1941. W discusses the composition of *TMBV*, a projected series of historical novels on "the urbanization of a feudal folk," *NS*, Chicago writers, and prospective changes in fiction in the forties.

8721. Vreeland, Frank. "*Native Son*." *Bob Wagner's Script*, 25 (19 April 1941), p. 27. Confesses to not having attended the play because he is racially prejudiced, but admits that it was well received. Reprinted: 1986.

8722. Anon. "Historical News and Notices." *The Journal of Mississippi History* 4 (July 1942), 179–183. Contains a notice of *The Best Short Stories, 1941* mentioning briefly "Almos' a Man."

8723. Anon. "Big Gambles Saved the Face of the Face of Show Business in 1941." *The Chicago Defender* (10 January 1942), p. 20. One of the gambles was the decision of the Mercury Theatre to stage *NS* in spite of Southern racism.

8724. Anon. "'Bigger Thomas' Visits City." *The Chicago Defender* (31 January 1942), p. 21. Photograph of Canada Lee and others in Chicago.

8725. Anon. "Billikens Greet 'Native Son' Star." *The Chicago Defender* (3 January 1942) p. 19. Photograph of children with Canada Lee, "star of the dramatic hit, "Native Son."

8726. Anon. "Life Is Endless Training for Star of 'Native Son.'" *Minneapolis Morning Tribune* (12 January 1942), p. 5 Article on Canada Lee.

8727. Anon. "Historical News and Notices." *The Journal of Mississippi History* 4 (July, 1942), 179–183. Contains a notice of *The Best Short Stories, 1941* mentioning briefly "Almos a Man."

8728. Anon. "'Native Son' Plays at Lyceum Three Nights January 12, 13, and 14." *Minneapolis Spokesman* (9 January 1942), p. 1. Announces the play's Minneapolis stand; reviews careers of W, Green, and Welles; lists the cast; and calls the theme "an eloquent and moving appeal for race tolerance."

8729. Appel, Benjamin, "People of Crime." *The Saturday Review of Literature*, 25 (18 April 1942), 7. Favorable review of Algren's *Never Come Morning*, in which he has made his characters "terrifying and important as Bigger" was made terrible and important by Wright."

8730. DuBois, W.E.B. "A Chronicle of Race Relations." *Phylon: The Atlanta University Review of Race and Culture*, 3 (Fourth Quarter) (1942), 433. Notes that W is not mentioned in a *Saturday Review of Literature* issue on the Deep *South*.

8731. DuBois, W.E.B. "A Chronicle of Race Relations." *Phylon: The Atlanta University Review of Race and Culture*, 3 (Third Quarter 1942), p. 334. Compares Ted Poston's "The Revolt of the Evil Fairies" with *NS* with respect to racial self-criticism. Reprinted 1980.

8732. Locke, Alain Leroy. "Negroes (American)," in *1942 Britannica Book of the Year*. Chicago: Encyclopaedia Britannica, p. 472. Includes favorable comment on *NS*, the novel and the play.

8733. Newman, Cecil. "This World." *Minneapolis Spokesman* (2 January 1942), p. 1. Mentions unfavorable responses to *TMBV* by Harry P. Felgate and John Selby.

8734. _____. "This World." *Minneapolis Spokesman* (29 May 1942), p. 1. Notes that Nelson Algren's *Never Come Morning* is reminiscent of *NS*. W contributed the introduction.

8735. _____. "This World." *Minneapolis Spokesman* (16 January 1942), p. 1. Criticizes W.J. McNally's review of the play *NS* for minimizing its social message.

8736. Scott, Helen M. "Inquisitive Sal." *Minneapolis Spokesman* (16 January 1942), p. 4. Contains an interview with Canada Lee, saying almost nothing about the play *NS*.

8737. Anderson, M. Margaret. "Open Letter to the Reader's Digest." *Common Ground*, 3 (Spring 1943), 107–108. Mentions W briefly (p. 107).

8738. Anon. "Wright, Richard," in *Webster's Biographical Dictionary*. Ed. William Allan Neilson. Springfield, MA: G.S.C. Merriam, 1943, p. 1600. Brief biographical entry. Reprinted: 1966, 1980.

8739. Downs, Karl E. *Meet the Negro*. Pasadena: Login Press, 1943, 96 pp. Includes brief discussion of *NS* (pp. 22–23) and mentions *TMBV* (p. 74).

8740. Hughes, Langston. "The Future of Black America. "*Negro Digest*, 1 (July 1943), 3–6. Mentions W briefly. Reprinted: 2002.

8741. Sandburg, Carl. "Negro Opportunity," in his *Home Front Memo*. New York: Harcourt, Brace, 1943, pp. 204–207. Mentions briefly *NS* (p. 205).

8742. Anon. "*13 Against the Odds* by Edwin R. Embree." *The American Historical Review*, 49 (July 1944), 801. Review mentioning W briefly.

8743. Anon. "*Thirteen Against the Odds*, by Edwin R. Embree." *The New Republic*, 110 (13 March 1944), 358. Notice mentioning W briefly.

8744. Anon. "Wright, Richard," in *The Columbia Encyclopedia*. Ed. Clarke F. Ansley. New York: Columbia University Press, 1944, p. 48 of supplement. Very brief biographical entry.

8745. Cayton, Horace R. "Robert Park." *The Pittsburgh Courier* (26 February 1944, p. 7. Cayton recalls a dinner at his Chicago apartment with Park, who praised W as "a great writer."

8746. Davie, Maurice R. "Success Stories of Negro Americans." *The Yale Review*, 33 (March 1944), 547–549. Review of Edwin R. Embree's *13 Against the Odds* calling W "portrayer of the forces that create hatred and strife."

8747. Flanagan, John T. "The Middle Western Historical Novel." *Journal of the Illinois State Historical Society*, 37 (March 1944), 7–47. Mentions W briefly (pp. 30–44).

8748. Hansen, Harry. "New Novels on Social Issues." *Survey Graphic*,

33 (April 1944), 221–222. Review of Lillian Smith's *Strange Fruit* mentioning favorably *NS*.

8749. Redus, M.W. "*Thirteen Against the Odds* by Edwin Embree." *Southwest Review*, 29 (Autumn 1943–Summer 1944), 597–599. Favorable review calling W the "author of bitter and brilliant writings."

8750. Thorp, Willard, and Margaret Farrand Thorp. "Biographical Notes," in their *Modern Writing*. New York: American Book Company, 1944, pp. 448–460. Includes biographical sketch of W (p. 460). An excerpt *from TMBV* is included in this collection.

8751. Anon. "Historical News and Notices." *The Journal of Mississippi History*, 7 (April 1945), 121–126. Contains a brief notice of *BB*.

8752. Anon. "News and Comment." *Journal of the Illinois State Historical Society*, 38 (December 1945), 492–508. Contains a notice of *Black Metropolis* stating that W's introduction "is emotional rather than historical."

8753. Coan, Otis W., and Richard G. Lillard. *America in Fiction*. Revised edition. Stanford, CA: Stanford University Press, 1945, p. 135. Reprint of 1941.

8754. Himes, Chester. *If He Hollers Let Him Go*. Garden City, NY: Doubleday, Doran, 1945, pp. 105–106. Characters in the novel discuss W and *NS*.

8755. Roy, Claude. "Air d'Amérique." *Les Lettres Françaises* (17 March 1945), p. 3. Mentions W briefly.

8756. Anon. "Historical News and Notices." *The Journal of Mississippi History*, 8 (January 1946), 51–53. Contains a notice of *Black Metropolis* mentioning W's introduction.

8757. Anon. "Historical News and Notices." *The Journal of Mississippi History*, 8 (April 1946), 103–107. Notes that an abridgement of *BB* was published in the August 1945 issue of *Omnibook Magazine*.

8758. De Kay, Drake. "Literature," in *The Americana Annual: An Encyclopedia of the Events of 1945*. Ed. A.H. McDannald. New York: Americana, 1946, pp. 456–460. Mentions briefly *BB* (p. 456).

8759. Gannet, Lewis. "Books," in *While You Were Gone: A Report on Wartime Life in the United States*.

Ed. Jack Goodman. New York: Simon and Schuster, 1946, pp. 447–463. Mentions briefly *BB* (p. 458).

8760. Hughes, Langston. "Culture Via the Back Door." *Negro Digest*, 5 (July 1946), 47–48. Notes that W "is widely read and cordially applauded at lectures."

8761. _____. "Culture Via the Back Door." *Negro Digest*, 5 (July 1946), pp. 263–265. Notes that the fame of W and others does not insulate them from racial discrimination. Reprinted: 2002.

8762. _____. "Here to Yonder." *The Chicago Defender* (6 April 1946), p. 18. Notes that although W "is widely read and cordially applauded at lectures, he is still a victim of Jim Crow.

8763. _____. "The See-Saw of Race." *The Chicago Defender* (20 April, 1946), p. 18. Notes the cultural success of W and others. Reprinted.

8764. Maltz, Albert, "What Shall We Ask of Writers?" *New Masses* (12 February 1946), 19–21. Mentions W briefly while criticizing politicized literary criticism.

8765. Quinn, Kerker, and Charles Shattuck. "Contributors," in their *Accent Anthology*. New York: Harcourt, Brace, and Company, 1946, pp. 679–687. Includes a brief note on W, whose "The Man Who Lived Underground" is included in the volume.

8766. Anon. "The Talk of the Town." *The New Yorker*, 23 (22 February 1947), 19–23. Includes an interview with Simone de Beauvoir in which she mentions W (p. 20).

8767. Cowley, Malcolm. "'Not Men': A Natural History of American Naturalism." *The Kenyon Review*, 9 (Summer 1947), pp. 415–435. Mentions briefly *NS* (p. 430). Partially reprinted: 1970.

8768. Fisc[sic]her, Dorothy Canfield. "Preface," in *Black Boy — Jeunesse Noire*. Paris: Gallimard, 1947, p. 13. French translation of 1945. 899.

8769. Gagey, Edmond, *Revolution in American Drama*. New York: Columbia University Press, 1947, pp. 95, 157. Comments briefly on the play *NS*.

8770. Geismar, Maxwell. *The Last of the Provincials: The American Novel, 1915–1925*. Boston: Houghton Mifflin, 1947, pp. 358, 374. Mentions W briefly.

8771. Gunther, John. *Inside U.S.A.* New York: Harper, 1947, pp. 666, 691, 801. Brief mentions of W and *BB*.

8772. Hexter, Margaret B. "From Altar-Boy to Killer." *The Saturday Review of Literature*, 30 (24 May 1947, p. 13. Compares Willard Motley's *Knock on Any Door* favorably to *NS*.

8773. Anon. "Historical News and Notices." *The Journal of Mississippi History*, 10 (October 1948), 353–355. Contains a brief notice of the Modern Library edition of *NS*.

8774. Codman, Florence. "*The Living Is Easy. Dorothy West.*" *The Commonweal*, 48 (25 June 1948), 264–265. Mentions W briefly.

8775. Desternes, Jean. "Nouvel age litteraire." *Les Études Américaines*, No. 10 (1948), pp. 1–12. Mentions W briefly (pp. 9, 10).

8776. Gorer, Geoffrey. *The American People: A Study in the National Character*. New York: W.W. Norton, 1948, p. 199. Mentions favorably *BB*.

8777. Harrison Smith. "American Literature and the Party Line." *The Saturday Review of Literature*, 31 (10 April 1948), 20. Quotes the Soviet critic M. Mendelson attacking W: "It is highly characteristic that Wright, like the other American decadents, begins to represent negroes as hopeless people, idiotic and incapable of any protest against evil...."

8778. Hyman, Stanley Edgar. *The Armed Vision: A Study in the Methods of Modern Literary Criticism*. New York: Knopf, 1948, pp. 162–163, 165, 355. Comments on Frederic Wertham and Kenneth Burke on W.

8779. O'Connor, William Van. *Sense and Sensibility in Modern Poetry*. Chicago: The University of Chicago Press, 1948, p. 244. Mentions W briefly.

8780. Walrond, Eric. "Reviews of Books." *Life and Letters* (November 1948), pp. 176, 178, 180. Favorable review of *TMBV*, a book of "power and brilliance." Also mentions favorably *BB*, *UTC*, and *NS*. Reprinted: 1998.

8781. _____. "*Twelve Million Black Voices*. Richard Wright." *Life and Letters*, 59 (November 1948), 176, 178, 180. Highly favorable review contrasting the elitism of Du Bois to W, who "bases himself upon the broad masses. Also comments favorably on *UTC* and *NS*. Reprinted: 1998.

8782. Wecter, Dixon. *The Age of the Great Depression 1929–1941.* New York: Macmillan, 1948, pp. 253, 260. Mentions *NS* and notes that W was on the Federal Writers' Project.

8783. West, Dorothy Herbert, and Estelle A. Fidell, eds. *Essay and General Literature Index: 1941–1947.* New York: H.W. Wilson, 1948, pp. 1839–1840. Lists s.v. W six primary and six secondary items.

8784. Anon., "America's Top Negro Authors." *Color* (June 1949), p. 30. Comments on "the power and fury of *NS*, which was denied the Pulitzer Prize because of racism.

8785. Coan, Otis W., and Richard G. Lillard. *America in Fiction: An Annotated List of Novels That Interpret Aspects of Life in the United States.* Third edition. Stanford: Stanford University Press, 1949, p. 161. Reprint of 1941.

8786. Hook, Sidney. "Report on the International Day Against Dictatorship and War." *Partisan Review*, 16 (July 1949), 722–732. Attacks W's relation to the R.D.R. and Sartre. "If any additional commentary were needed about the character of left-wing French political thought, the emergence of Wright and Garry Davis as political figures would be sufficient" (p. 732).

8787. Humboldt, Charles. "Communists in Novels: II." *Masses & Mainstream*, 2 (July 1949), 44–65. Mentions briefly Benjamin Davis's review of *NS*.

8788. Schlesinger, Arthur M., Jr. "The Life of the Party: What It Means to Be a Communist." *The Saturday Review of Literature*, 32 (16 July 1949), 6–7, 34. Mentions W briefly. Reprinted: 1957.

8789. Anon. "American Literature," in *The Columbia Encyclopedia.* Eds. William Bridgwater and Elizabeth J. Sherwood. Second edition. New York: Columbia University Press, 1950, p. 61. Mentions W briefly. Reprinted in revised form: 1963.

8790. Anon. "James Baldwin." *Commentary*, 9 (March 1950), 257. Headnote to Baldwin's story "The Death of the Prophet" mentioning W briefly.

8791. Anon. "Negro," in *The Columbia Encyclopedia.* Eds. William Bridgwater and Elizabeth J. Sher-

wood. Second Edition. New York: Columbia University Press, 1950, pp. 1371–1373. List *TMBV* in the bibliography. Reprinted in revised form: 1963.

8792. Brown, Lloyd. "Not So Simple." *Masses & Mainstream*, 3 (June 1950), 81–84. Review of Langston Hughes's *Not So Simple* containing a brief, unfavorable mention of W.

8793. Cowley, Malcolm. "Naturalism in American Literature," in *Evolutionary Thought in America.* New Haven: Yale University Press, 1950, pp. 300–333. Mentions briefly *NS*.

8794. Gassner, John. "Bertolt Brecht," in his *A Treasury of the Theatre from Henrik Ibsen to Arthur Miller.* New York: Simon and Schuster, 1950, pp. 456–458. Mentions briefly *NS*. Reprinted: 1963.

8795. Hicks, Granville. "The Appeal of Communism." *Commentary*, 9 (March 1950), 291–294. Review of *The God That Failed* noting that W was a victim of racist exploitation and that his disillusion with Communism resulted from "the boundless hatred of the free mind" that permeates it.

8796. Hughes, Langston. "Some Practical Observations: A Colloquy." *Phylon*, 11 (Winter 1950), pp. 307–311. Mentions W briefly. Reprinted 2002.

8797. _____., et al. "Some Practical Observations: A Colloquy." *Phylon*, 11 (Winter 1950), 307–311. Hughes mentions W favorably. Reprinted: 2002.

8798. Qualls, Youra. "The Bookshelf: Simple — New Observer of U.S. Scene." *The Christian Science Monitor* (12 September 1950), p. 14. Mentions W and Bigger Thomas.

8799. Stone, Irving, "Richard Wright," in his *We Speak for Ourselves: A Self-Portrait of America.* Garden City, NY: Doubleday, 1950, p. 39. Brief headnote to *BB*.

8800. Yezierska, Anzia. *Red Ribbon on a White Horse.* New York: Charles Scribner's, 1950, pp. 157, 158, 161–163, 165, 178, 184–185, 186, 194–196. Frequent favorable mention of W in this autobiographical account of the New York Writers' Project. Includes W's winning the W.P.A. Writers' Contest. Excerpted in 1991.

8801. Brown, Sterling A. "Athletics and the Arts," in *The Integration*

of the Negro Into American Society: Papers Contributed to the Fourteenth Annual Conference of the Division of the Social Sciences. Ed. E. Franklin Frazier. Washington: Howard University Press, 1951, pp. 117–147. Mentions W's collaboration with Green on the play *NS* (p. 136) and mentions also W as a successful novelist (p. 147).

8802. Cowie, Alexander. *The Rise of the American Novel.* New York: American Book, 1951, p. 292. Mentions *NS* favorably, comparing it to Richard Heldreth's *The Slave: or Memoirs of Archy Moore.*

8803. DeVoto, Bernard. "The Ex-Communists." *The Atlantic Monthly*, 187 (February 1951), 61–65. Essay-Review of Richard Crossman's *The God That Failed* including sharp criticism of W's political credulity. Reprinted: 1955.

8804. Gassner, John. "Bertolt Brecht," in his *A Treasury of The Theatre.* Vol. 2. New York: Simon and Schuster, 1951, pp. 456–458. Reprint of 1950.

8805. Gunther, John. *Inside U.S.A.* Revised edition. New York: Harper & Row, 1951, pp. 723, 754, 883. Reprint of 1947.

8806. Hughes, Langston. "Prelude to Our Age: A Negro History Poem." *The Crisis*, 58 (February 1951), 87–90. Mentions briefly *NS*. Reprinted: 1995.

8807. Locke, Alain. "L'Apport intellectuel et Culturel du noir américain." *Les Ètudes Américaines*, No. 29 (1951), pp. 3–6. Mentions briefly *UTC* and *NS* as leftist literature (p. 5). Reprinted: 1960.

8808. Rosenthal, M.L. "On the Dissidents of the Thirties." *The University of Kansas City Review*, 17 (Summer 1951), 294–300. Includes comment on "Between the World and Me." Reprinted: 1990.

8809. Simkins, Francis Butler. *The South Old and New: A History 1820–1947.* New York: 1951, pp. 415, 426. Mentions briefly W and *NS*. Reprinted: 1963.

8810. Baldwin, Leland D. *The Stream of American History.* Vol. Two. New York: American Book, 1952, p. 831. Mentions briefly *BB*.

8811. Bell, Daniel. "The Background and Development of Marxian Socialism in the United States," in *Socialism and American Life.* Vol. 1. Eds. Donald Drew Egbert and Stow Persons. Princeton: Princeton

University Press, 1952, pp. 215–405. Mentions W briefly (pp. 354, 365).

8812. Breit, Harvey. "Talk with Ralph Ellison." *The New York Times Book Review* (4 May 1952), p. 26. Ellison comments on his friendship with W, in whose poetry he found "Eliot's kind of sensibility." Reprinted: 1995.

8813. Hays, H.R. "Nicolás Guillén y la poesia afrocubana." *La Ultima Hora* (10 July 1952), pp. 89. Claims that with the publication of *Sones para turistas* Nicolás Guillén deserves to be placed with W as an interpreter of the black race. Reprinted: 1972.

8814. Abrahams, Peter. *Return to Goli.* London: Faber and Faber, 1953, p. 30. States that W "was strongly attracted to existentialism and took me to lunch with Sartre once."

8815. Ames, Russell. "Social Realism in Charles W. Chesnutt." *Phylon*, 14 (March 1953), 199–206. Mentions W briefly (p. 203). Reprinted: 1999.

8816. Anon. "Banned, Branded, Burned." *Masses and Mainstream*, 6 (August 1953), 10–13. Lists *BB*.

8817. Anon. "Historical News and Notices." *The Journal of Mississippi History*, 15 (October 1953), 289–302. Mentions briefly William Gardner Smith's "Black Boy in France."

8818. Anon. "Life in Harlem." *The Nation*, 176 (6 June 1953), 488. Review of Langston Hughes's *Simple Takes a Wife* mentioning *O* briefly. Reprinted: 1997.

8819. Lawson, John Howard. "McCarthyism and Culture." *Masses and Mainstream*, 6 (May 1953), 19–27. Includes criticism of W and *O* for an "intellectual justification of murder."

8820. Murray, William. "Books Are Burning: The Spreading Censorship." *The Nation*, 176 (2 May 1953), 367–368. Mentions briefly Catholic censorship of W.

8821. Ruth, Kent. "Breaking Out of the 'Cage' of Negro Writing." *Louisville Courier-Journal* (21 June 1953), Sec. 3, p. 12. Mentions briefly Cross Damon and *O*.

8822. Simkins, Francis Butler. *A History of the South.* Second edition. New York: Knopf, 1953, pp. 453, 515, 526. Mentions briefly W and *NS*.

8823. Blair, Walter. "American Literature," in *Encyclopedia Britannica*. Chicago: Encyclopedia Britannica, 1954, vol. 1, pp. 784–794. Notes W's racial protest in *UTC* and *NS* (p. 793). Reprinted: 1954. 80.

8824. _____. "American Literature," in Encyclopedia Britannica. Chicago: Encyclopedia Britannica, 1954, Vol. 1, pp. 784–794. Compares W to James T. Farrell, mentioning *UTC* and *NS*.

8825. Reisman, David. "Marginality, Conformity, and Insight," in his *Individualism Reconsidered and Other Essays.* Glencoe, IL: Free Press, 1954, pp. 166–178. Reprint of 1953. 211.

8826. Smith, William Gardner. *South Street.* New York: Farrar Straus and Young, 1954, p. 17. A fictional character called the Old Man states that "Negroes are not unhappy, son. That's a myth created by Richard Wright."

8827. Brièrre, Annie. "Entretien avec Chester Himes." *France U.S.A.*, No. 80 (January 1955), 8, 12. Mentions W briefly. Reprinted: 199?.

8828. DeVoto, Bernard. "The Ex-Communists," in his *The Easy Chair.* Boston: Houghton Mifflin, 1955, pp. 177–189. Reprint of 1955.

8829. Kempton, Murray. *Part of Our Time: Some Ruins and Monuments of the Thirties.* New York: Simon and Schuster, 1955, pp. 126–127, 128, 138, 145. In a chapter entitled "The Social Muse," Kempton discusses W's early association with *Left Front* and the Communists. Reprinted: 1967.

8830. _____. *Part of Our Time: Some Ruins and Monuments of the Thirties.* New York: Simon and Schuster, 1955, pp. 106–107, 126–127, 128, 138, 145, 196. Comments on W as a Communist writer. Reprinted: 1967.

8831. Riesman, David, and Nathan Glazer. "The Intellectuals and the Discontented Classes." *Partisan Review*, 22 (Winter 1955), 47–72. Mentions briefly *BB* (p. 57). Reprinted: 1955, 1963, 1964.

8832. _____. "The Intellectuals and the Discontented Classes," in *The New American Right.* Ed. Daniel Bell. New York: Criterion Books, 1955, pp. 56–90. Reprint of 1955.

8833. West, Dorothy Herbert, ed. *Essay and General Literature Index: 1948–1954.* New York: H.W. Wilson, 1955, p. 2221. Lists s.v. W

two primary and six secondary items.

8834. Anon. "Historical News and Notices." *The Journal of Mississippi History*, 18 (July 1956), 237–242. Mentions briefly *BP* (p. 238).

8835. Brièrre, Annie. "Lectures américaines." *France U.S.A.*, No. 91 (January 1956), p. 6. Contains a notice of the French translation of *CC*, "un reportage intéressant mais quoique partial."

8836. _____. "Lectures américaines." *France U.S.A.*, No. 93 (March 1956), pp. 2, 8. Contains a review of the French translation of *O.* Compares its power to that of *Crime and Punishment.*

8837. _____. "Lecture américaines." *France U.S.A.*, No. 94 (April 1956), pp. 2, 7. Contains a review of the French translation of *SH* noting its suspense and use of psychology.

8838. Coan, Otis W., and Richard G. Lillard. *America in Fiction: An Annotated List of Novels That Interpret Aspects of Life in the United States.* Fourth edition. Stanford, California: Stanford University Press, 1956.

8839. Hughes, Langston, and Milton Meltzer. *A Pictorial History of the Negro in America.* New York: Crown, 1956, pp. 281, 286. Quotes from *TMBV* and mentions briefly W and *NS*. Reprinted: 1963, 1968, 1973.

8840. Jelliffe, Robert A., ed. *Faulkner at Nagano,* Tokyo: Kenkyusha, 1956, pp. 171–172. Includes Faulkner's comments on W.

8841. Barnes, Lois. "Letter." *Mainstream*, 10 (June 1957), 64. Includes a comment critical of W.

8842. Carpenter, Frederic I. "The Adolescent in American Fiction." *The English Journal*, 46 (September 1957), 313–319. Mentions briefly *BB* (p. 319).

8843. Howe, Irving. Untitled Headnote. *Dissent.* 4 (Autumn 1957), p. 358. Comments on W's lecture tour in Scandanavia as an introduction to a selection from *WML*.

8844. Hughes, Langston. "Langston Hughes' Speech at the National Assembly of Authors and Dramatists Symposium: 'The Writer's Position in America.'" *Mainstream* (July 1957), pp. 46–48. Mentions W among other black expatriate writers. Reprinted 2002.

8845. _____. "The Writer in

America." *Mainstream*, 10 (July 1957), 46–48. Mentions briefly *NS*.

8846. _____. "Where's the Horse for a Kid That's Black?" *Masses and Mainstream*, 10 (July 1957), pp. 46–48. Short essay mentioning briefly *NS*. Reprinted: 1993.

8847. Knox, George. *Critical Moments*: Kenneth Burke's *Categories and Critiques*. Seattle: University of Washington Press, 1957, pp. 39, 89. Quotes from *A Grammar of Motives* mentioning W.

8848. Levin, Harry. "A Gallery of Mirrors," in his *Contexts of Criticism*. Cambridge: Harvard University Press, 1957, pp. 234–250. Reprint of 1949.123.

8849. Merrill, Francis E. *Society and Culture: An Introduction to Sociology*. Englewood Cliffs, NJ: Prentice-Hall, 1957, pp. 287–288. Cites favorably *BB*.

8850. Schlesinger, Arthur M., Jr. "The Life of the Party," in *The Saturday Review Treasury*. Ed. John Haverstick, et al. New York: Simon and Schuster, 1957, pp. 333–343. Reprint of 1949.

8851. Smith, Bradford. *Why We Behave Like Americans*. Philadelphia: J.B. Lippincott, 1957, p. 219. Notes that W "describes the effects of discrimination upon the Negro" (p. 218).

8852. Starobin, Joseph. "More Comments on Howard Fast." *Mainstream*, 10 (April, 1957), 51–54. Mentions W briefly.

8853. Strong, Augusta. "Negro Culture." *Mainstream* 10 (February 1957), pp. 62–64. Review of Margaret Just Butcher's *The Negro in American Culture* mentioning W briefly.

8854. Anon. "Les Américains." *France U.S.A.* No. 123 (December 1958), p. 7. Review mentioning W briefly.

8855. Anon. "Wright, Richard," in *Everyman's Dictionary of Literary Biography: English and American*. Ed. D.C. Browning. London: J.M. Dent, 1958, p. 740. Brief biographical sketch mentioning *UTC, NS, BB, O*, and *BP*. Reprint of 1962.43.

8856. Brièrre, Annie. "Lectures américaines." *France U.S.A.*, No. 120-121 (September-October 1958), pp. 2, 7. Contains a brief review of the French translation of *PS*.

8857. Browning, D.C., after John W. Cousin. *Everyman's Dictionary of Literary Biography, English & Amer-*

ican. London: J.M. Dent, 1958, p. 756. Entry for W lists six of his works.

8858. Foley, Martha, and David Burnett. "Biographical Notes," in their *The Best American Short Stories 1958*. Boston: Houghton Mifflin, 1958. W's note appears on p. 352. The volume contains "Big, Black, Good Man" (pp. 337–347).

8859. Fox, Maynard. "*College English*." *Abstracts of English Studies*, 1 (1958), 332–333. Abstract of an article on W and others by Stanley Edgar Hyman.

8860. Jameson, R.D. "*Die Neueren Sprachen*." *Abstracts of English Studies*, 1 (1958), 131. Abstract of an article on W by Heinz Rogge.

8861. Lowery, Raymond. "Sometimes Bitter But More Often Humorous." *Raleigh News and Observer* (2 November 1958), Part 3, p. 5. Review of *The Langston Hughes Reader* mentioning W briefly. Reprinted: 1997.

8862. Mphahlele, Ezekiel. "*Black Orpheus*: *A Journal of African and Afro-American Literature*. Edited by Ulli Beier," *Ibadan*, No. 2 (1958), pp. 36–37. Mentions W briefly.

8863. Patrick, J. Max. "*La Revue de Paris*." *Abstracts of English Studies*, 1 (1958), 1348. Abstract of an article on W by Raymond Las Vergnas.

8864. Schumann, Hildegard. *Zum Problem Des Kritischen Realismus Bei John Steinbeck*. Halle (Saale): Max Niemyer Verlag, 1958, p. 37. Mentions W briefly.

8865. Bettersworth, John K. *Mississippi: A History*. Austin: Steck, 1959, p. 508. Comments on W, mentioning briefly *NS*.

8866. Jones, Le Roi. "Langston Hughes' *Tambourines to Glory*." *The Jazz Review*, 2 (June 1959), 33–34. Calls *NS* "among the three greatest novels ever written by a Negro in America" along with *Cane* and *Invisible Man*.

8867. Kristensen, Tom. "De NYE BØGER: Richard Wrights Sanhed." *Copenhagen Politiken*, 29 December 1959. Review of *LD* as a shocking novel of corruption and racism. Provides a plot summary.

8868. Perrin, Porter G. *Writer's Guide and Index to English*. Third edition. Chicago: Scott, Foresman, 1959, p. 288. Quotes three paragraphs describing a bullfight from *PS* to illustrate good paragraph

movement and effective use of active verbs.

8869. Rubinstein, Annette T. "American Negro Fiction." *Mainstream*, 12 (October 1959), 54–56. Review of Robert A. Bone's *The Negro Novel in America* mentioning briefly W and *NS*.

8870. Shannon, David A. *The Decline of American Communism: A History of the Communist Party of the United States Since 1945*. New York: Harcourt Brace, 1959, p. 56. Mentions W briefly.

8871. Woodson, Carter G., and Charles H. Wesley. *The Story of the Negro Retold*. Washington: The Associated Publishers, 1959, pp. 244, 393. Comments briefly on W and includes a photograph.

8872. Blair, Walter, "American Literature," in *Encyclopedia Britannica*. Chicago: Britannica, 1960, vol. 1, pp. 784–794. Reprint of 1954.80.

8873. Franklin, John Hope, and Rayford Logan. "Negro, American," in *Encyclopedia Britannica*. Chicago: Encyclopedia Britannica, 1960, vol. 16, pp. 194–201. Notes that W "gained wide recognition" for *UTC, NS, BB*, and *O*.

8874. Gassner, John. "Bertolt Brecht," in his *A Treasury of the Theatre from Henrik Ibsen to Arthur Miller*. New York: Simon and Schuster, 1960, pp. 456–458. Reprint of 1950.

8875. Harris, William O. "*Texas Studies in Literature and Language*." *Abstracts of English Studies*, 3 (1960), 35. Abstract of an article on W and others by Richard Lehan.

8876. Jones, Joseph, Ernest Marchand, H. Dan Piper, J. Albert Robbins, and Herman E. Spivey, comps. *American Literary Manuscripts: A Checklist of Holdings in Academic, Historical and Public Libraries in the United States*. Austin: University of Texas Press, 1960, pp. 419–420. Lists letters and a manuscript at Yale and, mistakenly, Hartford Theological Seminary.

8877. Kinney, Arthur F. "*Phylon*." *Abstracts of English Studies*, 3 (1960), 557–558. Abstract of an article on W and others by Harold R. Isaacs.

8878. Lamming, George. *The Pleasures of Exile*. London: Michael Joseph, 1960, p. 26. Mentions W's introduction to Lamming's *In the Castle of My Skin*. Reprinted: 1992.

8879. Locke, Alain. "L'Apport Intellectuel et culturel du noir américain." *Les Études Américaines*, No. 71 (1960), 1–4. Reprint of 1951.

8880. Reddick, L.D. "The Negro as Southerner and American," in *The Southerner as American*. Ed. Charles Grier Sellers, Jr. Chapel Hill: The University of North Carolina Press, 1960, pp. 130–147. Comments briefly on W and Bigger Thomas.

8881. Schlesinger, Arthur M., Jr. *The Age of Roosevelt: The Politics of Upheaval*. Boston: Houghton Mifflin, 1960, p. 168. Mentions W briefly as a signer of the call for the American Writers' Congress.

8882. Waller, John O. "*New Leader*." *Abstracts of English Studies*, 3 (1960), 20. Abstracts an article on *LD* by William S. Poster.

8883. Adler, Betty. *H.L.M.: The Mencken Bibliography*. Baltimore: The Johns Hopkins Press, 1961, p. 291. An entry on BB notes that Mencken was an early influence on W.

8884. Anon. "Obituaries," in *1961 Britannica Book of the Year*. Chicago: Britannica, pp. 509–522. Contains an obituary of W, "one of the most important Negro writers and spokesmen," mentioning *UTC, NS, TMBV, O, CC, WML,* and *LD*.

8885. Anon. "Necrology … 1960," in *The Americana Annual: An Encyclopedia of the Events of 1960*. Ed. John J. Smith. New York: Americana, 1961, pp. 839–852. Includes W with a biographical sketch.

8886. Bernstein, Abraham. *Teaching English in High School*. New York: Random House, 1961, p. 265. Mentions briefly *BB*.

8887. Burress, Lee A., Jr. "*Reporter*." *Abstracts of English Studies*, 4 (1961), 514–516. Abstract of an article on W by James Baldwin (p. 515).

8888. Dawson, Lawrence R., Jr. "*Encounter*." *Abstracts of English Studies*, 4 (1961), 369–372. Abstract of an article on W by James Baldwin (p. 372).

8889. De Andrade, Mario. "Richard Wright," in his *Letteratura Negra: La poesia*. Rome: Editori Riuniti, 1961, p. 441. Brief biographical note. An Italian translation of "I Have Seen Black Hands" is included on pp. 424–426.

8890. _____. "Richard Wright," in his *Letternatura Negra: La prosa*. Rome: Editori Riunti, 1961, p. 371. Note on W and his work focusing

on *BB* and *NS*. Provides an Italian translation of excerpts from "Big Boy Leaves Home" and *NS* (pp. 373–382).

8891. Golden, Harry. *Carl Sandburg*. Cleveland: World, 1961, p. 214. Mentions briefly *NS*.

8892. Hicks, Granville. "Commitment Without Compromise." *Saturday Review*, 44 (1 July, 1961), 9. Review of *Nobody Knows My Name*. Includes discussion of Baldwin's tripartite essay on W. Reprinted: 1970.

8893. Hughes, Langston. *Ask Your Mama: 12 Moods for Jazz*. New York: Alfred A Knopf, 1961. Mentions W in exile in Paris. Reprinted: 1995, 2001.

8894. Kaplan, Louis, ed. *A Bibliography of American Autobiographies*. Madison: The University of Wisconsin Press, 1961, p. 322. Lists *BB* with very brief annotation.

8895. Kinney, Arthur F. "*Phylon*." *Abstracts of English Studies*, 4 (1961), 80–81. Abstract of the second part of an article on W and others by Harold R. Isaacs.

8896. Levin, Gerald. "*Midstream*." *Abstracts of English Studies*, 4 (1961), 383–384. Abstract of an article on W by Gloria Bramwell.

8897. Lomax, Louis E. "It's Like This." *Saturday Review*, 44 (9 December 1961) 53–54. Notice of John Howard Griffin's *Black Like Me* mentioning W briefly.

8898. Mallory, T.O. "*Nation*." *Abstracts of English Studies*, 4 (1961), 338. Abstract of an article on W by Nelson Algren.

8899. Mayfield, Julian. "A Love Affair with the United States." *The New Republic*, 145 (7 August 1961), 25. Review of Baldwin's *Nobody Knows My Name* concluding with a paragraph on "Alas, Poor Richard." Reprinted: 1988.

8900. Sainville, Leonard. "Nota editoriale," in his *Letteratura negra: La prosa*. Rome: Editori Reuniti, 1961, pp. 9–10. Mentions briefly *NS* (p. 9).

8901. Schorer, Mark. *Sinclair Lewis: An American Life*. New York: McGraw-Hill, 1961, pp. 742, 812. Mentions Lewis praising W at South Carolina State College for Negroes and notes Lewis's influence on W.

8902. Agee, James. *Letters of James Agee to Father Flye*. New York: George Braziller, 1962, pp. 145–147. In a letter dated 21 May 1945 Agee

highly recommends *BB* to Father Flye.

8903. Bradley, Sculley. "The Twentieth Century: Literary Renaissance and Social Challenge," in *The American Tradition in Literature*. Eds. Sculley Bradley, Richard Croom Beatty, and E. Hudson Long. Revised edition. Vol. 2. New York: Norton, 1962, pp. 870–880. Mentions W briefly (p. 879). Reprinted: 1967, 1974.

8904. Congdon, Don. "Major Novelists," in his *The Thirties: A Time to Remember*. New York: Simon and Schuster, 1962, pp. 499–505. Mentions W and *NS* s.v. "The Next in Line."

8905. Hughes, Langston. *Fight for Freedom: The Story of the NAACP*. New York: W.W. Norton, 1962, pp. 68, 117. Mentions W briefly as a Spingarn Medal recipient and quotes briefly from *TMBV*. Reprinted: 2001.

8906. _____. "Old Customs Die Young." *The Chicago Defender* (29 September 1962), p. 10. Relates a conversation with a hotel manager in New York who considered *NS* "a disgraceful book."

8907. _____. "The Woes of a Writer." *Authors Guild Bulletin* (1962), p. 8. Mentions W briefly. Reprinted: 2002.

8908. Montgomery, Robert L., Jr., and William O.S. Sutherland, Jr. "Questions: Books and Men in Memphis," in their *Language and Ideas*. Boston: Little, Brown, 1962, p. 198. Study questions for an excerpt from *BB*.

8909. Mphahlele, Ezekiel. *Down Second Avenue*. Berlin: Seven Seas, 1962, p. 194. Mentions W briefly (p. 194).

8910. Smith, Hubert W. "*New Republic*." *Abstracts of English Studies*, 5 (1962), 32–34. Abstract of an article on W by Irving Howe.

8911. Webster, Harvey Curtis. "Pity the Giants." *The Nation*, 195 (1 September 1962), 96–97. Mentions W briefly. Reprinted: 1996.

8912. Yackshaw, Robert. "*Critic*." *Abstracts of English Studies*, 5 (1962), 298–299. Abstract of an article on W and others by Thomas McDonnell.

8913. Anon. "Negro," in *The Columbia Encyclopedia*. Eds. William Bridgwater and Seymour Kurtz. Third edition. New York: Columbia University Press, 1963, pp. 1473–1475. Revised reprint of 1950.

8914. Anon. "American Literature," in *The Columbia Encyclopedia*. Eds. William Bridgwater and Seymour Kurtz. Third edition. New York: Columbia University Press, 1963, pp. 64–65. Revised reprint of 1950.

8915. Anon. "Wright, Richard," in *Lexikon der Weltliteratur*. Ed. Gero von Wilpert. Stuttgart: Alfred Kröner Verlag, 1963, p. 1445. Biographical sketch naming W's books, and their German titles through *EM*.

8916. Blake, Nelson Manfred. *A History of American Life and Thought*. New York: McGraw-Hill, 1963, p. 568. Mentions briefly *NS*.

8917. _____. *A History of American Life and Thought*. New York: McGraw-Hill, 1963, p. 568. Mentions briefly *NS*.

8918. [Brièrre, Annie]. L'Amérique à travers ses livres." *France U.S.A.*, No. 165 (January 1963), p. 2. Contains a notice of the French translation of *EM* with a photograph of W.

8919. Brièrre, Annie. "Les U.S.A. à travers les romans et les essais." *France U.S.A.*, No. 168 (October 1963). Contains a notice of Paul Oliver's *Le monde du blues* with a favorable quotation from W.

8920. Ezell, John Samuel. *The South Since 1865*. New York: Macmillan, 1963, p. 294. Mentions briefly *UTC* and *NS*.

8921. Fallaci, Oriana. "Sammy Davis, Jr.: The Luck to Be Ugly," in her *The Egotists: Sixteen Surprising Interviews*. Chicago: Henry Regnery, 1963, pp. 225–238. Davis mentions W briefly (p. 231).

8922. Gassner, John. "Bertolt Brecht," in his *A Treasury of the Theatre from Henrik Ibsen to Arthur Miller*. New York: Simon and Schuster, 1963, pp. 456–458. Reprint of 1950.

8923. Hashimoto, Fukuo. "James Baldwin: A New Avenue in Black Literature." *Asahi Journal*, 5 (July 1963), 94–98. Discusses Baldwin's youth, his experience with racial prejudice, his feud with W, and finally his exile [Y.H. and T.K.].

8924. Hughes, Langston, and Milton Meltzer. *A Pictorial History of the Negro in America*. Second edition. New York: Crown, 1963, pp. 281, 286. Reprint of 1958.161.

8925. Lehan, Richard. "Existentialism in Recent American Fiction: The Demonic Quest," in *Recent American Fiction: Some Critical Views*. Ed. Joseph J. Waldmeir. Boston: Houghton Mifflin, 1963, pp. 63–83. Reprint of 1959.112.

8926. Leuchtenburg, William E. *Franklin D. Roosevelt and the New Deal, 1932–1940*. New York: Harper & Row, 1963, p. 127. Mentions briefly W, *UTC*, and the *Story* magazine prize.

8927. Riesman, David, and Nathan Glazer. "The Intellectuals and the Discontented Classes," in *The Radical Right*. Expanded edition. Ed. Daniel Bell. Garden City, NY: Doubleday, 1963, pp. 87–134. Reprint of 1955.68.

8928. Ruoff, James. "Katherine Anne Porter Comes to Kansas." *The Midwest Quarterly*, 4 (July 1963), 305–314. In an interview Porter cites W, Ellison, and Baldwin as examples of the danger to a writer of becoming "so involved in one corner of society as to lose his perspective" (p. 310).

8929. _____. "Katherine Anne Porter Comes to Kansas." *The Midwest Quarterly*, 4 (July 1963), 305–314. Porter castigates W (and Ellison and Baldwin): "I'm so tired of all that hatred and poison..." (p. 310). Reprinted: 1987.

8930. Simkins, Francis Butler. *A History of the South*. Third edition. New York: Knopf, 1963, pp. 453, 515, 526. Reprint of 1951 with an additional brief mention of W (p. 453).

8931. Watkins, George T., III. "*CLA Journal*." *Abstracts of English Studies*, 6 (1963), 417–423. Abstract of an article on W and others by A. Russell Brooks.

8932. Wrenn, John N. "*American Quarterly*." *Abstracts of English Studies*, 6 (1963), pp. 318–324. Abstract of an article on W and Baldwin by Maurice Charney (p. 324).

8933. Aaron, Daniel. "The Hyphenate Writer and American Letters." *Smith Alumnae Quarterly* (July 1964), pp. 213–217. Comments on W as outsider and discusses the relation of Ellison and Baldwin to W in the context of the Irving Howe-Ellison exchange.

8934. Bohner, Charles H. *Robert Penn Warren*. New York: Twayne, 1964, p. 18. Mentions W briefly.

8935. Daniel, Bradford. "William Faulkner and the Southern Quest for Freedom," in his *Black, White,* *and Gray*. New York: Sheed and Ward, 1964, pp. 291–308. Quotes from Faulkner's 1955 speech mentioning W briefly at the Southern Historical Association meeting in Memphis.

8936. Evans, Oliver. "The Case of Carson McCullers." *The Georgia Review*, 18 (Spring 1964), 41–42. Quotes W's "enthusiastic criticism" of McCullers. Reprinted: 1996.

8937. Heard, J. Norman. *Bookman's Guide to Americana*. Third edition. New York: Scarecrow Press, 1964, p. 421. Lists *NS* at $5.50 and $4.00 and *TMBV* at $4.75.

8938. Horne, Lewis B. "*Phylon*." *Abstracts of English Studies*, 7 (1964), 82–83. Abstract of an article on W and others by Esther Merle Jackson.

8939. Jones, LeRoi. "Black Writing." *American Dialog*, 1 (July-August 1964), pp. 32–33. Mentions briefly *BB* and *NS*

8940. Lewis, R.W.B. "Ellison's Essays." *The New York Review of Books* (28 January 1964), p. 2. Comments on the Ellison-Howe controversy over W. Reprinted: 1987.

8941. Moran, Fernando. *Nación y alienación en la literatura negro-africana*. Madrid: Taurus, 1964, pp. 48–51. Argues that in *BP* W's reaction to Africa was similar to that of a white liberal. Mentions also *NS* and notes W's connection with *Presence Africaine*.

8942. Nye, Russel B. "Insight on Fiction." *The Progressive*, 28 (March 1964), 42–43. Mentions W briefly.

8943. Renek, Morris. "'Sex Was Their Way of Life': A Frank Interview with Erskine Caldwell." *Cavalier* (March 1964), pp. 12–16, 40–42. Mentions briefly W and *NS* (p. 16). Reprinted: 1988.

8944. Riesman, David, and Nathan Glazer. "The Intellectual and the Discontented Classes," in *The Radical Right*. Garden City, NY: Doubleday/Anchor, 1964, pp. 106–135. Reprint of 1955.

8945. Strode, Hudson. "Comments," in *The Deep South in Transformation: A Symposium*. Ed. Robert B. Highsaw. University of Alabama Press, 1964, pp. 166–171. Mentions briefly *NS* (p. 168).

8946. Algren, Nelson. *Notes from a Sea Diary: Hemingway All the Way*. New York: G.P. Putnam's, 1965, p. 15. Mentions W briefly.

8947. Appel, Alfred, Jr. *A Season of Dreams: The Fiction of Eudora*

Welty. Baton Rouge: Louisiana State University Press, 1965, p. 154. Mentions briefly *NS* (p. 154).

8948. Baldwin, James, Colin MacInnes, and James Mossman. "Race, Hate, Sex, and Colour: A Conversation." *Encounter*, 25 (July 1965), 55–60. Mentions W briefly (p. 59). Reprinted: 1989.

8949. Bracy, William. "Wright, Richard," in *Encyclopedia Americana*. Ed. David C. Whitney. Vol. 29. New York: Americana, 1965, p. 555. Biographical sketch mentioning all of W's books through *WML*. "His fame rests upon his championing of the Negro cause, chiefly through his skill as a novelist." Reprinted: 1969.

8950. Cargill, Oscar. *Toward a Pluralistic Criticism*. Carbondale: Southern Illinois University Press, 1965, p. 139. Comments briefly on W's interest in Mencken.

8951. Daridan, Jean. *Noirs et blancs de Lincoln à Johnson*, Paris: Calmann-Lévy, 1965, pp. 25, 26, 87, 163. Comments on W as a leader of the black intellectual left and cites a letter from W dated 30 June 1946.

8952. Davies, Robert A. "*Massachusetts Review*." *Abstracts of English Studies*, 8 (1965), 509. Abstract of an article on W and others by Saunders Redding.

8953. Fidell, Estelle A., ed. *Essay and General Literature Index: 1960–1964*. New York: H.W. Wilson, 1965, p. 1518. Lists s.v. W five secondary items.

8954. Fohlen, Claude. *Les Noirs aux Etats-Unis*. Paris: Presses Universitaires de France, 1965, pp. 38–39, 126. Mentions *UTC*, comments on *NS*, and lists *NS* and *BB* in the bibliography. Reprinted: 1994.

8955. Hughes, Langston. "*Ebony's* Maturity: An Evaluation from Birth." *Ebony*, 20 (November 1965), pp. 425–429. Mentions briefly *BB*. Reprinted: 2002.

8956. Maruya, Sajichi. "From Baldwin's Three Books." *Shukan Dokushin* [*Weekly Reader*] (8 January 1965). Mixed review of three of Baldwin's works. The best piece in *Nobody Knows My Name* is "Alas, Poor Richard," *Giovanni's Room* is reminiscent of Mauriac's *Another Country*, though reminiscent of Graham Greene's *The Fallen Idol*, lacks dynamism [Y.H. and T.K.].

8957. Mossman, James. "Race, Hate, Sex and Colour: A Conversa-

tion with James Baldwin and Colin Mac Innes." *Encounter*, 25 (July 1965), 55–60. MacInnes asks Baldwin if there is a danger that he, like W. will become more "an emblematic figure" that an artist, Baldwin answers affirmatively. Reprinted: 1989.

8958. Ozawa, Fumio. "What Sustains the Essence of Negro Literature, VI: Between Richard Wright and James Baldwin." *Showa Joshi Daigaku Gakuen* [*Showa Women's College Instruction*], 304 (April 1965), 58–67. Compares the lives and literary stances of the two writers [Y.H. and T.K.].

8959. Swanberg, W.A. *Dreiser*. New York: Charles Scribner's, 1965, pp. 473, 474, 502. Notes that W was a vice-president of American Peace Mobilization, mentions that W heard a speech by Dreiser on 28 February 1941 and attended a cocktail party in his honor on 2 June 1944.

8960. Walters, Dorothy. *Wisconsin Studies in Contemporary Literature*, 8 (1965), 107–109. Abstract of an article on *O* by Kingsley Widmer (p. 108).

8961. Alford, Norman W., and John S. Phillipson. "*Preuves*." *Abstracts of English Studies*, 9 (1966), 184–189. Abstracts of two articles on W by James Baldwin (pp. 185–186, 187).

8962. Anon. "Wright, Richard," in *Webster's Biographical Dictionary*. Ed. William Allan Neilson. Springfield, MA: G.& C. Merriam, 1966, p. 1600. Reprint of 1943.

8963. Anthony, Mother Mary. "*Ramparts*." *Abstracts of English Studies*, 9 (1966), 607. Abstract of an article on Baldwin and W by Eldridge Cleaver.

8964. Ari, Jiro. *Amerika no Negro Sakka Tachi* [*America's Negro Writers.*]. Tokyo: Taiyosha, 1966. Book of essays, including "The Appearance of the Mutation Writer Baldwin," "Wright's Family and Baldwin's Room," "Why Aren't the Happenings in the Room Described?" and "Returning to America" [Y.H. and T.K.].

8965. Belinga, M.S. Eno. "La Culture négro-afticaine." *Démocratie nouvelle* Nos. 7–8 (July-August 1966), pp. 73–88. Calls Peter Abrahams "le 'Richard Wright de l'Afrique australe.'"

8966. Bontemps, Arna. "Preface,"

in his and Jack Conroy's *Any Place but Here*. New York: Hill and Wang, 1966, p. v. Mentions briefly W on the Illinois Writers project.

8967. Crouzet, Maurice. *Histoire général des civilisations*. vol. 7: *L'époque contemporaine*. Paris: Presses universitaires de France, 1966, pp. 175, 460. Mentions W briefly.

8968. Dent, Tom. "The Free Southern Theater: An Evaluation." *Freedomways*, 6, no. 1 (1966), 26–30. Mentions W briefly. Reprinted: 1991.

8969. Erzgräber, W. *Zeitschrift für Anglistik und Amerikanistik*, 9 (1966), 126–133. Abstract of an article on Baldwin and W by Heinz Wüstenhagen (p. 133).

8970. Floan, Howard R. *William Saroyan*. New York: Twayne, 1966, p. 114. Mentions briefly the play *NS*.

8971. Gerber, Helmut E. *Bulletin of Bibliography*, 9 (1966), 141–143. Abstract of a bibliography of W by Michel Fabre and Edward Margolies (p. 141).

8972. Huttar, Charles. "*Princeton University Library Chronicle*." *Abstract of English Studies*, 9 (1966), 649. Abstract of an article by Willard Thorp on the Whit Burnett papers mentioning W briefly.

8973. Jones, Howard Mumford. *Jeffersonianism and the American Novel*. New York: Teacher's College Press, 1966, p. 55. Mentions briefly *NS*.

8974. Miller, James E., Jr. "The New Negro Writer," in *The Literature of the United States*. Eds. Walter Blair, Theodore Hornberger, Randall Stewart, and James E. Miller, Jr. Third Edition, vol. 2, Chicago: Scott Foresman, 1966, pp. 1357–1358. Mentions W briefly.

8975. Sackett, S.J. "*Vlaamse Gids*." *Abstracts of English Studies*, 9 (1966), 541. Abstract of an article on W and others by Wm. Toebasch.

8976. Williams, John A. "Introduction to the First Edition," in his *Beyond the Angry Black*. New York: Cooper Square, 1966, pp. xvii–xix. Reprint of 1962.107.

8977. _____. "Introduction to the Second Edition," in his *Beyond the Angry Black*. New York: Cooper Square, 1966, pp. xi–xvi. Contains a paragraph on the continuing relevance of W (p. xv).

8978. _____. "Richard Wright," in his *Beyond the Angry Black*. New York: Cooper Square, 1966, p. 173.

Reprint of 1962.108 with an additional sentence mentioning *PS*, *LT*, *SH*, and *WML*.

8979. Woodson, Carter G., and Charles H. Wesley. *The Negro in Our History*. Eleventh edition. Washington: Associated, 1966, p. 695. Mentions briefly W, *NS*, and *BB*.

8980. Bell, Daniel. *Marxian Socialism in the United States*. Princeton: Princeton University Press, 1967, pp. 142n, 153. Reprint of 1952.

8981. Bendiner, Robert, "When Culture Came to Main Street," *Saturday Review*, 50 (1 April 1967), 19–21. Mentions W briefly (p. 20).

8982. Boardman, Fon W., Jr. *The Thirties: America and the Great Depression*. New York: Henry Z. Walck, 1967, p. 94. Mentions briefly W on the Writers' Project.

8983. [Bradley, Sculley]. "The Twentieth Century: Literary Renaissance and Social Challenge," in *The American Tradition in Literature*. Eds. Sculley Bradley, Richmond Croom Beatty, and E. Hudson Long. Third edition. Vol. 2. New York: Norton, 1967, pp. 1025–1037. Reprint of 1962.

8984. Butcher, Philip. "Baldwin, James (Arthur)," in *Encyclopedia of World Literature in the 20th Century*. Ed. Wolfgang Bernard Fleischmann. Vol. 1. New York: Ungar, 1967, pp. 91–92. Mentions briefly W and *NS*.

8985. Cannon, Steve, Lennox Raphael, and James Thompson. "A Very Stern Discipline: An Interview with Ralph Ellison." *Harper's Magazine*, 234 (March 1967), 76–95. Ellison discusses Jewish and black writers, W, the heroic strain in black life, politics and literature, Hemingway, and other topics. Reprinted: 1995.

8986. Coan, Otis W., and Richard G. Lillard. *America in Fiction: An Annotated List of Novels That Interpret Aspects of Life in the United States, Canada, and Mexico*. Fifth edition. Palo Alto, CA: Pacific Books, 1967, p. 194. Reprint of 1941 with an additional entry for *LD*.

8987. Converse, Margaret. "Black, White Bound Together — Ellison." *The Champaign-Urbana Daily Illini* (14 September 1967) p. 11. Mentions briefly Bigger Thomas.

8988. Corodimas, Peter, and Robert L. Joyce. "*CLA Journal*." *Abstracts of English Studies*, 10 (1967), 70–74. Abstract of an article on James Baldwin mentioning W by Therman B. O'Daniel (p. 71).

8989. Forgue, Guy Jean. *H.L. Mencken: l'homme, loeuvre, l'influence*. Paris: Menard Lettres Modernes, 1967, pp. 65, 343, 392. Paraphrases a passage from *BB* on Mencken, relates how W first became aware of Mencken, and counts W among the many writers who have praised Mencken's style.

8990. Gassner, John. "Realism in the Modern American Theatre," in *American Theatre*. New York: St. Martin's Press, 1967, p. 19. Mentions Paul Green's dramatizations of the Richard Wright novel *Native Ground* (sic), p. 19.

8991. Giammanco, Roberto. *Black Power, Potere Negro: Analisi e testimonianze*. Bari: Editori Laterza, 1967, pp. 263, 374. Quotes Floyd McKissick mentioning briefly *BP* and Etheridge Knight mentioning briefly W.

8992. Hicks, Granville. "Writers in the Thirties," in *As We Saw the Thirties: Essays on Social and Political Movements of a Decade*. Ed. Rita James Simon. Urbana: University of Illinois Press, 1967, pp. 78–101. Mentions briefly W and *NS* (p. 93).

8993. Hughes, Langston. "Introduction," in his *The Best Short Stories by Negro Writers: An Anthology from 1899 to the Present*." Boston: Little, Brown, 1967, pp. xi–xiii. Mentions briefly W and *NS* (p. 2).

8994. Johnson, Robert. "Negro Reactions to Minority Group Status," in *The Substance of Sociology: Code, Conduct, and Consequences*. Ed. Ephraim M. Mizruchi. New York: Appleton-Century-Crofts, 1967, pp. 27–46. Quotes from *BB* (p. 44).

8995. Katz, William Loren. *Eyewitness: The Negro in American History*. New York: Pitman, 1967, p. 399. Mentions briefly W's attraction to communism.

8996. Kempton, Murray. *Part of Our Time*. New York: Dell, 1967, pp. 126–127, 128, 138, 145. Reprint of 1955.

8997. Marx, Gary T. *Protest and Prejudice: A Study of Belief in the Black Community*. New York: Harper & Row, 1967, pp. 84, 145. Mentions W briefly and quotes from *BB* on black anti–Semitism. Reprinted: 1970.

8998. Moore, Geoffrey, and R.W. Willett. "American Literature," in *The Year's Work in English Studies — 1965*. London: John Murray, 1967, pp. 336–392. Mentions W briefly (p. 359).

8999. Ottley, Roi, and William J. Weatherby, eds. *The Negro in New York: An Informal Social History*. New York: The New York Public Library, and Dobbs Ferry, NY: Oceana, 1967, pp. x, 257, 261, 291. Edited from materials written by the Federal Writers Project of New York City, including W. Mentions *UTC*, praises W's craft, and quotes W on Harlem celebrating a Joe Louis victory.

9000. Salzman, Jack. Untitled footnote, in his *Years of Protest: A Collection of American Writings of the 1930's*. New York: Pegasus, 1967, p. 354. Biographical sketch. "I Have Seen Black Hands" is included on pp. 354–355.

9001. Turner, Darwin T. "The Literary Presumptions of Mr. Bone." *Negro Digest*, 16 (August 1967), 54–65. Reprint of 1966.

9002. Algren, Nelson. "City on the Make," in *Law and Disorder: The Chicago Convention and Its Aftermath*. Ed. Donald Myerus. Chicago: American Civil Liberties Union, 1968, pp. 10–11. Mentions W briefly.

9003. Ames, Karl. "*Midway*." *Abstracts of English Studies*, 11 (May 1968), 231–233. Abstract of an article on W and others by Seymour L. Gross (p. 233).

9004. Anon. "Historical News and Notices." *The Journal of Mississippi History*, 30 (May 1968), 166–172. Mentions W briefly (p. 168).

9005. Berman, Ronald. *America in the Sixties: An Intellectual History*. New York: Free Press, 1968, pp. 246, 253. Quotes Ezekiel Mphahlele mentioning W and comments on the Howe-Ellison debate over W.

9006. Couch, William, Jr. "Introduction," in his *New Black Playwrights*. Baton Rouge: Louisiana State University Press, 1968, pp. ix–xxiii. Mentions W briefly (p. x). Reprinted: 1969.

9007. Davies, Phillips G. "*Poet and Critic*." *Abstracts of English Studies*, 11 (October 1968), 423. Abstract of an article on W and others by Martha Ellison.

9008. Drimmer, Melvin, ed. *Black History: A Reappraisal*. Garden City, NY: Doubleday, 1968, pp. 198, 373. Mentions briefly W, *BB* and *NS*.

9009. Early, James, Robert Freier,

Emily Ellison, A.R. Gurney, Jean Sisk, with Louis Eisenhauer and Thomas M. Folds, eds. *Adventures in American Literature*. Classic edition. New York: Harcourt, Brace, 1968, pp. Notes James Baldwin's meeting with W and mentions briefly *NS* and *BB*.

9010. Farrell, James T. "Themes in American Realism," in *The Annals of America*. Vol. 16. Chicago: Encyclopaedia Brittanica, 1968, pp. 395–400. Reprint of 1946.194.

9011. Gurko, Leo. *The Angry Decade*. New York: Harper & Row, 1968, pp. 3, 63, 67, 94, 270–271. Reprint of 1947.206.

9012. Harding, Vincent. "You've Taken My Nat and Gone," in *William Styron's Nat Turner: Ten Black Writers Respond*. Ed. John Henrik Clarke. Boston: Beacon Press, 1968, pp. 23–33. Mentions W briefly (p. 29). Reprinted: 1995.

9013. Handlin, Oscar. *America: A History*. New York: Holt, Rinehart and Winston, 1968, p. 1056. Partial reprint of 1968.

9014. _____. *The History of the United States*. Vol. Two. New York: Holt, Rinehart and Winston, 1968, pp. 502, 514. Mentions W briefly. Partially reprinted: 1968.

9015. Lindfors, Bernth. "A Decade of *Black Orpheus*," 42 (Autumn 1968), 508–510, 512–516. Notes that the first number contains a review of *BP* (p. 508). Partially reprinted: 1986.

9016. Moore, Geoffrey, and R.W. Willett. "American Literature," in *The Year's Work in English Studies — 1966*. London: John Murray, 1968, pp. 331–390. Mentions briefly Warren French on *NS* (p. 362).

9017. Murray, Edward. *Clifford Odets: The Thirties and After*. New York: Frederick Ungar, 1968, p. 32. Compares Odets's disillusion with communism with W's.

9018. Reed, Rex. "Carson McCullers," in his *Do You Sleep in the Nude?* New York: New American Library, 1968, pp. 38–43. Mentions W briefly (p. 39).

9019. Saito, Tadatoshi. "The Problems of Race in James Baldwin's Writing." *Hitotsubashi Ronso [Hitotsubashi University Review]*, 1 (January 1968), 16–31. Baldwin's treatment of race makes a great contribution to the advancement not only of black people but also of mankind. His approach, critical of W's con-

frontational tactics, calls for unity and harmony between the two races [G.H. and T.K.].

9020. Sire, James W. "*Denver Quarterly*." *Abstracts of English Studies*, 11 (January 1968), 16–18. Abstract of an article on W and others by Nathan A. Scott, Jr. (p. 17).

9021. Stevens, Shane. "The Best Black American Novelist Writing Today." *Washington Post Book World* (27 April 1969), pp. 4–5. Review of Chester Himes's *Blind Man with a Pistol* mentioning "the long shadow of Richard Wright." Reprinted: 1999.

9022. Straumann, Heinrich. "Literature," in *American Civilisation: An Introduction*. Eds. A.N.J. den Hollander and Sigmund Skard. London: Longman, Green, 1968, pp. 389–438. Mentions briefly the "terrifying novel *Native Son*."

9023. Wager, Willis, *American Literature: A World View*, New York: New York University Press, 1968, pp. 197, 263. Quotes W on Gertrude Stein's appeal to uneducated black workers and mentions *NS*, *BB*, *O*, and *LD*.

9024. Baldwin, James, Eve Auchinloss, and Nancy Lynch. "Disturber of the Peace: James Baldwin," in *The Black American Writers*, Vol. 1. Ed. C.W.E. Bigsby. Deland, FL: Everett/Edwards, 1969, pp. 199–215. Interview mentioning *NS* briefly (p. 202). Reprinted: 1971, 1989.

9025. Boorkman, Charles J. *Black Bibliography: A Selected List of Books on Africa, Africans, and Afro-Americans*. Long Beach: California State College, 1969, p. 83. Lists *LD*, *NS*, and *O*.

9026. Bracy, William. "Wright, Richard," in *Encyclopedia Americana*. Ed. George A. Cornish. Vol. 29. New York: Americana, 1969, p. 555. Reprint of 1965.45.

9027. Burger, Nash K. "Eudora Welty's Jackson." *Shenandoah: The Washington and Lee University Review*, 20 (Spring 1969), 8–15. Contains a paragraph noting that W and Welty were in school in Jackson at the same time. Reprinted: 1985.

9028. Coles, Robert. "The Words and Music of Social Change." *Daedalus*, 98 (Summer 1969), 684–698. Mentions W briefly (p. 692). Reprinted: 1972.

9029. Dabbs, James McBride. *Civil Rights in Recent Southern Fiction*. Atlanta: Southern Regional

Council, 1969, pp. 10–14, 15–16. Criticizes W for the harshness of his view of the South while endorsing W's criticism of life in Chicago. Compares W and Ellison.

9030. Ekirch, Arthur A., Jr. *Ideologies and Utopias: The Impact of the New Deal on American Thought*. Chicago: Quadrangle Books, 1969, p. 168. Mentions briefly W and the Writers' Project.

9031. Fitz Gerald, Gregory, and Peter Marchant. "An Interview: Ernest J. Gaines." *The New Orleans Review*, 1 (Summer 1969), 331–335. Gaines disavows W's influence (p. 335). Reprinted: 1991.

9032. Goncalves, Joe. "When State Magicians Fail: An Interview with Ishmael Reed." *Journal of Black Poetry*, 1 (Summer-Fall 1969), 72–77. Mentions briefly Max and *NS* (p. 77). Reprinted: 1991.

9033. Graver, Lawrence. *Carson McCullers*. Minneapolis: University of Minnesota Press, 1969, p. 2. Mentions W briefly. Reprinted.

9034. Howe, Irving. "Books: New Black Writers." *Harper's Magazine*, 239 (December 1969), 130–137, 141. Mentions W briefly (p. 130). Reprinted: 1991.

9035. [Kinnamon, Keneth]. "Wright Richard." *American Literature Abstracts*, 3 (December 1969), 73. Abstract of 1969.145.

9036. _____. "Wright, Richard, 'The Pastoral Impulse in Richard Wright'." *American Literature Abstracts*, 3 (December 1969), 73. Abstract of 1969.145.

9037. Lee, Don L. "Black Writing: this is u, thisisu." *Negro Digest*, 18 (March 1969), 51–52, 78–81. Mentions briefly "bigger thomas." Reprinted: 1991.

9038. Major, Clarence. "Vague Ghost After the Father." *Nickel Review*, 4 (3 October 1969), 4. Compares W favorably to Willard Motley and Frank Yerby. Mentions *BB* and *NS*.

9039. Moers, Ellen. *Two Dreisers*. New York: Viking Press, 1969, p. 231. Claims that Clyde Griffiths is the model for Bigger Thomas.

9040. Phillips, Cabell. *The New York Times Chronicle: From the Crash to the Blitz, 1929–1939*. New York: Macmillan, 1969, pp. 393, 402. Mentions briefly W, *BB*, and *NS*.

9041. Pinckney, Darryl. "Blues for Mr. Baldwin." *The New York Review of Books*, 26 (6 December

1969), 32–33. Comments on the W-Baldwin conflict and Eldridge Cleaver's criticism of Baldwin and praise of W.

9042. Redding, Saunders. *Of Men and the Writing of Books.* Lincoln, PA: Vail Memorial Library of Lincoln University, 1969, 8 pp. Comments briefly on the scene in *NS* in which Bigger rapes and murders Bessie. Reprinted: 1992.

9043. Rees, Robert A., and Barry Menikoff. *A Manual to Accompany the Short Story: An Introductory Anthology*, Boston: Little, Brown, 1969, p. 6. Contains a paragraph on "The Man Who Lived Underground" as "an ironic and mordant treatment of the Christian theme of rebirth."

9044. [Rubin, Louis D., Jr.]. "Notes and Reports on Southern Literary Study." *S.S.S.L.: The News-Letter of the Society for the Study of Southern Literature*, 2 (May 1969), 4–8. Lists Dan McCall's *The Example of Richard Wright*.

9045. Rühle, Jürgen. *Literature and Revolution: A Critical Study of the Writer and Communism in the Twentieth Century.* Trans. Jean Steinberg. London: Pall Mall Press, 1969, pp. 441, 442, 465, 474. Quotes from *The God That Failed* and mentions W elsewhere.

9046. Shepperd, Walt. "Dusting the Front Shelves." *Nickel Review*, 4 (21 November 1969), 7. Notes that W is included in Joseph North's anthology of *New Masses* writings.

9047. Smith, Marcus. "*South Atlantic Quarterly.*" *Abstracts of English Studies*, 12 (May 1969), 263–265. Abstract of an article on W and others by James D. Graham (p. 264).

9048. Stevens, Shane. "The Best Black American Novelist Writing Today." *Washington Post Book World* (27 April 1969), Sec. 9, pp. 4–5. Mentions briefly W's influence on Himes (p. 5). Reprinted: 1999.

9049. _____. "The Best Black American Novelist Writing Today." *Washington Post Book World* (27 April 1969), pp. 4–5. Review of Chester Himes's *Blind Man with a Pistol* mentioning "the long shadow of Richard Wright." Reprinted: 1999.

9050. [Sutton, Walter]. "Fiction Between the Wars," in *American Literature: Tradition and Innovation.* Eds. Harrison T. Meserole, Brom Weber, and Walter Sutton. Lexington, MA: D.C. Heath, 1969, pp.

3080–3082. Mentions favorably W, *NS* and *BB*.

9051. _____. "Richard Wright 1909 ([sic]–1960) "in *American Literature: Tradition and Innovation.* Eds. Harrison T Meserole, Brom Weber, and Walter Sutton. Lexington, MA: D.C. Heath, 1969, pp. 3315–3316. Biographical-critical headnote (not always accurate), followed by "The Man Who Went to Chicago."

9052. Thorpe, Earl E. *The Central Theme of Black History.* Durham, NC: Seeman Printery, 1969, pp. 15, 98, 100, 106, 159, 162. Mentions briefly W, *The God That Failed*, and *NS.*

9053. Tinkle, Lon. "Reading and Writing: Africans Cherish American Authors." *The Dallas Morning News* (2 February 1969), p. 7B. Notes that African students have read W and other African American authors.

9054. Toch, Hans. *Violent Men: An Inquiry Into the Psychology of Violence.* Chicago: Aldine, 1969, pp. 186–187. Quotes from and comments on the scenes in *NS* of the murders of Mary and Bessie. Reprinted: 1992.

9055. Waldmeir, Joseph J. *American Novels of the Second World War.* The Hague: Mouton, 1969, 51, 52. Mentions briefly W and *NS.*

9056. Watkins, Mel. "Confession by Proxy." *Nickel Review*, 3 (June 1969), 12. Mentions briefly W and Bigger Thomas.

9057. Weinig, Sister Mary Anthony. "*Richard Wright.*" *Abstracts of English Studies*, 13 (November 1969), 195. Abstract of an article by Keneth Kinnamon.

9058. _____. *Southern Humanities Review*, 12 (March 1969), 164–165. Abstract of an article on W and others by Darwin T. Turner.

9059. Welburn, Ron. "New Slave Journals." *Nickel Review*, 3 (June 1969), 10. Mentions briefly *BB.*

9060. Williams, John A. "Introduction to the First Edition," in his *Beyond the Angry Black.* New York: Cooper Square, 1969, p. xix. Calls W "the first angry man."

9061. _____. "Introduction to the Second Edition," in his *Beyond the Angry Black.* New York: Cooper Square, 1969, pp. xii–xvi. Includes comment on W and Max's summation during Bigger's Trial in *NS.*

9062. Aaron, Daniel, and Robert Bendiner. "Document 44: 'Joe Louis

Uncovers Dynamite' Richard Wright," in their *The Strenuous Decade: A Social and Intellectual Record of the 1930s.* Garden City, NY: Anchor Books, 1970, p. 392. Headnote to a reprinting of W's essay.

9063. Anon. "Wright, Richard," in *A Dictionary of Literature in the English Language From Chaucer to 1940.* Ed. Robin Myers. Oxford: Pergamon Press, 1970, p. 933. Very brief biographical note followed by a list of his works.

9064. Aptheker, Herbert. "Racism and Historiography." *Political Affairs*, 49 (May 1970), 54–57. Mentions W briefly (p. 56). Reprinted: 1987.

9065. Blair, Walter. "American Literature," in *Encyclopedia Britannica.* Chicago: Encyclopedia, 1970, Vol. 1. pp. 773. Reprint of 1954.

9066. Bone, Robert. "The Novels of James Baldwin," in *The Black Novelist.* Ed. Robert Hemenway. Columbus, OH: Charles E. Merrill, 1970, pp. 113–133. Reprint of 1965. 43.

9067. _____." Zora Neale Hurston," in *The Black Novelist.* Ed. Robert Hemenway. Columbus, OH: Charles E. Merrill, 1970, pp. 57–61. Partial reprint of 1958.

9068. Bottorff, William K. "*Richard Wright*," *Abstracts of English Studies*, 14 (November 1970), 196. Abstract of an article by Stanley Edgar Hyman.

9069. Brennan, Sister Mary Ann. "Brown, Lloyd W. *Black Entitles: Names as Symbols in Afro-American Literature.*" *Abstracts of English Studies*, 14 (December 1970), 255. Abstract of an article on W and others.

9070. Burton, Dwight L. *Literature Studies in the High Schools.* New York: Holt Rinehart and Winston. Third Edition, 1970, pp. 275–276, 278–279, Includes a brief discussion of *NS* as a protest novel.

9071. _____. *Literature Study in the High Schools.* Third edition, New York: Holt, Rinehart and Winston, 1970, pp. 275–276, 278–279. Discusses W's social purpose in his fiction, especially *NS.*

9072. Calder, Angus. "Chester Himes and the Art of Fiction." *Journal of Eastern African Research and Development*, 1 (1970–1971), 1–18. Calls *NS* "a classically simple and direct modern reworking of *Crime and Punishment.*

9073. Chambers, Bradford. "Introduction," in *Right On!: An Anthology of Black Literature*. Eds. Bradford Chambers and Rebecca Moon. New York: New American Library, 1970, pp. 11–21. Comments on W and quotes from the introduction to *CC*.

9074. _____, and Rebecca Moon. "Richard Wright," in their *Right On!: An Anthology of Black Literature*. New York: New American Library, 1970, p. 52. Headnote to "Big Boy Leaves Home."

9075. Clark, Marden J., Soren F. Cox, and Marshall B. Craig. "Introduction," in their *About Language: Contexts for College Writing*. New York: Charles Scribner's, 1970, pp. vi–vii. Mentions W briefly.

9076. Clipper, Lawrence J. "Folkloric and Mythic Elements in *Invisible Man*." *CLA Journal*, 13 (March 1970), 229–241. Disclaims influence by W on Ellison (p. 230).

9077. Collins, L.M. *Books for Black Americans*. Nashville: Fisk University Library, 1970, pp. 6, 7, 30, 32–34. Lists *NS*, *BB*, "The Ethics of Living Jim Crow," Constance Webb's biography, and Edward Margolies's *Native Sons*. Also includes an evaluative sketch of W's life and career.

9078. Couch, William, Jr. "Introduction," in his *New Black Playwrights*. New York: Anon Books, 1970, pp. xxiii. Reprint of 1968.

9079. Cowley, Malcolm. "A Natural History of American Naturalism," in his *A Many-Windowed House: Collected Essays on American Writers and American Writing*. Ed. Harry Dan Piper. Carbondale: Southern Illinois University Press, 1970, pp. 116–152. Partial reprint of 1947.

9080. _____. "A Natural History of American Naturalism," in his *A Many Windowed House: Collected Essays on American Writers and American Writing*. Carbondale: Southern Illinois University Press, 1970, pp. 116–152. Reprint of 1950.

9081. Darling, Edward. *When Sparks Fly Upward*. New York: Ives Washburn, 1970 pp. 37–55. Paraphrases substantial passages from *BB* to emphasize W's stubborn integrity. Concludes with W "leaving Memphis to realize "his impossible dream of becoming a writer." Mentions *BB*, *UTC*, and *WML*.

9082. Erzgräber, Willi. "*Ralph Ellison*." *Abstracts of English Studies*,

14 (October 1970), 124. Abstract of an article by William Goede treating "The Man Who Lived Underground" as well as *Invisible Man*.

9083. Fidell, Estelle A., and Norma Freedman, eds. *Essay and General Literature Index: 1965–1969*. New York: H.W Wilson, 1970, p. 1518. Lists s.v. W two primary and seven secondary items.

9084. Franklin, John Hope, and Sterling A. Brown. "Negro, American," in *Encyclopedia Britannica*. Chicago: Encyclopedia, 1970 Vol. 16. pp. 189–201. Calls W "the watershed of Negro fiction, its most influential single figure" (p. 200A). Includes a photograph of W (p. 200).

9085. Garraty, John A. "A Century of American Fiction: John A. Garraty Interviews Alfred Kazin." *American Heritage*, 21 (June 1970), 12–15, 86–90. Kazin mentions W briefly (p. 89).

9086. Geismar, Maxwell. "The Shifting Illusion: Dream and Fact," in *American Dreams, American Nightmares*. Ed. David Madden. Carbondale: Southern Illinois University Press, 1970, pp. 45–57. Includes discussion of W, "almost the best symbol of social concern and social protest being molded into literary masterworks" (p. 55). Comments briefly on *UTC*, *NS*, and *BB*.

9087. Genet, Jean. "Introduction," in *Soledad Brother: The Prison Letters of George Jackson*. New York: Coward-McCann, 1970, pp. [i–ix]. Mentions W briefly (p. [v]).

9088. Genet, Jean. "Introduction," in *Soledad Brother: The Prison Letters of George Jackson*." New York: Bantam Books, 1970, pp. 1–8. Mentions W briefly (p. 4). Reprinted: 1973.

9089. Guttmann, Allen. "Focus on Ralph Ellison's *Invisible Man*: American Nightmare," in *American Dreams, American Nightmare*. Carbondale: Southern Illinois University Press, 1970, pp. 188–196. Mentions W briefly (pp. 188, 192).

9090. Halsell, Willie D. "A Bibliography of Theses and Dissertations Relating to Mississippi, 1969." *The Journal of Mississippi History*, 32 (February 1970), 81–88. Lists dissertations on W by Russell Carl Brignano and Edward L. Margolies.

9091. Hand, John T. "*Ralph Ellison*." *Abstracts of English Studies*, 14 (September 1970), 60. Abstract of an article containing Ellison's views on W's work.

9092. Hayden, Robert. "Words in the Mourning Time," in his *Words in the Mourning Time*. New York: October House, 1970, pp. 41–51. Mentions briefly *BB* and *NS* (p. 48).

9093. Hemenway, Robert. "James Baldwin: 'Everybody's Protest Novel,'" in his *The Black Novelist*. Columbus, OH: Charles E. Merrill, 1970, pp. 218–219. Headnote to the Baldwin essay. Mentions W briefly.

9094. _____. "Nathan A. Scott, Jr.: 'The Dark and Haunted Tower of Richard Wright," in his *The Black Novelist*. Columbus, OH: Charles E. Merrill, 1970, pp. 72–73. Headnote to the Scott essay with comment on W and on Scott.

9095. _____. "Richard Kostelanetz: "The Politics of Ellison's Booker: *Invisible Man* as Symbolic History," in his *The Black Novelist*. Columbus, OH: Charles E. Merrill, 1970, pp. 88–89. Headnote to the Kostelanetz essay. Mentions W's help to Ellison and comments on the Ellison-Howe controversy.

9096. _____. "Richard Wright: 'How "Bigger" Was Born,'" in his *The Black Novelist*. Columbus, OH: Charles E. Merrill, 1970, p. 166. Headnote to W's essay.

9097. _____. "Robert Bone: The Novels of James Baldwin," in his *The Black Novelist*. Columbus, OH: Charles E. Merrill, 1970, pp. 111–112. Headnote to Bone's essay (1965.43). Mentions W briefly.

9098. _____. "William Gardner Smith: The Negro Writer — Pitfalls and Compensations," in his *The Black Novelist*. Columbus, OH: Charles E. Merrill, 1970, pp. 196–197. Headnote to Smith's essay. Mentions W briefly.

9099. Hicks, Granville. "Nobody Knows My Name," in his *Literary Horizons: A Quarter Century of American Fiction*. New York University Press, 1970, pp. 91–95. Reprint of 1961.

9100. Itofuji, Hiroshi. "The Essence of James Baldwin's Writing." *Kaijo Hoan Daigako Kenkyu Hokoku* [*Coast Guard Academy Study Report*], 16 (September 1970), 87–103. As *Moby-Dick* and Tiro Nitta's writing cannot be confined to sea literature and mountain literature, respectively, Baldwin's writing cannot be regarded as black literature. Compares Baldwin's work with W's protest literature, Japanese proletarian literature, and writings about the problems of Koreans living in Japan [Y.H. and T.K.].

9101. Lee, Brian. "American Literature: The Twentieth Century," in *The Year's Work in English Studies—1968*. London: John Murray, 1970, pp. 379–417. Comments briefly on work on W by Edward Margolies (p. 382), John Milton Hughes (p. 398), and Constance Webb (p. 414).

9102. Legris, Maurice. "*Richard Wright*." *Abstracts of English Studies*, 13 (March 1970), 536. Abstract of an article by Phillipe Séjourné.

9103. Lewis, Allan. *American Plays and Playrights of the Contemporary Theatre*. Revised edition. New York: Crown, 1970, p. 252. Describes briefly the play *NS*.

9104. Lingeman, Richard R. *Don't You Know There's a War On?: The American Home Front, 1941–1945*. New York: Putnam's, 1970, p. 330. Mentions *BB* briefly.

9105. Madden, David. "Introduction: True Believers, Atheists, and Agnostics," in his *American Dreams, American Nightmares*. Carbondale: Southern Illinois University Press, 1970, pp. xv–xxxii. Includes brief mentions of W (pp. xxxii).

9106. Margolies, Edward. "Introduction," in *Blood on the Forge*. By William Attaway. New York: Collier Books, 1970, pp. vii–xviii. Mentions briefly *NS* (p. xviii).

9107. Marx, Gary T. "The Social Context of Militancy," in *Americans from Africa: Old Memories, New Moods*. Ed. Peter I. Rose. New York: Atherton Press, 1970, pp. 149–181. Reprint of 1967.

9108. Millet, Kate. *Sexual Politics*. Garden City, NY: Doubleday, 1970, pp. 15–16, 147. Compares briefly Mailer's Stephen Rojack and Bigger Thomas. Also notes the "bitterness and anger" in *BB*.

9109. Nemanich, Donald D. "*Richard Wright*." *Abstracts of English Studies*, 13 (January 1970), 399–400. Abstract of an article by Ronald Sanders.

9110. Paden, John N. "African concepts of Nationhood," in his and Edward W. Soja's *The African Experience*. Vol I: Essays, Evanston: Northwestern University Press, 1970, pp. 418, 421. Notes Senghor's application of negritude to W and quotes from W's "Tradition and Industrialization."

9111. Paden, John N., and Edward W. Soja, eds. *The African Experience*. Vol. III, A Bibliography. Evanston: Northwestern University Press, 1970, p. 1098. Lists *BP*.

9112. Pearce, Howard. "Robert McDowell. *Mothers and Sons*." *Abstracts of English Studies*, 14 (November 1970), 198. Abstract of an article on W and others.

9113. [Rubin, Louis D., Jr.]. "*A Bibliographical Guide to the Study of Southern Literature*." *S.S.S.L.: The News-Letter of the Society for the Study of Southern Literature*, 3 (May 1970), 9–10. Quotes a reviewer in Mississippi making a disparaging remark about W.

9114. _____. "*Southern Humanities Review*." *S.S.S.L.: The News-Letter of The Society for the Study of Southern Literature*, 3 (May 1970), 14. Notes a symposium in the fall 1969 issue including Darwin Turner on W.

9115. Sire, James W. "*Fiction*." *Abstracts of English Studies*, 14 (November 1970), 143. Abstract of an article treating W and others.

9116. Storms, Gilbert. "Gross, Theodore L. *The Idealism of Negro Literature in America*." *Abstracts of English Studies*, 13 (April 1970), 579. Abstract of an article treating W and others.

9117. _____. "*Richard Wright*." *Abstracts of English Studies*, 13 (April 1970), 597. Abstract of an article by Keneth Kinnamon.

9118. Szabo, Andrew, ed. *Afro-American Bibliography*. San Diego: Library, San Diego State College, 1970, pp. 27, 148, 196, 241. Lists *BB*, *TMBV*, *EM*, *LD*, *NS*, *O*, *UTC*, and *WML*.

9119. Tees, Arthur T. "*Richard Wright*." *Abstracts of English Studies*, 13 (September 1970), 659. Abstract of an article by James Nagel.

9120. Turnage, Maxine. "*Bibliography of Mississippi Writers, 1966*." *Abstracts of English Studies*, 13 (February 1970), 468. Abstract of a bibliography including W.

9121. _____. "*1968 Bibliography of Mississippi Writers*." *Abstracts of English Studies*, 13 (April 1970), 598. Abstract of a bibliography including W.

9122. Turner, James, "Afro-American Perspective," in *The African Experience*: Vol. I: Essays. Eds. John N. Paden and Edward J. Soja. Evanston: Northwestern University Press, 1970, p. 604. Mentions briefly W's "anguish of culture conflict" in his attitude toward Africa.

9123. Walker, Alice. "The Black Writer and the Southern Experience." *New South*, 25 (Fall 1970), pp. 23–26. Mentions W briefly (p. 25). Reprinted: 1983.

9124. Webb, Constance W. "Wright, Richard," in *Encyclopedia Britannica*. Chicago: Encyclopedia Britannica, 1970, p. 817. Biographical sketch with commentary on *UTC*, *NS*, *TMBV*, *BB*, and *O*, with mention of his other books through *LD*.

9125. Weinig, Sister Mary Anthony. "*James Baldwin*." *Abstracts of English Studies*, 14 (October 1970), 123. Abstract of an article by Fred L. Standley mentioning W and *NS*.

9126. _____. "*Richard Wright*." *Abstracts of English Studies*, 14 (October 1970), 131. Abstract of an article by Darwin T. Turner.

9127. Anon. *No Crystal Stair: A Bibliography of Black Literature*. New York: The New York Public Library, 1971, pp. 28, 29, 38. Lists *NS* and three critical works.

9128. Aptheker, Herbert. "Afro-American Superiority: A Neglected Theme in the Literature," in *Black Life and Culture in the United States*. Ed. Rhoda L. Goldstein. New York: Thomas Y. Crowell, 1971, pp. 165–179. Mentions W briefly (p. 166).

9129. Baldwin, James, Eve Auchinloss, and Nancy Lynch. "Disturber of the Peace: James Baldwin," in *The Black American Writer*. Ed. C.W.E. Bigsby. Baltimore: Penguin, 1971, pp. 199–215. Reprint of 1969.

9130. Bessy, Maurice. *Orson Welles*. New York: Crown, 1971, p. 21. Mentions briefly Welles's direction of the play *NS*.

9131. Bishop, Jim. *The Days of Martin Luther King, Jr*. New York: G.P. Putnam's, 1971, p. 432. Mentions briefly *BP*.

9132. Blackwell, Louise, and Frances Clay. *Lillian Smith*. New York: Twayne, 1971, p. 114. Mentions briefly *NS*.

9133. Branch, Edgar M. *James T. Farrell*. New York: Twayne, 1971, p. 165. Mentions W as one influenced by Farrell.

9134. Brennan, Sister Mary Ann. "*Richard Wright*." *Abstracts of English Studies*, 14 (January 1971), 333. Abstract of an article by Kenneth T. Reed.

9135. Calder, Angus. "Chester

Himes and the Art of Fiction." *Journal of Eastern Africa Research and Development*, 1 (1970–71), 3–18. Includes comparison of *NS* and *Crime and Punishment* (p. 11) and Himes and W (pp. 11, 13). Reprinted: 1999.

9136. Cornish, Sam. "Bigger Thomas Says Some Bad Niggers Is Over Thirty," in his *Generations*. Boston: Beacon Press, 1971, pp. 76–77. Poem associating W's protagonist with black life in the sixties.

9137. Cunningham, James. "Incest for Brothers: A Criticism," in *Jump Bad: A New Chicago Anthology*. Ed. Gwendolyn Brooks. Detroit: Broadside Press, 1971, pp. 151–156. Mentions W several times while criticizing Calvin Hernton and Eldridge Cleaver. Cf. 1969.63.

9138. Davis, George. *Coming Home*. New York: Random House, 1971, p. [vii]. The epigraph to this novel is from *NS*. Reprinted: 1984.

9139. Editors of *Ebony*. *Ebony Pictorial History of Black America, Vol. III: Civil Rights Movement to Black Revolution*. Chicago: Johnson, 1971, pp. 267–269, 275, 282. Sketches briefly W's life, mentioning *NS* and *BB* and noting his relation to Ellison and Baldwin. Also mentions the play *NS*.

9140. Ellison, Ralph. "Hidden Name and Complex Fate," in *Some Modern Writers*. Ed. Robert Scholes. New York: Oxford University Press, 1971, pp. 365–382. Reprint of 1964.

9141. Fabre, Michel J. "Wright, Richard, 'Richard Wright: The Man Who Lived Underground.'" *American Literature Abstracts*, 5 (December 1971), 156–157. Abstract of 1971. 108.

9142. Fiedler, Leslie A. "The Two Memories: Reflections on Writers and Writing in the Thirties," in his *The Collected Essays of Leslie Fiedler*. New York: Stein and Day, 1971, pp. 235–255. Reprint of 1968.99.

9143. Fleming, Alice. "Richard Wright," in her *Pioneers in Print: Adventures in Print*. Chicago: Reilly & Lee, 1971, pp. 61–75. Biographical sketch for juvenile readers. Derives mainly from *BB*, but mentions briefly *UTC*, and *NS*.

9144. Foley, Martha. "Foreword," in her *The Best American Short Stories 1971*. Boston: Houghton Mifflin, 1971, pp. ix–xi. Mentions W briefly.

9145. Fredrickson, George M. *The Black Image in the White Mind: The Debate on Afro-American Char-*

acter and Destiny, 1817–1914. New York: Harper & Row, 1971, p. 329. Mentions W briefly. Reprinted: 1972.

9146. Gayle, Addison, Jr. "Cultural Nationalism: The Black Novelist in America." *Black Books Bulletin*, 1 (Fall 1971), 4–9. Quotes from "Blueprint for Negro Writing" and discusses *NS* in terms of the "concentration camp metaphor" (p. 9).

9147. Halsell, Willie D. "A Bibliography of Theses and Dissertations Relating to Mississippi, 1970." *The Journal of Mississippi History*, 33 (February 1971), 59–68. Lists a dissertation on W by Steven J. Rubin.

9148. Heard, J. Norman, and Jimmie H. Hoover. *Bookman's Guide to Americana*. Sixth edition. Metuchen, NJ: Scarecrow Press, 1971, p. 863. Lists *BB* at $12.50, *BP* at $8.50, *NS* at $14 *and* $5, *O* at $10, and *TMBV* at $13.50.

9149. Ihde, Horst. "Der Beitrag der Negersklaven zur Kultur in den USA." *Zeitschrift für Anglistik und Amerikanistik*, 19 (1971), pp. 5–35. Quotes from *WML*: "It was through the door of religion that the American Negro first walked into the house of Western Culture" (p. 20).

9150. Katz, William Loren. *Eyewitness: The Negro in American History*. Revised Edition. New York: Pitman, 1971, p. 399. Mentions briefly W's attraction to communism.

9151. Kikuchi, Akira. "A Statistical Analysis of Black Literature: An Approach to Baldwin (in comparison with Wright and Faulkner)." *Otaru Shoka Daigaku Tinbun Kenkyu* [*Liberal Arts Study of Otaru College of Commerce*], 43 (November 1971), 249–270. A statistical analysis of diction in *Another Country* and *NS* indicates that Baldwin's thrives in a cheerful style while W's is characterized by a gloomy style. Frequent appearances of such words as *fear*, *hate*, *proud*, and *despise* in *Go Tell It* suggest that the insults black people receive from whites are far more detrimental to the black psyche than the anger black people feel toward white people. Finally, a statistical analysis of the use of conjunctions in such novels as *Another Country*, *NS*, and *Light in August* shows that Baldwin's novel is more akin to Faulkner's than W's, for Baldwin's and Faulkner's style reflects the authors' retrospective atti-

tude, while W's echoes the author's confrontational voice [Y.H.] and T.K.].

9152. Kimball, William J. "Richard Wright." *Abstracts of English Studies*, 15 (September 1971), 193. Abstract of an article by Blyden Jackson.

9153. Kline, Herbert. "On John Steinbeck." *The Steinbeck Quarterly*, 4 (Summer 1971), 80–92. Notes that his and his brother Mark's friend W showed up in Mexico City during the filming of Steinbeck's *The Forgotten Village*. "John liked him, and sometimes this fine writer joined our talk-fests on the film plans."

9154. Ladner, Joyce. *Tomorrow's Tomorrow: The Black Woman*. Garden City, NY: Doubleday, 1971, p. 47. Mentions briefly *BB*. Reprinted: 1972, 1995.

9155. Lee, Brian. "American Literature: The Twentieth Century," in *The Year's Work in English Studies — 1969*. London: John Murray, 1971, pp. 395–424. Comments on work on W by Nelson Manfred Blake (p. 406), Donald Gibson (pp. 417–418), and Keneth Kinnamon (p. 418).

9156. Lee, Don L. "Introduction: Explanations, Insights, Hindsights, Goings-on," in his *Dynamite Voices: Black Poets of the 1960's*. Detroit, Broadside Press, 1971, pp. 13–27. Mentions W briefly. Reprinted: 1991.

9157. _____. *Dynamite Voices*. Detroit Broadside Press, 1971, pp. 20, 38. Mentions W briefly and quotes from a poem about W by Conrad Kent Rivers.

9158. Lutwack, Leonard, *Heroic Fiction and American Novels of the Twentieth Century*. Carbondale: Southern Illinois University Press, 1971, pp. 125, 129, 142. In a chapter on *Invisible Man*, Lutwack comments on *NS* and *O*.

9159. Maddock, Lawrence H. "Richard Wright." *Abstracts of English Studies*, 15 (December 1971), 400. Abstract of an article by Dan Donlan.

9160. Mphahlele, Ezekiel. *The Wanderers*. New York: Macmillan, 1971, p. 92. Mentions briefly *UTC*.

9161. Nin, Anaïs. *The Diary of Anaïs Nin 1944–1947*. Ed. Gunther Stuhlmann. New York: Harcourt Brace Jovanovich, 1971, pp. 102, 145, 186, 189–191. Notes that she visited W when he moved to Greenwich Village, states that she "had in mind Richard Wright and Helen [sic], and their child in her story "The Child Born Out of the Fog," Records that W disliked Howard Fast for some personal injury he had done him," and described her dinner party for W, who spoke of his desire to go to Europe to escape racism. Nin supports such a move, which might make him less neurotic, "I have tried to be his friend, but I find him reserved and full of mistrust" (p. 191).

9162. Peavy, Charles D. *Go Slow Now: Faulkner and the Race Question.* Eugene: University of Oregon Books, 1971, pp. 42, 43–44. Comments briefly on *TMBV* and "Man of All Work."

9163. Piper, Henry Dan. "Social Criticism in the American Novel of the Nineteen Twenties," in *The American Novel and the Nineteen Twenties.* Eds. Malcolm Bradbury and David Palmer. London: Edward Arnold, 1971, pp. 59–83. Mentions briefly W and *NS* (pp. 60, 61, 64–65).

9164. Rexroth, Kenneth. *American Poetry in the Twentieth Century.* New York: Herder and Herder, 1971, p. 155. Comments favorably on W's haiku as well as his protest poetry.

9165. [Rubin, Louis D., Jr.]. "The Annual Checklist." *S.S.S.L.: The News-Letter for the Society for the Study of Southern Literature,* 4 (December 1971), 2–3. Notes that eight items on W appear in the checklist.

9166. _____. "Essays and Articles." *S.S.S.L.: The News-Letter of the Society for the Study of Southern Literature,* 4 (December 1971), [6–10]. Lists articles on W by John M. Reilly, Keith [sic] Kinnaman [sic], Russell C. Brignano, and John Timmerman.

9167. _____. "Essays and Articles." *S.S.S.L.: The News-Letter of the Society for the Study of Southern Literature,* 4 (May 1971), 8–11. Lists articles on W by Blyden Jackson and Edward Kearns.

9168. _____. "Notes on the Current Scene." *S.S.S.L.: The News-Letter of the Society for the Study of Southern Literature,* 4 (May 1971), 4–5. Mentions correspondence between Mencken and W at the New York Public Library.

9169. _____. "Notes on the Current Scene." *S.S.S.L.: The News-Letter of the Society for the Study of*

Southern Literature, 4 (December 1971), [3–6]. Mentions essays on W by Warren French and Darwin T. Turner.

9170. Simpson, Deborah M. "*Ralph Ellison.*" *Abstracts of English Studies,* 14 (March 1971), 463. Abstract of an article mentioning W.

9171. Steves, Edna L. "*Gilmore Millen.*" *Abstracts of English Studies,* 15 (July 1971), 58. Abstract of an article by Clayton Robinson mentioning W.

9172. Suda, Minoru. "Visionless Catharsis: Fern Marja Eckman's *The Furious Passage of James Baldwin.*" *Kokujin Kenkyu [Negro Studies],* 41 (June 1971), 14–16. Review. *The Furious Passage* deals with Baldwin's antipathy to W [Y.H. and T.K.].

9173. Thorpe, Earl E. *Black Historians: A Critique.* New York: William Morrow, 1971, p. 12. Mentions W briefly.

9174. Tischler, Nancy M. "The Metamorphosis of the Brute Negro." *Recherches Anglaises et Américaines,* 4 (1971), 3–11. Contains a paragraph on *UTC, EM,* and *NS,* emphasizing W's development of "the innocence and ignorance of the "Brute Negro" type.

9175. Turner, Darwin T. *In a Minor Chord: Three Afro-American Writers and Their Search for Identity.* Carbondale: Southern Illinois University Press, 1971, pp. xx, 99, 124, 136. Mentions W briefly and comments briefly on *NS* and Bigger Thomas.

9176. Vidal, Gore. "Taking a Grand Tour of Anaïs Nin's High Bohemia Via the Time Machine." *Los Angeles Times Book Review* (26 September 1971), pp. 1, 5, 23. Mentions W briefly (p. 1). Reprinted: 1993.

9177. Walker, Alice. "*The Autobiography of Miss Jane Pittman.*" *The New York Times Book Review* (23 May 1971), pp. 6, 12. Reprinted: 1991.

9178. West, Hollie I. "The Black Bard of Revolution." *The Washington Post* (26 December 1971), pp. F1, F6–7. Mentions W as an important influence on Don L. Lee. Reprinted: 1991.

9179. Anon. "Biblio 1." *Black Books Bulletin,* 1 (Winter 1972), 66–76. Mentions W briefly in an annotated listing of George Kent's *Blackness and the Adventure of Western Culture.*

9180. Anon. "Publications Relating to Mississippi." *The Journal of Mississippi History,* 34 (May 1972), 184–187. Lists the special W issue of *New Letters.*

9181. Anon. "Publications Relating to Mississippi." *The Journal of Mississippi History,* 34 (August 1972), 298–300. Lists an essay on W by John M. Reilly.

9182. Anon. "Publications Relating to Mississippi." *The Journal of Mississippi History,* 34 (November 1972), 409–410. Lists an essay on W by Harold T. McCarthy.

9183. Bandler, Michael J. "Portrait of a Man Reading." *The Washington Post Book World* (9 April 1972), p. 2. Interview with Chester Himes, who recalls reading *BB, NS, UTC,* and *O.* Praises highly *NS* and *BB,* but names Faulkner and Dashiell Hammett, not W, as influences on his own work. Reprinted: 1995.

9184. Baumbach, Jonathan. "Amerikanische Existenz Als Alptraum," in *Amerikanische Literatur* des 20 Jahrhunderts. Ed. Gerhard Hoffmann. Frankfurt am Main: Fischer Taschenbuch Verlag, 1972, pp. 129–148. Mentions W briefly (p. 129).

9185. Beauford, Fred. "A Conversation with Ernest J. Gaines." *Black Creation,* 4 (Fall 1972), 16–18. Gaines comments briefly on *NS* as an urban novel. Reprinted: 1995.

9186. Blake, Nelson Manfred. *A History of American Life and Thought.* Second edition. New York: McGraw-Hill, 1972, pp. 590, 599, 678. Mentions W's difficulty with the Communist Party, notes his literary achievement, and mentions *NS.*

9187. Bowles, Paul. *Without Stopping: An Autobiography.* New York: G.P. Putnam's Sons, 1972, p. 233. Mentions W's move into the Middagh Street house in Brooklyn. Reprinted: 1985.

9188. Brown, Dorothy S. "*Black Literature.*" *Abstracts of English Studies,* 15 (March 1972), 597. Abstract of an article on W and others by John O'Brien.

9189. _____. "*Richard Wright.*" *Abstracts of English Studies,* 15 (March 1972), pp. 593, 594. Abstracts of articles by Keneth Kinnamon, John M. Reilly, David Bakish, Raman K. Singh, and Michel Fabre.

9190. _____. "*Richard Wright.*" *Abstracts of English Studies,* 16 (November 1972), 196. Abstract of an article by Campbell Tatham.

9191. Canaday, Nicholas, Jr. "Black Fiction at Home and in Exile." *The CEA Critic*, 35 (November 1972), 34. Mentions W briefly.

9192. Christadler, Martin. *Ellison: Invisible Man.* Düsseldorf: August Bagel Verlag, 1972, pp. 333–369. Mentions briefly W and Bigger Thomas (pp. 335, 338) and *BB* (p. 336).

9193. Coles, Robert. "The Words and Music of Social Change," in his *Farewell to the South.* Boston: Little, Brown, 1972, pp. 266–284. Reprint of 1969.

9194. Cowley, Malcolm. "*Native Son,*" in *The Critic as Artist: Essays on Books 1920–1970.* Ed. Gilbert A. Harrison. New York: Liveright, 1972, pp. 96–99. Reprint of 1940. 614.

9195. E., J.V. "*Black.*" *Abstracts of English Studies*, 15 (April 1972), 671–672. Abstract of an article on W and others by Michel Fabre.

9196. Eastman, Arthur M. "Literature of the Melting Pot." *The CEA Critic*, 35 (November 1972), 30–32. Mentions W briefly.

9197. Erzgräber, Willi. "*Black Literature.*" *Abstracts of English Studies*, 15 (March 1972), 596. Abstract of an article on W and others by Stephen B. Bennett and William W. Nichols.

9198. Forman, James. *The Making of Black Revolutionaries.* New York: Macmillan, 1972, pp. 4, 35, 75. Mentions reading W. Reprinted.

9199. Fredrickson, George M. *The Black Image in the White Mind: The Debate on Afro-American Character and Destiny, 1817–1914.* New York: Harper & Row, 1972, p. 329. Reprint of 1971.

9200. Gaga [Mark S. Johnson]. "Interview with Ishmael Reed." *MWENDO*, No. 4 (Fall 1973), pp. 32–35. Reed notes the influence of Western culture on W. Reprinted: 1995.

9201. Gold, Michael, "The Second American Renaissance," in *Mike Gold: A Literary Anthology.* Ed. Michael Folsom. New York: International, 1972, pp. 243–254. Includes a brief comparison of W and Steinbeck (pp. 244–245).

9202. _____. "The Second American Renaissance," in his *Mike Gold: A Literary Anthology.* Ed. Michael Folsom. New York: International, 1972, pp. 243–254. Gold comments

briefly on W in this speech to the Fourth Congress of American Writers in 1941.

9203. Gotimer, Sister Mary Eugene. "*Black.*" *Abstracts of English Studies*, 15 (April 1972), 672. Abstract of an article on W and others by Raman K. Singh.

9204. _____. "*Richard Wright.*" *Abstracts of English Studies*, 15 (April 1972), 669–670. Abstract of an article by John M. Reilly.

9205. Greenlee, Sam. "*The Quality of Hurt* by Chester Himes." *Black Books Bulletin*, 1 (Spring/Summer 1972), 52–57. Review discussing the troubled friendship between Himes and W.

9206. Hays, H.R. "Nicolas Guillén y la poesía afrocubana," in *Recopilación de textos sobre Nicolás Guillén* Ed. Nancy Morejón. Havana: Casa de los Americas, 1972, pp. 91–99. Reprint of 1952.

9207. Holman, C. Hugh. *A Handbook to Literature.* Third edition. New York: Odyssey Press, 1972, pp. 9, 621, 622. Mentions W briefly s.v. Afro-American literature and includes *NS* and *BB* in an "Outline of Literary History: English and American." Reprinted.

9208. Kraus, Alan. Untitled questions, in his *The Nature of Work: Readings for College Students.* New York: John Wiley, 1972, p. 204. Study aids for a selection from *BB*.

9209. Ladner, Joyce. *Tomorrow's Tomorrow: The Black Woman.* Garden City, NY: Doubleday/Anchor, 1972, p. 57. Reprint of 1971.

9210. Lee, Don L. "Preface: Gwendolyn Brooks: Beyond the Wordmaker—The Making of an African Poet," in *Report from Part One.* Detroit: Broadside Press, 1972, pp. 13–30. Mentions W briefly (p. 15). Reprinted: 1996.

9211. Lynch, Acklyn R. "Blueprint for Change." *Black Books Bulletin*, 1 (Winter 1972), 16–20. Mentions W briefly (p. 18).

9212. Magee, William H. "*Richard Wright.*" *Abstracts of English Studies*, 15 (March 1972), 593. Abstract of an article by Michel Fabre.

9213. Maddock, Lawrence H. "*Richard Wright.*" *Abstracts of English Studies*, 16 (November 1972), 196. Abstract of an article by Donald R. Merkle.

9214. May, John Richard. "Apocalypse in the American Novel." *Dissertation Abstracts International*, 32

(1972), 4009A–10A. Applies eschatology to *NS* and other works.

9215. McCarthy, Harold T. "Wright, Richard, 'The Expatriate as Native Son." *American Literature Abstracts*, 5 (June 1972), 194. Abstract of 1972.149.

9216. Moramarco, Fred, *Edward Dahlberg.* New York: Twayne, 1972, p. 51. Mentions that W was on the National Council of the League of American Writers.

9217. Nelson, Raymond. "Domestic Harlem: The Detective Fiction of Chester Himes." *Virginia Quarterly Review*, 48 (Spring 1972), 260–276. Mentions W briefly (p. 261). Reprinted: 1999.

9218. Ozick, Cynthia. "Literary Blacks and Jews." *Midstream*, 18 (June/July 1972), 10–24. Comments on and quotes from Irving Howe's "Black Boys and Native Sons" (p. 14). Reprinted: 1983, 1994.

9219. Rekrut, Martha D. "*Black Literature.*" *Abstracts of English Studies*, 16 (September 1972), 49. Abstract of an article on W and others by Alfred Kazin.

9220. Reynolds, Paul R. *The Middle Man: The Adventures of a Literary Agent.* New York: William Morrow, 1972, pp. 117–121, 133–134, 174. W's agent relates how W's effort to obtain a commission in the army was unsuccessful and how he terminated his lecture tour because "he was a sensitive, high-strung, extremely nervous man" (p. 118). Reynolds also prints W's inscription to him in a gift copy of *LD*.

9221. [Rubin, Louis D., Jr.]. "Annual Checklist." *S.S.S.L.: The News-Letter of The Society for the Study of Southern Literature*, 5 (November 1972), [5]. Notes that thirteen items on W appear in the checklist.

9222. _____. "Articles on Southern Literature." *S.S.S.L.: The News-Letter of The Society for the Study of Southern Literature*, 5 (November 1972), [9–13]. Lists articles on W by Lewis Leary, Eugene E. Miller, Phyllis R. Klotman and Melville Yancey, Blyden Jackson, Ronald Primeau, and Louis Graham.

9223. _____. "New Books." *S.S.S.L.: The News-Letter of The Society for the Study of Southern Literature*, 5 (November 1972), [7–9]. Mentions briefly Sam Bluefarb's *The Escape Motif in the American Novel: Mark Twain to Richard Wright.*

9224. Schmitz, Neil. "Al Young's

Snakes: Words to the Music." *Paunch*, 35 (February 1972), 3–9. Mentions W briefly (p. 4).

9225. Schroeder, Sister Rose Mary. "*Black Literature*." *Abstracts of English Studies*, 15 (March 1972), 597–598. Abstract of an article on W and others by Lance Jeffers.

9226. Snelling, Paula. "Three Native Sons," in *From the Mountain*. Eds. Helen White and Redding S. Sugg, Jr. Memphis: Memphis State University Press, 1972, pp. 203–210. Reprint of 1940.930.

9227. Sollors, Werner. *A Bibliographic Guide to Afro-American Studies*. Berlin: John F. *Kennedy-Institut für Nordamerikstudien*, Freie Universität Berlin, 1972, pp. 159, 187–189, 204. Mentions W and lists his works and four books about him.

9228. Spady, James G. "The Cultural Unity of Cheikh Anta Diop, 1948–1964." *Black Image*, 1 (Autumn and Winter 1972), 14–22. Discusses Baldwin's treatment of W's debate with Senghor at the Congress of Black Writers and Artists in Paris in 1956.

9229. Starobin, Joseph R. *American Communism in Crisis, 1943–1957*. Cambridge, MA: Harvard University Press, 1972, pp. 136, 137. Mentions W briefly.

9230. Taylor, Walter. "Faulkner's Pantaloon: The Negro Anomaly at the Heart of *Go Down, Moses*." *American Literature*, 44 (November 1972), 430–444. Quotes W'd dictum that the Negro is "America's metaphor." Reprinted: 1989.

9231. Tees, Arthur T. "*James Baldwin*." *Abstracts of English Studies*, 16 (October 1972), 124. Abstract of an article on W, Baldwin, and Eldridge Cleaver by Morris Dickstein.

9232. _____. "*Richard Wright*." *Abstracts of English Studies*, 16 (October 1972), 133–134. Abstracts of articles by Katherine Sprandel, Thomas Cripps, John Houseman, Edward A. Watson, Daniel Aaron, Michel Fabre, Margaret Walker Alexander, Henrietta Weigel, and Fabre and Edward Margolies.

9233. Terrell, Angela. "Nikki Giovanni: 'Vision and Space.'" *The Washington Post* (23 July 1972), sec. H, pp. 1, 7. Mentions W briefly. Reprinted: 1992.

9234. Tritt, Carlton S. "*Black Literature*." *Abstracts of English Studies*, 15 (March 1972), 596. Abstract of

an article on W and Camara Laye by Joseph Bruchac.

9235. _____. "*Richard Wright*." *Abstracts of English Studies*, 15 (March 1972), 593–594, 594–595. Abstracts of articles by Lloyd W. Brown and Paul C. Sherr.

9236. Turner, Darwin. "Frank Yerby: Golden Debunker." *Black Books Bulletin*, 1 (Spring/Summer 1972), 4–9, 30–33. Mentions W briefly (p. 5).

9237. Walker, Jim. "*The Quality of Hurt*. By Chester Himes." *Black Creation*, 3 (Spring 1972), 53–54. Review quoting Himes on W.

9238. Washington, Cleve. "Lerone Bennett, Jr.: Exploring the Past/Creating a Future." *Black Books Bulletin*, 1 (Spring/Summer 1972), 16–19. Compares briefly Bennett's childhood to that depicted in *BB*.

9239. Watkins, Mel. "The Fire Next Time This Time." *The New York Times Book Review* (28 May 1972), pp. 17–18. Review of James Baldwin's *No Name in the Street* noting Bigger Thomas's "pathological and decidedly unrevolutionary violence." Reprinted: 1988.

9240. White, Helen, and Redding S. Sugg, Jr. "Introduction," in their *From the Mountain*. Memphis: Memphis State University Press, 1972, pp. xxv, 15. Mentions *NS* and David Cohn's unfavorable view of it.

9241. Willis, William S., Jr. "Skeletons in the Anthropological Closet," in *Reinventing Anthropology*. Ed. Dell Hymes. New York: Pantheon Books, 1972, pp. 121–152. The "skeletons" are what W called "frog perspectives" (p. 121). Cites *WML* (pp. 144, 152).

9242. Young, Al. "Interview: Ishmael Reed." *Changes*, November 1972, pp. 12–13, 33. Mentions W briefly.

9243. Anon. "*From Apology to Protest: The Black American Novel* Noel Schraufnagel." *The CEA Forum*, 4 (December 1973), 17. Publisher's notice mentioning briefly *NS*.

9244. Anon. *Notable Names in American History: A Tabulated Register*. Clifton, NJ: James T. White, 1973, p. 611. Lists W as a winner of the Spingarn Medal.

9245. Anon. "University Press Books." *The CEA Forum*, 3 (February 1973), 5. Lists Kinnamon's *The Emergence of Richard Wright*.

9246. Aptheker, Herbert. *Anno-*

tated Bibliography of the Writings of W.E.B. Du Bois. Millwood, NY: Kraus-Thomson, 1973, items 291, 315, 1075, 1224. Includes all items concerning W written by Dubois.

9247. Baldwin, Leland D., and Erling A. Erickson. *The American Quest*. Vol. II. Belmont, CA: Wadsworth, 1973, p. 589. Mentions briefly *NS*.

9248. Belfrage, Cedric. *The American Inquisition, 1945–1960*. Indianapolis: Bobbs-Merrill, 1973, pp. 23, 99, 142, 267. Mentions W as protest writer, notes his participation in conferences in Paris, and calls his exile a relief from a "double nightmare, racism and the Communist Party." Reprinted: 1989.

9249. Bjornstad, William B. "*Subjects*." *Abstracts of English Studies*, 16 (April 1973), 526. Abstract of an article on W and others by Rodrigue E. Labrie.

9250. Borden, Morton, and Otis L. Graham, Jr., with Roderick W. Nash and Richard E. Oglesby. *Portrait of a Nation: A History of the United States*. Lexington, MA: D.C. Heath, 1973, p. 148. Mentions briefly *NS*.

9251. Bracy, William. "Wright, Richard," in *Encyclopedia Americana*. Ed. Bernard S. Cayne. Vol. 29. New York: Americana, 1973, p. 555. Reprint of 1965.45.

9252. Brown, Dorothy S. "*Richard Wright*." *Abstracts of English Studies*, 16 (May 1973), 610. Abstract of an article by Louis Graham.

9253. Brown, Lloyd W. "Introduction," in his *The Black Writer in Africa and the Americas*. Los Angeles: Hennessy & Ingalls, 1973, pp. 1–10. Mentions briefly *NS* (p. 6) and W (p. 7).

9254. Bullins, Ed. *The Reluctant Rapist*. New York: Harper & Row, 1973, pp. 144–145. Describes the immensely powerful effect of reading *BB*.

9255. Burns, Edward, ed. *Staying on Alone: Letters of Alice B. Toklas*. New York: Liveright, 1973, pp. 14–15, 16, 78, 256. In a letter to Carl Van Vechten after Stein's death, Toklas recounts a dispute over a picture of Francis Rose. She also mentions W in letters to W.G. Rogers (1947) and again to Van Vechten (1952).

9256. Caute, David. *The Fellow-Travellers: A Postscript to the Enlightenment*. New York: MacMillan,

1973, p. 75. Mentions W briefly. Reprinted: 1988.

9257. Cook, Mercer A. "Some Literary Contacts: African, West Indian, Afro-American," in *The Black Writer in Africa and the Americas.* Ed. Lloyd W. Brown. Los Angeles: Hennessey & Ingalls, 1973, pp. 119–140. Discusses W's important role in *Présence Africaine* and his general stimulus to black writers (pp. 132–133). Mentions *NS, BB,* and *UTC.*

9258. Clarke, Austin C. "Some Speculations as to the Absence of Racialistic Vindictiveness in West Indian Literature," in *The Black Writer in Africa and the Americas.* Ed. Lloyd W. Brown. Los Angeles: Hennessey & Ingalls, pp. 165–194. Mentions W briefly (p. 191).

9259. Chapman, Abraham. "Concepts of the Black Aesthetic in Contemporary Black Literature," in *The Black Writer in Africa and the Americas.* Ed. Lloyd W. Brown. Los Angeles: Hennessey & Ingalls, 1973, pp. 11–43. Quotes from W's speech at the First International Conference of Negro Artists and Writers in Paris.

9260. Davis, Bonnie M. *Comprehensive Dissertation Index 1861–1972.* Ann Arbor: Xerox University Microfilms, 1973. Vol. 30, p. 826. Lists dissertations treating W by Kathryn Osburn Cowan, David Bakish, Raman Kumar Singh, Steven Joel Rubin, David Dobbs Gritt, Edward Robert Zeitlow, John Reilly, Yomah Gray, Keneth Kinnamon, Russel Brignano, Edward Margolies, and Hugh Gloster.

9261. Emanuel, James A. "The Challenge of Black Literature: Notes on Interpretation," in *The Black Writer in Africa and the Americas.* Ed. Lloyd W. Brown. Los Angeles: Hennessey & Ingalls, 1973, pp. 85–100. Mentions briefly "Fire and Cloud," *NS,* and the W special issue of *Negro Digest* (p. 96).

9262. Fine, Elsa Honig. *The Afro-American Artist: A Search for Identity.* New York: Holt, Rinehart and Winston, 1973, p. 170. Mentions W briefly.

9263. Fleming, Robert E. "Willard Motley's Urban Novels." *Umoja,* 1 (Summer 1973), 15–19. Notes that the defense lawyer for Nick Romano in *Knock on Any Door* is similar to Boris Max in *NS.*

9264. Ford, Nick Aaron. "Black Literature and the Problem of Eval-

uation," in *The Black Writer in Africa and the Americas.* Ed. Lloyd Brown. Los Angeles: Hennessey & Ingalls, 1973, pp. 45–68. Mentions briefly *NS* (p. 63).

9265. [Frederick, John T.] "Richard Wright," in *A Treasury of American Literature.* Eds. Joe Lee Davis, John T. Frederick, and Frank Luther Mott, eds. *A Treasury of American Literature,* Vol. 2 New York: Grolier, 1973, p. 913. Reprint of 1949.95.

9266. Gaga [Mark S. Johnson]. "Interview with Ishmael Reed." *MWENDO,* No. 4 (Fall 1973), pp. 32–35. Reed notes the influence of Western Culture on W. Reprinted: 1995.

9267. Gayle, Addison. "*Under Western Eyes*: A Review Essay." *Black World,* 22 (July 1973), 40–48. Includes a quotation from W at the African Writers' Conference in 1956.

9268. Genet, Jean. "Revolution and the Writer," in *Person to Person: Rhetoric, Reality, and Change.* Eds. Irving Deer, Harriet A. Deer, and James A. Gould. New York: Holt, Rinehart and Winston, 1973, pp. 325–331. Reprint of 1970.

9269. Hagen, Lyman B. "*Richard Wright*." *Abstracts of English Studies,* 16 (April 1973), 544. Abstracts of articles by John Timmerman and Lewis A. Lawson.

9270. Halsell, Willie D. "A Bibliography of Theses and Dissertations Relating to Mississippi, 1972." *The Journal of Mississippi History,* 35 (February 1973), 83–90. Lists theses on W by Melissa M. Freeman and Katherine A. Martin and a dissertation on W by Raman K. Singh.

9271. Hart, Robert C. "Black-White Literary Relations in the Harlem Renaissance." *American Literature,* 44 (January 1973), 612–628. Mentions W briefly (p. 628). Reprinted: 1996.

9272. Henley, Elton F. "Richard Wright." *Abstracts of English Studies,* 17 (November 1973), 194. Abstracts an article by James G. Kennedy.

9273. Hoffman, Frederick J. "Gertrude Stein," in *Seven American Stylists from Poe to Mailer.* Minneapolis: University of Minnesota Press, 1973, pp. 124–161. Notes that W was impressed by "Melanctha" (p. 150).

9274. Hornsby, Alton, Jr. *The Black Almanac.* Revised edition. Woodbury, NY: Barron's Educa-

tional Series, 1973, p. 65. Reprint of 1972.

9275. Hughes, Langston, Milton Meltzer, and C. Eric Lincoln. *A Pictorial History of Blackamericans.* Fourth edition. New York: Crown, 1973, pp. 281, 286, 356. Revised reprint of 1958.161.

9276. Jordan, June. "Gorilla, My Love." *Black World,* 22 (July 1973), 80. Favorable review of the Bambara work, comparing it to *UTC.* Partially reprinted: 1994.

9277. Kearns, Edward A. "*Richard Wright*." *Abstracts of English Studies,* 16 (May 1973), 610. Abstract of an article by Edward Kearns.

9278. Kent, George E. "Rhythms of Black Experience." *Chicago Review,* 25 (Fall 1973), 76–78. Mentions briefly W and *NS* (p. 76). Reprinted: 1999.

9279. Lee, Brian and David Murray. "American Literature: The Twentieth Century," in *The Year's Work in English Studies —1971.* London: John Murray, 1973, pp. 427–475. Comments on work on W by Eldridge Cleaver (p. 432), Martha Stephens (p. 465), and John W. Reilly (p. 465).

9280. Levy, Eugene. *James Weldon Johnson: Black Leader, Black Voice.* Chicago: The University of Chicago Press, 1973, p. 129. Mentions briefly *BB.*

9281. Light, Martin. "Robert Penn Warren, *Homage to Theodore Dreiser*." *Modern Fiction Studies,* 19 (Winter 1973), 611–612. Review mentioning W briefly.

9282. Mallory, Thomas O. "Particularism and Regionalism." *Abstracts of English Studies,* 17 (November 1973), 178. Abstracts an article by Jerry H. Bryant on W and others.

9283. Margolies, Edward. "The Letters of Richard Wright," in *The Black Writer in Africa and the Americas.* Los Angeles: Hennessey & Ingalls, 1973, pp. 101–118. Reviews W's letters, emphasizing his consciousness of historical perspective. His most important correspondents were Paul Reynolds, Edward Aswell, Margrit Sabloniere, and Gertrude Stein. W's letters reveal much about his relation with his agent and editors as well as about writing projects that did not reach print. Wright's politics and world view are often in the forefront of his letters, especially those concerning Communism and the West — both distrusted by W.

9284. Miller, Eugene E. "Some Black Thoughts on Don L. Lee's *Think Black!* Thunk by a Frustrated White Academic Thinker." *College English*, 34 (May 1973), 1094–1102. Includes comments on W's (and Du Bois's) notion of the "double vision" of African Americans (p. 1101). Also mentions *NS* (p. 1102). Reprinted: 1991.

9285. Nagel, James. "An Annotated Bibliography of Selected Recent Books on American Fiction." *Studies in American Fiction*, 1 (Spring 1973), 76–91. Mentions W briefly (pp. 77, 90).

9286. Ness, Verna M. "*Richard Wright.*" *Abstracts of English Studies*, 16 (May 1973), 610–611. Abstract of an article by Martha Stephens.

9287. Paulson, Barbara A. "Particularism and Regionalism." *Abstracts of English Studies*, 16 (June 1973), Abstract of an article on W and others by Morris Dickstein.

9288. Pearson, Norman Holmes. "American Literature: The Twentieth Century," in *Encyclopedia Americana*. Ed. Bernard S. Cayne. Vol. 1. New York: Americana, 1973, p. 706. Reprint of 1968.178.

9289. Perrett, Geoffrey. *Days of Sadness, Years of Triumph: The American People 1939–1945.* New York: Coward, McCann & Geoghegan, 1973, p. 146. Quotes briefly from the *Time* magazine review of *NS*.

9290. Primeau, Ronald. "*LeRoi Jones.*" *Abstracts of English Studies*, 16 (May 1973), 605. Abstract of an article on *BB* and Jones's *Home*.

9291. Rohlehr, F.G. "West Indian Poetry: Some Problems of Assessment: Part Two." *Bim*, 14, No. 55 (1973), 134–144. Mentions W briefly (p. 140). Reprinted: 1996.

9292. Rouse, Sarah A. "Literature, 1890–1970," in *A History of Mississippi*. Ed. Richard Aubrey McLemore. Vol. 2. Jackson: University and College Press of Mississippi, 1973, pp. 946–976. Contains a biographical paragraph on W, mentioning most of his books (p. 459).

9293. Rozwenc, Edwin C. *The Making of American Society.* Boston: Allyn and Bacon, 1973, p. 402. Mentions briefly *UTC* and comments on *NS*.

9294. [Rubin, Louis D., Jr.]. "Books." *S.S.S.L.: The News-Letter for The Society for the Study of Southern Literature*, 6 (April 1973), [5–6]. Lists Kenneth [sic] Kinnamon's *The*

Emergence of Richard Wright and Michel Fabre's *The Lonely* [sic] *Quest of Richard Wright.*

9295. _____. "Brooks, Warren, and Lewis." *S.S.S.L.: The News-Letter of The Society for the Study of Southern Literature*, 6 (April 1973), 2–3. Notes that W is included in *American Literature: The Makers and the Making.*

9296. _____. "Essays and Articles." *S.S.S.L.: The News-Letter of The Society for The Study of Southern Literature*, 6 (April 1973), [6–9]. Lists articles on W by Eugene E. Miller, Phyllis R. Klotman, and Sidonie Ann Smith.

9297. Smith, Sidonie Ann. "The Song of a Caged Bird: Maya Angelou's Quest After Self-Acceptance." *Southern Humanities Review*, 7 (Fall 1973), 365–375. Briefly compares *BB* and *I Know Why the Caged Bird Sings* (pp. 367–368). Partially reprinted: 1994.

9298. Smith, William Gardner. *South Street.* New York: Chatham Bookseller, 1973, p. 17. Reprint of 1954.

9299. Stephens, Martha. *The Question of Flannery O'Connor.* Baton Rouge: Louisiana State University Press, 1973, p. 74. Comments on *UTC* and the "race war."

9300. Tees, Arthur T. "Jack Conroy." *Abstracts of English Studies*, 17 (November 1973), 186. Abstracts an article by Michel Fabre mentioning W.

9301. Toklas, Alice B. *Staying on Alone: Letters of Alice B. Toklas.* Ed. Edward Burns. New York: Liveright, 1973, pp. 14–15, 16, 78, 256. Mentions a painting W bought through Gertrude Stein and a State Department diplomat (Miss Shipley) who "made so many difficulties for Richard Wright."

9302. Walker, I.M. "Wright, Richard," in *Webster's New World Companion to English and American Literature.* Ed. Arthur Pollard. New York: World, 1973, pp. 748–749. Biographical sketch with a list of W's works.

9303. Williams, Colin. "*Black and White Together: The Race Struggle in the U.S.A.*" Sydney: Angus and Robertson, 1973, p. 64. Mentions briefly W and his expatriation.

9304. Williams, John A. "Career by Accident," in his *Flashbacks: A Twenty-Year Diary of Article Writing.* Garden City, NY: Anchor Press,

1973, pp. 393–406. Comments favorably on W, mentioning *NS*, *SH*, and *PS*. Also comments on Ellison, Himes, and Baldwin.

9305. _____. "Chester Himes — My Man Himes," in his *Flashbacks: A Twenty-Year Diary of Article Writing.* Garden City, NY: Anchor Press, 1973, pp. 293–352. Reprint of 1970.366.

9306. _____. "Romare Bearden," in his *Flashbacks: A Twenty-Year Diary of Article Writing.* Garden City, NY: Anchor Press, 1973, pp. 280–291. Mentions W briefly (p. 290).

9307. Wolf, William D. "*Particularism and Regionalism.*" *Abstracts of English Studies*, 16 (January 1973), 320. Abstract of an article on W and others by Gerald W. Haslam.

9308. Aaron, Daniel. *Writers on the Left: Episodes in American Literary Communism.* New York: Octogon Books, 1974. Reprint of 1961.2.

9309. Anderson, David D. "Jack Conroy's Return." *Society for the Study of Midwestern Literature Newsletter*, 4 (Summer 1974), 6–8. Mentions W briefly (p. 7).

9310. _____. "A Major New Chicago Novel." *Society for the Study of Midwestern Literature Newsletter*, 4 (Fall 1974), 13–15. Mentions briefly *NS*.

9311. Anon. "Biblio 1." *Black Books Bulletin*, 2 (Winter 1974), 60–64. Lists *The Most Native of Sons* by John A. Williams.

9312. Anon. "Ellison, Ralph (Waldo) 1914–," in *Contemporary Authors.* Vols. 9–12 (first revision). Eds. Clare D. Kinsman and Mary Ann Tennenhouse. Detroit: Gale, 1974, pp. 268–269. Contains the following rubrics: Personal, Career, Writings, Work in Progress, Sidelights, and Bibliographical/Critical Sources.

9313. Anon. "*Five Black Writers: Essays on Wright, Ellison, Baldwin, Hughes, and LeRoi Jones* Donald B. Gibson, Editor." *Black Books Bulletin*, 2 (Winter 1974), 53. Publisher's announcement.

9314. Anon. "New Letters." *Society for the Study of Midwestern Literature Newsletter*, 4 (Spring 1974), 4–5. Mentions the special W issue of the journal.

9315. Anon. "Wright, Richard (1908–1960)," in *Webster's American Biographies.* Eds. Charles Van Doren and Robert McHenry. Springfield,

MA: G. & C. Merriam, 1974, pp. 1164–1165. Biographical sketch mentioning all of W's published books except *SH*.

9316. Anon. "Wright, Richard," in *Webster's American Biographies*. Springfield, MA: G. & C. Merriam, 1974, pp. 1164, 1165. Biographical sketch.

9317. Anon. "Wright, Richard," in *Webster's Biographical Dictionary*. Ed. William Allan Neilson. Springfield, MA: G. & C. Merriam, 1974, p. 1600. Biographical sketch.

9318. Blotner, Joseph. *Faulkner: A Biography*. New York: Random House, 1974. Vol. 1, p. 1190. Quotes from Faulkner's letter to W.

9319. [Bradley, Sculley]. "The Twentieth Century: Literary Renaissance and Social Challenge," in *The American Tradition in Literature*. Eds. Sculley Bradley, Richard Croom Beatty, E. Hudson Long, and George Perkins. Fourth edition. Vol. 2. New York: Norton, 1974, pp. 843–857. Reprint of 1962.

9320. Bullins, Ed. "Introduction," in his *The New Lafayette Theatre Presents*. Garden City, NY: Anchor Press/Doubleday, 1974, pp. 3–5. Compares briefly the protagonist of J.E. Gaines's play *What If It Turned Up Heads* to the protagonist of "The Man Who Lived Underground."

9321. [Core, George]. "*The American Tradition in Literature*." *The Newsletter of The Society for the Study of Southern Literature*, 7 (April 1974), 6. Notes that W is included in the fourth edition.

9322. _____. "Selected Checklist of Southern Articles in Current Periodicals." *The Newsletter of The Society for the Study of Southern Literature*, 7 (December 1974), [9–10]. Lists articles on W by Jean François Gounard, Mildred B. Everette, Robert Felgar, Kichung Kim, Sheldon Brivic, and Amritjit Singh.

9323. _____. Untitled Note. *The Newsletter of The Society for the Study of Southern Literature*, 7 (April 1974), [8]. Announces *Richard Wright: Impressions and Perspectives*, edited by David Ray and Robert M. Farnworth [sic].

9324. Dance, Daryl C. "You Can't Go Home Again: James Baldwin and the South." *CLA Journal*, 18 (September 1974), 81–90. Quotes Saunders Redding on W in *BP* (p. 82). Reprinted: 1988.

9325. Dash, Michael. "Marvelous Realism — The Way Out of Négritude." *Black Images*, 3 (Spring 1974), 80–95. Discusses Baldwin's treatment of Senghor's views on *BB* (p. 84).

9326. Editors of Ebony. *Ebony Pictorial History of Black America*. Vol. IV: The 1973 Year Book. Chicago: Johnson, 1974, pp. 225, 230. Mentions the film *NS* and includes a still shot of W as Bigger.

9327. Ellison, Ralph. "On Initiation Rites and Power: Ralph Ellison Speaks at West Point." *Contemporary Literature*, 15 (Spring 1974), 165–186. Responding to a question, Ellison disavows W's influence. Reprinted: 1986.

9328. Gayle, Addison, Jr. "The Black Aesthetic: Defender." *Black World*, 24 (December 1974), 31–43. Mentions W briefly (p.). Reprinted: 1991.

9329. Gelfand, Marvin. "Taking a Leaf: A Talk with Albert Murray." *West Side Literary Review*, 1, no. 2 (25 April 1974), p. 3. Murray states that "Baldwin is too derivative from Richard Wright." Reprinted: 1997.

9330. Graver, Lawrence. "Carson McCullers, 1917–1967," in *American Writers: A Collection of Literary Biographies*. Ed. Leonard Unger. Vol. II. New York: Charles Scribner's, 1974 pp. 585–08. Mentions W briefly as a resident of the house in Brooklyn Heights (p. 586).

9331. Gunn, Drewey Wayne. *American and British Writers in Mexico, 1556–1973*. Austin: University of Texas Press, 1974, p. 200. Mentions W briefly.

9332. Hagen, Lyman B. "Richard Wright." *Abstracts of English Studies*, 17 (March 1974), 462. Abstracts an article by Eugene E. Miller.

9333. _____. "Richard Wright." *Abstracts of English Studies*, 17 (March 1974), 462. Abstracts an article by Phyllis R. Klotman and Yancey Melville.

9334. Halsell, Willie D. "A Bibliography of Theses and Dissertations Relating to Mississippi, 1973." *The Journal of Mississippi History*, 36 (February 1974), 105–111. Lists Brian J. Benson's dissertation on W.

9335. Harper, Michael S. "Bigger's Blues." *Hambone*, 1 (Spring 1974), 92. Poem on *NS*. Reprinted.

9336. _____. "Afterword: A Film." *Hambone*, 1 (Spring 1974), 94. Poem on *NS*. Reprinted.

9337. _____. "Heartblow: Messages." *Hambone*, 1 (Spring 1974), 93. Poem on W and *NS*. Reprinted.

9338. Hatch, James V., and Ted Shine. "*Big White Fog 1938*," in their *Black Theater U.S.A.: Forty-Five Plays by Black Americans 1847–1974*. New York: Free Press, 1974, pp. 278–280. Mentions briefly the play *NS*.

9339. Hoffman, Frederick J. "Gertrude Stein," in *American Writers: A Collection of Literary Biographies*, Ed. Leonard Unger. Vol. IV. New York: Charles Scribner's, 1974, pp. 25–48. Notes W's favorable opinion of "Melanctha" (p. 40).

9340. Jackson, Blyden. "A Survey Course in Negro Literature." *College English*, 35 (March 1974), 631–636. Includes high praise for W: "The Age of Wright is, at least until now, the Golden Age of Negro Literature.... The greatest writer of this age ... is Richard Wright..." (p. 634).

9341. Kent, George. "Rhythms of Black Experience." *Chicago Review*, 25, No. 3 (1974), 73–79. Mentions briefly W and *NS*. Reprinted: 1999.

9342. Kimball, William J. "Richard Wright." *Abstracts of English Studies*, 17 (April 1974), 531. Abstracts an article by Sidonie Ann Smith.

9343. Lee, Brian and David Murray. "American Literature: The Twentieth Century," in *The Year's Work in English Studies—1972*. London: John Murray, 1974, pp. 434–477. Comments on work on W by Harold J. McCarthy, Phyllis R. Klotman, Melville Yancy, Laurie Leary, Eugene E. Miller, Louis Graham (p. 470) and Ralph J. Giblett (p. 475). Reprinted: 1998.

9344. Major, Clarence. "James Baldwin: A Fire in the Mind," in his *The Dark and the Feeling: Black American Writers and Their Work*. New York: The Third Press, 1974, pp. 73–83. Includes comments on Baldwin's first meeting with W.

9345. _____. "John A. Williams: The Black Writer Who Called I am," in his *The Dark and the Feeling: Black American Writers and Their Work*. New York: The Third Press, 1974, pp. 85–97. Includes comment on Williams's admiration of W.

9346. _____. "Willard Motley: Vague Ghost After the Father," in his *The Dark and the Feeling: Black*

American Writers and Their Work. New York: The Third Press, 1974, pp. 95–97. Reprint of 1969.

9347. Manchester, William. *The Glory and the Dream: A Narrative History of America, 1932–1972.* Vol. 1. Boston: Little, Brown, 1974, p. 372. Mentions briefly *BB*.

9348. Mathis, Sharon Bell. "Black Writers and Children: Lessons in Black Love," in *Theme: The Image of Black Folk in American Literature.* Washington: The Howard University Institute for the Humanities, 1974, pp. B, 1–19. Mentions *The Most Native of Sons* by John A. Williams.

9349. McMichael, George. "James Baldwin 1924– ," in his *Concise Anthology of American Literature.* New York: Macmillan, 1974, pp. 1810–1811. Reprint of 1974.125.

9350. _____. "Ralph Ellison 1914– ," in his *Concise Anthology of American Literature.* New York: Macmillan, 1974, pp. 1701–1702. Reprint of 1974.126.

9351. _____. "Richard Wright 1908–1960," in his *Concise Anthology of American Literature.* New York: Macmillan, 1974, pp. 1690–1691. Reprint of 1974.128.

9352. McQuade, Donald, and Robert Atwan, "Richard Wright/ *Black Boy*," in their *Popular Writing in America.* New York: Oxford Press, 1974, p. 632. Biographical headnote to an excerpt from *BB.* Reprinted: 1977.

9353. Mebane, Mary E. "Rules to Follow in Teaching Black Literature." *The CEA Forum,* 4 (April 1974), 3. Mentions W briefly.

9354. Mellow, James R. *Charmed Circle: Gertrude Stein & Company.* New York: Praeger, 1974, pp. 459, 462. Mentions Stein meeting W, "whose *Black Boy* she had admired." Also mentions W in regard to the racial issue (see 1945.1150).

9355. Neal, Larry. "A Profile: Zora Neale Hurston." *Southern Exposure,* 1 (Winter 1974), 160–168. Briefly contrasts Hurston and W (p. 161).

9356. [Perkins, George]. "Richard Wright (1908–1960)," in *The American Tradition in Literature.* Fourth edition (shorter edition). Eds. Sculley Bradley, Richmond Croom Beatty, E. Hudson Long, and George Perkins. New York: Grosset & Dunlap (distributed by Norton), 1974, pp. 1670–1671. Reprint of 1974.142.

9357. Perkins, George, Sculley Bradley, Richmond Croom Beatty, and E. Hudson Long. "The Twentieth Century: Literary Renaissance and Social Challenge," in their *The American Tradition in Literature.* Fourth edition. Vol. 2. New York: Grosset & Dunlap (distributed by Norton), 1974, pp. 843–857. Mentions W briefly (p. 855).

9358. Pinsker, Sanford. "About *Runner Mack*: An Interview with Barry Beckham." *Black Images,* 3 (Autumn 1974), 35–41. Pinsker mentions *UTC* and *EM* (p. 36).

9359. Plumpp, Sterling D. "*Sula* Toni Morrison." *Black Books Bulletin,* 2 (Winter 1974), 62–64. Review mentioning briefly *NS.*

9360. Presley, Delma Eugene. "Carson McCullers and the South." *The Georgia Review,* 28 (Spring 1974), 19–32. Mentions W briefly (p. 24). Reprinted: 1997.

9361. Prosen, Rose Mary. "'Ethnic Literature'— of Whom and for Whom; Digressions of a Neo-American Teacher." *College English,* 35 (March 1974), 659–669. Includes comments on *NS* and Bigger Thomas (pp. 666, 667).

9362. Randall, Dudley. "*How I Wrote Jubilee* Margaret Walker." *Black Books Bulletin,* 2 (Winter 1974), 50. Mentions briefly *How "Bigger" Was Born.*

9363. Rennert, Robert A. "Richard Wright." *Abstracts of English Studies,* 17 (March 1974), 462. Abstracts an article by Donald B. Gibson.

9364. [Rubin, Louis D., Jr.] "Selected Checklist of Southern Articles in Current Periodicals." *The Newsletter of The Society for the Study of Southern Literature,* 7 (April 1974), [17–20]. Lists articles on W in *CLA Journal and Studies in Black Literature.*

9365. Schmitz, Neil. "Neo-Hoo-Doo: The Experimental Fiction of Ishmael Reed." *Twentieth Century Literature,* 20 (April 1974), 126–140. Compares briefly Reed's *The Free-Lance Pallbearers* to *NS* and *BB.* Reprinted: 1991, 1999.

9366. Shrodes, Caroline, Harry Finestone, and Michael Shugrue. "Suggestions for Discussion, Suggestions for Writing," in their *The Conscious Reader.* New York: Macmillan, 1974, pp. 988–1989. Study aids for "The Ethics of Living Jim Crow." Reprinted: 1978, 1985.

9367. Smith, Barbara. "*The Last Days of Louisiana Red* by Ishmael Reed." *The New Republic,* 171 (23 November 1974), 53–54. Mentions briefly *NS.* Reprinted: 1999.

9368. Southerland, Ellease. "Zora Neale Hurston: The Novelist-Anthropologist's Life/Works." *Black World,* 23 (August 1974), 20–30. Mentions W briefly. Reprinted: 1991.

9369. Standley, Fred L. "The Use and Effects of the Study of Afro-American Literature." *CEA Forum,* 4 (April 1974), pp. 2–3. Quotes Darwin Turner mentioning W briefly.

9370. Stern, Frederick C. "Black Lit., White Crit.?" *College English,* 35 (March 1974), 637–658. Mentions W briefly (pp. 652, 653).

9371. Tarshis, Jerome. "The Other 300 Years: A Conversation with Ernest J. Gaines, Author of *The Autobiography of Miss Jane Pittman.*" *San Francisco Magazine* (June 1974), pp. 26–28. Mentions W briefly.

9372. Towns, Saundra. "Black Autobiography and the Dilemma of Western Artistic Tradition." *Black Books Bulletin,* 2 (Winter 1974), 17–23. Comments on W's isolation from his race in *BB* (pp. 18, 19).

9373. Tyce, Richard S. "Fiction." *Abstracts of English Studies,* 17 (February 1974), 385. Abstracts an article on "Racism, Formula, and Popular Fiction" by James Mellard mentioning W.

9374. Unger, Leonard, "Introduction," in his *American Writers: A Collection of Literary Biographies.* New York: Charles Scribner's, 1974, p. ix. Mentions W briefly.

9375. Walker, Alice. "In Search of Our Mothers' Gardens." *Ms.,* 11 (May 1974), pp. 64–70, 105. Mentions W briefly (p. 70). Reprinted: 1991.

9376. Ward, Jerry. "*A Poetic Equation: Conversations Between Nikki Giovanni and Margaret Walker.* Edited by Paula Giddings." *Southern Voices,* 1 (August/September 1974), 74–75. Comments on Walker's corrective to Fabre on her relation to W.

9377. Weisberger, Bernard A. "Reading, Writing, and History." *American Heritage,* 25 (February 1974), 98–100. Review of Jerre Mangione's *The Dream and the Deal: The Federal Writers' Project, 1935–1943,* mentioning W briefly.

9378. _____. "Reading, Writing, and History," *American Heritage*, 25 (February 1974, 98–100. Review of Jerre Mangione's *The Dream and the Deal* mentioning W very briefly.

9379. Westmoreland, Guy T., Jr. *An Annotated Guide to Basic Reference Books on the Black American Experience*. Wilmington, DE: Scholarly Resources, 1974, p. 54. Mentions W briefly.

9380. Abbott, Ruth, and Ira Simmons. "An Interview with Ismael Reed," *San Francisco Review of Books*, 1975, pp. 13–20. Reed claims that *Partisan Review* "put James Baldwin up to attacking Richard Wright."

9381. Allen, Samuel. *Paul Vesey's Ledger*. London: Paul Breman, 1975, 20 pp. Poem on African American history mentioning Bigger Thomas (p. 17).

9382. Anon. "American Literature," in *The New Columbia Encyclopedia*. Eds. William H. Harris and Judith S. Levey. Fourth edition. New York: Columbia University Press, 1975, pp. 87–88. Revised reprint of 1950.

9383. Anon, ed. *Essay and General Literature Index: 1970–1974*. New York: H.W. Wilson, 1975, pp. 1669–1670. Lists s.v. W three primary and thirty-seven secondary sources.

9384. Anon. "PS 3545, Wright, Richard," in *Books for College Libraries*. Vol. II: Language and Literature. Chicago: American Library Association, 1975, p. 422. Lists *NS*, *UTC*, *LT*, as well as Edward Margolies's *The Art of Richard Wright*.

9385. Anon. "WPA: It Wasn't All Leaf-Raking." *Newsweek*, 85 (20 January 1975), p. 57. Mentions W briefly.

9386. Anon. "Wright, Richard," in *The New Columbia Encyclopedia*. Eds. William H. Harris and Judith S. Levey. Fourth edition. New York: Columbia University Press, 1975, p. 3012. Revised reprint of 1950.

9387. Anon. "Wright, Richard," in *Great Soviet Encyclopedia*. Ed. A.M. Prokhorov. New York: Macmillan, 1975, pp. 748–749. Biographical sketch with a list of W's works. Notes that his books are "permeated with hate for the bourgeois system" (p. 749).

9388. Austin, James C. "Richard Wright." *Abstracts of English Studies*, 18 (February 1975), 400. Abstracts an article by Harold T. McCarthy.

9389. Berkoben, Lawrence D. "Poetry." *Abstracts of English Studies*, 19 (September 1975), 61. Abstracts an article by Lawrence Lieberman mentioning W.

9390. Bicket, Zenas J. "Ralph Ellison." *Abstracts of English Studies*, 18 (February 1975), 389. Abstracts an article by Jerold J. Savory treating W and Jones as well as Ellison.

9391. Brown, Dorothy S. "Richard Wright." *Abstracts of English Studies*, 19 (November 1975), 190. Abstracts an article by Amritjit Singh.

9392. Bruccoli, Matthew J. *The O'Hara Concern: A Biography of John O'Hara*. New York: Random House, 1975, p. 177. States that O'Hara was pleased when W said that his story "Bread Alone" was "the only story about Negroes by a white author that he liked."

9393. Caselli, Ron. *The Minority Experience: A Basic Bibliography of American Ethnic Studies*. Revised and enlarged edition. Santa Rosa, CA: Sonoma County Office of Education, 1975, p. 23. Lists *BB*, *NS*, and *O*.

9394. Cook, Richard M. *Carson McCullers*. New York: Frederick Unger, 1975, pp. 9, 43–44, 128. Quotes Rex Reed mentioning W, quotes from W's review of *The Heart Is a Lonely Hunter*, and comments on W's evaluation of McCullers.

9395. _____. *Carson McCullers*. New York: Frederick Ungar, 1975, pp. 9, 43–44, 129. Mentions W as a resident of February House and quotes from his review of *The Heart Is a Lonely Hunter*.

9396. Cooper, Carla M., and Teddie McFerrin, eds. *A Cumulative Index to MFS (1955–1975)*. West Lafayette, IN: Purdue Research Foundation, 1975, pp. 56, 60, 65, 103. Lists item by William Goede, David Bakish, Russell Carl Brignano, Keneth Kinnamon, and Edward Margolies.

9397. [Core, George]. "'A Climate for Genius.'" *The Newsletter of The Society for the Study of Southern Literature*, 8 (December 1975), [p. 6]. Reports that W is the subject of one part of a six part television series on Mississippi writers produced by the Mississippi Authority for Educational Television.

9398. _____. "Recent Bibliography." *The Newsletter of The Society for the Study of Southern Literature*, 8 (December 1975), [9–14]. Lists ar-

ticles on W by John Pyros and Jerrold [sic] J. Schoong [sic].

9399. Davies, Phillips G. "Richard Wright." *Abstracts of English Studies*, 19 (September 1975), 59. Abstracts an article by Paul N. Siegel.

9400. Davis, Robert R., Jr. *Lexicon of Afro-American History*. New York: Simon and Schuster, 1975, pp. 157–158. Biographical sketch mentioning most of W's books.

9401. Emerson, Donald. "American Literature Through World War II," in *Encyclopedia of World Literature in the 20th Century*. Ed. Leonard S. Klein. Vol. 1. New York: Continuum, 1975, pp. 57–67. Reprint of 1967.30.

9402. Engel, Bernard F. "*The Great Lakes Review* Reviewed." *Society for the Study of Midwestern Literature Newsletter*, 5 (Spring 1975), 7–9. Mentions W briefly.

9403. Fisher, Dexter. "Minority Literature: What Price Assimilation?" *The CEA Forum*, 6 (October 1975), 3–5, 15. Mentions W briefly.

9404. Fleischmann, Ulrich. "Native Son," in *Hauptwerke der Amerikanische Literatur*. Ed. Gertrud Baruch. Munich: Kindler Verlag, 1975, p. 283. Summary with evaluative comments and a brief bibliography.

9405. _____. "*The Outsider*," in *Hauptwerke der amerikanische Literatur*. Ed. Gertrud Baruch. Munich: Kindler Verlag, 1975, pp. 283–284. Summary with evaluative comments and a brief bibliography.

9406. Fox, Arnold B. "Richard Wright." *Abstracts of English Studies*, 19 (September 1975), 59. Abstracts an article by Sheldon Brivic.

9407. Gawronski, Donald V. *Out of the Past: A Topical History of the United States*. Second editon. Beverly Hills: Glencoe Press, 1975, p. 438. Mentions W briefly.

9408. Graham, D.B. "Art in *McTeague*." *Studies in American Literature*, 3 (Autumn 1975), 143–155. Notes that Graham is working on an article on W (p. 143).

9409. Gurin, Patricia, and Edgar Epps. *Black Consciousness, Identity, and Achievement: A Study of Students in Historically Black Colleges*. New York: John Wiley, 1975, pp. 370, 377, 379. Mentions the admiration of three students for W.

9410. Harrison, John William. "Richard Wright." *Abstracts of English*

Studies, 19 (October 1975), 124. Abstracts an article by John Timmerman.

9411. Ihde, Horst. *Von der Plantage zum schwarzen Ghetto.* Leipzig: Urania-Verlag, 1975, pp. 45, 142–146, 156. Quotes from *TMBV*, reviews W's career, and mentions W briefly.

9412. Jahn, Janheinz. "*Black Boy*," in *Hauptwerke der amerikanischen Literatur.* Ed. Gertrud Baruch. Munich: Kindler Verlag, 1975, pp. 282–283. Summary with evaluative comments and a brief bibliography.

9413. Kennedy, Ellen Conroy. "Notes on the Translators," in her *Negritude Poets: An Anthology of Translations from the French.* New York: Viking Press, 1975, pp. 275–276. The note on Samuel Allen mentions his acquaintance with W.

9414. Klinkowitz, Jerome. "Clarence Major's Superfiction," in *Yardbird Reader*, Volume 4. Ed. Ishmael Reed. Berkeley, CA: Yardbird, 1975, pp. 1–11. Includes comments on Major's essay on W in *The Dark and Feeling* (p. 3).

9415. Miller, R. Baxter. "'No Crystal Stair': Unity, Archetype, and Symbol in Hughes's Poems on Women." *Negro American Literature Forum*, 9 (Winter 1975), 109–113. Mentions W briefly (p. 109). Reprinted: 1989.

9416. Mitchell, Sally. "Richard Wright." *Abstracts of English Studies*, 19 (October 1975), 124–125. Abstracts an article by Mary Ellen Brooks.

9417. Nin, Anaïs. *A Woman Speaks: The Lectures, Seminars, and Interviews of Anaïs* Nin. Ed. Evelyn J. Hinz. Chicago: Swallow Press, 1975, p. 120. Comments on her first meeting with W, who spoke of going to Europe so that he would not be so obsessed by the racial theme.

9418. Paden, W.D. "James Baldwin." *Abstracts of English Studies*, 18 (June 1975), 665. Abstracts an article by Addison Gayle, Jr., mentioning W.

9419. _____. "*Particularism and Regionalism.*" *Abstracts of English Studies*, 18 (June 1975), 657. Abstracts an article by Abraham Chapman mentioning W.

9420. _____. "Ralph Ellison." *Abstracts of English Studies*, 19 (November 1975), 182–183. Abstracts an article on Ellison by Lawrence J. Clipper mentioning W.

9421. _____. "Richard Wright." *Abstracts of English Studies*, 19 (November 1975), 190. Abstracts articles by Thomas Le Clair and Raman K. Singh.

9422. _____. "Richard Wright." *Abstracts of English Studies*, 19 (October 1975), 124–125. Abstracts articles by Keneth Kinnamon, Darwin T. Turner, Donald B. Gibson (2), George E. Kent (2), and Blyden Jackson.

9423. Pérez Gállego, Cándido. *Literatura norteamericana.* Barcelona: Editorial Planeta, 1975, p. 152. Mentions W briefly.

9424. Petersen, Carl. *Each in Its Ordered Place: A Faulkner Collector's Notebook.* Ann Arbor: Ardis, 1975, p. 175. Lists Constance Webb's reprint of two paragraphs of a Faulkner letter to W.

9425. Pingree, Elizabeth E., ed. *Humanities Index April 1974 to March 1975.* New York: H.W. Wilson, 1975, p. 513. Lists eight items s.v. W.

9426. Pinsker, Sanford. "The New Carpetbaggers, Black Literature, and Academia's Revolving Door." *The CEA Forum*, 6 (October 1975), 2–3. Mentions W briefly.

9427. Pizer, Donald, Richard W. Dowell, and Frederic E. Rusch. *Theodore Dreiser: a Primary and Secondary Bibliography.* Boston: G.K. Hall, 1975, p. 288. Includes a reprint of Friederike Hajek's article on *An American Tragedy* and *NS*.

9428. Pogel, Nancy. "Society Sponsors at Pop Culture Convention." *Society for the Study of Midwestern Literature Newsletter*, 5 (Spring 1975), 14–15. Mentions a paper by Jennifer Banks treating the film *NS*.

9429. Reynolds, Barbara A. *Jessie Jackson: The Man, the Movement, the Myth.* Chicago: Nelson-Hall, 1975, p. 420. Mentions W briefly.

9430. Sequeira, Isaac. *The Theme of Initiation in Modern American Fiction.* Mysore: Geetha Book House, 1975, p. 80. Mentions briefly W and *NS* in a discussion of *Invisible Man*.

9431. Singh, Raman K. "Marxism in Richard Wright's Fiction." *Indian Journal of American Studies*, 3 (Fall 1975), 21–35. Argues that Marxism is W's main ideological orientation and analyzes *UTC*, *NS*, *O* to support this thesis. The three main categories are class, caste, and capitalism, the third being more important

than the first two. W's point of view is that of anti-communist Marxism.

9432. Spacks, Patricia Meyer. *The Female Imagination.* New York: Alfred A. Knopf, 1975, p. 32. Mentions briefly *BB*.

9433. Spivey, Herman E. "General." *Abstracts of English Studies*, 19 (September 1975), 61–62. Abstracts an article by Malcolm Cowley mentioning W.

9434. Stronks, James. "*Sherwood Anderson/Gertrude Stein: Correspondence and Personal Essays.* Edited by Ray Lewis White; *Theodore Dreiser.* By W.M. Frohock." *Journal of the Illinois State Historical Society*, 68 (June 1975), 296–297. Review mentioning W briefly.

9435. van den Berghe, Pierre L. *Man in Society: A Biosocial View.* New York: Elsevier, 1975, p. 22 Praises W as a social novelist.

9436. Walker, Alice. "Beyond the Peacock: The Reconstuction of Flannery O'Connor." *Ms.*, 4 (December 1975), 77–79, 102–106. Comments on Faulkner's house and O'Connor's house, but "no one even remembers where Richard Wright lived" (p. 106). Reprinted: 1983, 1985.

9437. Walton, Hanes, Jr. "*Black Activism: Racial Revolution in the United States 1954–1970.* By Robert N. Brisbane." *Journal of Negro History*, 60 (July 1975), 437–438. Mentions briefly *NS*.

9438. Webster, Ivan. "Really the Blues." *Time*, 105 (16 June 1975), 79. Review of Gayl Jones's *Corregidora* stating that "no black American novel since Richard Wright's *Native Son* (1940), has so skillfully traced psychic wounds to a sexual source."

9439. Willie, Charles V. *Oreo: A Perspective on Marginal Men and Women.* Wakefield, MA: Parameter Press, pp. 50–51. Includes a long quotation from *TMBV* with brief comments by Willie.

9440. Woodward, C. Vann. "Why the Southern Renaissance?" *The Virginia Quarterly Review*, 51 (Spring 1975), 222–239. Mentions W briefly (p. 228). Reprinted: 1989.

9441. Anderson, David D. "Anderson and Myth," in his *Sherwood Anderson: Dimensions of His Literary Art.* East Lansing, MI: Michigan State University Press, 1976, pp. 118–141. Mentions briefly W and Bigger Thomas. Reprinted: 1981.

9442. Anderson, James D. "Aunt

Jemima in Dialectics: Genovese on Slave Culture." *The Journal of Negro History*, 61 (January 1976), 99–114. Quotes from *BB* (p. 112).

9443. Anon. Untitled Note, in *Black Boy-Jeunesse Noire*. Paris: Gallimard, 1976, pp. 7–8. Critical-biographical note emphasizing the difficulties imposed by southern racism on black people. Mentions *NS* as well as *BB*, comparing W to Dostoevsky. Notes that W opened the way for Baldwin, Himes, and LeRoi Jones.

9444. Austin, James C. "William Faulkner." *Abstracts of English Studies*, 19 (May 1976), 596–597. Abstracts an article by Walter Taylor mentioning W.

9445. Bracy, William. "Wright, Richard," in *Encyclopedia Americana*. Ed. Bernard S. Cayne. Vol. 29. New York: Americana, 1976, p. 555. Reprint of 1969.

9446. [Core, George]. "A Climate for Genius." *S.S.S.L.: The News-Letter of The Society for the Study of Southern Literature*, 9 (December 1976), 15. Notes that a video on W is available on loan.

9447. _____. "Among Recent Periodical Essays." *S.S.S.L.: The News-Letter of The Society for the Study of Southern Literature*, 9 (December 1976), 17–18. Lists an article on W by Jeffrey A. Sadler.

9448. Cox, Oliver C. *Race Relations: Elements and Social Dynamics*. Detroit: Wayne State University Press, 1976, p. 164. Mentions W in a discussion of racial intermarriage.

9449. _____. *Race Relations*: Elements and *Social Dynamics*. Detroit: Wayne State University Press, 1976, p. 164. Mentions briefly W's interracial marriage.

9450. French, Warren, "The Thirties-Fiction, "in his *The Thirties: Fiction, Poetry, Drama, Second Edition*, Deland, FL: Everett/Edwards, 1976, pp. 5–10. Comments briefly on *UTC, NS*, and *LT*.

9451. Friedman, Melvin J. "*The Mortgaged Heart:* The Workshop of Carson McCullers." *Revue des Langues Vivantes*, 42 (1976), pp. 144–155. Mentions W as one of the residents in the house on Middagh Street in Brooklyn.

9452. Friedman, Melvin. "*The Mortgaged Heart*: The Workshop of Carson McCullers." *Revue des Langues Vivantes*, U.S. Bicentennial

Issue (1976), 143–155. Mentions W briefly. Reprinted: 1996.

9453. Garvin, Patricia Y. "Richard Wright." *Abstracts of English Studies*, 19 (May 1976), 604. Abstracts an article by Seymour L. Gross.

9454. Grund, Gary R. "Richard Wright." *Abstracts of English Studies*, 20 (November 1976), 195. Abstracts an article by James R. Giles.

9455. Hagen, Lyman B. "Richard Wright." *Abstracts of English Studies*, 19 (January 1976), 327. Abstracts an article by Lewis Leary.

9456. Hall, Donald, and D.L. Emblem. "Some Possibilities," in their *A Writer's Reader*. Boston: Little, Brown, 1976, p. 329. Study aids for an excerpt from *BB*. Reprinted: 1979, 1982, 1985, 1988, 1991, 1994.

9457. _____. "Richard Wright The Library Card," in their *A Writer's Reader*. Boston: Little, Brown, 1976, p. 321. Biographical headnote to an excerpt from *BB*. Reprinted: 1979, 1982, 1985, 1988, 1991, 1994.

9458. Hourcade, R. Caffin. *Black Boy de Richard Wright*. Paris: Pedagogie Moderne, 1976, 71 pp. In a series designed to inspire students to read, this pamphlet consists of questions and study aids on *BB* followed by exercises more or less related to the book; documents concerning slavery and its aftermath; black education and the civil rights movement; grammatical games; and poems related to racial issues.

9459. Jackson, Blyden. "Richard Wright in a Moment of Truth," in *The Thirties: Fictions, Poetry, Drama*. Ed. Warren French. Second Editions. Deland, FL: Everett/Edwards, 1976, pp. 81–87. Reprint of 1971. 178.

9460. Jago, David M. "Theodore Dreiser." *Abstracts of English Studies*, 20 (November 1976), 188–189. Abstracts an article by Friederike Hajek comparing Dreiser and W.

9461. Kato, Tsunehiko. "How Did James Baldwin Conquer 'Bigger.'" *Kochi Joshi Daigaku Kiyo* [*Kochi Women's College Bulletin*], 24 (March 1976), 22–31. Compares Baldwin's and W's treatment of "Bigger." Baldwin is able to transcend the problems of Bigger by reconciling acceptance and protest [Y.H. and T.K.].

9462. Larson, Charles R. *The Novel in the Third World*. Washington, DC: Inscape, 1976, pp. 90, 177.

Mentions W's introduction to *In the Castle of My Skin* and refers briefly to *BB*.

9463. Lee, A Robert. "Violence Real and Imagined: The World of Chester Himes's Novels." *Negro American Literature Forum*, 10 (Spring, 1976), 13–22. Includes brief mentions of W (p. 13) and an excerpt from W's *PM* review of *If He Hollers Let Him Go*. Reprinted: 1999.

9464. McGill, Raymond D. "Green, Paul," in his *Notable Names in the American Theatre*. Clifton, NJ: pp. 782–783. Biographical sketch mentioning the play *NS*.

9465. Messent, Pete, and Mark Leaf. "American Literature: The Twentieth Century," in *The Year's Work in English Studies—1974*. London: John Murray, 1976, pp. 505–569. Comments on W by Stephen Butterfield (p. 513), Harold McCarthy (p. 530), Paul M. Siegal (p. 552), Robert Felgar (p. 552), Don B. Graham (p. 552), Mildred W. Everette (p. 552), and Jean François Gounard (p. 552).

9466. Miura, Mitsuyo. "Baldwin's White God [in English]." *Junshin Joshi Tanki Daigaku Kiyo*[*Bulletin of Junshin Women's Junior College*], 17 (November 1976), 11–15. The protagonist's suicide in *Another Country* is a protest against the white God. Unlike white characters in *NS*, Vivaldo tries to understand black people [Y.H. and T.K.].

9467. Mootry, Maria K. "*The Way of the New World* Addison Gayle, Jr." *Black Books Bulletin*, 4 (Spring 1976), 47–48. Review noting Gayle's praise of W and *NS*.

9468. Nin, Anaïs. *The Diary of Anaïs Nin 1955–1966*. Ed Gunther Stuhlmann. New York: Harcourt Brace Jovanovich, 1976, p. 24. Nin recalls W "saying he could not expand as a writer because the race problem festered in him."

9469. Paden, W.D. "*Fiction*." *Abstracts of English Studies*, 20 (September 1976), 54. Abstracts an article by Warren French mentioning W.

9470. _____. "James Baldwin." *Abstracts of English Studies*, 19 (June 1976), 667–668. Abstracts an article by Michel Fabre mentioning W.

9471. _____. "*Poetry*." *Abstracts of English Studies*, 20 (September 1976), 55. Abstracts an article by A. Kingsley Weatherhead mentioning W.

9472. _____. "Richard Wright." *Abstracts of English Studies*, 19 (January 1976), 327. Abstracts an article by Richard Kostelanetz.

9473. Pearson, Norman Holmes. "American Literature: The Twentieth Century," in *Encyclopedia Americana*. Ed. Bernard S. Cayne. Vol. 1. New York: Americana, 1976, p. 706. Reprint of.

9474. Phillips, Robert L. "*A Climate for Genius.*" *S.S.S.L.: The News-Letter of The Society for the Study of Southern Literature*, 9 (December 1976), 15. Mentions the W segment on the video about Mississippi writers.

9475. _____. "*South Carolina Review.*" *The Newsletter of The Society for the Study of Southern Literature*, 9 (April 1976), [4]. Lists an essay on W by Jeffrey A. Sadler.

9476. Pingree, Elizabeth E., ed. *Humanities Index: April 1975 to March 1976.* New York: H.W. Wilson, 1976, p. 793. Lists three items s.v. W.

9477. Pratt, Phyllis I. "*Fiction.*" *Abstracts of English Studies*, 19 (April 1976), 534. Abstracts an article by David D. Anderson mentioning W.

9478. Sepamla, Sipho. "The Black Writer in South Africa Today: Problems and Dilemmas." *The New Classic*, No. 3 (1976), pp. 18–26. Mentions W briefly (p. 19).

9479. Taylor, Arnold H. *Travail and Triumph: Black Life and Culture in the South Since the Civil War.* Westport, CT: Greenwood Press, 1976, p. 212. Contains three paragraphs on W, mentioning *BB*, *NS*, *UTC*, and *LD*. Emphasizes the theme of racism, but states that W "painted a somewhat one-dimensional picture of Southern black life."

9480. Tooker, Dan, and Roger Hofheins. "Ernest J. Gaines," in *Fiction!: Interviews with Northern California Novelists.* New York: Harcourt Brace Jovanovich, 1976, pp. 86–99. Gaines makes a brief, unfavorable judgment on W's expatriate writing (p. 99). Reprinted: 1995. _____."Ernest J. Gaines." in their *Fiction!: Interviews with Northern California Novelists.* New York: Harcourt Brace, Jovanovich, 1976, pp. 87–99. Gaines states that W "did not write anything really great once he left the American scene."

9481. Turnage, Maxine. "William Attaway." *Abstracts of English Stud-*

ies, 20 (September 1976), 41. Abstracts an article by L. Moody Simms, Jr., mentioning W.

9482. Anderson, James D. "*This Species of Property.* By Leslie Howard Owens; *The Black Family in Slavery and Freedom 1750–1925.* By Herbert G. Gutman." *The Journal of Negro History*, 62 (July 1977), 289–294. Review quoting from and commenting on *TMBV* (pp. 289, 293) and *WML* (p. 294).

9483. Anon. "An Exhibit of Treasures Restored." *The Schomburg Center for Research in Black Culture*, 1 (Fall 1977), 6–7. Illustrated step-by-step explanation of the restoration of the manuscript of *NS*.

9484. Anon. "Gibson, Donald B. 1933– ," in *Contemporary Authors.* Vols. 25–28 (first revision). Ed. Christine Nasso. Detroit: Gale, 1977, p. 266. Lists Gibson's *Five Black Writers*, which treats W.

9485. Anon. "Interesting People." Cleveland *Call and Post* (2 July 1977), p. 38. Biographical sketch of W.

9486. Anon. "Wright a Pioneer in Rebellion of Literature." *Chicago Defender* (31 December 1977), p. 11. Biographical sketch including a photograph of W in the film role of Bigger Thomas.

9487. Baker, Houston A., Jr. "The Embattled Craftsman: An Essay on James Baldwin." *Journal of African-Afro-American Affairs*, 1, no. 1 (1977), 28–51. Mentions briefly W and *BB* (p. 30).

9488. _____. "Preface," in his *A Dark and Sudden Beauty: Two Essays in Black American Poetry by George Kent and Stephen Henderson.* Philadelphia: Afro-American Studies Program at the University of Pennsylvania, 1977, pp. 3–4. Mentions W briefly.

9489. Berger, Gertrude. "Island Trees, New York: Community in Conflict." *Indiana English*, 1 (Fall 1977), 19–22. Comments on *BB* as one of the books attacked in 1976 in a school censorship case.

9490. Blotner, Joseph, ed. *Selected Letters of William Faulkner.* New York: Random House, 1977, pp. 201, 393. Prints Faulkner's letter to W of 11 September 1945 preferring *NS* to *BB*. Also comments on Joe Brown, whose verse Faulkner is reading (p. 201). In a letter to Harold Ober about an essay Faulkner has written, he instructs him to "delete Richard Wright from the text" (p. 393).

9491. _____. Ed. *Selected Letters of William Faulkner.* New York: Random House, 1977, p. 393. Letter to Harold Ober concerning Faulkner's comment on the Emmett Till case asking him to delete Richard Wright from the text.

9492. Butcher, Philip, ed. *The Minority Presence in American Literature, 1600–1900: A Reader and Course Guide.* Vol. 2. Washington, DC: Howard University Press, 1977, pp. 289, 321, 368. Mentions W briefly, comparing him to Charles W. Chesnutt, Stephen Crane, and Dreiser. Mentions *NS*.

9493. Clecak, Peter. "Culture and Politics in the Sixties." *Dissent*, 24 (Fall 1977), 439–442. Review of Morris Dickstein's *Gates of Eden: American Culture in the Sixties* mentioning W briefly (p. 440).

9494. Cook, Bruce. *Dalton Trumbo.* New York: Scribner's, 1977, p. 250. Notes that Charles White was a friend of W in Chicago.

9495. Dance, Darryl. "*The Waiting Years: Essays on American Negro Literature.* By Blyden Jackson." *The Journal of Negro History*, 62 (April 1977), 189–191. Review mentioning two essays on W.

9496. Eckels, Jon. *Pursuing the Pursuit—The Black Plight in White America.* Hicksville, NY: Exposition Press, 1977, p. v. W is one of the dedicatees.

9497. Ezell, Macel. *Unequivocal Americanism: Right-Wing Novels in the Cold War Era.* Metuchen, NJ: Scarecrow Press, 1977, pp. 87–88. Mentions briefly Andrew Lytle's unfavorable review of *LD*.

9498. Fields, Perry. "*American Hunger* Richard Wright." *Black Books Bulletin*, 5 (Fall 1977), 34–35. Favorable review focusing on its relation to *BB*. *AH* is "an attack on the blind racism of America as well as an existential treatise of life in general" (p. 35).

9499. Fine, David M. *The City, The Immigrant and American Fiction.* Metuchen, NJ: Scarecrow Press, 1977, p. 142. Mentions briefly W and *NS*.

9500. Gavins, Raymond. *The Perils and Prospects of Southern Black Leadership: Gordon Blaine Hancock, 1884–1970.* Durham, NC: Duke University Press, 1977, pp. 87, 91. Quotes from *TMBV*. Reprinted: 1993.

9501. Gornick, Vivian. *The Ro-*

mance of American Communism. New York: Basic Books, 1977, p. 9. Quotes W on the appeal of the Communist Party.

9502. Graver, Lawrence, *"Carson McCullers"* in *Seven American Women Writers of the Twentieth Century: An Introduction,* Minneapolis: University of Minnesota Press, 1977, pp. 265–310. Mentions W briefly (p. 268).

9503. ____. "Carson McCullers," in *Seven American Women Writers of the Twentieth Century.* Minneapolis: University of Minnesota Press, 1977, pp. 265–310. Reprint of 1969.

9504. Hairston, Loyle. "Chester Himes—'Alien' in Exile." *Freedomways,* 7 (First Quarter 1977), 14–18. Mentions W briefly. Reprinted: 1999.

9505. ____. "Chester Himes 'Alien' in Exile." *Freedomways,* First Quarter, 1977), 14–18. Mentions W briefly (p. 15). Reprinted: 1999.

9506. Harrison, John W. "General." *Abstracts of English Studies,* 21 (September 1977), 65. Abstracts an article by William Cosgrove mentioning W.

9507. Harrington, Ollie. "Look Homeward Baby," in *A Freedomways Reader: Afro-America in the Seventies.* Ed. Ernest Kaiser. New York: International, 1977, pp. 94–112. Mentions W at the Café Monaco in Paris (p. 99).

9508. Henderson, Stephen. "The Question of Form and Judgment in Contemporary Black American Poetry: 1962–1977," in *A Dark and Sudden Beauty: Two Essays in Black American Poetry.* Ed. Houston A. Baker, Jr. Philadelphia: Afro-American Studies Program at the University of Pennsylvania, 1977, pp. 19–36. Mentions W briefly (p. 27).

9509. Hornsby, Alton, Jr. *The Black Almanac.* Fourth edition. Woodbury, NY: Barron's Educational Series, 1977, p. 86. Reprint of.

9510. Hornung, Alfred. "Richard Wright." *Abstracts of English Studies,* 21 (November 1977), 222. Abstracts an article by Dennis E. Baron.

9511. Kaiser, Ernest. "Recent Books." *Freedomways,* 17 (Second Quarter 1977), 117–129. Contains a notice of Addison Gayle's *Wayward Child* mentioning *BB* (p. 123).

9512. ____. "Recent Books." *Freedomways,* 17 (Third Quarter

1977), 182–191. Contains an unfavorable notice of *AH* (p. 190).

9513. Korenman, Joan S. "Richard Wright." *Abstracts of English Studies,* 21 (October 1977), 142. Abstracts an article by Jeffrey A. Sadler.

9514. Lampley, James T. "Autobiography of Little Value." *Freedomways,* 17 (Third Quarter 1977), 175–176. Review of Addison Gayle's *Wayward Child* mentioning W briefly.

9515. Levine, Lawrence W. *Black Culture and Black Consciousness: Afro-American Folk Thought From Slavery to Freedom,* New York: Oxford University Press, 1977, p. 256, 340. Quotes from *TMBV* and *BB.*

9516. Madsen, Axel. *Hearts and Minds: The Common Journey of Simone de Beauvoir and Jean-Paul Sartre.* New York: Morrow, 1977, pp. 134, 136, 139, 159, 161. Comments on de Beauvoir's visits with W in New York and W's support of the R.D.R. Reprinted: 1979.

9517. Martin, Jay. "National Development and Ethnic Poetics: The Function of Literature in the Liberation of Peoples," in *The Study of American Culture: Contemporary Conflicts.* Ed. Luther S. Luedtke. DeLand, FL: Everett/Edwards, pp. 219–240. Mentions W briefly and quotes from "Blueprint for Negro Writing" (p. 220).

9518. McConnell, Frank D. *Four Postwar American Novelists: Bellow, Mailer, Barth, and Pynchon.* Chicago: The University of Chicago Press, 1977, p. 9. Mentions briefly W, *NS,* and Bigger.

9519. McQuade, Donald, and Robert Atwan. "Richard Wright/ *Black Boy,*" in their *Popular Writing in America.* New York: Oxford University Press, 1977, p. 393. Reprint of 1974.

9520. Nagel, James. "A Conversation in Boston," in his *American Fiction: Historical and Critical Essays.* Boston: Northeastern University Press and Twayne, 1977, pp. 174–202. Mentions W briefly (p. 198).

9521. Nielson, David Gordon. *Black Ethos: Northern Urban Negro Life and Thought, 1890–1930.* Westport, CT: Greenwood Press, 1977, pp. 4–5, 15, 110, 123–124, 125–126. Comments on *NS* and *BB*; quotes from *TMBV* and *NS.*

9522. Phillips, Robert L. *"Negro American Literature Forum." S.S.S.L.:*

The News-Letter of The Society for the Study of Southern Literature, 10 (April 1977), 20. Lists an article on W by A. Robert Lee.

9523. ____. "Negro American Literature Forum." *S.S.S.L.: The News-Letter of The Society for the Study of Southern Literature,* 10 (April 1977), 9. Mentions an article on W by P. Jay Delmar.

9524. ____. "Obsidian: Black Literature in Review." *S.S.S.L.: The News-Letter of The Society for the Study of Southern Literature,* 10 (April 1977), 9. Mentions W briefly.

9525. ____. Untitled note. *S.S.S.L.: The News-Letter of The Society for the Study of Southern Literature,* 10 (November 1977), 6. Mentions an article on W by Mary Ann Witt in *The Comparatist.*

9526. ____. Untitled note. *S.S.S.L.: The Newsletter of The Society for the Study of Southern Literature,* 10 (April 1977), 11. Mentions David Bakish's *Richard Wright.*

9527. ____. Untitled note. *S.S.S.L.: The News-Letter of The Society for the Study of Southern Literature,* 10 (April 1977), 16. Mentions briefly *AH* and *BB.*

9528. ____. Untitled note. *S.S.S.L.: The News-Letter of The Society for the Study of Southern Literature,* 10 (November 1977), 14. Announces *A Richard Wright Reader.*

9529. ____. Untitled note. *S.S.S.L.: The News-Letter of The Society for the Study of Southern Literature,* 10 (November 1977), 14. Notes the inclusion of W in *First Printings of American Authors.*

9530. Pingree, Elizabeth E., ed. *Humanities Index: April 1976 to March 1977.* New York: H.W. Wilson, 1977, p. 821. Lists one item s.v. W.

9531. Plessner, Monika. *Ich bin der dunklere Bruder: Die Literatur der schwarzen Amerikaner.* Hagen: von der Linnepe, 1977, pp. 121, 141, 153, 155, 167, 184, 206, 214, 215, 223, 234, 240–257, 260, 261, 263, 265, 267, 272, 273, 292, 293, 296, 297, 300, 306. The chapter on W begins with emphasis on the increasing influence of the Communist Party in the thirties, then examines W's childhood, his emergence as a writer, and finally his expatriation. Plessner analyzes "Big Boy Leaves Home," and *NS,* and discusses W's influence on Ellison and Baldwin.

9532. Portelli, Alessandro. *Bianchi e neri nella letteratura americana: la dialletica dell'identità*. Bari: DeDonato, 1977, pp. 17, 85–89, 90, 91, 92, 97–98, 142, 143, 337, 338, 343, 369. Discusses Bigger as "the victim as agressor," focusing on his relation to Mary and comparing him to Frederick Douglass (pp. 85–89). Also comments on Ellison's disagreements with *NS* (pp. 89–91). Elsewhere mentions *O* (pp. 92, 142) and comments briefly on "Big Boy Leaves Home" (pp. 97–98).

9533. Reckley, Ralph. "The Use of the Doppelganger or Double in Chester Himes' *Lonely Crusade*." *CLA Journal*, 20 (June, 1977), 448–458. Compares Himes's treatment of his aggressive tendencies to W's. Reprinted: 1999.

9534. _____. "The Use of the Doppelganger or Double in Chester Himes' *Lonely Crusade*." *CLA Journal*, 20 (June 1977), 448–458. Mentions W briefly (p. 457). Reprinted: 1999.

9535. Redding, J. Saunders. "The Black Arts Movement: A Modest Dissent." *The Crisis*, 84 (February 1977), 50–52. Mentions W briefly. Reprinted: 1992.

9536. Reed, Ishmael, Quincy Troupe, and Steve Cannon. "The Essential Ellison," *Y'Bird Magazine* 1 (Autumn 1977), 126–159. Ellison discusses his early literary friendship with W. Reprinted: 1995.

9537. Sewell, George A. "Richard Nathaniel Wright, Novelist," in their *Mississippi Black History Makers*. Jackson: University Press of Mississippi, 1977, pp. 287–312. Biographical essay based mainly on the Fabre and Webb biographies. The period of W's expatriation is virtually ignored, but his family background is given in some detail. Reprinted: 1984.

9538. Simon, Linda. *The Biography of Alice B. Toklas*. Garden City, NY: Doubleday, 1977, p. 187. Mentions W briefly.

9539. Smith, Barbara. "Toward a Black Feminist Criticism." *Conditions*, 2 (1977), 25–44. Mentions briefly *BB* (p. 30). Reprinted: 1998.

9540. Smith, Jessie Carney. *Black Academic Libraries and Research Collections: An Historical Survey*. Westport, CT: Greenwood, 1977, pp. 166, 193. Notes that W papers are at the Schomburg Collection.

9541. Titon, Jeff Todd. *Early Downhome Blues: A Musical and Cultural Analysis*. Urbana: University of Illinois Press, 1977, p. 192. Quotes from W's foreword to *Blues Fell This Morning*. Reprinted: 1999.

9542. Turner, Darwin T. "Black Fiction: History and Myth." *Studies in American Fiction*, 3 (Spring 1977), 109–126. Mentions briefly W and *UTC* (pp. 116–117). Reprinted: 1977.

9543. _____. "Black Fiction: History and Myth," in *American Fiction: Historical and Critical Essays*. Ed. James Nagel. Boston: Northeastern University Press and Twayne, 1977, pp. 109–126. Mentions briefly *UTC* (p. 116) and W (p. 117).

9544. _____. "Faulkner and Slavery," in *The South and Faulkner's Yoknaptawpha: The Actual and the Apocryphal*. Jackson: University Press of Mississippi, 1977, pp. 62–103. Notes that W never suggested that black-white friendships in the South were possible (p. 73). Also mentions W elsewhere (p. 89).

9545. Um'Rani, Munir. "Richard Wright *American Hunger*: A Review." *Bilalian News* (4 November 1977), pp. 28–29. Emphasizes W's "psyche pain" inflicted by racism. Discusses his difficulties with the Communist Party.

9546. Urcia, Ingeborg. "*Particularism and Regionalism*." *Abstracts of English Studies*, 20 (June 1977), 653. Abstracts an article by Manfred Puetz mentioning W.

9547. Vanleer, Jay. "Book Reviews." Cleveland *Call and Post* (23 July 1977), p. 3B. Includes a brief, favorable review of *AH* with mention of Michel Fabre's "Afterword."

9548. Watkins, Floyd C. *In Time and Place: Some Origins of American Fiction*. Athens: The University of Georgia Press, 1977, p. 203. Mentions W briefly.

9549. Watkins, Mel. "Talk with Toni Morrison." *The New York Times Book Review* (11 September 1977), pp. 48, 50. Mentions briefly W and *NS* (p. 48). Reprinted: 1994.

9550. Whitlow, Roger. "Baldwin's *Going to Meet the Man*: Racial Brutality and Sexual Gratification." *American Image*, 34 (Winter 1977), 351–356. Mentions briefly *NS* (p. 351). Reprinted: 1988.

9551. Yamada, Hiroyasu. "James Baldwin's *Go Tell It*: A Road to the Advent and Its Meaning," in his *Amerika Shosetsu—Kenkyu to Kon-*

satsu [*American Fiction: Studies and Observations*]. Osaka: Sogensha, 1977, pp. 134–150. Compares *Go Tell It* with *NS*. John Grimes and Bigger Thomas are prototypes of black men.

9552. Allen, Samuel. "*Song of Solomon* by Toni Morrison." *Boston University Journal*, 26 (1978), 67–69. Mentions W briefly (p. 69). Reprinted: 1988.

9553. Anon. "Lest We Forget: Richard Wright (1908–1960)." *Bilalian News* (8 December 1978), 1 p. Relates W's encounters in the South with racism and comments briefly on W's later life. Mentions briefly *UTC*, *TMBV*, *BB*, and *BP*.

9554. Anon. *Materials and Human Resources for Teaching Ethnic Studies: An Annotated Bibliography*. New York: Arno Press, 1978, p. 24. Lists *NS*.

9555. Anon. "'Native Son' Premieres at Goodman," *Chicago Defender* (5 August 1978), Accent sec., p. 2. Announces the opening of the revival of the play *NS* on 12 October 1978.

9556. Anon. "*Richard Wright Reader*." *Black Books Bulletin*, 6 (Spring 1978), 1. Full-page publisher's announcement with a photograph of W.

9557. Austin, James C. "William Melvin Kelley." *Abstracts of English Studies*, 21 (May 1978), 657. Abstracts an article by Phyllis R. Klotman mentioning W.

9558. Bateman, Beverly. "Albert Murray: Up Tempo or 'The Velocity of Celebration.'" *Off Peachtree*, 1, no. 8 (September 1978), pp. 40–41. Mentions briefly *NS*. Reprinted: 1978.

9559. Benston, Kimberly W. "Introduction," in his *Imamu Amiri Baraka (Leroi Jones): A Collection of Critical Essays*. Englewood Cliffs, NJ: Prentice-Hall, 1978, p. 13, 15. Mentions W briefly and quotes from Baraka mentioning W and Bigger Thomas.

9560. Carter, Purvis M. "The Negro in Periodical Literature, 1970–1972, Part I." *The Journal of Negro History*, 63 (April 1978), 161–189. Lists items on W by Ronald Ridenour and Darwin T. Turner.

9561. _____. "The Negro in Periodical Literature, 1970–1972, Part II." *The Journal of Negro History*, 63 (July 1978), 262–306. Lists items on W by Robert Farnsworth and

David Ray, Blyden Jackson, Griffith J. Pugh, Steven J. Rubin, and Martha Stephens.

9562. Cassata, Mary B. "Profiles of the Users and Usage of Afro-American Literature: A Unification of Communications and Library Research Strategies." *Journal of Black Studies*, 9 (September 1978), Quotes Fred Standley mentioning W briefly. See 1974.

9563. Cassill, R.V. "Richard Wright," in his *The Norton Anthology of Short Fiction*. New York: Norton, 1978, p. 1434. Biographical sketch. "The Man Who Was Almost a Man" is included on pp. 1374–1384, followed by five study questions. Reprinted: 1981.

9564. Coleman, Larry G. "LeRoi Jones' *Tales*: Sketches of the Artist as a Young Man Moving Toward a Blacker Art," in *Imamu Amiri Baraka (Leroi Jones) A Collection of Critical Essays*. Ed. Kimberly W. Benston. Englewood Cliffs, NJ: Prentice Hall, 1978, pp. 84–95. Comments on Baraka's use of W in "The Screamers," Mentions Bigger and *NS*.

9565. Demby, William. *Love Story Black*. New York: Reed, Cannon & Johnson, 1978, pp. 31–32. Classroom scene in this novel in which the professor lecturing on W is interrupted by a diatribe delivered by a militant Puerto Rican student.

9566. Donald, Miles. *The American Novel in the Twentieth Century*. Newton Abbot: David & Charles, 1978, pp. 143–146. Favorable treatment of *NS*, praising its style and W's "ability to convey the subtleties of the social situation" (p. 144).

9567. Downing, David B. "Al Young." *Abstracts of English Studies*, 22 (November 1978), 116–117. Abstracts an article by Neil Schmitz mentioning W.

9568. Elder, Arlene A. *The "Hindered Hand": Cultural Implications of Early African-American Fiction*. Westport, CT: Greenwood Press, 1978, p. xii. Quotes W that "the Negro is America's metaphor."

9569. _____. *The "Hindered Hand": Cultural Implications of Early African-American Fiction*. Westport, CT: Greenwood Press, 1978, p. xii. Mentions W briefly.

9570. Ellison, Ralph. "Wright, Richard 1908–1960," in *Contemporary Literary Criticism*. Ed. Dedria

Bryfonski. Detroit: Gale, 1978, p. 583. Partial reprint of 1945.890.

9571. El'Zabar, Kai. "*Nappy Edges* Ntozake Shange." *Black Books Bulletin*, 6 (Winter 1978), 75–76. Quotes Shange's poem on Bigger Thomas, "The suspect is black and in his early 20's."

9572. Ezell, John Samuel. *The South Since 1865*. Second edition. Norman: University of Oklahoma Press, 1978, p. 294. Mentions briefly *UTC* and *NS*.

9573. Fields, Raymond. "*Richard Wright Reader*." *Black Books Bulletin*, 6 (Summer 1978), 54–55. Favorable review.

9574. Finholt, Richard. *American Visionary Fictions: Mad Metaphysics as Salvation Psychology*. Port Washington, NY: Kennikat Press, 1978, pp. 102–103. Comments on and quotes from Ellison's "Richard Wright's Blues."

9575. Fleming, Robert E. *James Weldon Johnson and Arna Wendell Bontemps: A Reference Guide*. Boston: G.K. Hall, 1978, p. 84. Lists and summarizes W's review of Bontemps's *Black Thunder*.

9576. _____. *Willard Motley*. Boston: Twayne, 1978, pp. 9, 46, 55, 59, 61, 63, 64, 119, 128, 139, 142, 144, 145, 146, 149–150. Mentions briefly W, *NS*, Bigger Thomas, and *SH*.

9577. Fontenot, Chester J., Jr. "Fanon and the Devourers." *Journal of Black Studies*, 9 (September 1978), 93–114. Mentions W briefly (pp. 107, 108).

9578. Jackson, Jocelyn Whitehead. "The Problem of Identity in Selected Early Essays of James Baldwin." *The Journal of the Interdenominational Theological Center*, 6 (Fall 1978), 1–15. Discusses Baldwin's critique of W in *Notes of a Native Son*. Reprinted: 1988.

9579. Jago, David M. "Black." *Abstracts of English Studies*, 21 (February 1978), 425. Abstracts an article by Nancy M. Tischler mentioning W.

9580. Johnson, Abby Arthur. "Literary Midwife: Jessie Redmon Fauset and the Harlem Renaissance." *Phylon*, 39 (June 1978), 143–153. Quotes from "Blueprint for Negro Writing."

9581. Kaiser, Ernest. "Recent Books." *Freedomways*, 18 (Fourth Quarter 1978), 230–231. Contains an unfavorable notice of Ellen Wright

and Michel Fabre's *Richard Wright Reader*.

9582. Kanaseki, Hisao. "American Influence on Japanese Literature," in *Other Voices, Other Views*. Westport, CT: Greenwood Press, 1978, pp. 45–58. Mentions W briefly (p. 48).

9583. Larson, Charles R. *American Indian Fiction*. Albuquerque: University of New Mexico Press, 1978, pp. 10, 169. Mentions briefly W, *UTC*, and *NS*.

9584. Lea, Sydney, and Jay Parini. "Interview with Eleanor Clark and Robert Penn Warren." *New England Review* (March 1978), 49–70. Clark believes that expatriation damaged W as a writer (p. 63). Reprinted: 1978.

9585. Littlejohn, David. "Wright, Richard 1908–1960," in *Contemporary Literary Criticism*. Ed. Dedria Bryfonski. Detroit: Gale, 1978, pp. 583–585. Partial reprint of 1966.97.

9586. Lynch, Acklyn R. "Reflections on Black Culture in the Early Forties." *Black Books Bulletin*, 6 (Spring 1978), 30–37, 76–78, 81. Mentions briefly Bigger Thomas (p. 31) and *NS*, *TMBV*, and *BB* (p. 37).

9587. M., L.H. "Black." *Abstracts of English Studies*, 21 (January 1978), 361–362. Abstracts an article by James Page mentioning W.

9588/9. MacDonald, Scott. "An Evaluative Check-List of Erskine Caldwell's Short Fiction," *Studies in Short Fiction*, 15 (Winter 1978), 81–97. Mentions briefly *UTC* (p. 81). Reprinted: 1981.

9590. Marszalek, John F. "*Mississippi Black History Makers*. By George Alexander Sewell." *The Journal of Mississippi History*, 40 (November 1978), 380–381. Review mentioning W briefly.

9591. Miller, R. Baxter. *Langston Hughes and Gwendolyn Brooks: A Reference Guide*. Boston: G.K. Hall, 1978, p. 18. Includes a synopsis of W's "Forerunner and Ambassador."

9592. Mitchell, Sally. "Ralph Ellison." *Abstracts of English Studies*, 21 (February 1978), 438. Abstracts an article by Jerry Wasserman mentioning W.

9593. Mphahlele, Ezekiel. *Down Second Avenue*. Gloucester, MA: Peter Smith, 1978, pp. xi, 183. Reprint of 1968.

9594. Okadigbo, Miriam. "Consciencism as the Key to Nkrumah." *Umoja*, 2 (Spring 1978), 41–52. Notes that Nkrumah's "*Dark Days in Ghana* opens with a quote from Richard Wright's *Black Power*" (p. 51).

9595. Parker, Bettye J. "BBB Interviews Ngugi Wa Thiongo." *Black Books Bulletin*, 6 (Spring 1978), 46–51. Thiongo disavows influence of *BB* on *Weep Not Child* (p. 47) and notes that George Lamming, who had recently visited the University of Nairobi, was "very fond of Richard Wright and some of the more revolutionary writers" (p. 49).

9596. Phillips, Robert L. "Alabama Symposium." *S.S.S.L.: The News-Letter of The Society for the Study of Southern Literature*, 11 (November 1978), 9. Lists a paper by Jack B. Moore on "The View from the Broom-Closet of the Regency Hyatt: Richard Wright as Southern Writer."

9597. _____. "*Black American Literature Forum*." *S.S.S.L.: The News-Letter of The Society for the Study of Southern Literature*, 11 (November 1978), 19. Lists articles on W by Charles De Arman and Diane Long Hoeveler.

9598. _____. "Charles T. Davis." *S.S.S.L.: The News-Letter of The Society for the Study of Southern Literature*, 11 (November 1978), 1. Notes Davis's work on W.

9599. _____. "*The Literary South*." *S.S.S.L.: The News-Letter of The Society for the Study of Southern Literature*, 11 (November 1978), 26. Lists authors included in the Rubin anthology, including W.

9600. _____. "*Modern Language Association Meeting 1978*." *S.S.S.L.: The News-Letter of The Society for the Study of Southern Literature*, 11 (November 1978), 4–5. Lists a paper by John Wideman on "*Lawd Today*: Richard Wright and Urban Lore."

9601. _____. "*Studies in Short Fiction*." *S.S.S.L.: The News-Letter of The Society for the Study of Southern Literature*, 11 (November 1978), 23. Lists an article on W by Joseph T. Skerrett, Jr.

9602. _____. Untitled note. *S.S.S.L.: The News-Letter of The Society for the Study of Southern Literature*, 11 (April 1978), 5. Lists a paper by Ella Lees Brown on "Four Versions of Hell: Dante, Wright, Ellison, and Baraka" at a meeting of the Tennessee Philological Association.

9603. _____. Untitled note. *S.S.S.L.: The News-Letter of The Society for the Study of Southern Literature*, 11 (April 1978), 6. Mentions a paper by Dean McWilliams on "Richard Wright's Adaptation of *Native Son*" at a meeting of the Popular Culture Association.

9604. _____. Untitled note. *S.S.S.L.: The News-Letter of The Society for the Study of Southern Literature*, 11 (April 1978), 10. Announces publication of John M. Reilly's *Richard Wright: The Critical Reception*.

9605. _____. Untitled note. *S.S.S.L.: The News-Letter of The Society for the Study of Southern Literature*, 11 (November 1978), 12. Notes the publication of the paperback edition of Michel Fabre's *The Unfinished Quest of Richard Wright*.

9606. Pingree, Elizabeth E., ed. *Humanities Index: April 1977 to March 1978*. New York: H.W. Wilson, 1978, p. 761. Lists six items s.v. W.

9607. Robinson, Cedric J. "The Emergent Marxism of Richard Wright's Ideology." *Race and Class*, 19, no. 3 (1978), pp. 221–237. Contrasts W to Ellison, Himes and Baldwin, who rejected Marxism. W, on the other hand combined social ideology, racial consciousness, and left political analysis. *NS* and "How Bigger Was Born" "underscored the absolute character of revolutionary commitment" and also spoke to Marxian class analysis. Robinson also mentions *UTC*, *BB*, *O*, and *LD*.

9608. Salzman, Jack. *Albert Maltz*. Boston: Twayne, 1978, pp. 42, 47, 53, 90, 94, 140. Mentions briefly "Fire and Cloud," Maltz's review of *NS*, and W's politics.

9609. Seifullah, Abdul Aleem. "'Native Son' Message Still Powerful." *Bilalian News* (17 November 1978), p. 28. Favorable review of the play *NS* as staged in the Goodman Theater in Chicago. Lists members of the cast.

9610. Shrodes, Caroline, Harry Finestone, and Michael Shugrue. "Richard Wright," in their *The Conscious Reader*. Second edition. New York: Macmillan, 1978, p. 1000. Reprint of 1974.157.

9611. _____. "Suggestions for Discussion, Suggestions for Writing," in their *The Conscious Reader*. New York: Macmillan, 1978, p. 951. Reprint of 1974.

9612. Smith, Barbara. "Sexual Politics and the Fiction of Zora Neale Hurston." *The Radical Teacher*, No. 52 (May 1978). Mentions W briefly. Reprinted: 1998.

9613. Smith, Lillian, "A Trembling Earth," in her *The Winner Names the Age*. Ed. Michelle Cliff. New York: W.W. Norton, 1978, pp. 121–125. A speech for Paris radio including praise for W (pp. 123–124).

9614. Sossaman, Stephen. "Ishmael Reed." *Abstracts of English Studies*, 21 (February 1978), 445. Abstracts an article by Neil Schmitz mentioning W.

9615. Steeves, Edna L. "Characters." *Abstracts of English Studies*, 21 (April 1978), 577. Abstracts an article by Blanche Gelfant mentioning W.

9616. Stepto, Robert B. "Teaching Afro-American Literature: Survey or Tradition: The Reconstruction of Instruction," in his and Dexter Fisher's *Afro-American Literature: The Reconstruction of Instruction*. New York: Modern Language Association, 1978, pp. 8–24. Mentions briefly W and *NS* (pp. 9, 19). Reprinted: 1992.

9617. Szwed, John F., and Roger D. Abrahams. *Afro-American Folk Culture*. Philadelphia: Institute for the Study of Human Issues, 1978, pp. 402–403. Contains annotated listings for *BB*, *TMBV*, and *WML*.

9618. Williams, Jerry, ed. *Southern Literature 1968–1975*. Boston: 1978, p. 216. Lists items on W by Daniel Aaron, Richard Abcarian, Margaret Walker Alexander, Lola J. Ames, David D. Anderson, Herbert Aptheker, Houston Baker, David Bakish, Richard E. Baldwin, Bernard W. Bell, Stephen B. Bennett, Faith Berry, C.W.E. Bigsby, A.G. Billingsley, Nelson M. Blake, Sam Bluefarb, Piero Boitanic, H. Philip Bolton, Robert Bone, G.N. and L.A. Boyd, Russell C. Brignano, Sheldon Brivic, Mary Ellen Brooks, Cecil Brown, Lloyd Brown, Joseph Bruchac, Jerry H. Bryant, Earl Cash, Horace Cayton, Michael G. Cooke, Robert A. Corrigan, William Cosgrove, Ralph Ellison, Malcolm Cowley, Thomas Cripps, Robert M. Crundin, David P. Demarest, Jr. Morris Dickstein, Melvin Dixon, Dan M. Donlan, Sister Ann Edward, James A. Emanuel,

O.B. Emerson, Seymour Epstein, M.W. Everette, Michel Fabre, Robert Felgar, Robert E. Fleming, Warren French, Gayle Gaskill, Addison Gayle, Donald B. Gibson, J.R. Giles, William Goede, Malcolm Goldstein, Jean-François Gounard, G.B. Graham, Seymour L. Gross, Doris Grumbach, Friedrike Hajek, Gerald W. Haslam, Robert Hemenway, Mildred A. Hill, John Houseman, Irving Howe, S.E. Hyman, Blyden Jackson, Charles L. James, Lance Jeffers, Lola Jones, June Jordan, Ernest Kaiser, Edward Kearns, James G. Kennedy, George E. Kent, John Killinger, Kichung Kim, Keneth Kinnamon, Phyllis R. Klotman, Richard Kostelanetz, R.B.V. Larsen, Lewis A. Lawson, Lewis Leary, Thomas LeClair, Richard Lehan, Valentina Libman, Arthur Liebman, S. Longstreet, Jerre Mangione, K.H. Mann, Loretta V. Monucci, Edward Margolies, Clifford Mason, John R. May, Dan McCall, Harold T. McCarthy Robert E. McDowell, Donald R. Merkle, Shirley Meyer, Eugen E. Miller, Louis D. Mitchell, James Nagel, Larry Neal, Blake Nevius, John O'Brien, Carole W. Oleson, Dorothy Padmore, William Peden, R.H. Pells, George Perkins, Donald Petesch, Marcia Pitcale, P.R. Plante, Ronald Primeau, Linda Prior, John Pyros, David Ray, Robert Farnsworth, Kenneth T. Reed, John M. Reilly, Milton and Patricia Rickels, Ronald Ridenour, Roger Rosenblatt, Ronald Sanders, Jerald J. Savory, Noel Schraufagel, Nathan A. Scott, Carl Senna, Paul C. Scherr, Paul N. Siegel, Lewis P. Simpson, Amritjit Singh, Raman K. Singh, Dwight L. Smith, Sidonie Ann Smith, Theodore Solotaroff, Katherine Sprandel, Alvin Starr, Martha Stephens, Campbell Tatham, Michel Terrier, John Timmerman, Darwin T. Turner, Melvin and Margaret Wade, Marilyn W. Waniek, Edward A. Watson, Constance Webb, Henrietta Weigel, Adrian Weiss, John A. Williams, James Woodress, and James O. Young.

9619. Anon. "*Celebrations and Attacks: Thirty Years of Literary and Cultural Commentary.*" *Dissent*, 26 (Summer 1979), 303. Publisher's announcement of a book by Irving Howe. Mentions W briefly. Reprinted: 1980.

9620. Anon. "Richard Wright," in *Obituaries from the Times 1951–1960.* Comp. Frank C. Roberts. Reading: Newspaper Archive Developments Limited, 1979, pp. 767–768. Reprint of 1961.9.

9621. Anon. "Richard Wright," in *Obituaries from the Times 1951–1960.* Reading: Newspaper Archive Developments Limited, 1979, pp. 767–768. Reprint of the obituary of W in *The London Times* on 22 February 1960. Reviews W's life emphasizing his "restless critical spirit."

9622. Bennett, Lerone, Jr., and Margaret G. Burroughs. "A Lorraine Hansberry Rap." *Freedomways*, 19 (Fourth Quarter 1979), 226–233. Mentions W briefly (p. 227).

9623. Bigsby, C.W.E. "The Divided Mind of James Baldwin." *Journal of American Studies*, 13 (December 1979), 325–342. Discusses Baldwin's quarrel with W (pp. 333–334, 336–339). Bigsby defends *NS* vigorously against Baldwin's attack. Reprinted: 1988.

9624. Bracy, William. "Wright, Richard," in *Encyclopedia Americana*. Ed. Bernard S. Cayne. Vol. 29. New York: Americana, 1979, p. 555. Reprint of 1969.

9625. Burress, Lee. "A Brief Report of the 1977 NCTE Censorship Survey," in *Dealing with Censorship*. Ed. James E. Davis. Urbana, IL: National Council of Teachers of English, 1979, pp. 14–47. Lists *BB* as one of the books to which objections were made (pp. 20, 24).

9626. Clark, VéVé. "Restaging Langston Hughes' *Scottsboro Limited*: An Interview with Amiri Baraka." *The Black Scholar*, 10 (July-August 1979), 62. Baraka mentions W materials at the Beinicke Library at Yale. Reprinted: 1994.

9627. Dickinson, Donald C. "Langston Hughes, 1902–1967" in *American Writers: A Collection of Literary Biographies*. Supplement I, Part 1. New York: Charles Scribner's, 1979, pp. 320–348. Notes W's approval of *The Big Sea*.

9628. Dowling, Colette. "The Song of Toni Morrison." *The New York Times Magazine* (20 May 1979), pp. 40–42, 48, 52, 54, 56, 58. Mentions briefly W and *NS* (p. 40). Reprinted: 1994.

9629. Emerson, O.B., and Marion C. Michael, eds. *Southern Literary Culture: A Bibliography of Masters' and Doctors' Theses*. Revised and enlarged edition. University, AL: The University of Alabama Press, 1979, 195–196. Lists twenty theses on W.

9630. Fohlen, Claude. *Les Noirs aux Etats-Unis*. Paris: Presses Universitaires de France, 1979, pp. 38–39, 126. Comments briefly on *NS*, mentions briefly *UTC*, and includes *NS* and *BB* in the bibliography. Reprinted: 1994.

9631. Francis, Claude, and Fernande Gontier. *Les ecrits de Simone de Beauvoir: La vie–L_écriture*. Paris: Gallimard, 1979, pp. 55, 71, 144, 153, 356. Notes that de Beauvoir translated a speech by W on 13 December 1948 at a R.D.R. rally, mentions W's death, and cites mentions of W by de Beauvoir in 1947 in *The New Yorker* and *The New York Times*.

9632. Galloway, David. *Edward Lewis Wallant*. Boston: Twayne, 1979, p. 149. Mentions W briefly.

9633. Green, Paul. "An Interview with Paul Green." *Southern Exposure*, 7 (Winter 1979), 139–140. Mentions W briefly.

9634. Gresham, Jewell Handy. "Lorraine Hansberry as Prose Stylist." *Freedomways*, 19 (Fourth Quarter 1979), 192–204. Mentions briefly W (p. 193) and *NS* (p. 194).

9635. Gunter, McArthur. "Baldwin Deserves Nobel Award." *The Baltimore Afro-American* (10 February 1979), p. 4. Letter to the editor mentioning W, Hughes, and Baldwin as "the three greatest black writers."

9636. Hairston, Loyle. "Black Writers' Views of America." *Freedomways*, 19 (Third Quarter 1979), 151–157. Mentions W briefly (p. 154).

9637. Hall, Donald, and D.L. Emblem. "Considerations," in their *A Writer's Reader*. Second edition. Boston: Little, Brown, 1979, pp. 491–492. Reprint of 1976.

9638. _____. "Richard Wright The Library Card," in their *A Writer's Reader*. Second edition. Boston: Little, Brown, 1979, p. 483. Reprint of 1976.

9639. Halpern, Shelly. "Valuable Information Seriously Flawed." *Freedomways*, 19 (Third Quarter 1979), 170–173. Review of *Black American Writers* by M. Thomas Inge, Maurice Duke, and Jackson R. Bryer mentioning W briefly.

9640. Holland, Laurence B. "American Literature Between the

Wars, 1914–1945," in *The Norton Anthology of American Literature*. Eds. Ronald Gottesman, Lawrence B. Holland, David Kalstone, Francis Murphy, Hershel Parker, William H. Pritchard, and Holland. New York: W.W. Norton, 1979, pp. 1015–1024. Mentions briefly W as expatriate.

9641. _____. "Richard Wright," in *The Norton Anthology of American Literature*. Eds. Ronald Gottesman, David Kalstone, Francis Murphy, Hershel Parker, William H. Pritchard, and Holland. New York: W.W. Norton, 1979, p. 2575. Bibliographical note.

9642. _____. "Richard Wright, 1908–1960," in *The Norton Anthology of American Literature*. Eds. Ronald Gottesman, David Kalstone, Francis Murphy, Hershel Parker, William H. Pritchard, and Holland. New York: W.W. Norton, 1979, pp. 1720–1723. Biographical-critical headnote to "Long Black Song."

9643. Jackson, Blyden. "Wright, Richard," in *The Encyclopedia of Southern History*. Eds. David C. Roller and Robert W. Twyman. Baton Rouge: Louisiana State University Press, 1979, pp. 1363–1364. Biographical sketch with a brief secondary bibliography.

9644. Jackson, Richard L. *Black Writers in Latin America*. Albuquerque: University of New Mexico Press, 1979, pp. 9–10, 142. Quotes from "Blueprint for Negro Writing" and *AH*.

9645. Jenkinson, Edward B. "Dirty Dictionaries, Obscene Nursery Rhymes, and Burned Books," in *Dealing with Censorship*. Ed. James E. Davis. Urbana, IL: National Council of Teachers of English, 1979, pp. 3–13. Cites W and *BB* as targets of censorship (pp. 8, 9).

9646. Kaiser, Ernest. "Recent Books." *Freedomways*, 19 (First Quarter 1979), 54–64. Contains a notice of Carol Fairbanks and Eugene A. Engeldinger's *Black American Fiction: A Bibliography* mentioning W briefly.

9647. Kazin, Alfred. "The Self as History: Reflections on Autobiography," in *Telling Lives: The Biographer's Art*. Ed. Marc Pachter. Washington: New Republic Books, 1979, pp. 74–89. Mentions briefly *BB*. Reprinted.

9648. Kinnamon, Keneth. "James Baldwin, 1924– " in *American Writers: A Collection of Literary Biographies*. Ed. Leonard Unger. Supplement I, Part 1. New York: Charles Scribner's, 1979, pp. 47–71. Includes discussion of the W-Baldwin relationship (pp. 51, 52, 64).

9649. Lindfors, Bernth. *Black African Literature in English: A Guide to Information Sources*. Detroit: Gale, 1979, p. 47. Lists Chukwudi T. Maduka's dissertation on Achebe, Peter Abrahams, Flaubert, and W.

9650. Madsen, Axel. *Hearts and Minds: The Common Journey of Simone de Beauvoir and Jean-Paul Sartre*. New York: Morrow Quill, 1979, pp. 134, 136, 139, 159, 161. Reprint of 1977.

9651. Mason, Elizabeth B., and Louis M. Starr, eds. *The Oral History Collection of Columbia University*. New York: Columbia University, 1979, p. 137. Entry for Jean B. Hutson mentions W as one of her interview topics.

9652. Naison, Mark. "Richard Wright and the Communist Party." *Radical America*, 13 (January-February 1979), pp. 60–63. Discusses *AH* and W's assessment of the Communist Party. In Chicago W depicts accurately the Party's repression of individualism, but in New York he enjoyed much more intellectual and cultural freedom.

9653. Nash, Gerald D. *The Great Depression and World War II: Organizing America, 1933–1945*. New York: St. Martin's Press, 1979, pp. 78, 87. Mentions briefly W and *NS*.

9654. Pearson, Norman Holmes. "American Literature: The Twentieth Century," in *Encyclopedia Americana*. Ed. Bernard S. Cayne. Vol. 1. New York: Americana, 1979, pp. 703–709. Reprint of 1973.

9655. Petillon, Pierre-Yves. *La grand-route: Espace et écriture en Amérique*. Paris: Éditions du Seuil, 1979, p. 126. Mentions W briefly.

9656. Pinckney, Darryl L. "Blues for Mr. Baldwin." *The New York Review of Books* (6 December 1979), pp. 32–33. Mentions briefly *NS* and W's quarrel with Baldwin. Reprinted: 1988.

9657. Phillips, Robert L., Jr. "SCMLA." *S.S.S.L.: The News-Letter of The Society for the Study of Southern Literature*, 12 (November 1979), 5. Lists a paper by William E. Tanner on "The Metaphor of the Underground Man in Richard Wright's *The Outsider*."

9658. _____. Untitled note. *S.S.S.L.: The News-Letter of The Society for the Study of Southern Literature*, 12 (April 1979), 16. Notes the publication of John M. Reilly's *Richard Wright: The Critical Reception*.

9659. _____. Untitled note. *S.S.S.L.: The News-Letter of The Society for the Study of Southern Literature*, 12 (April 1979), 17. Notes a reprint of *WML*.

9660. _____. Untitled note. *S.S.S.L.: The News-Letter of The Society for the Study of Southern Literature*, 12 (November 1979), 8. Notes that W is included in the fifth edition of David Madden's *Studies in the Short Story* and that "Margaret Walker has received a Ford Fellowship for her study of Richard Wright.

9661. _____. Untitled note. *S.S.S.L.: The News-Letter of The Society for the Study of Southern Literature*, 12 (November 1979), 15. Lists Evelyn Gross Avery's *Rebels and Victims: The Fiction of Richard Wright and Bernard Malamud*.

9662. _____. Untitled note. *S.S.S.L.: The News-Letter of The Society for the Study of Southern Literature*, 12 (November 1979), 18. Lists a paperback edition of *AH*.

9663. Pingree, Elizabeth E., ed. *Humanities Index: April 1978 to March 1979*. New York: H.W. Wilson, 1979, p. 710. Lists four items s.v. W.

9664. Pritchard, William H. "James Baldwin, 1924– ," in *The Norton Anthology of American Literature*. Eds. Ronald Gottesman, Laurence B. Holland, David Kalstone, Francis Murphy, Hershel Parker, and Pritchard. New York: W.W. Norton, 1979, pp. 2113–2114. Headnote mentioning W briefly. Reprinted: 1985, 1989, 1994, 1998.

9665. _____. "Ralph Ellison, 1914– ," in *The Norton Anthology of American Literature*. Eds. Ronald Gottesman, Laurence B. Holland, David Kalstone, Francis Murphy, Hershel Parker, and Pritchard. New York: W.W. Norton, 1979, pp. 1929–1931. Headnote mentioning W briefly. Reprinted: 1985, 1989, 1994, 1998.

9666. Pujols, Carmen. "The Omission." *Freedomways*, 19 (Second Quarter 1979), 100–102. Article on the actor Lou Gilbert noting that he was a friend of W.

9667. Pyros, John. *Mike Gold: Dean of American Proletarian Literature.* New York: Dramatika Press, 1979, p. 130. Mentions W briefly.

9668. Saffioti, Carol Lee. "Stephen Crane." *Abstracts of English Studies*, 23 (November 1979), 103. Abstracts an article by Alvin Starr mentioning W.

9669. Sandiford, Keith A. "Ralph Ellison and George Lamming: Two Episodes, One Myth." *Minority Voices*, 3 (Fall 1979), 19–25. Quotes from W's introduction to Lamming's *In the Castle of My Skin* (pp. 19, 24).

9670. Shorter, Eric. "Points West: Dublin, Chicago, New York." *Drama: The Quarterly Theatre Review*, No. 131 (Winter 1979), 21–27. Contains a mixed review of the revival of the play *NS* at the Goodman Theatre in Chicago. Stylistically dated, the play nevertheless retains "its force as a lesson in racialism" (p. 27).

9671. Skates, John Ray. *Mississippi: A Bicentennial History.* New York: Norton, 1979, pp. 17, 139, 140, 143–144. Sketches W's career, stressing his rage, hatred, and bitterness (pp. 143–144). Mentions W elsewhere.

9672. _____. *Mississippi: A Bicentennial History.* New York: W.W. Norton, 1979, pp. 16, 139, 140, 143–144. Comments on W and Ann Moody (p. 16) and contrasts the perspectives of W and Faulkner (pp. 143–144).

9673. Udosen, Willye Bell. *Image of the Black Woman in Black American Drama, 1900 to 1970.* Ann Arbor, MI: UMI, 1979, pp. 125–126, 269. Comments on Mrs. Thomas, Vera, and Clara Mears.

9674. Wynter, Sylvia. "Sambos and Minstrels." *Social Text*, 1 (Winter 1979), 149–156. Includes analysis of the Pease and Reynolds episode in *BB* in terms of the Sambo stereotype (pp. 153–155).

9675. Anon. *Biographical Books 1950–1980.* New York: R.R. Bowker, 1980, pp 1300–1301. Lists *BB* and biographies by Constance Webb and Michel Fabre.

9676. Anon. "*Celebrations and Attacks: Thirty Years of Literary and Political Commentary.*" *Dissent*, 27 (Summer 1980), 307. Reprint of 1979.

9677. Anon. "Interview with Eleanor Clark and Robert Penn Warren," *in Robert Penn Warren Talking: Interviews 1950–1978.* Eds. Floyd C. Watkins and Jolen J. Hiers. New York: Random House, 1980, pp. 260–277. Reprint of 1978.

9678. Anon. "Ph.D. Program in Afro-American Literature." *Afro Scholar Newsletter*, 1 (October 1980), 8. Mentions W briefly.

9679. Anon. "Publications Relating to Mississippi." *The Journal of Mississippi History*, 42 (November 1980), 388–389. Lists 1980.247.

9680. Anon. "Wright, Richard," in *Webster's Biographical Dictionary.* Ed. William Allan Neilson. Springfield, MA: G. & C. Merriam, 1980, p. 1600. Reprint of 1943.

9681. Avery, Evelyn Gross. "Wright, Richard, 1908–1960," in *Contemporary Literary Criticism.* Eds. Dedria Bryfonski and Laurie Lanzen Harris. Detroit: Gale, 1980, pp. 597–599. Partial reprint of 1979.

9682. Banks, Ann. *First-Person America.* New York: Alfred A. Knopf, 1980, p. xviii. Notes that the Federal Writers Project gave W the time to write *NS.* Reprinted: 1981.

9683. Baraka, Amiri. *In the Tradition (for Black Arthur Blythe).* Privately published, 1980, p. [5]. Refers to "Blue Black Boys & Little Richard Wrights." Reprinted: 1987, 1995.

9684. _____. "Letter to the Editor." *The Black Scholar*, 11 (November/December 1980), 84–85. Mentions W briefly.

9685. Binder, Wolfgang. "James Baldwin, an Interview." *Revista/Review Interamericana*, 10 (Fall 1980), 326–341. Baldwin comments on "Man of All Work" (p. 332) and discusses his attitude toward W. He rejects the "Stalinist garbage" of *NS* but thinks that *LT* is "just a fantastic book ... full of niggers! ... full of life" (pp. 336–338). Reprinted: 1989.

9686. Blake, Susan L. "Old John in Harlem: The Urban Folktales of Langston Hughes." *Black American Literature Forum*, 14 (Fall 1980), 100–104. Mentions W briefly (p. 104). Reprinted: 1993.

9687. _____. "Old John in Harlem: The Urban Folktales of Langston Hughes." *Black American Literature Forum*, 14 (Fall 1980), 100–104. Mentions W briefly (p. 104).

9688. Craig, E. Quita. *Black Drama of the Federal Theatre Era: Beyond the Formal Horizons.* Amherst: The University of Massachu-setts Press, 1980, p. 182. Quotes Owen Dodson mentioning W briefly.

9689. Dixon, Melvin. "Richard, Richard." *The Black Scholar*, 11 (March–April 1980), p. 80. Poem on W's death with emphasis on the cremation with allusions to *NS.*

9690. DuBois, W.E.B. "A Chronicle of Race Relations," in *Writing in Periodicals Edited by W.E.B DuBois: Selections from Phylon.* Ed. Herbert Aptheker. Millwood, New York: Kraus-Thomson Organization Limited, 1980, p. 209. Reprint of 1942.

9691. _____. "A chronicle of Race Relations," in *Writings in Periodicals Edited by W.E.B. DuBois: Selections from Phylon.* Ed. Herbert Aptheker. Millwood, New York: Kraus-Thomson Organization Limited, 1980, p. 191.

9692. Egejuru, Phanuel Akubueze. "Who Influenced the Writers?" in his *Towards African Literary Independence: A Dialogue with Contemporary Writers.* Westport, CT: Greenwood Press, 1980, pp. 71–81. Ezekiel Mphahlele acknowledges W's influence, especially in *UTC* (p. 79).

9693. Enekwe, Ossie Onuora. "An Interview with Amiri Baraka." *Okike: An African Journal of New Writing*, 16 (February 1980), pp. 97–108. Baraka comments on W as a self-made petit bourgeois idealist despite his lower-class background. He also criticizes W's bookishness and his estrangement from black culture (pp. 97–108). Reprinted: 1994.

9694. Foley, Martha. "Autobiography: Paris in the Twenties." *The Massachusetts Review*, 21 (Spring 1980), 67–79. Abridged version of a section of 1980.98.

9695. Fowler, Carolyn. *A Knot in the Thread: The Life and Work of Jacques Roumain.* Washington, DC: Howard University Press, 1980, p. 206. Mentions briefly W's attendance at a banquet-reception for Jacques Roumain at the Harlem YWCA on 15 November 1939.

9696. Franklin, John Hope. *From Slavery to Freedom: A History of Negro Americans.* Fifth ed. New York: Knopf, 1980, pp. 376–377, 499. Reprint of 1956.158.

9697. Gérard, Albert. "The Study of African Literature: Birth and Early Growth of a New Branch of Learning." *Canadian Review of Comparative Literature*, 7 (Winter 1980),

67–92. Mentions briefly W's dislike of negritude (p. 78).

9698. Gerson, Steven M., and Lou Kelly. "Bigger Thomas: Realistic or Existential Hero?" *Iowa English Bulletin* (Fall 1980), pp. 15, 17–18. Mostly plot summary of *NS* with comments on relevance to student readers. *NS* transcends social criticism in its "vision of the existential agony of the individual" (p. 18).

9699. Gregory, Carole E. "Hurston Revisited." *Freedomways*, 20 (Fourth Quarter 1980), pp. 305–307. Review of *I Love Myself When I Am Laughing ... and Then Again When I Am Looking Mean and Impressive: A Zora Neale Hurston Reader* mentioning W briefly.

9700. Hakutani, Yoshinobu. *Young Dreiser: A Critical Study.* Rutherford-Madison-Teaneck, New Jersey: Associated University Press, 1980, p. 19. Mentions W briefly.

9701. Harris, William J. "An Interview with Amiri Baraka." *The Greenfield Review*, 8 (Fall 1980), 19–31. Baraka comments on reading *BB* at age twelve. "I loved Richard Wright because of *Black Boy*. I never liked *Native Son*. I read *Uncle Tom's Children* in the last ten years and to me that's a great book" (p. 27). Reprinted: 1994.

9702. Hart, John E. *Albert Halper.* Boston: Twayne, 1980, p. 125. Mentions W briefly.

9703. Howard, Lillie P. "*The Diaries of Willard Motley* by Jerome Klinkowitz." *The Black Scholar*, 11 (November/December 1980), 81–82. Review mentioning W briefly.

9704. _____. "*The Diaries of Willard Motley* by Jerome Klinkowitz." *The Black Scholar*, 11 (November/December 1980), 81–82. Review mentioning W briefly.

9705. _____. *Zora Neale Hurston.* Boston: Twayne, 1980, pp. 110, 155. Mentions W briefly and quotes from his "scathing" review of *Their Eyes Were Watching God.*

9706. Jordan, June. "Wright, Richard 1908–1960," in *Contemporary Literary Criticism.* Eds. Dedria Bryfonski and Laurie Lanzen Harris. Detroit: Gale, 1980, pp. 595–596. Partial reprint of 1979.

9707. Kaiser, Ernest. "Recent Books." *Freedomways*, 20 (Second Quarter 1980), 113–123. Contains a notice of *Propaganda and Aesthetics* by Abby Arthur Johnson and Ron-

ald Maberry Johnson mentioning W briefly (pp. 116–117).

9708. _____. "Recent Books." *Freedomways*, 20 (Fourth Quarter 1980), 311–320. Contains a notice of Addison Gayle's *Richard Wright: Ordeal of a Native Son* emphasizing United States government surveillance of W (p. 319). Also contains a notice of Dexter Fisher and Robert B. Stepto's *Afro-American Literature: The Reconstruction of Instruction* mentioning W briefly (p. 317).

9709. Kennedy, Randall. "An American Dissident." *The New York Times Book Review* (3 August 1980), pp. 10, 27. Review of Addison Gayle's biography of W emphasizing the political persecution W suffered as revealed by previously unavailable F.B.I. reports. Kennedy criticizes Gayle's fictionalizing and inaccuracy.

9710. Kertesz, Louise. *The Poetic Vision of Muriel Rukeyser.* Baton Rouge: Louisiana State University Press, 1980, p. 58. Mentions W briefly.

9711. Kirby, John B. *Black Americans in The Roosevelt Era: Liberalism and Race.* Knoxville: University of Tennessee Press, 1980, pp. 67, 153. Mentions W briefly.

9712. Lee, A. Robert. "Making New: Styles of Innovations in the Contemporary Black American Novel," in *Black Fiction: New Studies in the Afro-American Novel Since 1945.* Plymouth and London: Vision Press, 1980, pp. 222–254. Mentions W briefly (pp. 223, 224, 225. Also mentions *NS* (p. 223).

9713. McWilliams, John P., Jr. "Innocent Criminal or Criminal Innocence: The Trial in American Fiction," in *Law and American Literature: A Collection of Essays.* Chicago: Commission on Undergraduate Education in Law and the Humanities of the American Bar Association, 1980, pp. 1–109. Discusses *Native Son* in the context of American legal history and in comparison to *The Pioneers*, *Billy Budd*, and *An American Tragedy.* Most similar to Dreiser's novel, *Native Son* differs in its portrayal of the liberating psychological effect of the act of killing on the protagonist. Reprinted: 1983.

9714. Miller, Bobbie Jean. "Claude Brown." *Abstracts of English Studies*, 23 (March 1980), 279. Abstracts an article by Robert M. Goldman and William D. Crano mentioning W.

9715. _____. "Richard Wright." *Abstracts of English Studies*, 23 (March 1980), 283. Abstracts an article by J.F. Gounard.

9716. Mitterling, Philip I. *U.S. Cultural History: A Guide to Information Sources.* Detroit: Gale Research, 1980, p. 196. Mentions W briefly in an entry for *Black Writers of the Thirties.*

9717. Morison, Samuel Eliot, Henry Steele Commager, and William E. Leuchtenburg. *The Growth of the American Republic.* New York: Oxford University Press, 1980, Vol. 2, p. 504. Mentions briefly W on the Writers' Project.

9718. Nolan, Charles J., Jr. *Aaron Burr and the American Literacy Imagination.* Westport, CT: Greenwood Press, 1980, p. 178. Comments on Bigger Thomas as an "image of man as victim."

9719. O'Meally, Robert G. *The Craft of Ralph Ellison.* Cambridge: Harvard University Press, 1980, pp. 1, 4, 11, 30, 32, 37, 38, 41, 44–49, 54, 57, 60, 77, 78, 106, 163–165, 180. Comments on Ellison's early friendship with W and his subsequent sharp criticism of *NS*, but he praised *BB* and was influenced by "The Man Who Lived Underground."

9720. Phillips, Robert L., Jr. Untitled note. *S.S.S.L.: The News-Letter of The Society for the Study of Southern Literature*, 13 (November 1980), 14. Lists Addison Gayle, Jr.'s *Richard Wright: Ordeal of a Native Son.*

9721. Pingree, Elizabeth E., ed. *Humanities Index: April 1979 to March 1980.* New York: H.W. Wilson, 1980, p. 750. Lists three items s.v. W.

9722. Reilly, John M. "Wright, Richard (Nathaniel)," in *American Writers Since 1900.* Chicago: St. James Press, 1980, pp. 646–649. Reprint of 1979.213.

9723. Robinson, Cedric. "Richard Wright: Marxism and the Petite-Bourgeoisie." *Race and Class*, 21, no. 4 (1980), pp. 353–368. Rejecting Stalinist anti-intellectualism, W worked in the tradition of Lenin to "transform a 'renegade petite bourgeoisie' into a revolutionary vanguard" which would reject Christianity and critique Marxism as practiced by the Communist Party. *O* is Robinson's main source for working out these ideas.

9724. Rosenberg, Ruth. "Black." *Abstracts of English Studies*, 23 (January 1980), 178. Abstracts an article by Donald A. Petesch mentioning W.

9725. Salaam, Yusef A. "Books: Addison Gayle's Timely Bio on the Legendary Native Son." *New York Amsterdam News* (20 December 1980), p. 51. Favorable review: "colorfully written, graphically detailed." Emphasizes CIA intrigue.

9726. Smith, Barbara. *Toward a Black Feminist Criticism*. Brooklyn: Out & Out Books, 1980, p. [5]. Reprint of 1977.

9727. Sternburg, Janet. "Notes on Contributors," in her *The Writer on Her Work*. New York: W.W. Norton, 1980, p. 264. Notes that Margaret Walker is writing a biography of W.

9728. Strandberg, Victor. *A Faulkner Overview: Six Perspectives*. Port Washington NY: Kennikat Press, 1980, p. 80. Mentions briefly *NS* and *TMBV*.

9729. Wade-Gayles, Gloria. "She Who Is Black and Mother: In Sociology and Fiction, 1940–1970," in *The Black Woman*. Ed. La Frances Rodgers-Rose. Beverly Hills, CA: Sage, 1980, pp. 89–106. Comments on W's introduction to *Black Metropolis* (p. 89) and briefly analyzes the characterization of Mrs. Thomas in *NS*.

9730. Walker, Warren S. *Twentieth Century Short Story Explication*. Supplement I to Third Edition. Hamden, CT: Shoe String Press, 1980, p. 225. Lists thirteen items on W.

9731. Warner, Keith Q. "Introduction," in *Black Shack Alley*. By George Zobel. London: Heinemann, 1980, pp. [i–xii]. States that "Zobel himself claims that his novel was inspired by Richard Wright's *Black Boy*" (p. i).

9732. W[atkins], T.H. "*First-Person America*." *American Heritage*, 32 (December 1980), 108. Review mentioning W briefly.

9733. Wideman, John. "Wright, Richard 1908–1960," in *Contemporary Literary Criticism*. Eds. Dedria Bryfonski and Laurie Lanzen Harris. Detroit: Gale, 1980, pp. 596–597. Partial reprint of 1978.256.

9734. Winslow, Henry F., Sr. "Two Black Poets and Their Legacy." *The Crisis*, 87 (November 1980), 365–370, 372. States that "Mr.

Winslow ... is at work on a biography of Richard Wright" (p. 365). Reprinted: 1996.

9735. Yarborough, Richard. "Afro-American Literature Without Books?" *CAAS Newsletter*, 5 (November 1980), 4–5. Notes that *LD*, *WML*, *LT*, *SH*, and *EM* were all out of print in paperback editions and unavailable for his undergraduate W seminar, though they had been available in 1974.

9736. Zinn, Howard. *A People's History of the United States*. New York: Harper & Row, 1980, pp. 437–438. Quotes from *BB* and notes that W joined the Communist Party but became disillusioned. Reprinted: 1995.

9737. Anderson, David D. "Anderson and Myth," in his *Critical Essays on Sherwood Anderson*. Boston: G.K. Hall, 1981, pp. 267–283, p. 271. Reprint of 1976.

9738. Anon. *Bibliographic Guide to Black Studies: 1980*. Boston: G.K. Hall, 1981, p. 419. Lists two primary (translations) and three secondary items concerning W in the New York Public Library.

9739. Anon. "Black Books Round-up." *The Black Scholar*, 12 (March/April 1981), 63–69. Lists *Richard Wright Reader* edited by Ellen Wright and Michel Fabre (p. 65).

9740. Anon. *Index to Periodical Articles by and About Blacks: 1979*. Boston: G.K. Hall, 1981, p. 413. Lists four items about W.

9741. Anon. "Kenneth [sic] Kinnamon." *Afro Scholar Newsletter*, 3 (February 1981), 3–4. Note on Kinnamon's work on W.

9742. Anon. "Main Selections of the Book-of-the-Month Club," in *American Novelists 1910–1945. Part 3: Mari Sandoz-Stark Young*. Ed. James J. Martine. Vol. 9 of *Dictionary of Literary Biography*. Detroit: Gale, 1981, pp. 297–303. Lists *NS* and *BB*.

9743. Anon. "Publishers Listings of Black Interest Books." *The Black Scholar*, 12 (March/April 1981), 35–62. Lists Addison Gayle's *Richard Wright: Ordeal of a Native Son* (p. 41), *AH* (p. 44), *Richard Wright's Hero: The Faces of a Rebel-Victim* by Katherine Fishburn (p. 54), and *Richard Wright* by Robert Felgar (p. 57).

9744. Anon. "Wrights [sic] 'Native Son' Under Attack; Parents Say

Remove from Bookshelf." *The Baltimore Afro-American* (25 July 1981), p. 3. Despite a petition with sixty-two signatures, a high school in North Adams, Massachusetts, refuses to ban *NS*.

9745. Ashley, Leonard R.N. "American Short Fiction in the Nineteenth and Twentieth Centuries," in *Critical Survey of Short Fiction*. Ed. Frank N. Magill. Englewood Cliffs, NJ: Salem Press, 1981, pp. 528–562. Contains a paragraph on W stating that his short stories lack "the full force" of the novels and *BB* (p. 555).

9746. Banks, Ann. *First-Person America*. New York: Vintage Books, 1981, p. xviii. Reprint of 1980.

9747. Bell, Bernard. "The Image of Africa in the Afro-American Novel." *Commonwealth*, 5 (1981–1982), 53–69. States that W "accepts conventional white-black symbolism and the negative white image of Africa" (p. 62) in *LD* and elsewhere.

9748. Billops, Camille. "An Interview with Charles Griffin — Actor, Director, Archivist," in *Artists and Influences: Hatch-Billops Collection* (1981), pp. 137–153. Comments on W, the John Reed Club, and the play *NS* (p. 151).

9749. Butler, David L. "Edgar Allan Poe." *Abstracts of English Studies*, 24 (April 1981), 64. Abstracts an article by Linda T. Prior mentioning W.

9750. Butler, Johnnella E. *Black Studies: Pedagogy and Revolution*. Washington: University Press of America, 1981, pp. 68–72, 74, 108–109, 110, 116, 149. Criticizes W for his "acceptance of the Western idea of culture being subservient to economics, politics, and social reality" (p. 69). Quotes from "Blueprint for Negro Writing" and mentions *BB*, *UTC* (with discussion), and *NS*.

9751. Calder, Angus, "Chester Himes and the Art of Fiction." *Journal of Eastern African Research and Development*, 1, No. 1 (1981), 3–18. Mentions W briefly. Reprinted: 1999.

9752. Cassill, R.V. "Richard Wright," in his *The Norton Anthology of Short Fiction*. Second edition, shorter. New York: Norton, 1981, p. 716. Reprint of 1978.

9753. Christian, Barbara. "The Contrary Women of Alice Walker: A Study of Female Protagonists in *In Love and Trouble*." *The Black*

Scholar, 12 (March–April 1981), 21–30. Mentions W briefly (p. 22). Reprinted: 1985.

9754. Clift, Arlene. "Literature: Folklore," in *Encyclopedia of Black America*. Eds. W. Augustus Low and Virgil A. Clift. New York: McGraw-Hill, 1981, pp. 507–512. Mentions W briefly (p. 509).

9755. Cripps, Thomas R. "Motion Pictures," in *Encyclopedia of Black America*. Eds. W. Augustus Low and Virgil A. Clift. New York: McGraw-Hill, 1981, pp. 571–582. Mentions briefly the film *NS*.

9756. Davis, Thadious M. "Southern Writers: Notes Toward a Definition of Terms." *The Southern Quarterly*, 19 (Winter 1981), 10–16. Includes comments on W (pp. 12, 14).

9757. De Beauvoir, Simone. *La Cérémonie des adieux, suivi Entretiens avec Jean-Paul Sartre*. Paris: Gallimard, 1981, p. 308. Mentions meeting W and his wife in New York. Reprinted: 1984.

9758. Dennis, Frank Allen. "A Bibliography of Theses and Dissertations Relating to Mississippi, 1981." *The Journal of Mississippi History*, 43 (February 1981), 65–71. Lists a dissertation by Mary Frances Sisney including treatment of *NS* (see 1980. 231).

9759. Faulkner, Howard. "Black Short Fiction," in *Critical Survey of Short Fiction*. Ed. Frank N. Magill. Englewood Cliffs, NJ: Salem Press, 1981, pp. 575–583. Includes a discussion of *UTC* and *EM* emphasizing the theme of achieving manhood by resisting racism (pp. 578–580).

9760. Fischer, William C. "Amiri Baraka, 1934.," in *American Writers: A Collection of Literary Biographies* Supplement II, Part 1. Ed. A. Walton Litz. New York: Charles Scribner's, 1981, pp. 29–63. Mentions briefly "The Man Who Lived Underground" (p. 40).

9761. French, Warren. "American Fiction and the 1930s," in *American Novelists, 1910–1945. Part 3: Mari Sandoz — Stark Young*. Ed. James J. Martine. Vol. 9 of *Dictionary of Literary Biography*. Detroit: Gale, 1981, pp. 247–271. Contains a paragraph on W, a photograph of W, and a facsimile of the title page of *NS* (pp. 268–271).

9762. Gallagher, Brian. "'About Us, for Us, Near Us': The Irish and Harlem Renaissances." *Éire-Ireland: A Journal of Irish Studies*, 16 (Winter 1981), 14–26. Mentions briefly *NS* (p. 25). Reprinted: 1996.

9763. Galloway, David. *The Absurd Hero in American Fiction*. Austin: University of Texas Press, 1981, p. 108. Mentions briefly *NS*.

9764. Gayle, Addison, "Zora Neale Hurston: The Politics of Freedom," in *A Rainbow Round Her Shoulder: The Zora Neale Hurston Symposium Papers*. Ed. Ruthe T. Sheffey. Baltimore: Morgan State University Press, pp. 21–27. Discusses W's review of *Their Eyes Were Watching God* and analyzes the difference, existential and philosophical, between Hurston and W.

9765. Gill, Glenda. "Careerist and Casualty: The Rise and Fall of Canada Lee." *Freedomways*, 21 (First Quarter 1981), 15–27. Includes discussion of Lee's performance of Bigger in the play *NS* (p. 19).

9766. Hatch, James. "An Interview with John A. Williams," in *Artists and Influences: Hatch-Billops Collection* (1981), pp. 183–198. Williams comments on W and on the relation of *NS* to the media. He prefers *O* to *NS*.

9767. Hicks, Jack. *In the Singer's Temple: Prose Fictions of Barthelme, Gaines, Broutigan, Piercy, Kesey, and Kosinski*. Chapel Hill: The University of North Carolina Press, 1981, pp. 96, 97, 115, 130. Includes comparison of W and Gaines. Different in many ways, they both foresee "an indigenous black American literature" (p. 96). Mentions *UTC*.

9768. Hooks, Bell. *Ain't I a Woman: Black Women and Feminism*. Boston: South End Press, 1981, p. 101. Attributes to W himself the proprietary attitude toward black women expressed by Silas in "Long Black Song."

9769. Joyce, Joyce Ann. "Change, Chance, and God in *Their Eyes Were Watching God*," in *A Rainbow Round Her Shoulder: The Zora Neale Hurston Symposium Papers*. Ed. Ruthe T. Sheffey, pp. 69–78. Contrasts W and Hurston to reveal "the diversity of sensibility, philosophy, and craft of the "Black American Writer."

9770. Kaiser, Ernest. "Recent Books." *Freedomways*, 21 (First Quarter 1981), 69–80. Mentions W briefly in a review of Lillie P. Howard's *Zora Neale Hurston*, commenting unfavorably on works by Russell Brig-nano, Michel Fabre, and James Baldwin on W (p. 70). Also mentions W briefly in a notice of Charles D. Peavy's *Afro-American Literature and Culture Since World War II* (p. 77).

9771. Kaplan, Harold. *Power and Order: Henry Adams and the Naturalist Tradition in American Fiction*. Chicago: The University of Chicago Press, 1981, pp. 129–130, 142. Includes a brief discussion of *NS* as an example of "redemptive violence" in fiction.

9772. _____. *Power and Order: Henry Adams and the Naturalist Tradition in American Fiction*. Chicago: The University of Chicago Press, 1981, pp. 129–130, 142. Discusses the murder of Mary Dalton in *NS*, the role of Max, and Bigger's "personal need for a redemptive act of self-assertion."

9773. Kazin, Alfred. "The Self as History: Reflections on Autobiography," in *The American Autobiography: a Collection of Critical Essays*. Ed. Albert E. Stone. Englewood Cliffs, NJ: Prentice-Hall, 1981, pp. 31–43. Reprint of 1979.

9774. _____. "The Self as History: Reflections on Autobiography," in *The American Autobiography: A Collection of Critical Essays*. Ed. Albert E. Stone. Englewood Cliffs, NJ: Prentice-Hall, 1981, pp. 31–43. Reprint of 1979.

9775. Keyssar, Helene. *The Curtain and the Veil: Strategies in Black Drama*. New York: Burt Franklin, 1981, pp. 116, 153. Mentions briefly *NS* and "The Man Who Lived Underground."

9776. Kiernan, Robert F. "American Literature," in *Encyclopedia of World Literature in the 20th Century*. Revised edition. Ed. Leonard S. Klein. Vol. 1. New York: Frederick Ungar, 1981, pp. 57–76. Mentions briefly *UTC* (p. 63) and *BB* (p. 69).

9777. Koster, Donald N. *American Literature and Language: A Guide to Information Sources*. Detroit: Gale Research, 1982, pp. 24 120, 309–311. Bibliography of secondary sources on W.

9778. Lacey, Henry C. *To Raise, Destroy, and Create: The Poetry, Drama, and Fiction of Imamu Amiri Baraka (Le Roi Jones)*. Troy, New York: Whitston, 1981, pp. ix, 114. Mentions W briefly and quotes from a poem by Baraka commenting on Bigger Thomas.

9779. Layman, Richard. *Shadow Man: The Life of Dashiell Hammett.* New York: Harcourt Brace Jovanovich, 1981, p. 173. Lists W among the signers of a statement issued by the American Friends of Spanish Democracy.

9780. Lipsitz, George. *Class and Culture in Cold War America: "A Rainbow at Midnight."* New York: Praeger, 1981, p. 188. Quotes briefly *AH.*

9781. Lloyd, James B. "Introduction: Mississippians and their Books," in his *Lives of Mississippi Authors.* Jackson: University Press of Mississippi, 1981, pp. xi–xvi. Mentions briefly *BB* (p. xii).

9782. Long, Terry L. *Granville Hicks.* Boston: Twayne, 1981, p. 44. Mentions briefly Hicks's praise of *UTC.*

9783. Low, W. Augustus, and Virgil A. Clift. "Black Power," in *Encyclopedia of Black America.* Eds. W. Augustus Low and Virgil A. Clift. New York: McGraw-Hill, 1981, p. 183. Notes that W had used the term before Stokely Carmichael.

9784. _____. "Cayton, Horace Roscoe," in *Encyclopedia of Black America.* Eds. W. Augustus Low and Virgil A. Clift. New York: McGraw-Hill, 1981, pp. 221–223. Notes that Cayton died while working on a biography of W.

9785. _____. "Harsh, Vivian G.," in *Encyclopedia of Black America.* Eds. W. Augustus Low and Virgil A. Clift. New York: McGraw-Hill, 1981, p. 421. Mentions W briefly.

9786. _____. "Lee, Canada (Leonard Lionel Cornelius Canegata)," in *Encyclopedia of Black America.* Eds. W. Augustus Low and Virgil A. Clift. New York: McGraw-Hill, 1981, pp. 501–503. Mentions Lee's role as Bigger Thomas.

9787. _____. "Wright, Richard," in *Encyclopedia of Black America.* Eds. W. Augustus Low and Virgil A. Clift. New York: McGraw-Hill, 1981, p. 869. Biographical sketch.

9788. MacDonald, Scott. "An Evaluative Check-List of Erskine Caldwell's Short Fiction," in his *Critical Essays on Erskine Caldwell.* Boston: G.K. Hall, 1981, pp. 342–360. Reprint of 1978.

9789. _____. "An Evaluative Check-List of Erskine Caldwell's Short Fiction," in *Critical Essays on Erskine Caldwell.* Boston: G.K. Hall, 1981. Reprint of 1978.

9790. Magistrale, Anthony Samuel. "The Quest for Identity in Modern Southern Fiction: Faulkner, Wright, O'Connor, Warren." *Dissertation Abstracts International,* 42 (1981), 4001A–02A. Includes discussion of W's rejection of the past.

9791. Marable, Manning. *Blackwater: Historical Studies in Race, Class Consciousness, and Revolution.* Dayton: Black Praxis Press, 1981, pp. 14–21. Mentions W briefly (p. 16).

9792. Martin, Ronald E. *American Literature and the Universe of Force.* Durham: Duke University Press, 1981, p. 256. Mentions W briefly.

9793. Materassi, Mario. "James Baldwin," in *I Contemporanei: Novecento Americano.* Ed. Elémire Zolla. Vol. 3. Rome: Lucari Editore, 1981, pp. 209–216. Mentions W briefly (p. 210).

9794. McCollum, Kenneth G. "Nelson Algren," in *American Novelists, 1910–1945. Dictionary of Literary Biography.* Vol. 9. Detroit: Gale, 1981, pp. 10–15. Quotes from W's introduction to *Never Come Morning.*

9795. Mendelson, Edward. "W.H. Auden, 1907–1973," in *American Writers: A Collection of Literary Biographies.* Supplement II, Part 1. Ed. A. Walton Litz. New York: Charles Scribner's, 1981, pp. 1–28. Mentions W in the house in Brooklyn "in the midst of bohemian chaos" (p. 17).

9796. Moore, Jack B. *W.E.B. Du Bois.* Boston: Twayne, 1981, pp. 95, 111–112. Mentions W briefly and discusses Du Bois's review of *BB.*

9797. O'Meally, Robert. "Ralph Ellison, 1914– ," in *American Writers: A Collection of Literary Biographies* Supplement II, Part 1. Ed. A. Walton Litz. New York: Charles Scribner's, 1981, pp. 221–252. Discusses W's influence on Ellison's early career (pp. 221, 228) and Ellison's later unfavorable evaluations of W (pp. 235, 250).

9798. O'Neale, Sondra. "Speaking for Ourselves: Black Women Writers of the '80s." *Southern Exposure,* 9 (Summer 1981), 16–19. Notes W's eloquent denunciation of racism but criticizes his portrayal of black women.

9799. Patrick, Michael D. "Black." *Abstracts of English Studies,* 24 (April 1981), 54. Abstracts an article by Ronald Primeau mentioning W.

9800. Peden, William. "Short Fiction in English: 1910–1950," in *Critical Survey of Short Fiction.* Ed. Frank N. Magill. Englewood Cliffs, NJ: Salem Press, 1981, pp. 238–277. Includes discussion of *UTC* and *EM* recognizing their power but considering them "more important as social history than as creative literature" (p. 268).

9801. Perkins, George, Sculley Bradley, Richmond Croom Beatty, and E. Hudson Long. "The Twentieth Century: Literary Renaissance and Social Challenge," in their *The American Tradition in Literature.* Fifth edition (shorter edition). New York: Random House, 1981, pp. 1269–1282. Reprint of 1974.

9802. _____. "Richard Wright (1908–1960)," in *The American Tradition in Literature.* Fifth edition (shorter edition). Eds. Sculley Bradley, Richmond Croom Beatty, E. Hudson Long, and George Perkins. New York: Random House, 1981, pp. 1630–1631. Reprint of 1974.142.

9803. Philips, Robert L., Jr. "Editions and Reprints." *S.S.S.L.: The News-Letter of The Society for the Study of Southern Literature,* 14 (November 1981), 17–18. Lists W and Paul Green's *Native Son: The Biography of a Young American: A Play in Eleven Scenes to Be Performed Without an Intermission.*

9804. _____. "Film." *S.S.S.L.: The News-Letter of The Society for the Study of Southern Literature,* 14 (April 1981), 9–10. Lists the film version of "Almos' a Man."

9805. _____. "News, Projects, Research." *S.S.S.L.: The News-Letter of The Society for the Study of Southern Literature,* 14 (April 1981), 2–7. Mentions that Charles T. Davis and Michel Fabre are working on a descriptive bibliography of W.

9806. Pingree, Elizabeth E., ed. *Humanities Index: April 1980 to March 1981.* New York: H.W. Wilson, 1981, pp. 753–754. Lists five items s.v. W.

9807. Ramsey, Priscilla R. "*All Is Well,* or Is It?: Conflict as Motivating Force in Julius Lester's Autobiography." *The New England Journal of Black Studies,* 1 (1981), 45–54. Mentions briefly "Blue-Print for Negro Writing" (p. 46).

9808. Robinson, William H. "Earlier Black New England: The Literature of the Black I Am," in *American Literature: The New England Heritage.* Eds. James Nagel and

Richard Astro. New York: Garland, 1981, p. 81. Mentions briefly *BB*.

9809. Rosenfelt, Deborah. "From the Thirties: Tillie Olsen and the Radical Tradition." *Feminist Studies*, 7 (Fall 1981), 371–406. Mentions W briefly (p. 387). Reprinted: 1994.

9810. ____. "From the Thirties: Tillie Olsen and the Radical Tradition." *Feminist Studies* (Fall 1981), 371–387. Mentions W briefly.

9811. Saffioti, Carol Lee. "Black." *Abstracts of English Studies*, 24 (April 1981), 53. Abstracts an article by Marilyn Nelson Waniek mentioning W.

9812. ____. "Stephen Crane." *Abstracts of English Studies*, 24 (April 1981), 67. Abstracts an article by Alvin Starr mentioning W.

9813. Scholes, Robert. "Richard Wright 1908–1960," in his *Elements of Fiction: An Anthology*. New York: Oxford University Press, 1981, pp. 504–505. Headnote to "The Ethics of Living Jim Crow."

9814. Schraufnagel, Noel. "Literature: The Novel," in *Encyclopedia of Black America*. Eds. W. Augustus Low and Virgil A. Clift. New York: McGraw-Hill, 1981, pp. 523–530. Includes discussion of *NS* but not W's subsequent fiction.

9815. Schultz, Elizabeth. "To Be Black and Blue: The Blues Genre in Black American Autobiography," In *American Autobiography: A Collection of Critical Essays*. Ed. Albert E. Stone. Englewood Cliffs, NJ: Prentice-Hall, 1981, pp. 109–132. Reprint of 1975.

9816. ____. "To Be Black and Blue: The Blues Genre in Black American Autobiography," in *The American Autobiography: A Collection of Critical Essays*. Ed. Albert E. Stone. Englewood Cliffs, NJ: Prentice-Hall, 1981. Reprint of 1975.172.

9817. Smith, Thelma M., and Ward L. Miner. "[Transatlantic Migration]," in *Critical Essays on Erskine Caldwell*. Ed. Scott MacDonald. Boston: G.K. Hall, 1981, pp. 237–245. Partial reprint of 1955.78.

9818. ____. "[Transatlantic migration," in *Critical Essays on Erskine Caldwell*. Ed. Scott MacDonald. Boston: G.K. Hall, 1981, pp. 237–245. Excerpt from 1955.78.

9819. Snipes, Katherine. "Richard Wright," in *Critical Survey of Short Fiction*. Ed. Frank N. Magill. Englewood Cliffs, NJ: Salem Press, 1981, pp. 2462–2467. Analyzes "Fire and Cloud" and "The Man Who Lived Underground" as Marxist and existentialist respectively. Also comments on W's other works and his influence and provides a primary and secondary bibliography. Reprinted in revised form: 2001.

9820. Standley, Fred L. "James Baldwin," in *Twentieth-Century American Dramatists*. Ed. John MacNicholas. Vol. 7, Part 1, of *Dictionary of Literary Biography*. Detroit: Gale, 1981, pp. 45–49. Mentions Baldwin's first meeting with W (p. 46). Reprinted: 1988.

9821. Stone, Albert E. "Introduction: American Autobiographies as Individual Stories and Cultural Narratives," in his *The American Autobiography: A Collection of Critical Essays*. Englewood Cliffs, NJ: Prentice-Hall, 1981, pp. 1–9. Mentions briefly *BB* (p. 4).

9822. Sylvander, Carolyn Wedin. "Baldwin, James," in *Encyclopedia of World Literature in the 20th Century*. Revised edition. Ed. Leonard S. Klein. Vol. 1. New York: Frederick Ungar, 1981, p. 182. Mentions W briefly. Reprinted: 1981, 1989.

9823. ____. *Jessie Redmon Fauset, Black American Writer*. Troy, New York: Whitston, 1981, pp. 207, 209. Quotes W on "perspective" (p. 207) and mentions W elsewhere.

9824. Taylor, Clyde. "The Ordeal of Richard Wright." *The Black Collegian*, 11 (April/May 1981), 162–183. Favorable review of Addison Gayle's biography of W emphasizing his persecution by the U.S. government. Claims that W became an accommodationist, less radical than his popular image.

9825. Vowell, Faye Nell. "Minorities in Popular Culture," in *Handbook of American Popular Culture*, Vol. 3. Ed. M. Thomas Inge. Westport, CT: Greenwood Press, 1981, pp. 205–229. Mentions W briefly (p. 221).

9826. Wald, Alan. "Remembering the Answers." *The Nation*, 233 (26 December 1981), pp. 708–711. Notes that W reacted bitterly to the withdrawal of support for the John Reed Clubs (p. 708). Reprinted: 1992.

9827. Ward, A.C. "Wright, Richard," in his *Longman Companion to Twentieth Century Literature*. Third Edition revised by Maurice Hussey. Burnt Mill, Essex: Longman Group, 1981. Revised version of 1975.200.

9828. Washington, Mary Helen. "Afterword," in *Brown Girl, Brownstones*. Old Westbury, New York, 1981, pp. 311–324. Mentions briefly *BB* (p. 312).

9829. Weiss, Irving, and Anne de la Vergne Weiss. *Thesaurus of Book Digests: 1950–1980*. New York: Brown, 1981, pp. 139, 344–345. Mentions *EM* and provides a brief and critique of *O*.

9830. Wiehe, Roger E. "Richard Wright." *Abstracts of English Studies*, 24 (July 1981), 81. Abstracts an article by Jerry W. Ward.

9831. Wilson, Judith. "A Conversation with Toni Morrison." *Essence*, 12 (July 1981), 81, 86, 128, 130, 133–134. Mentions briefly W and *NS* (p. 81). Reprinted: 1994.

9832. Winslow, William. "Modernity and the Novel: Twain, Faulkner, and Percy." *The Gypsy Scholar*, 8 (Winter 1981), 19–40. Mentions briefly W and "Big Boy Leaves Home" (pp. 22, 39).

9833. Abraham, Kinfe. *From Race to Class: Links and Parallels in African and Black American Protest Expression*. London: Grassroots, 1982, pp. 74, 75, 76–78, 147–173. The sixth chapter, "Urban Protest 1930–1950," is an extended comparison of W and Peter Abrahams: their social backgrounds, their Marxism, and their writings. Elsewhere Abraham quotes from *TMBV* and *WML*.

9834. Anon. "Keneth Kinnamon." *Afro Scholar Newsletter*, 7 (April 1982), 10. Mentions W briefly.

9835. Anon. *Bibliographic Guide to Black Studies: 1981*. Boston: G.K. Hall, 1982, p. 187. Lists two primary and two secondary items concerning W in the New York Public Library.

9836. Anon. "Black Books Round-up." *The Black Scholar*, 13 (Spring 1982), 73–80. Lists Richard Wright: *A Primary Bibliography* (p. 73) and *Richard Wright* by Robert Felgar (p. 73).

9837. Anon. "Black Books Round-up." *The Black Scholar*, 13 (Spring 1982), 73. Contains a brief notice of Robert Felgar's *Richard Wright*.

9838. Anon. *Index to Periodical Articles by and About Blacks: 1980*. Boston: G.K. Hall, 1982, p. 173. Lists one item about W.

9839. Anon. *Index Translationum 31*. Paris: Unesco, 1982, pp. 123, 224, 486, 612, 820, 968, 1002. Lists translations of *BB* into German,

Danish, French, and Russian; *AH* into Danish, Japanese, and Swedish; and *O* into Serbo-Croatian.

9840. Anon. "1983 National Afro-American History Kit." *Negro History Bulletin*, 45 (October-November-December 1982), [87]. Lists "Richard Wright, His Life and Writings" by James R. King.

9841. Ansbro, John J. *Martin Luther King, Jr.: The Making of a Mind*. Maryknoll, NY: Orbis Books, 1982, pp. 211, 226. Mentions W's use of the term "Black Power" and mentions W briefly. Reprinted: 2000.

9842. Baldwin, James. "Richard Wright 1908–1960," in *Contemporary Literary Criticism*. Eds. Sharon Gunton and Gerard Senick. Detroit: Gale, 1982, pp. 438–439. Partial reprint of 1961.107.

9843. Beers, Henry Putney. *Bibliographies in American History, 1942–1978*. Vol. 1. Woodbridge, CT: Research Publications, 1982, pp. 366. Mentions W in listing of M. Thomas Inge's *Black American Writers* and in Michel Fabre's catalog of the W archive at Yale (1978. 96).

9844. Bennett, Lerone, Jr. *Before the Mayflower: A History of Black America*. Chicago: Johnson, 1982, pp. 533, 536, 560. In a chronology and milestones, Bennett lists *NS*, the award of the Spingarn Medal to W, and W's death.

9845. Bigsby, C.W.E. *A Critical Introduction to Twentieth-Century American Drama*. Vol. 1 Cambridge: Cambridge University Press, 1982, pp. 206, 244. Mentions W briefly.

9846. Bracy, William. "Wright, Richard," in *The Encyclopedia Americana*. Danbury, CT: Grolier, 1982, Vol. 29, p. 555. Reprint of.

9847. Brady, Owen. "Richard Wright 1908–1960," in *Contemporary Literary Criticism*. Eds. Sharon Gunton and Gerard Senick. Detroit: Gale, 1982, pp. 460–461. Partial reprint of 1978.47.

9848. Bramwell, Gloria. "Richard Wright 1908–1960," in *Contemporary Literary Criticism*. Eds. Sharon Gunton and Gerard Senick. Detroit: Gale, 1982, pp. 439–440. Partial reprint of 1961.129.

9849. Briscoe, Mary Louise, ed. *American Autobiography, 1945–1980*. Madison: The University of Wisconsin Press, 1982, p. 242. Lists *AH* with annotation.

9850. Bruck, Peter. "Introduction

A.: Protest, University, Blackness: Patterns of Argumentation in the criticism of the Contempory Afro-American Novel," in his and Wolfgang Karrer's *The Afro-American Novel Since 1960*. Amsterdam: B.R. Grüner, 1982, pp. 1–27. Includes discussion of *NS* "as both a model and … 'a roadblock' for black thinkers" (p. 5). Numerous critics are cited.

9851. _____. "Returning to One's Roots: The Motif of Searching and Flying in Toni Morrison's *Song of Solomon* (1977)," in *The Afro-American Novel Since 1960*. Eds. Peter Bruck and Wolfgang Karrer. Amsterdam: B.R. Grüner, 1982, pp. 289–305. Mentions the motif of flying in *LT* and *NS* (p. 297).

9852. Bruck, Peter, and Wolfgang Karrer. "A Chronological Checklist of Afro-American Novels 1945–1980," in their *The Afro-American Novel Since 1960*. Amsterdam: B.R. Grüner, 1982, pp. 307–325. Includes *O, SH, LD, LT*, and "Five Episodes of an Unfinished Novel."

9853. _____. "Preface," in their *The Afro-American Novel Since 1960*. Amsterdam: B.R. Grüner, 1982, p. vii. Mentions W briefly.

9854. Burks, Ruth Elizabeth. "*Black American Literature and Humanism*: A Review." *CAAS Newsletter*, 7 (November 1982), pp. 9, 15. Notes that an essay in this collection by Chester Fontenot treats W.

9855. Butler, David L. "Richard Wright." *Abstracts of English Studies*, 25 (June 1982), 93. Abstracts an article by Michel Fabre.

9856. Carby, Hazel V. "The Racism Behind the Rioting." *In These Times*, 27 (January 1982), p. 18. Mentions W briefly. Reprinted: 1999.

9857. Cell, John W. *The Highest Stage of White Supremacy: The Origins of Segregation in South Africa and the American South*. Cambridge: Cambridge University Press, 1982, pp. 243, 246, 273. Comments on W's experience with segregation and quotes from *NS*.

9858. Collins, Marva, and Civia Tamarkin. *Marva Collins' Way*. Los Angeles: J.P. Tarcher, 1982, p. 41. Collins relates reading *BB* and *NS* as a child.

9859. [Conley, Larry]. "Calendar." *The Southern Register*, 1 (Spring 1982), 2. Announces "Richard Wright and the Mid-South," a photographic and narrative exhibit in Memphis, March-December 1982.

9860. Daniel, Walter C. *Black Journals of the United States*. Westport, CT: Greenwood Press, 1982, pp. 7, 35, 115, 262. Notes that *Abbott's Monthy* published a story by W, *Amistad 2* was dedicated to W, and *Negro Digest* published him. Daniel also discusses *Challenge and New Challenge*, mentioning "Blueprint for Negro Writing."

9861. Dennis, Frank Allen. "A Bibliography of Theses and Dissertations Relating to Mississippi, 1982." *The Journal of Mississippi History*, 44 (February 1982), 83–88. Lists a dissertation on W by William J. Barnette (see 1982.16).

9862. Dickstein, Morris. "Richard Wright 1908–1960," in *Contemporary Literary Criticism*. Eds. Sharon Gunton and Gerard Senick. Detroit: Gale, 1982, pp. 458–460. Partial reprint of 1977.110.

9863. Drake, St. Clair. "Diaspora Studies and Pan-Africanism," in *Global Dimensions of the African Diaspora*. Ed. Joseph E. Harris. Washington, DC: Howard University Press, 1982, pp. 341–402. Mentions W briefly (p. 356).

9864. _____. "Diaspora Studies and Pan-Africanism," in *Global Dimensions of the African Diaspora*. Washington: Howard University Press, 1982, pp. 341–402. Mentions W briefly (p. 356).

9865. Du Bois, W.E.B. "Richard Wright 1908–1960," in *Contemporary Literary Criticism*. Eds. Sharon Gunton and Gerard Senick. Detroit: Gale, 1982, pp. 434–435. Partial reprint of 1945.883.

9866. Duffus, R.L. "Richard Wright 1908–1960," in *Contemporary Literary Criticism*. Eds. Sharon Gunton and Gerard Senick. Detroit: Gale, 1982, p. 435. Partial reprint of 1945.885.

9867. Dunlea, William. "Richard Wright 1908–1960," in *Contemporary Literary Criticism*. Eds. Sharon Gunton and Gerard Senick. Detroit: Gale, 1982, p. 437. Partial reprint of 1958.109.

9868. Ellison, Ralph. "Richard Wright 1908–1960," in *Contemporary Literary Criticism*. Eds. Sharon Gunton and Gerard Senick. Detroit: Gale, 1982, pp. 441–442. Partial reprint of 1963.77.

9869. Ensslen, Klaus. "Collective Experience and Individual Responsibility: Alice Walker's *The Third Life of Grange Copeland*, in *The*

Afro-American Novel Since 1960. Eds. Peter Bruck and Wolfgang Karrer. Amsterdam: B.R. Grüner, 1982, pp. 189–217. Mentions briefly *LD*.

9870. Fabre, Michel. "Richard Wright, Négritude and African Literature," in *Global Dimensions of the African Diaspora.* Ed. Joseph E. Harris. Washington, DC: Howard University Press, 1982, pp. 210–218. Discusses W's relationship to Alioune Diop, Peter Abrahams, George Padmore, the First Congress of Negro Artists and Writers, and various African writers. W served as an intermediary between Africans and African Americans. He supported the political struggle against colonialism but showed little interest in African literature. Includes comments on or mentions of *NS*, *LD*, *WML*, and *BP*. Reprinted 1985 in revised and much expanded form.

9871. _____. "Richard Wright, Negritude," and African Literature," in *Global Dimensions of the African Diaspora.* Ed. Joseph E. Harris. Washington: Howard University Press, 1982, pp. 210–218. Discusses W's role in *Présence Africaine* and his friendship with Alioune Diop, Peter Abrahams, and George Padmore. Recounts W's disagreements with Senghor and with the American Society for African Culture. In general, W's approach to Africa was political rather than cultural or literary. Reprinted in revised form: 1985, 1986.

9872. Fiedler, Leslie, *What Was Literature?: Class Culture and Mass Society.* New York: Simon and Schuster, 1982, pp. 69, 168, 217, 220–22, 222. Mentions W briefly and comments on Bigger as "a kind of crypto-good bad nigger." Mentions briefly W's first collection of stories, *Uncle Tom's Chillun* [sic].

9873. French, Warren. "Richard Wright 1908–1960," in *Contemporary Literary Criticism.* Eds. Sharon Gunton and Gerard Senick. Detroit: Gale, 1982, pp. 447–449. Partial reprint of 1969.

9874. Giles, James R. "Richard Wright 1908–1960," in *Contemporary Literary Criticism.* Eds. Sharon Gunton and Gerard Senick. Detroit: Gale, 1982, pp. 452–455. Partial reprint of 1973.157.

9875. Gilman, Richard. "Richard Wright 1908–1960," in *Contemporary Literary Criticism.* Eds. Sharon Gunton and Gerard Senick. De-

troit: Gale, 1982, p. 440. Partial reprint of 1961.160.

9876. Graham, Don. "Naturalism in American Fiction: A Status Report." *Studies in American Fiction*, 10 (Spring 1982), 1–16. Mentions briefly *NS* (p. 3) and W (p. 16).

9877. Griffith, Kelley, Jr. *Writing Essays About Literature: A Guide and Style Sheet.* New York: Harcourt Brace Jovanovich, 1982, p. 19. Contains a paragraph on *NS* s.v. "Literature is Affective." Reprinted: 1986, 1990, 1994.

9878. Gunton, Sharon R. "Richard Wright 1908–1960," in her *Contemporary Literary Criticism.* Detroit: Gale Research, 1982, pp. 434–462. Biographical sketch followed by critical excerpts from W.E.B. Du Bois, R.L. Duffus, Raymond Kennedy, Granville Hicks, Robert Hatch, William Donlea, Irving Howe, James Baldwin, Gloria Bramwell, Richard Gilman, Ralph Ellison, Ronald Sanders, Edward Margolies, Warren French, Keneth Kinnamon, Darwin Turner, James R. Giles, Robert Stepto, Morris Dickstein, Owen Brady, and Steven J. Rubin.

9879. Hall, Donald, and D.L. Emblem. "Considerations," in their *A Writer's Reader.* Third edition. Boston: Little, Brown, 1982, p. 488. Reprint of 1976.

9880. _____. "Richard Wright The Library Card," in their *A Writer's Reader.* Third edition. Boston: Little, Brown, 1982, p. 479. Reprint of 1976.

9881. Hansen, Klaus P. "William Demby's *The Catacombs 1965*: A Latecomer to Modernism," in *The Afro-American Novel Since 1960.* Eds. Peter Bruck and Wolfgang Karrer. Amsterdam: B.K. Grüner, 1982, pp. 123–144. Mentions briefly "the Wright school of naturalistic protest" (p. 140).

9882. Harris, Joseph E. "Introduction," in his *Global Dimensions of the African Diaspora.* Washington, DC: Howard University Press, 1982, pp. 3–14. Contains a paragraph on W in relation to Michel Fabre's essay in this collection.

9883. _____. "Introduction," in his *Global Dimensions of the African Dispora.* Washington: Howard University Press, 1982, pp. 3–14. Comments on Michel Fabre's contribution to this collection.

9884. Hatch, Robert. "Richard

Wright 1908–1960," in *Contemporary Literary Criticism.* Eds. Sharon Gunton and Gerard Senick. Detroit: Gale, 1982, p. 436. Partial reprint of 1958.146.

9885. Hicks, Granville. "Richard Wright 1908–1960," in *Contemporary Literary Criticism.* Eds. Sharon Gunton and Gerard Senick. Detroit: Gale, 1982, pp. 435–436. Partial reprint of 1953.150.

9886. Hicks, Granville. "Richard Wright 1908–1960," in *Contemporary Literary Criticism.* Eds. Sharon Gunton and Gerard Senick. Detroit: Gale, 1982, pp. 440–441. Partial reprint of 1963.105.

9887. Howe, Irving. "Richard Wright 1908–1960," in *Contemporary Literary Criticism.* Eds. Sharon Gunton and Gerard Senick. Detroit: Gale, 1982, pp. 437–438. Partial reprint of 1961.178.

9888. _____. *A Margin of Hope: An Intellectual Autobiography.* San Diego: Harcourt Brace Jovanovich, 1982, pp. 156, 240. Mentions W briefly and comments on his expatriation.

9889. Hudson Withers, Clenora. "The Legitimacy of Violence in Richard Wright's Fiction: An Anthropological Perspective." *Umoja*, 6 (Summer 1982), 21–28. Drawing on Houston Baker's concept of the "anthropology of art," Hudson Withers argues that the protagonists of *UTC* and *NS* "engage in symbolic acts of inversion" (p. 22) by defying white culture and affirming rebellion. Similarly, black critics should reject white norms and affirm black cultural values.

9890. Isserman, Maurice. *Which Side Were You On?: The American Communist Party During the Second World War.* Middletown, CT: Wesleyan University Press, 1982, p. 38. Mentions W briefly.

9891. Janssens, G.A.M "Styron's Case and *Sophie's Choice*," in *Critical Essays on William Styron.* Eds. Arthur D. Casciato and James L.W. West III. Boston: G.K. Hall, 1982, pp. 269–283. Reprint of 1980.

9892. Jones, Harry L. "*Arna Bontemps-Langston Hughes Letters, 1925–1967.* Selected and Edited by Charles H. Nichols." *The Langston Hughes Review*, 1 (Spring 1982), 25–26. Review mentioning W briefly.

9893. _____. "*Arna Bontemps-Langston Hughes Letters, 1925–1967.*" *The Langston Hughes Review*,

1 (Spring 1982) 25–26. Notes that there are forty-two references to W.

9894. Joyce, Joyce Ann. "Ann Petry." *Nethula Journal*, 2, No. 2 (1982), 16–20. Mentions W, *UTC*, and *NS* and compares *NS* and Petry's *The Steet*. Reprinted: 1994.

9895. Kaiser, Ernest. "Blacks and the Mass Media: A Bibliography." *Freedomways*, 22 (Third Quarter 1982), 193–209. Mentions briefly Canada Lee's appearance in the play *NS*.

9896. _____. "Recent Books." *Freedomways*, 22 (Second Quarter 1982), 121–127. Includes comment on *Richard Wright: A Primary Bibliography* and announces this secondary bibliography and an editon of W's letters as forthcoming. Also notes Fabre's biography of W.

9897. _____. "Recent Books." *Freedomways*, 22 (First Quarter 1982), 120–127. Praises *Richard Wright's Primary Bibliography* and comments on other bibliographical works by Keneth Kinnamon, Joseph Brown, and Craig Werner. Also comments on Donald Gibson's *The Politics of Literary Expression: A Study of Major Black Writers*, noting that it treats W among others.

9898. _____. "Recent Books." *Freedomways*, 23 (Fourth Quarter 1982), 297–304. Contains a notice of Ladel Payne's *Black Novelists and the Southern Literary Tradition*, noting that it treats W (p. 298).

9899. Karrer, Wolfgang B. "Integration or Separation: The Social History of the Afro-American Dilemma After World War II," in his and Peter Bruck's *The Afro-American Novel Since 1960*. Amsterdam: B.R. Grüner, 1982, pp. 29–52. Mentions W briefly (p. 34).

9900. _____. "The Novel as Blues: Albert Murray's *Train Whistle Guitar* (1974)," in his and Peter Bruck's *The Afro-American Novel Since 1960*. Amsterdam: B.R. Grüner, 1982, pp. 237–262. Quotes Ellison on *BB* (p. 259).

9901. _____. "Multiperspective and the Hazards of Integration: John William's *Night Song* (1961), in his and Peter Bruck's *The Afro-American Novel Since 1960*. Amsterdam: B.R. Grüner, 1982, pp. 75–101. Quotes Williams on W (p. 76).

9902. Kennedy, Raymond. "Richard Wright 1908–1960," in *Contemporary Literary Criticism*. Eds. Sharon Gunton and Gerard Senick. De-

troit: Gale, 1982, p. 435. Partial reprint of 1945.976.

9903. Kinnamon, Keneth. "Richard Wright 1908–1960," in *Contemporary Literary Criticism*. Eds. Sharon Gunton and Gerard Senick. Detroit: Gale, 1982, pp. 451–452. Partial reprint of 1971.204.

9904. Margolies, Edward. "Richard Wright 1908–1960," in *Contemporary Literary Criticism*. Eds. Sharon Gunton and Gerard Senick. Detroit: Gale, 1982, pp. 443–447. Partial reprint of 1969.

9905. Mberi, Antan Sudan Katara. "Landmark Novel of Social Protest." *Freedomways*, 22 (Fourth Quarter, 1982), 256–259. Mentions W briefly (p. 256).

9906. McCluskey, John, Jr. "Paradise Valley: Black Writers and Midwestern Cities, 1910–1950." *Journal of American Culture*, 5 (Fall 1982), 93–103. Includes substantial discussion of W's response to Chicago and his treatment of urban themes in *AH, LT, NS, O*, and *TMBV*. W insists that the human condition in modern society is one of estrangement and alienation.

9907. Meyers, Jeffrey. "Introduction," in his *Hemingway: The Critical Heritage*. London: Routledge & Kegan Paul, 1982, pp. 1–62. Quotes Ellison on the influence of W and Hemingway on his own work (pp. 10–11).

9908. Miller, R. Baxter. "The 'Etched Flame' of Margaret Walker: Biblical and Literary Re-Creation in Southern History." *Tennessee Studies in Literature*, 26 (1982), pp. 157–172. Mentions W briefly (p. 157). Reprinted: 1986.

9909. Morgenstern, Dan. "Jazz — The Jewish-Black Connection," in *Creators and Disturbers: Reminiscences by Jewish Intellectuals of New York*. Eds. Bernard Rosenberg and Ernest Goldstein. New York: Columbia University Press, 1982, pp. 95–112. Mentions reading W (p. 103).

9910. Morse, Lucile M. "Richard Wright." *Abstracts of English Studies*, 25 (March 1982), 101. Abstracts an article by H. Philip Bolton.

9911. Muller, Gilbert H. "Questions," in his *The McGraw-Hill Reader*. New York: McGraw-Hill, 1982, p. 228. Study questions to accompany "The Psychological Reactions of Oppressed People." Reprinted: 1985, 1988.

9912. _____. "Richard Wright, The Psychological Reactions of Oppressed People," in his *The McGraw-Hill Reader*. New York: McGraw-Hill, 1982, p. 224. Biographical headnote. Reprinted: 1985, 1988, 1991.

9913. Ogunyemi, Chikwenye Okonjo. "The Old Order Shall Pass: The Examples of 'Flying Home' and 'Barbados.'" *CLA Journal*, 25 (March 1982), 303–314. Mentions briefly Bigger Thomas (p. 303).

9914. Ostendorf, Berndt. *Black Literature in White America*. Brighton, Sussex: The Harvester Press, 1982, pp. 11, 24, 32, 59, 126–127, 129, 133, 145, 147. Mentions or comments on Bigger Thomas, "Blueprint for Negro Writing," *BB*, and Ellison's "Richard Wright's Blues."

9915. Painter, Nell Irvin. "Social Equality, Miscegenation, Labor, and Power," in *The Evolution of Southern Culture*. Ed. Neuman V. Bartley. Athens: The University of Georgia Press, 1982, pp. Reprinted 2002.

9916. Paquet, Sandra Pouchet. *The Novels of George Lamming*. London: Heinemann, 1982, pp. 5, 9, 46. Quotes from "How 'Bigger' Was Born" and mentions briefly "The Man Who Lived Underground."

9917. Pérez Gállego, Cándido. *Gùia de la Literatura Norteamericana*. Madriel: Editorial Fundamentos, 1982, p. 150. Mentions W briefly.

9918. Phillips, Robert L., Jr. "News, Projects, and Research." *S.S.S.L.: The News-Letter of The Society for the Study of Southern Literature*, 15 (April 1982), 5–9. Mentions an article on *SH* by John Vassilovitch.

9919. _____. "SAMLA." *S.S.S.L.: The News-Letter of The Society for the Study of Southern Literature*, 15 (November 1982), 4–5. Lists a paper by Joyce Ann Joyce on "Richard Wright's 'Long Black Song': A Moral Dilemma."

9920. _____. Untitled note. *S.S.S.L.: The News-Letter of The Society for the Study of Southern Literature*, 15 (April 1982), 9–10. Notes that W is included in a series of "Audio Sketches of American Writers" from National Public Radio.

9921. _____. "Literary Criticism and Scholarship." *S.S.S.L.: The News-Letter of The Society for the Study of Southern Literature*, 15 (November 1982), 7–9. Mentions Charles

T. Davis's bibliography of W and Margaret Walker's biography.

9922. Pickering, James H. and Jeffrey D. Hoeper. "The Elements of Fiction," in their *Literature*. New York: Macmillan, 1982, pp. 11–67. Comments on "The Man Who Lived Underground" in relation to plot conflict (p. 12) and unreliable narrators (p. 43).

9923. _____. "Richard Wright 'The Man Who Was Almost a Man,'" in their *Instructor's Manual: Literature*. New York: Macmillan, 1982, pp. 22–23. Brief analysis of the story emphasizing the protagonist's immaturity and the role of the gun.

9924. Pingree, Elizabeth E., ed. *Humanities Index: April 1981 to March 1982*. New York: H.W. Wilson, 1982, p. 786. Lists four items s.v. W.

9925. Pizer, Donald. *Twentieth-Century American Literary Naturalism: An Interpretation*. Carbondale: Southern Illinois University Press, 1982, p. xiii. Calls W "a major figure," but considers *NS* "a seriously flawed work."

9926. Poenicke, Klaus. *Der amerikanische Naturalismus: Crane, Norris, Dreiser*. Darmstadt: Wissenschaftléche Buchgesellschaft, 1982, p. 136. Mentions briefly *NS*.

9927. Riese, Utz. *Zwischen Verinnerlichung und Protest: McCullers, Salinger, Malamud, Bellow, Capote*. Berlin: Akademie-Verlag, 1982, pp. 12, 85, 190. Mentions briefly W and *NS*.

9928. Rive, Richard. "The Ethics of an Anti-Jim Crow," in *Design and Intent in African Literature*. Eds. David F. Dorsey, Phanuel A. Egejuru, and Stephen H. Arnold. Washington, DC: Three Continents Press, 1982, pp. 7–15. Recalls reading *UTC* and *NS* as a boy in Cape Town (pp. 7, 12).

9929. Roch, John H. "Martha Foley." *Abstracts of English Studies*, 25 (September 1982), 84. Abstracts an article by Martha Foley mentioning W.

9930. _____. "Ralph Ellison." *Abstracts of English Studies*, 25 (September 1982), 82. Abstracts an article by Joseph T. Skerritt mentioning W.

9931. Rubin, Louis D., Jr. "Trouble on the land: Southern Literature and the Great Depression," in his *A Gallery of Southerners*. Baton Rouge: Louisiana State University Press,

1982, pp. 152–173. Reprint of 1979. 223.

9932. _____. "Trouble on the Land: Southern Literature and the Great Depression," in *Literature at the Barricades: The American Writer in the 1930's*. Eds. Ralph F. Bogardus and Fred Hobson. University, Alabama: The University of Alabama Press, 1982, pp. 37, 38. Mentions briefly *UTC* and W.

9933. Rubin, Steven J. "Richard Wright 1908–1960," in *Contemporary Literary Criticism*. Eds. Sharon Gunton and Gerard Senick. Detroit: Gale, 1982, pp. 461–462. Partial reprint of 1981.119.

9934. Saffioti, Carol Lee. "Richard Wright." *Abstracts of English Studies*, 25 (March 1982), 101. Abstracts an article by Robert Fleissner.

9935. Sanders, Ronald. "Richard Wright 1908–1960," in *Contemporary Literary Criticism*. Eds. Sharon Gunton and Gerard Senick. Detroit: Gale, 1982, pp. 442–443. Partial reprint of 1963.192.

9936. Schoen, Carol B. *Anzia Yezierska*. Boston: Twayne, 1982, pp. 108–109. Comments on Yezierska's friendship with W when they were on the Writers Project together.

9937. Schultz, Elizabeth. "Search for 'Soul Space': A Study of Al Young's *Who Is Angelina?*(1975) and the Dimensions of Freedom," in *The American Novel Since 1960*. Amsterdam: B.R. Grüner, 1982, pp. 263–287. Mentions briefly Bigger Thomas and *NS* (p. 263).

9938. Shankman, Arnold. *Ambivalent Friends: Afro-Americans View the Immigrant*, Westport, CT: Greenwood Press, 1982, pp. 132, 134, 147. W comments on black antisemitism.

9939. Stepto, Robert B. "Richard Wright 1908–1960," in *Contemporary Literary Criticism*. Eds. Sharon Gunton and Gerard Senick. Detroit: Gale, 1982, pp. 455–458. Partial reprint of 1977.294.

9940. Suggs, Jon Christian. "An Interview with Jack Conroy," in *Dictionary of Literary Biography Yearbook: 1981*. Eds. Karen L. Rood, Jean W. Ross, and Richard Ziegfeld. Detroit: Gale, 1982, pp. 186–188. Conroy states that W's disaffection with the Communist Party began with the disbanding of the John Reed Clubs.

9941. _____. "Jack Conroy," in *Dictionary of Literary Biography: 1981*. Eds. Karen L. Rood, Jean W. Ross, and Richard Ziegfeld. Detroit: Gale, 1982, pp. 182–186. Mentions W briefly (p. 184).

9942. Towers, Robert. "Good Men Are Hard to Find." *The New York Review of Books*, 29 (12 August 1982), 35–36. Briefly contrasts W's women in *NS* to Alice Walker's in *The Color Purple*.

9943. Turnage, Maxine. "Richard Wright." *Abstracts of English Studies*, 25 (June 1982), 93. Abstracts an article by John Vassilovitch, Jr.

9944. Turner, Darwin T. "Richard Wright 1908–1960," in *Contemporary Literary Criticism*. Eds. Sharon Gunton and Gerard Senick. Detroit: Gale, 1982, pp. 450–451. Partial reprint of 1969.239.

9945. _____. "Thoughts About Literature, the Diaspora, and Africa," in *Global Dimensions of the African Diaspora*. Ed. Joseph E. Harris. Washington: Howard University Press, 1982, pp. 136–141. Mentions the inclusion of W in college courses (pp. 139, 141).

9946. ten Harmsel, Larry. "Ellison, Ralph," in *Encyclopedia of World Literature in the 20th Century*. Ed. Leonard S. Klein. Revised edition. New York: Frederick Ungar, 1982, pp. 22–23. Mentions W briefly. Reprinted: 1989.

9947. Turner, Darwin T. "Appendix One: Uses of the Antebellum Slave Narratives in Collegiate Courses in Literature," in *The Art of Slave Narrative: Original Essays in Criticism and Theory*. Macomb: Western Illinois University, 1982, pp. 127–134. Mentions briefly *NS* (p. 127).

9948. _____. "Thoughts About Literature, the Diaspora and Africa," in *Global Dimensions of the African Diaspora*. Ed. Joseph E. Harris. Washington, DC: Howard University Press, 1982, pp. 136–141. Mentions W briefly (pp. 138, 141).

9949. Wall, Cheryl A. "Zora Neale Hurston: Changing Her Own Words," in *American Novelists Revisited* by Fritz Fleischmann. Boston: G.K. Hall, 1982, pp. 371–393. Mentions W briefly (p. 372). Reprinted: 1993.

9950. Washington, Ida H. *Dorothy Canfield Fisher: A Biography*. Shelburn, Vermont: New England Press, 1982, p 202. Discusses the Book-of-the-Month Club debate over *NS*

and quotes Fisher's favorable opinion of it.

9951. _____. *Dorothy Canfield Fisher: A Biography.* Shelburne, Vermont: New England Press, 1982, pp. 202–203. Discusses Fisher's support of *NS* as a Book-of-the-Month Club selection although it was not suitable for young readers. Fisher states that her introduction was written at the request of the publisher.

9952. _____. *Dorothy Canfield Fisher: A Biography.* Shelburne, Vermont: New England Press, 1982, pp. 202–203. Discusses the selection of *NS* by the Book-of-the-Month Club an act of "mild heroism." Quotes Canfield on the matter, including her view that *NS* is not suitable for adolescent readers.

9953. Wixson, Douglas. "Jack Conroy, The Sage of Moberly." *Book Forum*, 6 (Spring 1982), 201–206. Mentions W briefly (p. 202).

9954. Zamora, Lois Parkinson. "The Myth of the Apocalypse and the American Literary Imagination," in her *The Apocalyptic Vision in America: Interdisciplinary Essays on Myth and Culture.* Bowling Green, OH: Bowling Green University Popular Press, 1982, pp. 97–138. Mentions W briefly (p. 111).

9955. _____. "The Myth of Apocalypse and the American Literary Imagination," in her *The Apocalyptic Vision in America.* Bowling Green, OH: Bowling Green University Popular Press, 1982), pp. 97–138. Mentions W briefly (p. 111).

INDEX

To preserve the fidelity of the citations, author and title are indexed exactly as they appear on each work. Each published variant of an author's name or title has a separate entry.